THE LIFE AND GAMES OF CARLOS TORRE

Second edition 2023 by Thinkers Publishing

All sales or enquiries should be directed to Thinkers Publishing, 9850 Landegem, Belgium.

Email: info@thinkerspublishing.com

Website: www.thinkerspublishing.com

Managing Editor: Daniël Vanheirzeele

Typesetting: Primož Žerdin, Primož Riegler

Cover Design: Mieke Mertens

Graphic Artist: Philippe Tonnard

Production: BESTinGraphics

ISBN 9789464201727
D/2023/13732/5

The Life and Games of Carlos Torre

by

Gabriel Velasco and

Taylor Kingston

Thinkers Publishing 2023

Thinkers Publishing

Key to symbols

!	a good move	±	White has a serious advantage
?	a weak move	∓	Black has a serious advantage
!!	an excellent move	+–	White has a decisive advantage
??	a blunder	–+	Black has a decisive advantage
!?	an interesting move	→	with an attack
?!	a dubious move	↑	with initiative
□	only move	⇄	with counterplay
=	equality	∆	with the idea of
∞	unclear position	⌓	better is
=/∞	with compensation for the sacrificed material	N	novelty
⩲	White stands slightly better	+	check
⩱	Black stands slightly better	#	mate

Frequently Used Abbreviations

ACB: *American Chess Bulletin*
CA: chess association
CB: ChessBase (Mega Database 2017)
CC: chess club
CF: chess federation
Ch: Championship
CL: Chess Life magazine
CM: Candidate Master (a/k/a Expert)
FIDE: Fédération Internationale des Échecs, i.e. the International Chess Federation
GM: Grandmaster
IM: International Master
TN: theoretical novelty, i.e. a new move in the opening
WCh: World Championship
WSZ: Wiener Schachzeitung (Vienna Chess Magazine)

Table of Contents

Preface to the First Edition (2000)

In 1993, *Vida y Partidas de Carlos Torre* appeared, published by Incaro. The current work began as a straightforward translation of that work, but the author, working closely with the translator Taylor Kingston, expanded the original manuscript and the result is this English edition. This book is offered to chessplayers and enthusiasts of all Spanish-speaking countries as an homage to one of the greatest Latin American chess players of all time: grandmaster Carlos Torre Repetto, originally from Yucatán, Mexico. In recognition of Torre's formidable accomplishments and triumphs during the years 1924-1926, the Fédération Internationale Des Echecs (FIDE, the International Chess Federation) in 1977 bestowed on Torre the title of International Grandmaster.

The author visited Torre in the town of his birth, Mérida, where he passed away a year later. Though Torre knew the intent of this book, it is sad that he did not live to see it realized. Those who knew Carlos Torre recall him as an unaffected person of noble sentiments. His health was always fragile and he suffered constantly from insomnia. In his book *The Psychology of the Chess Player*, Reuben Fine described some of Torre's eccentricities, as well as the nervous breakdown he suffered in October 1926, which forced him to retire permanently from chess at the age of 21. Fine related that Torre could never sleep more than two hours a day and described some of his strange habits, such as eating 12 pineapple ice cream sundaes in a day and other such extravagances.

In this book we will make no attempt to psychoanalyze Torre, nor will we indulge in theorizing about his untimely and unexpected retirement from chess, in which respect he was similar to some other grandmasters. Our major concern will be to present Torre's great games, his beautiful combinations and his strategic and tactical concepts. The author was able to compile about 170 games of the Yucatan grandmaster, which were narrowed to a selection of 100 of the best, though, in fact, the final total turned out to be 105. We have included four losses and a number of draws, but the great majority of games offered were, logically, won by Torre. Naturally, many trips, letters, and inquiries were necessary to assemble the games.

The author would like to express his gratitude to all those who assisted in the collection of the games, the biographical data, and the tournament tables, including Dale Brandreth, the late Alice N. Loranth, Julieta viuda de Gilberto Repetto Milán, Alejandro Báez and Taylor Kingston. To all these people, my sincere thanks.

Gabriel Velasco León, Guanajuato, Mexico, March 2000

Preface to this Second Edition

Serving as the translator for Gabriel Velasco's *Vida y Partidas de Carlos Torre* was my first big job in chess book writing and editing, and one of my most enjoyable. Besides the interesting work of turning Spanish into English, it introduced me to Carlos Torre as a chess player and as a person.

It has been twenty-three years since the first edition of this book went to press. It was well received critically, and I felt proud of what Dr. Velasco and I had worked hard to produce. Still, over the years, as my skill and experience with chess databases and analytical software increased, I realized it could have been much better. Better for one in its technical aspects, especially game annotations and notation. Also as I continued research into chess history (a lifelong interest), new things related to Torre would turn up, things that would have made worthwhile additions to the book. These kept accumulating in my files.

But they just stayed there until I saw the film *Torre x Torre*, a documentary by Mexican film-makers, released in 2019. It inspired me to think seriously about a new edition. Dr. Velasco was unable to contribute further, and even went so far as to suggest that the new edition should be credited to me as sole author, but there is still enough of his original work here that I could not accept that.

Here is what has been added to this edition:

- ♖ More accurate and more extensive annotations, computer-assisted. Every game has been examined under Stockfish 14, probably the best analytical engine available for home computers at this time. For the first edition we had only Fritz 4 and 5, which compare to Stockfish like a Model T Ford to a Ferrari, and many games were given no computer examination at all. Thus owners of the first edition will find most annotations here substantially different (and substantially better). However, many general assessments and heuristic notes proved valid and have been retained.
- ♖ Torre's own annotations to several games have been unearthed and added. These come from several sources: the *American Chess Bulletin*, his book of the 1926 Mexican Championship tournament, and his instructional booklet *Development of Chess Ability*.

- Several games have been added. Some, frankly, are Torre losses, which are given in the interest of presenting a more complete, balanced picture of his play. The first edition, to some extent, looked at Torre through rose-colored glasses; here the aim is only for untinted clarity. Also added are the six games between players other than Torre that he annotated for the Mexican Championship tournament book (see Chapter VIII).
- There are many more diagrams and photographs than in the first edition. Also more thumbnail bios of Torre's opponents.
- More ancillary material about Torre's life and career: pictures, anecdotes, interesting facts, opinions, bits of trivia etc., drawn from the *American Chess Bulletin*, the *Wiener Schachzeitung*, the film *Torre x Torre*, and other sources.
- A 1927 interview with Torre, published in the Yucatán magazine *Anahuac*, in Chapter III.
- Chapter IV, excerpts from the book *64 Variaciones Sobre un Tema de Torre* by his friend Germán de la Cruz.
- Chapter V, "Remembrances of Carlos Torre," which consists of columns and articles from newspapers in his home town of Mérida.
- Chapter VI, "A Clash of Opposites," an article originally published in the British magazine *Kingpin*, comparing and contrasting Torre with the notorious Norman Tweed Whitaker, whom he played at Detroit 1924.
- Chapter VII, the full text of Torre's 1926 instructional booklet *Development of Chess Ability*, which has become a very rare collector's item.
- Chapter IX, a review of *Torre x Torre*, a film by turns fascinating, informative and misleading.
- A more extensive, more fully informed overall assessment of Torre as a chess player in Chapter X.

I have preserved Dr. Velasco's biographical portrait of Torre much as it was, though with several additions and some minor corrections. Also some of our original game annotations (at least those not overturned by Stockfish!). And the vast majority of the games are the same ones he chose for the first edition. Some are readily available on ChessBase, but others, especially the non-tournament games from Torre's 1926 sojourn in Mexico, are known today only because of his diligent research.

Besides Dr. Velasco, I would like to thank Juan Obregón, co-director of *Torre x Torre*, for sending me various Mexican newspaper articles about Torre, and along with his fellow director Roberto Garza, for providing information about their film; Edward Winter for two letters about Torre written by E.Z. Adams; Jeremy Spinrad for news reports of Torre's 1926 breakdown; and also Guy van Habberney of Belgium, for providing scans of Torre's book on the 1926 Mexican Championship. Also my junior high school Spanish teacher, the late Felipe Chacón, for all he taught me about that beautiful language so that I could translate those texts. And finally my beloved wife Emily, who is about the most supportive helpmate a chess writer could want, even though she doesn't know the game.

Taylor Kingston, Pas Robles, California, November 2022

Chapter I

Biographical Portrait of Carlos Torre

Little is known of Carlos Torre's childhood and early adolescence, the years which gave rise to his love for chess. He was born the 29th of November, 1904, in Mérida, Yucatán province, Mexico. Carlos was the sixth of seven siblings (four boys and three girls). It is known that his father, Egidio Torre, taught him to play chess at an early age. According to Carlos, he learned the moves of the pieces at age six, by observing the games between his father and his older brother, Raúl. In 1916, when Carlos was not yet 12, the Torre family moved to the United States, settling in the city of New Orleans, Louisiana, birthplace of the legendary Paul Morphy. The reason for choosing this particular city was perhaps merely geographical, as the distance between Mérida and New Orleans is relatively short, even less than that separating Mérida from Mexico City. Of course, in those days it was relatively easy for a Mexican to enter the United States and settle there for short, long or indefinite periods. The problem of undocumented or illegal aliens did not then exist.

Within a few months of his arrival in New Orleans, Carlos quickly learned to read and write English, and he began to frequent that city's chess circles. His first chess books were those of James Mason (*The Art of Chess* and *The Principles of Chess*). In one of those appears a great number of combinational exercises and brilliant games with colorful tactical themes, which undoubtedly influenced the style Torre would eventually acquire. At age 13 his chess talent became apparent to Edwin Z. Adams (1885-1944), a chess organizer well-known in the United States. At that time, Adams served as vice-president of the New Orleans Chess, Checkers and Whist Club and he gladly took on the role of guide and mentor to the talented youth.

It was natural that under such conditions young Torre made very swift progress. At age 14 he was already considered the second best chessplayer in New Orleans, after the veteran Leon Labatt. That year, the magazine *The Good Companion* dedicated an entire page to the Mexican prodigy, along with a photograph

244 *The Good Companion*

A second Paul Morphy discovered i[n] the old French City.

Master CARLOS REPERTO, fourteen years of age, solves eight of our Washington Birthday Problems in less than one hour.

In simultaneous play against ten of the leading players of New Orleans, he wo[n] eight and drew two games.

Our Vice-President, E. Z. Adams, discovered the youthful star who hails fro[m] Yucatan, Mexio.

showing the boy Carlos and Edwin Adams at the board, surrounded by the leading players and personalities of the New Orleans chess world. The title ran "A second Paul Morphy discovered in the old French City" (as New Orleans is sometimes called). The article further said "Master Carlos Reperto *[sic]*[1], 14 years of age, solved eight of the most difficult chess problems from the *Washington Birthday Problems* in less than an hour," and added "In a simultaneous exhibition against 10 of the best chessplayers in New Orleans, he won eight games and drew two. Our vice-president, E.Z. Adams, discovered the young star, who comes from Yucatán, Mexico."

In a 1920 letter to Hermann Helms, publisher of the magazine *American Chess Bulletin*, Adams wrote about Torre as follows:

> I have just received a visit from C. Torre, R., and I have obtained the following information from him. He was born in Merida, Yuc. Mex. 29 November 1904 and came with his parents to this country in 1916. He has been playing chess with his father and brothers for about six years and about two years with all comers. He learned the game from his father and brothers and became so efficient at it that he soon left them far behind. He has played the following with the strongest players to a finish in N.O. but I am sorry to say there is *[sic]* no records kept of the games.
>
> | | |
> |---|---|
> | James McDonnell | 2 games, he won 1 and lost 1 |
> | Prof. Dixon | 8 games, he won 5 and lost 3 |
> | Chas. Rosen | 4 games, he won 2 and lost 1, draw 1 |
> | Percy Moise | 5 games, he won 4 and lost 1 |
>
> His simultaneous exhibition at the chess club, he won eight and drew two games. In a lightning game with Mr E. Laker *[sic; apparently Edward Lasker]* of Chicago played in April 1920 the game was given up as a draw.

1 Besides misspelling "Repetto," the article makes a mistake often seen in English-language publications, of taking the matronymic for the surname. With Spanish names, the mother's surname, in this case Repetto, is often appended after the father's surname. This will be seen with many names in this book, e.g. Agustín Garza Galindo and Raúl Ocampo Vargas. English speakers often mistakenly assume the paternal surname is just a middle name, as in, say, Edgar Allan Poe or Franklin Delano Roosevelt, and take the matronymic for the surname.

> The little fellow is very modest and unassuming and his success in chess has not given him the swell head. He has a very extensive knowledge of the openings also the end games. He is also a very good problem solver. If he had some professionals to play with, I think in a short time he would be very strong.

Edwin Ziegler Adams was described as "The Sponsor of Carlos Torre" in an article on pages 110-111 of the May-June 1927 *American Chess Bulletin*:

> On the second page of Carlos Torre's *Development of Chess Ability*, reserved for the dedication, appears the name of Edwin Z. Adams of New Orleans quite properly heading the list. We say quite properly because it was due to this Southern gentleman more than to anyone else that the little Mexican, now among the grand-masters of the game, started out upon the great adventure that took him first to New York and then overseas to his European successes.

Further on in the article, Adams looked back on his association with young Carlos:

> "My chess career," Mr Adams modestly wrote us many moons ago, "consists principally of my interest in Carlos. I commenced to study the game about ten years ago. I had a hard time of it, as I had to batter my way along and get whatever pointers I could pick up by watching the others play, and finally I learned the code and played over the games in the books. It was over two months before I was able to win a game from the poorest player I could find at the club (and the only one who would play with me), and it was only by 'bucking the line' and being 'thrown for many losses' and taking my medicine like a man that I finally learned to play a little.
>
> "About eight years ago I met Carlos. I think he was then about 14 years old. He was a small, dark-skinned, thin little fellow, very polite, quiet and serious for a boy of his age. He had learned to play chess from his father and brothers and soon was able to make short work of them over the chessboard. Dr Ainsley (now deceased) was their family physician, a member of the chess club and also a very good player, well above the average. When visiting the family one day they mentioned to him that they had a small member who could play a good game and asked him to play with the little chap and see if he really could play well. I think Carlos won two out of the three games to the surprise of all. Dr Ainsley then suggested that he play Mr Percy Moise, a very strong player. Carlos showed his strength with him also. Next, I think, he played with Mr C. Rosen, also one of the best here, with the same results.
>
> "Things, however, drifted along until I received a letter from his older brother telling of Carlos' chess ability, when I arranged to have him come to

the club and show what he could do. None of the old dignitaries with chess reputations wanted to play with the child, so a Dr Sternberg, a visitor, volunteered to play him. The latter had been toppling us all over, and that, I figured, would be a real test. I will never forget that day. As one of the gentlemen remarked, 'You felt more like petting the little fellow than trying to beat him a game of chess'. Carlos electrified the crowd, and Dr Sternberg enjoyed his rout also.

"Next, Carlos gave a peripatetic exhibition, playing six games at once, winning four and drawing two. The chess club was so impressed with his play that they gave him *carte blanche*, and from that time on he visited the rooms very often, until he could not get anyone to play with him, for they were all tired of being beaten. So he had nothing to do but come to my home occasionally, when we would play a few games and go over the openings together. His next feat was to win the city championship in 1923, which he did with ease.

"During all these years he worked and attended night school, so he was driven very hard. After a very severe case of pneumonia he was out of a position, and I suggested that he go to New York, with an introduction to the *American Chess Bulletin*. He also took an interest in problems and endgames and, of course, was excellent in these branches. He won several prizes in *Good Companion* tourneys. This is about all I can give you concerning Carlos. To you, better than to anyone else, is known the rest[1]."

After winning the city championship of New Orleans, Torre in 1923 won by a wide margin the Louisiana state championship, a double round-robin 8-man tournament. For unknown reasons, this tournament's games were not published by any New Orleans newspaper. The *New Orleans Times-Picayune* had had an excellent chess column, but this ceased in 1919. Only one game from the event is known to have survived (Game 1 of this collection, Labatt-Torre), thanks to Torre himself, who included it in his booklet *Development of Chess Ability*. The oldest known game of Torre's dates from 1920, when he was 15 years old, that being the famous loss to Adams in a game featuring an amazing combination with repeated Queen sacrifice offers and threats of back-rank mate. However, there is considerable doubt that such a game was actually played. The score is given as Game 107 of this collection, together with a discussion of its historical validity.

---

1 The text of this and the previous letter were obtained from Edward Winter's article "Adams v Torre – A Sham?" at *https://www.chesshistory.com/winter/extra/adamstorre.html*. They appear here with his permission.

Here it is pertinent to note a peculiar trait of Torre's character, and of his attitude toward chess, one which partly explains the enigma of his unexpected and premature retirement from competition. This trait was identified by the master Alejandro Báez, who lived with Torre for years and was able to observe many details of his personality. Ironic though it might seem, Torre never cared for the idea of struggle and competition inherent in chess. For Torre there never was "the thrill of victory, the agony of defeat," because for him chess was foremost, perhaps solely, an art form. Torre's pleasure in a game came from its artistic, aesthetic value, independent of whether he had won or lost. In his later years, well after retiring from international competition, he was in the habit of playing offhand games with friends, obtaining a won position, and then surprising his opponent with a draw offer. When Torre won a beautiful game he would still sometimes feel regret, even actual suffering, at having inflicted a defeat on his opponent. Many of the great chess champions, such as Alekhine, Fischer, Tal, Karpov, Kasparov *et al*, have been characterized at the board by a confrontational indomitability, the aggressive attitude of a gladiator. Carlos Torre had a comparable degree of chess talent, but was lacking this competitive malice, often bordering on cruelty, seen in some of the greatest chessplayers. It was not an exaggeration when Boris Spassky said of Anatoly Karpov that he radiated an aura of enmity comparable to a crocodile. No such thing was ever said of Carlos Torre. In contrast to Alekhine, who was known occasionally to falsify game scores and notes to make himself appear stronger, in the 1920 Adams game incident Torre may have changed a game score for the sake of beauty, even if it meant portraying himself as the loser.

In June of 1924, Torre traveled to New York in search of stronger opposition. He soon joined the Marshall Chess Club and took part in its Friday afternoon blitz tournaments. In his first six such tournaments Torre took first place in five (once tied with Smirka, then New York state champion) and second place in the other, behind Tholfsen, then champion of the Marshall Club. The *ACB*, in its July-August 1924 issue, made mention of Torre's strong play and the ease with which he defeated the Marshall's most experienced veterans. Page 156 read:

> Carlos Torre, the young Mexican expert who for several years has made his home in New Orleans, where he outranked all others interested in chess, recently came to New York and affiliated himself with the Marshall Chess Club. Like Capablanca, he has shown himself to be almost invincible in rapid transit play[1],although primarily he prefers slow, studious play.

1 A form of speed chess then popular, played at ten seconds per move.

At that time, the best players then living in New York City were the Cuban José Raúl Capablanca, champion of the world, and the eponymous Frank J. Marshall, for 20 years one of the ten best in the world, but neither took part in club championships. After them, the best players were considered to be Abraham Kupchik and Morris Schapiro, both members of the Manhattan Chess Club. Naturally, after Torre's easy victories over the Marshall's best, curiosity grew about how he would measure up against the Manhattan's strongest players. In July 1924 the club directors organized a closed championship to which Torre was invited. This proved a profitable experience for the young Mexican master; despite losing to Kupchik and Shapiro, he took a noteworthy third place.

1924 Manhattan Chess Club Championship:

		1	2	3	4	5	6	7	8	9	10	total
1	Kupchik	*	0	1	1	1	1	1	1	1	0	7
2	Shapiro	1	*	1	½	1	1	1	0	1	0	6½
3-4	**Torre**	**0**	**0**	*	**½**	**1**	**½**	**1**	**1**	**1**	**1**	**6**
3-4	Frink	0	½	½	*	½	½	1	1	1	1	6
5-7	Beihoff	0	0	0	½	*	1	1	0	0	1	4
5-7	Katz	0	0	½	½	1	*	1	0	0	1	4
5-7	Tenner	0	0	0	1	0	0	*	1	1	1	4
8	Samuels	0	1	0	0	0	1	0	*	½	1	3½
9	Ross	0	0	0	0	½	1	0	½	*	1	3
10	Norwood	1	1	0	0	0	0	0	0	0	*	2

For this book we have selected five of Torre's games from this tournament: wins against Beihoff, Tenner, Frink, and Samuels, and his loss to Schapiro in an interesting pawn ending. Not long after the Manhattan event Torre was to demonstrate his superiority over Kupchik and Shapiro, defeating them brilliantly in exhibition games. From those successes came a growing desire to face Marshall and Capablanca.

In August of 1924, Alrick H. Mann, president of the Marshall Chess Club, announced an attractive prize fund for seven of New York's best chess players, including Torre, Marshall, and the young Anthony Santasiere, to compete in two special invitational double round-robin tournaments. These were thematic events: in the first the Vienna Gambit (1.e4 e5 2.♘c3 ♘f6 3.f4) was obligatory, and in the second the romantic Ponziani Gambit (1.e4 e5 2.♗c4 ♘f6 3.d4, also known as the Urusov). The purse for the second tournament was donated by Mr. Edwin Dimock, who also chose the thematic opening. Five of the seven competitors were the same in both events; in the second Norwood and Gustafsson took the place of Santasiere and Fosberg. These two thematic tourneys demonstrated convincingly that Marshall and Torre were in a class by themselves among New York masters (with the exception of Capablanca). In the first they drew their two games against each other, and in the second they won one apiece, oddly each with the black pieces. In both tournaments they left the rest of the field well behind. For this book, we have selected four games from these events.

In August the New York State Championship took place at the Rochester Chess Club. The nine contestants played a round robin. Neither Marshall nor Kupchik took part, but there was still strong competition. The *American Chess Bulletin* reported as follows:

NEW YORK STATE MEETING AT ROCHESTER

With nine competitors in the Championship Tournament and six in Class A of the General Tournament, the New York State Chess Association held a very successful meeting at the rooms of the Rochester Chess Club from August 18 to 22. The championship competition was noteworthy for the participation of Carlos Torre of New Orleans, who made his debut in the North on that occasion. The circumstances that he and Harold E. Jennings of Rochester, State champion in 1916, tied for first place without losing a game, in the face of the fact that an expert of high repute like Roy T. Black of Syracuse was competing, speaks volumes for the ability of these two young men who bid fair to blossom out into the master class. Both made scores of 7-1, leaving the question of the championship undecided. Later, they agreed to meet at the Marshall Chess Club in New York, on September 13 and 14, to play off the tie.

New York State Championship, Rochester 1924:

		1	2	3	4	5	6	7	8	9	total
1-2	**Torre**	*	**½**	**½**	**1**	**1**	**1**	**1**	**1**	**1**	**7**
1-2	Jennings	½	*	½	1	1	1	1	1	1	7
3	Black	½	½	*	0	1	1	1	1	1	6
4	Adams	0	0	1	*	0	1	1	1	1	5
5	Lear	0	0	0	1	*	½	1	1	1	4½
6	Searle	0	0	0	0	½	*	1	1	0	2½
7-8	Gluckemus	0	0	0	0	0	0	*	½	1	1½
7-8	Weiss	0	0	0	0	0	0	½	*	1	1½
9	Palmer	0	0	0	0	0	1	0	0	*	1

The playoff match was indeed held as reported. Torre won by a score of 3-1, making him Champion of the State of New York.

Playoff Match, September 13-19, 1924

	1	2	3	4	total
Torre	0	1	1	1	3
Jennings	1	0	0	0	1

From these we have chosen two games from the tournament (against Lear and E.B. Adams, not the same man as E.Z. Adams of New Orleans), and the last three games of the Jennings match.

In those days, though Marshall would not put his US Champion title at stake except in match play, a tournament sponsored by the Western Chess Association functioned as a *de facto* United States tournament championship, the Western Championship. An invitational event limited to the strongest masters and state champions, in 1924 it took place in Detroit, Michigan, with contestants coming from as far south as Memphis, Tennessee, and as far west as Los Angeles, California. The program called for a tough two-games-per-day schedule, with a time limit of 20 moves per hour.

Carlos Torre attended as the representative of New York, and instead of Jennings another even younger master on the rise was invited: Samuel Reshevsky, then but 12 years old. Though in 1924 Reshevsky had not reached anywhere near the strength and maturity that made him one of the world's best from the mid-1930s to the late 1960s, he still managed to take an honorable 5th place.

The Western Championship resulted in a convincing triumph for Torre, who took clear first 2½ points ahead of the field. With an undefeated 12 wins and four draws in 16 games, Torre showed that, apart from Marshall and Capablanca, no other master then living in the USA could compare with him. The *ACB* wrote:

> As was the case in the ever-memorable tournament at New York in 1857, which has gone down in history as the First American Chess Congress, a youth came out of the South, from New Orleans to surprise an unexpectant chess world. Carlos Torre, who had been in New York only three months and was sent to the State meeting at Rochester by the Marshall Chess Club, which he joined, set the pace from the start.
>
> Displaying throughout the sort of invincibility which marked the career of Paul Morphy, he went straight through without losing a game and finished well in the lead as winner of the first prize and the Western championship. He accomplished it with the total score of 14-2, representing 12 wins and 4

drawn games. This astonishing performance unquestionably places the young Mexican in the first ranks of American experts, and, doubtless, he will be heard from again in the not far distant future.

Western Chess Association Championship, Detroit 1924:

		1	2	3	4	5	6	7	8	9	10	11	12	13	14	15	16	17	Total
1	**Torre**	*	1	½	1	1	1	½	1	1	1	1	½	1	½	1	1	1	14
2-4	Factor	0	*	1	½	1	½	0	1	0	1	½	1	1	1	1	1	1	11½
2-4	Hahlbohm	½	0	*	0	0	½	1	½	1	1	1	1	1	1	1	1	1	11½
2-4	Whitaker	0	½	1	*	1	½	1	1	1	0	½	1	0	1	1	1	1	11½
5	Reshevsky	0	0	1	0	*	1	½	0	1	1	½	1	1	1	1	1	1	11
6	Banks	0	½	½	½	0	*	½	½	½	1	1	½	1	1	1	1	1	10½
7	Ruth	½	1	0	0	½	½	*	0	1	½	0	1	1	1	1	1	1	10
8	Mlotkowski	0	0	½	0	1	½	1	*	½	½	½	1	0	½	1	1	1	9
9-10	Stolzenberg	0	1	0	0	0	½	0	½	*	1	1	0	1	1	0	1	1	8
9-10	Scrivener	0	0	0	1	0	0	½	½	0	*	1	1	1	1	1	0	1	8
11	Spero	0	½	0	½	½	0	1	½	0	0	*	½	0	½	1	1	1	7
12	Palmer	½	0	0	0	0	½	0	0	1	0	½	*	0	1	1	1	1	6½
13	Winter	0	0	0	1	0	0	0	1	0	0	1	1	*	0	0	0	1	5
14	Margolis	½	0	0	0	0	0	0	½	0	0	½	0	1	*	1	0	1	4½
15-16	Erdeky	0	0	0	0	0	0	0	0	1	0	0	0	1	0	*	1	1	4
15-16	Jenkines	0	0	0	0	0	0	0	0	0	1	0	0	1	1	0	*	1	4
17	Goerlich*	0	0	0	0	0	0	0	0	0	0	0	0	0	0	0	0	*	0

** Goerlich withdrew after losing his first five games. His remaining games were scored as wins for his opponents.*

The September-October 1924 issue of the *American Chess Bulletin* was devoted almost completely to articles on Torre, his playing style and triumphs. Hermann Helms and C.S. Howell even compared him to Capablanca, and filled page after page with praise for the young Mexican master. Here is what Howell had to say:

A NEW CHAMPION

When the publisher of the *American Chess Bulletin* asked me to annotate "briefly" several games by Carlos Torre in Rochester and Detroit, it is possible he selected me because Torre is a Mexican and Mr. Helms knows that I have spent years in Latin-American countries and have a very keen realization that much that is good in the Western Hemisphere lies south of the Rio Grande and that the term American is rightly used as far away as Puntas Arenas.

> Americans have every reason to be proud of Carlos Torre as they already had reason to be proud of Capablanca. Both of these chessists are American and products of Western Hemisphere progress. They and the Latin Americans who will surely come after them in chess affairs are very welcome, too, especially now when there are no signs whatever of young North Americans coming very far forward in the royal game.
>
> I have played over Torre's games very carefully and with great interest. They show very clearly that he is developing a real chess talent. It is very evident that he has imagination and skill and that he possesses self-confidence and courage of conviction. He lacks technique and for the sake of his chess future, I hope that he will not hasten too much in cultivating it. Acquired naturally and as a result of the experience of play, technique is a valuable asset but the attempt to acquire it before one's ability to combine has been fully developed has stopped permanently the improvement of a good man young players.

At the end of the games annotated by Howell, he wrote "Altogether a study of the Mexican's games leaves one with the impression that he may go far. There is a directness and energy about his play that I have not seen in the games of other young American players for some years and that is very refreshing as a change from the many attempts I have seen the part of other young players to imitate (usually without understanding) the so-called hyper-modern style of play. Evidently Torre has no fetishes and no dogmatic notions. It is to be hoped that he will let the 'Books' alone for a while and go on developing his natural style. The technique will come when he needs it."

Due to the high caliber of Torre's play in the Western Championship, we have chosen ten of his games from that event, games which show the vigorous and artistic style of the young Yucatecan, his impressive imagination and characteristic abundance of ideas. At only 19 years of age, quite young for a chess master of that time, he had reached an extraordinary level of ability and maturity.

In mid-December, an exhibition game between Carlos Torre and Morris Schapiro came about under unusual circumstances. On December 15th it was announced at the Manhattan Chess Club that Torre would give a simultaneous exhibition against all comers. It was expected that there would be 30 or 40 opponents, but when only 10 turned up, the club directors decided to change from a simul to an exhibition game between Torre and Schapiro, who had finished second, ½-point ahead of Torre, in the club championship some months earlier. In retrospect it was a providential decision, as it resulted in an excellent and exciting game in which Torre delighted the spectators with a series of brilliant combinations culminated by a Queen sacrifice. A true jewel of the art of attack. Even the greatest attacking masters are seldom able to realize a proper Queen sacrifice more than every ten years or so in serious tournament or match games. Nevertheless, Torre would do this with much greater frequency. In the Western Championship, for example, he sacrificed his Queen in two games, against Reshevsky and against N.W. Banks. Even at the highest levels of serious competition he was able to do this, as shown by his brilliancies against Lasker and Verlinsky at Moscow 1925.

Torre's attitude toward exhibition games was to seek, above all, to delight the spectators with an interesting, exciting, yet high-quality game. For Torre, this kind of chess was entertainment. In contrast, his opponents often were more tense and cautious, taking few risks, treating it as they would a decisive tournament game. Oddly, Torre's more light-hearted approach brought out a more agile, fluent style than in his tournament games and he in fact won every exhibition game he ever played, except for two with Reuben Fine in 1934.

Late in December 1924, an exhibition game was arranged between Torre and the Franco-Polish master Dawid Janowski, who had been living in New York since 1915. Janowski had once been one of the top players in the world, even playing a world championship match with Emanuel Lasker in 1910. Though Lasker had defeated him soundly, and his skills had clearly declined since then, Janowski was still an opponent worthy of respect. The exhibition game was held at the Manhattan Chess Club on December 28. Torre had the black pieces and played his favorite variation of the French Defense. The game was adjourned, and resumed the next day. Torre finally prevailed in a hard fight of 62 moves.

The great publicity given to Torre's victories in the *American Chess Bulletin* soon opened a new chapter in his career, as his games and style rapidly became known in Europe. First veteran German grandmaster Siegbert Tarrasch and later, former world champion Emanuel Lasker, commented positively on Torre's style of play. From Berlin, Dr. Lasker sent a lengthy letter to Herman Helms, editor of the *ACB*. The letter, dated October 25, was published in the November 1924 issue. Lasker touched on various matters, responding to some attacks by Capablanca, discussing philosophy, and finally mentioning Torre. He wrote: "C. S. Howell's article on Carlos Torre hits the nail on the head: Carlos Torre's games are interesting, his style is promising, his combinations are chessy."

At the start of 1925 an important international competition was announced, to be held in the German city of Baden-Baden. Dr. Tarrasch, age 62, would serve as tournament organizer and director. It was hoped to bring together for this event all the best chess players of the world. Alekhine, Rubinstein, Nimzovich, and Spielmann confirmed their participation, but Dr. Lasker announced he would not take part. Invitations were extended to the most eminent New World players: Capablanca, then world champion, and Frank J. Marshall. When Capablanca declined, it was decided to invite in his place either Torre or Kupchik. To make the final choice, a match between the two was organized. In addition to the tournament bid and expenses for travel to Germany, the winner would collect $500. The match was set at ten games, to begin the 3rd of March, games to be played on Tuesday, Thursday, Saturday and Sunday in two sessions from 2:00 PM to 6:00 PM. In the event of adjournment, play was to be resumed the same day, going from 8:00 PM until midnight, if necessary. Naturally, both masters were eager to win the right to attend such a strong tournament. Ironically, this very desire to win, and the unambivalent "either-or" nature of the situation, caused Torre for the first time to think in terms of achieving a definite result and playing with premeditated caution, rather than give free rein to his natural artistic qualities.

This attempt to control his imaginative talents and change his concept of "chess as art" to one of "chess as competitive sport" caused Torre to play in a strange, artificial way against an opponent he would in other circumstances probably defeat with relative ease. Kupchik won the first game and Torre the second. Then came four consecutive draws characterized by positional struggle and great caution on both sides. Then, unexpectedly, on March 13th, as preparations were under way for the seventh game, came a telegram from Dr. Tarrasch saying that two places in the tournament had been reserved, for Marshall and Torre. Naturally these tidings did not please Abraham Kupchik, but he had no choice but to accept the final decision of the Baden-Baden organizers.

Following the suspension of their match, Torre and Kupchik both took part in New York Metropolitan League play, a club team competition. As luck would have it, eight days after the end of the match, they faced each other as first board for their respective clubs. The game excited considerable interest, as it was seen as a sort of unofficial decision to their inconclusive match. This time Torre, free of external pressures, defeated Kupchik in a beautiful game.

At the end of March 1925, Torre and Marshall left for Germany aboard the Cunard liner *Antonia*. During the trip the two became fast friends and played a great many informal games in which each tried out various openings and experimented with unusual systems of attack and defense. In one of these Torre tried out the double-edged line 1.d4 ♘f6 2.c4 ♘c6!?, which he would later use at Baden-Baden against the German master Sämisch. In one blitz game Marshall tried to refute this strange move outright and lost in nine moves:

1.d4 ♘f6 2.c4 ♘c6 3.d5 ♘e5 4 b3(?) e6! 5.♗b2 ♗b4+ 6.♘d2?? ♘e4(–+) 7.♗c1 ♕f6 8.♘f3 ♘g4 9.♖b1 ♘e×f2, 0-1.
White's Queen is lost in three more moves: 10.♕c2 ♘e3 11.♕b2 ♗c3 12.♕a3 ♘c2+.

The opening ceremonies of the Baden-Baden tournament were held April 15th, 1925. Play was conducted in the lavish salons of the city's casino. The prize fund, in German gold marks, was: 1st place, DM 1,500; 2nd, 1,000; 3rd, 700; 4th 500; and 5th, 300. Also, players would receive 20 marks for every game won and 10 for every draw in addition, of course, to meals and lodging in first-class hotels. The tournament concluded May 15th in an impressive victory for the future world champion, Alexander Alekhine. Carlos Torre played somewhat nervously in his international debut. While attaining a respectable 10th place (out of 21), he clearly was more concerned with not losing rather than trying to win.

Baden-Baden, 17 April to 14 May, 1925:

		1	2	3	4	5	6	7	8	9	10	11	12	13	14	15	16	17	18	19	20	21	total
1	Alekhine	*	½	1	½	½	1	1	½	1	½	1	1	½	½	1	1	½	1	1	1	1	16
2	Rubinstein	½	*	½	½	0	½	½	½	½	1	½	1	1	1	1	½	1	1	1	1	1	14½
3	Sämisch	0	½	*	1	½	0	½	½	1	½	1	1	1	½	1	0	½	1	1	1	1	13½
4	Bogoljubow	½	½	0	*	1	0	0	0	1	1	1	1	1	½	0	½	1	1	1	1	1	13
5-6	Tartakower	½	1	½	0	*	½	½	½	1	½	½	½	½	½	1	½	1	½	1	½	1	12½
5-6	Marshall	0	½	1	1	½	*	1	½	½	½	0	½	½	½	½	1	½	1	½	1	1	12½
7	Rabinovich	0	½	½	1	½	0	*	½	0	½	½	½	1	1	½	1	1	1	½	½	1	12
8	Grünfeld	½	½	½	1	½	½	½	*	½	0	0	1	½	1	0	1	½	0	1	1	1	11½
9	Nimzovich	0	½	0	0	0	½	1	½	*	½	1	0	½	1	½	½	1	1	1	½	1	11
10	**Torre**	**½**	**0**	**½**	**0**	**½**	**½**	**½**	**1**	**½**	*	**½**	**0**	**½**	**0**	**1**	**½**	**½**	**½**	**1**	**1**	**1**	**10½**
11-13	Réti	0	½	0	0	½	1	½	1	0	½	*	½	1	1	½	½	½	0	1	0	1	10
11-13	Treybal	0	0	0	0	½	½	½	0	1	1	½	*	½	1	0	½	½	1	1	½	1	10
11-13	Spielmann	½	0	0	0	½	½	0	½	½	½	0	½	*	1	1	0	1	1	½	1	1	10
14	Carls	½	0	½	½	½	½	0	0	0	1	0	0	0	*	0	1	1	½	1	1	1	9
15	Yates	0	0	0	1	0	½	½	1	½	0	½	1	0	1	*	0	0	0	1	0	1	8
16-17	Tarrasch	0	½	1	½	½	0	0	0	½	½	½	½	1	0	1	*	0	½	0	0	½	7½
16-17	Rosselli	½	0	½	0	0	½	0	½	0	½	½	½	0	0	1	1	*	1	0	½	½	7½
18	Colle	0	0	0	0	½	0	0	1	0	½	1	0	0	½	1	½	0	*	0	1	1	7
19	Mieses	0	0	0	0	0	½	½	0	0	0	0	0	½	0	0	1	1	1	*	1	1	6½
20	Thomas	0	0	0	0	½	0	½	0	½	0	1	½	0	0	1	1	½	0	0	*	½	6
21	te Kolsté	0	0	0	0	0	0	0	0	0	0	0	0	0	0	0	½	½	0	0	½	*	1½

The Baden-Baden area's newspapers regularly published games and accounts of the tournament, along with interesting facts and opinions about the players. For example, on April 28th, after the ninth round, a local journal discussed Torre in the following terms:

> The American prodigy Carlos Torre is without doubt an excellent player of whom we will surely hear much in the future, but he has, nevertheless, an obvious character defect, in that he plays too fearfully and nervously, offering draws just when the game is reaching its decisive point, even in positions of advantage for him. He has now gained 5½ points in the first 9 games. We would hope that with the years he is able to master his nervousness and play with more self-confidence and with greater facility.

Immediately after the Baden-Baden event, many of its players moved on to the Czechoslovakian city of Marienbad (also known as Marianske Lazne) for another tournament which began only eight days later. Though its luster was somewhat dimmed by the absence of Alekhine, the field was of similar quality, with 11 of Baden-Baden's players also among the 16 at Marienbad. The tournament ended with Nimzovich and Rubinstein equal 1st. Torre improved greatly to share 3rd and 4th places with Marshall, who had won five games, drawn 10 and lost none, the only undefeated player. Carlos Torre won six, drew eight, and lost one, to Spielmann in the 13th round.

It was gratifying to see Torre return to his natural style of play: more vigorous, bold, and enterprising. Ironically, at Baden-Baden he attempted to play safely and cautiously, and lost four of his 20 games, while at Marienbad he returned to his natural energetic risk-taking style, thereby losing only one of 15 games. As the Mexican saying goes, "When Juan imitates Pedro he is neither Juan nor Pedro."

The Marienbad tournament ended June 8, 1925. Over the next four or five months Carlos Torre was relatively inactive, taking a rest from serious chess. He mostly played exhibition games and simultaneous displays in various parts of the United States, and annotated games for the *ACB*. Then he and Marshall sailed across the Atlantic again.

Marienbad, 20 May to 8 June, 1925:

		1	2	3	4	5	6	7	8	9	0	1	2	3	4	5	6	total
1	Nimzovich	*	1	0	½	½	1	½	1	½	1	½	1	1	1	1	½	11
2	Rubinstein	0	*	½	½	1	½	1	½	1	0	1	1	1	1	1	1	11
3-4	Marshall	1	½	*	½	½	½	½	½	1	1	½	½	½	1	½	1	10
3-4	**Torre**	**½**	**½**	**½**	*	**½**	**1**	**0**	**1**	**1**	**1**	**1**	**½**	**½**	**½**	**½**	**1**	**10**
5-6	Tartakower	½	0	½	½	*	1	0	1	1	½	½	½	1	½	1	1	9½
5-6	Réti	0	½	½	0	0	*	1	0	½	1	1	1	1	1	1	1	9½
7	Spielmann	½	0	½	1	1	0	*	0	½	½	0	½	1	1	1	1	8½
8	Grünfeld	0	½	½	0	0	1	1	*	1	½	½	½	½	½	½	1	8
9	Yates	½	0	0	0	0	½	½	0	*	1	1	½	½	½	1	1	7
10	Opocensky	0	1	0	0	½	0	½	½	0	*	0	½	1	½	1	1	6½
11-12	Przepiórka	½	0	½	0	½	0	1	½	0	1	*	1	0	1	0	0	6
11-12	Thomas	0	0	½	½	½	0	½	½	½	½	0	*	½	1	1	0	6
13-14	Sämisch	0	0	½	½	0	0	0	½	½	0	1	½	*	0	1	1	5½
13-14	Janowski	0	0	0	½	½	0	0	½	½	½	0	0	1	*	1	1	5½
15	Michell	0	0	½	½	0	0	0	½	0	0	1	0	0	0	*	1	3½
16	Haida	½	0	0	0	0	0	0	0	0	0	1	1	0	0	0	*	2½

On November 10 began the great Moscow 1925 tournament, in which Lasker, Capablanca, Bogoljubow, Rubinstein, Réti, and practically all the world's best players with the exception of Alekhine, took part. Marshall and Torre were invited. The tournament would be a much stronger event than Baden-Baden or Marienbad, due not only to the participation of Lasker and Capablanca, but also of the best Russian chess players, who were just beginning to reach their later extraordinarily high level of mastery. Noteworthy Soviet masters included Romanovsky, Levenfish, the veteran Dus-Chotimirsky and USSR champion Boris Verlinsky.

The Moscow tournament was won in emphatic and surprising style by the Ukrainian master Efim Bogoljubow, who had the advantage of prior familiarity with the Russian players, whom he dominated (+7 =2 -0) and against whom he gained the majority of his points. Lasker gained 2nd place with 10 wins, 8 draws and 2 losses (to Levenfish and Torre). Capablanca had a very weak start, playing some games like a sleepwalker. Belatedly, he awoke and finished like a cyclone, winning seven and drawing two of his last nine games, but even so he could not overtake Lasker and much less Bogoljubow, though he did have the satisfaction of defeating the latter in a brilliant game.

Moscow, 10 November to 9 December, 1925:

		1	2	3	4	5	6	7	8	9	0	1	2	3	4	5	6	7	8	9	10	11	total
1	Bogoljubow	*	½	0	½	1	1	0	½	1	1	½	1	1	½	1	1	1	1	1	1	1	15½
2	Lasker	½	*	½	1	½	0	½	1	½	1	1	1	1	1	0	½	1	½	½	1	1	14
3	Capablanca	1	½	*	1	1	½	½	½	½	0	1	0	½	½	½	½	1	1	1	1	1	13½
4	Marshall	½	0	0	*	½	0	1	1	½	0	1	1	1	1	1	1	½	0	½	1	1	12½
5-6	Tartakower	0	½	0	½	*	½	1	½	½	½	½	1	1	1	½	1	1	½	½	½	½	12
5-6	**Torre**	**0**	**1**	**½**	**1**	**½**	*	**½**	**0**	**½**	**½**	**0**	**1**	**½**	**½**	**1**	**½**	**0**	**1**	**1**	**1**	**1**	**12**
7-8	Réti	1	½	½	0	0	½	*	1	0	1	1	½	0	½	½	1	1	½	1	½	½	11½
7-8	Romanovsky	½	0	½	0	½	1	0	*	1	0	½	1	0	0	1	1	1	½	1	1	1	11½
9-10	Grünfeld	0	½	½	½	½	½	1	0	*	1	½	½	½	0	½	1	1	½	½	½	½	10½
9-10	I.-Zhenevsky	0	0	1	1	½	½	0	1	0	*	½	0	1	½	0	½	1	½	½	1	1	10½
11	Bohatirchuk	½	0	0	0	½	1	0	½	½	½	*	½	½	1	½	1	½	½	½	½	1	10
12-14	Verlinsky	0	0	1	0	0	0	½	0	½	1	½	*	1	1	1	½	0	1	½	1	0	9½
12-14	Spielmann	0	0	½	0	0	½	1	1	½	0	½	0	*	1	1	½	½	1	½	0	1	9½
12-14	Rubinstein	½	0	½	0	0	½	½	1	1	½	0	0	0	*	1	0	0	1	1	1	1	9½
15	Levenfish	0	1	½	0	½	0	½	0	½	1	½	0	0	0	*	1	1	½	½	1	½	9
16	Rabinovich	0	½	½	0	0	½	0	0	0	½	0	½	½	1	0	*	1	½	1	1	1	8½
17	Yates	0	0	0	½	0	1	0	0	0	0	½	1	½	1	0	0	*	1	½	0	1	7
18-19	Sämisch	0	½	0	1	½	0	½	½	½	½	½	0	0	0	½	½	0	*	0	1	0	6½
18-19	Gotthilf	0	½	0	½	½	0	0	0	½	½	½	½	½	0	½	0	½	1	*	0	½	6½
20	D.-Chotimirsky	0	0	0	0	½	0	½	0	½	0	½	0	1	0	0	0	1	0	1	*	1	6
21	Zubarev	0	0	0	0	½	0	½	0	½	0	0	1	0	0	½	0	0	1	½	0	*	4½

In contrast, Torre had a phenomenal start, standing clear first after nine rounds. Later he lost to Bogoljubow in a very instructive game and fell back a bit. Even so, entering the 13th round the standings at the top were: 1. Bogoljubow 9½-2½, 2. Torre 8½-2½, 3. Lasker 8-3, 4. Marshall 7½-3½, 5. Tartakower 7-4, 6. Ilyin-Zhenevsky 7-5, 7. Rubinstein 6½-4½, 8. Capablanca 6½-5½. In the last rounds, Torre gave way under the nervous pressure and could not keep up with the pace set by Bogoljubow and Lasker. The Mexican lost inexplicably to players in the lower half of the table and fell to 5th place, being overtaken by Capablanca and by Marshall, who also had a good closing rush. Still, Torre's overall performance fully merited the high praise it received in the Soviet press, and he produced in the process some worthy additions to any "greatest games" anthology.

Torre remained in Moscow for the New Year festivities, and later was invited to Leningrad (now St. Petersburg) to play in a small quadrangular tournament with three of the best chess players of that beautiful city. A professor of the University of Leningrad, Konstantin Derzavin, proposed to Torre that he write a short essay on chess development, or on the educational value of chess. Torre spent two weeks writing. The manuscript was quickly published in Russian under the title *Carlos Torre and Latin American Chess Creativity*. Later this was the basis for a booklet which Torre published in Spanish as *El Desarrollo de la Habilidad en el Ajedrez*, and in English under the name *Development of Chess Ability*. At Leningrad, Torre won both games against Abram Model, who later would be mentor to future world champion Mikhail Botvinnik. His games against Yakov Rokhlin were drawn, while Solomon Gotthilf had the opportunity to avenge his loss to Torre at Moscow by taking both games. It is clear that Moscow had tired Torre more than it had Gotthilf. At Leningrad, Torre also was more concerned with trying out certain experiments with closed opening systems, and with other ideas that he would later detail in his booklet.

After more than ten years' absence, Torre returned to the land of his birth, Mexico. He arrived at Veracruz the 19th of April, 1926, where he was received with great warmth and enthusiasm by the local people. Two days later he moved on to Mexico City, where he stayed more than two months. At the end of July he went north from there to Zacatecas, in central Mexico, and later he traveled southeast to Progreso and Mérida (his birthplace) on the Yucatán peninsula.

During his stay in the capital, Torre played in another double-round quadrangular tournament with three of the best chess players of the Federal District[1]. This time his opposition was considerably less dangerous than in Leningrad, and Torre won all six of his games, most with relative ease.

Mexican Championship, Mexico City 1926:

		1	2	3	4	total
1	**Torre**	**	**11**	**11**	**11**	**6**
2	Araiza	0 0	**	½ 1	1 ½	3
3	Soto Larrea	0 0	½ 0	**	1 0	1½
4	Freyria	0 0	0 ½	1	**	1½

Torre spent almost four months in Mexico. Finally, on August 11 1926 he took ship at the port city of Progreso and sailed back to the United States aboard the Norwegian steamer *Gunni*. After a few days in New Orleans he traveled by train to Chicago, to take part in a strong tournament. This included many of the best North American players as well as Hungarian grandmaster Geza Maróczy, then living in the U.S. The front page of the September-October *ACB* reported:

1 Mexico's equivalent of the USA's District of Columbia.

Chicago, accustomed to doing things in a big way, surpassed herself in the matter of the 27th annual convention of the Western Chess Association, held in that city from August 21 to September 2 in the Red Room on the 19th floor of the Hotel La Salle, and the result was a memorable meeting which will take high rank in American chess history. Aside from the several tournaments of the first rank held in this country, no more important competition has ever been held here than the national masters' tournament in which the best talent available, 13 players in all, competed ...

After what may properly be termed a hair-raising finish, Frank J. Marshall emerged as the winner of the first prize of $650 in the masters tournament ...

During the first few rounds of the masters' tournament the pace was set by Charles Jaffe of New York, and A.J. Fink of San Francisco also gave a good account of himself. Both Marshall and Maróczy were in fine fettle and early gave promise of finishing well up in the list. Torre started poorly by losing to Jaffe in the opening round, but then settled down to serious work and did not lose again until the thirteenth and final round. At that time the Mexican, with a lead of half a point, seemed to be the likely winner, but the cup of victory was snatched from his lips at the very last moment.

Going into the last round, Torre held the lead, but then he unexpectedly stumbled against German-American master Edward Lasker and finished equal second (with Maróczy), ½-point behind Marshall.

Western Masters Tournament, Chicago 1926:

		1	2	3	4	5	6	7	8	9	10	11	12	13	total
1	Marshall	*	0	1	1	½	1	½	½	1	0	1	1	1	8½
2-3	**Torre**	**1**	*	**1**	**½**	**0**	**½**	**1**	**0**	**½**	**1**	**½**	**1**	**1**	**8**
2-3	Maróczy	0	0	*	½	½	1	1	½	1	1	1	1	½	8
4-5	Kupchik	0	½	½	*	1	½	1	1	0	1	1	0	1	7½
4-5	Jaffe	½	1	½	0	*	½	0	1	1	1	1	1	0	7½
6	Kashdan	0	½	0	½	½	*	1	1	½	0	1	1	1	7
7	Factor	½	0	0	0	1	0	*	1	1	½	½	1	1	6½
8	Ed. Lasker	½	1	½	0	0	0	0	*	1	1	1	0	1	6
9	Fink	0	½	0	1	0	½	0	0	*	1	½	½	1	5
10	Banks	1	0	0	0	0	1	½	0	0	*	½	½	1	4½
11	Chajes	0	½	0	0	0	0	½	0	½	½	*	1	1	4
12	Showalter	0	0	0	1	0	0	0	1	½	½	0	*	0	3
13	Isaacs	0	0	½	0	1	0	0	0	0	0	0	1	*	2½

After this tournament, Torre returned to New York, where he suffered a nervous breakdown which put an end to his short but brilliant career. This episode is discussed in more detail in the narrative following Game 106, and in the 1927 *Anahuac* interview with Torre in Chapter III. The November 1926 issue of the *ACB* reported on page 140:

> On October 23, Carlos Torre, Mexican chess champion, sailed from New York on board the steamship *Monterey* of the Ward line bound for his home in Mérida, Yucatán, by way of Havana and Progreso. The young international expert returned to this country in August in order to play in the national tournament at Chicago, where he finished second on a level with Maróczy and just below Marshall. Since his return to New York, Torre has been in poor health and has gone home to rejoin his parents. In the milder climate of his native land he hopes for early recovery.
>
> Antonio Canto, another native of Mérida, and Emilio Deymeier, both members of the Philidor Chess Club of New York, were passengers on the same ship. Before leaving Mexico City, where he won the national championship in a tournament, Torre obtained strong backing for a match with Marshall for the Pan-American championship, but negotiations that were set afoot were discontinued.

After returning to Mexico, Torre lived for a while on a friend's ranch in the state of Tamaulipas, then lived several years in the city of Monterrey, capital of the state of Nuevo León. He was employed there by his brother, a pharmacist, working in his drugstore. For more about Torre's post-1926 life in Mexico, see Chapters III and IV; for now we give just a brief summary.

Later, around 1950, Torre moved to Mexico City. Except for a few people, such as chess master Alejandro Báez, who treated him with sincerity and friendship, most were indifferent or interested only in taking advantage of him. Torre took the occasional odd job, but lived mostly in poverty. He had little or no concern for money, women, or mundane pleasures, and developed an interest in Buddhism. There were recurrences of his nervous breakdowns, sometimes requiring hospitalization. Around 1960 he left Mexico City and returned to the town of his birth.

Finally, in 1973, his friend Báez arranged for him to enter a home for the aged in Mérida. There he lived in clean and peaceful surroundings. An amusing anecdote stems from those years. Torre would receive the occasional visitor, some like Báez true friends, others merely local players who were just interested in getting their games analyzed for free. Torre became increasingly annoyed with these. One such, a minor master but a very conceited man, insisted on showing Torre

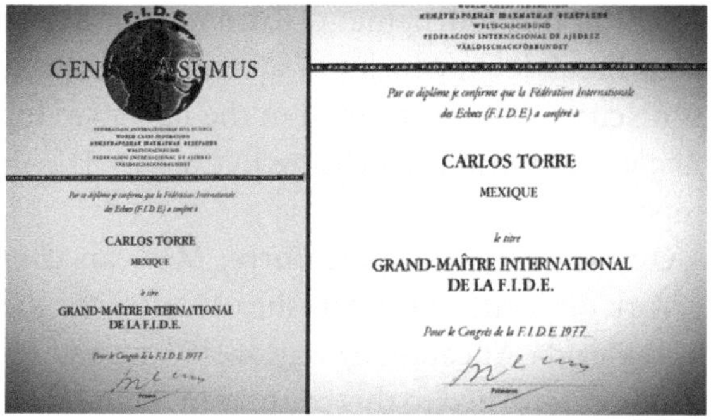

Torre's GM certificate (screen print from the film Torre x Torre)

his latest "brilliancy." Torre reluctantly agreed, on condition that upon spotting his first mistake, the session was over. The vain master, confident he had made no error, agreed. The game, with him playing Black, began 1.e4 e6 2.d4 d5 3.♘c3 ♘f6 4.e5 ♘g8. "What kind of a move is that, ...♘g8?" Torre broke in severely. "Why, it's a move of great subtlety, even Nimzovich played it!" came the indignant reply. "Ah," said Torre calmly, "but Nimzovich was a genius; he could afford to make such bizarre moves and still win. You and I are just ordinary people. Therefore we must respect the principles of development." End of analysis.

In contrast to the way he was lionized in 1926, Torre in his final years was little remembered by his country, except in Mérida and the Yucatán, where he had the status of a beloved elder statesman, and in Mexico City, where he still had friends. The international chess community still remembered him intermittently. He had been granted the honorary title of International Master by FIDE in 1963, and in late 1977 his title was upgraded to the more fitting one of International Grandmaster. However, this news was reported little if at all in Mexico, and to the authors' knowledge, Torre never learned of it in the few months remaining to him. Given his outlook on life and the game he might not have cared, deserved though the honor was. Torre died in Mérida on March 19, 1978. For more on that, see "Don Carlos Torre Repetto: A Chess Player Until Death" in Chapter V.

Chapter II

The Games Section

Analytical Methodology and Technical Details

Before getting to the games themselves, a description of our analytical method is in order. As a scientist must explain his experimental technique in a detailed way that will allow others to replicate it and check the validity of his results, so we do here with our methodology.

All games here, and any notes by human annotators, were examined using Stockfish 14, among the strongest of all analytical engines, rated about 3500 Elo, running on a Dell Inspiron 17 7000 Series with an Intel Core i7-7500U CPU at 2.90 GHz with 16 GB RAM and a 64-bit operating system. The games were accessed via ChessBase 14 with the engine running in "kibitzer" mode.

Informator symbols (*e.g.* +−, −+, ±, ∓, etc.) are used sometimes, but these can be somewhat vague, and so we have generally used the engine's numerical assessments — *e.g.* 28.♖f5 (+2.58), or 35.♘×f3 ♖g7 (-2.25) — to indicate the status of a position, as we consider this more precise and informative. The numbers represent Stockfish's evaluation of the position to the nearest hundredth of a pawn, *e.g.* a difference of exactly one pawn, with no other relevant non-material differences, has the value +1.00 when in White's favor, or -1.00 when in Black's. A position where White is considered better by 3½ pawns (or the equivalent, such as a minor piece) would get the value +3.50, the advantage of a Rook +5.00, etc. With the symbols, a position where White is up Knight for pawn, and another where he's up a Queen, would both get a "+−", but there is obviously a big difference. Most evaluations are also followed by a whole number, *e.g.* "+1.57/30". This means that Stockfish reached a search depth of 30 ply, *i.e.* it looked 30 half-moves beyond the end of the variation. Generally we tried to reach at least 25 ply deep before accepting the evaluation. With very one-sided evaluations the ply depth is usually irrelevant and is not given.

These numbers should not always be taken entirely at face value, especially to the right of the decimal point, and they will vary some from one machine to another, or with the time allowed for analysis, but they are generally valid and reliable, and serve as useful shorthand for assessments and comparisons that would otherwise require extensive detailed explanation.

Diagrams of actual game positions are in 14-point type, while diagrams of analysis variations are in smaller, 12-point type.

Modern engines such as Stockfish can show supposed masterpieces to be seriously flawed, and make players and analysts of the past look quite bad, somewhat like what the Chief of the Nazgûl described in Tolkien's *Lord of the Rings*: "Thy flesh shall be devoured, and thy shriveled mind be left naked to the Lidless Eye."

It is not our intention to devour or shrivel anyone, least of all our hero Torre, for whom we have great admiration and sympathy. We simply aim for analysis that is objectively correct. True, sometimes Stockfish shows that a Torre game did not deserve all the praise it received, but on the other hand it can reveal important, sometimes wonderful possibilities never noticed by the annotators of his day. The point is to find chess truth. Torre himself repeatedly stressed how this was his highest goal. It could not be done in his time, when all analytical engines were inside human skulls. Therefore we like to think he would approve of our using today's technology to come closer to his long-sought, elusive goal.

Game 1

Labatt-Torre

Louisiana Championship, New Orleans 1923

Queen's Gambit Declined [D67]

Leon L. Labatt (1854-1928), a graduate of prestigious Georgetown University, was a prominent New Orleans jurist, and a strong chess amateur who won the Louisiana Championship in 1917. Among his laurels were a 3-1 victory over Adolf Albin in a thematic Evans Gambit match in 1895, a remarkable win over Marshall in 1913,

> That game is worth presenting here.
>
> **Labatt-Marshall**, New Orleans, 1913: 1.e4 e5 2.♘f3 ♘f6 3.♘×e5 d6 4.♘f3 ♘×e4 5.c4 d5 6.♘c3 ♘×c3 7.d×c3 ♗e6 8.♕b3 ♘c6 9.♕×b7 ♘a5 10.♕a6 c6 11.c×d5 ♕×d5 12.♗e3 ♗e7 13.♗e2 0-0 14.♕d3 ♖ab8 15.b3 ♗a3 16.♖d1 ♕×d3 17.♗×d3 ♗b2 18.c4 ♗c3+ 19.♔e2 ♖fe8 20.h3 ♖bd8 21.g4 c5 22.♔f1 f5 23.♗×c5 ♘×c4 24.g×f5 ♘b2? 25.f×e6 ♘×d3 26.e7 ♖d7 27.♗a3 a5
>
> Now begins one of the most extraordinary King walks on record.
>
> 28.♔e2! ♘f4+ 29.♔e3! ♘d5+ 30.♔e4! ♘f6+ 31.♔f5! ♖d5+ 32.♔e6! ♖b5 33.♖d8 ♗b4 34.♗×b4 ♖×b4 35.♖hd1 h6 36.♘e5 ♔h7 37.♔f7 ♘e4 38.♔×e8 ♖b7 39.♔f8 ♘g5 40.e8♕ ♔h8 41.♖1d7 1-0.

and wins against Lasker and Capablanca in simuls and casual games *ca.* 1907-1915. Here we see a changing of the guard as the 18-year-old Torre beats

Leon L. Labatt

Labatt, age 69, on his way to becoming state champion himself.

1.d4 d5 2.♘f3

The use of this move, instead of the thematic 2.c4, is usually prompted by two motives:

(a) White wishes to avoid the dubious but contentious Albin Countergambit (2.c4 e5?!) or,

(b) White wishes to walk more tranquil paths, such as the Colle System (2.♘f3 ♘f6 3.e3 c5 4.♘bd2), the Zukertort System (*e.g.* 2.♘f3 e6 3.e3 ♘f6 4.♗d3 c5 5.b3), or the Torre System (2.♘f3 ♘f6 3.♗g5, of which we will see many examples in this book).

2...♘f6 3.c4 e6 4.♗g5?!

In the first decades of the 20th century this move, seemingly so natural, was recommended and played by Capablanca, who held that White did well to wait until Black moved his c-pawn to either c5 or c6, and that in the latter case the Queen's Knight stood much better on d2 than on c3, the c3 placement being advisable only if Black plays ...c7-c5. According to the great Cuban grandmaster, White should therefore defer the development of his Knight at b1 in favor of 4.♗g5. In contrast, Alekhine strongly criticized 4.♗g5, stating that 4.♘c3 first was correct, as after 4.♗g5 Black plays neither ...c6 nor ...c5, but rather 4...h6!, obliging White to exchange his Bishop, since if 5.♗h4 there follows 5...♗b4+!, and if 5.♗f4, then 5...c5! is a good response.

4...♗e7

An invitation to enter the well-worn paths of the Orthodox Defense. Apart from 4...h6, the text is in fact the only viable alternative in this position;
4...c6? will not do, because then Capablanca's idea 5.♘bd2! works well, and Black cannot enter the famous Cambridge Springs Defense. The Cambridge-style trap attempt 5...♕a5? 6.e3 ♘e4 avails nothing after 7.♗f4. (This book's first edition gave the line 7.♗e2 d×c4 8.♗f4 g5 9.♗c7!, but instead Black can play 8...c3! 9.b×c3 ♘×c3∓.)

5.e3 ♘bd7

Or 5...c6? 6.♘bd2! ♘bd7 7.♗d3 d×c4 8.♘×c4! when White has control over the square e5, as in numerous games of Capablanca's, for example Capablanca-Janowski, New York 1918.

6.♘c3 0–0 7.♖c1

A position seen thousands of times during the first three decades of the 20th century. The principal alternative is 7.♕c2, used various times by Rubinstein with the idea of castling long and later launching a pawn-storm on the King's flank. There were several famous games between Rubinstein and Teichmann with this classic theme. In the late 1930s the Yugoslavian master Pirc discovered that after 7.♕c2 the reply 7...h6! 8.♗h4 c5! is very strong.
Also 7.♗d3 is answered by ...c5!, either immediately or after 7...h6 8 ♗h4. In contrast, the text move is aimed directly at meeting ...c5 with advantage.

7...c6

The classical reply, probably played first in Zukertort-Schiffers at Frankfurt 1887, then by Steinitz against Lasker in their 1894 title match, four times by Showalter in his 1897 match with Pillsbury, and innumerable times since. Mason essayed it against Marshall at Hannover 1902 (it should be remembered that Mason was the author of the first books Torre studied). Today, it is preferred to insert first the moves 7...h6 8 ♗h4 before 8...c6. On the other hand, the so-called "Argentine Variation" 7...a6 was played several times by Alekhine in his 1927 world championship match with Capablanca.

8.♗d3

Rubinstein's move 8.♕c2 was much discussed in the first half of the century. Before 1923 (the year of the present game), Alekhine recommended against 8.♕c2 the reply 8...a6, to which he even appended an exclamation mark in his book *My Best Games of Chess 1908-1923*, game 80. At that time he was unaware of Ståhlberg's strong reply to 8...a6, *i.e.* 9.c5!. In his second volume of best games, Alekhine had a different opinion (a wise man knows when to change his mind) and gave the correct response as 8...♘e4! (*1924-1937*, game 89). This strong reply was introduced to high-level international play in Grünfeld-Wolf, Mährisch-Ostrau 1923, though it had been seen nearly two years earlier in Illa-Reca, Montevideo 1922.

8...d×c4 9.♗×c4 ♘d5 10.♗×e7 ♕×e7

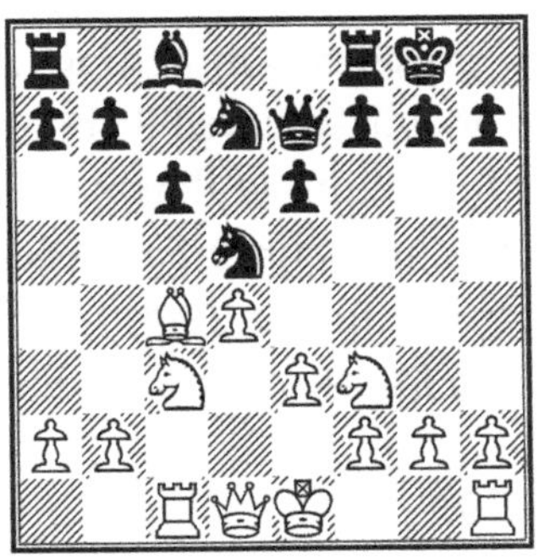

11.0–0

An interesting alternative is 11.♘e4!?, a favorite of Alekhine for a time (*e.g. 1924-37*, Game 7 vs. Treybal).

Even so, Alekhine himself later recognized that 11.0–0 was more correct and less risky. In the 6th game of the 1927 Buenos Aires match, Alekhine played 11.♘e4, to which Capablanca responded 11...♕b4+ 12.♕d2 ♕×d2+ 13.♖×d2 ♖d8. However, in the 16th game Capablanca found the most accurate defense: 11...♘5f6! 12.♘g3 ♕b4+ 13.♕d2 ♕×d2+ 14.♔×d2 b6! 15.e4 ♖d8 16.e5 ♘e8, which produced a draw in 24 moves.

11...♘×c3 12.♖×c3

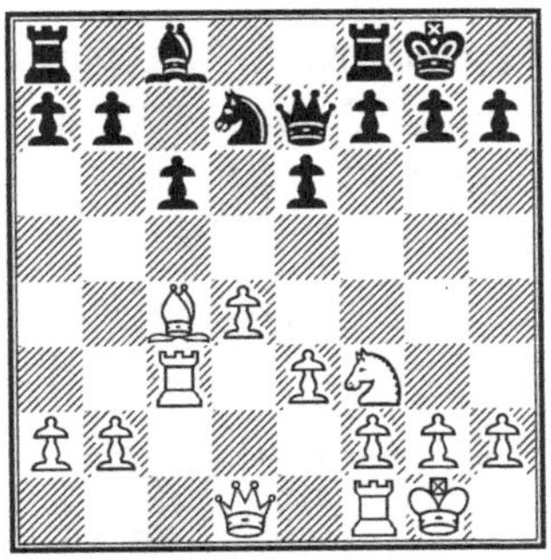

This is the critical position of the old Orthodox Defense, rarely encountered these days, but which at the time of this game was practically a chess player's daily bread. The position is ripe for change because Black can free his game with 12...e5, which he usually does at this point.

12...b6

A somewhat passive move, though on the whole not bad. Dusting off the theory of those bygone days, one finds the normal line to be 12...e5 13.♕c2 e4 14.♘d2 ♘f6 15.♖c1, or alternatively 13...e×d4 (somewhat better than

13...e4) 14.e×d4! ♘f6 15.♖e1 ♕d6 16.♘g5 ♗g4 (??; better 16...g6),

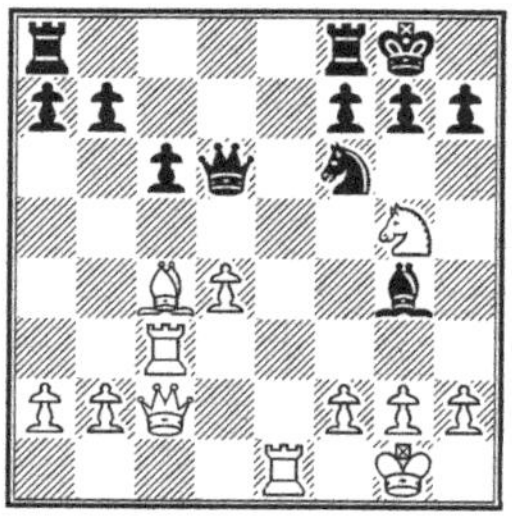

followed usually by 17.♕b3 or 17.♖g3. It is surprising that this was accepted theory for decades; it is not until Müssig-Müller, Wallertheim 1993, that ChessBase shows White playing the refutation 17.♗×f7+! (17.♘×f7 works equally well) 17...♖×f7 18.♘×f7 ♔×f7 19.♕b3+ ♔f8 20.♕×b7 ♖b8 21.♕×a7 ♖×b2 22.♖×c6! ♕×c6 23.♕a3+ ♔g8 24.♕×b2,

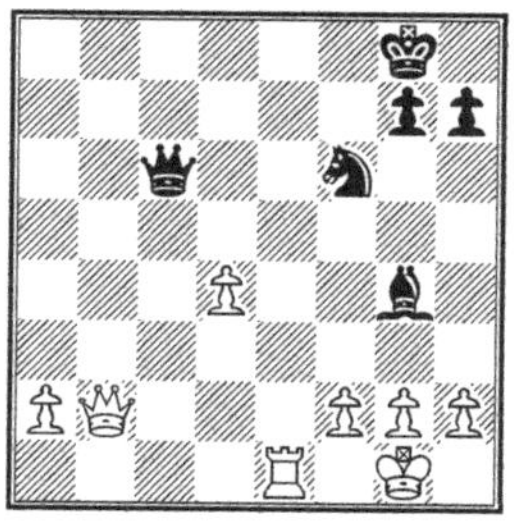

and with ♖+5♙ vs. ♗+♘+2♙, White should have a winning endgame.

The text move 12...b6 appears to have been a favorite of the young Torre (we will see it again in Game 12, Lear-Torre). However, though the Mexican master won both games, it is clear he was by no means content with the passive positions thus obtained. After the Lear game, Torre never again returned to the Orthodox Defense, and it is evident that it was ill-suited to his enterprising and vigorous style. Returning to the game:

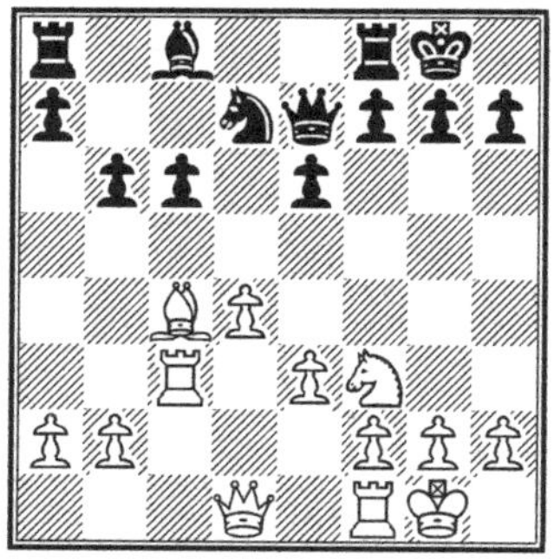

13.♕e2

The normal line, played also by Lear in Game 12. In the same position, however, Capablanca preferred 13.♕c2 (*e.g.* vs. H. Steiner, Budapest 1928). That game continued 13...c5 (13...♗b7 is also playable) 14.d×c5 ♘×c5 15.b4 ♘a6?! 16.a3, and the Cuban won in 37 moves. Correct was 15...♘d7! 16.a3 ♘f6, followed by ...♗b7, with equality. The idea behind 13.♕e2, logically, is to reply to ...♗b7 with 14.♗a6!, a well-known maneuver intending an exchange of light-squared Bishops, so as later to exploit the weaknesses of those squares. Many games have been won using this simple strategy introduced by Oldrich Duras in the early 1900s.

13...♖d8

A move never played before, according to the databases. Deserving attention was 13...a5!?, so as to prevent White's planned maneuver 14.♗a6.

Also possible, albeit more passive, was 13...♗b7, a move that had been played before at least four times. A likely continuation would be 14.♗a6 ♗×a6 15.♕×a6 c5 16.♖fc1 ♖fd8 17.♕b5, and White has only a very slight edge.

14.♗d3

A move difficult to explain. 14.♗a6! immediately is indicated.

14...♗b7

Black can instead reply 14...c5 15.♗e4 ♖b8 16.♖fc1 ♘f6! (but not 16...♗b7? 17.♗×b7 ♖×b7 18.♕a6 ♘f6 19.♘e5!. However, Torre decides on a different course, less active and energetic.

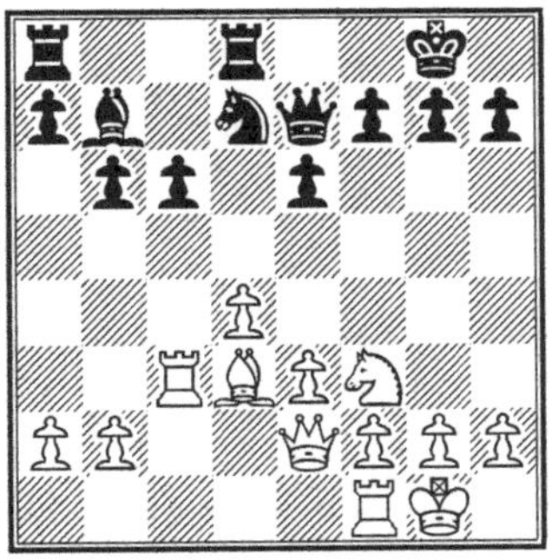

15.♗a6

But this is inconsistent with his previous move. Now 15.♗e4! seems clearly best. If 15...♖ac8 (what else?) 16.♖fc1 ♘b8 17.♘e5 the c-pawn is doomed, *e.g.* 17...c5 18.♗×b7 ♕×b7 19.♕f3! ♕×f3 20.g×f3 f6 21.♘d3 etc. The text move entails a loss of time allowing Torre a respite.

15...♗×a6 16.♕×a6 c5

Finally Black appears to have equalized, or nearly so, though White retains a slight initiative on the queenside.

17.♕e2?

Planless play. The Queen stood well on a6.

17...♖ac8 18.♖fc1 ♖c7?!

Correct was 18...e5 with equality.

19.d×c5?!

Letting Torre off the hook. White could have regained his queenside initiative with 19.b4 ♖dc8 20.b×c5 b×c5 21.♕a6±.

19...♖×c5

Better than 19...♘×c5 20.b4 ♘a6 21.♖×c7 ♘×c7 22.♘d4 △ 23.♘c6.

20.a3

The most logical move, since b2-b4 is necessary to deny the black Knight access to c5. The position is very even and with correct play should soon result in a draw. However, now comes the truly interesting part of the game, the only reason we have included it in this collection. Torre notices a potential weakness which he exploits in a very instructive manner. It is clear that both contestants want to make an outlet for their Kings, to avoid unpleasant surprises on the back rank. Both ...g7-g6 by Black and g2-g3 by White will be perfectly safe, though careless play by White can leave the hole created by g2-g3 open to exploitation. This in fact does happen when White allows Black to advance his e-pawn with impunity.

20...g6 21.g3

After 21.h3 a draw was the probable result. This is also playable, but requires a bit more care on White's part.

21...e5!

22.b4

The dangers of neglecting silicon-based advice are illustrated by our note to this move in the first edition. We wrote "now 22.e4 was insufficient due to 22...f5! *[s/b ??]* 23.e×f5 g×f5 24.♖×c5 ♘×c5 25.♕c4+ ♔f8 26.b4 ♘d3 27.♖c2 e4 and Black's position is superior." Kingston likes to call this sort of multi-error note a Charlie Fox. Instead of 22...f5??, any reasonable move, *e.g.* 22...♖×c3, 22...♔g7, 22...f6, or 22...♖dc8, keeps the game dead even. The flaw in 22...f5?? shows up several moves later, after 23.e×f5 g×f5 24.♖×c5 ♘×c5,

when White plays not 25.♕c4+?! but 25.♘×e5! (25.♕×e5 is also quite good.) 25.♖d4 (if 25...♘d7? 26.♕c4+) 26.b4 ♖e4 27.♕a2+ ♕e6 28.♕×e6+ ♘×e6 29.♘c6 and Black will be two pawns down after either 30.♘×a7, or 29...a6 30.♘e7+ ♔f7 31.♘×f5. The original line has other errors the reader may wish to work out.

Returning to the actual game:

22...♖×c3 23.♖×c3 e4 24.♘d4 ♘e5 25.♘c6 ♕c7

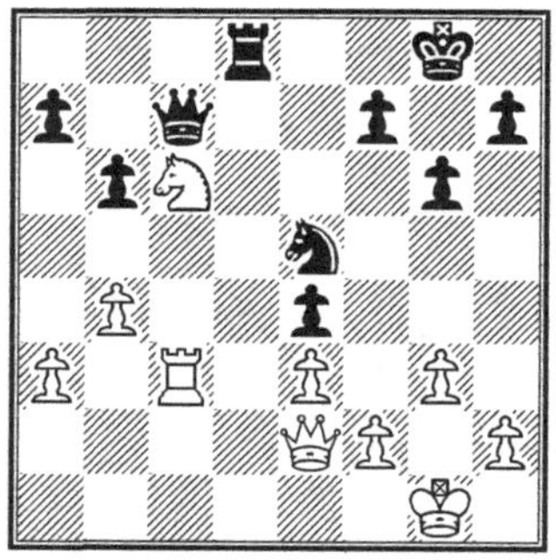

26.♕c2??

A major blunder. Two better alternatives were available:

(a) 26.♘×d8, when Black may still be able to eke out a win, but with difficulty in a position where both attack and defense require considerable precision, *viz.* 26...♕×c3 27.♕b5□ ♔f8 28.♕d5□ ♔e7 29.a4 ♕c7!□ (threatening 30...♕d6 31.♕×e4 ♔×d8−+), and now either:

(a1) 30.b5 ♕d6, and White has nothing better than 31.♘c6+ ♘×c6 32.♕×e4+ ♘e5 33.f4 f5 34.♕×e5+ ♕×e5 35.f×e5 with a pawn ending Black should win because of his superior King position (-4.85/32); or

(a2) 30.♘b7 f5! 31.♕g8 Forced; Black threatened 31...♕c1+ 32.♔g2 ♘f3 and after a few spite checks White will have to give up his Queen to prevent mate (-9.87/31). 26.♔g2 ♕×b7 27.♕×h7+ ♘f7 28.♕×g6 ♕d7, and with a Knight for two pawns Black should eventually win the ending;

(b) Best, however, was 26.♔g2! (preventing the threatened 26...♖d2! 27.♕×d2 ♘f3+ −+) 26...♖d6 (26...♖d3 27.♖c1 ♖d6 lacks independent significance) 27.b5□ ♘d3 (27...♘×c6? 28.♕c4+−) 28.♕g4, and Stockfish sees Black as having a slight advantage but no clear way to win (-0.40/37). But after 26.♕c2?? this is all academic. Torre now wraps up efficiently.

26...♘f3+ 27.♔f1 ♖d3!

Not 27...♘×h2+?? 28.♔g2 ♘f3 29.♘×d8+−.

28.h3

If 28.♖×d3 e×d3 and the Knight is lost.

28...♕d7 0–1

White resigns in the face of the threat of 29...♖d1+ followed by mate. If 29.♖×d3 e×d3 30.♕c3 ♕×h3#.

Game 2

Torre-Beihoff

Manhattan CC Championship, New York 1924

Queen's Gambit Declined [D30]

German immigrant George Beihoff (1879-1937) was a regular at the Manhattan Club, though never one of its top players. Despite an early opening inaccuracy, Torre has little trouble with him here.

1.d4 d5 2.c4 e6 3.♘f3 ♘f6 4.♗g5 ♗e7

As mentioned in the previous game, correct here is 4...h6.

5.e3 0–0

More flexible than 5...♘bd7, which we saw in the previous game. Now Black can enter the Lasker Defense after 6.♘c3 ♘e4 7.♗×e7 ♕×e7 8.♖c1 etc., or the Orthodox Defense after 6.♘c3 ♘bd7.

6.♘bd2?!

A timid, naïve move which works well only if Black replies 6...c6?. The move ♘b1-d2 is in fact feasible if White has not already moved his c-pawn, as then against the natural ...c7-c5 he can play c2-c3, entering the Torre Attack, a line which months later the Yucatán master would perfect. The correct move in this position is, naturally, 6.♘c3.

6...h6

Also worthwhile is 6...c5 immediately, but its effect is heightened by the interpolation of 6...h6 first.

7.♗h4 c5

Black has already equalized, perhaps even has a slight advantage.

8.♗d3

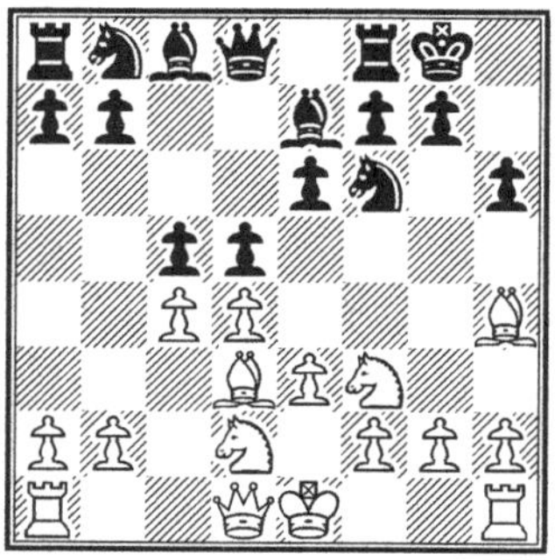

8...d×c4

There was no need to resolve the central tension so quickly. An enterprising alternative would be, for example, 8...♘c6!?, or safe and sound was 8...♘bd7, *viz.* 9.0–0 d×c4 10.♗×c4 (10.♘×c4 is also good, as White need not fear 10...b5?! 11.♘ce5 ♕b6? 12.♗e4! ♘×e4 13.♗×e7 ♖e8 14.♘×d7 ♗×d7 15.♗×c5±) 10...b6 11.♕e2 (if 11.♕a4 a6!) 11...♗b7 (not now 11...a6 12.a4!) 12.♗a6 ♗×a6 13.♕×a6 ♘d5 with good play for Black.

9.♘×c4

Torre follows Capablanca's idea of controlling e5 with the two Knights (see notes to previous game).

9...♘bd7

The attempt to stir up complications by 9...b5? fails to 10.♗×f6! and after either 10...g×f6, 10...♗×f6, or 10...b×c4, 11.♗e4! wins the Exchange.

10.0–0 b6 11.♕e2 ♗b7 12.♖fd1

It is said that in such positions one always moves the wrong Rook. The obvious moral, therefore, is to decide after long reflection which Rook to move, then move the other. Joking aside, more sensible would be to play first 12.♖ac1, then decide whether the King's Rook belongs at d1 or e1, since there is the chance that White may be saddled with an isolated d-pawn.

12...c×d4

Now White must recapture with the Knight, to justify placing his Rook on d1.

13.♘×d4 ♘d5?

A number of other moves were preferable, including 13...a6, 13...♘c5, 13...♖c8, and 13...♘e4.

14.♗g3!

Excellent. Torre now plays the remainder of the game with his accustomed energy, though gaining the point will still require a few more mistakes by his opponent. White has pursued his strategic theme of control of e5; in addition his Bishop on g3 controls an important diagonal without opposition. The threat of ♘c4-d6 hangs in the air, awaiting an appropriate moment.

14...♘7f6?

Relatively best was 14...♘c5 15.♗c2 ♕e8 (if 15...♗a6 16.♘c6 with the same result) 16.♘d6 and White gains the Bishop pair. Other moves are much worse, *e.g.* 15...♗f6? 16.♘d6 ♗a6 17.♕e1 with e4-e5 looming. The text is a serious mistake.

15.♖ac1

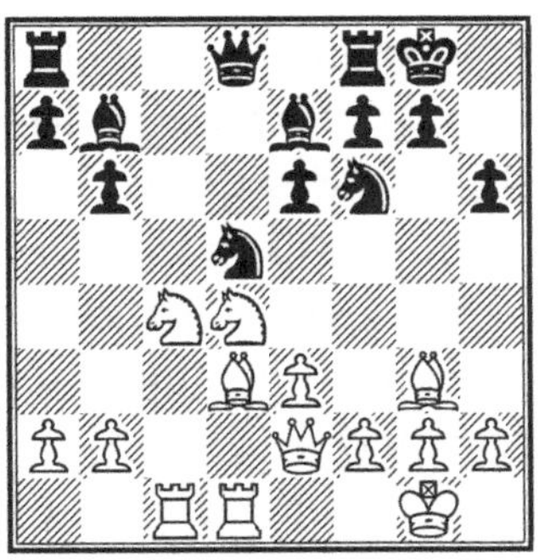

Also very strong was 15.♘b5 threatening 16.e4 ♘b4 17.♗b1 ♕c8 18.♘cd6 ♗xd6 19.♘xd6 ♕d7 20.♘xb7 ♕xb7 21.♗d6 winning the Knight or the Exchange.

15...a6

It is superfluous to give this move a question mark. Black hopes to create a haven for his discomfited Queen by a7-a6, b6-b5 and ♕d8-b6, but he has no time for such a slow plan. Still, there is nothing better, *viz.* 15...♘b4 16.♗b1 ♕d5 17.e4! ♘xe4 18.♘e3 ♘xg3 19.hxg3 ♕e5 20.f4 ♕a5 21.♖c7 ♗a6 22.♕g4 ♗f6 23.♘xe6! etc. (+4.13/25), or 15...♖c8 16.e4 ♘b4 17.♗b1 ♕e8 18.a3 ♘c6 19.♘b5 and Black cannot cope with the multiple threats of 20.♘d6, 20.♘c7, or 20.e5 (+3.97/27).

16.e4 b5

If 16...♘b4 17.♗b1 ♘d7 (White threatened 18.♘xe6. 17...♕e8 would meet with the same reply.) 18.♘d6 ♗c8 19.♘xf7!! ♖xf7 20.♘xe6 ♕e8 21.♘c7+–.

17.♘e5

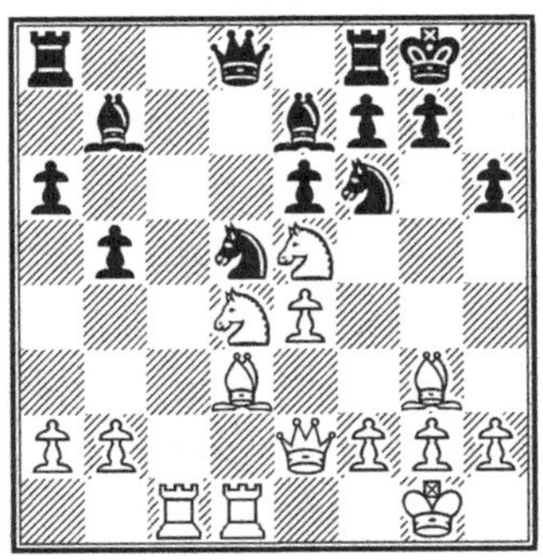

17...♘b4

Objectively no worse than other moves, and less bad than some, but Black is lost whatever he tries. Attempts to complicate and "fish in troubled waters" fall short, *e.g.* 17...♘f4 18.♗xf4! ♕xd4 19.♖c7! (much stronger than 19.♘c6) 19...♗d6 20.♘f3 ♗xf4 21.♘xd4 ♗xc7

22.e5 ♘d5 23.♕e4 ♖fd8 (if 23...g6? 24.♘×e6!) 24.♕h7+ etc.

18.♗b1 ♖c8

Less bad but still inadequate was 18...♕b6 19.a3 ♖ad8 20.♘g6! f×g6 21.♗c7! ♕a7 22.♗×d8 ♖×d8 23.e5 ♖×d4 24.e×f6 ♗×f6 25.♕×e6+ ♔h7 26.a×b4+−.

19.♖×c8

In later years Torre might well have gone for the even stronger 19.♘×e6, but the text, though less flashy, is quite sufficient.

19...♕×c8 20.a3 1-0

After 20...♘c6 21.♘d×c6 ♗×c6 22.♖c1 White wins the pinned Bishop and more. A game which began interestingly, but was tarnished at the end by Beihoff's mistakes.

Game 3

Tenner-Torre

Manhattan CC Championship, New York 192

French Defense [C12]

Though born in what is now the Ukraine, Oscar Tenner (1880-1948) was of German extraction. Playing in the reserve section of the Mannheim 1914 tournament at the outbreak of World War I, Tenner was for a while interned there with Alekhine and Bogoljubow, and made a chess set out of bread to pass the time. Joining the Austrian Army, he was twice wounded. After the war he emigrated to America, and became a fixture at the Manhattan Chess Club, where his skill at speed chess provided him with a small income. He was an outspoken man of unshakeable self-confidence and a brash, romantic style of play that gained him brilliancy prizes and victories over such noteworthy masters as Isaac Kashdan, Al Horowitz, and Fedor Bohatirchuk (Denker, p. 45). He also may have been the earliest known victim of Alekhine's occasional carelessness with facts. A 1911 game between the two, which Tenner claimed was drawn (see Fred Reinfeld's *The Unknown Alekhine*, p. 93), was reported as being played in 1907 and won by Alekhine in his book of *Best Games 1908-1923* (gm. 90, note to move 7)[1]. Here Torre handles Tenner in a style of which Alekhine himself would be proud.

---

1 The alleged game went 1.e4 e5 2.♘c3 ♘c6 3.♗c4 ♘f6 4.d3 ♗c5 5.f4 d6 6.♘f3 ♗g4 7.♘a4 e×f4 8.♘×c5 d×c5 9.♗×f4 ♘h5 10.♗e3 ♘e5? 11.♘×e5 ♗×d1 12.♗×f7+ ♔e7 13.♗×c5+ ♔f6 14.0-0+ ♔×e5 15.♖f5#.

1.e4 e6 2.d4 d5 3.♘c3 ♘f6 4.♗g5 ♗b4

The McCutcheon variation, though probably ultimately sound, is one of the more difficult lines for Black in the French Defense. Today few GM-level French experts venture this old system, which grants White too many positional concessions. However, it has a certain appeal to those who thrive on adversity. It had quite a vogue in the first three decades of the 20th century, for example being played four times by Marshall (1907) and three times by Tarrasch (1908) in their world title matches with Lasker, and later by such luminaries as Capablanca, Alekhine, Bogoljubow, and Réti. It was a favorite of Torre's; this is only the first of several examples in this book.

5.♘ge2

Suggested by Viennese master Heinrich Wolf, and introduced in master play by Jacques Mieses of Leipzig in 1907.
However, 5.e5! presents Black with the most difficulties: 5...h6 6.♗d2 ♗×c3 7 b×c3 (Fischer once recaptured with the Bishop against Petrosian at Curaçao 1962, the Armenian grandmaster winning instructively.) 7...♘e4 8 ♕g4

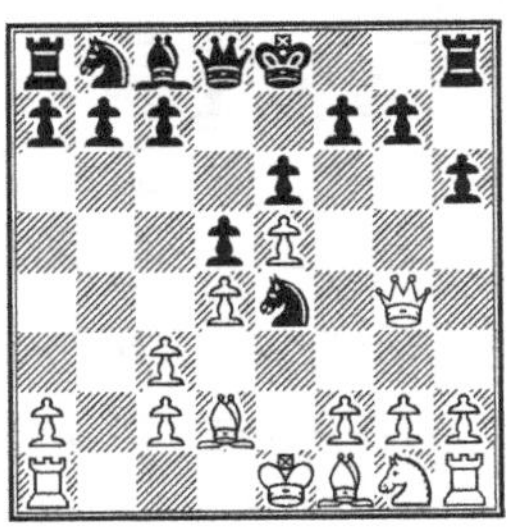

and now Black must choose between 8...g6 and 8...♔f8, in either case making his second positional concession (the first being exchange of his good Bishop). In compensation Black gets somewhat uncertain queenside attacking chances, which nevertheless on occasion do grant him a strong initiative.

5...d×e4 6.a3 ♗e7

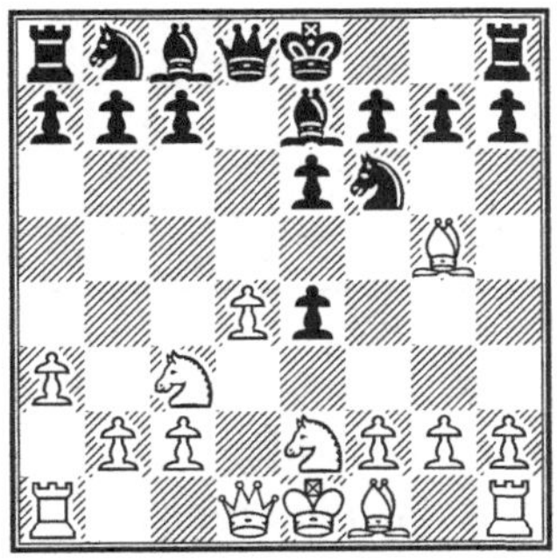

This creates a position very similar to the Burn (or delayed Rubinstein): variation: 3...♘f6 4.♗g5 d×e4 5.♘×e4 ♗e7. In such lines, after ♗×f6 Black can recapture with the pawn to open the g-file, then develop his Queen's Bishop on b7 and castle queenside, obtaining a dynamic position with chances for counterplay, though not without danger.

7.♗×f6 g×f6 8.♘×e4 b6

At New York 1924, Réti essayed the immediate 8...f5 against Emanuel Lasker; there followed 9.♘4c3 ♗d7 10.♕d2 ♗d6 11.0–0–0 ♕e7 12.♘g3 with the better game for White.

9.♕d2

More common is 9.♘2c3, as we will see elsewhere in the book, *e.g.* Samuels-Torre (Game 5) or te Kolsté-Torre (Game 34).

9...♗b7 10.♘2c3 c6!

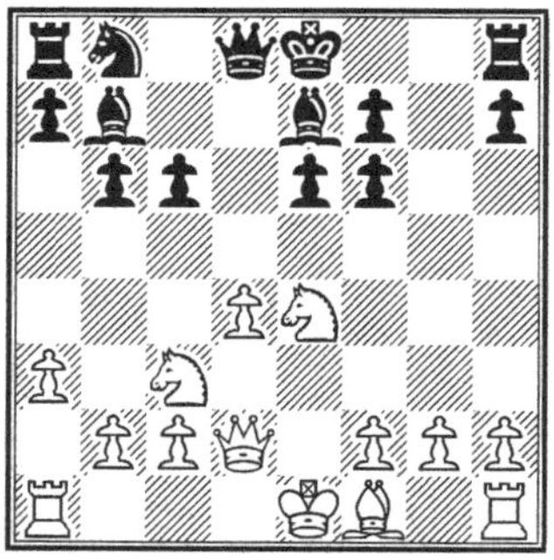

A move virtually necessary at this point, in order to play ...♘b8-d7 without fear of d4-d5 in reply. This type of position is relatively easy for Black to play, in the sense that only one very clear plan is open to him. After completing his development, he will expel the central white Knight with ...f6-f5, then apply pressure on the kingside (whether or not White has castled there), often with the advance of the h-pawn. This game is in fact a model realization of that strategy.

11.f4

If 11.0–0–0 there follows 11...f5 12.♘g3 ♕d6 with equality. Not 12...f4? 13.♘h5! ♕c7 (worse is 13...♖g8 14.♕d3 ♖g6 15.♕f3 ♘d7 16.♘×f4 +–) 14.♘g7+ ♔f8 15.♘h5 and White both denies Black castling and wins a pawn. With the text, White decides to restrain Black's pawns. However, now Black's strategy becomes crystal-clear: he will pressure the f4-pawn with his pieces until White is obliged to defend it by g2-g3, at which point the g-pawn becomes a perfect target for the h7-h5-h4 advance. White cannot stem this advance by h2-h4 without incurring serious weakness on the g-file.

11...f5 12.♘g3 ♘d7 13.♗e2

Taking advantage of the fact that for the moment the black Knight obstructs the Queen, thus 13...c5 can be answered by 14.d5.

13...♘f6 14.♗f3 ♕c7 15.0–0–0 0–0–0 16.♕e3 ♗d6 17.♘ge2 ♔b8

It is interesting to see how Torre is attentive to possibilities on both flanks, not just on his intended target the kingside. With the text Black prepares the eventual maneuver ...c5 followed by ...c×d4 in combination with ...♘g4. It is essential during this maneuver that White not be able to capture on b7 with check.

18.g3 h5 19.♔b1 ♘g4

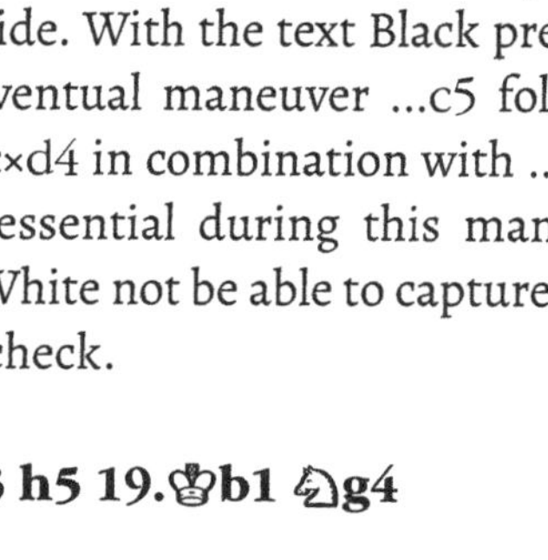

Stronger than the immediate 19...h4, because White would not be obliged to respond with 20.g×h4. Black sees that his kingside action will be much more effective if he can first induce White to trade off his light-square Bishop before opening the position.

20.♗×g4?

Tenner falls in with Torre's plan. Essential was 20.♕g1!, when after 20...a6 (not 20...c5?! 21.♘b5!=) 21.♘c1 c5 22.♗×b7 c×d4 23.♕×d4 we reach this position:

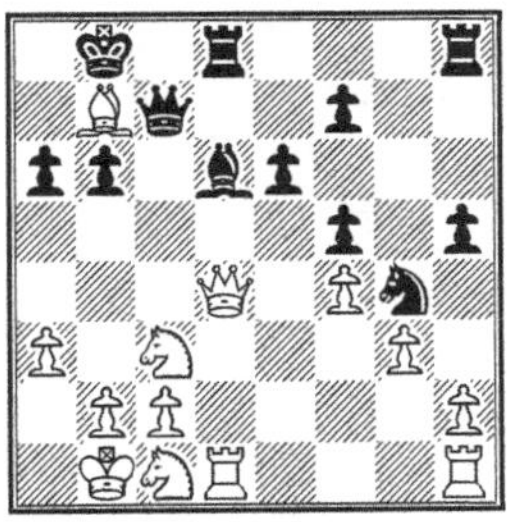

And now:

(a) Of course not 23...♗×a3?? 24.♕a4+−;

(b) if 23...♔×b7 24.♕d3 ♕c6 25.♕e2 ♗×a3 26.♘d3 (26.b×a3?? ♕×c3−+) 26...♗d6 White has lost a pawn but by no means the game (-0.28/27);

(c) 23...♕×b7 24.♕d2 ♗e7 (24...♗×a3?? 25.♕×d8+) 25.♘d3, and Black does not even get the pawn.

In either (b) or (c), his kingside pressure may yet bear fruit, but it will be a long road.

20...h×g4

White is seriously weak on the light squares and his position very delicate. He now tries to free himself, but this serves only to accelerate Black's advance.

21.h4

The least evil. After the next-best move, 21.♖d2, play might continue 21...a6 22.♘a4 ♗e7 23.♕f2 c5 24.♖hd1 c4 25.d5!? ♗×d5 26.♘×b6 ♗c5 27.♘×d5 ♗×f2 28.♘×c7 ♖×d2 29.♘×a6+ ♔a7 30.♖×d2 ♔×a6 31.♖d6+ ♔b7 32.♖d7+ ♔c6 33.♖×f7 ♖×h2, and though at the moment White is a pawn up, Stockfish indicates the ending is clearly won for Black (-5.40/28).

21...g×h3 22.♘g1 h2

Black augments his kingside pressure. The weak, immobile g3-pawn is the target.

23.♘f3 ♖h3

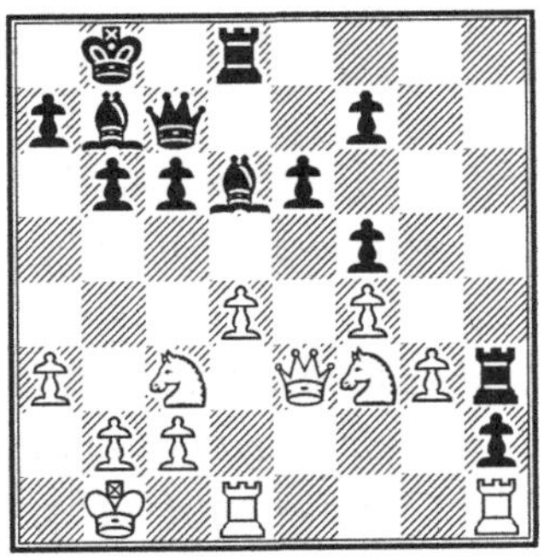

24.♘e2?

Though seemingly reinforcing White's defenses, this meets with a surprising refutation.

Necessary was 24.♕f2 when best play for both sides proceeds 24...♖g8 25.♖×h2 ♖g×g3 26.♘e5 f6 27.♘e2

♖×h2 28.♕×h2 ♖g8 29.♘d3, when Black with his extra pawn and Bishop pair stands better, but the engines indicate White can hold on for quite a while (-1.36/27).

A more speculative continuation is 24...♗×f4!? 25.g×f4 ♕×f4 26.♖d3 c5 27.d5□ ♖dh8 28.♘e2 ♕h6 29.c4□, when Black's potential kingside majority of three passed pawns may be adequate compensation for the sacrificed piece (-0.59/29). In any event, after the text White is lost.

24...♖×g3!

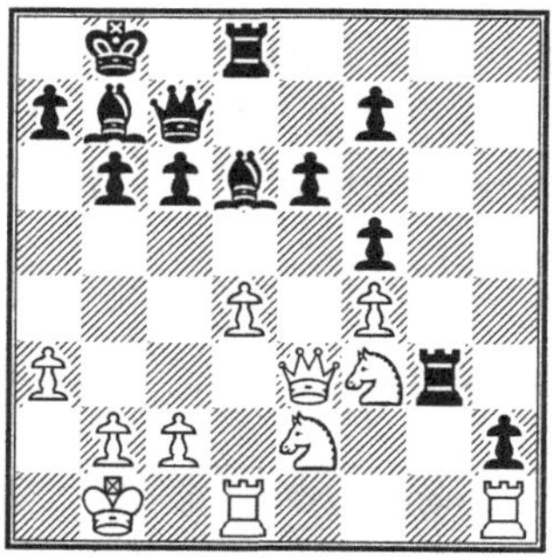

A wrecking-ball move! At the outset of Black's attack against the g3-pawn at move 18, few would suspect that it would fall in such spectacular fashion. But in fact this was just one of three ways Black could win. Perhaps even stronger were

(a) 24...c5! 25.♖×h2 c×d4 26.♘e×d4 ♖×g3 27.♘b5 (forced; if, say, 27.♖f2 ♗c5 28.♕e2 ♖×f3 29.♖×f3 ♗×d4 30.♖h3 ♕×f4−+) 27...♖×f3 28.♕d2 ♕c5 29.♘×d6 ♗e4 30.♘×e4 ♖×d2 31.♘×d2 ♕d4 △32...♖×f4−+; or

(b) 24...♖dh8 25.♕f2 c5 26.♖×h2 ♖×h2 27.♘×h2 ♕c6! 28.♖f1 ♕g2 29.♘f3 ♕×f2 30.♖×f2 ♖h1+ 31.♔a2 f6 (-2.92/30).

25.♘×g3 ♗×f4 26.♕e2 ♗×g3 27.♘×h2

There was no salvation in 27.♖hf1 c5 28.d×c5 ♖×d1+ 29.♖×d1 b×c5 and White has nothing better than 30.♘×h2 ♗×h2−+.

27...c5 28.♘f3

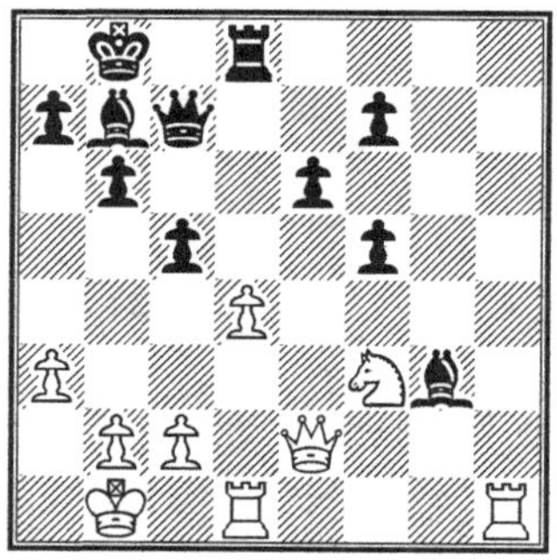

28...c×d4?!

Black has more than ample compensation for the Exchange; his Bishops literally sweep the board. But much stronger was 28...♕f4! 29.♖hf1 ♕e4! 30.♕d2 (or 30.♕×e4 f×e4 31.♘g1 f5−+) 30...f4 and Black can win as he pleases (-2.59/26).

29.♖h7?

This allows Torre to wrap up decisively. White missed a chance to resist strongly with 29.♖h3!□ ♗e4 30.♘×d4 ♔b7 (to prevent 31.♖×g3 ♕×g3 32.♘c6+ ♗×c6 33.♖×d8+, when a draw is likely

(0.00/35)) 31.Ka2 Be5 32.Nb5 Qe7 33.R×d8 Q×d8 and if Black can still win, he has quite a long way to go (-0.24/28).

29...e5 30.Ng5 Bd5
White could well have resigned here.

31.b3
A last-ditch swindle attempt was 31.Qb5, inviting 31...Rc8 32.Q×d5 Q×c2+ 33.Ka2 Q×d1?? (33...Qc4+! −+) 34.Q×f7 and mate in four. But 31...Bf4 would preserve the win.

31...Bf4 32.Nh3 Be3 33.Rf1 Be4
Threatening 34...d3.

34.Nf2 B×f2 35.Q×f2 d3 0-1
White resigns in view of the double threat of 36...d×c2+ and 36...d2. An excellent example of positional attack by Torre.

Game 4

Torre-Frink

Manhattan CC Championship, New York 1924

Barry Attack [D00]

1.d4 Nf6 2.Nf3 g6
Orrin Frink, Jr., a native of Brooklyn, New York, graduate of Columbia University, was famous in the United States as an openings expert and correspondence player. He won the 1923 Brooklyn CC championship. The defensive system he employs here was rather a novelty in those days, though today it is common knowledge.

3.Nc3
Today 3.c4 is considered best, but at that time opinions were divided. The text is by no means an error; for example it was played by Edward Lasker against Maróczy at New York 1924. In his excellent and entertaining book *Chess Secrets I Learned From the Masters* he describes (page 293) everything that went through a master's head when confronted in those days with 2...g6.

3...d5!
Best, and first seen in Tartakower-Wahltuch, London 1922. It is curious that Alekhine criticized this move in his book of the New York 1924 tournament. Annotating Capablanca-Yates, he wrote: "This reaction against 3.Nc3 does not seem positionally opportune, because the King's Bishop thereafter may be given an outlet only by means of time-robbing efforts." He added "More in the spirit of the fianchetto is the move 3...d6 employed by Maróczy in two games in this tournament with the object of attacking as soon

as possible White's center with ...c5." Alekhine's summary judgement today appears overly dogmatic, but what we regard now as "modern chess" was then still under development; his comments should not suffer unduly severe criticism. After 3...d6, 4.e4 would enter one of the main lines of the Pirc Defense.

4.♗f4

In recent years this deployment has come to be called the Barry Attack[1]. It came highly recommended in GM Aaron Summerscale's 1998 book *A Killer Chess Opening Repertoire*. Though never as popular as lines where White plays c2-c4 before moving his Queen's Knight, it has had some distinguished adherents over the years, such as Marshall, Colle, Bogoljubow, Tartakower, Bondarevsky, Kholmov, Yusupov, Aronian, and especially England's Mark Hebden.

4...♗g7 5.e3 0–0 6.♗d3

In this kind of position the move h2-h3 is sometimes played, with the idea of making a retreat for the Queen's Bishop in the event of ...♘f6-h5. But here it is not a good idea: 6.h3 c5 7.♗e2 b6 8.0–0 ♗b7, and the tempo lost by 6.h3 in this case enables Black to play a Catalan with colors reversed. The maneuver h2-h3 and ♗f4-h2 works better in situations where White has not moved his Queen's Knight, as then he can reinforce his center with c2-c3 and develop the Knight at d2, as in the London System. More often seen in later years is 6.♗e2, about which Summerscale gushes "White has a crude, almost barbaric plan from this position: shove the h-pawn up the board and attempt to tear the black King limb from limb!" However, the present game develops along quite different lines.

6...c5 7.0–0

Colle-Euwe, 5th match game, Amsterdam, 1928, continued 7.d×c5 ♘bd7 8.0–0 ♘×c5 9.♗e5 ♗g4 10.h3 ♘×d3 11.c×d3 ♗×f3 12.♕×f3 e6, which is no particular improvement on the text.

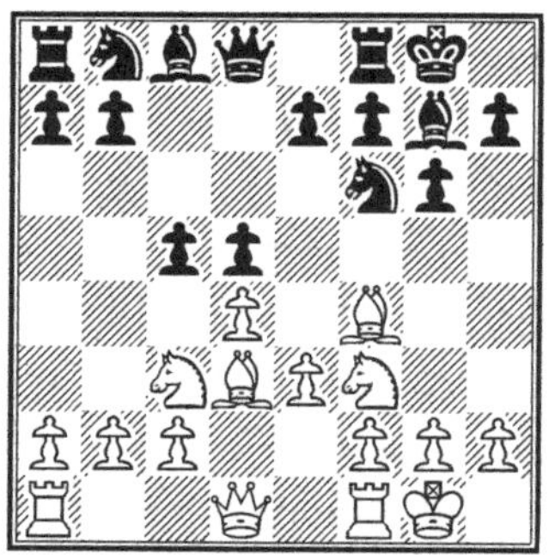

7...c4?!

1 Oddly, the name does not derive from anyone named Barry playing the line. According to IM Gary Lane, when British GM Julian Hodgson was playing it in the 1980s, he was acquainted through his younger brother with someone named Barry, who habitually pretended to greater knowledge than he actually had. The opening having some elements of bluff, Hodgson thought this Barry's name fit it well. Another version says it comes from Cockney rhyming slang, the phrase "Barry White, load of shite."

A superficially attractive advance, but in fact dubious, even sloppy. The advanced pawn can be easily attacked with b2-b3, leaving Black nothing better than to launch a premature attack on the queenside. It was preferable to maintain the central pawn tension, for example 7...♘bd7 8.d×c5 ♘×c5 with an even game. Smyslov-Anagnostopoulos, London 1989 (yes, even Smyslov played the Barry once!) continued 8.a4 b6 9.a5 ♗b7 10.a6 ♗c6 11.♘e5 ♘×e5 12.♗×e5 ♘d7 13.♗×g7 ♔×g7 14.f4 and White eventually won (1-0, 44).

8.♗e2 ♘c6 9.♘e5!

This, in combination with White's next move, is the best way to refute the imprudent 7...c4?!. If now 9...♗f5 there follows 10.♘×c6 b×c6 11.♗e5! with a clear superiority, but Black chooses an even worse line.

9...♕b6?

Black's Queen will find nothing to do on b6, and the move prompts White to play what he intended anyway.

10.b3 c×b3 11.a×b3 ♗f5

Naturally not 11...♘×e5?? 12.d×e5 ♘d7 13.♘×d5+-.

12.♘a4! ♕d8

Demonstrating the uselessness of 9...♕b6.

13.♘×c6 b×c6 14.♗a6!

White's last several moves aim at immobilizing Black's weaknesses before attacking them, in keeping with the precepts of Nimzovich: first restrain, then blockade, and finally destroy. The weak pawns at a7 and c6 are now fixed and will soon both be blockaded, before White proceeds to the third stage. The text move forces Black to retreat his only active piece, the Queen's Bishop, due to the threat of 15.♗b7.

14...♗c8 15.♘c5 ♘d7

Black hurries to trade off the annoying blockaders, but White's heavy pieces are ready to take their places, in accordance with Nimzovich's maxim *Changez les bloqueurs*.

16.♘×d7 ♕×d7

Of course not 16...♗×d7? 17.♗b7.

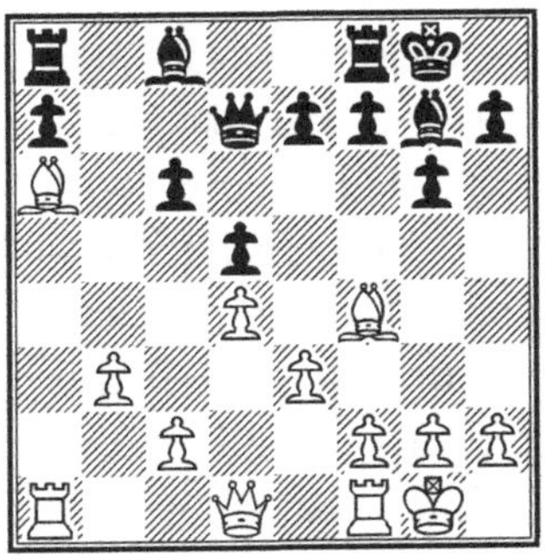

17.♖a5?!

Torre hastens to bring a Rook to bear on c5, keeping the blockade in force, but he overlooks a finesse available to Black. Correct was 17.♗e2!, avoiding an exchange of Bishops, and if 17...c5 then 18.♖a5 forcing 18...c×d4 19.e×d4, and though the black c-pawn is no longer there to be blockaded, White has inescapable long-term pressure on the a-pawn, and after it disappears White's passed b-pawn will be the key to victory.

17...♖e8?

Black could have solved his most pressing problems by 17...♗×a6! 18.♖×a6 c5.

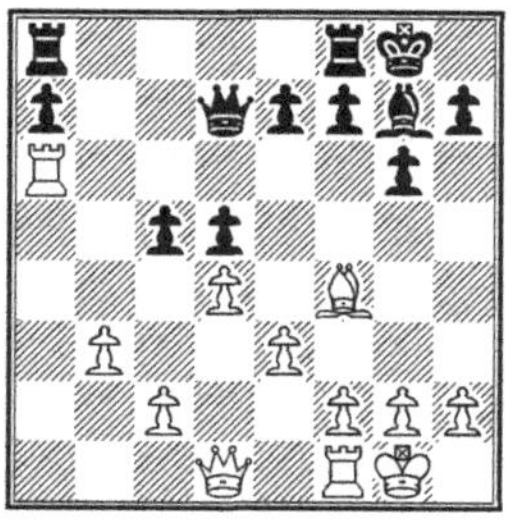

The key difference between this and the note line above is that now the exchange of light-squared Bishops is a definite plus for Black. It removes an active, attacking white piece, while getting rid of an encumbrance that hindered Black's piece coordination. With the useless Bishop off the board, Black could have connected his Rooks and conducted a much better defense of his queenside. And if 19.d×c5 ♕b5! 20.♖a4 ♕×c5 the game is quite even (+0.11/39).

18.♕d3

Best still was 18.♗d3 or 18.♗e2, but after the text the Bishop exchange would not be especially good for Black, *viz.* 18...♗×a6 19.♖×a6 (19.♕×a6 is also good) 19...c5? 20.d×c5 and White will keep the pawn. And if 19...♕b7 20.♖a5 the c-pawn stays blockaded (+1.56/25).

18...e5!?

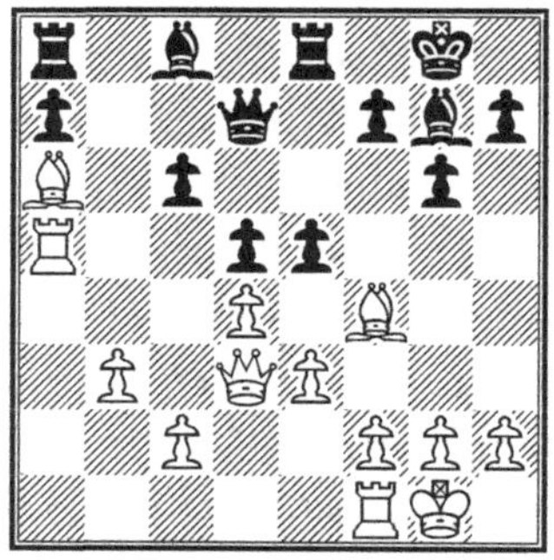

Relatively best now that Black has missed his chance to equalize. The only way to resist White's queenside assault is by energetic action in the center, otherwise Black will soon die of suffocation.

19.♗×e5

19.d×e5 would just transpose, since if Black tries 19...♖e6(?) to lessen the scope of White's Bishop, he happily plays 20.♕c3! and stays a pawn ahead, *viz.* 20...♕e7? 21.♗×c8 ♖×c8 22.♖×d5!, or 20...♗×a6 21.♖×a6 and if 21...♖ae8 22.♖fa1 etc. (+3.16/26), or 21...c5 22.♖a5 ♗f8 23.♖d1 (+2.69/23).

19...♗×e5 20.d×e5 ♗×a6

Somewhat better was 20...♖×e5, which would induce White to play 21.♗×c8 ♖×c8 when Black's Rook has developed with tempo compared to the game, and if 22.♕c3? d4! 23.e×d4 ♖×a5 24.♕×a5 ♕×d4=.

21.♖×a6

Also worth consideration was 21.♕×a6, to occupy c5 with the Rook before Black can advance and sacrifice the c-pawn. On the other hand, a6 is a better post for a Rook than a Queen. All things considered, White is one tempo short of being able to obtain an ideal blockading position and thereby a won game.

21...♖×e5 22.♕c3
Preparing ♕c3-c5 and ♖f1-a1, with a severe bind.

22...♖e6 23.♖fa1
White apparently did not give serious thought to Black's upcoming pawn sacrifice. In hindsight, more precise was 23.♕c5! to prevent it (blockade first, then destroy).

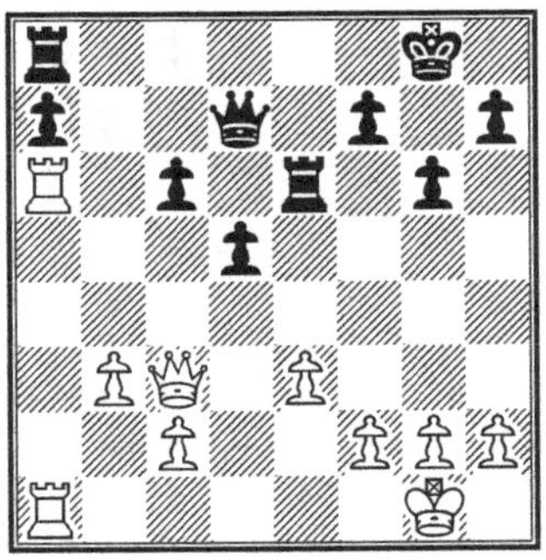

23...c5?!
he wrong pawn to sacrifice! Better counterplay came from 23...d4!? 24.e×d4 (not 24.♕×d4? ♖d6 25.♕c4 ♖d1+ 26.♖×d1 ♕×d1+ 27.♕f1 ♕×c2=) 24...♖d8 25.♖d1 (if 25.♖×a7? ♕×d4=) 25...♕b7 26.♖aa1 ♕b6 27.♖d3 ♖e4 28.♖ad1 h5 and suddenly it's Black who is pressuring a weak pawn. White still stands better (+1.65/26), and objectively should still probably win, but the task has become harder because of the suddenly active black Rooks. After the text White's superiority remains unquestioned.

24.♖×e6
After 24.♕×c5?! ♖c8! (better than 24...♖×a6 25.♖×a6 ♖c8 26.♖×a7 ♖×c5 27.♖×d7 ♖×c2±) 25.♕×a7 ♕×a7 26.♖×a7 ♖×c2 we would have a difficult "all Rook endings are drawn" kind of position.

24...♕×e6 25.♕×c5 ♖c8 26.♕×a7 ♖×c2 27.♕d4!□

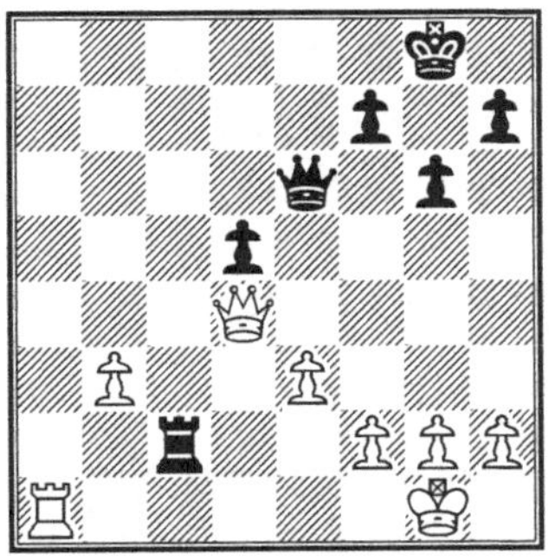

The only move to retain mastery of the position.

27...♕c6?!
Somewhat better was 27...♖c8, in keeping with the principle that in the endgame the side down in material should seek to exchange pawns, not pieces. However, White's advantage would then still be great (+2.84/32).

28.g3
The best way to forestall back-rank mate.

28...♖c1+?

It was still not too late to steer away from the Rook exchange by, say, 28...♕b7.

29.♖×c1 ♕×c1+ 30.♔g2 ♕c6

The Rook exchange has pushed Stockfish's assessment up to +6.06. A passed pawn advances much more easily when supported by a Queen, as here, rather than by a Rook.

31.b4

Passed pawns must be pushed!

31...h5

All Black can do is hope to stir up some trouble on the kingside, perhaps finding a perpetual check.

32.h4 ♕b5 33.♕c5 ♕d3 34.b5 ♕e4+

35.♔h2

In the previous edition we gave this a "?" and mistakenly flagged it as the move that let the win slip away. In fact it is perfectly playable. Still, 35.♔f1, as we recommended back then, might have made things a bit easier: if 35...♕h1+ 36.♔e2, or 35...♕b1+ 36.♔e2 ♕b2+ 37.♔f3 ♕f6+ 38.♔g2, or 35...♕d3+ 36.♔e1 ♕b1+ 37.♔e2. In each case Black quickly runs out of checks.

35...♕f5 36.e4

Not strictly necessary; 36.♔g2 or 36.♔g1 would win too. But though the text gives up a pawn, Stockfish likes it best.

36...♕×e4 37.b6 d4 38.♕c8+

38.♕c4, 38.♕c7, and 38.♕b4 were a bit better (about +11 to +12), but the text also wins (+6.27/27).

38...♔h7

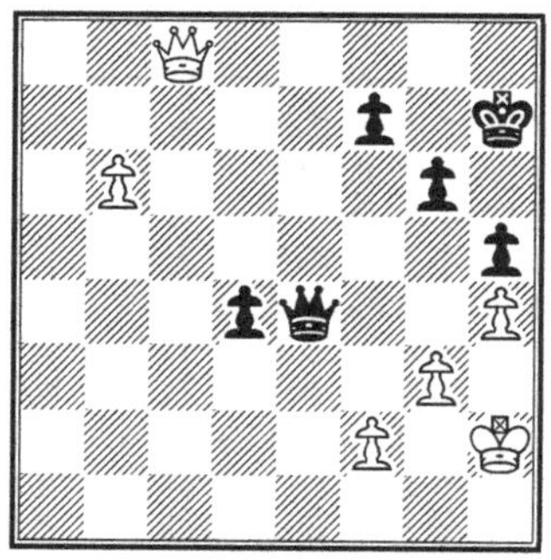

39.b7?

A lamentable mistake, probably induced by time pressure, that throws away the win. Instead, victory was to be had by 39.♕d7! ♕f3 40.♕×d4, or 39.♕c4! ♔g7 40.♕b4!□ ♕b7 41.♕×d4+ etc.

39...♕e2!

The only move that draws! Black in fact now finds a series of "only" moves to salvage the half-point.

40.♕c6 ♕b2□ 41.♕d5 ♔g7□
Not 41...♕xf2+?? 42.♕g2+–.

42.♕e5+ ♔h7□ 43.♕d5 ♔g7□ 44.♔g2 d3□ 45.♔f3 ♕e2+
45...d2 also draws.

46.♔g2 ♕b2□ 47.♕×d3 ♕×b7+ 48.♕f3 ♕b4 ½-½
Despite Torre's error at move 39, a truly interesting game, both for his well-conducted queenside attack, and Black's stubborn, courageous defense.

Game 5

Samuels-Torre

Manhattan CC Championship, New York 1924

French Defense [C12]

Though many of the players Torre faced at the Manhattan CC in 1924 did not have international reputations, they should by no means be considered weak. While Lester Samuels, a prominent New York attorney, was never much more than a casual club player, he was strong enough to defeat future U.S. Champion and International Master Herman Steiner in match play in 1931, losing not a single game in the process. The first eight moves of this game are identical to those of Game 3.

1.e4 e6 2.d4 d5 3.♘c3 ♘f6 4.♗g5 ♗b4 5.♘ge2 d×e4 6.a3 ♗e7 7.♗×f6 g×f6 8.♘×e4 b6 9.♘2c3
This seems better than 9.♕d2 as in Game 3. Another playable alternative is 9.g3 ♗b7 10.♗g2 c6 11.♕d2 f5 12.♘4c3 ♘d7 etc.

9...♗b7
Bogoljubow-Alekhine, New York 1924 continued 9...f5 10.♘g3 ♗b7. Ironically, Alekhine later criticized his own 9...f5, pointing out that after 10.♘g3 ♗b7 the advance 11.d5! is very strong. Bogoljubow, nevertheless, did not see this opportunity, playing 11.♗b5+ c6 12.♗c4 ♘d7 13.♕e2, and the game ended in a draw after 85 moves.

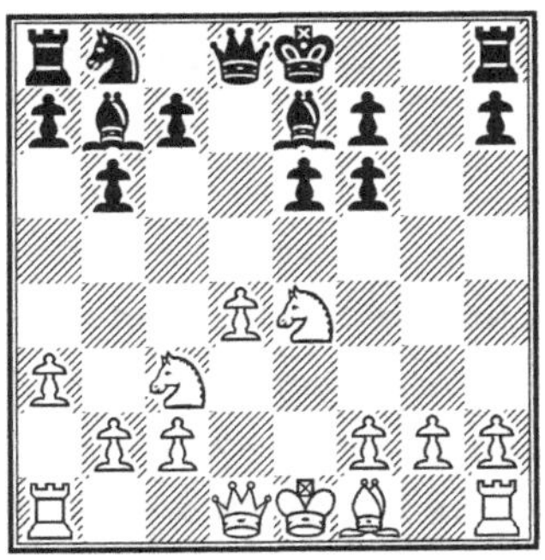

10.♗b5+?
At Baden-Baden 1925, the Dutch master te Kolsté played the much better 10.♕f3. That will be examined in Game 34. The text allows Black to play with tempo a move he intended already, and ultimately win material.

10...c6

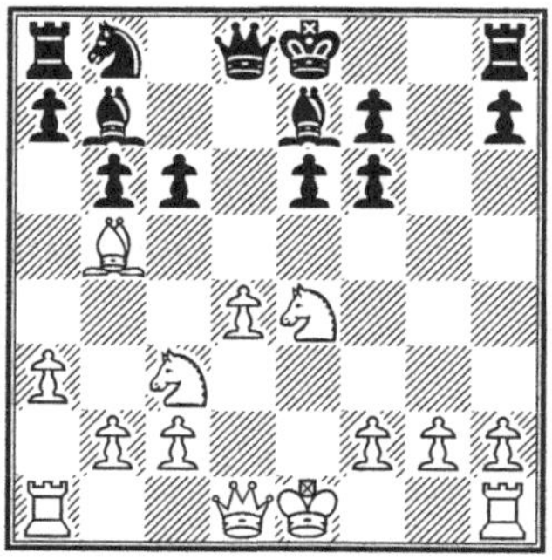

11.♗e2

Alternatives are no better, *e.g.* 11.♗c4 f5 12.♘g3 b5 (not 12...♗f6?! 13.♕e2! ± △14.♘xf5 or 14.0–0–0) 13.♗b3 ♖g8 14.♕d3 a5 (discouraging queenside castling) 15.0–0 ♘a6 16.♖fe1 ♘c7 (-1.72/29).

If 11.♗a4 f5 12.♘g3 b5 13.♗b3 transposes to the same variation.

11...f5 12.♘g3 ♗f6

This works better than in the previous note because the white Queen cannot get to e2.

13.♗f3?

Compounding his previous error. There was some hope of counterplay with 13.♘h5, *e.g.* 13...♗xd4 14.♕d3 ♗e5 15.♕e3 ♕d4 16.♕h6 ♖g8 17.f4 ♗h8 18.♖d1 ♕c5 19.♕xh7.

13...♕xd4

Not 13...♗xd4? 14.♘b5 ♗xb2 15.♘d6+ ♔e7 16.♘xb7 ♗c3+ 17.♔f1 ♕c7 18.♘xf5+! exf5 19.♕e2+∞. Besides avoiding that trap, the text forces an exchange of Queens, much to Black's advantage now that he is a pawn up.

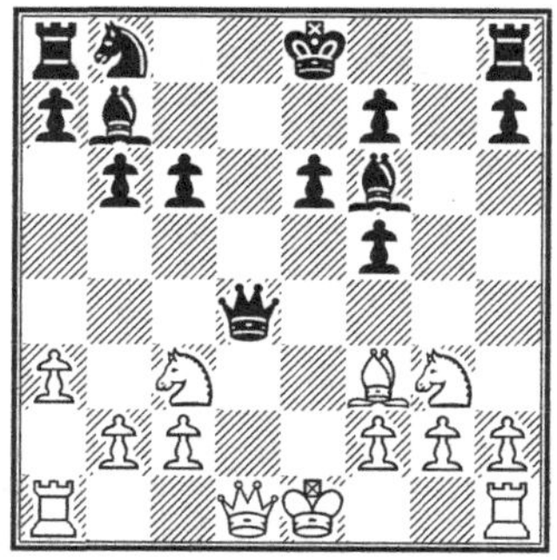

14.0–0

Better may have been 14.♕xd4, as after 14...♗xd4 15.0–0–0 [not 15.♘b5? ♗xb2 16.♘c7+ (or 16.♘d6+ ♔e7 17.♘xb7 ♗xa1 –+) 16...♔d8 17.♘xa8 ♗xa1 –+] 15...♗xc3 16.bxc3 ♘d7 we reach the same position as in the game, except that White's King is on not g1 but c1, where it can help defend the weak queenside pawns.

14...♕xd1 15.♖axd1

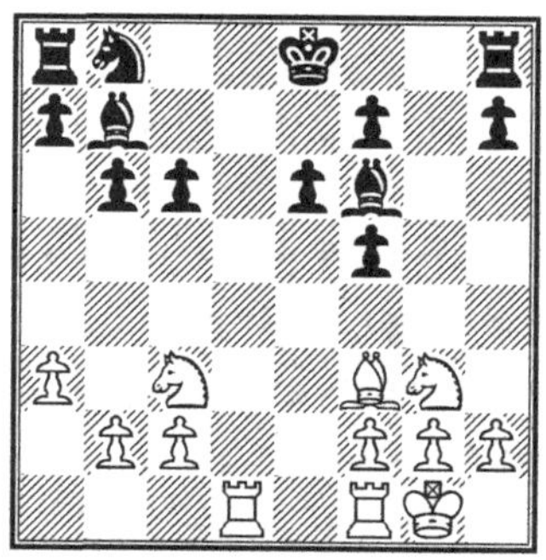

15.♗xc3!

A difficult and important decision. Black trades an excellently posted Bishop for a less active Knight, to weaken the enemy pawn structure.

One sees this theme occasionally in the games of great masters, perhaps the most notable example being Quinteros-Fischer, Buenos Aires 1970, when the American grandmaster exchanged his fianchettoed Bishop for a Knight at c3 on the sixth move and won in masterly fashion.

Quinteros-Fischer, Buenos Aires 1970
1.c4 g6 2.♘c3 ♗g7 3.♘f3 c5 4.d4 c×d4 5.♘×d4 ♘c6 6.♘c2 ♗×c3+!

7.b×c3 ♘f6 8.f3 d6 9.e4 ♗e6 10.♗e2 ♖c8 11.♘e3 ♕a5 12.♗d2 ♘e5 13.♕b3 ♘fd7 14.f4 ♘c5 15.♕c2 ♘c6 16.0–0 ♕a4 17.♕b1 ♘a5 18.e5 d×e5 19.f×e5 0–0 20.♖f4 ♘d7 21.♘d5 ♖fe8 22.♕e4 b5 23.♖×f7 ♔×f7 24.♕h4 ♔g7 25.♘×e7 ♕c2 26.♕h6+ ♔h8 27.♖c1 ♕×c1+ 28.♗×c1 ♖×e7 29.c×b5 ♘c4 30.♕h4 ♖f7 31.♕d4 ♔g8 32.♗f4 ♖c5 33.♗f3 ♖×b5 34.h3 ♘c×e5 35.♗a8 ♖f8 36.♗×e5 ♘×e5 37.♕×a7 ♗d5 38.♗×d5+ ♖×d5 39.♕e3 ♖a5 40.♕e2 ♖fa8 41.a4 ♘f7 42.h4 ♖×a4 0-1.

Lesser mortals are often hesitant to trade Bishops for Knights, but the great masters do not hesitate to do so when an important advantage is gained.

16.b×c3 ♘d7 17.♖d6 ♔e7 18.♖fd1 ♘e5!

Defending the Knight by 18...♖hd8 was also good, *viz.* 19.♗×c6 ♗×c6 20.♖×c6 ♖ac8 21.♖×c8 ♖×c8 and the doubled c-pawn is already under siege.

19.♗×c6?

It is superficially attractive for White to regain his lost pawn this way, but it comes at the price of serious positional concessions. Black in fact hoped to provoke this response, having seen that he can more easily capitalize on White's doubled, isolated c-pawn after the c-file is opened, exposing it to pressure by the black Rooks. Correct for White here was 19.♗e2, keeping his pieces active. Now the reverse will occur, Black's pieces becoming active and White's passive. In Rook endings in particular, passivity is almost always fatal.

19...♗×c6 20.f4 ♘c4 21.♖×c6

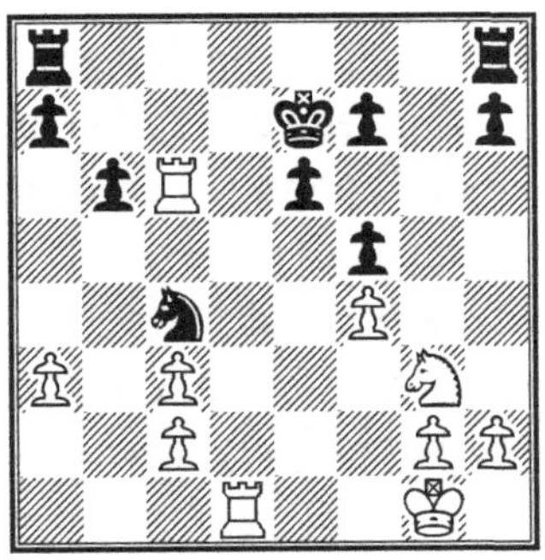

21...♖hc8

Much better than 21...♘×a3?! 22.♖c7+ ♔f6 23.♖dd7 ♖hf8 24.♖×a7 ♖×a7

25.♖×a7 ♘b5 26.♖a4 ♘×c3 27.♖c4 ♘d5 when getting the win is much more difficult for Black.

22.♖×c8 ♖×c8 23.♖a1

If 23.♖d4, best is 23...b5. The alternative 23...♘×a3 is playable, but leads to pawn rather than piece exchanges, *e.g.* 24.♖a4 ♘b5 (much better than 24...♘×c2?! 25.♖×a7+) 25.c4 ♘c3 26.♖×a7+ ♔f6 27.♖a6 ♖×c4 28.♖×b6. The drawback of 23.♖a1 is that it reduces the Rook to a purely passive role.

23...♘e3 24.♘e2 ♘d5!

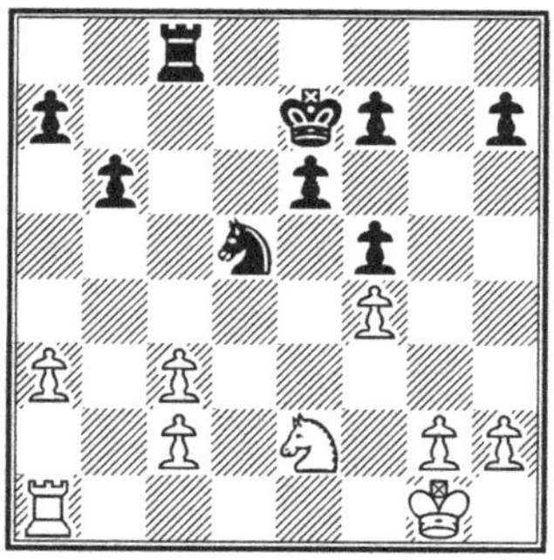

As Tarrasch wrote, weak pawns are undesirable not so much because they may be captured, but rather because they demand too much care and protection from one's pieces.

24...♘×c2 was quite playable, but the text leads to getting the Knights off the board and simplifying Black's task.

25.♔f2 ♘×c3 26.♘×c3 ♖×c3 27.♖a2 ♔d6

White is at a severe disadvantage in this Rook ending. The rest is a matter of technique.

28.♔e2 ♔c5 29.♔d2 ♔c4 30.a4 h5 31.a5 b5!□

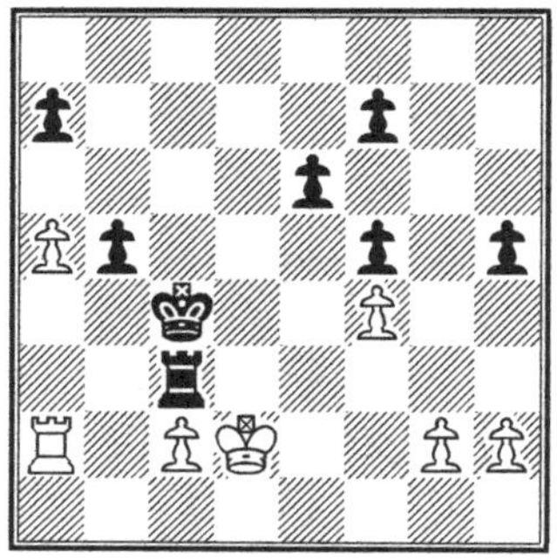

Allowing the Rook no scope. Any other move would enable White to draw.

32.♖a1 h4 33.♖g1 ♖a3 34.g4 h×g3 35.h4

White finally gets a passed pawn and some room for his Rook to roam, but it is too little, too late.

35...♖f3 36.h5 a6 37.h6 ♖×f4 38.♖×g3 ♖h4 39.♖g7 ♖×h6 40.♖×f7 ♔b4 0-1

An exemplary game, demonstrating Torre's strategic acumen and endgame technique, this time unmarred by a late error.

Game 6

Torre-Schapiro

Manhattan CC Championship, New York 1924

Queen's Gambit Accepted (in effect) [D53]

Lithuanian-born Morris A. Schapiro (1903-1996), just age 21 at the time of this game, would become a respected investment banker and America's leading expert on government bonds. He negotiated several major bank mergers in the 1950s. He became quite wealthy, something unusual among chess players. A Manhattan CC regular, he was also of master strength in chess, winning the club championship in 1921 and 1922, leading the Columbia University team to four national collegiate championships, and in match play defeating the strong American players Charles Jaffe and Oscar Chajes. Here he demonstrates similar strength against Torre. The opening moves are of no particular note, and are given without commentary. Our main focus will be on the interesting endgame which arose after the first 24 moves.

1.d4 d5 2.c4 e6 3.♘f3 d×c4 4.♘c3 ♘f6 5.♗g5 ♗e7 6.e3 0–0 7.♗×c4 c5 8.0–0 ♘c6 9.♕e2 c×d4 10.♖fd1 e5 11.e×d4 e×d4 12.h3 h6 13.♗e3 ♗c5 14.♘b5 ♕e7 15.♘b×d4 ♗d7 16.♖ac1 ♘×d4 17.♗×d4 ♕×e2 18.♗×e2 ♗×d4 19.♘×d4 ♖ac8 20.♗f3 b6 21.♗b7 ♖×c1 22.♖×c1 ♖d8 23.b3 ♗e6 24.♘×e6 f×e6

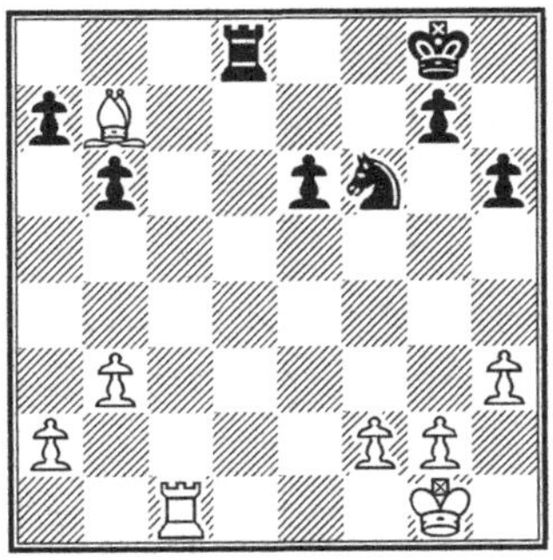

An evaluation of the position is in order before proceeding. In the first place, White has the more solid pawn structure, with two pawn islands vs. three for Black. Furthermore, his combination of Rook and Bishop is generally superior to Rook and Knight in open positions with pawns on both wings, as in this case. It therefore seems strange that Black intentionally ceded both these apparent advantages with his 23rd move. However, moving from generalities to specifics, Black has in fact decent chances in this endgame, due to the fact that his central pawn provides his Knight with a well-supported outpost. The lack of any central White pawns guarantees that Black stands no worse.

25.♗c8

White tries to induce the advance of the e-pawn, which would give his Bishop complete freedom of the board. Black in turn wishes to maintain the pawn at all costs on e6, so as not to concede control of d5 to his opponent. Also, for Black an exchange of Rooks is obviously advantageous, and he will seek one at the first opportunity.

25...♖e8

25...♖d6 was also playable; if 26.♖c7 a5=.

But of course not 25...♔f7? 26.♖c7+ ♔g6 27.♗×e6+−.

26.♖c6

White insists on trying to provoke advance of the e-pawn, but it cannot be forced. 26.♖c7 can be met by 26...♔f8 △27...♖e7, or by 26...♘d5 and the rash Rook must retreat.

Better was 26.♔f1, starting to get the King into the game. White will pay dearly for his tardiness on this score!

26...♔f7 27.♗a6 ♘d5

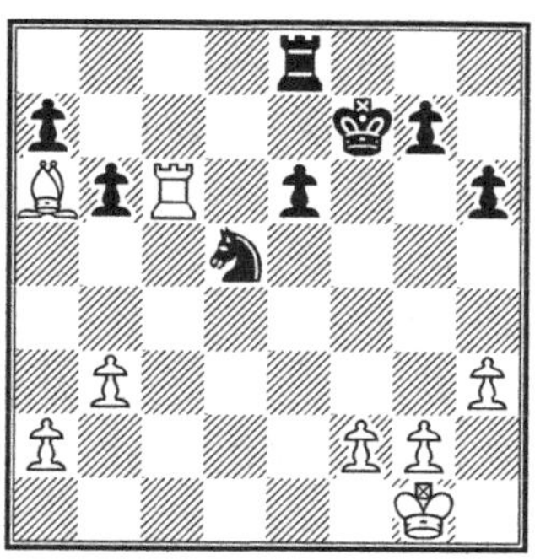

Definitely Black's best chance, as will be seen. He takes advantage of the lack of white central pawns to post his Knight strongly.

28.♗c4?!

It is natural that White should want to remove the powerful centralized Knight, but this was not the moment to try, as now Black can either win a pawn or force a favorable exchange of Rooks. Correct was 28.a3, a sample continuation being 28...♖e7 29.♗c4 ♖d7 30.g3 (against a centralized Knight an important counter-measure is to use pawns to deny it further inroads) 30...♔e7 31.♔f1 ♖d6 32.♖c8 and now if 32...♖d8?! (△32...♖d7=) 33.♖×d8 ♔×d8 34.♗×d5 e×d5 and White will have the better chances in the pawn ending (though contrary to our claim in the first edition, there is no clear win, Stockfish saying only +0.82 at 40 ply). After the text move, the question is not how White can win, but whether he can draw.

28...♘b4 29.♖c7+

Better may have been 29.♖d6 ♘×a2 30.f4 (threatening 30.f5, regaining the pawn) 30...♔f6 31.♔f2 ♘c3 32.♔f3 b5 33.♗d3 with an even game despite White's pawn deficit (-0.12/30).

29...♖e7 30.♖×e7+

And here it was better to avoid the Rook exchange by 30.♖c8.

30...♔×e7 31.a4?

Effectively, the losing move.

Correct was 31.a3! ♘c2 32.a4 ♔d6 33.f4 ♘e3 34.♗d3=.

31...♘c6!

The only winning move. After, say, 31...♘d5, White can draw with either 32.♔f1 32...♔d6 33.♔e2 ♔e5 34.h4 ♘f4+ 35.♔f3=, or 32.♗×d5 e×d5 33.♔f1 ♔d6 34.♔e2 ♔c5 35.♔d3 ♔b4 36.♔c2=.

32.♔f1?

From bad to worse, as now ♔g1-h2-g3 etc. has become the right way to activate the King.

Relatively best was 32.♗e2 with slim drawing chances if White errs. But after 32...♘d4!,

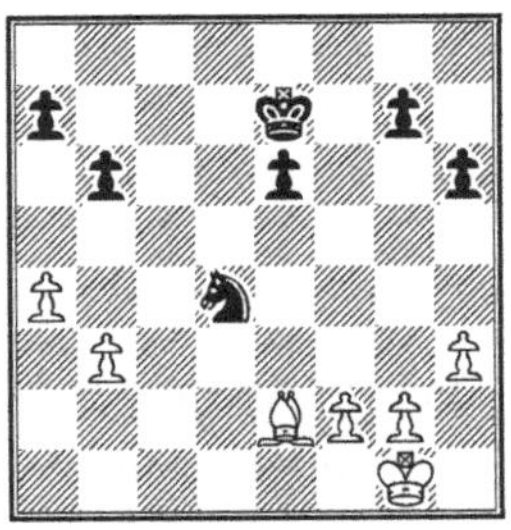

Black will win after either 33.♗d1 ♔d6 34.b4 b5 35.♔h2 ♔d5 36.♔g3 ♔c4 37.a×b5 ♔×b5 38.♔f4 ♔×b4 39.♔e5 ♔c3 etc., or 33.♗c4 e5 34.♔h2 ♔d6 35.♔g3 ♔c5 36.♔g4 ♔b4 37.♔h5 ♘×b3 38.♗b5 ♘c5 39.♔g6 ♘×a4 40.♗e8 ♘c5 41.♔×g7 ♘e4−+.

And if 32.♗d3, not 32...♘a5 as in our first edition, but 32...♔d6! 33.f4 ♔c5 34.♔f2 and now 34...♘a5! wins. In all these lines, White's problem is his King's backward position, allowing him into the fray too late.

32...♘a5!

Schapiro shows remarkable precision. Again the only winning move.

33.♔e2 ♘×c4 34.b×c4 ♔d6

The position can be described as "White to play, Black wins." For readers who enjoy a scientific approach to the endgame, with regard to the Theory of Corresponding Squares, one could assign the number 1 to the points c3 and c5, 2 to d3 and c6, 3 to d2 and d6, and finally 4 to e2 and c7. However in this case such subtleties are unnecessary, the winning plan being quite clear.

35.♔d3 ♔c5 36.♔c3 e5!

Again the best move; Black now has control of the critical invasion points, b4 and d4. 36...h5 would also win, but 36...g5 and 36...a6 are problematic, both only about -1.00 per Stockfish, compared to -7.15 for the text.

37.f3 a6 38.g3

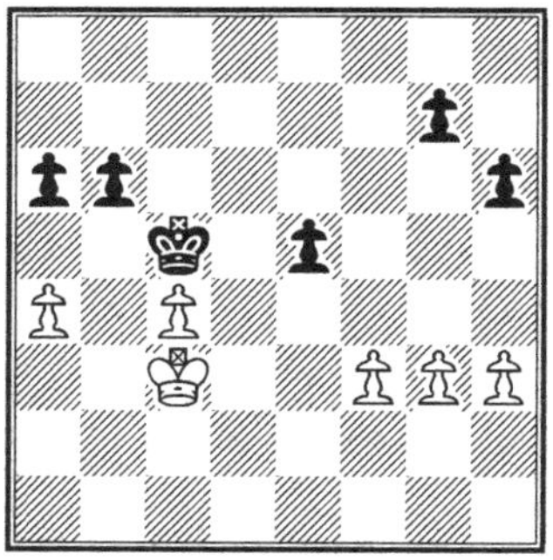

38...a5

38...h5 was equally good, but an error would be 38...g5? 39.♔d3! ♔b4 40.♔e4 ♔×a4 41.♔×e5 ♔b3 42.f4 g×f4 43.g×f4 a5 (most definitely not 43...♔×c4?? 44.f5 and White queens first and wins) 44.f5 a4 45.f6 a3 46.f7 a2 47.f8♕ a1♕+ 48.♔d5 with an even Queen ending (0.00/33).

39.h4 h5!□

Black is showing astute, precise management of his reserve tempi.

40.g4 e4!!

Yet again the only winning move. Further comment is unnecessary.

41.f×e4 h×g4 42.♔d3 ♔d6 43.♔d4 ♔e6 44.e5 ♔f5 45.e6 ♔×e6 46.♔e4 ♔d6 47.♔f4 ♔c5 48.♔×g4 ♔b4 0–1

An endgame with many instructive points. Though he lost here, Carlos Torre would soon have the opportunity to exact revenge, and in brilliant fashion (see Game 11).

Game 7

Torre-Marshall

Vienna Gambit thematic, New York 1924,

Vienna Gambit C29

As of 1924 Frank James Marshall (1877-1944, historical Elo 2570) had been among the world's ten best players for twenty years, since his victory at Cambridge Springs 1904 ahead of Lasker, Janowski, Schlechter, Pillsbury, Teichmann, Chigorin, and other all-time greats. He loved chess as much as any man who ever lived, rarely if ever letting a day pass without playing, and his games were generally full of interest and excitement. It was a benchmark of Carlos Torre's strength that he more than held his own against Marshall, scoring +2 -0 =2 against him in serious games lifetime. The following game, being from a thematic tournament where the Vienna Gambit was obligatory, is not counted in their "serious" score, but is, like most Torre-Marshall games, highly interesting.

1.e4 e5 2.♘c3 ♘f6 3.f4 d5

The only way for Black to equalize. If, for example 3...e×f4 4.e5 ♕e7 5.♕e2 ♘g8 6.♘f3, and White quickly develops a dangerous attack.

4.f×e5

In the 19th century, Steinitz recommended the solid but passive 4.d3. On the other hand, 4.e×d5 e4 transposes to the Falkbeer Counter Gambit.

4...♘×e4

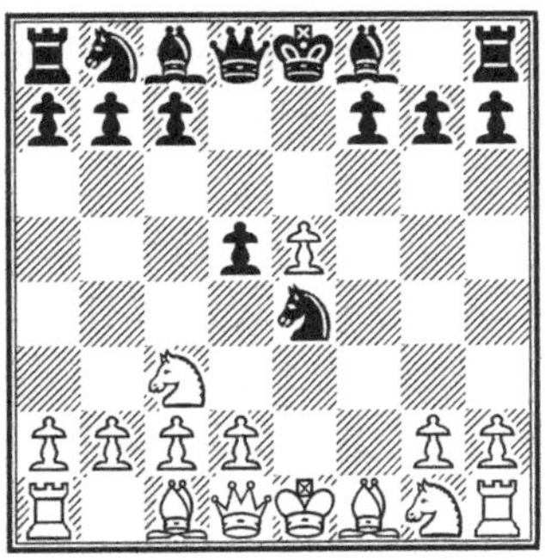

5.♘f3

Best, though there are several trappy lines suitable to informal games, such as 5.d3!? ♕h4+?! 6.g3 ♘×g3? (△6...♘×c3) 7.♘f3 ♕h5 8.♘×d5! ♗g4 9.♗g2 ♘×h1 10.♘×c7+ ♔d7 11.♘×a8 ♘c6 12.♗e3! f6 13.d4 f×e5? 14.d5+−, as in Milner-Barry–Sergeant, Ramsgate 1938.

5...♗c5

Interesting, and typically Marshall. The circumspect 5...♗e7 is safer.

6.♕e2!

An idea of Alekhine's which foils Black's aggressive plans.

In contrast, if 6.d4 ♗b4 7.♗d2 c5 8.♘×e4?! (△8.d×c5) 8...d×e4 9.♗×b4 c×b4! 10.♘g1 0–0 Black would stand better.

6...♗f2+ 7.♔d1 ♘×c3+ 8.b×c3

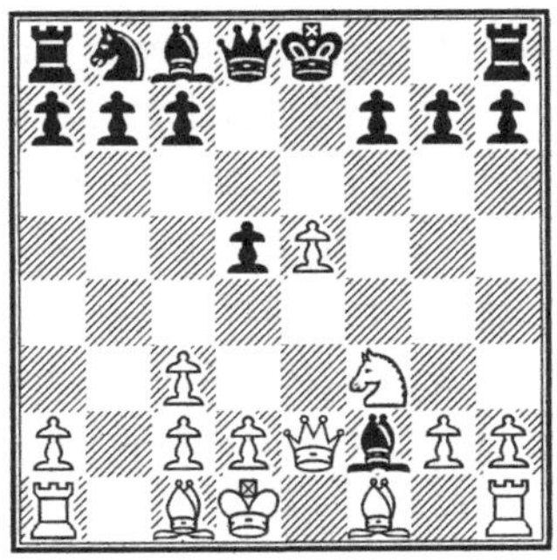

8...♗b6?!

After the obvious reply 9.d4 the Bishop will be out of play. Instead after 8...♗c5 9.♕b5+ (9.d4 ♗e7∓) 9...♘d7 10.d4 c6 11.♕b3 ♗e7 White would stand only slightly better, if at all.

9.d4 ♗f5 10.♗g5 ♕d7 11.♕e3

It is important to restrain a potential ...c7-c5, which would reactivate Black's Bishop at b6.

11...h6

The pawn sacrifice 11...c5 would complicate the game, but not favorably for Black, *e.g.* 12.d×c5 ♗a5 13.♖b1 0–0 14.♗b5 ♘c6=.

12.♗h4 ♘c6 13.♗d3 ♗×d3 14.♕×d3

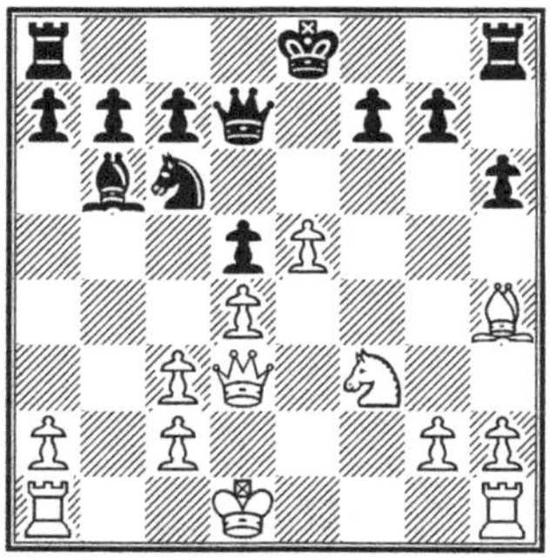

The correct decision. Recapture with the pawn would fortify the central squares, but would also open the d1-a4 diagonal leading to the white King. The text puts the Queen in a dominant position; for starters White threatens 16.e6! with a violent attack.

14...♕e6 15.h3

A prophylactic move, further limiting the scope of the black Queen, and restraining the potential advance ...g7-g5-g4, after which Black could castle queenside.

15...♘a5 16.♖f1 ♘c4

Threatening a disagreeable fork at b2.

17.♖b1 0–0 18.♘d2 f5

A double-edged move. On the one hand, Black cedes his opponent a protected, passed pawn at e5, which may become dangerous in the endgame. On the other hand, White must now worry about a general advance of the kingside black pawns, in which Black runs little risk due to the static center. White also must try to connect his Rooks as soon as possible.

19.♘×c4 d×c4 20.♕f3

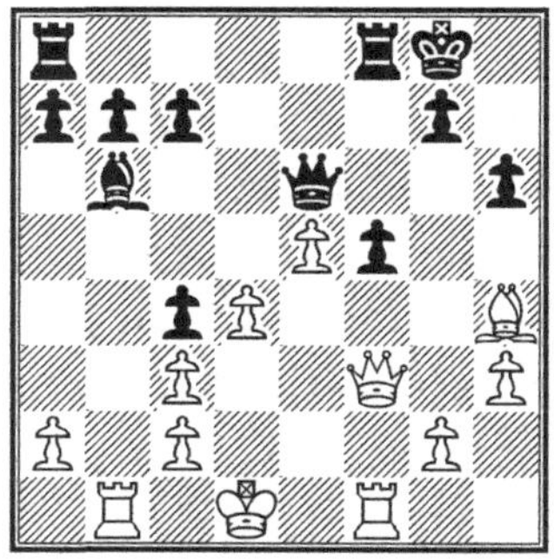

20...c6

Trying to stir up complications by 20...c5? would backfire, *viz.* 21.d5! (not 21.♕×b7? c×d4 22.♖b5 d×c3 23.♗e7 ♖fe8 24.♗d6 ♖ad8 25.♕d5 ♗c7 26.♕×e6+ ♖×e6 27.♖d5 ♗×d6 28.e×d6 ♖e×d6 29.♖×d6 ♖×d6+ and Black will win (-4.32/31)) 21...♕×e5 22.♖e1 ♕c7 23.♗e7! ♖f7 24.d6 and though Black is nominally a pawn ahead, White's advanced d-pawn is what matters, and the white King can safely "castle by hand": ♔d1-e2-f2-g1 (+2.58/25).

After the text move, White's safe haven for his King is at a1.

21.♔c1 ♖f7 22.♔b2 ♗d8 23.♗×d8 ♖×d8 24.♔a1 ♖d5

More reasonable and consistent would seem 24...♖df8. On d5 the Rook makes a poor blockader.

25.g4

A somewhat impetuous advance, which nevertheless works out well. More prudent and conserving of White's slight advantage was 25.♕e3.

25...f4?
A mistake that could have lost the game. Correct was 25...f×g4 forcing 26.♕×f7+ ♕×f7 27.♖×f7 ♔×f7 28.♖×b7+ ♔e6 29.h×g4 c5□ 30.♖×g7 c×d4 31.c×d4 ♖×d4 with an even game (+0.25/32).

26.♕e4! g5
Some brilliant possibilities begin to surface. If 26...♕e7 (to prevent an eventual ♖×b7), then 27.e6 ♖f6 28.♖×b7! (anyway!) 28...♕×e6 (28...♕×b7?? 29.e7+–) 29.♖×f4 ♕×e4 30.♖×e4 ♖f3 31.♔b2 ♖×h3

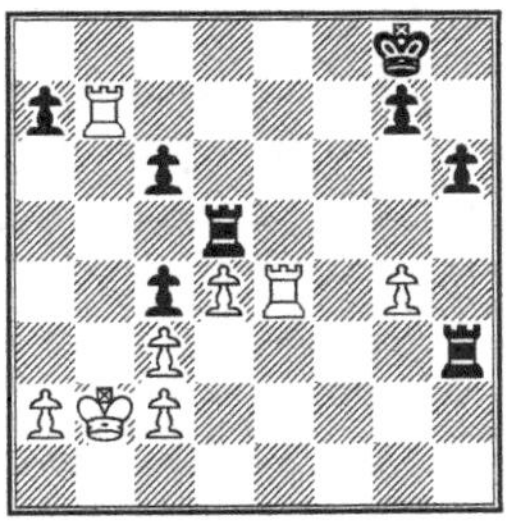

32.a4! (not 32.♖×a7? ♖b5+ 33.♔c1 ♖h1+ 34.♔d2 ♖bb1 ∞) 32...a5 33.♖e6 and White is winning (+3.10/25).

27.h4!

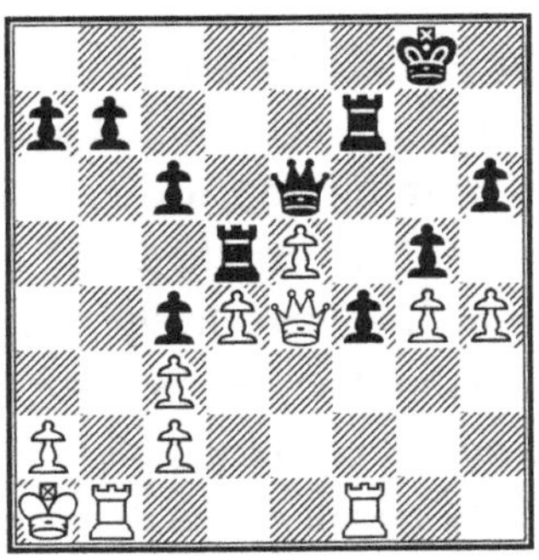

27...♔g7?
Marshall compounds his previous error. Relatively best was 27...♖dd7.
Definitely bad was 27...♕×g4? 28.e6 ♖e7 29.♕g6+ ♖g7 (if 29...♔f8 30.♕f6+ ♔g8 31.♕×e7 and mate shortly) 30.e7!! ♖×g6 31.e8♕+ ♔h7 32.♖×b7+ ♖g7 33.♖fb1 +–.
Or if 27...g×h4? 28.♖×f4 ♖×f4 29.♕×f4 ♖d7 30.g5 ♕h3 (to prevent 31.♖h1) 31.♔b2 (preventing 31...♕×c3) 31...♖f7 32.♕e4 ♕f5 (if 32...h×g5 33.♕g6+ ♖g7 34.♕e8+ ♔h7 35.e6+–) 33.♕×h4 h×g5 34.♖g1 ♖g7 35.♕h5 etc. (+4.84/25).

28.h×g5 h×g5 29.♖h1 ♕g6 30.♕e2 f3?!
A move typical of Marshall when under duress, unsound but aggressive. He always preferred counter-attack to passive defense, and in this case his bluff works. Objectively least bad was 30...♖d8, but after 31.♖h5 ♖e8 32.♖bh1 White is obviously winning.

31.♕h2 ♖d8

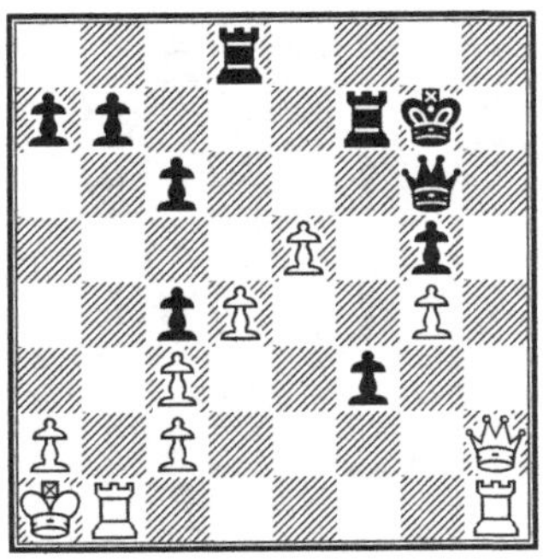

32.♖bf1?
Marshall's gamble at move 30 has had the desired psychological effect:

suddenly Torre is paralyzed by fear of Black's advancing pawn! Though the text leaves White still with the advantage, it is so far from best that it deserves at least one question mark, if not two.

Instead, crushing was 32.e6!!,

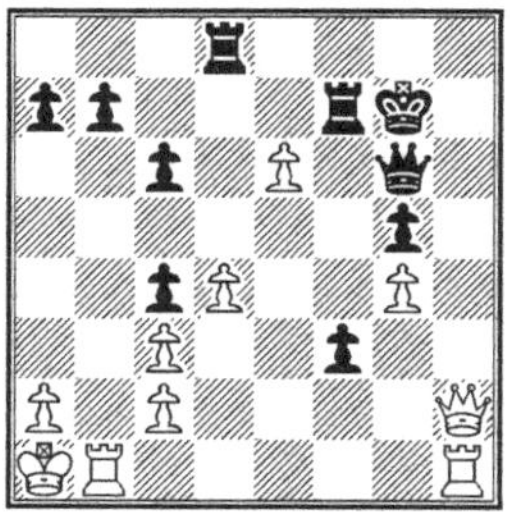

when if 32...♕×e6 33.♕h7+ ♔f8 (or 33...♔f6 34.♖h6+) 34.♕h8+ ♔e7 35.♖×b7+ ♖d7 36.♖b8! and mate in at most eleven more moves.

And if 32...♖e7 33.♕e5+ ♕f6 34.♖h7+ ♔×h7 35.♕×f6 etc. The only move not allowing a quick mate, 32...♖f4, succumbs to 33.♖×b7+ ♔f6 34.♕h6! ♖g8 35.e7+-.

32...♖f4 33.♕h3 f2 34.♔b2 ♖df8

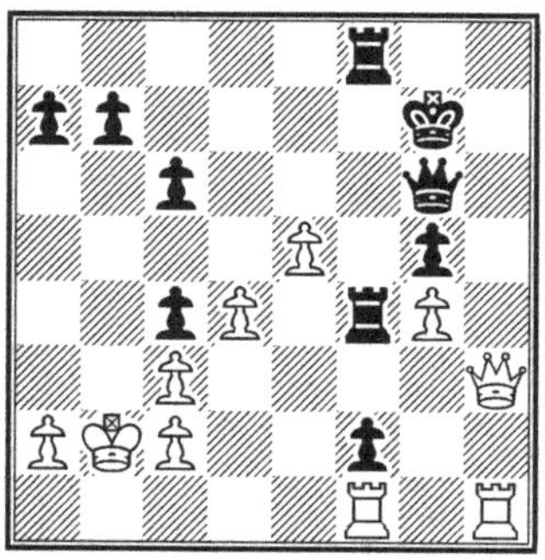

35.♕e3?

And now the game is definitely drawn. The last chance to play for a win lay in 35.♕h2, when best play goes along the lines of 35...♖×g4 36.e6 ♖gf4 (not 36...♕×e6?? 37.♕h7+ ♔f6 38.♖h6#) 37.e7 ♖e8 38.♖×f2 ♖×f2 39.♕×f2 ♖×e7

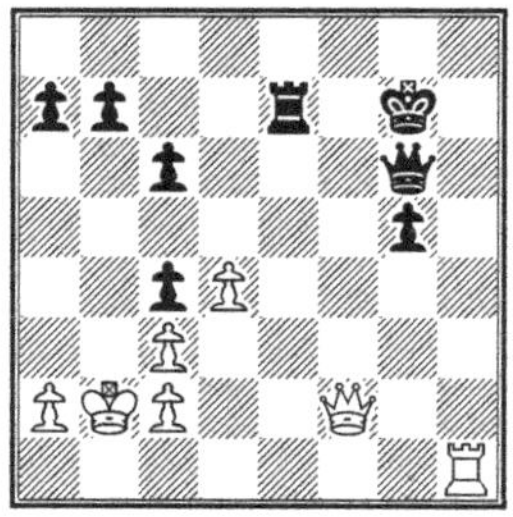

40.d5 c×d5 41.♕d4+ ♔f7 42.♕×d5+ ♔g7 (if 42...♕e6 43.♕×g5) 43.♕d4+ ♔f7 44.♖f1+ ♔g8 45.♕d8+ ♖e8 46.♕d5+ ♔g7 47.♕×b7+ ♔g8 48.♕d5+ ♔g7 49.♕d7+ ♔g8 50.♖f5 and Stockfish says White will win (+4.71/25).

35...♕e4?

But Marshall gives Torre another chance. Correct was 35...♖f3±.

36.♕h3 ♕g6 37.♕e3?

Again, 37.♕h2! would have entered the winning line above.

37...♕e4 38.♕h3 ♕g6 ½-½

Now though 39.♕h2 would again enter the winning line, a threefold repetition has been reached and a draw was agreed. A very lively game, but one showing that Torre's tactical ability had not reached full potential. Thus he became one of the many victims of a "Marshall swindle."

Game 8

Marshall-Torre

Dimock thematic tournament, New York 1924

Ponziani Gambit [C24]

1.e4 e5 2.♗c4 ♘f6 3.d4

This romantic gambit dates from about 1750 (about one hundred years before Morphy). It was discovered by the Italian, Domenico Lorenzo Ponziani, and analyzed and played in the 1850s by the Russian prince Sergey Semyonovich Urusov (hence its alternate name, the Urusov Gambit).

3...e×d4

The coffee-house style 3...♘×e4 4.d×e5 ♕h4

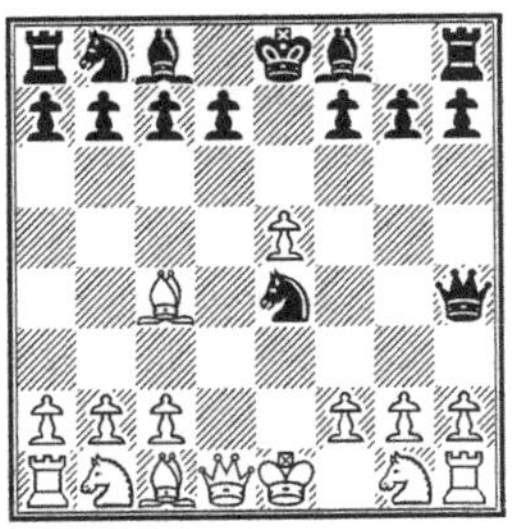

can lead to extremely sharp play, but Larsen's recommendation 5.♕f3 ♘g5 6.♕f4 (even better perhaps is 6.♕e2) 6...♕×f4 7.♗×f4 ♘e6 8.♗g3 seems to give White an edge.

4.♘f3 ♘×e4

Usually 4...♘c6 is played here, transposing to what can be considered either the Scotch Gambit or a variation of the Two Knights Defense; however that could be considered a tacit admission of the Ponziani Gambit's worth. Apart from the text, also worthwhile is 4...d5 5.e×d5 ♗b4+ 6.c3 ♕e7+ with good play.

5.♕×d4

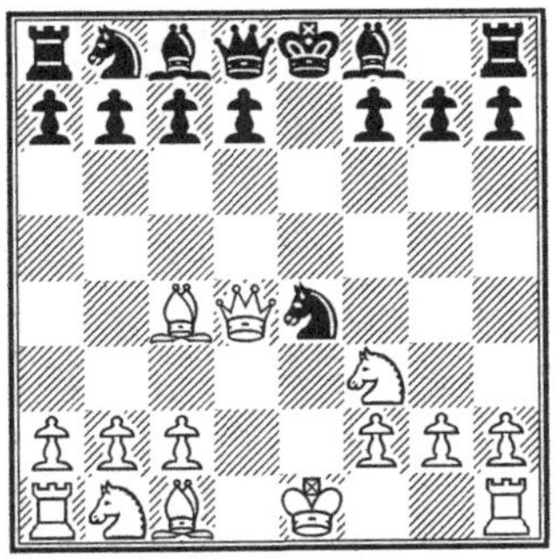

5...♘f6

Against 5...♘c5, 6.♗g5! is an idea of Keres. Urusov recommended 6.♘e5, but this fails to 6...♘e6! 7.♕e4 (other moves are worse, per Stockfish) 7...d6 and White is forced into 8.♘×f7 ♔×f7∓.

5...♘d6?? runs into 6.0–0 f6 [if 6...♕f6 7.♖e1+ ♗e7 8.♖×e7+! ♕×e7 9.♕×g7 ♖f8 10.♘c3 f6 (10...♘×c4?? 11.♘d5 ♕d6 12.♘f6+ ♔d8 13.♗f4! (+12.25)) 11.♕g4 ♘×c4 12.♘d5+−] 7.♖e1+ ♗e7 and Black is already lost (+4.44/25).

6.♘c3

The main line ran 6.♗g5 ♗e7 7.♘c3 c6! 8.0–0–0 d5 9.♖he1 ♗e6 10.♗d3

♘bd7 11.♕h4 ♘c5 12.♘d4 ♘g8!=. From that point the game Torre-Tholfsen from the same tournament continued 13.f4!? ♔f8?? (△13...♗×g5 14.f×g5 ♘e7=):

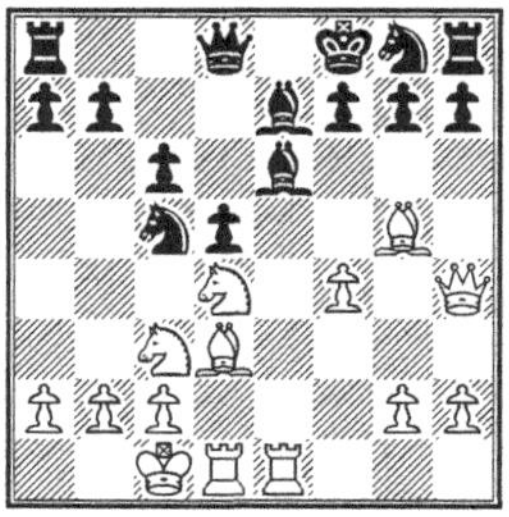

Here Torre played 14.♖e5?! and eventually lost (0-1, 32). Instead he could have won brilliantly with 14.b4! ♘×d3+ (14...♘a6?? 15.♗×a6 b×a6 16.♖×e6!) 15.♖×d3 and:

(a) 15...♗d7 16.♖×e7! ♘×e7 17.♖e3 f6 18.♗×f6! etc.; or

(b) 15...h6 16.♖×e6! ♗×g5 (16...f×e6?? 17.♘×e6+) 17.f×g5 ♕×g5+ 18.♕×g5 h×g5 19.♖e5+−; or

(c) 15...♕c8 16.♗×e7+ ♘×e7 17.♖de3 etc.

Besides 6...♗e7, the move 6...♘c6

is an interesting experiment of Torre's, a sample being 7.♕h4 d5! 8.♗d3 (or 8.♗b3 ♕e7+! 9.♔f1 ♗e6∓) 8...♘b4 9.0–0 ♘×d3 10.c×d3 ♗e7 11.♘bd2 0–0, as in Tholfsen-Torre, from this same event (0-1, 34).

6...♘c6 7.♕h4 ♗b4

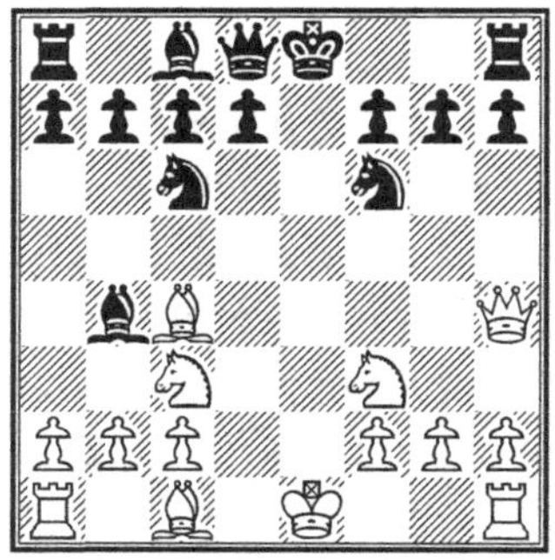

8.0–0

In view of his pawn minus, Marshall decides to seek rapid mobilization of his pieces, despite the weakening of his pawn structure that entails.

But if 8.♗d2?! ♕e7+! and either 9.♔d1 ♕d8 10.♖e1+ ♗e7, or 9.♗e2 0–0 10.0–0–0 ♗×c3 11.♗×c3 ♘e4 12.♕×e7 ♘×e7 is favorable to Black. Best probably was 8.♗g5, when if 8...♕e7+ 9.♔d1 ♗×c3 10.b×c3 d5 11.♖e1 ♗e6 12.♗b5 the game is even.

8...♗×c3 9.b×c3 0–0 10.♗d3

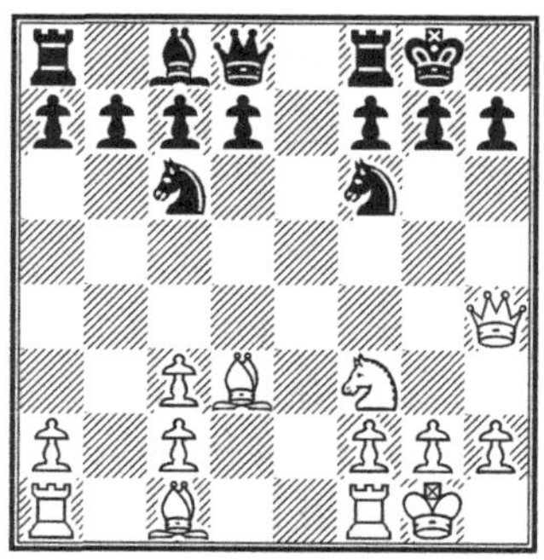

10...♘e7!

It is important to bolster the kingside defenses. If instead 10...d5 11.♗g5 h6 12.♗f4 (not 12.♗×h6? g×h6 13.♕×h6 ♘e4!□ 14.♗×e4 d×e4 15.♘g5 ♗f5−+) 12...♘e4 13.♕×d8 ♖×d8 14.♗×c7 and White recovers his pawn.

11.♗g5 ♘g6 12.♕g3

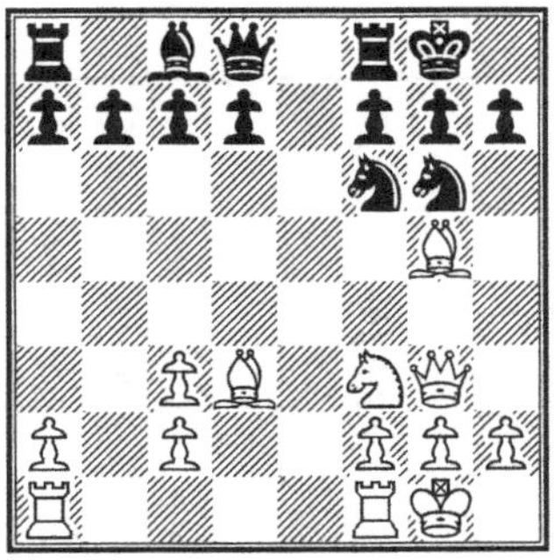

12...d5

Seeking to return the pawn in exchange for positional superiority.

The alternative 12...d6 would more or less force 13.♘h4 ♘e5 14.♖fe1 ♘×d3 15.c×d3 ♔h8 with about an even game. If instead 13.♖fe1?!, then 13...h6 forces wild, ultimately unclear complications:

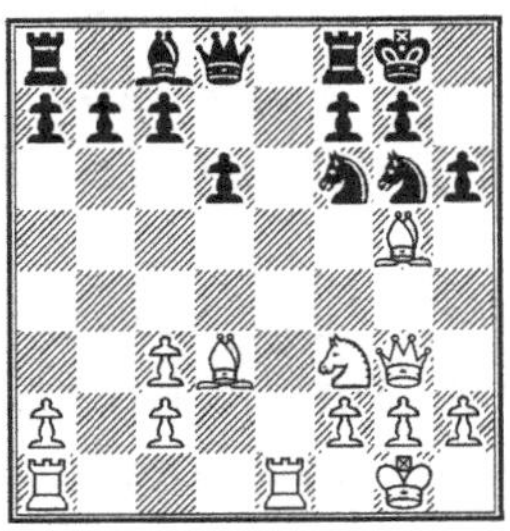

14.♗×h6 (if 14.♗d2?? ♘h5 wins the Queen) 14...g×h6 15.♗×g6 f×g6 16.♕×g6+ ♔h8 17.♕×h6+ ♘h7 18.♘h4 ♗f5 19.g4 ♖f6 20.♕h5 ♗d7 21.g5 ♖f7! 22.♕×f7 ♕×g5+ 23.♔f1 ♗h3+ 24.♔e2 ♕×h4 25.♔d1 ♖f8 26.♖e8 ♖×e8 27.♕×e8+ ♔g7 28.♔c1 ♕×f2∞. Stockfish now says -1.20/30, but this seems like the sort of position where, as in Bent Larsen's memorable phrase, "both sides stand worse."

With the text Torre's strategy becomes similar what he used against Samuels (Game 5).

In both cases White has a doubled c-pawn, and to attack it Torre seeks to sacrifice his own c-pawn. However, the situation here is more difficult for Black, due to White's strong Bishop at d3.

13.♖fe1 h6

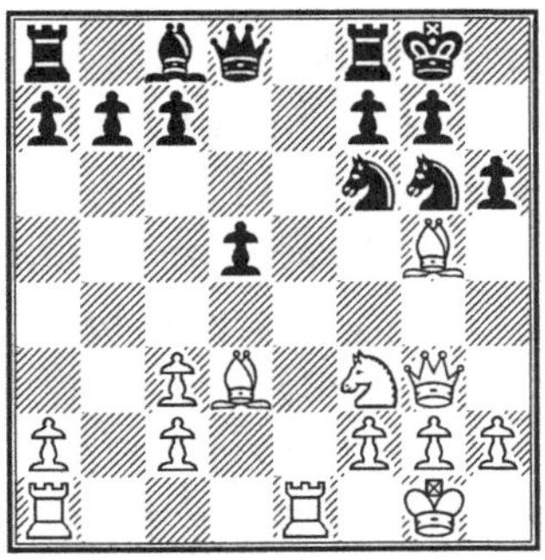

14.♗×f6

If 14.♗×h6 ♘h5! 15.♕g5 ♘hf4 16.♗×g6 ♘×g6 17.h4 (not 17.♘e5?? ♕×g5 18.♗×g5 ♘×e5 19.♖×e5 f6−+) 17...♕×g5 18.♗×g5 with only a slight advantage for Black, if any. And if 14.♗×g6 h×g5! 15.♗d3 g4 16.♘g5 g6, when Black's position is sound.

14...♕×f6 15.♕×c7 ♘f4 16.♕e5 ♕×e5 17.♖×e5 ♗e6 18.g3

Realizing his positional inferiority, Marshall tries to find the least disadvantageous line. If instead 18.♗f1 ♖ac8 with tremendous pressure on the doubled pawns, as in Samuels-Torre.

18...♘×d3 19.c×d3 ♖ac8 20.♖c1 ♖c5 21.♘d4 ♖fc8

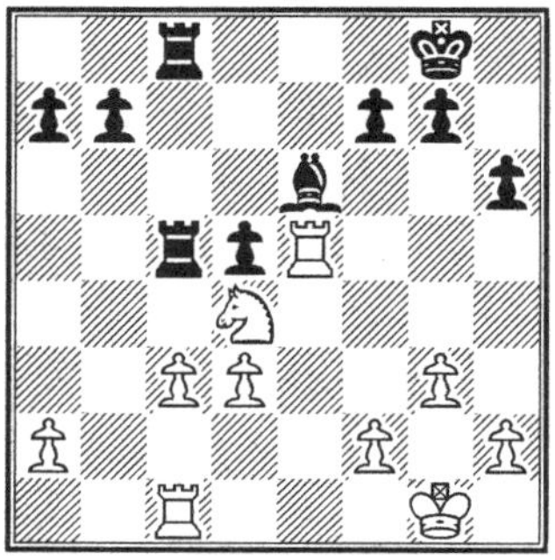

22.f4?!

The straightforward 22.♘×e6 f×e6 23.♖×e6 ♖×c3 24.♖×c3 ♖×c3 25.♖e7 ♖×d3 26.♖×b7 ♖a3 was dead even. With 22.f4, Marshall may have been hoping to bring off another swindle by 22...♖×c3 23.♖×c3 ♖×c3 24.f5 ♖×d3? 25.f×e6 ♖×d4?? 26.e7+−, but Torre does not fall for that.

22...♗g4!

Also good was 22...♗d7.

23.c4?

The losing move. Instead 23.♔f2 would have kept the game close to even, *e.g.* 23...♖×c3 24.♖×c3 ♖×c3 25.♖e8+ ♔h7 26.♔e3!□ (-0.36/32).

23...f6!

The only winning move, to enable ...d×c4 without fear of ♖e5×c5. Torre now closes out flawlessly.

24.♖e7 d×c4

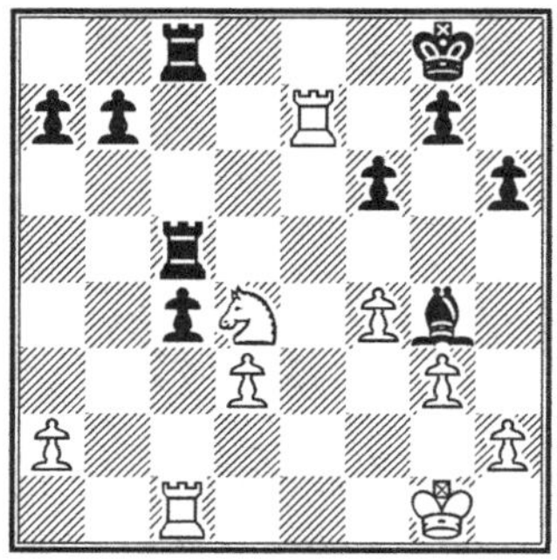

25.d×c4

25.♖×b7 loses to either 25...c×d3 26.♖×c5 ♖×c5 27.♖b2 ♖c4 28.♘b3 ♖c2−+, or 25...♖d5 26.♘b5 c×d3! 27.♖×c8+ ♗×c8 28.♖b8 ♖c5−+. No further comment is necessary.

25...♖×c4 26.♖×c4 ♖×c4 27.♘b3 ♖c2 28.h4 ♖×a2 29.♖×b7 a5 30.♘d4 a4 31.f5 ♖d2 32.♘e6 ♗×f5 33.♘×g7 ♖d7 34.♖b5 ♗d3 0-1

A very hard-fought game, mostly positional on the surface, but with hidden tactical eruptions lurking just below.

Game 9

Torre-Bigelow

Dimock thematic tournament, New York 1924

Two Knights Defense (by transposition) [C56]

Swiss-born Horace Ransom Bigelow (1898-1980) had already established himself as a strong player in Europe before immigrating to the USA in 1921. There he became a prominent member of the Manhattan Club. He was one of the chief organizers of the great New York 1924 tournament, won by Lasker ahead of Capablanca and Alekhine. He also edited a chess column in the *New York Evening Post* and *Liberty* magazine. Here against Torre he is blown away by a powerful attack.

1.e4 e5 2.♗c4 ♘f6 3.d4 e×d4 4.♘f3 ♘c6 5.e5

Also playable is 5.0–0 ♘×e4 6.♖e1 d5 7.♗×d5 (or also 7.♘c3!?, the Canal variation, *e.g.* 7...d×c3 8.♗×d5 ♗e6 9.♗×e4 ♗b4 10.b3 ♕×d1 11.♖×d1 h6 12.♗f4 etc.) 7...♕×d5 8.♘c3 ♕a5 9.♘×e4 etc., a line seen in both coffee-houses and master tournaments alike. As an alternative to 8...♕a5, there is David Bronstein's interesting suggestion 8...♕d8.

5...d5 6.♗b5

Generally considered best. The game Tholfsen-Marshall, from this same tournament, proceeded 6.♗b3?! ♘e4 7.c3 ♗g4 8.c×d4 ♗b4+ 9.♔f1□ 0–0 10.h3 ♗e6 11.♗e3 f6 12.♕d3? (△12.♘bd2∓) 12...f×e5 13.d×e5

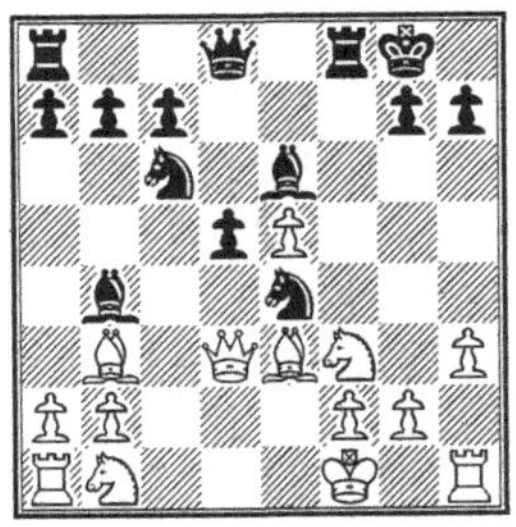

13...♔h8?! Missing a chance to win brilliantly by 13...♕d7! 14.♔g1 ♖×f3!! 15.g×f3 ♘×e5 16.♕e2 ♖f8! 17.f×e4 ♘f3+ 18.♔g2 ♗×h3+! 19.♖×h3 ♕g4+ 20.♖g3 ♘h4+ 21.♔f1 ♕×g3 etc.
But Marshall soon wins brilliantly anyway: 14.♘c3 ♗×c3 15.b×c3 ♕d7 16.♗a4? ♗f5! 17.♔g1?? (△17.♕d4 ♘×d4 18.♗×d7∓) 17...♘×f2! 18.♕b5 ♘×h1 19.♕×b7 ♗×h3!! 20.♗×c6 ♕g4 21.♕b2 ♖ab8 22.♘h2 ♕e4 23.♕d2 ♘g3 0-1.

6...♘e4 7.♘×d4 ♗c5

More energetic than 7...♗d7, which is nonetheless quite playable, *e.g.* 8.♗×c6 b×c6 9.0–0 ♗c5 10.f3 ♘g5 11.♗e3 ♗b6 etc.

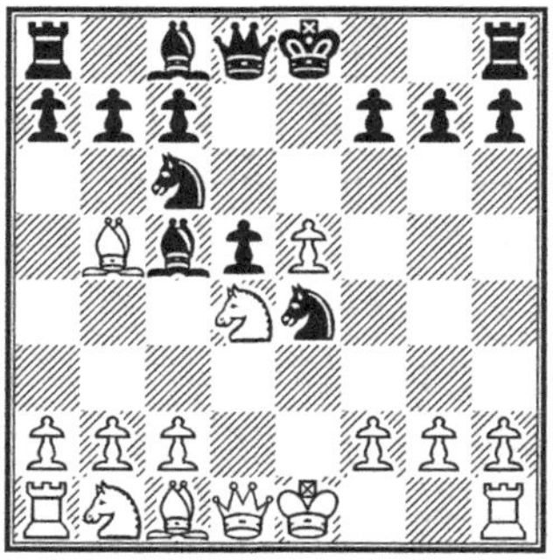

8.♗e3
One of the best moves at White's disposal.
Messy but ultimately even is 8.♘×c6 ♗×f2+ 9.♔f1 ♕h4 10.♘×a7+ c6 11.♘×c8 ♖×c8 12.♗e2=.
The other alternative is 8.0–0 0–0 9.♗×c6 b×c6 and:
(a) 10.♗e3 ♕e8 11.♘d2=, or
(b) 10.♘×c6?! ♕d7 11.♘d4 ♖e8! (stronger than 11...♗a6 12.♖e1=) 12.f3 f6 13.e6 ♕×e6 14.f×e4 ♕×e4 15.c3 ♗a6 16.♘d2 (forced; if, say, 16.♖f4?? ♕e1+ 17.♕×e1 ♖×e1+ 18.♔f2 ♖×c1–+) 16...♗×d4+ 17.♔h1 ♕e3 18.c×d4 ♗×f1 19.♕×f1 ♕×d4 with an unbalanced, unclear position.

8...♗d7
Interesting is 8...0–0 9.♘×c6 b×c6 10.♗×c5 ♘×c5 11.♗×c6 ♖b8 12.♕×d5 (12.♕d4? ♘e6 13.♕d2 ♖×b2∓) 12...♕e7 13.0–0 ♖d8 14.♕f3 ♖×b2, when Black's active pieces compensate for his pawn minus.

9.♗×c6 b×c6 10.0–0

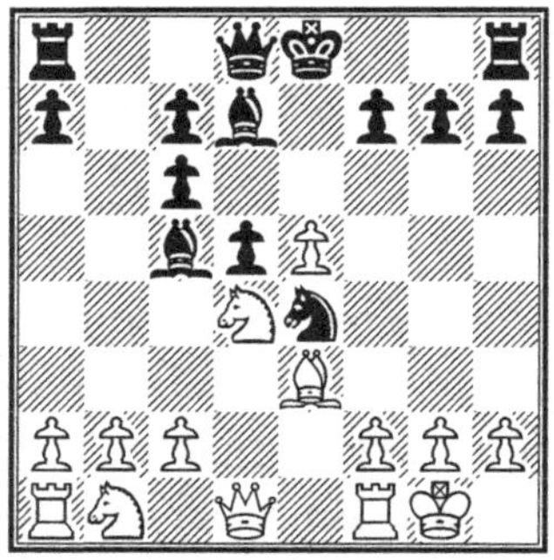

10...♕e7
Also playable is 10...0–0, for example 11.f3 ♘g5 12.♕d2 f6 13.e×f6 ♕×f6 14.b4 ♗b6 15.♘c3 with an even game.

11.f3 ♘g5 12.f4 f6?!
A questionable combination. Its drawback is that Black has not yet castled, thus opening the position entails considerable risk. 12...♘e6 was safer.

13.f×g5 f×e5
Black recovers his piece one way or another.

14.♘c3

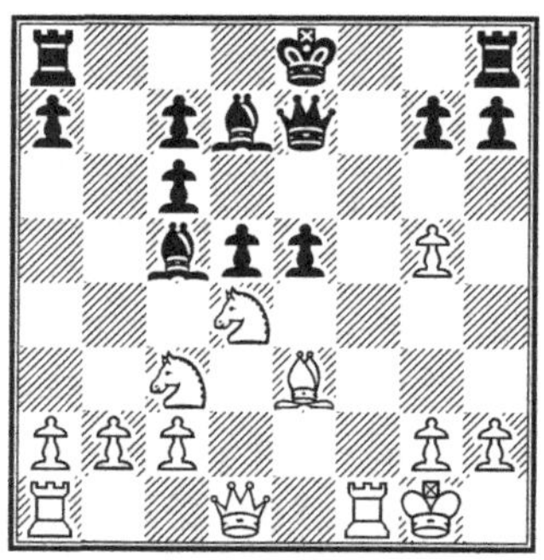

14...e×d4
There was no need to hurry with this

recapture, as White's attacked pieces cannot run away.

Preferable was 14...0–0–0, *viz.* 15.♕d3 e×d4 16.♗×d4 ♗b6 (reinforcing the disjointed pawn structure) 17.♘a4 ♖de8 18.♘×b6+ a×b6 19.a4 c5 20.♗f2 d4 with a roughly even position (+0.27/25).

15.♗×d4 ♗e6?

Black believes his King will be safe on d7, but this proves too optimistic in this open position. 15...0–0–0 again was preferable, or 15...♗b6 and 16...0–0–0.

16.♕d3 ♔d7 17.♘a4

Preparing to open more lines with c2-c4. White's plan is simply to expose Black's King wherever he is.

17...♗d6 18.♕e3!

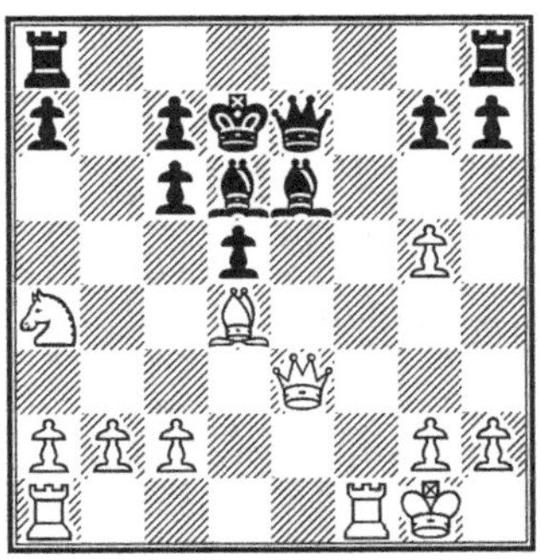

White must prevent ...c6-c5. The move also applies veiled pressure on the e-file.

18...♖he8?

Natural-looking but calamitous. Black was already hard pressed, but less egregious were 18...♗g4 19.♕×e7+ ♔×e7 20.♖ae1+ ♔d8, or 18...♖af8 19.♘c5+ ♗×c5 20.♗×c5 ♖×f1+ 21.♖×f1 ♕e8, or 18...h6 19.♖ae1 ♖ae8 20.h4 h×g5 21.♘c5+ ♗×c5 22.♗×c5 ♕d8 23.♕d3 g4.

In each case Black stands definitely worse (about +2.00) but he can still fight on. After the text his situation is hopeless.

19.♖ae1 ♗g4

Vainly hoping to exchange Queens, which would relieve Black's plight. Torre says "No way."

20.♕d2 ♗e6 21.c4

With the unpleasant threat of 22.c5. The reply is practically forced.

21...♗b4 22.♗c3 ♗×c3

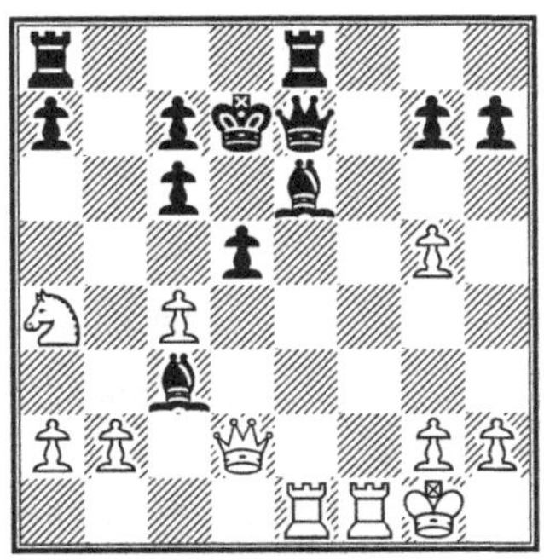

23.b×c3

Good enough to win, but much the strongest was 23.♕×c3 intending 24.c×d5 c×d5 25.♘c5+ etc.

23...♕a3 24.c×d5!

White gives no respite to his opponent, who may have been hoping to get his King off the hot seat after 24.♕c2 ♖ad8 △25...♔c8.

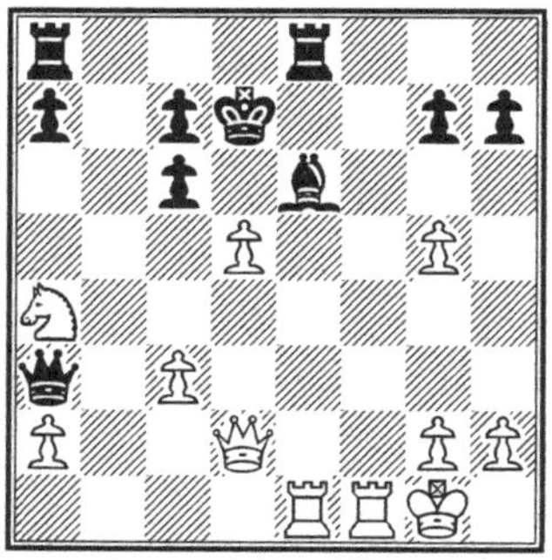

24...♗×d5

If 24...c×d5 25.♕d4! threatening, among other things, 26.♘c5+. And of course if 24...♕×a4?? 25.d×e6+ ♔c8 26.♕d7+ ♔b7 27.♖b1+ and mate soon.

25.♕d4 ♖×e1 26.♖×e1 ♕f8

If 26...♖e8 27.♘c5+ forces 27...♕×c5 28.♕×c5 ♖×e1+ 29.♔f2+–, because if 27...♔d8 28.♖b1 and 28...♕×c5 is forced anyway.

27.♘c5+ ♔d6?? 1-0

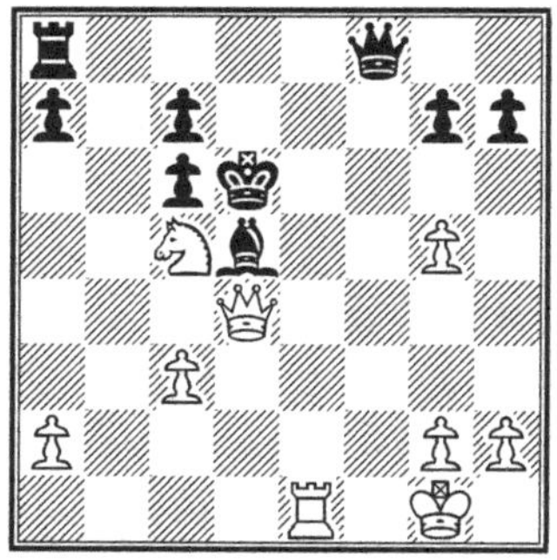

An oversight, though the position was clearly lost. Black stopped the clock when he realized his move allowed 28.♖e6#. In any event, the only way to forestall a quick mate was to give up the Queen by 27...♕×c5. One of Torre's better attacking games.

Game 10

Torre-Smirka

Dimock thematic tournament, New York 1924

Two Knights Defense (by transposition) [C56]

In the notes to Black's 7th move of the previous game it was mentioned that 7...♗d7 was playable. Here is one of Torre's games, from this same tournament, where his opponent played that move. Vienna-born Rudolph Smirka (1887-1947) was New York State Champion at the time, a title he would win again in 1927. He and Torre engage in a slam-bang fist fight, very much in keeping with the spirit of the gambit opening.

1.e4 e5 2.♗c4 ♘f6 3.d4 e×d4 4.♘f3 ♘c6 5.e5 d5 6.♗b5 ♘e4 7.♘×d4 ♗d7

Varying from Torre-Bigelow (Game 9), where 7...♗c5 was played. The first recorded instance of 7...♗d7 was, interestingly, Lichtenhein-Morphy, First

American Chess Congress, New York 1857. In subsequent years it was played by such worthies as Janowski, Napier (both in 1896), Réti, Spielmann (both 1914), and Yates (1923). After 1924 it was seen in games by Kashdan (1938), Reshevsky (1939), Lilienthal (1953), Taimanov (1957), Gligoric (1960), and Keres (1961), among other greats.

8.♗×c6

Lichtenhein-Morphy continued 8.♘×c6 b×c6 9.♗d3 ♗c5 10.♗×e4 ♕h4 11.♕e2 d×e4 12.♗e3 ♗g4 13.♕c4 ♗×e3 14.g3 ♕d8 15.f×e3 ♕d1+ 16.♔f2 ♕f3+ 17.♔g1 ♗h3 18.♕×c6+ ♔f8 19.♕×a8+ ♔e7 0-1.

8...b×c6 9.0–0 ♗e7

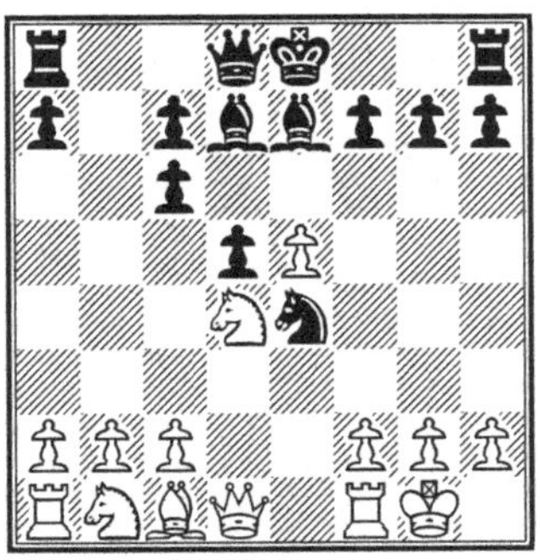

10.f3

Torre breaks new ground. In the only known earlier instance of this position, Bauer-Herland, Hauptturnier A, Breslau 1912, play continued 10.♘d2 ♘×d2 11.♗×d2 c5 12.♘e2 0–0 (0-1, 63).

10...♘c5 11.f4 ♘e4 12.♘d2 ♘×d2

Black has moved this Knight five times, only to exchange it for one that has moved once. Still, as bad as this seems on general principles, the position remains even.

13.♗×d2 c5 14.♘e2 ♖b8?

Intentionally trying to provoke White into an attack on Black's King, because in this case neither player's interest was served by a draw. Whatever the motivation, the move is objectively bad.

Better 14...f5 or 14...g6, both forestalling White's intended f4-f5.

15.f5!

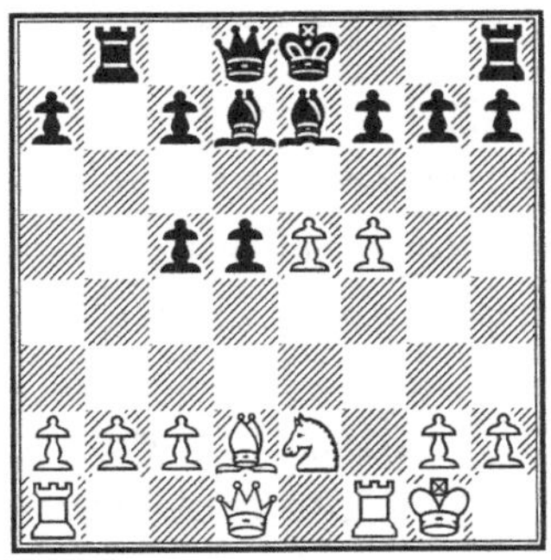

15...d4

If 15...♖×b2? 16.e6! f×e6 17.♗c3 ♖b6 18.♗×g7 ♗f6 19.♗×f6! (19.♗×h8 ♗×h8 20.♖b1 is also quite good) 19...♕×f6 20.f×e6 ♕×e6 21.♘f4 ♕e3+ 22.♔h1 ♕d4 23.♘×d5! (+4.69/23).

16.b3

With ♗d2-c3 no longer possible, the b-pawn needed protection.

16...0–0

If 16...♗c6 17.♘f4 and a strong attack is brewing (+3.08/24).

17.♖f3?
Letting White's advantage slip. Correct was 17.♘c1 ♗g5 18.♘d3 ±, or 17.♘g3 ♔h8 18.♕g4. But now the game is even once again.

17...♖e8! 18.♘g3 ♗c6

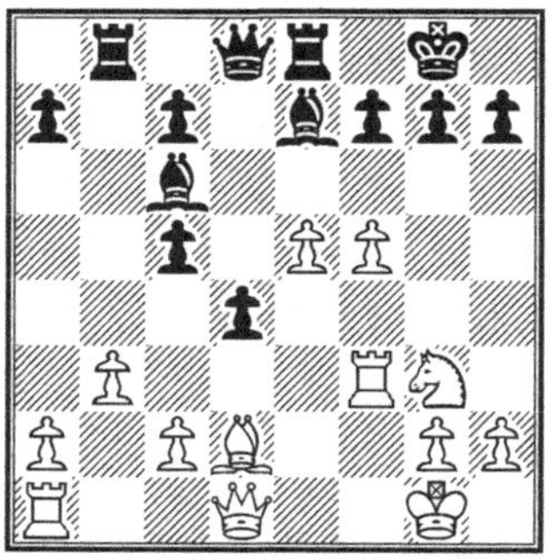

19.♘h5?!
The Exchange sac is a playable idea, but this is not the best way to carry it out. Correct was 19.f6 ♗×f3 (or 19...♗f8 20.f×g7 ♗×g7 21.♖f2 ♖×e5=) 20.f×e7 ♗×d1 21.e×d8♕ ♖b×d8 22.♖×d1 ♖×e5=. Or White could simply play 19.♖f2 with equality. But as indicated above, neither player wanted a draw.

19...♗×f3 20.♕×f3

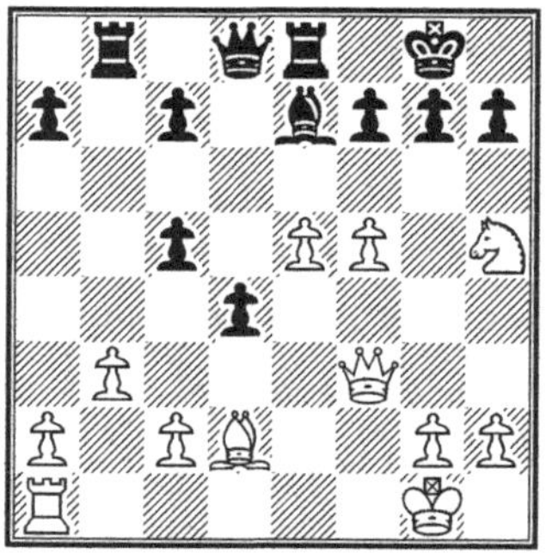

20...♗f8?
A serious mistake that puts Torre back in the driver's seat.
Better 20...g6 21.♗h6 d3! 22.c3□ (if 22.c×d3?? ♕d4+, or 22.♕×d3?? ♕×d3 23.c×d3 g×h5 −+) 22...♗h4! 23.e6 ♕e7 24.♕g4 ♖bd8, when after 25.♘g7 ♖f8 we have a weirdly complicated position somewhat in Black's favor (-1.04/27).
If instead 20...d3, White must play 21.♗c3 d×c2=, avoiding 21.♕×d3?? c4 22.♕×d8 ♖b×d8 23.♗e3 g6 24.♘g3 ♗f6 25.e×f6 ♖×e3 when Black has consolidated his material advantage (-5.20/24).

21.♕g3! ♔h8??
From bad to much worse. 21...d3 was the only remotely playable move.

22.♗g5!□ ♕c8
22...♕d5 is refuted by 23.♗f6 +−.

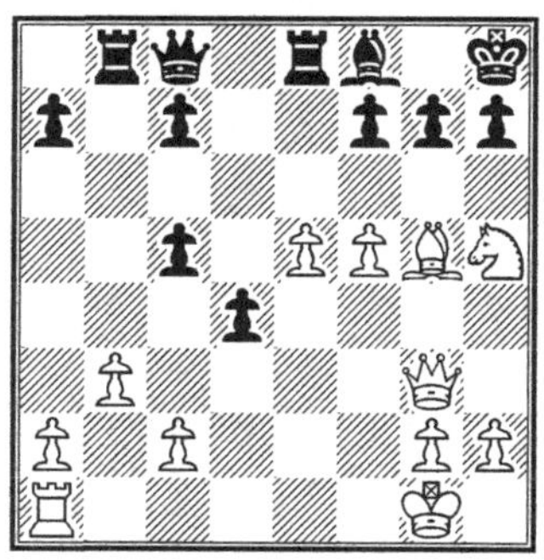

23.♖f1
Good enough to win, but Torre again misses his best shot. Deadly was 23.e6! f×e6 (if 23...♗d6 24.♕g4 ♗e5 25.♖e1 +−) 24.f6!□ e5 (if 24...♕d7 25.♕e5 ♔g8 26.f×g7 ♗×g7 27.♗f6 etc.) 25.f×g7+ ♗×g7 26.♘×g7 ♖g8 27.♗f6 etc., winning.

23...♖b6??

But Smirka errs in turn. There was some slight hope in 23...♖b7.

24.e6!

Now Torre has the right idea!

24...f×e6 25.f6! e5 26.f×g7+ ♗×g7 27.♘×g7 ♔×g7??

There was no good move, but this allows mate in 13.

28.♗f6+ ♔f7 29.♗×e5+

Mate could be forced by 29.♗d8+ ♔e6 30.♕g4+ ♔d6 31.♕×c8 etc. But the text wins too.

29...♔e6 30.♗×c7 ♖a6

Not 30...♖c6?? 31.♕e5+ ♔d7 32.♖f7+ ♖e7 33.♕×e7#.

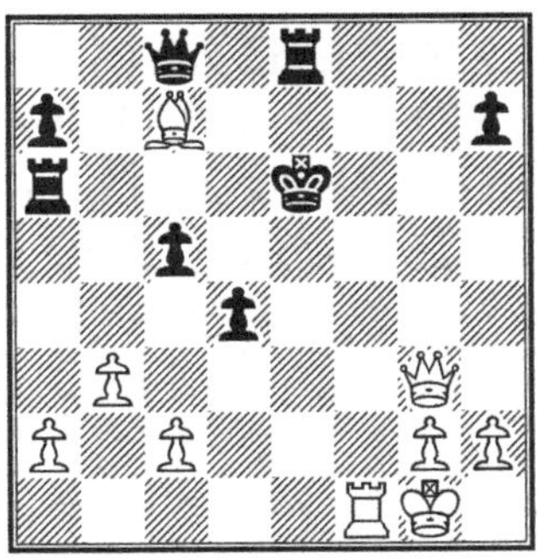

31.c4?

It's not clear what Torre had in mind with this move, but it could have allowed Black to draw. Best was 31.♕g4+ ♔d5 32.♕f3+ ♖e4 33.c4+ d×c3 34.♖d1+ ♔c6 35.♗e5 ♕g4 36.♖d6+ ♔b5 37.♕d3+ etc., winning.

Also good were 31.♕h3+, 31.♕d3, 31.♕f3, plus several other moves.

31...♔d7!□ 32.♖f5 ♖ae6!

Of course not 32...♕×c7?? 33.♖f7+ ♖e7 34.♖×e7+ ♔×e7 35.♕×c7+.

33.♖d5+ ♔c6□ 34.h3

Necessary to forestall back-rank threats.

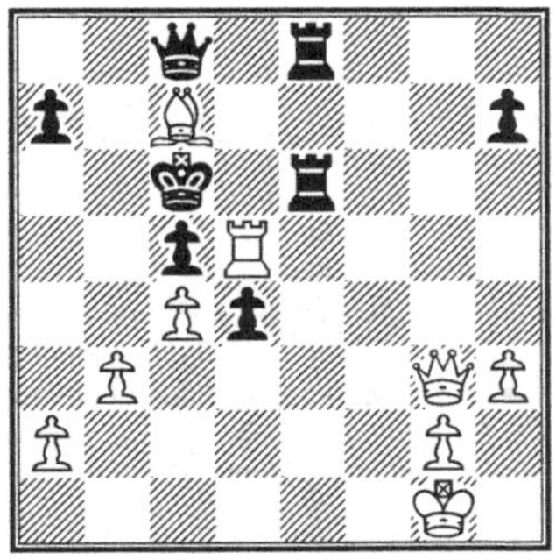

34...♖g8??

After finding all the right moves to draw, Black errs for the last time.

Correct was 34...♕×c7 35.♖×c5+ ♔×c5 36.♕×c7+ ♔b4, or 34...♖e1+ 35.♔h2 ♕×c7 etc., with an even ending either way (0.00/45).

35.♕f3!

Torre finds the only winning move.

35...♖e3

If 35...♔×c7 36.♖×c5+, or 35...♕×c7 36.♖e5+ ♔d7 37.♕f7+ etc.

36.♖×c5+ ♔×c5 37.♕d5+ 1-0

It's mate next move: 37...♔b4 38.♕a5#.

A good rough-and-tumble fighting game, imperfect but exciting.

Game 11

Torre-Schapiro

Exhibition game, New York, 15 December 1924

Queen's Gambit Declined [D43]

Torre's revenge for his loss to Schapiro in Game 6.

1.d4 d5 2.c4 e6 3.♘f3 ♘f6 4.♗g5 h6

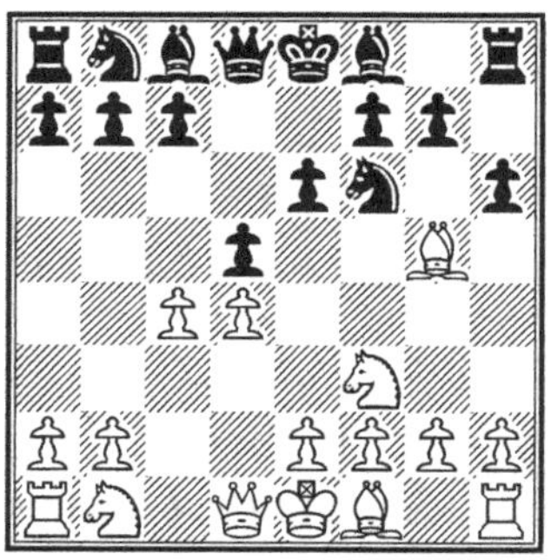

This reply casts the strongest doubt on the value of the 3.♘f3, 4.♗g5 system. White is now pretty much obliged to cede the Bishop pair without significant compensation, since if 5.♗f4 c5!, while after 5.♗h4 Black has either

(a) 5...d×c4 6.♕a4+ (not 6.e4? g5; if 6.e3 b5 7.♗e2 ♗b7∓, as in Makogonov–Ilyin-Zhenevsky, Tbilisi 1937 (½-½, 33)) 6...♘bd7 7.♕×c4 c5! 8.♘c3 a6 intending 9...b5 as in Freyman-Alekhine, St. Petersburg 1914 (0-1, 24); or

(b) 5...♗b4+ 6.♘c3 (or 6.♘bd2 d×c4, seen first in Stoltz-Gilg, Prague Olympiad 1931 (0-1, 28)) 6...d×c4 7.♕a4+ ♘c6 8.a3 ♗×c3+ 9.b×c3 ♕d5 10.♗×f6 g×f6 11.♕c2 f5 with at least equality.

5.♗×f6 ♕×f6 6.♘c3

More aggressive is 6.♕b3 c6 7.♘bd2 ♘d7 8.e4 d×e4 9.♘×e4 ♕f4 10.♗d3 and:

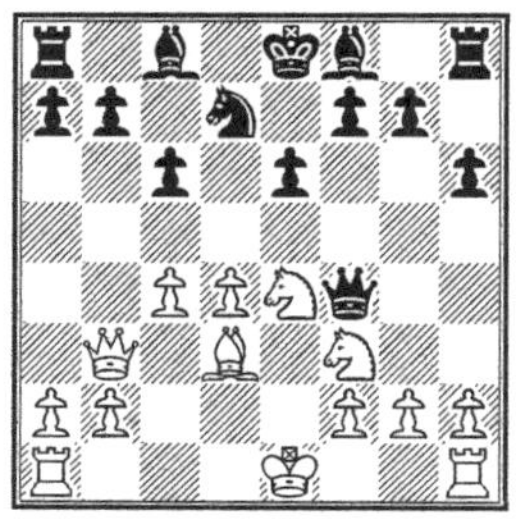

(a) 10...♘f6 11.♘×f6+ ♕×f6 12.0–0 ♗d6 13.♖fe1 0–0 14.c5 with complications, as in Capablanca-Ståhlberg, Buenos A. Olympiad 1939 (½-½, 30); or

(b) 10...e5 11.0–0 ♗e7 12.♖fe1 e×d4 13.♘×d4 (13.c5!?) 13...0–0 14.♗c2 ♘f6 15.♖ad1 g6 16.♘×f6+ ♗×f6 17.♖e4 ♕c7 18.♕e3 ♔g7∓, Euwe-Fine, AVRO 1938 (0-1, 44).

6...c6

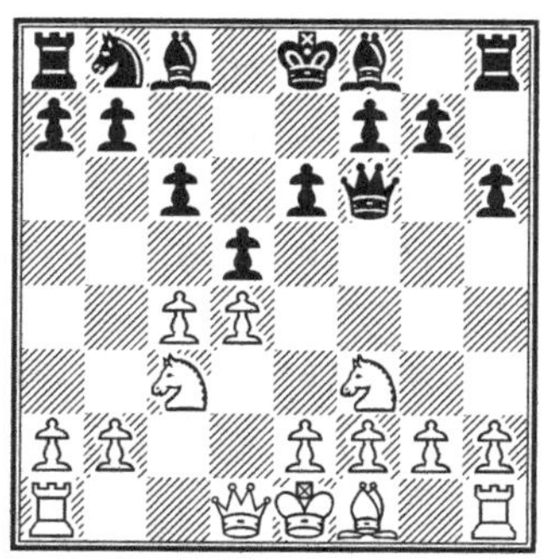

7.e3

Simplest and best. The thrust 7.♕b3 is now without basis, since the black d-pawn is well protected; furthermore Black can reply 7...d×c4 8.♕×c4 ♘d7 9.♖d1 g6! 10.e4 e5 11.d5 ♘b6 when he stands well.

7...♘d7 8.♗d3 ♕d8

The Queen retreat is necessary eventually; she has little to do on f6. Nevertheless, worth consideration was 8... ♗b4 9.0–0 ♕e7 10.♖c1 0–0 11.a3 ♗d6 so as to meet 12.c5 by 12...♗b8, with good play.

9.0–0 ♗e7 10.e4

White capitalizes on his advantage in development with this central push. If now 10...d×e4 11.♘×e4 0–0 12.♘g3 b6?! (△12...c5) 13.♗c2 ♗b7 14.♕d3 g6 15.♖ae1 with a strong initiative. Black prefers to capture the c-pawn, but this will give White a central preponderance.

10...d×c4 11.♗×c4 0–0 12.♕e2 b5!?

Seeking to launch a quick queenside offensive with ...♕b6, ...a6 and ...c5, but this is not without risk, because White controls the center.

13.♗d3 ♕b6?!

Seemingly natural, but not the best follow-up. Better either 13...♗b7, or; 13...b4 14.♘d1 c5=.

14.e5!

A first-class move, the best counter to Black's strategy. The weakening of the d5-square is unimportant for the time being, as Black is in no position to exploit it, either with his Knight or his Bishop. In contrast, the move opens for White the e4-square, which will serve as a transfer point for his pieces en route to a rapid and explosive kingside assault.

14...♖d8 15.♕e4 ♘f8

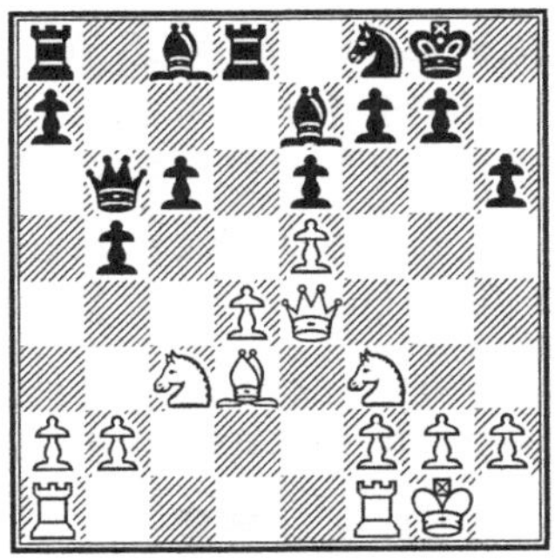

16.♖fd1

The immediate 16.♕g4!? was interesting and perhaps preferable, *viz.* 16...f5? 17.e×f6 ♗×f6 18.♖ad1 and Black dare not take the d-pawn: 18...♗×d4?? 19.♘×d4 ♖×d4 20.♕×d4 ♕×d4 21.♗h7+ ♘×h7 22.♖×d4+–. And if 16...c5 17.♘e4 much as in the game.

16...♗b7 17.♕g4 c5!

Finally the long-awaited liberating advance. This book's first edition gave the move some mild disparagement by putting "liberating advance" in quotes, but it is in fact Black's best choice. Where Black starts to go wrong is with his next move.

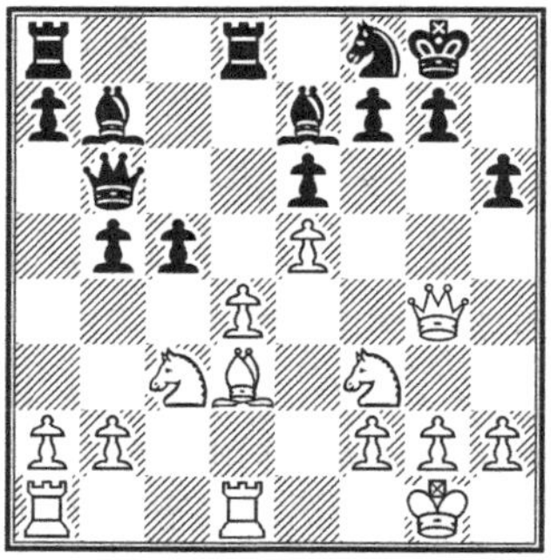

18.♘e4!

Torre is not attracted to the bait of the b-pawn, which would prove somewhat toxic after 18.♘×b5 (of course not 18.♗×b5?? ♗×f3 19.♕×f3 c×d4−+) 18...c×d4 [Not bad is 18...a6 19.♘c3 ♕×b2 (also good is 19...c×d4 20.♘e4/♘e2 ♘d7) 20.♖ab1 ♕×c3=.] 19.♘b×d4 ♖d7 20.♘b3 ♖ad8 and suddenly White is on the defensive.

18...c4?!

This impetuous advance shows that Black is oblivious to the growing danger. He is playing for the endgame, speculating about white weaknesses at d4 and d5, but the game never gets to such a point. Best here was 18...♘d7, preventing 19.♘f6+. Also good were 18...♗×e4 or 18...♔h8.

19.♘f6+!

Black will lose his way in the complications stirred up by this move.

19...♗×f6 20.e×f6 g6 21.♕h4

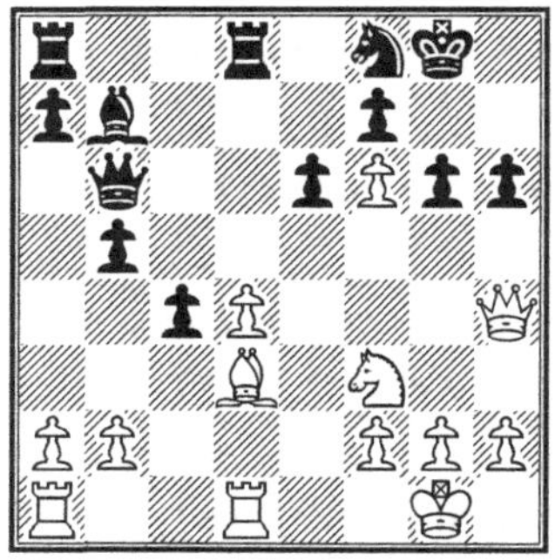

21...e5?

With the idea of vacating e6 for the Knight, from where it can defend the vital point g7. But objectively Black had only two playable moves:

(a) 21...h5 22.♕f4 ♔h7 (if 22...♘h7? 23.♕h6 ♘×f6 24.♗×g6! with a stronger attack than in variation **(b)** below) 23.♘g5+ ♔g8 24.♘e4 ♔h7□ 25.♗c2 ♖d5 (25...♖×d4?? 26.♘g5+) 26.♘g5+ ♔g8 27.♗e4 ♖d7 28.♗×b7 ♕×b7 with advantage to White (+1.40/27), but no clear win in sight;

(b) 21...♘h7 22.♗×g6!? with two main variations:

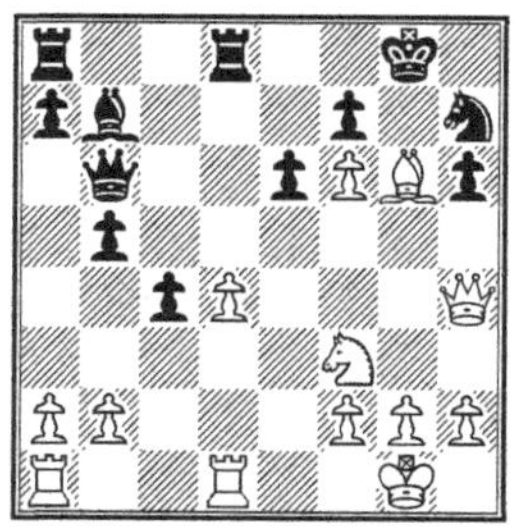

(b1) 22...f×g6 23.♕×h6 ♖d7 [if 23...♕c7?! 24.♕×g6+ ♔h8 25.♘e5 ♖d7 (forced) 26.f7 ♗d5 (defending the e-pawn) 27.♕h5 ♔g7 (+1.24/30)] 24.♘e5 ♘×f6 (not 24...♖c7?? 25.f7+) 25.♘×d7 ♘×d7 26.♕×g6+ ♔f8 27.h4 and the complications will continue indefinitely. Whether the material imbalance of ♖+♙-vs-♗+♘ is in White's or Black's favor remains to be seen. Stockfish says 0.00 at 30 ply; **(b2)** 22...♗×f3 23.♕×h6 ♘×f6 24.g×f3 ♕b7□ 25.♗e4 ♘×e4 26.♔g2! f6□ (not 26...♘d6?? 27.♖g1! and mate in at most four.) 27.♕g6+ ♕g7 28.♕×g7+ ♔×g7 29.f×e4 and the dust has finally settled with White up a pawn, but Stockfish considers the position virtually even (+0.23/30).

22.d×e5!

Torre's knack for finding the only winning move is seen again. If instead 22.♕×h6? ♕×f6 23.d×e5 ♕g7 (any other reasonable Queen move is also satisfactory) 24.♕×g7+ ♔×g7 25.♗e2 ♘e6= (0.00/32).

22...♗×f3

The white Bishop is untouchable: 22...c×d3?? 23.♕×h6 ♘e6 24.♘g5 and mate in short order. 22...♖×d3?? 23.♕×h6 is no better.

23.♕×h6 ♘e6

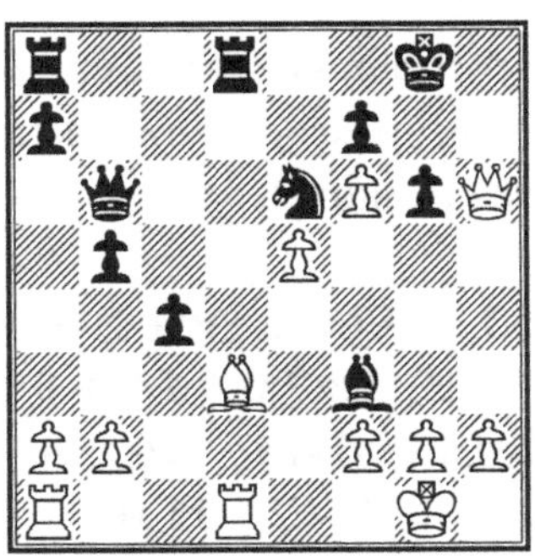

24.♗×g6!!

Again, the only winning move. In postgame analysis, several strong Manhattan Club players suggested here 24.♗f5 (threatening ♗×e6), giving the variation 24...g×f5 25.g×f3 ♕b7 26.♕h5 followed by ♔h1 etc. However, as Torre himself wrote in the *ACB*, 24.♗f5? fails to 24...♖×d1+ 25.♖×d1 ♖d8! (the kibitzers had considered only 25...♕c5??) 26.♖f1 g×f5 27.g×f3 ♕c6! 28.♔g2 ♖d4! and it is Black who would win. It bears mentioning that the kibitzers' 25...♕b7?? was a blunder that is refuted not by 26.♕h5? but 26.♔g2!, preparing for the Rook to dispense death on the g-file.

24...f×g6

Anything else allows mate in eight at most.

25.♕×g6+ ♔f8

25...♔h8 is no better, merely transposing to the game continuation.

26.g×f3 ♕b7 27.f4!

Threatening 28.f5.

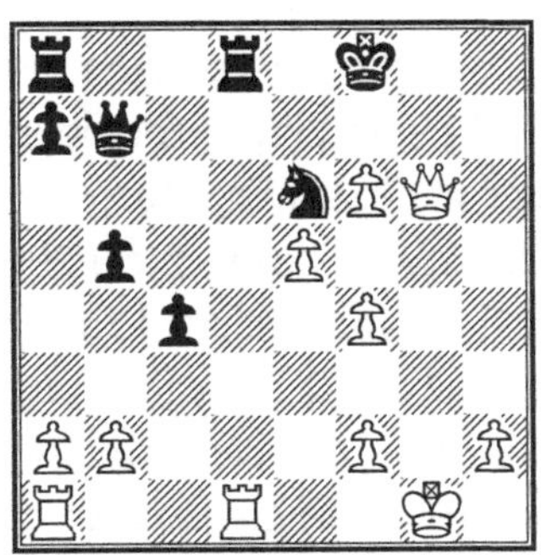

27...♘d4

This allows a beautiful finish, but there was no satisfactory defense. If, say, 27...♕f7 28.♕h6+ ♔e8 29.f5 ♕g8+ 30.♔h1 ♘f8 31.e6 ♖×d1+ 32.♖×d1 ♕g4 33.♕g7+−. Or 27...♖d3 (relatively best) 28.♖×d3 c×d3 29.♖d1 ♕f3 30.♖×d3 ♕×f4 31.♕h7 ♕g4+ 32.♔f1 ♖c8 33.♕h8+ ♕g8 34.♕h6+ ♔e8 35.♖g3 etc. And of course if 27...♘×f4 28.♕h6+ ♔g8 29.♕×f4+−.

28.♖×d4! ♖×d4 29.e6 ♖d7

Thinking that he can perhaps salvage the endgame resulting from 30.e×d7 ♕×d7, but in fact 31.♖e1 then forces mate in ten at most.

30.♖e1

Simplest, and just as good as 30.e×d7.

30...♖e8

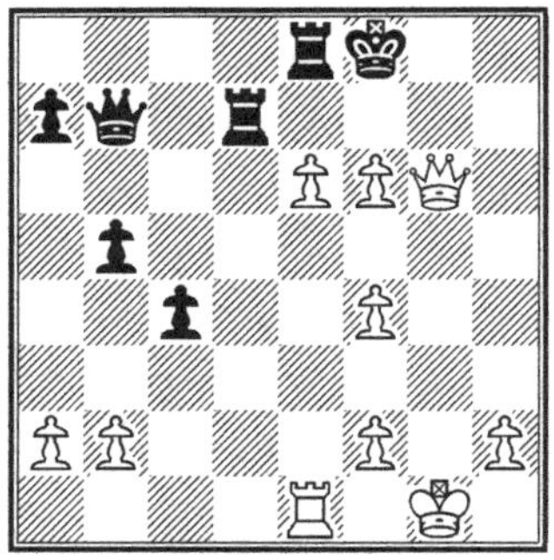

31.♕×e8+!! 1–0

A beautiful climax to a great attacking game. After 31...♔×e8 32.e×d7+ ♔×d7 (or 32...♔d8 33.♖e8+ etc.) 33. ♖e7+ brings the curtain down, hence Black resigns. Definitely a "best of" game, and indicative of the progress Torre was making in late 1924.

Game 12

Lear-Torre

New York State Championship, Rochester 1924

Queen's Gambit Declined [D67]

In this game we see Torre on the defensive. Playing White was Joseph D. Lear, a strong master from Buffalo, New York, who played the opening in excellent style, leaving Torre in a difficult, passive position. Realizing this, the Mexican master tried for complications, seeking a kingside counterattack that, in objective terms, was not justified. One might say that Torre was lucky to win a game he was on the point of losing, but as Capablanca was fond of saying in such cases, "Good players are often lucky." Partly as a result of this game, Torre never again played such a passive line as the Orthodox Defense; the only other example in this book is Game 1.

1.d4 d5 2.c4 e6 3.♘c3 ♘f6 4.♗g5 ♘bd7 5.e3 ♗e7 6.♘f3 0–0 7.♖c1 c6 8.♗d3 d×c4 9.♗×c4 ♘d5 10.♗×e7 ♕×e7 11.0–0 ♘×c3 12.♖×c3 b6

It is this move that leads to such a passive and difficult position for Black. Pachman's book on the Queen's Gambit (1964) says of the text merely that it is "used less often than 12...e5, but not bad." Nevertheless, Pachman does not say how to proceed against 13.♕e2, a perfectly logical and playable response. He cites only 13.♕c2, from Capablanca-H. Steiner, Budapest 1928, as noted in Game 1. We find essentially the same comment in Ståhlberg's *The Queen's Gambit* (1957). This is perhaps not surprising as in many cases opening books are to an extent merely copies of each other, much like Spanish-English dictionaries. We do not know what (if anything) the opening manuals of Torre's time were saying about 12...b6, but in fairness it should be mentioned that the move did not have a bad track record as of 1924. According to ChessBase, the line had suffered two losses: Marshall-Lowcki, Breslau 1912 (1-0, 26), and Euwe-Fontein, Scheveningen 1923 (1-0, 47); but also three wins: Euwe-Vidmar, London 1922 (0-1, 46), Davidson-Euwe, match 1924 (0-1, 26), and of course Labatt-Torre, New Orleans 1923 (0-1, 28). And also one draw, Sterk-Kostic, Budapest 1921 (½-½, 36). Eventually, though, ChessBase shows 12...b6 scoring only +14 -34 =34 in 82 games through 2016. So on both theoretical and practical grounds it must be considered wanting.

13.♕e2

First played in the aforementioned games Sterk-Kostic and Euwe-Vidmar.

The move certainly appears strong and logical, but it has been seen much less often than Capablanca's 13.♕c2, and has performed notably worse statistically, with ChessBase showing a record of just +2 -6 =8, compared to 13.♕c2's +18 -5 =9 through 2016.

13...♖d8 14.♖fc1

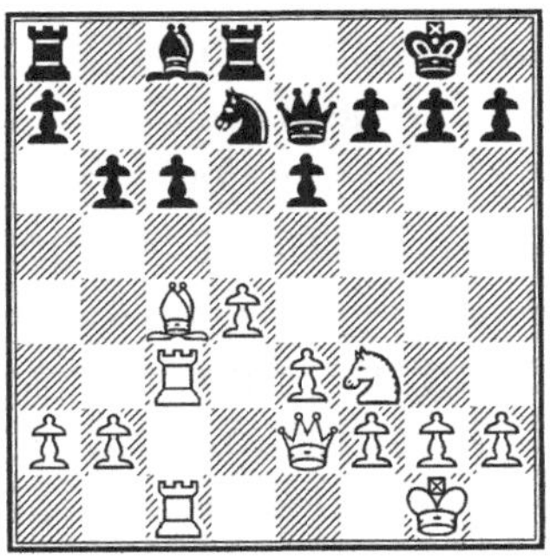

14...♗b7

A good alternative was 14...c5 15.♗b5 (if 15.♗a6?! ♗×a6 16.♕×a6 e5 with definite equality) 15...♗b7 16.d×c5 ♘×c5 17.b4 ♘e4 18.♖c7 ♕×b4 19.♖×b7 ♘d6 20.♗c6 ♘×b7 21.♗×b7 ♖ab8 with another even (0.00/27) ♗+♘-vs-♖+♙ situation as in Game 11, note to move 21, variation b1).

15.♗a6 ♗×a6 16.♕×a6

Curiously, we have arrived at a position identical to Game 1, except that White is a move ahead, as his King's Rook already occupies c1.

16...c5 17.♕a3

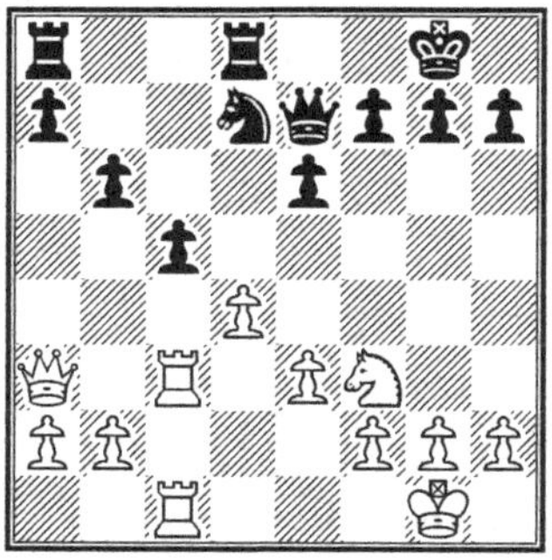

At this point, in the book's first edition we opined that Black's position "begins to deteriorate seriously." Yet Stockfish says that after 17...e5 matters would be dead even (0.00/31)! Optically, White does look better, with his doubled Rooks, his more advanced Knight, and his Queen both pinning Black's c-pawn and preventing Black's Queen's Rook from moving. Yet there is no organic weakness on the black side, nor any organic superiority on the white.

17...h6

One of eight moves Stockfish assesses as no worse than +0.30. It considers 17...e5 best, giving the continuation 18.d×c5 (18.d×e5?! ♘×e5 19.♘×e5 ♕×e5 is seen as better for Black (-0.78/26), possibly because of his queenside pawn majority) 18...♘×c5 19.b4 ♘e4 20.♖c4 ♘d2 21.♘×d2 ♖×d2 with an evaluation no worse than dead even after any reasonable white move. The text is quite sensible, giving the King an escape hatch in the event of the c-file opening and a white Rook invading the 8th rank.

18.h3 ♕f6

With this move Torre starts to go astray. Though not posted very actively at e7, the Queen was performing a valuable function, keeping the queenside stable. Better was 18...a5, preventing 19.b4 and clamping down on potential queenside action, besides freeing the ♖a8 from defense of the a-pawn.

19.b4 c×d4 20.♘×d4

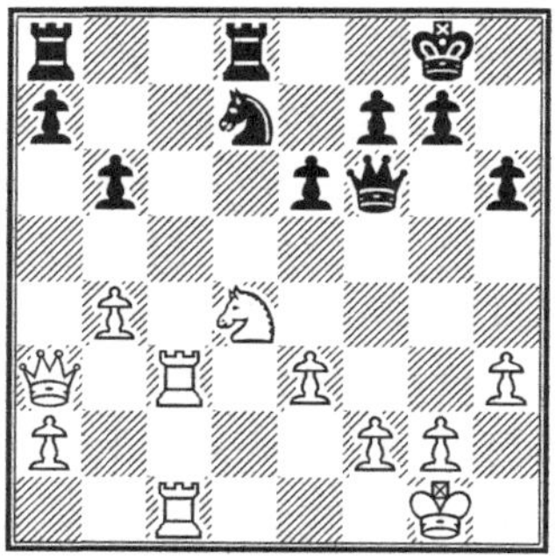

In the first edition we wrote: "Positionally, the game is almost won for White: he has absolute domination of the only open file and invasion of the seventh rank by his Rooks is imminent; he also has a strong centralized Knight, and is close to winning Black's a-pawn." Nevertheless, as dominant as White's position might appear, translating his positional advantage into a tactical win is very problematic against best play, which Stockfish gives as 20...a5 and:

(a) 21.b×a5 ♖×a5 22.♕b2 ♘c5 23.♕×b6 ♖×a2 (threatening mate) 24.♖3c2 ♖×c2 25.♖×c2 ♘e4=;

(b) 21.b5 ♘c5 and the best White has is 22.♖×c5!? b×c5 23.♕×c5 and though the passed b-pawn looks like a potential threat, the game is actually even (0.00/30 after 23...a4, 23...♖d5, or 23...e5;

(c) 21.♖3c2 (defending the a-pawn against 21...a×b4 22.♕×b4 ♖×a2) 21...♘e5 (not 21...a×b4? 22.♕×b4 ♖a6 23.♘c6 ♖da8 24.♕d6! ♘c5 25.♘b4 ♖a4 26.♕×b6±) 22.b×a5 b×a5 23.♖c5 a4 with only a slight edge for White (+0.44/30).

20...♘e5

Rather than purely defensive play, Torre tries for complications, beginning an action against the enemy King with his Queen and Knight. This proves risky, but by now Torre had surely learned from Marshall the psychological impact of aggressive counterplay, even when not entirely sound.

21.♕a6!

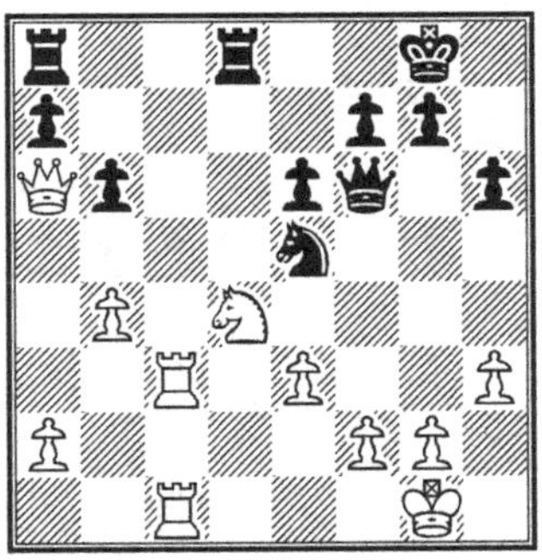

Blockading the a-pawn before invading the 7th rank.

21...♔h7!?

This move is based more on perceptive intuition than concrete considerations. The Yucatán master seeks to confuse his opponent and provoke him to an excessive optimism. A computer programmed to make only "correct" moves would play 21...♖d7 and after, say, 22.♖c7 ♖×c7 23.♖×c7 ♖d8 24.♖c8 (if 24.♕×a7?! ♘d3 25.♖c2 ♘×b4=, or 24.♖×a7?! ♘c6 25.♖a8 ♘×b4=) 24...♖×c8 25.♕×c8+ ♔h7 26.♕c7 ♘d3 27.♕c2 ♕g6 28.♘c6 e5 would find itself still on the defensive (+0.37/37). But Torre is playing the man, not the board.

22.a3

Not bad, though the strongest reply was 22.♖c7.

22...♘g6?!

Black abandons the a-pawn to its fate, and sends the Knight off to muddy the waters and fish, but objectively this is too risky. Best was 22...♕g6 and if 23.♖c7 as in the game, then 23...♘d3 24.♖f1 ♘f4!? 25.e×f4 ♖×d4∞.

23.♖c7

Straightforward and best.

23...♘h4

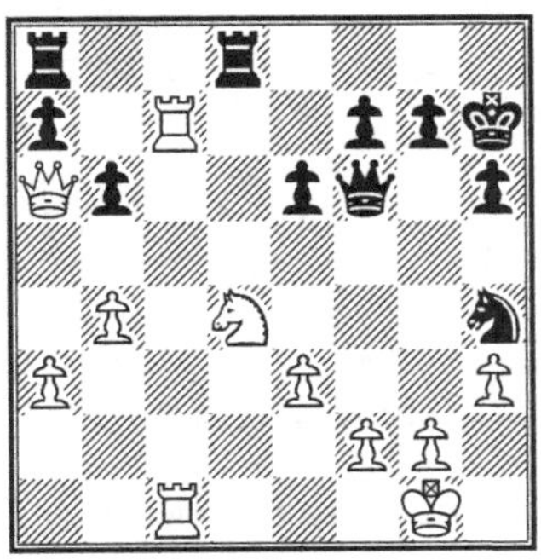

A trap, inviting White into ambush via 24.♖×a7?? ♖×a7 25.♕×a7 ♖×d4!! 26.e×d4 ♕g5 and 27...♕×c1 –+. A swindler's delight! White avoids this particular trap, but Black has more in store.

24.♕b7

White could have squelched Black's would-be attack by 24.♕d3+! ♔g8 25.♕e4 ♘g6 26.♘c6 ♖d5 27.b5! ♕b2 (not 27...♖×b5?? 28.♘e7+ ♘×e7 29.♕×a8+) 28.♘d4 (△29.♘×e6) 28...♖e8 29.a4 with a terrific positional bind that must soon bear tactical fruit, *e.g.* 29...♕a3 30.♖1c6! ♘e7 [if 30...♕×a4?? 31.♖×e6! ♖×e6 (31...f×e6?? 32.♕×g6 and mate shortly.) 32.♕×d5 ♖f6 33.♖c8+ ♔h7 34.♕d8+–) 31.♖c4 ♕d6 32.♖×a7+–.

24...♕g6!?

Throwing out the fishing line once again, and this time the opponent bites.

25.♖×f7?!

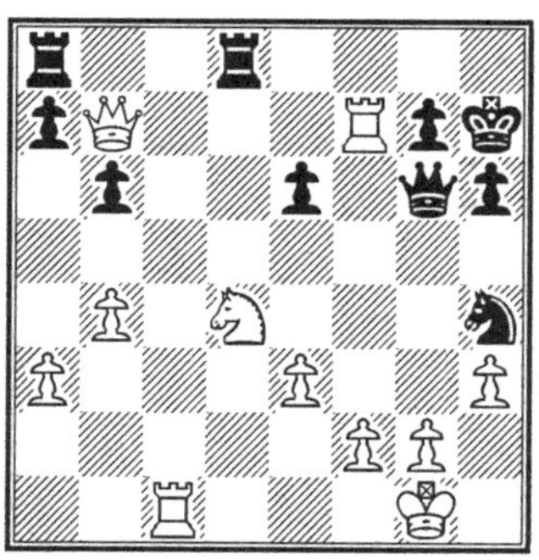

This capture may not be objectively a losing move, but it leads to very sharp complications not in White's favor. Sounder and more correct was 25.g3!, which would have shown Black's speculative attack to have the worth of a 3-dollar bill. After the text move, the position becomes unclear.

25...♖db8!

One of the two good moves at this point. The other was 25...♖×d4! 26.e×d4 (or 26.♖×g7+ ♕×g7 27.♖c7 ♖d1+ 28.♔h2 ♖g8 29.♖×g7+ ♖×g7 30.♕e4+ ♘g6 31.♕×e6∓) 26...♖b8 27.♖×g7+ ♕×g7 28.♕e4+ ♘g6 29.♕×e6 ♖f8∓. The text forces White into some hair-raising tactics, since now the Queen cannot defend both g2 and f7 simultaneously.

26.♖×g7+ ♕×g7 27.♕e4+ ♘g6 28.♘×e6 ♕f6

Only this or 28...♖e8 will do, due to the threat of 29.♖c7+.

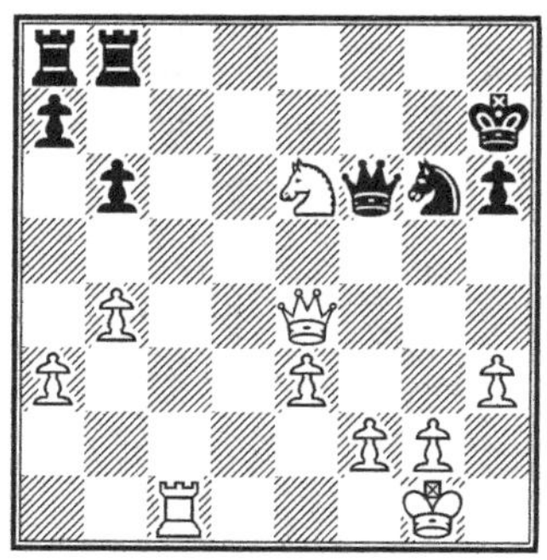

29.♘f4?

White finally goes astray. His only playable move was 29.♖c7+, forcing 29...♔h8 30.♘f4 (30.♖g7?? ♖g8–+) 30...♖g8 31.♖c6 ♕a1+ 32.♔h2 ♕e5 33.♕f3□ ♖ae8 34.♕g3 ♕g5 35.♘×g6+

♔h7 36.♘f4 ♕×g3+ 37.f×g3 ♖c8, when though White has three pawns for the Exchange, the endgame appears even as long as White avoids a Rook exchange (0.00/26). If he does exchange Rooks, his Knight and King will be unable to defend his scattered pawns.

29...♖g8?
This could have thrown the game back in White's favor.
Correct and winning was 29...♖c8! 30.♖d1 ♖d8 31.♖c1 ♖ac8 and the Rook exchange is forced.

30.♖c7+
Missing 30.♕b7+! ♔h8 31.♖c6 ♖ab8 (anything else is much worse) 32.♖×f6 ♖×b7 33.♘×g6+ ♔h7 34.♘f4 when, unlike the note to White's previous move, his pawn structure is much better and with ♘+3♙-vs-♖ he has good winning chances. After the text, the position is even once again.

30...♔h8 31.♕b7 ♖gb8 32.♕e4□

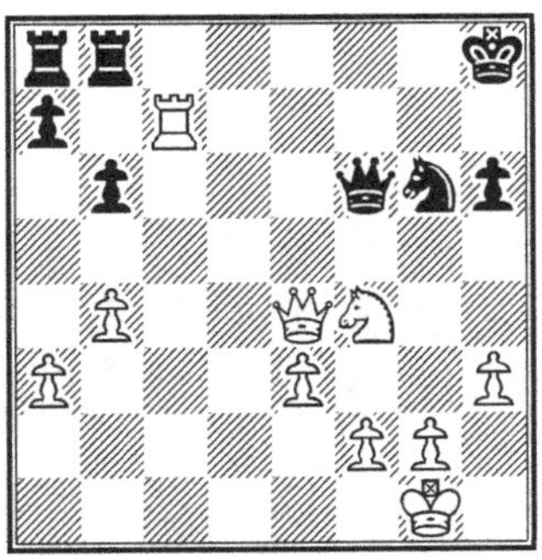

32.♖h7+ ♔g8 33.♕c7 fails to 33...♖c8 34.♕b7 ♘×f4. With his next move Black invites a draw by repetition, which White, either overestimating his position or angry with himself for missing earlier chances, mistakenly refuses.

32...♖g8 33.♖c6
Only this or 33.♕b7 keeps the draw in hand.

33...♕a1+□ 34.♔h2 ♕e5

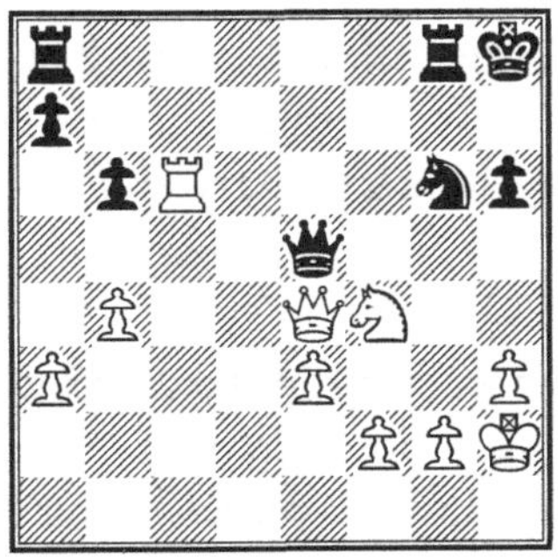

35.♕×g6?? 0-1
With the "brilliant" idea of 35...♖×g6 36.♘×g6+, recovering the Queen with a piece and three pawns to the good. A fabulous finish, but for the minor detail that the Knight is pinned. White stopped the clock and resigned
He could have retained the draw with 35.♕f3 or 35.♕c2. The only other perhaps playable line was 35.♕×e5+ ♘×e5 36.♖×h6+ ♔g7 37.♖h5 ♘c4 38.a4, when the endgame would have been highly problematic, as White has four connected passed pawns for the Rook. We venture to say that Black would have good chances, and Stockfish agrees (-1.98/26), but we hope the reader will understand if we do not provide exhaustive analysis.

Game 13

Torre-Adams

New York State Championship, Rochester 1924

Ruy López [C60]

The player of Black in this game was not related to the aforementioned Edwin Ziegler Adams of New Orleans. Edward Bradford Adams (1878–1972), alumnus of Yale, was a New York master. Neither should be confused with other chess worthies such as Edward Beckley Adams of Maryland or Weaver W. Adams of Massachusetts.

1.e4 e5 2.♘f3 ♘c6 3.♗b5 g6

An old variation, now seldom seen, introduced by the Danish master Martin From at Paris 1867. Steinitz liked it for a while, playing it four times at London 1883. It was a particular favorite of Pillsbury, and was also played by Alekhine, Euwe, Réti, Spielmann and other early 20th century greats, though usually more with the idea of surprising the opponent than from belief in its objective merits. Still, it has had its later adherents, especially Smyslov, who scored +17 -6 =24 with it over 1975-2000. B. Spassky also played it twelve times 1985-1993, scoring +4 -2 =6.

4.d4

Not bad, though 4.c3 is more often played.

4...e×d4

The best reply. In 1920, Rubinstein recommended 4...♘×d4, with the following idea: 5.♘×d4 e×d4 6.♕×d4 ♕f6 7.e5 ♕b6. However, all of Rubinstein's analysis was based on the premise that White would now play 8.♕×b6. Some years later, the Hungarian GM Maróczy showed that with 8.♕d3! White gains an advantage, for example 8...c6 9.♗c4 ♕a5+ 10.♘c3 ♕×e5+ 11.♗e3 d5 12.0–0–0! with a strong lead in development for the pawn.

5.♘×d4?!

Indicating that Black's choice of opening has had its intended surprise effect. The correct continuation is 5.♗g5! f6 6.♗f4 (if 6.♗h4 ♗g7 7.♘×d4 ♘ge7 8.♗c4?! (△8.♘c3) 8...♘a5 9.♗e2 d5 10.e×d5 ♘×d5 11.♕d2 c5! with initiative, as in Dely-Smyslov, Szolnok 1975) 6...♗g7 7.0–0±.

5...♗g7=

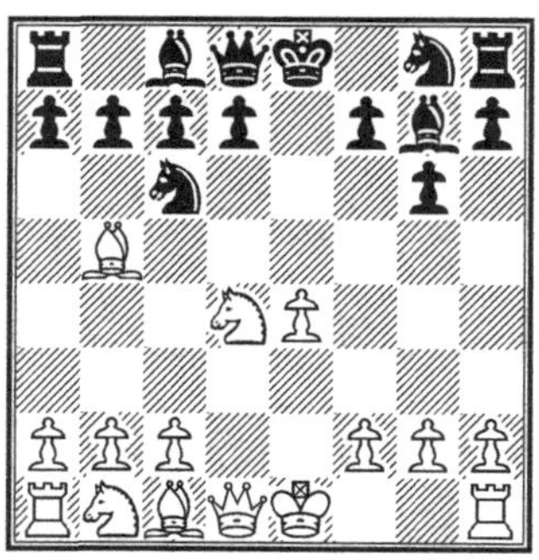

6.♗e3
Or 6.♘×c6 b×c6 7.♗c4 ♘e7 8.♘c3 d6 9.0–0 ♗e6 10.♗b3 0–0 11.♗e3 c5 12.♗×e6 f×e6 with advantage to Black as in Lasker-Pillsbury, Hastings 1895 (1-0, 40).
The text move was seen in Teichmann-Pillsbury from the same event (0-1, 30).

6...♕e7?!
But this is wrong. Against Teichmann, Pillsbury played here 6...♘f6 7.♘c3 0–0 8.f3 ♘e7 9.0–0 c6 10.♗d3 d5∓.

7.♘c3 ♘f6 8.0–0 ♘×d4 9.♗×d4

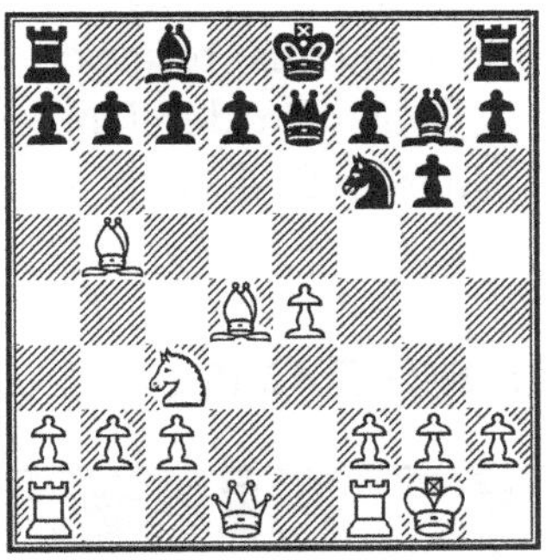

9...c6?
Necessary was 9...0–0 10.e5 ♘e8 11.♘d5 ♕d8 12.♗c5 d6 13.e×d6 c×d6 14.♗d4, when though Black has been forced into a truly Steinitzian retreat (see Lasker-Steinitz, Hastings 1895, after Black's 18th move), he may yet survive (+0.91/25).

10.e5! ♘h5
The simplest way to refute Black's strategy. Now Black cannot capture the Bishop: 10...c×b5?? 11.e×f6 ♗×f6 12.♖e1+–.

11.♗c4
Good, but even stronger was 11.f4, when relatively best is 11...d5 [not 11...c×b5?? 12.♘d5 ♕d8 13.♗c5 (△14.♗e7 winning the Queen) 13...♗f8 14.♗d6 ♗×d6 15.e×d6 0–0 16.♕d4 and Black can resign (+5.20/25)] 12.g4 c×b5 13.g×h5 ♗e6 14.♘×b5 0–0 15.♕d2 (+2.05/25).

11...0–0 12.♖e1
White has emerged from the opening with clear advantages in space and development.

12...b5 13.♗e2
It's not clear why Torre chose this less effective retreat, shifting the Bishop from the a2-g8 diagonal to the a8-h1. Best was 13.♗b3, maintaining pressure on Black's kingside.

13...♘f4 14.♗f3

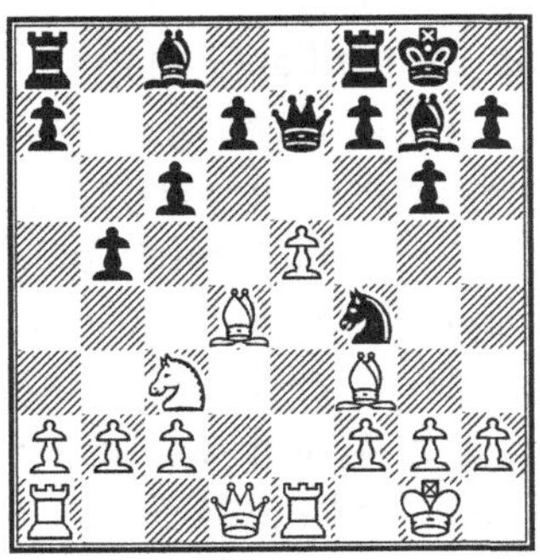

14...♗a6?
But Black hands the advantage right back. With 14...♘e6! the game would have been even, best play continuing 15.♘×b5 ♕b4 16.a4 ♘×d4 17.♘×d4 ♕×b2=, or 15.a4 b4 16.♘b5 ♘×d4

17.♕×d4 d5! 18.e×d6 ♕×e1+ 19.♖×e1 ♗×d4 20.♘×d4 ♗d7 21.♖d1= (21.♘×c6?! ♗×c6 22.♗×c6 ♖ac8 23.♗b5 ♖×c2∓)

15.a4

More precise and energetic was 15.♘e4!, since if 15...♗×e5?? (△15...♘e6) 16.♘c5 wins material. The text allows activation of the Bishop at a6.

15...b4 16.♘e4

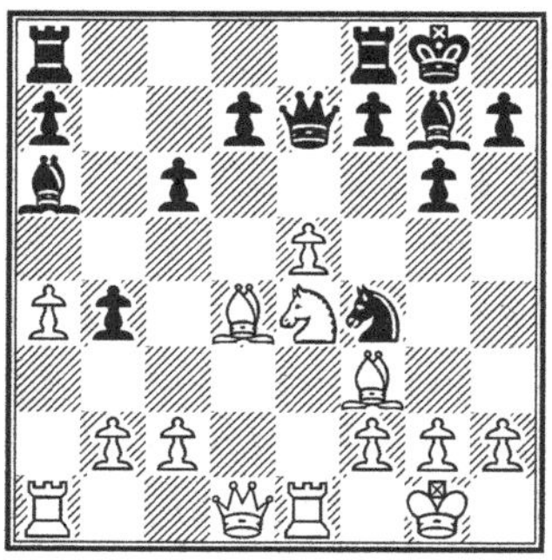

16...♗×e5?

Black sees he can now take this pawn without immediate material loss, due to the *Zwischenschach* 17...♘e2+. However, he does not see that in doing so he lets all White's pieces develop rapidly to their best squares. The excellent teacher, International Master and World Correspondence Champion Cecil Purdy once wrote an interesting article titled "The Tyranny of the Pawn," discussing how chessplayers are too often willing to cede positional or other advantages for the sake of a single pawn. Black here would have benefitted from Purdy's advice. Correct was 16...♘e6, to answer 17.♘f6+ with 17...♔h8 18.♗e3 d6 when White must walk a narrow path to retain his advantage: 19.♗×c6 ♖ad8 20.♘d5 ♕h4 21.♕d2 d×e5 22.♕×b4 ♕c4 23.♕×c4 ♗×c4 24.♘b4 ♖b8 25.♘d3 (+1.39/25). However, White can do a bit better than this by playing 17.c3 (+1.66/26).

17.♘c5

Also good was 17.♘f6+ ♕×f6 18.♗×e5 ♕g5 19.♕×d7+−.

17...♘e2+ 18.♗×e2 ♗×d4 19.♕×d4 ♗×e2 20.♖ad1

Playable was 20.♘×d7 ♖ad8 21.♘f6+, but Torre disdains recovery of the pawn in favor of a developing move which brings him a decisive advantage in short order.

20...♖fe8 21.♖d2 ♕g5

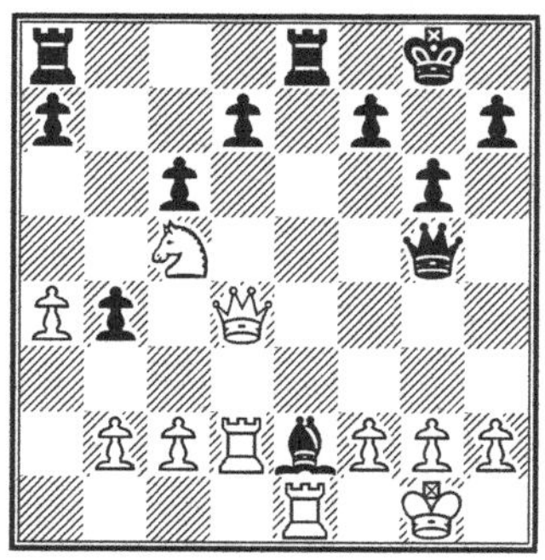

Setting a trap: if now 22.♖d×e2?? ♖×e2 23.♖×e2 ♕c1+ and mate next. True, it is a bit obvious, but does it not at least get the Queen out of her awkward situation on the e-file? Perhaps, but White's reply shows that Black pays one way or another.

22.f4!

Showing that Black actually had no way of extricating the threatened piece. The final moves were

22...♕f5 23.♖d×e2 ♖×e2 24.♖×e2 d6 25.♘e4 ♖e8 26.♘f6+ ♕×f6 27.♖×e8+ ♔g7 28.♖g8+ 1-0

Game 14

Torre-Jennings

New York State Championship playoff match, game 2, New York, 1924

Queen's Gambit Declined [D30]

Rochester-born Harold Evans Jennings (1898-1990) did not have to travel far to play in this tournament, and this "home court advantage" may have helped him share first place with Torre. However, the playoff match in New York City was another story.

1.d4 ♘f6 2.♘f3 d5 3.c4 e6 4.♗g5 ♘bd7 5.e3 c6 6.♘bd2

This strong idea of Capablanca's, as mentioned earlier, refutes Black's strategy in this line.

6...♕a5

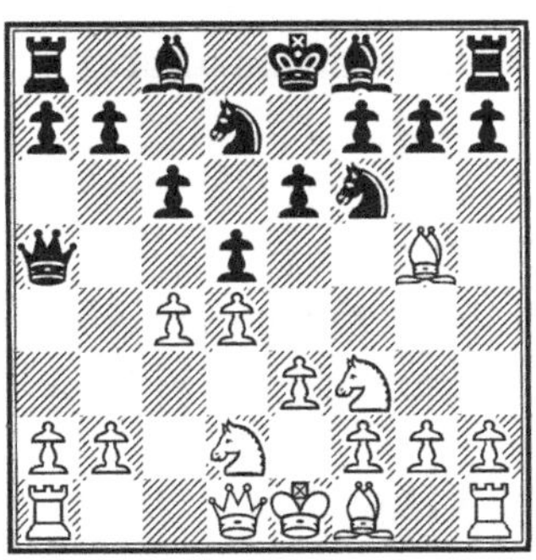

This move is not as effective here as it is in the Cambridge Springs Defense (6.♘c3 ♕a5). White has two good replies at his disposal: 7.a3 and 7.c×d5. Interestingly, the originator of the 6.♘bd2 system had the opportunity to test both replies to 6...♕a5 in tournament play:

(a) 7.c×d5 e×d5 8.♗d3 ♘e4 9.0–0 (△9.♗f4±) 9...♘×g5 10.♘×g5 ♘f6 11.h3 h6 12.♘gf3 ♗d6 13.♘e5 0–0 14.f4=, Capablanca-Tartakower, Moscow 1925 (1-0, 73);

(b) 7.a3 ♗e7 8.b4 ♕d8 9.♗d3 0–0 10.0–0 d×c4 11.♘×c4 ♘d5 12.♗×e7 ♕×e7 13.♕c2 g6 14.h4 ♘5b6 15.♘a5 e5 16.h5 e×d4 with complications, Capablanca-Kupchik, Lake Hopatcong 1926 (½-½, 41). Incidentally, the present game Torre-Jennings appears to be the first occurrence of 7.a3, but it is unlikely that Capablanca knew of it in 1926. The logical moves are continually rediscovered in tournament practice.

7.a3 d×c4 8.♗×c4 ♗d6 9.0–0 e5?

A dubious idea, opening the position before castling. However, even after

9...0–0 10.♗d3 White stands better, according to Torre's notes of the time. Stockfish concurs: +2.24/26.

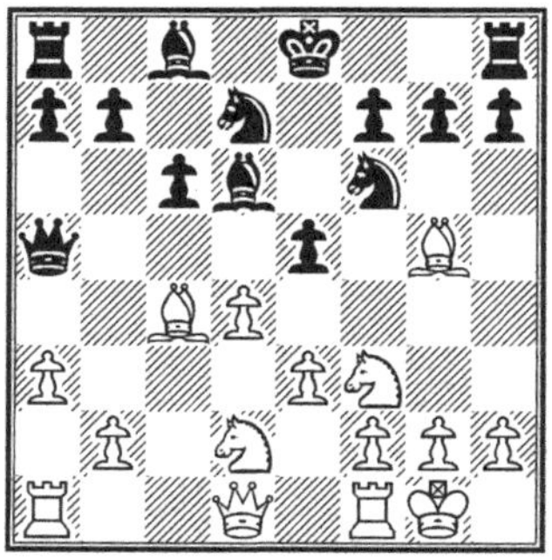

10.♕b3

A natural and reasonable move, but much stronger was the quietly lethal 10.♗a2! △11.♘c4. The key to victory for White lies in possession of the Bishop pair. He does obtain this soon, but only because Black allows it. On the other hand, 10.♗a2 virtually forces it, *viz.*:

(a) 10...e4 11.♘c4 ♕c7 12.♘×d6+ ♕×d6 13.♘d2;

(b) 10...♕c7 11.♘c4 e×d4 (11...e4 merely transposes to (a), while if 11...♗e7?? 12.d×e5 ♘e4 13.♗×e7 ♔×e7 14.♕d4 ♘dc5 15.♘d6+–) 12.♘×d6+ ♕×d6 13.♗f4 ♕e7 14.♕×d4;

(c) If 10...♗b8, to avoid the fork of Queen and Bishop, then 11.♘c4 ♕d8 12.d×e5 ♘×e5 13.♘c×e5 0–0 14.♗×f7+! etc.;

(d) And 10...b5, to prevent 11.♘c4, is a cure worse than the disease, allowing White several ways to win, *e.g.*

(d1) 11.♕b3 0–0 12.♗×f6 ♘×f6 13.d×e5 ♗×e5 14.♘×e5 ♕×d2 15.♖ad1 ♕a5 16.♘×f7 etc.;

(d2) 11.d×e5 ♗×e5 12.♘×e5 ♘×e5 13.♗×f6 g×f6 14.f4 ♗g4 15.♕c2 ♘d7 (or 15...♘c4 16.♘×c4 b×c4 17.f5! etc.) 16.♕×c6+–;

(d3) 11.♗×f6 g×f6 (11...♘×f6? 12.d×e5) 12.♘e4 ♗e7 13.d×e5 (13.♘h4 △14.♘f5 is also very strong) 13...f×e5 14.♘fg5 (equally good is 14.♘d6+ ♗×d6 15.♕×d6 ♕d8 16.♘×e5+–) 14...♗×g5 15.♘×g5 0–0 16.♕h5 ♘f6 17.♕h6 ♕d8 18.♗b1 with a crushing attack.

Strong though 10.♗a2 would have been, it is a type of move that does not readily occur to a human player, being both quiet and a backward retreat.

10...0–0 11.d×e5 ♗×e5?

The power of the Bishops will be so great that it was better not to worry about kingside pawn structure, and play 11...♘×e5 12.♗×f6 g×f6, when Black has the two ♗'s.

12.♘×e5 ♕×e5 13.♘f3

Torre prefers to aim for a slightly advantageous endgame, rather than risk 13.f4 with uncertain attacking chances.

13...♕c7?

13...♕e7 was much the better retreat, avoiding the exchange of Queens.

14.♗f4 ♕b6

If 14...♕d8 White can continue to pile on positional pressure with 15.♖fd1.

15.♗d6 ♕×b3 16.♗×b3 ♖e8

The white Bishops have a lion's share of the board. Black's only advantage lies in his queenside pawn majority, but it will be extremely difficult to use that until he can develop his Queen's Bishop and connect his Rooks.

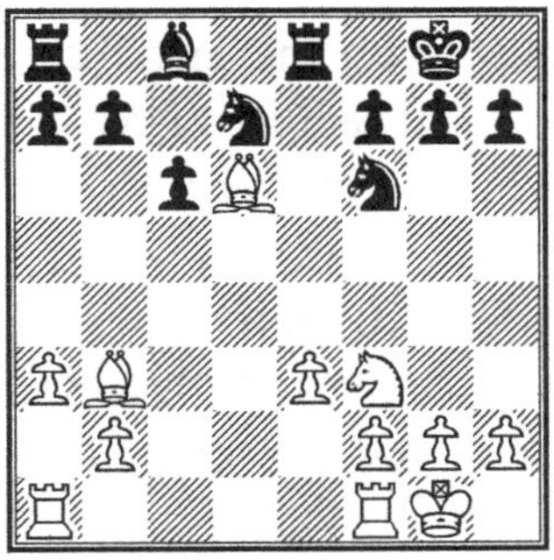

The correct strategy to follow with the Bishop pair was described in the 19th century by Dr. Tarrasch: restrict the range of the enemy pieces and augment that of one's own. The present game is as instructive in this regard as any of Steinitz, Tarrasch, or Lasker. Perhaps the three most notable such games of the 19th century are Englisch-Steinitz, London 1883; Richter-Tarrasch, Nuremberg 1888; and Blackburne-Lasker, London 1892. Later grandmasters have also produced masterful examples of Bishop pair technique, a prime example being Fischer-Ibrahimoglu, Siegen 1970.

17.♘g5!

The Bishops' long-range bite is already felt; Black cannot defend the f-pawn by 17.♖f8/♖e7.

17...♘d5□ 18.e4 h6□ 19.e×d5

Not 19.♘×f7? ♖×e4!=.

19...h×g5 20.♖fe1!

Torre demonstrates a fine knowledge of the precepts of Tarrasch. 20.d×c6 b×c6 is attractive because it leaves a black pawn weak; nevertheless, this weak pawn would serve as a support to the black Knight once it reaches d5. To restrict Black's mobility it is essential to deny the Knight any central outpost.

20...♘f6 21.♖×e8+ ♘×e8 22.♗e7 c×d5 23.♗×d5

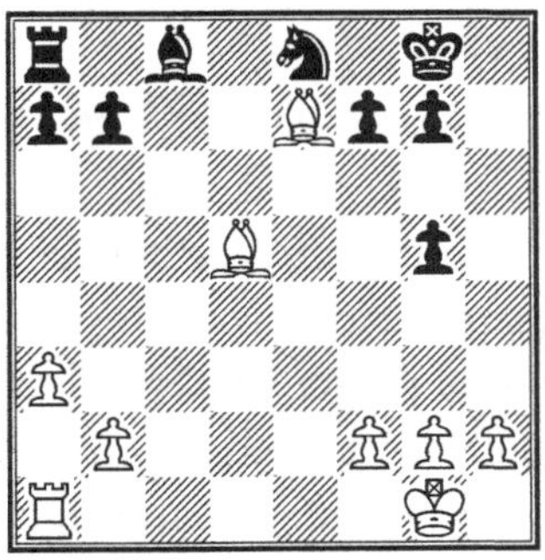

23...♘c7?!

Better was 23...♘f6, which would force White either to give up a Bishop with 24.♗×f6, or allow Black to develop his Bishop, *e.g.* 24.♗f3 g4 25.♗e2 ♗d7 etc. After the text Black's Bishop will not enter the game for some time yet.

24.♗e4!

Hindering development of the ♗c8. No good now is 24...♖b8?? 25.♗d6!.

24...f6 25.♖c1

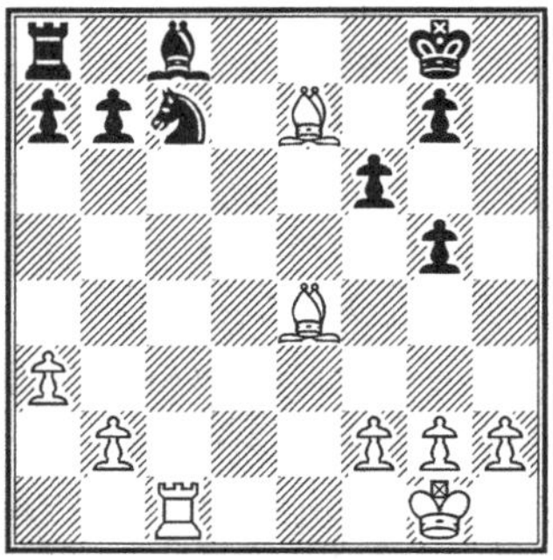

25...♘e8

Black's pieces are being pushed to the edge of the board. If 25...♘b5 26.♗d5+ ♔h7 27.h4 g4 (if 27...g×h4? 28.♖c4 etc., or 27...♘d4 28.♖e1 g×h4 29.♗c5 ♘c6 30.♖e8+−) 28.♖c4 a5 29.a4 ♘a7 30.♖c7+−.

Probably best was 25...♘e6 26.♗b4 ♘d8 27.♖c7 ♗e6 28.♖e7 (not 28.♗×b7? ♘×b7 29.♖×b7 and the opposite-color Bishops make a draw likely (+0.24/30)) 28...♗f7 29.f3 ♖c8 30.♔f2 when Black has finally developed his Bishop and Rook. But White's greater control of the board persists, and he will be able to bring his King into the game much sooner than Black (+2.35/31).

26.♗d5+

Pushing Black's King back as well. Of the board's 64 squares, White now controls 44 to Black's 20.

26...♔h7 27.b4

Putting the kibosh on 27...♗f5 28.♗×b7 ♖b8 etc.

27...♔g6 28.♖c4

Capitalizing on the fact that Black's pieces are far removed from the king-side, White begins to harass that flank.

28...♖b8 29.h4 g4?!

Making this pawn an object of attack. Preferable was 29...g×h4, as Torre pointed out in the *ACB*.

30.h5+!

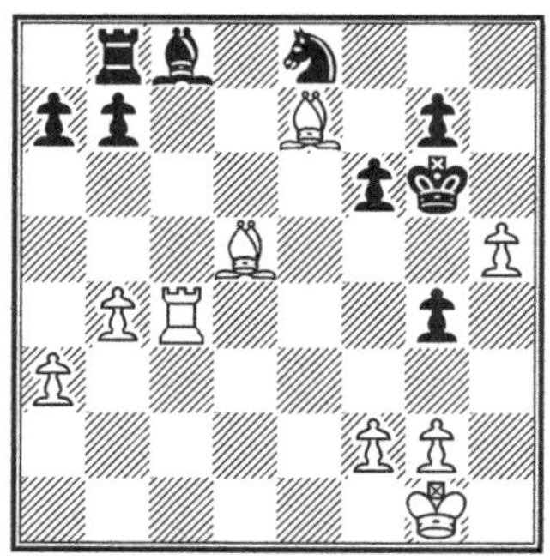

30...♔h7

Not 30...♔×h5?? 31.♗f7+ ♔h6 32.♖c5! (if 32.♗×e8? ♗e6) 32...f5 33.♗×e8+−. But least unpleasant was 30...♔h6 31.♗f7 ♗f5.

31.♗f7

"The idea behind White's maneuver is to invite the advance ...g6, which will accentuate Black's weaknesses on the King's flank." — Torre.

31...♗f5

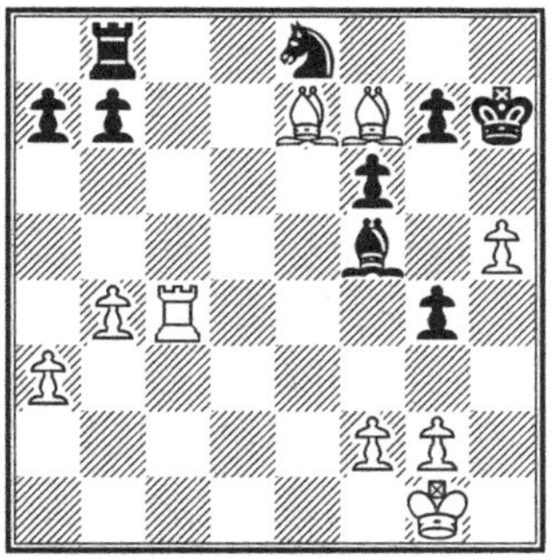

32.♖c5
Good, but better was 32.♖f4! finally forcing material gain, *viz.*
(a) 32...♗c2 33.♖×g4;
(b) 32...♗d7 33.♖d4 and either 33...♗f5?? 34.♗d8 winning the Knight, or 33...♗b5 34.♖×g4;
(c) 32...g6 33.h×g6+ ♗×g6 34.♗×f6 ♘×f6 (if 34...♗×f7? 35.♗e5 ♖c8 36.♖×f7+ ♔g6 37.♖×b7+−) 35.♖×f6 etc.
Though Torre missed this shot, he now continues to extend his control of the board, playing almost as if he had no opponent, slowly but inexorably reaching a winning position. And his technique is so artistic that we may perhaps be glad he did not win so quickly.

32...g6
Black might try 32...♗e4 33.♖c4 ♗f5 34.♖f4 ♗d7, with the idea of maintaining what Reuben Fine called "a philosophical defense," but that fails to 35.♖d4 as in variation (b) of the previous note.

33.h×g6+ ♗×g6 34.♗e6!
Much better than exchanging Bishops.

34...b6 35.♖c4 ♖b7
Threatening to complete his development, rather like the septuagenarian who hoped to complete his education, take up a profession and eventually marry.

36.♗d8 ♗h5 37.♖d4!
The g4-pawn is poison: 37.♗×g4? ♗×g4 38.♖×g4 ♖d7 and the Bishop is trapped.

37...♔h6 38.♔h2 ♔g5 39.♗d7
Threatening 40.♖d5+ ♔h6 41.♖×h5+ ♔×h5 42.♗×e8+ etc.

39...♖b8 40.♗e7 ♔h6 41.b5 ♔g7 42.♗c6
Preparing invasion of the seventh rank, against which Black has no defense.

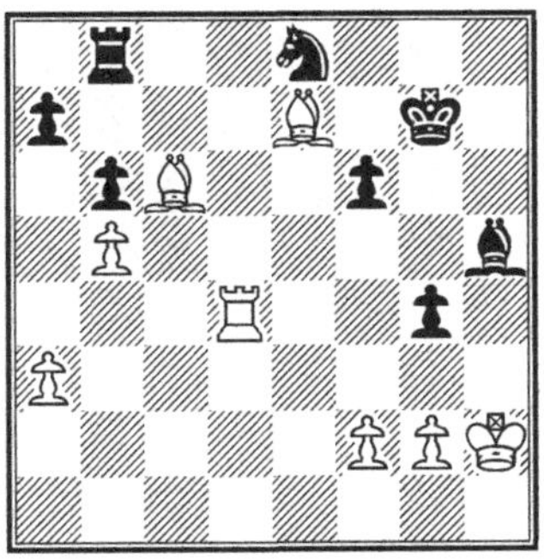

42...♗g6
Black sacrifices the g4-pawn in order to transfer his Bishop to defense of the queenside, which White menaces with three pieces while Black defends with only two. The alternatives were

42...♔g6 43.♗e4+ ♔f7 44.♗b4 ♔e6 45.♗c6 ♘g7 46.♖e4+ ♔f5 47.♖e7, or 42...♔f7 43.♖d7 ♔e6 44.♖×a7, White winning anyway in either case.

43.♖d7!

Torre never was much subject to the aforementioned "tyranny of the pawn," and here he rightly rejects the offer of one. After 43.♖×g4 ♔f7 44.♗b4 ♖d8 the win is more problematic.

43...♗f5 44.♖×a7

The capture of this pawn does not allow Black any counterplay. 45.♗d6+ is now threatened.

44...♔g6

The least evil for Black. If 44...♔g8 45.♗d5+ ♔h8 46.♔g3 ♗c8 47.♔f4 f5 48.a4 with *Zugzwang*.

45.a4! ♘g7

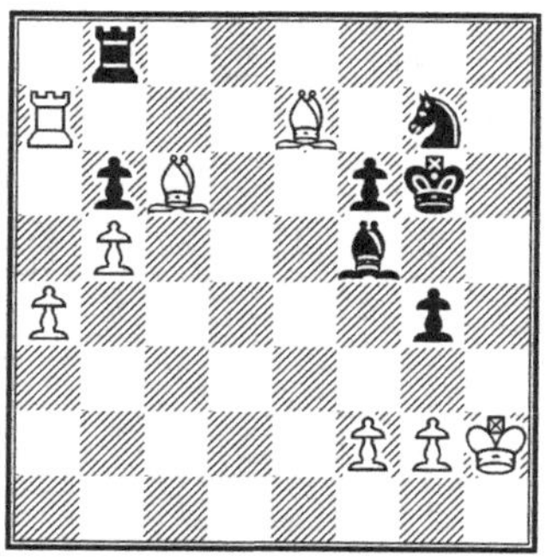

46.♗d6

Also good was 46.♖a8 ♖×a8 47.♗×a8 ♘e6 48.a5 b×a5 49.b6 and the pawn can be stopped from queening only at terrible cost.

46...♖h8+

Desperately hoping White will fall for the trap 47.♔g3? ♘h5+ 48.♔h2 ♘f4+ 49.♔g1 (49.♔g3?? ♘e2#) 49...♘e2+ 50.♔f1 ♘d4 and White's advantage is greatly reduced (+0.91/26).

47.♔g1 ♖d8 48.♗c7 ♖d1+ 49.♔h2 ♗e6 50.a5

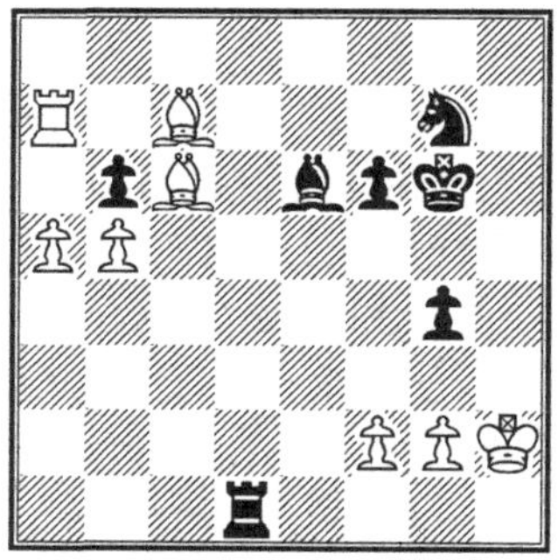

About as good as 50.♗×b6.

50...♘f5

Or 50...b×a5 51.b6, winning quickly.

51.a×b6 ♖d3 52.b7 g3+ 53.♗×g3 1–0

Torre demonstrated excellent technique, practically taking the entire board away from his opponent. Wilhelm Steinitz would have been delighted with this game.

Game 15

Jennings-Torre

New York State Championship playoff match, game 3, New York, 1924

French Defense [C13]

The idea of "the tyranny of the pawn," mentioned in the previous game, proves very relevant here. Torre again is immune to it, while his opponent proves all too susceptible, to such an extent that for the sake of capturing one he completely misses a winning variation, and for the sake of another lays himself open to a crushing attack.

1.e4 e6 2.d4 d5 3.♘c3 ♘f6 4.♗g5 d×e4

Known as the Burn or Deferred Rubinstein variation, in Torre's time this was seen often in the games of Alekhine, Tartakower, Réti, and Sämisch. Despite being one of the best and most solid lines of the French, it fell into disuse at the highest levels by the 1970s. Petrosian was one of its few adherents, using it to defeat the Brazilian Henrique Mecking in a memorable game at San Antonio 1972. Petrosian also employed it in the third game of his Candidates Match with Fischer at Buenos Aires, 1971, obtaining a won endgame, but inadvertently allowing Fischer to draw by threefold repetition. The line has enjoyed a resurgence in the 21st century, played often by such high-ranking GMs as Korchnoi, Ivanchuk, Bareev, Ehlvest, Morozevich, M. Gurevich, and even Carlsen and Anand now and then. Torre's choice of this line was highly unusual, as he almost invariably played the McCutcheon variation, 4...♗b4.

5.♘×e4 ♗e7 6.♘g3?!

A dubious move, perhaps even wrong; its only point is to avoid simplification. It is clear that Mr. Jennings was not eager to enter another early endgame against Torre after his experience of the previous game. 6.♗×f6 or 6.♘×f6+ are book.

6...c5 7.♘f3

Other continuations are no better, for example 7.d×c5 ♕c7 8.♘f3 ♘bd7 9.♕d4 h6 10.♗f4 ♕×c5∓.

7...♕b6 8.♗d3 c×d4

Taking the proverbially poisoned b-pawn is playable but not especially advantageous: 8...♕×b2 9.0–0 c×d4 10.♖b1 ♕×a2 11.♘e5[a].

9.♘×d4 ♗d7

Now the b-pawn is a bit more appealing, but Torre is not interested in having to thread through the complications that might ensue, *e.g.* 9...♕×b2 10.0–0 0–0 11.♘b5 a6 12.♖b1 ♕e5 13.♗×f6 ♕×f6 14.♘e4 ♕h6 15.♘bd6 ♖a7 16.♖b6 ♘c6 17.♗×a6 ♖×a6

18.♖×a6 b×a6 19.♘×c8 ♖×c8 20.♕d7 etc. As in the previous game, no "tyranny of the pawn" for him. Fortunately, it does afflict his opponent soon.

10.♘b3 ♘c6 11.0–0 ♘d5

Psychological play. Torre has noticed that his opponent is avoiding simplification and uses that to his own advantage.

12.♗d2

Torre's ploy pays off; White loses time. It was better to exchange on e7.

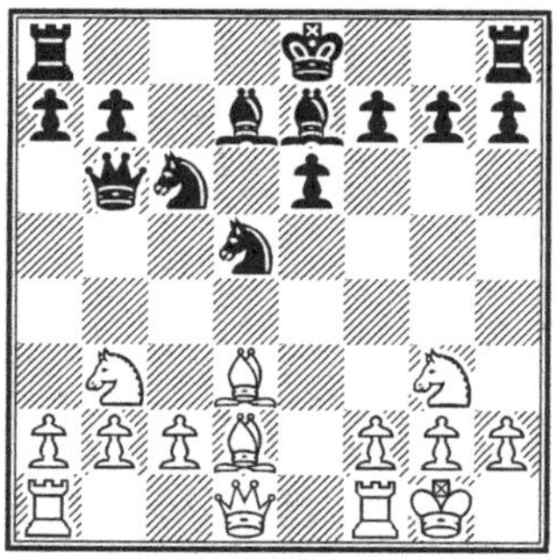

12...f5?!

If, as the sequel shows, Torre was intent on attack along the h- and g-files, it was far better to play 12...h5 now, *e.g.* 13.♘×h5 0–0–0 14.♘×g7? (⌓14.♗e4 or 14.c4) 14...♘f6 15.♕f3 ♖dg8 16.♗c3 ♕c7 17.h3 ♘e5 18.♕g3 ♘×d3 19.c×d3 ♗d6 20.f4 ♘d5 with a strong attack. The text not only delays that advance needlessly, but it creates a positional weakness, the backward e-pawn.

13.♖e1

White naturally aims at the backward pawn.

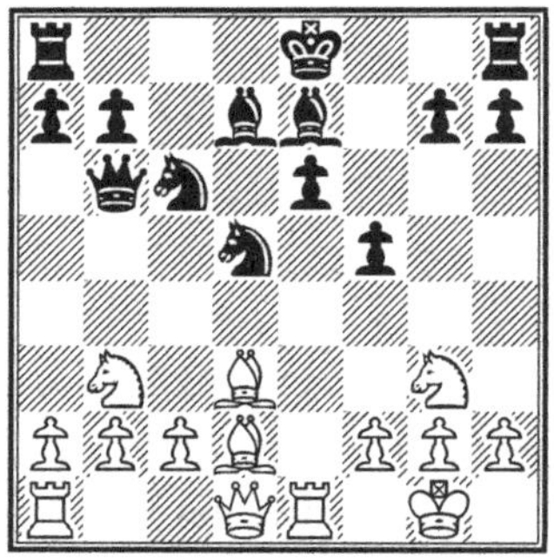

13...h5?

In the first edition we game this an exclam, but that was quite wrong. Objectively, this could have backfired badly on Torre. Relatively best was 13...♘f6, and if 14.♗c4 e5 △15...0–0–0, or if 14.♕e2 0–0–0 15.♗b5 ♖he8 16.♕c4, with advantage for White in either case, but not nearly so great as after the text.

14.♘×h5?

Talk about a poisoned pawn! While not lethal, this one will surely give White indigestion, especially in the postmortem when he finds out he could have gained a probably winning advantage with 14.♗c4!:

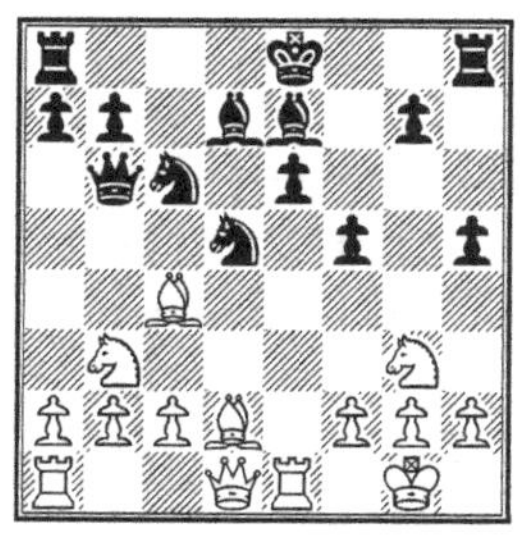

Some representative continuations then are:

(a) 14...0–0–0 15.♘×f5! e×f5 16.♗×d5

♗f6 17.♗e3 ♕c7 18.♕d2 ♖he8 (18...♗×b2? 19.♖ab1 would just give White the b-file as an added avenue of attack) 19.c4 (+4.33/27);

(b) 14...g6 15.♗×d5 e×d5 16.♘e2 0–0–0 17.♘f4 ♗e8 (the only move that defends both the d- and g-pawns) 18.♖×e7 ♘×e7 19.♗a5 ♕d6 20.♗×d8 ♕×d8 21.♕d4 ♗f7 and White is winning after either 22.♕×a7 or 22.♘a5 ♔b8 23.♕g7 ♖f8 24.♖e1 (△ 25.♕e5+) 24...g5 25.♕×g5 +–;

(c) 14...♘c7 15.a4 a5 16.c3 (△ 17.♗e3 winning the Queen) 16...♗c5:

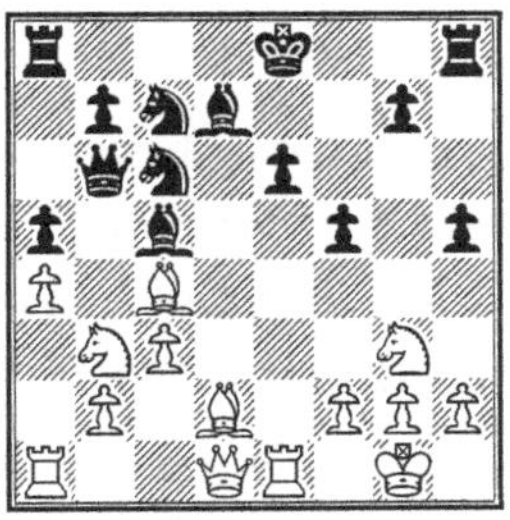

(c1) 17.♘×c5 ♕×c5 18.♗g5!! ♕×c4 19.♕d6 ♕d5 20.♕×c7 ♖c8 21.♕×b7 +–;

(c2) White could even play 17.♘×f5 ♗×f2+ 18.♔h1 forcing 18...0–0–0 [18...♗×e1?? 19.♘d6+ ♔d8 20.♕×e1 ♘e7 (or 20...♖f8 21.♗e3 +–) 21.♘f7+ ♔c8 22.♘×h8 +–] 19.♘d6+ ♔b8 20.♘f7 ♗×e1 21.♕×e1 ♘d5 22.♘×h8 ♖×h8 23.♕g3+ ♔c8 24.♕×g7 +–.

And of course if 14...♘f6 simply 15.♗×e6 +–. But fortunately for Torre, Jennings saw none of this. Returning to the actual game:

14...0–0–0!

Audaciously sacrificing a second pawn to open another file. Contrary to Jennings' earlier fears, Torre is obviously not aiming for the endgame.

15.♘×g7?

If the h-pawn was indigestible, the g-pawn is positively toxic. Better 15.♕e2, 15.h3, or 15.♗c4 with a game still playable for White.

15...♖dg8

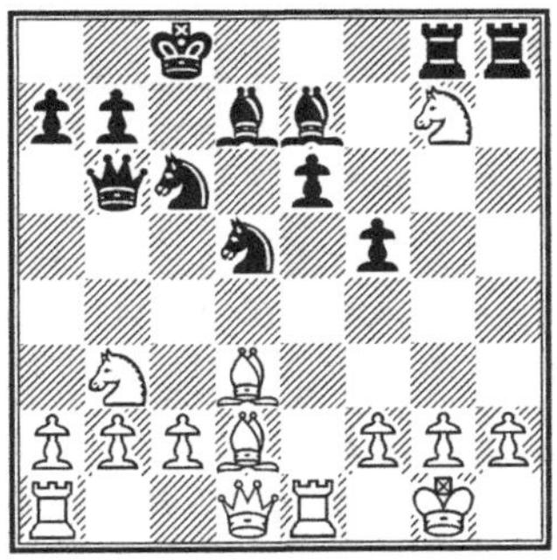

16.♘×e6

Apparently White was taught to eat whatever was set before him. Paradoxically, it was better to give up the Knight by 16.♘×f5 e×f5 17.♕f3 ♗h4 18.g3 f4 19.♗×f4 ♘×f4 20.♕×f4 ♖f8 21.♕e3 and White might yet mount a viable defense (-1.49/25).

16...♖×h2!!

The decisive blow. We have one of those Reinfeld-style quiz combinations; if now 17.♔×h2 ♕×f2 18.♕f3 ♖h8+ and mate shortly. The denouement is highly entertaining.

17.♕f3□ ♖gh8 18.g3

Or 18.♔f1 ♖h1+ 19.♔e2 ♖×e1+ 20.♖×e1 ♗×e6 etc.

18...♗d6
Also good was 18...♖h1+.

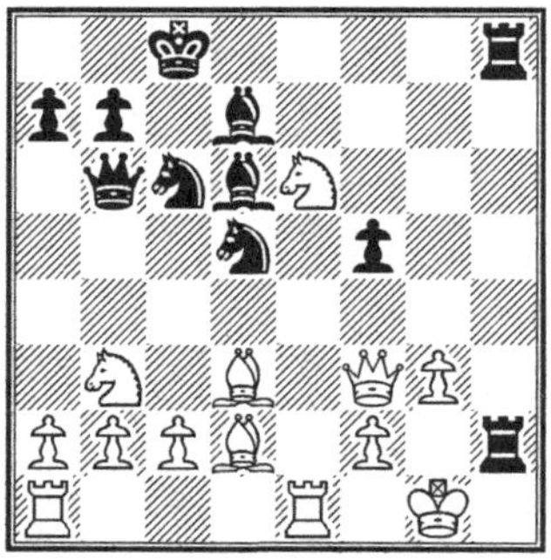

19.c4?
The least evil was 19.♔f1, when 19...♖h1+ is not as effective, and Black must find 19...f4! 20.g×f4 ♖8h3 21.♕e2 ♘e5! 22.f×e5 ♖h1+ 23.♔g2 ♗c6! 24.f3 ♖3h2+ 25.♔g3 ♗×e5+! 26.♔g4 (if 26.♕×e5 ♕f2+ 27.♔g4 ♕h4+ 28.♔f5 ♘e7#) 26...♖×e2 27.♖×e2 ♖×a1 −+.

19...♖h1+ 20.♕×h1 ♖×h1+ 21.♔×h1 ♕×f2 22.♘g5
Taking the Knight makes no real difference: 22.c×d5 ♕f3+ 23.♔g1 ♕×g3+ 24.♔f1 ♕×d3+ 25.♖e2 ♕×d5 −+. Further comment is unnecessary.

22...♕×g3 23.♖e2 ♕×d3 24.♖g2 ♘f6 25.♘f7 ♘e5 26.♘×d6+ ♕×d6 27.c5 ♕d5 28.♘a5 f4 29.♔h2 ♘f3+ 0–1

Playing through this game, co-author Kingston could not help but think of Emanuel Lasker and the Breslau 1889 *Hauptturnier*. Had Lasker not won that event and gained the title of *Deutscher Schachmeister*, his biographer Hannak says he intended to give up serious chess. The outcome hinged on the game Feyerfeil-Lipke in the *Siegergruppe* (Winners' Section). Had Feyerfeil won or drawn, he, not Lasker, would have won the *Siegergruppe*, and Lasker's great chess career might have never happened. Fortunately for chess, Lipke won (quite laboriously, in 121 moves!).

If Torre had lost this game, a definite possibility if Jennings had played 14.♗c4, then Jennings, who had already won the first game of their playoff, could have won the match and become New York State Champion. Would Torre then have gotten invitations to the 1924 Western Association Championship, and the prestigious European tournaments of 1925 in which he did so well? Or would his chess career, like Lasker's might have, arrive stillborn? An intriguing but imponderable "what if?"; we can only be glad it did not turn out so. As it was, this loss seems to have left Jennings completely demoralized, and he put up a pitiful effort in the final game of the match.

Game 16

Torre-Jennings

New York State Championship playoff match, game 4, New York, 1924

Queen Pawn's Game, Double Fianchetto Defense [A48]

1.d4 ♘f6 2.♘f3 g6 3.♘c3 b6?

Unsound, already ceding the center. Better 3...d6, entering the Pirc, or 3... d5, entering the Barry Attack as in Game 4.

Torre proceeds here very much in Barry Attack style.

4.e4 ♗b7 5.♗d3 ♗g7 6.♗f4

White could already build up a dominant central superiority by 6.e5 ♘d5 7.♘×d5 ♗×d5 8.c4.

6...0–0 7.♕d2 ♖e8?

Getting some pressure on the center by 7...c5 was vital.

8.0–0–0 d5?

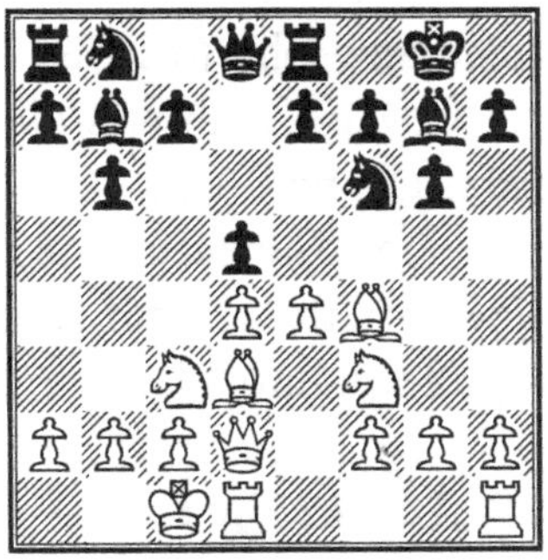

Good at move three, dismal here. Perhaps Jennings thought he was playing in Hypermodern style, delaying the advance of his center pawns, but this is just bad chess.

9.e5! ♘fd7?

Better, though not at all salvational, was 9...♘e4.

10.♗h6 ♗h8?

Jennings seems intent on suicide.

11.h4 c5 12.e6

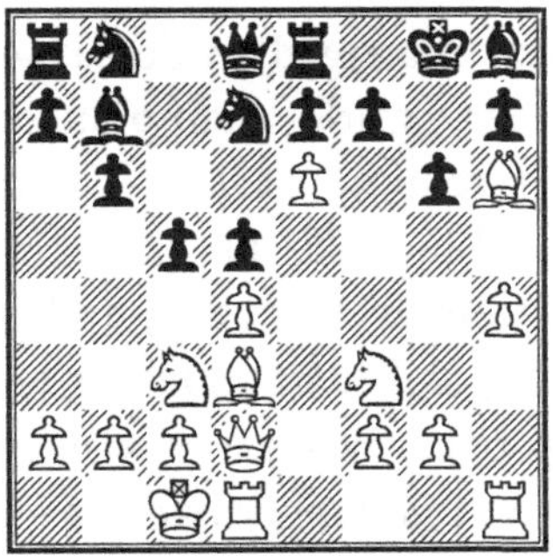

12...♘f6

If 12...f×e6 13.h5 c×d4 14.h×g6! ♗f6 (if 14...d×c3?? 15.g×h7+ ♔f7 16.♘g5+ ♔f6 17.♕f4#, or 14...h×g6 15.♕g5 and mate shortly) 15.♕e2 e5 16.♘g5 ♗×g5+ 17.♗×g5 ♘f6 18.♕×e5 ♕d6 19.g×h7+ ♔h8 20.♕×d6 e×d6 21.♗×f6#.

13.♘e5 ♖f8 14.♗×f8 ♕×f8 15.e×f7+ ♔g7 16.h5 ♘×h5 17.♖×h5 1–0

Mate in at most seven follows.

Game 17

Janowski-Torre

Exhibition game, New York, 1924

French Defense [C12]

The Franco-Polish master Dawid Markelowicz Janowski (1868-1927, historical Elo 2570), was at this time in the twilight of his life and career. He had been a regular in the highest-level events, in both Europe and America, since about 1894. Around 1900-1905 he was among the best six players in the world, and is one of the few chess masters who managed to defeat at least once every world champion he ever faced (Steinitz, Lasker, Capablanca and Alekhine). In his prime his play was extremely energetic, and he was especially skilled at attacking with the Bishop pair. By 1924 he was in poor health and no longer had the stamina required for success in a lengthy tournament (he finished last in the great New York tournament held March-April 1924), but in any given game he could still be very dangerous.

1.e4 e6 2.d4 d5 3.♘c3 ♘f6 4.♗g5 ♗b4 5.e5 h6 6.♗e3

Janowski had a dangerous attacking style fraught with tactical traps, for which the 6.♗e3 variation is well-suited, as White sacrifices two queenside pawns to obtain a kingside attack. However, Torre manages to find an interesting, well-coordinated defensive plan.

6...♘e4 7.♕g4 ♔f8 8.♗d3 ♘×c3 9.♗d2 ♘×a2 10.c3

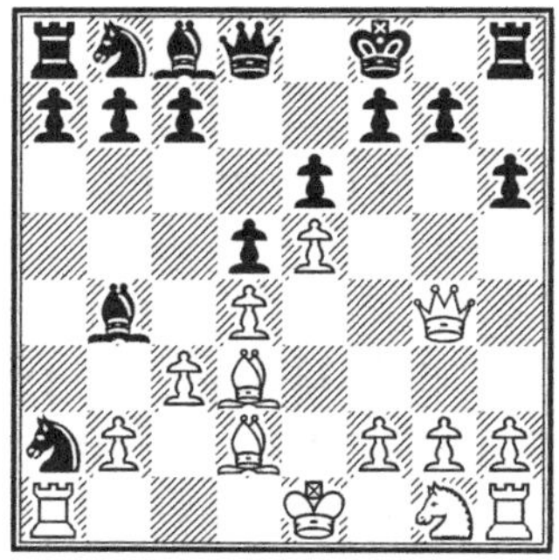

10...♘×c3

Something new at the time. In earlier games, from Ostend 1907, Black had played 10...♗e7 in Janowski-Burn (1-0, 40), Spielmann-John (0-1, 45), and Spielmann-Süchting (½-½, 31); and 10...♗a5 in E. Cohn-John (0-1, 31) and Teichmann-John (0-1, 76). And at Karlsbad 1907 10...♗a3 was played in Spielmann-Olland, (1-0, 38). ChessBase then shows no occurrence of the 10.c3 line until the present game, nor anything after it until 1964!

11.b×c3 ♗e7 12.♘e2

White has compensation for the two pawns in his better development, his greater control of space, the open lines for his pieces, and the awkward state of Black's kingside.

12...c5 13.0–0 c4

In a similar position in the aforementioned game Janowski-Burn, Black tried to keep the queenside fluid by ...♘c6 and ...♕b6, but Janowski devised a blistering attack.
With the text, Torre starts an interesting and ingenious defensive plan involving the transfer of his King to the queenside, in order to escape the concentration of white forces on the other wing.

14.♗c2 ♘c6 15.♕h5

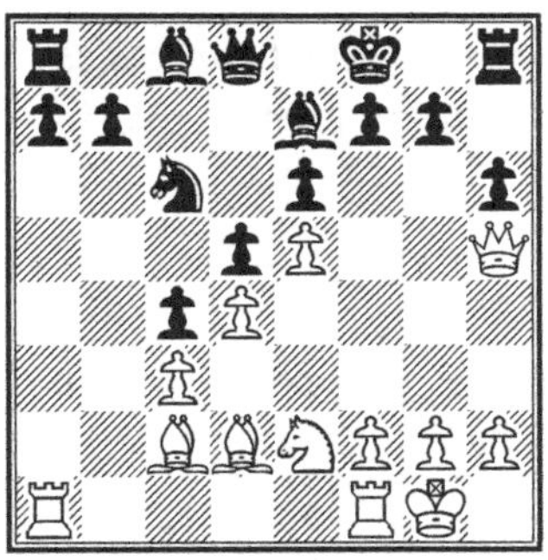

A textbook example of IM Jeremy Silman's "pawn-pointing" rule, *i.e.* that one should advance and attack in the direction one's pawn chain points. Clearly here that means Black should aim queenside, while White must attack on the kingside, *e.g.* with f2-f4-f5 etc. But now Torre begins removing his King from that wing, leaving Janowski no real target.

15...♔e8! 16.♖ab1 g6 17.♕h3 ♔d7 18.♕f3 ♖h7 19.♘f4 ♔c7?!

Best first was 19...a6, as will shortly be seen.

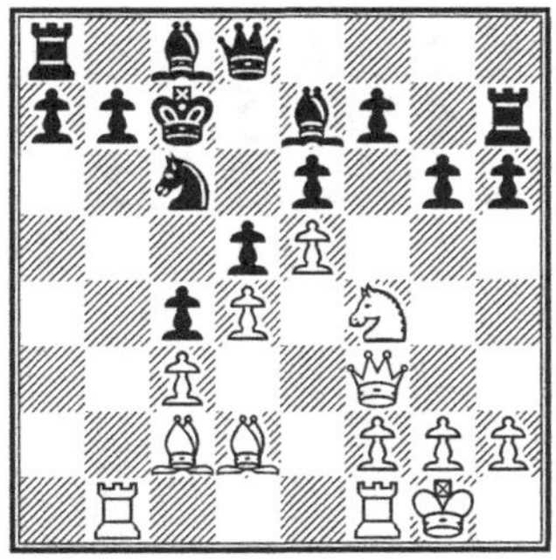

20.♘h5?!

Janowski keeps trying to get somewhere on the kingside, but here he missed a promising opportunity for a central breakthrough with 20.♖b5!?, made possible by Black's neglect of 19...a6. If then 20...a6 21.♘×d5+!? e×d5 22.♖×d5⩲.
Though White has sacrificed an entire Knight, he has considerable compensation in the lines suddenly opened for his Bishops to aim queenside, on the a8-h1 and b8-h7 diagonals. Janowski would have had considerable scope for his beloved rabbis (as his Bishops were called). Stockfish rates the resulting position at -1.00 at 31 ply. With the text move, Janowski missed his only real chance to make a fight of this game.

20...a6 21.♘f6

Though it is generally a great advantage to post a Knight on the sixth rank, in this position the cavalryman has no real targets.

21...♖h8 22.♗f4 b5 23.♘g4 h5 24.♘f6 ♗b7 25.♕e3 ♘b8!

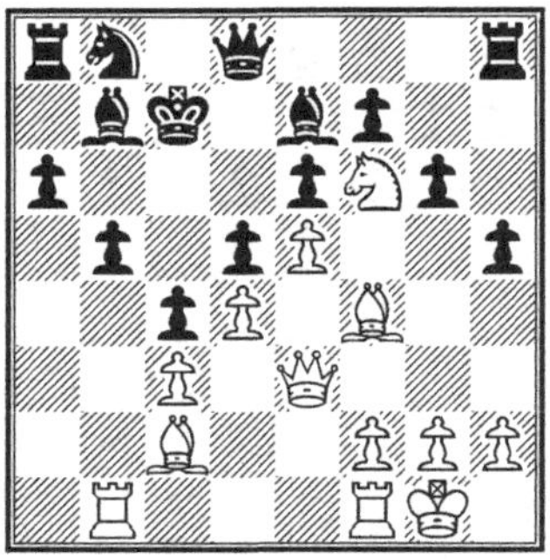

It would be extremely dangerous for Black to trade off the Knight by ...♗×f6 due to the consequent severe weakness of his dark squares. Therefore he maneuvers to take at f6 with his Knight and preserve his dark-squared Bishop.

26.♗h6 ♘d7 27.♗g7 ♘×f6!
Black is willing to give up the Exchange if in return he gets White's dark-squared Bishop. The move involves a trap: 28.♗×h8? ♘g4!.

28.e×f6 ♗d6
Of course not 28...♗×f6?? 29.♕f4+.

29.f4
White decides not to take the Rook after realizing that it would leave him with a rather undynamic position. Even so, it appears that the supposed attack for which he gave up two pawns has been reduced to nothing.

29...♖g8
Though materially Black is up only two pawns, his positional superiority is now so great that Stockfish evaluates it at about -5.00, *i.e.* the value of a full Rook. Janowski seems to have lost the thread of the game, and engages in aimless wood-shifting. Black, on the other hand, has a clear plan: push the queenside pawns!

30.♖f3 ♕e8 31.♗h6 a5
Black now takes the initiative with this queenside advance. The game is essentially decided already.

32.♕d2 ♕c6 33.♖ff1 ♗c8
The immediate 33...b4 was strong, but Torre may have wanted to reach time control at move 40 before committing himself; thus he engages in some inconsequential maneuvering for a while.

34.f5
To retrieve his exiled Bishop. White had no better move.

34...g×f5 35.♗f4 ♗d7
35...♖b8 was best to keep the situation firmly under control.

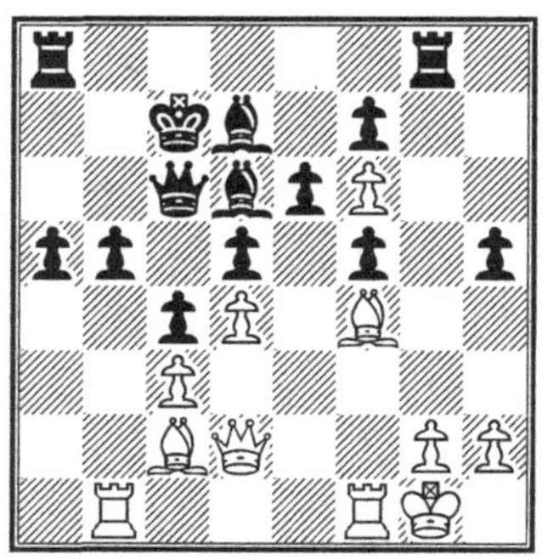

36.♗d1
White might have tried 36.♖×b5!? ♕×b5 37.♗×d6+ ♔×d6 38.♖b1, hoping

for 38...♕c6?? 39.♕f4+ e5 40.♕×e5#, or 38...♕a6?? 39.♕f4+ ♔c6 40.♗a4+ ♕b5 41.♗×b5+ ♔b6 42.♗×d7+ ♔a7 43.♕c7+ ♔a6 44.♕b6#. But after 38...♕×b1+ 39.♗×b1 a4 Black is still winning (-2.81/24).

36...♗×f4 37.♕×f4+ ♕d6 38.♕d2 ♖gb8 39.♗×h5
The fact that this gives White a passed h-pawn is of no importance.

39...♗e8 40.♗f3 b4

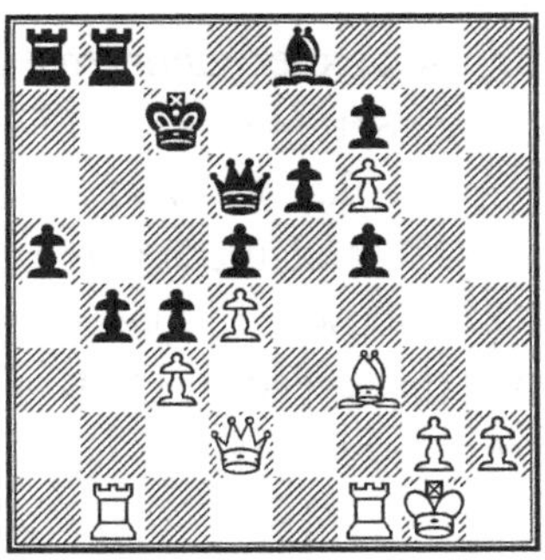

Here the game was adjourned. Janowski, who famously said "I detest the endgame," must surely have detested this one. Though the position is obviously hopeless for White, Janowski, perhaps applying the precept of his Polish countryman Savielly Tartakower, that "no one has ever won a game by resigning," carried on to the bitter end.

41.c×b4 a×b4 42.♖fc1 b3 43.h4
If 43.♖b2 ♕b4 etc.

43...♗c6 44.h5 ♖a2 45.♕g5 b2 46.♖e1 c3 47.♗d1 ♗a4 48.♕e3 c2 49.♕c3+
The spite check in its purest form.

49...♕c6 50.♕a5+ ♔d7 51.♗×c2 ♕×c2 52.♕a6 ♕c6 53.♕a5 ♗b3 54.♕d2 ♗c2 55.♕g5 ♗×b1 56.♕g7 ♗e4!

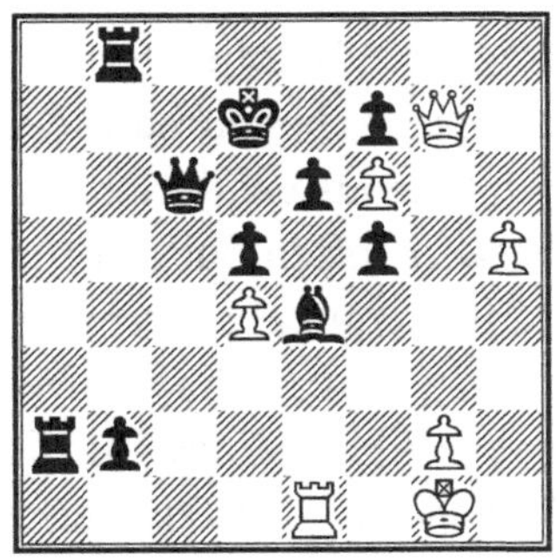

The threat to the f-pawn can be ignored, in fact if 56...♔e8?! 57.♕h8+.

57.♕×f7+ ♔c8 58.♕g8+ ♔c7 59.♕g7+ ♔b6 60.♕g3 ♔a7 61.f7 b1♕ 0-1
Mate follows in at most five moves. An impressive and dominant performance by Torre against a fading all-time great.

Game 18

Torre-Banks

Western CA Championship, Detroit 1924

Old Indian Defense [A46]

While Newell W. Banks of Detroit (1887-1977) was good at chess, about middling national master strength, he was extremely good at checkers (a/k/a draughts), winning the US championship in 1908 and holding it for 24 years, and barely losing a world title match in 1922 to Scotland's Robert Stewart +1 -2 =37. For decades he toured widely, giving simultaneous exhibitions in chess and checkers, often both in the same event, and frequently *sans voir*: it was said in 1953 that he had played over 80,000 blindfold games. In his book *Banks' Blindfold Checker Masterpieces* (Philadelphia, 1947) he mixed both chess- and checkers-related anecdotes[1]. In chess his most noteworthy victims were Marshall and Kashdan at Chicago 1926. In this game he was the victim of one of Carlos Torre's most spectacular moves.

1.d4 ♘f6 2.♘f3 d6 3.♘c3 ♗f5

An unusual form of the Old Indian, first seen in Jaffe-Capablanca, match, New York, 1912. In Torre's time it was occasionally played by Réti, Tartakower, Nimzovich, and the Czech, Karel Hromadka. In the 1980s it popped up as a surprise weapon in games by Spassky and Tal. In the form 1.d4 ♘f6 2.c4 d6 3.♘c3 ♗f5 it is sometimes called the Janowski Indian, after the game Alekhine-Janowski, New York 1924.

4.♗g5 ♘e4?!

An ill-advised experiment, making its debut here. Better is 4...♘bd7, as in Brach-Hromadka, 7th Czech Ch, Brno 1921 (0-1, 37), and most games since. ChessBase shows 4...♘e4 having a very poor track record, +3 -12 =4 in 19 games over 1924-2015.

5.♘×e4 ♗×e4 6.♘d2! ♗g6

Black must retreat his Bishop and cede control of e4, as 6...d5? 7.♘×e4 is advantageous to White.

7.e4 f6?!

Another oddity from Banks. Though it entailed loss of time, best probably was 7...d5 when if 8.e5 ♕d7 9.c3 e6 Black would have a reasonably sound sort of French Defense with his Queen's Bishop already developed outside his pawns. The text instead just increases Black's cramp.

1 This information comes mainly from an article by Edward Winter, at https://www.chesshistory.com/winter/extra/banks.html.

8.♗e3 e6
If 8...e5 9.d5 c6 10.c4± or 10.♗c4±.

9.♗d3 ♗e7
The only move this piece will make. The problems caused by this *very* bad Bishop will beset Black throughout the game.

10.♕g4!?
An indication that Torre is in an adventurous mood.

10...♕d7 11.0–0
Black's play to this point might have had Torre thinking he was facing an "Apertura China" (Chinese Opening) or "Sistema Barrerovsky" (Barrerovsky System), Mexican coffeehouse slang for irregular hedgehog-style openings. However, while White has a considerable advantage in space and development, in such a closed position that is not necessarily quickly decisive.

11...e5
Returning to Old Indian methods. Black is playing in a style reminiscent of the Indian master Mir Sultan Khan (1905-1966), who in the 1930s was wont to say that a "bad Bishop" was not necessarily so bad, because it defended its pawns from behind, a rather strange chess philosophy. Sultan Khan was enamored of blockaded positions with "bad" Bishops, baffling opponents with strange maneuvers born of his idiosyncratic philosophy. Banks, however, is no Sultan Khan.

12.♕g3
Torre prefers to deny exchanges to his cramped opponent, and to keep Queens on the board.

12...e×d4
Trying to maintain the pawn on e5 by 12...c6 followed by ...♕c7 and ...♘d7 fails to 13.♘f3 0–0 (if 13...♕c7? 14.♘h4!) 14.♘h4 ♗h5 (14...♗f7? 15.♗h6) 15.d×e5 f×e5 16.f4 with a strong attack (+2.90/24).

13.♗×d4 ♘c6 14.♗c3
As C.S. Howell pointed out in the *ACB*, White is little concerned by the prospect of an eventual ...♘e5, as he will then simply retreat his Bishop to e2 and later expel the Knight with f2-f4.

14...0–0–0
Castling kingside was no safer, as White is prepared to advance pawns and open lines on either wing.

15.b4 ♖df8?
Black is thinking defensively, making a retreat square for his Knight, but he should have recalled the axiom that a flank attack should be countered in the

center, in this case by 15...d5!. Necessary then would be 16.a3, because if 16.b5?! ♘b4 17.a4 (if 17.♗e2 ♘×c2) 17...♖he8 and suddenly the initiative is in Black's hands (-2.07/24).

16.b5 ♘d8 17.♕e3 b6

Preferable was 17...♔b8. White will now find it easier to open a queenside file.

18.a4 ♕g4??

Banks can't seem to make up his mind about what kind of game to play. First he crouches behind his barricades, but now he makes a wild, unsound kingside sortie. It was still not too late for 18...d5, with some slight chance of survival (+2.53/27). After the text Stockfish's assessment jumps to over +6.00.

19.a5 ♘e6 20.a×b6 a×b6

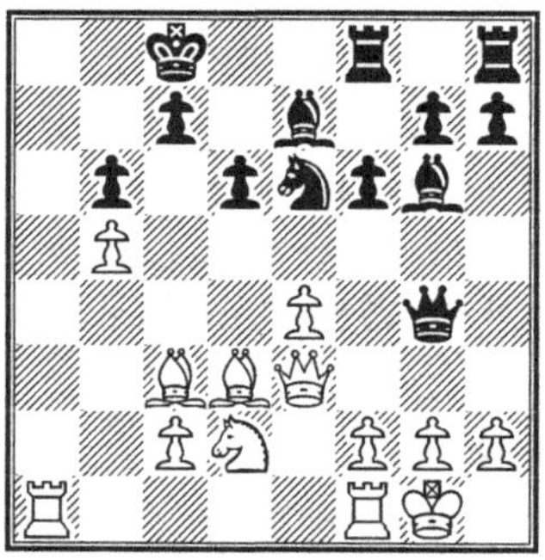

Hoping perhaps to induce 21.♖a8+ ♔b7 followed by liquidation of all the Rooks, but even this would be fine for White, *viz.* 22.♖×f8 ♖×f8 23.♗c4 ♘f4 24.g3 ♘h3+ 25.♔g2 ♗f7 26.♗×f7 ♖×f7 27.♕d4 ♖f8 28.♕d5+ ♔b8 29.♕c6 etc. (+8.23/27).

21.♗c4

One of many very strong moves; others include 21.♗e2, 21.h3, 21.♖a7, 21.♗b4, and 21.♗d4.

21...♘f4

Threatening an unsubtle mate. Perhaps Black expected his opponent to cross himself, say "Hail Mary" and resign.

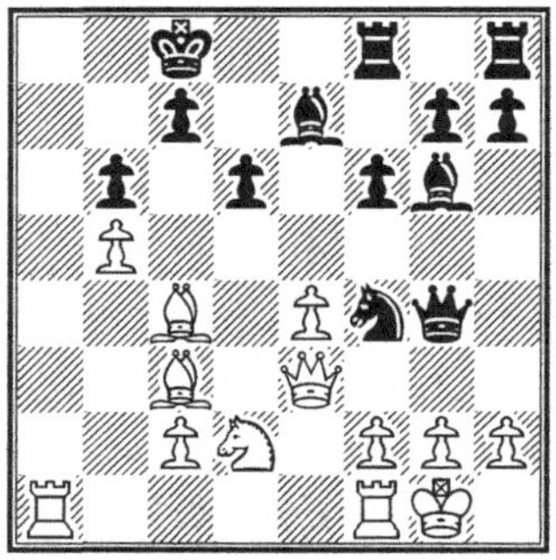

22.♕×f4!!

Instead of genuflecting, White throws a bomb: a spectacular and fascinating (if not entirely necessary) Queen sacrifice. Surely a player of Torre's caliber could see that the simple, straightforward 22.♕g3 would give White a decisive advantage, *viz.*:

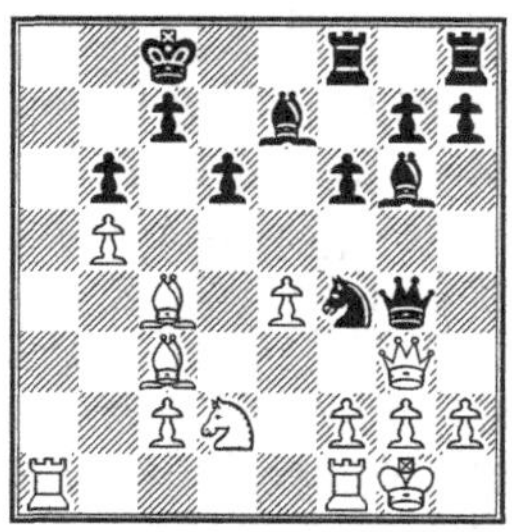

(a) 22...♕×g3 23.h×g3 ♘h5 24.♗e6+ ♔b8 25.♖a6 etc.;

(b) 22...h5 23.h3 ♕×g3 24.f×g3 d5 25.e×d5 +−;

(c) 22...♕g5 23.♕×g5 f×g5 24.g3 d5 25.e×d5 ♘h3+ (or 25...♘h5 26.d6 ♗×d6 27.♗d5 ♘f6 28.♗c6 ♔d8 29.♖fe1 etc.) 26.♔g2 ♘×f2 27.♖×f2 +–; **(d)** 22...♘e2+ 23.♗×e2 ♕×e2 24.♕h3+ f5 (if 24...♔b8 25.♕d7! △ 26.♕c6 +–) and White can win with 25.♗×g7, 25.♖fe1 or almost any other reasonable move.

Apparently Carlos Torre was feeling his oats that day and wanted to set himself the task of analyzing a forest of complicated variations, or perhaps he felt a strong intuitive inspiration. In either case we can be grateful that he made a dramatic addition to the list of great Queen sacrifices.

22...♕×f4 23.♗e6+!□

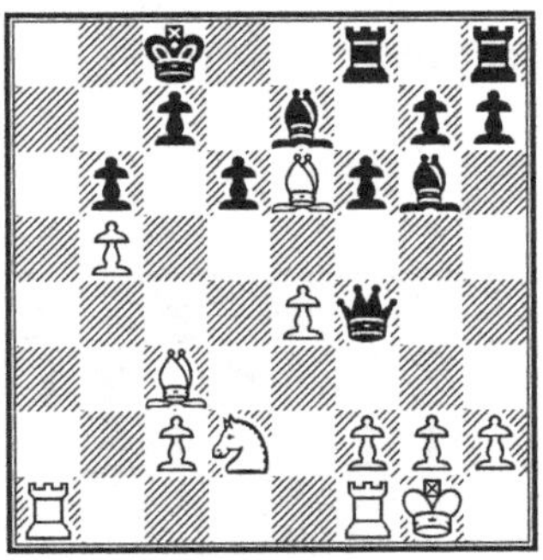

Demonstrating the point of the Queen sac: Black's Queen has been deflected off the c8-h3 diagonal.

23...♔b7??

Banks makes it easy for Torre. The critical line was 23...♔b8, so that 24.♗d5 would not be check. Working on this book's first edition in 1999, the best analysis engine we had was Fritz5, and it was rather out of its depth here. We spent days agonizing over how White should proceed after 23...♔b8, at first despairing when it looked like the sacrifice was unsound. Finally we laboriously churned out 2½ pages demonstrating the soundness of the Queen sac. For this edition, much less ink and sweat need be spilled. First, let's look at the line given by C.S. Howell in the *ACB*, 24.♖a4:

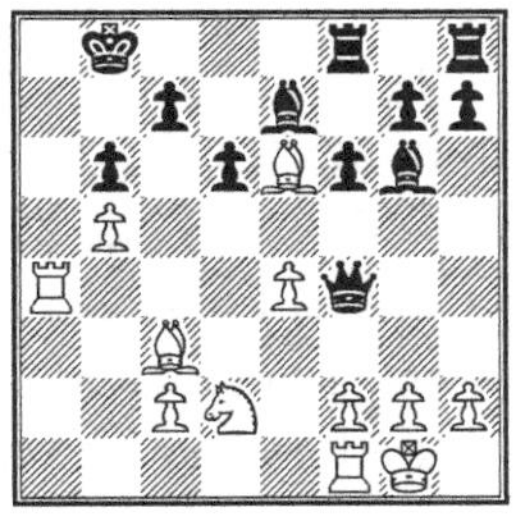

This serves two purposes, defending the e-pawn and preparing to double Rooks. Howell continued 24...c6 25.♖fa1 d5 26.g3 ♕g5 27.h4 ♕h5 28.g4 ♕×h4 29.e5 ♕×f2+ (if 29...c×b5 30.♖a8+ ♔c7 31.♖1a7+ ♔c6 32.♗d7+ ♔c5 33.♖c7#) 30.♔×f2 f×e5+ 31.♔g3 ♗f6 32.♖a7 ♗e8 33.g5 d4 34.♘e4 "and mate soon."

Howell's analysis proves on the whole quite sound; about the only nit worth picking is that 27.b×c6 was much stronger than 27.h4 (though both moves win).

In the first edition we considered his analysis wanting, however, because it appeared to be refuted right at the start if Black replied to 24.♖a4 with a move Howell did not consider, 24...♕g5:

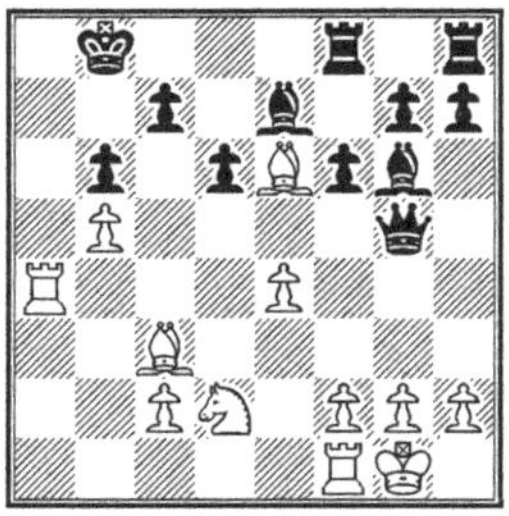

If then 25.♗d5, Black can give the Queen back and gain equality: 25...♕×d5! 26.e×d5 ♗f7=. However, Fritz5 somehow never saw the efficacy of 25.♗d7!, threatening a quick mate starting with 26.♗c6, and forcing 25...♕×b5 26.♗×b5 ♗e8 27.♗×e8 ♖×e8, when White is up Knight for pawn with an easily won game. So, belatedly, Howell is vindicated.
Also vindicated is the alternative to 24.♖a4 we endorsed, 24.♗d5:

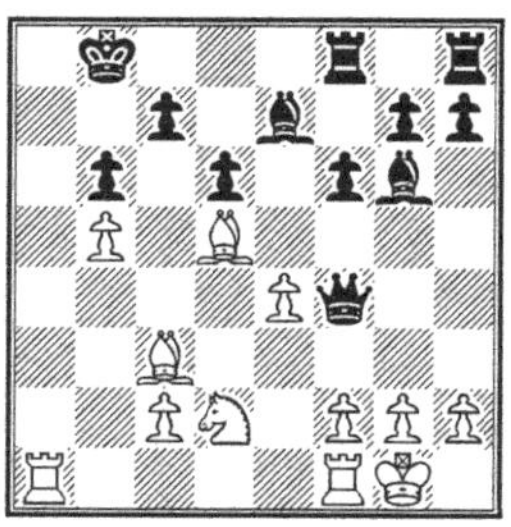

This turns out to be the second-strongest continuation, after 24.♖a4. Forced is 24...c6 25.b×c6! (Not 25.♗×c6? ♖c8! and the would-be mating net is torn apart: 26.♖a6 ♖×c6! 27.b×c6 ♔c7 with about an even game.) 25...♖c8 26.♖fb1! ♖×c6 (if 26...♔c7? 27.♖×b6! ♔×b6 28.♗a5+ ♔c5 29.♘b3+ ♔b5 30.c4+ ♔a6 31.♗c7#) 27.♗×c6 ♔c7 28.♗d5 ♖b8 29.♘b3 (△30.♘d4) 29...♗×e4 30.♗×e4 ♕×e4 31.♖e1 and Back must either allow 32.♖×e7+ or give up Queen for Rook (+5.84/28).
Whether the advantage White enjoys after 22.♕×f4 is greater than what he might have had after the simpler 22.♕g3 is debatable, perhaps ultimately a question of style. Capablanca, Petrosian or Karpov would have almost certainly played 22.♕g3, while Alekhine, Spielmann, Bronstein or Tal might well have chosen the sacrifice. Posterity can only be grateful to Torre that by trusting his intuition he left us such a fascinating position. It is a pity that all these brilliant variations are confined to the notes. After 23...♔b7?? White has a forced mate.

24.♗d5+

This being check puts White a tempo ahead of the 23...♔b8 24.♗d5 line analyzed above.

24...c6

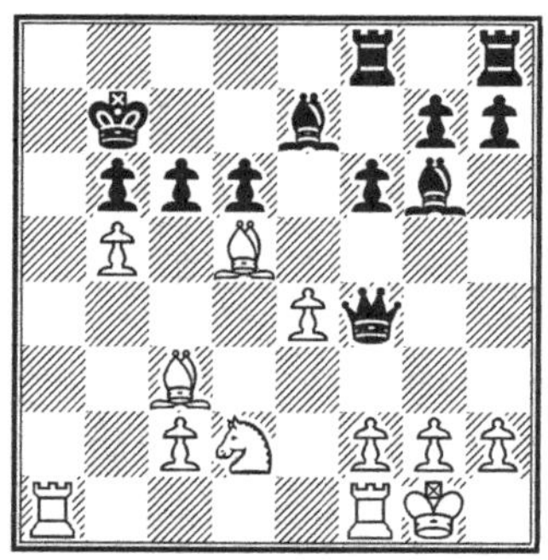

25.♗×c6+

Quickest (and prettiest) was 25.b×c6+ ♔b8 26.♖a8+!! ♔c7 (if 26...♔×a8 27.c7+ ♔a7 28.♖a1#) 27.♖a7+ ♔d8 28.♖d7+ ♔e8 29.♖a1 etc.

25...♔c8 26.♖a8+ ♔c7 27.♖a7+ ♔c8 28.g3 ♕g4 29.♖fa1 ♔d8 30.♗d4 1-0

There is no escape: if 30...♕d7 31.♗×d7 and 32.♗×b6#. A strange game culminated by a difficult and fascinating combination. C.S. Howell wrote "While it is true that Black played the early part of this game weakly and thus gave Torre an opportunity to play brilliantly, the manner in which the young Mexican took advantage of the opportunity is highly interesting and shows that he has a keen 'sense' of the positions that justify sacrifice of mere material."

Game 19

Scrivener-Torre

Western CA Championship, Detroit 1924

Ruy López [C68]

Robert Silas Scrivener (born Mobile, Alabama, 1881, died Memphis, Tennessee, 1969) was highly respected as both a player, organizer, and administrator at the time of this game. He had placed high in the US Opens of 1913 and 1920, and served for many years as president of the Western Chess Association. At various times he won the state championships of Alabama, Louisiana and Florida. He was awarded the honorary title of Master Emeritus by the USCF in 1963 (*CL*, 5/1969, p. 212). Here Torre proves to be the master.

1.e4 e5 2.♘f3 ♘c6 3.♗b5 a6 4.♗×c6 d×c6 5.d4

This advance is very good, perhaps as good as 5.0–0, the move recommended by Fischer. At the time of this game, the famous victories of Dr. Lasker in 1914 over Tarrasch and Capablanca, in both of which he played 5.d4, were still fresh in players' minds. The 5.0–0 line is advisable for White if he is familiar with its sharp variations, such as 5.0–0 ♗g4 6.h3 h5 7.d3 ♕f6 8.♘bd2! ♘e7 9.♘c4 ♗×f3 10.♕×f3 ♕×f3 11.g×f3 ♘g6 12.♗e3 ♗e7 13.♔h1 ♗f6 14.a4 0–0–0 15.a5, as in Spassky-Hort, Candidates Match, Reykjavik, 1977, 16th game. In Torre-Whitaker, from the same tournament as the present game, White chose a third playable alternative, 5.♘c3 (see Game 22).

5...e×d4 6.♕×d4 ♕×d4 7.♘×d4

A simplified position, but rather comfortable for White and difficult for Black. Dr. Lasker was very fond of the white side, and in later times GM Bent Larsen also won more than a few endgames in which White's kingside pawn majority was the decisive factor, a prime example being the 7th game of the Candidates Match Larsen-Portisch,

Rotterdam 1977. Black's compensation is his pair of Bishops.

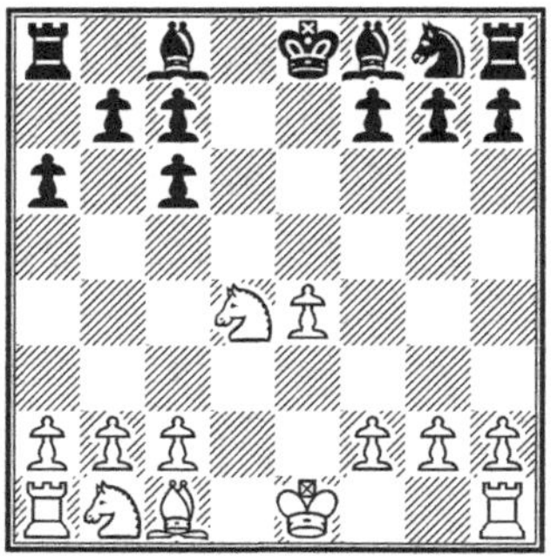

7...♗d6

Recommended by Capablanca. Some years later Alekhine stated that 7...♗d7 was more precise, with the idea of castling long. He applied this idea successfully in several games, against Post (Mannheim 1914), Golmayo de la Torriente (Hamburg Olympiad 1930), and Petersson (Örebro 1935). Capablanca, on the other hand, held that Black should castle short, so that his King would stand ready to defend the wing where White would be advancing his pawns. In this game, Torre follows the Cuban's advice.

8.♗e3 ♘e7 9.♘d2

CB shows only three earlier games reaching this position.

9...♘g6

Apparently a new move. 9...f5 was played in Köhnlein-P. Johner, match 1909, and Forgacs-Teichmann, Hamburg 1910, while Meyer-Black, NY Rice CC Ch 1913 saw 9...c5. In terms of theory and precedent, both players are already on their own; in its nearly seven million games, ChessBase shows no occurrence of this position before, and very few since.

10.0–0–0

Which side White should castle on has also been the subject of much debate. Some theoreticians have even held that White should not castle at all. Dr. Lasker preferred to castle queenside in this position.

10...0–0 11.h3 ♖e8 12.g3

Preparing his next move, which turns out to be an error. White should not be overly hasty in advancing his kingside pawns when the time is not yet ripe.

12...f6

For Black, the correct policy is one of restriction. For this, his pawns belong on dark squares (f6, b6, c5), so that White's Bishop has as little scope as possible. Furthermore, it is advisable for Black to overprotect the critical e5 square. It is instructive to see how Torre does this over the next several moves, bringing every available piece to bear on e5.

13.f4?

Premature. Perhaps White hoped to emulate the famous game Lasker-Capablanca, St. Petersburg 1914, in which White played f2-f4 in a similar position. However, there are critical differences. Firstly, Lasker knew he could force the exchange of dark-squared

Bishops, here for the moment impossible. Secondly, Lasker was able to make the advance f4-f5 in a situation where Black could not maneuver his Knight to e5 (Capablanca's being at e7, not g6). After the text, Black rapidly seizes the initiative and never gives it up. The rest of the game gives an excellent illustration of Black's resources in the Ruy López Exchange variation.

13...c5!

Ending White's chance of playing f4-f5 followed by ♘d4-e6 (as in Lasker-Capablanca). The Knight must now retreat and White must concern himself with defending his e-pawn with pieces, as the advance e4-e5 will be impossible.

14.♘4f3 b6 15.♗f2 ♗b7 16.♖he1 ♖e7

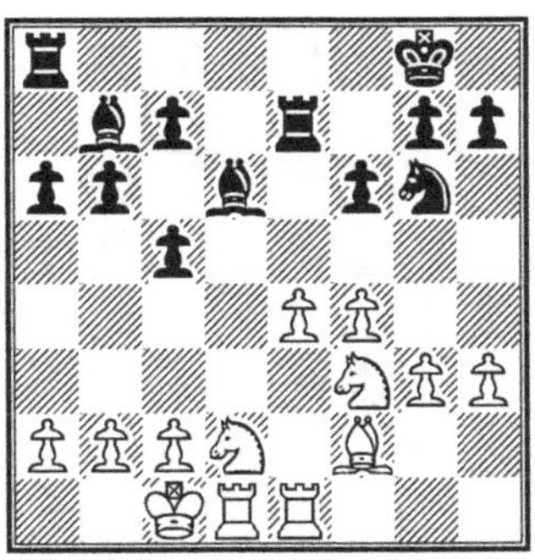

17.♖e2?

With Black obviously intending to double Rooks, this seems perfectly natural, aiming to do the same. But best was 17.h4 h5 18.♖e3 ♖ae8 19.♖de1, when if 19...♗×f4 as in the game, then 20.g×f4 ♘×f4 21.♖a3 ♗×e4 22.♖×e4 ♖×e4 23.♘×e4 ♖×e4 24.♖×a6 and White is better (+1.45/25). Or 19...♘×f4 20.g×f4 ♗×f4 21.♖3e2 ♖×e4 22.♖×e4 ♗×e4 with equality rather than advantage for Black.

Also coming into consideration was the pawn sac 17.♘c4 ♗×e4 18.♘fd2 ♗g2 19.♘×d6 c×d6 20.♘c4 ♖×e1 21.♖×e1 ♖b8 22.♘×d6 ♗×h3 when White's game is very much freer, and the opposite-color Bishops may provide drawing chances (-0.57/28).

If White wants to double Rooks immediately, the better way was 17.♖e3, when if 17...♖ae8 18.♖de1 ♗×f4? 19.g×f4 ♘×f4 Black gets no gain of tempo for the fork by ...♘g2. Black could try expediting his sacrifice and using a different piece, by 17...♘×f4!? 18.g×f4 ♗×f4 19.♖e2 ♖×e4:

Now not 20.♖×e4? ♗×e4 21.♘h2 (21.♘g1? ♖d8−+) 21...♗f5 22.♘hf1 ♗×h3 and with the Bishop pair and four pawns for the piece, three of them connected and passed, Black's prospects are excellent (-2.83/26).

Correct instead is 20.♘g1 ♖d8 21.♖de1, when Black's edge is minimal (-1.18/36).

17...♖ae8 18.♖de1 ♗×f4!

An unexpected strike, typical of Torre. The Belgian grandmaster Alberic O'Kelly used to say that a combination was like the joke that ends a serious conversation. Here ends conversation on the topic of sustaining the e-pawn.

19.g×f4 ♘×f4

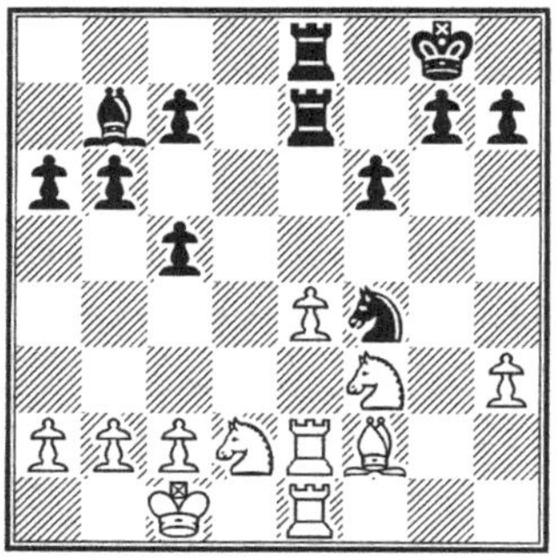

If now 20.♖e3 ♘g2. In any case, Black gets a Rook and two pawns for two minor pieces. Usually this is not quite sufficient compensation, but here the fall of the e-pawn is imminent, giving Black three pawns, one of them passed.

20.♗g3?

White greatly worsens his plight with this move, which allows a wholesale liquidation of pieces that will put Black's advantage in its clearest form. Far less injurious were:

(a) 20.e5 ♘×e2+ 21.♖×e2 h6 (probably not as strong is 21...f×e5 22.♖e3 e4 23.♗h4 ♖e6 24.♘h2 (-1.13/25)) 22.h4 (-1.62/25); or

(b) 20.♖e3 ♘g2 21.e5 ♘×e3 22.♖×e3. Then 22...f×e5 is definitely not best (-0.83/25), a key difference compared to the game continuation being that Black's e-pawn, though passed, is isolated, and therefore more readily blockaded. Better again 22...h6 (-1.61/25).

20...♘×e2+ 21.♖×e2 ♗×e4

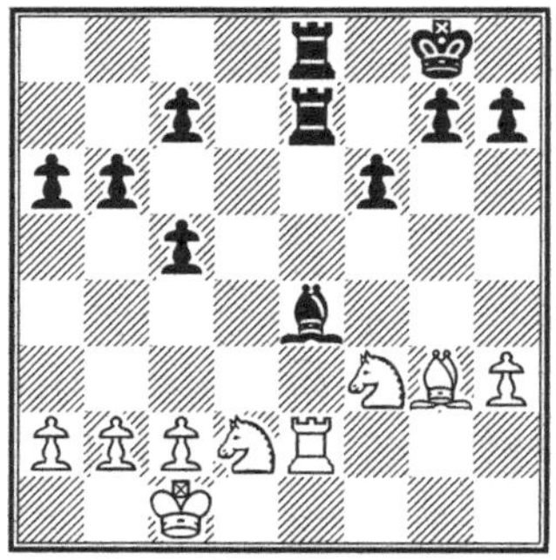

22.♘×e4

Trying to avoid exchanges does not help White now, *e.g.* 22.♖g2 ♗c6 23.♖g1 ♖e3 24.♖f1 ♖8e7 (-5.12/25), or 22.♖h2 ♗×f3 23.♘×f3 ♖e3 24.♖f2 ♖8e7 (-4.73/25).

22...♖×e4 23.♖×e4 ♖×e4

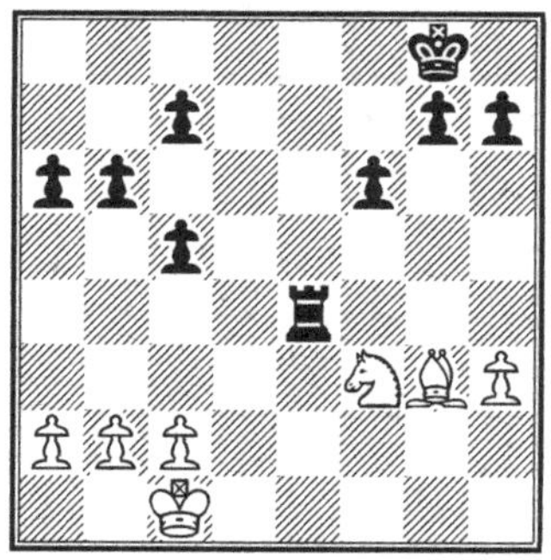

Reaching an ending clearly favorable to Black. If now 24.♗×c7 ♖e3 25.♘h4 ♖×h3 26.♘f5 b5 and Black's three passed pawns will quickly decide matters.

24.♔d2 ♖e7

The ending is won, but Black has a few minor pitfalls to avoid. If, for example 24...c6?! 25.♗c7 b5 26.♔d3 and

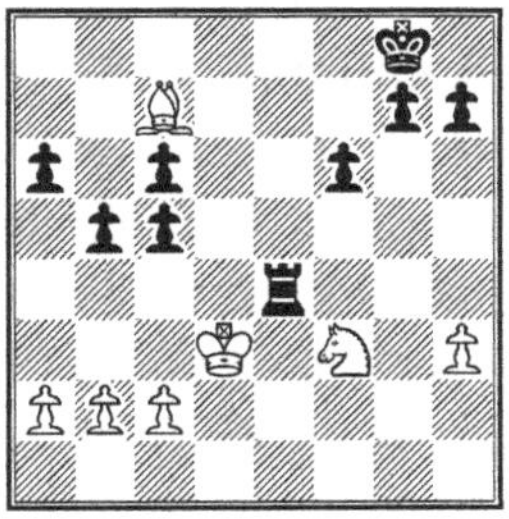

(a) 26...♖e6 27.♗b6 c4+ 28.♔d2 and the ending has become much more problematic due to the Bishop's suddenly greater mobility, or

(b) 26...♖e8 27.b3! intending either 28.c4 ♔f7 29.♗b6 b×c4+ 30.b×c4 ♖b8 31.♗×c5, or 28.♗b6 c4+ 29.b×c4 b×c4+ 30.♔×c4, and Black's queenside is suddenly vulnerable in either case. The Mexican master's technique here is a model of its kind.

Torre recognizes that correct technique involves restricting the Bishop by keeping his pawns on dark squares. His methods here resemble those used against Jennings in Game 14, where the enemy pieces were practically pushed off the board.

25.c4 g5 26.a4

An important move, to fix the queenside pawns. Otherwise Black would have mobile majorities on both flanks. Furthermore White needs to place his pawns on light squares, otherwise his Bishop, already considerably hemmed in by black pawns, would have even less scope.

26...a5 27.b3 ♔f7 28.♔d3

No good is the maneuver 28.♗f2 ♔g6 29.♗e3 h5 30.♔e2 f5! (not 30...g4?! 31.h×g4 h×g4 32.♘h4+) 31.♔f2 (if 31.♘×g5?? f4–+) 31...f4 32.♗d2 ♔f5 and Black's King invades the kingside. An essential part of Black's winning procedure is to maintain the e-file as a *cordon sanitaire* over which the white King may not pass. In most endgames, the King is the most effective blockader of passed pawns. The white King's inability to go past the e-file denies the defender his best tool.

28...♔g6 29.♔d2 f5 30.♘e5+ ♔f6 31.♘d3

31.♘c6 might get White's King across the e-file, *e.g.* 31...♖d7+ 32.♔e2 f4 33.♗e1 ♔f5 34.♔f3, but would still leave him utterly lost (-10.73).

31...f4 32.♗f2

Sacrificing a piece for two pawns by 32.♘×f4/♗×f4 provides no relief (-9.23/27).

32...♔f5
The King threatens to penetrate to f3. White's pieces are without useful squares.

33.♘e1 h5 34.♘g2 g4 35.h×g4+ h×g4 36.♘e1 g3 37.♗g1 ♔g4
White now wishes the board would suddenly grow an extra back rank.

38.♘g2 f3 39.♘e3+ ♔h3
Another way to win was 39...♖×e3! 40.♗×e3 ♔h3 41.♔e1 ♔g2.

40.♘d1 ♖d7+ 41.♔e1 ♖×d1+! 0-1
A textbook example of endgame technique.

Game 20

Torre-Reshevsky

Western CA Championship, Detroit 1924

Queen's Gambit Declined [D63]

Samuel Herman Reshevsky (1911-1992), born Szmul Rzeszewski in Poland but an American resident from 1920 on, was to have one of the longest chess careers of all time. A child prodigy, he was playing master-level chess and giving simultaneous exhibitions as early as age six, and was by the late 1940s one of the five or six strongest players in the world. He won the U.S. Championship six times, was a FIDE Candidate as late as 1967, and was still winning tournaments in his seventies. At the time of the 1924 Western Championship he was not quite 13 years old and had been playing in master tournaments for only two years. Still, against a tough field he scored 11-5 (+10 -4 =2) to finish in 5th place, certainly an outstanding achievement. Had he won this game, which he nearly did, he would have finished clear second.

The young Reshevsky resorted to the oldest line of the Orthodox Defense (7...b6), and Torre decided to counter it with the dangerous Pillsbury Attack, named for the famous game Pillsbury-Tarrasch, Hastings 1895.

1.d4 d5 2.♘f3 ♘f6 3.c4 e6 4.♘c3 ♘bd7 5.♗g5 ♗e7 6.e3 0–0 7.♖c1 b6
Arriving at the same position as Game 1. Today this system of defense is considered inferior, due not so much to the Pillsbury Attack, as to the rapid incursion it allows White into the queenside light squares. This technique, pioneered by Oldrich Duras, was seen in Games 1 and 12. In recent decades the line has virtually disappeared from the highest levels, the only examples we could find being Gelfand-Short, Candidates Match 1991 (0-1, 66), and

Ivanchuk-Ljubojevic, Roquebrune rapid 1992 (½-½, 36).

8.c×d5 e×d5

If 8...♘×d5? 9.♘×d5 e×d5 (or 9...♗×g5 10.♘×c7) 10.♗×e7 ♕×e7 11.♖×c7, White wins a pawn.

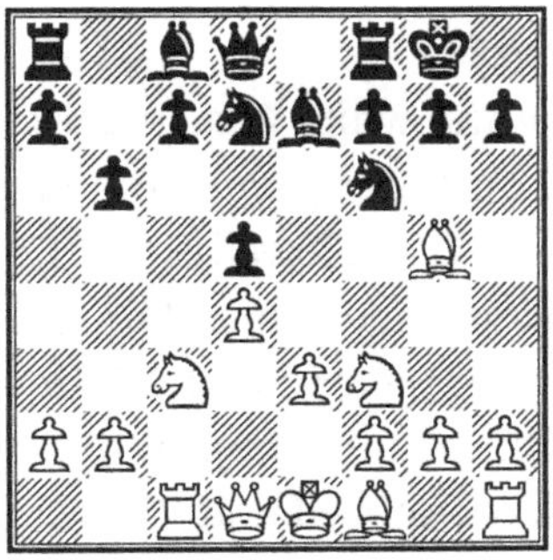

9.♘e5

This advance, combined with f2-f4, characterizes the start of the Pillsbury Attack. Another version is the famous "Vidmar System," in which these moves are delayed for greater effect. In a lengthy article in the magazine *Ajedrez Canario*, July 1974, the Spanish master R. Calvo analyzed the pros and cons of various systems used against the Orthodox Defense, concluding that the Vidmar System was probably the most effective. The stem game of that line was Vidmar-Yates, London 1922: 9.♗d3 ♗b7 10.0–0 c5 (if 10...♘e4 11.♗f4! c5 12.♕e2 etc.) 11.♕e2 c4 12.♗b1 a6 13.♘e5 b5 14.f4, and Vidmar won with a brilliant kingside attack. For those preferring quiet positional play, there is the Duras System, characterized by 9.♕a4. A fourth alternative is 9.♗b5, attributed to Capablanca. Annotating that move, from Capablanca-Teichmann, Berlin 1913, in *Chess Fundamentals*, the Cuban wrote "An invention of my own, I believe. I played it on the spur of the moment simply to change the normal course of the game. Generally the Bishop goes to d3, or to a6 after ♕a4. The text move is in the nature of an ordinary developing move, and as it violates no principle, it cannot be bad."

9...♗b7

Obviously, 9...♘×e5? would lose a pawn after 10.d×e5 and 11.♗×e7.

10.f4

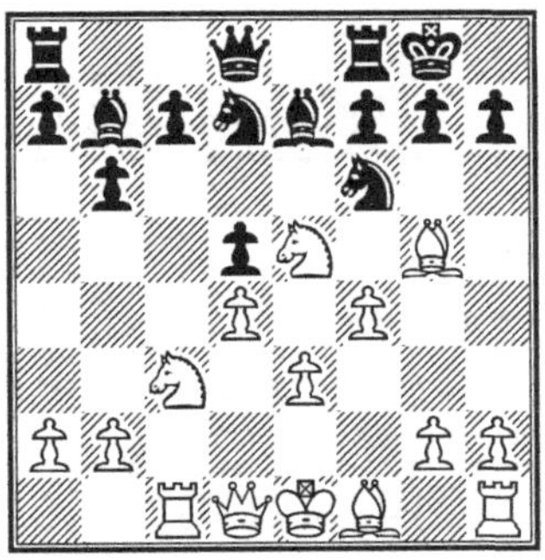

10...♘e8

A maneuver invented by Teichmann in the early 1900s. The idea is that after the exchange of Bishops, the Knight returns to f6 or d6 to pressure the hole at e4. An alternative was

10...c5 11.♗d3 h6 [if 11...♘e4 12.♗×e4 d×e4 13.♗×e7 ♕×e7 14.♘×d7 c×d4? (14...♕×d7=) 15.♘×f8 d×c3 16.0–0?! (△16.♕h5! ♖×f8 17.♖×c3 +–) 16...c×b2 17.♖b1 ♖×f8 18.♕a4 ♕c5 19.♖fe1 ±, Rubinstein-Yates, Bad Pistyan 1912]

12.♗×f6 ♘×f6 13.♕f3 ♗d6 14.0–0 a6 15.♔h1 ♕e7=, Vidmar–Znosko-Borovsky, Nuremberg 1906.

11.♗×e7 ♕×e7 12.♕f3 ♘ef6

Or 12...♘×e5 13.f×e5 ♖d8 14.♗d3 f6 15.0–0 g6=, Teichmann-Swiderski, Ostende 1906.

13.♗d3 ♘e4?!

13...c5 would equalize.

14.♗×e4

Dubious is 14.♘×d7?! ♕×d7 15.♘×e4 d×e4 16.♗×e4 ♗×e4 17.♕×e4 ♖fe8 18.♕d3 ♖×e3+! 19.♕×e3 ♖e8 20.♕×e8+ ♕×e8+ 21.♔f2∓.

Losing would be 14.♘×e4?? d×e4 15.♗×e4 ♘×e5! and either 16.f×e5 ♕h4+ or 16.d×e5 ♕b4+.

Probably best was 14.0–0 ♘df6 15.♕h3 (+0.88/24). The text and White's next few moves do not improve his position.

14...d×e4 15.♕e2

Again not 15.♘×e4?? ♘×e5 etc. 15.♕g4 was a good alternative.

15...♘×e5 16.f×e5 a5

Preventing White from castling: 17.0–0? ♗a6.

17.♕c2

Again 17.♕g4 suggests itself, intending 18.0–0 (but not 18.♘×e4?! h5 19.♕f5 ♕b4+ 20.♔d1 ♕×b2.

17...♕g5

Forcing the white Queen back by the attack on the e-pawn. Annotating in the *ACB*, C.S. Howell said "17...f6 at once is stronger," but then gave only 18.♘×e4(??) f×e5 "and White's King will soon be uncomfortably exposed." Howell overlooked that White can play 18.♕b3+ ♔h8 19.e6 ♖ad8 20.0–0 ♖fe8 21.♕c4 ♕×e6 22.♕×c7 with equality; thus his recommendation is no stronger than the text.

18.♕d2

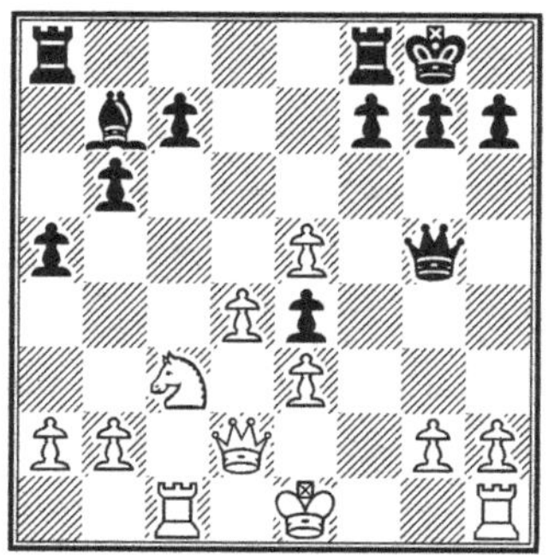

18...f6

Black had a promising pawn sac in 18...♗a6!? 19.♘×e4 ♕g4 20.♘c3 ♖ad8, intending to open lines against White's King by ...f6 and/or ...c5. Stockfish indicates ample compensation for the pawn (-0.93/25).

19.e6?!

Now was the next-to-last chance for 19.0–0!=.

Other moves beside that and the text lose quickly, *viz.*

(a) 19.d5? f×e5 20.♘×e4 ♕h4+ 21.♘g3 ♖ad8 22.e4 c6 23.♕e3 c×d5 24.♕×b6 ♕g5 25.♖c2 (25.♖c7? d×e4! -7.75/24) 25...♖c8;

(b) 19.♘b5? f×e5 20.♖×c7 ♗a6 21.a4 ♗×b5 22.a×b5 e×d4 23.♕×d4 (if 23.e×d4 e3−+) 23...♕×g2 24.♕c4+ ♔h8 25.♖f1 ♖×f1+ 26.♕×f1 ♕×h2−+;

(c) 19.e×f6? ♕×f6 20.♖c2 ♗a6 21.♕f2 (21.♘×e4?? ♕f1+ 22.♖×f1 ♖×f1#) 21...♕e6 22.♕g3 ♗d3 etc. (-6.00/24).

19...♖fe8 20.d5?

This gives White a lost position. Necessary was 20.0–0, or 20.h4 ♕g3+ 21.♕f2 ♕d6 22.0–0.

20...♖ad8!□ 21.♖d1

White now has no really good defense. Though this is objectively insufficient, on psychological grounds it appears to be his best chance.

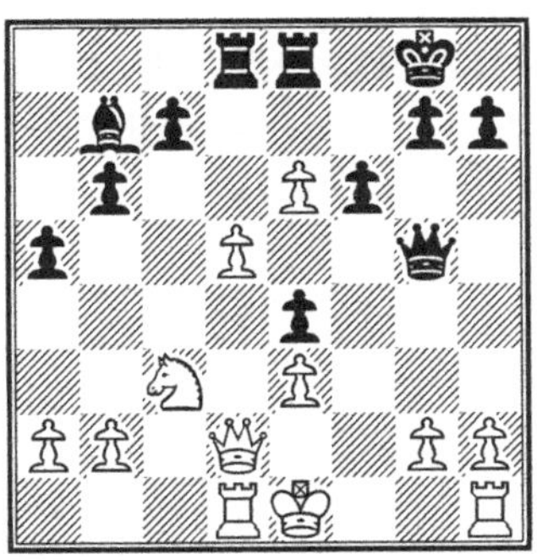

21...♖×e6

Also winning was 21...♗×d5! 22.♘×d5 c6 23.♘×f6+ ♕×f6 24.♕c3 ♖×d1+ 25.♔×d1 ♕×e6 26.♔c2 ♖f8 with a not very difficult ending (-3.11/27). Though this is not quite as great an advantage as Stockfish gives the game continuation, it has the virtue of greater simplicity and lack of complication, which as we will see becomes significant.

22.d×e6 ♖×d2 23.♖×d2 ♕×e3+

23...♔f8 would also have been unpleasant for White.

24.♔d1 ♔f8!□ 25.♖d7 ♕f2?!

This somewhat reduces Black's advantage. Best instead were 25...♕f4, 25...♕c5, or 25...♕g5.

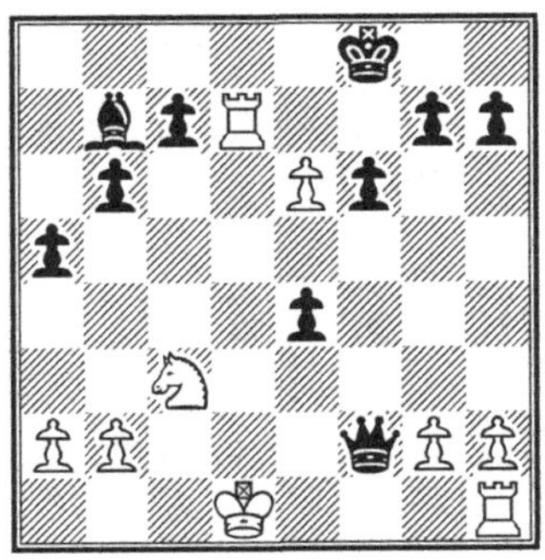

26.♔c1

White might have tried 26.♖f7+, hoping for 26...♔e8? 27.♘b5! ♗c6□ 28.♘×c7+ ♔d8 29.♔c1! ♔c8 30.♖d1 and Black must accept a draw by repetition, *e.g.* 30...♕e3+ 31.♔b1 ♕e2 32.♖c1 ♕d3+ 33.♔a1 ♕d2 34.♔b1 ♕d3+ etc.

But 26...♔g8 keeps Black winning, *viz.* 27.♖d7 h6 28.♖d8+ ♔h7 29.e7 ♗c6 30.♔c1 (worse is 30.e8♕ ♗×e8 31.♖×e8 ♕×b2 when White loses a

Knight or Rook) 30...♕×g2 31.♖e1 f5 32.e8♕ ♗×e8 33.♖×e8 ♕×h2, and though Black now has a Knight and two Rooks for the Queen, Black has five extra pawns, four of them connected and passed (-3.55/23).

26...♗a6??

In a position where any of at least a half-dozen moves secure the win, young Reshevsky snatches defeat from the jaws of victory. Instead 26...♗c6, 26...♕f4+, 26...♕c5, 26...♕×g2, and 26...♕f5, among others, would all win handily.

27.♘d5!!

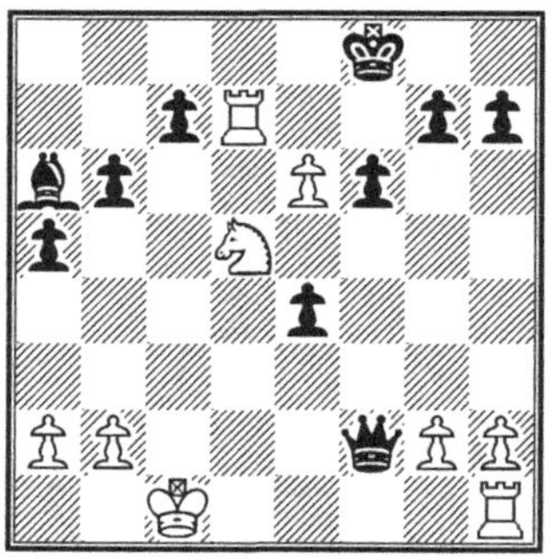

Reshevsky had intended 27...♗d3 throwing a mating net around the white King, but he failed to consider this reply, threatening mate in one. Now it is White with the advantage, and from here on Torre is remorselessly accurate in converting it into a full point. One wonders if this error was induced by the sort of time trouble Reshevsky was famously prey to later, for most of his adult career.

27...♕c5+ 28.♔b1 ♗b5 29.♖f7+ ♔e8

If 29...♔g8 30.♘e7+ etc.

30.♘×c7+ ♔d8 31.e7+ ♔c8

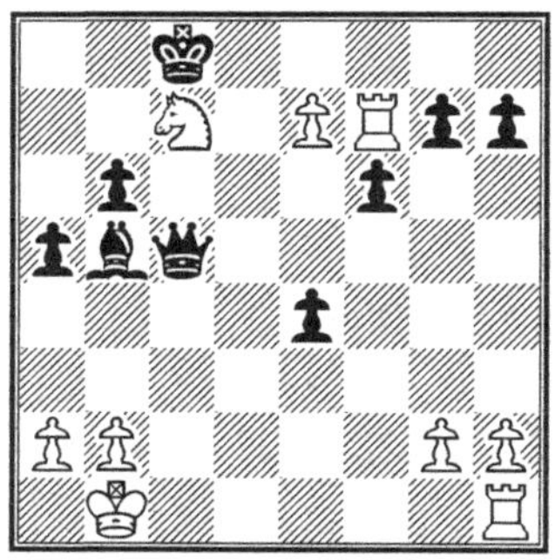

31...♕×e7 was equally hopeless: 32.♖×e7 ♗d3+ 33.♔c1 ♔×e7 34.♔d2 and White wins easily.

32.♘×b5 1–0

After 33...♕×b5 34.♖d1 is curtains. An emotional game between two ascendant young masters.

Game 21

Torre-Winter

Western CA Championship, Detroit 1924

French Defense [C10]

Detroit native John Winter (1874-1950) was Torre's opponent here. Not to be confused with the British master William Winter or journalist Edward Winter. Quite a crowd gathered to watch this game, but saw little excitement over the first 25 moves. Like Reshevsky in the previous game, Winter gave Torre quite a hard time, at first holding his own and then getting an opportunity to win, until errors at moves 27 and 28 turned the tide.

1.e4 e6 2.d4 d5 3.♘c3 c5?!

A line played fairly often by Marshall in the years 1905-1915, with which he did quite well, scoring +4 -0 =4 against strong opponents in major events. Among these was his most famous win, against Levitsky at Breslau 1912, with its shocking 23...♕g3!! climax. However, the line is considered positionally unsound due to the isolated d-pawn Black is usually burdened with, and its track record since Marshall's day is quite poor, with ChessBase showing a score of +284 -748 =173 from 1920 on.

4.e×d5 e×d5 5.♘f3 ♗e6

A typical isolated d-pawn position, dating as far back as Green-Steinitz, London 1862, and before that to games between Paulsen and Kolisch in 1861! (Though in all those cases it was reached by 1.e4 c5 2.♘f3 e6 3.♘c3 d5 4.e×d5 e×d5 5.d4 ♗e6.) Apparently it was not seen again in the intervening six decades until the present game. Black must seek active play for his pieces, or his positional weakness will leave him without counterplay.

6.♗e2 ♘c6 7.0–0 ♗e7 8.♗f4 ♘f6 9.d×c5 ♗×c5 10.♘b5

Aiming to occupy the weak square d4.

10...♖c8 11.♘bd4 0–0 12.♘×c6 ♖×c6

Black cannot try to bolster his d-pawn with 12...b×c6 due to 13.♗a6 ♖a8 14.♗b7 winning the Exchange.

13.♘d4

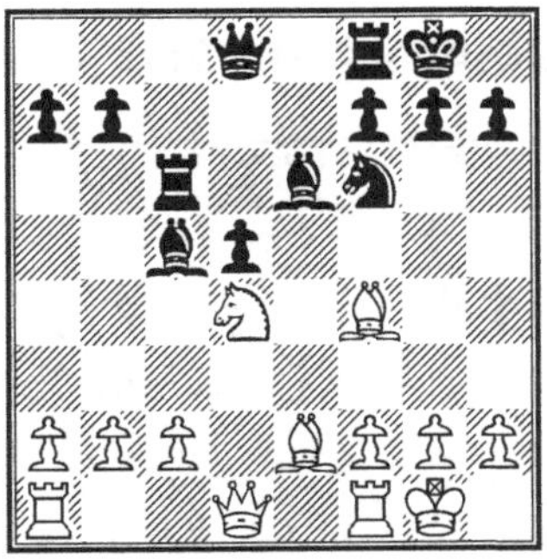

Gaining a tempo, since if now 13...♗×d4 14.♕×d4 ♖×c2 15.♗d3 ♖c8

16.♕×a7 and Black has not one weak pawn but two.

13...♖c8 14.♗g5 h6 15.♗h4 a6

Black might like to bring his Rook to the e-file but as yet cannot: 15...♖e8 16.♗b5 ♗d7 17.♗×f6 etc. Torre, capitalizing on such tactical details, gradually takes the life out of Black's position, though without adding much to his own.

16.c3 ♖e8 17.♗f3 ♗e7 18.♖e1 ♕b6

As good a way as any to prevent 19.♘×e6 f×e6 20.♖×e6. Also playable was 18...♕d7.

19.♖b1

An alternate plan was 19.♘×e6 f×e6 20.♕c2, intending ♖e1-e2, ♖a1-e1 and ♗h4-g3, shifting pressure from the d-pawn to the newly created backward e-pawn.

19...♗d8 20.♕d3 ♘h7 21.♗×d8

An exchange of Bishops is unavoidable; if 21.♗g3 ♗c7.

21...♖c×d8 22.♖e2 ♘g5 23.♖be1

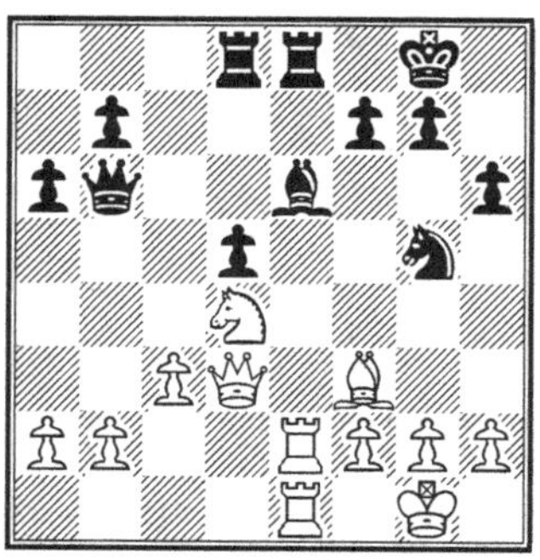

23...♘e4!?

Interesting, if perhaps not objectively best. Stockfish suggests two alternate plans for Black.

In one he gives up the d-pawn: 23...♗d7 24.♗×d5 ♖×e2 25.♖×e2 ♗g4 26.f3 ♗e6, but the engine considers the resulting position virtually equal (+0.30/29).

In the other he aims at exchanges: 23...♘×f3+ 24.♕×f3 [or 24.♘×f3 ♗d7 25.♕d4 (not 25.♕×d5?? ♖×e2 26.♖×e2 ♗b5) 25...♕b5 26.♖×e8+ ♖×e8 27.♖×e8+ ♗×e8 28.♕d2 (+0.50/29)] 24...♗d7 25.♖×e8+ (25.♕×d5?! ♕×b2∓) 25...♖×e8 26.♖×e8+ ♗×e8 27.♕e2 (27.♕×d5?? is even worse now: 27...♕×b2 and 28...♕×c3−+) 27...♗d7 with only a small advantage for White (+0.49/28). With Rooks off the board, the isolated d-pawn is not a big liability unless White can manage to trade off the remaining pieces, which seems unlikely.

24.h3

If 24.♗×e4 d×e4 25.♕×e4 ♗×a2 26.♕×e8+ ♖×e8 27.♖×e8+ ♔h7 28.b3 ♕c5 (28...♗×b3?? 29.♖b1+−) 29.♖8e3 (△30.♖a1+−) 29...♕a3 30.c4, and again we reach a position nominally favorable to White (+0.86/34), but it is not clear how he might win. The text is the sort of move usually necessary in such positions to forestall back-rank mate, and it might as well be made now.

24...♗d7

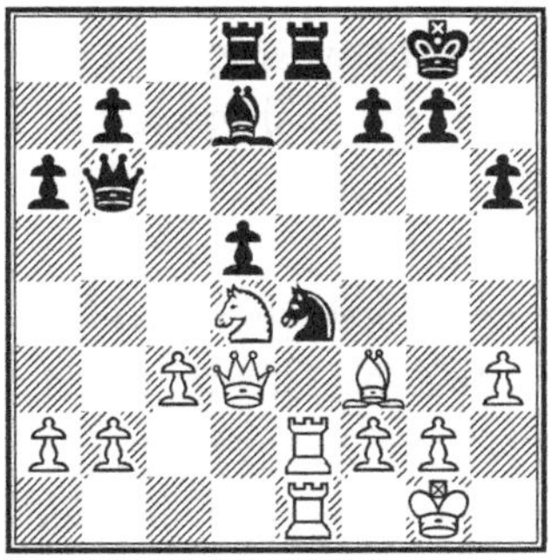

25.♗×e4

With this the game becomes very drawish. The main alternative was 25.♕c2, but after 25...♘f6 neither side is making any progress.

25...d×e4 26.♖×e4?!

A careless move by Torre, due perhaps to the tension surrounding this game. This pawn now carries a drop of poison. After 26.♕g3, 26.♕d2, or 26.♕e3 the game would be quite even.

26...♖×e4

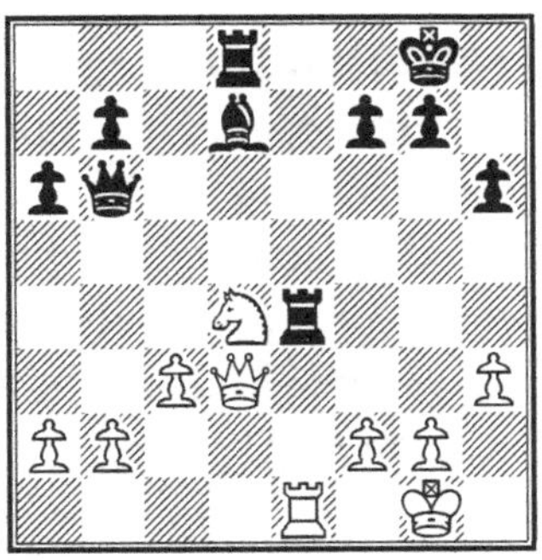

27.♖×e4??

This could have lost the game for Torre. Necessary was 27.♕×e4 ♖e8 28.♕b1 ♖×e1+ 29.♕×e1 ♕×b2 30.♕e7 ♗a4 31.♘f3 ♕×a2 32.♕×b7, when the game has turned slightly in Black's favor (-0.45/30), but is still likely drawn.

27...♕×b2?

Black is too intent on his original thought, begun with 23...♘e4, of trading his weak d-pawn for White's b-pawn, and he misses the chance to win the Exchange with 27...♗f5. According to Torre's account, there were some 80 spectators to this game, and all 80 immediately saw the chance of 27...♗f5 while the two contestants somehow did not. Black would have been clearly winning after 27...♗f5, *viz.* 28.b4 (this or 29.b3 is necessary, or the b-pawn is also lost) 28...♕c7 29.f3 ♗×e4 30.f×e4 b5 etc. (-6.16/26). With the text the game is again even.

28.♘f5

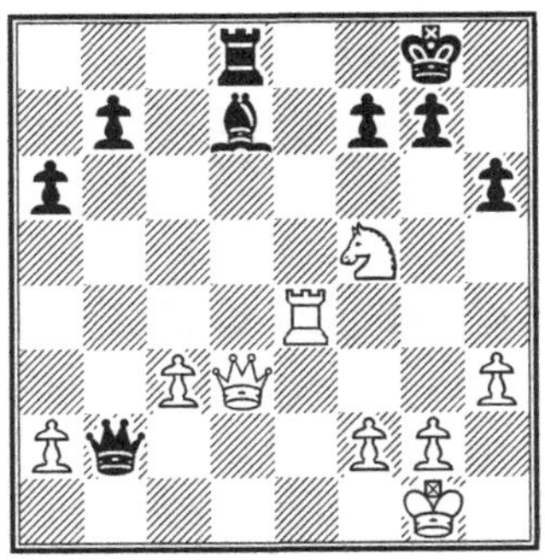

28...♕c1+?

A serious error, in fact the losing move. Necessary was either 28...♕b5 when White will be unable to double his heavy pieces on the d-file (0.00/28), or 28...♖f8, unpinning the Bishop, when if 29.♕×d7?? ♕b1+ 30.♔h2 ♕×e4−+

29.♔h2 ♕g5
Because of his 28th move, Black is a tempo short of being able to throw off the bothersome pin.

30.♖d4 g6 31.♘e3

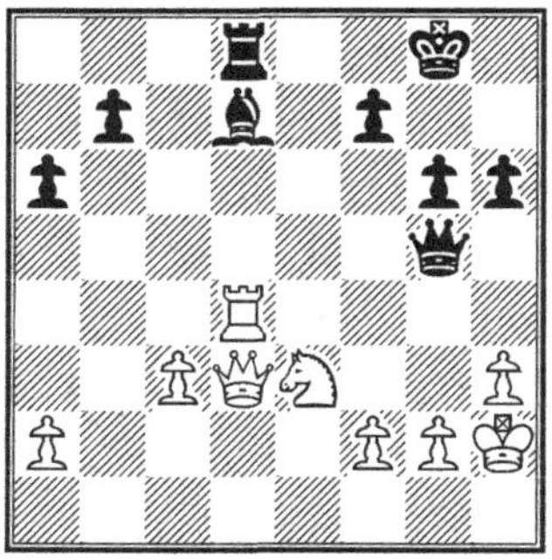

If now 31...♕b5 32.c4! (not possible after 28...♕b5 because the ♘f5 was hanging) 32...♕a4 33.♘g4 ♔f8 34.♘f6 and if Black still tries to defend the pinned Bishop, he gets in worse trouble, *e.g.* 34...♔e7 35.♘d5+ ♔e8 36.♖e4+ ♗e6 37.♖×e6+! f×e6 38.♕×g6+ and mate shortly.

31...♕e7 32.♘g4 ♔g7 33.♖d6!
The pin on the d-file has Black practically paralyzed, and now White threatens 34.♘f6+. Black sees no remedy but to sacrifice the Exchange.

33...♗×g4 34.♕d4+
This *Zwischenschach*, forcing 34...f6, will leave Black vulnerable on the seventh rank.

34...f6 35.♖×d8 ♗e6 36.♕d6 ♕f7

37.c4
Gaining maneuvering space by capitalizing on the Bishop's enforced immobility (37...♗×c4? 38.♖d7).

37...g5 38.c5 ♔g6 39.c6
Very instructive. Torre gives away a pawn to clear out the queenside, in order to gain the space needed to utilize the Queen and Rook to their full capacities.

39...b×c6 40.♕×c6 ♗×a2 41.♕c2+ f5
41...♔g7 would have been answered forcefully by 42.♖c8. However, this advance merely opens another window in Black's already too well ventilated position.

42.♖d6+ ♗e6
Now, by triangulation, White aims to transfer his Queen to e5 without loss of tempo.

43.♕c8 ♔f6 44.♕h8+ 1-0
After 44...♔g6 (44...♔e7 45.♕d8#) 45.♕e5 the Bishop is lost. Howell wrote "A good example of the energetic chess which Torre plays. Any technical faults are counter-balanced by the directness of the play."

Torre's opponent in the next game was one of the great rogues of chess history, one of the few masters to be also an habitual felon. Well educated, with fine manners (when he wanted to use them), Philadelphia-born Norman

Tweed Whitaker (1890-1975, IM title 1965, historical Elo 2420) was, at least early in his adult life, a lawyer by profession. He was also a liar, draft-dodger, check-bouncer, thief, and swindler who served several prison terms, including one in Alcatraz alongside Al Capone. Dubbed "Caïssa's Conman" by Arnold Denker[1], he was an accomplished chess player as well, twice winning the Western Open (1923 and 1927) and placing =4th-6th (of 16) in the 1928 FIDE Amateur World Championship. Over his long career he defeated such prominent players as Showalter, Janowski, Marshall, Reshevsky, Kashdan, and Lajos and Herman Steiner.

For a full examination of the sharply contrasting personalities of Whitaker and Torre, see "A Clash of Opposites" in Chapter V. For now we concentrate on their game. Owners of the first edition will find the notes here rather different, as Stockfish uncovered many errors and missed opportunities that passed unnoticed before. There were also positions where Stockfish itself seemed perplexed, unable to reach any solid evaluation. This is one of the most difficult, problematic games of its era, one truly exemplifying Tartakower's dictum that "the winner of a chess game is he who makes the next-to-last mistake."

Game 22

Torre-Whitaker

Western CA Championship, Detroit 1924

Ruy López [C68]

1.e4 e5 2.♘f3 ♘c6 3.♗b5 a6 4.♗×c6 d×c6 5.♘c3

A logical alternative to the more usual 5.d4 or 5.0–0. It renews the threat to Black's e-pawn, capture of which at the moment is premature (5.♘×e5 ♕d4).

5...f6 6.d4 e×d4 7.♕×d4 ♕×d4 8.♘×d4

Arriving at the classic imbalance of the exchange Spanish: White has a strategic advantage in his kingside majority, which bodes well for his chances in the endgame, while Black has the Bishop pair and must seek to attack in the middle game. Oddly, though, it is White's queenside pawns that will be the decisive factor in this game.

1 Denker devotes thirteen pages to Whitaker in his memoir. Not everything there is accurate; for example he claimed that Whitaker had been Assistant Secretary of the Interior in the Harding administration. In fact Whitaker never held any federal post higher than minor patent attorney.

8...♗d6 9.♗e3 ♗d7

9...♘e7 is considered most precise. However, Black here intends queenside castling, which is perfectly playable and should lead to equality.

10.0–0–0 0–0–0

The *ACB* remarked "Both Kings have gone to the wrong side!", though in Schlechter-Rubinstein, Berlin 1918, 10.0–0 ♘e7 11.♖ad1 c5 12.♘de2 ♘g6 13.♘d5 0–0–0 led to a Black win. The text line goes back at least to Von Bardeleben-Salwe, Prague 1908; overall it has produced mainly draws.

11.♔b1

This appears to be an unnecessary loss of time. More usual is 11.♘b3 or 11.f3.

11...♘e7 12.♘b3

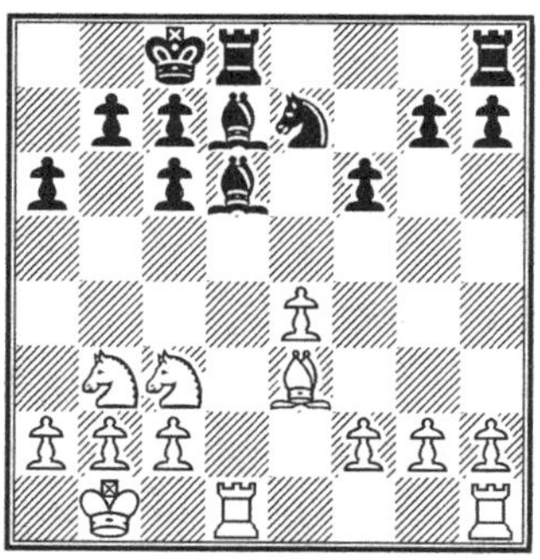

12...♗e6

If 12...b6?, to deny c5 to the Knight, then either 13.♗×b6! ♗g4 14.♖×d6 (14.f3?! ♗×f3 is equal after either 15.♗×c7 ♗×d1 16.♗×d8 ♗×c2+ 17.♔×c2 ♖×d8, or 15.g×f3 c×b6) 14...♖×d6 15.♗c5 ♖d7 16.♗e3±, or even better 13.♖×d6! c×d6 14.♗×b6 ♖de8 15.♖d1 d5 16.♘c5 etc. (+2.23/26).

13.♘c5 ♗f7 14.♘d3

The Knight is much better posted here than at b3.

14...b6 15.f3 ♘g6 16.h3

So that the King's Rook can move without leaving the h-pawn *en prise*.

16...♖he8 17.♖he1

With this move White begins drifting into a difficult position. Better perhaps was 17.g4, intending ♖h1-f1 and f3-f4, expanding on the kingside. Black is soon able to lock down that side of the board.

17...♘h4 18.♖e2 c5 19.♖ed2 g5!

Well played positionally. Black realizes that the Knight at d3 is vital to White for its control of the dark squares. He wants to evict it by c5-c4, but first makes sure it cannot escape to f4.

20.a3 h6 21.♗g1 c4 22.♘b4 ♗f4

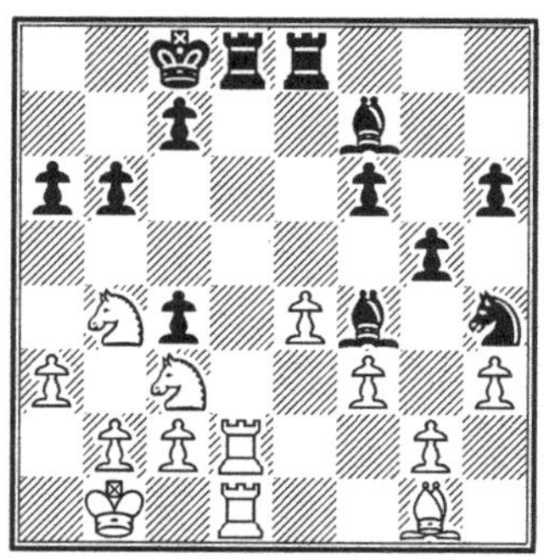

23.♖e2?

This could have led to a lost game.

Correct was 23.♖×d8+ ♖×d8 24.♘bd5 [not 24.♖×d8+? ♔×d8 25.♗d4 (if 25.♘×a6 c5 eventually trapping the Knight) 25...♘×g2 26.♗×f6+ ♔d7 27.♗g7 h5 (-3.07/26)] 24...♗d6 25.♘e3 with only a slight edge for Black (-0.61/27).

23...♖×d1+ 24.♘×d1

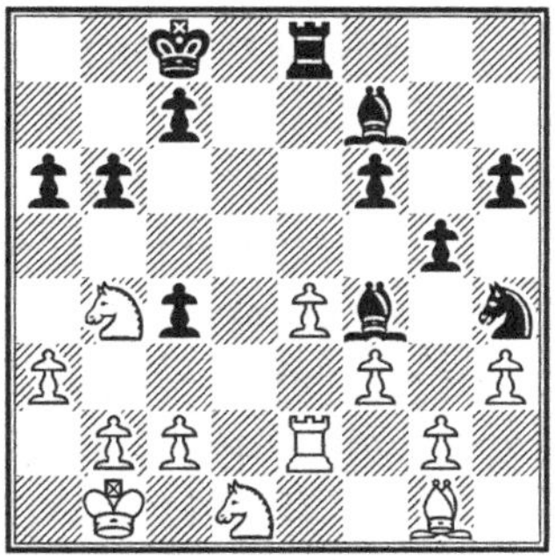

24...c5

Not bad, but only third- or fourth-best. Strongest was 24...a5 25.♘a2 f5 26.♘dc3 f×e4,

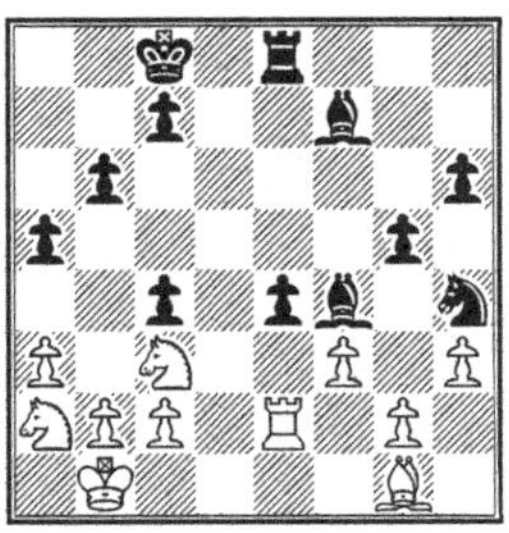

and if:

(a) 27.♖×e4? simply 27...♘×g2−+; or

(b) 27.♘×e4? ♗h5 28.♘ac3 (if 28.♘ec3?? ♖×e2 29.♘×e2 ♘×g2−+) 28...♘×g2!−+ (if 29.♖×g2 ♗×f3 etc.); or

(c) 27.f×e4 and while material is even, Black has achieved his goal of opening up the position for his Bishops and has a definite, perhaps winning advantage (-2.88/30).

25.♘a2

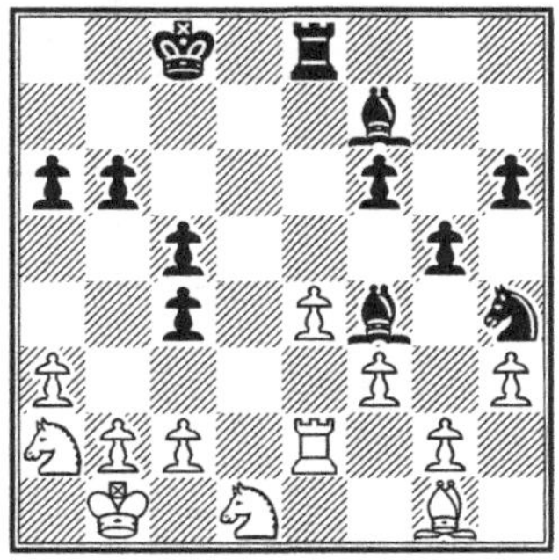

25...♖d8

Again, less than best. Whitaker never seems to realize the vulnerability of White's kingside pawns, which again could be exploited by 25...f5! 26.♘ac3 ♗h5 27.♘d5 f×e4 28.g4 ♗f7,

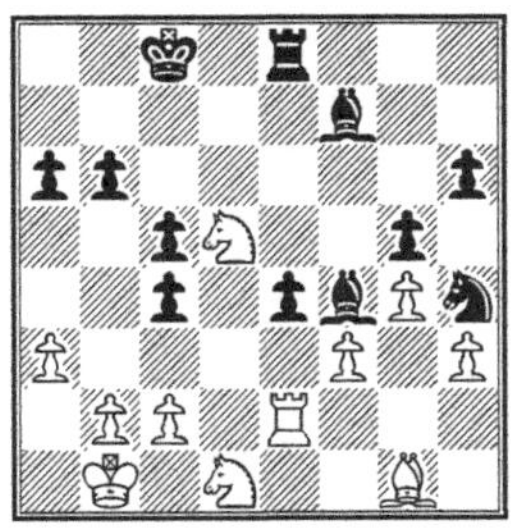

and either

(a) 29.♘×b6+ ♔c7 30.♘a4 ♖d8 31.♘dc3 ♘×f3 32.♗×c5 ♘d2+ 33.♔a2 ♔c6 34.♗e3 ♗g6 (-2.27/28), or

(b) 29.♘×f4 g×f4 30.f×e4 ♘f3 31.♗h2 [if 31.♗f2 h5! 32.g×h5 c3! 33.b3 (if 33.♘×c3? or 33.b×c3?, then 33...♗c4−+) 33...♘d2+ 34.♔c1 ♗×h5 35.♖e1 ♘×e4 (-2.77/25)] 31...♘×h2 32.♖×h2 ♖×e4 (-1.66/26).

26.♘e3

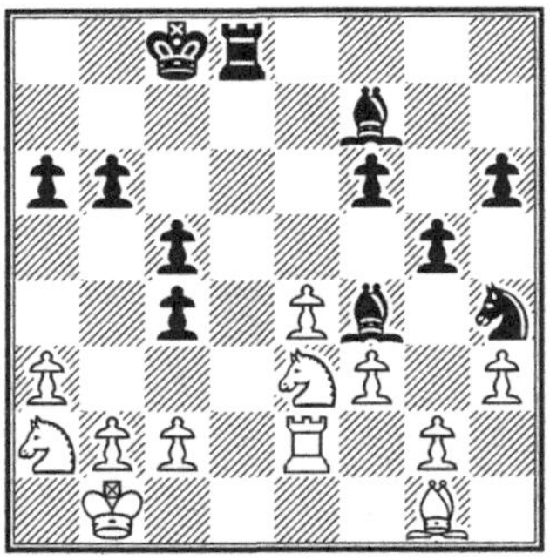

Torre too is making mistakes. Correct was 26.♘ac3∓.

26...f5?!

Too late! Yet again Whitaker misses the best line, which was 26...♗×e3! 27.♗×e3 ♖d1+ 28.♘c1 c3 29.b×c3 (if 29.b3 ♖h1 △30...♖h2 and 31...♖×g2) 29...♗c4 30.♖f2 (if 30.♖d2? ♖×d2 31.♗×d2 ♗f1 △32...♗×g2) 30...♖e1 31.g3 ♖×e3 32.g×h4 g×h4 33.♔b2 ♔c7 when White is badly tied up and Black should win the ending (-2.67/25). After the text Black's advantage is almost gone (-0.44/26).

27.♘c3! f×e4 28.f×e4

With this, White solves his problems on the King's flank, and is finally in position to play g2-g4. True, the e-pawn is weak, but it controls important central squares, supporting White's Knights and giving him dynamic possibilities.

28...♗h5 29.g4

Finally ending the g-pawn's time as a target.

29...♘f3 30.♗f2

With this move Torre offered a draw, as he had already clinched first place in the tournament. Whitaker also ought to have been amenable to a half-point, since thereby he would be virtually assured of second place, plus it would have given him the moral victory of three points against his four strongest opponents. Nevertheless, Whitaker refused the draw, a decision he would regret. Recalling the game to Velasco 53 years later, Torre said "I then decided to steel myself and exploit to the maximum any small imprecision by my opponent. From there developed a tense and hard-fought struggle." Indeed!

30...♗f7 31.♘ed5 ♔b7 32.♗e3

Trying to exchange or evict Black's strong ♗f4 without giving up the well-posted ♘d5.

32...♗g3 33.♖g2

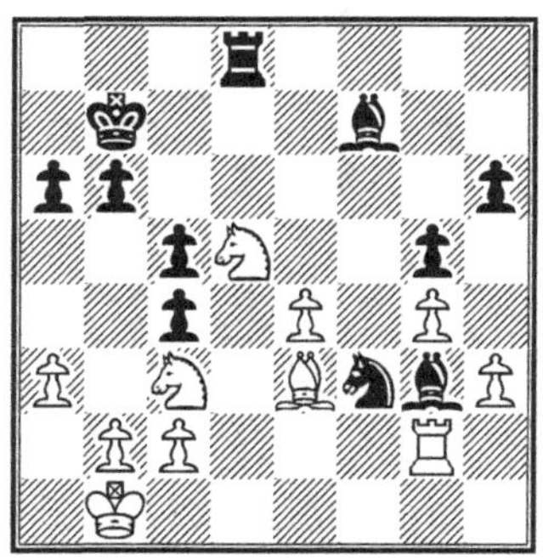

33...♗e1

Best. If 33...♗d6 34.♖f2 ♗×d5 (34...♘e5? 35.♖f6) with advantage to White after either 35.e×d5 ♖f8 36.♘e4, or 35.♖×f3 ♗c6 36.♖f6.

34.♖e2

According to Torre's brief notes, at this point both players were very short of time, explaining this repetition.

34...♗g3 35.♖g2 ♗e1 36.♖e2

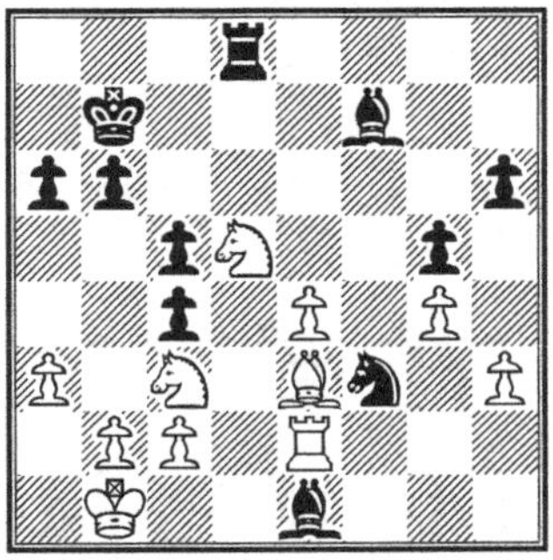

36...♔c6?!

The text lets White gain an important tempo. Black could have claimed a draw by repetition with 36...♗g3 but imprudently avoids doing so.

Slightly better alternatives included 36...♖d7∓, 36...♗e6∓, and 36...♗×d5 37.♘×d5 ♗g3∓.

37.♘e7+! ♔d7 38.♘f5

The game is quite even now.

38...♗e6 39.♗f2

Not 39.♘×h6 ♖h8∓.

39...♗×f2?!

A perhaps better exchange was 39...♗×c3 40.b×c3 ♖e8 41.♘g3=.

40.♖×f2

Now 40...♘d4? would lose the h-pawn without compensation: 41.♘×h6 ♖h8 42.♖f6 ♔e7 43.e5±.

If 40...♘e5 though, better 41.♘e3 (41.♘×h6? ♖h8 42.♖f6?? ♔e7−+).

40...♘g1

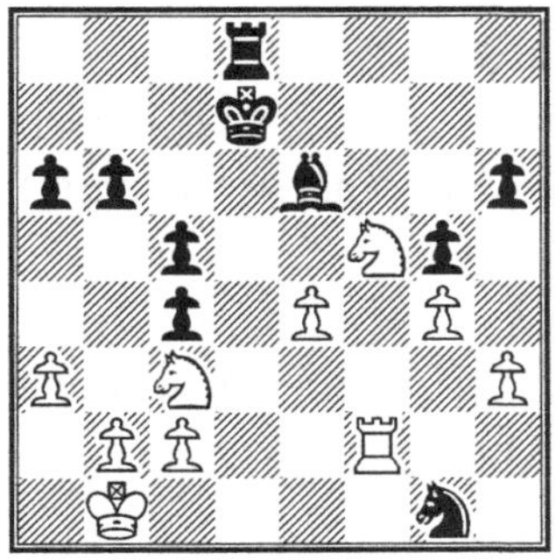

41.♖g2

The position is extremely difficult to analyze. Stockfish initially likes two other moves better, but neither leads to anything conclusive:

(a) One is the mysterious-looking 41.a4, apparently to prevent 41...b5 and 42...b4, driving the Knight off its valuable post at c3. If Black nabs the h-pawn, 41...♘×h3, then 42.♖h2 ♘f4 43.♖×h6 ♔c7 with a thin edge for White (+0.41/32), but a draw likely;

(b) The other is 41.h4, when best play proceeds 41...g×h4 42.♘×h4 b5 (42...♗×g4?? 43.♖g2) 43.♖f6 ♗×g4 44.♘d5 (△45.♖f1 ♘e2 46.♘f6+ winning the Bishop) 44...♗e6 45.♘f4 ♗g4 46.♖×h6 ♘e2 47.♘×e2 ♗×e2 48.♖×a6, a position rated even despite White's pawn plus.

In a nutshell, this has become a very difficult, problematic game, one that abounds in ways to lose but shows no clear way to win against correct defense. Since neither player is content with a draw, the outcome will hinge on whoever makes fewer or less serious mistakes.

41...♘f3

41...♘×h3 42.♖h2 ♘f4 43.♖×h6 ♔c7 44.a4 would transpose to line (**a**) above.

42.♖g3

42.♖f2 ♘g1 43.h4 would transpose to line (**b**) above.

42...♗×f5

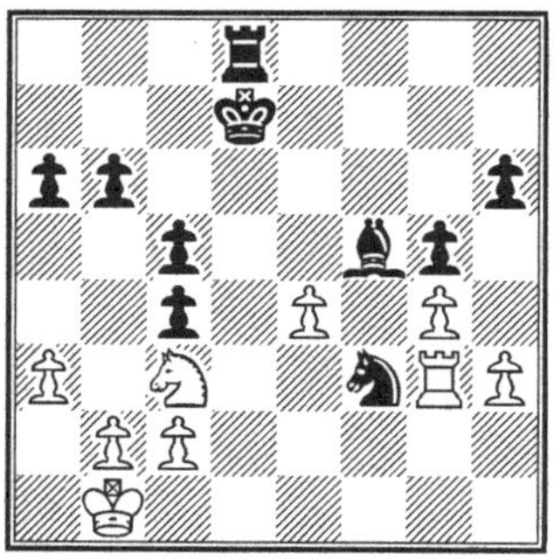

43.♖×f3

In the first edition we gave this an exclam, saying "[White demonstrates] fine positional judgement. The black Knight is a more important piece than the Bishop in this position, due to its ability to occupy the vital dark squares; in contrast the Bishop is a 'paper tiger,' because White's pawns, especially the e-pawn, greatly limit its mobility." This assessment hinges, however, on the premise that White wins if Black plays ...♔×d5 three or four moves from now. As we will see, this is not true. Therefore White was better off playing 43.e×f5 ♘d4 44.♖e3, when the protected, passed f-pawn would seem to give him whatever winning chances there may be. Though the game may then still be a draw with best play by both sides — Stockfish churned out to 40 ply without its evaluation ever rising as high as +1.00.

43...♗e6 44.♘d5 ♗×d5 45.e×d5 ♔d6 46.♖f6+

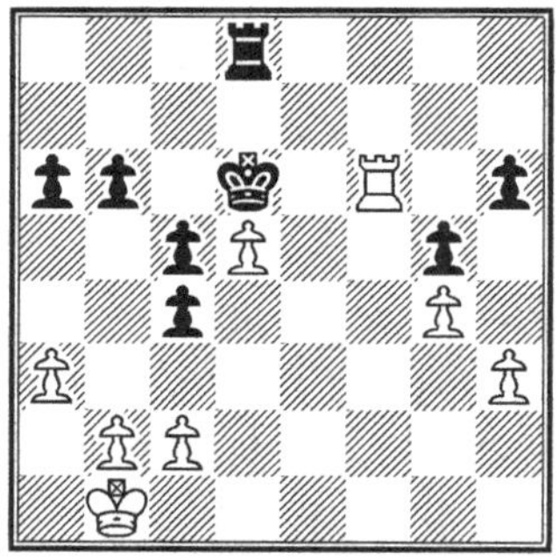

46...♔e5

In the first edition we gave 46...♔×d5 47.♖×h6 ♖d6 48.♖h5 ♖g6 49.h4 ♔e6 50.♖×g5 ♖×g5 51.h×g5 ♔f7 52.♔c1 ♔g6 53.♔d2 ♔×g5 54.♔e3 ♔×g4 55.♔e4 as winning for White:

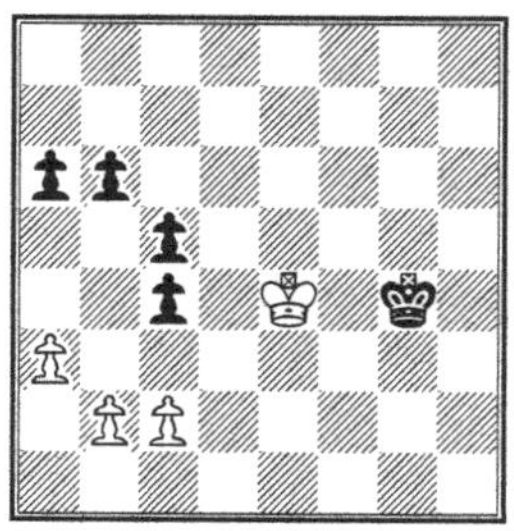

It is, if Black plays what we then gave, 55...c3⁈, but Black can draw with 55...♔g3!, *viz.* 56.♔d5 ♔f3 57.♔×c4, and either

(a) 57...♔e2 58.♔d5 ♔d2 59.c4 ♔d3 60.♔c6 ♔×c4 61.♔×b6 a5!□ 62.♔×a5 ♔b3 63.♔b5 ♔×b2 64.a4 ♔b3 65.♔×c5 ♔×a4, or
(b) 57.♔c6 ♔e2 58.♔×b6 ♔d2 59.♔×c5 ♔×c2 60.♔×c4 ♔×b2 61.♔b4 a5+ 62.♔a4 ♔a2 63.♔×a5 ♔×a3.

47.♖e6+ ♔f4?
Black takes a step toward losing. Correct was 47...♔×d5 48.♖×h6 and Black can split the point with either 48...♖d6 as in the previous note, or 48...c3 49.♖×b6 ♖h8 50.b×c3 (if 50.♖×a6 ♖b8! 51.b3 ♖f8 52.♖g6 ♖f1+ 53.♔a2 ♖c1=) 50...♖×h3 51.♖g6 ♔c4.

48.♖×h6
If 48.♖×b6, not 48...♖×d5? 49.♖×a6+−. Necessary would be 48...♔g3 49.♖×h6 ♖×d5 50.♔c1, when White stands slightly better (+1.18/34), but it is unclear, even unlikely, that he can win against best play.

48...♖×d5 49.♖×b6 ♖d1+ 50.♔a2

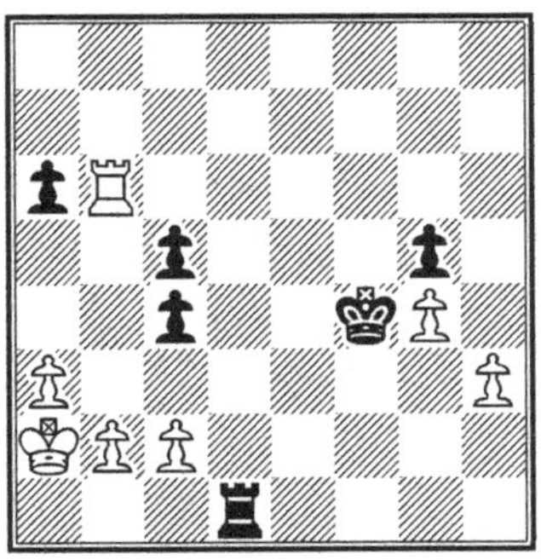

50...♖d2?
Correct was 50...♔g3 51.♖g6 ♖d5, and again we have a position slightly better for White but not won (+1.46/33). After the text Black is lost.

51.c3?!
But White does not find the winning line, which is 51.♖×a6 ♖×c2 52.♔b1 ♖h2 53.♖a4 ♔e5 (if 53...♖×h3? 54.♖×c4+ ♔f3 55.a4+−) 54.♖×c4 ♔d5 55.♖c3 c4 56.a4 ♔c5 57.a5 ♔b5 58.♔a2 ♔×a5 59.♖×c4 ♖×h3 60.♖c5+ ♔b4 61.♖×g5 ♖h8 and after 62.♖e5/♖f5/♖h5 White is clearly winning (+6.40/31).

51...♖h2?
Black errs again! Once more, 51...♔g3 was necessary, *e.g.* 52.♖g6 ♔h4 53.a4 (if 53.♖×a6?! ♔×h3 draws) 53...a5 54.♖h6+ ♔g3 55.♖h5 ♔f4!□ 56.h4 g×h4 57.♖×h4 ♔e5! when if White can win, it will be with great difficulty (+3.08/44).

52.♖f6+!
Finally Torre finds the best move. 52.♖h6 might also win, but the text is strongest.

52...♔g3

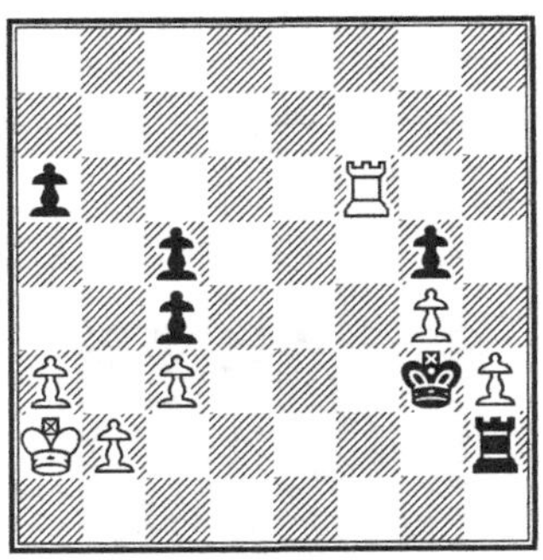

This offered salvation at moves 50 and 51, but now it is only the least evil.

53.♖×a6?
Oh no! Torre again lets the win slip. Correct was 53.♖f5! ♔h4 54.♖×c5 ♖×h3 55.♖×c4 ♖g3 56.b4 ♖×g4 57.♖c6!,

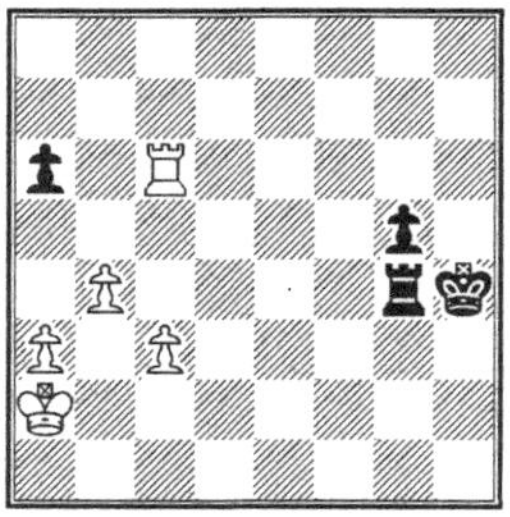

and now if
(a) 57...a5 58.b5! ♖g2+ 59.♔b3 g4 60.b6 ♖f2 61.b7 ♖f1 62.♔a4 ♖b1 63.♖c7 g3 64.♖g7 g2 65.c4 g1♕ (if 65...♖×b7 66.♖×b7 g1♕ 67.♖h7+ ♔g3 68.♖g7+ etc.) 66.♖×g1 ♖×b7 67.c5 etc., winning; or
(b) 57...♖g2+ 58.♔b3 g4 59.♖×a6 ♖f2 60.♖h6+ ♔g5 61.♖h1! This gets White's Rook in front of Black's passed pawn, and behind his own, a winning combination (+12.56/28).
After the text Black finds a series of "only" moves that keep the game even.

53...♖×h3□ 54.♖a4 ♔×g4□ 55.♖×c4+ ♔f3
Only this or 55...♔f5 holds the draw.

56.♖×c5 g4
This or 56...♔f4 are the only moves.

57.a4 g3 58.♖g5
Now any reasonable move holds the draw for Black.

58...♖h4 59.a5 g2 60.♖×g2!
This and 60.a6 are the only moves that do not lose.

60...♔×g2 61.b4 ♔f3 62.♔b3 ♔e4 63.♔c4 ♔e5+ 64.♔c5 ♔e6 65.a6

65...♖h8??
Finally, Black commits a fatal error from which White does not let him recover.
65...♖h3! would have still held the draw, *viz.* 66.a7 ♖×c3+ 67.♔b6 ♖a3 68.♔b7 ♔d6 69.b5 ♔c5 70.b6 ♖a1 etc. (0.00/40), or 66.c4 ♔d7 67.b5 ♔c8 68.b6 ♖a3 69.a7 ♔b7=.

66.a7!
From here on Torre finds the only moves that win.

66...♔d7 67.♔b6!□ ♖c8

Now not 68.♔b7? ♖c7+ 69.♔b6 ♖c6+ 70.♔a5 ♖×c3 71.♔b6 ♖a3=, nor 68.c4? ♖c6+ 69.♔a5 ♖c8 70.♔a6 ♔c7 71.b5 ♖h8 72.b6+ ♔c6 73.b7 ♖h3 74.b8♘+ (74.b8♕?? ♖a3#) 74...♔c7 75.♘c6 (75.a8♕ ♖a3+ 76.♔b5 ♖×a8=) 75...♖h8 (0.00/50).

68.b5!□

Preventing 68...♖c6+ and ensuring that Black will have to give up his Rook for the a-pawn while White still has his other two pawns. Therefore: **1-0**.

Perhaps the most difficult game of Torre's career, and one in which he showed admirable perseverance.

Game 23

Torre-Stolzenberg

Western CA Championship, Detroit 1924

Dutch Defense [A80]

An intriguing minor footnote in chess history comes from Torre's opponent in this game. Though in 1924 a resident of Detroit, Leon Stolzenberg (1895-1974) was born in Tarnopol, Russia. In 1916, during World War I, he was serving there at a military hospital to which future world champion Alekhine was sent to recover from shell shock. There he saw the blindfold exhibition in which the famous game Alekhine-Feldt, with its stunning moves 15.♘f7!! and 16.♕×e6+!!, was played. However, Stolzenberg wrote in *Chess Review* in 1951 that Alekhine's opponent was not "Feldt" but a Dr. Martin Fischer (not the only time Alekhine fiddled with the facts; see Game 3). Stolzenberg was himself a strong master-strength player who played several blindfold games with Alekhine during their time at Tarnopol.

1.d4 f5 2.♗g5!?

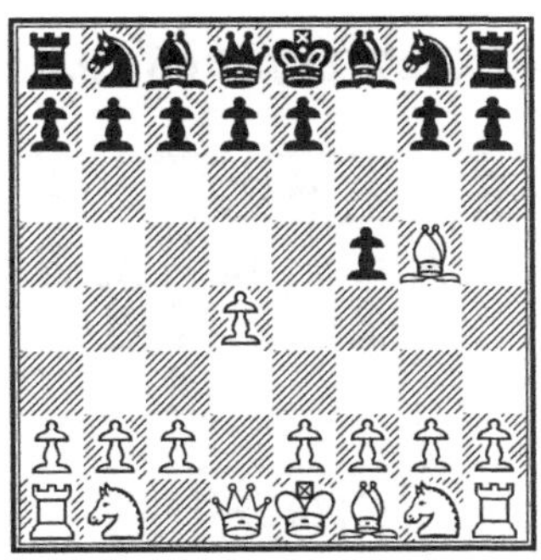

An interesting (and as far as we could determine, nameless) deployment against the Dutch, going back at least to Göring-Berger, Graz 1870. It was subsequently played by Schiffers, Mackenzie, Chigorin and Alapin in the 19th century. Some years later it was played by Bogoljubow, and is occasionally seen even today. Black should avoid the temptation of trying to trap the Bishop: 2...h6 3.♗h4 g5 4.♗g3 f4?? 5.e3! h5 6.♗e2! ♗h6 7.e×f4 g×f4 8.♗h4+–.

2...♘f6

This or 2...g6 are considered the only good replies. The attempt to avoid doubled pawns or ...g7-g6 by 2...d6 3.e3 ♘d7 △4...♘gf6 fails to 4.♗d3, attacking the f-pawn.

3.♗×f6 e×f6 4.e3 d6?

Too passive. Correct is 4...d5, as first played in Schiffers-Chigorin, 6th match game, St. Petersburg, 1878 (½-½, 52).

5.c4 ♘c6 6.♘c3 g6 7.♗d3 ♗g7

7...♗h6 appears more active, since sooner or later Black will have to play f5-f4.

8.♘ge2 ♘e7 9.♕c2 c6 10.h4

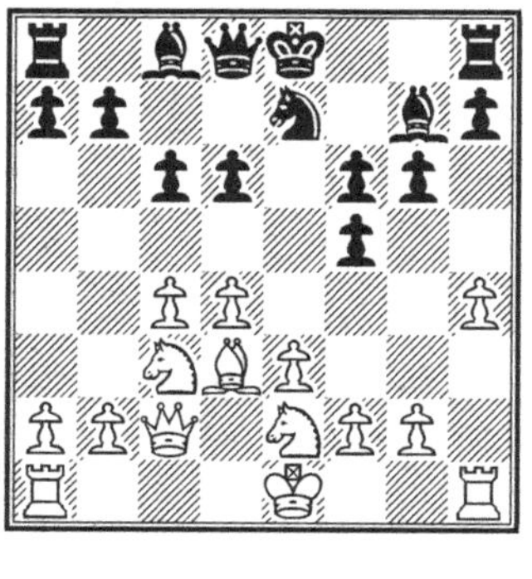

White follows a natural plan of attack, intending to castle queenside and open the h-file.

10...♗e6 11.h5 ♗f7 12.0–0–0 d5

Belatedly trying to make up for his omission at move 4. Of course not 12...g×h5? 13.♘f4! etc.

13.c5?!

This closes the position somewhat, thus making it harder for White to reap the benefits of his lead in quality development. Stronger was 13.c×d5, *viz.* 13...♘×d5 14.h×g6 h×g6 15.♖×h8+ ♗×h8 16.a3 (+2.55/24), or 13...c×d5? 14.♘f4 g5 15.h6 ♗×h6 (15...♗f8?? 16.♗b5+ ♘c6 17.♘f×d5 (+6.90/23)) 16.♘f×d5 (or 16.♖×h6 g×f4 17.♗×f5+–) 16...♗×d5 17.♖×h6+–.

13...♕d7 14.h×g6 h×g6 15.♖×h8+ ♗×h8 16.♖h1

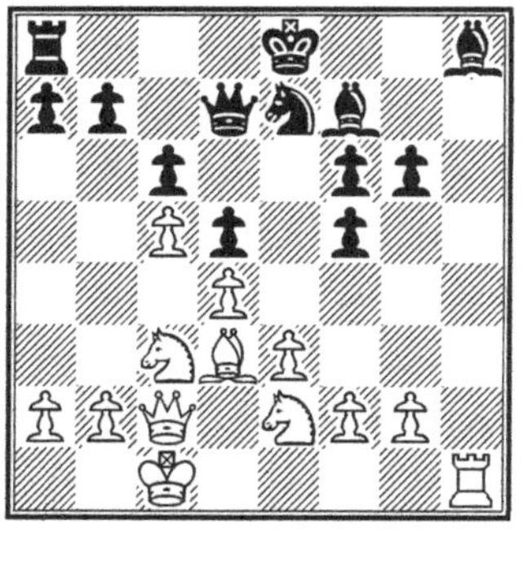

16...♗g7

In case of 16...0–0–0 17.♖h7 ♕e8 (not 17...♗e6?? 18.♘f4 ♖g8 19.♕a4 ♔b8 20.♘b5! c×b5 21.♗×b5+–) 18.b4 ♔b8 19.b5 with a winning attack (+4.42/23).

17.♖h7

Forcing the black King to remain on the kingside.

17...♔f8 18.♘f4 ♔g8 19.♖h1 ♕e8 20.f3

The central advance and break envisioned with this move is probably not best, for reasons that will become clear in a few moves. Stockfish, while not especially liking the text, seems to want just to sit on White's positional advantage, recommending mainly waiting moves leading to no clear progress. This is not unusual for engines in the sort of closed position White created with his 13th move.

20...g5 21.♘fe2

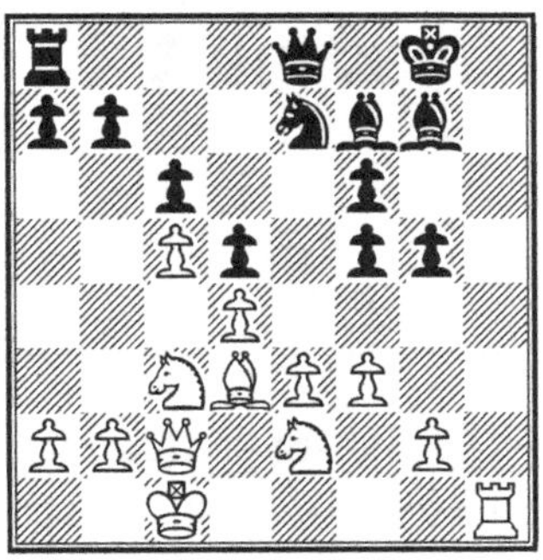

21...♗g6

Black need not have bothered to defend his f5-pawn. Best was 21...b6, when if 22.♗×f5?? ♘×f5 23.♕×f5 ♗g6 24.♕h3 ♕×e3+ and wins. White's best course after 21...b6 would have been 22.♘d1, so that if 22...b×c5?! 23.♕×c5, when White has a definite positional advantage, but Black is not in immediate danger of an attack.

22.e4?!

Consistent, but this could have lost most of White's advantage. Stockfish, oddly, recommends 22.f4, which to a human player looks horribly anti-positional, rendering as it does the e-pawn backward on an open file. However, Black is not in a position to exploit this, *viz.* 22...♘c8 23.♔d2 ♕e6? 24.g4 ♘e7 25.♖f1 ♖e8 26.f×g5 f×g5 27.g×f5 ♘×f5 28.♗×f5 ♕×e3+ 29.♔e1, and while Black has won the pawn, White has won a piece.

22...f4?

A serious mistake, in fact the losing move. There were two much better continuations:

(a) 22...d×e4 23.f×e4 f×e4 24.♘×e4 ♗×e4 25.♗×e4 f5 26.♗d3 ♖d8, and
(b) 22...f×e4 23.f×e4 ♖d8 (or 23...d×e4 as before) 24.e×d5 ♗×d3 25.♕×d3 ♘×d5 26.♘×d5 ♖×d5.

In either case, White's advantage has been much reduced, and Black has broken out of his cramped position and gotten some play for his pieces. Stockfish evaluates both lines at about +1.00 to +1.35, whereas the text boosts it up to +2.95 at 25 ply.

23.e×d5 ♗×d3 24.♕×d3 c×d5 25.♘b5!

Threatening 26.♘c7.

25...♕g6

Neither 25...♕c6, 25...♖d8, nor 25...♖b8 were any better.

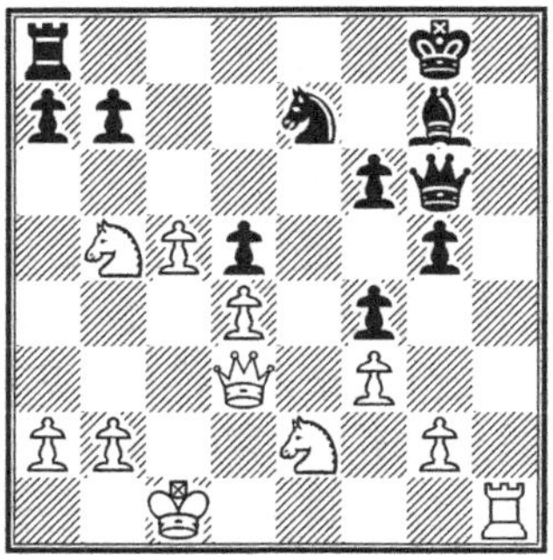

26.♕×g6

Perhaps stronger was 26.♕b3 ♖d8 27.♘d6 f5 28.♖e1 (threatening 29.♘×f4) 28...♕e6 29.♔d2, when forced is 29...♕e3+ 30.♕×e3 f×e3+ 31.♔×e3 (+3.50/24). But Torre has foreseen that after the Queens are gone he can start picking off pawns and reach a won endgame.

26...♘×g6 27.♘ec3 f5 28.♖d1!

Best. Much less good was 28.♘×d5?! ♖d8 29.♘d6 ♗×d4 and White's advantage is minimal (+0.88/26).

28...♘e7

29.♘c7

One of several winning lines. Another was 29.b4 ♘c6 30.♘×d5 ♖d8 31.♘d6 ♗×d4 32.b5 ♗×c5 33.♘×b7 ♗a3+ 34.♔b1 ♖c8 35.b×c6 (+4.11/25).

29...♖d8 30.♘e6 ♖d7?

30...♖e8 was better, so that after 31.♘×g5 ♘c6 32.♘×d5 ♘×d4 with some counterplay.

31.♘×g5 ♗f6

If now 31...♘c6 32.♘e6! ♗f6 33.♘e2 △34.♘6×f4.

32.♘e6

Also good was 32.♘h3 △33.♘×f4.

32...♔f7 33.♘×f4

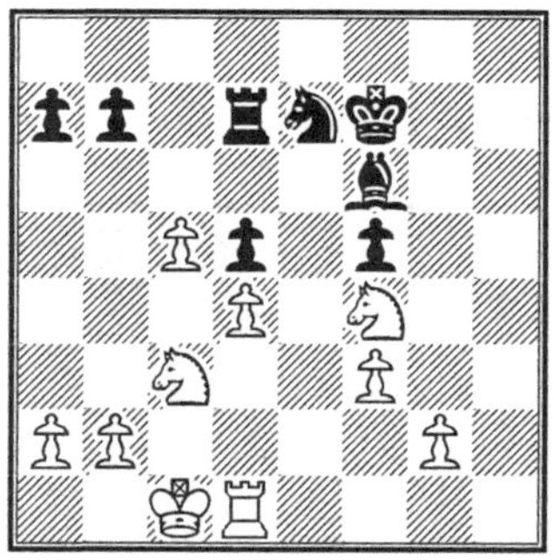

The dust has mostly settled with White up two pawns. The only question now is: how best to advance them?

33...♗g5 34.g3 ♘g6 35.♖e1

It's not clear why Torre gives up a pawn here; perhaps he just wanted to exchange a couple of minor pieces. Best was 35.♘ce2. However, White is still winning after the text.

35...♘×f4?

Superficially it would seem logical

to retain the Bishop rather than the Knight, but correct was 35...♗×f4+ 36.g×f4 ♘×f4 when Black's Knight defends his d-pawn, freeing his Rook from that burden. Stockfish rates that position at about +3.25, while after the text it's about +5.75.

36.g×f4 ♗×f4+ 37.♔c2 ♗g3 38.♖e2 ♔f6 39.♔d3 ♗f4 40.b4

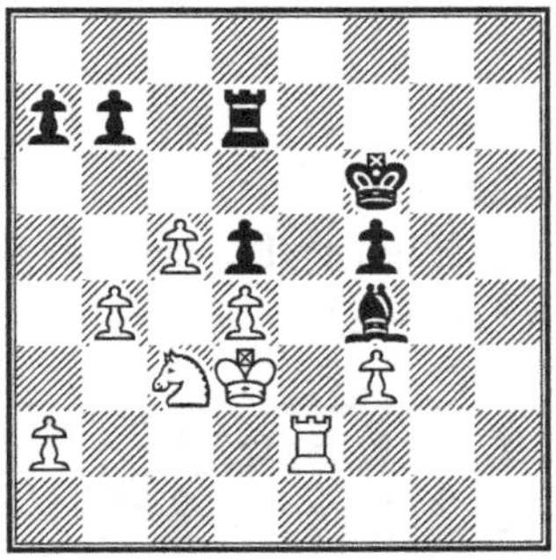

White finally mobilizes his queenside pawn majority. The ending is relatively easy to win, as in addition to the pawn plus, White has his pieces on excellent squares. Torre here, as in Game 19 (Scrivener-Torre), uses his Rook on the e-file to bar the enemy King from the wing where Torre's pawns will advance.

40...a6 41.a4 ♔f7 42.b5 a5 43.b6!
Beginners are often advised that the pawn most likely to Queen is the one to advance first. Here the c-pawn is clearly the most likely candidate for promotion, but this case is an exception to the rule. Such subtle contradictions are often baffling to beginners. Capablanca, author of several books for novices, would advise "with a majority, first advance the pawn that has no enemy pawn in front of it." However in some of his games he did the opposite (for example the last game of his 1909 match with Marshall). Every position must be examined individually. In this case the point of advancing the b-pawn is to isolate Black's a-pawn, maneuver the Rook to b5 and capture it. That White ends up not actually using this idea does not detract from its correctness.

43...♖d8
This and Black's 45th move are to enable ...♖d8-a8 in the event of the white Rook going to b5.

44.♖e1 ♔f6 45.♖b1 ♔e6 46.♖h1
Best. 46.♖b5 would be pointless now. From here the game is easily won, and little further commentary is necessary.

46...♗g5 47.♖h7 ♖b8 48.♘b5 ♗f4 49.♘c7+ ♗×c7 50.♖×c7 f4 51.♖h7 ♖g8
Desperation.

52.♖×b7 ♖g3 53.c6 ♖×f3+ 54.♔d2 ♔d6 55.c7 ♖f2+ 56.♔e1 ♖h2
If 56...♖c2 57.♖b8 ♔d7 58.♖d8+ ♔e7 59.c8♕ etc.

57.c8♕ ♖e2+ 58.♔×e2 f3+
Hoping for 59.♔×f3?, stalemate.

59.♔f1 1–0

Game 24

Spero-Torre

Western CA Championship, Detroit 1924

Two Knights Defense [C58]

Irving Hersh Spero (1892-1955) was born in Poland, but later lived in the USA, first in Ohio, where he was state chess champion and chess and checker columnist for the *Cleveland News*, and later in Los Angeles, where he was chess columnist for the *California Jewish Voice*. He had finished 6th (of 12) in the 1922 WCA Ch, and would come 5th (of 14) in 1926. Here he and Torre engage in a spirited debate about the merits of a seldom-seen opening variation.

1.e4 e5 2.♘f3 ♘c6 3.♗c4 ♘f6 4.♘g5 d5 5.e×d5 ♘a5 6.d3

An interesting move that goes back to Kieseritzky-Anderssen, match, London, 1851. It was played later by Morphy, Chigorin, and Tartakower. In the 1950s it was seen in games by Bronstein and Korchnoi. Bronstein's game with Rojahn, XII Olympiad 1956, was a veritable Morphy-style jewel. Spero had played this line before, against Showalter in the 1922 Western CA Championship (½-½, 33). More usual is 6.♗b5+.

6...h6

Taking the pawn is a mistake: 6...♘×d5? 7.♕f3 ♗e6 8.♘×e6 f×e6 9.♕h5+ g6 10.♕×e5 winning easily. Once 6...e4? was tried against Morphy, but the Louisianan found a prompt refutation: 7.♕e2 ♕e7? (△7...♘×c4 8.d×c4 ♗f5±) 8.♘×e4 ♘×e4 9.d×e4 ♕b4+ 10.♘d2 ♘×c4 11.♕×c4+−, Morphy-Maude, London, 1859.

7.♘f3 e4

Best. Also playable is 7...♘×c4, as in Rossetto-Gligoric, Buenos Aires 1960: 8.d×c4 ♗d6 9.h3 0–0 10.♘c3 c6=.

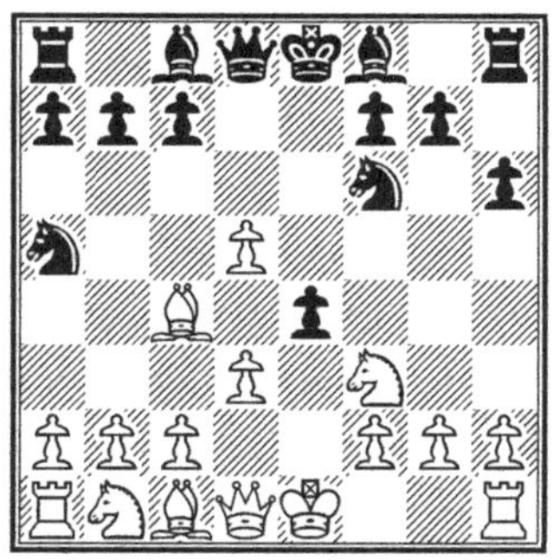

8.♕e2

In the aforementioned game Bronstein-Rojahn, the Soviet grandmaster audaciously sacrificed his Bishop with 8.d×e4 ♘×c4 9.♕d4 ♘b6 (interesting would have been 9...♘d6 10.e5? ♘f5 11.♕a4+ ♕d7−+) 10.c4. White gained two pawns and a powerful mobile center for his piece. However, such a sacrifice is usually correct only if played by a Bronstein. For those who are not geniuses, the text move is more advisable.

8...♘×c4 9.d×c4 ♗c5!

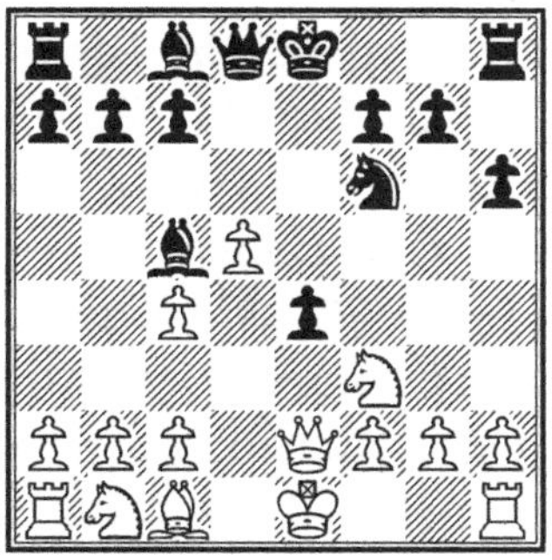

It is important to prevent 10.♘d4. The wrong way is 9...♗g4 10.h3 ♗h5 11.g4 ♗g6 12.♘h4 (Korchnoi-Suetin, Minsk 1952 continued 12.♘d4 c6 13.♘c3 ♗b4 14.♗d2 c×d5 15.0–0–0 0–0±) 12...♗h7 13.♘c3 (+1.86/24).

10.h3

Usual here is 10.♘fd2 0–0 11.♘b3 ♗g4 12.♕f1 ♗b4+ 13.c3. Tartakower-Bogoljubow, Hamburg 1927, then continued 13...♗d6 14.h3 ♗h5 15.g4 ♗g6 16.♗e3 ♘d7 (1-0, 61).

> The game **Spero-Showalter** had an amusing finish. In this position,
>
> 
>
> Black had to play 33...♖e5 with an even game. Instead, Showalter played 33...♔g8(??) and offered a draw, which Spero accepted.
> Actually White had mate in two: 34.♘×f6+ and 35.♖b8#. According to the *ACB* both players suddenly realized it two minutes later.

10...0–0 11.♘h2 e3

Torre varies from the aforementioned Spero-Showalter game (*see right*), which continued 11...b5.

The text leads to a more or less even game. 11...♘h7?! was played three times by Morphy as Black in this position, losing once against a consultation team and winning twice against de Rivière. It is curious that Morphy, so expert in central pawn breaks, never played the text.

Best probably is 11...c6, and then if 12.d×c6 e3! 13.♗×e3 ♗×e3 14.f×e3 ♘e4 with a powerful attack for Black, as in Kondratiev-Kopylov, Leningrad Championship 1955.

12.♗×e3 ♗×e3 13.f×e3 ♘e4

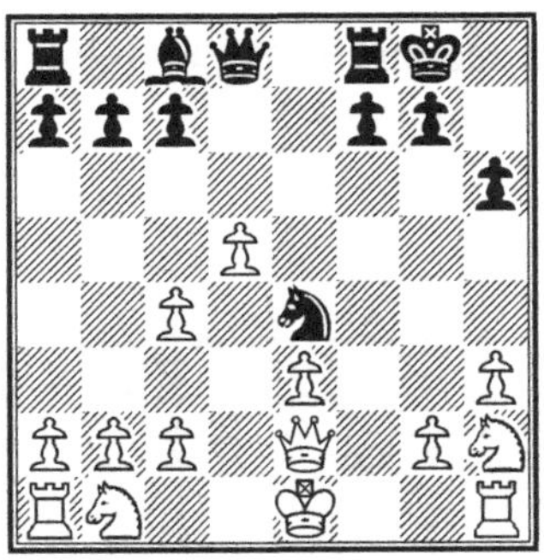

White is ahead two pawns, but his position is not enviable. Hanging in the air are threats of a Knight fork at g3 and a Queen check at h4, among other things. However, this position was not new at the time of this game. In the previous century, the aging Steinitz explored it in home analysis. Later he asked several masters their opinion of the position and almost all considered it better for Black. But Steinitz held that White had the advantage after the interesting exchange sacrifice 14.0–0!?, a very subtle move not at all easy to counter. Steinitz's suggestion has been tried several times in tournament play, starting with Matteucci-Porecca, 15th Italian Ch, Ferrara 1952 (0-1, 28), then in Rosenfeld-Heuer, 12th Estonian Ch, Tallinn 1955 (0-1, 31), and Rakic-Ivkov, Sombor 1957, which continued 14.0–0 ♘g3 15.♕d3 ♘xf1 16.♘xf1 ♕g5 17.e4, draw. Despite the move's poor record in actual play, Stockfish considers 14.0–0 objectively best, though good only for equality, and not the advantage Steinitz claimed. In 1954, the young Korchnoi encountered this position against Sliwa at Bucharest. After long reflection he decided on 14.♘f1, as does Spero in the present game.

14.♘f1?!

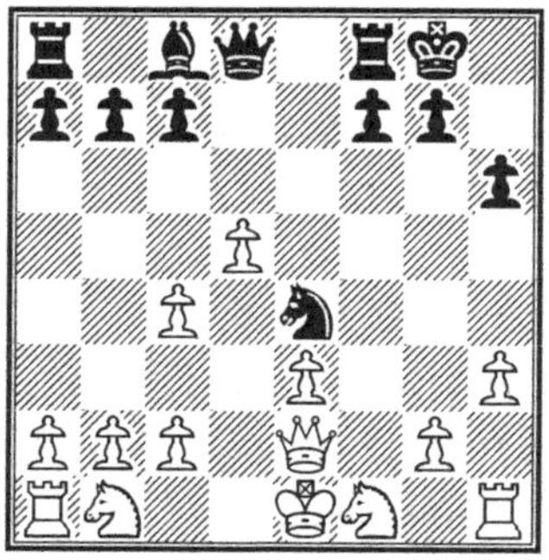

14...♕f6

After the game, the strong master Stasch Mlotkowski of Los Angeles told Torre that here 14...♕h4+ looked stronger. Indeed it seems the obvious move, and it was also the move played by the Polish master Sliwa in the aforementioned game with Korchnoi, which continued 14...♕h4+ 15.g3 ♕f6 16.c3 ♗f5 17.♕f3 ♘g5 (better perhaps is 17...♘c5 18.♘bd2 ♘d3+ 19.♔e2 ♘e5 20.♕f4 ♖ae8 21.e4 ♘xc4 22.♘e3 ♘xe3 23.♔xe3 ♖xe4+ 24.♘xe4 ♖e8 25.♖h2 ♖xe4+ 26.♕xe4 ♗xe4 27.♔xe4, reaching a ♖+♖-vs.-♕ ending favorable to Black -1.57/30) 18.♕f4 ♕g6 19.♘bd2 ♘xh3 20.♕xc7

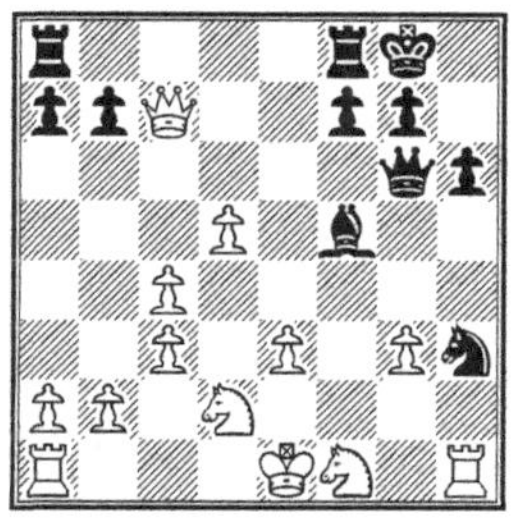

with an unclear position, though White won after 20...♗g4?! 21.♖xh3! ♗xh3 22.0–0–0.

Stockfish indicates 14...♕h4+ is stronger, and that the text leads only to equality or at most a slight advantage against best play.

15.c3 ♗f5

Best was 15...♕b6 △16...♖e8 and 17...♘g3–+.

16.♕f3

Better 16.♘bd2 ♘c5 17.♘g3=.

16...♖ae8 17.♘bd2

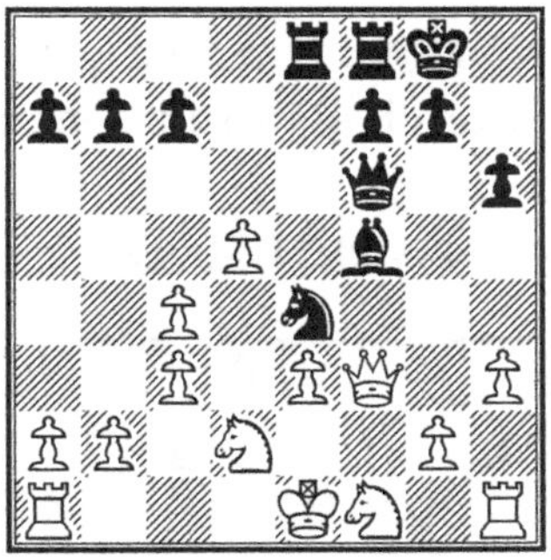

17...♕e5
17...♘c5 looked attractive, but after 18.♘g3 ♕h4 (18...♘d3+? 19.♔e2 ♗g6 20.♕×f6 g×f6 21.♘h5! ♗×h5+ 22.♔×d3 ♗g6+ 23.♔e2 +4.89/24) 19.0–0 ♗d3 20.♖f2 the danger of attack has faded and White can begin to realize his material advantage (+2.05/24).
Best was 17...♕g6∓.

18.♘×e4 ♗×e4 19.♕e2 ♗h7

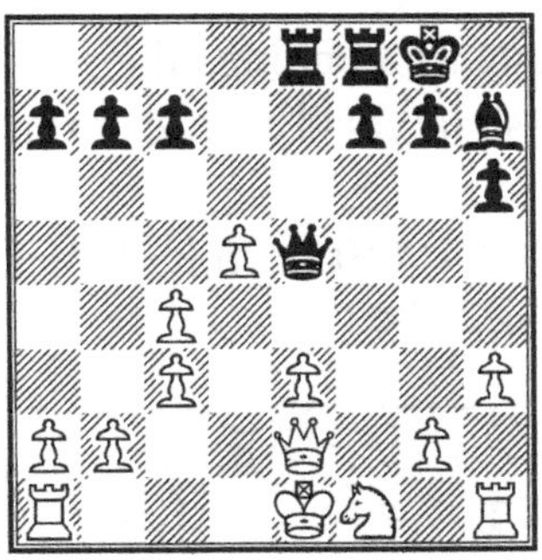

Impeding castling, since now if 20.0–0–0? ♕e4 21.b4 (21.♔d2? f5 △22...f4–+) 21...a5 22.b5 ♕b1+ 23.♔d2 ♕×a2+ 24.♔e1 ♕b3 (-2.39/25).

20.♔d2?
The first of several errors over the next few moves that change the game from about equal to lost for White. Correct was 20.♔f2! when the game is almost dead even (+0.25/25).

20...c6
One of several good moves for Black. Most direct was 20...f5 21.g3 f4 22.g×f4 ♖×f4 23.♖g1 ♕f6! 24.e×f4 ♖×e2+ 25.♔×e2 ♕b6 (△26...♕×g1) 26.♘d2 ♕×b2 27.♖af1 ♕×c3 28.♖f3 ♕d4 and the ending definitely favors Black (-2.12/24).

21.♘h2?
If White wants to give back a pawn or two to improve his precarious situation, a better way was 21.♖d1 c×d5 22.c×d5 ♕×d5+ 23.♔e1 ♕×a2 24.♔f2, finally putting the King where he should have gone at move 20, though even then Black stands better (-1.57/24).
No good is 21.♕f3? c×d5 22.c×d5 ♗e4 23.♕f2 ♕×d5+ etc.

21...c×d5 22.♘f3 ♕e4
Much stronger was 22...♕g3 23.c×d5 f5 △24...f4. It is strange that Torre never hits on the idea of advancing his f-pawn, a logical way to pressure the pinned e-pawn.

23.c×d5 ♕×d5+ 24.♘d4?
Again, 24.♔e1 △25.♔f2 was correct.

24...♖e5 25.♖hf1 ♗e4 26.♖f2 ♖fe8 27.a3

Removing the pawn from attack by Black's Queen, so that the Queen's Rook can finally be developed. But White fails to notice an important nuance.

27...b5 28.♖af1??
Too soon! Necessary first was 28.b3. The text may be considered the losing move.

28...♕a2!

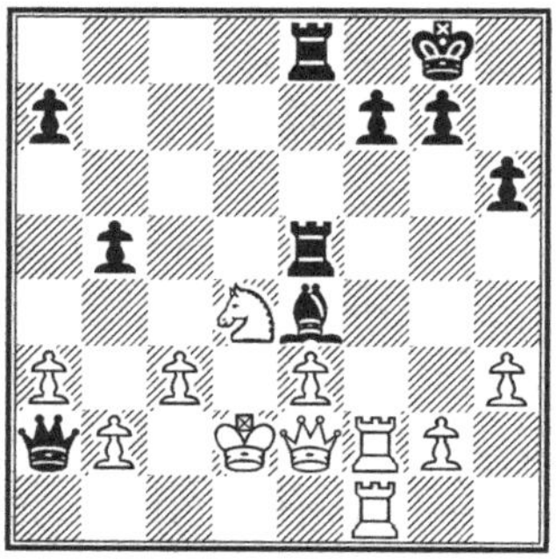

Showing that it was not just the pawn on a2 that needed defending, but the square a2 itself.

29.♔e1
If 29.♖×f7 ♕×b2+ 30.♔e1 ♕×a3 31.♘×b5 ♖×b5! 32.♕×b5 ♕×c3+ 33.♔f2 ♗c6 34.♕e2 ♔×f7 −+.

29...♗×g2!?

Flashy but unnecessary. Strong and straightforward was 29...♗d5, with threats of 30...♗c4 and 30...♖×e3. Still, the text is quite sufficient to win.

30.♖×g2 ♖×e3 31.♖×g7+

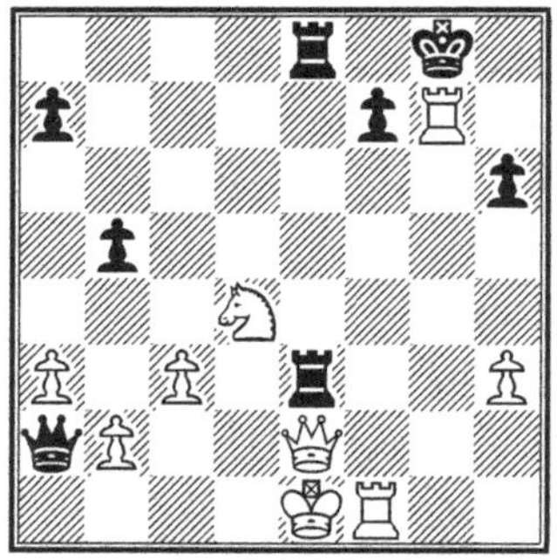

A desperate defense. If now 31...♔×g7?? 32.♘f5+.

31...♔h8
Better was 31...♔f8 when after 32.♖g×f7+ ♕×f7 33.♖×f7+ ♔×f7 34.♕×e3 ♖×e3+ 35.♔f2 ♖e5 Black has an easily won ending. The text allows White some small chance of survival.

32.♖f×f7 ♕b1+ 33.♔f2 ♖×e2+ 34.♘×e2 ♕c2

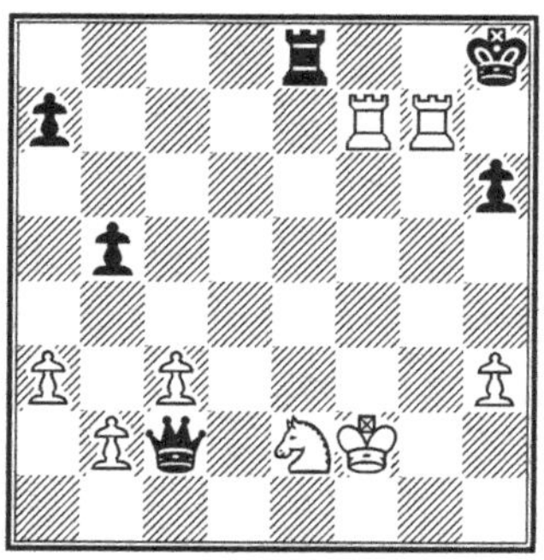

35.♖h7+?

35.♖e7! would have made the win more difficult: 35...♖×e7 36.♖×e7 ♕f5+ 37.♔e1 ♕×h3 38.♖×a7 (-1.88/28).

35...♕×h7 36.♖×h7+ ♔×h7

Reaching a very interesting ending, Black up the Exchange but down a pawn. The technique by which Carlos Torre capitalizes on his small advantage is highly instructive.

37.♘f4 ♔g7 38.♔f3 ♔f6 39.♘d5+ ♔g5 40.♘e3

If 40.♘c7 ♖e5 is strong. Or if 40.b3 ♔h4 41.♔g2 ♖g8+ 42.♔h2 ♖g3 and wins.

40...♖d8 41.c4 b×c4 42.♘×c4 ♖d3+ 43.♔e4

43.♔g2 is insufficient due to 43...♔h4 etc.

43...♖×h3 0–1

And White resigned.

A game of importance for opening theory.

Game 25

Ruth-Torre

Western CA Championship, Detroit 1924

Max Lange Attack [C56]

With William Allen Ruth (1886-1975), we have an example of the vagaries of chess opening nomenclature. The line 1.d4 ♘f6 2.♗g5, called by most of the world the Trompowsky Attack, should instead be known as the Ruth Opening, according to the 13th edition of *Modern Chess Openings* (1990), which states that the line was "consistently propagated" by Ruth "long before" Octavio Trompowsky (1897-1984) began advocating it in the 1930s. ChessBase provides only slight support for this, showing just two instances of Ruth playing it, in 1935, only a year before the first of many examples by Trompowsky. Furthermore, Levitsky, Bogoljubow, Sämisch, Dus-Chotimirsky, and Mattison all played it by 1925, and Janowski played it four times in in a single tournament, Semmering 1926. So who knows, who should get the credit? However, we digress. Here Ruth chooses a line from the Romantic Era, playing it well enough to be one of the few participants in this tournament to hold Torre to a draw.

1.e4 e5 2.♘f3 ♘c6 3.♗c4 ♘f6 4.d4 e×d4 5.0–0 ♗c5

Torre invites his opponent to enter the complicated labyrinth of the Max Lange Attack. If Black wants to avoid complications, he may play 5...♘×e4 6.♖e1 d5, arriving at a position mentioned in the notes to Game 10.

6.e5

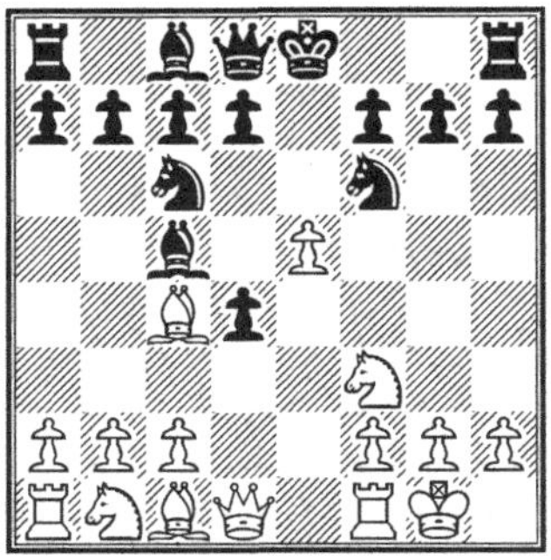

6...d5

In Morphy-Domínguez, Havana, 1864, Black played 6...♘e4??, and there followed 7.♗d5 (⌓7.♕e2 d5 8.e×d6 f5 9.♗g5 ♕×d6 10.♘bd2 ♕g6 11.♖fe1 etc. (+5.67/25)) 7...f5 8.e×f6?! (⌓8.♘bd2!) 8...♘×f6 9.♗g5?! (⌓9.♖e1+) 9...♗e7 10.♗×f6 ♗×f6 11.♖e1+ ♘e7?? (⌓11...♔f8□, +1.21/25) 12.♘e5 ♗×e5 13.♕h5+ g6 14.♕×e5 ♖f8 15.♘d2 c6 16.♘c4! d6 17.♘×d6+ ♔d7, and White announced mate in three.

7.e×f6 d×c4 8.♖e1+ ♗e6 9.♘g5

In what was probably the Max Lange Attack's debut, Lange-von Schmidt, Magdeburg, 1853, its inventor continued 9.f×g7 ♖g8 10.♘g5 ♕e7 11.♘×e6 f×e6 12.♕h5+ ♔d7 13.♗h6 ♖ae8 14.♘d2 d3 15.c3 b5 16.♘e4 ♗b6 17.♗g5 ♕×g7 18.♘f6+ ♔c8 19.♘×e8 ♕×g5 20.♕×g5 ♖×g5 21.♖×e6 ♔d7 22.♖ee1 d2 23.♖ad1, 1-0.

However, the text came to played far more often and is the main line.

9...♕d5 10.♘c3 ♕f5 11.♘ce4

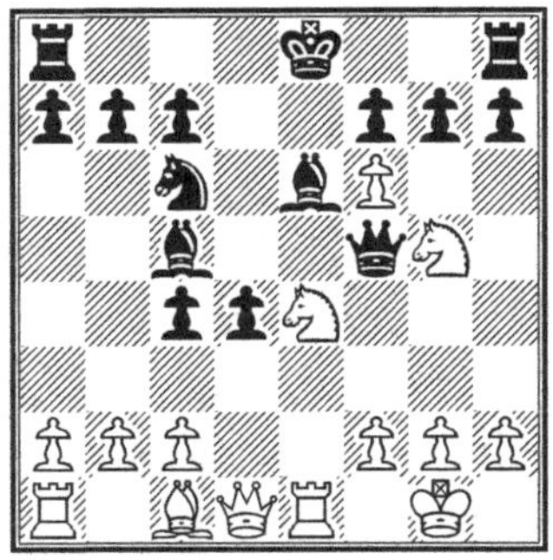

The critical position of the Max Lange Attack, which despite being played in hundreds of tournament games for over 150 years is still considered to have unresolved complications. The main line, and considered best here, is 11...0–0–0 12.g4 ♕e5 13.♘×e6 f×e6 14.f×g7, but theoretical analyses have then gone as far as move 30 only to reach a verdict of "unclear."

The antiquated alternative Torre chooses, 11...♗f8!?, is not entirely bad, and was in fact played regularly in the previous century. It has never been clearly refuted; rather it has passed out of fashion, due to its apparently counter-productive retreat of a developed piece, compared to 11...0–0–0 which does not lose a tempo and which connects Black's Rooks. The paradoxical idea of the Bishop retreat is to complicate the game even further, by inviting the sacrifice 12.♘×f7!?. This produces such a profusion of tactical possibilities that they usually can be handled in OTB play by those with analytical abilities are far above the norm (*e.g.* Kasparov). It bears mentioning that while this paragraph was being written,

Stockfish analyzed the diagram position out to 34 ply. It concluded that 11...0–0–0 was best, at +0.27, with 11...♗f8 next at +0.74.

11...♗f8

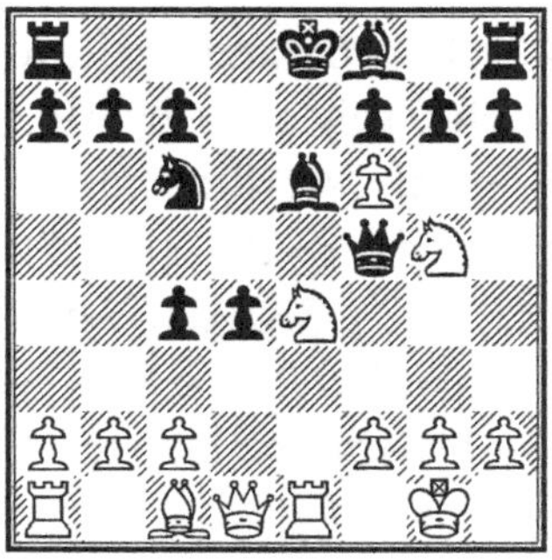

12.♘×e6

Preferring not to disturb the lion. After 12.♘×f7 ♔×f7 13.♘g5+,

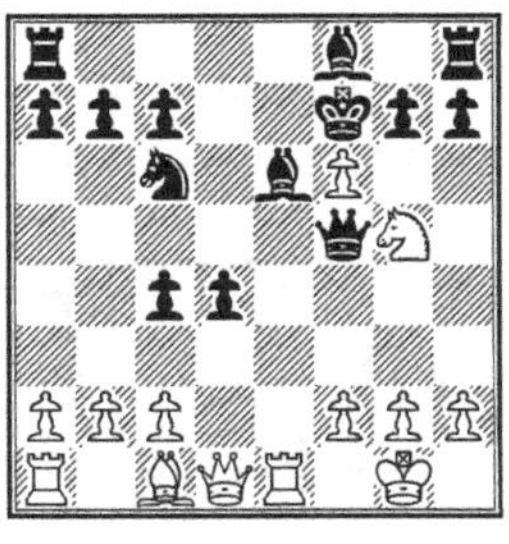

the theory of the time recommended 13...♔g8 14.g4 ♕g6 (14...♕×g4+?? 15.♕×g4 ♗×g4 16.f7#) 15.♖×e6 [If 15.f×g7 Rubinstein suggested 15...♗d5!□ 16.g×h8♕+ ♔×h8 17.♘h3, when 17...♗d6 (or 17...♗h6) leads to equality after 18.♘f4 ♗×f4 (if 18...♕h6 19.♘h5±) 19.♗×f4 ♖f8 20.♗g3=.] 15...g×f6 16.♕f3 ♔g7 (suggested by Tartakower), with an unclear position, though the Soviet theoretician Estrin believed that White would stand better after 17.♗f4. Stockfish disagrees, deeming that position even, and recommending 17.h4! with a big advantage for White (+1.99/28). And going back one move, Stockfish prefers 16...♗e7±.

In the first edition, Velasco wrote that "More recently, theoreticians have analyzed the problematic continuation 13...♔g6, which leads to an extremely sharp game after 14.f×g7 ♗×g7 15.♖×e6+ ♗f6 16.g4 ♕d5 17.♘h3 ♔f7 18.♘f4 ♕c5 19.♕f3 ♖hf8 20.♕e4 ♔g8 21.♘h5 ♗e5 22.♗h6 d3!, and again we have a verdict of 'unclear.'" Stockfish validates every move of that line as best play all the way, but disagrees on the final verdict, saying that after 23.♗e3! ♕b5 24.c×d3 c×d3 25.f4! ♗g7 26.♖d1! ♕×b2 27.♖×d3 Black is busted (+4.59/27).

12...f×e6

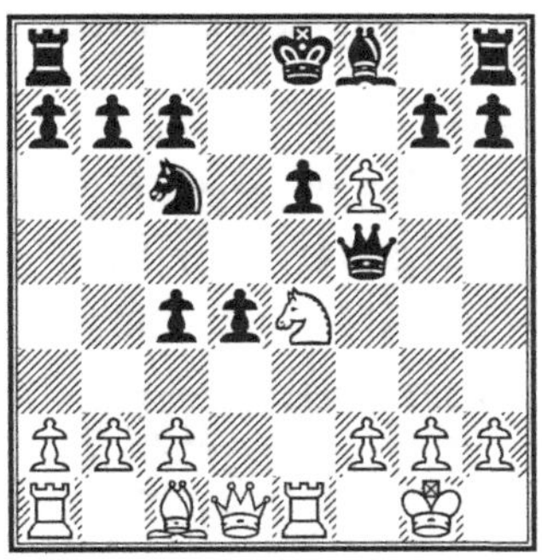

13.f7+

Better perhaps was 13.♗g5, when if 13...h6 14.♗h4 g5 15.♕h5+ ♔d7 16.♗g3±, or 13...0–0–0 14.f×g7 ♗×g7 15.♗×d8 ♖×d8=, Black's big center compensating for the loss of the Exchange. The text allows Black some advantage.

13...♔×f7 14.g4?

A mistake that could have lost the game. 14.♕e2 was necessary.

14...♕d5! 15.♘g5+ ♔g8

Preferable was 15...♔e8, and after either 16.♖×e6+ or 16.♘×e6, then 16...♔d7 followed by ...♗f8-d6 and development of the Rooks, with a big edge for Black.

16.♘×e6

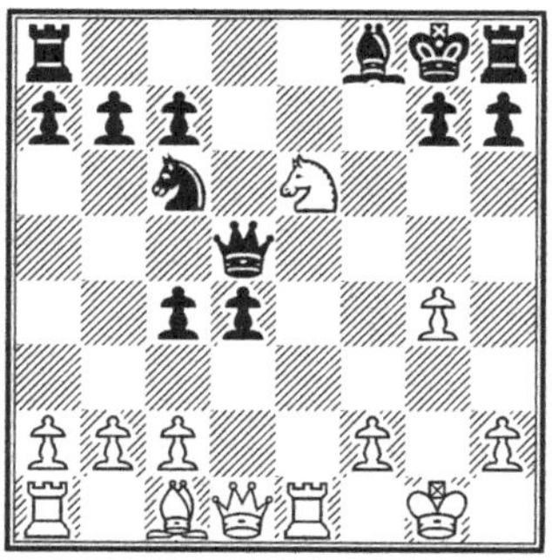

16...♗d6?!

Apparently fearing the Knight fork at c7, Torre misses a big chance. Winning was 16...♘e5! 17.♘×c7 ♘f3+!,

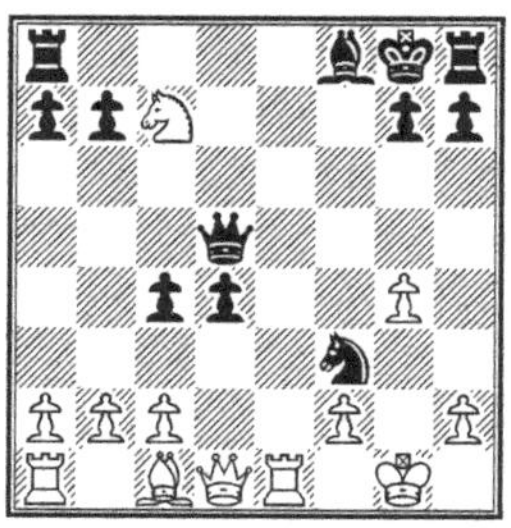

and either

(a) 18.♔f1 ♘×h2+ 19.♔g1 ♘f3+ 20.♔f1 ♕f7 21.♘×a8 h5! 22.g5 ♕f5, when to avoid catastrophe starting with 23...♕h3+, White must submit to 23.♖e3 d×e3 24.♗×e3 ♘h2+ 25.♔g2 ♘g4, and Black is clearly winning (-5.87/24); or

(b) 18.♔h1 ♕c6!, and again to avoid catastrophe, this time by 19...♘h4+, White must sacrifice by 19.♖e6 ♗d6 20.♖×d6 ♕×d6 21.♕×f3 ♕×c7 22.♕d5+ ♕f7 23.♕×d4, when Black will soon get his Rooks into play and reap the benefits of his material advantage (-1.89/26).

17.♗f4!

The only non-losing move. Having been let off the hook, Ruth, champion of the state of Pennsylvania, now shows no fear of his opponent and plays very well for the next several moves.

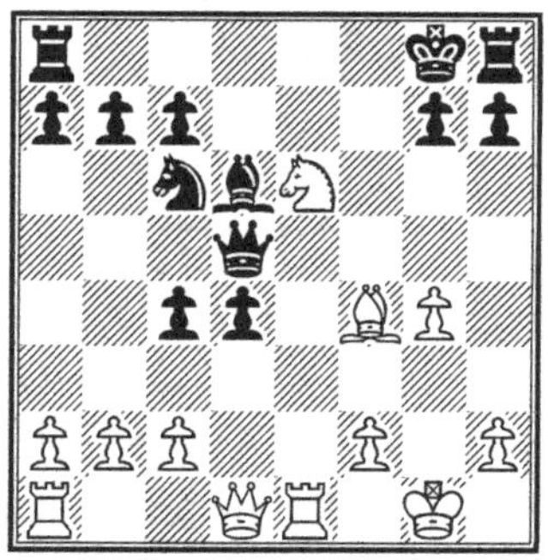

17...♘e5?!

With this the last of Black's advantage disappears. Best was 17...♗e5 18.♗×e5 (if 18.♘×c7? ♗×c7 19.♗×c7 ♔f7∓) 18...♘×e5, when things develop along the lines of variation (a) in the previous note: 19.♘×c7 ♘f3+

20.♔f1□ ♘×h2+ 21.♔g1 ♘f3+ 22.♔f1 ♕c6 23.♘×a8 ♘h2+ 24.♔g1 h5 25.g5□ ♘f3+ 26.♔f1 ♘×e1 27.♔×e1 ♔f7 28.♕×d4 ♖×a8, when though material is even, Black has a slight edge due to his passed h-pawn (-1.01/24).

18.♗×e5!□
If 18.♘×d4? ♕×d4! 19.♕×d4 ♘f3++–. And if 18.♘g5?! h6! 19.♗×e5 ♗×e5 20.♘e4 h5 21.g5 ♕f7 (-2.27/27).

18...♗×e5 19.f4! ♗d6 20.♘×d4 ♖d8

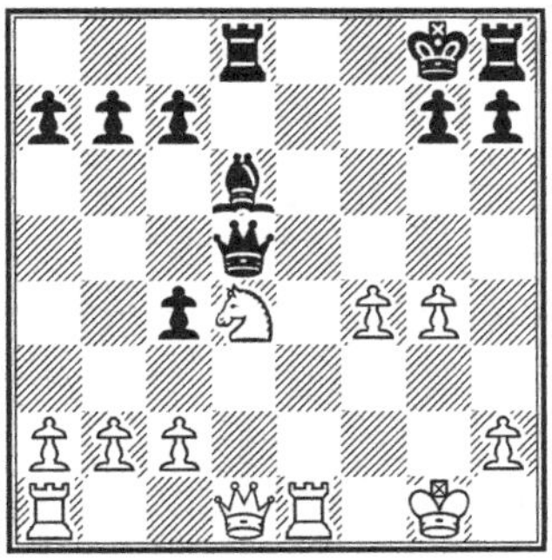

21.c3?
Correct was 21.♘f3, with the game staying even after either 21...♕c6 22.♕e2 or 21...♕×d1 22.♖a×d1. The text gives the initiative back to Black.

21...h5!
While 21...♗×f4 looks natural and obvious, it leads to no advantage (0.00/29 after either 22.h4 or 22.♕e2). The text enables Black to open the h-file and activate his King's Rook, since if now 22.g5? ♗×f4 *is* strong.

22.♕e2 h×g4 23.♕×g4 ♖h6
Preventing an exchange of Queens by 24.♕e6+.

24.♖e3 ♕f7 25.♖g3 ♖f6
Also good was 25...♗×f4 26.♘f5 ♖f6 27.♕×f4 ♖×f5 28.♕g4 ♖f8.

26.♔h1 ♗×f4 27.♖f3 ♖f8 28.♖af1 ♕d5 29.♕g2□
It was crucial to unpin the ♖f3, since Black threatened 29...c5 30.♘e2 ♗×h2 31.♔g2 (or 31.♔×h2 ♖×f3 etc.) 31...♗b8 (-7.35). If now 29...c5 30.♘e2 ♗×h2?? 31.♖×f6+–.

29...♕h5

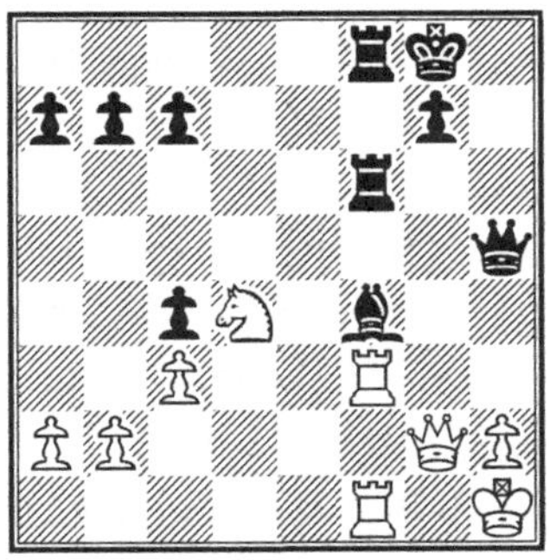

30.♖g1
If 30.♖h3, most definitely not, as we wrote in the first edition, 30...♗e3??. It works great against 31.♖×h5?? ♖×f1+ 32.♕×f1 ♖×f1+ 33.♔g2 ♖f2+ 34.♔g3 ♖×b2–+, but fails badly to 31.♖g1! ♗×g1 32.♖×h5 ♗×d4 33.♕d5+ ♖6f7 34.♕×d4+–.
Rather 30...♕e5! 31.♖g1 ♖8f7 32.♖h4 ♖e7 33.♖g4 ♗h6 34.♘f3 ♕e2 35.♕×e2 ♖×e2 36.♖4g2 ♖×g2 37.♔×g2, and Black has reached the optimal sort of ending for him, one of Rook and

Bishop against Rook and Knight. The Rook and Bishop, both being long-distance pieces, work well together. In contrast, the Rook and Knight do not cooperate very dynamically.

30...♕h7?!

Torre must have been having an off day, or he would have played 30...♖g6! 31.♕e2 (31.♕×g6?? ♕×h2#) 31...♖h6 32.♕×c4+ (if 32.♖g2 ♕d5 △33...c5−+) 32...♖f7 33.♖g2 ♗×h2 34.♖g5 ♕×g5 35.♕×f7+ ♔h7 36.♕f5+ ♕g6 37.♕×g6+ ♔×g6, and Black should win (-2.76/27). But after the text the game becomes irrevocably even.

31.♖h3 ♖h6 32.♖×h6 ♕×h6 33.♘e6 ♖f7 34.♘×f4 ½-½

Here White offered a draw, which Torre accepted. A game of some importance for the theory of the Max Lange Attack.

Game 26

Factor-Torre

Western CA Championship, Detroit 1924

Dutch Defense (Staunton Gambit) [A83]

Polish-born Samuel D. Factor (1892-1949) was yet another east European émigré who became one of America's best players. He scored quite well in this event, +10 -3 =3, to tie for = 2nd-4th with Hahlbohm and Whitaker. He was a frequent contestant in major open tournaments, and participated in one U.S. Invitational Championship, the first in 1936, where he finished 10th (out of 16), but only ½-point behind Al Horowitz and ahead of Arnold Denker and Herman Steiner, future GM and IM respectively. In his long career he notched victories over Reshevsky and Edward Lasker (twice each), Horowitz, Kupchik, and H. Steiner. Edo Chess Ratings pegs him at about 2450 at the time of this game (edochess.ca/players/p7185.html). He tries to bowl Torre over here, but instead becomes the pin instead of the ball.

1.d4 f5 2.e4

A gambit that debuted in Staunton-Horwitz, match, London, 1846, and was promulgated by Staunton in his *Chess Player's Chronicle*. It was later employed by such worthies as Anderssen, Blackburne, Pillsbury, Gunsberg, Lasker, Capablanca, Marshall, Tarrasch, Réti, Rubinstein and Euwe. The veteran Factor was probably hoping to find young Torre unprepared for it, but the reverse turns out to be true.

2...f×e4 3.♘c3 ♘f6 4.♗g5 c6 5.♗×f6

White decides to recover his pawn at once, which is somewhat contrary to the spirit of the opening. More often 5.f3 has been played here, making it a true gambit.

5...e×f6 6.♘×e4 ♕b6

Seen first in Goldsmith-Fisher, match, Melbourne, Australia, 1875 (0-1, 30), and later in Kürschner-Tarrasch, match, Nuremberg, 1887 (0-1, 20), and Marshall-Chigorin, Ostend 1905 (1-0, 30). 6...d5 has been by far most frequent, and our game quickly transposes back to that.

7.♖b1

As in Marshall-Chigorin. Kürschner played 7.b3. Stockfish indicates White's best course is to disregard the threat to the pawn and continue developing by 7.♘f3 or 7.♗d3, with an even game.

7...d5 8.♘g3 ♗d6 9.♗d3 0–0

Reaching a position seen only once before, in the aforementioned Goldsmith-Fisher. It seems unlikely either Factor or Torre knew such an obscure game, yet they follow it through move 11.

10.♕h5

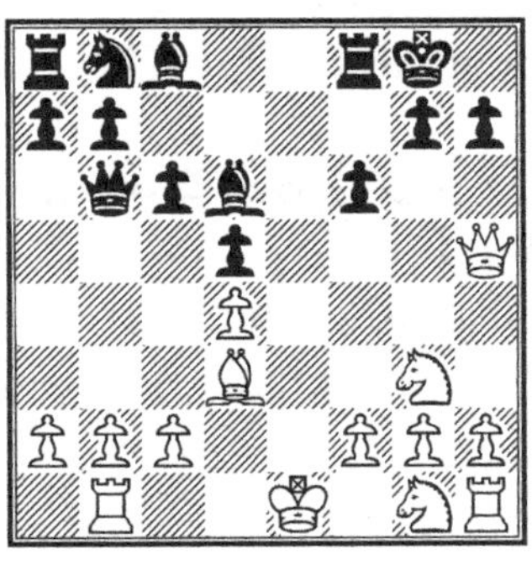

10...f5!

Best. If 10...g6? 11.♗×g6! h×g6 12.♕×g6+ ♔h8 13.♕h6+ ♔g8 14.♘h5 ♕c7□ 15.♘×f6+

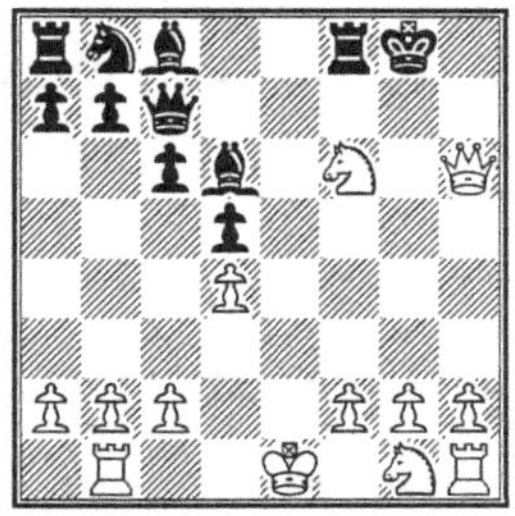

15...♖×f6 [or 15...♔f7 16.♘h7 ♗f5 (not 16...♖g8? 17.♘f3! ♗f4 18.♘fg5+ ♗×g5 19.♘×g5+ ♔e8 20.0–0 ♕g7 21.♖be1+ ♔d7 22.♕×g7+ ♖×g7 23.h4 +4.93/26) 17.♕f6+ ♔e8 18.♘×f8 ♕e7+□ 19.♕×e7+ ♔×e7 (+0.82/28)] 16.♕×f6 ♕e7+ More or less forced, as otherwise the King will be in too much danger. 17.♕×e7 ♗×e7 18.♘f3, and with an ending of ♖+3♙-vs-♗+♗ in prospect, White's chances are good (+0.87/26).

11.♘×f5?

Already the losing move! Best was 11.♘f3, when after either 11...g6 or 11...♘d7, White incurs only a slight disadvantage (-0.46/27). Now at this critical juncture, Torre plays perfect defense, finding the only good line over the next five moves.

11...g6!

Excellent. If instead 11...♗×f5? 12.♗×f5 h6 13.♘f3 ♕d8 14.0–0, White is safely a pawn ahead, with good attacking chances as well.

12.♘e7+

Goldsmith-Fisher continued 12.♘h6+?? ♔g7 13.♕g5 ♕×d4 (-6.07/25). If Factor knew of that game, this may have been his prepared improvement. Though not nearly as bad as 12.♘h6+, Torre shows that Black is still winning after the text.

12...♗×e7 13.♗×g6

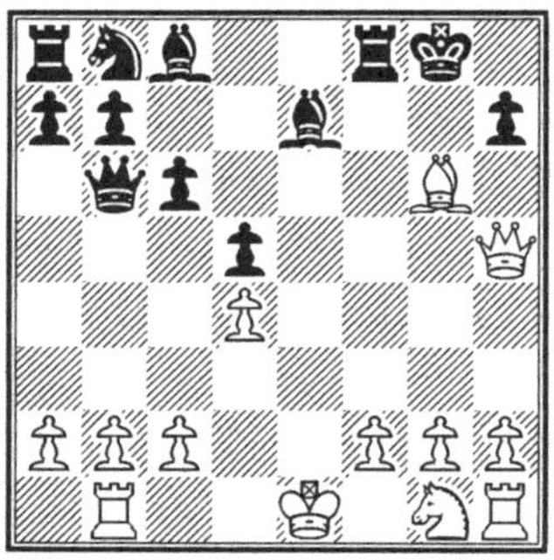

13...♗b4+!□

Again, the only correct defense. 13...h×g6? 14.♕×g6+ ♔h8 15.♕h6+ ♔g8 16.♕g6+ etc. is a draw. The point of the text is to clear the second rank so that Black's Queen can defend against the mate threat.

14.c3 ♕c7!□

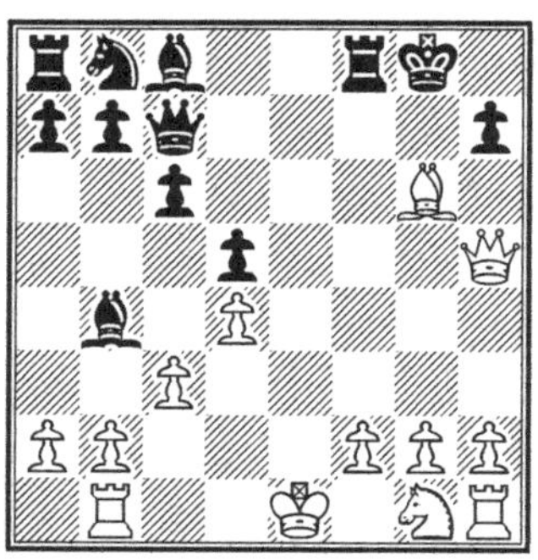

15.♗d3?

Making it easier for Black. Relatively best was 15.c×b4 h×g6 16.♕×g6+ ♕g7

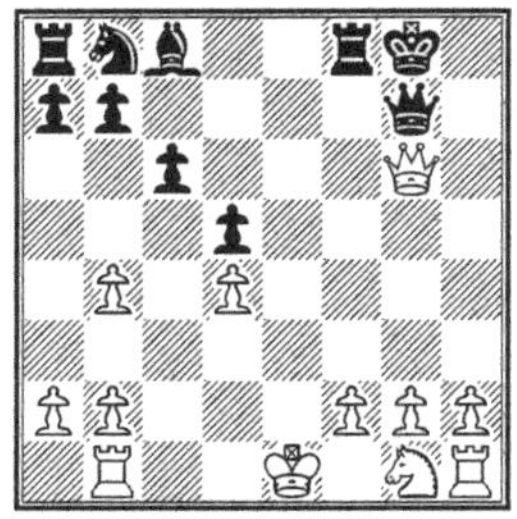

when, with a bit of luck, White's kingside pawns might prove adequate compensation for the sacrificed Bishop. Less good was 15.♗×h7+ ♕×h7 16.♕×h7+ ♔×h7 17.c×b4 (-3.09/26).

15...♗d6! 16.♘e2 ♕f7 17.♕h6 ♗f5

17...♕×f2+ 18.♔d1 ♗f5 was best, but the text is still quite good enough to win.

18.♗×f5 ♕×f5 19.0–0

If 19.♕×d6? ♕×b1+.

19...♗f4 20.♘×f4 ♕×f4 21.♕h3 ♕f5 22.♕h4 ♘d7 23.♕g3+ ♔h8 24.♕c7 ♖g8 25.f3

If instead 25.♕×b7?? ♖×g2+!! and mate in three at most.

25...♖ae8 26.♖be1 ♖×e1 27.♖×e1 ♕×f3 0–1

A dominating win for Torre over a solid, experienced master at his peak.

Game 27
Erdeky-Torre

We discuss now a fragment from **Detroit 1924**. The game was presented in its entirety in the first edition, with, unfortunately, several analytical errors. We correct those here. Erdeky-Torre reached this position after **15.g2-g3?**:

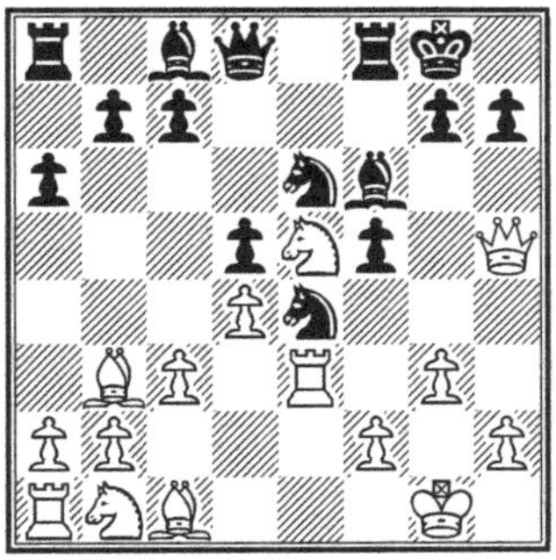

This was perhaps intended to prevent ...♘e6-f4, but was a serious mistake. Torre could have capitalized with 15...c5!, winning at least a pawn, since White can neither play 16.d×c5 nor further defend the now twice-attacked d-pawn (16.♖d3?? c4−+). There might ensue 16.♖e1 c×d4 17.♘d3,

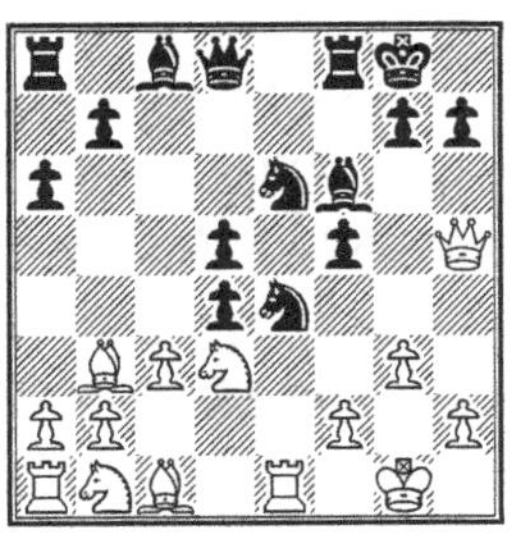

and now not 17...d×c3 18.♘×c3 ♘×c3 19.b×c3 ♗×c3 20.♗a3 ♖f6 21.♖ad1 ♗×e1 22.♘×e1 ♘c7 23.♗×d5+! ♘×d5 24.♖×d5! ♗d7 (24...♕×d5?? 25.♕e8+ ♖f8 26.♕×f8#) 25.♕d1 ♖f7 26.♘f3 △27.♘e5, when White has considerable counterplay, but 17...♔h8! 18.c×d4 ♗×d4 when besides being up a pawn, Black has a strong attack (-3.67/26).

Actual play (from previous diagram), continued

15...♗g5?! 16.f4 ♗×f4?

Given an exclam in the first edition, this is actually unsound.

Better the retreat 16...♗f6 when Black still retains some advantage. White cannot reply 17.♕×f5?? because of 17...♘×d4−+ or 17...♘6g5−+.

17.g×f4 ♘×f4 18.♕f3!□

Relatively best now for Black is 18...♕h4 19.♕f1! ♗e6 20.♖f3 ♘g6 21.♘×g6 h×g6 when he does not have enough for the piece, but may still draw (+0.88/25).

18...♕g5+?

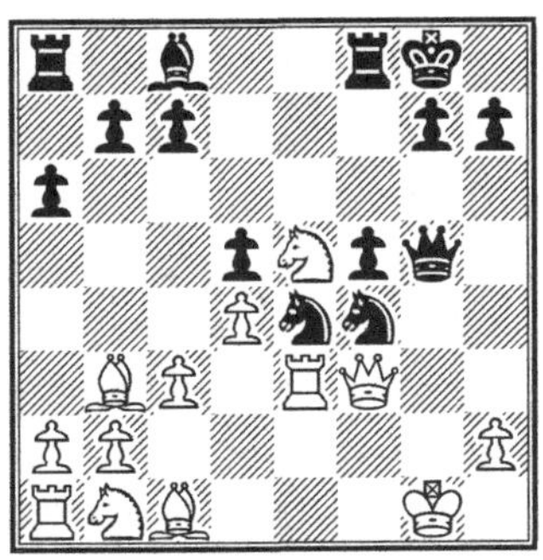

19.♔h1??

It's commonly said that given a choice of moving either of two Rooks to a certain square, one will invariably choose the wrong Rook. The same might be said about a choice of moving one's King to h1 or f1.

Here 19.♔f1! would have preserved the win, *viz.* 19...♕h4 20.♖e1! — Not, as we said in the first edition, 20.♘d2? ♖f6? (20...♗e6!∓) 21.♘×e4 f×e4 which neither forces mate nor wins the Queen after 22.♖×e4 ♗h3+ 23.♔g1=. — 20...♘e6 21.♗×d5+−.

19...♘h3!

Finally the real Torre shows up. Not only the single winning move, but the only move that does not lose!

20.♗×d5+ ♔h8 0-1

White resigns, as Black threatens mate two ways and they cannot both be stopped except at great material cost. A game exemplifying the adage "good players are lucky."

Game 28

Torre-Kupchik

2nd match game, New York, 1925

Old Indian Defense [A55]

Though Reuben Fine called Rudolf Spielmann "the meekest and most retiring of men," that distinction may rightly have belonged to Abraham Kupchik of New York City. Born in Brest-Litovsk, Russian Poland, Kupchik (1892-1970) stood barely five feet tall and weighed less than 115 pounds, and the assertiveness of his personality was in proportion to his size. Arnold Denker called him a "timid, tiny whisper of a man" and a "frightened little rabbit." Nonetheless this diminutive introvert was one of the best players in America at the time (historical Elo 2480), especially at speed chess; he once won a 10-seconds-per-move tournament ahead of Capablanca. In keeping with his personality, his style was thoroughly defensive and non-aggressive: he would erect a staunch bulwark and invite his opponent to dash himself to bits against it (which many did: among the scalps he took were those of Janowski, Bogoljubow, Maróczy, Marshall, Kashdan, Denker, Fine, and Bisguier). Here Torre manages to stir up enough complications that Kupchik could not cope.

1.♘f3 ♘f6 2.d4 c6 3.c4 d6

Black declines to enter the Slav Defense by 3...d5. The "Old" Indian was not so old at this time, its first appearance in master play being Schlechter-Tarrasch, Monte Carlo 1903 (1-0, 26).

After that initial failure it was played successfully by Chigorin, Nimzovich, Mieses, Tartakower, Burn, and Capablanca. Kupchik may have been influenced to adopt it by the game S. Rubinstein-Capablanca, New York 1913.

4.♘c3 ♘bd7 5.e4 e5 6.♗e2 ♗e7

The distinctive difference between the Old Indian and King's Indian is the development of the Bishop to e7. Black still might have transposed to one of the more common lines of the King's Indian by 6...g6 7.0–0 ♗g7 etc.

7.0–0 0–0 8.h3 ♕c7 9.♗e3 ♖e8 10.♕c2 ♘f8

Another difference between the King's Indian and Old Indian is that Black does not intend a rapid attack on the kingside; rather he seeks to develop his pieces quietly and wait for an opportune moment to attack White's center. This was very much in keeping with Kupchik's style.

11.♖ad1 ♘g6 12.♖d2 ♗d7 13.♖fd1 ♖ad8 14.a3 h6 15.b4

It might have been advisable for Black to play ...a7-a5 somewhere in the last few moves, to inhibit this advance. White has been able to come out of the opening with an advantage in space on the queenside. His plan now consists of trying to open a queenside file in order to apply pressure with his Rooks.

15...♗f8 16.♕b1! b6

This move makes it harder for White to breach the queenside. At the same time, it prepares to strike at the center with ...c6-c5, which here would have been premature due to 17.b×c5 d×c5 18.d5±.

17.a4 ♗c8 18.♖a2

Preferable was 18.d5 c5 and only then 19.♖a2, when White can prepare a queenside breakthrough without worry over central counterplay.

18...e×d4

Liquidating the central tension before striking out with ...c6-c5.

19.♘×d4 c5?!

Perhaps eventually necessary at some point if Black is to have any counterplay, but it may have been better to defer this and play 19...♗b7. The downside of the text is that it makes holes at b5 and d5, and leaves the d-pawn backward on an open file.

20.♘db5 ♕b8

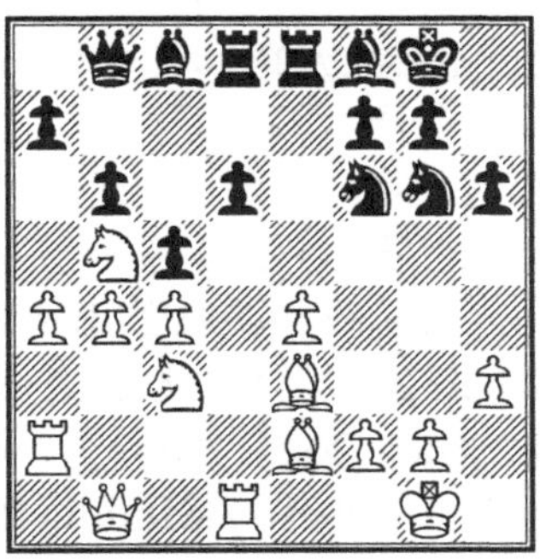

21.♖ad2?!

Torre considered this is the only move

that allows White to regroup his pieces and continue to fight in the center. Furthermore, it seems only natural to increase the pressure on the d-pawn. However, it turns out this allows Black a path back to equality.

Strongest was 21.♘d5! from which stem a number of interesting variations, all favorable to White:

(a) 21...♘×d5 22.c×d5 ♕b7 23.b×c5, and if

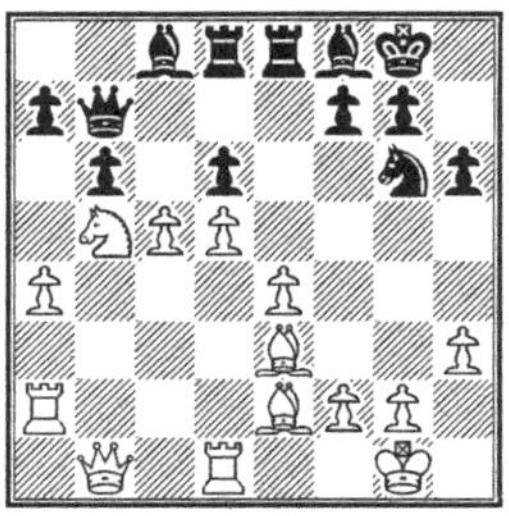

(a1) 23...d×c5 24.f4 ♕e7 25.e5 and the threat of 26.d6 and 27.♘c7 virtually forces 25...♘×e5 26.f×e5 ♕×e5 27.♗f2 (+1.65/24), or

(a2) 23...b×c5 24.a5 a6 25.♘c3 ♕e7 (not 25...♕×b1? 26.♖×b1 ♖d7 27.♖b6 ♖a7 28.f3 with dominant long-term queenside pressure (+2.85/28)) 26.f4 f5 27.♗h5 ♕f6 28.♖a3 (+1.14/29);

(b) 21...♘×e4?! 22.♗d3 f5 23.♗×e4 ♖×e4 (if 23...f×e4? 24.♘bc7 ♖e5 25.f4 ♖f5 26.♕×e4 +3.86/28) 24.b×c5 b×c5 (24...d×c5?? 25.♘f6+ g×f6 26.♖×d8+−) 25.♖b2 ♕a8 26.f3 ♖e5 27.f4 ♖e4 28.♘bc3 ♖e6 29.♘c7 winning the Exchange.

21...c×b4

A good alternative was 21...a6, when likely is either

(a) 22.♘a3 ♗b7 23.b×c5 ♘×e4! 24.♘×e4 ♗×e4 25.♕×b6 d×c5 26.♕×b8 ♖×b8∓, or

(b) 22.b×c5!? a×b5 and either

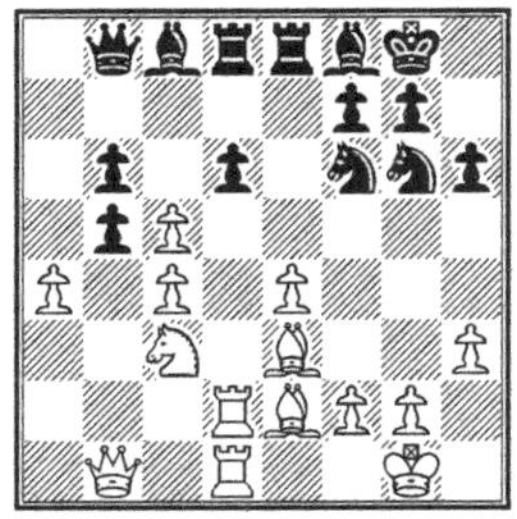

(b1) 23.♕×b5 ♘×e4 24.♘×e4 ♖×e4 25.♕×b6 ♗d7 26.♕×b8 ♖×b8=, or

(b2) 23.c6 b4 24.♘d5 ♕a8□ 25.♗×b6 ♘×e4 26.♗×d8 ♘×d2 27.♖×d2 ♕×c6 (27...♖×d8?! 28.c7 ♖e8 29.♕×b4 ♗b7 30.a5 ♘e7□ 31.♕b5 +0.98/26) 28.♗a5 ♕×a4 29.♕×b4 ♕×b4 30.♗×b4 ♗e6=.

22.♕×b4

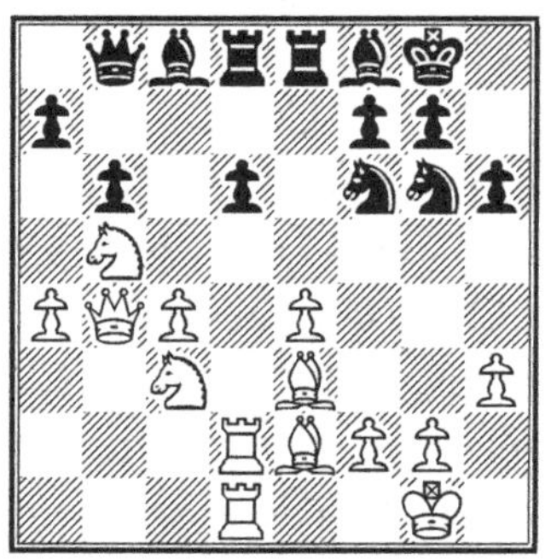

22...♘×e4

Best. If 22...d5?! 23.♕b1 ♕e5 (not 23...♘×e4? 24.♘×e4 ♖×e4 25.♕×e4! d×e4 26.♖×d8 ♔h7 27.♗g4 and with two Rooks and a Bishop for the Queen,

White is clearly winning (+5.74)) 24.c×d5 ♗c5 25.♕d3 ♘×e4 26.♘×e4 ♕×e4 27.♕×e4 ♖×e4 28.♗×c5 b×c5 29.♘×a7 ♖×a4 30.♘c6 ♖d6 31.♖c2 when White wins the c-pawn and has the better endgame prospects (+0.89/25).

23.♘×e4 ♖×e4 24.♘×d6

Torre comments "This move has the appearance of being risky, but it was played with the intention of exchanging the Queen for the two Rooks."

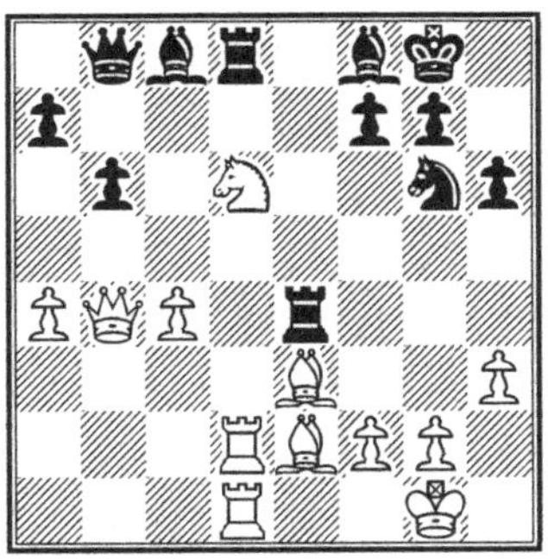

24...♖×d6?

This reflex recapture is natural and wrong. The Knight is pinned, so recapture can be delayed, best by 24...♔h7 25.♗f3 ♖×e3 [Necessary; if the Rook retreats anywhere along the e-file, then 26.c5!+−, while if 25...♖h4 26.g3 ♘e5 (26...♖×h3? 27.c5!) 27.♕b1+ g6 28.♗e2 (28.g×h4?? ♘×f3+) 28...♖×d6 (28...♖×h3?? 29.♘×c8 ♖×c8 30.♔g2 wins the Rook) 29.♖×d6 ♗×d6 30.g×h4 and White has won the Exchange.] 26.f×e3 a5□ 27.♕a3□ ♘e5□ 28.♗e2 ♗a6 29.♔f2 ♘×c4 30.♗×c4 ♗×c4 31.♖d4 ♗a6 and the game is virtually even (+0.51/28).

25.♖×d6 ♗×d6

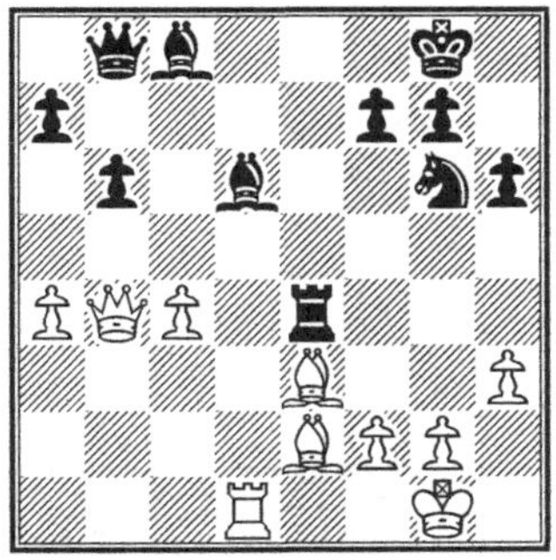

26.♖×d6

Another wrong recapture! Much stronger was 26.♕×d6! ♕×d6 (26...♕b7/♕a8?? 27.♗f3+−) 27.♖×d6 (threatening 28.♖d8+) 27...♔f8 28.c5! ♔e7□ (not 28...b×c5?? 29.♖d8+ ♘e8 30.♗×c5+ ♘e7 31.♖d2 ♗e6 32.♗×a7+−) 29.♖c6 ♔d7 30.♗b5 a6 31.♖×g6+ a×b5 32.♖×g7 b×a4 33.♖×f7+ ♔c6 34.c×b6 ♗d7 35.♗×h6 a3 36.♗g7 a2 37.♔h2 and despite the opposite-color Bishops, White's winning prospects, with four pawns to only one for Black, are quite good (+2.91/26). White may even be able to afford giving up his Bishop for Black's last pawn and still win.

26...♕c7

White's sub-optimal 26th move notwithstanding, the result of this skirmish is that Black's pieces are somewhat disorganized, while White's cooperate harmoniously. Stockfish now recommends 27.♗d3 ♘e5 28.♗×g6 f×g6 29.♖×g6, winning a pawn, but this idea seems questionable because it creates opposite-colored Bishops. Torre prefers to move on the queenside. Judging by the quality of play over the next five moves, one suspects time pressure was already a factor. Or perhaps the complexities were just too much for the human antagonists.

27.a5

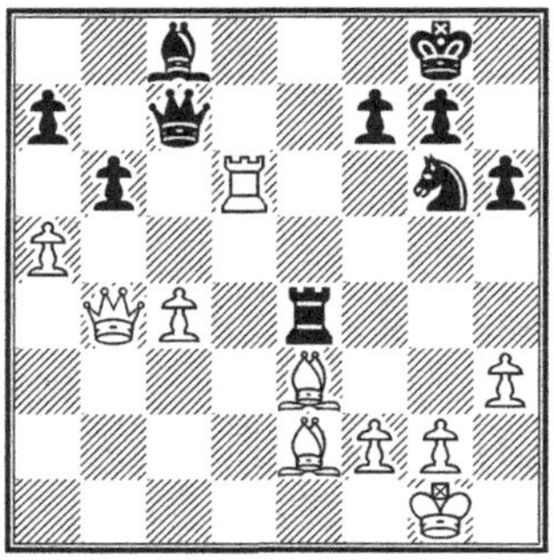

27...b×a5
Taking the pawn is obligatory, as after 27...♖e6 28.♖×e6 ♗×e6 29.a×b6 a×b6 30.♗×b6, the c-pawn will bring White a quick victory.

28.♕d2 ♗e6?
Black needed to play his only trump card: 28...a4! 29.c5 a3 30.♗d3 (or 30.♗f3 ♖e6 31.♗d5 ♖×d6 32.c×d6 ♕d7=) 30...♖e6 31.♖d4 ♘e5 32.♗b1 ♖e8=.

29.c5! ♘e5?
This and the previous move have cut off any retreat for the Rook back down the e-file. Much better were 29...♕e7 or 29...♖b4.

30.f3?!
This attack is premature, as the Rook still has an escape route. That should have been closed first with 30.♗d4! △31.f3.

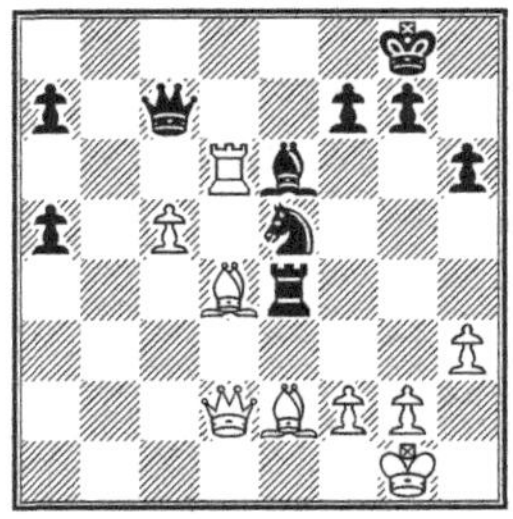

Knight moves are no good then, *viz.* 30...♘d7/♘g6 31.♗f3 ♖h4 32.g3 ♖×h3 33.♖×e6 f×e6 34.♔g2, or 30...♘c4 31.♗×c4 ♗×c4 32.♗×g7!! ♔×g7 33.♕×h6+ ♔g8 34.♕g5+ ♔f8 35.♖d8+ ♖e8 36.♕h6+ ♔e7 37.♕h4+ f6 38.♖×e8+ ♔×e8 39.♕×c4+−.
And on most other moves 31.f3 or 31.♗f3 forces 31...♖×d4 32.♕×d4+−.

30...♖b4 31.f4

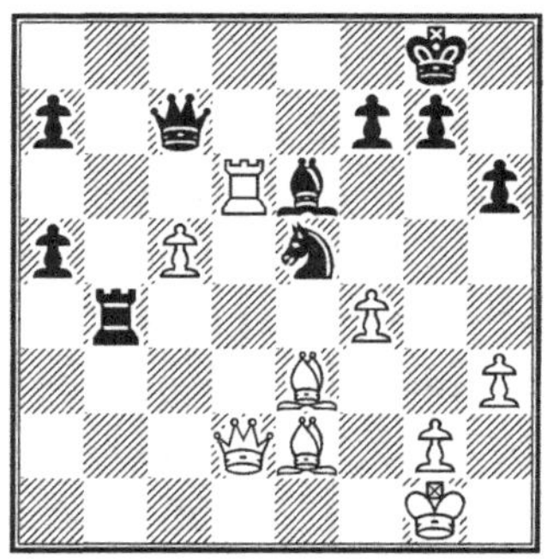

31...♘d7?
Now Black is irrevocably lost, and Torre starts finding the best moves. The least evil was 31...♘g6 32.♗d3 ♘e7 33.♖d8+ ♕×d8 34.♗h7+ ♔×h7 35.♕×d8 ♘f5, with some hopes of a draw (+1.79/26).

32.c6! ♘f8 33.♖d8
Also very good was 33.♗c5 ♖b8 34.♕d4 ♖e8 35.♗d3 △ 36.♗×a7.

33...♕e7?
The least evil this time was 33...♖b8, but after 34.♖×b8 ♕×b8 35.♕×a5 White is still in control (+2.47/26).

34.♖a8! ♗f5 35.♕c3! ♔h7 36.c7
Somewhat better was 36.♖×a7, but it is academic by now. Torre prefers to keep his Rook where it supports queening of the pawn.

36...♘g6 37.♗g4 ♖b1+ 38.♗c1 ♗×g4 39.h×g4 ♘×f4 40.♖h8+! ♔g6
Kupchik seems to consider this safer than 40...♔×h8 41.c8♕+, but it actually allows mate in nine.

41.c8♕
Quickest was 41.♕c2+ ♔g5 42.♕f5+ ♔h4 43.g3+ ♔×g3 44.♕×f4+ etc., but it hardly matters.

41...♘e2+
A worse than useless spite check.

42.♔f2 1–0
If 42...♘×c3 43.♕f5#.
A good win over a man very hard to beat.

Game 29

Kupchik-Torre

3rd match game, New York, 1925

Ruy López [C99]

In this game the opening followed the best-known line of the Closed Ruy López.

1.e4 e5 2.♘f3 ♘c6 3.♗b5 a6 4.♗a4 ♘f6 5.0–0 ♗e7 6.♖e1 b5 7.♗b3 0–0 8.c3 d6 9.h3 ♘a5 10.♗c2 c5 11.d4 ♕c7 12.♘bd2
A well-known position of the Chigorin System. During the years 1961-73, Anatoly Karpov had this position 11 times as Black in serious events, scoring +1 -3 =7. Later he abandoned it in favor of the Breyer System, which gave him better results in his early years: +3 -0 =9 as Black. As White he did better from this position, scoring +6 -0 =5 through 1988. It is interesting to note that Fischer in his career (through 1972) arrived 21 times at this position (always as White), of which he won 16, drew 3 and lost only 2 (to Letelier in 1959 and Kholmov in 1965). For Fischer this position was, apparently, "White to play and win." For Kupchik, however, we cannot say, as this is the only instance where ChessBase shows him playing the line.

12...♗d7

The most flexible move. Other frequently played alternatives include 12...c×d4, 12...♘c6, and 12...♖e8, each with its own merits.

13.♘f1

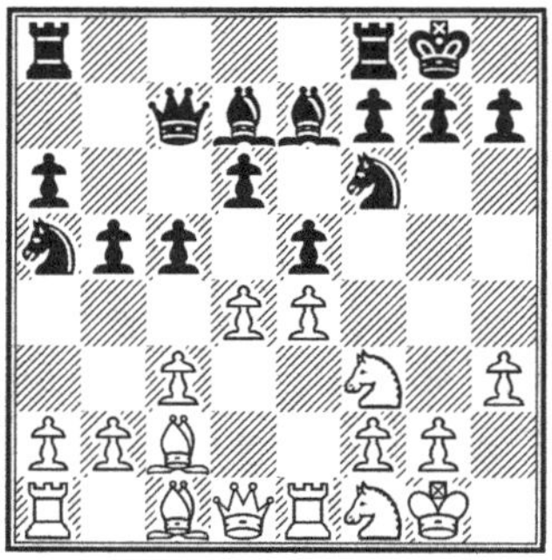

13...♖fc8

A novelty at the time. In earlier games ChessBase shows Black playing 13...♖ac8 three times, and 13...c×d4 once. The latter became the most commonly played move, followed by 13...♘c4, 13...♖fe8, and 13...♖ac8.

14.♘e3 c×d4 15.c×d4 ♘c6

16.♗b3

An interesting alternative is 16.♘d5!?, which Stockfish indicates either wins a pawn or gives White a significant positional advantage, *viz.*

(a) 16...♕d8 17.♘×e7+ ♕×e7 18.♗e3 (+1.32/24), or

(b) 16...♘×d5 17.e×d5 ♘b4 18.♗b1 ♘c2 (if 18...f6?! 19.d×e5 f×e5 20.♗g5 ♗×g5 21.♘×g5 ♘c2 22.♕d3 g6 23.♗×c2 ♗f5 24.♕e3 ♗×c2 25.♖ac1 (+2.35/26)) 19.♗×c2 ♕×c2 20.d×e5 ♕×d1 21.♖×d1 d×e5 22.♘×e5 ♗e8, when White is up a pawn but there is still a lot of play left in the position (+0.81/25).

In Fischer-Bisguier, US Ch 1958-59, 16.a3 was played. The position is closed enough that one cannot say with certainty a given move is "best"; in such cases, more important than any one move is an overall plan of attack or defense.

16...♘a5 17.♘d5 ♘×d5 18.♗×d5 ♗c6

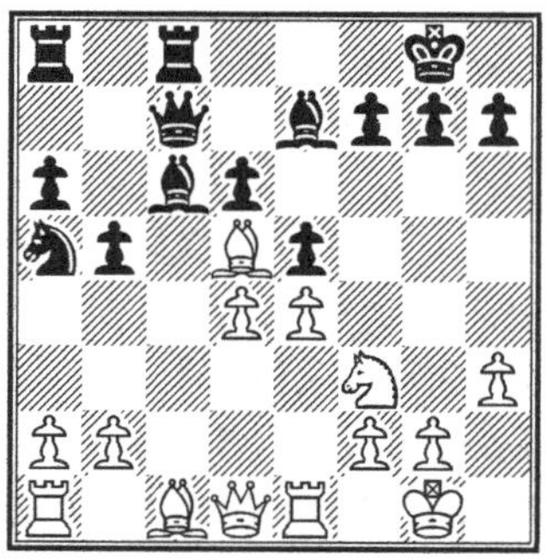

19.♗×c6

This exchange deadens the position somewhat. A perhaps better plan was 19.b3 ♗×d5 20.e×d5 f6 21.♘h4 intending to pressure Black further with f2-f4, ♕d1-f3-g3, ♘h4-f5, and possibly ♗c1-a3.

19...♘×c6 20.♗e3 ♕b7

In his own comments on the game, Carlos Torre wrote "A detailed examination of the position reveals that this is the best square for the Queen." Stockfish concurs.

21.♖c1 ♖c7?!

Torre's only clearly weak move of the game. With a draw appearing ever more likely, Black does best to expedite it, simplifying matters with 21...♘×d4 22.♘×d4 e×d4 23.♗×d4 ♖×c1 24.♕×c1 ♖c8=.

22.♕d2?!

A move that highlights Kupchik's trademark timidity.

It was more aggressive to force Black's Knight out of play by 22.d5!, when either 22...♘d8, 22...♘a7, or 22...♘a5 leaves White standing better (about +1.50 to +2.00), and 22...♘b8 allows White to seize control of the c-file: 23.♕b3 ♘d7 24.♖×c7 ♕×c7 25.♖c1 ♕b7 26.♕c3±.

22...♖ac8 23.d5

Too late! This is less effective now because after the Knight's retreat to b8 White will not be able to take control of the c-file as in the note above.

23...♘b8 24.♘h2

A characteristic of the Closed Ruy López is the interminable coming and going of the Knights in search of better squares, by both Black and White. Some masters dislike the opening for that reason. For example, Bent Larsen was known to detest the Ruy López with either White or Black. Observing Keres-Gligoric, San Antonio 1972 (a Breyer System), after 16 moves Larsen commented "Both players have a bad game!".

24...♘d7 25.♘f1 ♗h4

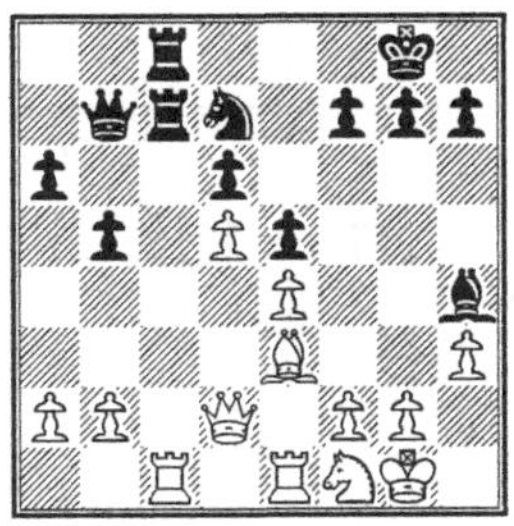

White's Knight has been dancing around for some time seeking an oasis on g3, but now Black moves to exchange his bad Bishop for the terpsichorean steed should it venture there. Kupchik must have frowned to see this move.

26.♖ed1

So that the f-pawn can advance to defend the e-pawn after Black's next move.

26...♘c5 27.f3 ♘a4 28.♕b4 ♗e7

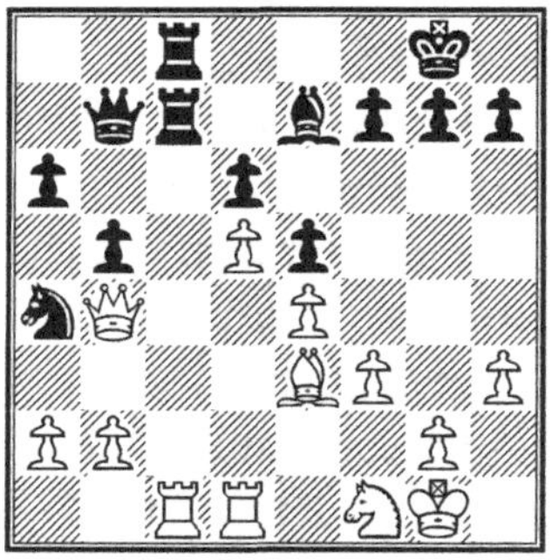

29.♖×c7

Or 29.♘g3 ♖×c1 30.♖×c1 ♖×c1+ 31.♗×c1 ♕b6+ 32.♔h2 ♕c5 with a very drawish game.

29...♖×c7 30.♖c1 ♖×c1 31.♗×c1 ♕c7 32.♗e3

32...g6

Also playable was 32...♕c2 33.♕a5 ♕×b2 34.♕×a6 ♘c3 with deadeye equality. The seeming threat of ♕a6-c8+ is not to be feared.

33.♕d2 ♗d8

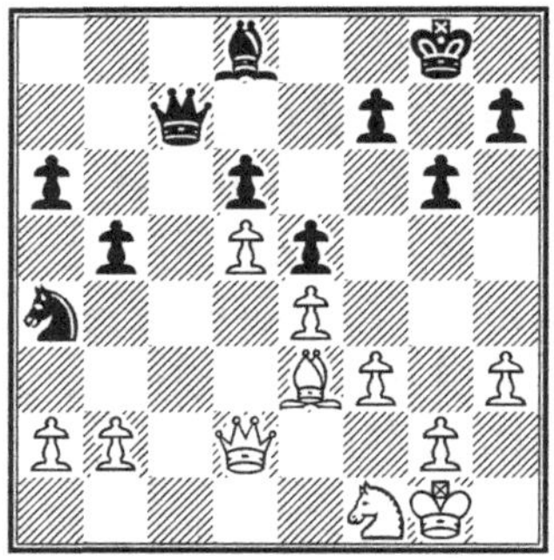

34.♘g3

Trying to contest the open file with 34.♕c1?! is dubious due to 34...♕×c1 35.♗×c1 ♗b6+ 36.♔h2 ♗d4 37.b3 ♘c3 38.a3□ ♘e2 39.♗d2 ♗c5 40.a4 (40.b4? ♗g1+ 41.♔h1 ♗d4 △42...♗b2 and 43.♗×a3) 40...b4 41.♗h6 f6 and Black has the better posted pieces.

34...♕a5 35.♕c1

White could also have exchanged Queens, *e.g.* 35.♕×a5 ♗×a5 36.♗c1 ♘c5 37.♔f1 ♘d3 38.♘e2=. But keeping Queens on the board does nothing to enhance his winning chances.

35...♗b6 36.b3 ♘c3 37.♗×b6 ♕×b6+ 38.♔h2 b4 ½-½

And a draw was agreed. Stockfish quite concurs, rating the position at 0.00 to 33 ply and beyond. A game conducted with caution (if anything with too much by White at moves 16, 19, and 22) and, possibly excepting Black's 21st move, with correctness by both players, producing the logical result.

Game 30

Kupchik-Torre

5th match game, New York, 1925

Grünfeld Defense [D94]

1.d4 ♘f6 2.♘f3 g6

The match with Kupchik marked the beginning of a sudden new phase in Torre's concept and handling of the opening. In those days many of the modern lines of play were in their early development, and there is ample reason to include Carlos Torre among the "Hypermodern" vanguard, along with Réti, Nimzovich, Tartakower, Grünfeld et al. While we do not know the exact reasons prompting the Mexican master to abandon his heretofore classical focus so abruptly, certainly it must have stemmed in part from his passionate desire to try new variations and enrich his repertoire. It was precisely this spirit of self-criticism and his aptitude for experimentation that sped his rise from the level of the amateur to a grandmaster of the first magnitude. Torre never worried much about winning or losing; rather he sought truth and originality. He was anxious to learn and evolve, to satisfy his curiosity, even though it cost him a game.

3.c4 ♗g7 4.♘c3 d5

Introduced by Ernst Grünfeld in his match with Albert Becker, Vienna, 1922. Grünfeld considered this the only playable form of the King's Indian Defense. It was quickly taken up by Alekhine, Réti, Colle and other adventurous masters.

5.c×d5 ♘×d5 6.e3

6.e4 had been more usual from the start; in fact, of the twelve earlier games reaching this position in ChessBase, 6.e4 was played in all but one, Moritz-Grünfeld, Frankfurt 1923.

6...0–0 7.♗c4 ♘×c3

Also playable is 7...♘b6 8.♗b3 c5.

8.b×c3 c5 9.0–0 ♘c6

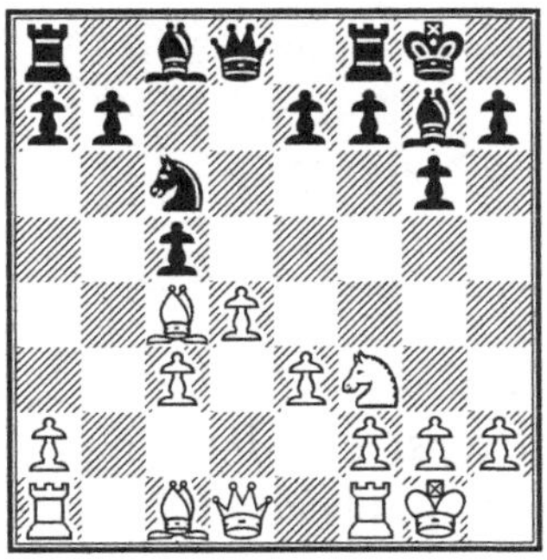

10.♗a3

Already seen twice before, in Rubinstein-Alekhine, Vienna 1922 (1-0, 28), and Prochaska-Prokes, 8th Czech Ch, Pardubice 1923 (1-0, 21). Perhaps Kupchik knew those games and expected another quick win.

10...c×d4 11.c×d4 ♗f5

Varying from the aforementioned games. Alekhine had played 11...a6, Prokes 11...♕a5. It bears mentioning that Stockfish considers Torre's choice best by a slight margin. It begins a maneuver intended to blunt the pressure White's Bishops are exerting on their parallel diagonals.

12.♖c1 ♖c8 13.♗c5 ♗e4 14.♘d2?!

This allows Black equality. Better was 14.♕e2±.

14...♗d5 15.♕a4

Of course not 15.e4?? ♗×c4 16.♘×c4 ♗×d4–+.

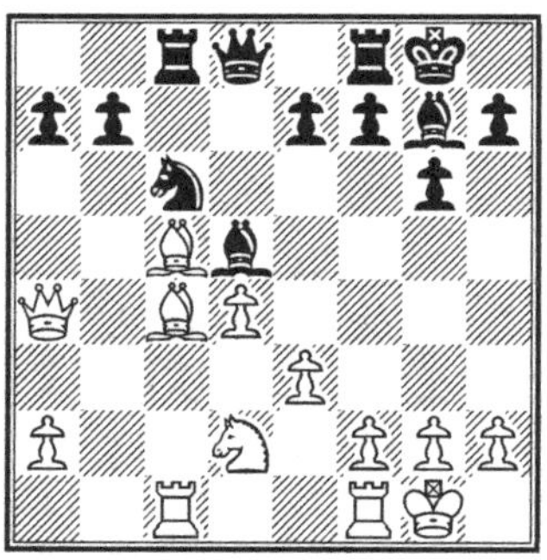

15...♖e8

Central tension is building up, with potential complications neither player seems to appreciate fully. The text is intended to support a break with 16...e5, but better was 15...♗×c4 and either 16.♘×c4 b6 17.♗a3 ♕d5=, or 16.♖×c4 ♕d7 17.♖fc1 ♖fd8 △ 18...e5!=.

16.f4?!

White, logically, wants to prevent the break 16...e5. This method should do that, but it has drawbacks that make it a remedy worse than the disease. Better 16.♖fd1, and if then 16...e5? 17.♗×d5 ♕×d5 18.e4 ♕d8 19.d5±.

16...e5?!

Torre is counting on the unprotected state of the Knight at d2 to make this work, but he needed to see one move beyond 19...♕×d2 to evaluate the line properly. Stockfish recommends instead 16...e6, with best play then continuing 17.h3 a6 18.♗×d5 e×d5 when Black is at least equal, and with a strategic target in the suddenly weak white e-pawn.

An attempt to trap the ♗d5 fails, *e.g.* 17.♗d3 b6 18.♗a3 a6!

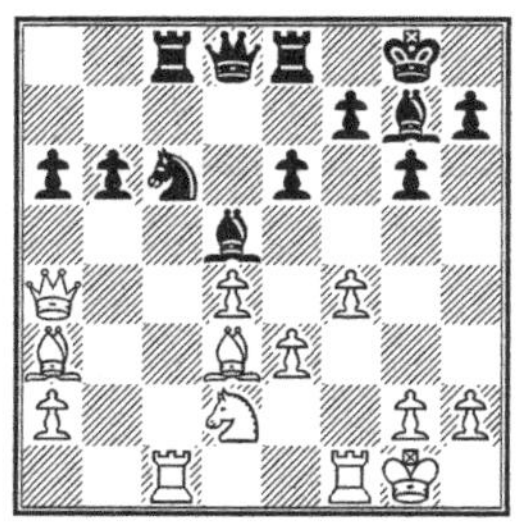

19.e4? (not 19.♕×a6?? ♖a8–+) 19...b5 20.♕c2 ♘a7 21.♕b1 ♗×a2!! 22.♕×a2 ♕×d4+ 23.♔h1 ♕×d3–+.

17.f×e5?!

As in the above note, best here was 17.♗×d5 ♕×d5 18.e4 ♕d7 19.d5±.

17...♘×e5 18.♗×d5 ♕×d5 19.d×e5

If 19.♘b3?? ♘d3 and either 20.♖c2 ♖×e3–+, or 20.♕c4 ♕×c4 21.♖×c4 b6–+.

19...♕×d2

Completing the tactical finesse Torre envisioned with his 15th and 16th moves. But he did not realize White too had a finesse at this disposal.

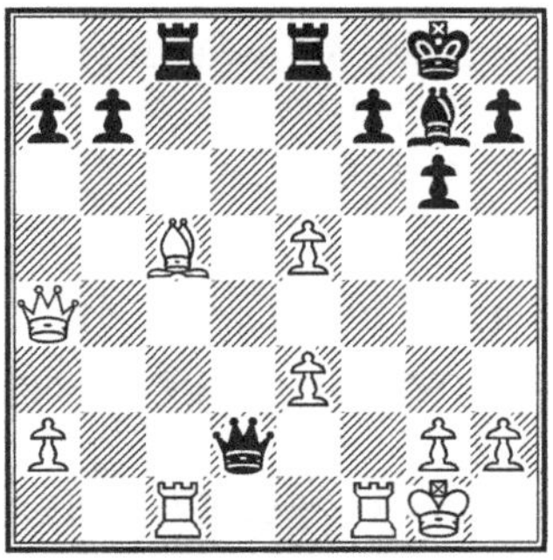

20.♗d4?!

This makes the game completely level. A more enterprising move both players missed was 20.e6!?, and either

(a) 20...f×e6 21.♖fd1 ♕e2 22.♕d7 a6 23.a4 ♗h6 24.♔h1 ♖cd8 (not 24...♗×e3?? 25.♗×e3 ♕×e3 26.♖×c8+−) 25.♕×d8 ♖×d8 26.♖×d8+ ♔f7 27.♖d7+ ♔f6 28.♖×h7 ♗×e3 29.♗×e3 ♕×e3 30.♖f1+ ♔e5 31.♖×b7 and White has the better of it in the ♕-vs-♖+♖ ending (+1.61/26), though a draw is likely; or

(b) 20...♖×e6 21.♖cd1 ♕×d1□ (if 21...♕e2?? 22.♕d7 ♖ec6 23.♕×f7+ ♔h8 24.♖d7 forcing 24...♕×f1+ 25.♕×f1+−, since if 24...♖g8 25.♕×g8+ ♔×g8 26.♖d8+ ♗f8 27.♖d×f8+ etc.) 22.♖×d1 ♖×c5 23.♖d8+ ♗f8 and again White stands better, this time in an ending of ♕+♖-vs-♖+♖+♗.

20...♕×c1

20...♗×e5 was also quite playable.

21.♖×c1?!

Another wrong reflex recapture. Correct was 21.♕×e8+ ♖×e8 22.♖×c1 ♗×e5 23.♗×a7 ♖a8 24.♗d4 ♗×d4 25.e×d4 ♖×a2 26.♖b1 ♖d2 27.♖×b7 ♖×d4 with an even, virtually certain drawn ending (-0.09/30).

21...♖×c1+ 22.♔f2

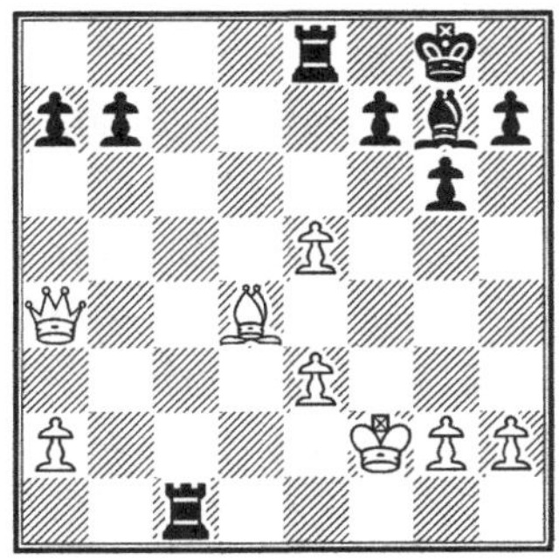

22...♖c6

If Torre was trying to play for a win, preferable was 22...♖cc8 23.♕×a7 ♗×e5 24.♗×e5 ♖×e5 25.♕×b7 ♖c2+ 26.♔f3 ♖f5+ 27.♔g3 ♖×a2, when Black has the better chances in the ♕-vs-♖+♖ ending.

23.♕×a7 ♖c7 24.h3 ♖ce7 25.e6

25...♖×e6

More promising was 25...♗×d4, and either 26.e×f7+?? ♖×f7+ and mate in six, or 26.e×d4 ♖×e6 27.♕×b7 ♖e2+ 28.♔f3 ♖×a2 (-3.36/30), or 26.♕×d4 ♖×e6 when Stockfish again says Black is winning (-3.62/34).
However, if so it will be a long process. We leave it to the interested reader to explore further.

26.a4
Despite the relatively scant material, there is still a lot of danger lurking. For example 26.♗×g7 ♔×g7 27.♕×b7 ♖×e3 28.a4 (-3.14/25), or 26.♗b6 ♗h6 27.h4? (better 27.♕×b7 ♗×e3+ 28.♗×e3 ♖×e3 29.a4 -3.14/25) 27...♖×b6! 28.♕×b6 ♗×e3+ 29.♕×e3 ♖×e3 30.♔×e3 f6 and Black wins the pawn ending (-6.01/27).

26...♗×d4 27.e×d4

27...b6
Best was 27...♖a6, by which Black might, with luck, eventually reach an ending of two Rooks and three pawns against Queen and two pawns. However, it appears this cannot be forced against best play, *e.g.* 28.♕×b7 ♖×a4 29.♕b5 ♖a2+ 30.♔f3 ♖a3+ 31.♔f2 ♖d8 32.♕b6 ♖d5 33.♕c6 ♖aa5 34.♔e3 ♖d8 35.♔e4 ♖a1 36.♕b6 ♖e1+ 37.♔f3 ♖d5∞.

28.♕d7 ♖e2+
The game is now clearly drawn, and further comment is superfluous.

29.♔g1 ♖e1+ 30.♔h2 h5 31.d5 ♖a8 32.d6 ♖d1 33.♕e7 ♖a5 34.♕d8+ ♔g7 35.♕×b6 ♖×a4 36.♕c5 ♖e4 37.♕c3+ ♖ed4 38.♕b2 h4 39.♕c3 f6 40.♕c7+ ♔h6 41.d7 ½-½

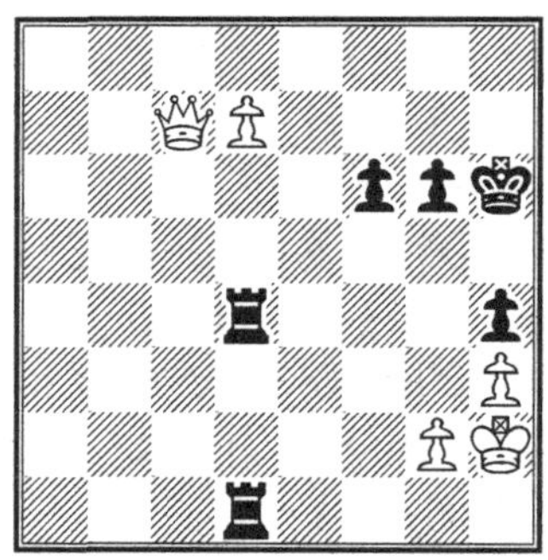

Draw agreed. If 41...♖×d7 42.♕f4+ and 42...♔g7 43.♕×h4= or 42...♔h5 43.♕×f6=.

Game 31

Torre-Kupchik

6th match game, New York 1925

Ruy López [C90]

In this final game of the match, we see most clearly the tendency noted in the introductory chapter, that Torre's "attempt to control his imaginative talents and change his concept of 'chess as art' to one of 'chess as competitive sport' caused Torre to play in a strange, artificial way against an opponent he would in other circumstances probably defeat with relative ease." Kupchik plays here in an entirely passive style, like a boxer in a crouch, never throwing a punch. Yet unlike the second game of the match, Torre never found a way to break through his defenses. The result was a tedious, interminable draw. We limit our notes mainly to the few points where Torre had winning chances.

1.e4 e5 2.♘f3 ♘c6 3.♗b5 a6 4.♗a4 ♘f6 5.0–0 ♗e7 6.♖e1 b5 7.♗b3 d6 8.c3 ♘a5 9.♗c2 c5 10.d4 ♕c7 11.♘bd2 ♘c6

All book so far. This position was first seen in the 1908 Lasker-Tarrasch world title match, twice, Lasker playing White both times, losing once and winning once. Now 12.h3 0–0 would reach the same position as those two games, and as in our Game 29, Kupchik-Torre. But Torre instead chooses what had already become, and would remain, the main line.

12.d5 ♘d8 13.a4 ♖b8 14.♘f1

Finally breaking new ground. 14.h3 was played in Michell-Yates, Hastings 1918 (0-1, 58).

14...h6 15.a×b5 a×b5 16.♘g3 ♘h7 17.♗e3 ♘g5 18.♗d3 g6 19.♘d2

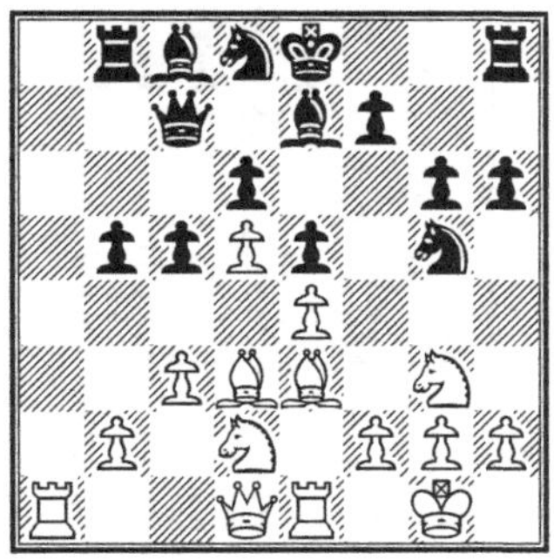

19...f6?

Kupchik takes passivity to a new extreme. Better was 19...c4, with a position evaluated at +1.35 to +1.75, whatever retreat the ♗d3 takes. The drawback of the text, besides making the ♗e7 even a worse Bishop than it already was, is that it leaves Black's g-pawn undefended, a weakness White can exploit to force further concessions.

20.f4?!

In a position as crowded and opaque as this, the best move is often not at all obvious, and so it is understandable that Torre would want to open things up a bit. But he missed a winning opportunity in 20.h4!:

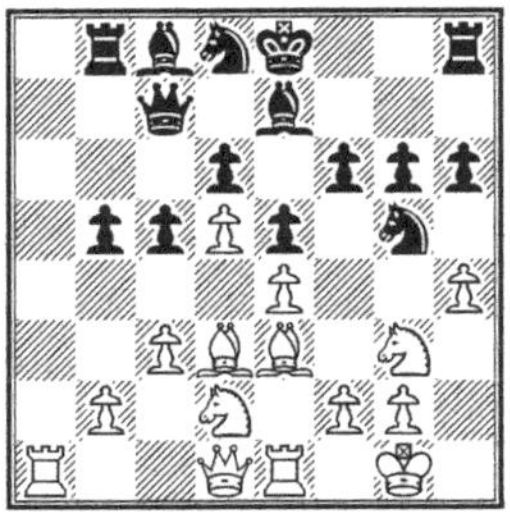

This leaves Black only three alternatives:

(a) 20...♘gf7 21.h5! c4 22.♗e2,

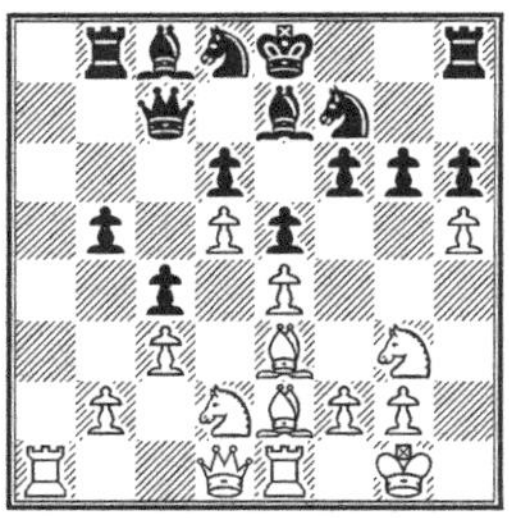

(a1) 22...g5 23.♗g4 0–0 24.♕f3 ♗×g4 25.♕×g4 ♘b7 26.♖a7 ♕c8 27.♘f5 ♔h7 28.♖ea1 ♗d8 29.♖1a6 (+9.25/24);

(a2) 22...f5 (relatively best) 23.h×g6 f4 24.g×f7+ ♘×f7 25.♘df1 f×e3 26.♘×e3 (+6.26/24);

(b) 20...♘h7 21.h5 g5 22.♗e2:

(b1) 22...0–0 23.♗g4 ♘f7 24.b4 ♖e8 25.♗f5 ♗d7 26.♕e2 ♖ec8 27.♘b3 ♗×f5 28.♘×f5 ♗f8 29.♘a5 ♘d8 30.c4 b×c4 31.b×c5 d×c5 32.♘×c4 and White is obviously winning (+6.69/ 27);

(b2) 22...f5 About the only way to get a decent square for the ♘h7. 23.e×f5 ♘f6 24.♘de4

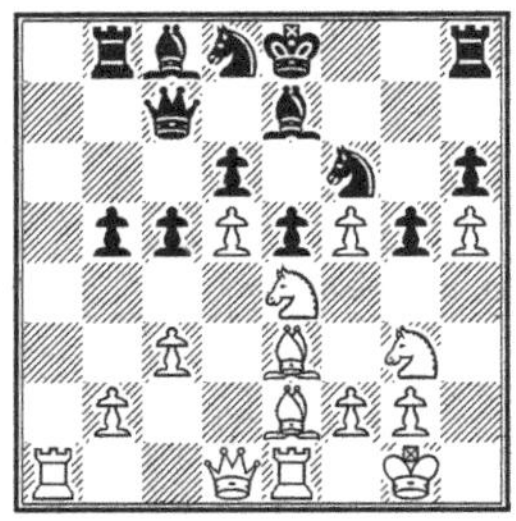

(b2a) 24...♘×e4 25.♘×e4 ♗×f5 26.♘g3 ♗h7 27.♗d3 0–0 28.♗×h7+ ♔×h7 29.♕d3+ ♔h8 30.b4 (+6.47/28);

(b2b) 24...0–0 25.♘×f6+ ♗×f6 26.b4 c4 27.♖a7 ♖b7 28.♖a6 ♘f7 29.♘e4 ♔g7 30.♗g4 (+5.73/24);

(c) 20...c4:

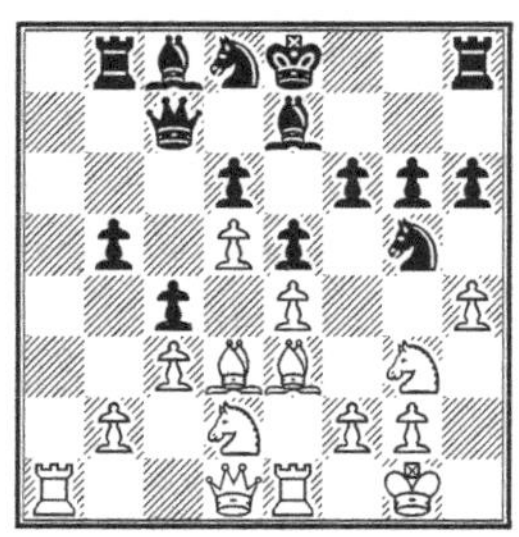

(c1) 21.♗e2 ♘gf7 22.h5, and now 22...g5 would transpose to (a1), 22...f5 to **(a2)**;

(c2) Perhaps simplest is 21.♗×c4!? b×c4 22.h×g5 h×g5 23.♕a4+ ♗d7 24.♕×c4 ♕×c4 25.♘×c4,

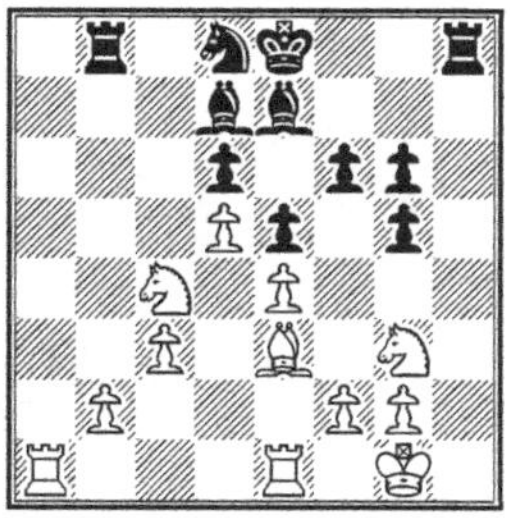

and White's queenside pawn majority guarantees a winning ending (+3.82/25).

The above variations are presented more as illustrative sample possibilities than as conclusive analysis. The attentive reader may have noticed that in several of them Stockfish gives very high evaluations (in the case of (a1), extremely so) when material is even and no mating attack or winning combination seems imminent. Still, White's positional advantage is so great, the black forces so cramped and ultimately unable to defend against various threats, that White's victory must be considered inevitable. For example, in the end position of variation (a1):

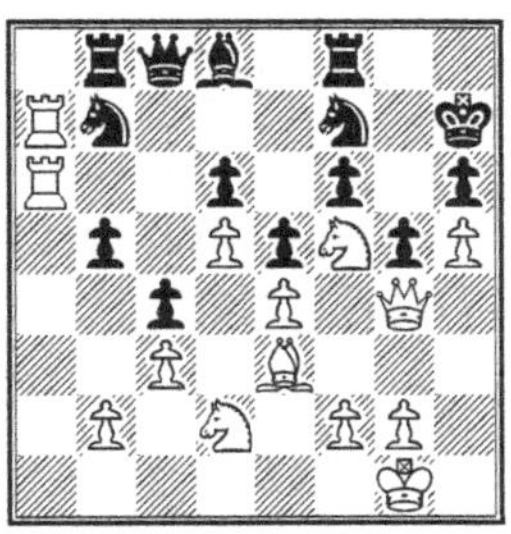

Black can do nothing while White leisurely regroups his forces for a decisive breakthrough, *e.g.* 29...♔h8 30.♘f1 ♕d7 31.♕d1 ♗e7 32.♘h2 ♖fc8 33.♘g4 ♔h7 34.♕f3:

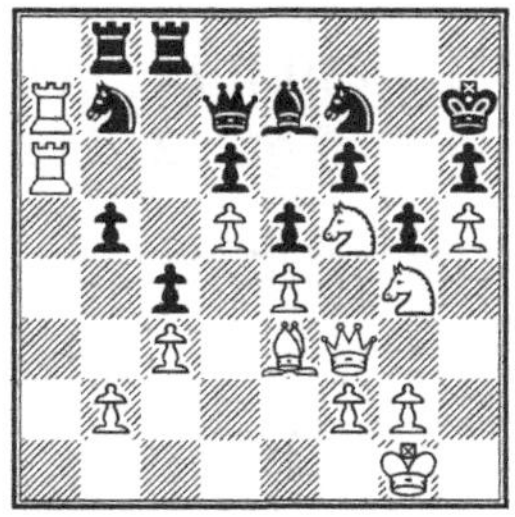

White threatens 35.♘×e7 ♕×e7 36.♕f5+ ♔g8 37.♕g6+ ♔f8 38.♘×f6 etc. If Black tries to prevent this with 34...♗d8, then 36.♗b6! ♕e8 (36...♗×b6?? 37.♘×f6+) 36.♗×d8 ♕×d8 37.♖c6 ♔h8 38.♘fe3, when Stockfish announces mate in 11.

But, alas, Torre did not find 20.h4!.

Returning to the actual game, after **20.f4**:

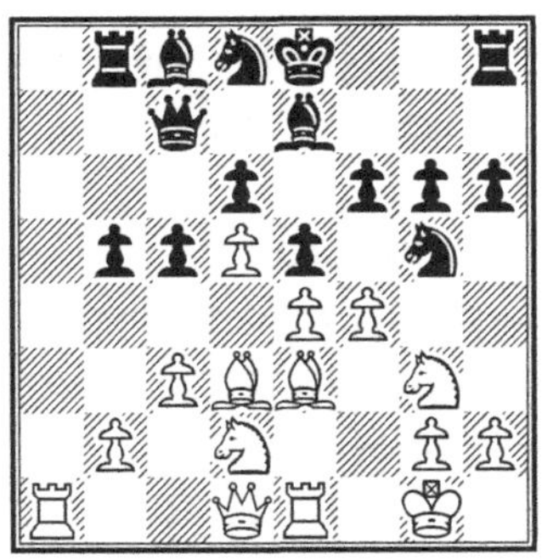

20...e×f4 21.♗×f4 ♘gf7 22.♘f3 ♘e5 23.♘×e5 f×e5 24.♗e3 ♘f7 25.♖f1 ♗d7 26.♘h5 0–0□
26...g×h5?? 27.♕×h5 ♖f8 28.♗×h6+–.

27.♘f6+ ♔g7 28.♘×d7 ♕×d7 29.b4 c4 30.♗e2 ♗d8? 31.♗g4! ♕e7 32.♖a6 ♘g5 33.♖×f8 ♕×f8

34.♖a7+ ♗e7 35.♗×g5 h×g5 36.♕f3 ♕×f3 37.g×f3 ♔f8 38.♗d7 ♗d8 39.♔f1 ♗b6 40.♖a6 ♗e3 41.♔e2 ♗g1 42.♖a1! ♗×h2

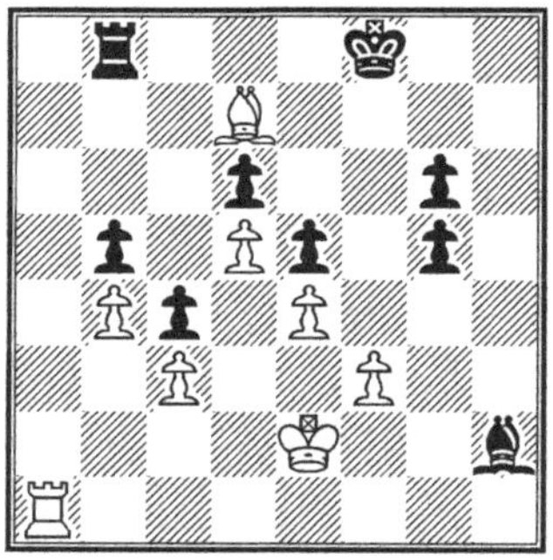

43.♗c6?
Torre may have missed another winning opportunity here: 43.♖a5! ♗g1 44.♗×b5 ♗b6 45.♖a1 ♔e7 46.♖h1 (if 46.♗×c4 ♖c8 47.♔d3 ♖f8) 46...♔f6 47.♗×c4 and despite the "bees of opps" White should have good winning chances (+3.30/37). The text creates an even game, which the subsequent moves do nothing to alter.

43...♔e7 44.♖a8
With this Torre makes a draw inevitable. One wonders why play continued another 33 moves.

44...♖×a8 45.♗×a8 g4 46.f×g4 g5 47.♗c6 ♗g1 48.♗×b5 ♔d8 49.♗×c4
With Rooks no longer on the board, even this two-pawn advantage is not enough to win. The remaining moves are all pointless wood-shifting.

49...♔c7 50.♗b5 ♔b6 51.c4

♔c7 52.♗e8 ♗d4 53.♔d3 ♗g1 54.♔c3 ♗f2 55.♗a4 ♗g1 56.♗e8 ♗f2 57.♔b3 ♗e3 58.♔a4 ♔b6 59.♔b3 ♔c7 60.♗a4 ♗f2 61.♔c3 ♗g1 62.♗c2 ♗f2 63.♔b3 ♗e3 64.♔a4 ♔b6 65.♔a3 ♗c1+ 66.♔b3 ♗e3 67.♔c3 ♔c7 68.♗a4 ♗f2 69.♗e8 ♗e3 70.♗f7 ♗f2 71.♗e6 ♗e3 72.♔b3 ♗f2 73.♔a4 ♔b6 74.c5+ d×c5 75.b5 ♔c7 76.♔b3 c4+ 77.♔×c4 ♔d6 ½-½
A stultifying game, interesting only for its might-have-beens.

A few days after the inconclusive match with Kupchik, Carlos Torre played on Board 1 for the Marshall Chess Club in the New York Metropolitan League, the city's inter-club team championship. Torre obtained the highest percentage of all first-board players, however this was not enough to give his team the championship. The Stuyvesant Chess Club (captained by Kupchik) and the Columbia University team (led by M.A. Schapiro) occupied the top two spots, leaving the Marshall CC a half-point behind, though still well ahead of the Brooklyn CC, International CC, Hungarian CC, Staten Island CC, and New York University (which lost all seven of its matches).

The strongest New York club, the Manhattan, did not field a team, but their members played on other teams. Particularly exciting was the last-round contest between Kupchik and Torre, played March 21st, one week after the suspension of their match. Though Torre's team lost the match 3½-4½, Torre defeated his counterpart Kupchik, a victory many took as the unofficial conclusion to their indecisive match.

Game 32

Kupchik-Torre

Metropolitan Chess League team match, New York, 21 March 1925, Grünfeld Defense [D71]

1.d4 ♘f6 2.c4 g6 3.♘c3 ♗g7 4.g3 d5 5.c×d5 ♘×d5 6.♗g2 ♘×c3 7.b×c3 c5 8.♘f3

This move gives White a less solid center than the plan of 8.e3 and 9.♘e2, as played in the first game with this line, J. Bernstein-Alekhine, Carlsbad 1923 (0-1, 43), and recommended by later theory and practical results.

8...♘c6 9.♗b2?!

Better 9.0–0, 9.♖b1, 9.e3, or 9.♗e3.

9...♕b6!

Hitting strongly at the d-pawn with all available forces, and aiming for a transition to a favorable endgame.

10.♕b3 ♗e6 11.♕×b6?!

Positionally suspect, even though superficially it looks better, as it gives Black a doubled, backward pawn on an open file. Better was 11.♕a3=.

11...a×b6 12.a3 0–0 13.0–0 ♗d5

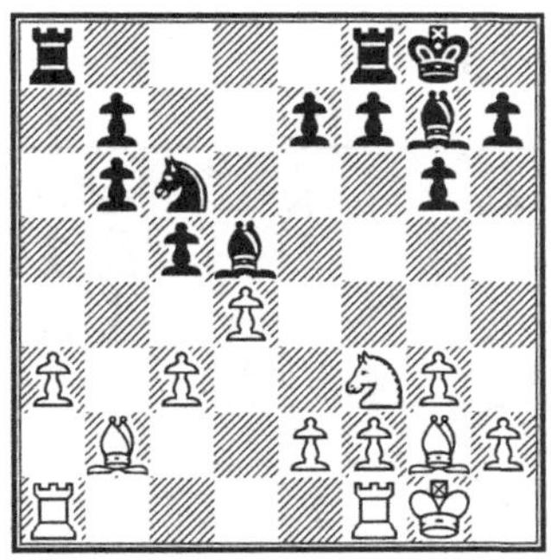

14.♖fd1

If 14.♖fb1 △15.♗c1 to attack the b-pawn, then 14...♗e4 forces the Rook back. Or Black can just continue 14...♖fd8, since if 15.♗c1 ♗e4 16.♖×b6? c×d4 17.c×d4 ♗×f3 18.♗×f3 ♗×d4 forking White's Rooks. And if 14.♖ab1 ♗e4 again forces the Rook off the b-file.

14...♖fd8 15.e3 ♘a5

Torre commented "The threat of playing this Knight to c4, which would be unpleasant for White, forces the exchange of light-squared Bishops, and also allows Black to take control of the d-file." Better, though, was the immediate 15...e5, or 15...♗b3 16.♖e1 e5.

16.♘d2 ♗×g2 17.♔×g2 e5
Continuing to strike at the d4-pawn, a major theme of the Grünfeld Defense.

18.d×c5?
A serious misjudgement. Better 18.♖ab1, now playable due to the light-squared Bishop's absence, or 18.♘f3 ♘c4 19.♖ab1, in either case with only a small advantage for Black.

18...b×c5

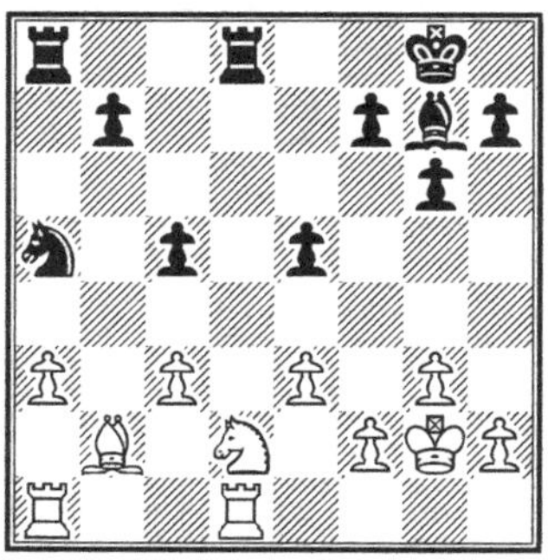

19.♖ab1?!
Apparently played from fear of 19...♖×d2 20.♖×d2 ♘b3, but that would only squander Black's advantage. Less bad was 19.c4 f5 20.♗c3 ♘c6 21.♖db1 ♖d3 22.♖b3 ♖×c3 23.♖×c3 e4 24.♖ac1 ♗×c3 25.♖×c3 ♖d8 26.♘f1 ♘e5 27.♖b3, when Black's advantage is not overwhelming (-0.99/26).

19...f5!
By far the best move, threatening 20...e4 –+.

20.c4
"In order to free his Bishop, White must now confine his Knight." – Torre.

20...♖d3! 21.♔f1 ♖ad8 22.♔e2 e4
Torre is in his element, finding one optimal move after another.

23.♗×g7 ♔×g7

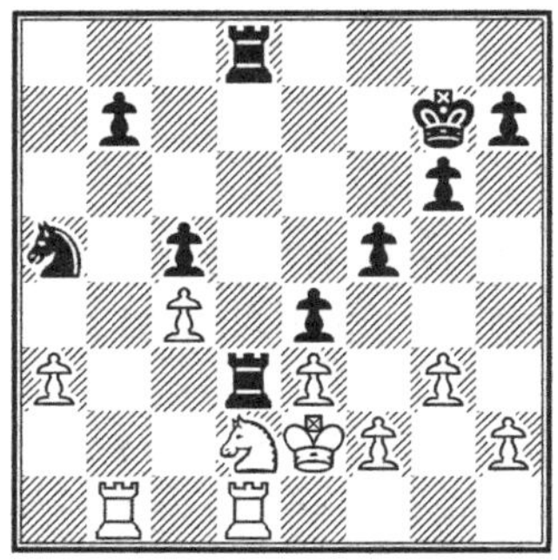

24.♖a1?
Kupchik spent nearly 45 minutes on this move, only to come up with a lemon. It is generally inadvisable to tie a Rook down to this sort of menial defensive task; furthermore, as will be seen, the move has a definite tactical drawback. Relatively best was 24.a4, when Black must avoid 24...♖a3? 25.♖b5! (not 25.♖a1?? ♖×d2+ 26.♔×d2 ♘b3+ etc.),

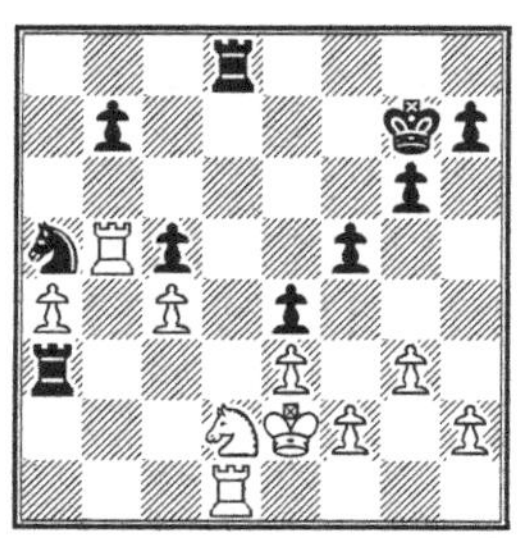

and after 25...♖×a4 26.♖×c5 ♖a2 27.♔e1 the game is almost dead even (-0.34/26), or if 25...b6 26.♖×b6 ♖a2 27.♔e1 ♖a×d2 28.♖×d2 ♖×d2 29.♔×d2 ♘×c4+ 30.♔c3 ♘×b6 31.a5 ♘c8 32.♔c4 ♔f6 33.♔×c5 it's definitely a draw (0.00/35).
After 24.a4, correct would be 24...b6 25.g4 ♔f7 26.g×f5 g×f5 when Black stands better (-2.52/28) but he still must work to bring home the point.

24...♔f6
A natural move, and not at all bad, but Black could have capitalized fully on White's last move with 24...b5!,

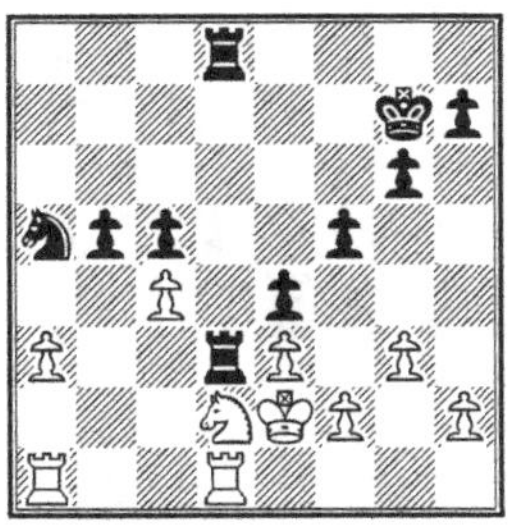

forcing 25.c×b5 c4 26.♖ac1 c3 27.♘f1 (worse is 27.♘b1?? c2) 27...♘b3 28.♖×c3 ♖×d1 29.♖×b3 ♖a1,

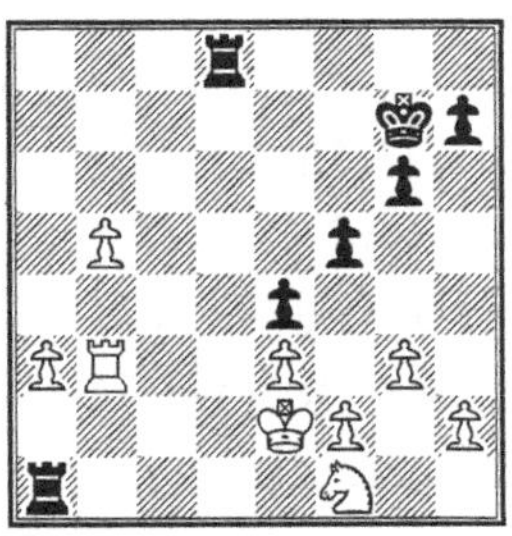

and now 30.g4 is forced; otherwise, say, 30.b6 ♖a2+ 31.♔e1 ♖c8 and either 32.♔d1 ♖a1+ 33.♔d2 ♖×f1−+, or 32.♖b1 ♖cc2 33.b7 ♖e2+ 34.♔d1 ♖×f2 35.♔e1 ♖ae2+ 36.♔d1 ♖×f1+ 37.♔×e2 ♖×b1−+. After 30.g4 Black continues 30...h5! 31.g×h5 ♖a2+ 32.♔e1 ♖c8 33.♖b1 ♖cc2 34.♘g3 ♖×f2 35.b6 ♖fb2−+.

Returning now to the actual game (after **24...♔f6**):

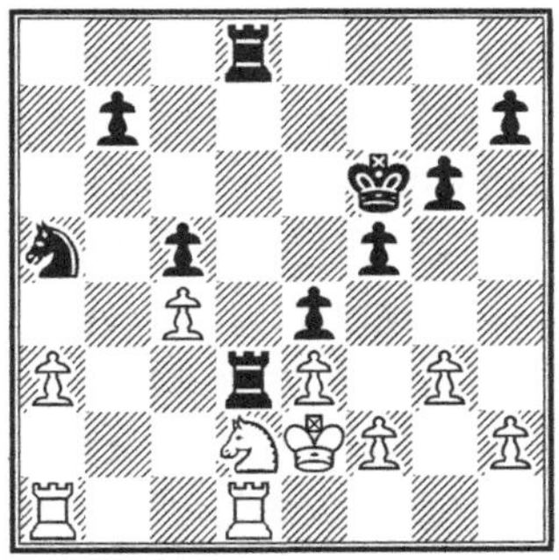

25.♔e1?!
Though it would be a tacit admission that his previous move was wrong, better was 25.♖ac1. Then not 25...♖×a3? 26.♘×e4+! ♔e7 27.♖×d8 ♔×d8 28.♘×c5 with a virtually even game, but 25...♔e5! 26.♖c2 ♖×a3 27.f4+ ♔e6 28.♘×e4 ♖×d1 29.♘g5+ ♔e7 30.♔×d1 ♖a4 (not 30...♖×e3? 31.♔d2 ♖a3 32.♘×h7 ♖a4 33.♔d3=) 31.♘×h7 ♘×c4 and Black, with his passed b- and c-pawns, should win, but White can still make a fight of it (-2.80/27).
The text reduces White to just shuffling his King between e1 and e2, while Black keeps increasing the pressure.

25...♔e6 26.♔e2 ♖8d7 27.♔e1 b5!
Finally Torre hits on the winning idea! White is now doomed.

Amazingly, though, in his notes to this game, Torre called 27...b5 "entirely wrong," and commented further "Black has played a fine positional game and has built a winning position; now he should simply continue with 27...♖c3. But he will play a combination, his knowledge to the contrary notwithstanding. That is probably why the great masters — Capablanca, Lasker, Alekhine — lose so few games. Regardless of the judgment of other masters, they will seldom play against their own judgment." Yet as computer-assisted analyses have shown, Lasker, Capablanca and Alekhine were usually better players than they were annotators, and Torre here follows in their steps. 27...♖c3 was good, and should eventually win, but 27...b5! is best, far stronger. Though Torre was unduly hard on himself here, at least this comment shows his passionate desire for perfection in every move.

28.c×b5 c4 29.♖ac1 c3 30.♘f1 ♘b3!

Just as in the note to Black's 24th move.

31.♖×d3 ♖×d3!□ 32.♖c2 ♔d5

33.g4

This book's first edition, falling in with Torre's criticism of 27...b5, gave this an exclam and called it "a tactical resource that must have escaped Torre's calculations ... [that] puts Black's pawn chain under strong pressure." But in fact White had no good move, and the text is not at all to be feared.

33...♔c4

ChessBase gives 33...♔c5 here, but Torre has ...♔c4. In any event, it is immaterial after Black captures on b5.

34.g×f5

34.b6, which Torre may have been trying to tempt White into when he played his King to c4 rather than c5, fails to any number of replies, best of which is 34...♖d6 35.♘g3 ♔d3 36.♔d1 ♘a1! 37.b7 ♖b6 and now 38.♖×c3+ ♔×c3 is virtually forced, since if 38.♖c1 c2+ 39.♔e1 ♖×b7 followed by 40...♖b1. And if 38.♖a2?? ♖b1#.

34...g×f5 35.♘g3 ♔×b5 36.♘×f5 ♔a4?

This is where Torre should have really been hard on himself, as this move could have thrown the win away. The a-pawn is nothing. Correct was 36...♔c4–+.

37.♘g3 ♘d2

38.♔d1??

Torre wrote "The position has been very difficult for the last ten moves and now White makes a surprising move, running into a discovered check." Apparently White thought this was his chance to cross the *cordón sanitaire* and blockade the dangerous passed pawn, but it fails badly. He missed 38.♘e2!,

when if

(a) 38...♔b3 39.♖×c3+! ♖×c3 40.♔×d2! ♖c2+ 41.♔e1 ♔×a3 42.♘g3 and White has definite drawing chances in the ♘+3♙-vs-♖+2♙ ending (-0.63/36), or

(b) 38...♘f3+ 39.♔f1 ♔b3 (39...♖d1+?! 40.♔g2 ♘e1+ 41.♔g3 ♘×c2?? actually *loses* to 42.♘×c3+ ♔×a3 43.♘×d1+–, so Black is forced into 41...♖d6 42.♖×c3 ♖g6+ 43.♔f4=) 40.♖×c3+ ♖×c3 41.♘×c3 ♔×c3 42.♔g2!□ ♔b3 43.♔g3 ♔×a3 44.♔f4 ♘d2 45.♔g5 which is definitely drawn (0.00/41). But after the text he is once again doomed.

38...♘f1+ 39.♔c1 ♘×g3 40.h×g3 ♔×a3 41.♖e2 ♔b3 1-0

White resigns. For example after 42.♖c2 ♖d5 43.♖e2 ♖a5 44.♔b1 ♖h5 45.♖e1 c2+ 46.♔c1 ♔c3 it's mate in three more moves.

Torre was not done with needlessly chastising himself. His final comment was "If we are to learn anything from this game, let it raise our appreciation of beauty in chess. Let us endeavor to curb our impulse for forced brilliancy; for to give it rein would retard our development if not altogether deform it. Furthermore, we may render incongruous that which is inherently beautiful." One must wonder if this tendency toward overly harsh self-criticism contributed to Torre's eventual breakdown and withdrawal from chess.

Games from the International Tournament at Baden-Baden

The front page of the February 1925 *American Chess Bulletin* announced:
Copies of the program of the forthcoming international chess masters' tournament at Baden-Baden, Germany, have been received from Dr. S. Tarrasch of Munich, the director of the congress. The competitors, of whom it is planned to have twenty, will meet on April 15 to draw their numbers on which the pairings will be based. Play will begin on Thursday, April 16, and will continue until May 15. The tournament will take place in the rooms of the Casino under the auspices of the Municipal Health Administration ... In addition, all participants will receive free board and lodging in first class hotels.

The March 1925 *ACB* went on at greater length:
With a full entry list of twenty competitors assured, not to mention a number that are on the waiting list, and about fifteen different countries represented, the stage is all set for the opening of the international chess masters' tournament at Baden-Baden on April 15. Excepting Capablanca and Dr. Lasker, the pick of the talent of Europe and America will be engaged and for a full four weeks, up to May 15, when it is expected the congress will end, enthusiasts in the four quarters of the globe will look with forward with eager expectancy to the results as cabled from the scene of action.

As this is being written, Frank J. Marshall and Carlos Torre, who sailed from New York on the good Steamship Antonia of the Cunard Line on March 28, have about completed their ocean voyage and are due to land at Cherbourg, whence, by way of Paris, they will travel to Baden-Baden, to be on hand in ample time for the opening of the congress. The doings of these two representatives of the Western Hemisphere will be followed closely from day to day with especial interest and the reason for this one need not go far to seek.

It is an open secret here that Marshall, in view of his long experience and particularly because of his splendid showing in the New York tournament of 1924[1] is favored strongly to win the contest at Baden-Baden. It is a good deal to expect of the United States champion, for the cream of European skill will be pitted against him but he has accomplished even greater things before. So far as Torre is concerned, this youth makes his international debut under most auspicious circumstances. He certainly earned his spurs before leaving

1 Marshall scored 11-9 (+6 -4 =10) to place 4th of 11, behind only Lasker, Capablanca and Alekhine.

New York and, after what he accomplished in one short year after his arrival from New Orleans, no one can deny that he of all American players next to Marshall is well qualified to contend for international honors and to do it with credit to himself and the company of devotees that believed in him and sent him over.

Lacking in the hard experience so essential as a rule to success in a meeting of the masters, Torre went over about as well equipped in the matter of theoretical knowledge of the game as could well be expected. It will not surprise those who have watched him the closest if he readily holds his own at this first attempt to view with the leaders of the chess world, or even carry off one of the prizes. Of all the twenty entered this talented player seems to be the man of destiny and, in a measure, recalls the departure from these shores, nearly seventy years ago, of an illustrious son of New Orleans, whose praises are being sung until this very day.

Game 33

Torre-Alekhine

Baden-Baden 1925, round 1,

English Opening [A39]

The level of competition faced by Torre took a quantum leap upwards at Baden-Baden, where he met most of the world's best. Of the 21 contestants, ten — Alekhine, Rubinstein, Bogoljubow, Tartakower, Marshall, Nimzovich, Spielmann, Réti, Grünfeld, and Tarrasch — were, would be, or had been among the world's top ten.

Chief among them was Alexander Alekhine (1892-1946, historical Elo 2690), who would win the world title from Capablanca in 1927. He had ranked among the world's elite since his 3rd place at St. Petersburg 1914 (behind Lasker and Capablanca), but as of 1925 he had not yet had a truly dominating performance in a major international tournament. Baden-Baden was to be the first of many such for him. But Torre gives him a surprisingly tough time, refuting *extempore* a dubious opening novelty.

1.d4 ♘f6 2.♘f3 c5

Inviting White to play 3.d5 and establish a Benoni-style formation. In the earliest games reaching this position — Schlechter-Blackburne, Vienna 1898, and Charousek-Chigorin, Cologne 1898 — 3.e3 was played, but 3.d5 soon became the norm after Capablanca-Mieses, 1st match game, Berlin, 1913 (1-0, 27), and Rubinstein-Tarrasch,

Berlin 1918 (1-0, 51). With his next move, Torre shows he prefers to transpose into a variation of the English.

3.c4

Seen only once before, in Michell-Blake, 17th British Ch, Southport 1924 (½-½, 44). Alekhine seems to have liked what he saw here, as he reached the same position, by 1.c4 c5 2.♘f3 ♘f6 3.c4, in a later round of this tournament, against Sämisch (1-0, 52).

3...c×d4 4.♘×d4 ♘c6

Other moves are perfectly playable here, for example 4...g6 5.♘c3 d5 6.c×d5 ♘×d5 7.♘db5 ♘×c3 8.♕×d8+ ♔×d8 9.♘×c3 ♘c6, and though he cannot castle, Black has a satisfactory position (Szabó-Benko, 10th Hungarian Ch, Budapest 1954, ½-½, 16).
Also playable are 4...e6 and 4...d5. Against Alekhine in the 11th round, Sämisch played 4...b6 5.♘c3 ♗b7 6.♗g5 ♘e4.

5.♘c3 g6 6.g3 ♕b6?!

A move never seen before in master play, nor would it be seen again until Konstantinov-Stankov, Bulgarian Ch, Sofia 1973! And with good reason: in 31 games, ChessBase shows White scoring +16 -5 =10 against it. The black Queen will not be entirely happy on this square, as will quickly be seen. Better 6...d6 or 6...♗g7.

7.♘b3 ♘a5?!

Alekhine, somewhat typically for him, still avoids the routine and natural 7...♗g7.
But his experiment here might well have blown up in his face.

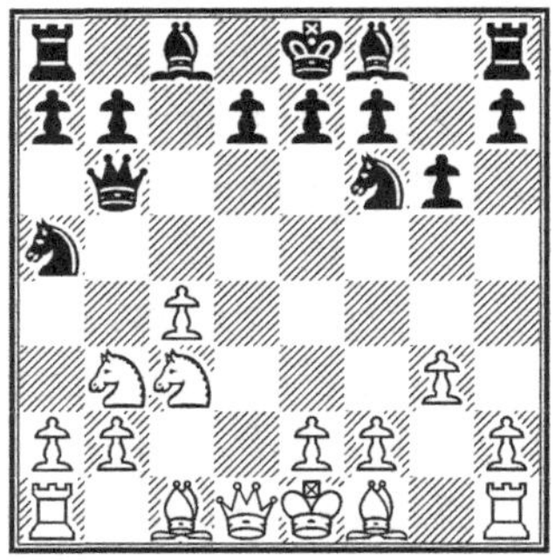

8.♗e3

Not bad, but much stronger was 8.♗g5! ♘×b3 9.a×b3 ♕c6 10.♕d4!:

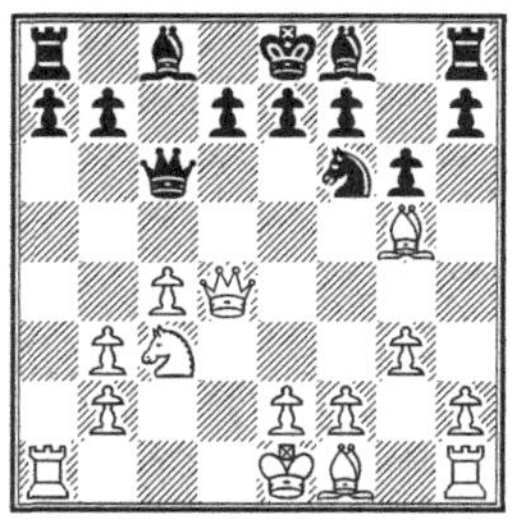

Now not 10...♕×h1? 11.♗×f6 e×f6 12.♕×f6 d6 (Forced; if 12...♖g8?? 13.♕e5+ ♔d8 14.♘d5 and Black has no defense against 15.♕f6+ ♔e8 16.♘c7# except at grievous material cost.) 13.♕×h8 ♗h3 14.0–0–0 ♗×f1 15.♕d4 and wins (+4.12/22).
Necessary would be 10...♗g7 11.♘d5 ♔f8□ 12.♗×f6 ♗×f6 13.♘×f6 e×f6 14.♖g1 and White might be said to have a strategically won game due to Black's weak d-pawn (+1.72/24).

8...♕d8?

Correct was 8...♕c6 9.♘×a5 (9.♖g1? ♘×c4∓) 9...♕×h1 10.♘b5

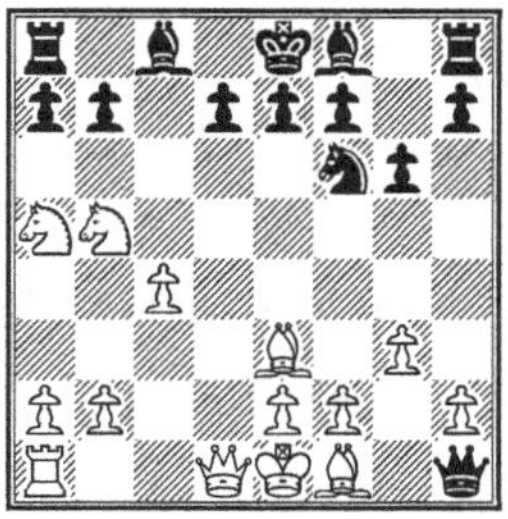

Trying now to save the Queen's Rook is worse than futile: 10...♔d8? 11.♕d2 ♗g7 12.♗×a7 d6 13.0–0–0 ♘e4 14.♕e3 and White's multiple threats force Black to give up the Rook anyway: 14...♖×a7 15.♕×a7 ♕×h2 16.♘×b7+ etc. (+5.68/25).

Therefore Black must play 10...♗g7 11.♘c7+ ♔f8 12.♘×a8 b6 with a complicated, roughly even game (+0.30/24).

9.♘×a5 ♕×a5

All Alekhine's ill-advised experiment has accomplished is to give White a nice lead in development.

10.♗g2 ♗g7 11.0–0 0–0

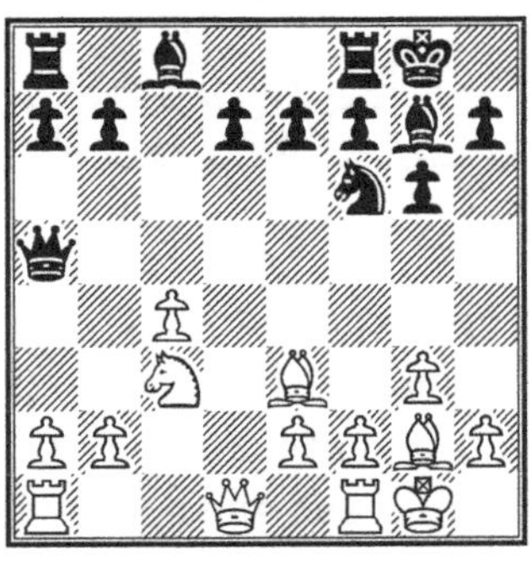

12.♗d4

This indicates Torre is playing for a draw. He could have retained or even increased his lead in development with, say, 12.♕d2 d6 13.♖fd1 ♕c7 14.♖ac1 (+1.72/24).

12...d6 13.♘d5

Definitely drawish. Worth considering was 13.♗×f6 ♗×f6 14.♘d5 △ 15.♘×f6+ e×f6, damaging Black's pawn structure.

13...♘×d5 14.♗×d5 ½-½

Here Torre offered a draw. His position is good enough that Alekhine did not hesitate an instant to accept.

In the Baden-Baden press, and later in the tournament book, the young Mexican master was severely criticized for his tendency to offer draws in superior positions, which some labeled "a lack of self-confidence on Torre's part." However, it is natural that a youth of barely 19 years would play somewhat nervously in his first strong international tournament. Torre also offered draws in superior positions against Réti, Marshall, and Rosselli.

It is worth noting that after this round, Alekhine won nine consecutive games to take an insurmountable lead. This was one of the best tournaments of his life, along with San Remo 1930 and Bled 1931. It would prompt Tartakower to write "Lasker was champion, Capablanca is champion, and Alekhine plays like a world champion ought to play."

Game 34
te Kolsté-Torre

Baden-Baden 1925, round 2

French Defense [C12]

Jan Willem te Kolsté (1874-1936) was a Dutch master whose playing career was mainly confined to his own country. He played in close to a dozen Dutch Championships, and actually won the title in 1907. However, he had relatively little impact outside the Netherlands. His impact was perhaps least at Baden-Baden, where he finished dead last, 4½ points behind the next lowest competitor. Out of 20 games he managed 3 draws and stoically suffered 17 losses, including the following game, which, interestingly, he might have won.

The first nine moves are identical to Games 3 and 5 of this book.

1.e4 e6 2.d4 d5 3.♘c3 ♘f6 4.♗g5 ♗b4 5.♘ge2 d×e4 6.a3 ♗e7 7.♗×f6 g×f6 8.♘×e4 b6 9.♘2c3 ♗b7

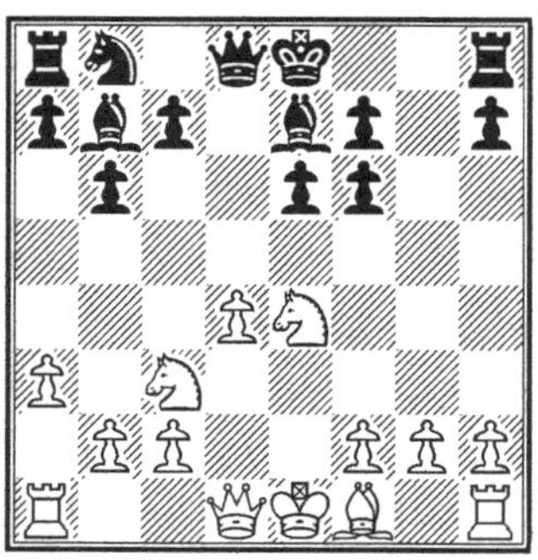

So far as in Game 5, Samuels-Torre, which continued 10.♗b5+. White here tries something new.

10.♕f3

This is the strongest line available to White in this variation of the McCutcheon. The manner in which Torre counters White's scheme of development has long been considered classic, and furthermore is mentioned in opening manuals as the model method against Wolf's idea of 5.♘ge2. But as we will see, this reputation is unwarranted.

10...c6 11.0–0–0

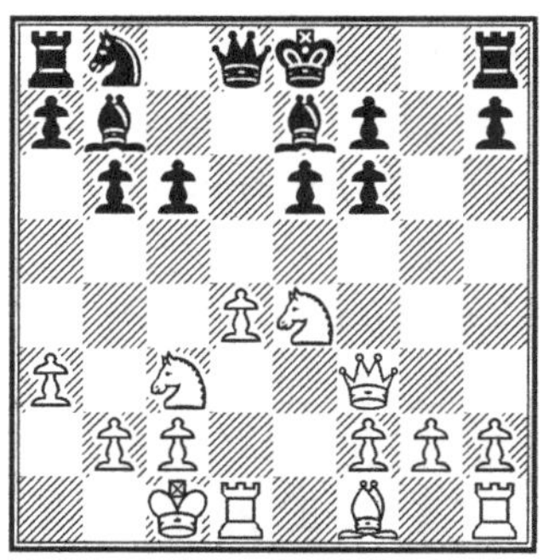

11...f5?!

Prematurely committal. It might have been preferable to temporize with 11...♘d7, a move Black is going to make in any event, and not advance the f-pawn until White has developed his King's Bishop. If 12.♗c4, then 12...f5, but if 12.♗d3 then 12...♕c7 and castling queenside.

12.♘g3 ♘d7

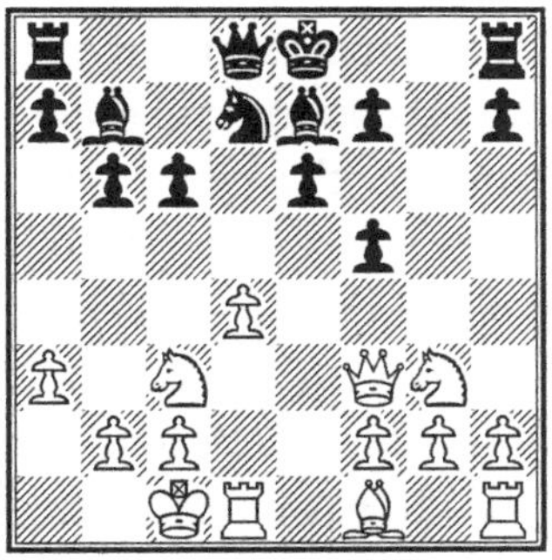

13.♗c4

More aggressive was 13.♗d3!, to be followed in most variations by 14.♗×f5!. For example 13...♘f6 14.♗×f5 and Black dare not play 14...e×f5? in view of 15.♖he1 ♔f8 16.♘×f5 ♗d6 17.d5! ♘×d5 (or 17...c×d5? 18.♘b5 +4.82/23) 18.♘e4 ♗e5 19.c4+– (+4.60/26). Relatively best after 13.♗d3 would be 13...♕c7 14.♗×f5 0–0–0 15.♗d3 ♘f6, stoically accepting the loss of the pawn (+1.22/24).) ChessBase shows only three games in which 13.♗d3 was played. Black replied 13...♕c7 in all three, but in none did White then dare 14.♗×f5!. With the text White envisions a different Bishop sacrifice, on e6, but this proves unsound.

13...♕c7?

At this point in the first edition, we wrote "Black's play in this game is considered, even today, virtually impossible to improve upon." Alas, under the cold scrutiny of the Lidless Eye, we know now this is no longer true. Stockfish much prefers 13...♘f6 with a nearly even game, and finds considerable fault with the text, as will be explained next note.

14.♖he1 ♘f6

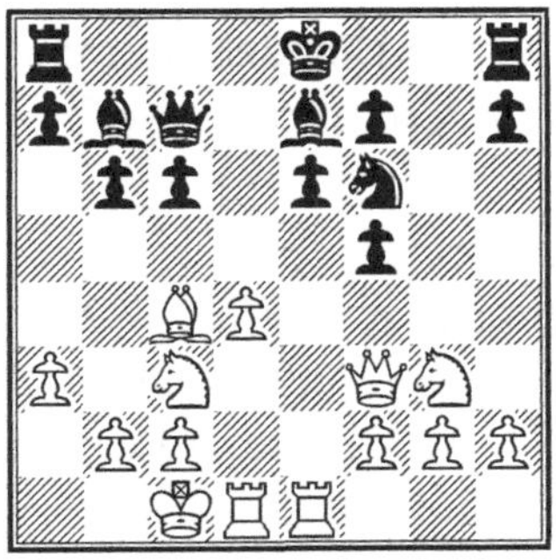

15.♕e2?![1]

Te Kolsté waits a move too long! Now was the time for his Bishop sac: 15.♗×e6! f×e6 16.♖×e6. If then 16...0–0–0? 17.♘×f5 ♘d5 18.♘×d5 ♗g5+ 19.♘de3+–. Therefore Black must play 16...0–0 17.♘×f5 ♗d8 18.d5! c×d5 19.♘b5,

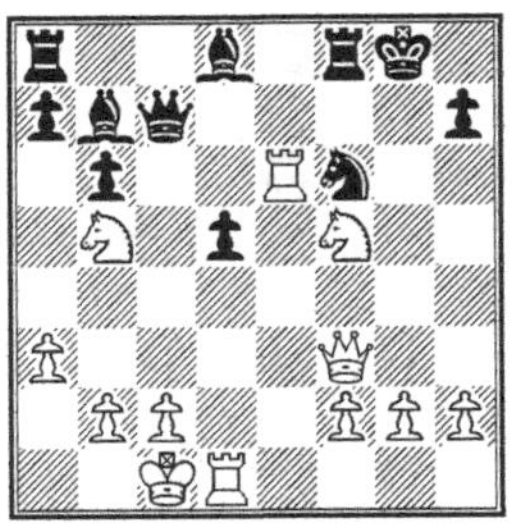

1 The first edition erroneously gave 15.♕e3 here. That of course is bad due to 15...f4 16.♕e5 ♕×e5 17.d×e5 f×g3 18.e×f6 g×f2 19.♖f1 ♗×f6 20.♘e4 ♗e7 21.♖×f2 ♖g8∓.

when he has only the unpleasant choice between 19...♕×h2 20.♘bd6 ♗c8 21.♖×f6 ♗×f6 22.♕×d5+ ♗e6 23.♕×e6+ ♔h8 24.♘f7+ ♖×f7 25.♕×f7 ♕f4+ 26.♔b1 ♕×f5 27.♖d6 ♕×f2 28.♖×f6 ♕×g2 29.♕c7 (+4.66/23), or 19...d4 20.♘×c7 ♗×f3 21.♘×a8 ♗×d1 22.♔×d1 ♘g4 23.f3 ♘e3+ 24.♘×e3 d×e3 25.c4 (+2.30/24).

15...0–0–0?
Another non-model move. Better 15...♖g8 △16...♔f8.

16.♗×e6+?
The losing move. Rather than this now unsound sac, White could have tried 16.♘×f5, which leads to considerable complications, *viz.* 16...♕f4+ 17.♘e3 ♖×d4 18.♗d3 ♕×h2 19.♘f5 ♕f4+ (19...e×f5?? 20.♗×f5+) 20.♔b1 ♖d7 21.g3 ♕c7 22.♘×e7+ ♖×e7 23.♕f3 ♘e8, when White has compensation for the pawn (+0.70/24) but the issue is still in doubt.

16...f×e6 17.♕×e6+ ♖d7 18.♘×f5 ♗d8

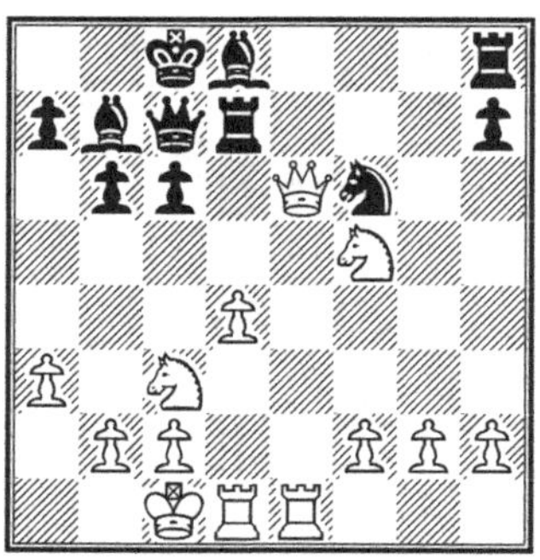

Generally speaking, it is inadvisable to trade a minor piece for three pawns unless one's extra pawns can then quickly take an active part in the game. Such an exchange is generally considered advantageous in the endgame, but this is the middle game. Even in the endgame there are exceptions; for example, the 22nd game of the 1927 Capablanca-Alekhine match, which was adjourned with Alekhine having Rook, Knight and six pawns against Rook, two Knights, and three pawns. Alekhine even had three passed pawns and Capablanca none. Everyone thought Alekhine would win, but when the Cuban was asked if he did not fear the extra pawns he replied "Oh, no big deal, I'll eat them all!" When the game was resumed, Capablanca recovered his pawns one by one, reaching an ending of Rook versus Rook and Knight which Alekhine almost lost. In the game at hand, White is in no position to advance his extra pawns any time soon, while Black has excellent open lines for his Rooks and Bishop pair. Black's game now practically plays itself, making lengthy commentary superfluous.

19.♘e4 ♘×e4 20.♖×e4 ♔b8! 21.g3
More logical, in terms of both advancing pawns and supporting the Knight, was 21.g4, but it would make little difference.

21...♗c8 22.♕h6 ♖f7 23.♘e3
If 23.g4 ♖hf8 △24...♗×f5 25.g×f5 ♖×f5.

23...♖×f2

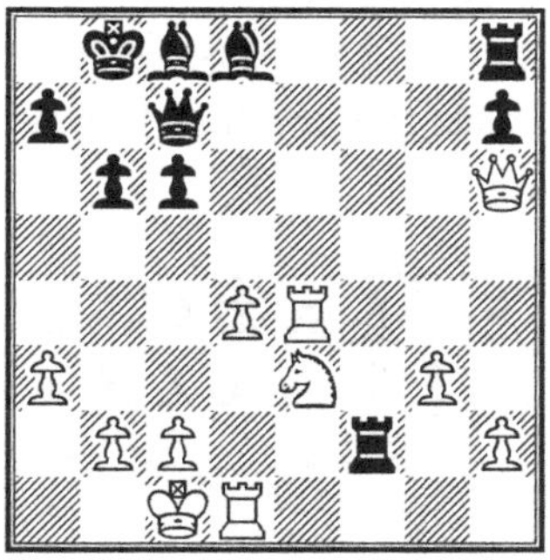

24.c3??

Such a move with an enemy Rook on one's second rank is like jumping into a lake from fear of rain. The *Deutsche Schachblätter* suggested here 24.♘g4, but even so White loses quickly via 24...♖g8! (△25...♗g5+) 25.♕e3 ♖ff8 26.♕e2 ♗f5 27.♖f4 ♗g5 etc.

24...♖g8 25.d5 ♗g5 26.♕×c6 ♕×c6 27.d×c6 ♗f5 0-1

So Torre's first two games at Baden-Baden were almost exact opposites: one where he refuted an unsound opening novelty and drew against a top grandmaster, and this, where he played unsoundly but won due to the incompetence of his low-ranking opponent.

Game 35

Torre-Réti

Baden-Baden 1925, round 3,

Alekhine's Defense [B02]

Torre might have had a kindred spirit in Richard Réti (1889-1929) of Czechoslovakia, like him a player to whom artistry and beauty were more important than winning or losing. Réti once lost by letting his clock expire, because he was absorbed in composing in his head an endgame study, rather than attending to the game at hand. Despite this occasional impracticality, Réti was a formidable opponent, his peak strength estimated at 2550. The year before, at New York 1924, he had dealt world champion Capablanca his first loss in eight years. A seminal openings theoretician and an excellent writer as well as player, Réti's life and career were tragically short; he died of scarlet fever at age 40. As we will see, his absentmindedness surfaced again in this game, which our analysis reveals to be rather a comedy of errors by both contestants, as well as by Tartakower, whose annotations we quote at certain points.

1.e4 ♘f6 2.e5 ♘d5 3.♘c3

A very aggressive variation, which opens up the game with gain of tempo, and eliminates the black King's Knight, so that if Black castles short his King will be less well protected and more exposed to attack. Torre had a great liking for openings in which his own queenside pieces were exchanged for his opponent's kingside pieces. For example, the opening he chose for Game 23 (Torre-Stolzenberg), 1.d4 f5 2.♗g5 ♘f6 3.♗×f6, shows this tendency. It is even more evident in an opening of which we will see several examples, his own Torre Attack, 1.d4 ♘f6 2.♘f3 e6 3.♗g5, in which White trades his Bishop for the ♘f6, then plays ♘b1-d2 to transfer his Queen's Knight to the kingside. All these development schemes produce a middle game in which White has more pieces than Black on the King's wing.

3...♘×c3 4.d×c3

Capture with the b-pawn produces a different kind of position, with which the late Mikhail Tal was very successful at prosecuting attacks involving a rapid advance of the f-pawn. See for example Tal-Podgaets, Sochi 1970, and Tal-Gedevanishvili, Poti 1970.

4...♘c6

More natural and effective would be 4...d6 immediately, as Réti himself played in later games in this line in this same tournament. Other alternatives are 4...d5 (Capablanca) and 4...g6 (Korchnoi). It bears mentioning that the text was played by a young Boris Spassky, against Nezhmetdinov in the 26th USSR Ch, Tbilisi 1959 (0-1, 40).

5.♘f3 d6 6.♗b5!

A TN from Torre. In the 1920s the theory of Alekhine's Defense was in its infancy, and it was possible to produce many novelties within the first ten moves.

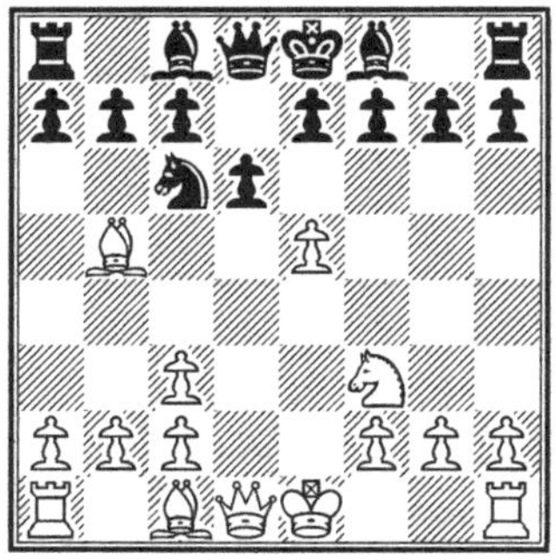

6...a6

In Keres-Schmid, Zürich 1961, the German GM tried 6...♗d7, but with no better result after 7.♕e2 ♘×e5 (△7...a6) 8.♘×e5 d×e5 9.♕×e5 c6?! 10.♗c4 ♕b8?! 11.♕e4 e6 12.♗g5! h6 13.♗h4 ♗d6 14.0–0–0 ♕c7 15.♕d4± (1-0, 29).

7.♗×c6+ b×c6 8.♗f4 ♖b8 9.b3 e6

Black has an uncomfortable game. As a solution Stockfish proposes the odd-looking 9...f6 10.e×f6 g×f6, when it sees White as having nothing better than 11.♘e5!? f×e5 12.♕h5+ ♔d7 13.♗×e5, and now not 13...♖g8? 14.♕×h7 ♖b5 15.f4±, but 13...♖b5! and a draw by perpetual check: 14.♕g4+ ♔e8 (14...e6?? 15.♗×h8+−) 15.♕h5+ ♔d7 16.♕g4+ etc.

White need not play into this line, but the engine indicates Black will be at least even, whatever White tries.

10.♕d3!

White's play is very instructive: on the one hand he prevents 10...♗d7, on the other he threatens 11.♕c4 and 12.♕a4, striking at Black's weak pawns. This obliges Réti to advance his d-pawn, ending the central tension and leaving White with an excellent game.

10...d5

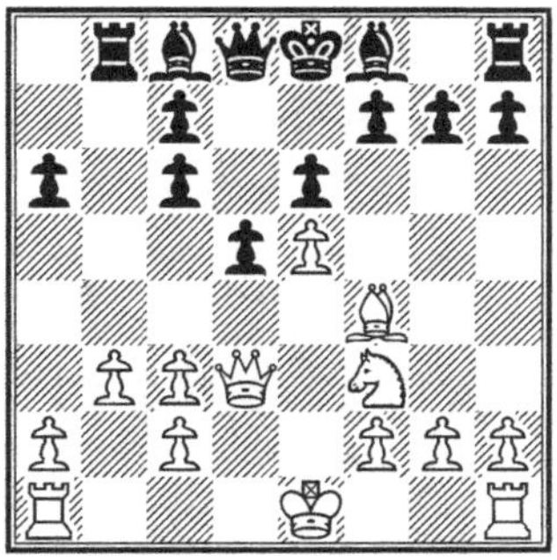

11.0–0?!

An old saying goes "Castle because you must or because you will, but not just because you can." Seemingly natural, this move will make it hard for the King's Rook to take any meaningful part in the game.

A more aggressive possibility was 11.h4, intending 12.♖h3 or 12.h5 and 13.♖h4, in either case bringing the Rook by this unorthodox route into a strong kingside attacking position. A sample continuation: 11...♗e7 12.♖h3 f5 13.♖g3 0–0 14.♗h6 ♖f7 15.♘g5 ♗×g5 16.♗×g5 ♕e8 17.h5 with good prospects (+1.68/27). White's King will be perfectly safe on his home square for the foreseeable future.

11...♕d7 12.♖ad1 a5

Within the confines of his difficult position, Réti tries to avoid any further deterioration in the short term. The text aims at a regrouping of his pieces, starting with ...♖a8 and ...♗a6. Somewhat better perhaps was 12...c5 △ 13...♗b7.

13.♖fe1

This will be, alas, the last move this Rook makes. Still, White's position is much the better one.

13...♖a8

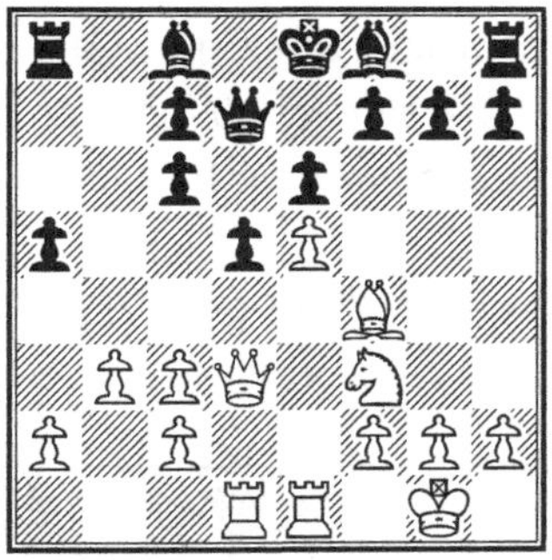

14.♘g5

White has a great advantage in development, but in this kind of position that does not count for much unless there is a way to crack the center rapidly and open up the game. The only pawn break available to White is c3-c4, which he could have essayed immediately: 14.c4 and

(a) 14...♗a6 15.♘d4 c5 16.♘e2 ♗e7 17.♕g3 g5□ 18.♗e3 (if 18.♗×g5?! ♖g8) 18...♗b7 19.f4 with a strong initiative (+2.15/23); or

(b) 14...h6 15.h4 ♗b7 16.♘d4 ♗e7 17.♕g3 g6 18.♘f3 (+1.81/27); or
(c) 14...♗b7 15.♘g5 h6 16.♘e4 ♖d8 17.♕h3 ♕e7 18.♘c3 ♖d7 19.♖d3 intending, based on circumstances, either ♖d3-g3, or ♖e1-d1 (+1.93/26).

However, Torre prefers to defer the c-pawn advance, and when he makes it, the aim is not to open the game, but to blockade the queenside. This proves an ineffective strategy.

14...h6 15.♘h3
Also playable was 15.♘e4, since if 15...d×e4?? 16.♕×e4 ♕e7 17.♕×c6+ etc. However, after 15...♕e7 White would have to play 16.♘g3, and Torre wants that square for his Queen.

15...♗a6 16.♕g3 g6 17.♗e3 ♗e7 18.♘f4 c5?

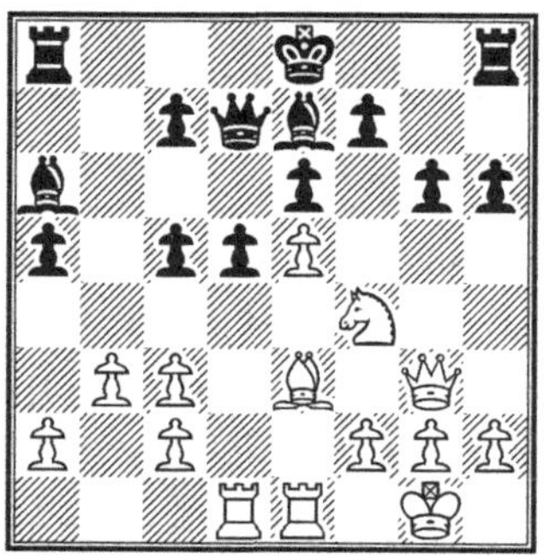

Aside from putting a piece *en prise*, this is about the worst move Black could have made. Almost anything else was better.

19.f3?
But Torre does not see his chance. This innocent-looking move loses most of his carefully crafted advantage. Why he played it is not clear; perhaps he felt it was a wise prophylactic measure against the impending possibility of Black forming a mate-threatening ♕c6-and-♗b7 battery. Also he soon uses f2 as a retreat for his Bishop. But why think defensively in such a dominant position? The time for the c-pawn's advance was now: 19.c4!, and if 19...d4? 20.c3 ♕c6 21.c×d4 c×d4 22.♖×d4 (+3.86/24). Relatively best would be 19...c6 20.♘d3,

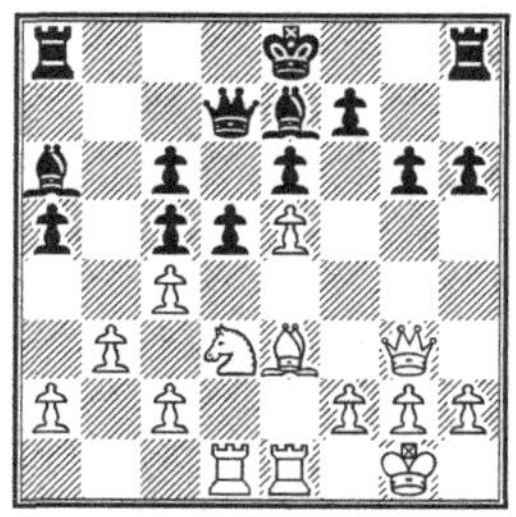

and now not 20...d4? 21.♗c1 ♔f8 22.h4 ♔g7 23.h5 g5 24.♖e4 ♖h7 25.♖g4 ♔h8 26.f4 ♖g8 27.♘f2 ♖hg7 28.♘e4 g×f4 29.♕×f4

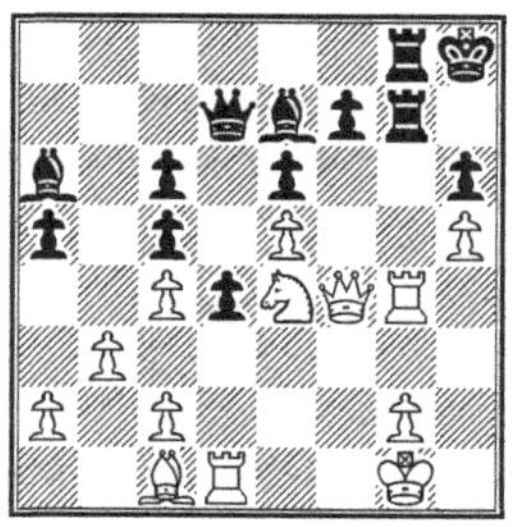

29...♕d8 (if 29...♖×g4?? 30.♕×h6#, or 29...♖h7?? 30.♖×g8+ ♔×g8 31.♘f6+ ♗×f6 32.e×f6 ♔f8 33.♗a3 and mate in 12) 30.♕×h6+ ♖h7 31.♕f4 ♖×g4 32.♕×g4 (+7.86).

Best instead is (from previous diagram) 20...♕a7 21.h4 ♔d7 22.c3 ♔c7 23.♘b2 Suddenly the queenside has become the theater of action. 23...♖ad8 24.♕f3 ♖h7 25.♘a4 g5 26.h5 ♖g7 27.♕g4,

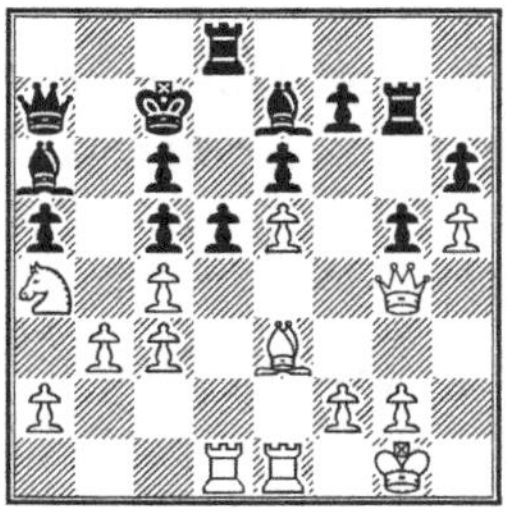

and now not 27...d×c4?? 28.♖×d8 ♔×d8 (28...♗×d8 29.♗×c5+−) 29.♖d1+ ♔c7 30.♖d6!! ♗×d6 31.e×d6+ ♔b8 (31...♔×d6?? 32.♗×c5+) 32.♘×c5 and it's a slaughter (+7.23). Relatively best is 27...♖gg8, and while no immediate breakthrough is apparent, White's increased positional advantage most definitely is, and victory a virtual certainty. Stockfish rates this at +3.55/25.

Returning to the game:

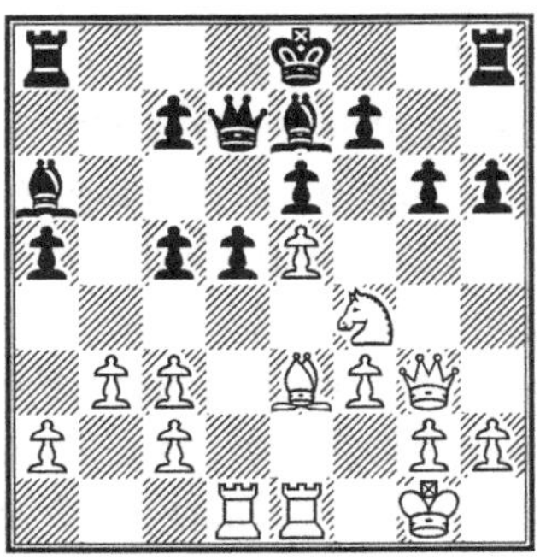

19...♕c6 20.c4

This now has nothing like the effect it would have had one move earlier. Tartakower, annotating the game in the Belgian magazine *L' Echiquier*, completely missed the potential impact of 19.c4!, and now comments fatuously "Marvelous! This move begins a notable blockading maneuver by the conductor of the white pieces." Among world-class masters, there has been perhaps no worse annotator than Tartakower.

20...d4

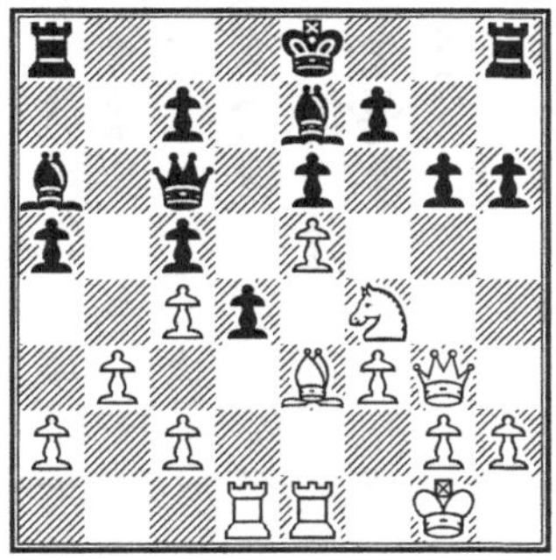

And this move has much more effect, because with the black Queen on c6 the d-pawn is no longer pinned. At least Tartakower did see that 20...d×c4?? would lose to 21.♘×g6! f×g6 22.♕×g6+ ♔f8 23.♗×h6+ etc., and he correctly observes that "In his following moves, Black must be very alert to the possibility of the Knight sacrifice at g6."

21.♗f2

Here 21.♘×g6? would fail: 21...f×g6 22.♕×g6+ ♔d7 23.♗×h6 ♖ag8 24.♗g7□ ♕a8 25.c3 ♖h4! 26.c×d4 c×d4 27.g3 c5! 28.g×h4 ♕e8 29.♕×e8+ ♔×e8 30.♖e4 ♖×g7+ with advantage to Black (-1.84/25).

21...♗b7?!

This could have thrown the advantage back to White. Best was 21...♖d8.

22.a4?!

Missing 22.c3! g5 23.♘e2 d3 (if 23...d×c3 24.♘×c3 (+1.95/24), and White stands better after either 24.♖×d3 ♖d8 25.♘c1 (+1.61/24) or 24.♘c1 ♖d8 25.♘×d3 (+2.37/27). After the text the game is quite even.

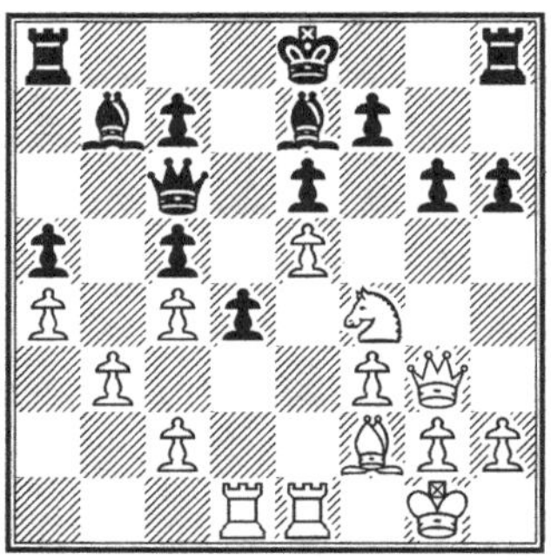

22...♔f8?

Black was right to avoid 22...0–0?? 23.♘×g6 f×g6 24.♕×g6+ ♔h8 25.♕×h6+ ♔g8 26.♕g6+ ♔h8 27.♖e4 etc., but the text move brings out more fatuity from Tartakower. Giving the text an exclam, he writes "In this difficult position, Black evolves a profound plan, the purpose of which is to safeguard the King by transferring him to h7." As we will soon see, this "profound" plan is anything but; correct again was 22...♖d8.

However, Réti, forgetting that his Queen's Rook had already been moved, actually castled long here. Were this legal, it would have been Black's best move, but being illegal, he was obliged by rule to move his King. But of the three moves then available to Black, best was not 22...♔f8 but 22...♔d7!, with the likely continuation 23.c3 g5 24.♘e2 ♖ad8 25.c×d4 ♔c8 26.♖d3 c×d4 27.♖ed1 ♕e8, when Black has "castled by hand," and though he will soon lose a pawn, he has freed his position and has a fighting chance (+0.95/27).

23.♖d3

Again, 23.c3 was best.

23...♔g7?

And again 23...♖d8 was best.

24.♘h5+ ♔h7

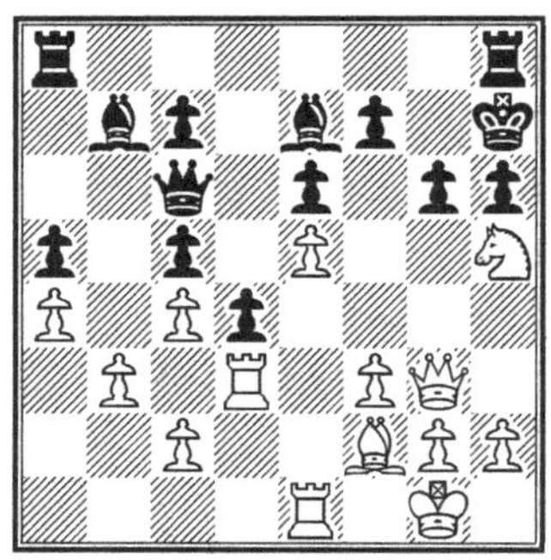

25.♕f4?!

Torre again misses a win, which could be had by 25.♘f6+! ♗×f6 26.e×f6 ♖hg8 27.♖e5 (Finally getting this Rook into the fight!) 27...g5□ (This must be played before White gets 28.h4 in.) 28.c3 (a bit stronger than 28.h4 g×h4 29.♕×h4 ♖g6) 28...d×c3 29.♖×c3 ♖ad8 30.♖c1□ ♕d7 31.♖×c5 and White is winning (+4.28/28).

25...♖hf8?

Giving White another chance to win! The best defense was 25...f5 26.♘f6+ ♔g7 (if 26...♗xf6? 27.exf6 g5 28.♕e5+−) 27.c3 g5 28.♕c1 ♖hd8 29.h4 ♔g6 30.cxd4 cxd4 31.♖xd4 ♖xd4 32.♗xd4 and though Black has lost a pawn, his King is safe and he can still fight.

26.♘f6+! ♗xf6

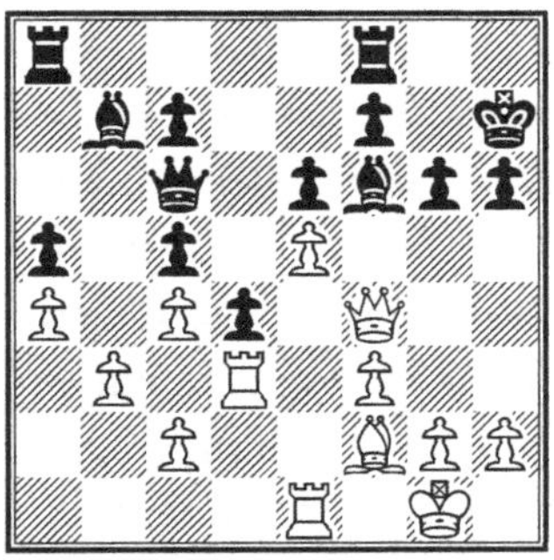

27.♕xf6?

Missing White's last chance to win. We quote Tartakower again, for once making sense: "White expects to win a pawn by the transfer of his ♖e1 to e4 and h4. Nonetheless, 27.exf6! would have been more effective, because despite the fact that it results in a position with Bishops of opposite color, White would have excellent winning chances by attacking Black's weak pawns (a5, c7, and c5)."

After 27.exf6 the two least evils are 27...♖g8 28.♕e5 ♕b6 (discouraging 29.c3) 29.g4 g5 30.♗g3 ♖ac8 31.♔f2 ♗a8 32.♖h1 ♕d6 33.♕e2 ♕c6 34.h4 ♖g6 35.♗e5+− (+6.61/24), and 27...g5 28.♕e5, which will eventually enter lines similar or identical to 27...♖g8.

27...g5! 28.♗g3 ♖g8! 29.♕xf7+ ♖g7 30.♕h5 ♖f8 31.h3 ½-½

The game's final outcome has a story behind it. The tournament schedule called for the game to be adjourned two hours for dinner and a brief rest. 31.h3 was Torre's sealed move. Certainly it is not a very good move (better was 31.♖e4), as it increases the incipient danger to the white Queen, which can now be threatened with a maneuver such as 31...♖f5 32.♕g4 ♕e8! followed by ...h6-h5. Torre, worried over this detail, proposed a draw, which Réti immediately accepted, not without some surprise, for the Czech master had done a quick adjournment analysis and concluded that his game was irretrievably lost. As it turns out, the danger to White's Queen is more apparent than real. After 31...♖f5 32.♕g4 ♕e8 33.♗f2! h5 34.♕g3 she would have been out of danger, but despite being a pawn ahead White had virtually no chance to win (-0.38/29). Considering the many errors by both sides, a draw seems the fair outcome.

Game 36

Treybal-Torre

Baden-Baden 1925, round 4

French Defense [C00]

The Czechoslovakian jurist Dr. Karel Treybal (1885-1941, historical Elo 2490) had quite an eventful life. During World War I he was a captain in the Czech Legion, a volunteer force fighting for the Entente against the Central Powers, with the goal of political independence from the Austro-Hungarian Empire for the Czech and Slovak peoples. After the Bolshevik Revolution and Russia's surrender, the legion was stranded there while civil war between the Reds and Whites raged. Unable to return home by the shorter western route, Treybal and the legion eventually made it by rail across Siberia to Vladivostok on the Pacific coast, and finally returned home by ship via Suez. In chess Treybal was Czech champion in 1907 and co-champion in 1921. An avid amateur, he played in many tournaments, and though not usually a high prize-winner he defeated such greats as Tarrasch, Janowski, Maróczy, Marshall, Spielmann, Nimzovich, Vidmar, Ståhlberg, Euwe, Tartakower, and even Alekhine. He was, alas, a victim of the Nazis soon after they occupied his briefly independent country, a sad and unjust end for a good man.

In this tournament the Czech masters seemed to have cast a spell on Torre, as once again he obtained a better position a pawn ahead, and this time he not only failed to win, but lost badly.

1.e4 e6 2.♕e2

Chigorin's brainchild, which he played almost exclusively against the French over the years 1893-1907, scoring +26 -15 =10, with many top players among his victims. After his death it was taken up by the Czech master Hromadka, whose influence may explain his countryman Treybal trying it here. Though considered less than best by theory, it is still seen in high-level competition to this day, popping up in the games of Bronstein, Gheorghiu, Romanishin, Short, Morozevich, Karjakin, Bologan, Ivanchuk, Nakamura and Nepomniatchi, among others. Its main virtue is that it prevents 2...d5; its main drawback that on e2 the Queen hinders White's development.

2...♘c6 3.♘f3 e5

First seen in Chigorin-Teichmann and Chigorin-Albin, Hastings 1895, and later in Geus-te Kolsté, Scheveningen 1913. In slightly different form (3.♘c3) it appeared in Chigorin-Lasker, London 1899 (0-1, 42). Though the text seems a loss of tempo, that is offset by the fact that White must fianchetto his

King's Bishop, with equal or greater loss of time.

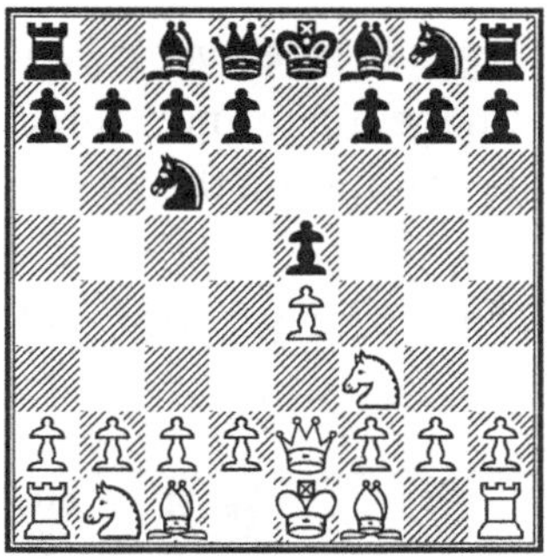

4.g3 ♗c5 5.♗g2 ♘ge7
Both players are winging it now; we could find no earlier game with this position, though of course Treybal may have analyzed it in his home preparation. In any event, the game is quite even.

6.d3 d6 7.♗e3 ♗g4 8.h3 ♗e6 9.♘bd2 ♘g6 10.♘b3 ♗b6

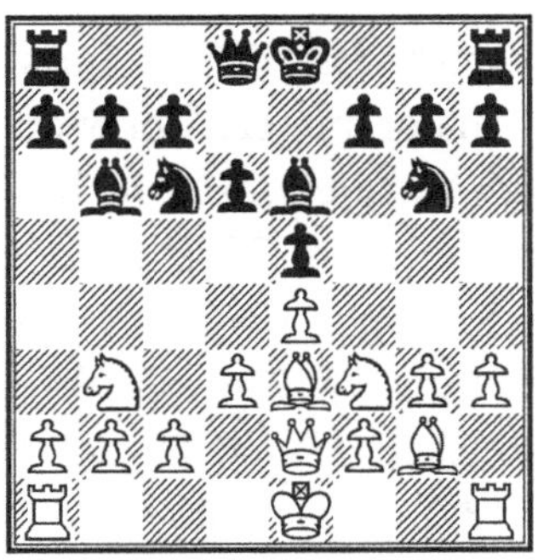

11.d4?
Difficult to explain, as it costs White a pawn with little apparent compensation. Better were 11.c3, 11.♖d1, 11.0–0, or even 11.0–0–0.

11...♗×b3 12.a×b3
A better way to lose a pawn was 12.d5 ♗×e3 13.f×e3 ♗×c2 14.♕×c2∓.

12...e×d4 13.♗g5 f6 14.♗d2 ♕e7
Giving Black the option of castling on either wing.

15.h4 ♘ge5 16.♘×e5 ♘×e5?!
Torre's first incomprehensible move in this accident-prone game. Obviously, after 16...d×e5 Black remains a pawn up with a sounder pawn structure.

17.♕b5+
White could have seized the initiative with 17.f4.

17...♕d7 18.♕×d7+ ♘×d7 19.f4 0–0 20.b4

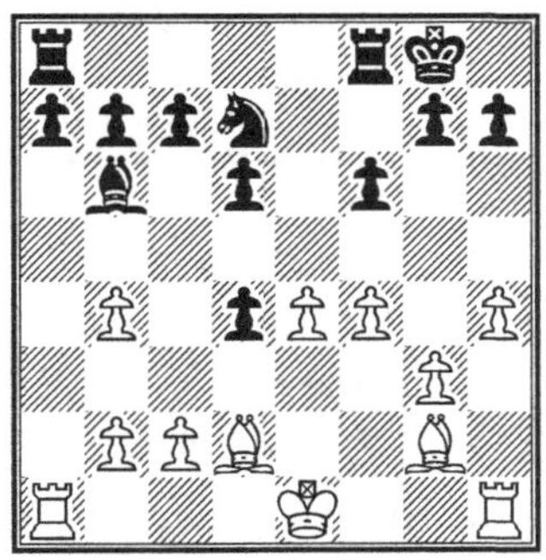

20...♖ae8
Better 20...f5, and if 21.e×f5 ♖ae8+ 22.♔f1 c6 23.g4?! ♘f6 24.♗f3 h5 25.g×h5 (25.g5?! ♘e4∓) 25...d5∓.

21.0–0–0 ♘b8?!
Apparently Torre's head was none too clear that day. The aimless peregrinations of this Knight waste time, accomplish nothing, and give

White the chance to activate his light-square Bishop.
Better, say, 21...♖e7 22.g4 ♖fe8 23.g5 c6 24.♖he1 (24.g×f6? ♘×f6 loses the e-pawn) 24...♗c7=.

22.g4 c5 23.♖de1 ♘c6 24.b5 ♘d8?
The Knight has spent three moves going from a bad square to a worse one. 24...♘a5, 24...♘e7, and 24...♘b4 were marginally better.

25.♗f1!

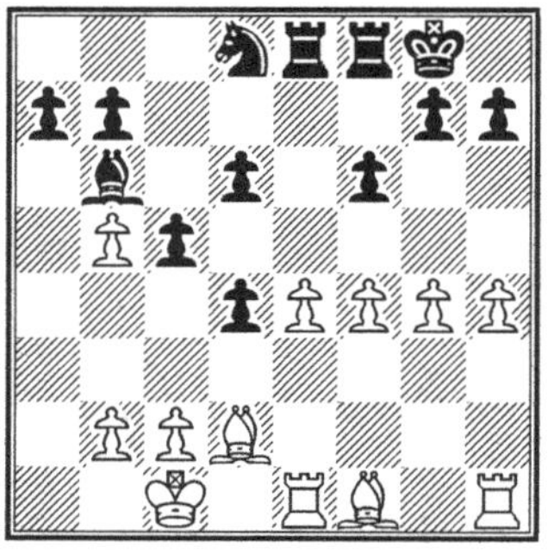

25...♔h8
25...d5!? would force the Bishop back to g2, since if 26.e×d5 ♖×e1+ 27.♗×e1 ♘f7 △28...♘d6 and Black is finally getting the Knight to a halfway-decent square.

26.♗c4 ♘e6?! 27.f5
Good, though 27.g5! was most energetic (+2.76/25).

27...♘d8 28.g5 ♘f7 29.g×f6 g×f6 30.♗d5 a6?!
Another subpar move. 30...♖e7 was a better way to defend the pawn.

31.b×a6 b×a6 32.♖h3!
Threatening to slide this Rook like an MX missile along the third rank to the a-, b- or g-file, wherever it can do the most damage. Torre's next three moves just pour gasoline on the fire.

32...♗d8? 33.♖g3 a5? 34.♖eg1 ♗e7

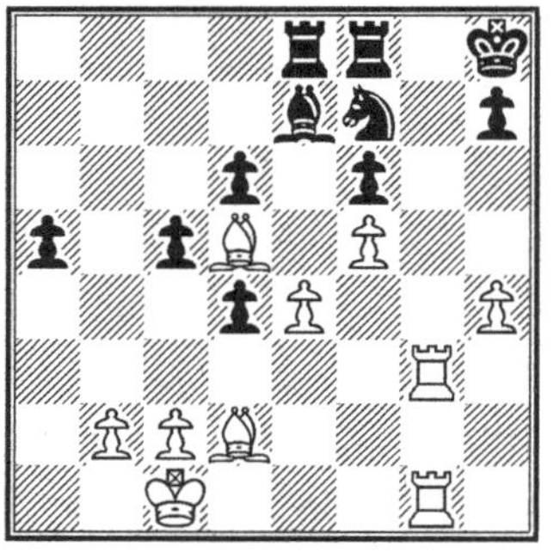

Stockfish's assessment has gone from about +2.50 to +6.50.

35.b3
Most direct was 35.♖g7 forcing the win of major material or worse, *viz.* 35...♘g5 36.♖×e7 ♖×e7 37.h×g5 f×g5 38.♗×g5+−, or 35...♖g8 36.♗×f7 ♖×g7 37.♖×g7 ♔×g7 38.♗×e8+−, or 35...♘e5 36.♗h6 ♗d8 37.♖d7 ♖g8 38.♖×g8+ ♖×g8 39.♗g7+ ♖×g7 40.♖×d8+ ♖g8 41.♖×g8#.
But White's position is now so strong that he can temporize before landing the *coup de grace*.

35...♖b8 36.♗×f7 ♖×f7 37.♗h6
Lack might as well have resigned now. Further comment is unnecessary.

37...d5 38.♗g7+ ♖×g7 39.♖×g7 ♗d6 40.e×d5 a4 41.♔d2 ♗h2 42.♖1g2 ♗f4+ 43.♔d3 a×b3 44.c×b3 ♖×b3+ 45.♔c4 ♖b8 46.♖d7 ♗h6 47.d6 ♗f4 48.♖a2 ♗h6 49.♖a3 ♗e3 50.♖aa7 ♖b4+ 51.♔×c5 ♖b8 52.♔c4 h5 53.♖h7+ ♔g8 54.♖ag7+ 1-0

One of Torre's worst performances. One wonders what was wrong that day, it is so far below his usual standard.

The young Mexican master recovered quickly from this unfortunate misstep, as in the 5th round he won a marvelous game against the English master Sir George Thomas.

Game 37

Torre-Thomas

Baden-Baden 1925, round 5

Pirc Defense [B08]

Sir George Alan Thomas (1881-1972, historical Elo 2470, IM title 1950) was, along with F.D. Yates, one of the few significant English chess players of the 1920s and '30s. Of aristocratic background (a baronet), Thomas was twice British champion (1923 and 1934), and represented England in Olympiads for both chess (seven times) and athletics, in the sport of badminton. He also excelled at tennis, playing at Wimbledon 1919-26. He was respected even more for his exemplary sportsmanship and sense of fair play (he even refused to analyze adjourned games as a point of honor). Though not usually a high prize-winner in international chess, he occasionally rose to great heights, as when he tied for first with Euwe and Flohr at Hastings 1934-35, ahead of Capablanca, Botvinnik, Lilienthal and four others.

1.d4 ♘f6 2.♘f3 g6 3.♘c3

Relatively new at the time (the first instance seems to have been Tartakower-Wahltuch, London 1922), this move had quite a vogue in the early 1920s, for example being played by Capablanca, Marshall and Edward Lasker at New York 1924. We already saw it played by Torre in games 4 and 16.

3...♗g7

Black chooses to enter the Pirc Defense, rather than play 3...d5 and prevent 4.e4.

4.e4 d6

At the time this opening did not really have a name; Alekhine in the New York 1924 tournament book called it just "Indian Defense," then a catch-all for almost anything that began 1.d4 ♘f6. Though it had been seen as far back as Schallop-Paulsen, Nuremberg

1883, it had received scant attention from theorists; for example the sixth edition of *Modern Chess Openings* (1939) gave it only one minor footnote, citing Tarrasch-Davidson, Semmering 1926, which had continued 4...0–0 5.♗g5 h6 6.♗f4 d6. So both players are now already on their own, and Sir George soon finds himself rather confused.

5.♗c4
Apart from the text White has at least three other good alternatives: 5.♗f4, 5.h3 and 5.♗g5.

5...0–0
Here 5...♘×e4 would be premature due to 6.♗×f7+ ♔×f7 7.♘×e4 ♖f8 8.h4 ♔g8 9.h5 etc. If White wants to avoid such complications he can retreat his Bishop to b3 at this point.

6.0–0
Later theory came to recommend 6.♕e2, to prevent what Black might have done next move.

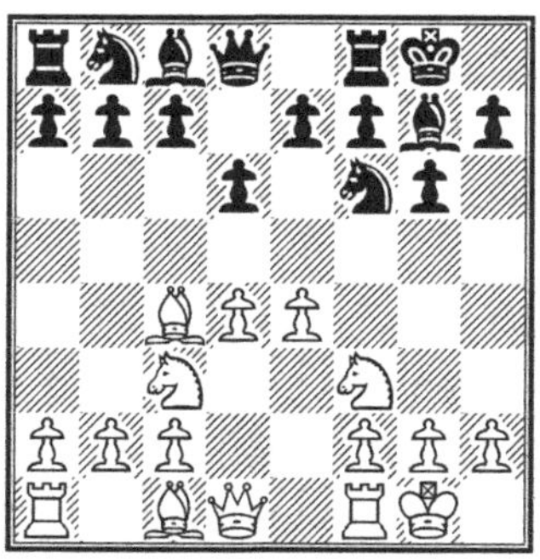

6...♘bd7?
Already, a serious mistake. Best was 6...♘×e4!. Bad one move before, it would now lead to equality after either 7.♘×e4 d5 8.♗d3 d×e4 9.♗×e4 or 7.♗×f7+ ♖×f7 8.♘×e4.

7.e5!

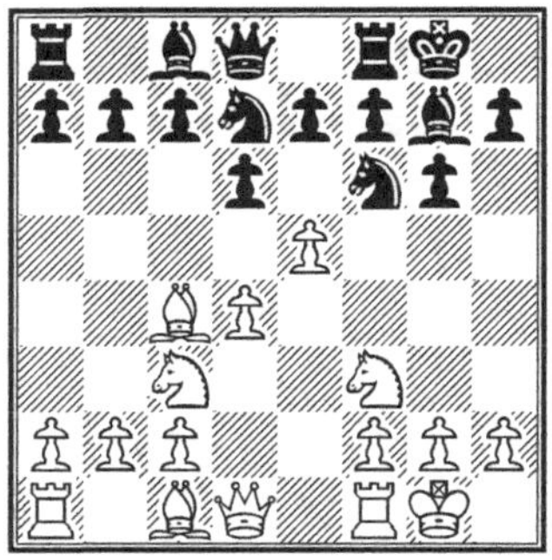

7...♘h5
The least evil. If instead 7...d×e5 8.d×e5 ♘g4 9.e6 ♘de5 (9...f×e6?? 10.♗×e6+ ♔h8 11.♗×g4) 10.e×f7+ ♘×f7 11.♗×f7+ ♔×f7 12.♕e2 (+3.37/24), or 7...♘e8? 8.e6 f×e6 9.♘g5 ♘df6 10.♗×e6+ ♔h8 11.♘f7+ ♖×f7 12.♗×f7 +–.

8.♖e1
8.e6 was a bit stronger, but this is also good. Against the precipitous 8.g4? Black replies 8...♘b6! with good play.

8...♘b6 9.♗d3

9...f5?

This merely blocks the action of Black's pieces, especially his Queen's Bishop, and helps White consolidate his center. Better 9...d×e5 10.d×e5 c6±. But not 9...c5? 10.d×c5 d×c5 11.h3 (△12.g4+−) 11...♗h8 12.♗h6 ♘g7 and Black's position is ridiculous (+3.50/21).

10.♗g5 d5?

A lesser evil was 10...d×e5 11.♘×e5 c6 (11...♕×d4?? 12.♗c4+) 12.a4 a5 13.♕d2 when Black is lost strategically, but not yet tactically.

11.♕d2

Torre now begins a strategy of blockade, to deprive Black of any dynamic potential and leave him cramped and without counterplay.

11...c6

Black's only remaining hope for active play lay in 11...f4 intending 12...♗f5/♗g4. For example if then 12.♘e2?! ♗g4 13.♘×f4 ♘×f4 14.♗×f4 ♗×f3 15.g×f3 Black has greatly lessened his cramp at the cost of a pawn (+1.37/25).

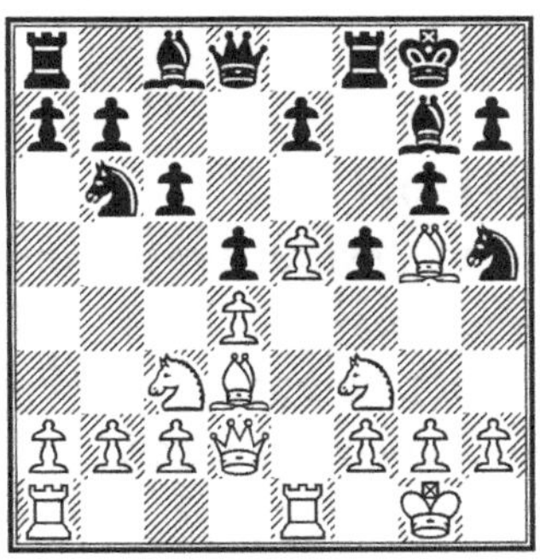

12.♘e2!

Torre pursues the blockade methodically, aiming the Knight toward f4. The move is also prompted by his previously mentioned penchant for trading queenside pieces for kingside ones, so that the opposing King's field will be less well protected.

12...♔h8 13.♘f4 ♘×f4 14.♕×f4

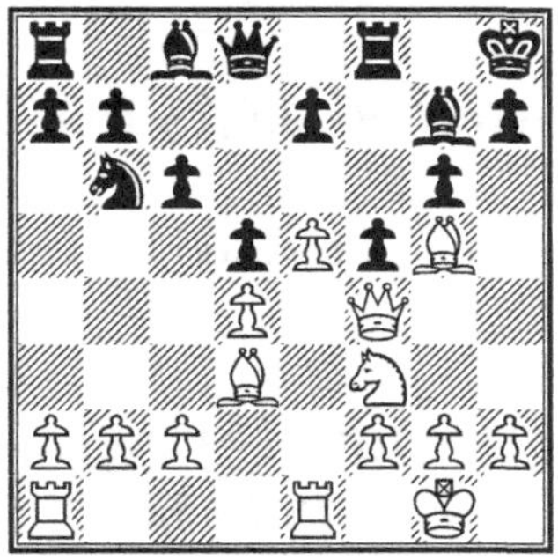

14...♕e8

The English master seems unaware that his young opponent is working systematically to leave him with the mobility of a pinned insect, so as later to deliver the final blow at will. But he had no significantly better move.

In the Russian book of the tournament, Nikolay Grigoriev recommended 14...♗e6, but this loses quickly to 15.♕h4, *viz.* 15...♖f7 16.♗d2 ♕g8 17.♘g5 ♖ff8 18.♖e3 h5 19.♖h3 ♗f7 20.♖e1 ♘c4 21.♗b4 a5 22.♗×e7 etc., or 15...♘c8 16.♖e3 ♗g8 17.♖ae1 h5 18.g4! ♕e8 (18...f×g4?? 19.♗×g6 and mate in 8 at most.) 19.g×h5 g×h5 20.♔h1 ♗h7 21.♗f4 ♖g8 22.♖g1 ♗f8 23.♘g5 etc.

15.e6! ♘c4 16.♗×c4 d×c4

17.♖ad1 b5

This costs a pawn, but there was hardly anything better. Grigoriev mentioned 17...♕d8 (to prevent 18.♕c7) 18.♕h4 ♖e8 19.♗f4 ♗f6 20.♘g5 ♗×g5 21.♕×g5 △ 22.♗e5+ ♔g8 23.♕h6 and 24.♕g7#.

18.♕c7 ♕d8

If 18...♗f6 19.d5! c×d5 20.♖×d5+−.

19.♕×c6 ♖b8 20.♕c5 ♖e8 21.d5! ♖b6

If 21...♗×b2 22.d6 e×d6 23.♖×d6 ♕a5 24.♖e5! (+13.61).

22.♗f4 ♖b7 23.♘g5 ♕b6 24.♘f7+ ♔g8 25.♕×b6

Stockfish says 25.♕b4 or 25.♕a3 was best, but from a human perspective this simplification is appealing, prudent, and strong. With Queens off the board, Black will have nothing to stop the decisive advance of the d-pawn.

25...♖×b6

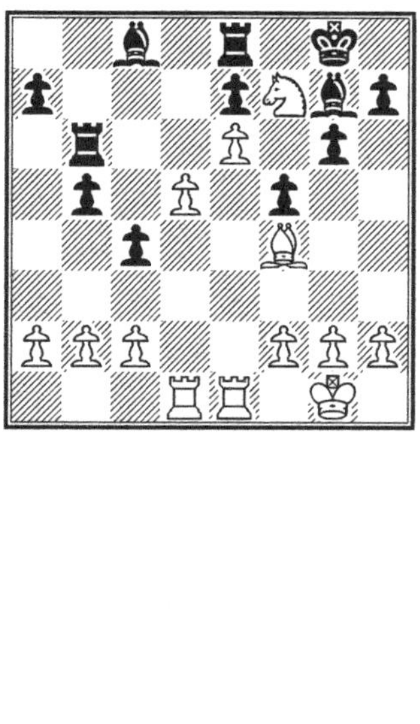

26.♗e5

26.d6 was most direct, *viz.* 26...e×d6 27.♘×d6 ♖×d6 (27...♖d8?? 28.e7) 28.♗×d6+−, or 26...♗×e6 27.♘g5! ♗d7 28.♖×e7+−.

26...♗b7

If there was any hope, it lay in 26...♖a6 or 26...♗×e5.

27.♗c7! ♖a6

Torre now permits himself the luxury of leaving two queenside pawns *en prise*.

28.d6 e×d6 29.♘×d6 ♖×d6 30.♗×d6 ♗×b2 31.♗e5 ♗×e5 32.♖×e5 a6 33.f3

To let his King enter the game.

33...♔g7 34.♖d6

34.♖d7+ ♔f6 35.f4 ♖e7 was playable, but no better.

34...♔f6 35.♖e2 ♖e7 36.♔f2 ♗c8 37.♔e1 c3

After 37...♗×e6 38.♖×a6 or 37...♖×e6 38.♖e×e6+ ♗×e6 39.♖×a6 the Exchange-up ending is an easy win for White.

38.♖c6 1–0

"The young Mexican master conducted this game marvelously, demonstrating an excellent command of positional play." — Nikolay Grigoriev.

Game 38

Sämisch-Torre

Baden-Baden 1925, round 6

Mexican Defense [A50]

The German master Friedrich Sämisch (1896-1975, GM title 1950, historical Elo 2490), one of Europe's most active players circa 1920-43, lived an intermittently harrowing life. As a soldier in World War I he was wounded and nearly killed. During World War II he was interned briefly in a concentration camp for speaking out against the Nazi regime, and he then survived the lengthy Russian siege of Königsberg in 1945. In the period 1928-30 he won several strong tournaments, but his 3rd place in this event is considered the best overall performance of his career. His great love in chess was opening theory, for example variations of the Nimzo-Indian and King's Indian are named for him, and he once said "If I could play the first 20 moves, I would not mind someone else finishing the game for me." This game was then to his taste: it was of theoretical interest, and it went only one move beyond his preferred limit. (His name, by the way, is not pronounced SAY-mish as is commonly supposed, but ZEH-mish, rhyming with blemish.)

1.d4 ♘f6 2.c4 ♘c6

It's not clear whether Torre got the idea for this defense from Alexander Kevitz of the Manhattan CC, or vice versa. Walter Korn, editor of *Modern Chess Openings*, says Kevitz played it frequently in the 1920s, though ChessBase shows no instance before 1955. It was later played by the Yugoslavian correspondence master Mihajlo Trajkovic, and became known as the Kevitz-Trajkovic Defense, though according to IM Georgi Orlov its original name was the Mexican Defense, in honor of Torre and this game, which was its debut in top-level play. More recently it has been the subject of a monograph and a book by Orlov, who calls it the Black Knights' Tango. Considered extravagant in 1925 (the *Deutsche Schachzeitung* commented "In our day, many strange things happen."), it has today achieved respectability, being played by such grandmasters as Yermolinsky, Shabalov, Benjamin, Bologan, Blatny, Christiansen, Nakamura and Caruana.

3.d5 ♘e5 4.e4 ♘g6

Not 4...♘×e4?? 5.♕d4. Considered best today is 4...e6, according to Orlov, who adds that Black should avoid moving the Knight from e5 as long as possible.

5.f4

5...e5?!
The only move, said Mieses, who in the *Leipzig Neue Nachrichten* analyzed White as winning a piece after 5...e6 6.♗d3 e×d5 7.e5 ♘e4 8.c×d5 ♕h4+ 9.g3 ♘×g3 10.♘f3 ♕h5(??) 11.♖g1 ♘f5 12.♖g5. However, Orlov points out that instead of 10...♕h5?? Black can improve with 10...♕h3! when he "is very much alive," or even earlier, with ...♗f8-b4+! at move 7, 8, or 9.

6.f5 ♘×e4
"A piece sacrifice designed to confuse White," says Orlov. Instead, better is 6...♗b4+, "when White has a space advantage but nothing concrete." Stockfish is very fond of space advantages, and after 6...♗b4+ 7.♗d2 ♗×d2+ 8.♘×d2 ♘e7 9.g4 rates White's advantage at about +1.85.
On psychological grounds, however, Torre's sacrifice has some justification, due to the fact that Sämisch, who was habitually prone to time trouble, will now have to think even harder than usual.

7.♕f3?!
Sämisch over-thinks! Best was the plain and straightforward 7.f×g6 h×g6 8.♘f3 (+1.81/27).

7...♗b4+ 8.♔d1

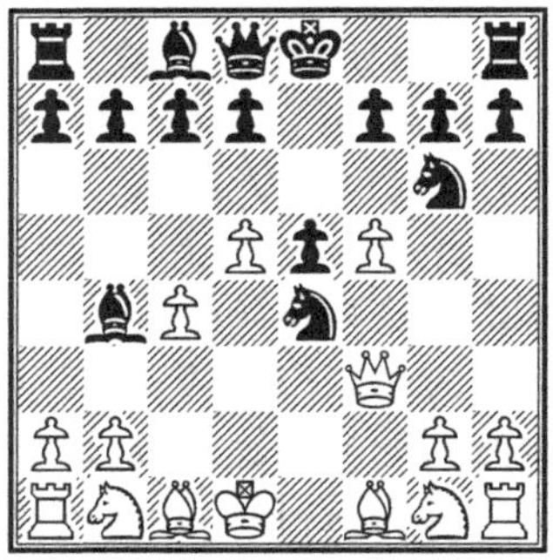

8...♕h4?
Torre, clearly in one of his experimental moods, further muddies the waters, but unsoundly.
Best was simply 8...♘f6 9.f×g6 f×g6 and 10...0–0 when Black has two pawns and other compensation for the lost piece (+1.13/23).

9.g3
The position is quite complicated, and the German master has already spent an inordinate amount of time on his first nine moves (something not unusual for Sämisch, who once forfeited at move 13, and at Linköping 1969 was to lose 13 out of 15 games on time).

9...♕g4 10.♕×g4 ♘f2+ 11.♔e2 ♘×g4 12.h3! ♘f6 13.f×g6 h×g6
At this point White's *Zeitnot* was extreme, with less than two minutes to

make time control at move 30. The position is objectively won for White, but can Sämisch find the winning continuation at less than seven seconds per move?

14.a3! ♗c5 15.♗e3 d6?
15...♗×e3 16.♔×e3 was better, though still winning for White.

16.♗×c5 d×c5 17.♘c3 ♗f5 18.♗g2 0–0–0 19.g4!
Objectively best, says Stockfish, though in the first edition we wrongly gave it a question mark.

19...♗c2 20.♖c1
Best was 20.♘f3 (+4.24/24).

20...♗b3 21.♘e4
With his flag about to fall, Sämisch moves the first piece he sees to the first unoccupied square he finds. And lo, this was his best choice.

21...b5 ½-½
Torre accompanied this move with his now customary offer of a draw. Sämisch understandably accepted at once, though his position is still winning (+3.43/34).

Game 39

Torre-Spielmann

Baden-Baden 1925, round 7

Queen's Gambit Declined [D03]

Austrian master Rudolf Spielmann (1883-1942, historical Elo 2560) had been a fixture on the European tournament scene since about 1904. At first given mainly to gambit play, by the mid-1920s he was changing to a more rounded style, which during the period 1926-29 was to make him one of the top ten players in the world. He was highly variable over his tournament career, low finishes alternating with high. Baden-Baden was a relative low for him (equal 11th out of 21), but next year at Semmering he was to take clear first, ahead of Alekhine and many other greats.

The game is one of the most complicated in this book, and both players lose their way several times in the confusing maze of possibilities. Owners of the first edition will find our notes here substantially different, as Stockfish uncovered various mistakes and improvements previously undetected (or even undreamed of!). Still, despite its flaws, this is a terrific fighting game. Spielmann, known more as an attacker, put up a valiant defense against Torre's queenside onslaught until an imprecision by Torre at move 38 allowed Spielmann to save himself. But for that mistake, this game would probably be considered one of the best of Torre's career. That is the nature of chess; as GM Ludek Pachman, misquoting Stefan Zweig, wrote: "Even eternity cannot repair the damage of a second." [1]

1.d4 ♘f6 2.♘f3 d5 3.c4 e6 4.♗g5 ♘bd7 5.e3 c6 6.♘bd2

Following in the footsteps of Capablanca-Janowski, New York 1918, mentioned in Game 1. The great Cuban considered this best if Black played his c-pawn to c6 instead of c5.

6...h6

Apparently a novelty of Spielmann's, which he would also play against Tartakower at Semmering 1926 (0-1, 49). After that it was seen rather seldom, though it was played by Yusupov in 1982 and Smyslov in 1986.

7.♗h4 ♗e7 8.♗d3 0–0 9.0–0 ♖e8

More active would be to play 9...c5 and 10...b6 (or vice versa). Spielmann in fact did so in the same position against Tartakower at Semmering 1926. Until about 1978 the continuation approved by theory was that of Capablanca-Thomas, Carlsbad 1929: 9...c5 10.♖c1 b6 11.c×d5 e×d5 12.d×c5 ♘×c5 13.♗e2 etc. Then the game Mikhalchishin-Raicevic, Vrnjacka Banja 1978, showed a 10th-move improvement for White: 9...b6 10.♕e2! ♗b7 11.♖ac1 c5 12.♖fd1 c×d4 13.♘×d4 ♘e5 14.♗b1 ♗a6 15.f4 with initiative.

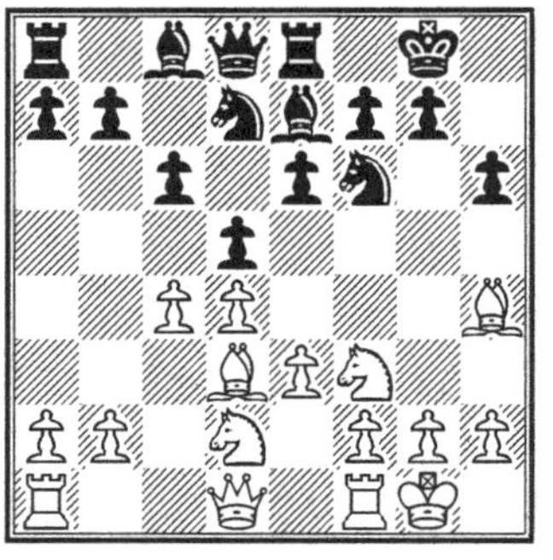

10.♖c1 c5 11.♕e2 c×d4 12.e×d4 ♘h5 13.♗×e7 ♖×e7

Black does not want to let White's Rook invade the 7th rank, which recapture with the Queen would allow.

14.g3

To keep the black Knight off f4, though better perhaps was 14.♗b1, when if 14...♘f4? 15.♕e3! ♘h5 (if 15...♘g6? 16.♗×g6 f×g6 and Black's pawn structure is ruined) 16.c5 when White's queenside advance gets going while Black's Knight is dim on the rim.

14...♘hf6 15.♖fe1 ♘f8?!

1 That is found on page 57 of Pachman's memoir *Checkmate in Prague*. It seems to be a faulty memory of something in Zweig's account of the 1453 fall of Constantinople: "Aber in die Geschichte wie im menschlichen Leben bringt Bedauern einen verlorenen Augenblick nicht mehr wieder, und tausend Jahre kaufen nicht zurück, was eine einzige Stunde versäumt." This translates as "But in history, as in human life, regret does not bring back a lost moment, and a thousand years do not buy back what a single hour has missed."

Black should have played 15...d×c4!, with equality whichever way White recaptures.

16.♘e5
Now was the time to punish Black for his negligence, with 16.c5!±. But Spielmann again does not seize his counter-chance, 16...d×c4.

16...♗d7?! 17.c5!

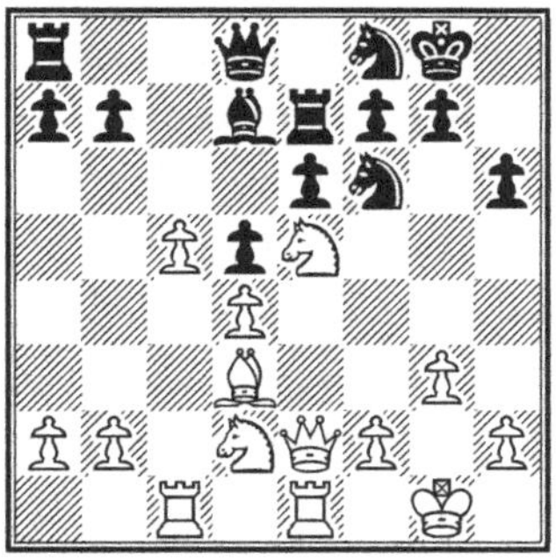

Now Torre has the right idea. Having assumed control of the center, he mobilizes his queenside pawn majority, which soon becomes very threatening.

17...♖c8 18.b4 a6 19.♘b3

19...♗e8
Getting the Bishop out of the way, since the b-pawn will soon need protection.
Another possibility, though hardly any better, was 19...♗a4, *e.g.* 20.♘a5 ♖ec7 21.c6! b×c6 22.♗×a6 ♗b5 23.♗×b5 c×b5 24.♖×c7 ♕×c7 25.♘ec6! and 26.♕×b5. But not 25.♘ac6?! ♘e4 26.♕×b5? f6−+.

20.♘a5! ♖ec7
If 20...b6, White has at least two good continuations: 21.c×b6 ♖×c1 22.♖×c1 ♕×b6 23.a3 (Grigoriev), or 21.♗×a6 b×a5 22.♗×c8 ♕×c8 23.b5 and the two connected passed pawns are formidable.

21.c6!

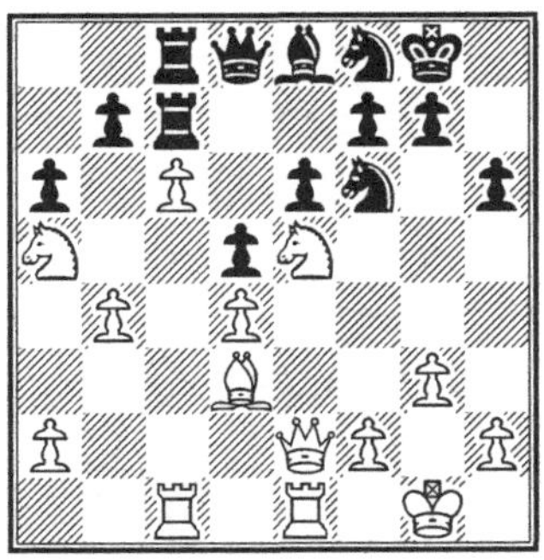

Not exactly a case of "now or never," but patient preparation of the advance by ♖c1-a1, followed by a2-a4 etc., would be too slow.
However, a good alternative was 21.a3 △22.♘×b7 ♖×b7 23.♗×a6 ♖bb8 24.♗×c8 ♕×c8. In any event, the text move is very strong, threatening to destroy Black's queenside.

21...♕d6?

A serious mistake. Relatively best was 21...b6, which White can answer with either 22.♘b7 ♕e7 23.♗×a6 ♕×b4 24.♖b1 ♕a4 25.♘d6 ♖d8 26.♗b5 (+1.82/24), or 22.♗×a6 b×a5 23.♗×c8 ♖×c8 24.b5 (+2.09/26).

22.c×b7?!

Far stronger was 22.♘×b7! ♕×b4 23.♘c5 ♖a7 (not 23...♗×c6?? 24.♘×a6) 24.♗×a6 ♖cc7 25.♗b7 (+3.91/26). The text seriously lessens White's advantage (+1.77/24).

22...♖×c1 23.b×c8♕ ♖×c8 24.♗×a6 ♖a8

This is the position Spielmann envisioned when he played 21...♕d6.

25.♗b7

About equally good was 25.b5 ♗×b5 26.♗×b5 ♖×a5 27.a4±.

25...♖a7

25...♖b8 was somewhat better.

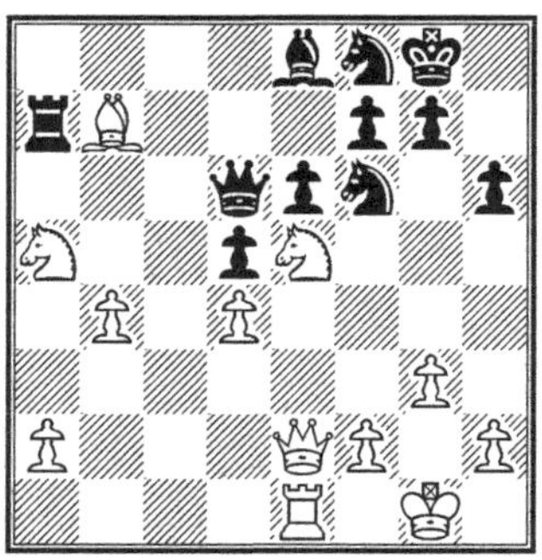

26.♕b2?!

Another less-than-best move. Optimal was 26.a3, when best play then proceeds 26...♕b6 27.♗c6 ♘8d7 28.♕e3 (also good is the straightforward 28.♘×d7 ♗×d7 29.♗×d7 ♘×d7 30.♖c1 +2.90/24) 28...♖c7 29.♗×d7 ♘×d7 30.♘×d7 ♗×d7 31.♘b3 △32.♘c5 (+3.19/25).

26...♕b6!

The only reasonable defense. The threat, obviously, is 27...♖×a5. This forces White to let Black have two pieces for a Rook, but in return White's passed pawns are rapidly mobilized, supported from behind by the heavy pieces. After the game, various grandmasters, among them Alekhine and Nimzovich, analyzed this position with Torre and Spielmann. None found a way for Black to save the game, though his chances are much better now than a few moves ago.

27.♖b1□

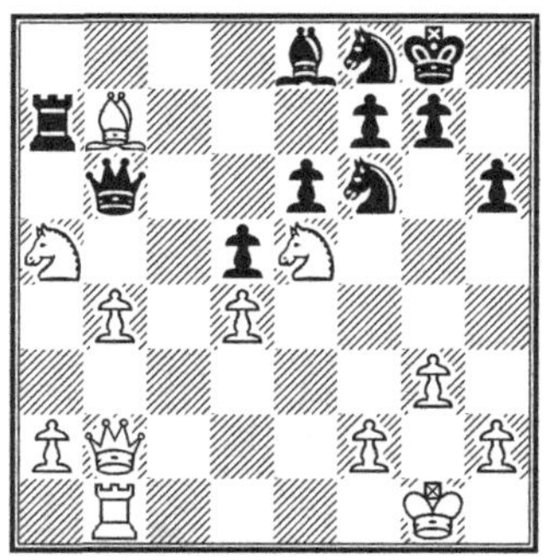

27...♖×b7?!

Not strictly necessary. Better 27...♘g6 28.♗c6 (not 28.♘×g6? f×g6 29.♗c8 ♖a8 30.♗b7 ♖a7 etc., draw.) 28...♘e7 29.♗×e8 ♘×e8 30.♕c1 ♖c7 31.♕e1 ♘d6 32.b5 ♖a7 33.♘ac6 ♘×c6 and after either 34.♘×c6 ♖×a2 35.♕b4 ♘e4

36.♖b2 ♖×b2 37.♕×b2 g5 (+2.24/33), or 34.b×c6 ♕×d4 35.♘d7 g5 (+1.39/34), there is still fight in Black's position.

28.♘×b7 ♕×b7 29.b5 ♘8d7

This is not bad, but Black might have optimized his piece placement by 29...♘e4 30.a4 ♘d7 31.♘c6 ♘df6 32.♖c1 ♘d6.

30.♘×d7

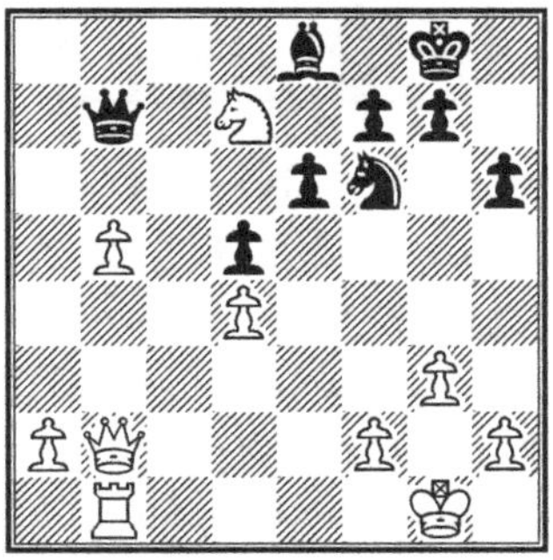

30...♗×d7

30...♘×d7 would just leave the Bishop out of play after 31.a4. If then 31...♘b6? 32.a5 ♘c4 33.♕b4 ♕a8 34.a6 ♘b6 35.♕e7 ♗d7 36.♖c1 ♕b8 (36...♗×b5?? 37.♖c7 +−) 37.♕c5 △ 38.♕c7 +−.

31.a4?!

The complications continue to puzzle both players. Best now was 31.b6 ♗c6 32.♖c1 ♘d7 33.♕c3 ♘b8□ 34.♕a5 (△35.♕a7) 34...♘a6 35.♖×c6 ♕×c6 36.♕×a6 +−.

31...♘e8?

Necessary was 31...♘e4, when the best White has is 32.b6 (if 32.a5 ♘d6 33.b6 ♘c4) 32...♗×a4 33.♖a1 ♗c6 34.♖a7 ♕b8 35.♖c7 ♗a8 36.h4 ♘d6 37.♕b4 ♕d8 38.h5 ♔h7 39.♕a3 ♘f5 and though White definitely stands better (+1.72/25), it is not clear how he can break through to win.

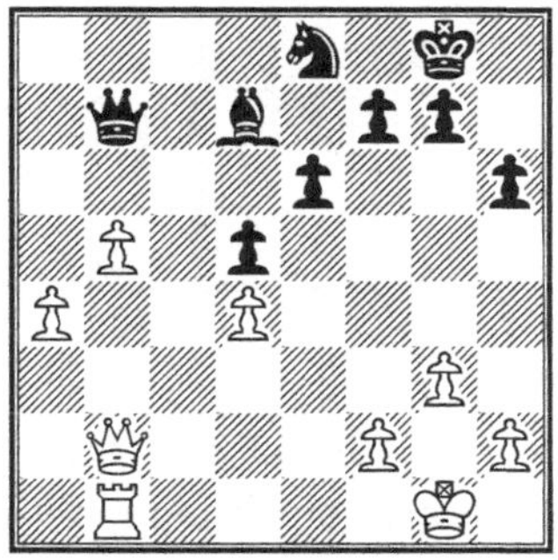

32.♕b4!

This or 32.♕a3 is best. 32.a5?! leads to little or nothing, *viz.* 32...♘d6□ 33.b6 (33.a6? ♕b6 0.00/28) 33...♗c8! (+1.59/26).

32...e5!?

Spielmann finds a remarkable defensive resource, the best available under the difficult circumstances. With this surprising move he decides to sacrifice his two central pawns with the object of clearing the light-squared diagonals and counter-attacking with Queen and Bishop. If now 33.d×e5? d4! 34.♕e7 (if 34.♕×d4? ♗h3 35.f3 ♕×f3 36.♕d2 ♕e4∓) 34...♕d5=.

33.♕e7!

This or 33.b6 is the best reply.

33...e×d4 34.a5!□ d3 35.a6!

After so much muddling, Torre is now finding the best moves.

35...♕c8

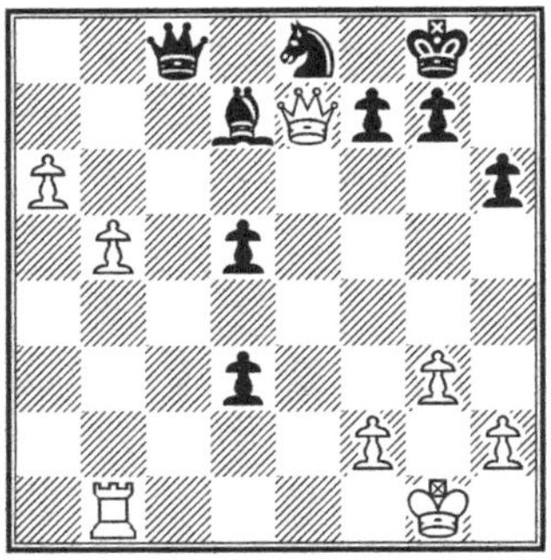

36.b6!

In the first edition we gave this a question mark, but it is in fact one of White's two best moves.

The other, only slightly better, was pointed out by Alekhine in the post-mortem: 36.a7, when if:

(a) 36...♗h3 37.b6 d2 38.♕e2!□ ♕c1+ 39.♕d1+–;

(b) 36...♗f5 37.b6 d2 38.♖d1 ♗d3 39.♕e3 ♗a6 40.♕×d2 ♗b7 41.♕f4 d4 42.♖e1! (42.♕×d4? ♕c6=) 42...♔h7 43.♕b8 ♕c6 44.♕×b7!! ♕×b7 45.♖×e8 etc.;

(c) 36...d2 (relatively best) 37.♕e2 ♘d6 38.b6 ♕c1+ 39.♕d1 ♕×d1+ 40.♖×d1 ♗c6 41.♖×d2 ♘c4 42.♖a2 ♗a8 43.♖a4 △44.♖b4 and 45.b7+–.

36...d2

If 36...♕c2, then not 37.♖a1? ♗b5! 38.a7 d2 39.♕×e8+ ♗×e8 40.a8♕ d1♕+ 41.♖×d1 ♕×d1+ 42.♔g2 ♕e2 43.b7 ♕e4+ 44.♔f1 (44.♔h3?? ♔h7!–+) 44...♕b1+ 45.♔g2 ♕e4+ 46.♔g1 ♕e1+ etc., draw., but 37.♖f1!□,

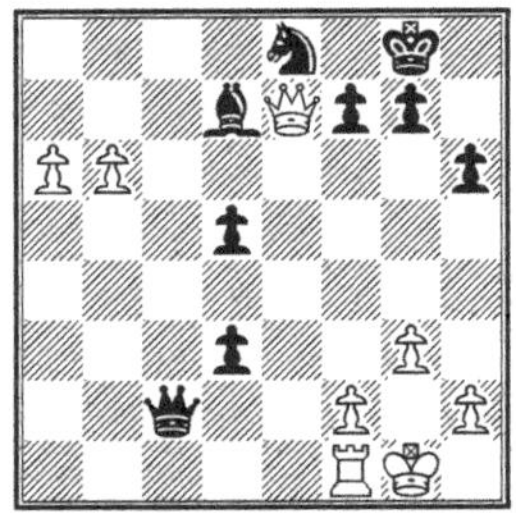

and either 37...♗h3 38.♕×e8+ ♔h7 39.♖a1 d2 40.♕e2+–, or 37...♗c6 38.b7 d2 39.b8♕ d1♕ 40.♕e×e8+ ♗×e8 41.♕×e8+ ♔h7 42.a7! ♕de2 43.♕×e2 ♕×e2 44.a8♕+–.

Continuing the actual game:

37.♕e2□ ♕c2

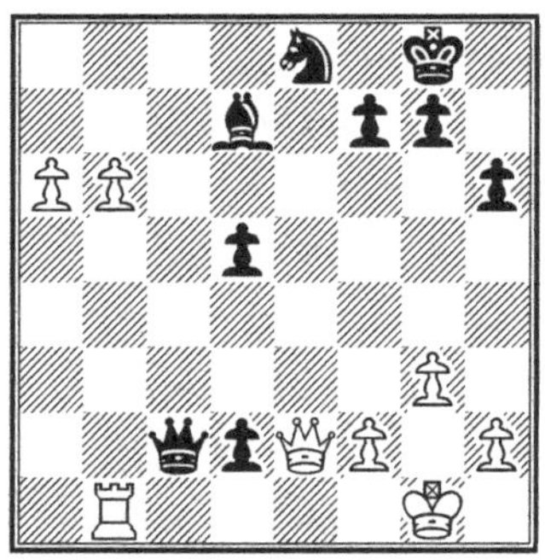

38.♕d1?

After playing so well for seven consecutive moves, Torre tragically lets the win slip irrevocably. Victory could have been his by 38.♖d1 ♗b5 (relatively best) 39.♕×d2 ♕×d2 40.♖×d2 ♗×a6 41.♖×d5,

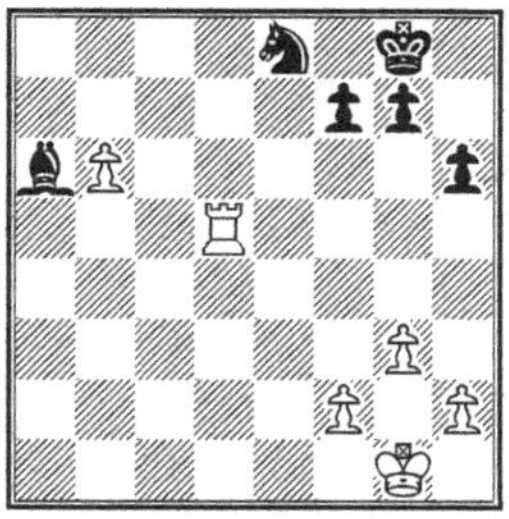

and

(a) 41...♗b7 42.♖d8 ♔f8 43.♖b8 ♗c6 44.b7 ♗×b7 45.♖×b7+−;

(b) 41...♘f6 42.♖d8+ ♔h7 43.♖a8 ♗b7 44.♖a7 ♗d5 45.♖c7 and 46.b7 etc. (not 45.b7? ♘d7); or

(c) 41...♔f8 42.♖d7 ♘f6 43.♖a7 ♗b5 44.b7 ♘d7 45.♖a8+ ♔e7 46.b8♕ ♘×b8 47.♖×b8 and White should have little trouble winning the ♖-vs-♗ ending. But after the text Black can force a draw.

38...♕e4!□ 39.f3□ ♕d4+ 40.♔g2 ♗a4!

And a draw was agreed (½-½).

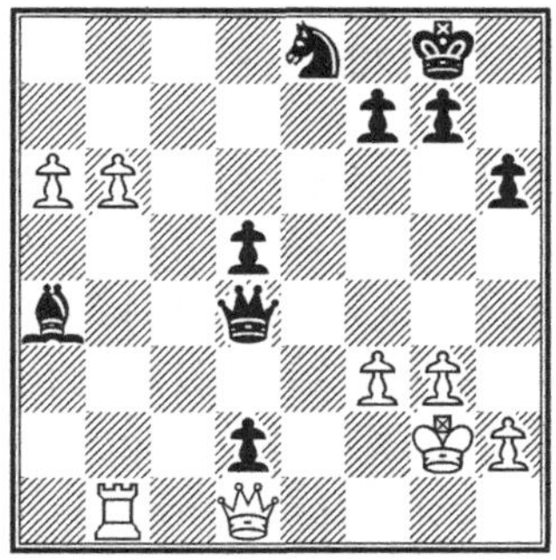

Now 41.♕×a4?? loses to 41...♕×a4 42.b7 ♕c2 and mate shortly.

The best White can do is 41.♕e2 d1♕ 42.♖×d1 ♗×d1 43.♕×e8+ ♔h7 44.b7 ♕d2+ 45.♔f1 ♗b3 46.b8♕ ♗c4+ 47.♔g1 ♕d1+ 48.♔f2 ♕d2+ etc., draw.

So, an imperfect but still dramatic, prodigious and engrossing struggle between two giants of the board, even if neither of them stood at full stature in this case.

Game 40

Rabinovich-Torre

Baden-Baden 1925, round 8

King's Indian Defense [E77]

Russian master Ilya Leontyevich Rabinovich (1891-1942) was, like Oscar Tenner (Game 3) a graduate of the "Mannheim school." Imprisoned as an enemy alien by the Germans 1914-17, he played frequently against Bogoljubow and other strong internees, winning two "prison tournaments" and developing a solid positional style. Returning to Russia, he became one of the Soviet Union's strongest masters, winning (jointly with Levenfish) the 1935 USSR Championship, and playing an important role in training future grandmasters, in particular Botvinnik. It was a signal honor for Rabinovich to be at Baden-Baden: he was the first Soviet master to play in an international tournament outside the USSR.

1.d4 ♘f6 2.c4 g6 3.♘c3 ♗g7 4.e4 d6 5.f4

The Four Pawns Attack is the most overtly aggressive line against the King's Indian. The earliest known games with it come from a long series between the English master John Cochrane and the strong Bengali player Moheshunder Bonnerjee in Calcutta, 1853-54 (indicating the King's Indian actually did originate in India!). It was not seen in Europe until Schwarz-Paulsen, match, Leipzig, 1879, and seldom after that until it became fashionable in the 1920s.

5...0–0 6.♗e2 c5 7.d5 e6 8.d×e6

This capture is somewhat premature. Better 8.♘f3 transposing to the normal line, but White for some reason wants to save f3 for his Bishop.

8...f×e6

As in several earlier games, within the first few moves Torre reaches a position never seen before in master play, reflecting the many experimentations (if not convulsions!) in opening theory during the 1920s. The relatively few games reaching this position are about equally divided between this recapture and 8...♗×e6, in either case with an even game.

9.♗f3 ♘c6 10.♘ge2 e5!

Superficially seeming bad for leaving the d-pawn backward on the open file, this is actually an energetic move by which Black takes control of the important square d4.

11.0–0 ♘d4 12.f×e5 d×e5 13.♗g5?!

Pursuing a dubious plan. Trading off this Bishop will leave White weak on the dark squares.

13...h6 14.♗×f6 ♕×f6 15.♘d5 ♕g5!

An instructive exploitation of the Bishop's absence.

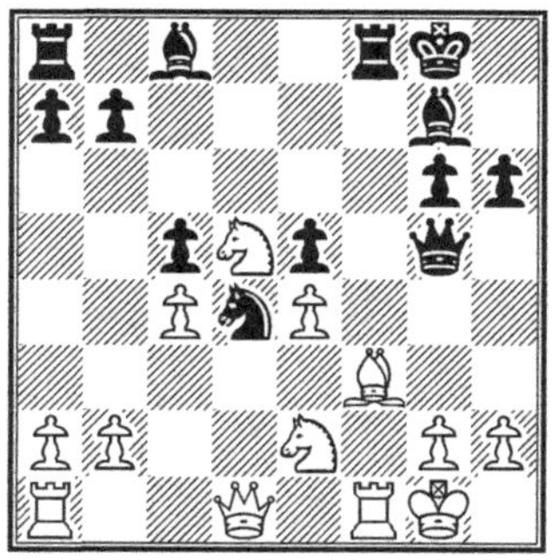

16.♔h1

Relatively best. If instead, say, 16.♘×d4? e×d4 17.b4 c×b4 18.♘×b4 ♗e6 19.♘d5 ♖ac8 20.♖c1 ♗e5! 21.♕b3 ♖f7 22.♗e2 (not 22.♖fd1?? ♖cf8 23.♗e2 ♖f2 24.♗f1 ♗g4 △25...♗f3–+) 22...♖cf8 23.♖cd1 (23.♖×f7 ♕×c1+) 23...h5 with a slowly building attack (-2.32/24).

16...♗d7 17.♘×d4?!

Better 17.♘g1 or 17.♘ec3.

17...e×d4 18.♕c1 ♕e5

Black's Queen will not be able to maintain this seemingly strong post.
Better 18...♗e5!, and if 19.♕×g5 h×g5 20.♖ad1 ♔g7 21.♔g1 ♖h8 22.g3 ♖h7, again with a strong attack building (-2.56/25).

19.b4 c×b4 20.♘×b4 ♖ac8 21.♘d3

Displacing the Queen and blockading the passed pawn.

21...♕c7

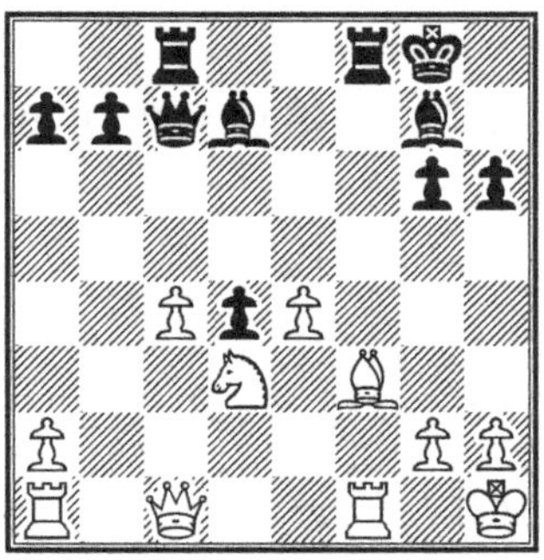

22.♖b1

Not 22.♘b2? b5! 23.c×b5 ♕×c1 24.♖a×c1 ♗×b5 25.♖×c8 ♖×c8 26.♖d1 ♖c3 and the d-pawn will soon become a serious threat in most variations (-4.00/26).

22...♕×c4

The first edition gave this a ?, but Stockfish considers it the best move on the board, though good only for a small advantage against best play (-1.03/25).

23.♕×c4+ ♖×c4 24.♖×b7 ♗c6

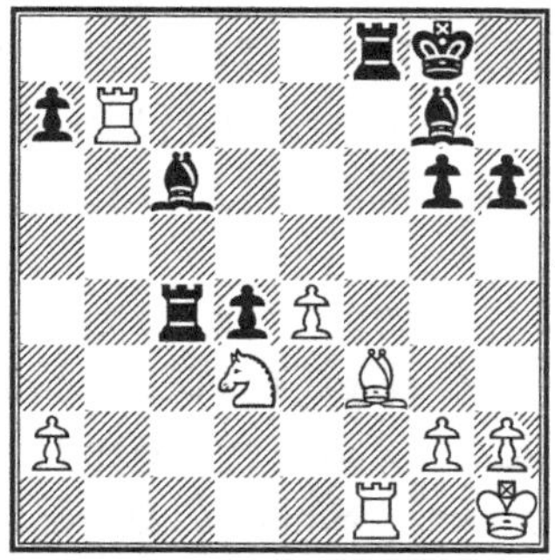

25.♖bb1?

This should have lost the game. Correct was 25.♖×a7! ♗×e4 26.♘f2 ♗×f3 27.g×f3 ♖×f3 28.♔g2 ♖f7 29.♖×f7 ♔×f7 30.♘d3+ and White should be able to salvage a draw (-1.12/25).

25...a5?

A useless move and, as with Réti and Spielmann, another case of Torre missing a win.
Correct was 25...♖c3!,

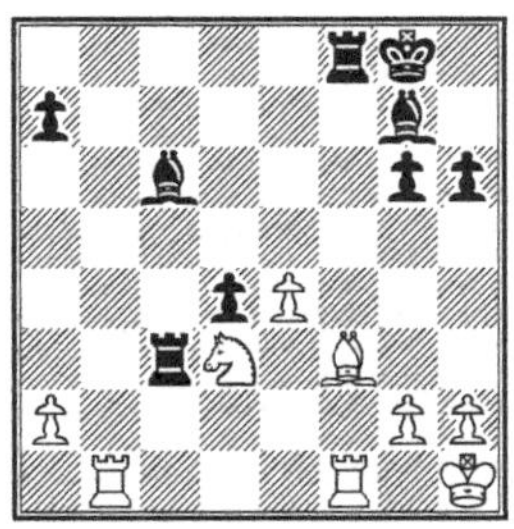

winning in all variations, *e.g.*:
(a) 26.♖fd1 ♗a4 27.♖d2 ♗c2 (-4.33);
(b) 26.♖bd1 ♗a4 27.♖d2 ♗b5 28.♖fd1 h5 (△29...♗h6−+) 29.♘f2 d3 30.e5 ♗h6 (30...♗×e5?! 31.♘×d3) 31.♖b2 ♗a4 32.♖g1 d2 33.h3 ♖c1 34.♗d1 ♖×f2 35.♗×a4 ♖×g1+ 36.♔×g1 d1♕+ 37.♗×d1 ♖×b2−+;
(c) 26.♘b4 ♗b5 27.♖f2 d3 28.♖d2

h5 29.♘d5 ♖c5 30.♔g1 a6 (30...♗h6 31.♖xb5 ♖xb5 32.♖xd3 ♗g7 is also good) 31.♖dd1 ♗a4 32.♖xd3 ♗c2 33.♖bb3 ♗xd3 34.♖xd3 ♗e5 (-4.37/25).

And of course if 26.♗e2, simply 26...♗xe4−+, or if 26.e5?? ♗xf3 27.♖xf3 ♖xf3 28.gxf3 ♖xd3−+.

26.e5!□
This takes White out of danger.

26...♗xf3
Forced; if 26...♗a4/♗d7?? 27.♗d5+.

27.gxf3 ♖c3
Without the light-square Bishop to harass the white Rooks, this move now is ineffective.

28.♖bd1 g5 29.♖d2 ♔f7 30.♖b1 ♖e8 31.♖b5!
The game is now completely even (0.00/25).

31...a4 32.♖d5 ♖a3 33.♔g2 ♖e7 34.♔g3 ♔e6 35.♖xd4 ♔f5 36.f4 ♖xe5
Hoping for 37.fxe5?? ♗xe5+ 38.♔g2 ♗xd4−+, but Rabinovich avoids that swindle.

37.♔f2 ♖e2+ 38.♔xe2 ♗xd4 ½-½

Game 41

Torre-Mieses

Baden-Baden 1925, round 9

Dutch Defense [A83]

By 1925 Jacques Mieses (pronounced MEE-zezz, rhymes with "cheeses") had 40 years of master play behind him, and another 20 ahead of him. Born Jakob Mieses in Leipzig in 1865, in his early 20s he changed his first name to the French "Jacques" because it better fit his outgoing personality, stylish dress and colorful, combinative style of play. Though not one of the world's top-rank players (historical Elo 2490), he was a veteran of many high-level tournaments and matches, and was also very active as a chess organizer, journalist, and editor. His peak had come around 1907, but as late as 1923 he won a tournament at Liverpool ahead of Maróczy, Thomas and Yates. He once said of himself "I may be accused of playing bad chess, but I can never be accused of playing dull chess!" His constant dedication to chess was recognized in 1950 when he was named to FIDE's initial list of international grandmasters.
Torre's game with Mieses is very instructive, in that it shows how time can be the decisive factor in chess. It is

a textbook example of how to proceed when one has two or three extra tempi in a position too simplified to warrant any mating attack. White played an audacious gambit in the opening but gained from it only a slight advantage in development. Still, with great ability, Torre was able to maintain that advantage into a won endgame, where his technique, though not perfect, was better than Mieses'.

1.d4 f5 2.e4

Apparently at this tournament someone spread the rumor that Mieses was a sucker for the Staunton Gambit. This was reinforced when Tartakower used it to crush Mieses in the 7th round in a mere 15 moves. Only two rounds later, the young Mexican tried his luck with it, but by this time the experienced veteran was well prepared.

2...f×e4 3.♘c3 ♘f6 4.♗g5

Here Tartakower had played 4.g4, but it would have been absurd for Torre to think that line had any further surprise value.

4...♘c6 5.d5 ♘e5 6.♕d4 ♘f7 7.♗×f6 e×f6 8.0–0–0

8.♘×e4 has come to be the main line, but the text is also seen fairly often. In two games with Mieses, Réti played 8.0–0–0 at Kaschau 1918, and 8.♘×e4 at Berlin 1920, winning both times.

8...f5

Now entering *terra incognita*. ChessBase shows no earlier example of this move, nor any later until 1978! Stockfish considers it best.

9.f3

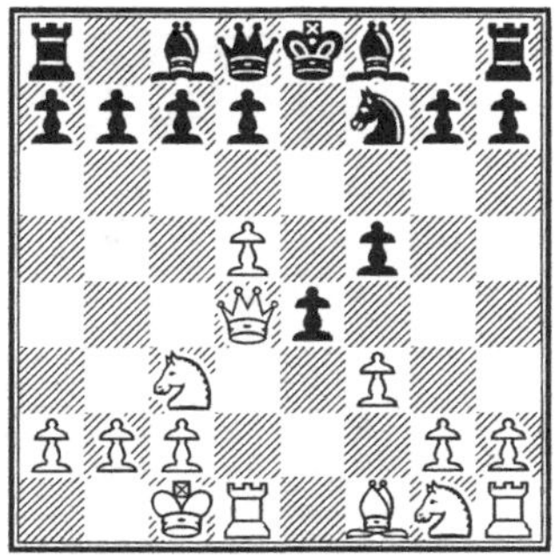

9...♕g5+?!

Mieses had been doing fine so far, but now he starts to go astray. As an alternative, Stockfish proposes this astounding continuation: 9...c5!? 10.♕f2 b5!? Suddenly it's Black who's playing a gambit. 11.♗×b5 ♗d6 12.f×e4 0–0 13.e×f5 ♖b8 14.♘f3 ♕a5 15.f6 g6 16.♕e2 ♗a6 17.♗×a6 ♖×b2! 18.♔×b2 ♕b4+ 19.♔c1 ♗f4+ 20.♘d2 ♕×c3 21.♕b5□ (else 21...♕a1#) 21...♖b8 22.♗b7 ♘e5 (△23...♘c4–+) 23.♕b3 ♕a1+ 24.♕b1 ♕c3 25.♕b3 ♕a1+ etc., draw. It is hard to imagine a human being playing like that, though.

10.♔b1 ♗d6

A difficult decision. White threatened 11.f×e4 f×e4 12.♖e1 ♗e7 13.♘×e4+–. The text does not prevent 11.f×e4, but greatly lessens its impact because Black can reply 11...♗e5.

11.♘h3

Natural and stronger was 11.f×e4 ♗e5 (if 11...f×e4? 12.♘×e4 ♕e7 13.♘×d6+ ♘×d6□ 14.♘f3 0–0 15.♗d3 with a serious attack looming) 12.♕d3 f4 13.♘f3 ♕f6±.

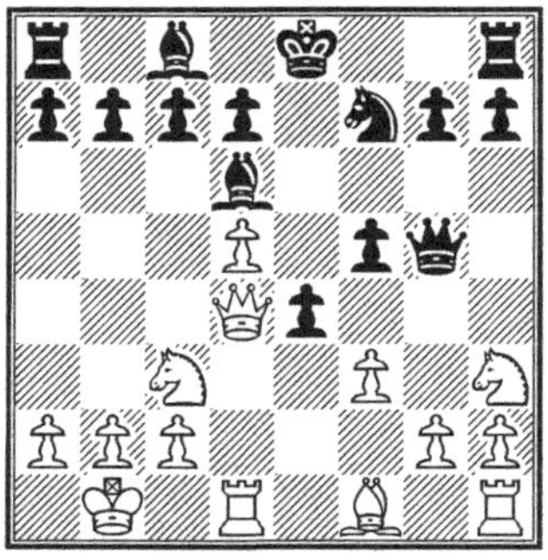

11...♕f6

The exchange of Queens will dampen White's chances for an immediate attack, but Black's development problems will remain.

Slightly better was 11...♕h6 12.f×e4 ♗e5 13.♕c4 f4, denying White's Knight its hoped-for post on f4. Then after, say, 14.♘f2 a6 (to prevent ♘c3-b5) 15.d6 ♗×d6 16.♘d5 0–0 17.♘×c7 b5 18.♕c3 ♖b8 19.♘d5 ♗b7 Black has gotten "back to normalcy." Still, the text is only about a half-pawn worse.

12.♕×f6 g×f6 13.f×e4 f×e4 14.♘×e4 ♗e5

Exchanges have greatly simplified the position, but White maintains a considerable advantage in development. In particular his Rooks stand ready to take the field, while Black's cannot for some time yet. White's task is to capitalize on this as quickly as possible; any delay will permit Black to equalize.

15.g3

This will be necessary eventually if the white King's Rook is ever to move, but there was no need to play it right now. Better 15.♖e1 or 15.♗d3.

15...d6 16.♗b5+ ♗d7?

Mieses is trying to connect his Rooks as quickly as possible, but an exchange of these Bishops is not to his advantage. Correct was 16...♔e7 or 16...♔f8, with a near-even game in either case.

17.♗×d7+ ♔×d7 18.♖hf1 ♔e7 19.♖de1

Renewing the threat of 20.♘×f6. With a developmental advantage every move should, ideally, contain a threat which keeps the opponent from completing his development.

19...♘h6

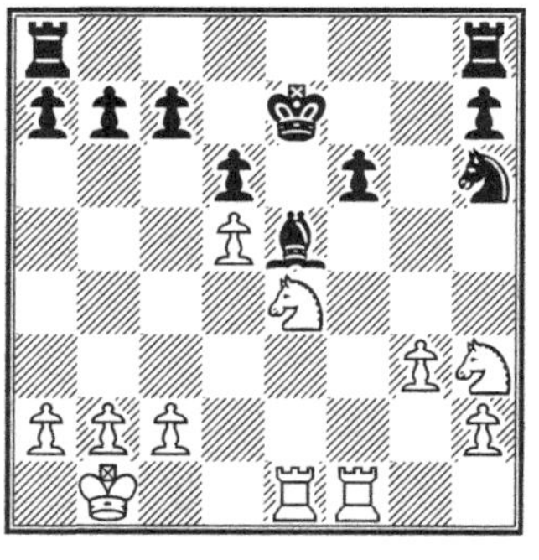

Expecting to get his Rooks in play after 20.♘×f6 ♖af8 21.♘e4 ♖×f1 22.♖×f1 ♘g4, forcing White to play 23.♖h1 if he wants to keep the pawn. There would follow 23...♖f8, and the now great activity of Black's pieces would more than compensate for the pawn given up. However, as noted earlier, Torre was little subject to "the tyranny of the pawn." For him, piece activity mattered more than material advantage.

20.♘f4!

Discouraging Black from playing a Rook to f8 due to the response 21.♘e6. At the same time it invites Black to trade off his only active piece, after which the f-pawn will be a permanent weakness.

20...f5 21.♘c5

Threatening 22.♘fd3, striking at the pinned piece.

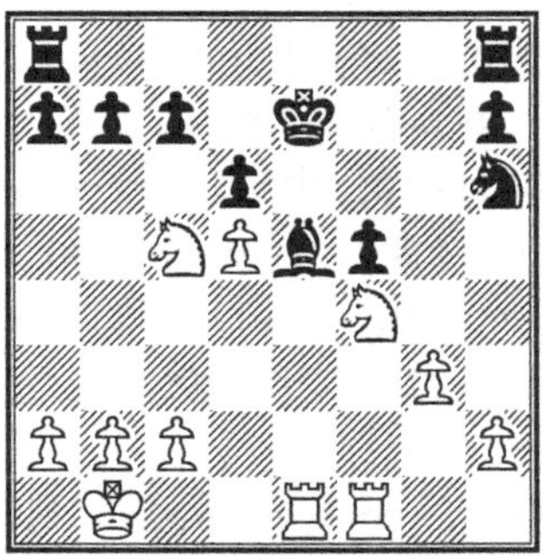

21...♘g4?!

If 21...d×c5?? 22.♖×e5+ ♔d7 23.♖e6 ♘f7 24.♘d3 b6 25.♖×f5 +−. But better was 21...♖ae8.

22.h3 ♘f6? 22...d×c5 23.h×g4 ♔d6 24.g×f5 ♖ag8 was a far lesser evil (+1.49/25).

23.♘fd3!

Not 23.♘cd3?, which would allow Black to centralize his Knight with 23...♘e4 and solve the worst of his problems. The principle governing White's strategy was exemplified masterfully in the play of Rubinstein and Capablanca, and enunciated by Tarrasch: "When one has a positional advantage, one should simplify the position, exchanging only those pieces that do not contribute to the strategic imbalance." In this case, White's advantage is not truly positional, resting as it does on the greater activity of his Rooks compared to Black's. This is a temporary advantage, and only by a series of threats can it be prolonged. However, Tarrasch's principle applies, in that White must seek to exchange the minor pieces in ways that do not otherwise affect the favorable (to him) imbalance. Generally, this is the most difficult type of advantage to exploit, as a lax move or two can let it evaporate. White's move here is not lax, but in fact winning.

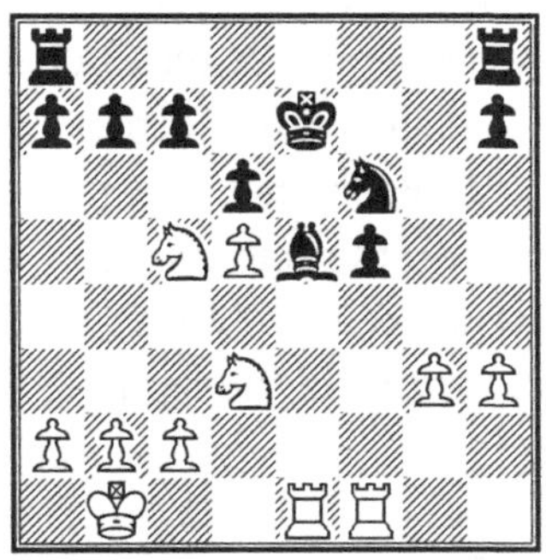

23...♘×d5??

The best Black could have done was 23...♘e4 24.♘×e4 f×e4 25.♖×e4 ♖hf8 26.♖fe1 ♖f3 27.♘×e5 d×e5 28.♖×e5+ ♔d6 29.♖h5 ♖×g3 30.♖e6+ ♔c5 31.b3 ♖g7 32.♖eh6 (+3.37/25). The text allows much worse material loss.

24.♘×e5 d×e5 25.♖×e5+

Good, winning a pawn, but considerably stronger was 25.♖×f5! ♔d6 26.♘×b7+ ♔c6 27.♘a5+ ♔b6 28.♘c4+ ♔b7 29.♖f×e5, and White is two pawns up, with Black's pieces still uncoordinated (+6.12/23). The text still leaves White in control and on course for victory, though as will be seen, with rather greater difficulty.

25...♔d6 26.♖f×f5 ♔×c5 27.♖×d5+ ♔b6

The first edition commented here "White's strategy has triumphed: he has not only maintained the superior mobility of his Rooks but has won a pawn as well. He can no longer prevent Black from developing his Rooks, but that is now not essential, as the developmental advantage has been transformed into a won endgame, a matter of technique." However, it turns out that near-perfect technique is required, which neither Torre nor Mieses possessed. Back then we made little comment on the remaining 27 moves, but now we can show the interesting turns of fortune hidden among them.

28.b3

Some *Luft* for the King, to forestall any chance of back-rank mate. If instead, say, 28.♖h5, 28...♖he8 would force this or 29.a4 anyway.

28...♖ae8 29.♖f6+ c6 30.♖d7 h5 31.♖ff7 ♖b8 32.♖g7 ♖hd8 33.♖df7 ♖d5 34.h4 a5 35.♔b2 ♔a6 36.♖g5 ♖×g5 37.h×g5 ♖e8

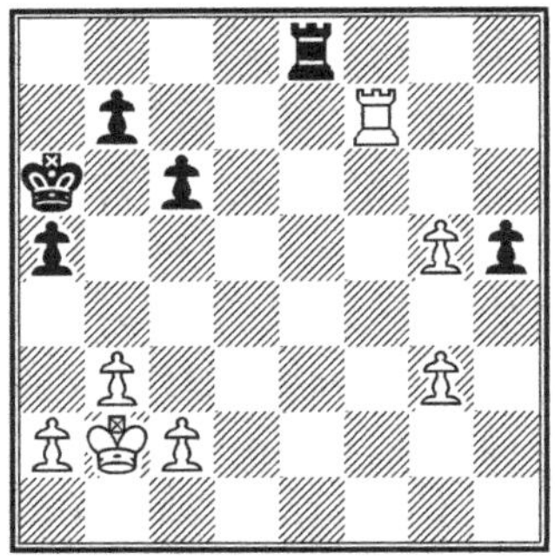

38.♖h7?!

This puts the win in jeopardy. Correct was 38.g4! and either

(a) 38...h×g4 39.♖f4 ♖g8 40.♖×g4 (+4.91/25), or

(b) 38...♖g8 39.g×h5 ♖×g5 40.h6 ♖h5 41.h7 ♖h3 42.♔c1 and the white King will eventually arrive at the g-file to start harassing the black Rook, thus forcing Black to give it up for the h-pawn, or make other concessions that win for White (+4.80/29).

38...♖e3! 39.g4 ♖g3 40.g×h5 ♖×g5 41.h6 ♖g3?

Better 41...♖h5, observing the rule that "Rooks belong behind passed pawns." The game then would very probably be drawn (+0.88/33).

42.♖g7 ♖h3 43.h7

Arriving at a position like variation (b) in the note to move 38, though Stockfish rates it not nearly so favorable to White (+2.26/25).

43...b5 44.♔c1 ♔b6 45.♔d2 ♔c5 46.a3

Preventing ...♔c5-b4-a3, but 46.c3 was the better way to do it.

46...b4?

Much better was 46...♔d4/♔d5/♔d6, all +1.69/36.

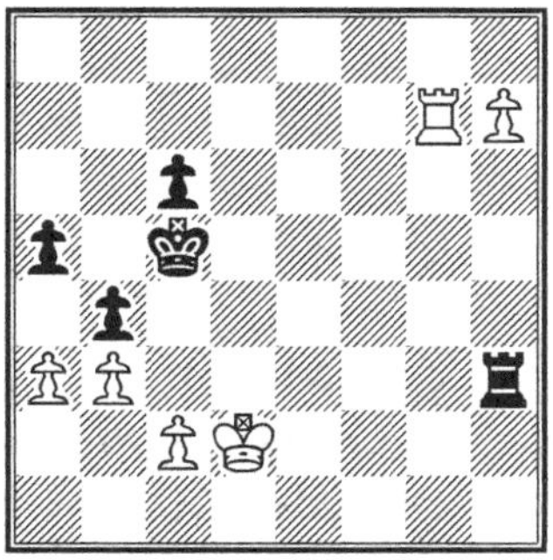

47.a4?

This lets Black draw. Correct was 47.a×b4+! and either

(a) 47...a×b4 48.♖d7 ♔b5 49.♔e2 ♔b6 50.♔f2 c5 51.♔g2 ♖h6 52.♔f3 ♔c6 53.♖f7 ♔d6 54.♔g4 ♔e6 55.♔g5 ♖h2 56.♖f6+ ♔e5 57.♖h6 ♖g2+ 58.♔h5 ♖h2+ 59.♔g6 ♖g2+ 60.♔f7 etc., or

(b) 47...♔×b4 48.♖b7+ ♔a3 49.♔e2 ♔b2 50.c4 ♔c3 51.♔f2 c5 52.♔g2 ♖h5 53.♔g3 etc., winning in either case.

47...♔d4□ 48.♖d7+

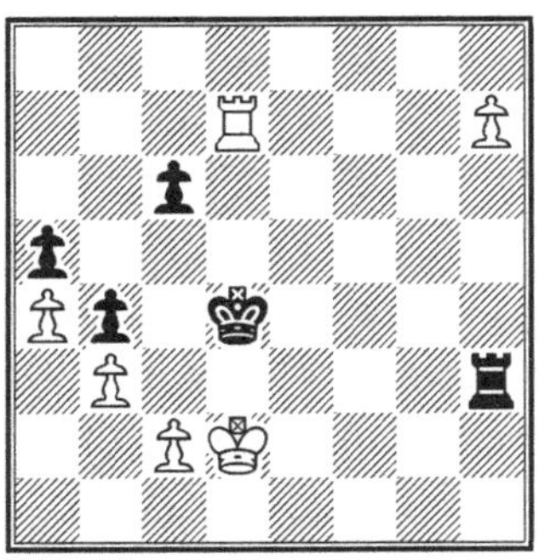

48...♔e5??

To paraphrase Dinah Washington, what a difference one square makes. 48...♔e4! could have drawn, *viz.* 49.♔e2 ♖h2+□ 50.♔f1 ♔f3 51.♔g1 ♖h6 52.♖f7+ ♔e3□ 53.♔g2 ♔d2□ 54.♖f2+ ♔c1 55.♖f1+ ♔×c2 56.♖h1 ♖×h7!!□

57.♖×h7 ♔×b3 58.♔f3 ♔×a4 0.00/44. Even so, that variation is so difficult that one wonders if Mieses could have found his way through such a gauntlet of "□" moves.

In any event, the text does not allow Black such an invasion, and Torre gives him no further chance.

49.♔e2 ♔e6 50.♖a7 ♔d5 51.♖×a5+ ♔d4 52.♖a7 ♔c3 53.a5 ♔×c2 54.a6 1-0

Though Torre's endgame technique here was sometimes flawed, he showed admirable resourcefulness, positional judgement, and perseverance.

In the interest of giving a balanced, objective picture of Torre's chess, we have added some of his worst losses, games not included in the first edition. This is the first such:

Game 42

Carls-Torre

Baden-Baden 1925, round 10

Position after **15.♗d2-c3**:

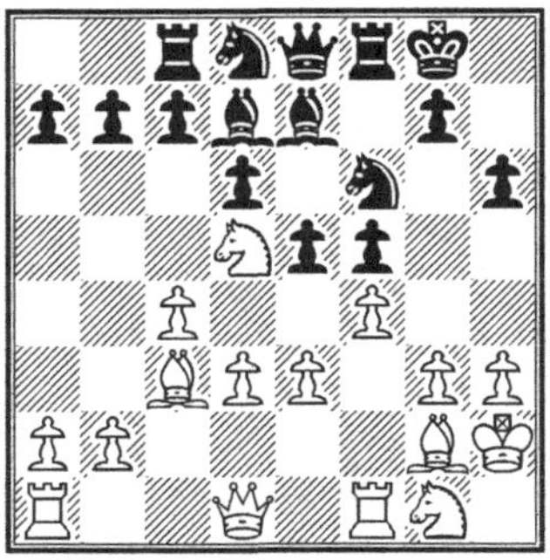

The German master Carl Carls (1880-1958, historical Elo 2450, IM title 1951) has here a position somewhat better, but hardly decisively so. Best now was 15...♘×d5 16.♗×d5+ ♗e6 17.♗g2±.

Instead came
15...c6? 16.♘×e7+ ♕×e7 17.f×e5 d×e5 18.♘f3

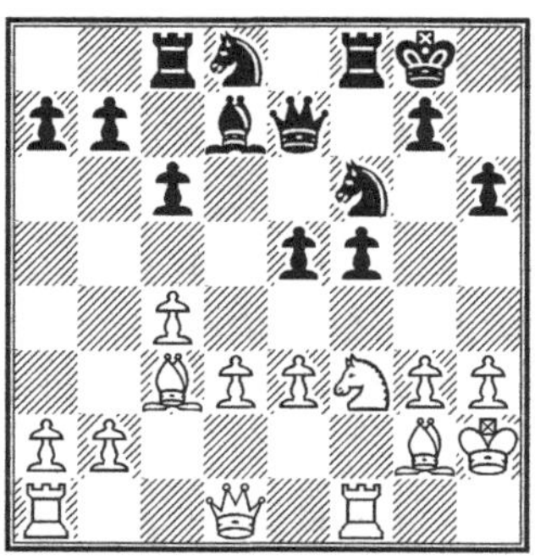

Now the least evil was 18...♘f7 19.♘h4 ♕d6 20.♘×f5, losing a pawn.

18...e4??
This will lose much more.

19.♘e5
Threatening 20.♘g6, winning the Exchange.

19...♖e8??
Trying to lose neither the f-pawn nor the Exchange, but allowing worse. 19...♗e8 was necessary, though then after 20.♖×f5 e×d3 21.♕×d3 Black is in bad shape.

20.d×e4 f×e4 21.♖×f6! ♕×f6
21...g×f6 22.♘×d7 is worse.

22.♕×d7

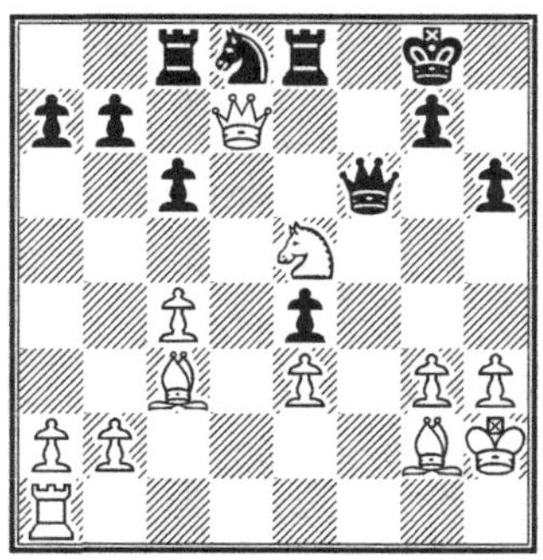

Superficially White's advantage is not much, two Bishops for a Rook, but Stockfish sees further material loss is inevitable and rates it at +6.69/25. Torre played on to move 34, but might well have resigned here (**1-0**).

Game 43

Marshall-Torre

Baden-Baden 1925, round 12

Stonewall Attack [A45]

1.d4 ♘f6 2.e3 g6 3.♗d3 ♗g7 4.f4

Something new already. While the Stonewall Attack already had a long pedigree, back at least to Hanham-Showalter, New York 1889, this seems to be the first time it was played against a King's Indian deployment.

4...c5 5.c3 b6

Torre goes full hypermodern. Since the Stonewall does not exert much pressure on Black's position in the early stages, he can afford the luxury of a double fianchetto.

6.♘f3

The only attempt to refute Black's fifth move would be 6.e4, but after, say, 6...♗b7 7.♘d2 c×d4 8.c×d4 d6 9.♘gf3 0–0 10.0–0 ♘c6 Black is fully equal.

6...♗b7 7.0–0 0–0 8.♘bd2 ♘c6 9.♘e4 ♘×e4 10.♗×e4

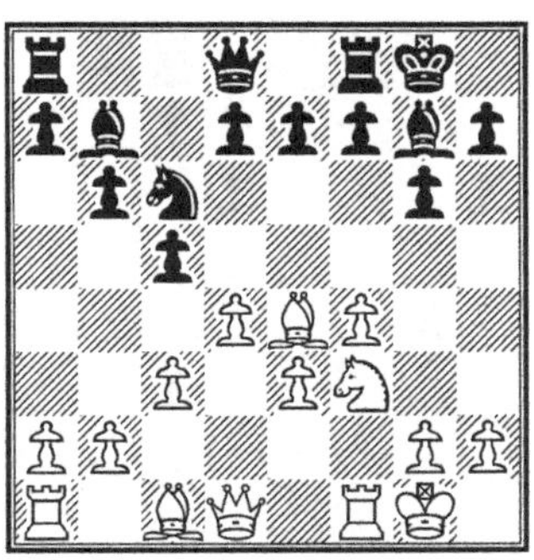

10...♘a5

10...e6 was preferable, when a likely continuation is 11.♕e2 ♕c7 12.♗d3 c×d4 13.e×d4 ♘e7 △ 14...♘d5∓.

11.♗d3?!

Marshall wishes to preserve his King's Bishop so as not to be weakened on the light squares. Still, this needlessly loses a tempo. Better was 11.♗×b7 ♘×b7 12.e4±.

11...♖c8 12.♕e2 c×d4 13.e×d4 ♗d5?!

Rabinovich praises this in the tournament book, but best was 13...e6 to prevent White's next move.

14.f5!

Suddenly both White's Bishops are activated, and aimed kingside.

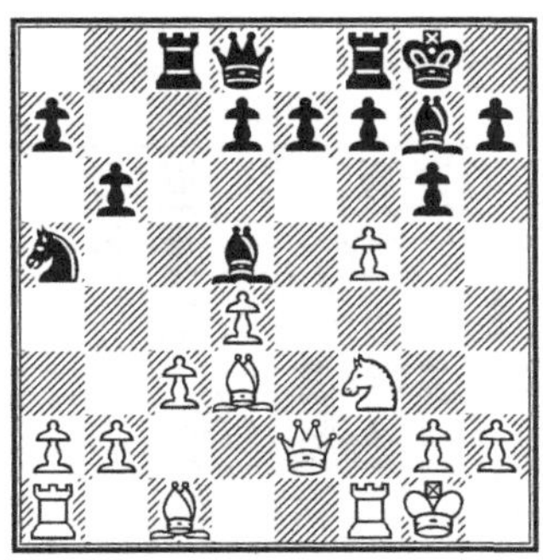

14...e6□

Necessary. Suicidal would be 14...g×f5?

15.♗×f5 e6 (if 15...♗c4?? 16.♕e4 h6 17.♘e5 ♗×f1 18.♗×h6! ♗×h6 19.♕g4+ ♔h8 20.♕h5 ♔g7 21.♖×f1 etc. +7.49) 16.♗×h7+! ♔×h7 17.♘g5+ ♔g6 18.h4 etc. (+2.66/23).

15.f×g6 f×g6 16.♗d2?!

Surprising to see the normally attack-minded Marshall so timid.
Much stronger was 16.♗g5! ♗×f3 17.♕e3! ♕c7 18.♖×f3 ♘c4 19.♖×f8+ ♖×f8 20.♕e2 ♘d6±.

16...♘c4 17.♗c1?!

Timidity again! 17.♗g5 was still better, or 17.♘g5, with equality either way. The text puts White at a disadvantage.

17...♘d6

If Black wanted to play for a win, 17...b5 was worth a thought, with the idea of a queenside minority attack. Our first edition says Torre offered a draw here, which Marshall accepted. ChessBase adds a few repetitive moves:

18.♗d2 ♘c4 19.♗c1 ♘d6 20.♗d2 ♘c4 ½-½

A strange game.

Game 44

Torre-Bogoljubow

Baden-Baden 1925, round 13

Since Bogoljubow was one of the top five or six players in the world at this time, losing to him was no shame. But Torre did so in a rather ignominious fashion. This is the position after

15...d6-d5:

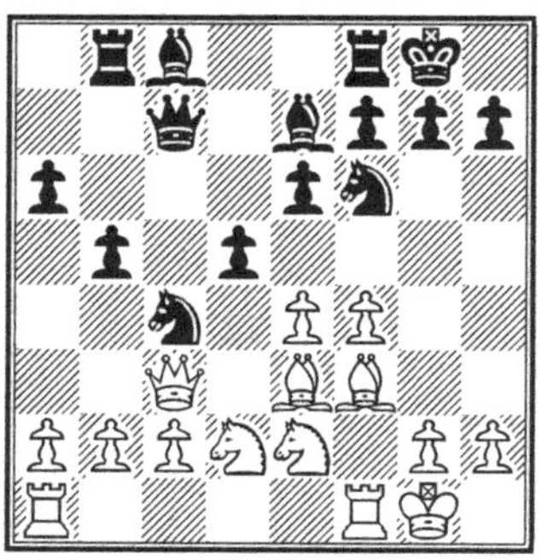

16.♗d4??

16.♘×c4 b×c4 17.e5 would have maintained an even game, but this loses a piece after a series of forced moves.

16...b4 17.♕d3 ♘×d2 18.♕×d2 d×e4 19.♗×f6 e×f3 20.♗e5 ♕b6+

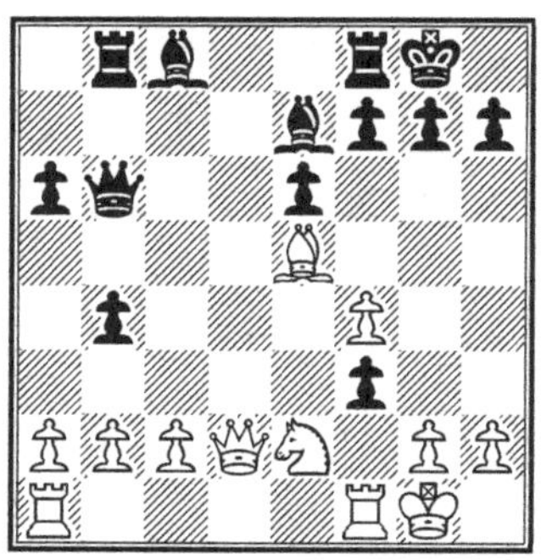

21.♘d4
21.♗d4 f×e2 22.♗×b6 e×f1♕+ 23.♖×f1 ♖×b6 leaves Black up ♖+♗+♗-for-♕.

21...♖b7 22.♖×f3 f6
The finishing touch, winning the trapped Bishop (0-1, 29).

Game 45

Rubinstein-Torre

Baden-Baden 1925, round 14

Akiva Rubinstein (1882-1961, historical Elo 2640, GM title 1950) was another all-time great to whom Torre might be expected to lose, but he did so here in the most lamentable fashion of all his Baden-Baden games. The position after

23.♖c1×d1:

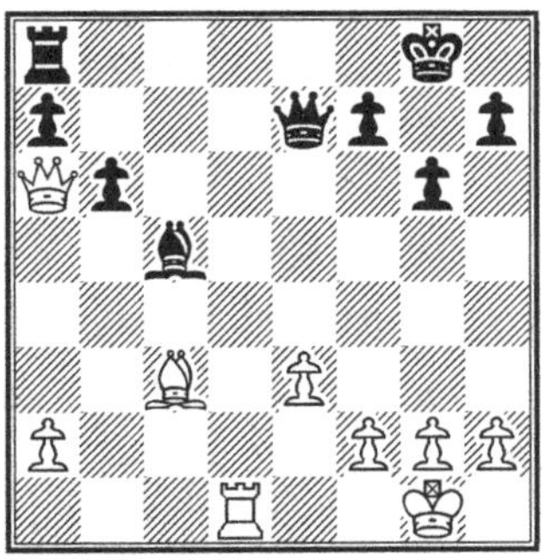

The game is dead even, and almost any reasonable move would keep it so, but now comes Torre's blunder.

23...♗×e3??
Apparently expecting 24.f×e3 ♕×e3+ 25.♔f1 ♕×c3−+, but White has other options.

24.♖e1

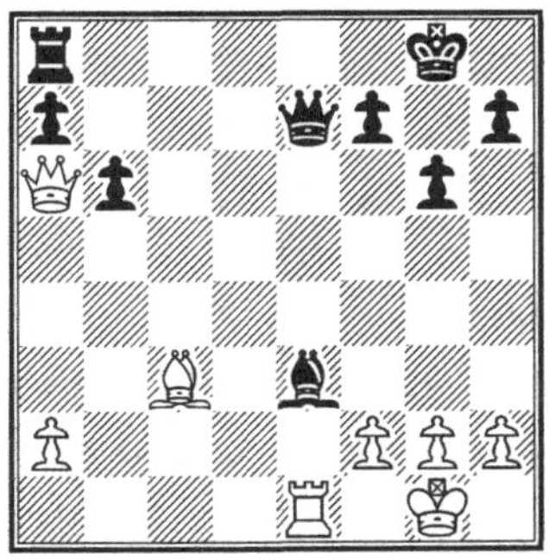

Of course!

24...♗×f2+ 25.♔×f2 ♕c5+ 26.♖e3 ♖e8 27.♕d3
and 1-0, 47.

Game 46

Torre-Tartakower

Baden-Baden 1925, round 15

Sicilian Defense [B42]

The cynically brilliant, Polish-born Savielly Tartakower (1887-1956, historical Elo 2560, GM title 1950) contributed more memorable witticisms and aphorisms to chess literature than perhaps all other writers combined. He was a prolific author, of both books and magazine articles, and a very active player, needing frequent income from chess to support his frequent losses in card games. At the time of Baden-Baden 1925 he was reaching his peak strength, and he would be considered one of the top ten players in the world until about 1930. One his famous sayings, from *Die Hypermoderne Schachpartie* (1924) was "Die Fehler sind dazu da, am gemacht zu werden," *i.e.* "The mistakes are there, that they may be made." It certainly applies to this arduous, baffling, even maddening game, one as rich in errors as it is in complications, and one of this collection's most difficult to analyze.

1.e4 c5 2.♘f3 e6 3.♘c3 a6 4.d4 c×d4 5.♘×d4 ♕c7

The Paulsen variation, one of oldest of Sicilian lines, and named not so much for Louis Paulsen, as for his less famous older brother Wilfried, who played it close to two dozen times 1879-1892. In the 1920s, Tartakower and Sämisch were among its more frequent devotees. Torre here seems well acquainted with it up to a point, and plays the main line for White.

6.♗d3

By far the most common reply. Next most frequent are 6.♗e2, 6.g3 and 6.♗e3.

6...♘f6 7.0–0 ♗e7 8.♕e2

Relatively rare; most common is 8.♔h1. The text had been seen only once before, in Znosko-Borovsky–Maróczy, London 1922.

8...d6 9.♗e3 ♘bd7

The aforementioned game continued 9...0–0 10.h3 ♘bd7 11.f4 b5 12.♔h1 ♗b7 13.♗d2 b4 14.♘d1∓. Torre avoids Znosko-Borovsky's tempi-losing line, but his play is not that much better.

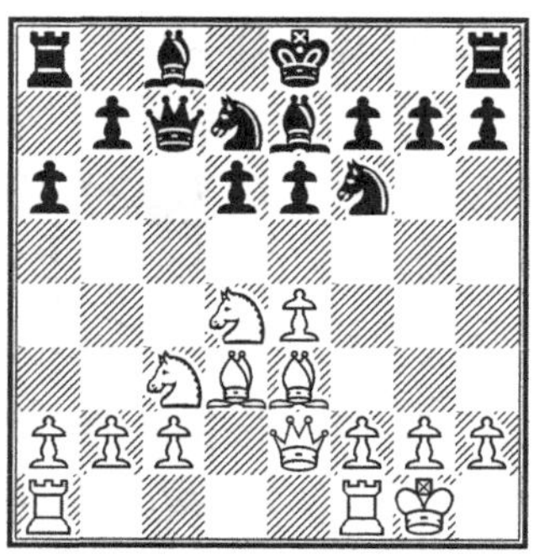

10.♖fd1

Using a deployment similar to what Torre played against Colle (Game 48 below), with similarly ineffective results. Today this seems a very strange move for White to play in a Sicilian Defense. The idea of playing ♖f1-d1, and then ♖a1-c1 to oppose Black's pressure on the c-file, has practically disappeared from master play.

White's Rooks are better placed at e1 and f1 to support central and kingside action, as in Yates-Opocensky, Marienbad 1925, which continued 10.f4 b5 11.♖ae1 ♗b7 12.a3 ♖c8 13.♔h1 ♘c5 14.♗f2 ♘fd7, and now White could have initiated an attack with 15.♘d5!? e×d5 16.e×d5 ♘f6 17.♘f5 ♘×d5 18.♗h4 ♘e6 19.♗×e7 ♘×e7 20.♘×e7 ♕×e7 21.f5.

10...b5 11.♖ac1

Continuing the aforementioned plan. An interesting alternative was 11.a4 b4 12.♘a2 forcing 12...♕b7, interfering with Black's intended queenside fianchetto.

11...♗b7 12.f3 0–0 13.a4?!

This is ineffective compared to move 11; in fact it is now downright disadvantageous. Better 13.♗f2 or 13.♔h1, awaiting developments. The text is the first of three bad moves out of four by Torre, after which begins a series of alternating mistakes that turn the game into a comedy of errors, where it seems Torre is repeatedly trying to lose and Tartakower refuses to win.

13...b4

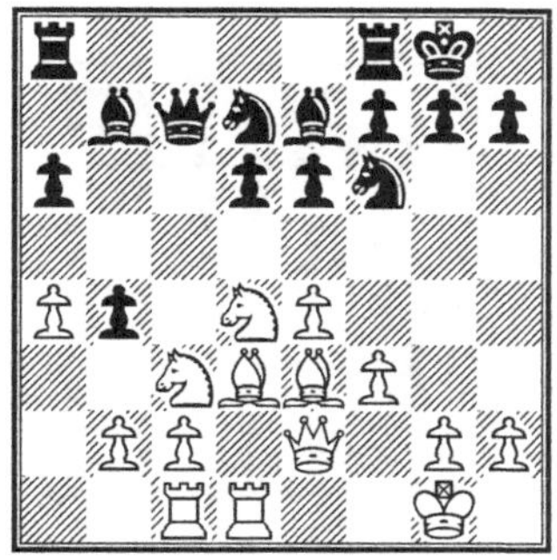

14.♘a2?

Torre compounds his mistake. 14.♘b1 was the a better retreat. Then after 14...d5 15.c3 b3! 16.♘d2 ♗d6 17.g3 d×e4 18.♘×e4 ♘×e4 19.♗×e4 ♗×e4 20.f×e4 ♘c5 White still stands worse (-1.02/25), but not nearly as bad.

14...d5! 15.c3

Just about White's only playable move. Not 15.e×d5? ♘×d5 16.♗f2 (else after 16...♘×e3 17.♕×e3 ♗d6/♗c5, the absence of White's dark-square Bishop will give Black an attack) 16...♘c5 and it is the absence of the light-square Bishop that will be felt (-2.68/25).

15...d×e4?

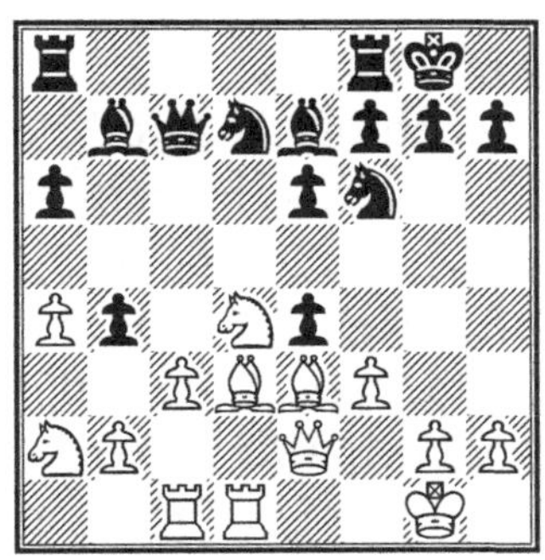

Tartakower starts his own series of errors! Just about winning was 15...b3!,

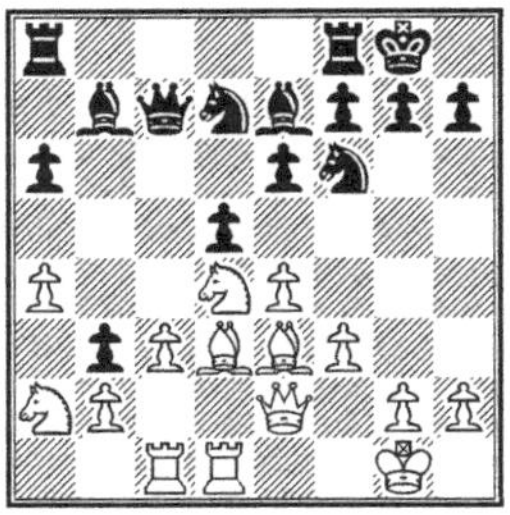

forcing either:

(a) 16.♘b4 d×e4 17.♗×e4 (if 17.♗×a6 e×f3 18.♘×f3 ♗×a6 19.♘×a6 ♕b7 20.♘b4 ♖×a4 21.♘d3 (-2.18/25)) 17...♘×e4 18.f×e4 ♘c5 (less good is 18...♗×e4 19.♘×a6 or 19.♘×b3) 19.e5 ♖fd8 (playable but less good is 19...♕×e5 20.♘dc6 ♕c7 21.♘×e7+ ♕×e7) 20.♗f2 ♘×a4 21.♘×b3 a5 22.♘d3 ♗×g2! 23.♔×g2 ♕b7+ 24.♔g1 ♕×b3 (-2.60/25); or

(b) 16.♘×b3 d×e4 17.♗×e4 (if 17.f×e4? ♘e5 18.♗f4 ♕b6+ 19.♘d4 ♘×d3 20.♖×d3 ♗×e4 -2.94/27) 17...♗×e4 18.f×e4 ♗d6 19.g3 ♗×g3! 20.a5 (not 20.h×g3? ♕×g3+ 21.♔h1 ♘e5 22.♘d2 ♘fg4 23.♗d4 f5! △ 24...♖f6 etc. with a lethal attack -4.47/24) 20...♗e5 21.♘b4 ♘×e4 (-2.09/27).

16.f×e4?

But Torre returns the favor! He could have clawed back to equality with 16.♗×e4! ♘×e4 (or 16...b3 17.♗×b7 ♕×b7 18.♘b4=) 17.c×b4 ♕e5 18.f×e4 ♘f6 19.♘f3 ♕×e4 20.♖c4 ♕f5□ (not 20...♕g6? 21.♘h4 ♕h5 22.♕×h5 ♘×h5 23.♖c7 ♗×h4 24.♖×b7±) 21.♖c7 ♗d5 22.♖×e7 ♗×a2=.

16...b×c3?!

The march of folly continues. 16...b3! 17.♘×b3 ♘e5 would transpose to variation (b) of the note to Black's 15th move, the parenthetical line beginning with 17.f×e4? ♘e5. The text ends Black's serious attacking chances for the time being, taking the assessment down from about -3.00 to -1.00.

17.♖×c3

This or 17.♘×c3 are about equally good.

17...♕a5

17...♕b8 was better.

18.b4!?

A fighting counter-stroke, which Black's reply makes more effective.

18...♕×a4

Grabbing the pawn allows Black to regain full equality. Best was 18...♕e5, and if 19.♘f3 ♕b8 putting the Queen back where she belonged anyway.

19.♖c7!□ ♖ab8 20.♖b1?

Missing 20.e5!:

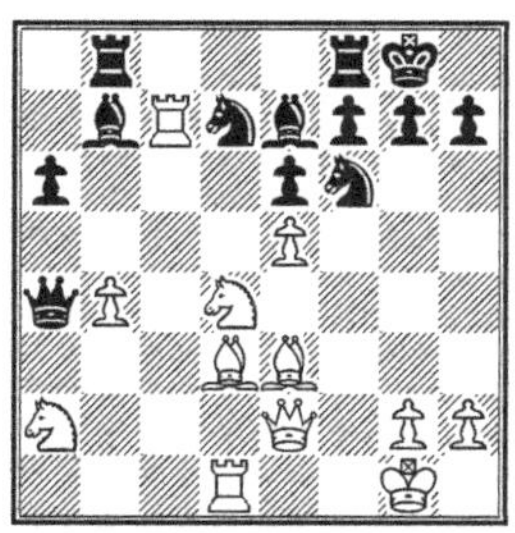

This forces either:

(a) the unclear 20...♘d5 21.♗c2! ♕a3 22.♗c1 ♕×a2 23.♗×h7+ ♔×h7

24.♕×a2 ♘×c7 25.♕c2+ ♔g8 26.♕×c7 ♖fd8 when though White has won the Queen for Rook and Bishop, Black has considerable compensation (+0.17/33); **(b)** the complicated 20...♘×e5 21.♖×e7 ♘×d3 22.♖×d3 ♘d5 (△23...♘×e7)

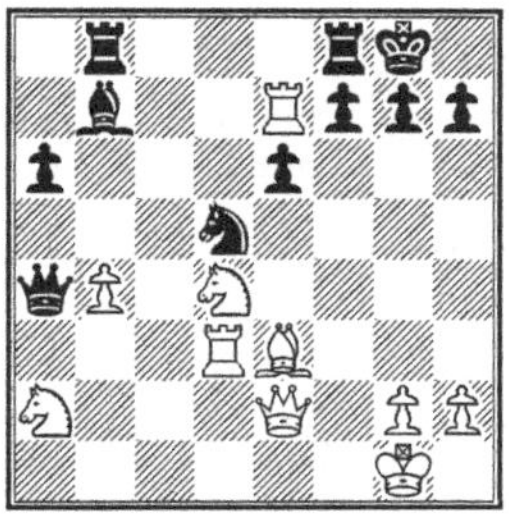

and now either

(b1) 23.♗g5 ♘×e7 24.♗×e7 ♖fe8 25.♖g3 ♖×e7 (25...g6 26.♗f6=) 26.♕e5 g6 27.♕×b8+ ♖e8 28.♕×b7 ♕d1+ 29.♔f2 ♕×d4+ 30.♖e3=, or

(b2) 23.♘×e6 ♘×e7 24.♘×f8 ♘d5 (if 24...♔×f8/♖×f8?? 25.♗c5) 25.♗h6!? ♕e8 (not 25...g×h6?? 26.♘e6 f6 (26...f×e6 27.♕×e6+ and mate shortly) 27.♖g3+ ♔h8 28.♘c5 ♕e8 29.♕×e8+ ♖×e8 30.♘×b7+−) 26.♕×e8 ♖×e8 27.♘d7 g×h6=.

The text revives Black's winning chances. Returning to the game (**20.♖b1?**):

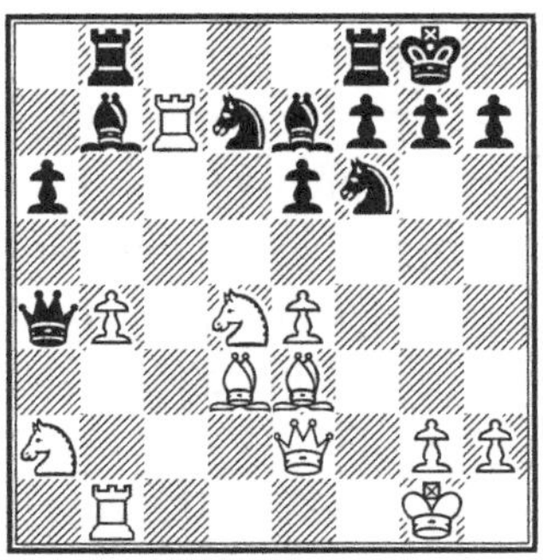

20...♘e5?!

Tartakower continues the cavalcade of confusion.

With 20...♖fc8! he could have regained the upper hand, *viz.* 21.♘c3 — This and 21.♖×b7 ♖×b7 22.♗×a6 ♖bc7 23.♗×c8 ♖×c8 are White's only remotely playable continuations; if 21.♖×c8+?? ♖×c8 △22...♘e5−+. — 21...♕a3 22.♘c2 ♖×c7 23.♘×a3 ♖×c3

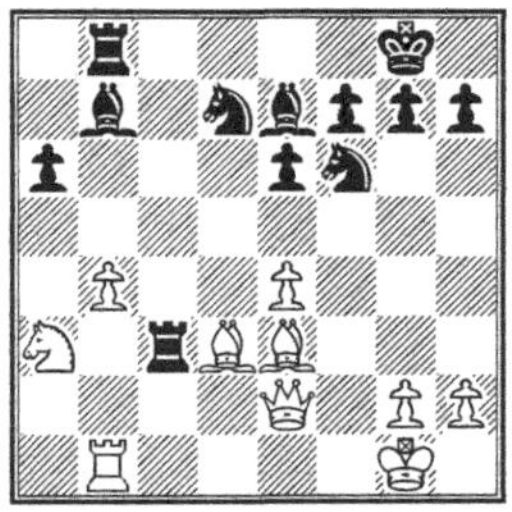

and

(a) 24.♘c4 ♖×d3 25.♕×d3 ♗×e4 26.♕d1 ♗×b1 27.♕×b1 ♖×b4 with ♖+♘+3♙ for the ♕; or

(b) 24.♘c2 ♘e5 25.♖d1 ♖d8 26.♘e1 ♗c6 △27...♘×d3 28.♘×d3 ♗b5; or

(c) 24.♖a1 ♗×b4 25.♘c2 ♗e7 and Black has two pawns and other compensation for the nominal ♕-vs-♖+♘ material deficit (-1.73/25).

Continuing the game, from previous diagram:

20...♘e5 21.♖×e7 ♘×d3 22.♘c3!□

The game is now completely even (0.00/23), though it won't stay that way for long!

22...♕a3□ 23.♘b3??

A terrible blunder that should have lost the game. Correct was 23.♖c7=.

23...♕×b4 24.♖c7

One move too late now. Stockfish's evaluation has gone from 0.00 to -6.50. Black now begins making optimal moves, forcing White's reply at all times.

24...♗×e4 25.♘d2 ♕d6 26.♖×b8 ♖×b8 27.♘d×e4 ♘×e4 28.♘×e4 ♖b1+ 29.♖c1

White's only slim hope; obviously 29.♕f1 ♖×f1+ or 29.♗c1 ♕×c7 are far worse.

29...♘×c1?!

Though both this and 29...♖×c1+ get the same computer evaluation, close to -7.00, the Rook capture is far better in human terms, because it forces 30.♗×c1 ♘×c1, taking two more pieces off the board and thus simplifying Black's task. The importance of this will be seen after move 32.

30.♕c2

An amazing position: all of Black's pieces are *en prise*, yet he is still winning.

30...♘e2+ 31.♔f2 ♕b8 32.♕×e2

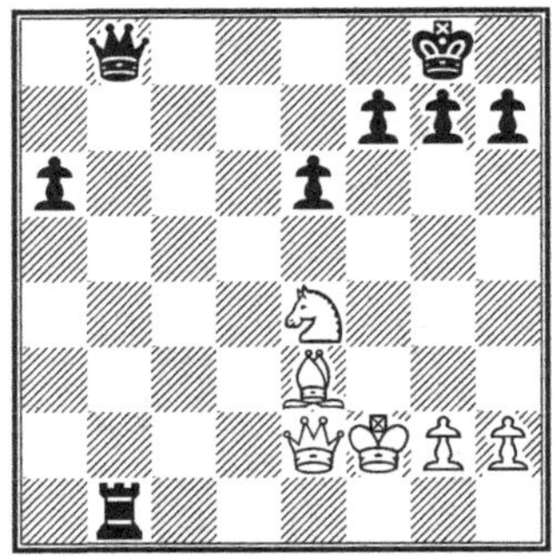

32...♕×h2?!

With this Black throws away his trump card (the a-pawn) and cuts his advantage almost in half.

Best was 32...♖b2 33.♘d2 ♕d6 34.♕c4 h6 (Also good is 34...♖×d2+ 35.♗×d2 ♕×d2+ 36.♔f1 g6 37.♕×a6, and with two extra pawns the Queen ending should not be too hard to win.) 35.♕c3 ♖a2 36.h3 a5

and stopping the pawn's advance will be unbearably costly (-6.38/26).

After the text, however, Black loses the a-pawn and his advantage dips to about -3.75. Which while still good enough to win, will require much more work and many difficult calculations.

33.♕×a6 ♕h4+ 34.♔f3 ♕h5+ 35.g4 ♕h1+ 36.♔g3

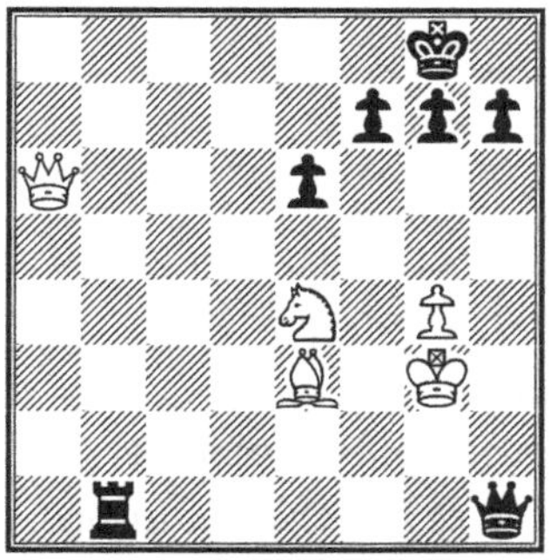

36...h6?

Tartakower blows his last chance to win! Correct was 36...♕e1+ (36...♖b8 was also good) 37.♗f2 ♖b3+ 38.♔h2 ♕b4□ 39.♕c8+ ♕f8 when exchanging Queens obviously loses, while if, say, 40.♕c2 ♕b8+ 41.♗g3 ♖b2! 42.♗×b8 ♖×c2+ with an easy ♖+4♙-vs-♗+♘+♙ endgame, or 40.♕c6 h6 41.♔g2 ♕d8 42.♘g3 ♖b4 43.♔h3 ♕b8 (-4.49/27), or 40.♕d7 h6 41.♗g3 ♕a8 (-4.53/27). It bears mentioning, however, that while Stockfish projects a Black win, with Queens on the board as in those last two variations, many moves are required before a position clearly winning to human perception can be realized. This is because the win will entail the advance of Black's king-side pawns, which can be very problematic and dangerous when a hostile Queen, Knight and Bishop still roam the steppe.

37.♕c8+!

Torre's eyes must have lit up at this unexpected deliverance. He now finds the only moves that force a draw.

37...♔h7 38.♕c2! f5 39.g×f5 e×f5 40.♘g5+!

This Tartakower probably did not foresee.

40...h×g5 41.♕×f5+

and perpetual check (½-½).

Had Black played 40...♔g6, then 41.♘f3! holds the draw, *e.g.* 41...♖f1 42.♘h4+ ♔h7 43.♕d3=, or 41...♖b4 42.♘e5+ ♔f6 43.♘d7+ ♔e6 (if 43...♔e7 44.♕c5+ ♔×d7 45.♕×f5+ etc.) 44.♘f8+ ♔f7 45.♕×f5+ etc.

According to ChessBase, though Tartakower played the Sicilian another 59 times in high-level events, it seems that after this he never again chose the Paulsen variation. Was that due to a bitter taste left by this failure? All we can say is: chess is a devilishly hard game.

Game 47

Grünfeld-Torre

Baden-Baden 1925, round 16

Dutch Defense [A90]

Here Torre faced Austrian grandmaster Ernst Grünfeld (1893-1962, GM title 1950, historical Elo 2550), who only a few months earlier was victor at the strong Merano 1924 tournament, scoring 10½-2½ to finish ahead of Spielmann, Rubinstein, Tarrasch, Colle and other famous masters. As such, he appeared to Torre a most formidable adversary. He was, furthermore, a great authority on openings, an area in which he clearly surpassed the young Mexican.

What should Torre play against the Viennese opening expert's 1.d4? It seemed foolish to attempt the Grünfeld Defense against Grünfeld himself. Finally, Torre decided on a complicated, double-edged system which, due to the fact that Torre had never played it before, Grünfeld would not expect. If furthermore Torre could leave established lines early and complicate the game, that would probably level the playing field. Psychologically this was highly advisable against Grünfeld, who disliked unclear complications in the opening. As it turned out, Torre's chosen plan worked to perfection. After the first few moves Grünfeld felt uncomfortable and began to show uncertainty. On move 12 he committed a serious error and on move 14 found himself forced to resign.

1.d4 e6

Torre avoids the immediate 1...f5, perhaps to rule out the Staunton Gambit, though Grünfeld was never known to essay it in serious play.

2.♘f3 f5 3.g3 ♘f6 4.♗g2

An old line, seen twice way back in the Steinitz-Zukertort match of 1872, where Steinitz won both games as White. Lasker played it twice in his 1890 match with Bird, winning and losing once each. Grünfeld had played it four times circa 1920-22, defeating Walter John, and drawing three times with Tartakower.

4...d5

This Stonewall variation also has an ancient lineage, going back to Somacarana-Cochrane, Calcutta, 1856, though there it was reached by 1.g3 d5 2.d4 f5 3.♗g2 ♘f6 4.♘f3 e6. Most commonly seen here is 4...♗e7 (2,648 games on CB), but the text is a close second with 2,252.

5.0-0 ♗d6

This was not really a new move; it had been seen in Lee-Bird, London 1891, and Mieses had played it twice, against Tarrasch at Teplitz-Schönau 1922 (½-½, 82), and Bogoljubow in the 5th round here at Baden-Baden (1-0, 35). But it seems to have escaped Grünfeld's notice, for he thought long on his next move.

6.c4 c6

All as in the games mentioned last note. Those now continued 7.e3, 7.♘bd2, and 7.♘c3, respectively (the last eventually becoming theory's main line), but Grünfeld has other ideas.

7.♕c2

White aims at the e4-square, a common target for White in the Dutch. However, in the Stonewall line it is very difficult for White to enforce the advance e2-e4. We are still not yet in uncharted seas, as Norman-Mieses, Hastings 1923-24 reached this by transposition (0-1, 34). It is not especially better or worse than the moves mentioned last note.

7...0–0 8.b3

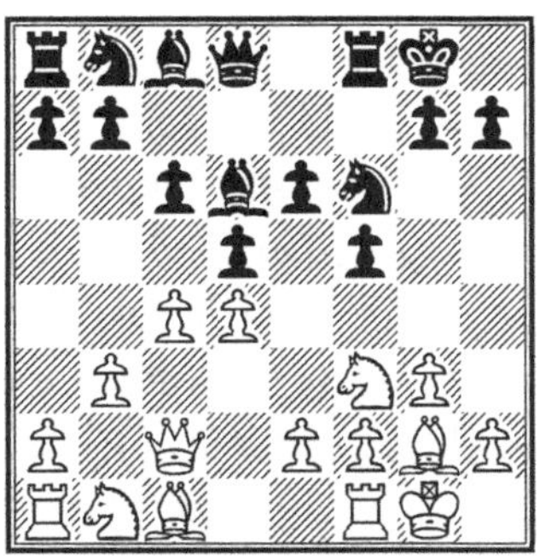

Finally breaking new ground. White decides on a common anti-Dutch deployment, but the formation chosen by Black is designed precisely to meet that deployment with a "stone wall." Most reasonable here, to capitalize on the unusual placement of Black's Bishop, would be 8.♗f4!, for example 8...♘e4 9.♘c3 ♘d7 10.♘×e4 ♗×f4 11.♘c5 ♘×c5 12.g×f4 ♘e4 13.♘e5 ♗d7 14.f3 ♘f6 15.c5 ♗e8 16.e3 ♖c8 17.♔h1 ♘h5 18.♕f2, with equality, as in Tarrasch-Torre in the 19th round, with a draw in 31 moves. Perhaps because of its strategic inappropriateness, the text move would not be seen again until Moisieev-Khasin, USSR Ch semi-final, Moscow 1949.

8...♘e4 9.♗b2 ♘d7 10.♘e5?!

A dubious move, showing that White is disoriented in this opening.
Better 10.♘c3, or 10.♘bd2 with the idea of ♘f3-e1-d3 and ♘d2-f3, overprotecting e5.

10...♕f6 11.f3?

Consistent, but tactically flawed. Better to retreat the Knight back to d3 or f3.

11...♘×e5!

We reverse here the judgement of the first edition, which said this was "anti-positional and could have been severely punished." In fact it is the best move on the board. The alternative suggested by the magazine *Czekoslovensky Sach*, 11...♘g5, is slightly better for White after 12.♘d3.
The text (**11...♘×e5!**) is actually a good try for the win, especially against someone like Grünfeld, who favored

a positional style and disliked tactical complications.

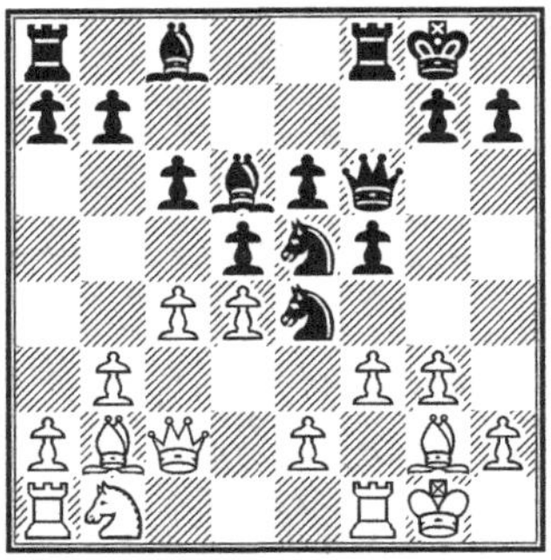

Best now was 12.c5, which both Torre and *Czekoslovensky Sach* thought would win, or at least be advantageous for White, because it puts three Black pieces under attack, and they cannot all be saved. But Black then has 12...♘g4! (not considered by the Czech magazine). Best then is 13.c×d6 (if 13.f×g4 ♗e7 White gets no material advantage to compensate for the attack he will come under, and if 13.f×e4?? ♕h6 and he can resign) 13...♘×h2! 14.♔×h2 ♕h6+ 15.♔g1 ♘×g3 16.♘c3, and now not 16...♘×f1? 17.♖×f1 ±, but 16...f4!:

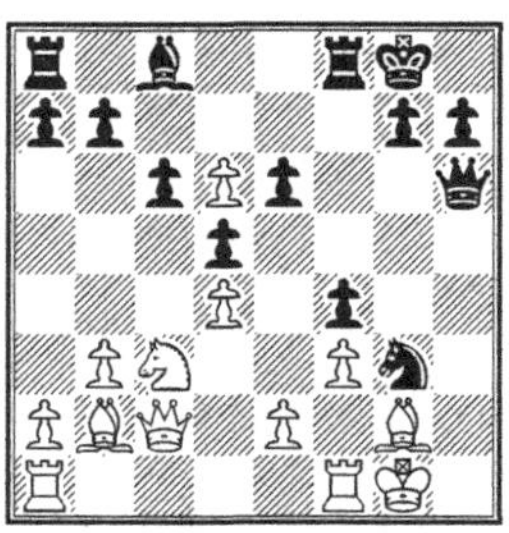

This throws the board into utter chaos. Two main lines ensue:

(a) 17.♖fe1? ♘f5 18.♘d1 ♘h4 19.e4□ ♕g5 20.♕f2 ♖f6 21.♔f1 b6! (△22...♗a6+) 22.♔e2,

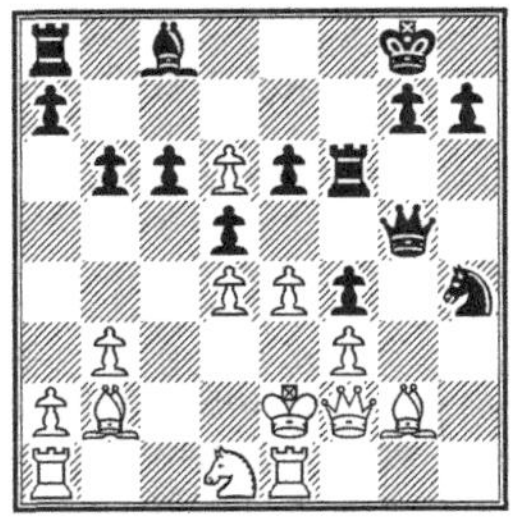

and Black wins with either 22...d×e4 23.♗h1 e3 24.♘×e3 f×e3 25.♕×e3 ♕g3, or 22...♗a6+ 23.♔d2 ♘×g2 24.♖g1 ♖g6, or simply 22...♘×g2 23.♖g1 ♖g6;

(b) 17.♖ae1□ ♖f6 18.e4□ ♗d7! 19.♘e2 ♕h4 20.♗c1 ♖af8 21.♘×g3 f×g3 22.♗h1□ g5 23.e5 ♖h6 24.♕g2□ c5 25.a4 (if 25.d×c5? ♗b5) 25...c×d4 26.♖d1□ ♖c8 27.♖d3□ ♖c3∞ and the struggle rages on. Though no clear win for Black is apparent, this line requires White to find so many "only moves" that it seems unlikely any human player could put up an adequate defense. We leave further analysis to the reader.

Torre himself did not fully appreciate the strength of his 11th move. Writing about the game later, he said "Black's move is showy, and it sets a trap by inviting White to recapture with the d-pawn. Unfortunately for Grünfeld, he suffered an instant of confusion and did not analyze that with 12.c5 he would have three enemy pieces under attack. He falls instead for a swindle."

Returning to the game and its sudden conclusion:

12.d×e5??
An unspeakable blunder, amazing for a player of Grünfeld's stature. Now it, instead of 11...♘×d5, is "severely punished."

12...♗c5+ 13.♔h1 ♘×g3+ 0–1
Swift mate follows: 14.h×g3 ♕h6+ 15.♗h3 ♕×h3#, another combination for those Reinfeld-style quiz books.

Irving Chernev relates that Grünfeld was extremely upset and swore to friends that the next time he faced Torre he would take drastic vengeance.

Game 48

Torre-Colle

Baden-Baden 1925, round 18

Sicilian Defense [B83]

Edgard Colle (1897-1932, historical Elo 2490) was Belgium's top player in the 1920s. Despite perennially poor health, Colle was a very active player, averaging about four or five tournaments per year. He was always a gentlemanly, courteous opponent, and was popular with both chess fans and organizers because of his bright combinative style. Though in events of such caliber as Baden-Baden 1925 he was usually somewhat outclassed, he did win six Belgian championships and several international tournaments before his premature death brought on by complications of a gastric ulcer. Those interested in his career and games may wish to obtain Kingston's book *Edgard Colle: Caïssa's Wounded Warrior* (Russell Enterprises, 2021). Colle was at any time capable of stellar attacking play, as in his series of brilliant sacrifices against Grünfeld at Berlin 1926, but here he is seen mainly on the defensive, in what seems superficially like an uneventful draw, but which nonetheless has several interesting unplayed possibilities below the surface.

1.e4 c5 2.♘f3 ♘c6 3.d4 c×d4 4.♘×d4 ♘f6 5.♘c3 d6 6.♗e2 e6
Colle chooses the Scheveningen variation, rather than the Dragon with 6...g6.

7.0–0 ♗e7

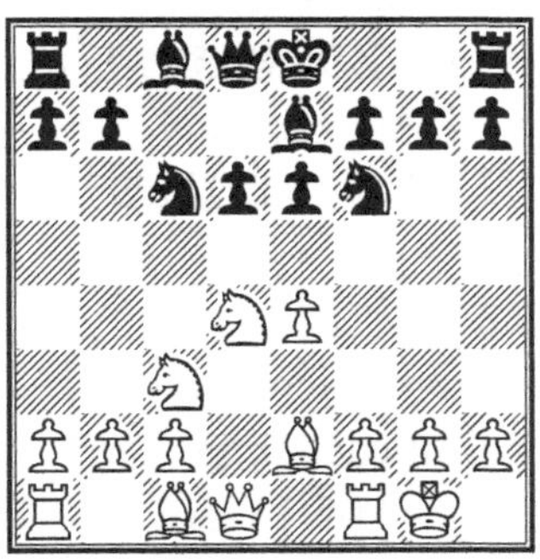

8.b3

A most unusual continuation, found in less than one percent of games reaching the above position. Far more common are 8.♗e3, 8.♔h1, and 8.f4. The text had been played twice before, in Michell-Maróczy, Hastings 1923-24 (0-1, 49), and Geus-Euwe, Scheveningen 1925 (1-0, 40), and it would crop up again in the games of some high-ranking players: Alekhine-Euwe, exhibition match 1926-27 (½-½, 40), Taimanov-Panov, Baku 1944 (1-0, 31), and Ragozin-Benko, Moscow-Budapest team match, 1949 (½-½, 39). While not a bad move, objectively there is little to recommend it beyond surprise value.

8...0-0 9.♗b2 a6

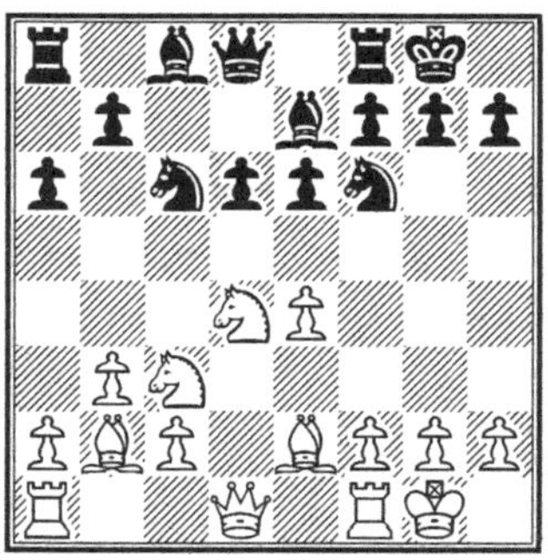

About 18 months later, Alekhine-Euwe continued 9...♕a5 10.♕d2 ♖d8 11.♖ad1 ♘xd4 12.♕xd4 ♘e8 13.♕e3 ♗d7 14.a3 ♗f6 15.f4 ♖ac8=.

10.♕d2

Varying from Michell-Maróczy, which had continued 10.g3 ♕c7 11.♗f3 ♗d7 12.♘ce2 b5 13.♖c1 ♘e5 14.♗g2 ♕b6∓. Taimanov-Panov would proceed 10.♔h1 ♗d7 11.f4 ♕a5 12.♗f3 ♖fd8 13.g4 ♘xd4?! (△13...d5!) 14.♕xd4 ♖ac8 15.g5, and White eventually got a decisive kingside attack.

10...♕c7 11.♖fd1 ♗d7 12.♖ac1 ♖ac8 13.♕e3 ♖fd8 14.♕g3 ♘e8

To oppose Bishops on the long diagonal with ...♗e7-f6, but a better Bishop deployment was 14...♘xd4 15.♖xd4 ♗c6∓.

15.♘b1

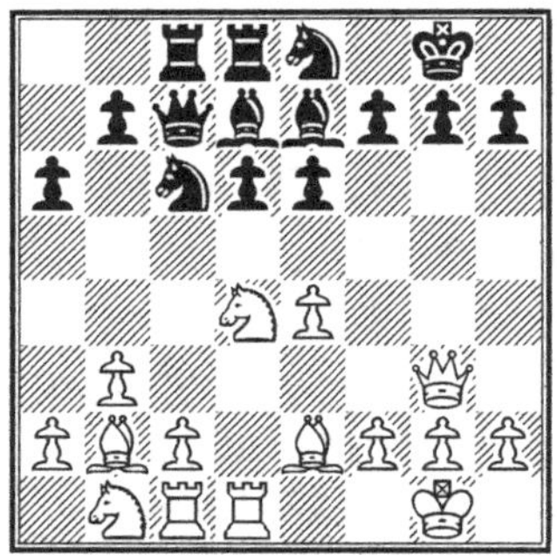

15...♗f6

Interesting would have been 15...♘b4. The threat of 16...♘xa2 forces the white Knight right back: 16.♘c3 (if 16.a3?? ♘a2 wins the Exchange) 16...♗f6 17.a3 ♘c6, and if White persists in trying to force c2-c4, then 18.♘b1 ♗e5 19.♕f3 (if 19.f4?! ♘xd4 20.♗xd4 ♗xd4+ 21.♖xd4 e5∓ (-1.08/25)) 19...d5! 20.exd5 ♘xd4 21.♗xd4 ♗xh2+ 22.♔f1 ♗f4 23.♗b6□ ♕xb6 24.dxe6 ♗xe6 25.♕xf4 ♖xd1+ 26.♗xd1 (26.♖xd1? ♖xc2) 26...♕c5∓.

16.c4

Arriving by a roundabout route at a Maróczy Bind sort of position.

16...♕b6 17.♕e3 d5?!

This premature counter-thrust enables White to summon up threats. Better a waiting move such as 17...♕c5, 17...♕a5, 17...h6, or 17...g6, with an even game in each case.

18.c5!?

The only move with potential advantage for White.

Not 18.c×d5?? ♗×d4 19.♗×d4 ♘×d4 20.♕×d4 (or 20.♖×c8 ♘×e2+ etc.) 20...♕×d4 21.♖×d4, allowing 21...♖×c1+−+. The other d5 capture, 18.e×d5 e×d5 19.c5 (again not 19.c×d5?? ♘×d4 etc.) 19...♕c7 would be quite even (+0.25/28).

18...♕a5

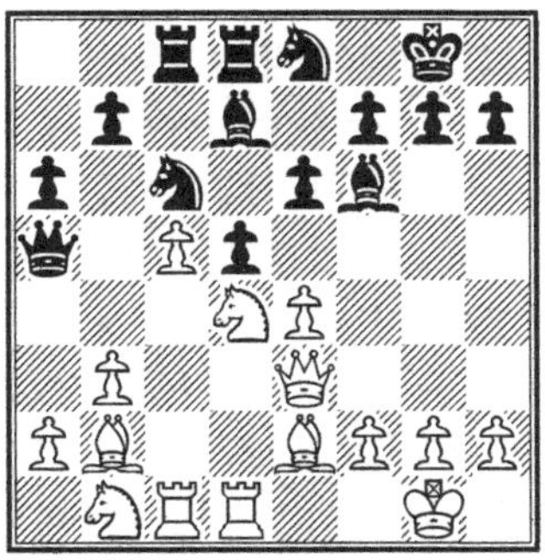

19.e×d5

A good alternative was 19.♘×c6!? ♗×c6 20.e5 ♕×a2□ (if 20...♗e7? 21.a3 △22.♗d3 and ♘b1-d2-f3 etc. with excellent attacking prospects (+2.06/25)) 21.♗d4 ♗e7 22.♘c3 ♕a5 (not 22...♕×b3?? 23.♖b1 ♕a3 24.♖a1 ♕b4 25.♖db1+−) 23.♗d3 and again White has attacking prospects, if not so strong as in the 20...♗e7 variation.

19...e×d5 20.a3

The position is approximately equal, though Black's isolated d-pawn can become a liability.

20...♘×d4?!

This series of exchanges has the net effect of Black trading a kingside piece (the ♗f6) for a queenside piece (the ♗b2). As such it is very much to Torre's taste.

Better were 20...♕c7, 20...g6, or 20...h6.

21.♗×d4 ♗×d4 22.♕×d4 ♘f6 23.b4 ♕c7 24.♘c3 ♗f5?

A mistake that might have lost the game. Best was 24...♗c6±.

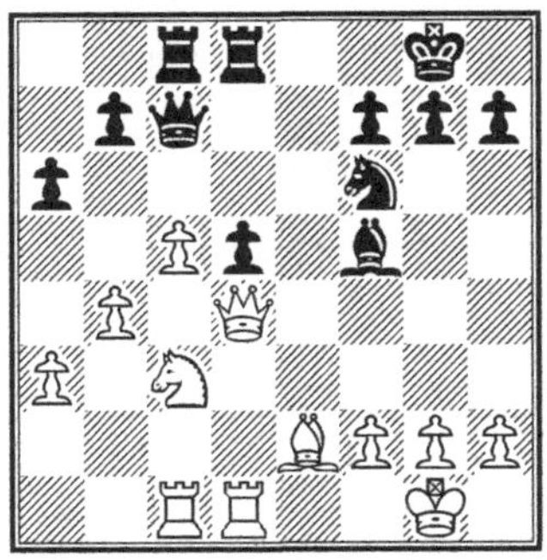

25.♗d3

Not bad, but much stronger was 25.g4! ♗e6 26.g5,

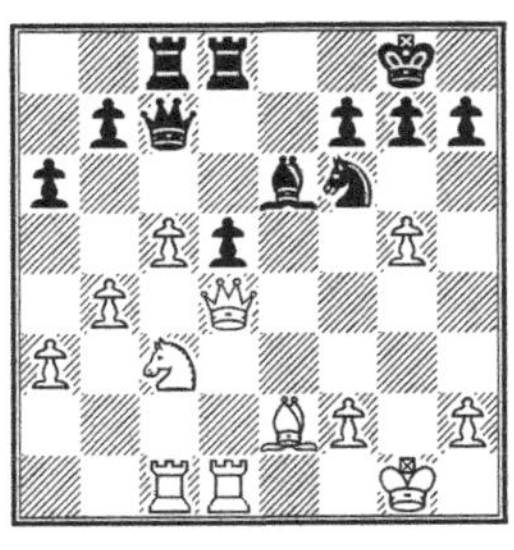

and Black has the unpleasant choice between

(a) 26...♘e4, losing a pawn to 27.♘×e4 d×e4 28.♕×e4; or

(b) 26...♘d7, a worse way to lose a pawn: 27.♘×d5 ♗×d5 28.♕×d5, or

(c) 26...♘e8 27.♗f3 ♕e7 28.♕e5 (not 28.♘/♗×d5?? ♕×g5+ −+) 28.h4 ♘c7 29.♖d3 △30.♖cd1 with maximal, nearly paralyzing pressure on the d-pawn (+2.75/25). If 29...♖d7 30.♘a4 △31.♘b6 prevents Black from bringing both Rooks to the pawn's defense.

Returning to the game (from previous diagram - **25.♗d3**):

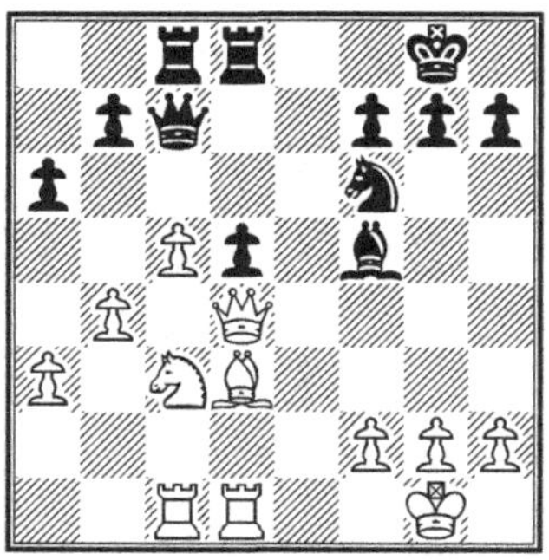

25... ♕d7?!

Better 25...♗×d3 and after either 26.♖×d3 or 26.♕×d3 the worst is over for Black (about +1.00 in either case).

26.h3

Stronger was 26.♗e2 △27.♗f3 in most lines.

26...h6 27.a4?!

This lets most of White's advantage slip away. Best again was 27.♗e2, with a definite plus for White (+1.80/25).

27...♗×d3 28.♖×d3

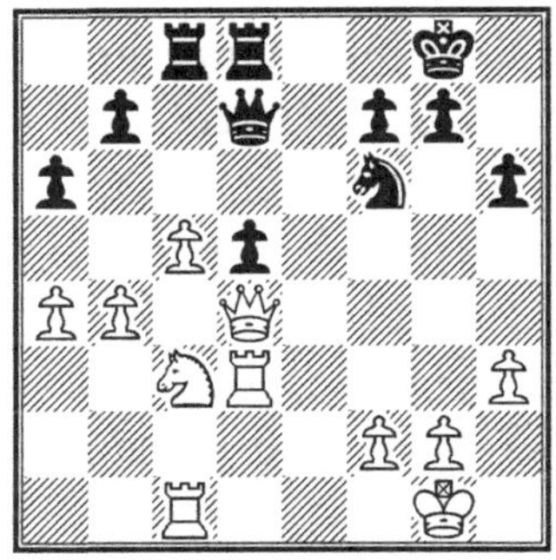

28... ♕c7

Somewhat better was 28...a5, and after either 29.♖b1 a×b4 30.♖×b4 or 29.b×a5 ♕e7 30.♘a2 ♘e4, Black is out of the woods with an even game. Even so, it soon becomes apparent that though his isolated d-pawn is weak, Black can muster as many pieces in defense of it as White can in attack. The classic technique against such an isolani requires as the final blow the advance of a pawn to c4 or e4, capitalizing on the pin along the d-file. But here, White has no such pawn available. Another technique that sometimes works is for the attacker to centralize his King prior to forcing a general exchange of pieces, whereupon the King can pick up the pawn. But that is not feasible here either.

29.a5 ♕c6 30.♖e1

If 30.♖cd1 intending ♕d4-f4-f3 so that the Queen is not the lead attacker of the pawn, Black simply plays 30...♖d7 and 31...♖cd8.

31...♖c7 31.♘e4

This leads to a major simplification, but it is not clear that White has any better move.

31...♖e7 32.♘×f6+ ♕×f6 33.♖×e7 ♕×e7 34.♖e3 ♕d7 35.♖g3 g6 36.♖e3 ♖e8 37.♖×e8+ ♕×e8 ½-½

It is a pity this was the only game between Torre and Colle. One suspects two such tacticians could have produced some sparkling battles, like those between Colle and Spielmann, who in nine exciting games scored four wins each, with only one draw.

Game 49

Torre-Yates

Baden-Baden 1925, round 20

Barry Attack [D00]

Fred Dewhirst Yates (1884-1932, historical Elo 2470) had been Britain's foremost player since 1913. Quitting his job as an accountant around 1909, he became a chess professional and made a small but adequate living from play and journalism. Like Colle his full potential was perhaps unrealized due to chronic ill health. Still, he was six times British champion, played in three Olympiads, and in tournament play he defeated many of the greatest players of his time, including Alekhine twice and Rubinstein and Bogoljubow three times each. His tournament results had an odd inconsistency: a disproportionate number of his wins were against the best players, and a high percentage of his losses were to the weaker ones. Here he may have taken newcomer Torre for one of the latter and played accordingly

1.d4 ♘f6 2.♘f3 g6 3.♘c3 d5 4.♗f4 c6

As mentioned earlier, this was first seen in Tartakower-Wahltuch, London 1922 (1-0, 32). Apparently intended to prevent ♘c3-b5, it is prematurely committal and needlessly passive. Correct was 4...♗g7 followed by 5...0–0, as in Game 4, Torre-Frink, with an eye to 6...c7-c5. Interestingly, Yates had already played that way against Capablanca at New York 1924, getting a reasonably good game and losing only after 77 moves.

5.e3 ♗g7 6.♗d3

Some 60-odd years later, when the British masters Mark Hebden and Julian Hodgson began popularizing the Barry Attack, 6.♗e2 came to be preferred. But the text is playable.

6...0–0 7.0–0

Later theory recommends 7.♕d2 △8.0–0–0, followed soon by h2-h4-h5 and a kingside attack, the Bishop on e2 supporting the pawn advance.

7...♘bd7

It was better to get the Queen's Bishop into action by 7...♗g4, before making this move.

8.♖e1

White threatens 9.e4. This prompts Black's following advance, which shows that 4...c6 was a loss of time.

8...c5

Now not 9.e4? d×e4 10.♘×e4 ♘×e4 11.♗×e4 c×d4 winning a pawn, since if 12.♘×d4?? e5.

9.♕d2 a6 10.♘e5

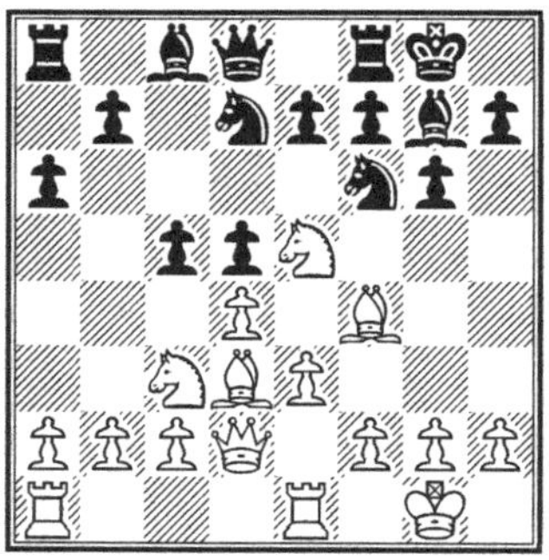

10...♘×e5

Worth considering was 10...♘h5, forcing 11.♘×d7 ♗×d7 12.♗e5 f6 13.♗g3 ♘×g3 14.h×g3∓. This variation shows another reason 6.♗e2 came to be preferred over 6.♗d3, as then 10...♘h5?! 11.♗×h5 would not be good for Black.

11.♗×e5 c4?!

This advance is not thematic. Now White will be able to transfer his Bishop to f3 to support the advance e3-e4, which will give him an enduring initiative. We saw a similar error in Game 4 (Torre-Frink), though in that case Black did not trade Knights on e5. That difference changes White's strategy. In the earlier game he exploited the weak move ...c5-c4 by striking at the advanced pawn with b2-b3. In the present case, it is much more effective to advance the e-pawn.

12.♗e2

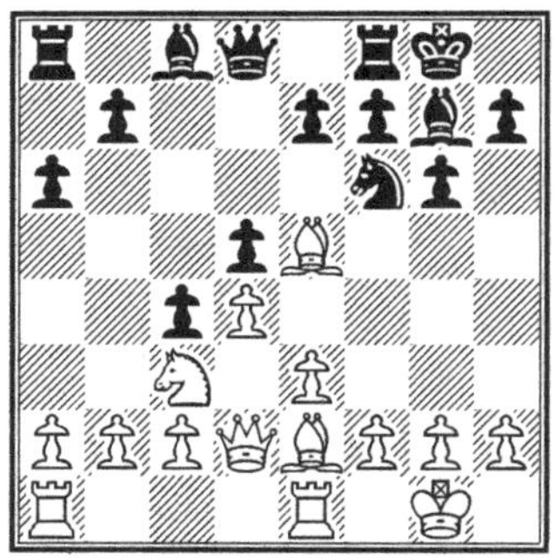

12...♗f5

The *Deutsche Schachblätter* commented "Black wishes to impede the advance e3-e4; nevertheless, the Bishop is ill-situated on f5, in consequence of which Black will soon find himself in a difficult situation. It was preferable to play 12...b5." The German annotator was perhaps too strong in his condemnation of the text; the only slightly better move was 12...e6, but he was quite wrong in his suggested alternative. After 12...b5? 13.♗×f6 ♗×f6 14.♘×d5! White wins a pawn, since if

14...♕×d5?? 15.♗f3 and 16.♗×a8 wins both a pawn and the Exchange.

13.♗f3 e6

This is undesirable in that it obstructs the mobility of Black's light-squared Bishop and excludes it from whatever might occur on the queenside, yet it is necessary to support the d-pawn so that Black can mobilize his queenside pawns.

14.♕e2 g5?

Apparently intended either to threaten the ♗f3, or give the ♗f5 a retreat square. Whatever Black's rationale, the text is a miscalculation that weakens his kingside and begins his downfall. Better either 14...h5 or 14...b5, with only a slight disadvantage.

15.e4! d×e4 16.♘×e4 ♘×e4 17.♗×e4

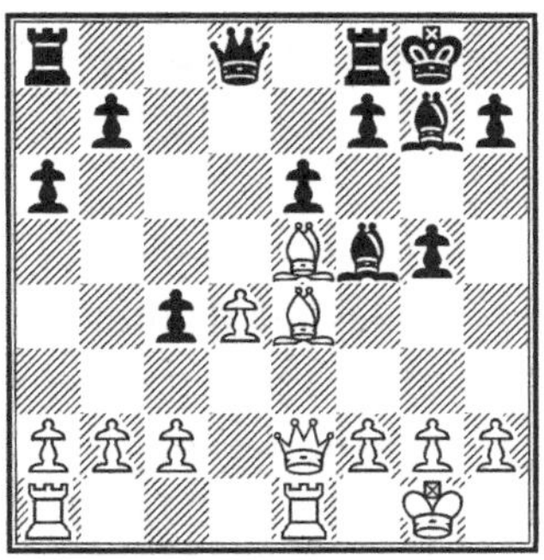

17...♗×e5

If 17...f6 18.♗g3, and either 18...♗×e4 19.♕×e4 ♖e8 20.♕×b7±, or 18...♖f7 19.d5! ♕c8□ (19...♗×e4? 20.d×e6 ♖e7 21.♕×e4+−) 20.d×e6 ♕×e6 21.♗×f5 ♕×f5 22.♖ad1±, a position where White commands all the open lines.

18.d×e5 ♕c7?

A serious error. Necessary were either 18...♗×e4 or 18...♗g6.

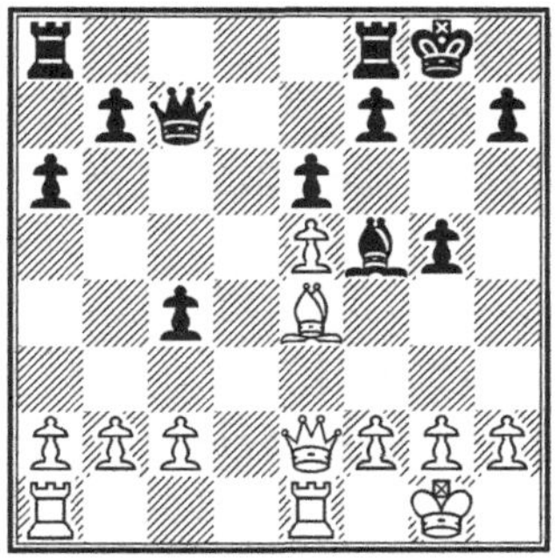

19.♕f3

Not bad, but Torre misses a chance to wrap things up early. Winning was 19.♗×f5 e×f5 20.♕h5 ♕e7 21.♖e3 f4 22.♖h3 f6 (this or 22...f5 is forced) 23.e×f6 ♖×f6 24.♕×g5+ ♔h8 25.♕d5,

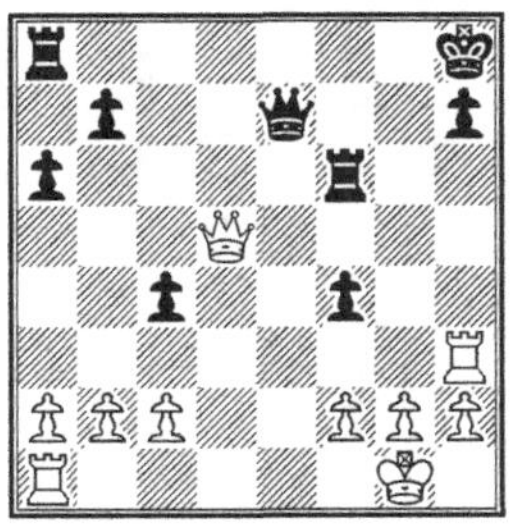

and now:

(a) 25...♖c8 26.♔f1 b5 27.♖e1 ♕g7 28.♖h5 (+4.15/29), or

(b) 25...♖e8 26.♕×c4 ♖c6 27.♕d4+ ♕e5□ 28.♕×e5+ ♖×e5 29.c3 ♖e2 30.b3 ♖c2 31.♖d1 ♖2×c3 32.♖×c3 ♖×c3 33.g4! ♖c2 (if 33...f×g3? 34.h×g3 +5.06/25) 34.♖d8+ ♔g7 35.♖d7+ ♔g6 36.♖×b7 ♖×a2 37.h4 (+3.82/30).

19...♗×e4?
This puts White in the driver's seat again. Necessary was 19...♗g6 with good drawing chances (+1.01/29).

20.♖×e4!
Much stronger than 20.♕×e4.

20...♖ac8?
Black had to play 20...♕e7 to have any hope (+2.48/23).

21.h4 ♕e7 22.h×g5
Almost any reasonable move wins for White now, for example 22.♖g4 f6 23.e×f6 ♕×f6 24.♕×f6 ♖×f6 25.♖×g5+ ♔h8 26.♖d1 (+4.41/27), or 22.♖d1 ♖c5 23.♕e3 ♔h8 24.h×g5 ♖g8 25.f4 ♖d5 26.♖×d5 e×d5 27.♖d4 ♕e6 28.♕f3 ♖d8 29.b4 (+3.92/24).

22...♔h8

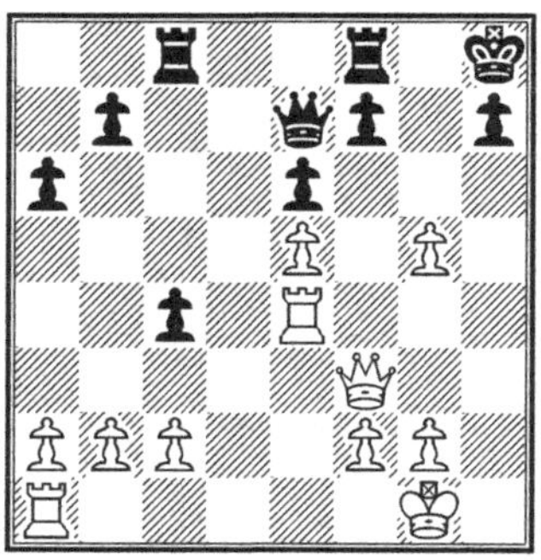

At this point in the first edition we gave the following note: "The play we will see from the diagrammed position is very instructive. White wants to avoid an exchange of Queens, because despite White's pawn plus, Black would then be able to draw with relative ease. Consequently, White's plan should involve an attack on the black King, however a straightforward piling up of forces will fail, because Black is in position to bring all his pieces to the King's defense. In such cases one must use a technique Capablanca called 'the sudden attack from a different sector.' Applied to the present situation, White must, by various threats and maneuvers, force his opponent to focus on the queenside, in such a way that Black will be unable to shift his forces and respond rapidly to a kingside emergency. In carrying out these diversionary queenside maneuvers, White must be sure to maintain the coordination of his pieces so that they are ready for a lightning-like, orchestrated shift to the kingside."
Effectively, that is how the game turns out, but only because of errors on both sides (time pressure was no doubt a factor). In fact White had a more direct path to victory, as we will show.

23.♕e3?!
With this and his next move, Torre almost gives away his winning chances. Contrary to the first edition's note, the immediate exchange of Queens was in fact best: 23.♕f6+! ♕×f6 24.g×f6. This both cages in the black King, and makes it impossible for Black to defend adequately all his weak points, which

include his back rank and his f- and h-pawns. The seriousness of White's threats arising therefrom, including mate, and queening his e- or f-pawn, enable White to disregard threats to his queenside pawns. Best play continues 24...♖fd8 25.g3! ♖c5 26.♔g2 ♖dd5 27.f4! ♖d2+ 28.♔f3 and:

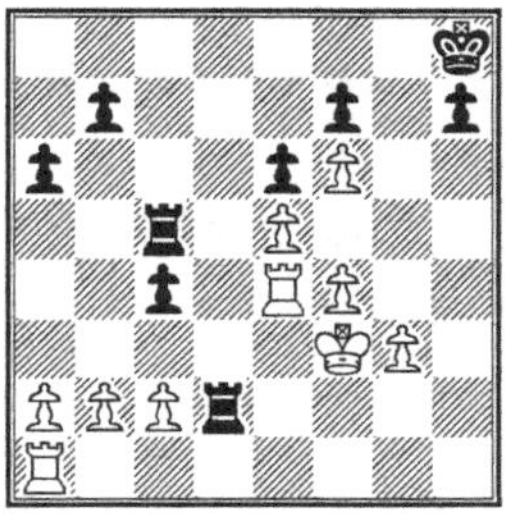

(a) 28...♖h2?? 29.♖d1 and either 29...♖c8 30.♖×c4! etc., or 29...h5 30.♖d8+ ♔h7 31.♖ed4 △ 32.♖4d7 +−; (b) 28...b5 29.♖h1 ♖cd5 30.♖e2 b4 31.♔e3 ♖×e2+ 32.♔×e2 ♖a5 33.♖d1 h5 34.♖d8+ ♔h7 35.♔e3 ♖×a2 36.♖f8 ♔g6 37.♖g8+ ♔h6 (if 37...♔h7 38.♖g7+ ♔h6 39.♖×f7 +−) 38.f5 ♖a5 39.♔f4 etc. (+12.84/22);
(c) 28...♖×c2?? 29.♖d1:

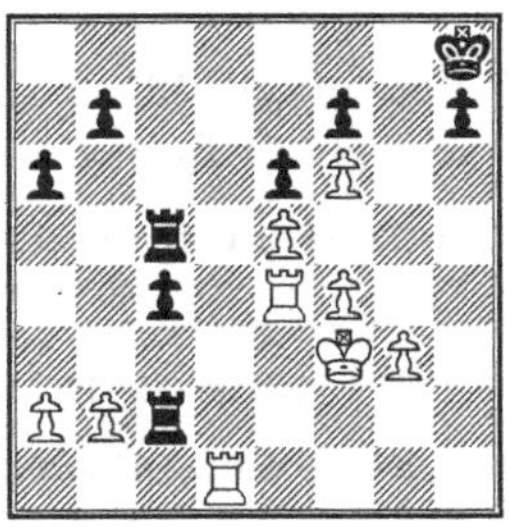

Now Black has only the ugly choice between

(c1) 29...♖d5 30.♖×d5 e×d5 31.♖d4 h5 32.♖×d5 ♔h7 33.f5 ♖×b2 34.♖d7 ♔g8 35.e6 and mate in ten, or
(c2) 29...♖c8 30.♖ed4 ♖g8 31.♖d8 h6 32.f5 ♖×d8 33.♖×d8+ ♔h7 34.♖f8 (+26.30), or
(c3) 29...h5 30.♖h1 ♖d5 31.♖×h5+ ♔g8 32.♖e1 ♖d3+ 33.♔g4 and Stockfish announces mate in 13.

Returning to the game:

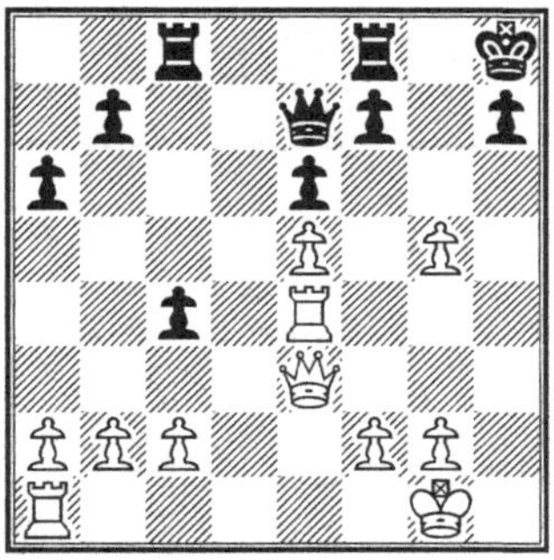

23...♖g8 24.f4?
This could have thrown the win away. Better 24.♖g4 and White may still have a shot (+1.98/32).

24...b5?!
But Yates misses his chance, which was 24...♖gd8! 25.♖e1 c3!? 26.b×c3 ♕a3 27.c4 ♕×e3+ 28.♖1×e3 ♖d2 29.♖c3 ♖c5, and though White is now two pawns up, his Rooks have lost their mobility and his advantage has shrunk badly (+0.75/30). A draw seems likely with best play by both sides.

25.♖d1 ♖cd8 26.♖ed4 26...♕c5?
The first of three bad moves in a row, each worse than the last, by which Yates seals his fate.
Necessary was 26...♖×d4 27.♕×d4 h6!? 28.♔f2! (28.g×h6?! ♕h4 ⇄) 28...♔g7

29.g×h6+ ♔×h6 30.♖h1+ ♔g7 31.♕e3 ♔f8 and Black can still fight on.

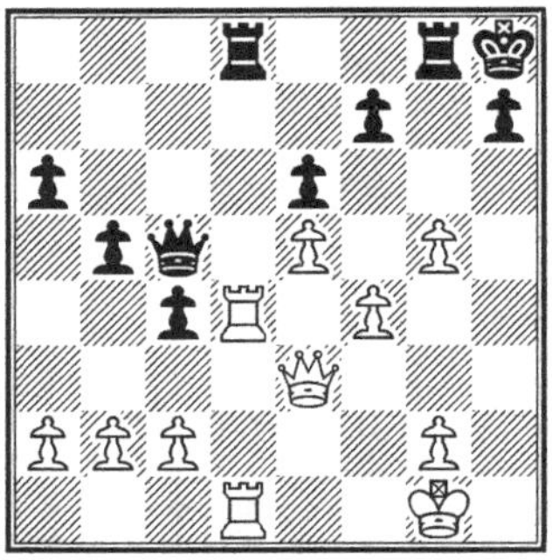

27.♔f2 ♖c8??

27...♖×d4 28.♕×d4 ♕c7 was the least evil.

28.♖h1! ♕e7??

28...♕f8 would have prevented mate, but still lost to 29.f5 e×f5 30.e6 ♕g7 31.♖dh4 ♖gf8 32.♕h3 etc. (+9.92/26).

29.♖×h7+! ♔×h7 30.♕h3+ ♔g6 31.♕h6+ ♔f5 32.♕h7+ ♖g6 33.♕h3# 1-0

An imperfect but hard-fought and entertaining game.

Game 50

Nimzovich-Torre

Baden-Baden 1925, round 21

Nimzovich Attack [A06]

So much has been written about and by Riga-born Aron Nimzovich (1886-1935, historical Elo 2615) that we hardly need elaborate much here. The Baden-Baden tournament, in which he finished 9th, ½-point ahead of Torre, was not one of his best, but immediately afterwards he began scoring triumphs that brought him recognition as probably the third-best player in the world, behind only Capablanca and Alekhine. These included an equal 1st with Rubinstein at Marienbad 1925 (+8 -1 =6 against many of the same players as at Baden-Baden, though without Alekhine), clear firsts at Dresden 1926 (+8 =1, well ahead of Alekhine and Rubinstein), and Hanover 1926 (+6 =1, ahead of Rubinstein), an equal 1st with Tartakower at London 1927 (+7 -2 =2), and clear first at Carlsbad 1929 (+10 -1 =10) ahead of almost all the world's best. So much has been made of Nimzovich's theoretical originality and personal eccentricity that his resourcefulness and qualities as a chess fighter are sometimes overlooked. Both his and Torre's are strongly in evidence here, but so is their fallibility, resulting in a difficult and perplexing, yet engrossing game.

1.♘f3 ♘f6 2.b3 d5 3.e3

Nimzovich's innovations on the white side of opening theory often involved playing as if he had Black. Here, for the first time, he deploys in a reverse

Queen's Indian, which he would repeat three times over the next few years, twice at New York 1927 and once at San Remo 1930. It would also be taken up later by Tartakower, Fine, and even Capablanca. Though this came to be called the Nimzovich Attack, it was first seen in three games by Joseph Henry Blackburne, vs. Minckwitz at Berlin 1881, Weiss at Vienna 1882, and Jacobs at Scarborough 1909. In this particular line, with 3.e3, Blackburne did better than Nimzovich, scoring +2 -1 to the Latvian's +0 -1 =3.

3...♗f5

Also possible is 3...♗g4, as seen in Nimzovich's games with Marshall and Vidmar at New York 1927. Torre here uses a deployment considered good even today, the London System, involving pawns at c6, d5, and e6, with the Queen's Bishop developed outside the pawns and the King's Bishop on d6. This scheme is also possible against a white kingside fianchetto.

4.♗b2 e6 5.♗e2 ♗d6 6.c4 ♘bd7 7.♘c3 c6 8.0–0 ♕e7

Arriving at a position typical of the Nimzovich Attack. White has intentionally avoided the advance d2-d4 (in fact the white d-pawn will never move at all in this game), so as to have available the thematic maneuver ♘f3-d4 followed by f2-f4. This maneuver is also playable when the King's Bishop is fianchettoed, an example being Nimzovich-Rubinstein, Berlin 1928 (1-0, 32).

9.c×d5 e×d5 10.♘d4 ♗e6?!

Why Torre played this, instead of safeguarding his Bishop by 10...♗g6, is not clear. In combination with his next move, it puts him under considerable positional pressure.

11.f4 ♘c5?!

Compounding his mistake. Black had to do something about the threat of 12.f5, but 11...♘b6 was much the lesser evil.

12.b4!

The author of *My System* hopes to prepare an attack against the base of Black's pawn chain. This move not only intends the advance b4-b5, but also is designed to limit the scope of the ♗d6, specifically keeping it out of a3.

12...♘ce4

The only playable move; if 12...♘a6? 13.♗×a6 b×a6 14.♘×c6.

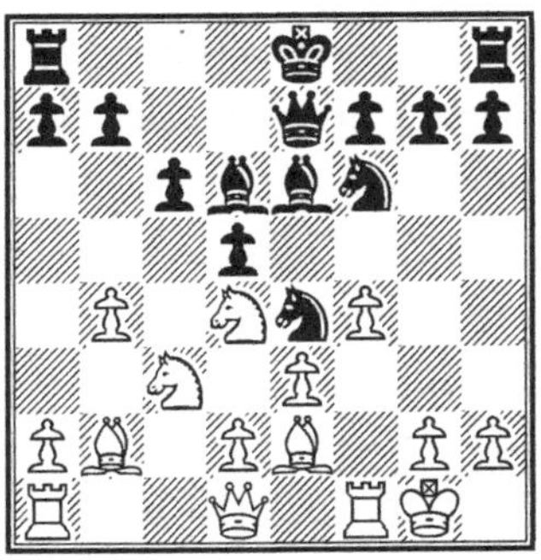

13.♘×e4

Also good was 13.♘×e6 ♕×e6 14.♘×e4: (a) 14...♘×e4 15.♗×g7 ♖g8 16.♗d4 ♗×b4 17.♖b1 ♕e7 18.♖b2 ♗c5 19.♕a4±;

(b) 14...d×e4 15.b5 0–0 [if 15...c5 16.♕a4 0–0 17.♗c4 ♕e7 18.♗×f6 ♕×f6 (18...g×f6 19.g4 with attack) 19.♗d5 winning a pawn] 16.b×c6 b×c6 and the isolated c-pawn is weak on the open file;
(c) 14...♕×e4 15.b5 c5 16.♗×f6 g×f6 17.♗f3 with a clear positional superiority.

13...d×e4?!
Torre keeps going from bad to worse. Better was 13...♘×e4, transposing to variation (a) above.

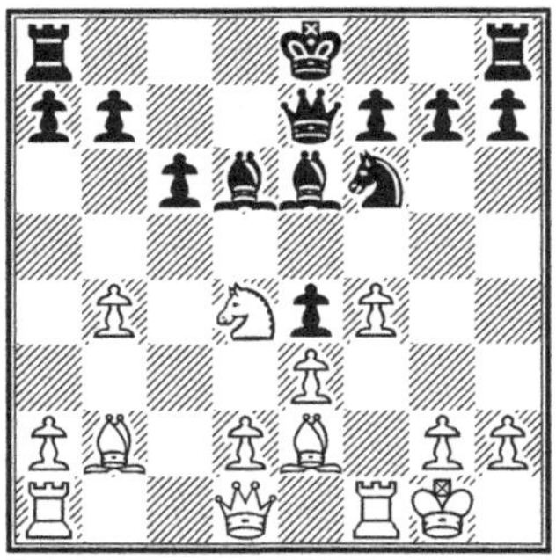

14.a3?!
But Nimzovich lets him off the hook. 14.b5! would present Black with difficult choices, *e.g.*
(a) 14...♗d7 15.b×c6 b×c6 16.♖c1 with strong pressure on the weak pawn (+1.60/24);
(b) 14...c5 15.♘×e6 ♕×e6 16.♕a4 0–0 17.♗c4 ♕e7 18.♗×f6 etc. as in the parenthetical sub-variation in line (b) in the note to White's 13th move above;
(c) 14...0–0 15.b×c6 b×c6 16.♘×c6 ♕b7 17.♗×f6 ♕×c6 18.♗d4±;
(d) 14...c×b5? 15.♗×b5+ ♔f8 (forced; if 15...♘d7?? 16.f5, or 15...♗d7?? 16.♘f5 ♕e6 17.♘×g7+) 16.♘×e6+ ♕×e6 17.♕a4 (+2.29/26);
(e) 14...♖c8 15.b×c6 b×c6 16.♕a4 ♗d7 17.♖ac1 etc. (+2.23/24).

By defending rather than advancing the b-pawn, Nimzovich takes much of the pressure off Black's position. In *Dynamic Chess* (1966), British writer R.N. Coles noted that Nimzovich's theory of prophylaxis often emphasized reducing the opponent's dynamic possibilities instead of enhancing his own; this may be a case where the theory was misapplied.

14...0–0
This or 14...♗d7 are Black's best available moves; it matters little in which order they are played.

15.♕c2
If 15.♘×e6 ♕×e6 White has no particularly strong follow-up, unlike at move 13. Black is still on the defensive, but he is not nearly as hard-pressed as he would have been after 14.b5.

15...♗d7 16.♘b3 b6
Best, preventing 17.♘c5/♘a5.

17.♗a6
A move accomplishing nothing. Better was 17.♗×f6, forcing 17...g×f6 in reply, when White might eventually be able to make something out of Black's disrupted kingside pawn structure.

17...♖ab8 18.♗c4

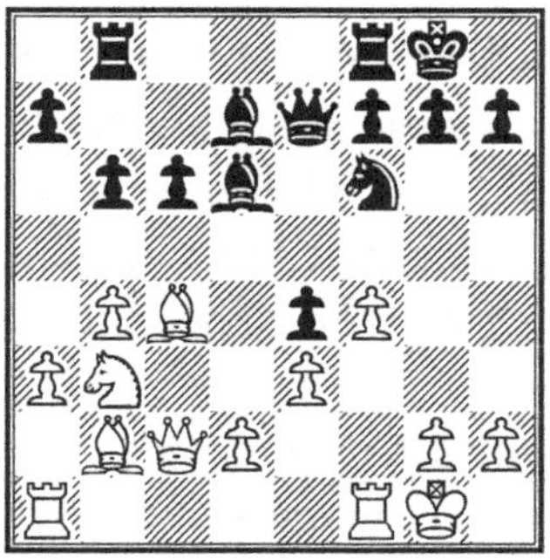

Admitting the pointlessness of his previous move. The game is now virtually even. Still, Nimzovich has placed his Bishops on excellent diagonals, and they stand ready at any moment to strike at f7 or g7. This forces Black to keep his Queen near his King, so as to go to f8 in the event of threats against g7.

18...♖fc8

In view of Torre's tendency in this tournament to seek early draws against his stronger opponents, one might have expected him to play 18...♖bc8. If then 19.♗a6 ♖b8, repeating. The text indicates a change in that policy.

19.♖fc1 ♘d5

Recognizing that the ♗b2 now looms large, Torre conceives a plan to neutralize it. After ...b6-b5, the Knight will head to b6, and from there to a4 or c4 to strike at the Bishop. While fine in principle, this plan however has a practical flaw.

20.♘d4 b5?!

It was more prudent to play 20...♘f6, indicating a willingness to draw by repetition.

21.♗a2?!

Nimzovich falls in with Torre's plan! More problematic for Black was 21.♗×d5 c×d5 22.♕d1 △ 23.♕h5, with unclear complications. But Nimzovich probably did not want to eliminate the backward c-pawn as a target.

21...♘b6 22.♕c3

This or 22.♘b3, 22.♘e2, or 22.♗b1 all maintain an even game.

22...♕f8

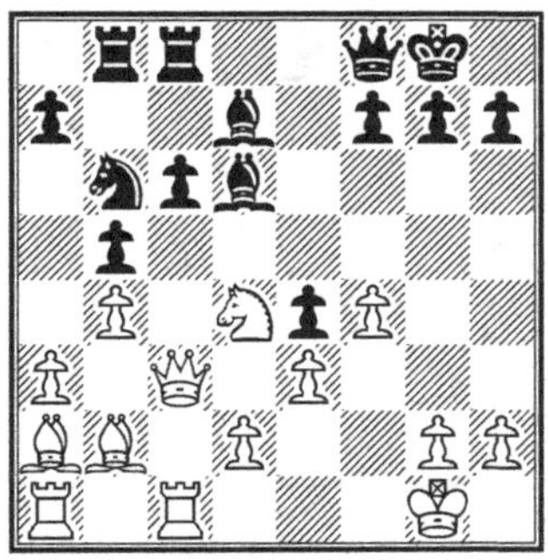

With this move Torre reaffirms what he announced with his 18th move, a preference for a prolonged fight, rather than a quick draw, which he might have obtained with 22...♘a4. The reason behind Torre's choice is simple: this was the last round of the tournament, and Torre had 10 points to Nimzovich's 10½. Just ahead was Grünfeld with 11, playing Black against Alekhine. Thus with a win Torre had a chance to reach as high as 8th place out of 21 participants, but Nimzovich held the advantage of “draw odds.” 22...♘a4 would have forced 23.♘f5 ♘×c3 24.♘×e7+ ♗×e7 25.♗×c3 with a very even game (0.13/25).

23.♘b3 ♘c4

This and 23...♘a4 are equally good.

24.♘c5 ♗×c5□ 25.b×c5

Stockfish indicates 25.♗×c4 was preferable, play continuing 25...b×c4 26.b×c5=. The text allows Black to gain an edge.

25...♘×b2 26.♕×b2

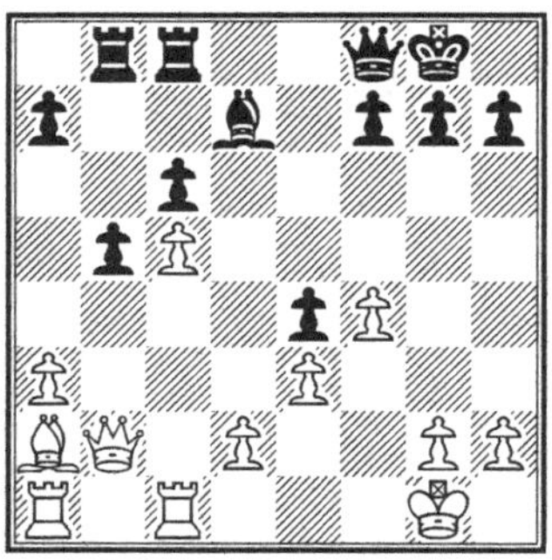

Stockfish now envisions 26...a5 as best. Play might then continue 27.♗b1 ♕e8 28.♕c3 ♗f5 29.h3 [or 29.♕×a5 b4 30.♖a2 (not 30.a×b4?? ♖a8−+) 30...♖b5 31.♕a4 ♖a8 32.♕d1 b3 33.♖b2 ♖×a3∓] 29...h5 30.♕×a5 b4 31.♖a2 ♗e6 (if now 31...♖b5 32.♕a4 ♖a8 33.♕d1 b3 34.♖b2 ♖×a3 35.♕×h5=) 32.♖b2 ♖b5 33.♕a7 ♖a8 34.♕c7 b×a3 35.♖×b5 c×b5 36.♗×e4 ♖c8 37.♕a5 a2 38.♔h2, a position rated at -0.75/33. While of some interest, this line does not seem notably better for Black than the game continuation.

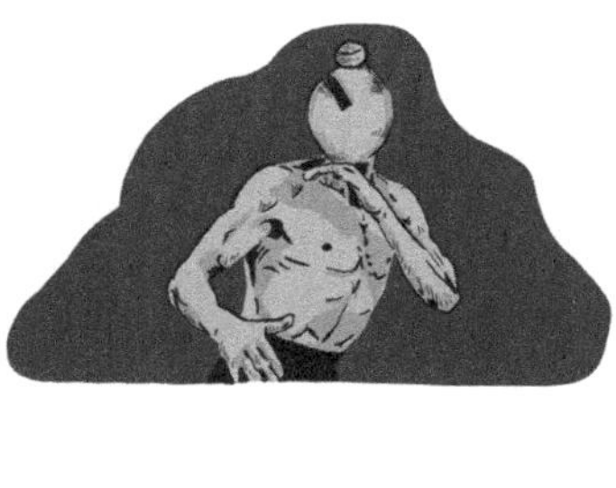

26...♕e7 27.♕c3 ♗f5

Ending any thoughts of d2-d4 for the time being. As Zubarev noted in the tournament book, Black has skillfully assumed the initiative.

28.♖f1?

This might appear to be one of Nimzovich’s “mysterious” Rook moves, but its purpose is to defend the d-pawn with one Rook at f2 and the other at c2 or d1, if necessary. However, there is a tactical flaw. Better was to move either Rook to b1.

28...♖d8! 29.♖f2

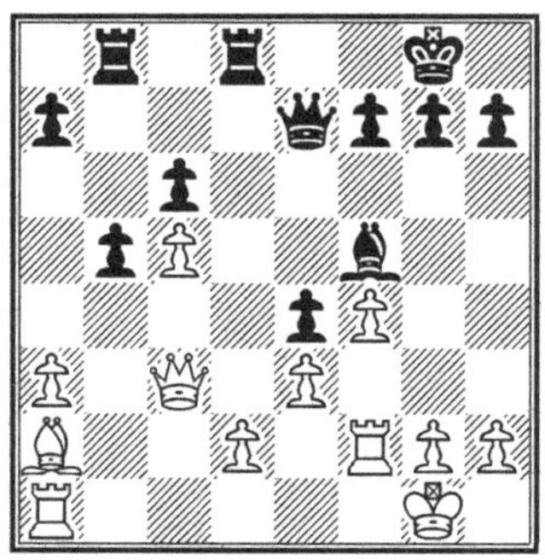

The game now enters a phase where Torre misses some strong moves, but Nimzovich’s defense is less than best, giving Torre new opportunities.

29...♖d3?!

A strange thing about this part of the game is that natural, seemingly strong moves like the text turn out to be far from best. It's not at all obvious, but Black could have had a great, likely winning advantage with 29...h5!,

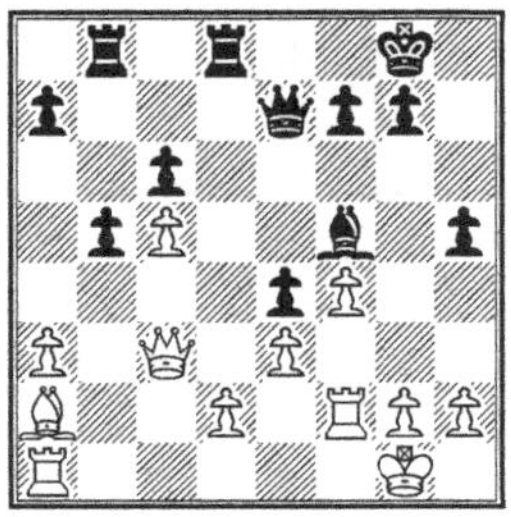

the point of which is to maintain the Bishop on its current diagonal by preventing h2-h3 and g2-g4. Some likely continuations then are:

(a) 30.h3 h4 31.♕b4 ♖d7 32.♖c1 ♕d8 33.♗b1 a5 34.♕c3 b4 35.a×b4 a×b4 36.♕b2 (-3.98/36);

(b) 30.♕e5 ♕×e5 31.f×e5 g6 32.h3 h4 33.♖f4 ♖×d2 34.♖×h4 ♖e8 35.e6 ♗×e6 (if 35...f×e6 36.g4) 36.♖×e4 a5 37.♗×e6 ♖×e6 38.♖×e6 f×e6 and White must lose a crucial pawn, by either 39.♔h2 ♖c2 40.♔g3 ♖×c5, or 39.♖c1 ♖d3, with a winning ending for Black in either case;

(c) 30.♕a5 ♖d7 (if 30...♕×c5?! 31.♕c7⇄) 31.♖c1 ♕d8 32.♕c3 ♕f6 33.h3 (or 33.♕×f6 g×f6 34.h3 h4 35.♗b1 a5 36.♔f1 b4 -4.64/26) 33...h4 34.♕c2 ♖d3 35.♗b3 a5 36.a4 b4 and with a protected passed pawn and enduring pressure on the d-file, Black's superiority is obvious (-4.34/26).

Returning to the game:

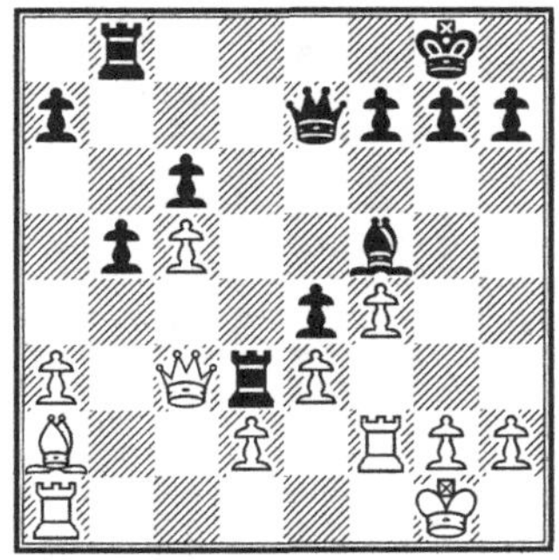

30.♕a5?

Nimzovich fails to see his opportunity to get back to near equality, which was 30.♕e5! ♕×e5□ 31.f×e5 ♗e6 (Notice the difference here without the pawn on h5: if 31...g6 32.g4! ♗×g4 33.♖×f7 forces a draw.) 32.♗b1 ♖d5 33.♗×e4 ♖×e5 34.♗×c6 ♖×c5 35.♗f3 a5 36.d4 ♖c3 37.d5 ♗d7 38.e4 and White has decent drawing chances (-0.69/25).

30...♖bd8

The text seems a natural way to increase the d-file pressure, but White's defensive resources are adequate.

30...h5 was still best. And not 30...♕×c5?! 31.♗×f7+! ♔f8 (31...♔×f7?? 32.♕c7+) 32.♗h5 ♕b6□ 33.♕b4+ c5 34.♕b2 and Black's advantage is not great (-1.47/25).

31.♖c1 ♕d7 32.♖c2 ♗e6?!

Having established his strategic advantage, Black logically seeks to exchange the one piece not contributing to it. Yet this is another seemingly natural but sub-optimal move. Again, 32...h5 was best, though not as effective as before (-2.08/25).

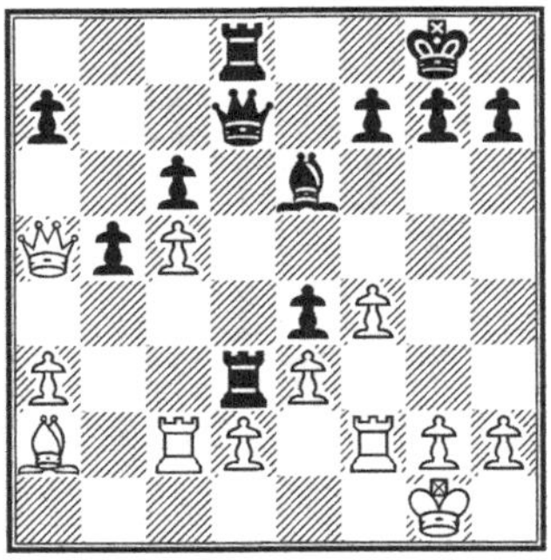

33.♗b1!

White in turn avoids trading off his Bishop, the one piece able to bother the Rook on d3. This is much better than 33.♗×e6? ♕×e6 34.♕×a7 ♕b3 35.♖c1 ♖×d2 36.♖e1 ♖2d3 37.♕b6 ♕d5 and more white pawns must eventually fall (-3.32/23).

33...f5?!

This allows some major wood-chopping that takes all the pressure off White. Stockfish's assessment suddenly becomes dead even, 0.00/25. If Black still wanted to play for a win, 33...♗f5 was necessary, though then his edge would be slight (-0.99/26).

34.♖b2 ♖b3 35.♗a2! ♖×b2 36.♗×e6+ ♕×e6 37.♕×d8+ ♔f7 38.♕c7+ ♔f6 39.h3

39.♕×a7 was perfectly playable, *viz.* 39...♕c4 40.h3 ♕c1+ 41.♔h2 ♖×d2 42.♖×d2 ♕×d2 43.♕b7 forcing 43...♕d5, since if 43...♕×e3?? 44.♕×c6+ ♔f7 45.♕d7+ ♔f6 46.♕d6+ ♔f7 47.c6+−.

39...♖c2 40.♕d8+

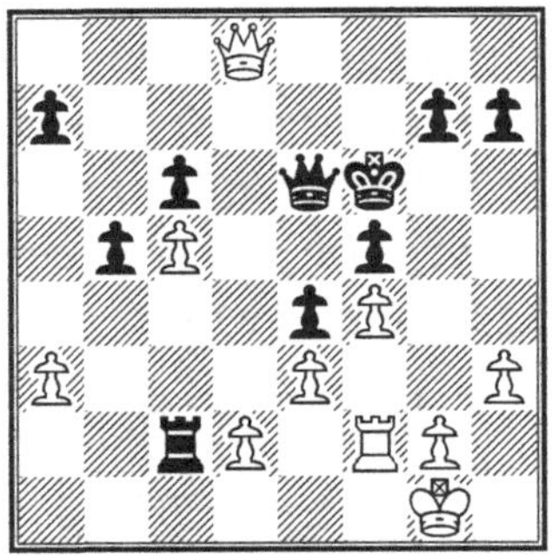

40.♕×a7 was again playable, but by now almost any reasonable move will draw.

40...♔f7 41.♕c7+ ♔f6 42.♕d8+

Seeking to draw by repetition, to which Black is still disinclined, though he does allow two iterations of this position.

42...♔f7 43.♕c7+ ♔f6 44.♕d8+ ♕e7 45.♕g8 h5 46.♕h7 ♖×c5 47.♕×h5 a5 48.g4

48...b4

Slightly better was 48...f×g4. But 48...♖c1+? would be a serious mistake, *viz.* 49.♔h2 f×g4 50.♖g2! ♔e6 (50...g×h3?? 51.♕g6#) 51.♖×g4 ♔d6 52.a4 ♖b1 53.♖g6+ ♔c7 54.♕h7 ♔b6 55.♖×g7 etc. (+3.76/26).

49.a×b4 a×b4 50.♖g2

50...♕f7?

Correct was 50...f×g4 51.♕×g4 g5□ 52.♕d1 (if 52.f×g5+ ♔g7 and, appearances notwithstanding, Black is OK (-0.74/25)) 52...♖f5 53.♕a1+ ♔e6 54.♕a6 ♔d6=. The text might well have lost the game.

51.♕h4+ ♔e6 52.♕h8?!

52.♕d8!, threatening 53.♕d4+−, would have made real trouble for Black,

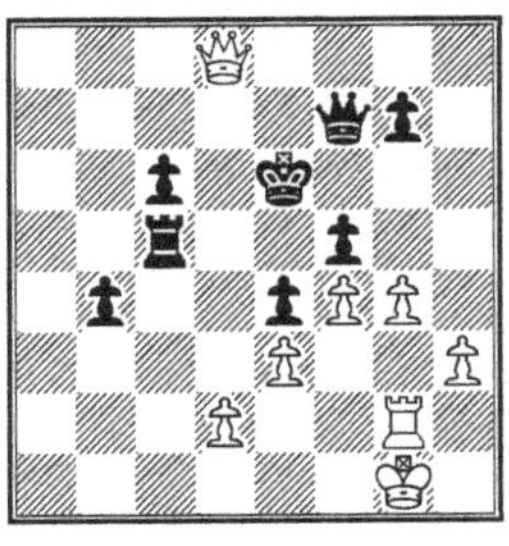

(a) 52...g6 53.g×f5+ ♖×f5 54.♕b6 ♕e8 55.♕×b4 ♔f7 56.♕c4+ ♔g7 57.♖g4 (+4.15/27);

(b) 52...f×g4 53.♖×g4 ♖b5 54.f5+! ♖×f5 (not 54...♔×f5?? 55.♖f4+, or 54...♕×f5?? 55.♖×g7 ♕h5 56.♖e7+ ♔f5 57.♕f8+ etc.) 55.♖×e4+ ♖e5 56.♕c8+ ♔d5 57.♖g4 (+4.19/23).

Returning to the game (**52.♕h8?!**):

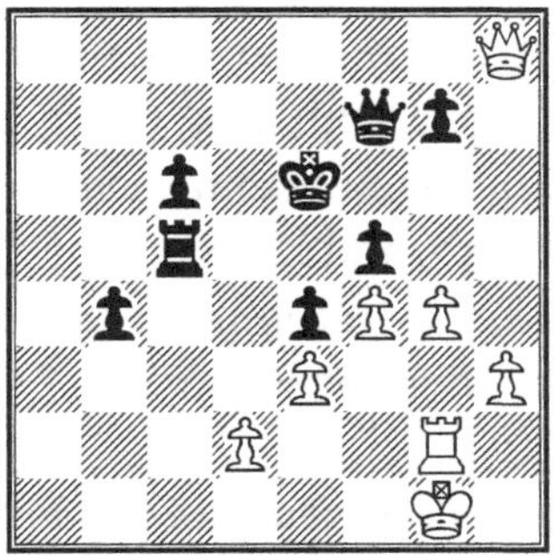

52...b3?!

Better was 52...♔d5=.

53.♕b8

The last slim winning chance was 53.♕a8 f×g4 54.♖×g4 g5 55.f×g5, but probably nothing much would come of it after 55...♖c1+ 56.♔h2 ♕f3 (+1.50/31).

53...♖b5!□

Torre finds the only saving move. White must now resort to perpetual check.

54.g×f5+ ♔d7 55.♕a7+ ♔e8 56.♕a8+ ♔d7 57.♕a7+ ♔e8 58.♕a8+ ♔d7 59.♕a7+ ♔e8 ½-½

A hard back-and-forth struggle, with both players in over their heads at certain points. Both had winning chances, but failed to find the clinching moves. A draw seems a fair outcome.

So, what sort of report card can we give Torre's performance at Baden-Baden? There were, in some ways, more negatives than positives. Against Rubinstein, Bogoljubow and the German master Carls, Torre lost through serious miscalculations if not outright blunders, uncharacteristic for him. Against Treybal he lost through aimlessness. He had losing positions against te Kolsté, Sämisch, Tartakower, Nimzovich, and possibly Tarrasch (another game not included here), but he managed, with luck, to score +1 =5 in those games. He missed wins against Réti, Spielmann, Rabinovich and Nimzovich. His wins against Mieses and Yates were sloppy, and his win over Grünfeld was something of a fluke, made possible only by an incomprehensible blunder. Only against Thomas did Torre play a smoothly dominant game.

But not everyone can be a Pillsbury or Capablanca, winning his first major international tournament. And even such greats as they have their lucky moments where a lost game suddenly turns into a draw or win. By whatever means, Torre still managed a plus score, +5 -4 =11, and against such a field as Baden-Baden 1925 had, that must be considered a highly respectable result for a young man's international debut. The *Wiener Schachzeitung*, in its concluding overview of the tournament, dated 14 May 1925, would say:

> The tenth and final prize-winner was Carlos Torre, America's much-touted new genius, from whom such heroic deeds were often expected that his relatively brilliant success may not be properly appreciated everywhere. But when one considers Torre's youth, when one considers that this was his first big tournament, when one considers how mature is his position judgment and how serene his style, then one must congratulate this serious and humble youth, and can only prophesy great future success.

Games from the International Tournament at Marienbad

The front page of the *American Chess Bulletin* for May-June 1925 announced:

> With an interval of only eight days between the close of the congress at Baden-Baden, Germany, and the opening of the international masters tournament at Marienbad, eleven of the experts with five others added, began play at the famous Czechoslovakian health resort on the morning of May 21, and, playing at the rate of five rounds per week, wound up another highly successful competition on June 8th. This gathering of the masters was held in one of the rooms of the handsome kurhaus under the auspices of the Municipal Health Committee, with Dr. Hans Turba, the Mayor of Marienbad, as chairman of the tournament committee. Isidor Gunsberg of London, one of the most famous of the older masters and, despite the fact that he is a septuagenarian, as keen an enthusiast as ever, was the organizer of the tournament and acted as tournament director.

Time limits were 30 moves in two hours, then 15 moves per hour after that. Cash prizes for first to sixth place, ranging from 5,000 to 1,000 Czech crowns, were to be awarded, plus 4,000 crowns to be divided among the non-prizewinners. Now, on to Torre's games!

Game 51

Torre-Opocensky

Marienbad 1925, round 1,

Slav Defense [D13]

Karel Opocensky (1892-1975, historical Elo 2460, IM title 1950) was not among the world's elite, but was still one of Czechoslovakia's strongest players of the period 1925-45, winning the national title five times in that span. After WW II he became active in FIDE, and was chief arbiter of the 1951 and 1954 world championship matches. He is also remembered for an odd incident involving Nimzovich, which must have occurred at this very tournament, as that seems to be the only time they met over the board. It was related by Reuben Fine in his book *The World's Great Chess Games*. Knowing Nimzovich's aversion to smoke, Opocensky walked some distance away during their game to light up a cigar. He was calmly studying the position from afar when Nimzovich suddenly rose and shouted “Stop shaking your belly!” (Nimzovich won in 48 moves.)

Torre's game with Opocensky was remarkable for the fact that the young Mexican master refuted what had been thought a sound line in the Slav Defense. Through move 21 his play was near-perfect. But the Czech master resisted stubbornly, and inaccuracies by Torre at moves 22, 34 and 39 evened the game. Finally a late blunder gave Torre the victory his exemplary opening play merited.

1.d4 d5 2.♘f3 ♘f6 3.c4 c6 4.♘c3 ♗f5(?)

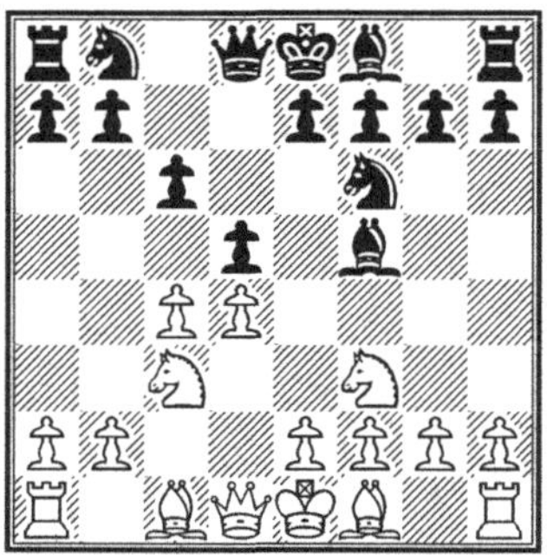

Considered sound at the time; in fact this had been played by Capablanca, Euwe, Sämisch, Treybal, Spielmann and other strong masters. Yet it is seldom seen any more in master practice. The reason is that it was effectively refuted by Carlos Torre in this very game, a performance he repeated soon after, against the Leningrad master Gotthilf at Moscow 1925. It is one of his lasting contributions to opening theory, recognized for example in *The Queen's Gambit* by Swedish GM Gideon Ståhlberg. As a result of this and the Gotthilf game it was established that Black must play 4...d×c4 or 4...e6 (the Semi-Slav Defense).

5.c×d5 ♘×d5

Gotthilf was to play 5...c×d5 but was refuted in virtually identical style (see Game 72).

6.♕b3

This position had been reached a few times before, in Kostic-Banks, New York 1916 (1-0, 57), Hakansson-Sämisch, Gothenburg 1920 (½-½, 31), and Romanovsky-Bohatirchuk, 3rd USSR Ch, Moscow 1924 (0-1, 57). From this point, only Hakansson played in a manner resembling Torre's here, and though he gained a clear advantage he let it slip away later.

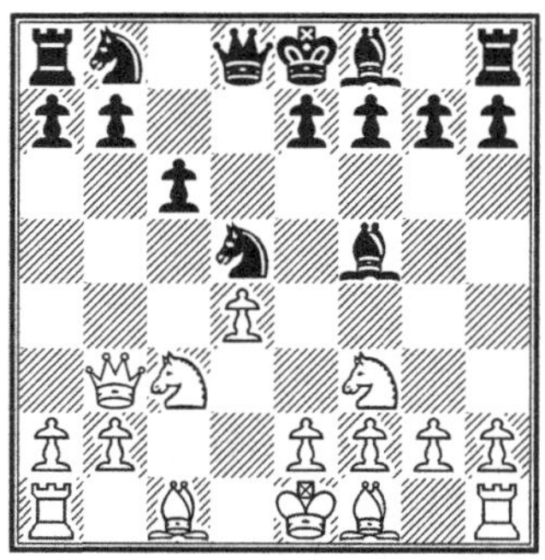

6...♕b6

If 6...♘×c3 7.b×c3 ♕b6 (not 7...♕c7? 8.♗f4! ♕b6 9.♘d2, or 8.♘g5! e6 9.e4) 8.♘d2 e5 9.♘c4 (9.e4 ♗e6 10.♘c4 ♕c7 11.a4± is also good) 9...♕×b3 10.a×b3 ♘d7 11.e3 and White has a central superiority and a potential target in Black's a-pawn (+0.80/26). These lines show that White's advantage in this variation can be positional rather than material, but no less real.

7.♘×d5 c×d5?

Better was 7...♕×b3 8.♘c7+ ♔d8 9.a×b3 ♔×c7 10.♗f4+ ♔c8 (so far as in Bohatirchuk-Romanovsky) 11.♘d2 ♘d7 12.e4 ♗g6 13.h4 h5 14.♗d3 with a positional plus for White (+1.01/24), but as yet no material gain.

8.♕×d5 e6 9.♕b3

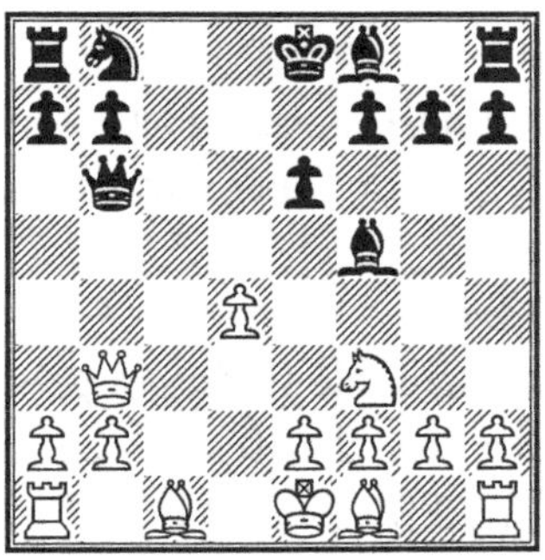

The statistics ChessBase shows for this position are remarkable: out of 165 games reaching it, White's record is +100 -22 =43, a winning rate of nearly 74%. And after this and the Gotthilf game, it was very seldom seen, the next instances not being until 1954, 1967, and 1981.

9...♘c6

If 9...♕×b3 10.a×b3 ♗c2 11.♗d2! ♗×b3 12.e4! ♗e7 (if 12...a6 13.♗b5+! anyway, or 12...♗d6 13.♗c3 0–0 14.♘d2 ♗c2 15.f3 and the ♗c2 will eventually be lost (+2.90/26)) 13.♗b5+ ♘c6 14.♘e5 0–0 (14...♖c8? 15.♖×a7) 15.♗×c6 b×c6 16.♘×c6 (+2.46/24).

10.♗d2

10.e3 was slightly stronger, but this is still very good.

10...♕×b3

If 10...♘×d4?? 11.♘×d4 ♕×d4 12.e3! (much stronger than 12.♕×b7) 12...♕d5 13.♕a4+! ♔e7 14.f3,

and neither the Queen nor the Bishop has any good retreat squares to avoid the threat of 15.e4, *viz.*:

(a) 14...♗g6?? 15.♗b4+ ♔f6 16.♗c3+ ♔e7 17.e4 ♕c6 (if 17...♕c5 18.♗b4, or if 17...♕g5 18.♖d1 and to prevent mate the Queen must give herself up: 18...♕e3+ 19.♗e2 ♕×c3+ 20.b×c3 +–) 18.♗b5 ♕c7 19.0-0-0 +12.66; or

(b) 14...♕c6?? 15.♗b5 ♕b6 16.e4 ♗g6 17.♗b4+ ♔f6 (if 17...♔d8 18.♗a5) 18.e5+ ♔×e5 19.♗c3+ and mate in 13.

Therefore Black would have to play, say,

(c) 14...♖c8 15.e4 ♕e5 16.♖d1 ♔f6 17.♗e2 ♗g6 18.h4 h6 19.g4! [Not the strong-looking but losing 19.♗g5+?? h×g5 20.h×g5+ ♔×g5 21.♖×h8 ♕g3+ 22.♔d2 ♕d6+ and either 23.♔e1 ♕b4+ 24.♕×b4 ♗×b4+ 25.♔f1 ♖×h8 –+, or 23.♔e3 ♕f4+ 24.♔d3 f5! with a winning attack (-4.81/23).] 19...♗d6 20.♕d7 and now forced is 20...♗×e4 21.f×e4+−.

11.a×b3 ♗c2

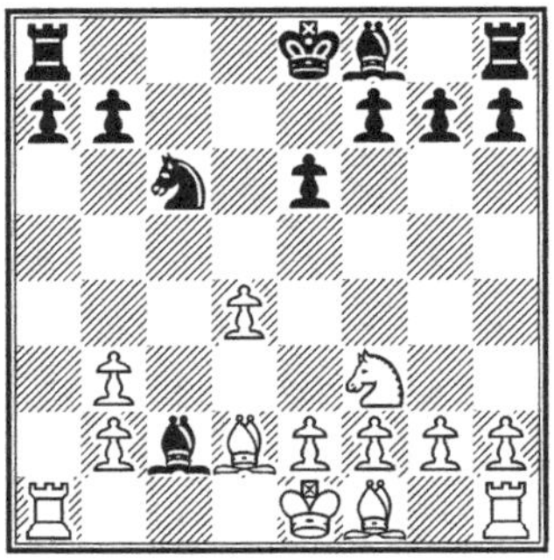

A position very similar to the later Gotthilf game, the only difference being that there Black's Knight stood at b8 instead of c6. Torre liked this position so much that it appears on the cover of his book *Development of Chess Ability*. Velasco once asked Torre why he was so partial to this position and to the Gotthilf game. He answered that for him, genuine beauty in chess consisted of a clear, simple concept, executed straightforwardly in the course of a game. This also corresponded to his definition of the term "classic." For this reason, Torre considered his games against Opocensky and Gotthilf to be the most classic of his career.
What is the idea behind White's play in these two games? Simply, exploitation of the premature sortie of the black Queen's Bishop. If this Bishop captures the b3-pawn, then White will surround and entrap it (as occurs in Torre-Gotthilf, wherein the Soviet master had to give up two pawns to rescue it). If, on the other hand, the Bishop retreats to g6 (as occurs here), then it will remain outside the main theater of action, the queenside, and Black will in effect be playing a piece down.
Months after this game, Capablanca was asked what Black should play after Torre's 6.♕b3. The Cuban thought a moment, then replied unequivocally that Black should retreat his Bishop to c8. This shows both the validity of Torre's concept and the deep intuition of Capablanca.

12.♗c3
Threatening 13.♘d2 and 14.e4, beginning to encircle the wayward Bishop.

12...♗b4?
Black has trouble finding a good plan, and here he chooses a bad one. If 12...♗×b3 13.♘d2 ♗c2 14.e4 f5 15.♗c4 ♔f7 16.f3 and the Bishop remains trapped (+2.08/23). Or White can be even more aggressive with 16.f4! f×e4 17.f5 ♔e8 18.f×e6, gaining connected passed d- and e-pawns (+2.75/24).
The least evil was 12...♗e7 13.♘d2 ♖c8 14.e3 a6 15.♗e2 0–0 16.♗f3 ♖c7 17.♔e2 ♘b4 18.♖hc1 (+1.73/27).

13.♘d2 ♗g6 14.e3 0–0 15.♗b5!
Gaining an important tempo due to the threat of 16.♗×c6. Black must now choose between two evils: either help White by rectifying his pawn structure with 16...♗×c3 17.b×c3, or retreat his Bishop to the less active post e7.

15...♗e7 16.♔e2 ♖fd8?!

Less bad was 16...♘b4.

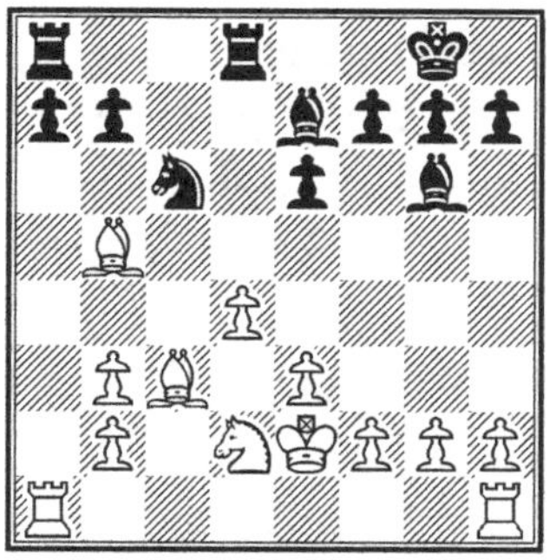

17.♖a4

For the first time in this so far exemplary game, Torre makes a notably less-than-best move. Strongest was 17.♗×c6 b×c6 18.♖a5! ♖d7 19.♖ha1 f6 (to prevent ♘d2-c4-e5) 20.f3 ♗f7 21.e4 ♖b7 22.♘c4 (+2.69/24).

However, the text is not bad, and still retains much of White's advantage.

17...♖dc8 18.♖ha1

A good alternative was 18.♖c4 △19.♗×c6 ♖×c6 20.♖×c6 b×c6 21.b4 f6 22.♖a1, when Black's Rook is tied down to defense of the a-pawn.

18...a6 19.♘c4!

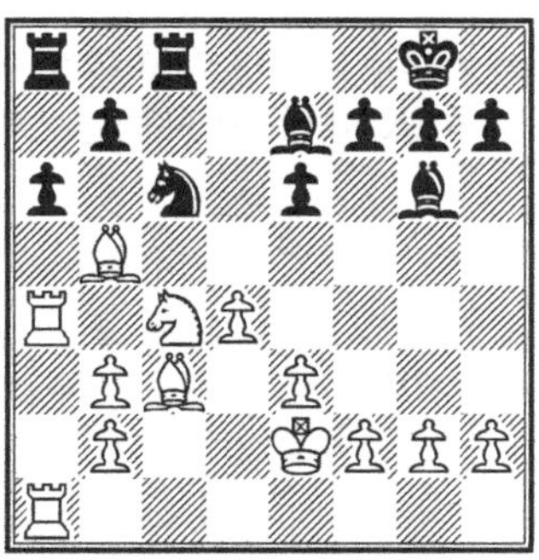

Simple but forceful. If now 19...♘a7?? 20.♗×a6! b×a6 21.♖×a6 ♖c7 22.♘b6 ♖b8 23.♖×a7 ♖×a7 24.♖×a7 ♖×b6 25.♖×e7+−.

19...♖ab8?

A rather serious error. Relatively best was 19...♖c7 20.♘b6 ♖d8 21.♗c4 ♖d6 when though Black is limited to passive defense, he can resist indefinitely (+1.61/28).

20.♗×c6 ♖×c6 21.♘e5 ♖c7

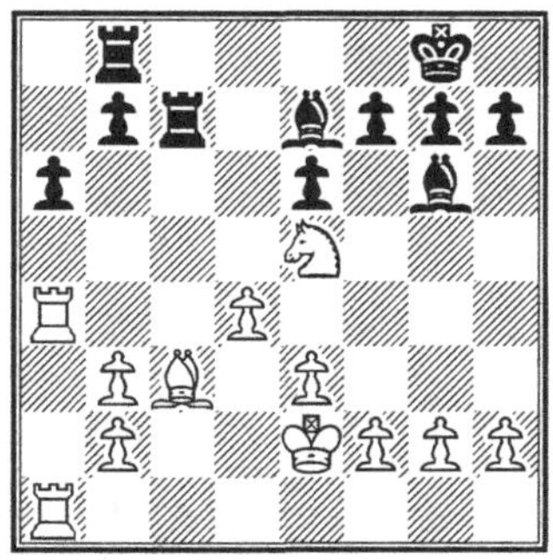

22.♘×g6

Torre believes the moment has arrived to simplify to a winning endgame. The plan is correct, but it appears that Torre may have slipped up slightly in the move order, because with 22.♖c4 ♖bc8 (22...♖d7?? is obviously not an option) and either 23.♖×c7 ♖×c7 24.♘×g6 h×g6 25.b4, or 23.♗a5 ♖×c4 24.b×c4 ♗f5 25.c5, the endgame would be an easier win.

As will be seen, the text allows Black a more tenacious resistance.

22...h×g6 23.♖c4 ♖d7!

A key move that 22.♘×g6 made

possible. It begins a defensive maneuver by which Opocensky tries to provoke the advance b3-b4, which would obstruct the mobility of White's pieces in that sector.

24.♖c1 ♖d5

Continuing the aforementioned maneuver. An alternative was 24...♖e8 25.♗d2 ♔f8 26.♖c7 ♖×c7 27.♖×c7 ♖b8 (+2.07/24).

25.♗d2 ♖b5

Completing the maneuver, which besides provoking b3-b4 shortly, also maximizes the Rook's mobility while it protects the b-pawn.

26.♖c8+ ♖×c8 27.♖×c8+

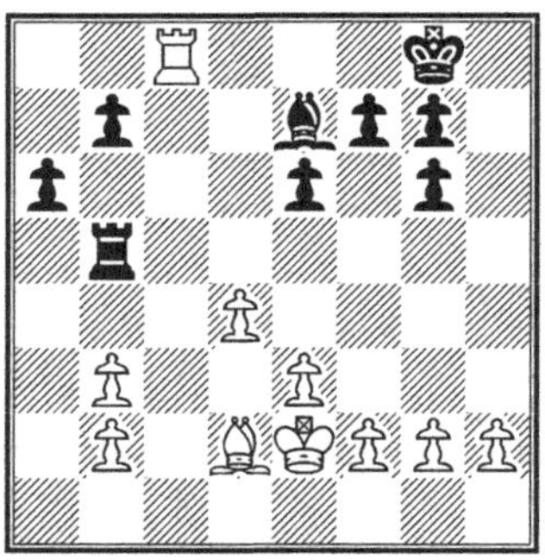

27...♗f8

Much better than 27...♔h7? 28.♖c7 ♗f6 29.b4 ♔g8 30.♖c8+ ♔h7 31.♔d3 g5 32.♖c7 ♔g8 33.e4 (△34.e5 ♗d8 35.♖c8 ♖d5 36.♗×g5+−), and now if 33...e5 34.d5+−, or 33...g4 34.e5 ♗d8 35.♖d7 ♖d5 36.♖×b7+−.

28.b4 f6 29.♔d3 ♔f7 30.♔c4

Preventing ...a5. Now White is able to advance his pawn majority on the other wing.

30...♗d6 31.e4 g5

Of course the h-pawn is immune to capture: 31...♗×h2? 32.g3 ♗g1 33.♗e3 and the Bishop is jailed.

32.h3 ♔e7 33.g3 ♔f7

Of course not 33...♔d7?? 34.♖g8+−.

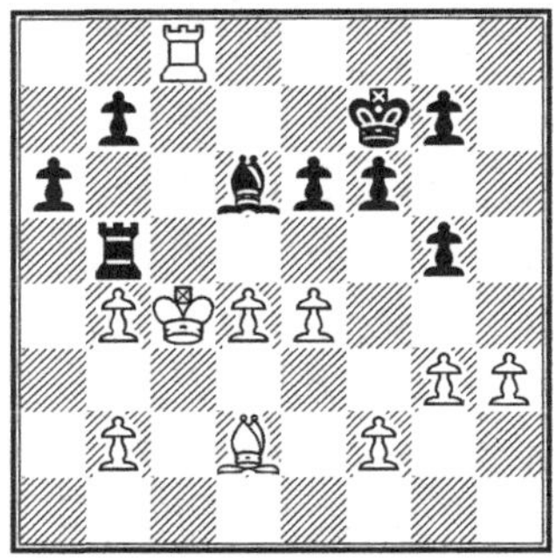

34.b3?

Torre's first major mistake. This does nothing for White except greatly reduce his winning chances. Better the more forceful 34.d5 (+2.83/30).

34...♔e7?!

34...f5! would have capitalized on White's wasted move. If then, for example 35.e5 ♗e7 36.♖c7 ♔e8 and it is not at all clear how White can make progress toward victory (+1.37/28).

35.♗e1

The first edition gave 35.f4 here. ChessBase has some repetitive moves before that, which we include here. Best actually was 35.d5, not only here but at moves 36, 37, 38, and 39.

35...Kf7 36.Bc3 Rb6 37.Be1 Rb5 38.Bd2 Ke7

39.f4?

Oh, how the cold gaze of the Lidless Silicon Eye sternly dispels illusions! In the first edition we gave this an exclam and called it "a masterful plan." Yet in fact Torre, after finding so many optimal moves throughout the game, finally makes an error, worse than at move 34, that definitely lets the win slip to a draw. Stockfish recommends 39.d5, evaluated at +2.07/27, though it does not see a clear path to victory for White. But the text takes the evaluation down to less than +0.50.

39...g×f4 40.g×f4 Rh5!

Torre erroneously thought he would gain an advantage by offering the h-pawn in order to lure the black Rook off its dominant position on the fifth rank. But in fact the game is now completely even. The next dozen moves are just inconsequential wood-shifting, doing nothing to affect that balance.

41.e5 Kd7 42.Rg8 b5+ 43.Kd3 R×h3+ 44.Kc2 Be7 45.R×g7 f×e5 46.d×e5 Rf3 47.Rg8 Bd8

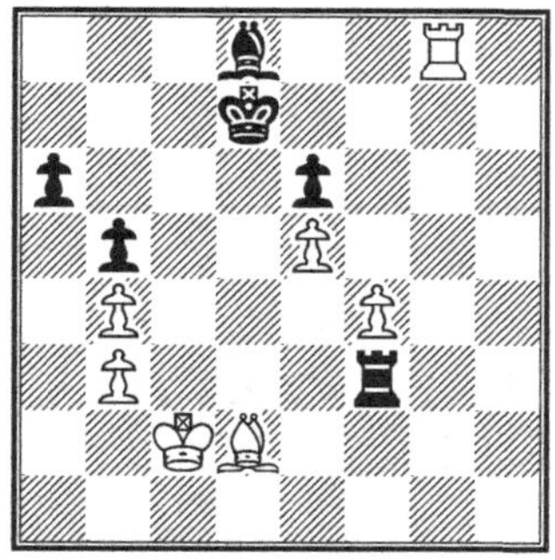

In the first edition, alas, we gave a completely mistaken evaluation of this position, stating that "if it were Black's turn to move, he would be in an insoluble *Zugzwang* predicament." Over the next few moves, Torre does in fact manage to bring about this same position, with Black to move, but it makes no difference.

48.Rh8 Rg3 49.Rf8 Ke7 50.Rf6 Rf3 51.Rg6 Kd7 52.Rg8

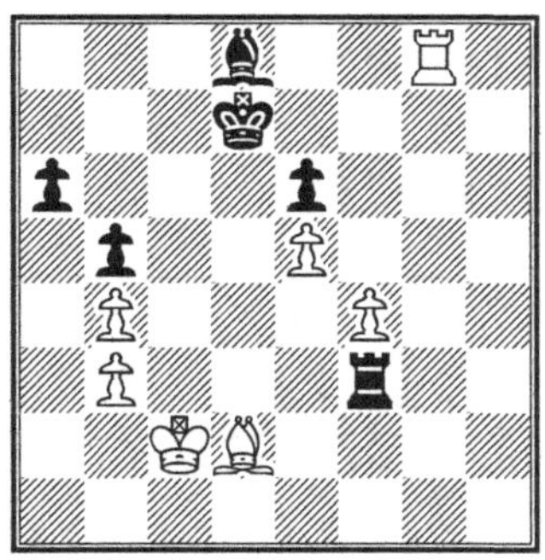

Reaching the same position as after move 47, but there is no "*Zugzwang* predicament." 52...Kc7 or 52...Bb6 would maintain deadeye equality, and 52...Bh4, 52...Rf2, 52...Rf1 and 52...Bc7 are also fine.

The move Black chooses is less good, but White does not capitalize.

52...♖h3?!

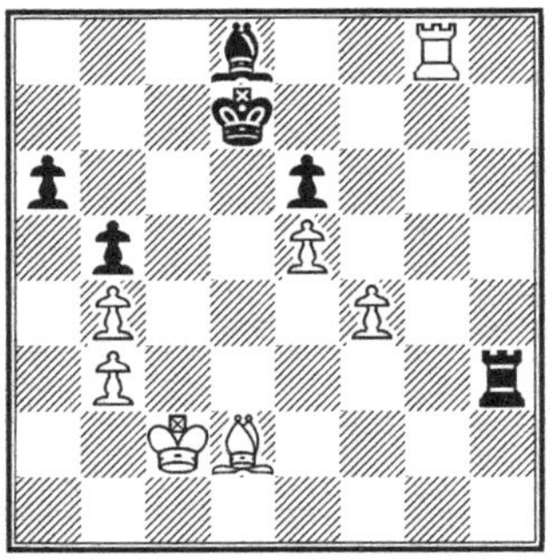

53.♖g7+
White might have tried 53.f5!?. If then 53...e×f5 54.e6+ ♔e7 (54...♔c7?? 55.♗f4+ ♔c6 56.♖×d8 and mate in nine) 55.♗g5+ ♔×e6 56.♖×d8 with winning chances. Relatively best for Black would be 53...♗c7 54.f6 ♖f3 55.♖g5 ♔c6 56.♔d1 ♗b6 57.♖g4 and while objectively the game may still be a draw, any winning chances are White's (+2.34/27).

53...♔c6 54.♖a7

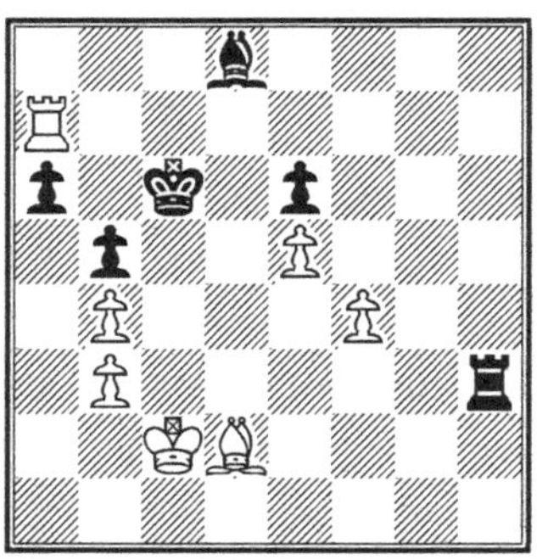

54...♔b6??
Finally, apparently influenced by "the tyranny of the pawn," Opocensky makes a fatal mistake that keeps his unimportant a-pawn but loses his essential e-pawn, and with it the game. He would have been fine after 54...♗c7 55.♖×a6+ ♔d5 (0.05/35).

55.♖d7! ♗c7
If 55...♖h8 56.♖d6+ ♔c7 57.♖×e6+−.

56.♖e7

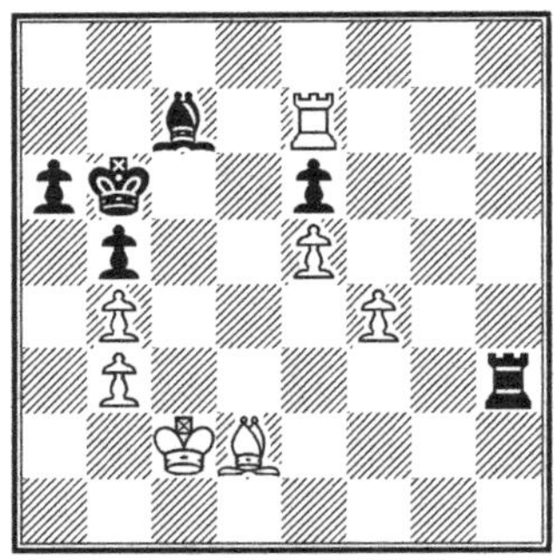

56...♔c6
And if 56...♖h6 57.f5 ♖h5 58.f6 ♗×e5 59.♖×e6+ ♔b7 60.f7 and either 60...♗g7 61.♖g6 ♗f8 62.♖g8 ♗d6 63.♖d8 ♖f5 64.♖×d6 ♖×f7+−, or 60...♖f5 61.♖e7+ ♔c6 62.♗h6 ♗d6 63.f8♕ ♖×f8 64.♗×f8+−.

57.♖×e6+ ♔d5 58.♖×a6 ♖f3 59.♖a7 ♗b6 60.♖b7 1–0
A remarkable game, both for its contribution to opening theory, and for Torre's exemplary play through the first 21 moves. Its luster is marred by Torre's errors at moves 22, 34 and 39, but he redeemed himself at the end by showing more tenacity and alertness than his veteran opponent.

Game 52

Nimzovich-Torre

Marienbad 1925, round 2

Queen's Gambit Declined (by transposition) [D06]

Another interesting draw between these two, though not as nerve-wracking and hair-raising as their first encounter. Torre tried a new opening idea, which seems to have taken Nimzovich aback. Once Black had attained equality, the game stayed even until a draw was agreed at move 30.

1.♘f3 ♘f6 2.e3 d5 3.c4

Varying from the queenside fianchetto of their Baden-Baden game.

3...♘c6

Surprise! Another Torre innovation. ChessBase has no earlier record of this move, and aside from Colle playing it against Crepeaux at Ghent 1926, it shows no later instance until 1994! Superficially it resembles the Chigorin Defense of the QGD, but White having already played 2.e3 gives it less impact.

4.d4

4.c×d5 ♘×d5 5.d4, as in Damljanovic-Insua Mellado, Seville Open 1994, was probably best.

4...♗f5 5.♕b3

Strong in Torre-Opocensky, this move has no such impact here. Again, best was 5.c×d5, as now semi-forced is 5...♕×d5 6.♘c3 ♕d6 7.♗b5 a6 8.♕a4 and Black must either allow his c-pawn to be doubled, or play 8...♗d7, when his further piece development will be awkward.

5...e6!

This apparently was the product of some advance preparation by Torre.

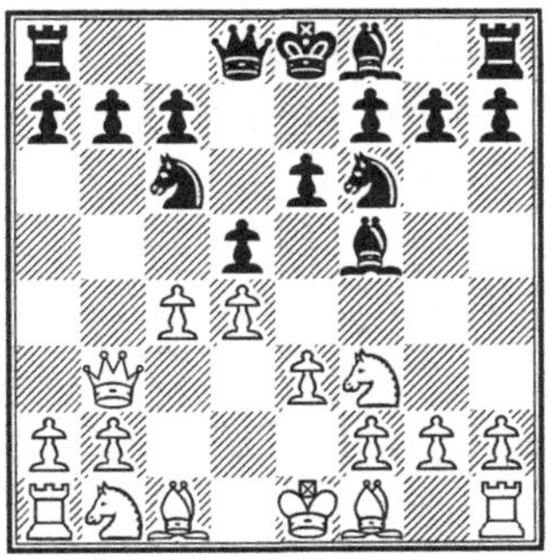

Now 6.♕×b7? would lose, *viz.* 6...♘b4! 7.c5 (if 7.♘a3?? a6! 8.♗d2 ♖b8 9.♕a7 ♕c8 etc. and White's Queen is lost) 7...♖b8 [Considerably stronger than the immediate 7...♘c2+ 8.♔d1 ♗e7 (8...♘×a1?? 9.♗b5+ ♘d7 10.♗×d7+ and White wins after either 10...♕×d7 11.♕×a8+, or 10...♔×d7 11.♘e5+ ♔e8 12.♕b5+ ♔e7 13.♘c6+, or 10...♔e7 11.♘e5! ♗×b1 12.♘c6+) 9.♗b5+ ♔f8 10.♘a3 ♘×a1 11.♘e5 ♘g4 12.♘c6 ♕c8 13.♕×c8+ ♖×c8 14.♔e2 -1.46/23.] 8.♕×a7 ♘c2+ 9.♔d1 ♘g4 10.♘a3 ♘×a1 11.♔e1 ♘c2+ 12.♘×c2 ♗×c2 and Black is up ♖-for-2♙ (-3.46/26).

6.c5
Best, preventing 6...♘b4.

6...♕c8 7.♗b5 ♘d7
To discourage 8.♘e5.

8.♗×c6 b×c6 9.0–0 ♗e7
Torre's TN has had the desired effect; Black now has an even game.

10.♗d2 0–0
10...♖b8!? might have changed the evaluation from = to ∓.

11.♗a5 ♗f6 12.♕c3 ♖e8 13.♘e5 ♗×e5 14.d×e5 f6!
The only way to prevent a central clamp-down by White.

15.f4 f×e5 16.f×e5 ♗×b1
Virtually forced positionally, otherwise the Knight would plant itself happily at d4.

17.♖a×b1 ♕d8 18.♕d4 ♖c8 19.♗c3 ♕g5 20.e4 ♕g4 21.♖bd1 ♖f8 22.e×d5 ♕×d4+ 23.♗×d4 e×d5
Either recapture maintains equality. The text enables Black to tie White down to the defense of his e-pawn, denying his Rooks the mobility to, say, threaten Black's a-pawn or penetrate to b7, until Black is prepared to respond.

In the first edition we opined that 23...c×d5 might lead to an ending of Knight vs. bad Bishop, favorable to Black, but in fact it is the Knight who turns out bad. After 23...c×d5 24.c6,

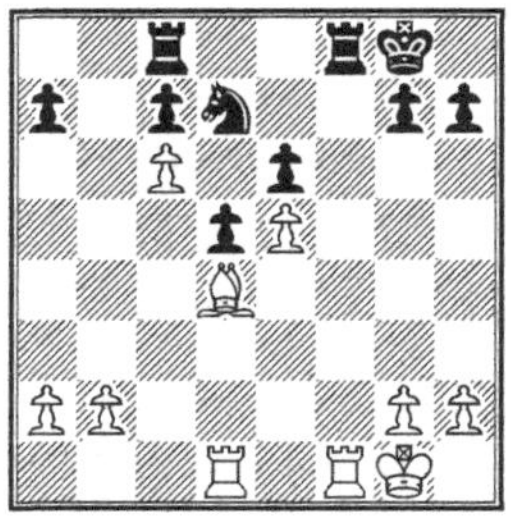

24...♘b8 is virtually forced (see analysis further on). If instead 24...♘b6?! 25.b3!,

keeping the Knight confined. If now 25...♖b8? 26.♖×f8+ ♖×f8 27.♗c5 ♖f5 28.a4 ♔f7 (28...♖×e5?? 29.♖f1 g5 30.a5 and the Knight is lost) 29.g4 ♖f4 30.♖f1 ♖×f1+ 31.♔×f1 ♘c8 32.b4

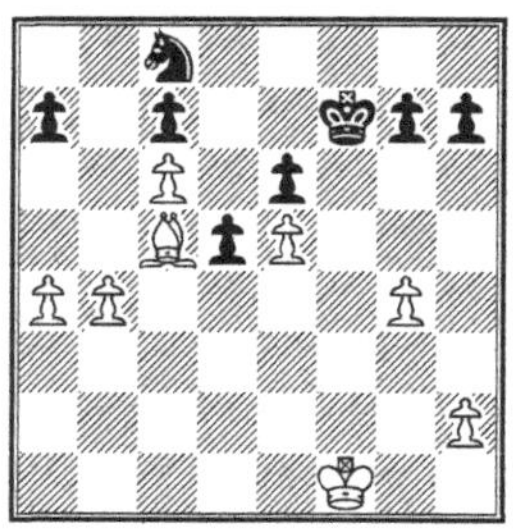

32...♔g6□ [if 32...♘e7? 33.b5 ♘c8 (else 34.♗×a7+−) 34.♔e2 +6.16/24] 33.b5 ♔g5 34.a5 ♔f4 35.♗d6!! +−:

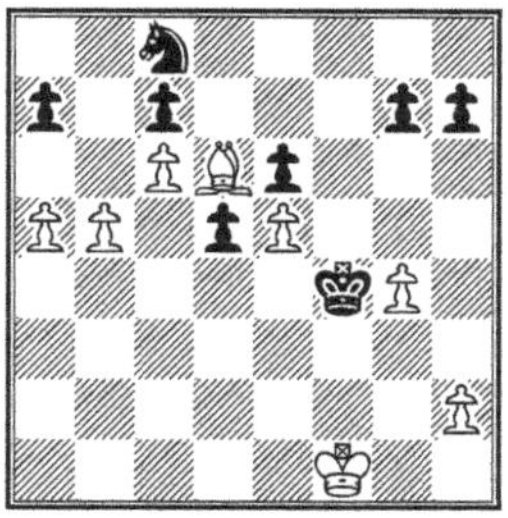

A remarkable turn of events.

Going back to the position after 24...♘b6?! 25.b3!:

a better try is 25...♖fe8 26.♖f4 ♖b8 27.♖df1 ♘c8 28.♖f7 ♘e7 29.♗c5 ♘×c6 30.♖×c7 ♖ec8 31.♖ff7 ♖×c7 32.♖×c7 ♘×e5 33.♗d4 ♘d3 34.♖×g7+ ♔f8 35.♖×h7 ♖b4 36.♗f6 e5 37.♖×a7

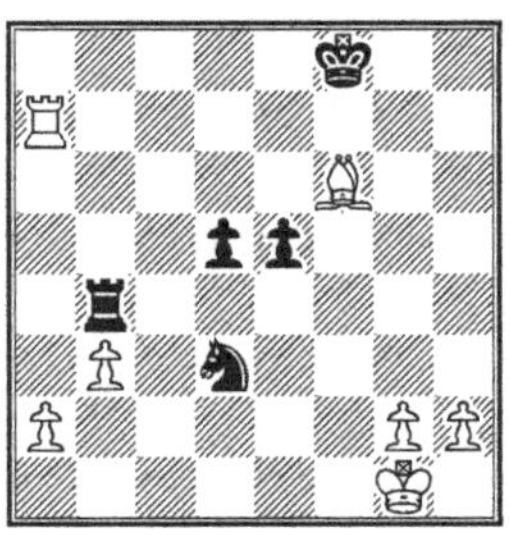

and while there is still a lot of play left, it looks like White's two passed pawn-pairs on the wings will eventually count for more than Black's central pair (+2.66/27).

So it behooves Black to avoid 24...♘b6, and instead after 23...c×d5 24.c6,

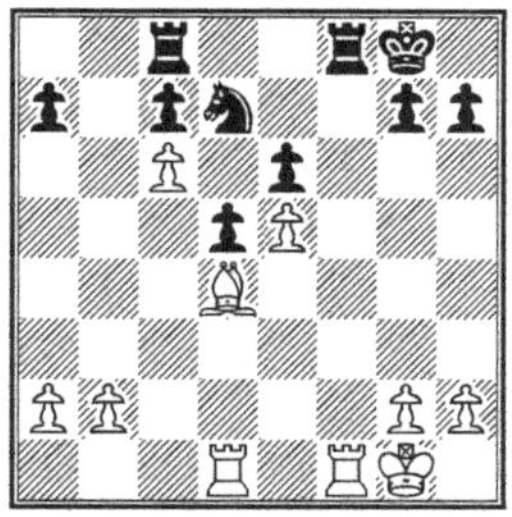

to play 24...♘b8, when a likely continuation is 25.♖c1 a5 26.♖c5 a4 27.♗c3 (not 27.♖a5? ♘×c6 28.♖×a4 ♘×d4 29.♖×d4 ♖a8 30.a3 ♖fb8 -2.16/24) 27...♖×f1+ 28.♔×f1 ♔f7 0.00/30.

Returning to the actual game (**23...e×d5**):

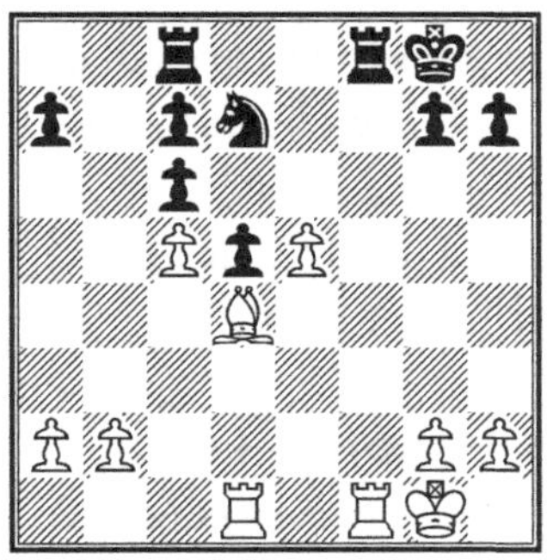

The remaining moves lock White into defending his e-pawn as Black attacks it, after which neither side can make progress and Stockfish says 0.00 *ad infinitum*.

24.♖fe1 ♖ce8 25.♖d3 ♖e6 26.g3 ♖fe8 27.♖de3 ♔f7 28.♔f2 ♔e7 29.♖1e2 ♖b8 30.♖a3 ♖b4 ½-½

After 31.♗c3 ♖b7 the game remains completely even. A less eventful game than the previous Nimzovich-Torre encounter, but one in which the young master demonstrated greater confidence and competence.

Game 53

Torre-Marshall

Marienbad 1925, round 3

Queen's Gambit Declined [D38]

Unlike their truncated 17-move draw at Baden-Baden, this Torre-Marshall game is a protracted, arduous, dramatic struggle that must have been very hard on the nerves of both players. Standing roughly even through the first 30 moves, Torre then made two bad moves that gave him a lost game. Yet the resulting ending of ♕+♘+2♙-vs-♕+♗+3♙ was so full of potential complications that Torre, like a gazelle evading a cheetah, kept dodging the inevitable for another 27 moves until a fatigued Marshall made an error that allowed Torre to draw.

1.♘f3 d5 2.c4 e6 3.d4

Torre opts for the classical QGD, rather than the hypermodern 3.g3, with which Réti won the 1st brilliancy prize against Bogoljubow at New York 1924.

3...♘f6 4.♘c3 ♗b4

Now called the Ragozin Defense, this was in fact already an old line going back to Blackburne-Gossip, New York 1889, and had been seen in dozens of games by Chigorin, Schlechter, Bernstein, Alekhine and other prominent players well before Ragozin's first use of it at Leningrad 1934. Marshall was particularly fond of it, playing it ten times over the years 1923-1931, and scoring +3 -1 =6, including draws with Lasker and Capablanca.

5.♗g5 h6

Ragozin's later idea was 5...d×c4, with which he scored 4-0 in Russian tournaments 1936-1945.

6.♗×f6 ♕×f6 7.e3

7.♕a4+ was played in Ed. Lasker-Marshall, 9th match game, US Ch, Cleveland 1923 (½-½, 63), and 7.♕b3 in Hodges-Ed. Lasker, Lake Hopatcong 1923 (0-1, 41). The text had been played once before, in Morrison-Ritchie, Canadian Ch, Hamilton 1924 (1-0, 45).

7...c5

As so often in Torre's games, we reach a position never seen before, though here the TN is Marshall's. 7...0–0 would come to be the main line, played about 75% of the time, compared to about 15% for the text. Among those favoring 7...0–0 has been Magnus Carlsen, playing it for example against Aronian, Ivanchuk, Giri, Mamedyarov, and Wesley So.

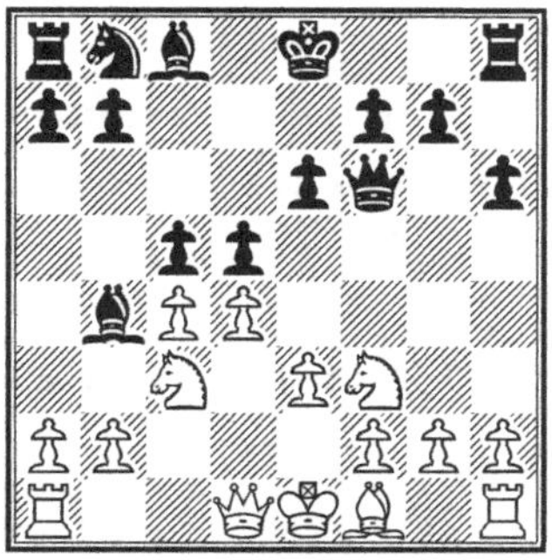

8.c×d5 e×d5 9.♗b5+ ♘c6

As will be seen, 9...♗d7 was preferable.

10.0–0 ♗×c3

This is virtually forced; if, say, 10...♗e6? 11.♘e2 0–0 (not 11...c×d4?? 12.♕a4+–) 12.a3 ♗a5 13.d×c5 winning a pawn and creating a fine Knight outpost at d4 (+2.40/24).

11.b×c3

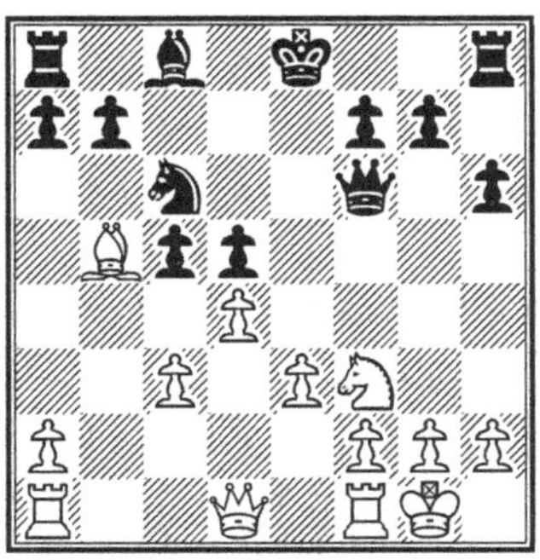

11...0–0

With this Black indicates his willingness to drop a pawn, at least temporarily, in return for freer development.

The main alternative is 11...c×d4 12.c×d4 ♗g4 13.♖c1 ♖c8 14.♗e2,

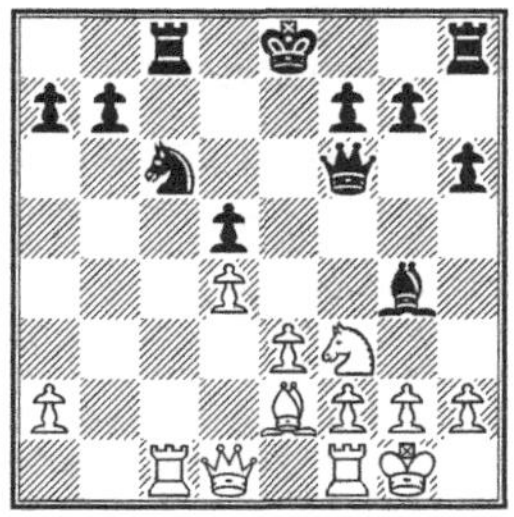

and now 14...0–0 15.♕b3 ♖c7 16.♕×d5 loses a pawn anyway (+1.21/27), while if 14...♖c7 15.h3 ♗f5 16.♕b3 ♕d6 17.♖c5 ♗e6 18.♖fc1 0–0 19.♕a4 ♗d7 20.♗b5 a6 21.♗×c6 ♖×c6 22.♖×c6 ♗×c6 23.♕b3 with enduring positional pressure (+1.20/25).

12.d×c5 ♕×c3 13.♕×d5 ♗e6 14.♕h5

An awkward square for the Queen, but the only one from which she still defends the c-pawn.

14...♖ad8 15.♖fc1 ♕b4 16.♗×c6 b×c6

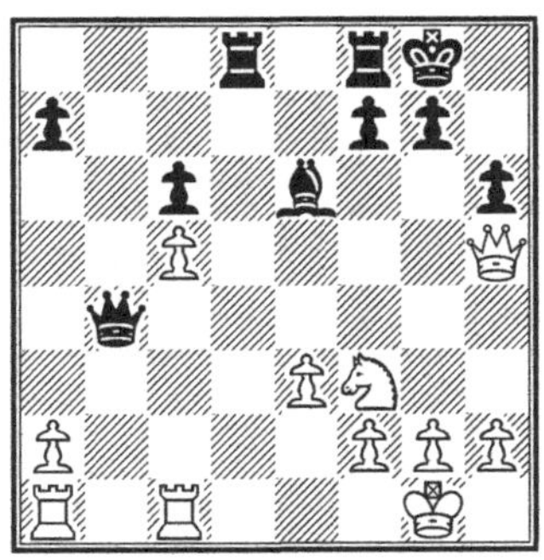

17.♘d4

Somewhat better was 17.a3 ♕a5 18.♘d4 ♖d5 19.♕f3 ♖×c5 20.♖×c5 ♕×c5 21.♕×c6, White remaining a pawn ahead.

17...♖d5 18.♕e2?!
It is unclear why Torre chose this instead of 18.♕f3, which would have retained the pawn advantage, as in the previous note.

18...♖×c5 19.♘×c6
While this retains the extra pawn for a while, White must eventually lose the a-pawn, restoring material equality.

19...♖×c1+ 20.♖×c1 ♕a3 21.♖c2 ♖c8
Black could also play the immediate 21...♗×a2, since if 22.♖×a2 ♕c1+ 23.♕f1 ♕×c6 24.♖×a7=.
With the text he aims to capture White's a-pawn while retaining his own.

22.h3 ♔h8

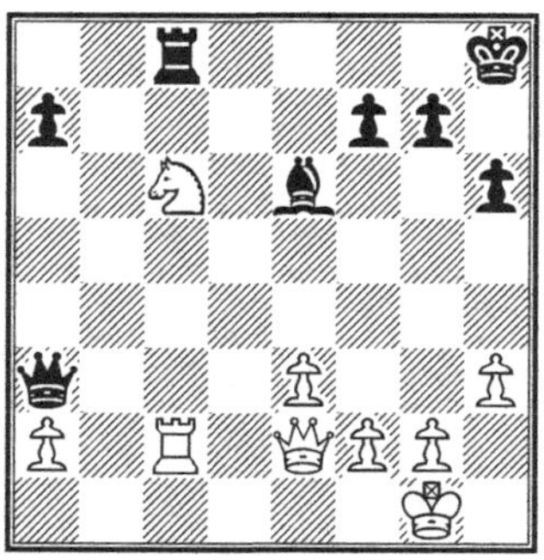

Forestalling any future threat of ♘c6-e7+. Black's threat now is not 23...♗×a2?!, which leads to nothing after 24.♖×a2 ♕c1+ 25.♔h2 ♕×c6 26.♖×a7, but 23...a5 △24...♕a4 25.♘d4 ♖×c2 26.♕×c2 ♕×c2 27.♘×c2 ♗×a2 with good winning chances for Black.

23.♘d4 ♖×c2 24.♕×c2 ♕×a2 25.♕c6
25.♕×a2 ♗×a2 would obviously favor Black, but probably not enough to win (only -0.55/28).

25...♕b1+ 26.♔h2 ♕b8+ 27.f4

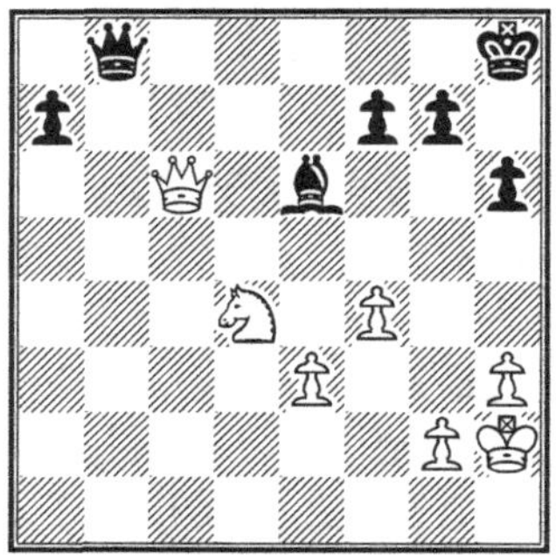

This advance looks somewhat more risky than the quiet 27.♔g1, as it appears to weaken the long white diagonal, but objectively it is equally good.

27...♕c8
Marshall would still like to exchange Queens.

28.♕a4 ♕d7 29.♕a5 ♗d5! 30.♘b5 ♗e4
Setting a cunning trap, one of Marshall's major stylistic traits.

31.♘×a7?
Falling into it. This hasty capture will cause White a great deal of trouble.

Better 31.♕b4 with a nearly even game (-0.47/32).

31...♕d3!

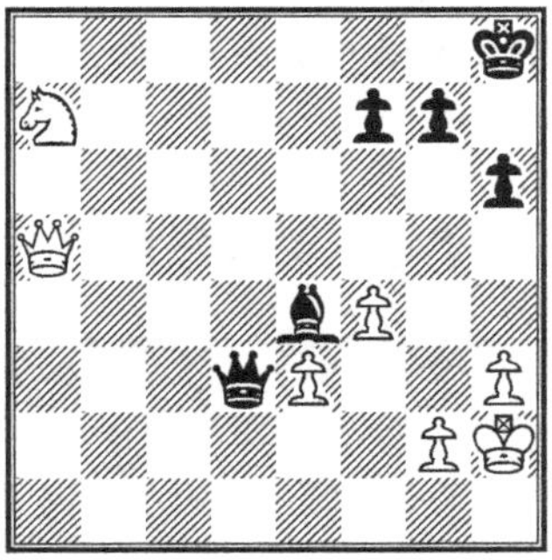

Springing the trap. Torre probably did not foresee this reply. White cannot defend the e-pawn; if 32.♕b6?? ♕e2 forces mate shortly, and if 32.♕e1?? ♕a6 33.♕b4 f5 34.♘b5 ♕a2–+.
The least evil was 32.♕b5, not because it draws, but because it makes Black's path to victory as difficult as possible. After 32...♕×e3□ 33.f5,

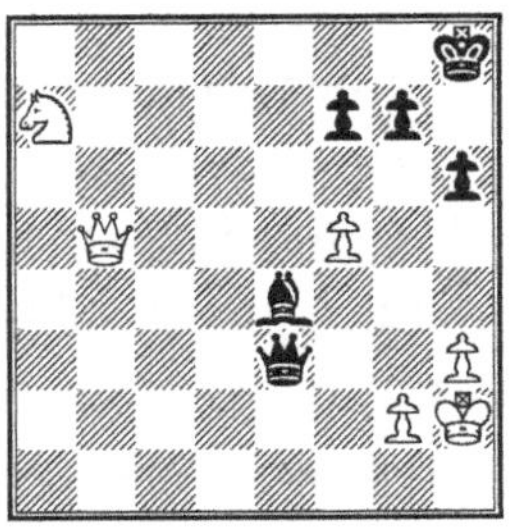

not 33...♕f4+ 34.♔g1 ♗×f5? (or 34...♕×f5? 35.♕×f5 ♗×f5 36.♘c6 with a book draw.) 35.♕e8+ ♔h7 36.♕×f7=, but 33...♔h7! 34.♕e5 ♕e2 35.♕g3 ♗b7! imprisoning the Knight, creating a virtual *Zugzwang*, and forcing eventual material loss, *e.g.* 36.h4 ♕f1,

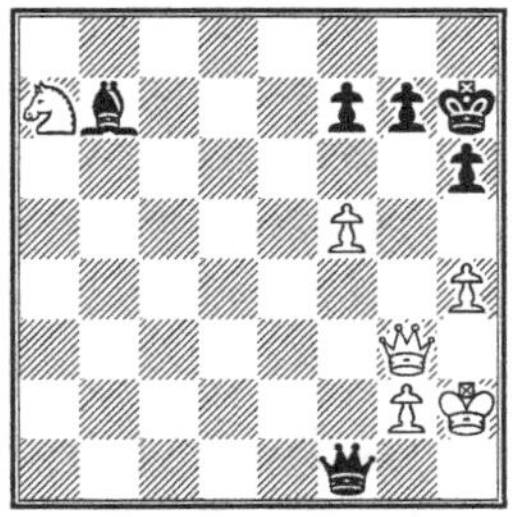

and either 37.♕g4? ♕a6 38.f6 (38.♕d4?? ♕e2 -8.65/29) 38...♕×f6 39.♕g3 ♕b6 40.♕b8 ♕a6 (-6.78/24), or 37.f6 g×f6 38.h5 f5 39.♕h3 ♕f2 40.♘b5 ♕f4+ 41.♔g1 ♕e4 42.♘c3 ♕c2 43.♔h2 (43.♕g3?? f4–+) 43...♗×g2 44.♕×g2 ♕×c3–+. Torre will have to find many such "least evil" moves to survive this ending.

Returning to the game (from diagram after **31...♕d3!**):

32.♕a2?
From bad to worse.

32...♕×e3 33.♘b5 ♕×f4+ 34.♔g1
As a result of his hasty play, White is a pawn down, plus the board is now clear for the Bishop to show its usual superiority to the Knight in an open position. However, even under these adverse conditions, Torre realizes that Black must keep Queens on the board, as the ending of ♘+2♙ -vs-♗+3♙, with all pawns on the same wing, is a draw. The presence of Queens greatly complicates matters and makes it difficult even for such a tactician as Marshall to find a way to win. Torre shows his mettle and works hard to save a half

point where a lesser player might have given up.

34...♕c1+ 35.♔h2 ♕f4+

Repetition to gain time on the clock.

36.♔g1 ♗c6 37.♘a3 ♕e3+ 38.♔h2 ♕e5+ 39.♔g1 ♕e3+ 40.♔h2 f5 41.♘b1 ♕e5+ 42.♔g1 ♕e1+ 43.♔h2

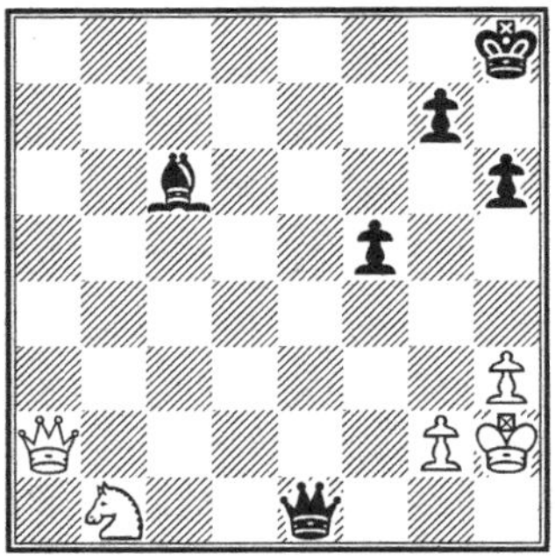

43...♗e4

43...f4 is also very strong. If then 44.♘a3 ♕g3+ (44...f3 also wins) 45.♔g1 ♕e1+ 46.♔h2 f3 47.g×f3 ♗×f3 and mate in 16.

44.♘a3 f4 45.♘c4

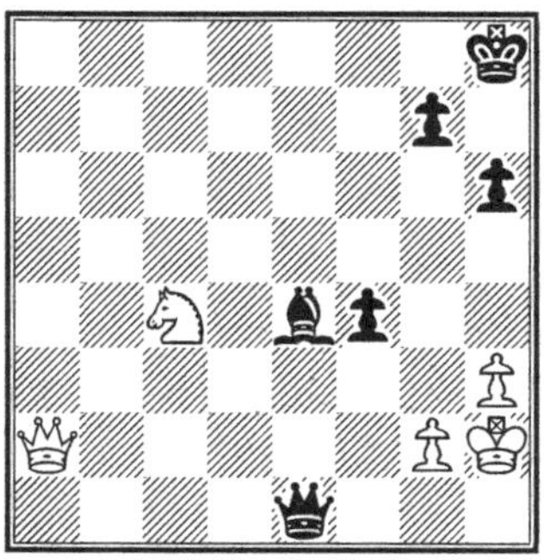

45...♗d5?!

Marshall's first notably sub-optimal move in the ending. Strongest was 45...♕g3+ 46.♔g1 ♕d3, when Black wins the Knight, either by 47...♗d5 if the white Queen does not move, or by an eventual ...♕×c4 if she does, the one exception being 47.♕a4 ♕e2 and mate in 11 at most.

46.♕c2! ♕g3+ 47.♔g1

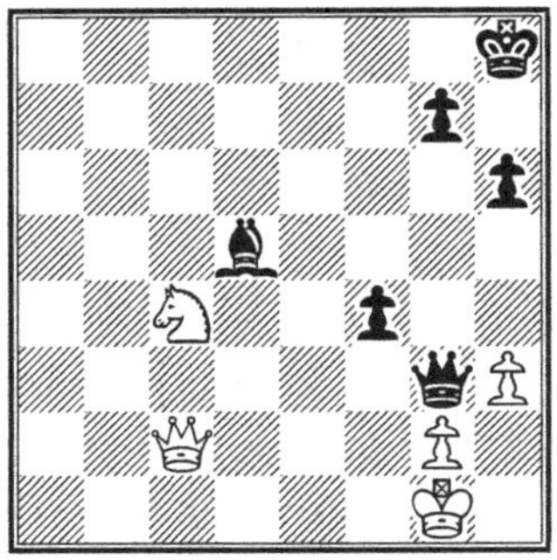

47...f3

A perhaps stronger alternative was 47...♕e1+ 48.♔h2 f3 49.g×f3 ♕h4, and now not 50.♘d2?? ♕f2+ 51.♔h1 ♗×f3+ 52.♘×f3 ♕×c2−+, but 50.♘b6 (another "least evil" move) 50...♕f4+ (not 50...♗×f3?? 51.♕c8+ ♔h7 52.♕f5+ ♔h8 53.♕×f3±) 51.♔g1 ♗×f3 52.♕f2 ♕g5+ 53.♔h2 ♕e5+ 54.♔g1 ♗b7

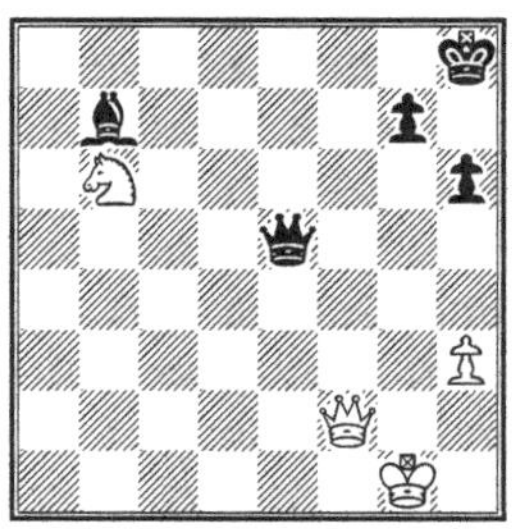

55.h4 [An interesting trap here is 55.♘c8 ♗×c8? (correct is 55...♕e6

56.♘a7 ♕×h3−+) 56.♕f8+ ♔h7 57.♕×c8=.] 55...♕e4 56.♔h2 ♕g4 57.♕f8+ ♔h7 58.♕f2 and somewhere in the fullness of time Stockfish sees Black winning (-13.81/28).

These and other analytical variations above demonstrate how, even though the untiring Lidless Eye glibly announces mates and overwhelming numerical evaluations, it can be a challenging, arduous, wearying task for a human brain to find the win. But the text should still do the job.

Continuing from the diagram after **47.♔g1**:

47...f3 48.♘e3 ♕e1+ 49.♘f1 ♗e4 50.♕f2

This or 50.♕d2 were the only remotely playable moves; if 50.♕c8+ ♔h7 51.g×f3 ♗d3 and the Knight goes.

50...♕×f2+ 51.♔×f2 f×g2

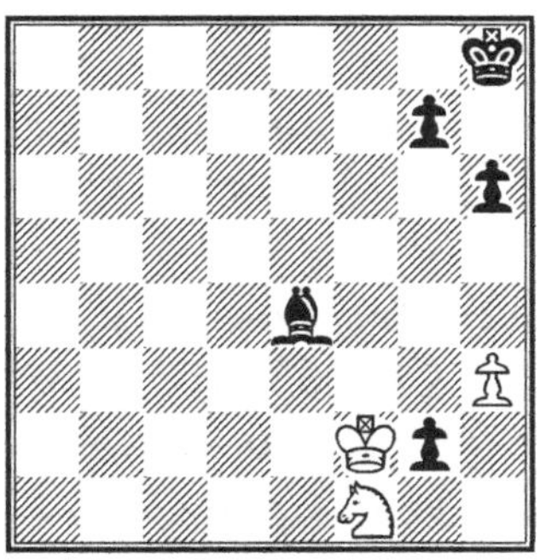

Earlier the exchange of Queens would have produced a draw, but now with Black having this pawn one square from queening, White seems doomed (-8.37/29).

52.♘g3 ♗b7 53.♘e2 g5?!

Another less-than-best move by Marshall. Better was 53...♔g8 intending to bring the King to the fore in advance of the pawns.

54.♔g3?

Torre too plays some sub-optimal moves. Not as bad was 54.h4, a trappy move inviting 54...g×h4? 55.♘f4 ♔g7 56.♔g1 ♔f6 57.♘×g2 when the game is suddenly drawn. However, 54...g4!□ would still win.

54...♔g7 55.h4 g×h4+

This or 55...♔g6 or 55...♔f6 all win. Torre is trying, and so far succeeding, to emulate his hero, Emanuel Lasker. In difficult or "hopeless" positions, the German champion almost invariably set the most difficult problems for his opponent, and by dint of a "miracle" often gained a precious half or even full point. Later we will see more examples in the art of successfully defending a very bad position, such as the famous ending against Capablanca in Moscow, 1925 (Game 73).

56.♔h2 ♔f6 57.♘f4 h3!□

A very astute move by Marshall, the only one that wins. If, say, 57...♔g5? 58.♘×g2!□ and Black will never be able to Queen an h-pawn.

58.♘×h3!

Stockfish announces mate now, but not for 25 moves. All other moves allow quicker mates, so this is best. Torre is still trying, like Lasker, to set his opponent the most difficult problems.

58...♔f5 59.♘f2

59...♔f4?

The game-decider. Marshall was in general a good endgame player, but now fatigue causes him to miss his last winning chance. Instead the winning line was 59...h5!, when Stockfish announces mate in 21, *e.g.* 60.♘d3 h4 61.♘e1 h3 62.♘d3 ♔g5 (not 62...♔g4? 63.♘f2+ ♔f3 64.♘×h3=) 63.♘f2 ♗c8!□ 64.♘d3 ♗f5 65.♘f2 ♔f4 66.♘d1 ♔f3 67.♘f2 ♔e2 68.♔g1 ♔e1 69.♔h2

69...♔f1! (not 69...♔×f2? stalemate) 70.♘×h3 ♗×h3 etc.

The text allows White a life-saving, tempo-gaining check.

60.♘d3+!□

Ensuring the draw, because now White will be able to take the g-pawn with impunity.

60...♔g4 61.♘e1

The Knight can now take the g-pawn, because Black will never be able to Queen his h-pawn, whether the minor pieces are traded off or not. Marshall decides to give it away.

61...g1♕+ 62.♔×g1 ♔g3

Marshall keeps probing, hoping for a mistake. But Torre makes none now.

63.♘g2 h5 64.♘e3!□ ♗e4 65.♘f1+ ♔f4 66.♔f2 h4 67.♘h2 h3 68.♘f1 ♗c6 69.♘h2 ♗b7 70.♘f1 ♗e4 71.♘h2 ½-½

What a struggle! This game is a great lesson in the practical value of tenacious and intelligent resistance.

Game 54
Torre-Grünfeld

Marienbad 1925, round 5
London System [D02]

This game was played May 26, 1925, only 20 days after the meeting of these same two players in the 16th round at Baden-Baden (see Game 47). Following that disastrous loss, Grünfeld had openly vowed that he would take "drastic vengeance" in his next confrontation with the young Mexican master. Furthermore, Grünfeld was now in top form, having won three games in a row (against Réti, Spielmann, and Haida), and he strongly wanted and expected to notch his fourth straight win at Torre's expense. But Torre had a surprise in store.

1.d4 d5 2.♘f3 c6 3.♗f4 ♘f6 4.e3 ♕b6 5.♗d3!?

Another Torre TN! In the only previous game in this line, Gibson-Speijer, Hastings 1919 minor tournament, White played the timid 5.♕c1. While that may have been more prudent, Torre's move has the distinct advantage of once again taking the great opening expert "out of book."

5...♕×b2

Black is practically obliged to take the proffered pawn, as otherwise White would have been in position to begin a queenside attack, with ♖a1-b1 and b2-b4-b5, targeting the pawn at c6.

6.♘bd2 ♕b6?!

Grünfeld starts going wrong already! 6...♕a3 was the better Queen retreat, keeping open the option of an eventual ...♕×a2.

7.0-0 e6 8.e4 d×e4 9.♘×e4 ♘×e4 10.♗×e4

Three tempi are normally considered adequate compensation for a pawn, and White now certainly has that, with three minor pieces already developed to none for Black, and his King already castled. Stockfish rates the current position at +1.66/26.

10...♘d7

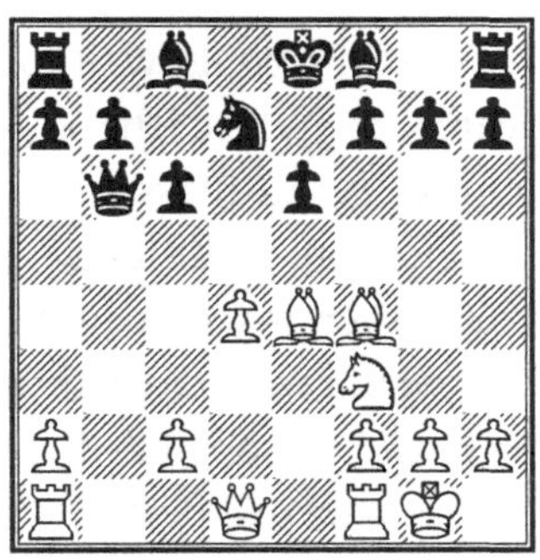

11.♕e2

Not bad, but White could have continued to build momentum with 11.♘e5! intending 12.♖b1 ♕a6 (not 12...♕d8? 13.♘×c6 b×c6 14.♗×c6 ♗a6 15.c4 and either 15...♗e7 16.♕a4+–, or

15...♗×c4 16.♖b7 ♗×f1 17.♕a4+−) 13.♕f3 etc. Black's best course after 11.♘e5 would then be 11...♘f6 12.♖e1! ♗e7 13.♖b1 ♕a6□ 14.♗d3 ♕a5 (if 14...♕×a2? 15.♘c4 forcing 15...b5 16.♖a1 ♕×a1 17.♕×a1 b×c4 18.♗×c4+−) 15.c4 0–0 with a very dominant position for White, with options to start a kingside attack with ♕d1-f3, ♖e1-e3 etc. (+2.32/25).
The text allows Black to start inching back toward equality.

11...♘f6 12.♗d3 ♗e7 13.♗e5
With this move White applies indirect pressure on the g-pawn, and immobilizes to some extent the ♘f6, which has the important function of defending h7. Perhaps better, though, was 13.c4 or 13.♖ab1 ♕d8 14.c4.

13...0–0
In his *Manual of Chess*, Emanuel Lasker commented "But here Black goes astray ... Castling could wait, because it indicates to White the direction in which he has to mass his pieces." While we hesitate to differ with such a great as Lasker, it seems improbable that Black would want to castle queenside, in view of the open b-file. Stockfish considers the text best.

14.♘g5 g6
Lasker says "The lesser evil was 14...h6 15.♘e4 ♘×e4 16.♕×e4 f5. The e-pawn would remain backward, but the King would be safe." Stockfish agrees, rating the resulting position at +0.33/25.

15.h4 ♕d8?!

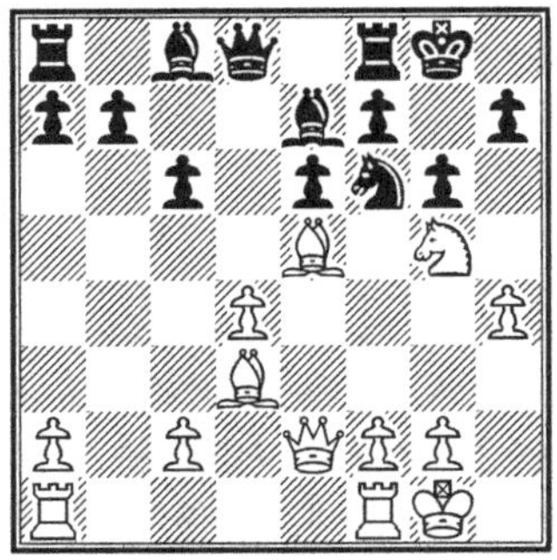

15...♘d7 was best, with equality (+0.29/25). Here Lasker commits an analytical howler, saying "The white h-pawn is no grave threat. If 16.h5, Black can now reply 16...♘×h5 because 17.♘×h7 ♖e8 leaves the white Knight endangered." As an annotator Lasker was often prone to superficiality (his book on St. Petersburg 1909 has many examples), and he certainly was not seeing deeply enough here, missing 18.♕g4!,

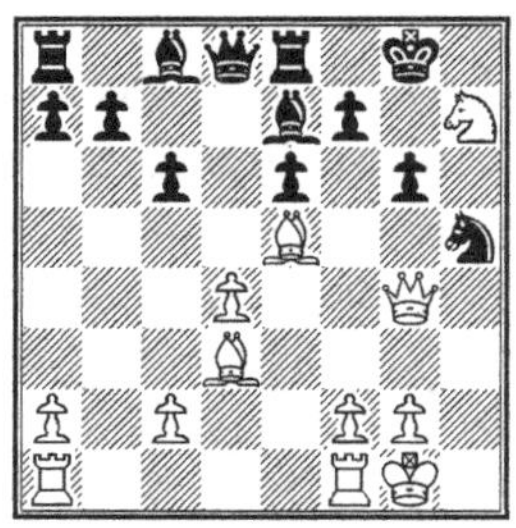

and Black can resign, as he cannot prevent 19.♗×g6 f×g6 20.♕×g6+ except at grievous cost.
After 16.h5, relatively best would be 16...♗d6, when 17.h×g6 f×g6 (if 17...h×g6? 18.♕e3 ♔g7 19.♖ae1 c5 20.♕g3/♕f4/20.♕h3 with attack) 18.♖ad1 ♕e7 19.f4 leaves White

very much in command (+1.56). Black would have to defend carefully for many moves to avoid catastrophe.

Returning to the game (from previous diagram):

16.♖ab1?!

Torre, perhaps psychically agreeing in advance with Lasker, misses 16.h5. In fact he will never play h4-h5, which is quite puzzling in view of his commanding kingside position. With his Knight and both Bishops poised to attack, his Queen ready to rush in, his Rooks not far behind, and Black cramped and undeveloped, h4-h5 would be just the nudge needed to start Black's position falling apart like a house of cards. After the text the game is even.

16...♘d7

This and 16...h5 are best.

17.♗f4

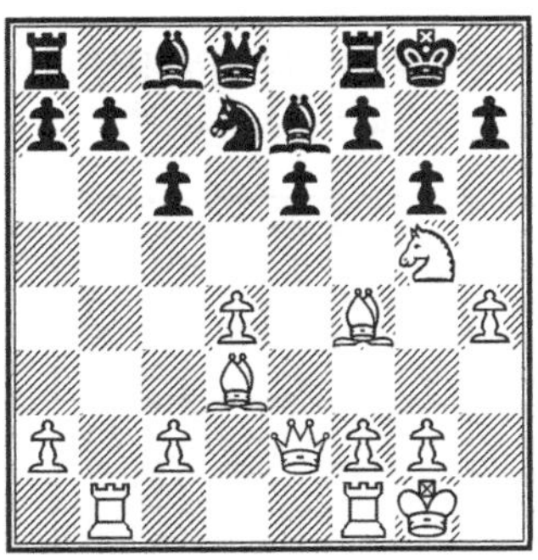

17...♗f6?!

Intending ...♗f6-g7 so that the Bishop defends both f6 and h6.

But best was moving the Knight right back, 17...♘f6. If then 18.♗e5 signals White's willingness to draw, or if 18.♘f3 ♘d5 forcing either 19.♗d2= or 19.♗h6 ♘c3 20.♕e3 ♘×b1 21.♖×b1 (if 21.♗×f8?! ♗×f8 22.♖×b1 ∓) 21...♗f6 (better than 21...♖e8 22.h5 ±) 22.♗×f8=.

The text keeps White's attacking chances alive.

18.♖fd1!

Lasker considered 18.c3 necessary, but the text is actually best.

18...♘b6

If 18...♗×d4? 19.♗×g6 h×g6 20.♖×d4 e5□ 21.♗×e5 ♕e7 22.♖e4 +−.

19.c4 ♗d7?

Lasker writes "Black does not judge right. He probably thought that a peaceful continuation would best preserve his advantage, but this is not so." This time Lasker is right. 19...♕e7 was relatively best.

20.♖b3

One of several strong moves at White's disposal.

Best was probably 20.♗c2 (about +3.35), followed by 20.♕e3, the text, 20.♗e5 and 20.♗d6, all with an evaluation of +2.00 or better.

20...♖c8?

Again, 20...♕e7 was the least evil.

21.♗e4

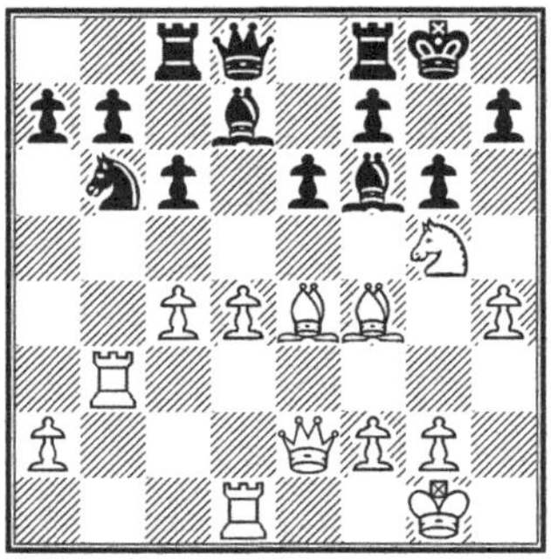

And again 21.♗c2 was best, intending 22.♖g3 and 23.h5 with a full-on and winning kingside attack.

The intent of the text is explained in Lasker's comment here: "White has discovered Black's weak spot: the b-pawn. That point plays a part in all the following combinations. Now 22.c5 threatens." Bluntly, no. While the b-pawn can become a target, to be successful an attack on it must be preceded by action on the other wing, in particular h4-h5, that will weaken Black's kingside and render his defense of the b-pawn futile. As will be seen, that defense is based on the idea that after his Knight is driven to d5, Black threatens ...♘d5-c3, winning the Exchange. But that threat can be made empty by proper preparation. And in fact, even if White were allowed an extra move in this position, after 22.c5 ♘d5 23.♗×d5 (presumably the reason for 21.♗e4) 23...e×d5 24.♖×b7, he really has nothing to show for it; all he has done is win back his gambit pawn while freeing Black's position considerably (+0.51/28).

21...h6 22.♘f3 ♗g7 23.♗d6 f5 24.♗c2

This and White's 22nd move are just strategic retreats, moving his Knight and Bishop to better squares with no diminution of his advantage, now calculated at +3.67 by Stockfish.

24...♖f7 25.♘e5

Better 25.♖e1, but Torre, again seeming to anticipate Lasker, retains notions of ♖d1-b1 (alas).

25...♗×e5 26.♗×e5 ♔h7

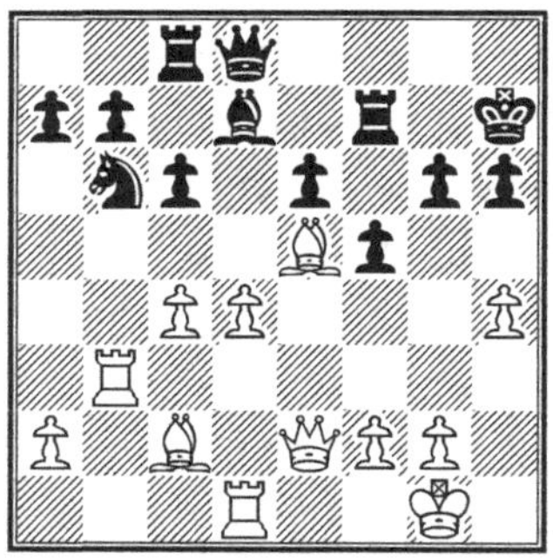

27.♖g3

Pretty good, but best — and in fact crushing — was 27.h5!, forcing 27...g5 (the aforementioned preparation) and now 28.c5! ♘d5 29.♖×b7!,

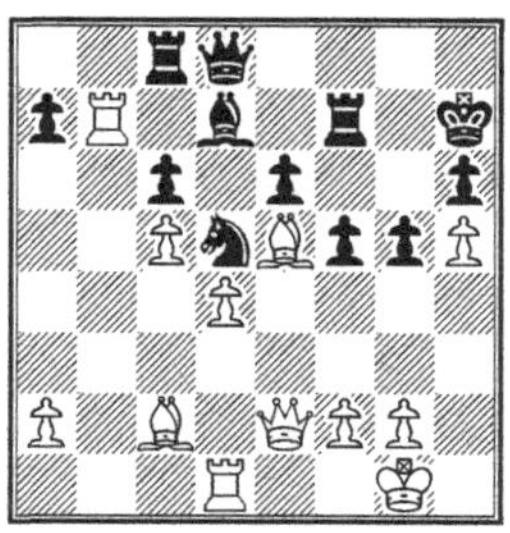

when if 29...♘c3? (which Lasker,

and apparently Grünfeld and Torre, thought was the refutation of 29.♖×b7) 30.♕c4 ♘×d1⁇,

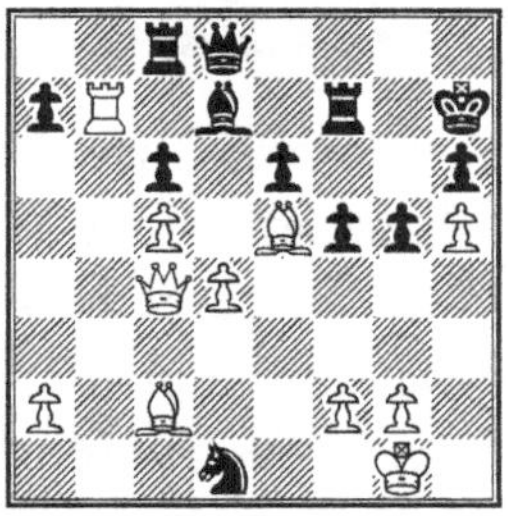

there comes 31.♗×f5+!! (showing why 27.h5 forcing 27...g5 was necessary before playing c4-c5) 31...♖×f5 32.♕×e6 and Black can resign.

Other 29th moves are little better, *e.g.* 29...♔g8 30.♕a6 ♘c7 31.♕×a7 (+5.57/23), or 29...a5 30.♖db1 ♕e8 (again if 30...♘c3? 31.♕c4 ♘×b1⁇ 32.♗×f5+ ♖×f5 33.♕×e6+−) 31.♕d2 ♖e7 32.♕×a5 ♕×h5 33.♕e1+−.

But Torre somehow never hits on the idea of h4-h5, which makes one wonder why he played 15.h2-h4 in the first place.

Returning to the game:

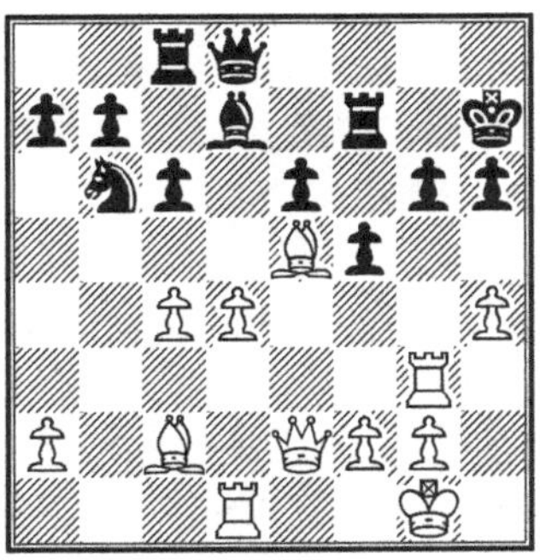

27...♕e7

27...♕×h4⁇ would be suicidal, *viz.* 28.♖h3 ♕g5 29.f4 ♕e7 30.♔f2 △31.♖×h6+ and mate shortly.

28.♖b1?!

This is actually not bad, but it is so sub-optimal that we must give it at least a "?!". Best again was 28.h5! g5 29.a4 (much less effective now is 29.c5 ♘d5 30.♖b1 b6) 29...♖e8 30.a5 ♘c8 31.♖e3 △32.d5+−.

28...c5□

Ending any thoughts of c4-c5 by White.

29.♗d3

We say again: 29.h5!, though its effect is diminished with each delay in its execution.

29...♗c6

Black's best defense was 29...c×d4 30.♗×d4 e5 31.♗×e5 ♕e6 32.♖c1 (the c-pawn was attacked three times) 32...♖e7 33.f4 ♗e8 with halfway-decent drawing chances (+1.33/24).

30.d5?

We must, unfortunately, consider this one of the most disappointing moves of Torre's brief career. Not that it is a gross error, or even close to one, but because it throws away White's advantage, and thus ruins the harmony of what could have been perhaps Torre's finest game to date. Before 30.d5? the game might still have demonstrated the impressive execution of a well-devised plan. But now it degenerates into a disorderly shambles ultimately decided by a blunder. Need we say what was best? Yes, still 30.h5, though by now it offered only a middling advantage (+1.20/25), and not a clear win. 30.♖e1 was also worth considering (+0.83/25).

30...e×d5!□

Another howler from Lasker here, saying "This is ill-advised. In any case 30...♗d7 was obligatory." Actually 30...♗d7?? loses to 31.d6 ♕d8 32.f4 intending 33.h5 with a decisive attack (+5.92/25). The text is in fact Black's only non-losing move, and the first in a series of nine perfect moves by Grünfeld.

31.♖×g6

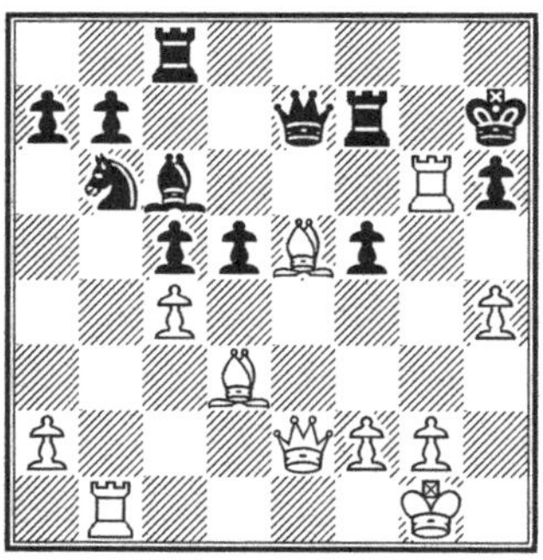

This looks stunning, and would be if Black replied 31...♔×g6?? 32.♕g4+! and either 32...♕g5 33.h×g5, or 32...♔h7 33.♗×f5+ ♖×f5 34.♕×f5+ ♔g8 35.♖b3 and mate in ten. But again Grünfeld finds the best defense.

31...♖g8! 32.♖×g8 ♔×g8 33.♗×f5?!

33.c×d5 ♗×d5 34.♖e1 would have retained a slight advantage (+0.43/26). After the text the game is completely even, and we enter a phase much like after move 39 in the Opocensky game, where Torre has let the win slip from his fingers, and he now must tack about haphazardly, hoping to provoke a mistake.

33...♖×f5 34.♕g4+ ♖g5!□

34...♔f8?? 35.♕×f5+ loses.

35.h×g5 ♕×e5 36.g×h6+ ♔h7□

Lasker comments "Black's defensive task is extremely difficult, because his King cannot find safety." Be that as it may, Grünfeld keeps finding the best moves (up to a point).

37.♖b3 ♗d7□ 38.♕h4 ♕e1+ 39.♔h2

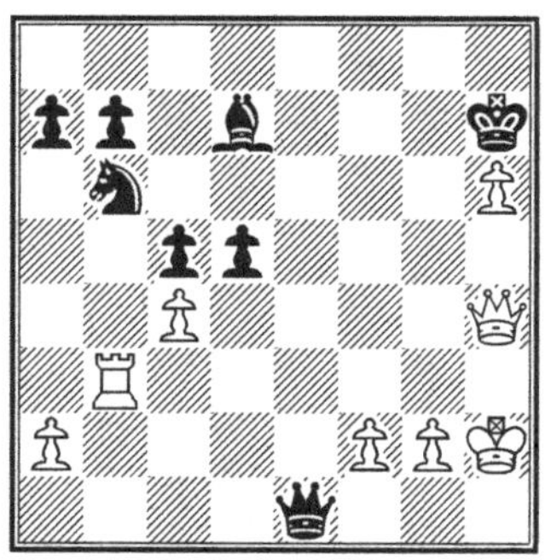

39...♕e4??

The mistake Torre needed. 39...♕e6 or

39...♕e5+ would have held the draw. One might glibly attribute this to time pressure, but in fact the TL was 30 moves in two hours, and 15 moves per hour after that, so *Zeitnot* seems unlikely.

40.♕f6!

Grünfeld must not have reckoned with this reply. It or 40.♕g5 win.

40...♕g6

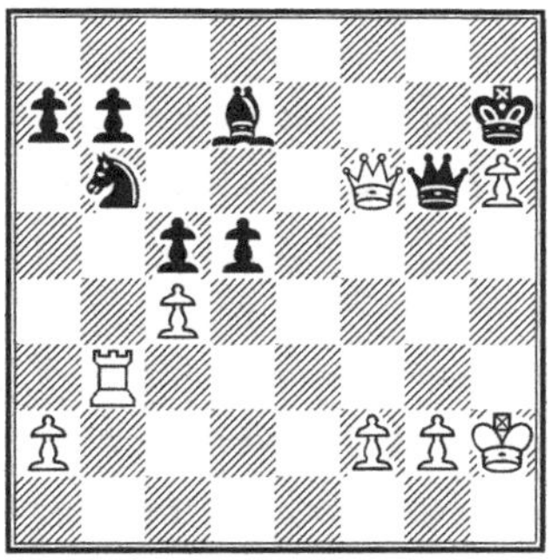

41.♕e7+

White must keep probing and avoid an exchange of Queens for the time being. The endgame after 41.♕×g6+ ♔×g6 42.c×d5 c4 43.♖c3 ♔×h6 is not promising, despite his passed f- and g-pawns (-1.87/25).

41...♔h8

If 41...♔×h6 42.♖f3! ♕h5+ 43.♔g1 d×c4 44.♖f6+ ♔g5 45.♕e5+ ♔h4 46.♕g3#.

42.♕f8+ ♔h7 43.♕e7+ ♔h8 44.♖e3

44.♔g1 ♕×h6 45.♕d8+ ♔g7 46.♖e3 might have been quicker.

44...♕×h6+ 45.♔g1 ♕g7 46.♕d8+ ♕g8 47.♕f6+ ♕g7 48.♕f4

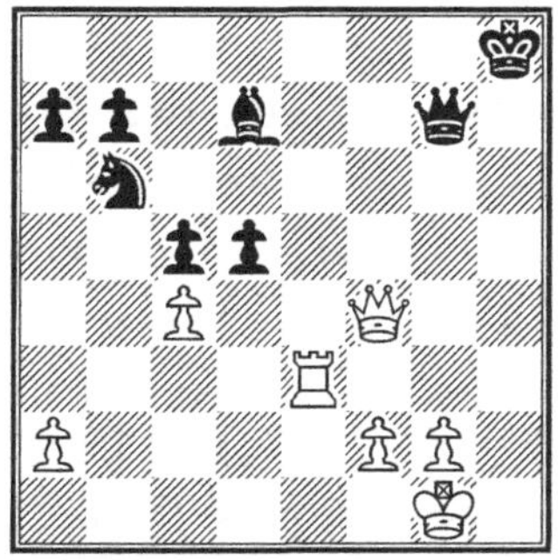

48...♗g4??

A further helpful mistake. Lesser evils (though offering no salvation) were 48...♕h7 or 48...♕a1+ 49.♔h2 ♕g7. If 48...♘×c4 49.♖g3! forces 49...♗g4 anyway, since if, say, 49...♕h7 50.♕f6+ ♕g7 51.♕×g7#.

49.♖g3

Natural and good, winning the Bishop. Stockfish finds lots of higher-rated moves, but the text not only wins a piece, but simplifies the position enough that a human player can be sure of where he is going. Most importantly, it makes a Queen exchange feasible.

49...♘×c4 50.♖×g4 ♕a1+ 51.♔h2 ♕e5 52.♕×e5+!

Now the exchange of Queens clinches the win for White.

52...♘×e5 53.♖g5!

The hungry Rook will feast on pawns. Grünfeld might well have resigned now, but perhaps feeling angry and frustrated at failing to get his "drastic vengeance," he stubbornly plays on almost to mate.

53...♘d3 54.♖×d5 c4 55.♖d8+ ♔g7 56.♖d7+ ♔f6 57.♖×b7
The b-pawn finally falls, 28 moves later than it might have.

57...a5 58.♖c7 ♘b2 59.♖c5 a4 60.g4 ♔e6 61.g5 ♔d6 62.♖c8 ♔e6 63.♔g3 a3 64.f4 ♔f5 65.♖c5+ ♔g6 66.♖c6+ ♔g7 67.f5 ♔f7 1-0
The game had been adjourned here, but Grünfeld resigned without resuming play. It's mate in nine at most after 68.♖c7+ or 68.g6+.

This game really threw a wet blanket on Grünfeld's hot start; after this he scored only +1 -1 =8 to wind up in 10th place with an 8-7 score. Interestingly, in its summary of the Marienbad tournament, the *Wiener Schachzeitung* wrote: "Grünfeld's morale has not yet recovered from his 13-move loss to Torre at Baden-Baden, and he played well below his class."

In the Vienna newspaper *Allgemeine Zeitung*, Richard Réti (who apparently did not understand it any better than Lasker did) described Torre-Grünfeld as "by far the most beautiful game of the Marienbad tournament." That misjudgement notwithstanding, Réti did add some very complimentary comments: "Notwithstanding his youth, Torre is a mature, self-controlled man who knows what he wants. He does not permit the allure of fame and gold to turn him from his path. He was asked he why did not take advantage of his sojourn in Europe in order to give exhibitions and to make tours, which would earn for him wide recognition. He replied 'Because I can learn nothing thereby.'"

The September-October *American Chess Bulletin* noted that at Marienbad, "something like eleven special prizes [for brilliancy] were distributed," then continued "Strangely enough, not one of these was awarded to Carlos Torre, whose fine game with Gruenfeld of Austria was a beautiful specimen of energetic and fearless play ... On his return here, Torre explained ... that the members of the committee making the award had been under the erroneous impression that one line of play in that game was unsound. Consequently, the game was left out of consideration."

The game was both interesting and frustrating. It continued a disappointing pattern, seen already in games 22 (Whitaker), 39 (Spielmann), 48 (Colle), 49 (Yates), and 51 (Opocensky), where Torre builds a winning position, only to err at a crucial point, throwing away his advantage, and ultimately drawing, or winning later only by a lucky happenstance. This not only affected his win-loss record, but marred his games aesthetically, like a mustache on the Mona Lisa.

Game 55

Thomas-Torre

Marienbad 1925, round 6

French Defense [C12]

Torre had little trouble with Sir George at Baden-Baden, but this game was quite a different story, as Torre tried another ill-advised opening novelty and was lost by move 14.

1.e4 e6 2.d4 d5 3.♘c3 ♘f6 4.♗g5 ♗b4 5.e5 h6 6.♗d2 ♗×c3 7.b×c3 ♘e4 8.♕g4 ♔f8 9.h4 c5 10.♗d3 ♘c6 11.♖h3 h5

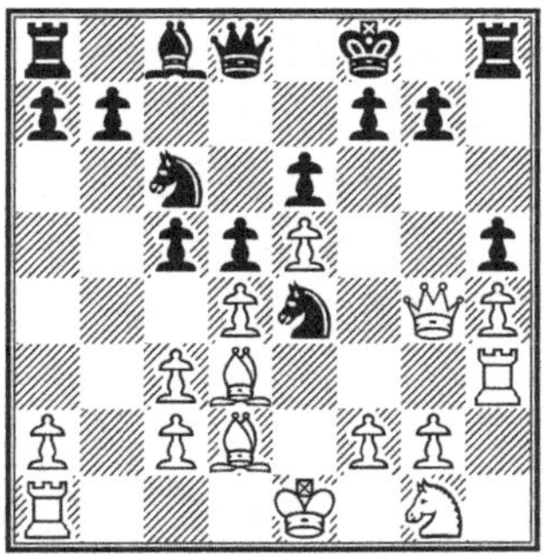

11...♘×d2, as in Thomas-Tarrasch, Karlsbad 1923 (0-1, 75), has been usual here. CB shows only five examples of the text move.

12.♕f4

CB has only one earlier instance of this position, in te Kolsté-John, Netherlands-vs-Berlin team match, 1922. There Black played 12...♘×d2 and eventually won. Torre tries a new path, which leads to disaster.

12...c×d4?

Better the aforementioned 12...♘×d2, or 12...♘e7, 12...♗d7, or 12.♕c7.

13.c×d4 ♘×d4??

Other than putting his Queen *en prise*, this is about the worst move Torre could make.

14.♖d1?!

White could have won with 14.♗×e4! d×e4 15.0–0–0!,

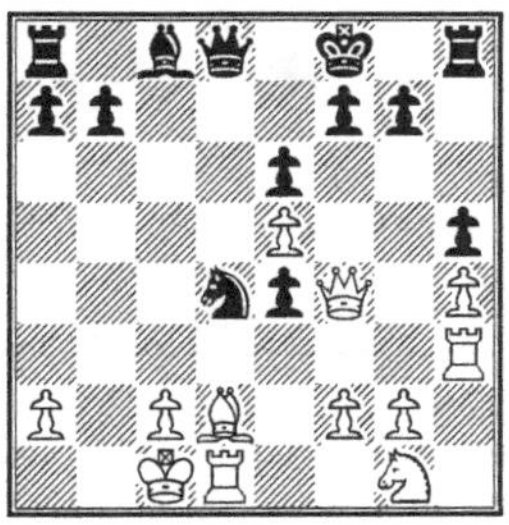

when he threatens 16.♗c3, winning the overly impetuous Knight. If it retreats, then 16.♗b4++–. If 15...♕b6 16.♗e3 and 17.♗×d4+–; or 15...♗d7 16.♗b4+ ♔g8 17.♖×d4+–. And if 15...♕e7 16.♕×e4 ♘c6 17.♗g5 ♕c7 18.♖hd3 ♔g8 19.♖d8+ ♘×d8 20.♖×d8+ ♕×d8 21.♗×d8+–.
Torre was fortunate that Sir George, not among the top tacticians of his day, missed this. But now Torre commits a second blunder.

14...♕b6??

14...♔g8 was best, with an even game. Now Sir George seizes his chance.

15.♗×e4 d×e4 16.♕×e4 f5 17.e×f6 g×f6 18.♕g6 e5□ 19.♗h6+ ♖×h6 20.♕×h6+ ♔e7

White has forced the win of the Exchange. He now gives a few quick checks to gain clock time.

21.♕g7+ ♔e8 22.♕g8+ ♔e7 23.♕g7+ ♔e8 24.♕h8+ ♔e7 25.♕h7+ ♔f8 26.♖g3 ♗g4

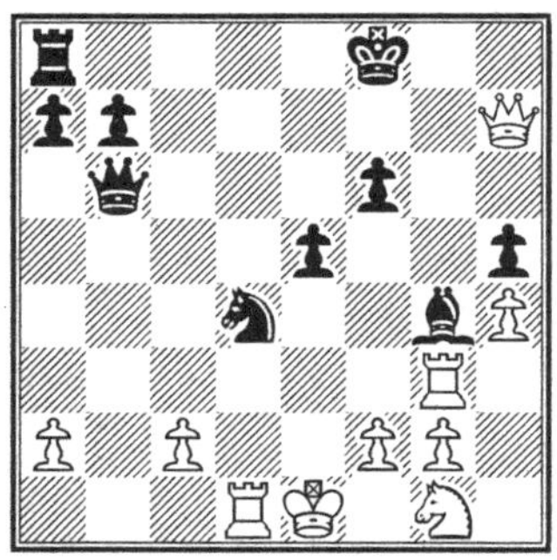

27.♖×g4?

Letting the win slip away. Correct was 27.c3! and

(a) 27...♗×d1?? 28.♖g8#;

(b) 27...♘c2+ 28.♕×c2 ♗×d1 29.♕×d1+−;

(c) 27...♘f5 28.♖×g4 h×g4 29.♕×f5+−;

(d) 27...♘c6 28.♖×g4 h×g4 29.♖d7+−;

(e) 27...♖e8 28.♖b1! (not 28.c×d4? e×d4+ 29.♘e2 ♖×e2+=) 28...♕a6 (if 28...♘b5 29.a4+−) 29.♕h8+ ♔e7 30.♖×b7+!! ♕×b7 31.♕g7++−.

27...♕b4+!□

Sir George neglected a cardinal rule: Always check for check! After this he must accept either perpetual check, or material loss that returns the game to equality.

28.♔f1 ♕b5+ 29.♕d3 ♕×d3+ 30.♖×d3 h×g4 31.c3 ♘b5 32.a4 ♘a3 33.♖d7 b5 34.a5 ♔e8 35.♖h7 ♖d8 36.♖×a7 ♖d1+ 37.♔e2 ♖×g1 38.a6 ♘b1?

Another error that might have lost the game for Torre. Correct was 38...♖a1=.

39.♖a8+?!

Stockfish indicates White could win as follows: 39.♖g7 ♔f8 40.a7 ♘×c3+ 41.♔d3 ♖a1 42.♖d7 ♘d5 43.♖d8+ ♔g7 44.a8♕ ♖×a8 45.♖×a8 ♘f4+ 46.♔e4 ♘×g2 47.♖a7+!□ ♔g6 48.h5+!□ ♔×h5 49.♔f5 ♔h6 50.♖f7 b4 51.♖×f6+ ♔h7 52.♔×e5 etc. (+10.82).

39...♔f7!□ 40.a7 ♘×c3+□ 41.♔d3 ♖a1□

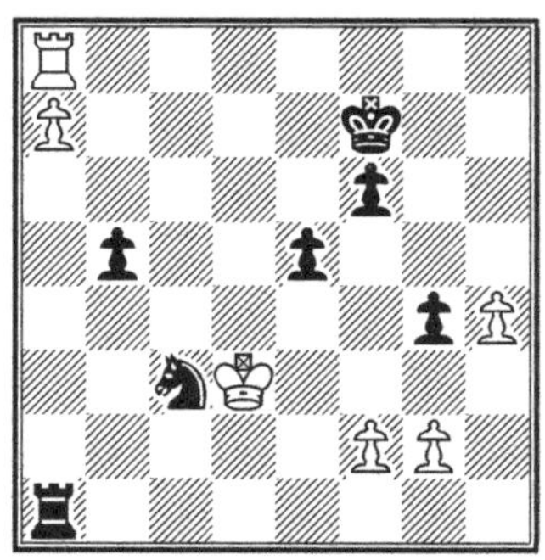

42.♔×c3

White might have tried 42.♖h8, when Black must find several "□"

moves to hold the draw: 42...♘d1□ 43.a8♕ ♖×a8 44.♖×a8 ♘×f2+ 45.♔e3 ♘h1!□ 46.♖a7+ ♔g6 47.h5+ ♔h6□ (47...♔×h5?? 48.♖h7+) 48.♖f7 b4 49.♖×f6+ ♔×h5 when though the ♖+♙-vs-♘+3♙ ending favors White slightly (+0.99/45), a split point is likely. Sir George tries for another 18 moves to find a win, without success.

42...♔g7 43.♔b4 g3 44.f×g3 e4 45.♔c3 ♖a3+ 46.♔b4 ♖a1 47.♔c3 ♖a3+ 48.♔d4 e3 49.♖e8 ♖×a7 50.♔×e3 ♖a3+ 51.♔f4 ♖a2 52.♖b8 ♖f2+ 53.♔g4 ♖×g2 54.♖×b5 ♔g6 55.♖b6 ♖c2 56.h5+ ♔g7 57.♖b5 ♖f2 58.♖f5 ♖b2 59.♖f3 ♖b5 60.♔h4 ♖a5 ½–½

A very lucky escape for Torre. Would he ever play a game that maintained a high technical and artistic level throughout? Our next game provides an answer.

Game 56

Torre-Yates

Marienbad 1925, round 7

Pirc Defense [B08]

Carlos Torre always considered this game the best he ever played. It is not a game of flashy, brilliant combinations of the kind that so delight the public. It is one for genuine connoisseurs of chess beauty. Here the Mexican master offers a marvelous example of imperturbability, discounting various opportunities to win material, instead carrying out his plan in direct, classic style. His opponent's error was to violate one of the principles of Steinitz: that to succeed with a flank attack it is necessary to have control of the center, or at least to ensure that it is permanently blocked. Yates launched a kingside attack contrary to this precept. Logically, Torre counterattacked in the center, and the black attack ended in an awkward tangle of pieces. Yates offered the Exchange to escape the tar pit, but Torre did not bother to accept. At last, almost desperate, Yates again offered the Exchange, now on the other side of the board, but Torre again paid no heed, and carried out his positional offensive as if he had no adversary playing against him. We include here Alekhine's notes from pages 198-199 of the 1925 *Wiener Schachzeitung*; these are labeled "AA:".

1.d4 ♘f6 2.♘f3 g6 3.♘c3 ♗g7
Yates varies from the Baden-Baden game, where he played 3...d5. With this we transpose to the Pirc Defense. AA: With this move Torre won against the same opponent at Baden-Baden.

Black can respond quite well with 3...d5; however, the deployment chosen here puts him at no disadvantage.

4.e4 d6 5.♗c4 0–0 6.0–0

So far as in Game 37, Torre-Thomas, which continued 6...♘bd7.

6...♘c6

Yates proceeds as he did against Olland in the Dutch-vs.-Foreigners Team Match, Scheveningen 1923 (0-1, 59). AA: But this is a "developing move" into thin air. Much closer to the spirit of the chosen defense was 6...c6 7.e5 ♘d7, so as to continue either ...d6-d5, or ...b7-b5 and ...a7-a5 to initiate queenside counterplay. White now obtains some advantage.

7.♗e3

Varying from Olland-Yates, which had continued 7.h3. With the text, as we have seen so often already, Torre breaks new ground. His choice, however, would not become mainstream theory; it would not be seen again until 1965, would not be adopted by any top-rank player, and Olland's 7.h3 would be preferred by a nearly 3-to-1 margin.

7...♘×e4

AA: Not entirely satisfactory, but Black was already embarrassed for a good move. If for example 7...♘g4 8.♗g5 h6 9.♗h4, or 7...e5 8.d×e5 ♘×e5 9.♘×e5 d×e5 10.♗c5! ♖e8 (if 10...♕×d1 11.♖a×d1 ♖e8 12.♘b5) 11.♕×d8 ♖×d8 12.♖ad1! ♖×d1 13.♖×d1 ♗d7 14.♘d5 ♘×d5 15.♗×d5±.

8.♘×e4!

Better than 8.♗×f7+ ♖×f7 9.♘×e4 d5 10.♘ed2∓.

8...d5 9.♗d3 d×e4 10.♗×e4 ♕d6?!

Beginning a strange and illogical deployment. Better was 10...♗g4. Presumably Yates was concerned then about 11.♗×c6 b×c6, doubling his pawns, but he is soon forced into that anyway. AA: The Queen stands exposed here. If ...f7-f5 was intended, it could have been played immediately. Black is playing imprecisely.

11.c3

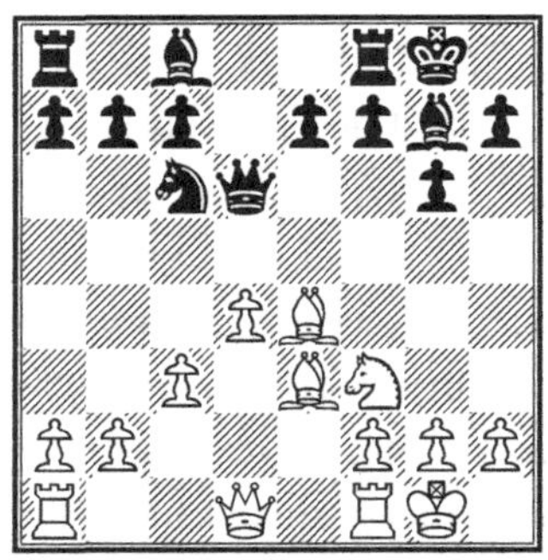

11...f5?!

The second strange move in a row. Better was either 11...a5, or 11...e5 12.♗×c6 e×d4 13.♘×d4 b×c6 14.♕a4 c5 15.♘b3 (if 15.♘f3 ♗b7=) 15...♗d7 16.♕a5 ♗c6, hoping for counterplay as compensation for the pawn Black is about to lose. Torre now spent more than 50 minutes contemplating the position. During that time he calculated a great many variations deriving from retreat of the attacked Bishop. Torre always liked to conserve his Bishops, and in preceding games we have seen his fine command of Bishop pair technique. Nevertheless, here he finally decided to trade it for a Knight, with the object of improving the mobility and harmony of his remaining pieces.

12.♗×c6!

The most difficult move of the game, according to Torre himself. Black must now recapture with the pawn, otherwise 12...♕×c6?! 13.♗f4! leaves Black with a strategically lost game due to this backward e-pawn.

12...b×c6

AA: Or 12...♕×d6 13.♕d2 with control of the c1-h6 diagonal and an eventual exchange of Bishops.

13.♖e1 f4

Apparently this is what Yates had in mind at his 11th move. As an attacking gesture, it lacks substance.

14.♕b3+!

This is not a case of the coffeehouse player's "See a check, give a check." The Queen in fact is excellently posted on b3, from where she dominates the

important a2-g8 diagonal, and inhibits Black's pieces from accessing the b-file.

AA: Not 14...♗e6 because of 15.♗×f4! etc.

14...♔h8

14...e6 was actually best, when after 15.♗d2 a5 16.a4 c5, Black stands worse but not lost (+1.21/25).

15.♗d2

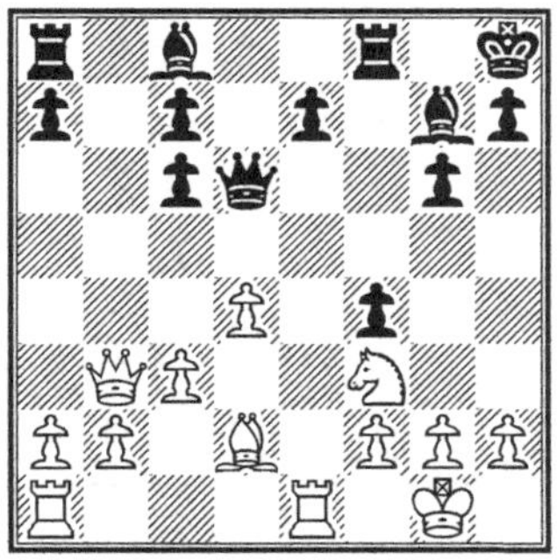

15...♖f5?

Yates intends to launch a pawn storm against White's King, but such an attack here lacks positional justification. Best was 15...♗d7 △16...♖ab8. Even 15...g5!? was better than the text; if then 16.♘×g5 ♕g6 17.♘e6 f3 18.g3 ♕h5 19.h4□ ♕f5 20.♘f4 Black might luck into some attacking prospects if White gets careless.

AA: After tiring one's self so long with thoughts of attack, one can no longer think about a defense which will be hopeless in the long run. Rather, one must continually try to keep the opponent occupied. Instead of the text, which parries the threat of 16.♘g5, 15...g5! should therefore be played, *e.g.* 16.♘×g5 (better 16.♘e5 ♗×e5 17.♖×e5 ♗f5 etc. with drawing prospects) 16...♕g6 17.♘e6 (or 18.♘f3 ♗h3) 17...f3 18.g3 ♕h5!∓.

Torre plays the concluding moves flawlessly. *(TK: Alekhine's evaluation of that last variation is incorrect; after* 19.h4! *White stands much better.)*

16.♖e4! g5 17.♖ae1

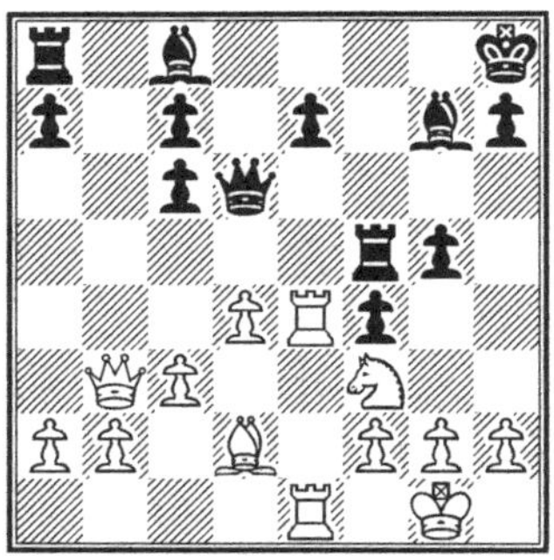

17...♗f6

Analysis of one variation is enough to show the incorrectness of Black's contemplated attack: 17...g4 18.♘e5 (also good is 18.♘h4 forcing 18...♖f8, since if 18...♖h5?? 19.♕f7! ♖×h4 20.♕e8+ ♗f8 21.♕×f8#) 18...♗×e5 19.♖×e5 ♖×e5 20.♖×e5 ♕f6 21.♖e4 (+5.06/24).

18.c4!

Torre continues inexorably building up his position.

AA: Threatening 19.♗b4.

18...a5 19.♗c3 ♗d7

19...a4 20.♕c2 accomplishes nothing.

AA: Here the King should have been taken off the enemy Bishop's line of fire by 19...♔g8.

20.♘e5!

Threatening 21.♘f7+.

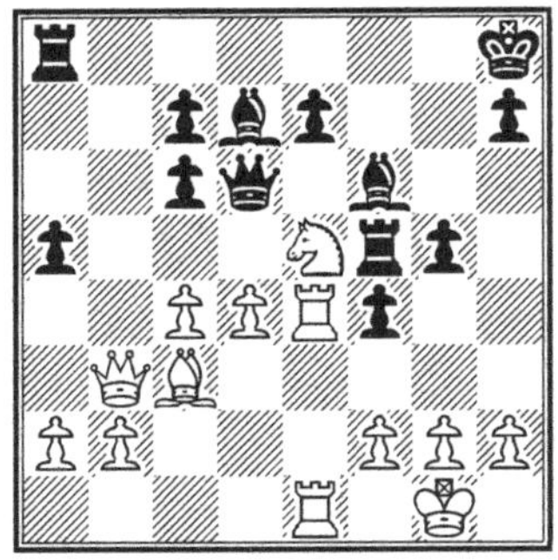

20...♗e8

If 20...♗×e5 21.♖×e5 ♖×e5 22.♖×e5 ♕g6 23.d5 ♔g8 24.h4! [The immediate 24.♖×e7 ♖e8 25.♖×e8+ (not 25.♖×d7?? ♕b1+ and mate shortly) 25...♗×e8 is playable but not quite as strong.] 24...g×h4 25.♖×e7 h3 (if now 25...♖e8 26.♖×d7 with impunity) 26.♖g7+ ♕×g7 27.♗×g7 ♔×g7+−.

21.♘g4

Threatening to trap the unfortunate Rook by 22.♘h6, but the most important aspect of this move is as the prelude to an invasion of the enemy camp by the white Rooks. If now 21...♗g7 22.♖×e7 ♖f8 23.♖×g7 ♔×g7 24.d5+ ♔g8 25.♖e6+−.

AA: Threatening simply 22.♘×f6 etc.

21...♗g6 22.♖e6

Best. Also good was the straightforward 22.♘h6, as any attack Black might hope to scrounge up by, say, 22...♖f8 23.♘×f5 ♗×f5 24.♖4e2 f3 25.g×f3 ♕f4 comes to nothing (+6.69/24).

22...♕d8
AA: 2...♕d7 also loses.

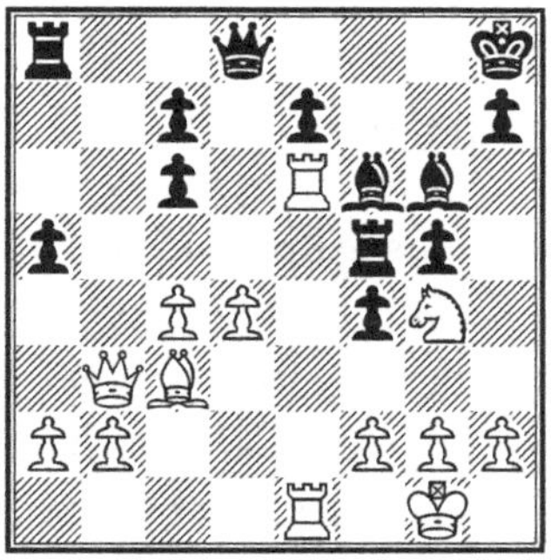

23.♖×c6
Torre sees the position not in material terms, and declines to win the Exchange with 23.♘h6. The Rook on f5 is actually doing nothing to make it worth the trouble, in fact it even helps White at the moment by obstructing its own Bishop on g6. Torre now concentrates on the focal point of his positional offensive, the square e7.

23...♖b8 24.♕a3
A very fine move. It creates the maximum difficulty for Black, who wants to disentangle his position without allowing an invasion by the white Rooks. Observe the lamentable situation of Black's pieces: the Queen's Bishop can hardly breathe because of the black Rook, which in turn cannot move due to obstruction by the other Bishop, which is in turn tied down to defense of the pawn at e7. Yates saw no remedy but to leave the pawn to its fate, placing his hopes on a tactical gamble we will soon see.

24...♗×d4 25.♖×e7
AA: 25.♖ed1 would also have sufficed, *e.g.* 25...e5 26.♘×e5! ♗×f2+ (or 26...♖×e5 27.♖×d4!) 27. ♔×f2 ♕×d1 28.♘f7+ ♔g8, 29.♘h8#.

25...♖b4

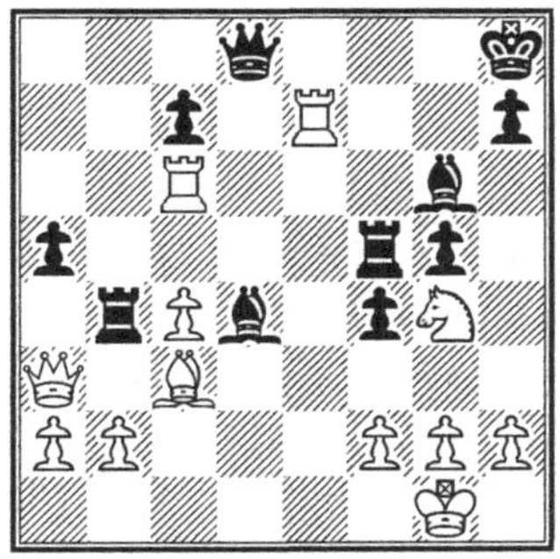

Playing his last card, albeit a weak one. Apparently Black hoped for 26.♗×b4 a×b4 27.♕×b4 ♗c5 when if 28.♕×c5?? ♕d1+ 29.♖e1 ♕×e1#. But this fails to 28.♕c3+ ♗d4 29.♕e1 (+9.94).
In any event, White's position is so strong that he can ignore this second desperate offer of the Exchange and play an even stronger line.

26.♖c×c7 ♔g8 27.♗×d4 ♕×d4 28.♖c8+ 1-0
Mate in four follows. A classic game.

According to Torre, Nimzovich closely followed the last moves. At the end he went over to a group of grandmasters and said in a loud voice, "A new genius has arisen in the world of chess!".

Game 57
Rubinstein-Torre
Marienbad 1925, round 8

Queen's Gambit, Baltic Defense [D06]

Until the rise of Capablanca, Akiva Rubinstein (1882-1961, GM title 1950, historical Elo 2640) was considered the prime contender for Emanuel Lasker's world title in the early 1900s. Title match negotiations were under way in 1914 but ended with the outbreak of World War I. Some chess writers see a significant decline in Rubinstein's strength after the war, but this is somewhat relative. His post-war tournament record continued to be stellar: 5 firsts, 6 seconds, and 3 thirds out of 18 events over 1920-25, including 2nd at Baden-Baden 1925 and equal 1st (with Nimzovich) in this tournament. However, in this game, Rubinstein does not demonstrate first-prize-worthy alertness, failing to capitalize on a blunder, and then committing one himself. However, Torre too failed to seize his chance, and so a draw was the logical outcome.

1.♘f3 ♘f6 2.d4 d5 3.c4 ♗f5

Another old off-beat line, going back to Burn-von Bardeleben, Breslau 1889 (1-0, 27). In the form 1.d4 d5 2.c4 ♗f5 it is known variously as the Baltic Defense or Grau variation. Historically it has not done well, ChessBase showing results nearly 70% in White's favor, though in what is probably the most famous game in this line, the Russian composer Sergei Prokofiev beat Capablanca in a 1914 St. Petersburg simul. Torre might have been influenced to try it after Marshall beat Thomas with it at Baden-Baden the month before.

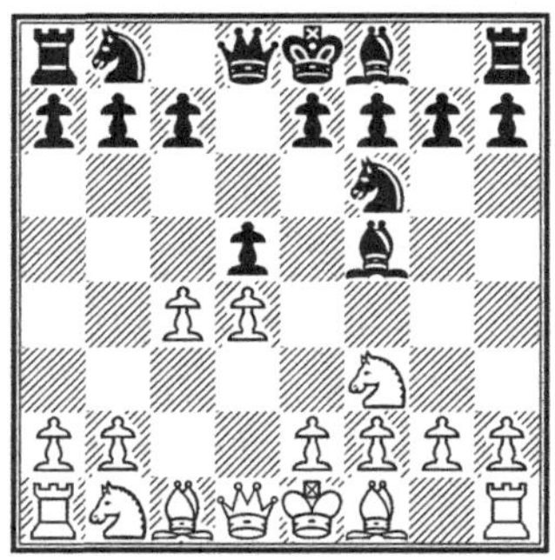

4.c×d5

It is not easy to say if this is the refutation of the strange move 3...♗f5. Bogoljubow suggested 4.♕b3, giving the line 4...d×c4 5.♕×b7 ♕d5 6.♕×d5 ♘×d5 7.♘c3 e6 8.♘e5 and concluding that "White has a clear advantage." However, his analysis is flawed: 5...♘bd7 is much better than 5...♕d5?, 7.♗d2 is better than 7.♘c3, and 7...e6? is refuted by 8.e4! ♘×c3 9.e×f5 ♘e4□ 10.♗×c4 (or 10.f×e6 ♗b4+ 11.♗d2 ♘×d2 12.e×f7+ ♔×f7 13.♘×d2+-) 10...♗b4+ 11.♔e2 ♘d6 12.♗b3 ♘×f5 13.d5 e×d5 14.♗×d5 c6 15.♗b3+-. On the other hand, at Moscow 1925,

Torre again tried 3...♗f5 against Marshall, and the American master made no effort to refute it, simply playing 4.♘c3 (which became by far the usual reply), though he did eventually lose.
What is the defect of 3...♗f5? Simply that it does nothing to preserve a central pawn for Black. On that basis, Rubinstein's 4.c×d5 appears the most logical reply, and if followed up properly might even be considered a refutation. But here Rubinstein does not find the right way.

4...♘×d5 5.g3?!
Letting Torre's risky opening pay off. Best was 5.♘bd2, threatening to win a piece. 5...♘b4?? would then blow up in Black's face, *viz.* 6.e4 ♗d7 (if 6...♗g6?? 7.♕a4+ ♘4c6 8.d5+−) 7.♕b3 c5 8.a3 ♘4a6 9.♘e5 e6 10.♕×b7 ♘c7 11.♘df3 (+4.61/23).
Thus forced is 5...♘f6 6.g3 e6 7.♗g2±.

5...♘b4!
Violating a basic opening principle, but in this case with ample justification, because the threat of 6...♘c2+ cannot be stopped by natural moves.

6.♘a3
Necessary. If 6.♕a4+ ♘8c6 7.♘a3 e5! turns the game in Black's favor.

6...♘8c6 7.♗g2 ♗e4
This second violation of opening principle is a bit much, and does nothing to further Black's development. Better 7...g6 or 7...e6.

8.0–0 e6 9.♘b5!
Excellent, getting the Knight back in the game.

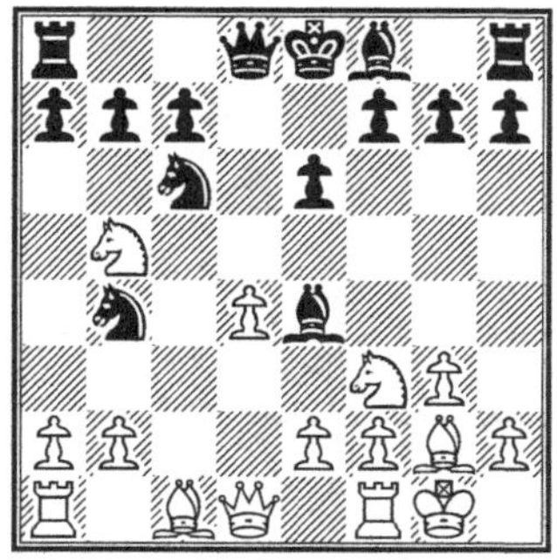

9...♘d5
Not 9...♘c2? 10.♗f4! ♗d6 [if 10...♘×a1?? 11.♘×c7+ ♔e7 12.♘×e6! ♔×e6 (12...f×e6?? 13.♗g5+) 13.♘g5+ ♔e7 14.♘×e4+−] 11.♘×d6+ c×d6 12.d5! e×d5 13.♖c1 ♘2b4 14.a3 ♘a6 15.♘d4 (+2.53/25).

10.♗d2
So as to capture on c3 with the Bishop. But preferable was 10.♘c3 ♘×c3 11.b×c3±.

10...♗e7 11.♘c3
The white Queen's Knight and black King's Knight have each lost about the same number of moves. Now the two peripatetic equines and their collective eight tempi disappear from the board.

11...♘×c3 12.♗×c3
The game is quite even now.

12...0–0
12...♕d5!? △13...0–0–0 was definitely worth a thought.

13.♘e1

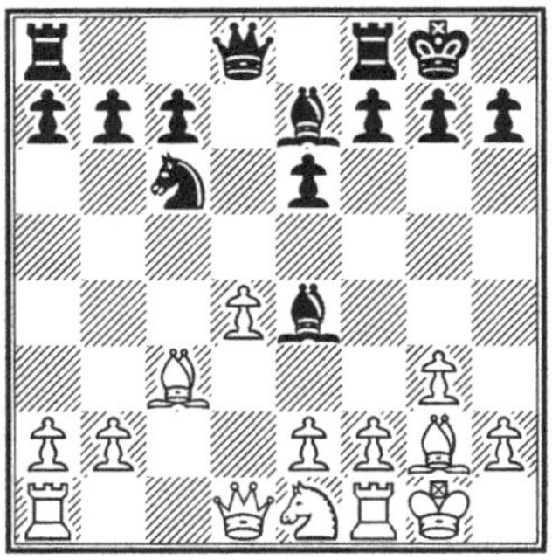

13...♗×g2

The sortie of the Bishop ends with little to show for it, but at least it has neutralized potential long-diagonal threats from White's ♗g2.

Worse were 13...♗g6 14.e4±, or 13...♗d5 14.e4 ♗c4 15.d5! ♗×f1 16.♔×f1 ♘b4 17.♕d4 e5□ 18.♕×e5 ♗f6 19.♕f4 ♗×c3 20.b×c3 ♘a6 21.e5 with tremendous central dominance as compensation for the Exchange (+1.08/23).

14.♘×g2 ♗f6 15.e3 ♕d5

Despite having no advanced center pawn, Black stands fairly well, his pieces occupying good squares. White's immediate problems are how to activate his Bishop, and how to enforce the advance e3-e4. Ideally, both goals should be part of the same plan. Rubinstein finds a way to enforce e3-e4 despite Black's strong pressure on the d-pawn.

16.♘f4 ♕f5

Somewhat better was 16...♕e4, making it harder for White to force e3-e4.

17.♘h5 ♖ad8 18.♕e2 ♖d7 19.e4 ♕g6 20.d5

Rubinstein's plan has been carried out well, but his center is not as dominant as it looks. 20.♘f4 was desirable before pushing the pawn.

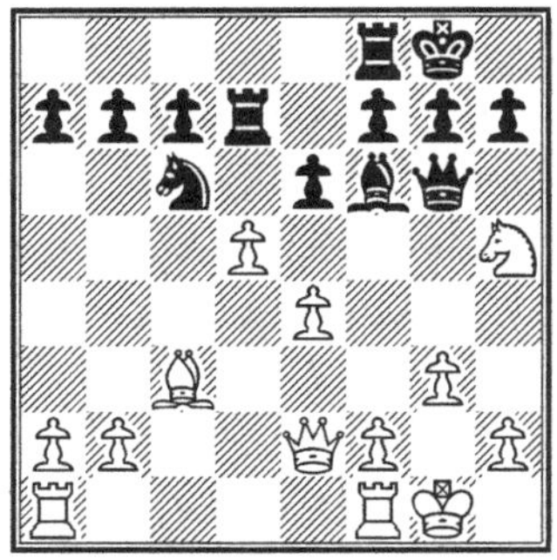

20...e×d5??

A grave blunder, which somehow escapes Rubinstein's notice. Necessary was 20...♗×c3□ 21.d×c6 ♖d2□ 22.♕e3 ♕×h5 23.♕×c3 ♖e2 24.c×b7 ♕b5□ with a dead-even game (0.00/32).

21.♗×f6 g×f6 22.e×d5?

One must wonder how two players of the caliber of Rubinstein and Torre both missed the simple combination 22.♘×f6+! ♕×f6 23.♕g4+ ♔h8 24.♕×d7+−. The game is now even, but does not stay so for long.

22...♘d4□ 23.♕d1?

Better either 23.♘×f6+ ♔h8□ 24.♕g4 ♕×g4 25.♘×g4=, or 23.♕g4 ♕×g4 24.♘×f6+ ♔h8 25.♘×g4=, or 23.♕e3=. The text apparently is Rubinstein's attempt to play for a win from a drawn position.

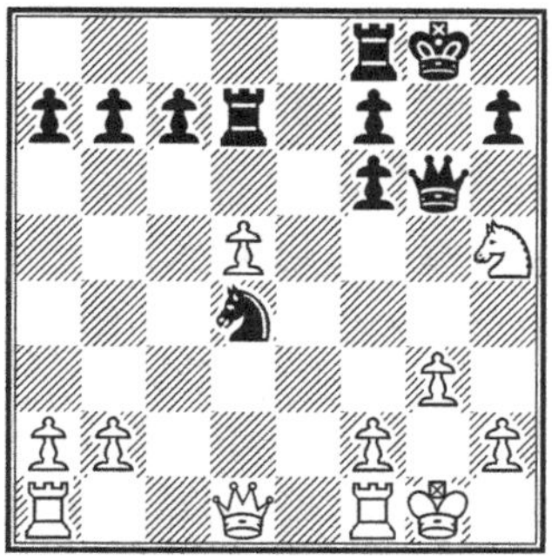

23...♖×d5

Rubinstein may have thought that Black could not play this because of the upcoming Knight fork. But Torre has seen a bit further.

24.♘f4 ♕e4!

There's the rub: if 25.♘×d5?? ♘e2+ wins the Queen. Now Rubinstein, a pawn down, must fight hard to salvage a draw.

25.f3?

25.♕b1 was the least evil.

25...♕e3+ 26.♔g2

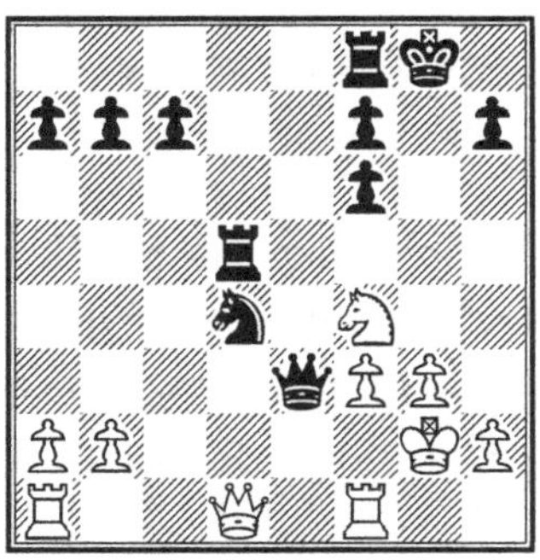

26...♖e5?!

This leads back to equality. 26...♖d6!, threatening 27...♘e6, was best. Necessary then would be 27.♕c1 ♘f5! and either

(a) 28.♖f2 ♖fd8 29.♕×e3 ♘×e3+ 30.♔h3, reaching an ending where White might be able to draw, but the winning chances are all Black's (-1.59/31), or

(b) 28.♕×c7 ♕d2+ 29.♖f2 ♘e3+ 30.♔h1 ♕×f2 31.♕×d6 ♕×b2 32.♖g1 ♕f2 33.♘g2 ♕×f3 34.♕f4 (forced; else 34...♘×g2 35.♖×g2 ♖c8 36.♕d2 ♕f1+ 37.♖g1 ♕f5+−) 34...♕×f4 35.g×f4 ♘×g2 36.♖×g2+ ♔h8, again reaching an ending where Black has all the winning chances (-2.53/35), difficult though it might be against perhaps the greatest Rook endgame player of all time.

27.♖e1 ♘f5 28.♕c2??

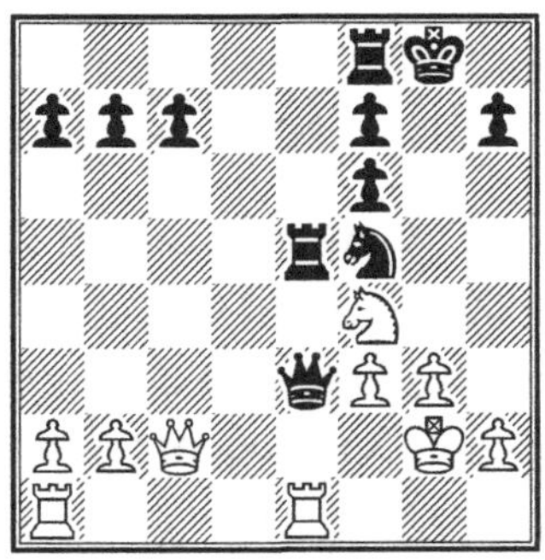

Strategically good, but tactically a serious oversight of the sort to which the post-WW1 Rubinstein was occasionally prone.

Correct was 28.♕d7 ♕d4 29.♕×d4 ♘×d4 30.♖ad1 and White should still be able to draw (-0.68/25).

28...♕c5

Amazingly Torre, perhaps in time pressure, does not see his chance. 28...♕×f3+! would win another pawn and probably the game, *viz.* 29.♔×f3 ♘d4+ 30.♔f2 ♘×c2 31.♖×e5 f×e5 32.♖c1 e×f4 33.♖×c2 f×g3+ 34.♔×g3 ♖c8, reaching an almost certainly winning Rook endgame with Black two pawns up (-3.36/26).

But now things are once again dead-even, and a peace treaty is soon signed.

29.♕×c5 ♖×c5 30.♖ac1 ♖×c1 31.♖×c1 c6 32.♘h5 ♘e3+ 33.♔f2 ♘d5 34.g4 ♖e8 35.♘g3 ♖e5 36.♖d1 ♔f8 37.♘f5 ½-½

Drawn on Rubinstein's offer. An interesting game, but one both players might wish to forget.

Game 58

Torre-Sämisch

Marienbad 1925, round 9

Torre Attack [A46]

As noted earlier, Torre would sometimes use tournament games for experimentation, without concern over whether the experiment would win or lose. This seems to be such a case. Playing his eponymous opening for the first time, Torre took an ill-advised turn down a theoretical dark alley that put him in a lost position after just 14 moves. But his opponent failed to capitalize, and Torre pulled off a combination that put him on top. But winning proved elusive, and by move 24 equality was restored, with a draw agreed soon thereafter.

1.♘f3 ♘f6 2.d4 e6

Inviting 3.c4, when Black can transpose to the Queen's Indian with 3...b6, the Bogo-Indian with 3...♗b4+, or the QGD with 3...d5.

3.♗g5

This, to our knowledge, was the first time Torre essayed the system that today bears his name. He was definitely not its originator; it was first seen in Albin-Noa, Dresden 1892 (0-1, 60), and in between then and the time of this game it had been played by Janowski, Jaffe, Alekhine, Kostic, Selesniev, Bogoljubow, Tartakower, Vidmar, Wahltuch, Kupchik, Marshall and Hromadka, among others. However, Torre deserves credit for successfully popularizing the system, hence his name is justly given to it. A few months later it was to bring him some resounding victories, against Dr. Lasker, the Soviet champion Boris Verlinsky, and against his present opponent, who in this game gets a completely winning position but ultimately only a draw.

The disadvantage of the Torre Attack is that by omitting the move c2-c4, it exerts less pressure on the center, but on the plus side it allows rapid development of White's pieces, which was very much to Torre's taste. The early sally of the Bishop leaves the b-pawn undefended, which Black may attempt to exploit by 3...c5 and 4...♕b6. In such cases, White will usually abandon the b-pawn to gain developmental tempi (as foreshadowed in Game 54). In that sense the Torre Attack may be considered a gambit.

3...c5 4.e4!?

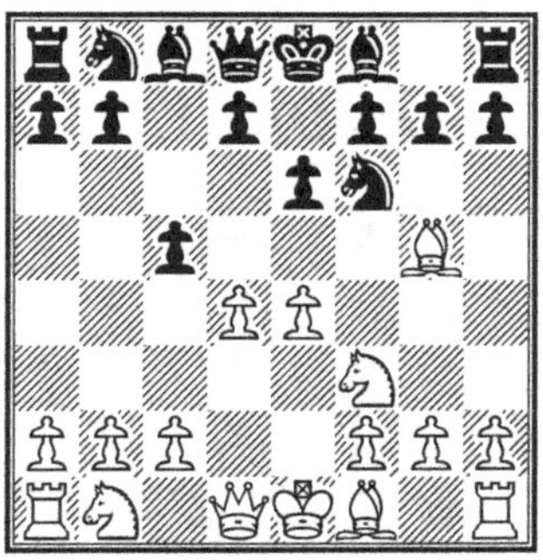

This advance, called the Heinrich Wagner Gambit after the German master who played it frequently *circa* 1921-1928, is very sharp, and seldom seen today. The normal move, by a factor of nearly 40-to-1, is 4.e3, which Torre employed in his later games, including the famous encounter with Lasker. Interestingly, the first instance of the text came in Wagner-Sämisch, Hamburg 1921 (0-1, 35). So Torre's opponent here was already prepared, which may explain how the opening turns out. In an earlier encounter, Tartakower-Sämisch, Vienna 1921, White played 4.c3.

4...h6

Theory today recommends 4...c×d4 5.e5 h6 6.♗h4 g5 7.♗g3 ♘e4 8.♕×d4 ♘×g3 9.h×g3 ♘c6 10.♕e4 ♗g7 11.♘bd2, with an unclear position.

5.♗×f6

Necessary, if White is to avoid losing the e-pawn. Torre was no doubt glad to play this, as it allows him to trade a queenside piece for a kingside one.

5...♕×f6 6.e5 ♕d8 7.♘c3?

Considered more energetic now, and played far more often, is the advance 7 d5!. The German grandmaster Burkhard Malich extensively analyzed this move and used it in his own games, for example 7.d5! e×d5 8.♕×d5 ♗e7 9.♘c3 0–0 10.0–0–0 with a nearly winning advantage in Malich-Zaitsev, East Berlin 1968; or 7.d5 d6 8.♗b5+! ♗d7 9.♗×d7+ ♕×d7 10.0–0 ♘a6 11.e×d6 ♗×d6 12.d×e6 f×e6 13.♘bd2±, Malich-Grünberg, Leipzig 1973.
7.c3 is also better than the text, though good only for equality.

7...c×d4 8.♘×d4?!

More in keeping with the spirit of the opening is 8.♕×d4 ♘c6 9.♕g4 or 9.♕e3. The text requires that White exchange his King's Knight for Black's Queen's Knight, quite inconsistent with aim 3.♗g5 pursued. This is the first notably inferior move in a stretch where Black makes several of them.

8...♘c6 9.♘×c6 b×c6

This opening of the b-file will prove advantageous for Black.

10.♗d3 ♖b8

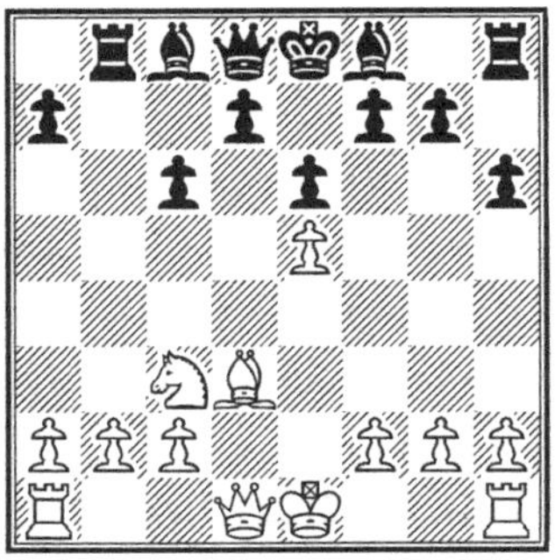

11.0–0

Abandoning the b-pawn is pretty much forced: if 11.b3?? ♗b4 12.♕d2 ♕a5–+, or 11.♖b1 ♕g5 12.0–0 ♕×e5, or 11.♕c1 ♕a5 12.f4 ♗c5 with attack. It is not as easy for White to capitalize on the pawn's capture when done by a Rook rather than by the Queen. The black Rook on b2 will be well posted and not as easily expelled as the Queen.

11...♖×b2 12.♕g4?

Another poor choice. Better 12.♕c1 or 12.♘e4. The text will allow Black to gain a crucial tempo.

It is curious that Torre would always play in such a risky fashion against Fritz Sämisch. The reason may have been Sämisch's tendency to use a great deal of time in the opening stage of the game. (As we noted earlier, he was known to say "If I could play the first 20 moves, I would not mind somebody else finishing the game for me.") Recall their encounter at Baden-Baden (Game 38), in which Torre ventured into extreme complications that nearly cost him the game. Against many other masters Torre would play in a more careful manner, but against Sämisch, despite the German's reputation as an established great of his day, Torre tended to recklessness.

12...♕a5 13.♘e4?

Very bad, needlessly giving up another pawn. Relatively best was 13.♘d1 ♖b4 14.♕e2∓.

13...♕×e5 14.♖fe1

14...♕a5?

A terrible move that squanders Black's tremendous advantage and puts White back in charge.

Winning was 14...h5! 15.♕f3 d5 (also very good are 15...♗b4, 15...♗e7, 15...h4 and several other moves) 16.♘g3 (The discovered attack 16.♘c5 leads nowhere: 16...♕f6 17.♕e3 ♗d6 18.♘b3 ♕f4 19.♕×f4 ♗×f4, and White has no way to attack the seemingly trapped Rook (-6.39/24).) 16...♕f6 17.♕e3 h4 18.♘e2 (18.♘f1 ♗b4 19.♘d2 h3 is no better) 18...♗d6 19.♕×a7 h3 20.g×h3 (20.♘g3 h×g2 is just as bad, and 20.g3?? ♕f3 is much worse) 20...♖×h3 21.♘g3 ♕h4 (-7.61/23).

15.♘d6+!
Presumably Sämisch did not see this *petite combinaison.*

15...♗×d6 16.♕×g7 ♖f8
One Rook or the other must die; this is the lesser evil.

17.♕×b2

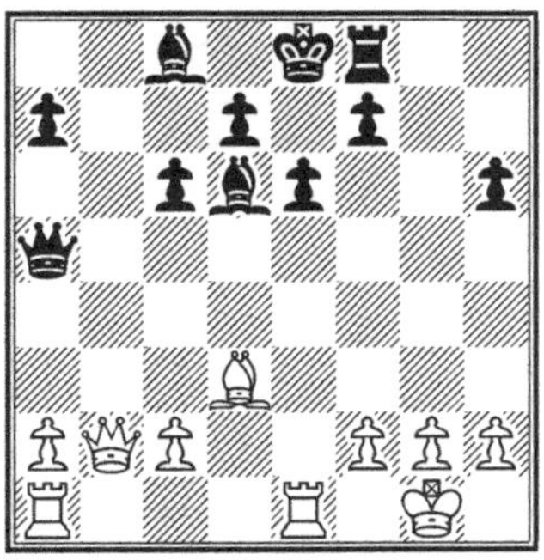

White is up ♖-for-♗+♙ for the moment, but the win is by no means assured, due to Black's active Bishops and his central superiority.

17...♕h5?!
17...♗b4 △18...♗c6 would have won back the Exchange: 18.♖e5 c5 19.♖d1 ♗c3 20.♕b8 ♗×e5 21.♕×e5 ♕b6 with a roughly even game. The mate threat made by the text is easily countered.

18.g3 f6?!
Played after 55 minutes' thought! Better first the obviously necessary and less committal 18...♔e7, retaining the option of ...f7-f5 in a single move.

19.♖ab1 ♔e7 20.♕d4
Best was 20.♖e4 △21.♖h4.

20...♗c5 21.♕f4 e5?!
Better 21...f5 or 21...♕g5, both about +1.15.

22.♗f5
22.c4 was worth a thought, perhaps with the idea of bringing pressure to bear along the d-file with the major pieces.

22...♔d8

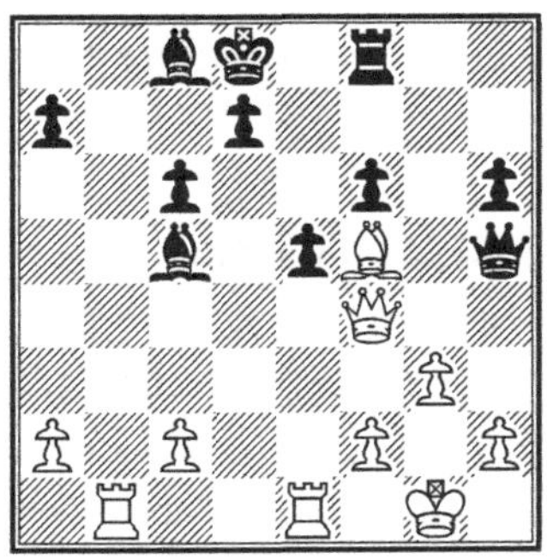

23.♕g4
While a Queen exchange might seem logical when one is up the Exchange, here it leads to complete equality. Torre might have tried 23.♕c4, but after 23...♗×f2+ 24.♔×f2 ♕×f5+ 25.♔g1 h5 his prospects are not especially bright.

23...♕×g4 24.♗×g4

The game now becomes just uneventful wood-shuffling.

24...♔c7 25.♖b3 ♗a6 26.♗e2 ♗c8 27.♗g4 ♗a6 28.♗e2 ♗c8 29.♖d1

29.♗e2 would have allowed Black to claim a draw by repetition.

29...d6 30.♖db1 ♗b6

Sämisch makes time control, presumably with his flag hanging by a fingernail.

31.a4 f5 32.♔g2 d5 33.♖a1 ♗a5 34.♖d1 ♗b6 35.♖a1 ♗a5 36.♖d1 ♗b6 37.♖a1 ♗a5 ½-½

Another strange, wild, but ultimately indecisive game between these two.

Game 59

Torre-Tartakower

Marienbad 1925, round 11

Réti Opening [A13]

We present this rather uneventful game as a counterpoint to the wild one these two played at Baden-Baden. Also it has a few points of interest for opening theory.

1.♘f3 d5 2.c4 e6 3.g3

Réti's brainchild, debuting in 1923 against Max Walter at Mährisch-Ostrau and Spielmann at Vienna, and famously played by Réti at New York 1924 against Yates, Ed. Lasker, and Bogoljubow, with White winning all five games. Though new back then, the line quickly entered mainstream theory, and ChessBase now shows over ten thousand examples.

3...d×c4 4.♗g2 ♘d7 5.♕a4 ♘gf6 6.0–0 ♗e7 7.♘a3

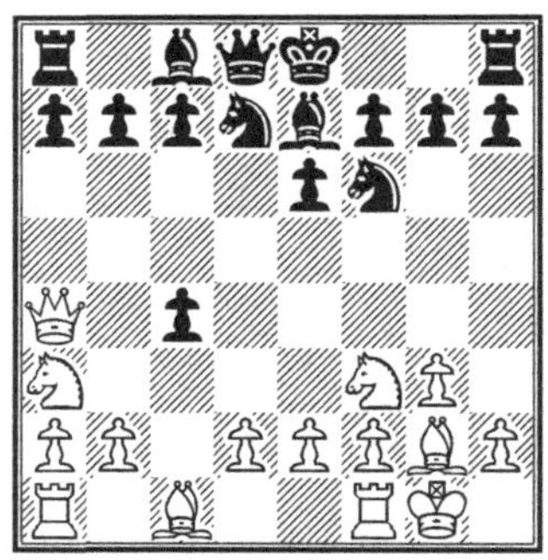

Another experimental novelty. Out of 87 games reaching this position on ChessBase, all but six continued 7.♕×c4. Besides this game, only two others have the text move: Jiménez-Letelier, Cárdenas/Matanzas/Santa Clara 1968 (½-½, 101), and Demitrijevic-Sos Andreu, Benidorm Open, U2000 section, 2010 (1-0, 37).

The idea of ♘b1-a3-×c4, in the form

of 1.♘f3 d5 2.c4 d×c4 3.♘a3, was introduced in Réti-Janowski, New York 1924, and was soon taken up by Euwe, Tartakower, Bogoljubow and Kostic, among others (including Torre himself; see Game 106). But it is somewhat out of place when White has already played ♕d1-a4. For one thing, after the Knight captures on c4, White may have to waste a tempo or two to avoid the pawn fork ...b7-b5. Another problem will become evident shortly.

7...0–0 8.♘×c4 c5 9.d3

9.b3 would be more in keeping with the spirit of the opening, intending ♗c1-b2 with Nimzovich-style overprotection of e5 (a theme Tartakower was fond of), perhaps strengthened further with ♘f3-e5 and f2-f4. But here 9.b3?! would leave the Queen out to dry, denying her any retreat back to b3, c2, or d1, and exposing her to potential attack by black pawns or minor pieces.

9...a6 10.♘ce5 ♗d6 11.♘×d7

Moving the Knight a fourth time to trade it for a piece that has moved only once. This cannot be optimal opening play.

11...♗×d7 12.♕h4

Any of the reasonable Queen retreats, to b3, c2, or d1, are equally playable. But White's opening advantage has gone with all the lost tempi, and the game is quite even.

12...♗c6 13.♗g5

Somewhat better was 13.b3, finally getting back into the hypermodern spirit.

13...♗e7 14.♖ac1 h6

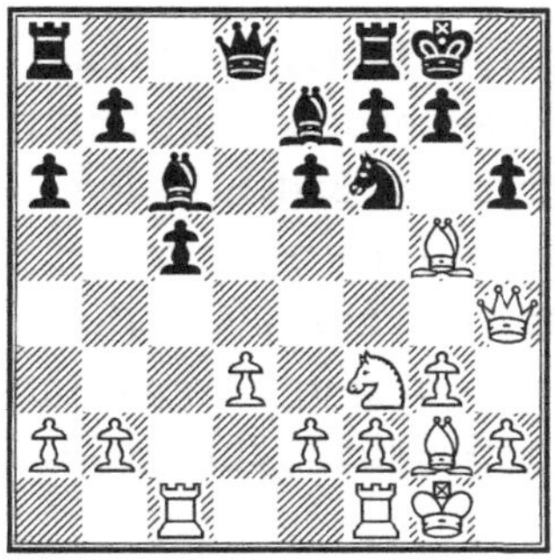

15.♗d2

15.♗×f6? ♗×f6 16.♕h5 ♗×b2 17.♖×c5 ♖c8 is obviously in Black's favor (-1.87/23).

15...♘e4

Superficially flashy, this move and the exchanges that follow take all the life out of the position. 15...♗d5 16.b3 a5 △... a5-a4 might have built on what slight advantage Black has now (-0.34/24).

16.♕h3 ♘×d2 17.♘×d2 ♗×g2 18.♕×g2

The remaining moves do nothing but polish the board with the felt bases of the pieces.

18...b5 19.♘b3 ♕b6 20.♖c2 ♖ac8 21.♕e4 ♖fd8 22.h4 ♖d5 23.♖fc1 ♕d6 24.♔g2 f5 25.♕f3 ♕d7 26.♕e3 ♕d6 27.♕f3 ♕d7 28.♕e3 ♕d6 29.♕f3 ♕d7 30.♕e3 ♕d6 31.♕f3 ♕d7 ½-½

Game 60
Réti-Torre
Marienbad 1925, round 12
English Opening [A20]

This game stands in brilliant contrast to the mistake-filled draw these two played at Baden-Baden. It is in fact one of Torre's best games ever, in Kingston's opinion better than his win over Yates in round 7, and far better than the Grünfeld game in round 5.

1.c4 e5 2.♘f3
Much as he did in Réti-Alekhine, Baden-Baden 1925 (which opened 1.g3 e5 2.♘f3), Réti turns the game into a sort of reversed Alekhine's Defense.

2...e4 3.♘d4 ♘c6
The anti-Alekhine-style 3...c5 did not work out well in Tartakower-Spielmann, Karlsbad 1923 (1-0, 44). The text would become the main line (if such a seldom played opening can be said to have a main line), played two-thirds of the time.

4.♘×c6
The most common reply, though 4.♘c2 has a slightly better track record (50% vs. 44.5%). Réti was fond of inflicting doubled pawns, going so far as to comment on te Kolsté-Réti, Baden-Baden 1925, that after 1.e4 ♘f6 2.e5 ♘d5 3.♘c3 ♘×c3 4.d×c3, Black had "a minute but clear positional advantage [that] can be easily converted into a win." Lasker, in his *Manual of Chess*, raked Réti over the coals for being "contrary to all proportion," concluding "The reader of Réti's remarks is led to think that an altogether new and profound strategy has recently arisen and is probably tempted to cast very deep strategic plans of the same order. He is in danger of losing his sound judgment, and neither he nor chess is well served thereby."

4...d×c6 5.♘c3 ♘f6

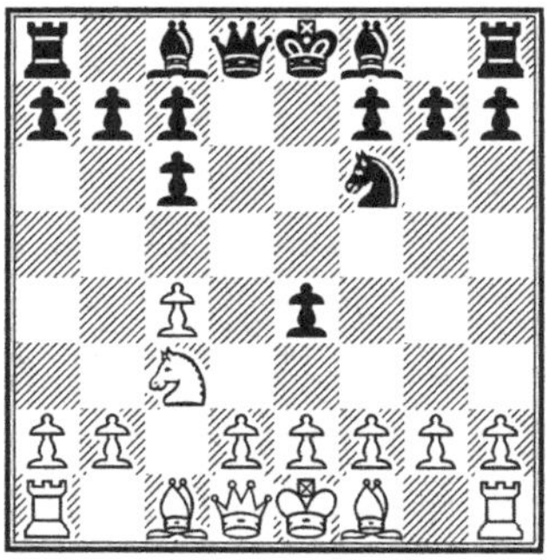

6.g3
Réti had a strong liking for the fianchetto, but better choices here were 6.d3 or 6.d4, likely followed in either case by 6...e×d3 7.e×d3 ♗c5 8.♗e2 0–0 9.♗e3 ♗×e3 10.f×e3, and White's central pawn majority may amount to something eventually. After the text, Black enjoys a free and normal development.

6...♗c5 7.♗g2 ♗f5 8.0–0 0–0 9.♔h1?

Intended, presumably, to unpin the f-pawn, but this could have backfired badly. White already is short of good moves; relatively best seems a different way to unpin, 9.♘a4 ♗e7 10.♕b3∓.

9...♕d4!

A strong move, though Stockfish prefers 9...♖e8,

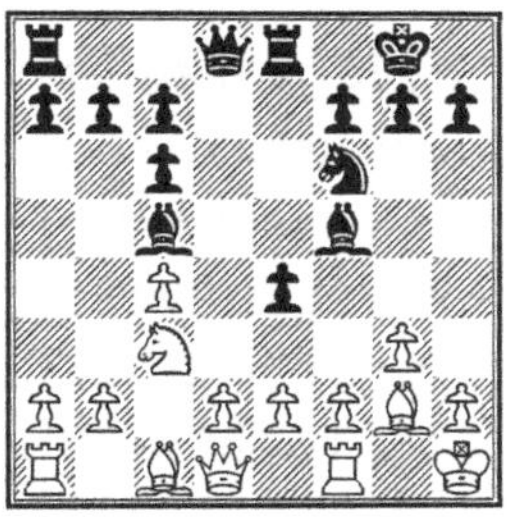

its evaluation suddenly jumping to -2.66 at 30 ply. However, it's hard to determine, without going through dozens of variations at considerable length, what exactly is the engine's basis for this evaluation, as nothing close to the win of a minor piece is evident in the lines it shows, and 9...♖e8 makes no immediate threat. We'll give a few samples:

(a) 10.♕c2 h5 11.f3 e×f3 12.♕×f5 f×g2+ 13.♔×g2 ♗d4 14.♕f3 ♕e7 15.♖e1 ♘g4 16.h3 ♘e5 17.♕×h5 g6 18.♕h4 ♕×h4 19.g×h4 ♘×c4;

(b) 10.♖b1 a5 (if 10...e3?! 11.f×e3 ♗×b1 12.♘×b1 and White's central pawn mass is at least partial compensation for the Exchange -1.12/23) 11.b3 ♕d7 12.♘a4 ♗b4 13.a3 ♗f8 14.♗b2 ♖ad8 15.♗c3 ♗×a3 16.♗×a5 b5 17.♘b2 h5 18.♗c3 ♘g4 19.d3 b4 20.♗d2 e×d3 etc. (-3.53/29); and

(c) 10.e3 ♕d7 11.♕c2 ♗g4 12.♘×e4 ♘×e4 13.f3□ ♘×g3+ 14.h×g3 ♗f5 15.e4 ♕d6! 16.d4 (not 16.e×f5?? ♕h6+ 17.♗h3 ♕×h3#) 16...♗×d4 17.♖d1 ♗e6 (-2.71/24).

Returning to the game:

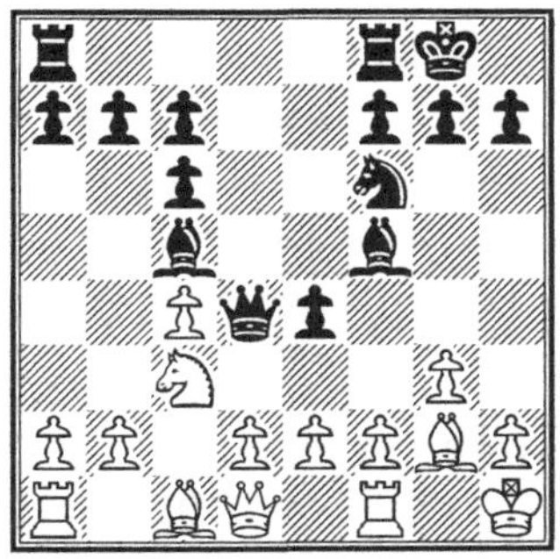

10.♕b3 ♖fe8?!

Torre's only questionable move of the game; it seems he just cannot resist gambitting his b-pawn. Better 10...b6 defending it, though as it turns out, Réti unwisely turns down the offer.

11.♘d1?

Beginning an ill-conceived reposting of the Knight that loses the game. Best was 11.♕×b7,

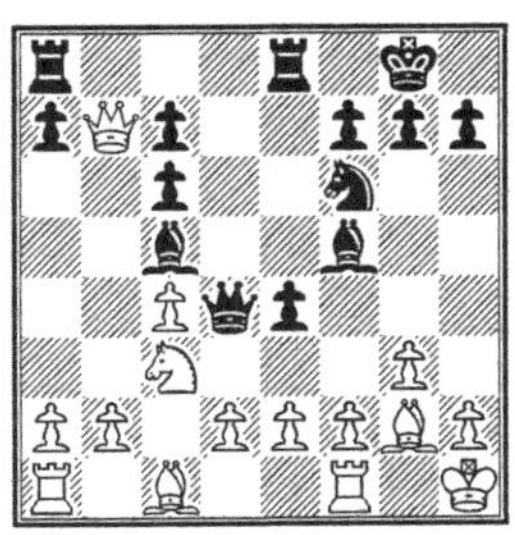

which either forces the black Queen to retreat to d7, d6 or e5, or else Black must gambit a second pawn by 11...♗b6 12.♕×c6 ♗d7 13.♕b7 a5 14.♘d5 ♖ab8 15.♘×f6+ ♕×f6 16.♕d5 ♗f5, and while he has developmental compensation for his material deficit (-1.32/25), he will need to make something out of it soon, or face a losing endgame.

And after 11.♕×b7 Black must avoid 11...♕×c4? 12.♕×c6 ♗d7, when either 13.♕×c7 ♖ac8 14.♕f4, or 13.d3 e×d3 (13...♗×c6? 14.d×c4 leaves Black two pawns down with nothing to show for it) 14.e×d3 ♕d4 (14...♕×d3?? 15.♕×c5) 15.♕f3 leave the game quite even.

11...♖ad8 12.♘e3?

Again, 12.♕×b7 was the least evil, though now it is more evil than at move 10, after 12...♕e5! (-2.18/26).

12...♗c8!

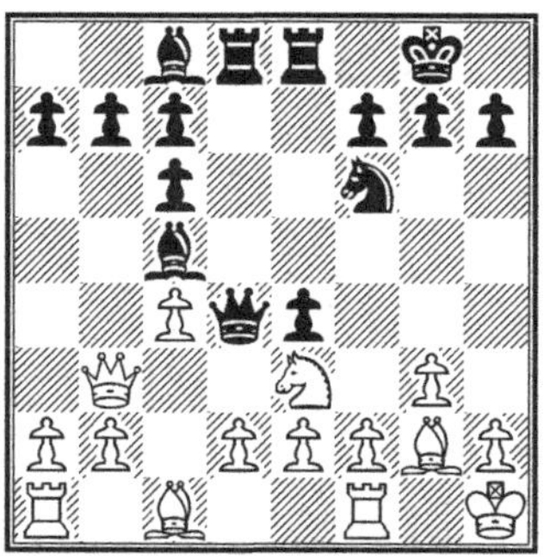

Best move on the board. The Bishop is not going to take part in the coming attack for some time, and so, considering that it must move anyway to avoid 13.♘×f5, it may as well defend the b-pawn.

13.♕c2

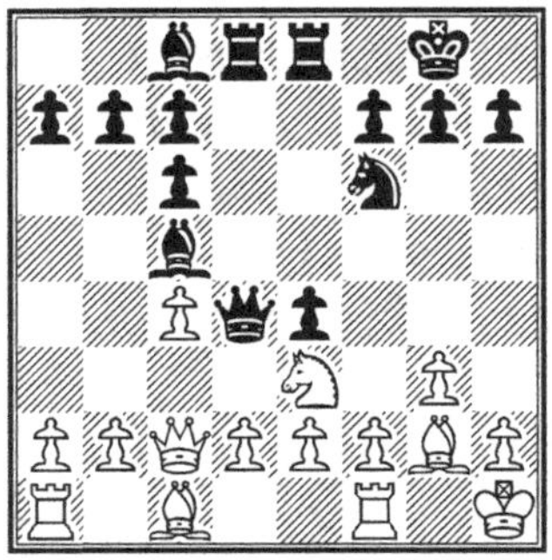

13...♕e5!

In his brief notes in *Development of Chess Ability*, Torre felt that here Black digressed somewhat, and should have played 13...h5 14.♖b1 h4 15.b4 ♗f8. But the text is actually best. 13...h5 is also quite good, but only if followed up differently, *i.e.* 13...h5 14.♖b1 ♕d6!,

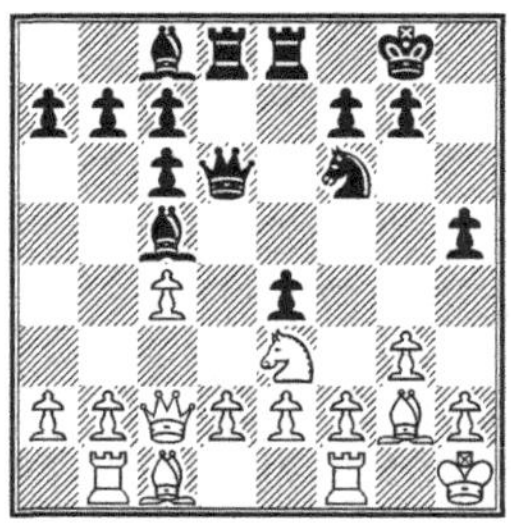

and White is virtually in *Zugzwang*, *viz.*

(a) 15.b4 ♗×b4;

(b) 15.d4 ♗×d4 (or 15...e×d3 16.e×d3 ♕×d3);

(c) 15.♖d1?? ♗×e3 16.f×e3 h4 (-8.53); or

(d) 15.h4 ♘g4! 16.♔g1 ♘×f2! 17.♔×f2 ♕f6+ 18.♔g1 ♕g6−+.

14.f3?

White already has nothing even close to a good move, but he might have tried

14.d3 e×d3 15.e×d3 ♘g4 16.♘×g4 ♗×g4 17.♗f4, though then 17...♕e2! is decisive (-4.17/23).

14...♕h5

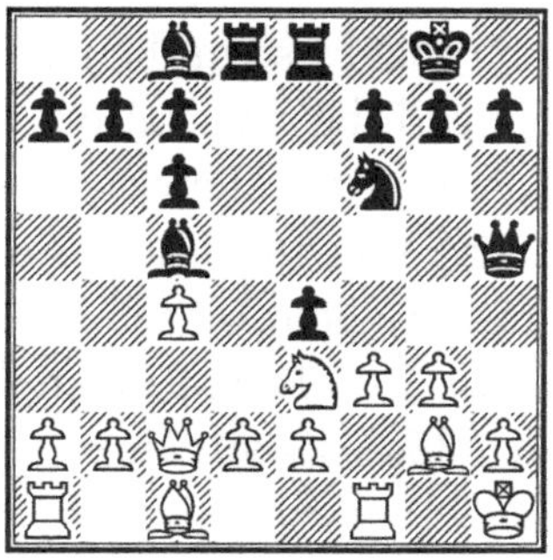

Even stronger was 14...e×f3 15.e×f3 h5 16.f4 ♕d4, but the text is a close second.

15.b4

Slightly less depressing was 15.b3, but after 15...♕g6 (threatening 16...♗×e3 17.d×e3 e×f3 18.♕×g6 f×g2+ 19.♔×g2 h×g6–+) 16.f×e4 ♘×e4 17.♗×e4 ♖×e4 18.♗b2 ♗h3 19.♖f3 h5 etc. Black's attack is unstoppable. In the first edition we wrote "From this point on, Black increases his advantage in a virtually flawless manner. Analysis by both human masters and computers has been unable to find any significant improvement for either side over the remaining moves." That still holds true today.

15...♗×b4 16.f×e4 ♕×e2 17.♗f3 ♕d3□ 18.♕×d3 ♖×d3 19.♗e2 ♖×d2!

Obtaining at least two pawns and a pair of very strong Bishops for the Exchange. 19...♖dd8 was playable, but not nearly as strong.

20.♗×d2 ♗×d2 21.♘f5 ♘×e4

Now Black has three pawns for the Exchange.

22.♗d3 g6

Forcing the retreat of White's only active piece.

23.♘h4 ♗h3 24.♘g2 ♘c5

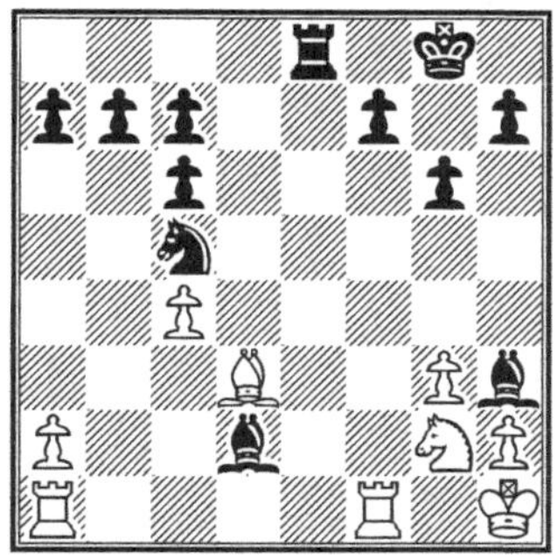

A magnificent square for the Knight; furthermore it clears the file for the Rook.

25.♖fd1

If 25.♖ad1 ♘×d3 26.♖×d2 ♘e1! winning back the Exchange.

25...♗c3 26.♖ac1 ♗g4 27.♖f1 ♗d2 28.♖c2 ♗a5

Now the white Bishop, despite being in the center of the board, has no escape square. Black wins back the Exchange, netting an overwhelming material advantage.

29.♘f4 ♘×d3 30.♘×d3 ♗e2 0–1

A game played in the style of Petrosian, but four years before he was born. One of the best by Carlos Torre in his short but brilliant career, and a great pleasure for this writer to play through and annotate.

Torre's fine performance in the above game was unfortunately followed by his only loss of the tournament, against Spielmann in round 13. That put the standings of the top half of the field as follows: 1. Nimzovich (9½-4½); =2-4. Rubinstein, Marshall, Réti (all 9-4); 5. Tartakower (8½-4½); 6. Torre 8-5 (+4 -1 =8); 7. Spielmann (7½-5½); 8. Grünfeld (7-6). With just two rounds to go, first place was almost certainly out of Torre's reach, but clearly he could rise in the standings. Equally clearly he could fall out of contention for prize money altogether; sixth place was the last cash prize, 1000 crowns (about US $30 in 1925, or $475 in 2022). So Torre had ample motivation in his last two games.

Game 61

Haida-Torre

Marienbad 1925, round 14

Slav Defense [D13]

One would think that if Torre could expect an easy game at Marienbad, it would be from the Czech player August Konrad Haida (1887-1940), the sort of minor master from the host country that tournament organizers bring in to round out the field. Never placing high in international events, Haida's best achievement (as near as we can determine from the skimpy record of his games) was finishing =5th-7th (of 12) in the 1921 Czech Championship. In the 1934 championship, he scored +0 -10 =1 to finish dead last. And last he was too at Marienbad, coming into this round with a score of +2 -12 =1, beating only the also-rans Thomas and Przepiórka. However, it bears mentioning that his draw was an arduous, hard-fought 59-mover against co-winner Nimzovich in the first round, where he held his own in an exhausting Knight ending lasting 26 moves. And in round 13 he had handled Przepiórka with great dispatch, driving the black King from g8 to e4 before delivering mate. If Torre had been paying attention, he might have known not to take this rabbit too lightly.

1.c4 ♘f6 2.♘c3 c6 3.♘f3 d5 4.c×d5 c×d5 5.d4 ♘c6

Reaching by transposition a standard position of the Slav Defense, the Exchange Variation, which had been known and frequently played since Jaffe-Capablanca, New York 1911. Historically this has proven a very drawish line, ChessBase showing 21.7% wins for White, 21.2% wins for Black, and 57.1% drawn in nearly 14,000 games reaching this position. This game does nothing to change that reputation. The next 27 moves are not very interesting, so our comments are minimal.

6.♗f4 e6 7.e3 ♗e7 8.♖c1 0–0 9.♗d3 ♘h5 10.0–0 f5 11.♗e5 ♗d7 12.♕e2 ♖c8 13.a3 ♘f6 14.h3 ♘e4 15.♗h2 ♘a5 16.♗×e4 f×e4 17.♘e5 ♘c4 18.♘×c4 ♖×c4 19.♗e5 ♕c8 20.♕g4

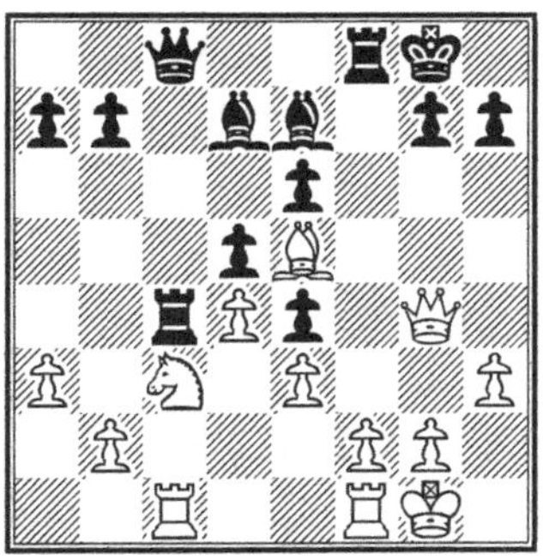

This attacking gesture is easily rebuffed.

20...♗f6 21.f4 ♗b5 22.♖f2 ♖c6 23.♖cc2 ♔h8 24.♔h2 ♗d3 25.♗×f6 ♖×f6 26.♖c1 ♖f7 27.♖g1 b5 28.♕h5 ♔g8 29.♕g4 a5 30.g3 ♖fc7

The tripling of the heavy pieces on the c-file and the advance of the queenside pawns look impressive, but should have no real effect against correct defense. The game could not be more even (0.00/27).

31.♕h5 b4 32.a×b4 a×b4

Play now enters a very interesting phase.

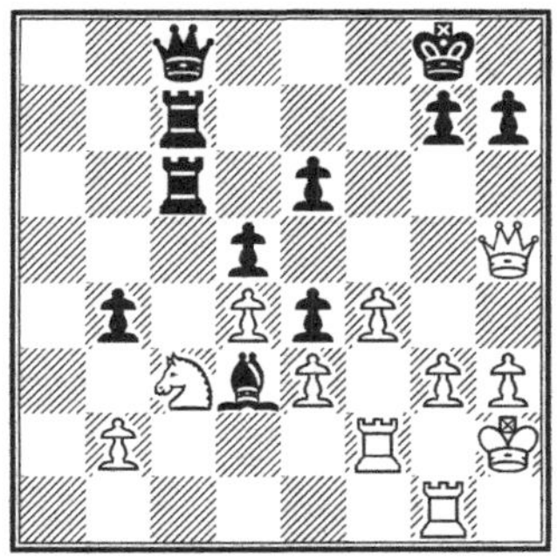

33.♘a4!□

Not (a) 33.♘d1? ♖c2 (△34...♖×f2+ 35.♘×f2 ♖c2 36.♖g2 ♖×b2–+) 34.♖gg2 ♖×f2 35.♘×f2 (if 35.♖×f2 ♖c1 36.♖d2 ♗b5 -5.57/26) 35...♖c2–+. Nor

(b) 33.♘b1? ♖c2 34.♘d2 (34.♖gg2?? ♖×f2 35.♖×f2 ♗×b1–+) 34...♖×b2–+. And not

(c) 33.♘a2? ♖c2 34.♖fg2 ♗e2! 35.g4 (35.♖×e2?? ♖×e2+ 36.♕×e2 ♖c2–+) 35...♗f3 36.♖×c2 ♖×c2+ 37.♔g3 ♖×b2–+.

33...♖c2 34.♖fg2 ♗e2 35.g4!□

Haida again finds the only correct move. If 35.♖×e2?? ♖×e2+ 36.♕×e2 ♖c2–+.

35...♗f3?

This could have lost the game for Torre. Necessary was 35...b3 or 35...♖f7, with equality in either case.

36.♖×c2 ♖×c2+ 37.♔g3

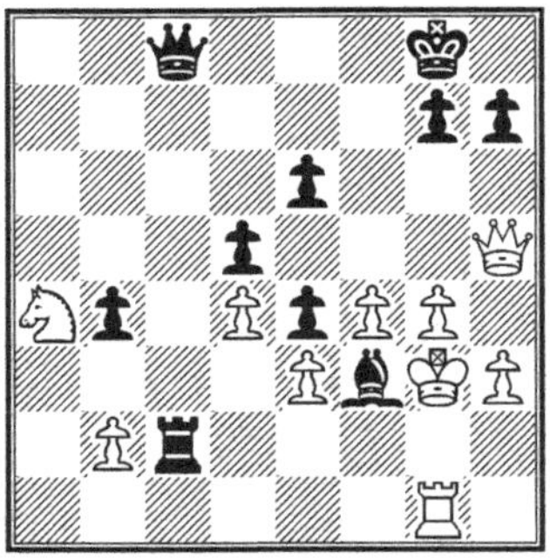

37...♖e2?

This and the last few moves look strong, invading White's third and second ranks and going after his e-pawn, but in fact this move compounds the problem move 35 created. Torre's sense of danger must have deserted him, and he fails to realize that his own e-pawn is actually under the greater threat. However, even after the relatively best move, 37...h6, White still wins with 38.♘c5! ♖×c5 (forced, either now or after 38...♔h7 39.♕e5) 39.d×c5 ♕×c5 40.♖e1 ♕c2 41.♕e8+ ♔h7 42.♕×e6 ♕×b2 43.♕f5+ ♔h8 44.♔h4! d4

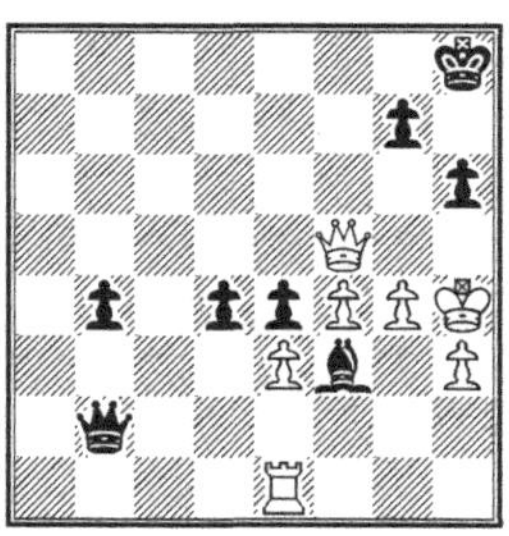

45.♔h5 (threatening 46.♔g6 and mate in six; somewhat simpler and also winning is 45.e×d4 e3 46.♕e5 e2 47.♕e3) 45...♕c3 46.e×d4 b3 47.♖e3! ♕×d4 (47...♕×e3?? 48.♔g6 and mate by ♕f5-c8 cannot be prevented.) 48.♖×b3 +−.

Returning to the game:

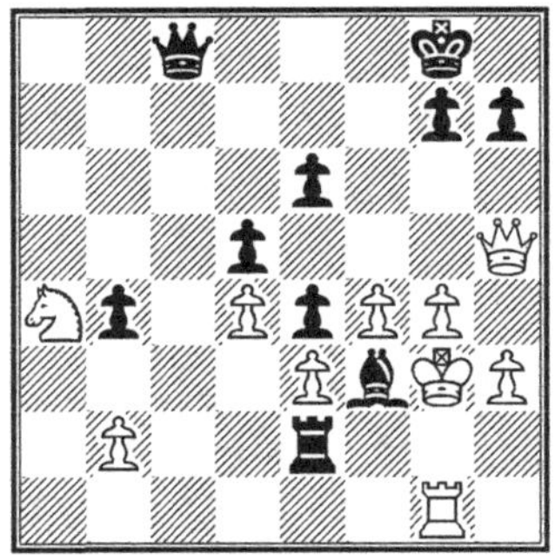

38.b3?

Haida does not recognize his golden opportunity! 38.♘c5! wins, *viz.*:

(a) 38...♖×b2 39.♕e5 ♖a2 40.♘×e6 ♖a7 41.♖b1 ♕b7 42.♘g5 ♖a8 43.♖×b4! and mate in nine;

(b) 38...♖×e3 39.♕e5 ♗d1+ (if 39...♔f7?? 40.♖a1 △41.♖a7++−) 40.♔h2 ♖e2+ 41.♖g2 ♖×g2+ 42.♔×g2 ♔f7 43.♔g3 ♗c2 44.f5 e×f5 45.♕×d5+ ♔f8 46.g×f5 e3 47.♘e6+ ♔e7 48.♕e5 and Black can resign (+6.47/21).

Equally good is 38.♕e5, transposing to this same line after 38...♖×e3 39.♘c5.

White could even win with 38.♖c1! ♕f8 (38...♕×c1?? 39.♕e8#) 39.♕e5 ♖g2+ 40.♔h4 ♕e7+ 41.♕g5 and Black is forced to allow the exchange of Queens by 41...♔f7 42.♕×e7+ ♔×e7 43.♖c7+ ♔d6 (if 43...♔f6?? 44.g5+ ♔g6 45.♘c5+−, or 43...♔f8 44.♘c5 ♖×b2 45.♘×e6+ etc.) 44.♖×g7 etc.

After the text White's winning chances have evaporated, though he can still draw.

38...♖×e3
This or 38...h6 equalizes.

39.♖c1?!
Now Haida begins to let things slide the other way. Best was 39.♘c5=, but he never hits on that idea.

39...♕b8
Of course not 39...♕×c1 40.♕e8#. 39...♕f8 was interesting, forcing 40.♕e5, but after 40...h5!? 41.♕×h5□ ♗h1+ 42.♔h2 ♕×f4+ 43.♔×h1 ♖×h3+ 44.♕×h3 ♕×c1+ 45.♔g2 ♕d2+ 46.♔g3 ♕×d4 47.♕h5 the game is still even.

40.♖c7 ♕f8!□ 41.♕e5□ h5
This or 41...♕f6 are the only non-losing moves.

42.♔f2 ♖e2+ 43.♔f1 e3 44.♕×e6+ ♔h7

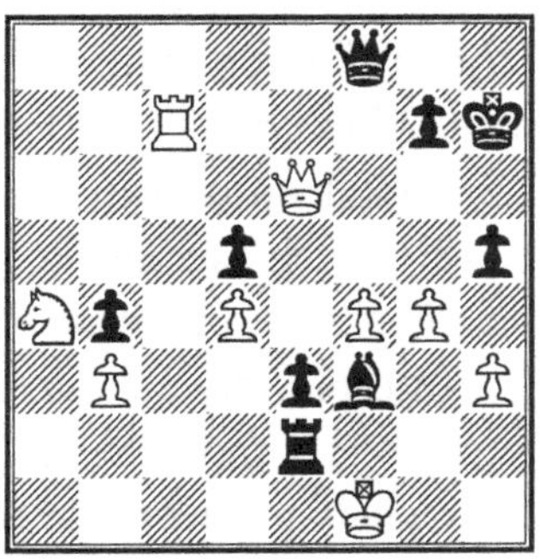

45.g×h5??
Just as he reaches the second time control, Haida blunders. The game would still be a draw after 45.♖f7 or 45.f5.

45...♖f2+
Torre jumps on his chance like a starved wolf on a T-bone steak.

46.♔e1 ♖g2 47.♕×e3 ♕f5!

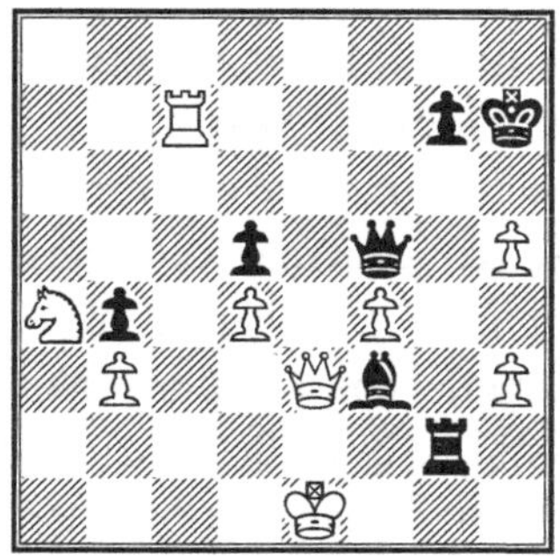

47...♖e2+ 48.♕×e2 ♗×e2 49.♔×e2 ♕×f4 would also win eventually, but Torre smells blood.

48.♔f1 ♕×h3 49.♕d3+ ♔h6 0-1
After a few spite checks, mate is inevitable. Baseball pitcher Lefty Gomez famously said "I'd rather be lucky than good." Here Torre certainly was.

Game 62

Torre-Przepiórka

Marienbad 1925, round 15

London System [A47]

Warsaw-born Dawid Przepiórka (1880-1940, historical Elo 2470, last name pronounced pshe-PURE-ka) came from a wealthy but non-chessplaying family. At age seven he taught himself to play, and by age nine he was declared a prodigy, already beating masters. As an adult his financial situation allowed him to concentrate on chess, and starting in 1905 he began professional tournament competition. None too successful at first, by the time of this game he had placed 2nd (of 15) in the 1924 Hungarian Master Congress, and tied for 1st (with E. Steiner) at Hastings 1924-25, ahead of Tartakower, Colle and others. In 1926 he would win the first Polish Championship. In 1930 he was a member of their gold medal-winning Olympiad team, and by 1935 he was deputy chairman of the Polish Chess Federation, taking major responsibility, as chairman of the Organizing Committee, for the 6th Chess Olympiad at Warsaw 1935. Sadly, as an ardent Polish patriot and a Jew, he was put in a concentration camp after the Nazis overran his country in 1939, and died soon thereafter.

1.d4 ♘f6 2.♘f3 b6 3.♗f4

Torre counters Black's Queen's Indian with the London System. This had first been tried twice by Jaffe against Janowski in a 1917 match, though White lost both games. Interestingly, it was also being played at the very same time as this game, by Marshall against Réti in this last round at Marienbad.

3...♗b7 4.♘bd2 e6 5.e3 ♗e7 6.♗d3 ♘h5 7.♗g3 d6 8.♕e2 ♘d7 9.c3

Torre and Marshall finally diverge; the latter played 9.0–0–0 and did not push his c-pawn until move 17. With the text, we again reach a position not seen before, and one that would not recur until Romih-Capablanca, Paris 1938.

9...0–0 10.0–0–0 c5 11.♘c4 ♘×g3

A very double-edged move. While it gives Black the Bishop pair, it also opens the h-file for White's Rooks, and since White has castled queenside their mobilization can be all the quicker. Stockfish seems to think Black's defensive resources or his potential counterplay are adequate, as it considers the text move best, conferring about a half-pawn's advantage on Black. But Przepiórka is no 21st-century computer engine.

12.h×g3

12.f×g3? b5 13.♘cd2 c4 14.♗c2 d5 and soon it will be Black attacking White's King, by ...b5-b4 etc., while White has no counterplay on the h-file.

12...h6 13.g4 b5 14.♘a3

14.♘cd2 was somewhat better.

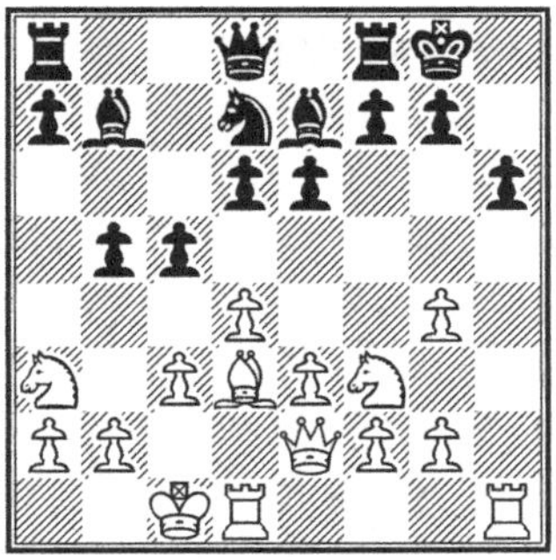

14...a6

An indication that Black is thinking defensively, when the position is clearly one where whoever "gets there firstest with the mostest" will win. He might have considered sacrificing a pawn by 14...♖b8 15.♗×b5 ♗×f3 16.g×f3 d5 (-0.93/23), or 14...♕a5 15.♗×b5 c×d4 (-0.83/24), in either case with open queenside lines as compensation.

15.♗c2

15...c4?!

By this advance, Black seals the Queen's wing, thereby depriving himself of counterplay.

Correct was 15...b4, when a likely continuation is 16.♘b1 a5 17.♕d3 (threatening 18.♕h7#) 17...f5 18.g×f5 e×f5 19.d5 b×c3 20.♘×c3 ♗a6 21.♕d2 ♘b6 when Black has good queeenside attacking prospects, while White's on the kingside are as yet undeveloped (-1.15/24).

16.♖h3 ♗f6

Perhaps preferable was 16...♖b8 17.♖dh1 ♖e8 (-0.49/26), which positions Black for defense on the kingside by ...♘d7-f8, or action in the center by ...e6-e5, or possibly action on the queenside with ...b5-b4.

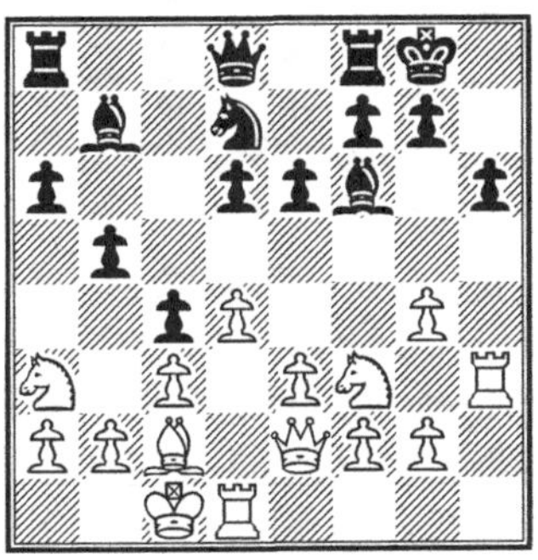

17.♖dh1

No doubt played automatically. In view of the fact that Black obviously intends 17...e5, an interesting alternative was

17.♘d2 e5 18.f4 e×f4 19.e×f4 ♖e8 20.♕f2 ♘f8□ 21.♖dh1 and the threat of 22.g5+− forces 21...♘e6 22.g5,

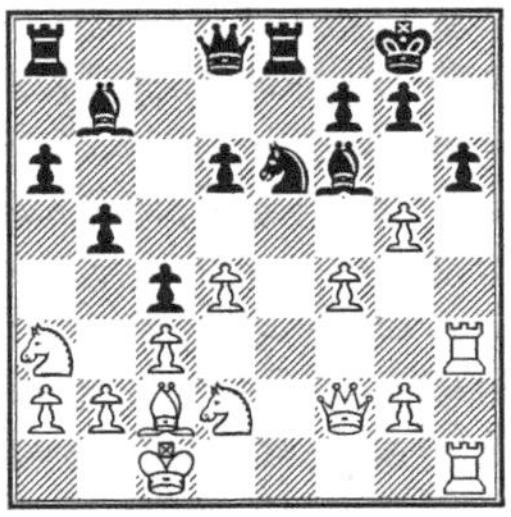

and Black must give up a piece by either 22...♘×f4 23.♕×f4 ♗×g5 24.♕f2, or 22...♗×g2 (gaining an extra pawn compared to 22...♘×f4) 23.♕×g2 ♘×f4 24.♕g4 ♗×g5 25.♖3h2 with an unclear, unbalanced position where White's winning chances depend on getting the ♘a3 back into the game.

17...e5 18.♗f5?!

This could have backfired slightly. Best was 18.g5 ♗×g5 19.♘×g5 ♕×g5 20.♖g3 ♕f6 21.♕g4 ♖fd8=.

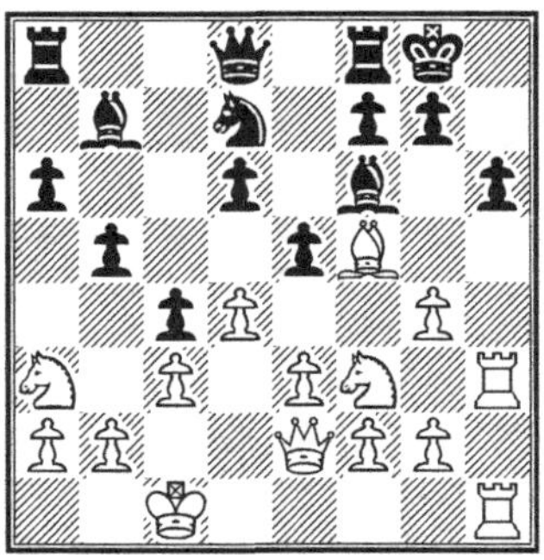

18...♖e8

18...g6! was the correct counter to White's less-than-best move, *e.g.*

(a) 19.♗×d7 ♕×d7 20.♖×h6 ♕×g4 (-0.62/27), or

(b) 19.g5 ♗g7 [not 19...♗×g5?? 20.♘×g5 ♗×g2 21.♘e6! ♕f6 22.♘×f8 ♕×f5 23.♘×d7 ♗×h3 24.f4 ♕×d7 25.♕f3 ♖e8 (not 25...♗f5?? 26.♕×a8+) 26.♖×h3] 20.g×h6 ♗f6 21.♗c2 ♖e8 (-0.65/25), or

(c) 19.♖×h6 (probably best) 19...♗g7 20.♖6h4 g×f5 21.g×f5 ♖e8 (0.00/26).

The text allows White's g-pawn to advance with tempo.

19.g5 ♗×f3?!

This serves only to activate White's Queen.

20.♕×f3 ♗×g5

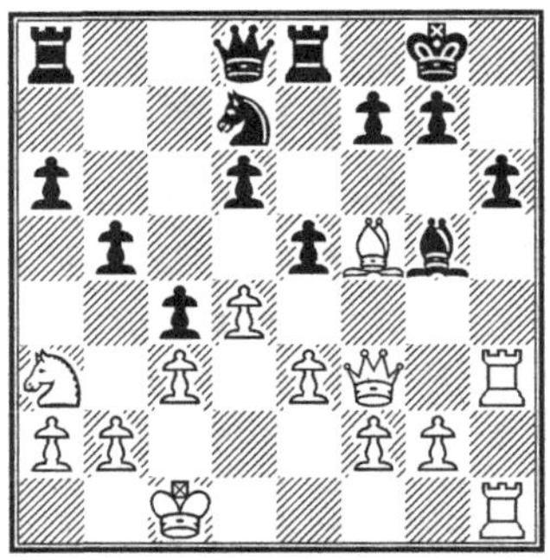

21.♕g4

A slight finesse here would have done more for White: 21.♕g3! e4 (virtually forced in view of the threatened 22.f4) 22.♕g4 with 23.♗×e4 to follow after 22...♘f8/♘b6/♖e8, and White has won an important pawn (+1.33/25). But Black's next move renders all that irrelevant.

21...♖a7??

As we said, Przepiórka was no analytical engine. Absolutely essential was

21...♘f8. The best White can do then is 22.f4 e×f4 23.e×f4 g6□ 24.♗c2 [if 24.f×g5 g×f5 25.♕f3 ♕×g5+ 26.♔d1 ♖e4 (26...♖e6?? 27.♕×a8) 27.♖×h6 ♕g4 28.♖×d6 ♖e3 29.♕×g4+ f×g4=] 24...♗f6 25.♖×h6 ♗g7□ 26.♖6h3 d5 27.f5 ♕d6 with a virtually even game (+0.19/30). But now Black's position collapses like the stock market in 1929.

22.f4! ♗f6

22...e×f4 makes little difference, *viz.* 23.e×f4 g6 24.f×g5 g×f5 25.♕g3 (+5.17/26).

23.♖×h6 ♔f8 24.♖h7

White's attack now plays itself, and further comment is superfluous.

24...♔e7 25.d×e5 d×e5 26.♖d1 ♕c8 27.f×e5 ♗×e5 28.♕e4 ♔d8 29.♘c2 ♕c7 30.♖×d7+ ♕×d7 31.♗×d7 ♖×d7 32.♘b4 1-0

With wins in the last two rounds, Torre's score rose to 10-5 (+6 -1 =8), passing Réti and Tartakower in the standings to finish tied with Marshall for 3rd-4th, a point behind Nimzovich and Rubinstein. This was much better than his result at Baden-Baden. Still, there was considerable room for improvement. Of his four draws with players in the lower half of the table, two — against Janowski and Michell — were humdrum affairs devoid of inspiration (and thus not included here), and in the other two, with Thomas and Sämisch, he played so recklessly that he could have lost. Of his four draws with upper-half finishers, the two with Nimzovich and Tartakower were solid efforts, while with Marshall and Rubinstein his play was uneven and inconsistent: in the former Torre was lost but got lucky late, while in the latter he went from equal to lost, then lost to winning, and finally winning to drawn.

A vexing inconsistency also marred three of his victories. Against Opocensky and Grünfeld, he let wins slip to draws, only salvaging full points with the help of late blunders. And against tail-ender Haida he was downright lost, but again his opponent's mistakes let him pull even and then win. His win over Przepiórka was somewhat messy, Torre standing somewhat worse for a while but gradually outplaying him, when the Pole's mistake allowed him a decisive attack. It was only in two games, against Yates and Réti, that Torre played strong, consistent, precise winning chess. Had all the breaks gone against him, had all the games he let slip to theoretical draws or losses stayed drawn or lost, Torre's score would have been only +3 -5 =7.

But that is to measure Torre against the absolute, unyielding standard of the Lidless Eye. That is not how a chess master is fairly gauged — the fair measure is how he does against his fellow competitors, in the rough-and-tumble struggle on the board with clocks ticking. The June 15, 1925 *New York Times* (presumably Hermann Helms) spoke along such lines:

So far as chess followers in this country are concerned, the player to emerge beyond question as the outstanding figure in the international chess masters' tournament, concluded June 8th at Marienbad, is Carlos Torre. The feat of the 20-year-old Mexican in tieing Frank Marshall, the United States champion, for third place, finishing only a point behind the two who deadlocked for first honors, and leading such renowned experts as Tartakower, Réti, Spielmann, and Gruenfeld, has provided chess devotees with one of those rare occasions where they may ask with sincerity and without appearing to be overenthusiastic: "Is this youth destined to become the foremost master of his day?"

Prodigies in chess are not infrequent. But like the little innovations which spring up from time to time in the game itself, they come and go, seldom contributing anything beyond passing entertainment and diversion. Their domain lies in simultaneous and even blindfold exhibitions, where, against mediocre players, they often perform with unusual brilliance. But, as the great Morphy once said, these things mean little. It is in the sound field of master play that the real test comes. And it is here that young Torre, without further ado, allowed himself to be measured and certainly has not been found wanting.

A year or so ago, Torre came to this city virtually unknown in the chess world. Forced to confine his activities for the time to tourneys in this country of only minor importance, he, nevertheless, quickly made his mark, and then, with no further experience in international play, he sailed forth to Baden-Baden. Here, for the first time in his brief career, he met the world's greatest players, thoroughly schooled from constant practice in the intricacies of international tournament competition. Finishing in the first division, he fulfilled all that had been expected of him. At Marienbad, finishing a single point behind the joint winners, Rubinstein and Niemzowitsch, he surprised the fondest hopes of his most ardent admirers.

Analysis of his games by experts also would indicate that a promising future lies in store for him. His style of play seems to combine a touch of originality and brilliance with soundness found only among the great experts and seldom among the average run of prodigies. It was that keen insight in the fundamentals, born in him, that enabled the young Capablanca to shoot like a meteor from the ranks a dozen years ago. The rise of young Torre may be even more spectacular. Who can tell?

And the *Wiener Schachzeitung* added:

> [Torre] fulfilled what he promised at Baden-Baden, and will hopefully fulfill what he promised at Marienbad, namely to be among the small number of top players in the world in a short time. Despite the fact that the masters tried very hard against him, only one, namely Spielmann, managed to defeat the boy, while other greats, including Rubinstein, were able to draw only with difficulty. And that says a lot.

From the interval between the Marienbad and Moscow tournaments, only two Torre games are known to us. He annotated the following game, played at the Manhattan CC soon after his return from Marienbad, in the September-October *ACB*. His consultation partner was C.E. Norwood, the opponents Leonard B. Meyer and Alfred Schroeder. All notes are his, except those in italics.

Game 63

Torre & Norwood - Meyer & Schroeder

Consultation, Manatan CC, New York, 1925

London System [D02]

1.d4 ♘f6 2.♘f3 d5 3.♗f4 e6 4.e3 ♗d6 5.♘bd2 ♗×f4 6.e×f4 c5 7.d×c5 ♕c7 8.♘e5 ♘bd7 9.♘df3 ♕×c5 10.c3 ♘e4 11.♕c2 f6 12.♘×d7 ♗×d7 13.♗d3 f5 14.0–0
White has a very good game, but the correct move is 14.♘e5.

14...0–0 15.♖ae1
15.♘e5 is still very good. Through their lack of exactness the White allies get into a bad, then into a lost position.

15...♖ae8 16.♘d4 g5(?)
The black pieces which should be quietly cooped in, are now liberated by this powerful rejoinder, and they certainly come to life with a vim.

The text is actually a mistake. Better, say, 16...♕c7, 16...♖f6, *or* 16...♕b6.

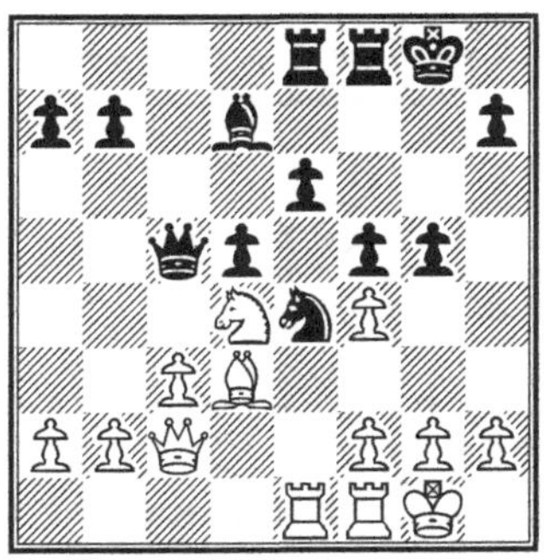

17.f3(?)
A pleasing analysis will show that Black always gets the best of it now.
Black would have had rather the worst of it after 17.f×g5! ♘×g5 18.♕d2!,

(see diagram next page)

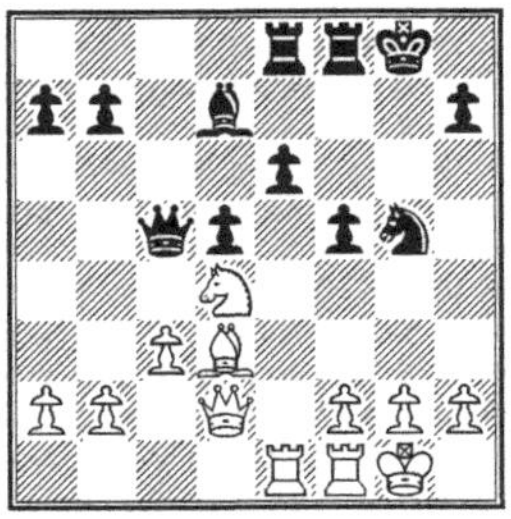

and either:

(a) 18...♘f7 19.♕e2 ♔h8 20.♕h5 ♕b6 21.♖e3 ♕d8 22.♖fe1± *with both pressure on the e-pawn and kingside attacking prospects;*

(b) 18...h6 19.♕f4 ♖f7 20.♖e2 ♕f8 21.♖fe1±, *or*

(c) 18...♘e4 19.♗×e4 d×e4 *[not* 19...f×e4?? 20.♕g5+ ♔h8 *(if* 20...♔f7 21.♖×e4+–*)* 21.♕e5+ ♔g8

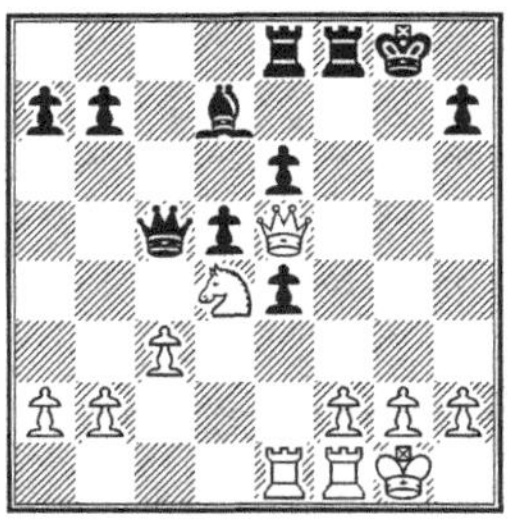

22.♖×e4! ♖f6 23.♖g4+ ♖g6 24.♖×g6+ h×g6 25.♕f6+–*]* 20.♘×f5! e×f5 21.♕×d7±, *winning a pawn.*

17...g×f4!

This brilliant move is the only one to maintain the advantage, but very sufficient for that purpose.

18.f×e4 f×e4 19.♗×e4 d×e4 20.b4

A wise attempt to avoid immediate loss, but the pawn position is very much weakened.

20...♕d6

The Black allies play with fine judgment. They perceive that 20...♕b6 is not so convincing after 21.♕×e4 ♗c6 22.♕e5 ♖f5 23.♕e2 ♖g5 24.♖f2.

21.♕×e4 e5 22.♘f3 ♗c6 23.♕c4+

To pass up this check and play 23.♕e2 at once would offer better resistance. That is all. For the rest Black plays a winning game very well. It is very instructive to note how the displacement of a Knight will lead to loss, even with a goood game.

23...♗d5 24.♕e2 e4 25.♘d4 e3 26.♕h5 ♖e5 27.♕g4+ ♕g6 28.♕×g6+ h×g6 29.♘f3 ♖e7 30.♘g5 ♗×a2

The ACB gives the impossible B-R5 *here, i.e.* ♗a4.

31.♘h3 ♖e4 32.♘g5 ♖e5 33.h4 ♗c4 34.♖f3 ♗d5 35.♖ff1 ♔g7 36.♘h3 f3! 37.g×f3 ♗c4 38.♘g5 ♗×f1 39.♔×f1 ♖f4 40.♔e2 ♖×h4 41.♘e4 ♖h×e4 0–1

Page 155 of the November *ACB* said "Owing to the departure for Europe of F.J. Marshall and Carlos Torre, their games in the Dimock tournament at the Marshall Chess Club were canceled." However, Torre must have played at least this one. *ACB* editor C.S. Howell probably could not resist the temptation to show off his upset win. The notes not in italics are his, and quite good.

Game 64

Howell-Torre

Dimock thematic, New York, 1925

Giuoco Piano [C54]

1.e4 e5 2.♘f3 ♘c6 3.♗c4 ♗c5 4.c3 ♘f6 5.d4 e×d4 6.c×d4 ♗b4+ 7.♘c3 ♘×e4 8.0–0 ♗×c3

The games played in this tournament would seem to indicate that 8...♘×c3 9.b×c3 d5 is Black's best line and gives him a theoretical advantage.

9.d5

The move which constitutes the Moeller Attack and first attracted wide attention when played by the winner of this game in one of the Anglo-American cable matches against R.P. Michell. The general opinion of analysts, confirmed by the games in this tournament, is to the effect that Black has no winning line of play against the Moeller.

9...♘e5

The Lasker defense. Probably not as good as 9...♗f6.

10.b×c3

Moeller himself recommends 10.♕e2 ♘×f3+ 11.g×f3 ♗f6 12.f×e4 followed by f2-f4, but I do not agree with him that White thus obtains the advantage, for, after 12...d6 13.f4 0–0 and White will have trouble in effectively developing his QB and QR.

Stockfish quite agrees, rating the resulting postion at about -2.25.

10...♘×c4 11.♕d4

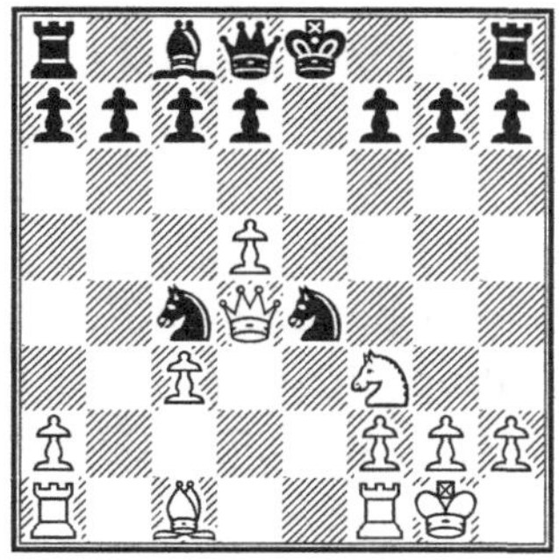

11...f5

If 11...♘cd6 12.♕×g7 ♕f6 13.♕×f6 ♘×f6 14.♖e1+ with advantage to White.

12.♕×c4 d6 13.♘d4 0–0 14.f3 ♘c5 15.♖e1

The move recommended in my original analysis and always heretofore played by me, 15.♗a3, is better, but I adopted the text as an experiment because it is favored by the "Larobok." *[One of the premier openings encyclopedias of the day.]* After 15.♗a3 b6 16.♗×c5 b×c5 17.♘c6 ♕f6 18.♖fe1 ♗d7 19.♖e7, and White should at least draw.

15...b6! 16.♘e6

Practically forced, for Black threatens 16...♗a6 and if 16.♘c6 ♕f6 or 16...♗a6, and White has no good way to proceed.

16...♗×e6

Not bad, but second best. Much better was 16...♕e8! 17.♗g5 ♗×e6 18.d×e6 ♕c6 *with advantage for Black (-1.27/26).*

17.d×e6 d5 18.♕d4 ♖e8 19.e7 ♕d6

Obviously not 19...♖×e7 20.♖×e7 ♕×e7 21.♕×d5+.

20.c4

Because of the inferior 15.♖e1, White is now hard put to it to find a good continuation. If 20.♗f4 ♕d7!, threatening ...♘e6. If 20.♗g5 ♘e6, and if 20.♗a3 c6.

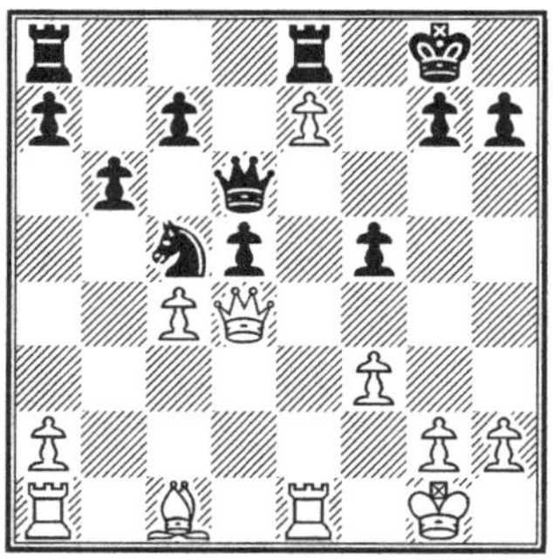

20...d×c4?

A bad slip. Torre did not play 20...c6, because of the continuation 21.♗b2 ♖×e7 22.c×d5 ♖d8 23.d×c6! ♖×e1+ 24.♖×e1 ♕×d4+ 25.♗×d4 ♖×d4 26.c7, overlooking that he might have played 23....♖ae8.

The game is now practically lost as White dominates the board and retains his strong passed pawn.

Also, in Howell's analysis variation, instead of 23...♖×e1+? *or* 23...♖ae8, *Black could play* 23...♕×d4+! 24.♗×d4 ♖c7∓.

21.♕×c4+ ♔h8 22.♗g5 ♘d3 23.♖ad1 ♘b2 24.♖×d6 ♘×c4 25.♖c6 b5 26.♖×c7 ♔g8 27.♖c5 a6 28.♖×f5

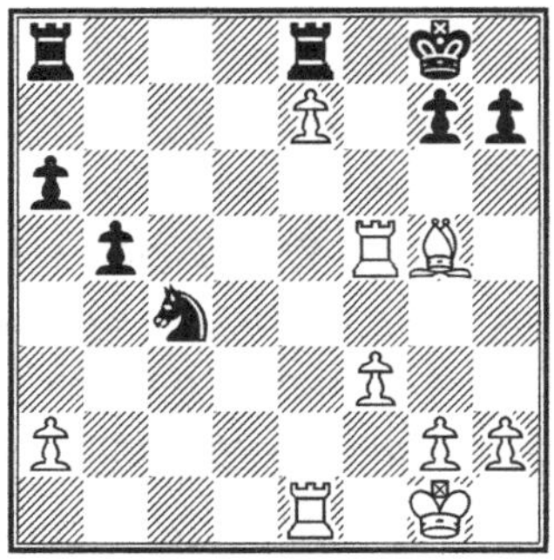

28...♖a7??

The least evil was 28...h6, *when after* 29.♗h4 ♖a7 *White cannot play* 30.♖d1? due to 30...g5 31.♗f2 ♖a×e7=. *But* 30.♖e6! *would keep him on the winning path, e.g. if* 30...g5?? 31.♖×h6! g×h4 32.♖f8+ ♖×f8 33.♖h8+ ♔×h8 34.e×f8♕+ *etc.*

29.♖d1 1–0

Black must lose the Exchange. If 29...♖aa8 30.♖d8, followed by 31.♖f8+. So 29...g6 30.♖f4 ♖a×e7 is all that Black has left and not promising enough to warrant continuance of the game.

Presumably such unimportant losses as these did not weigh on Torre, as he once again set off across the Atlantic to cross swords with the world's elite.

Games from the International Tournament at Moscow 1925

In the 1920s the Soviet Union, finally recovering from the ravages of World War I, the Bolshevik Revolution, and a civil war not ended until 1921, began promoting and sponsoring chess to such a degree and extent that the USSR would build the most dominant sports machine the world had ever seen. Under the leadership of Nikolai Krylenko, People's Commissar for Justice and one of the most powerful men in the government, the game was promoted in two major ways: (1) "Chess for the Masses," creating clubs and teams and teaching programs among schools, industrial and agricultural workers, civic and party organizations, the military etc., with 50- and even 100-board team matches and huge open tournaments; and (2) "Big Chess," major international tournaments in which the cream of Soviet players would compete against top players from around the world. The 1925 Moscow event was the first of those, the first state-sponsored chess tournament in history. The September-October *ACB* reported:

> In many respects the forthcoming international tournament scheduled to open at Moscow on November 5 bids fair to take as high a rank as the one held in New York early last year. No efforts apparently have been spared to obtain the best talent available, including José R. Capablanca and Dr. Emanuel Lasker, both of whom, contrary to general expectations, will once more be found together in the same competition.
>
> As we go to press, there is every likelihood that wo others will go from this side of the Atlantic — our own Frank J. Marshall and Carlos Torre, the talented young Mexican whose vaulting ambition led him to seek and obtain a place in the Russian congress. In addition, there will be on hand most of the outstanding European figures and ten Russians.

The November *ACB* added:

> Moscow, where in 1897 Steinitz battled with Dr. Lasker in a vain effort to recover his lost crown, is again the center of interest for chess players in all quarters of the globe. Steinitz has left us, but once more his conqueror is a

central figure in the drama being unfolded day by day as the cables send forth reports of what is happening at the new seat of government of the Union Soviet of Socialistic Republics *[sic]*.

The plan of the Soviet regime to bring to Moscow the pick of living experts has borne fruit, with the result that twenty-one masters started in the scheduled international tournament at the Hotel Metropole[1] on November 10 and are now engaged in playing through the twenty-one rounds at the rate of five a week, with Saturdays reserved for rest and Tuesdays for adjourned games ...

[Its roster of players] marks the Moscow congress as one of the greatest of such gatherings on record and about on a par with the one in New York in 1924 ... From dispatches to hand, it is understood that the undertaking cost approximately $25,000, but that the Soviet Government is behind it and that the financial burden, therefore, does not rest as heavily as usual upon the chess playing community.

The contestants held a preliminary meeting on November 9 at the Club of Nobles ... Here, it is reported, a reconciliation was effected between Capablanca and Dr. Lasker[2] ... At the meeting Capablanca is said to have protested vigorously against the short sessions of four hours each, and to have stood out for an extension to six hours. At any rate, he dislikes to play in a tournament where at least forty moves have not been made before the first adjournment. The committee decided that it was too late to make any change in the rules.

Of the topmost players at the time, only Nimzovich, Vidmar and Alekhine were missing, the latter because he was considered by the authorities "alien and hostile to Soviet power" (Soltis, p. 35). He continues:

Krylenko made the welcoming speech, November 9, at the overflowing Blue Hall of the House of Unions, just steps away from Red Square. Spectators stood on chairs to catch a glimpse of Capablanca, Emanuel Lasker and other stars. Clocks were started at 3:30 P.M. the next day ...

The Marienbad tournament having ended June 8, 1925, Carlos Torre had a more than 5-month respite from serious master competition until Moscow. Such lengthy periods between major competitions, rare today, were not unusual at that time; for example Capablanca's last serious game before Moscow was over a year

1 In Soviet Chess 1917-1991, p. 35, GM Andrew Soltis writes that play took place "in the Fountain Room of the House of Soviets, in what later became the restaurant of the Metropol Hotel."

2 Relations between the two had soured in the aftermath of their 1921 title match.

earlier than Torre's: March 17, 1924 against Bogoljubow at New York. (In fact Capablanca announced his retirement from chess after the New York tournament, his declaration to this effect being published in the *ACB* of September-October 1924. It was obviously reconsidered.) The long hiatus (during which Capa put on considerable weight) may explain the poor way in which the Cuban started the tournament, though in the second half he recovered the impeccable and dominating form which had made him world champion.

The tournament created a sensation among the Moscow public. Tickets to spectate in the playing hall sold out quickly each day, and crowds gathered outside, to such an extent that they blocked vehicle traffic. A movie crew filmed the players in action, these clips being combined with studio takes of actors to make the short feature *Chess Fever*, in which Capablanca had a starring role.

The unworldly Torre (at age 20 he was by far the youngest player) came unprepared for Russian weather. Velasco reports that he arrived wearing a t-shirt, and had nothing heavier than a suit coat; this when winter was approaching and temperatures were already below freezing. It is said that Torre thought about giving a simul to earn enough money to buy a decent coat, but asked Lasker if that might hurt his chances in the tournament. Lasker said it would, so Torre went without a proper winter coat. Finally Krylenko arranged for Torre to be taken to a shop where he was given a good one, of leather.[1]

Weather notwithstanding, and in contrast to Capablanca, Torre seemed unaffected or even energized by the long rest after Marienbad, as he began at Moscow (after a first-round bye) with victories against Dus-Chotimirsky, Marshall, and Levenfish, draws with Tartakower and Spielmann, then two more wins, over Zubarev and Sämisch. After seven rounds Torre found himself leading the tournament. Commented Capablanca, "It would not surprise me if this youngster soon begins beating everyone." Torre became something of a "media darling," with a whimsical caricature (above) by a Moscow artist published in the tournament reports.

1 This tale is related by Russian GM and historian Yuri Averbakh in the movie Torre x Torre (see Chapter IX). Unlike some others interviewed in that film, Averbakh may be considered a reliable source.]

Game 65

Torre–Dus-Chotimirsky

Moscow 1925, round 2

Polish Defense [A46]

Fedor Ivanovich Dus-Chotimirsky (1879-1965, IM title 1950, historical Elo 2440) rarely played abroad, but had been very active within Russia since 1900. GM Alexander Kotov called him "a chess fantasist, capable of losing to a beginner, but tomorrow crushing a world champion," a relevant example being the St. Petersburg 1909 tournament, in which he finished 13th but beat both co-winners Rubinstein and Lasker, reportedly infuriating the latter by pretending to be absorbed in a Japanese translation of Nietzsche's *Thus Spake Zarathustra* during the game. He generally tended to a sharp, risky style, though in this game his aims were more positional. It was Torre who took the risks that made this a rousing, entertaining game.

1.d4 ♘f6 2.♘f3 b5

With this move Black tries to steer into channels of the Polish Defense, so called after its debut by the Polish player Alexander Wagner in the 10th Swiss Correspondence Championship, and Wagner's 1914 analysis of it in the *Deutsches Wochenschach*. Though never a very popular line, many grandmasters have experimented with it: ChessBase shows it being tried around this time by Sämisch, Alekhine, Euwe, Tartakower and Bogoljubow. It was played many times by the German master Kurt Richter in the 1930s, and pops up later in games by Spassky and Miles. Its ideas are to impede the advance of White's c-pawn, to limit the developmental options of White's Queen's Knight, and to control the a8-h1 diagonal with the Bishop. However, it has the drawback of weakening Black's queenside.

3.♗f4

White proceeds with the London deployment, developing his pieces before concerning himself with the black b-pawn. Levenfish, in his game with Dus-Chotimirsky in this same tournament, played the Colle-style 3.e3 a6 4.♗d3 ♗b7 5.♘bd2 e6 6.a4 b4 7.0–0 c5 8.e4 c×d4 9.♘×d4 ♘c6 10.♘×c6 ♗×c6 11.e5 and won in 31 moves.

3...♗b7 4.♘bd2

After 4.e3 a6 5.h3 e6 6.♘bd2 Alekhine tried an interesting method to neutralize White's ♗f4: 6...♗d6!? 7.♗×d6 c×d6, Goldstein-Alekhine, Scarborough 1926 (0-1, 38).

4...e6 5.e3 a6

Yet again ChessBase indicates we reach a position not seen before in master competition.

6.♗d3 c5 7.c3 ♘c6

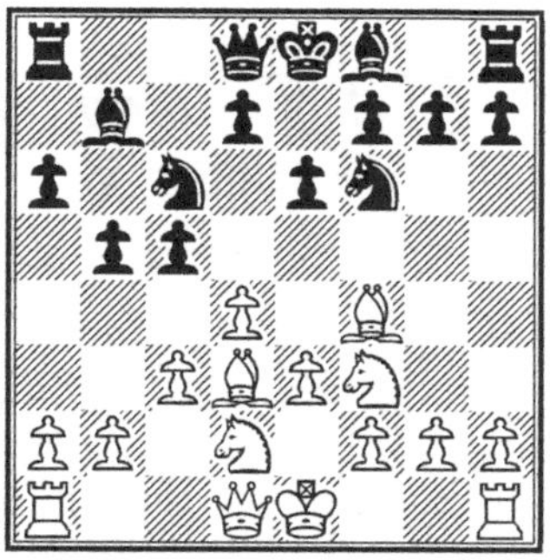

8.♕e2

As Dr. Tarrasch once noted, a characteristic of the new openings of the 1920s was the avoidance of contact and conflict in the early stages.

A somewhat more direct approach, in which White went badly astray, was seen in Gonzales-Kudrin, Las Palmas 1989: 8.h3 ♗e7 9.0–0 0–0 10.♖e1 ♕b6 11.♘e5 d6 12.♘g4?! ♘d7 13.♕c2?? f5! 14.d5 c4! 15.♗e2 e×d5 16.♘h2 g5, 0-1.

8...♗e7 9.h3 0–0 10.0–0 ♕b6

11.♗g5

This second move of the Bishop at this early stage is not very useful; better another developing move such as 11.♖fd1 or 11.♖fe1. Stockfish's top choice is 11.d×c5 ♕×c5 (better than 11...♗×c5 12.b4 ♗e7 13.e4) 12.e4 b4 13.♖ac1 b×c3 14.♖×c3 ♕a7 15.♖fc1 ±. After the text the game is even.

11...c×d4 12.e×d4 ♘d5 13.♗e4

White's 11th move has made impossible the Queen's Bishop's natural retreat to g3 or h2. 13.♗e3 would block the e-file, so Torre just lets it be exchanged, along with a pair of Knights.

13...♗×g5 14.♘×g5 ♘f6 15.♗d3 ♘e7 16.♘de4 ♘ed5 17.♖fe1 h6 18.♘×f6+ ♘×f6 19.♘e4

Further exchanges are not particularly in White's interest; somewhat better was 19.♘f3.

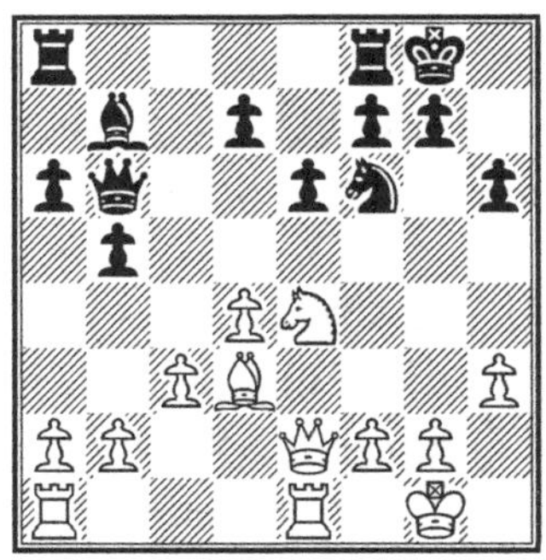

19...♘d5

Surprisingly, Black is now reluctant to exchange more pieces. He would have been no worse than equal after 19...♘×e4 20.♗×e4 ♗×e4 21.♕×e4. Instead he seems not to realize that he is removing defenders from his kingside just when White decides to aim his forces that way.

20.♕d2 d6

This is not expedient, since Black has little hope of enforcing ...e6-e5, and there is no prospect of a white piece being posted on e5. Black's best plan, which he hits on soon enough, is to organize a minority attack, first preventing c3-c4, then advancing ...a6-a5 and ...b5-b4 in conjunction with pressure on the c-file.

21.♘g3

By the same token, White does best to nip the minority attack idea in the bud with 21.b3 △ 22.c4.

21...♘f6 22.♖e2

22.b3 was still best. If White wants to double Rooks, 22.♖e3 was more efficient, both to expedite the Rook's eventual transfer to f3 or g3, and to add a defender to the c-pawn in some variations.

22...♖ac8 23.♖ae1

White clearly intends go all in on a kingside attack and not worry about his queenside. Anyway, if now 23.b3? ♕c6! (threatening mate) and 24...♕×c3.

23...♗d5 24.♗b1 ♖fd8

Now was the time to start the minority attack rolling with 24...a5. If Black wants to develop the King's Rook, better was first 24...♖c7 intending to bring it to c8 or b8. Since on d8 the Rook does not contribute to the intended strategy, the text is effectively a lost tempo. However, that is not crucial yet.

25.♖e3 a5!

Now Black has the right idea.

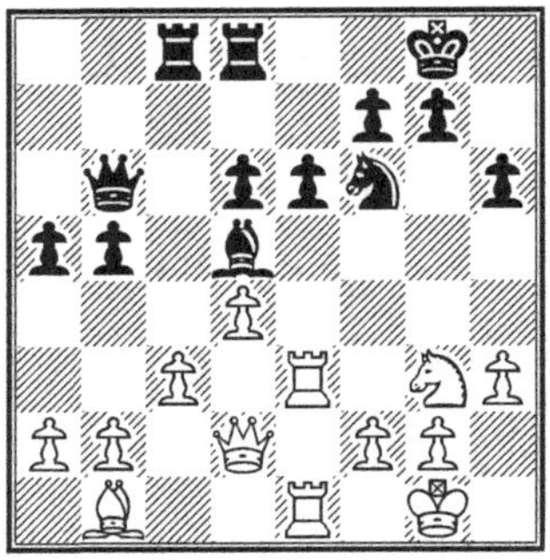

26.♘e2?!

A risky, objectively dubious move, something of a gamble, but if the gamble pays off then Torre will have his kingside attack.

The prudent but decidedly undynamic alternative was 26.♘e4, which after 26...♗×e4 27.♗×e4 b4 28.♗c2 b×c3 29.b×c3 d5 leads to an archetypal minority attack position that White can certainly hold (0.00/28), but with no chance of counterplay. Torre would rather fight than defend.

26...b4 27.♖g3!?

Continuing in the risky vein. More cautious was 27.b3 b×c3 28.♖×c3 ♖×c3 29.♘×c3, which creates the other face of the minority attack, where White has an isolated d-pawn instead of a backward c-pawn. Again probably something White could hold (-0.62/29), but dull and without counter-chances.

And though it is perhaps not immediately apparent, 27.♖g3!? abruptly has Black's position balancing on a knife edge.

27...♔f8!

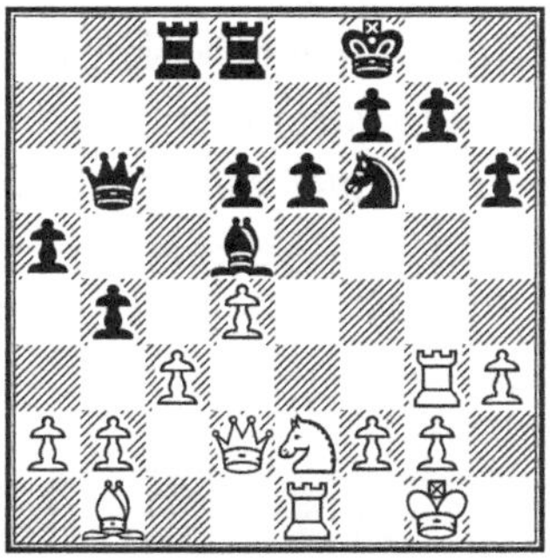

Definitely best; suddenly Black had only two moves that do not lose.

The other was 27...♔h8 28.♘f4 b×c3 29.♖×c3, when 29.b×c3 ♗c4 30.♕c2 would maintain the double-edged tension, while 29...♖×c3 30.♘×d5 ♘×d5 31.b×c3 ♖c8 32.c4 would be drawish.

Some of the losing alternatives are highly interesting and merit detailed examination:

(a) 27...♗e4 28.♕×h6 (not 28.♗×e4?? ♘×e4 29.♕×h6 ♘×g3−+) 28...♗g6 29.♕h4 ♗×b1 30.♕×f6 ♗g6 31.♖×g6! f×g6 32.♕×e6+ ♔h7 33.♘f4+−;

(b) 27...g5 28.♖×g5+! h×g5 29.♕×g5+ ♔f8 30.♕×f6 ♕b7 31.♘f4 ♔e8 32.♗f5 ♕e7 33.♕g7 ♗×a2 34.d5 e5 35.♘h5 (△36.♘f6+) 35...♕h4

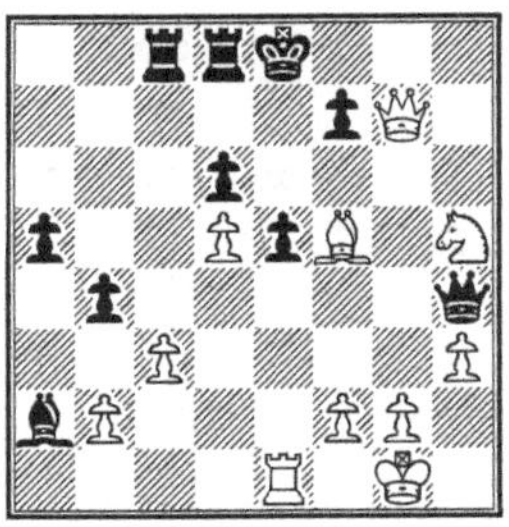

36.♗g4! ♖c4 37.g3 ♖×g4 38.h×g4 and Black has only the sorry choice between 38...♕×h5 or 38...♕e7 39.♘f6+ etc.;

(c) 27...♘h5 appears inviting by seeming to combine defense and attack. However, had Black played this, he would have been quickly disillusioned: 28.♕×h6! ♘×g3 29.♕h7+ ♔f8 30.f×g3,

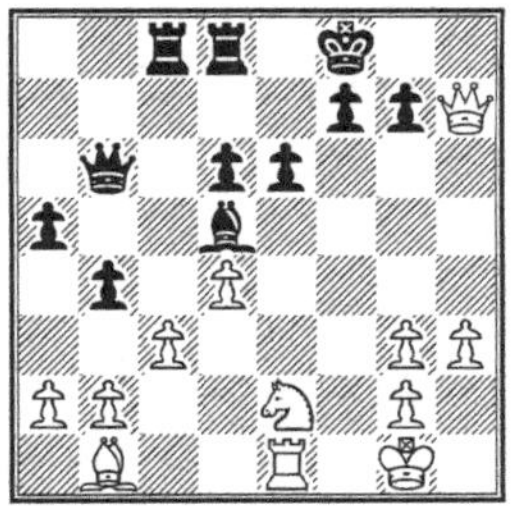

and he is lost in all variations, for example:

(c1) 30...♔e8 31.♘f4 ♕b7 32.♕×g7 ♖c7 33.♘×e6!!

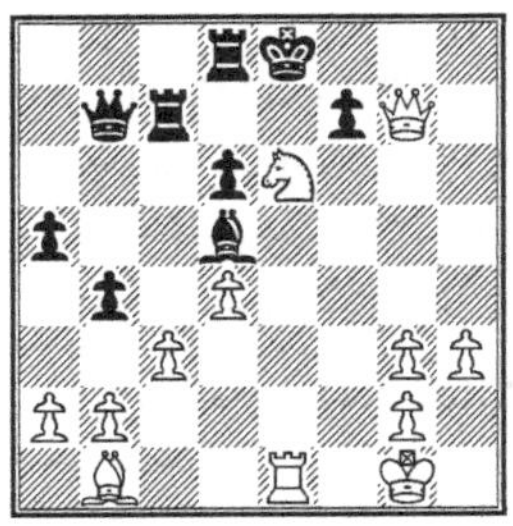

and either 33...♗×e6 34.♖×e6+ ♖e7 35.♖f6 ♔d7 36.♖×f7 ♖×f7 37.♕×f7+ ♔c8 38.♕e6+ etc. (+6.73/25), or 33...f×e6 34.♗g6+ ♖f7 35.♕g8+ ♔d7 36.♕×f7+ ♔c8 37.c4 ♗×c4 38.♖c1 ♕×f7 39.♗×f7 d5 40.♗×e6+ ♔b8 (+8.14);

(c2) 30...b×c3 31.b×c3 g5 (to prevent 32.♘f4) 32.♗g6!!:

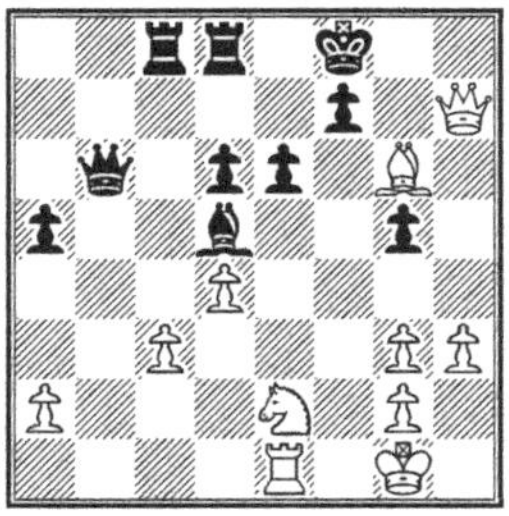

32...♕c7 (32...f×g6?? 33.♖f1+ ♔e8 34.♕f7#) 33.c4 ♗×c4 (33...f×g6 34.♖f1+ ♔e8 35.♕×g6+ ♔d7 36.♖f7+ ♔c6 37.♖×c7+ ♔×c7 38.c×d5+−) 34.♖f1 e5 35.♘c3!! e×d4 [35...♗×f1 36.♘d5! (△37.♕h8#) 36...f×g6 37.♘×c7+−] 36.♗×f7! ♗×f7 37.♘d5 ♔e8 (else 38.♕h8#) 38.♘f6+ ♔e7 39.♖e1+! ♔×f6 40.♖f1+ ♔e6 41.♕f5+ ♔e7 42.♕×f7#;

(d) 27...♘e4 28.♕×h6 ♘×g3 would transpose to line **(c)**.

These sample lines show the amazing tactical possibilities latent in the position. With 27...♔f8! Black avoids immediate danger, and he can still carry out his minority attack, but he must stay alert against such tactical shots by White.
Returning to the game (from diagram after (**27...♔f8**):

28.♘f4 b×c3 29.b×c3 ♕c6
Better 29...♗c4, to avoid 30.♘×d5.

30.♕d1
But Torre continues his risky play; if he must exchange his Knight, he wants it to be for Black's only kingside defender, the ♘f6. The text prepares 31.♘h5 for that purpose. Bogoljubow in the tournament book called this move a demonstration of Torre's great ability to conduct an attack, though that judgement is premature.

30...♗e4?

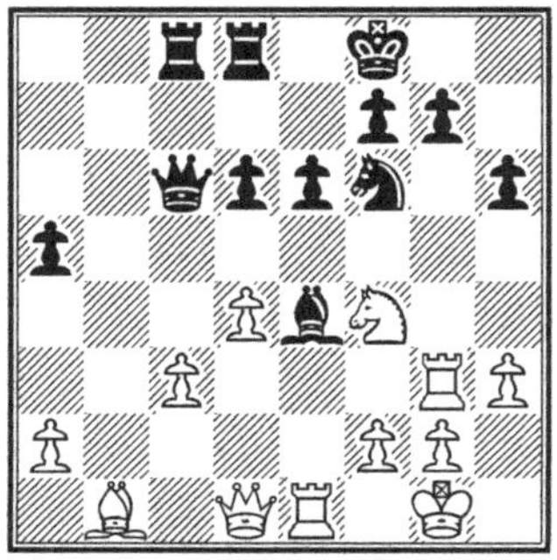

A mistake that could have had serious consequences. Best was 30...♖b8 intending 31...♖b2 to win the a-pawn. If then 31.♘×d5 ♕×d5 32.♕c1 ♕b5∓.

31.♘h5?!
Torre misses his first real opportunity. He could have gotten his attack rolling with 31.♗×e4 ♘×e4 32.♕f3 ♘f6 33.d5! e×d5 (33...♘×d5?? 34.♘×e6+ and mate shortly) 34.♖e6!!:

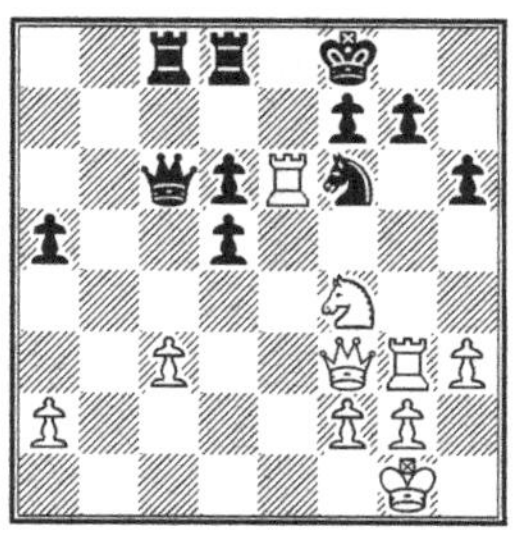

34...d4 (if 34...f×e6?? 35.♘×e6+ ♔e8 36.♘×g7+ ♔d7 37.♕f5+ ♔c7 38.♘e6+

♔b7 39.♘×d8+ ♖×d8 40.♕×f6+–) 35.♘g6+ f×g6 36.♖×f6+! ♔g8 (if 36...g×f6?? 37.♕×f6+ and mate in four) 37.♕d3! ♖d7 (not 37...g×f6?? 38.♕×g6+ ♔f8 39.♕g8+ ♔e7 40.♖g7#) 38.♕×g6:

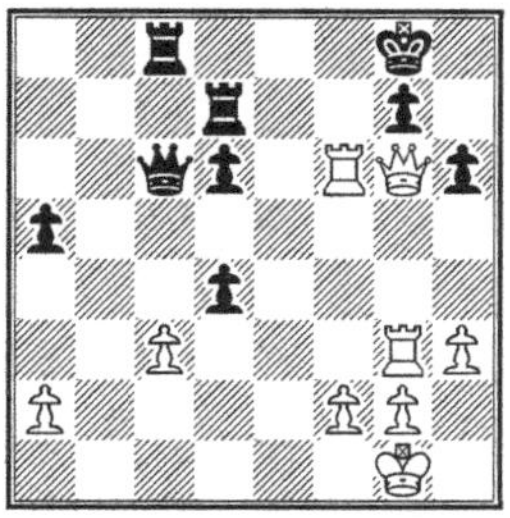

Now if 38...d×c3?? 39.♕f5 ♖e8 40.♖×h6 c2 41.♕h7+ ♔f8 42.♕h8+ ♔e7 43.♖e3+ ♔d8 44.♖×e8+ ♔c7 45.♖c8+ ♔b7 46.♖×c6 ♔×c6 47.♕c8+ and Stockfish announces mate in 13. Therefore Black must play 38...♔h8 39.c×d4 ♖g8 40.♖g4 ♕c4 41.♖h4 (not 41.♖×d6?? ♕c1+ 42.♔h2 ♕c7 winning the Rook) 41...d5 42.♖c6 and White must eventually pick up another pawn or two and win (+2.94/25).

31...♗×b1 32.♘×f6

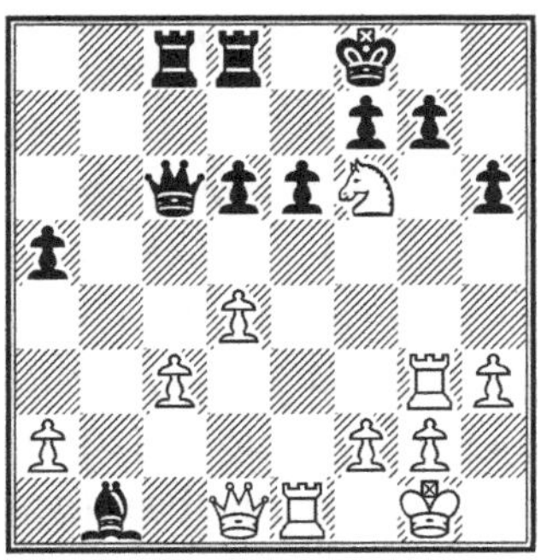

32...♗g6?

Dus-Chotimirsky gives Torre another chance!

32...♕b7 would have been even, *viz.* 33.♕×b1 [or 33.♘h5 ♗g6□! (now the only good move) 34.♘f4 ♗f5 (0.00/29)] 33...♕×b1 34.♖×b1 g×f6 (0.00/30). But not 32...♖b8?? 33.d5! e×d5 34.♕d4! (threatening 35.♘h7+ ♗×h7 36.♕×g7#) 34...g×f6 35.♕×f6 ♗e4 36.f3 ♕c5+ 37.♔h2 ♕c8 38.♕×h6+ ♔e8 39.f×e4 ♕e6 40.♕×e6+ f×e6 41.e×d5 e5 and White, two pawns up, has an easily won endgame.

33.d5!

An outstanding move, forcing Black to open the e-file.

33...e×d5 34.♘×d5?!

Another misfire; stronger was 34.♕d4 ♕c5 35.♕f4 (+2.16/25).

The text is a distant second-best.

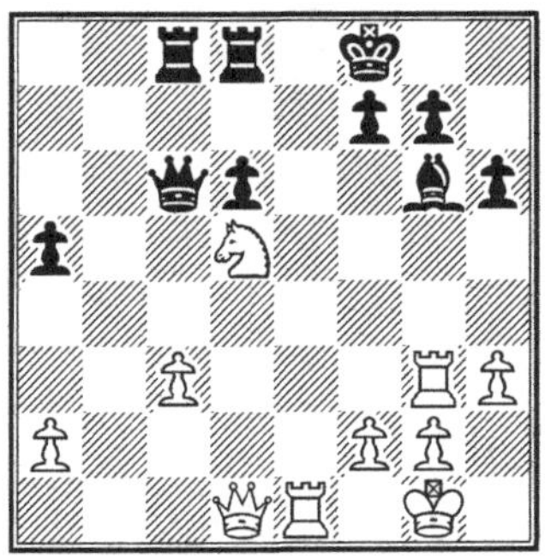

34...♖d7?

Torre's gambles have paid off; this is the losing move. White threatened 35.♘e7, but the correct way to prevent it was 34...♖e8□ 35.♖×e8+ ♕×e8□ (if 35...♖×e8?? 36.♖×g6 f×g6 37.♕f3+ ♔g8 38.♘f6+ loses the Queen, or if 35...♔×e8 36.♖e3+ ♔f8 37.♘e7+–) 36.♖e3 ♕b5 37.♘e7 ♖d8,

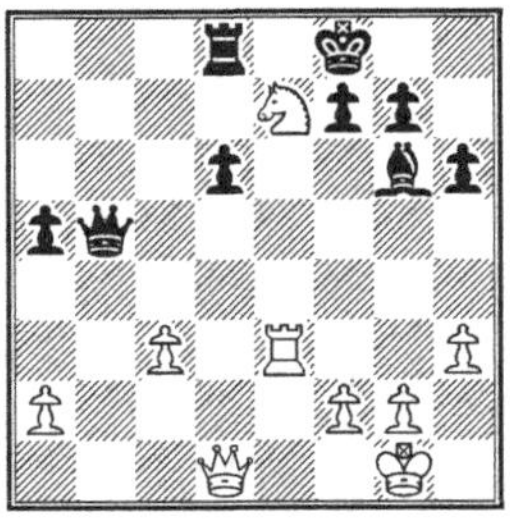

and after either 38.♘×g6+ f×g6 39.a4 ♕c6 40.♕g4 d5 41.♕d4 (+0.31/26), or 38.♕d4 ♗c2 39.c4 ♕c5 40.♕g4 ♕g5 41.♕e2 ♗f5 42.♘d5 (+0.58/25), White's advantage is very slight. But now Torre seizes control of the game and never lets go.

35.♖ge3!

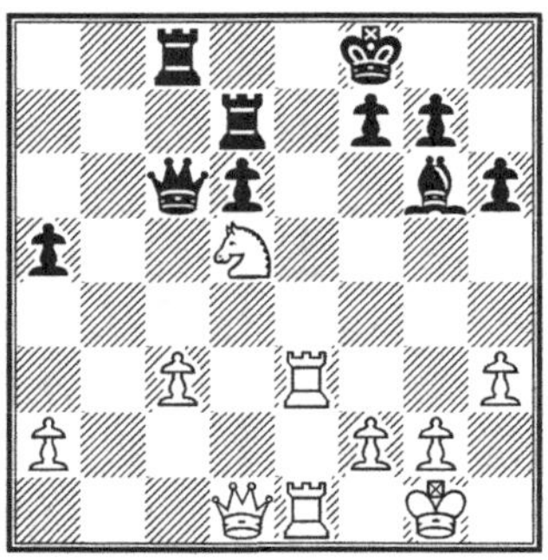

35...♖cd8
If 35...♖b8 36.♕g4! (again threatening 37.♘e7 with decisive effect) 36...♗h7 37.c4 ♖db7 38.♔h2 (to render 38...♖b1 ineffective) 38...a4 39.♕f4 and Black has no defense to such threats as 40.♖e6 ♖d8 41.♖×h6!!.

36.♕f3 ♕b7
If 36...f5 37.♖e6 ♗h7 38.♕e3!! ♕×d5 39.♖e8+ ♔f7 40.♖×d8 ♖×d8 41.♕e7+ ♔g6 42.♕×d8 +–.

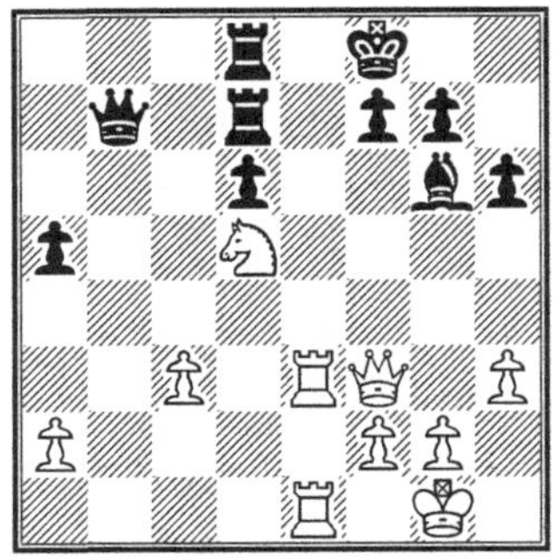

37.♘f6!!
A move at once beautiful and crushing. The immediate threat is 38.♖e8+ ♖×e8 39.♖×e8#.

37...♕c8
If 37...g×f6 38.♕×f6 and mate in at most four.

38.♖e8+
38.♘×d7+ was also winning, but the text leads to a general simplification and leaves Black without resource. The remainder needs no commentary.

38...♖×e8 39.♖×e8+ ♕×e8 40.♘×e8 ♔×e8 41.♕a8+ ♔e7 42.♕×a5 ♗e4 43.♕b4 f5 44.a4 ♖b7 45.♕d4 ♖b1+ 46.♔h2 ♖b2 47.♕×g7+ ♔e6 48.♕×h6+ ♔d5 49.♕e3 ♔c4 50.♕d4+ ♔b3 51.♕×d6 ♔×a4 52.h4 ♔b3 53.h5 ♔×c3 54.h6 ♖b7 55.f3 1-0
A wonderfully complicated, exciting struggle, with many beautiful combinations, both played on the board and hidden in the notes. One of Torre's best.

Game 66

Marshall-Torre

Moscow 1925, round 3

Queen's Gambit, Baltic Defense [D06]

In the second round Torre met his old friend Marshall, and, for the first time in international play, with a decisive result.

1.d4 ♘f6 2.♘f3 d5 3.c4 ♗f5

Torre repeats the line he played against Rubinstein at Marienbad. Marshall varies from Rubinstein's 4.c×d5.

4.♘c3

For a discussion of 4.♕b3, see Game 57.

4...e6 5.♗g5

Played at least twice before, in Von Scheve-Reggio, Monte Carlo 1902 (½-½, 35), and Esser-Loman, match, Amsterdam, 1913 (1-0, 31).

5...c6 6.♕b3 ♕b6

Still following the 1902 game. At London 1927, Marshall, on the black side of this position, played 6...♘bd7 against Fairhurst (½-½, 32).

7.c5

Most definitely a TN, not seen before, and not again until Nikolic-Klaric, Yugoslav Ch, Borovo 1981. Interestingly, Stockfish considers it White's best move at this point, by a small margin (+0.25).

7...♕c7

Probably better than 7...♕×b3 8.a×b3.

8.e3

Marshall might have tried 8.♗f4, but he probably had too much respect for Torre to think he would fall for 8...♕×f4?? 9.♕×b7+−. 8...♕c8 would maintain equality.

8...♘bd7 9.♗f4 ♕c8 10.h3 ♗e7 11.♖c1 0–0 12.♗e2 ♘e4 13.0–0

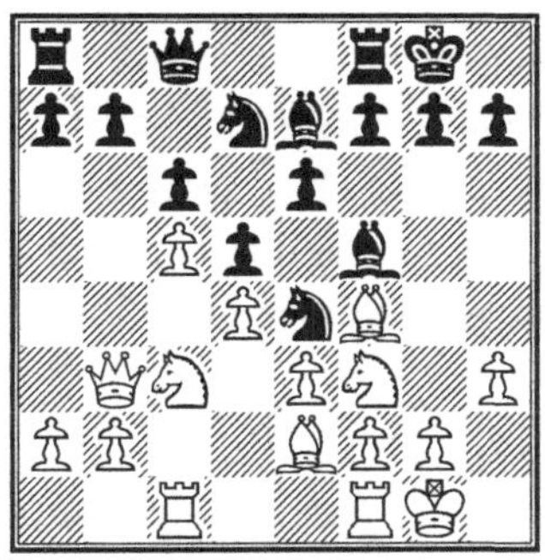

13...♖e8

13...e5!? was an interesting possibility here; if 14.d×e5 ♘d×c5=, or 14.♘×e5 ♘d2 15.♕d1 ♘×f1 16.♗×f1=, or 14.♗×e5 ♘×e5 15.d×e5 ♘×c5∓.

14.♕d1 ♗f6 15.♘×e4 ♗×e4

Not 15...d×e4? 16.♘d2 e5 17.♘c4! e×f4 18.♘d6 ♕c7 19.♘×f5±.

16.♘e5 ♗×e5

In a closed position it is no great matter to cede the Bishop pair.

17.d×e5

Marshall tries to preserve his Bishops, perhaps with the hope of opening the position later on. If 17.♗×e5 ♘×e5 18.d×e5=.

17...♕d8 18.b4 b6 19.c×b6 ♕×b6

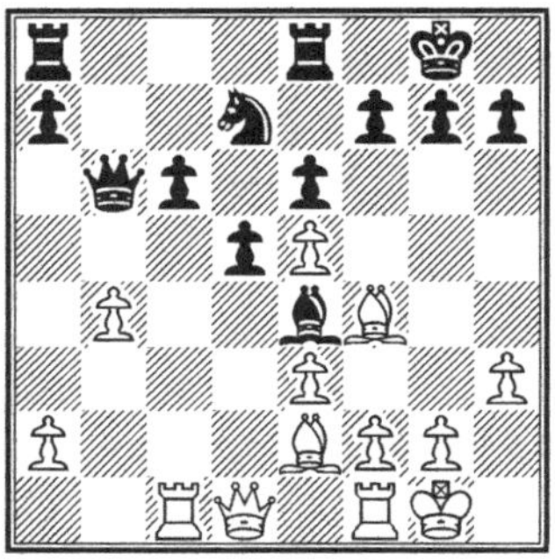

Superficially this looks bad for Black, with his c-pawn backward on the open file, but in fact White can make nothing of it against proper defense.

20.♕d4 ♖ab8

20...♖eb8 was perhaps slightly preferable, so that the a-pawn remains defended against the white Queen and Black can play ...♕×b4 in certain variations.

21.a3 ♖ec8 22.♖c3 a5

And perhaps slightly preferable here was 22...c5, though it was probably not to Torre's taste, as it could lead to a general exchange, 23.b×c5 ♖×c5 24.♖fc1 ♖bc8 25.♖×c5 ♖×c5 26.♖×c5 ♕×c5 27.♕×c5 ♘×c5, and an overall deadening of the game (0.00/29).

23.♕×b6 ♖×b6

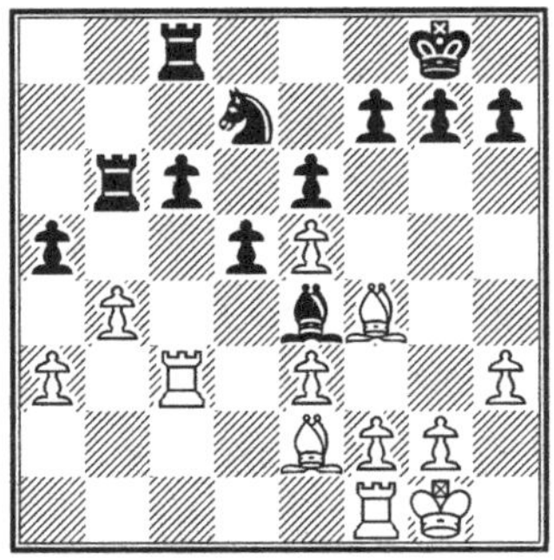

More certain to retain equality was 23...♘×b6, when if 24.b×a5 ♘a4 25.♖cc1 ♘b2 26.♖c3 ♘a4 draws, or Black can try for more with 26...c5.

The text enables White to enter a line where Black must defend precisely to avoid serious disadvantage: 24.b×a5!?. It does not seem to lead to a definite win for White, but it sets the most difficult problems for Black, in both number and degree. The complications are so tangled and profuse we cannot possibly examine them all, but a few sample lines should give the reader an idea of the possibilities. Forced then is 24...♖b2□ 25.♗a6, and then not 25...♖c7? 26.♖fc1 ♘b8 27.♗f1 ♖a7 when White keeps the extra pawn with either 28.a6 or 28.f3 ♗b1 29.♖c5, but 25...♖f8, reaching the first major branch:

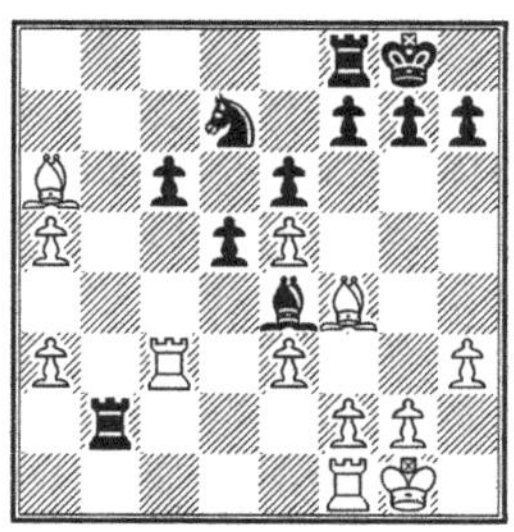

(a) Now not 26.♖×c6? ♘b8 27.♖d6 ♘×a6 28.♖×a6 ♗d3! forking the Rooks.

(b) 26.♖fc1 looks strong, and sets up some definite pitfalls, but seems to fizzle out against best defense. After 26...c5 27.a4 (△28.♗b5+−) 27...c4 28.f3, some sample lines are:

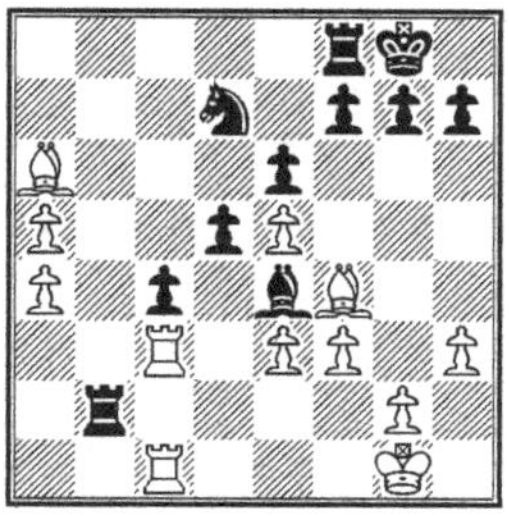

(b1) Illustrating how Black can easily go wrong is 28...♗b1? 29.e4! ♘c5 [if 29...d×e4?? 30.♗×c4 e×f3 31.g×f3 ♖b4 32.a6 ♗a2 (or 32...♘b6 33.♖b3 ♖×b3 34.♗×b3 ♗f5 35.a7 ♖a8 36.♖c7 etc. +6.47/24) 33.♗×a2 ♖×f4 34.♗b3 ♖b4 35.a7 etc. (+6.85/24)] 30.♗b5 ♘b3 31.a6

31...♘d4 (if 31...♘×c1? 32.♗×c1 ♖a2 33.e×d5 e×d5 34.a7 d4 35.♖×c4 ♗d3 36.♖c7 ♗f5 37.♗c6 etc. +4.47/26) 32.♗e3! ♘e2+ 33.♔h2 ♘×c3 34.♖×c3 ♖b3 35.♗d4 ♖×c3 36.♗×c3 ♖a8 and though Black is up ♖-for-♗+♙, the winning chances are White's (+2.99/30);

(b2) Correct is 28...♗g6! and either:

(b2a) 29.e4 (29.♗b5 ♘c5 30.e4 transposes) 29...♘c5 30.♗b5 ♘d3 31.♗e3 ♘×c1 32.♖×c1 ♖a8 33.a6 f6 34.e×d5 e×d5 35.a7 ♗e8□ 36.♗d4 ♖b3 37.♗×e8 ♖×e8 38.e6 ♖a8 with an almost certain draw (+0.38/27); or

(b2b) 29.♗×c4!? d×c4 30.♖×c4 ♖b1 31.♖×b1 ♗×b1 32.a6 ♖a8□ 33.♖c7 ♖×a6 34.♖×d7 h5 with the same verdict (+0.48/27).

(c) 26.♖d1 c5 27.♗f1 ♖a8 28.a6 ♖c2 29.♖×c2 ♗×c2 30.♖d2 ♗b3 31.e4 ♘b8 32.♗e3

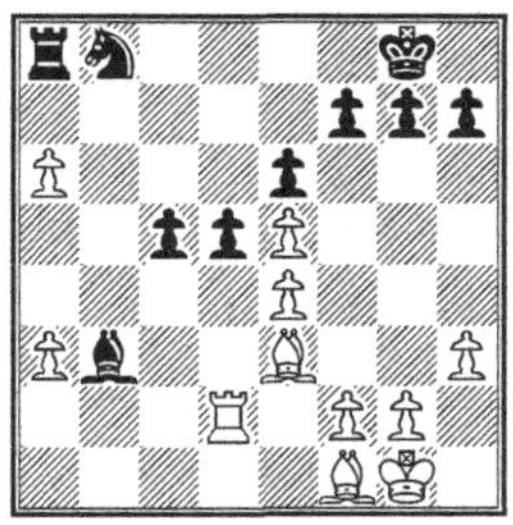

and:

(c1) 32...♘×a6 33.e×d5 e×d5 34.♗×a6 ♖×a6 35.♗×c5 (+0.86/24); or

(c2) 32...d4 33.♖b2 c4□ 34.♖d2 d3 35.♗×d3!? ♘×a6 (if 35...c×d3? 36.♖×d3 and 37.♖×b3+−) 36.♗e2 h6 37.♖d4 ♘c7 38.♗×c4 ♗×c4 39.♖×c4 ♘b5 40.a4 ♘a3 41.♖b4 ♘c2 42.♖c4 ♘a3 43.♖c1 ♖×a4 (+1.02/30). In either case it seems unlikely White can win.

(d) 26.f3 ♗c2□ (26...♗g6? 27.e4! d×e4 28.♖d1 ♘b8 29.♗c1 ♖b1 30.♗e2 e×f3 31.g×f3 h6 32.a6 and 32...♘×a6

33.♗×a6 is forced) 27.♖f2 ♖b1+ 28.♔h2 ♗a4 29.e4 and:

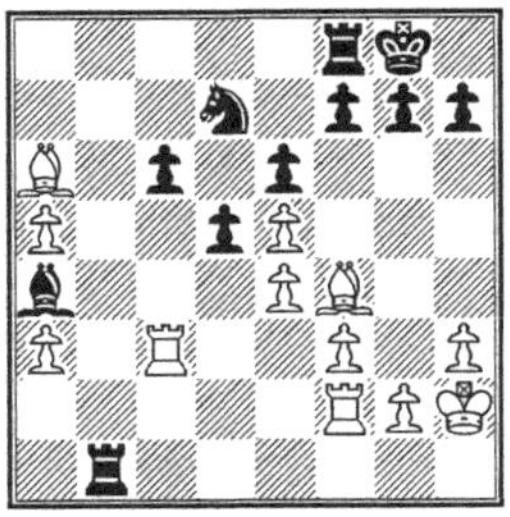

(d1) 29...d×e4? 30.♖d2 ♘b8 31.♗e2 e×f3 32.♗×f3 (+2.33/28);
(d2) 29...d4? 30.♖c4 ♗b5 31.♖×d4 (31.♗×b5 ♖×b5 32.♖×d4 ♘c5 transposes) 31...♘c5 32.♗×b5 ♖×b5 33.♗d2 (if 33.♖c2 ♖×a5 34.♖d6 ♘b7 35.♖d×c6 ♖×a3 +4.84/26) 33...♘b3 34.♖a4 ♖a8 35.♗c3 (+3.31/25);
(d3) 29...♖bb8! 30.e×d5 c×d5 31.♗d3 ♖a8 32.a6 ♘b8 33.♖b2 ♘×a6 and while Stockfish says White stands better (+1.05/29), winning seems highly problematic;
(d4) 29...c5! 30.e×d5 e×d5 31.♗d3 ♖b7 32.♖d2 c4:

(d4a) Now if 33.♗f5 ♗c6 (+1.11/28). Or White can try one of two sacrificial lines:
(d4b) 33.♗e2 ♗c6 34.♗×c4!? d×c4 35.♖×c4 ♘b8 ∞;
(d4c) 33.♗×c4!? d×c4 34.♖×c4 ♗b3 35.♖b4 ♖×b4 36.a×b4 ♗a4 with another complicated position Black should be able to hold (+0.73/31).

We hope we have not over-taxed the reader's patience. An old saying goes "Chess is a sea where a gnat may drink and elephant can bathe." The position after 24.b×a5 is one where an elephant could drown. Our analysis is by no means conclusive or exhaustive (even if it was mentally exhausting for this writer), but it does establish, we believe, that while 24.b×a5 did not win by force, it was White's best *chance* for a win, both on its objective merits, and the difficulty of the problems it sets. Returning to the actual game, this all became academic, because Marshall instead played

24.f3?!

allowing

24...a×b4!
This interpolation lets Black equalize.

25.a×b4 ♗g6 26.♖fc1 h6 27.♗g3

Trying to hold the b-pawn is fruitless: 27.♖b3? c5∓. And not 27.b5? c5∓.

27...♖×b4 28.♖×c6 ♖×c6 29.♖×c6 ♖b3 30.♖c8+ ♔h7 31.♖c7

31...♘b6
Black might have tried 31...♘×e5, hoping for 32.♗×e5? ♖×e3 33.♗×g7 ♔×g7 34.♔f2 ♖a3∓. But 32.e4 would keep things even.

32.♗f2?
The decisive mistake, ultimately losing a piece. 32.♗f4, 32.♔f2, or almost any reasonable move would have maintained equality. But now White is suddenly lost.

32...♖b1+! 33.♔h2 ♖b2!
Marshall either overlooked this sequence of check and skewer, or miscalculated that his winning the black Knight would compensate for the loss of a Bishop.

34.e4
The best try, making the winning sequence as long and complicated as possible. But Torre finds the way.

34...♘a8 35.♖a7 ♖×e2

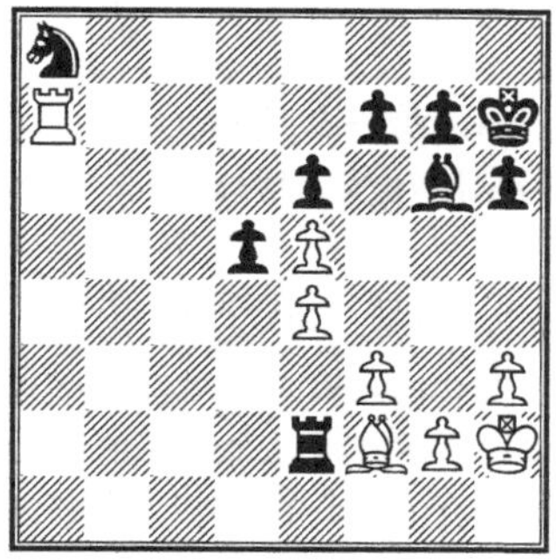

36.♔g3
The least evil was 36.♔g1 d×e4 37.♖×a8 e×f3 38.g×f3 ♖×e5, losing two pawns rather than a piece, with vague hopes for a draw.

36...d×e4 37.♖×a8
If 37.f×e4 ♗×e4 and the Knight is defended.

37...e3 38.♗g1 ♖e1 39.♗h2
Or 39.♔h2 e2 40.♗f2 ♖f1 −+.

39...♖h1

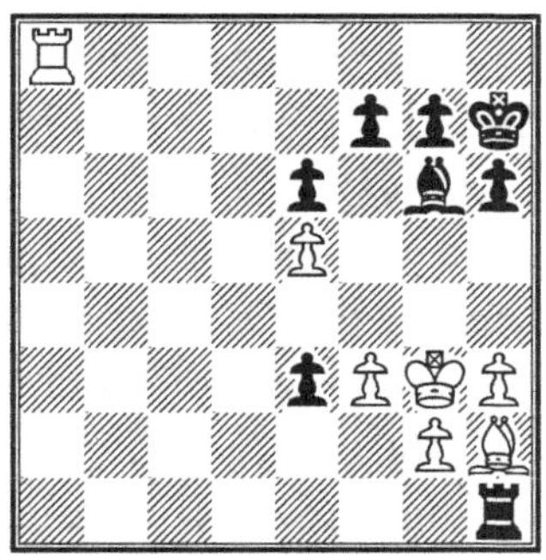

The plight of the white Bishop is tragicomic. Black's move ties the King to its defense, thus keeping both immobile.

40.♖a2 ♗d3 41.♔f4 e2

41...♖×h2 42.♔×e3 ♗f1 works well too.

42.♗g3 e1♕ 43.♗×e1 ♖×e1 44.h4 g5+ 45.h×g5 h×g5+ 46.♔×g5 ♖×e5+

Torre need only take care that he does not let all the pawns be traded off, since the ending of ♖+♗-vs-♖ is known to be a theoretical draw.

47.♔f4 ♖e2 48.♖a3 ♗c4 49.g4 ♔g6 50.♔g3 ♗d5 51.f4 ♖b2 52.♖a5 ♖b3+ 53.♔h4 ♗b7 54.f5+ e×f5 55.g×f5+ ♔f6 56.♖c5 ♗e4 57.♔g4 ♖b4 0-1

A game where just two moves made all the difference.

Game 67

Torre-Levenfish

Moscow 1925, round 4

Slav Defense [D15]

Leningrad's Grigory Yakovlevich Levenfish (1889-1961, GM title 1950, historical Elo 2540) was of the generation of Russian masters who reached maturity well before the 1917 revolution. He became one of the leading lights of Soviet chess in the 1920s and '30s, with high finishes in several USSR championships, *e.g.* 2nd in 1925 (to Bogoljubow, just before this event), =1st in 1935 and sole 1st in 1937. The sharp-tongued Levenfish later became a bitter rival of Botvinnik; they drew a match in 1937, after which Levenfish's career declined. At Moscow 1925, he and Torre were the only players to defeat the great Lasker. In this game, as he did with Dus-Chotimirsky, Torre again played in a risky fashion, but he took it too far, into recklessness. Levenfish might have forced a win at several points, but lost his way and allowed Torre to turn the tables.

1.d4 d5 2.c4 c6 3.♘c3 ♘f6 4.♘f3 d×c4

The main line of the Slav Defense, played tens of thousands of times, going back to Staunton-Cochrane, match, London, 1842 (0-1, 39), and taken up later by Winawer, Wolf, Schlechter and Alapin, to name just some early pioneers. By far the most common reply has been 5.a4, played about 84% of the time, followed by 5.e4 (7.5%) and 5.e3 (6.0%).

5.♘e5!?

But yet again, Torre comes up with something new. It is still quite rare, found in less than one percent of Slav games.

5...♘bd7

5...b5, first seen in Szekely-Pirc, Stubnanske Teplice 1930, would become the most frequent reply.

The text would be played by such latter-day greats as Akopian, Morozevich, Topalov, Bareev, and Shirov.

6.f4

Torre really ventures into the unknown with this audacious and interesting advance, which adds dynamic energy to the position and presages complications. CB has only seven other examples of this move, the most eminent names being Romanishin (twice), Knaak, and Langeweg.

6...e6

Inauspicious is 6...♘×e5?! 7.f×e5 ♘d5 8.e4 ♘×c3 9.b×c3.

Stockfish likes 6...b5, played only once, in Romanishin-Akopian, Linares Anibal Open 1996 (0-1, 74), rating things at about -1.00 after 7.♘×c6 ♕b6 8.♘e5. All other games on CB have used the text move.

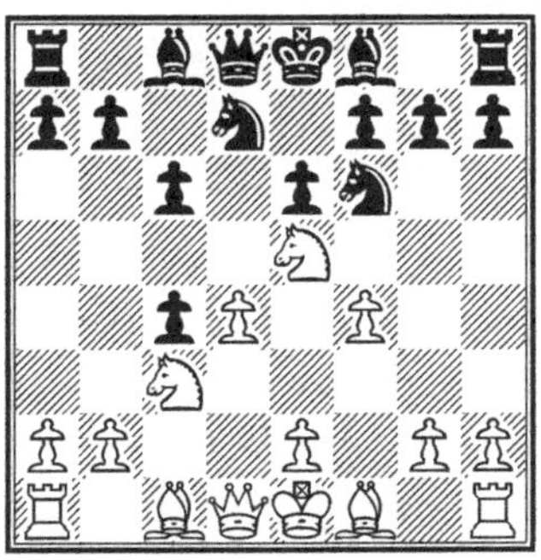

7.e3

Definitely going too far is 7.e4?, which met with swift correction in Langeweg-Welling, Netherlands Ch 1986: 7...♗b4 8.♕f3 c5 9.♗e3 ♕a5 10.♘×c4 ♗×c3+ 11.♔f2 c×d4 12.♗c1 ♕c5 13.♗d3 b5 14.e5 b×c4 15.e×f6 ♘×f6 0-1.

7...♘×e5?!

This is rather at odds with the strategic requirements of the position. There are two main flaws in White's deployment. One, he has loosened his pawn structure considerably.

Black could begin to exploit this with 7...c5 △...c5×d4, giving White an isolated d-pawn. Two, White has created a hole at e4. This invites 7...b5 8.♘×c6 ♕b6 9.♘e5 ♗b7, when the black Queen's Bishop has a wonderful diagonal and White will have some difficulty developing his own Bishops. The text, on the other hand, precludes that idea and actually forces Black to retreat his only well-placed piece.

8.f×e5 ♘d7

If 8...♘d5?! 9.♗×c4 ♗e7 10.0–0 0–0 11.♘e4±.

9.♕g4

Not 9.♗×c4? ♘×e5 10.♗b3 (if 10.d×e5? ♕h4+ 11.g3 ♕×c4 ∓/−+) 10...♘g6∓.

9...f5 10.♕g3 b5

So now it has become a real gambit. White must win in the middle game, or face an unfavorable endgame.

11.♗e2

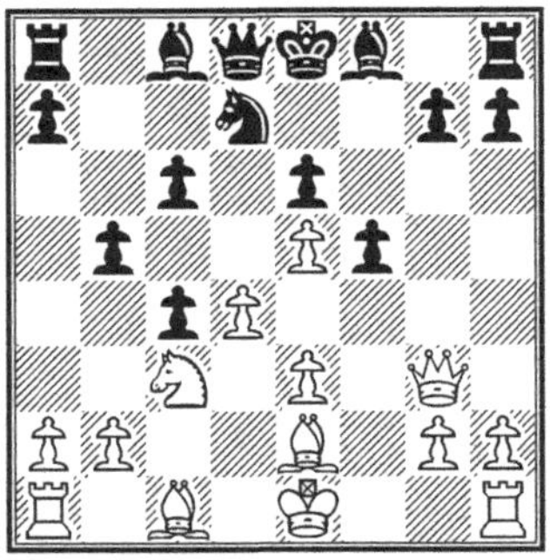

11...g6

It would be jejune to play 11...♘b6 and expect White to fall for 12.♗h5+?! g6 13.♗×g6+?? h×g6 14.♕×g6+ ♔d7 15.e4 ♕h4+ 16.g3 ♕h7 (-5.96/23). But Black clearly must play ...g7-g6 sooner or later, as otherwise White's Queen does not allow the Bishop at f8 to develop.

12.h4

Beginning an interesting (though ultimately rash) advance of both Rook pawns, a characteristic of Larsen's style decades later.

More prudent at the moment, however, might be 12.a3, to discourage ...b5-b4. Or 12.0–0, and if 12...b4 13.♘a4 ♗a6 14.b3 ♗b5 15.♗×c4 ♗×c4 16.b×c4 ♘b6 17.♘b2 ±.

12...♗e7 13.h5

Again, 13.a3 seems advisable. But as in his game with Dus-Chotimirsky, Torre is intent on aggression rather than prophylaxis, even if it entails risk.

13...g5 14.h6 0–0 15.a4?

But this is really over the top, risking loss of the game. Better sensible development by 15.0–0 or 15.♗f3.

15...b4 16.♘b1

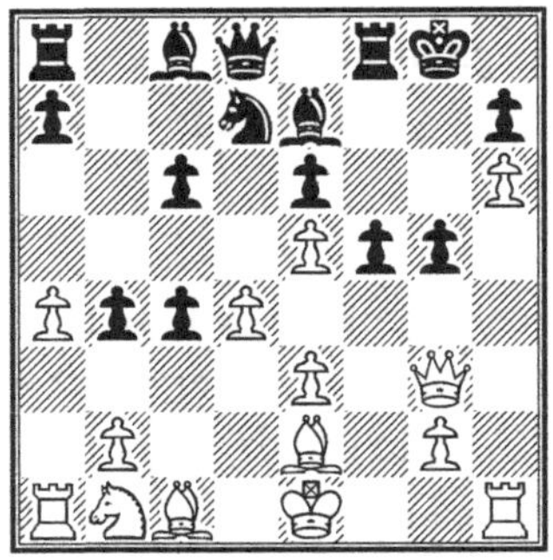

16...♘b6?!

A weak move that could have justified White's reckless 15th.

Instead, Black could have begun a successful kingside initiative in either of two ways:

(a) 16...c5! and:

(a1) 17.♘d2 c3 18.b×c3 b×c3 19.♘f3 ♔h8!

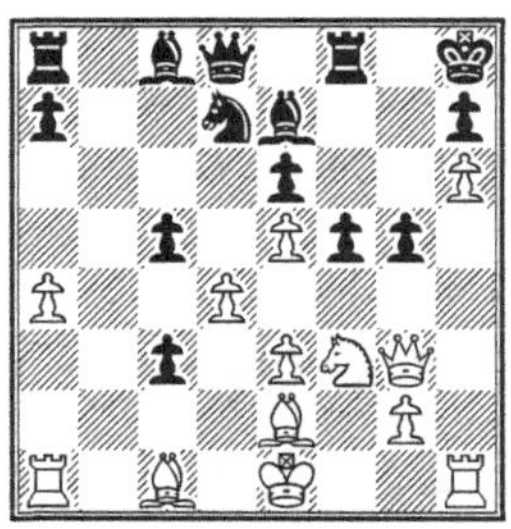

A quiet move preparing to make noise on the g-file. 20.d5 — The only remotely playable move. If instead, say, 20.0–0 ♖g8 21.d5 g4 22.d6 g×f3 23.d×e7 ♕×e7 24.♕×f3 ♖b8 25.e4 ♗b7 26.♕×c3 ♕h4 27.♖f2 ♗×e4 28.♗f1 ♘b6 29.♕×c5 ♖bc8 30.♕d6 ♖g6 31.♕d4 ♘d5 (-5.67/24). And of course 20.d×c5? ♘×c5 21.♗×c4 ♘e4 and 20.♗×c4? e×d4 21.e×d4 ♘b6 are very bad for White. — 20...e×d5 21.0–0 ♖g8 22.e6 ♘f8 23.♕e5+ ♗f6 24.♕×f5 ♘×e6! (not 24...♗×e6?? 25.♘e5!!+–) 25.♘×g5 ♘×g5 26.♕×f6+ ♕×f6 27.♖×f6 ♗h3! 28.♗f1 ♘e4 and the dust settles with Black up a pawn and with the better position (-2.12/25);

(a2) If 17.a5 to prevent ...♘d7-b6, then 17...♔h8 18.♗×c4 c×d4 19.e×d4 [if 19.♗×e6?? ♘c5 20.♗c4 (20.♗×c8 ♘d3+ 21.♔e2 ♖×c8 -10.14) 20...♘e4 21.♕h3 (or 21.♕f3 g4 22.♕f1 ♘g3–+) 21...f4 (-8.64)] 19...♘b8

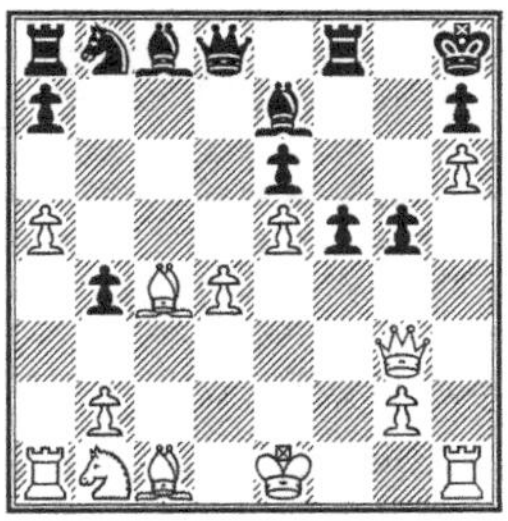

20.♘d2 (if 20.♕e3 ♘c6 and 21...♘×d4, or if 20.♕f3 ♕×d4! 21.♕×a8 ♕×c4 22.♕×b8 ♕×c1+ etc.) 20...♕×d4 21.♗e2 ♗a6 22.♘b3 ♕e4 23.♕f3 ♕×e5 24.♗e3 ♗×e2 25.♕×e2 ♔g8 (White threatened 26.♗d4; 25...♗f6 was also good) 26.♘d4 f4 27.♗f2 ♕×e2+ 28.♔×e2 e5 and again the smoke clears with Black ahead in both pawns and position.

(b) Also winning is 16...♔h8 17.0–0 c5 18.♘d2 c×d4 19.e×d4 f4 20.♕f2 ♗b7 21.♘×c4 ♖c8

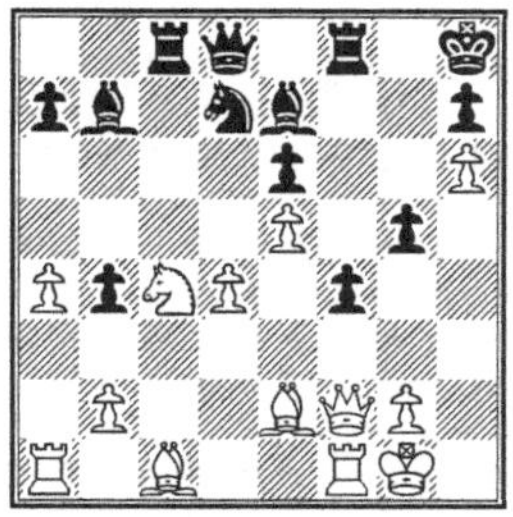

22.b3 [if 22.♕e1 ♘×e5! 23.d×e5 (23.♘×e5?? ♕×d4+ 24.♔h1 ♕×e5–+) 23...♕d5 24.♖f2 ♗c5–+] 22...♗d5 23.♗b2 g4! 24.♗×g4 ♗h4 25.♕e2 ♕g5

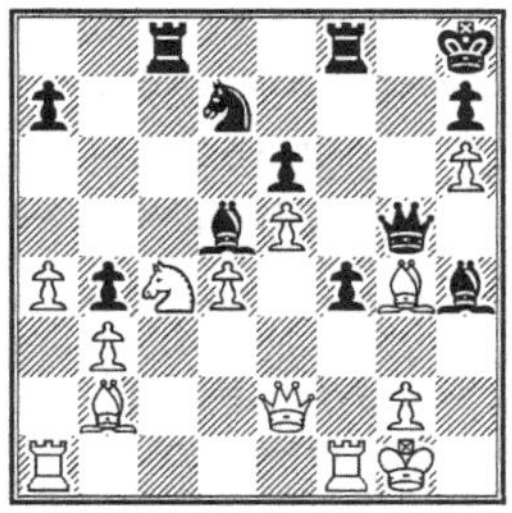

26.♗c1 (if 26.♗f3?? ♗g3 27.♖fd1 ♕h4 28.♕d3 ♗f2+ 29.♔f1 ♖×c4 30.b×c4 ♗e3 and mate soon) 26...♕×h6 27.♗d2 ♗g3 28.♗h3 ♘b6 29.♘d6 ♖c2 30.♖ac1 ♖b2 31.a5 ♘d7 32.♘c4 ♖×d2! 33.♕×d2 ♕h4 34.♘e3 (forced, otherwise 34...f3 in most lines) 34...f×e3 35.♖×f8+ ♘×f8 36.♕×e3 ♗f4 37.♕e1 (anything else is much worse) 37...♕g5 38.♖d1 (else 38...♗e3+ 39.♔h1 ♗×d3 in most lines) 38...♘g6,

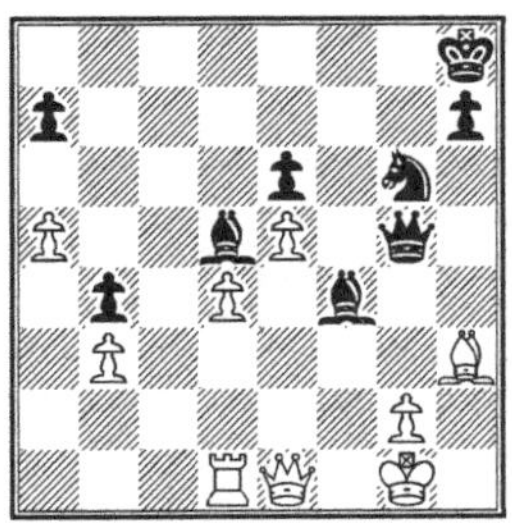

and though material is nominally even, ♖+♙-for-♗+♘, Black's far more active and dangerous pieces give him a winning advantage (-6.38/24). An example of the dangers: 39.♕×b4 ♗e3+! 40.♔f1 (if 40.♔h1 ♗×g2+ 41.♗×g2 ♕h4+ 42.♗h3 ♕×h3#, or 40.♔h2 ♕f4+ 41.♔h1 ♕g3 and after a few spite checks comes ...♕×h3#) 40...♕f4+ 41.♔e2 ♕f2+ 42.♔d3 ♘f4+ 43.♔c3 ♘e2+ 44.♔d3 ♗g5 and mate in ten at most.

The complexity of these variations, and the length of analysis required to establish their validity, explain why neither Torre nor Levenfish detected them at the board. In the first edition we were quite wrong to say this game was "easy to understand." Humbled again by the Lidless Eye!

Returning now to the game with (we hope) greater understanding, after

16...♘b6

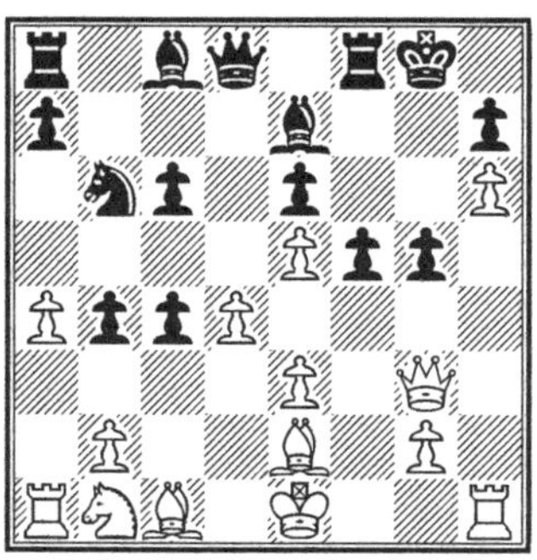

17.♘d2?

Now was the time for Torre to vindicate his impetuous 15th move with 17.a5, *viz.* 17...♘d5 18.♗×c4 c5 19.e4 f×e4 20.♘d2 when Black's advantage is much reduced and White can begin to fight back.

17...c3 18.b×c3 b×c3 19.♘f3

Best of the five possible Knight moves.

19...♔h8!

An indication Levenfish is now sensing his attacking possibilities.

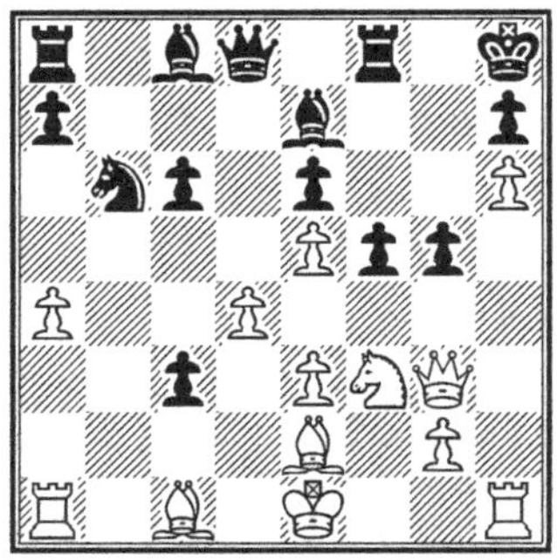

20.a5?

Torre's rook-pawn-pushing mania has gotten completely out of hand. This drives the Knight to where Black wants it anyway.

Necessary was 20.e4 f4 (not 20...f×e4? 21.♘×g5) 21.♕g4, when if Black makes trouble with 21...c5, White can muddy the waters and generate some counterplay with 22.♖h5 ♖g8 23.d×c5 ♘d7 24.c6.

20...♘d5 21.e4 f4!

21...f×e4?! 22.♘×g5 ♗×g5 23.♗×g5 ♖g8 24.♖h5 (-1.03/28) would squander Black's attacking chances.

22.♕g4

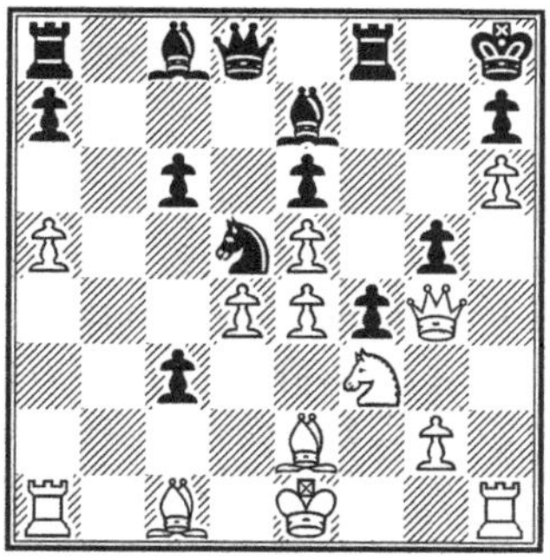

22...♘e3

Not bad, but a seriously second-best move.

Clearly winning was 22...♘b4! 23.0–0 ♖g8 24.♖d1 c5 25.d×c5 (if 25.d5 e×d5 26.e6 ♕d6 27.e×d5 ♘×d5 △28...♗×e6−+) 25...♗×c5+ 26.♔h1 ♕f8 (-5.94/26).

23.♗×e3 f×e3 24.0–0

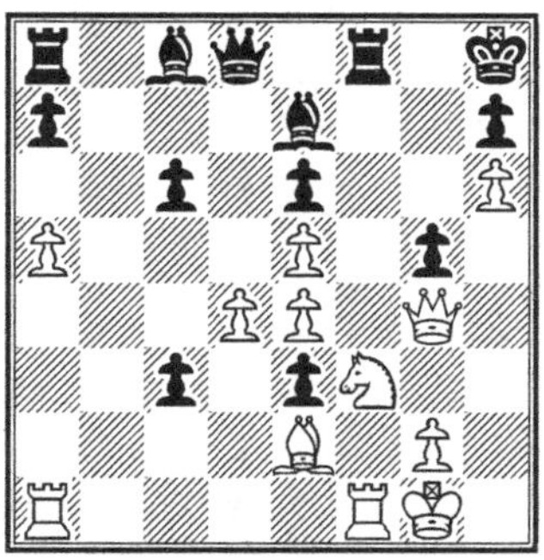

Apropos of nothing, the e-file seems to have become a palindrome.

24...♗d7?

With this inexplicably timid and pointless move, Black's advantage disappears.

Correct was 24...♖b8, when best play continues 25.d5□ e×d5 26.e6 ♖f4,

27.♘e5 — The least evil; if 27.♕g3 ♕d6! 28.e5 ♕×e6 29.♘×g5 ♖g4! 30.♗×g4 (30.♘×e6?? ♖×g3 -7.26) 30...♕×g4 31.♕×e3 ♖b2! 32.♖f2 ♖×f2 33.♔×f2 ♗×g5 34.♕×c3 ♗e6 (-6.55/22) — 27...♖×g4 28.♘f7+ ♔g8 29.♘×d8 ♖×e4! 30.♘×c6 ♖b7 31.♖ac1 d4 (-4.25/25).

With the text Levenfish misses his last chance to win.

25.♖ac1!

The game is now even.

25...♖f4 26.♕g3!□

Not 26.♕h3? g4 27.♕g3 ♕f8 28.♘h2 ♖×f1+ 29.♖×f1 ♕×h6 30.♘×g4 ♗h4! (-2.43/25).

26...♖×e4?!

This could have turned the game in White's favor. Best was 26...♖b8=.

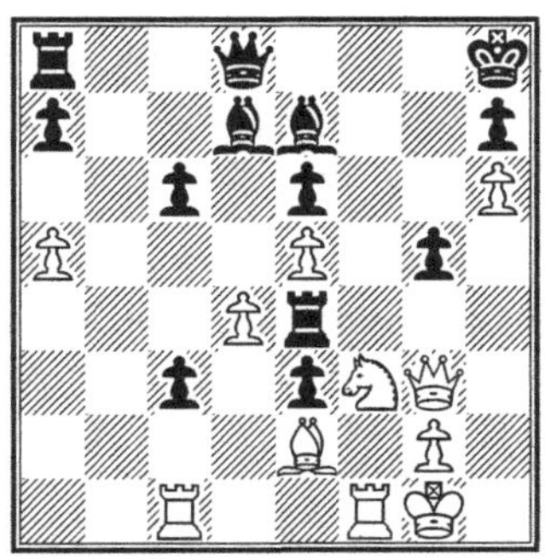

27.♖×c3

With this the game stays even.

Better, though not winning, was 27.♗d3! e2□ [if 27...♖f4? 28.♘×g5! ♖×f1+ 29.♖×f1 ♗×g5 30.♖f7!□ e2 (there is nothing better) 31.♖×h7+ ♔g8 32.♖g7+ ♔h8 33.♔h2 and wins (+6.53/26)] 28.♗×e4 e×f1♕+ 29.♖×f1 ♕g8□ 30.♘h2 ♖f8 31.♕×c3±.

27...♕g8?

Levenfish is beginning to falter.

Better were 27...♖f4, 27...♖b8, or 27...c5 28.d×c5 ♗c6, with about an even game.

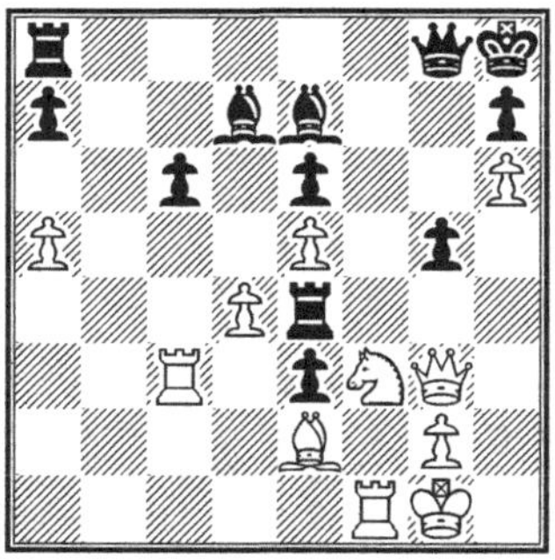

28.♖b1

Wrong Rook to the b-file! Correct and winning was 28.♖b3! ♖d8 — Relatively best; if 28...♖b8?? 29.♖×b8 ♕×b8 30.♘×g5 and mate shortly, showing one reason the Rook should stay on f1. — 29.♖b7 g4 30.♘h2 ♖×d4 31.♘×g4! ♕g6 32.♖f6! (Remember this move when comparing the next note.) 32...♗×f6 33.e×f6 ♖×g4 34.♗×g4 ♕×f6 35.♕×e3 a6 (if 35...♗c8 36.♖×a7+-, or 35...♕a1+ 36.♔h2 ♕×a5?? 37.♕d4+ e5 38.♕d6 and mate in four) 36.♕d3 ♕×h6 37.♖×d7+-. But do not despair for our hero, dear reader; the text is the proverbial next-to-last-mistake.

28...g4??

The losing move. Best was 28...♖d8 29.♖b7 g4! (now playable with impunity) 30.♘h2 ♖×d4 31.♘×g4 ♕g6 with only a small edge for White (+0.76/28), because he cannot play 32.♖f6.

29.♗d3! g×f3

If 29...♕g6 30.♘h4+-.

30.♕g7+

It's not clear why Torre chose this, which entails loss of the h-pawn, rather than the more direct 30.♕×g8+. However, it hardly matters.

30...♕×g7 31.h×g7+ ♔×g7 32.♗×e4 e2 33.♔f2!

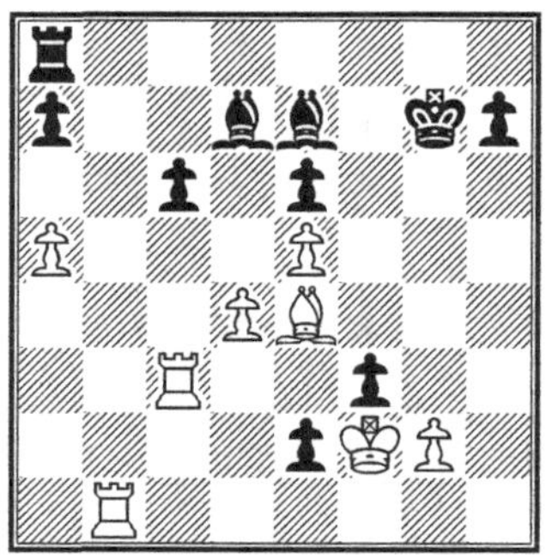

The only clearly winning move. 33.g×f3? allows 33...♗h4 34.♖e3 e1♕+ 35.♖e×e1 ♗×e1 36.♖×e1 when a white victory is much more problematic, if indeed attainable at all (+1.31/26).

33...♖b8

If 33...♗h4+ then of course 34.g3.

34.♖×f3
Avoiding the transparent trap 34.♖×b8?? ♗h4+ 35.g3 ♗×g3+ 36.♔×f3 e1♕–+.

34...♖×b1 35.♗×b1 c5 36.♖b3 ♗c6 37.♔×e2 c×d4 38.♔d3 ♗h4 39.♔×d4 ♗f2+ 40.♔d3 h5 41.♖b2 ♗g1 42.♗a2 ♔f7 43.♖c2 ♗a8
Black's Bishops appear dangerous, but as Petrosian was wont to say, "The advantage of the Exchange does not forgive."

44.a6 h4 45.♖c7+ ♔g6 46.♖c8
An instructive maneuver, the point of which is to transfer the Rook to the f-file, thus denying Black's King any access to the center (the by now familiar *cordón sanitaire*).

46...♗d5 47.♗×d5 e×d5 48.♖f8 ♗c5 49.♖f1 1-0
An exciting if ragged game, full of surprising unplayed possibilities. Neither player shone as a strategist, but Torre ultimately proved the better tactician.

Game 68

Torre-Spielmann

Moscow 1925, round 6

London System [D02]

In the fifth round Torre played a dull draw with Tartakower we do not include here. His next game, with Spielmann, was slightly more interesting, if only for the way Spielmann deftly rebuffed Torre's somewhat naïve attacking gestures.

1.d4 ♘f6 2.♘f3 b6 3.♗f4 ♗b7
We have seen this Queen's Indian deployment against the London System already in Game 62, Torre-Przepiórka, Marienbad 1925.

4.♘bd2 e6 5.e3 c5
By far the most common move here has been 5...♗e7, played about 62% of the time, starting with E. Cohn-Barasz, Breslau 1912, and by Réti and Przepiórka at Marienbad 1925. Later Kasparov would play it in two 1998 internet blitz games. This game seems to be the first instance of the text move; it would next occur in Tarrasch-Réti, Semmering 1926, and appear in about 14% of London System games. In a close opening like this, such minor difference are not usually important, the lines often transposing one to another.

6.♗d3 d5 7.c3 ♘bd7 8.0–0 ♗e7
Spielmann by this time no longer went in for wild gambits; his play here is sound and conservative. Interestingly

though, this position would not recur until Glienke-Yusupov, Plovdiv 1983.

9.♘e5
The first aggressive move.

9...♘×e5

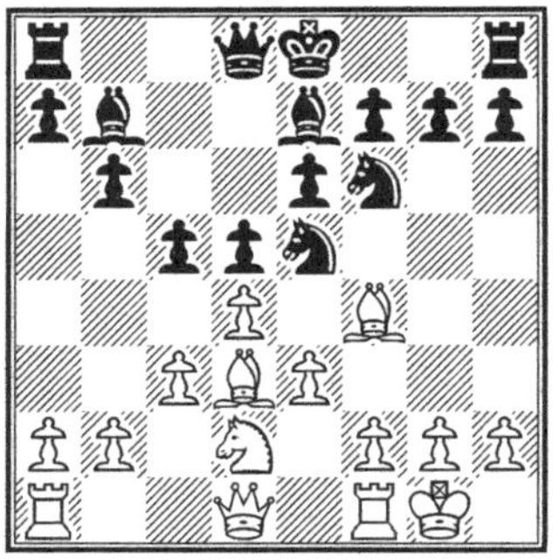

10.♗×e5
Stockfish prefers 10.d×e5 by about a half-pawn. Experience with it is scant; we found only one game with master-strength opponents, Dawidow-Talla, Czech Team Ch 2006, where play continued 10.d×e5 ♘d7 11.♗g3 h5 12.h3 ♕c7 13.f4 0–0–0 14.♕e2 h4 15.♗h2 f5 16.e×f6 g×f6 with a draw in 32 moves.

10...0–0 11.♕f3
With this Torre starts pursuing a kingside attack, intending to threaten h7 with Queen and Bishop, followed by f2-f4 and a Rook lift. However, this goal proves to be a mirage.

11...♘d7 12.♕h3
Continuing the plan of attack, but it may have been better to preserve the Bishop with 12.♗f4 or 12.♗g3.

12...f5!
By far the best defense against the mate threat, much better than 12...g6 or 12...h6.

13.f4?!
13.♗f4 was still preferable.

13...♘×e5 14.f×e5

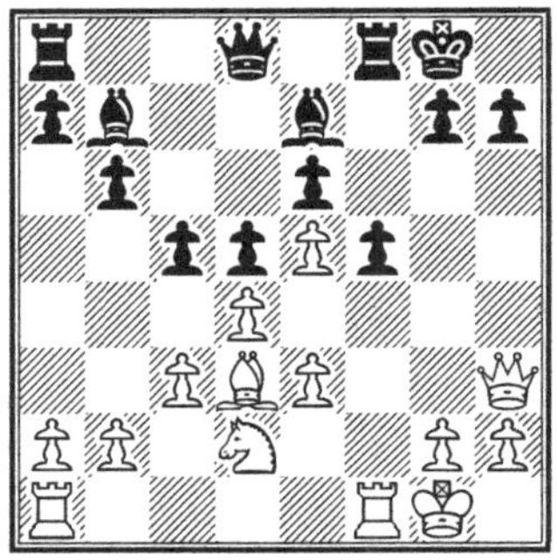

Torre has accomplished the initial deployment of his intended attack, getting a half-open f-file and a restrictive advanced pawn at e5. We saw Tore use this formation successfully against Levenfish in Game 67, and it would work out beautifully a few rounds later against Verlinsky, but here it is ineffective, mainly because of Black's solid pawn at f5.

14...♕e8!
A strong move, readying the Queen to play actively on either flank.

15.♖f3?!
A waste of time. Better 15.♗e2 or 15.♘f3. And definitely not 15.g4?, trying to challenge the f-pawn, due to 15...♕g6!∓.

15...h5!

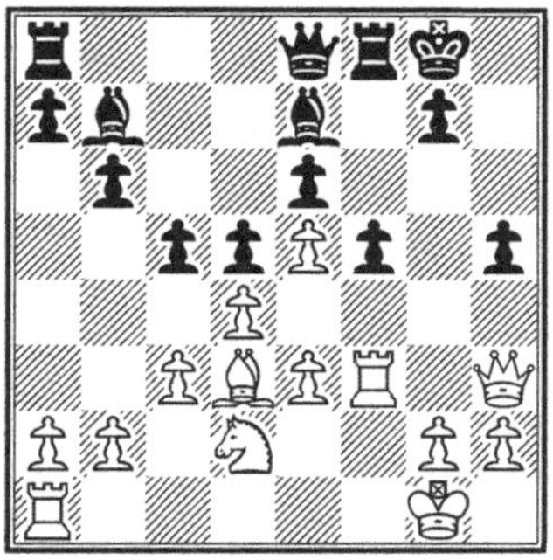

Outstanding. This turns White's would-be attackers into targets threatened by a kingside pawn advance. The game now begins to favor Black (-0.73/26).

16.♖f2

A regrettable but necessary retreat. Trying to press the attack would backfire, *e.g.* 16.♖af1 g5 17.♕g3 h4 18.♕e1 ♕h5∓, or 16.♖g3? g5

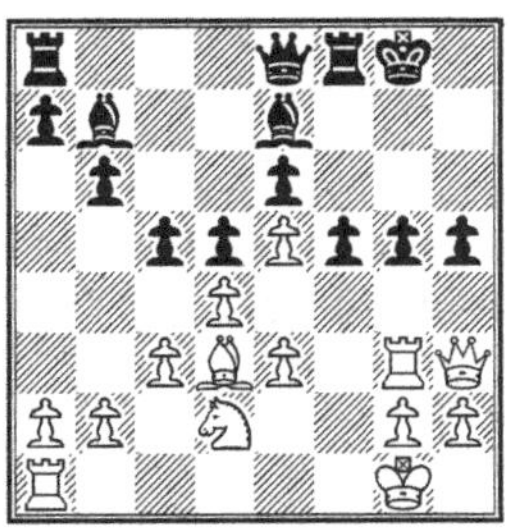

a nd to save his Queen White must give up the Rook: 17.♖×g5+ ♗×g5 18.♕g3 ♕g6 19.h4 ♗×e3+ 20.♕×e3.

16...g5 17.g3 g4 18.♕f1 c4

It is not clear why Spielmann committed to this queenside lockdown at this point. 19.d×c5? would have been bad for White, so there was no reason not to keep the queenside options open for the time being. Black does gain some space, but it is rather sterile space that he cannot utilize effectively as yet. Better, say, 18...♗g5 or 18...a5.

19.♗c2 b5 20.h3

To divert Black's forces from the queenside, Torre opens the h-file.

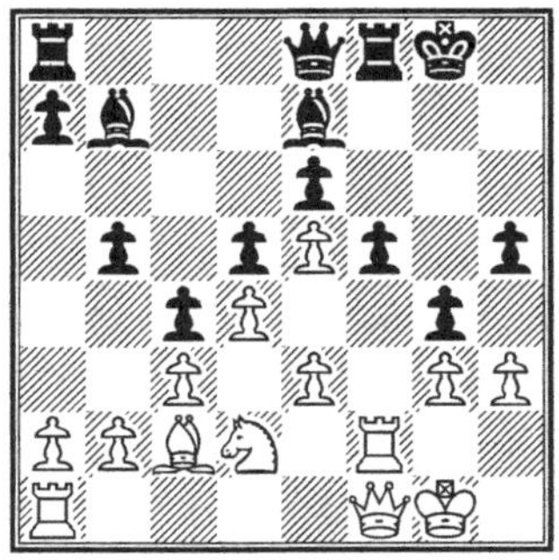

20...♕g6

If now 20...b4?! 21.c×b4 ♗×b4 22.♘b1 ♖b8 23.♘c3 ♗c6 24.h×g4 h×g4 25.♖h2 ♔g7 26.♘e2 ♖h8 27.♘f4 and White is solid enough on both wings (-0.52/25).

21.h×g4

21.h4 locking the kingside would have been OK; there does not seem to be any way that Black then could engineer a serious queenside breakthrough. Torre's pieces, especially his Knight, would be cramped, but his position should prove impregnable (-1.12/27).

21...h×g4 22.♖h2 ♔g7 23.♖e1

The only way to connect the Rooks and not lose control of the h-file.

23...♖h8 24.♖ee2 ♖h6 25.♕e1

♖ah8
Indicating a willingness to trade off all the Rooks. Instead 25...♗g5 would have been only a minor irritant, answered easily by 26.♘f1 or 26.♖×h6 ♕×h6 27.♘f1.

26.♘f1 a5 27.a3 ♗c6 28.♖×h6 ♖×h6 29.♖h2 ♖×h2 30.♘×h2 ♕h6 31.♘f1 ♕h8 32.♕d1 ½-½
So the last meeting between Torre and Spielmann proves rather an anti-climax.

Game 69,

Zubarev-Torre

Moscow 1925, round 7

Alekhine's Defense [B03]

Muscovite Nikolai Zubarev (1894-1951), once a friend of Alekhine, was important among the early Soviet masters. Of high but not topmost playing rank (his 10th place in the 1923 Soviet Championship and 11th-13th in 1925 were typical), he became an important administrator, helping devise the Soviet title system and working as a deputy to Krylenko in the 1930s. Later he headed a judges' panel for the famous 1945 USA-USSR radio match. In *Soviet Chess 1917-1991*, page 35, Soltis writes "At the board 'he personified common sense,' a cold-blooded rationalist, with high-arching skeptical eyebrows, Panov recalled ... Zubarev followed opening theory rigidly and sought conservative, clear-cut, low-risk plans — but was often helpless when positions became murky or the opening was new to him." We don't know if Soltis had this game in mind when he wrote that last sentence, but it certainly applies.

1.e4 ♘f6
This is the first time Carlos Torre ever played this defense, guided perhaps by the example of Capablanca, who used it in the 4th round to defeat Yates (the only time Capa was ever to use the defense named for his chief rival). Theoretically it was still rather *terra incognita*, the line having had its modern debut only four years earlier in E. Steiner-Alekhine, Budapest 1921.

2.e5 ♘d5 3.d4 d6 4.c4 ♘b6 5.e×d6
Seen first in Drewitt-Stephenson, Hastings 1921-22 (1-0, 39), and soon adopted by Grünfeld, Vukovic, Wolf, Tarrasch, Grigoriev, Opocensky, Spielmann and Maróczy among others. It seems also to have been a favorite of Soviet players at the time, with Bohatirchuk, Rozental, Rabinovich, Levenfish, Ilyin-Zhenevsky and Zubarev all playing it.

5...e×d6

In this exchange line Black may also capture with the c-pawn, *e.g.* 5...c×d6 6.♘f3 g6 7.♗e2 ♗g7 8.0–0 0–0 9.♗e3 ♘c6 10.♘c3 ♗g4=.

6.♗d3

Later theory came to favor 6.♘c3 by a wide margin, with 6.♘f3 a distant second and the text third.

6...♗e7 7.♗e3 d5?!

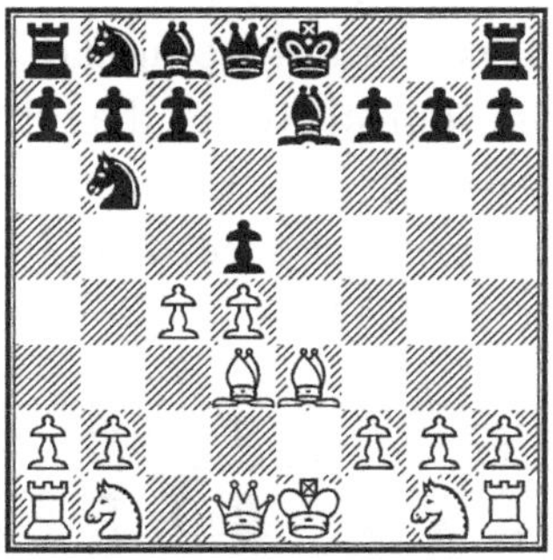

Torre comes up with another radically new move, one without precedent or posterity. CB shows only two other games with this move, from minor events in 2006 and 2012.

The few earlier games in this line saw 7...♘8d7 in Wolf-Grünfeld, Bad Pistyan 1922 (0-1, 50), 7...0–0 in Grigoriev-Vilner, 2nd USSR Ch, Petrograd 1923 (1-0, 38) and Rozental-Romanovsky, 3rd USSR Ch, Moscow 1924 (0-1, 44), and 7...♘6d7 in Levenfish-Réti, Moscow 1925, 3rd round (½-½, 51). 7...♘c6 would eventually become the main line.

8.c5

Zubarev finds the best reply.

8...♘6d7?

This could have landed Torre in serious trouble. Relatively best — and it does not speak well for Torre's novelty that we must already use that phrase — was 8...♘c4 9.♗×c4 d×c4 10.♕a4+ ♕d7 11.♕×c4 ♕e6 and White stands better after 12.♕×e6 ♗×e6 13.♘c3 (+0.72/25), though Black has some compensation for the lost pawn.

If this is the best that be expected from 7...d5, it explains why it was hardly ever played again. But perhaps Torre knew of Zubarev's slavish adherence to established theory, and so wanted to try something completely unorthodox, even if unsound.

9.♘f3 ♘f6

The Knight has gone a long way only to return to its natural square.

10.b4

Unnecessary and pointless. This might be desirable if Black plays ...b7-b6, but otherwise it can wait. White's advantage is his lead in development, and best were the natural developing moves 10.♘c3 or 10.0–0, or the prophylactic 10.h3, all rated about +1.50.

10...0–0 11.♕c2 ♖e8 12.♘bd2

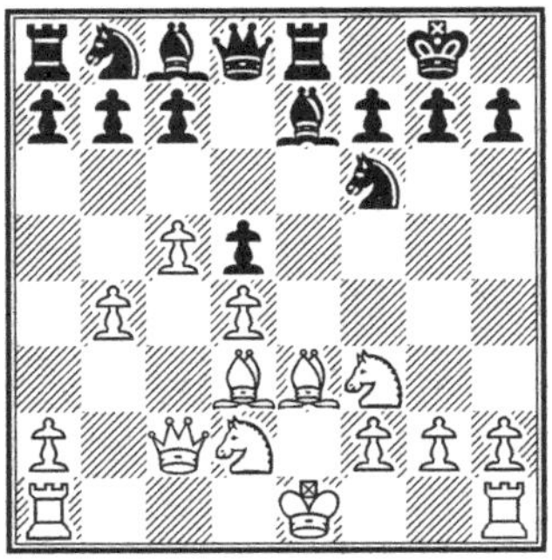

12...♗g4?

If this were poker, we would have to say that Torre just made a big raise on a nothing hand.

Best, to capitalize on White's poor 10th move, was 12...♘c6 13.a3 (not 13.b5?! ♘b4∓) 13...♘g4 and White's advantage is much reduced after 14.0–0 ♘×e3 15.f×e3 g6 (+0.63/24), or if 14.b5 ♘×e3 15.f×e3 ♗h4+ (if 15...♘b8? 16.♗×h7+ ♔h8 17.♘e5 +2.64/26) 16.g3 (not 16.♘×h4?? ♕×h4+ 17.♔d1 ♖×e3–+) 16...♘×d4□ 17.♘×d4 ♗g5 18.♘f1 ♕f6 19.0–0–0 g6 when the material balance favors White, but Black, with luck, may be able to net enough from the muddy waters to compensate for his sacrificed piece (+0.93/29).

13.♘e5

Torre in the *ACB* wrote "Herr Subarew *[sic; the* ACB *favored German-style transliterations]* has played very ably in the manner advocated by Lasker. But now he wants to choke Black too quickly. With Castling he would retain a very fine game." In the tournament book Romanovsky gave 13.0–0 ♗h5 14.♘e5 c6 15.b5 as equal; Stockfish says actually about +2.00. But much stronger is 15.f4! ♘bd7 16.h3 (△17.g4) 16...♘×e5 17.d×e5 d4 18.e×f6 d×e3 19.f×e7 ♖×e7 20.♘f3+–.

13...♘c6 14.♖b1?

This turns the game around completely. Correct was 14.♘×c6 b×c6 15.0–0 with still a big advantage for White (+1.50/32).

14...♘×e5 15.d×e5 d4!

"With his natural combinative talent, Torre quickly seizes the initiative" (Romanovsky). This is the only move that retains Black's newfound advantage.

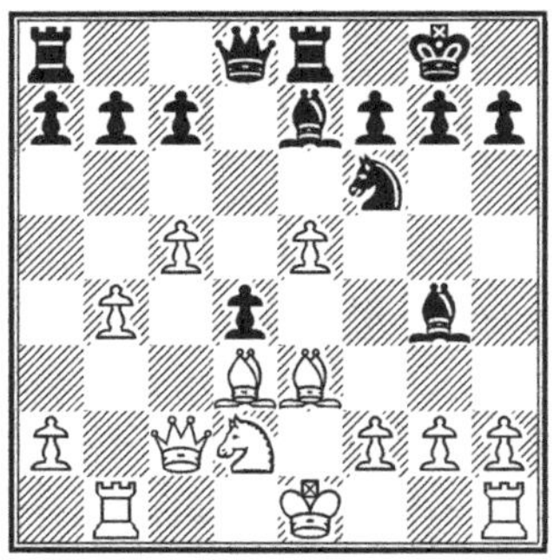

16.e×f6?!

Compounding the previous error. Less bad was 16.♘c4 d×e3 17.♘×e3 ♗×c5! (not 17...♘d5? 18.♗×h7+ ♔h8 19.♘×g4 g6 20.♗×g6 f×g6 21.♖d1 ♕d7 22.♕×g6±) 18.b×c5 ♖×e5 19.0–0 ♗c8 (-1.62/25).

16...d×e3 17.f×e3

Not 17.f×e7?? e×d2+ 18.♔×d2 ♕×e7–+. Even worse is 17.♗×h7+?? ♔h8 18.f×g7+ ♔×g7 19.f×e3 ♗h4+ 20.♔f1 (if 20.g3 ♖×e3+ 21.♔f1 ♕f6+ and mate soon.) 20...♕f6+ 21.♘f3 ♖×e3 (-11.00).

17...♗×f6

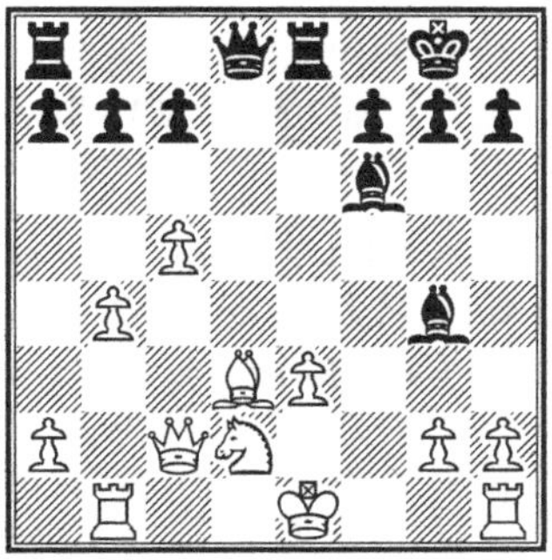

An amazing position. Material is even, and White still has time to castle, but Black is winning because his Bishops sweep the board, and even on g1 White's King will be none too safe because of his e-pawn's imminent demise and his complete lack of an f-pawn.

18.♗×h7+

The h-pawn is fool's gold, but White was lost anyway. Only slightly less bad was 18.♘c4 b5 19.c×b6 c×b6 20.0–0 ♖c8 (-3.86/23).

18...♔h8

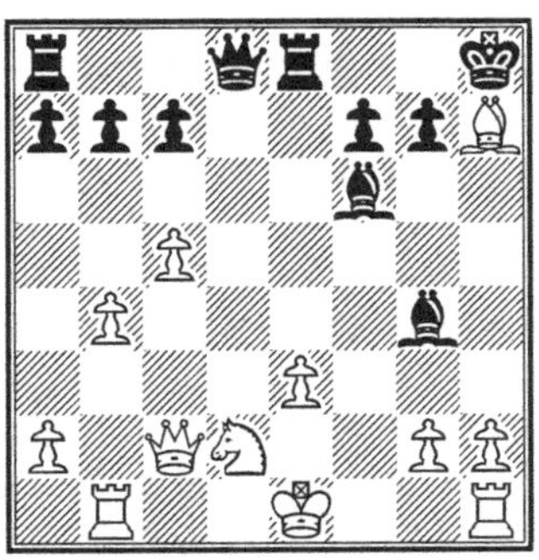

19.0–0

There is nothing better. If 19.♗e4 ♗h4+ and either 20.g3 f5! 21.0–0 ♗g5 22.♗×f5 ♗×e3+ 23.♔h1 ♕d5+ 24.♗e4 ♕×d2–+, or 20.♔f1 ♕g5 21.♖b3 ♖×e4! 22.♕×e4 ♖d8 23.♘f3 ♖d1+ 24.♔e2 ♖×h1 (-8.69).

19.♘e4 turns out much the same way: 19...♗h4+ 20.g3 f5 21.0–0 (21.♘f2?? ♖×e3+ 22.♔f1 ♕d5 -10.92) 21...f×e4 22.♗×e4 ♗g5–+. And if 19.♖b3 g6 20.♗×g6 f×g6 21.♕×g6 ♗h4+ 22.g3 ♕g5!! 23.♕d3 ♖ad8 24.♕c3+ ♔h7 25.0–0 ♕g6 26.e4 ♗h3 27.♖e1 (27.♖f2? ♖×e4!) 27...♗f6 etc. (-5.33).

19...♖×e3 20.♖f4

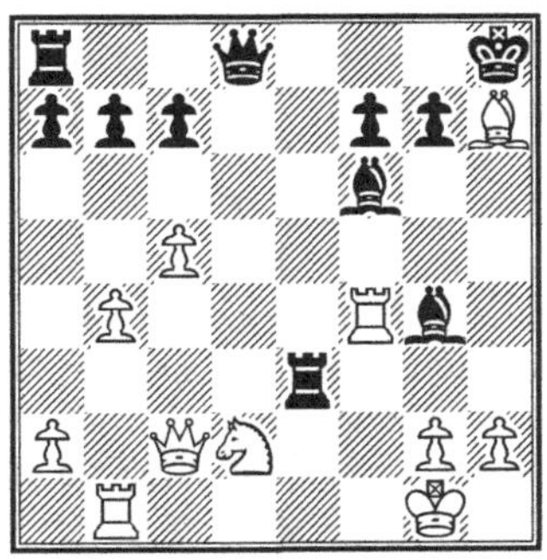

20...♖e2?

Having conducted the attack perfectly since move 14, Torre now errs in a way that could have thrown the win away. There were several winning moves, the best being 20...♖c3! and if

(a) 21.♕e4 ♕×d2 22.♖×g4 ♖e3 23.♕f5 and simplest is 23...♖e1+ 24.♖×e1 ♕×e1+ 25.♕f1 ♕×f1+ 26.♔×f1 ♔×h7–+; or

(b) 21.♕b2 ♖d3! and the best White has is 22.♕×f6 g×f6 23.♗×d3 ♕×d3

24.♖×g4 ♕×d2 leaving Black up ♕-for-♖.

21.♖×g4??

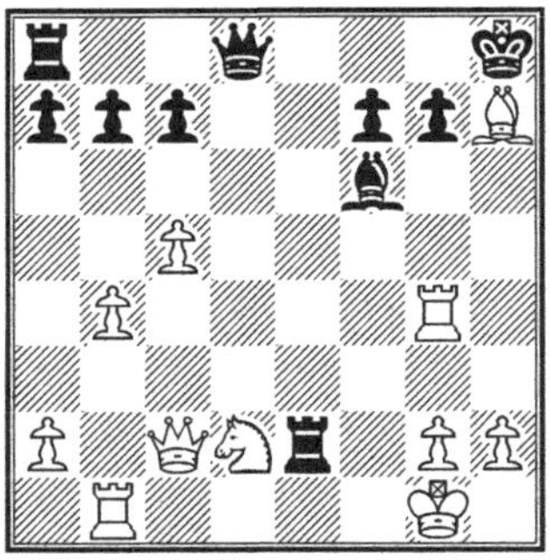

Losing the game all over again. With 21.♗d3! White might yet salvage a draw. Best play continues 21...♖e3 22.♘e4 ♕d4 23.♔h1□ ♖×d3 24.♖×g4 ♖d8 25.♖f1 ♖d1 26.♖gf4□ ♖×f1+ 27.♖×f1 ♗e7,

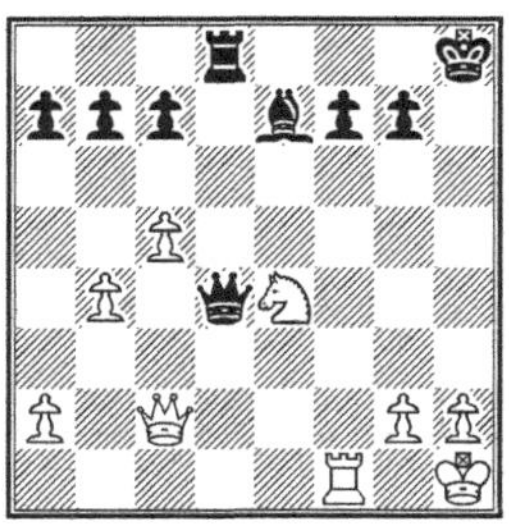

and now White has several playable lines, chief of which are:

(a) 28.h3 ♔g8 (28...♕×b4? 29.♖×f7) 29.♕b3 ♕d5 30.♕×d5 ♖×d5 and Black's only advantage is having ♗-for-♘ in an open position (-0.66);

(b) 28.a3 ♔g8 29.h3 ♖d5 30.♘c3 ♕c4 31.♖e1 ♗f8 (31...♗f6?? 32.♖e8#) 32.♖e3 (-0.95/27);

(c) 28.♘g3!? ♕×b4 29.♕e2 ♕×c5 30.♘f5 ♗g5 (if 30...♗f6?? 31.♕h5+ ♔g8 32.♘h6+ g×h6 33.♕×c5+−) 31.♕h5+ ♗h6 32.♕h4! ♕f8 33.♕g3 c5 34.h3 and though Black is two pawns up, Stockfish sees little prospect of him winning (-0.74/34).

Returning to the game (**21.♖×g4??**):

21...♖×d2 22.♕f5 ♖d1+ 23.♖×d1 ♕×d1+ 24.♔f2

Not 24.♕f1?? ♕×g4.

24...♖d8

Also very strong were 24...♖e8 or 24...♕d2+ 25.♔f3 ♕h6.

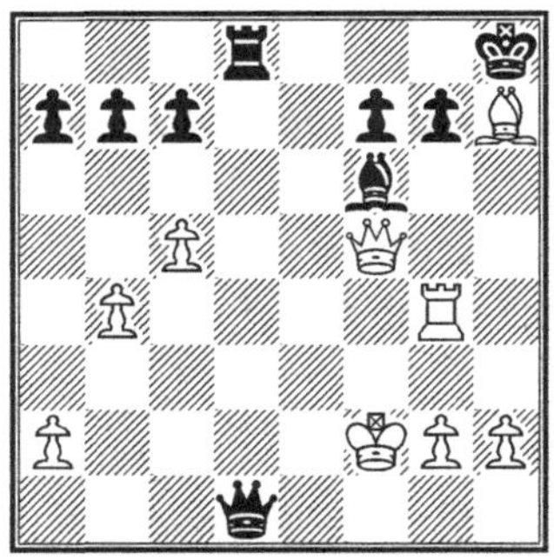

25.♖e4

Making it all the easier for Black, and unfortunately consigning a lovely variation to the notes: 25.♕h5 ♖d2+ 26.♔g3 ♖×g2+!! 27.♔×g2 ♕e2+ 28.♔h1 ♕f3+ 29.♔g1 ♗d4+ 30.♖×d4 ♕×h5−+.

25...♖d2+

Best, forcing mate in at most 14. Now come a few repetitious moves to gain clock time.

26.♔g3 ♖d3+ 27.♔f2 ♖d2+ 28.♔g3 ♖d3+ 29.♔f2 ♗h4+!

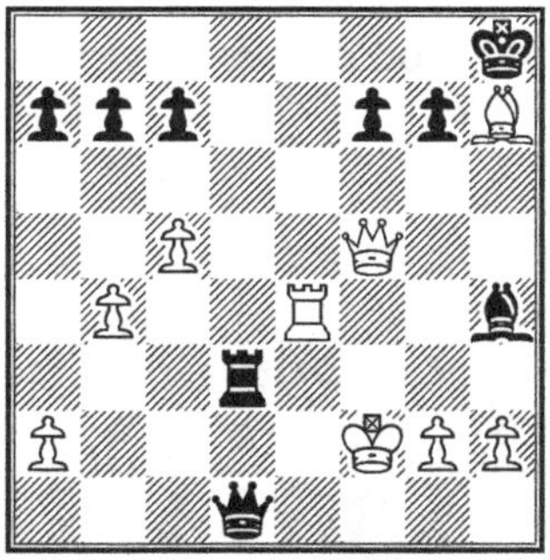

30.♖×h4

Somewhat longer resistance (mate in 8 instead of 4) was offered by 30.g3 ♖d2+ 31.♔e3 ♖e2+ 32.♔f3 ♖×h2+ 33.♔e3 ♕d2+ 34.♔f3 ♕f2+ 35.♔g4 ♕×g3+ 36.♔h5 ♗f6+ 37.♕h3 ♕g5#.

30...♕c2+

Missing the quick mate by 30...♕d2+ 31.♔f1 ♕c1+ 32.♔e2 ♕e3+ 33.♔f1 ♖d1#. But it hardly matters; the text wins the white Queen, and the rest is just unnecessary agony for White.

31.♔g1 ♖d1+ 32.♕f1 ♖×f1+ 33.♔×f1 ♕d1+ 34.♔f2 ♕d2+ 35.♔f1 g5 36.♖h3 ♔g7 37.a3 g4 38.♖h4 f5 39.g3 ♕d3+ 40.♔g1 ♕d1+ 41.♔f2 ♕f3+ 42.♔e1 ♕×a3 43.♖h5 ♕×b4+ 44.♔d1 ♕a4+ 45.♔c1 ♕e8 46.♖h4 ♕e3+ 47.♔b1 ♕×c5 48.♖h5 ♕b5+ 0-1

This game followed a pattern seen before against Dus-Chotimirsky and Levenfish: Torre attempts a dubious opening experiment or some risky middle-game moves and gets into a bad or even losing position, but one full of complications his opponent proves unable to fathom. A mistake or two is then all Torre needs to win. The resemblance to the play of the young Mikhail Tal is considerable. But how long could Torre get away with such risks? Would they work against the likes of Capablanca and Lasker?

Game 70

Torre-Sämisch

Moscow 1925, round 8

Torre Attack [A46]

This third and final encounter with Sämisch stands in sharp contrast to the other two. At Baden-Baden and Marienbad, Torre had taken wild chances in the opening and got himself into lost positions, but time pressure or clock-induced errors forced Sämisch to accept draws. But in this game we see a rather quiet opening and only one risky move by Torre. Another draw seemed likely, when Sämisch blundered in an even position, and Torre pounced. The flawed analysis by Bogoljubow at move 16 is a point of interest. We also found that this game was analyzed by Savielly Tartakower for the Russian magazine *Shakhmaty*, his notes then being translated into German in the *Wiener Schachzeitung*. These we were able to translate and add here, designated by "ST:".

1.d4 ♘f6 2.♘f3 e6 3.♗g5

ST: The young Mexican's strategy is built on the pursuit of maximum piece pressure. He therefore likes to choose this move, which theory considers less expedient than 3.c4.

3...c5 4.e3 ♘c6

Sharpest is 4...♕b6, for example 5.♘bd2 ♕×b2 6.♗d3 d5 7.c4 ♕c3 (△7...♕a3) 8.♘e5 ♘c6 9.♖c1 ♕a3=, Spassky-Miles, Tilburg 1978 (½-½, 37). On the other hand, a more sound, conservative continuation is 4...♗e7, as played by Lasker against Torre in round 12 (Game 74).

5.♘bd2 b6

Sämisch continues as he did against Janowski at Marienbad, as Taimanov would against Petrosian in the 1960 Leningrad Ch, and Caruana would against Hoang in the Mitropa Cup, Szeged 2007.

ST: A favorite deployment of the young German master, although in this position the transition to orthodox lines with 5.d5 seems easier.

6.c3 ♗b7 7.♗d3 c×d4 8.e×d4 ♗e7 9.♘c4

ST: A fine maneuver. White threatens 10.♗×f6, which would worsen Black's pawn position (10...g×f6) because 10...♗×f6 would have the fatal consequence 11. ♘d6+. Also with the text White prepares to occupy the strategically important point e5.

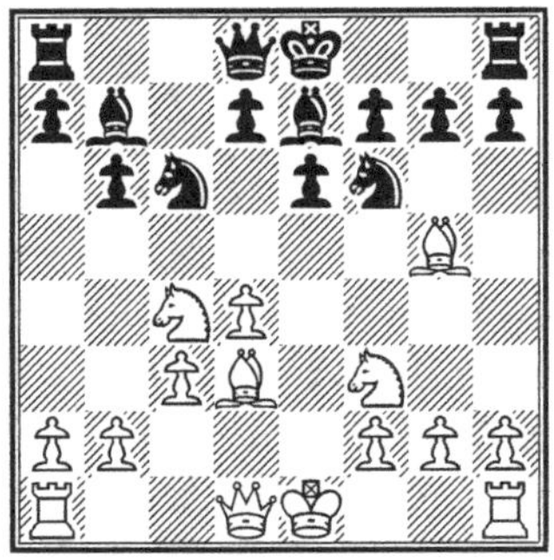

9...♕c7 10.♕d2

To enable ♗g5-f4.

10...♖c8 11.0–0 h6?!

Beginning an unnecessary and ultimately fatal weakening of the kingside. Better 11...♘d5 or 11...0–0.

ST: An offensive defense begins.

12.♗f4 d6

ST: In contrast to White's optimistic play, Black presents a cramped, cumbersome structure, entirely in the hypermodern spirit, whereby he still holds in his hands the key to the strategically important points.

13.♖fe1 ♘d8

ST: Tartakower quotes Réti: "A good move. The Queen's Bishop and Queen's Rook get open views, and the Knight covers the threatened points e6 and f7 on d8."

14.♕d1

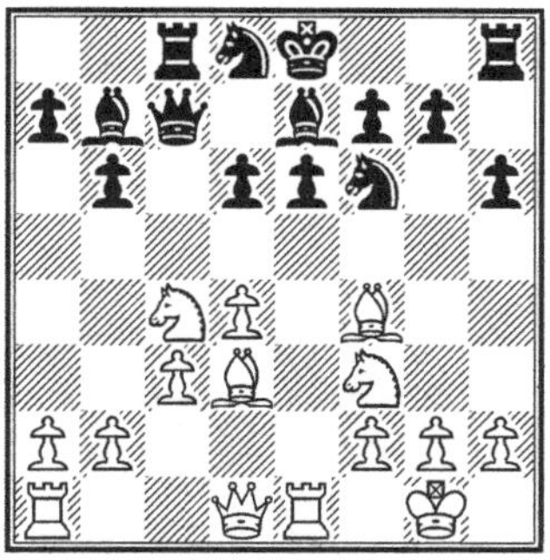

So that the Queen can recapture in the event of ...♗b7×f3.

14...♘d5 15.♗g3 0–0

ST: Better late than never. In anticipation of this moment, White now starts the direct attack.

16.♘h4?!

The aforementioned risky move. Better 16.h3, 16.a4, 16.♕e2, or 16.♘e3, all about +0.50 or better.

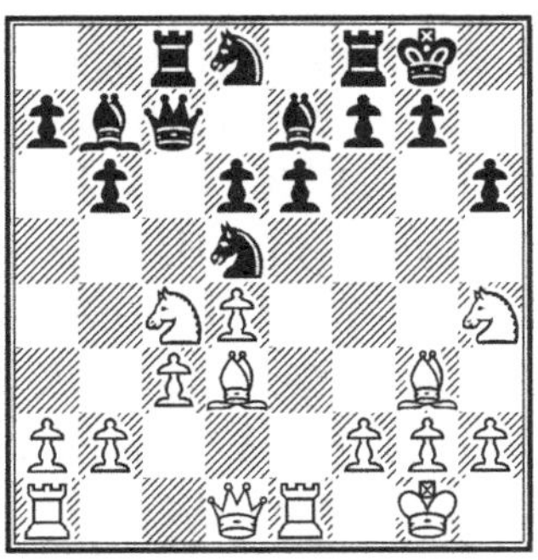

In the tournament book, Bogoljubow commented: "White has set an unusual trap with the move 16.♘h4. If now 16...♗×h4 17.♗×h4 ♘f4, Torre would not have continued with 18.♘e3, but rather with 18.♕g4!! ♘×d3 19.♗f6 g5 (if 19...g6, then 20.♕h4 ♔h7 21.♘e3!+–) 20.♕h5 ♔h7 21.♗×g5 f6, and from here Torre would surely have found the winning line." Bogo's analysis is badly flawed. After 16...♗×h4 17.♗×h4 ♘f4 his "!!" move 18.♕g4 turns out to be nothing brilliant,

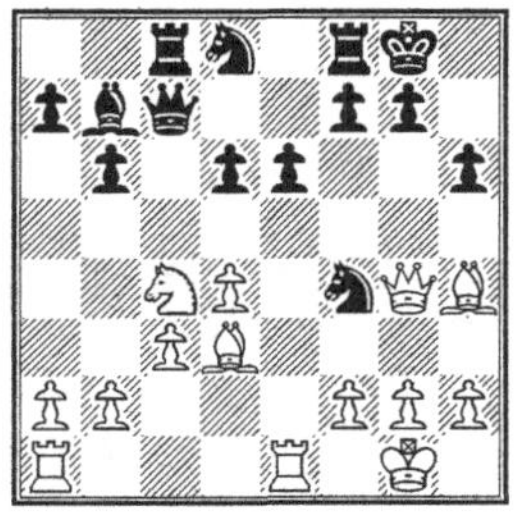

if instead of 18...♘×d3? Black meets it by 18...e5! 19.♗f6 ♘de6:

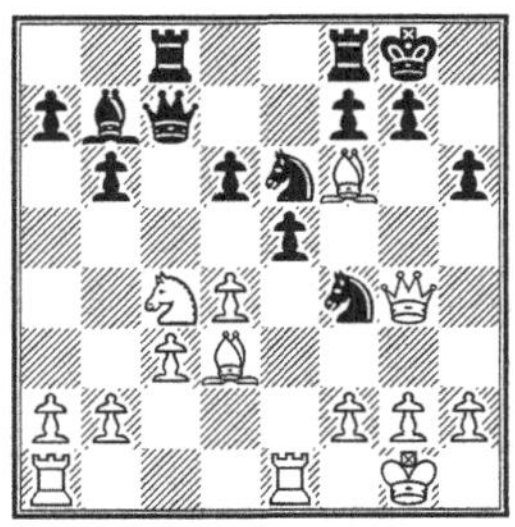

If now 20.♗f1? h5! 21.♕g3 ♔h8 22.♗g5 ♘×g5 23.♕×g5 f6 24.♕g3 ♗×g2 25.♗×g2 ♕×c4 (-3.13/27).

Therefore White must enter a very long forced line: 20.♘×d6 ♕×d6 21.♗×e5 f5 22.♗×f5 ♕d5 23.f3 ♖×f5 24.♕×f5 ♘×g2! 25.♔×g2 ♖f8 26.♕e4 ♕d7 27.d5 ♘g5 28.♕g4 ♕×d5 29.♖ad1 ♕f7 30.♖e3 ♗×f3+ 31.♖×f3 ♘×f3 32.♗d6 h5 33.♕e4 ♘h4+ 34.♔h3 ♖e8 35.♕d5 ♘f5 36.♕×f7+ ♔×f7, with a probable draw (-0.47/26).

However, there are so many hard-to-find, counter-intuitive moves in that line it seems very unlikely that human players could work their way through it with neither making a fatal misstep. In any event, it does show that, *pace* Bogoljubow, White has no forced win after 18.♕g4 e5!.

To examine Bogoljubow's line further, after 18.♕g4 ♘xd3?? 19.♗f6 g5?? (19...g6 is less bad),

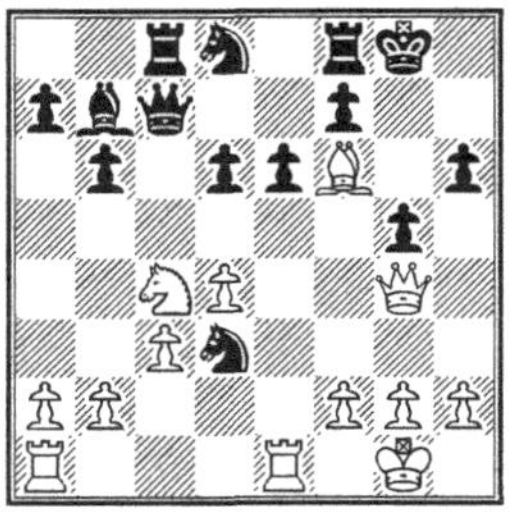

correct is 20.♕h3 ♕c6 21.♘e3 ♔h7 22.♗xg5 etc., winning. Bogo's 20.♕h5? ♔h7 21.♗xg5 hits a snag if instead of 21...f6? Black plays 21...♖h8! 22.♖e3 ♔g7 23.♖g3 hxg5 24.♖xg5+ ♔f8 25.♕xh8+ ♔e7 and Black may yet survive (+1.11/25).

From the diagram after **16.♘h4** we return to the game:

16...g5?!

A move only mildly bad, but if Black did not want to venture into the complications of 16...♗xh4, better was 16...♕c6, threatening 17...♗xh4 18.♗xh4 ♘xc3, which would have forced the Knight right back to f3, or the ♗d3 back to f1, with no further weakening of Black's kingside.

ST: A complete role reversal! Black impetuously chases away the uninvited guest.

17.♕h5

ST: Splendidly Answered!

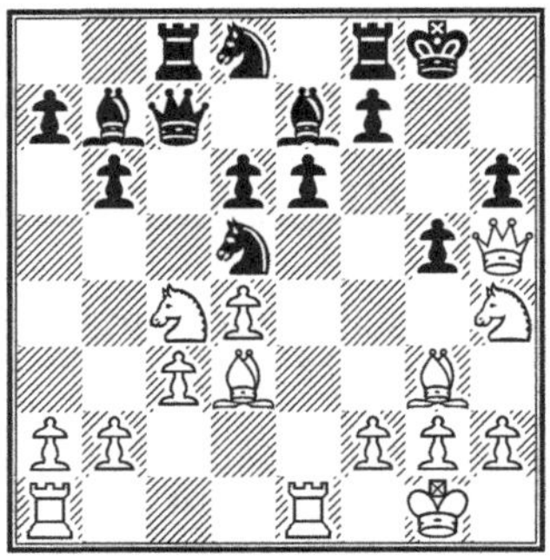

17...♔g7??

Necessary was 17...gxh4 18.♕xh6 f5!□ and White has nothing better than drawing by 19.♕g6+ ♔h8 20.♕h6+ etc. Now Torre concludes with a nice combination.

ST: It is an old failing of Sämisch that a small distraction disturbs the depth of his ideas so much. He who has said A must also say B. After the obvious reply 17...gxh4, White would have faced a difficult dilemma. He could either play for perpetual check: 18.♕xh6 f5 19.♕g6+ ♔h8 20.♕h6+ etc., or he had to consider and calculate a series of sacrifices which, however, would not have resulted in anything clear: 18.♕xh6 f5, 19.♖xe6 ♘xe6 20.♕xe6+ ♖f7, or 18.♖xe6 ♘xe6, 19.♕f5 ♘f6 20.♗xh4 ♘g7 and Black is rescued. The unfortunate text is followed by a thunderous finale.

18.♖×e6!! ♘×e6
If 18...♖h8 19.♖×h6 ♖×h6 20.♘f5+ ♔f8 21.♕×h6+ ♔e8 22.♘f×d6+ ♗×d6 23.♘×d6+ ♔d7 24.♕f8 and Stockfish announces mate in 17.

19.♘f5+ ♔g8 20.♘×h6+ 1-0
ST: After 19.♘f5+ ♔g8 20.♘×h6+ ♔g7 21.♘f5+ ♔g8 22.♘×e7+ ♔g7 23.♘×c8 ♖×c8 24.♘×d6 Black loses all his moveable goods. (Tartakower's line can be improved slightly at move 23 with the following forced mate: 23.♘f5+ ♔g8 24.♘c×d6 ♘df4 25.♗×f4 ♗e4 26.♗×e4 f6 27.♘h6+ ♔g7 28.♘df5+ ♔h8 29.♘f7+ ♔g8 30.♘5h6+ ♔g7 31.♕g6#.)

At the end of this round, Dr. Lasker commented: "These first steps of the young Torre are undoubtedly the first steps of a future world champion." The term "first steps" was highly appropriate, for Carlos Torre was still very much a work in progress, and his play still suffered from some obvious defects, which only time and experience could eliminate.

What were Torre's defects and weaknesses? Firstly, his poor preparation in the opening. It was clear that he still had found no sure and dependable defense against 1.d4. His constant improvisations and experiments showed that he still felt unsure of himself in this part of the game. Secondly, his sense of danger, a talent essential in top-rank competition, was insufficiently developed; too often he failed to discern dangerous possibilities that needed to be forestalled in advance, for example with Haida, Levenfish, and his first two games with Sämisch. Conversely, he sometimes failed to see attacking opportunities, *e.g.* with Opocensky, Dus-Chotimirsky, Levenfish again, and the second Grünfeld game. Another defect perhaps was his overly stereotyped play with the white pieces. He had not developed a sufficient variety of different schemes and systems of attack. Finally, he still needed to restrain his impetuosity and his desire to resolve every situation by tactical means, though if this was a defect it was one he held in common with other great players, such as the young Alekhine, Tal, and Kasparov.

In the ninth round of the Moscow tournament, the two front-runners, Torre, with a 6-1 score (five wins and two draws), and Bogoljubow at 6-2 (five wins, two draws, and a loss to Réti), faced each other. It was, therefore, a game of great importance. A win by Torre would in effect give him a more than one-point lead over his nearest rival, as he had already had the bye while Bogoljubow had not. After those two came Lasker, followed by Rubinstein, and the rest of the field. Capablanca stood well back (4½-3½, +2 -1 =5), though everyone expected he would make a closing rush as he did at New York 1924. However, the Bogoljubow game clearly pointed up other deficiencies in Torre's play.

Game 71

Bogoljubow-Torre

Moscow 1925, round 9

Queen's Pawn, Double Fianchetto Defense [A50]

Efim Dimitrijevic Bogoljubow (1889-1952, historical Elo 2610, GM title 1951), by birth a Ukrainian and subject of the Russian Tsar, was probably the most eminent "graduate" of the "Mannheim school." For him, more than anyone else, that 1914 tournament, and his subsequent internment as an enemy alien, constituted a turning point, as he won five of the eight tournaments staged by the internees, and attained the form that made him one of the world's top six players in the 1920s. Prior to the Moscow tournament he won the 1924 and 1925 Soviet Championships, but he soon came to feel his career was being hampered by Soviet officials. In 1926 he went back to Germany, where he already had a wife, and never returned to the USSR. Though his peak passed with his 1929 world championship loss to Alekhine, and his memory was sullied (mostly undeservedly) by association with the Nazis in the 1930s and '40s, Bogoljubow at Moscow 1925 was at the peak of his powers, playing in a style both positionally sound and tactically aggressive. He represented a very formidable adversary for the young Carlos Torre.

1.d4 ♘f6 2.♘f3 b6 3.c4 ♗b7 4.♘c3 g6

The double fianchetto, as we have seen a favorite of Torre's. Still, it would have been sounder to remain within normal Queen's Indian lines by 4...e6, so as to retain the option of contesting the e4 square by ...♗f8-b4 and/or ...d7-d5. The text had been seen twice before, in Réti-Blümich, Breslau 1925 (½-½, 63), and three rounds earlier at Moscow, in Réti-Zubarev (½-½, 61). It never gained much of a following, though it was played five times by the 2765-rated Shakhriyar Mamedyarov against comparably rated GMs in a 2014 blitz event in Beijing.

5.g3

White might have sought to capitalize on Black's 4th move more directly by 5.♕c2, intending a quick e2-e4. That and 5.d5 have been the usual replies since this game.

5...♗g7 6.♗g2 ♘e4

Torre again breaks new ground. Unlike some of his novelties, Stockfish actually considers this best. It would be seen later in games by such GMs as Portisch, Matanovic, Speelman, Tiviakov, and I. Sokolov, and it shows a plus score in the games on ChessBase, +16 -13 =23.

7.♕d3

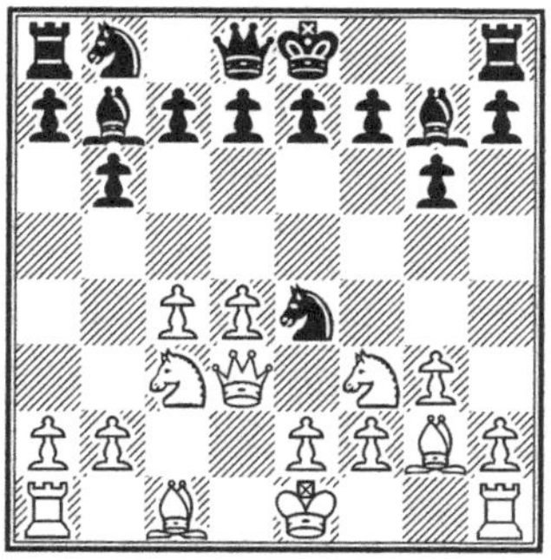

7...♘×c3

Best. 7...f5? runs into difficulties after 8.♘g5, when Black is forced into 8...♘c5 (of course not 8...♘×g5?? 9.♗×b7+−) 9.d×c5 ♗×g2 10.♖g1 ♗c6 11.g4! h6 12.♘f3 ♘a6□ 13.g×f5 ♘×c5 14.♕c2 g5 15.♘d5±.

8.b×c3 d6 9.h4

An instructive move, taking advantage of the fact that Black's ♘f6 has disappeared, thereby leaving his kingside more vulnerable. If Black tries to prevent further advance of the pawn by 9...h5?! he allows White an outpost at g5.

9...♘d7 10.h5 e5!

So far Torre is finding optimal moves in his new variation. The game is quite even.

11.♗g5 f6

White probably had hoped to provoke this reply with his 11th move. It weakens Black's support for his beleaguered g-pawn, but is still best if followed up properly. The alternative 11...♕c8, though playable, takes Black's Queen out of the game for a while.

12.♗d2 ♕e7

12...e4 accomplishes nothing after 13.♕e3.

13.h6

Ending the pressure on the g-pawn anyway.

13...♗f8 14.♕c2

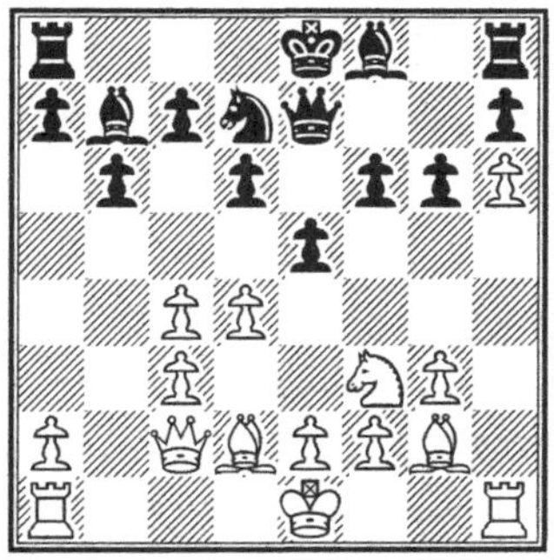

14...♖g8?!

Starting here, and through move 23, Torre plays as if in a daze. This move is the first step of a misconceived plan, intending ...g6-g5 and ...♖g8-g6 to target the h-pawn, which would seem to be easy prey. Yet this plan is time-consuming, and even if successful its fruits would be meager. Also, as will soon be seen, on g8 the Rook may come under attack from the white Queen after ♕c2-b3. Correct was 14...e4! 15.♘h2□ 0–0–0 16.♘g4 f5 17.♘e3 ♕f7 (-0.88/30):

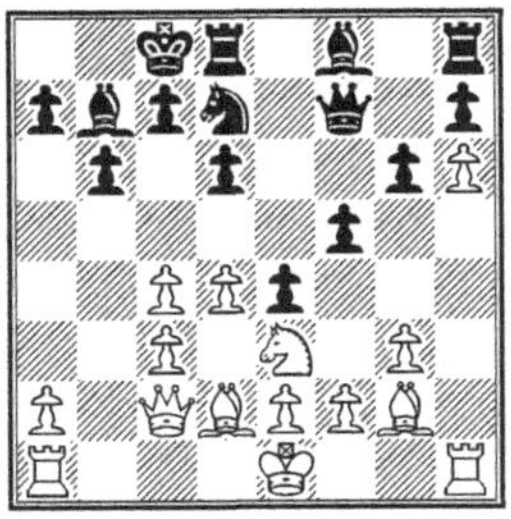

Black would then have several strategic options. For example if he still wanted to target the h-pawn, he could do so by ...♘d7-f6-g8, ...g6-g5 and ...♕f7-f6/g6. Or the King's Bishop could get back into action by ...d6-d5 and ...♗f8-d6, perhaps then intending ...f5-f4.

15.♗e3 a5?!

A move not intrinsically bad, but without apparent purpose, and completely unrelated to any preceding moves. Torre seems to have no clear idea of where to go, and with this and his next two moves he just tacks about randomly. 15...0–0–0 or 15...e4 would have maintained a slight positional edge for Black.

16.♖b1

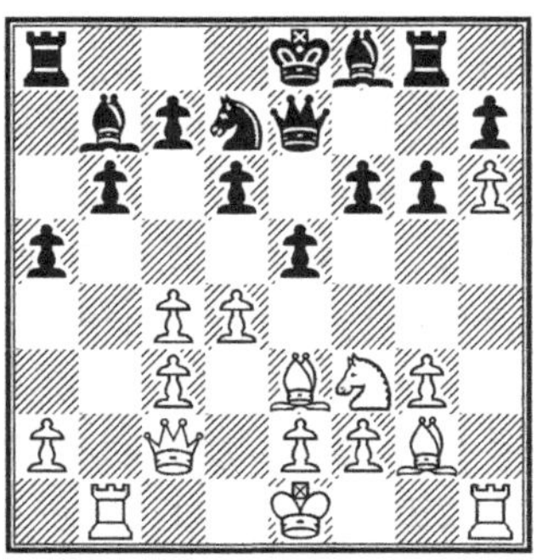

16...♖d8?

From here this Rook will not move for the rest of the game. Correct was 16...0–0–0, after which the Rook can be useful on the e-file. The King, left on e8, is nothing but an obstacle, or worse, a target.

At least Torre avoided the trap Bogoljubow set, the invitation to "win" the Exchange by 16...e×d4 17.c×d4 ♗e4 18.♕a4! ♗×b1? 19.♘d2 ♖c8 20.♘×b1:

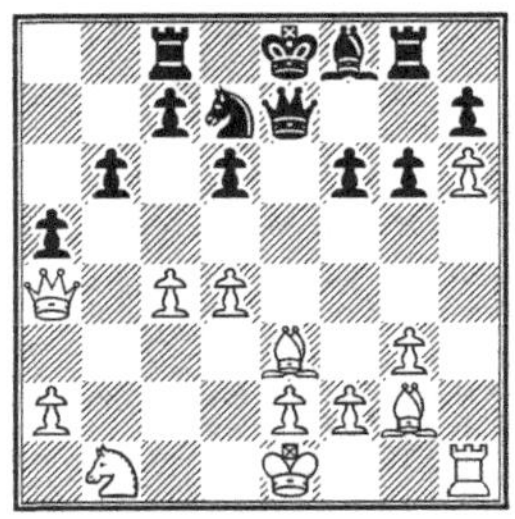

That would afflict Black with a severe case of leucopenia, Hans Kmoch's term for light-square weakness. A sample possibility then (one of the milder ones in fact) is 20...d5 (relatively best) 21.♗d2 (if 21.♗×d5?! ♕b4+ 22.♕×b4 ♗×b4+ 23.♔d1 ♖f8 much of the pressure is relieved) 21...c6 22.c×d5 c5□ (if 22...c×d5?? 23.♗×d5 ♖h8 24.e4 and Stockfish foresees what Harry Truman would call "a rain of ruin" falling on Black along the light-square diagonals and central files (+6.46/25)) 23.♘c3 c×d4 24.♘b5 ♘c5 25.♕c4 ♕d7 26.d6 ♘e6 27.♘c7+ ♖×c7 (27...♘×c7?? 28.♗c6) 28.d×c7 ♗c5 (28...♕×c7?? 29.♕×e6+) 29.♗b7 ♔e7 30.c8♕ ♖×c8 31.♗×c8 ♕×c8 32.♕d5 and White has come out ahead by the Exchange and a dominant position.

17.♕b3 ♗e4

Another seemingly random, unconnected move. As just shown, winning the Exchange is a devil's bargain for Black, even though White prevents it with his next move. Best still was 17...e4 18.♘d2 f5 with a reasonably tenable game (+0.66/77).

The text does at least avoid the Bishop getting shut in on b7 in certain lines, which is probably why Torre played it.

18.♖d1

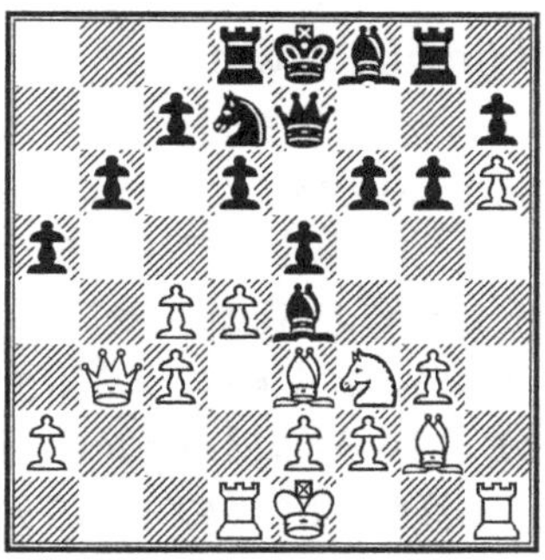

18...g5?

Proceeding belatedly with his original plan, but this is now a definite error. Best was 18...c5 19.♗h3 (19.d5 was not a concern now, with the Bishop outside the black pawns) 19...g5 20.♗g4 ♔f7 (20...f5?? 21.♗h5+) 21.d×e5 ♘×e5□ 22.♘×e5+ d×e5 23.♗h5+ ♗g6 24.♕×b6 ♖×d1+ 25.♔×d1 ♕d6+ 26.♕×d6 ♗×d6, and though Black is nominally down a pawn, he has freed his position, and the extra pawn is of little account because it's doubled, isolated, and blockaded.

19.c5!

Attacking the ♖g8 and forcing Black's reply.

19...d5 20.c×b6 c×b6 21.d×e5 f×e5

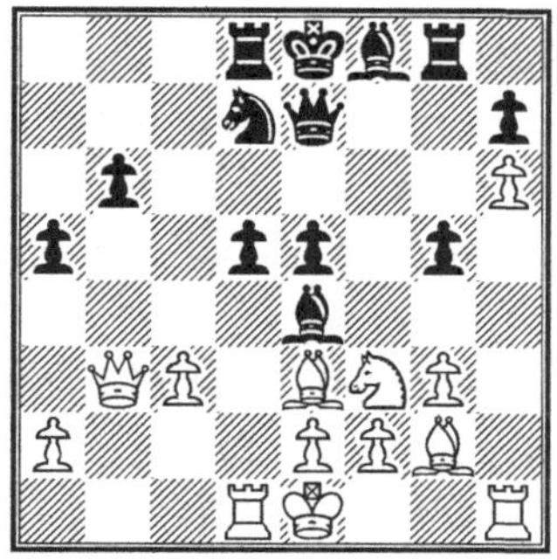

22.♖h5

This is strong, but with the hard-to-find 22.♔f1! White could have started a decisive continuation, *viz.* 22...g4 23.♘e1 ♖g6 (to defend the b-pawn; if instead 23...♗×g2+? 24.♔×g2 and either the d- or b-pawn must fall) 24.♖×d5! ♗×d5 25.♗×d5 ♕f6 26.♗e4 ♗c5 (the ♖g6 has no safe retreat square) 27.♘c2 (27.♘g2 ♔f8 28.♗×g6 is also good) 27...♔f8 28.♖h5! (much stronger than 28.♗×g6) 28...♗×e3:

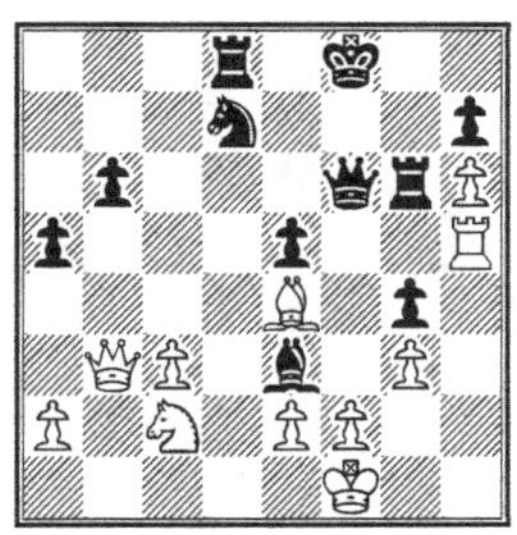

29.♘×e3 (also good is 29.♖f5 ♗c5 30.♕e6 ♗×f2 31.♖×f6+ ♖×f6 32.♕×g4 -2.38/24) 29...♘c5 30.♕b1 ♖g5 31.♖×g5 ♕×g5 32.♗c6 ♕×h6 33.♕×b6 ♕d6 34.♕×a5 with two pawns and other compensation for the Exchange (+2.39/23). However, White's failure to find this line becomes moot after Black's next two moves.

22...♖g6?

Torre continues the downward spiral. Necessary was 22...g4 23.♘h4 ♗×g2 24.♘×g2 ♕f7 25.♖g5 ♖×g5 26.♗×g5 ♖c8 27.♘e3 ♕g8 28.♕×d5 ♕×d5 29.♖×d5 ♖×c3 30.♘×g4 when the ending is likely lost for Black, but he may come up with some drawing chances (+2.04/26).

23.♔f1?!

Bogoljubow must have been under the impression that he had to defend his ♗g2 before capturing on g5. But in fact he could have gone right on ahead: 23.♗×g5 ♖×g5 24.♖×g5 ♗×f3 25.♖g7! (perhaps it was this move that Bogo's calculations missed) 25...♗×g7 26.h×g7 ♘f6 27.♗×f3 ♔f7 28.♗×d5+ ♔×g7 29.c4 with a won game (+2.75/30).

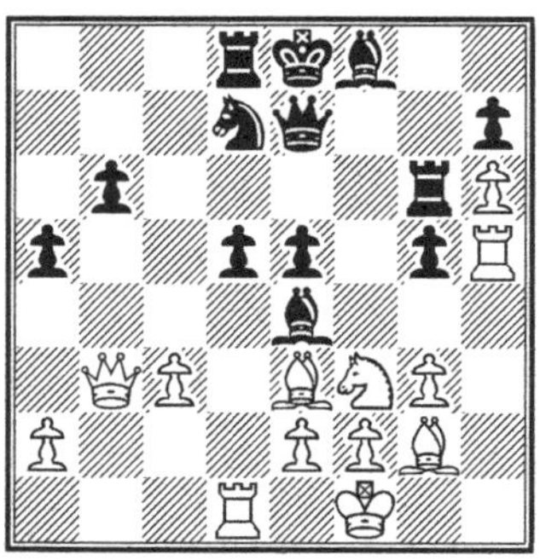

23...♘f6??

But now Torre caps all his previous errors with this blunder. The only hope lay in 23...♗×h6 24.♕b5 ♔f8 25.♘h4! g×h4 26.♗×h6+ ♖×h6 27.♖×h6 ♗c2 (+2.27/26), praying that White might go wrong in the complications, *e.g.* 28.♖×d5 ♕g5 29.♕b2□ ♕×h6 30.♕×c2 h×g3 31.f×g3? [Correct would be 31.♕f5+ ♔e8 32.♗h3 ♕c1+ 33.♔g2 g×f2 34.♕h5+ (34.♔×f2? ♕f4+ 35.♕×f4 e×f4=) 34...♔f8 35.♔×f2 +2.68/24.] 31...♔e7 △32...♖f8+ with a draw.

After the text the evaluation shoots up to about +6.00. Torre must have soon realized he was lost, but he plays on in hope of finding a swindle.

24.♗×g5 ♖×g5 25.♖×g5 ♗×f3 26.♗×f3 ♗×h6 27.♗h5+ ♔f8 28.♖f5 ♕e6 29.♗g4 ♔e7 30.♗h3 ♕d6 31.♕a4 ♘e4 32.♖d3 ♗g7 33.♗g2 ♘f6 34.♕h4 ♕e6 35.♖g5 ♔f7 36.♖f3 h6 37.♕h5+ ♔f8 38.♖×e5 ♕d6 39.♖×d5 ♔g8

A last attempt by Torre to reverse his sinking fortunes. Bogoljubow gave it two exclamation marks in the tournament book.

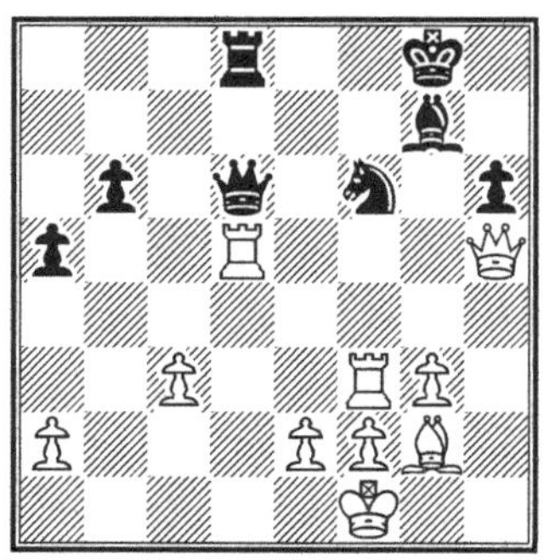

40.♖fd3

The swindle comes after 40.♖×d6?

♖×d6 (△41...♖d1#) 41.♖d3 (41.e4? ♘×h5) 41...♖×d3 42.♗d5+ Forced; if 42.e×d3 ♘×h5 and Black can certainly draw, perhaps even win (-1.46/24). 42...♖×d5 43.♕h3 and with ♖+♗+♘-for-♕, Black should be able to handle White's extra pawns (+1.21/25).
Besides the text, another swindle-avoiding and winning line was 40.♖×f6 ♕×f6 41.♖×d8+ ♕×d8 42.♗d5+ ♔h7 43.c4 and despite the opposite-color Bishops, White's extra pawns win (+8.62/25).

40...♘×d5
Torre wants to keep Queens on the board and avoid the obviously hopeless 40...♘×h5 41.♖×d6 ♖×d6 42.♖×d6, but the text allows White a quick finish.

41.♗×d5+ ♔h8 42.♗e4! ♕f6 43.♕g6! ♔g8 44.♕h7+ 1-0
After 44...♔f8/♔f7 54.♖f3 it's all over.

A disappointing effort by Torre, in which he completely lost the thread of the game during moves 14-23. Playing like this, how could he hope to survive against Capablanca and Lasker? But in the next round Torre seemed unaffected by his loss, as he easily handled the Leningrad master Solomon Borisovich Gotthilf (1903-1967), who had placed =6th-8th (of 20) in the recent Soviet Championship.

Game 72

Torre-Gotthilf

Moscow 1925, round 10

Slav Defense [D13]

1.d4 d5 2.c4 c6 3.♘c3 ♘f6 4.♘f3 ♗f5
This premature development of Black's Bishop was a common mistake in this line at the time. Correct is either 4...d×c4, or the Semi-Slav 4...e6. To Carlos Torre goes much of the credit for showing the critical defect of 4...♗f5 (see also Game 51, Torre-Opocensky).

5.c×d5 c×d5
If 5...♘×d5 6.♕b3,

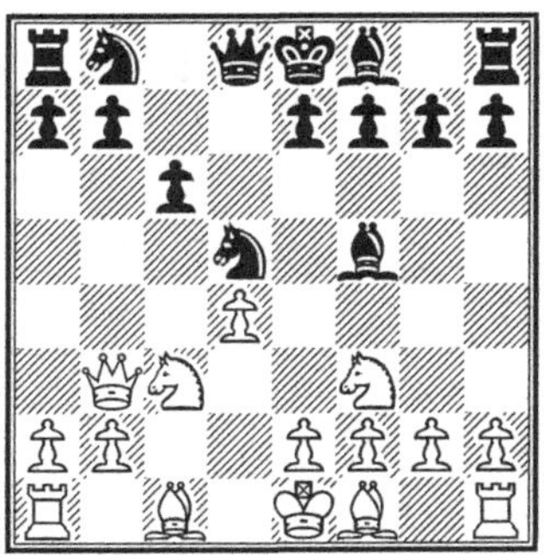

then either:
(a) 6...♕b6 7.♘×d5 c×d5 8.♕×d5 which would transpose back to the game, or

(b) 6...♘×c3 7.b×c3 ♕b6 with a choice of 8.♘d2 ♗g6 9.e4 ♘d7 10.f4±, Bogoljubow-Ståhlberg, match, Gothenburg, 1930 (1-0, 34), or 8.♗f4 ♘d7 9.♘d2 ♘f6 10.♗g3 ♘e4 11.♘×e4 ♗×e4 12.e3 e6 13.f3 ♕×b3 14.a×b3 ♗g6 15.e4±, Kostic-Banks, New York 1916 (1-0, 57).

6.♕b3 ♕b6

Though it would constitute a red-faced admission of error, correct here is Capablanca's recommendation 6...♗c8. Still not understanding what he's getting into, Black continues with his misconceived plan. Gotthilf seems oddly unaware of the Opocensky game from the Marienbad tournament several months earlier, or perhaps he thought he had found an improvement for Black.

7.♘×d5 ♘×d5 8.♕×d5 e6 9.♕b3

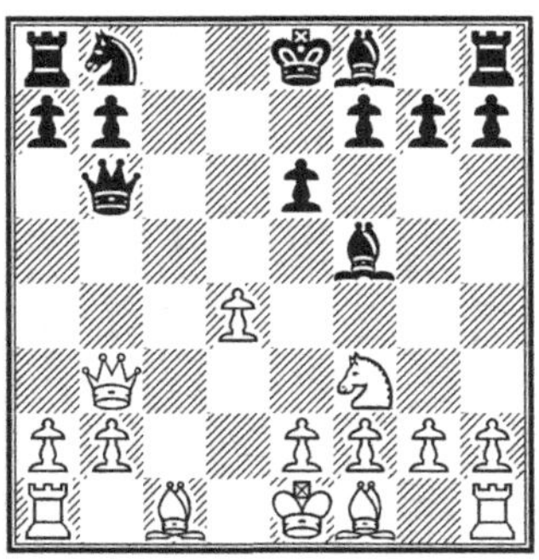

9...♕×b3

Or 9...♘c6 10.♗d2 ♕×b3 (if 10...♘b4 11.♖c1±) 11.a×b3 ♗c2 12.♗c3 b5? 13.e3 ♖b8 14.♖a6 ♘b4 15.♖×a7 ♗×b3 16.♘e5 ♘c2+ 17.♔d2 b4 18.♘d7 b×c3+ 19.♔×c3 ♖b4 20.♘×f8 ♖×f8 21.♗d3 1-0, Korchnoi-Ruderfer, Riga 1975. Clearly, the great Victor Korchnoi studied the games of Carlos Torre.

10.a×b3 ♗c2

Naturally enough, Black wants to recover his pawn, but he is now at a great positional disadvantage. In the first place, White has a solid command of the center; furthermore White has more mobility on the queenside, thanks to the half open a-file, and lastly, Black's light-squared Bishop is in danger of being trapped.

11.♗d2!

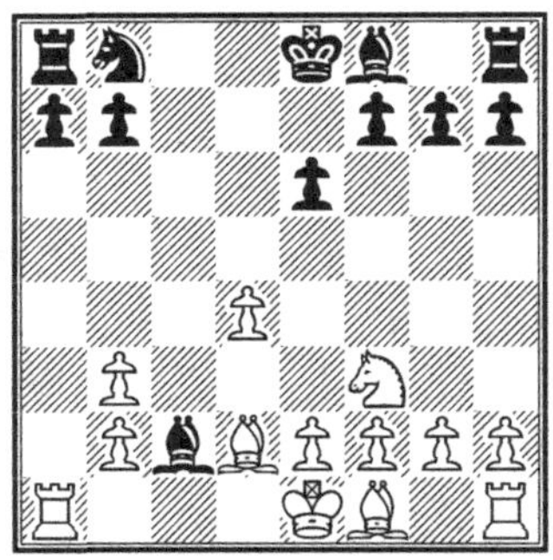

11...♗×b3

Thanks to this game (as well as Game 51), we are still within the realms of theory. The most important opening treatises give also 11...♘c6 12.♗c3, and then

(a) 12...♗b4 13.♘d2 ♗g6 14.e3 0–0 15.♗b5 ♗e7 16.♔e2! ♖fd8 17.♖a4± (Stockfish says +2.30/26), Torre-Opocensky, Marienbad 1925 (Game 51); or

(b) 12...♗e7 13.♘d2 0–0 14.e3 ♘b4 15.♗c4 (which the treatises put at just "±" but Stockfish says +1.98/25).

12.e4!

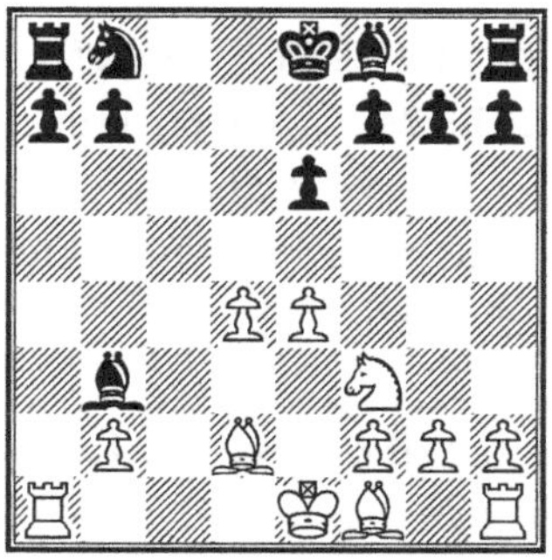

Threatening to trap the intruder by ♗d2-c3 and ♘f3-d2. Thus Black must take extreme measures.

12...f6?

The least evil was 12...♘c6 13.♗b5 (less good is 13.♗c3 a6 14.♘d2 ♗c2 15.♗b5 ♖d8 16.♗×c6+ b×c6 17.♖×a6 ♗d3 18.♖a5 +1.07/23) 13...♗e7 14.♘e5 0–0 15.♗×c6 b×c6 16.♘×c6, though that too is a losing proposition (+2.45/29).

13.♗c3 ♗c2 14.♘d2

The poor Bishop is like Paulus' army at Stalingrad: no way out!

14...♘d7 15.♗b5 a6

An empty threat, since the pawn is pinned.

16.♔e2 ♖c8 17.♗×d7+ ♔×d7 18.♖hc1 b5

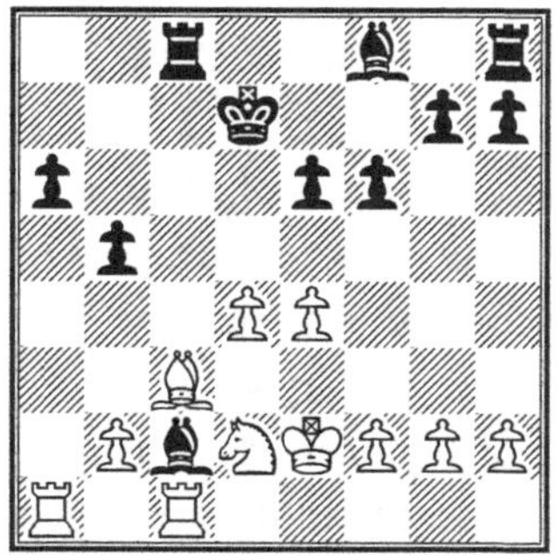

Trying to recover his piece, but White will remain with a decisive material advantage.

19.♖×c2 b4 20.♖×a6 b×c3 21.♖×c3 ♖×c3 22.b×c3 ♗d6 23.♘c4 1–0

A charming and very instructive little game. Carlos Torre made the following remark: "I consider this game to be the most classical one I have played so far. Basically it is a very simple game, but its beauty lies in its harmony. At the beginning White had a very simple plan: to take advantage of Black's dubious fourth move with his Bishop. The rest of the game is a natural unfolding of this idea."

Game 73

Capablanca-Torre

Moscow 1925, round 11

French Defense [C12]

World Champion José Raúl Capablanca (1888-1942, historical Elo 2725) had been almost unrecognizable early on at Moscow, scoring only 6½ points out of his first 12 games. However, the Cuban was in superb form during the latter part of the tournament, scoring 7 points in his last 8 games for a total of 13½, only a half-point short of Dr. Lasker, who ended in second place, and two points behind the winner Bogoljubow. In contrast, Carlos Torre had a superb performance in the first half (8½ points out of his first 11 games) but a surprisingly poor performance toward the end (only 3½ points out of his last 9 games). Torre's game with Capablanca came in the second half of the tournament, and the Cuban obviously was seriously determined to win, but the tremendous effort that he put into the task was in vain, as Torre defended very accurately throughout. To hold an inferior endgame against Capablanca, the "Chess Machine," was a very rare thing, and must be considered the supreme test for a master of those days. And with the exception of one move, Torre passed that test with flying colors.

1.e4 e6 2.d4 d5 3.♘c3 ♘f6 4.♗g5 ♗b4 5.e5

This advance is a stronger method against the McCutcheon French than 5.e×d5, which Capablanca played against Alekhine and Bogoljubow at New York 1924.

5...h6 6.♗d2 ♗×c3 7.b×c3 ♘e4 8.♕g4 g6

The alternative is 8...♔f8, Dr. Tarrasch's recommendation, which avoids the weakening effect of 8...g6 but forfeits the right to castle. It was played by Capablanca himself against Chajes at New York 1916 (1-0, 66), and by Torre against Thomas at Marienbad 1925 (Game 55, ½-½, 60).

9.♗d3 ♘×d2 10.♔×d2 c5

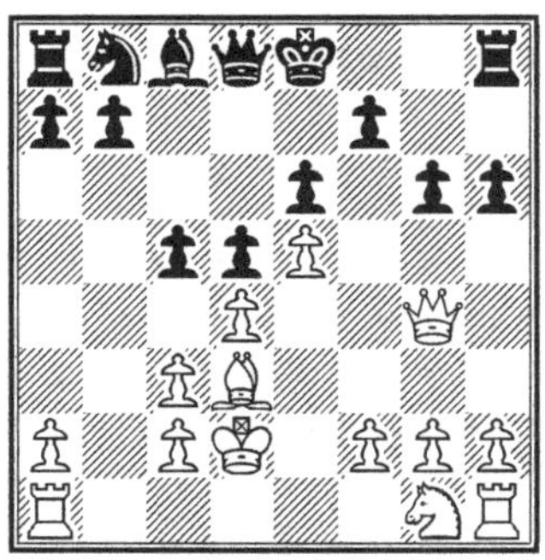

Arriving at a critical position of the McCutcheon variation, first seen in E. Cohn-Caro, match, Berlin, 1906 (0-1, 33). In 1925 experience with this line was meager; CB shows only two other games before this tournament: Griffith-Scott, Hastings 1920-21 (½-½, 39), and Bogoljubow-Réti, Breslau 1925 (1-0, 29).

11.h4

As in Bogoljubow-Réti. This would become the second-most frequent reply, after 11.♘f3. *Modern Chess Openings*, 13th edition, calls the text "The only other move [besides 11.♘f3] with any initiative," adding "for example 11...♘c6 12.♖h3 c×d4 13.c×d4, but after the solid 13...♗d7 Capablanca, against Torre, Moscow 1925, could find nothing better than 14.c3 ♕e7 15.♕d1 ♘a5 16.♕b1 ♖c8 17.♘e2 ♖c6=." Stockfish agrees, giving an evaluation of +0.33 at 28 ply.

11...♘c6 12.♖h3

A deployment known as the Maróczy System. This plan presents Black with definite difficulties, because the Rook is usually posted at f3, from where it hits Black's position at the most vulnerable point, f7. Furthermore, it hangs over Black the constant threat of a Bishop sacrifice at g6.

12...c×d4

The point of this move is that it prevents the potential ♗×g6 sacrifice, because after opening the a5-e1 diagonal Black can respond to the Bishop sac with ...♕a5+. Black then captures the Bishop and after ♕×g6+ his King flees to safety via d8 and c7. Without this detail, the exchange on d4 would be ill-advised until Black had developed his counter-attack considerably further.

13.c×d4

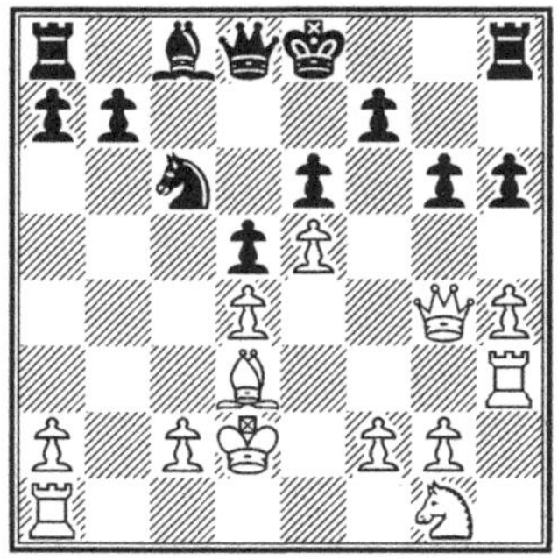

13...♗d7

Later games, starting with Lilienthal-Bondarevsky, Moscow 1937, showed 13...♕b6 to be quite strong. That game continued 14.♘f3 ♗d7 15.♕f4 0–0–0 16.g4 ♕b4+ 17.♔e2 f6 18.a3 ♕c3 19.♖b1 g5 20.♕d2? ♘×d4+ 21.♘×d4 ♕×d4 22.e×f6?? ♕×g4+ 23.♖f3 d4, 0-1.

14.c3 ♕e7 15.♕d1 ♘a5

15...0–0–0 may have been somewhat better. Stockfish sees no indication that White can generate a successful attack on the b-file (0.00/29).

16.♕b1 ♖c8

It becomes clear that queenside castling was never in Torre's plans. He prefers to pressure the weak c-pawn.

17.♘e2 ♖c6

Intending to drive the Queen off the b-file with 18...♖b6. Capablanca decides to get the Queens off the board.

This will have the side-benefit of turning his weak c-pawn into a healthy b-pawn.

18.♕b4

C.S. Howell in the *ACB* comments "This is not simply wood chopping ... Black's position is too secure for White to make any progress while the Queens are on the board. With them off, there are slight weaknesses that may be exploited in the end game."

18...♕×b4

Avoiding the Queen exchange by 18...♕d8 was playable, though Stockfish thinks it favors White slightly (+0.61/25).

19.c×b4 ♘c4+ 20.♗×c4 ♖×c4

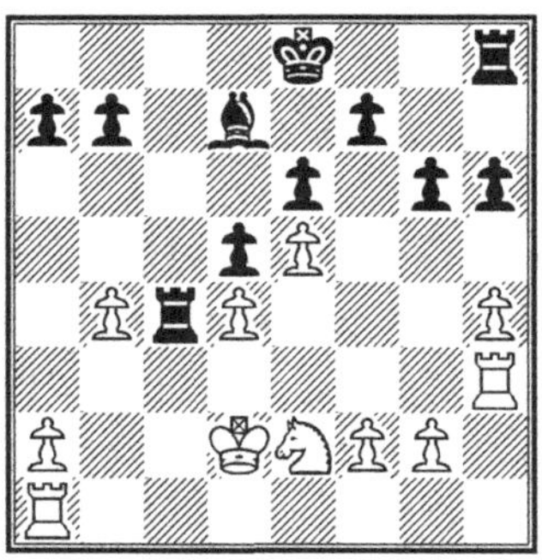

In his accustomed style, Capablanca has played with an eye to a favorable endgame. After these exchanges, White has a small but permanent and very clear advantage: the use of a Knight against his opponent's bad Bishop. As for the Rooks, it is plain they will end up all being traded off on the only open file. All those simplifications are inevitable in the near- or mid-term and, naturally, are favorable only to White, since the only pieces then remaining will be those which constitute White's advantage. As Sir George Thomas said, "Against Alekhine, one never knows what to expect; against Capablanca one always knows what to expect, but one can do nothing to avoid it."

21.a3 ♔e7 22.♖c3 ♖hc8 23.♖ac1 ♖×c3 24.♖×c3 ♖×c3 25.♘×c3

Reaching the aforementioned good-Knight-vs.-bad-Bishop ending, which Black could not avoid.

25...f6 26.♔e3 g5 27.e×f6+ ♔×f6 28.h×g5+

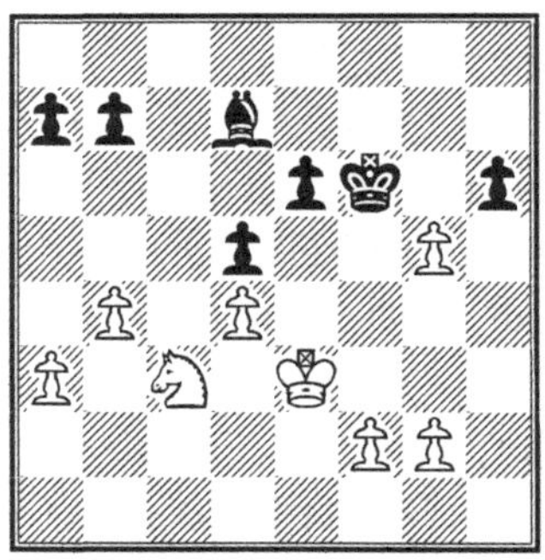

28...♔×g5!

Torre defends with precision. Recapture with the pawn would have made his defensive task more difficult if not impossible, for example 28...h×g5 29.g4 ♗c6 30.f4 ♗e8 31.♘e2 ♗b5 32.♘g1 ♔g6 33.♘h3 g×f4+ 34.♔×f4 (34.♘×f4+? ♔f6=) 34...♗f1 35.♘g5 ♔f6 36.♘f3 ♗d3 37.g5+ ♔e7 38.♔e5 etc., winning.

29.f3 ♗e8 30.g4 ♗c6 31.a4

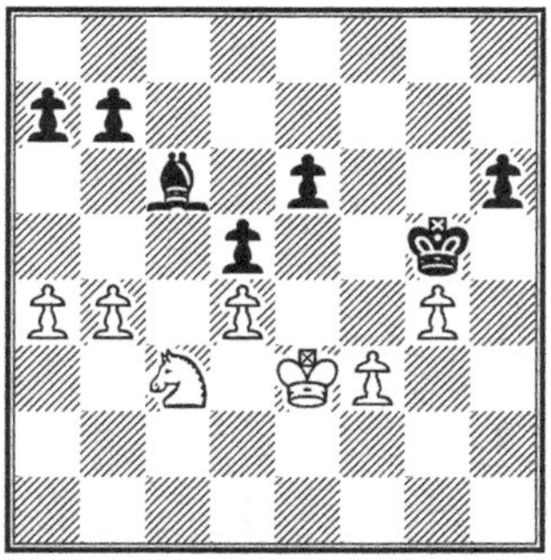

31...♗d7

Bogoljubow comments: "Black here follows a wait-and-see policy. I would suggest 31...♗e8, and if 32.b5 h5 33.g×h5 ♗×h5 (Black cannot capture with the King, as then the white King would invade the enemy camp via f4), and thus the dangerous g-pawn would be eliminated." This time Stockfish quite agrees with Bogo, rating the resulting position at +0.09/41.

32.b5!

The only move with any winning chances, +0.80/27.

32...♗e8 33.♘e2 h5?!

A perilous move. Better were 33...♔f6 or 33...♗g6.

34.♘f4!

This move is the key difference from Bogoljubow's analysis variation at move 31. It is no exaggeration to say that since the beginning of the game Capablanca has almost always made the very best moves at his disposal. At this point, however, some annotators have questioned the move 34.♘f4, the tournament book actually giving 34.g×h5

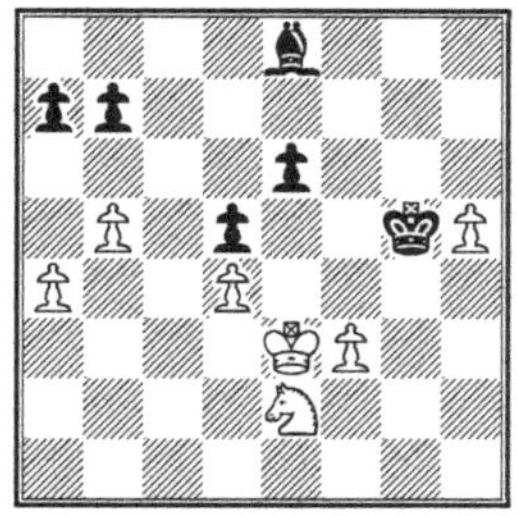

as a possible improvement for White. But computer analysis quickly dispels that illusion; after 34...♗×h5 35.♘f4 ♗f7□ 36.♘d3 b6!□ 37.♘e5 ♗e8 White is getting nowhere (+0.33/35).

34...h×g4□ 35.♘×e6+

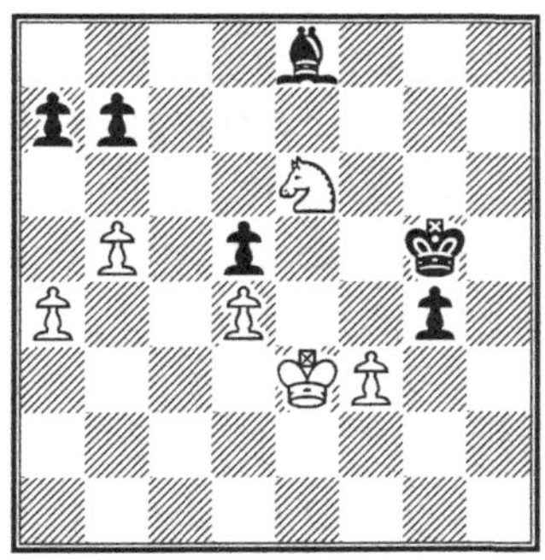

35...♔h4!

One of only two non-losing moves. The adroit endgame composer Richard Réti suggested 35...♔f6. In that case best play would proceed 36.♘d8 g×f3 (36...b6?? 37.f×g4+−) 37.♘×b7 ♔e7 38.♔×f3 ♗h5+!□ 39.♔f4 ♔e6 40.♘c5+ ♔d6□ and it's clear Black can hold (+0.91/45).

36.f×g4

If 36.f4?? ♔g3 etc. and *White* would lose.

36...♔×g4 37.♘d8

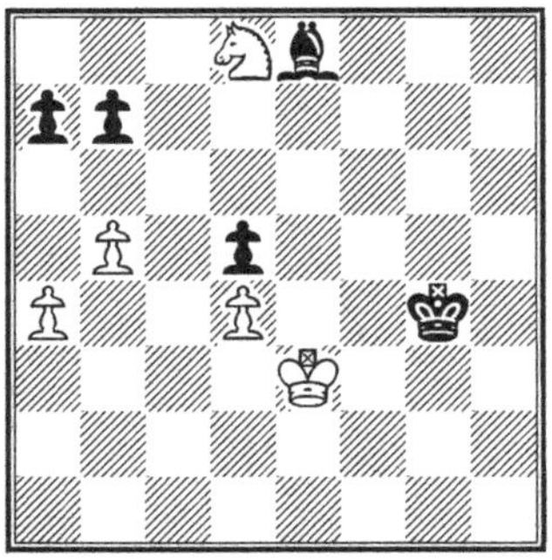

It must have been a nightmare to defend such a difficult ending against the patient technique of a Capablanca, who was ready to take all the time in the world to work very methodically in the gradual improvement of his position. For Black, the game is like a minefield through which there is only one path that avoids destruction, a path by no means obvious.

37...♔f5??

After finding his way carefully and ably though difficult variations for so long, Torre finally steps on a mine. Correct was 37...b6!□. The first edition had some analysis purporting to show it would lose, but that is not so. Black would have to continue finding "□" moves, but he could hold. Best play would continue 38.♘c6 a5□ 39.♘e7 ♗f7□ 40.♘c8 ♔f5□ 41.♘×b6 ♔e6□ 42.♘c8 ♗g6 (only this or 42...♔d7 hold) 43.♔d2 ♔d7!□ (not 43...♗e8?? as in the first edition) 44.♘a7 ♔c7□ 45.♘c6 ♔b6 and Stockfish, which sees especially deep in endgames, finds no way for White to make progress (+0.85/50).

38.♘×b7 ♔e6

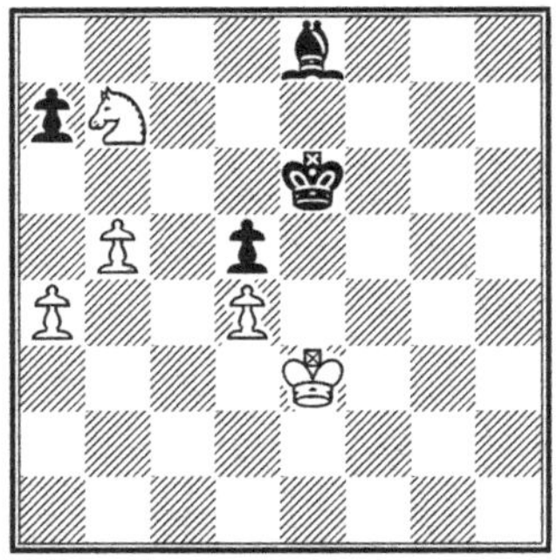

39.♔d3?

The Chess Machine malfunctions! Winning was 39.♘c5+! ♔d6 40.♘a6 ♗d7 41.♔d3 ♗c8 42.♘c5 ♔c7 43.a5! ♔b8 44.♔c3 ♔c7 45.♔b4 ♔d8 46.b6 a×b6 47.a×b6 etc. Quite rare for the great Cuban to miss such an opportunity.

39...♔d7!□

Reprieved, Torre makes no further errors, ensuring the draw.

40.♘c5+ ♔c7

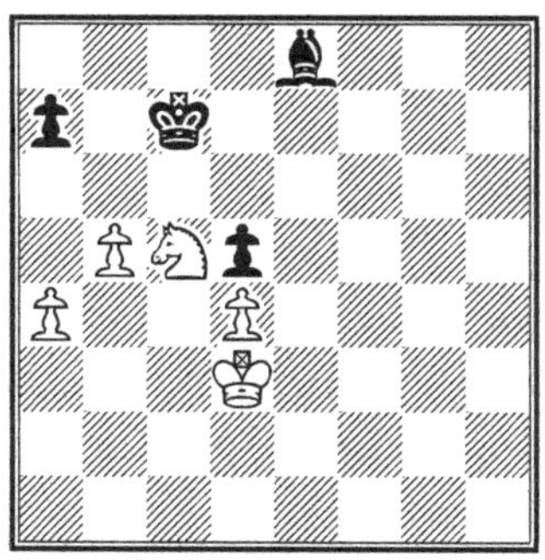

41.♘a6+

Immediately after the game, Capablanca indicated the variation 41.♔c3 ♔b6 42.♔b4 a5+, whereupon White's King would go to e5 and eventually win. In the tournament book, Bogoljubow disagreed, saying that Black might draw in that line by maneuvering his Bishop to d1 or f3. Our first edition gave further analysis purporting to vindicate Capablanca, but it erred early on. After 43.♔c3 ♔c7 44.♔d2, not 44...♔b6??, but 44...♗g6! (44...♗h5 *à la* Bogoljubow is also good) 45.♔e3 ♗c2 46.♔f4 ♔d6□, and the white King will obviously never get to e5 (+1.00/50).

41...♔b6□ 42.♔c3 ♔a5□ 43.♔b3 ♗h5

One of the few times in this ending where Torre had a choice of moves. 43...♗f7 should also draw.

44.♔a3 ♗d1 45.♘c5 a6!

An essential resource, often seen in this kind of ending. The idea behind such pawn breaks, naturally, is to dislocate the connected phalanx of enemy pawns and leave them uncoordinated. Also good was 45...♔b6 46.♔b4 a5+.

46.b×a6

If 46.♘×a6 ♗×a4=.

46...♔b6□ 47.♔b4 ♗e2 48.a5+ ♔a7□ 49.♘e6 ♗×a6 50.♘c7 ♗c4□ 51.♔c5

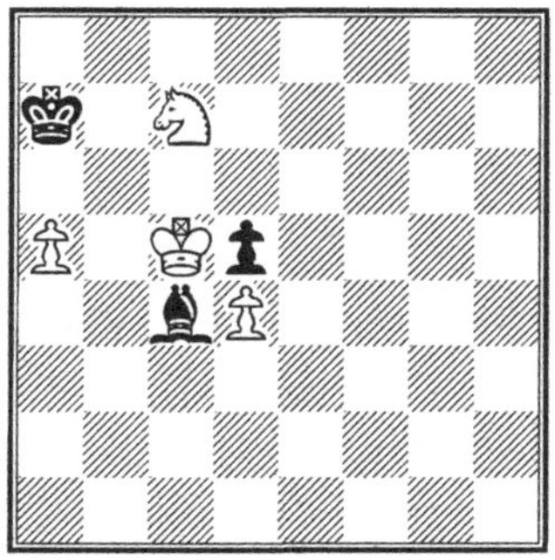

51...♗b3!□

Precision is still necessary! Now White cannot win with 52.♘×d5 ♔a6□ 53.♘b6 ♔×a5 54.♘c4+ ♔a6! 55.♘d6 ♗a2=.

52.♔c6 ♗c4□ 53.a6 ♗e2 54.♔×d5 ♔b6□ 55.♔d6 ♗g4 56.d5 ♗f3 ½-½

A very difficult endgame where Torre was able to survive only through the greatest ingenuity and exactitude, not to mention unflagging attention and perseverance. Aside from his 37th move (which was counter-balanced by Capablanca's 39th), it is one of Torre's finest achievements. We have seldom if ever seen a game in which a player had to find so many "□" moves, and did. Russian grandmaster Yuri Averbakh, with good reason, included this game in his book *Bishop and Knight Endgames*.

Game 74

Torre-Lasker

Moscow 1925, round 12

Torre Attack [A46]

Though he had lost his world title to Capablanca, Dr. Emanuel Lasker (1868-1941, historical Elo 2720), World Champion 1894 to 1921, was in 1925 still one of the most formidable opponents a chess player could face. After a two-year hiatus the devaluation of the German mark prompted his return to master competition, where he proved he was, arguably, still the #2 player in the world (the main argument coming from Alekhine), and perhaps still the #1 tournament player, based on his victory at New York 1924 (it was not until 1936 that Capablanca managed to finish ahead of Lasker in a tournament). While this game with Lasker is generally the only one of Torre's that is printed in anthologies of the "Compleat History of Chess" type, it is by no means the best game of either player. Still, like the Capablanca game, it showed that Torre could hold his own with the world's best, and its decisive combination is quite entertaining.

1.d4 ♘f6 2.♘f3 e6 3.♗g5 c5 4.e3 c×d4 5.e×d4 ♗e7 6.♘bd2 d6

An original idea of Lasker's, not seen before. He prefers to fight for control of the e5 square with the objective of obtaining a solid position along the lines of the Scheveningen Sicilian, in which Black avoids committing himself but reserves the option of advancing his central pawns as circumstances dictate or opportunity arises.

On the other hand, GM Reuben Fine, in *The World's Great Chess Games*, disliked Lasker's deployment and advocated 4...♕b6 rather than 4...c×d4. Interestingly, Fine's recommendation was used in two other game at Moscow 1925: Sämisch-Levenfish in round 11 (½-½, 53) and three rounds earlier in Dus-Chotimirsky–Zubarev (1-0, 58).

7.c3 ♘bd7 8.♗d3 b6

9.♘c4

The tournament book suggests 9.♕c2 ♗b7 10.0–0.

Another, perhaps better line is 9.0–0 ♗b7 10.♖e1 0–0 11.♘f1 ♖e8 12.♘g3 ♕c7 13.♗c2 ♘f8 14.♕d3, as Torre played against Grünfeld in round 14

(½-½, 30). But there is nothing wrong with the text.

9...♗b7 10.♕e2 ♕c7 11.0–0 0–0

At this point, Fine says "The great Lasker has been outplayed in the opening. White's pieces are freer and he has a strong initiative." Stockfish, on the other hand, considers the game quite even.

12.♖fe1

Here or at some point soon White might have considered 12.a4, to stabilize the position of the ♘c4. The desirability of this will become clear in a few moves.

12...♖fe8 13.♖ad1 ♘f8 14.♗c1

A move not in the spirit of the Torre Attack. 14.♗×f6 looks more natural, but Torre must have had his reasons for retreating the Bishop to c1. Fine gives 14.♗c1 an exclam, though he does not say why.
Stockfish suggests 14.♘e3, though the game then remains even after 14...♘d5 15.♘×d5 ♗×d5 16.♗×e7 ♖×e7.

14...♘d5 15.♘g5?!

Apparently the point of 14.♗c1 was to enable this, but it is another dubious move whose object is not readily apparent. It is probable that White had not hit on a concrete plan, but in such cases one is well-advised to remember Purdy's Rule: When you cannot think of a move, look for the piece that is least active, and find a plan to activate it. By this rule the least active white piece is the ♘c4, in that all the forward squares to which it might move are controlled by black pawns.
Worth considering, then, was 15.♘a3 intending 16.♘c2, and also opening the f1-a6 diagonal and hindering the queenside thrust Black now makes. 15.♘e3? was no longer desirable due to 15...♘f4!.

15...b5! 16.♘a3

And now of course not 16.♘e3?? ♗×g5 17.♘×d5 e×d5 –+.

16...b4!

Exploiting the misplaced Knight to force an isolated pawn on White.

17.c×b4

Worse of course is 17.♘b1 b×c3 18.b×c3 ♘×c3 19.♘×c3 ♕×c3, losing a pawn.

17...♘×b4 18.♕h5?!

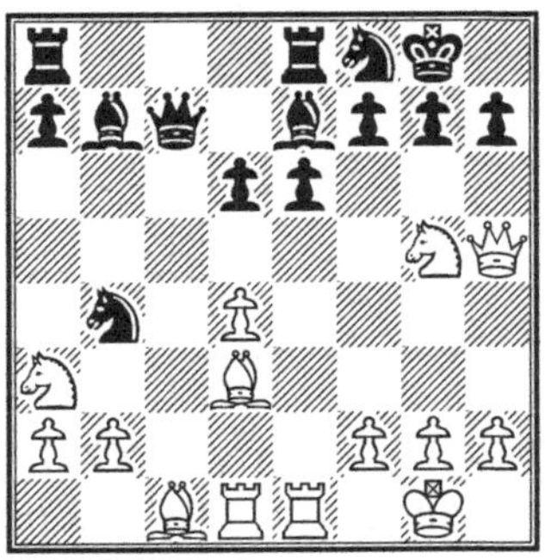

As in so many other games, Torre opts for audacity over prudence. Safer was 18.♗b1, retaining the Bishop and defending the a-pawn, though then after

18...♗d5 19.b3 a5 White, while not in serious danger, is thrown on the defensive (-0.52/26). Fine, on the other hand, calls the text "a bold idea."

18...♗×g5

Lasker for his part is not fully prudent either. Best was 18...g6, forestalling kingside threats. Then after 19.♕h3 Black stands better with either 19...♘×a2, 19...♖ac8, 19...♗d5, or 19...♘×d3 20.♕×d3, all about -1.00.

19.♗×g5?

Now Torre goes from boldness to recklessness.

Correct was 19.♕×g5 ♘×d3 (if 19...♘×a2 20.♗f4=) 20.♖×d3, and after 20...e5 21.d×e5 ♖×e5 22.♕d2 Black's edge is small (-0.36/27).

19...♘×d3 20.♖×d3 ♕a5!

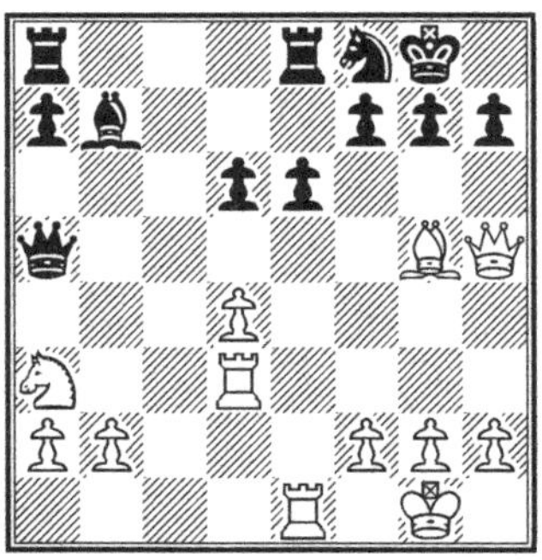

A very strong move which simultaneously attacks the ♖e1 and pins the ♗g5, threatening 21...f6/h6. White now offers a pawn in hopes of deflecting the Queen off the pinning rank.

21.b4□

Anything else loses the Bishop, e.g. 21.♖ed1 f6.

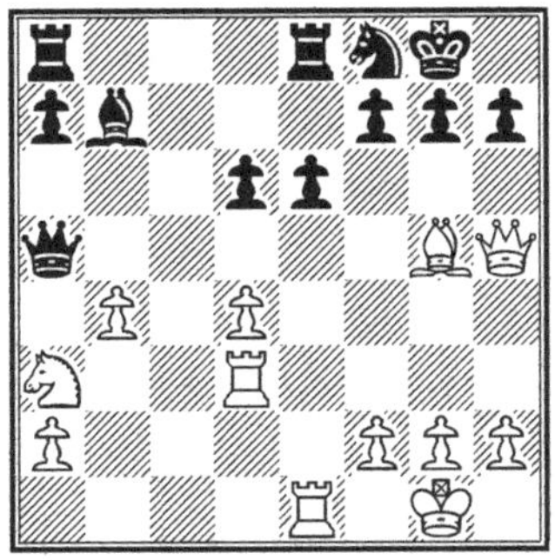

At least two explanations have been offered about what happens in the next few moves.

According to Hans Kmoch, Lasker was upset that day over some argument with Richard Réti, a dispute rancorous enough to affect his concentration.

However, a fuller explanation is offered by Lasker's biographer J. Hannak. According to Hannak, at or near this point Lasker "had much the better of a difficult game ... 'egging on' his opponent to an unsound attack which, ultimately, would seal the attacker's doom," when "a messenger entered the room and put a telegram" from Lasker's wife on the table. Lasker, who normally allowed nothing to intrude on his concentration at the board, "somewhat absentmindedly opened and read the telegram," and learned that a play he had written was to be produced for the stage. These tidings sent Lasker into a state of rapturous joy, "probably the happiest minutes of his life," and he went "pacing the lobby excitedly and telling all his friends the great news ...".[1] Then, returning to the board, Lasker sat down in a euphoric daze and committed a series of errors.

21...♕f5!

But Lasker is not erring yet; contrary to Romanovsky in the tournament book, and Nimzovich in *My System*, this is the best move, though the latter's suggestion 21...♕d5 is also quite good, *viz.* 22.♕g4 ♖ac8 23.♕g3 ♘g6 24.h4 h5 (-2.48/28).

22.♖g3??

Objectively we must give this the double-?, as it would have greatly aggravated the loss White must suffer had Lasker not been in his daze. Least bad was 22.♖h3, unpinning the Bishop so that 22...f6/h6 need not be feared. Black would still be winning after 22...♕d5 23.♖g3 ♘g6 24.♕d1 ♖ac8 25.♕b3 f6 26.♕×d5 ♗×d5 27.♗d2, about -3.00 per Stockfish, but as yet material is even and White may catch a break.

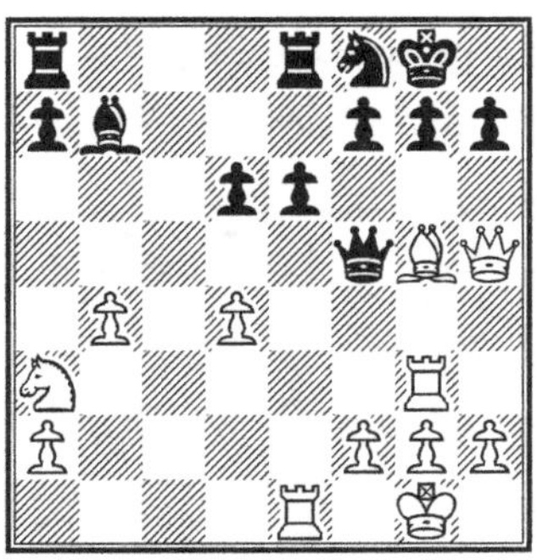

22...h6?

But catch a break he does anyway! This is a case of "wrong pawn," Lasker apparently thinking it makes no difference which pawn attacks the Bishop, but it most definitely does.

Crushing was 22...f6!, when White can do nothing to avoid major material loss, *e.g.* 23.♘c4 ♖e7! 24.♘e3 ♕b5 (also good is 24...♕g6 25.♕×g6 ♘×g6 and the Bishop has no escape square), and if 25.♗×f6 ♕×h5 with impunity, as g7 is defended.

23.♘c4!□

Nimzovich notes "This intervention of the Knight would have been impossible had the black Queen been at d5."

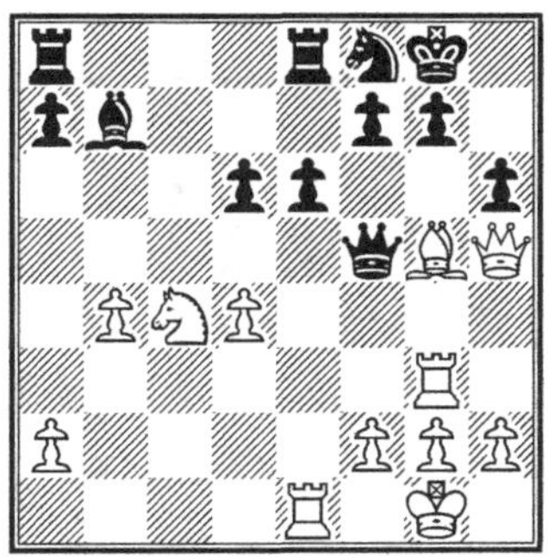

23...♕d5??

Lasker still thinks he can win the pinned Bishop and the game. Instead he should have settled for equality by 23...h×g5 24.♘×d6 ♕g6 25.♕×g6 ♘×g6 26.♘×b7=, or 23...♕g6 24.♕×g6 ♘×g6 25.♘×d6 h×g5 26.♘×b7, or 23...♘g6 24.♘×d6 ♕d5 25.♘×b7 ♕×b7 26.♗×h6 ♕×b4 (not 26...g×h6??

1 This account is basically confirmed in the definitive book on Lasker, *Emanuel Lasker: Denker, Weltenbürger, Schachweltmeister* (Berlin 2009).

27.♕×h6 ♕×b4 28.♖×g6+ f×g6 29.♕×g6+ ♔f8 30.♖e3 △31.♖f3++−.) 27.♖d1 g×h6 (27...♖ed8? 28.♗e3±) 28.♖×g6+ f×g6 29.♕×g6+ etc., draw.

Two seemingly minor inaccuracies have transformed a winning position into a hopelessly lost one. It is extremely unusual to see one of the greatest players of all time (some say *the* greatest) make two bad moves in a row; one is tempted to believe that the incident of the telegram must be the explanation. However, Torre certainly deserves some credit for having played boldly and energetically after he himself made some mistakes.

24.♘e3!

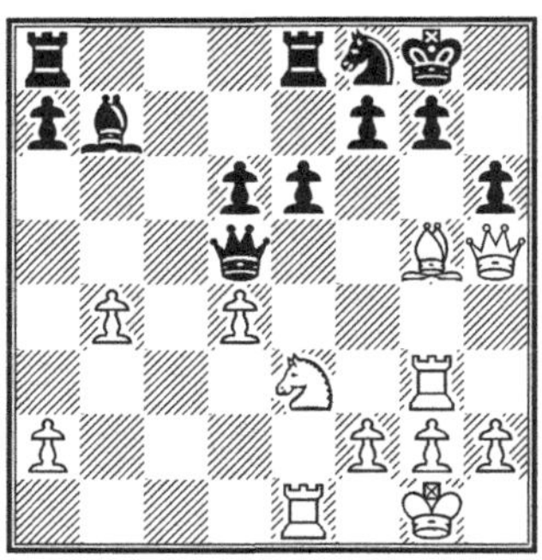

"Torre fights like a lion to break the pin, but without a point for the Bishop to fall back upon, it would have been impossible," says Nimzovich, who makes the further important point that now Black's Queen is driven to an unprotected square.

24...♕b5

Black is now lost in all variations. If instead

(a) 24...♕×d4 25.♗×h6 ♘g6 26.♗g5 ♘f4 27.♕g4 ♕d2 28.♘c2! ♕×c2 29.♗×f4 ♕g6 30.♕×g6 f×g6 31.♗×d6+−. Or

(b) 24...♕e4 25.♗×h6 ♘g6 26.♗g5 ♘f8 [if 26...♘f4 27.♗×f4 ♕×f4 28.♖h3 f6 (28...♕h6 29.♕b5+−) 29.♘g4 ♖e7 30.♕g6 ♗d5 31.♖h4 ♕g5 32.♕h7+ ♔f8 33.♘e3 ♖ae8 34.f4+−] 27.♗f6 ♘g6 28.♖g4 ♕c6

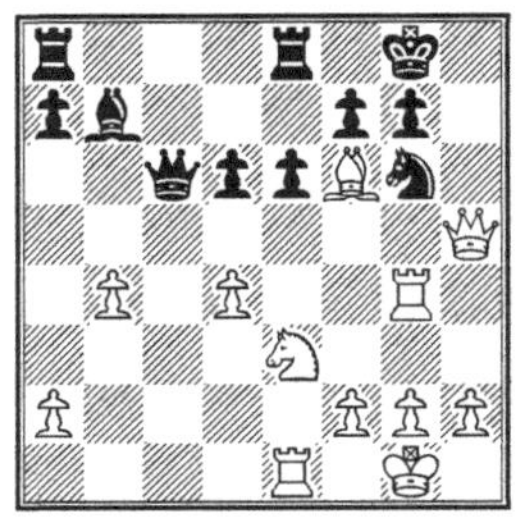

29.♖×g6 f×g6 30.♕×g6 ♕c7 31.♘g4 ♖f8 32.h3 ♗d5 33.♖e3 ♖f7 34.♘h6+ ♔f8 35.♕h7! ♖×f6 36.♕g8+ ♔e7 37.♕×g7+ ♔d8 38.♕×f6+ (+7.76/24).

After the text we are treated to Torre's most famous combination: the "windmill," or "see-saw check." Nimzovich writes: "The see-saw can be the scene of frightful devastation." Indeed:

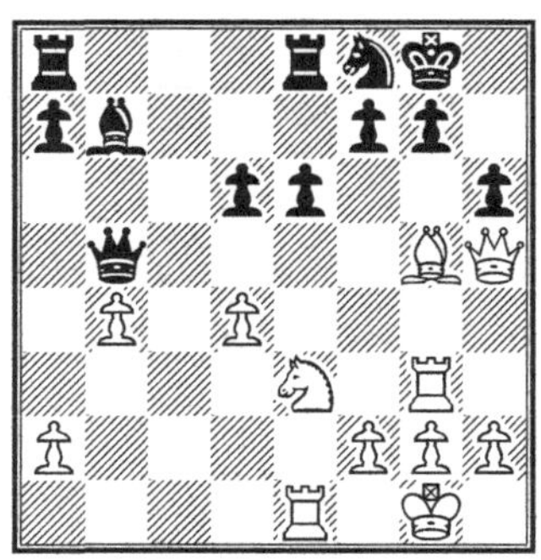

25.♗f6!! ♕×h5 26.♖×g7+ ♔h8

27.♖×f7+ ♔g8 28.♖g7+ ♔h8 29.♖×b7+ ♔g8 30.♖g7+ ♔h8 31.♖g5+

White follows the positional principle of not letting the opponent's pieces have open lines, hence he refrained from capturing the a-pawn. Closer analysis reveals that White could safely have taken that pawn as well, since it would be well-nigh impossible for Black to do anything useful with the ♖a8. However, it makes no real difference. The remainder of the game was perhaps unnecessary agony for Black, but Dr. Lasker was a stubborn and resourceful fighter, even when his position looked hopeless. Often he did indeed find a saving resource, but even he cannot find that which is not there.

31...♔h7 32.♖×h5 ♔g6 33.♖h3 ♔×f6 34.♖×h6+ ♔g5 35.♖h3 ♖eb8 36.♖g3+ ♔f6 37.♖f3+ ♔g6 38.a3 a5 39.b×a5 ♖×a5 40.♘c4 ♖d5 41.♖f4 ♘d7 42.♖×e6+ ♔g5 43.g3 1-0

In the *Wiener Schachzeitung*, Hans Kmoch commented humorously "By great misfortune [Lasker] lost to Torre. Showed no reaction. But the next day, apparently after speaking to Lasker, Torre went from room to room to his colleagues and repeated time after time in admiration: 'He is very philosophical, verrry philosophical!'"

Ironically, though this is perhaps the most famous of Torre's efforts (along with the apocryphal 1920 Adams game), objectively it must be considered one of lower quality. When Velasco asked Torre himself about it, he replied sharply "That was rather one of my worst games and, therefore, one of Dr. Lasker's worst."

After this game, Torre went into a tailspin, scoring only +1 -3 =5 in the last nine rounds. The first edition attributed this partly to an "experimental attitude," saying that Torre "avoided the cautious, classical openings he knew well, and instead began improvising and experimenting with lines he had never tried before ... Torre never worried much about winning or losing; rather he sought truth and originality." But close examination of the games shows that Torre simply played badly. His losses — to Romanovsky, Yates and Bohatirchuk — were dismal affairs, where the audacious tactician and precise technician of earlier rounds was unrecognizable. As Black against Bohatirchuk he did try an opening new for him, 1.e4 d5 2.e×d5 ♘f6 3.♗b5+ ♗d7 4.♗c4 ♗g4 5.f3 ♗f5, but this line is not unsound, and his loss was due to later blunders.

Game 75

Romanovsky-Torre

Moscow 1925, round 13

Ruy López [C88]

Petrograd-born Peter Arsenievich Romanovsky (1892-1964, IM title 1950) was one of the top Russian players at this time. He won the second Soviet Championship in 1923, placed second to Bogoljubow in the third in 1924, and at Moscow 1925 placed highest among Soviet players not named Bogoljubow (=7th-8th with Réti). Torre was playing him about even until a horrible blunder at move 18.

1.e4 e5 2.♘f3 ♘c6 3.♗b5 a6 4.♗a4 ♘f6 5.0–0 ♗e7 6.♖e1 b5 7.♗b3 0–0 8.a4

Forestalling the Marshall Gambit, which would occur after 8.c3 d5!?.

8...b4 9.d4 d6 10.h3 ♘×d4 11.♘×d4 e×d4 12.♕×d4 c5 13.♕d3 ♗b7 14.♘d2 ♖e8 15.♘f3 ♗f8 16.♗g5 h6 17.♗h4

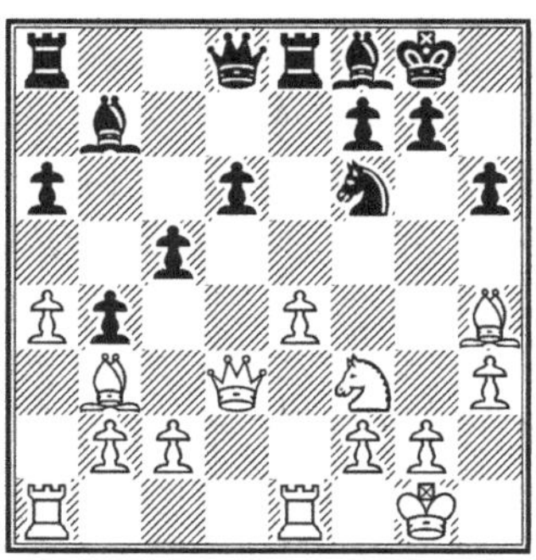

17...g5

This gives Black close to an even game. An interesting, probably better alternative was 17...♖×e4! 18.♖×e4 ♗×e4 19.♗×f6 ♕e8 20.♕d2 g×f6=.

18.e5

Clearly forced; if 18.♗g3? ♗×e4 19.♖×e4 ♖×e4 20.♗d5 ♖e7 21.♗×a8 ♕×a8 and Black is a clean pawn ahead (if 22.♕×d6?? ♖e1+).

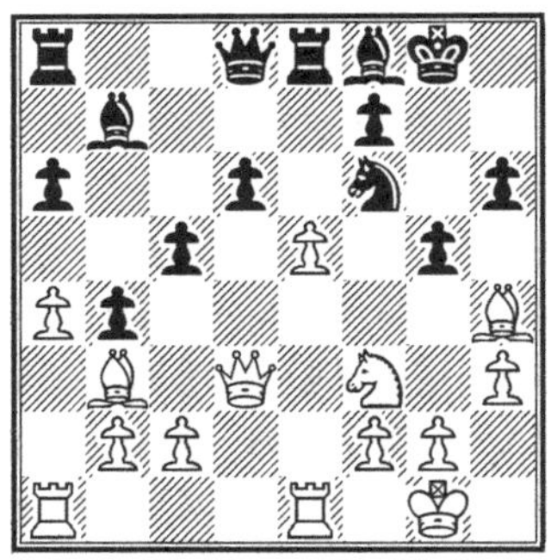

18...d5??

Apparently intended to ward off the threat of 19.♕g6+, but this is a dreadful miscalculation and a defense far worse than the threat. There were two playable continuations:

(a) 18...d×e5 19.♕g6+ ♔h8 20.♗×f7 ♗×f3 21.♗×g5 (if 21.♗×e8? ♗h5) 21...h×g5 22.g×f3 ♗g7 23.♖ad1 ♕e7 24.♗×e8 ♖×e8 25.♕×g5 and Black is not too bad off (+0.93/24);

(b) 18...c4 19.♗×c4 (19.♕×c4?! ♗d5) 19...d5 20.♗b3 g×h4 21.e×f6 ♕×f6 and while Black's pawn structure is a mess, it looks like he can survive (+0.68/25).

19.♘×g5!
How did Torre not foresee this? It is a standard motif in situations where the ♘f6 will remain pinned and under attack after the exchange on g5. Plus it is also a standard line-clearing sacrifice, allowing the Queen come in like thunder on the g-file.

19...h×g5 20.♗×g5 c4 21.♕f3!
Better than 21.♕g3 ♘h5.

21...♘e4
There is nothing better; if 21...c×b3 22.♗×f6 and 22...♕×f6 is forced.

22.♗×d8 ♖a×d8 23.♖×e4!

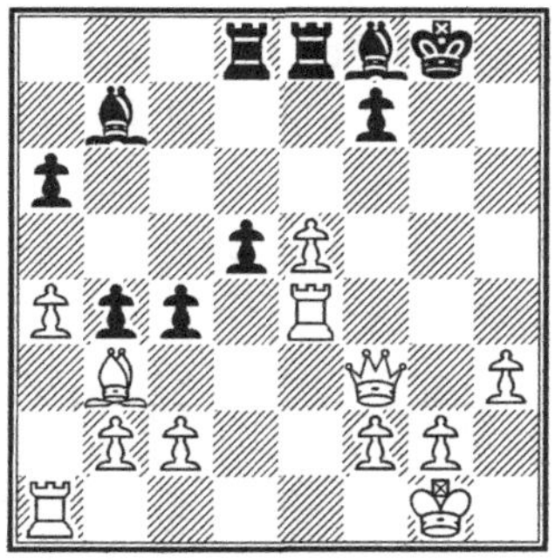

A good way to simplify a winning position.

23...d×e4 24.♕g3+ ♗g7 25.♗×c4 ♖×e5 26.♖e1 ♖d2 27.♗×f7+ ♔f8 28.♕f4 e3 29.♖×e3 ♖×e3 30.f×e3 ♔e7 31.♕×b4+ 1–0
Coming just after his heroic draw with Capablanca and his win over Lasker, this was an indication that all was not well with Torre.

Game 76

Yates-Torre

Moscow 1925, round 15

This game had gone along much the same lines as Capablanca-Torre (Game 73), the main difference being that Yates had adhered more closely to the Maróczy System's strategy of doubling heavy pieces on the f-file. Still, Torre had found counter-play on the queenside and was not too bad off in the position after

23.♖b1-b4:

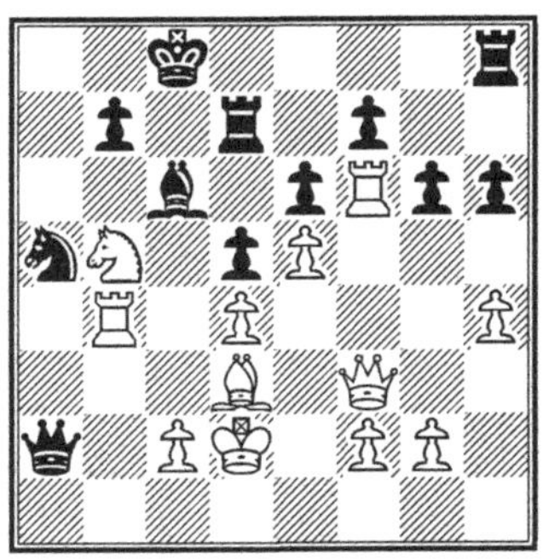

23...♘c4+?

Necessary was 23...♗×b5 and after either 24.♗×b5 ♖c7 25.♕d1 or 24.♖×b5 ♘c6 25.♖×f7 ♘×d4 Black is OK.

24.♗×c4 d×c4 25.♕c3! ♗×b5 26.♖×b5

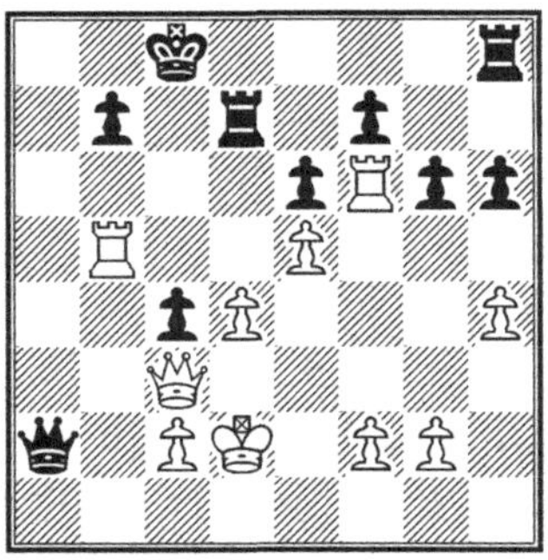

26...♖hd8??

A colossal blunder.

The only hope lay in 26...♔b8 27.♔e3 (if 27.♖a5 ♕b1 safely) 27...♖hd8 28.♖b4 ♖c7

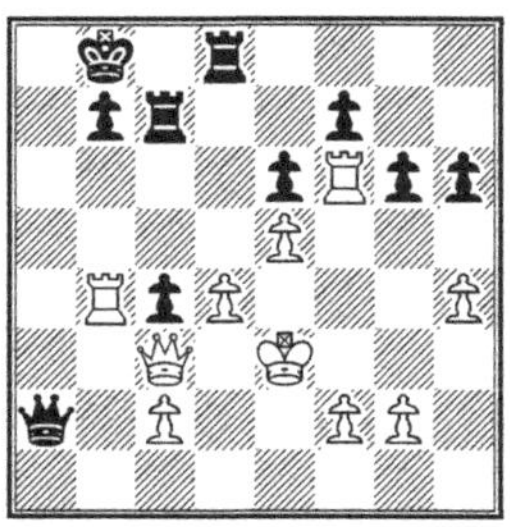

(+1.76/29).

27.♖a5 ♖×d4+

If 27...♕b1 28.♖a8+ ♔c7 29.♕×c4+ ♔b6 30.♕c5#.

28.♔e3 ♕b1 29.♖a8+

This is why 26...♔b8 was necessary.

29...♔c7 30.♖×f7+ ♔b6 31.♕a5+ 1–0

Torre's draws in this bad stretch were none too impressive either. In his 14th-round game with Grünfeld he committed an elementary oversight that should have lost a pawn. Torre-Rubinstein in round 16 was a perfunctory 21-move grandmaster draw. Against Rabinovich in round 17 Torre's experimental opening *was* unsound, so much so that he was lost by move seven (!), again at moves 13 and 17, and at several later points, but his opponent repeatedly let him off the hook. He was clearly winning against Ilyin-Zhenevsky in round 18 but a series of inferior moves let it slip away. And in his last-round draw with Réti, both players were obviously tired, and after some desultory fencing they just chopped wood down to a clearly drawn ending. We present the error-filled Rabinovich game as representative of Torre's draws in the second half at Moscow.

Game 77

Rabinovich-Torre

Moscow 1925, round 17

Queen's Fianchetto Defense [A50]

1.d4 ♘f6 2.c4 b6 3.♘f3 ♗b7 4.g3 c5

Something quite new at the time, seen only once before, in Havasi-Mattison, Debrecen 1925, just a few months earlier (1-0, 40).

5.d5 b5!?

This part of Torre's experiment was entirely new, and worthwhile. One can find some big names on the black side of later games with it, *e.g.* Klaman-Keres, 24th USSR Ch 1957 (½-½, 26), Johannessen-Fischer (yes, *that* Fischer), Havana Olympiad 1966 (0-1, 26), Rellstab-Keene, Hastings 1973-74 (0-1, 54), Hulak-Timman, Sarajevo 1984 (0-1, 73), and Pacey-I. Sokolov, Canadian Open 2013 (0-1, 25).

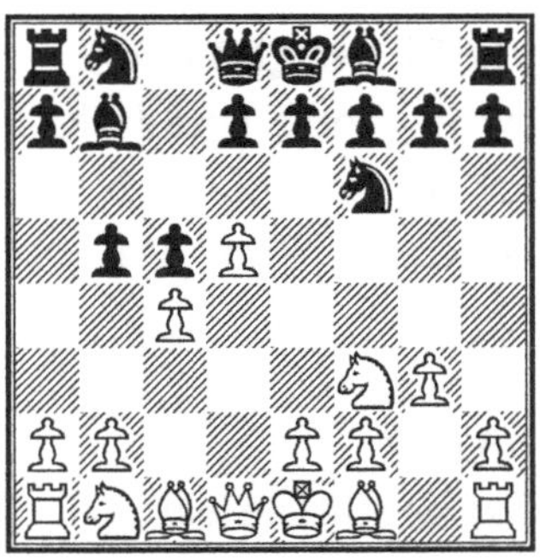

6.♗g2 e6?

But now Torre goes astray. Much better were 6...g6, 6...d6, or 6...b×c4.

7.♘h4

About the 5th-best reply. Stockfish rates 7.e4!,

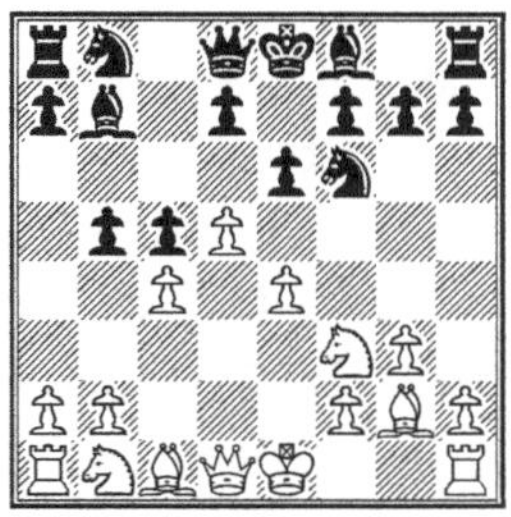

threatening 8.e5 ♘g4 9.0–0 b×c4 10.♘c3 e×d5 11.♘×d5 (-7.08/27), as virtually winning. Some sample lines:

(a) 7...♘×e4? 8.d×e6 f5 (if 8...d×e6? 9.♕×d8+ ♔×d8 10.♘g5 f5 11.♘f7+, or 8...f×e6 9.♘g5+–) 9.♘g5 ♗e7 [not 9...♘d6?? 10.♗×b7 ♘×b7 11.♘f7+– (11.♕d5 is also very strong)] 10.♗×e4 f×e4 11.♘f7+–;

(b) 7...♕a5+ 8.♗d2 ♕a6 9.c×b5 ♕×b5 10.♘c3 ♕a6 11.♘e5 ♗e7 12.♗f1 c4 13.♗×c4 ♕b6 14.0–0 (+3.84/29);

(c) 7...d6 8.d×e6 f×e6 9.c×b5 a6 (if 9...♘×e4 10.♘g5; 9...♗×e4 10.0–0 ♗e7 11.♖e1 ♘bd7 12.♘c3 ♗×f3 13.♕×f3 ♔f7 14.♗g5 ♖b8 15.♖ad1 with a killing attack (+6.00/23)) 10.♘c3 a×b5 11.♘g5 ♕e7 12.♘×b5 (+4.58/27);

(d) 7...b×c4 (relatively best) 8.0–0 e×d5 9.e×d5

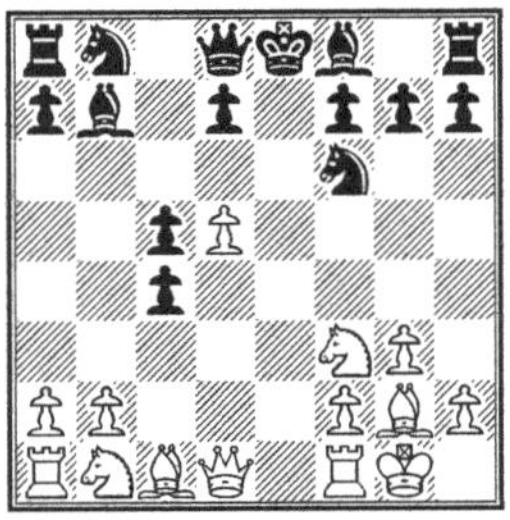

9...d6 (if 9...♗×d5? 10.♘c3 ♗c6 11.♖e1+ ♗e7 12.♕e2 d5 13.♘h4 and the best Black can do is give up the Bishop by 13...0–0, since if 13...♘e4 14.♘×d5 ♕×d5 15.♕g4+–) 10.♖e1+ ♗e7 11.♕e2 ♗×d5 (if 11...♘×d5 12.♘h4 0–0 13.♗×d5 ♗×d5 14.♕×e7+–) 12.♘c3 ♗b7 13.♗g5 ♘bd7 14.♖ad1 ♔f8 15.♘b5 ♗e4 16.♗×f6 ♘×f6 17.♘e5 ♗×g2 18.♔×g2 ♖c8 19.♘×a7 ♖c7 20.♘b5 ♖c8 21.♘×c4 d5 22.♘e3 g6 23.♘×d5 ♘×d5 24.♕f3 ♕b6 25.♕×d5 ♖d8 26.♕e5 ♗f6 27.♖×d8+ ♕×d8 28.♕×c5+ (+4.15/26).

Torre was fortunate that Rabinovich, primarily a positional player, did not have the tactical skill to find his way through these complications.

We return to the game after **7.♘h4**:

7...♕b6?

Torre steps in it again. Best now was 7...b×c4 8.d×e6 ♗×g2 9.e×f7+ ♔×f7 10.♘×g2 d5 11.♗g5 ♗e7 and Black should be able to castle by hand with ...♖h8-e8 and ...♔f7-g8 and reach an inferior but not lost game.

8.e4!

This time Rabinovich seizes his chance. This and his next four moves are all optimal.

8...b×c4 9.0–0 ♗e7 10.♘a3 ♕a6 11.♖e1 0–0 12.♗f1 ♖e8

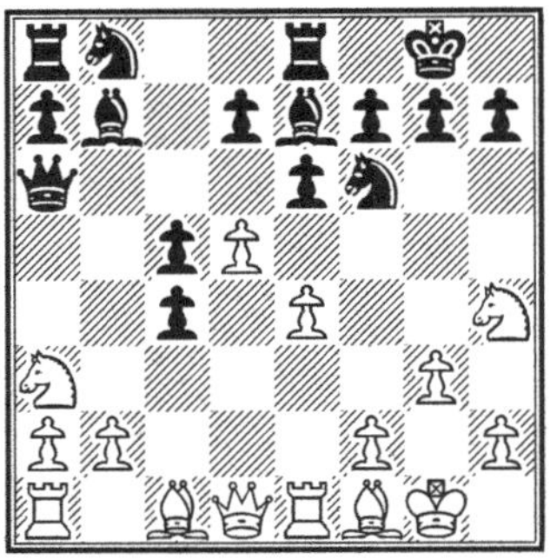

13.♗×c4?

But again Rabinovich shows his lack of tactical acumen.

Correct was 13.♘×c4! e×d5 14.e×d5 ♗×d5 15.♘e3 ♕b7 16.♘×d5 ♕×d5 (16...♘×d5?? 17.♘f5+–) 17.♕×d5 ♘×d5 18.♗g2 ♘c6 19.♗×d5 and White has won a piece. The text lets Black off the hook.

13...♕b6□ 14.♗b3 e×d5

But now it's Torre who lacks tactical acumen. Opening the e-file is counter-productive. Best was 14...♗f8 (+0.69/25).

15.e×d5 d6?

15...♗f8 was still the least evil.

16.♘f5

Not bad, but best was 16.♘c4 ♕c7 17.♗g5 ♘bd7 (forced) 18.♖×e7! ♖×e7 19.♘f5 ♖e5 (if 19...♖ee8? 20.♘c×d6

♖f8 21.♕f3 +6.10/28) 20.♘×e5 d×e5 21.♖c1 (+1.90/23).

16...♕d8??

An error more serious than 6...e6. Necessary was 16...♗f8±.

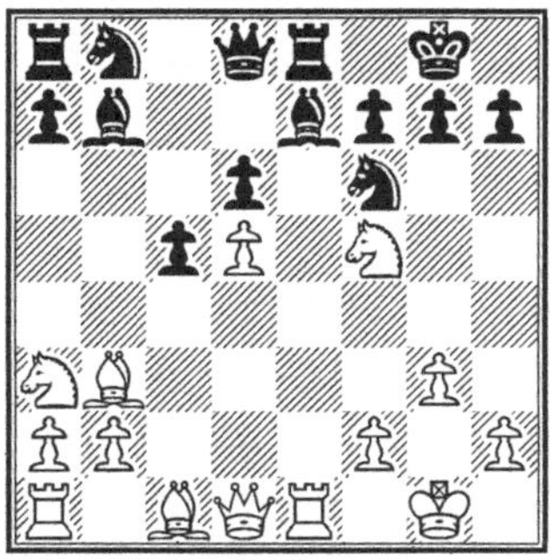

17.♗f4?

Rabinovich again does not see his chance. Winning was 17.♗a4! ♘bd7 (if 17...♘fd7 18.♘c4+−, or 17...♖f8?? 18.♘×e7+) 18.♗g5 and Black is helpless against the threats of 19.♕e2 or 19.♘c4. If 18...g6 19.♗×d7 ♕×d7 20.♘×e7+ ♖×e7 21.♗×f6+−.

17...♘bd7?

Yet again, 17...♗f8 was best (+0.91/25).

18.♘b5! ♘b6

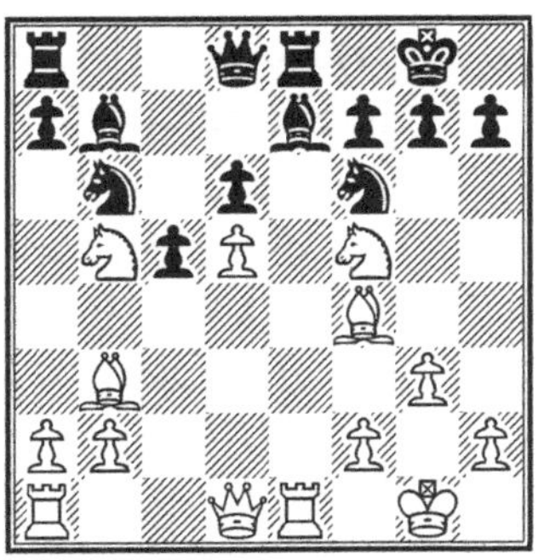

19.♘b×d6?!

Of the three ways the d-pawn could be captured, this is the least good. And in fact it was probably best not to capture it immediately, but finesse it by 19.♘c7! ♕×c7 20.♖×e7 ♖×e7 21.♗×d6 ♖e1+ 22.♕×e1 ♕d7 23.♘e7+ ♔h8 24.♗×c5 ♖e8 (not 24...♘b×d5? 25.♖d1) 25.♕b4 ♘f×d5 26.♘×d5 ♘×d5 27.♕a4 ♕c8 (if 27...♕×a4? 28.♗×a4 ♖e2 29.♖d1 h6 30.♗b3 ♘f6 31.♗×f7+−) 28.♗×a7 (28.♕×a7?? ♘f4−+) 28...♘f6 29.♕b5 (29.♗×f7?? ♕h3−+) 29...♖e7 30.♗d4 and with his passed pawns, White should win the endgame.

19...♗×d6 20.♘×d6 ♖×e1+ 21.♕×e1 ♗×d5 22.♗×d5 ♘b×d5

White has ended up not winning anything.

23.♕e5 ♕d7 24.♖c1 ♖d8?

Torre still seems determined to lose. Best was 24...♕h3 with a completely even game (if 25.♖×c5 ♘g4 26.♕d4□ ♘df6 forces a draw.

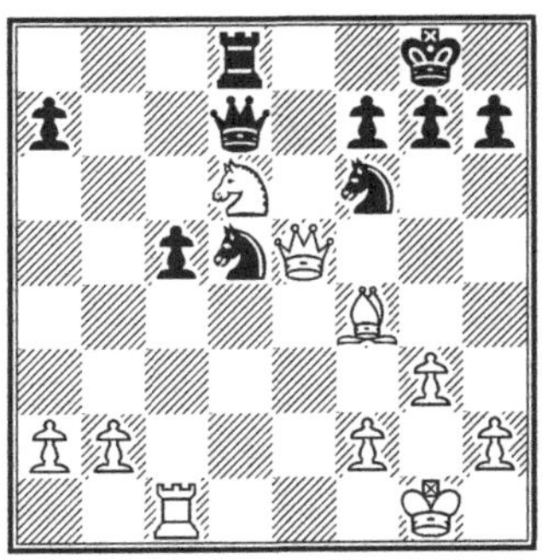

25.♖×c5 ♘b4?

Another serious error! Best was 25...♘×f4 26.♕×f4 ♕e6 (+0.75/26).

26.♖b5?!

But again Rabinovich is blind to opportunity.
Winning was 26.♕d4!

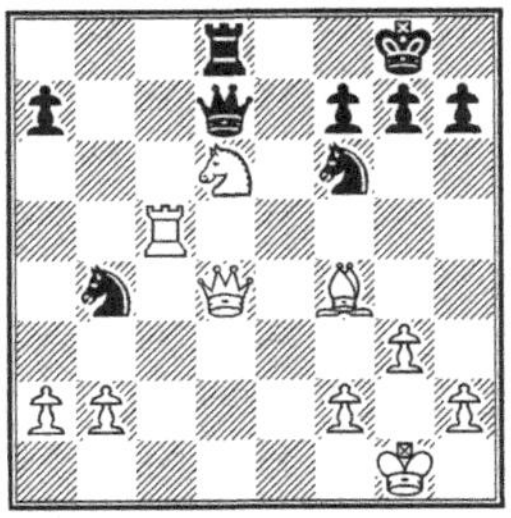

26...♘×a2 [if 26...♘c6? 27.♕c4 ♘b8 28.♖b5 (△29.♖b7) 28...♖f8 29.♘×f7!+−, or if 26...♘a6 27.♖a5 ♘c7 28.♖×a7+−] 27.♖a5 ♕e6 28.♖×a7 h6 29.♕b6! ♖f8 30.♕e3 ♕d5 31.♕d2 ♕×d2 (31...♕e6?? 32.b3+−) 32.♗×d2 ♖d8 33.♖a6 and wins (+3.92/25).

26...♘d3!□ 27.♕f5 ♘×f4

Better 27...♕×f5 28.♘×f5 ♘×f4 29.g×f4 g6 with an easier draw.

28.♕×d7 ♘×d7 29.g×f4 ♘b6 30.♘e4 ♖d4 31.f3 h6?!

Torre seems intent on finding the most difficult way to draw. Easier was 31...♔f8 or 31...♖d5.

32.b3 ♔f8?

Again, better 32...♖d5.

33.♖a5! ♖d7 34.f5! ♘d5 35.♔f2 ♔e7

⌓35...♘b4 36.♖a4 ♘c6

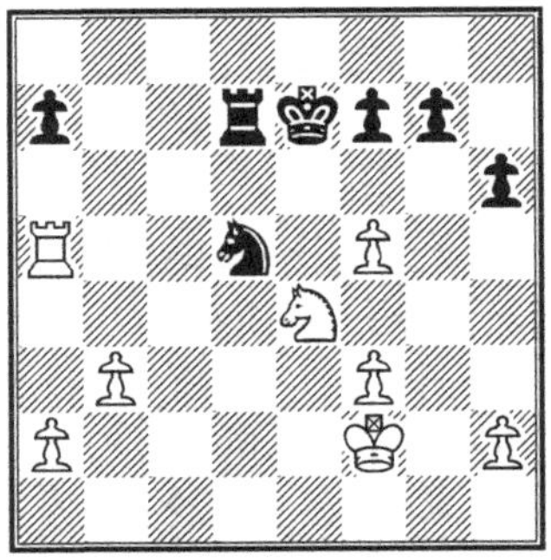

36.♖b5

It becomes abundantly clear that when it came to the endgame, Rabinovich was no Capablanca or Rubinstein. Despite repeated opportunities, he fails to make headway. White could have started something with 36.a3 ♔d8 37.b4 ♔c8 38.♘c5 (+3.28/25).

36...♘f4 37.♖b8 ♘d3+ 38.♔g3 ♘c1 39.a4 ♘e2+ 40.♔g4 ♘d4 41.b4 ♘c6 42.♖g8 ♘×b4 43.♖×g7 ♖d4 44.♖g8 ♘d5 45.♖b8 ½-½

The many mistakes in the above game clearly indicate that by round 13 at Moscow Torre was seriously fatigued, probably both mentally and physically. And perhaps after the euphoria of drawing with Capablanca and defeating Lasker, a psychological letdown was inevitable. It is unfortunate that Torre's bye at Moscow came at the beginning, rather than, say, after the Lasker game, when it might have helped him recover his energy and equipoise.

Game 78

Bohatirchuk-Torre

Moscow 1925, round 19

Of all the Soviet players at Moscow 1925, the Ukrainian Fedor Parfenovich Bohatirchuk (1892-1984, IM title 1954), of Kiev, might have had the most interesting life ahead of him. From 1923 to 1934 he played in six Soviet Championships, co-winning (with Romanovsky) in 1927, and sharing third place four other times. When in September 1941 Kiev fell to the Germans, Bohatirchuk, a radiologist, willingly joined a German medical facility. Working with the Red Cross, Bohatirchuk did a lot to help Soviet POWs held by the Germans under harsh conditions. This however irritated the Germans, and in February 1942 Bohatirchuk was arrested and spent about a month in a Gestapo detention centre in Kiev. Eventually he joined the Committee for the Liberation of the Peoples of Russia, an anti-communist, collaborationist militia organized by the Nazis in Prague in late 1944, headed by the turncoat Russian general Andrey Vlasov. In May 1945, after the defeat of Germany, Bohatirchuk was reunited with his family in American-occupied Bayreuth, and eventually emigrated to Canada, playing under that flag in the 1954 Olympiad. His wartime collaboration incurred the wrath of Soviet authorities, and until the 1976 defection of Victor Korchnoi, Bohatirchuk was the #1 *persona non grata* of Soviet chess, with many of his games expunged from the official records.

Torre's game with him is one both players might have wished to be expunged, as they traded errors until Torre made the last one. We pick up the action after

21.h4-h5?:

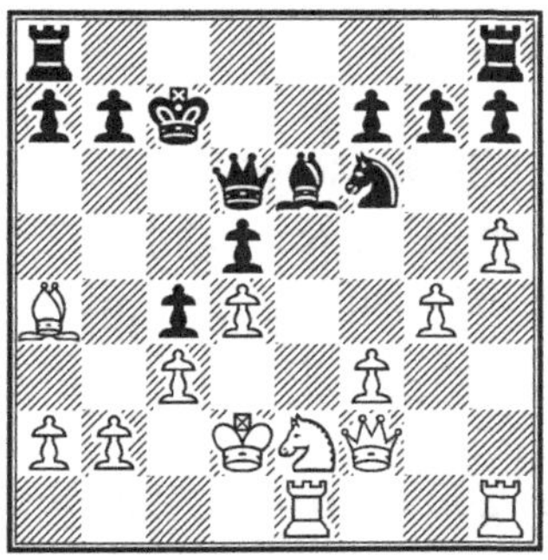

A rather elementary error; it is surprising both that Bohatirchuk played it and Torre failed to capitalize.

21...b5?!

Missing the simple 21...♗×g4! and either 22.f×g4?? ♘e4+, or 22.♘g3 ♗e6 (-1.81/23), or 22.♕g3 ♕×g3 23.♘×g3 ♗e6 (-1.25/23).

22.♗c2

Not 22.♗×b5?? ♖ab8 23.a4 (23.♗a4 ♖×b2+) 23...a6−+.

22...b4 23.g5 ♘d7 24.♕h4 ♖ab8 25.♖b1 a5 26.♘f4 ♖b6 27.♖he1 a4 28.♖e3?

⌓28.c×b4 ♕×b4+ 29.♔d1=

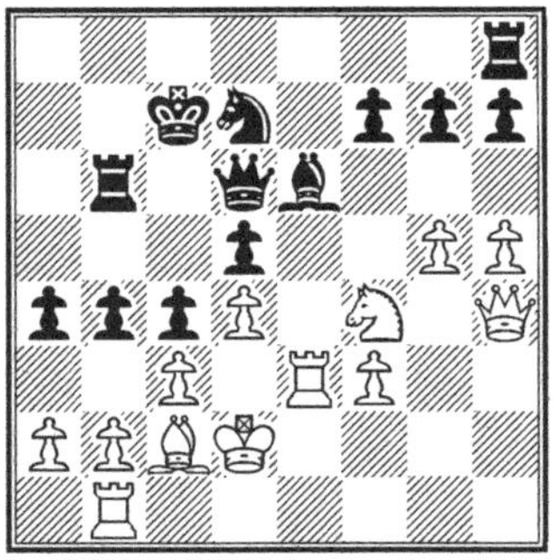

28...a3

Torre misses 28...b3! 29.a×b3 a×b3 30.♗d1 ♖a6 31.♘×e6+ f×e6 32.f4 ♖f8 33.♖f3 ♖aa8∓.

29.b3 ♖hb8? 30.g6?!

Bohatirchuk misses 30.♗×h7!, and if 30...g6 31.h×g6 ♗f5 32.g×f7! ♗×b1 33.♗×b1+−.

30...h×g6 31.h×g6 ♖c6 32.♖c1 b×c3+ 33.♖×c3

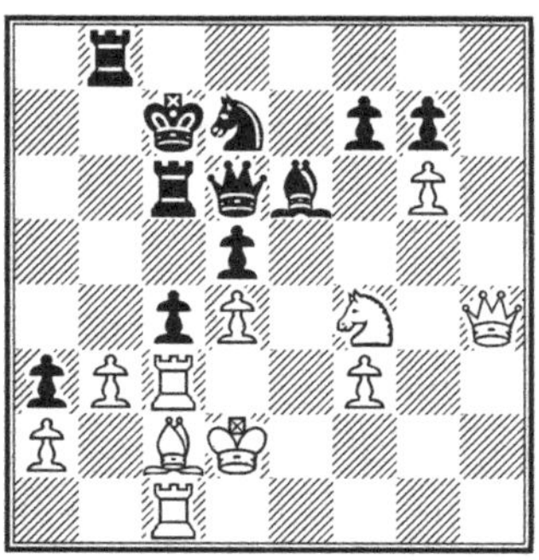

33...♕b4?

Natural-looking but wrong. Best was 33...♖h8! 34.♕g3 (if 34.♕×h8?? ♕×f4+ and Black wins the Rook back with interest after either 35.♔d1 ♕×d4+, or 35.♔e2 ♕×c1, or 35.♖e3 c×b3 36.a×b3 ♖c3) 34...♘b6=.

34.b×c4!

Bohatirchuk finally grabs an opportunity.

34...♖×c4?

Not quite so bad was 34...♘b6 35.c5 ♘c4+ 36.♔e2 ♖h8 (not 36...♕×c3?? 37.♘×d5+ ♗×d5 38.♕e7+ ♔c8 39.♗f5+ etc.) 37.♕g3 ♔c8 38.♗b3 (+1.96/23).

35.♗b3!□ ♖×c3 36.♖×c3+ ♔b6 37.♘d3 ♕a5 38.♕f4?!

38.g×f7 or 38.♕e7 would have been enough to compel resignation (both about +6.00).

38...♖c8 39.♕d6+

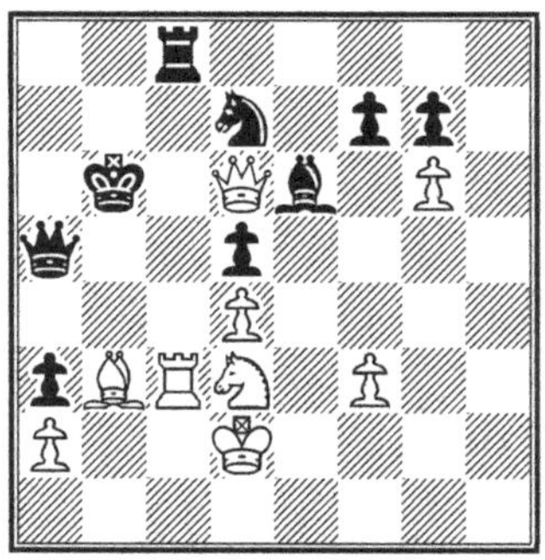

39...♔a7?

39...♔b7 was best, *viz.* 40.♘b4 ♖×c3 41.♔×c3 ♕c7+ 42.♕×c7+ ♔×c7 43.g×f7 [if 43.♘×d5+ ♗×d5 44.♗×d5 f×g6, and most importantly, if 43.♗×d5 ♔d6! (the crucial difference between this and the game continuation)

44.♗×e6 f×e6 (only +0.79/32)] 43...♗×f7 44.♘×d5+ ♗×d5 45.♗×d5 and Black may have an outside chance of holding the ♗-vs-♘ ending.
Torre had shown excellent awareness of such nuances against Capablanca, but not here.

40.♘b4 ♖×c3 41.♔×c3 ♕b6 42.♕×b6+ ♔×b6 43.♗×d5

With the black King one crucial square further away, this is decisive.

43...♗×d5 44.♘×d5+ ♔c6 45.♘b4+ ♔d6 46.g×f7 ♔e7 47.♘c6+ ♔×f7 48.♘e5+ ♘×e5 49.d×e5
Reaching an elementary pawn ending, easily won.

49...♔e6 50.♔d4 ♔e7 51.♔d5 ♔d7 52.f4 ♔e7 53.f5 ♔d7 54.f6 1–0

In the penultimate round, Torre did manage to produce a delightful minor masterpiece.

Game 79

Torre-Verlinsky

Moscow 1925, round 20

Torre Attack [D03]

Boris Markovich Verlinsky (1888-1950, historical Elo 2480, IM title 1950), though not well remembered today, was at the time of this tournament among the USSR's top 5 or 6 players, placing 4th in the 1925 Soviet Championship a few months earlier. At his peak, victories in the 1928 Moscow Championship and 1929 Soviet Championship made Verlinsky the first to receive the title "Grandmaster of the USSR." (According to Bronstein, he was later retroactively stripped of it so that Party favorite Mikhail Botvinnik could be officially "the first," though Soltis merely says the title was temporarily abolished 1931-35). Nearly deaf, Verlinsky understood speech by lip-reading, yet he loved to attend the symphony, and played the violin. Though in this event Verlinsky defeated among others Capablanca, Spielmann, Rubinstein, and Sämisch, against Carlos Torre he suffered a devastating defeat, in what is undoubtedly one of Torre's most beautiful games, and one of the more brilliant sacrificial attacks ever played.

1.d4 ♘f6 2.♘f3 b6 3.♗g5 ♗b7 4.♘bd2 d5

Yet again we reach a new position at a very early stage. Nenarokov-Grigoriev, Moscow Ch playoff, 1921, had the same moves through White's fourth, but then continued 4...d6.

5.e3 ♘bd7 6.♗d3 e6

ChessBase has only a few dozen games reaching this position. In the two with the highest-rated players, Mariotti-Tatai, 1st match game, Rome 1977, and Hort-Ljubojevic, Tilburg 1978, Black played 6...g6.

7.♘e5

An indication Torre is already thinking kingside attack.

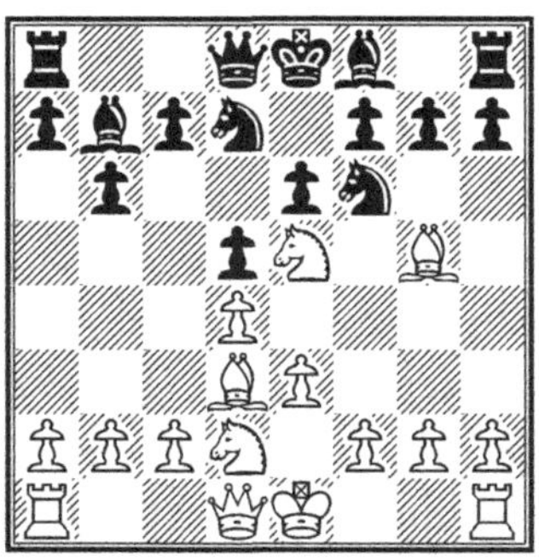

7...a6?!

Not a useful move. 8.♗b5 was a threat, but the way to counter it was 7...♘×e5. Black later trades off this Knight, but it was best done immediately: 7...♘×e5 8.d×e5 h6, with equality after either 9.♗f4 ♘d7, or 9.♗h4 g5 10.♗g3 ♘d7, and somewhat the better game after 9.♗×f6 g×f6 10.e×f6 ♕×f6, 9.♗×h6 ♖×h6 10.e×f6 ♕×f6, or 9.e×f6 h×g5 10.f×g7 ♗×g7. The game V. Sokolov-Matanovic, Yugoslav Championship 1965, continued 7...♘×e5 8.d×e5 h6 9.♗h4 g5 10.♗g3 ♘e4 11.♗×e4 d×e4 12.h4 ♖g8 13.h×g5 ♕×g5 14.♕e2 0–0–0 15.0–0–0 ♕g6 16.♕h5 ½-½.

8.f4!

In Torre's games one often sees the marked influence of Pillsbury, whose games Torre had enthusiastically studied since age 13, along with those of Morphy, Mason, and Tarrasch (whose *300 Chess Games* was almost obligatory reading in those days). While on some occasions Torre took on the style of Tarrasch, in his best attacks the stamp of Pillsbury is very evident. The present game is a clear example, White's last two moves resembling the 13th and 14th moves of Pillsbury-Tarrasch, Hastings 1895. 8...♘×e5?, good the move before when White had to recapture with the d-pawn, would now be distinctly disadvantageous, as White recaptures 9.f×e5.

8...♗e7 9.0–0 c5

While of course Black eventually needs to strike at White's center, right now it was more prudent to worry about the forces White is aiming kingside.

Best was 9...♘e4, forcing 10.♗×e7 ♕×e7, when Black stands only slightly worse (+0.63/25).

10.c3 0–0?

A prime example of "castling into it."

11.♕f3!

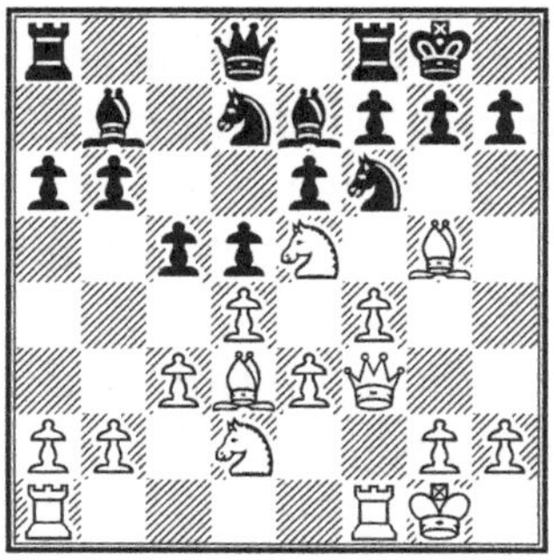

11...♘×e5?

Black was already in trouble, but this is nearly suicidal. There was no good alternative, but some less bad ones were:

(a) 11...a5 12.♕g3 c×d4 13.♕h4 ♗a6 Hoping to eliminate the threat of ♗×h7+, but allowing one just as bad: 14.♘c6 ♗×d3□ (not 14...♕e8?? 15.♗×h7+ ♘×h7 16.♘×e7+ ♔h8 17.♖f3 and mate in five) 15.♘×d8 ♖f×d8 16.e×d4 ♗×f1 17.♖×f1 and White is up ♕-for-♖+♗ (-1.79);

(b) 11...h6 12.♕h3! h×g5 13.f×g5 ♘×e5 14.d×e5 ♘e4 15.g6 f×g6 16.♕×e6+ ♔h7 17.♖×f8 ♗×f8 (if 17...♕×f8?? 18.♘×e4 d×e4 19.♕h3+ ♔g8 20.♗c4+) 18.♘×e4 d×e4 19.♗c4 ♗e7□ 20.♕h3+ ♗h4 21.g3 ♗d5 22.♗e2 ♔g8 23.♕×h4 ♕×h4 24.g×h4, and the precarious pawn structure notwithstanding, White should win the ending (+2.28/29);

(c) Probably best is 11...♘e8 12.♗×h7+ (Also 12.♗×e7 ♕×e7 13.♗×h7+ can be played, transposing. But if, say, 12.♕h5, then Black puts a damper on the attack with 12...f5.) 12...♔×h7 13.♕h5+ ♔g8 14.♗×e7! ♕×e7 15.♖f3 ♘×e5 16.♖h3 ♘f3+□ 17.♘×f3 f6 18.g4 ♘d6□ 19.♖f1 ♗c8 20.♖f2 c×d4 21.e×d4 ♕e8 22.♕h7+ ♔f7 23.♘e5+! ♔e7 (if 23...f×e5?? 24.f×e5+ ♔e7 25.♕×g7+ ♘f7 26.♖h7+–) 24.♕×g7+ ♖f7 (24...♘f7?? 25.♘g6+) 25.♘×f7 ♕×f7 26.♕×f7+ ♔×f7 27.g5 and the ending will favor White, but not greatly (+1.23/25).

12.f×e5

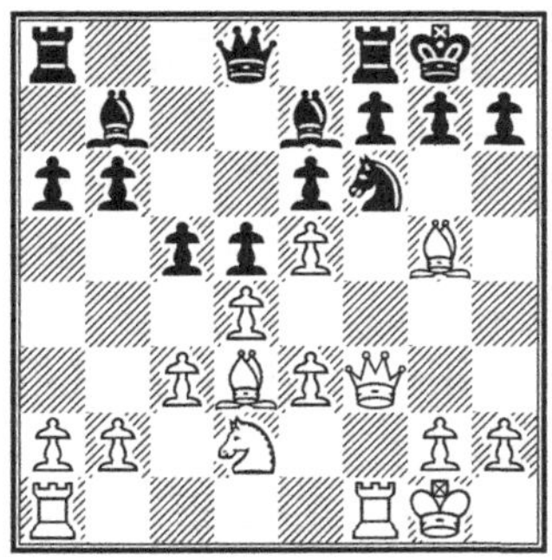

12...♘d7??

Though it is perhaps not obvious, this natural-looking move turns out to be the decisive mistake. Only after White unleashes some tremendously powerful and brilliant moves will it be clear that there is no possibility for Black to escape defeat.

As to alternatives, the Russian tournament book looked at 12...♘e8, concluding that White should win after 13.♗×h7+ ♔×h7 14.♕h5+ ♔g8 15.♘f3, which Stockfish sees as problematic after 15...f6, when White must find the tricky continuation 16.♘h4!

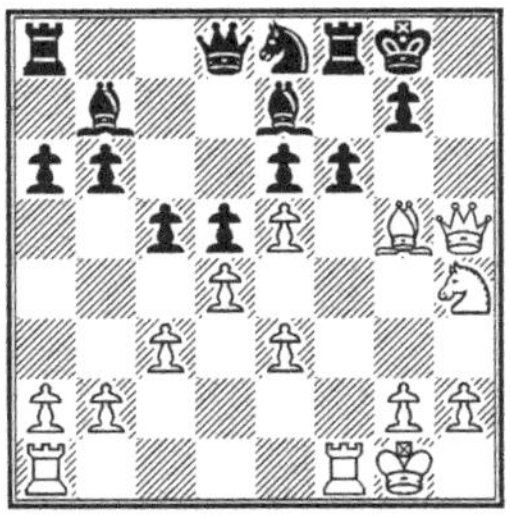

16...f×g5 17.♘g6 ♖×f1+ 18.♖×f1 ♘f6□ 19.e×f6 ♗×f6 20.g4 ♕d6 21.♔g2 (if 21.♖f3?! c×d4 22.e×d4 e5 23.d×e5 ♕c5+ and Black has counterplay (+1.44/23)) 21...♗c6 22.♖f3 ♗b5 23.♕h8+ ♔f7 24.♘e5+ (not 24.♕×a8? ♔×g6=) 24...♕×e5□ 25.♕h5+ ♔g8 26.d×e5 ♗e8 (if 26...♗×e5?? 27.♕f7+ ♔h8 28.♖h3#) 27.♕h3 ♗×e5, and though White has the Queen for two Bishops and a pawn, Black can resist a long time (+2.20/26).

In any event, that is all academic because after 12...♘e8 White has the much stronger 13.♕h3!,

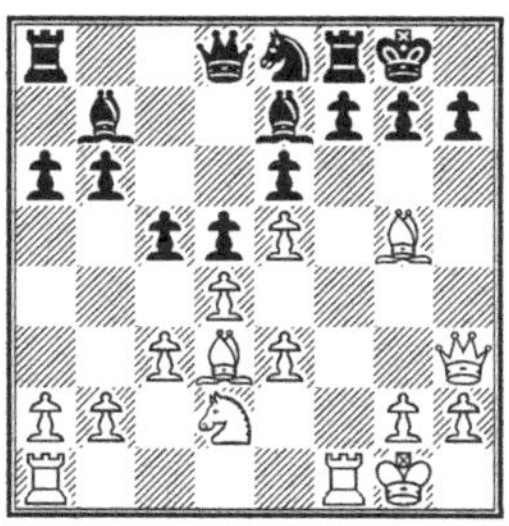

forcing 13...g6 14.♗h6 ♘g7 15.♖f2 ♗c6 (to enable ...♗c6-b5 or ...♗c6-e8 depending on circumstances) 16.g4 (16.♖af1 ♗b5 17.♗×b5 a×b5 is less good) 16...♗b5 17.♗c2 a5 18.a4 ♗a6 19.♘f3 ♖a7 with a long-term kingside siege in prospect, which White should win (+2.38/29).

The other playable alternative was 12...♘e4, forcing 13.♗×e7 ♕×e7 14.♘×e4 d×e4 15.♗×e4 ♗×e4 16.♕×e4, when White's attacking prospects have disappeared but he has gained a pawn. Stockfish sees White as ultimately winning (+2.48/25), but with all the major pieces still on the board, Black can fight on for some time.

But after the text, Black goes down in technicolor flames.

13.♕h3! g6

If 13...h6?? 14.♗×h6 g×h6 15.♕×h6 f5 (anything else allows mate in two) 16.e×f6 ♖f7 (if 16...♘×f6 17.♕g6+ ♔h8 18.♖×f6 ♖f7 19.♖×f7 ♕g8 20.♖h7+ ♕×h7 21.♕×h7#) 17.♕g5+ ♔f8 18.f×e7+ ♕×e7 19.♖×f7+ ♕×f7 20.♖f1 +−.

14.♗h6

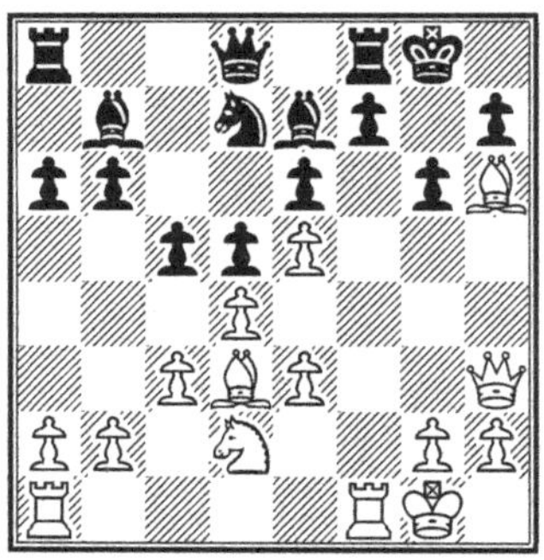

14...c4

By closing the center in this manner, Black only further justifies White's kingside attack. Now Black can only sit and wait to be crushed, but there was no adequate defense anyway.

Against 14...♖e8

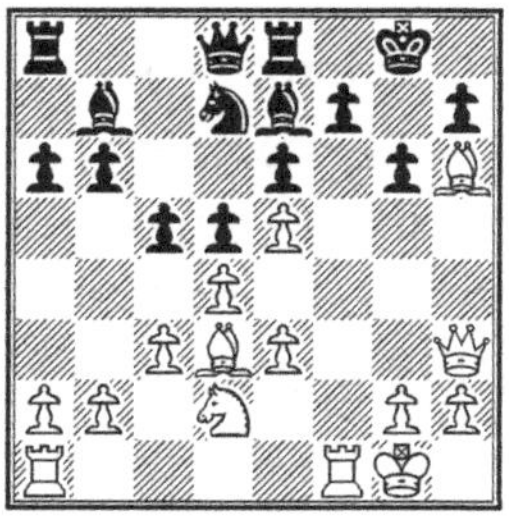

White would also have won brilliantly by 15.♖×f7!! ♔×f7 16.♖f1+ and either 16...♗f6 17.♗g5+−, or the sac-everything-but-the-kitchen-sink line 16...♔g8 17.♕×e6+ ♔h8 18.♗g7+!! ♔×g7 19.♖f7+ ♔h8 20.♖×h7+!! ♔×h7 21.♕×g6+ etc.

The least of evils may have been 14...♗g5 15.♗×f8 ♕×f8, but White would still have remained with a decisive advantage (+4.12/24).

15.♗c2 b5 16.♖f2

White can get a won game with the simple 16.♗×f8 here or in the next two moves, but Torre, emulating his idols Pillsbury and Morphy, wants to win with more panache.

16...♕b6 17.♖af1 f5 18.e×f6 ♖×f6 19.♘f3

As the Mexican saying goes, "Ya está toda la carne en el asador" — Now all the meat is on the grill.

19...♖e8 20.♕g3

The position is such that almost any move wins for White. Other possibilities: 20.♘e5! (+8.30), 20.♘h4 (+7.38), 20.♗f4 (+7.18), and 20.♗g5 (+5.88).

20...♘f8

The least evil was 20...♖f5, but that is like saying the guillotine is preferable to the gallows.

21.♘e5 ♕d8 22.h4

Of course, the prosaic 22.♘g4 would also have won very quickly, but as the late master Nicolas Rossolimo used to say: "I don't want just the point, I want my brilliancy!"

22...♖f5 23.♗×f5 ♗×h4

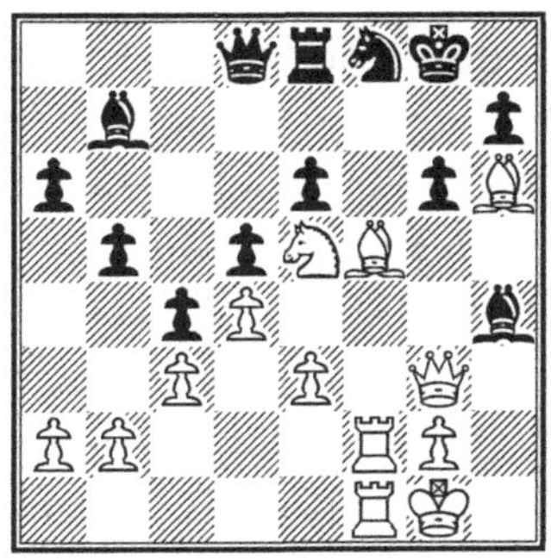

24.♗×g6!!

The best move on the board, and the one that makes this game such a gem.

24...♗×g3

Anything else allows mate in six or less.

25.♗f7+ ♔h8 26.♗×e8 ♗×f2+ 27.♖×f2 1–0

If Carlos Torre ever played an "immortal game" comparable to those of Morphy and Anderssen, this was it. It belies Capablanca's curious assertion that at Moscow "there were few good games," though he may have been thinking of Verlinsky's poor play here. In addition to Torre's effort here and against Dus-Chotimirsky and especially Gotthilf, the games Capablanca-Bogoljubow, Tartakower-Rubinstein, and Réti-Bogoljubow were also of very high quality. In fact, according to the February 1926 issue of the *Deutsche Schachzeitung*, there were so many tactically brilliant and/or positionally well-played games at Moscow 1925 that the prize judges had great difficulty choosing the most deserving.

The *ACB*, in its summary of the tournament in the December 1925 issue, would say:

> Apart from the feat of Bogoljubow, the showing of Carlos Torre of New York is generally regarded as the sensation of this tournament. After Baden-Baden and Marienbad, the chess world in a measure was prepared for what he did at Moscow. Starting with a bye in the first round, the talented young Mexican won his first three games and then drew two, after which he won two more. Bogoljubow checked him in the ninth round. He won in the tenth. Next came the ordeal which had been his chief reason for crossing the ocean. He encountered Capablanca and Dr. Lasker in the eleventh and twelfth rounds, drawing with the former and defeating the latter, gloriously! ...
>
> At this point in the tournament the finger of destiny seemed to point straight at Torre. However in the next nine rounds he experienced a reversal ... Disappointing as this was to him and his friends, he nevertheless enjoyed the satisfaction of dividing fifth and sixth prizes *[500 and 350 rubles, respectively]* with such a veteran campaigner as Dr. S. Tartakower, who again showed himself to be one of the hardest opponents to win a game from.

Torre's results at Moscow were mixed but on the whole promising. On the minus side was his slide in the second half. On the positive side was his =5th-6th place (in a field of 21) with a 60% score (+8 -4 =8), which included a net plus (+2 -1 =1) against the four players ahead of him in the final standings, two of them world champions and the other two past or future world championship challengers. After the tournament, Tartakower wrote "Even though Torre lost much of his physical strength in the second part of the tournament, because of his weak health, he still represents a great hope for the world of chess. The general opinion is that the future world champion has the right and obligation to play chess like Torre does."

Leningrad Quadrangular Tournament

In the February 1926 *American Chess Bulletin*, Torre himself reported on this event:

> Shortly after the big tournament in Moscow, my friend Mr. J. Rockline[1], secretary of the chess section of Leningrad and president of the Leningrad Chess Club, arranged to have me participate in a quadrangular tournament held in that city in January.
>
> The result was a great triumph for Gotthilf, who also played in the International Tournament in Moscow, finishing with a score of 4-2. Rockline and myself tied with 3-3, and Model, who played the higher chess, but was guilty of bad moves in some of his games, entirely reversing the value of the position, had to be content with 2-4.
>
> The conditions of play were most happily worked out with a time limit of 45 moves in 3 hours, with 6 hours straight play. As a result some very fine chess was developed, the fact that there were no adjourned games notwithstanding.

We present here two games from that event; two others appear in Chapter VII, where we reproduce *Development of Chess Ability*, with Torre's own notes.

Game 80
Model-Torre

Leningrad Quadrangular 1926
Queen's Indian Defense [E14]

Abram Yakovlevich Model (1896-1976) was a prominent Russian master. Soon after this tournament he played in the USSR's first international team match, Leningrad-Stockholm, 1926. He would place equal 3rd in the 1927 Soviet Championship, ahead of Botvinnik, whom he later helped train. Model was strong enough to beat Botvinnik as late as the 1930s.

1.c4 ♘f6 2.♘f3 b6 3.♘c3 ♗b7 4.d4 e6 5.e3 ♗e7 6.♗d3 d6 7.0–0 ♘bd7 8.e4 e5 9.♕e2 0–0 10.d5

1 Russian names, transliterated from the Cyrillic script, often get various spellings in other languages. Here the person Torre refers to is usually rendered as Yakov Rokhlin.

♘c5 11.♗c2 a5
The typical pawn advance securing the position of the Knight on c5.

12.♘e1 ♘fd7 13.♘d1
Heading for f5, though the trip involves a lot of time and ends up accomplishing little.

13...♗c8
Anticipating the Knight's arrival on f5. In any event, the Bishop no longer had much to do on the now clogged a8-h1 diagonal.

14.♘e3 ♗g5!
A typical maneuver in this sort of position. Black hopes to trade his bad Bishop for the opposite good one.

15.♘f5 g6

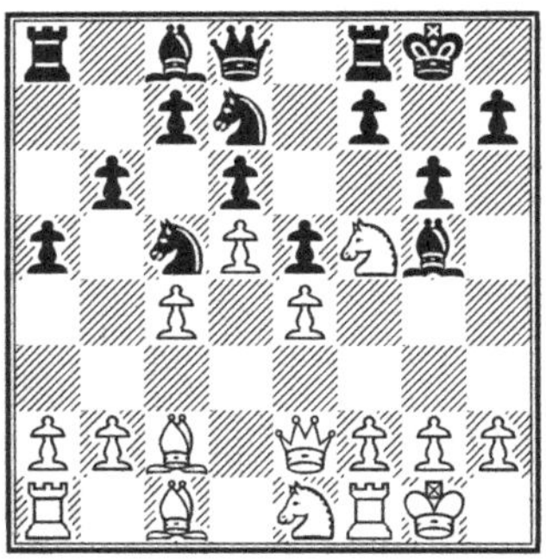

Played with a view to complications. After the automatic 15...♗×c1 16.♖×c1 the game would be quite even.

16.f4?
After 16.♘g3 ♗f4 the initiative would pass to Black, but better was 16.♗×g5 ♕×g5 17.♘f3 ♕f6 18.♘e3=.

16...e×f4
Slightly better was 16...♗×f4 17.♗×f4 e×f4 18.♘d4 ♕f6 19.♘ef3 ♘e5 20.♘×e5 d×e5, when Black can retain the pawn.

17.♘d4 ♘e5

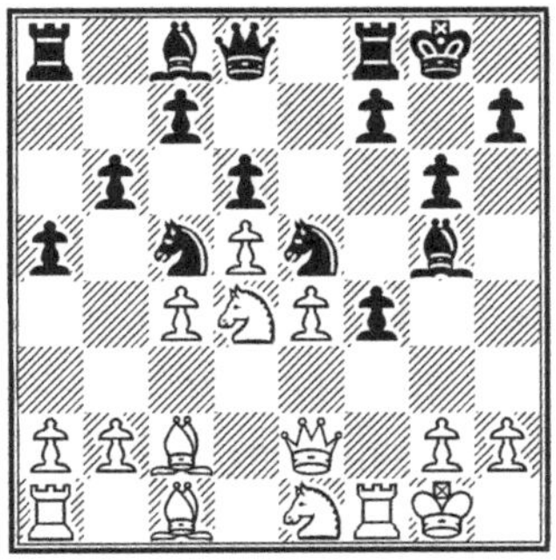

18.h3?!
White should have remembered the old Steinitz rule: "Do not create weaknesses on the side where your opponent is attacking!"
Slightly better was 18.♗×f4 ♗×f4 19.♖×f4, regaining the pawn, though then Black still stands better after 19...♕g5! 20.♖f1 ♗g4 21.♘ef3 (21.♕f2? ♘×c4) 21...♗×f3 22.♘×f3 ♘×f3+ 23.♕×f3 ♕e5∓.

18...♗d7 19.b3 ♕e7
Playable was 19...♕f6, retaining the pawn for the time being, and if 20.♗b2, with the idea of eventually threatening the black Queen, Black need not be concerned, *e.g.* 20...♖fe8 21.♘ef3 (not 21.♘df3?? ♘×f3+ 22.♘×f3 ♕×b2 23.♘×g5 h6 24.♘f3 ♘×e4−+) 21...♗h6 22.♖ab1 ♗g7 23.♘b5 ♕d8 24.♘fd4 g5∓.

20.♗×f4

White decides to recover his pawn, but Black remains in complete control of the dark squares. It is difficult to find a good plan for White. If 20.♗d2 there would follow 20...♗h6, threatening 21...g5, and White would then be compelled to take the pawn anyway. The drawback of White's position is not only that his kingside has been weakened by the advance 18.h3, but also that his pieces lack the coordination required for any middle game plan. As far as Black is concerned, he does have a clear plan: attack against White's weakened kingside. Also he has not only the advantage of good-vs.-bad Bishop, but magnificent posts for his Knights as well.

20...♗×f4 21.♖×f4 ♕g5

Of course not the hasty 21...♗×h3?? 22.g×h3 ♕g5+ 23.♘g2 and Black has no compensation for the sacrificed Bishop.

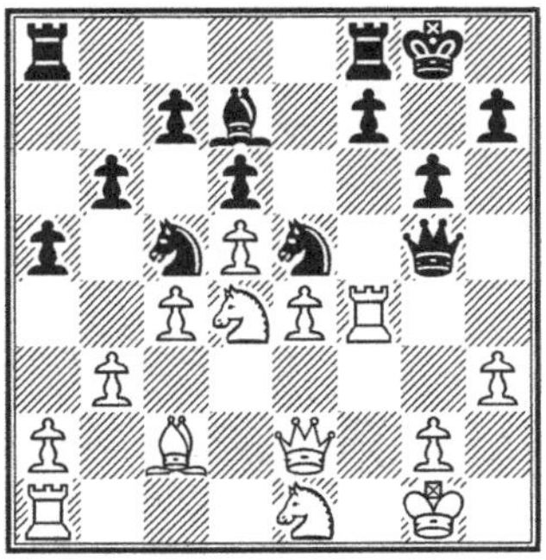

22.♖f2?

Critical was 22.♕d2, with complete equality. If then 22...♗×h3?? 23.♘df3 ♘×f3+ 24.♘×f3 ♕g3 25.♖h4+– (if 25...♗d7 26.♕h6!). By retreating the Rook back to the second rank, the text makes the Bishop sac possible.

22...♗×h3 23.♘ef3 ♘×f3+ 24.♘×f3 ♕g3 25.♕d2?

Good at move 22, this now worsens White's plight. Better was 25.♘d4.

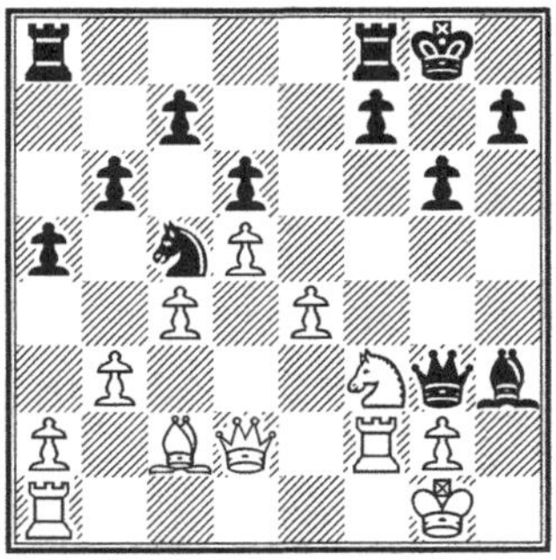

25...♗g4

Somewhat stronger was 25...♗×g2! 26.♕g5 (26.♖×g2? ♕×f3) 26...♕×g5 27.♘×g5 f6 28.♘×h7 ♔×h7 29.♖×g2 (+4.11/25).

26.♕g5?

Model is unable to fathom the complications. Less bad was 26.♘d4, keeping a Knight on the board (-2.07/25).

26...f6 27.♕h6 ♗×f3 28.♖×f3 ♕e5 29.♖e1 ♖ae8 30.♖h3

Though materially Black is up only one pawn, his positional advantages push Stockfish's evaluation up over -5.00. White has major, permanent dark-square weaknesses, "severe melanpenia" to use Kmoch's phrase, and this will prove decisive. White's apparent pressure along the h-file is temporary and irrelevant. Black need only apply reasonably good technique and the win is assured.

30...♖f7 31.♖ee3?

Either desperation, or White still has illusions of a counterattack by ♖e3-g3, with the threat of ♖×g6+ and so on. These are quickly dispelled.

31...♕a1+

Torre takes immediate advantage of the error.

32.♔h2 ♕c1 33.e5?

Running completely wild, but the prospect of exchanging Queens and going into a very inferior and hopeless ending was bleak.

33...♕×c2 34.e×f6 ♘e4! 35.♖h4 ♘×f6 36.♖×e8+ ♘×e8 0-1

Game 81

Rokhlin-Torre

Leningrad Quadrangular 1926,
Queen's Gambit, Baltic Defense [D06]

Yakov Rokhlin (1903-1996) was at this time an up-and-coming young Leningrad master. He would play in the 1927 and 1929 Soviet Championships, but was more important as an instructor, trainer, author, and organizer; for example he had put together the 4th Soviet Championship in 1925, just a few months before Torre came to Moscow. Notes in italics here are ours, those labeled "CT:" are by Torre, mostly from the January 1926 *ACB*.

1.d4 ♘f6 2.♘f3 d5 3.c4 ♗f5

Torre tries again the line with which he beat Marshall at Moscow (see Game 66).

4.♘c3 e6 5.♗g5 c6 6.e3 ♕b6 7.♕d2

CT: A fine move, for if Black plays 7...♘e4 8.♘×e4 d×e4 9.c5 ♕c7 10.♗c4 and 11.♘e5, with a magnificent game.

7...♘bd7

White does not fear 7...♘e4 due to 8.♘×e4 ♗×e4 9.c5 ♕c7 10.♗f4 etc. Or 7...♗b4 8.♗×f6 g×f6 9.a3 ♗×c3 10.♕×c3 ♘d7 11.c5 ♕c7 12.b4 with a considerable space advantage for White.

8.c5 ♕a5 9.a3

CT: Otherwise Black may continue with 9...b6.
The text prepares b2-b4 *in the event of* ...b7-b6.

9...♗e7 10.♗d3 ♕d8
Ending the Queen's somewhat inopportune adventure.
CT: An examination of the position will show this to be the best move.

11.0–0 0–0
Perhaps more prudent was 11...♘e4, *forcing* 12.♗×e4 d×e4 13.♗×e7 ♕×e7 14.♘e1, *though this creates a rather dull position of deadeye equality* (0.00/26).

12.♗×f6
CT: This exchange is not at all forced, but White does not fancy 12...♘e4.

12...♗×f6?!
Better was 12...♘×f6, *so that if* 13.♗×f5 e×f5 14.♕d3, *then* 14...♘e4 *is playable.*

13.e4
Again a space advantage could be had, by 13.♗×f5 e×f5 14.♕c2 g6 15.b4±.

13...d×e4 14.♗×e4 ♗g4
CT: A fine conception. White is to be left with his KB, which Black's pawn position renders ineffective.
The idea of this move is to break through in the center with ...e6-e5 as soon as possible. The alternative 14...♗×e4 15.♘×e4 ♕c7= *was perhaps equally good, but it seems that Torre was in the mood to play an open game instead of a closed one.*

15.♕f4 ♗×f3 16.♗×f3 e5 17.d×e5 ♗×e5 18.♕c4 ♕f6 19.♖ad1 ♖ad8 20.♕b4

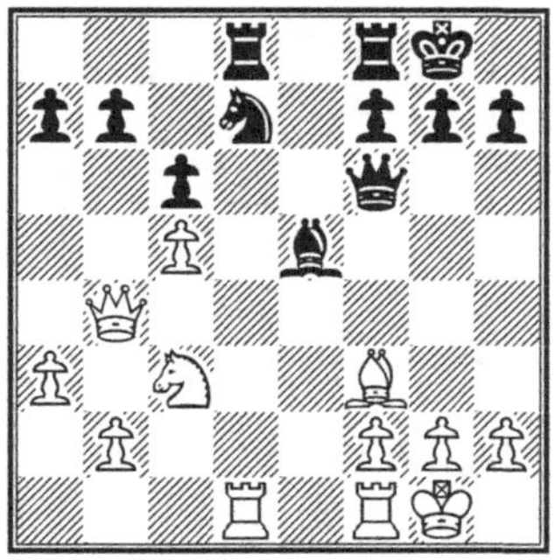

20...a5
CT: After forty minutes' deliberation Black commits himself to this advance. But the more exact move would be to improve his game with 20...g6, although it appears that White could likewise improve his game with 21.♖fe1. But such is not the case, as will be explained later.
The text is better than 20...g6 21.♕×b7 ♕f4 22.g3 ♕×f3 23.♖×d7 ♖b8 24.♕×a7 ♖×b2=, *which would be a continuation very similar to that of the actual game. However, after the text, Black keeps his a-pawn for a while, since if now* 21.♕×a5 ♕f4 22.♖fe1 ♕×h2+∓.

21.♕×b7 ♕f4 22.g3 ♕×f3 23.♖×d7 ♖b8 24.♕a6 ♖×b2
CT: Because now if the black pawn was at g6 and the white KR at e1, the correct continuation would be 24...♗×c3 and 25...♖b2, a point Black overlooked in his combination.
Of course, any effort by White to be parsimonious would be disastrous.

Let us say 20...g6 21.♖fe1 a5 22.♕×b7 ♕f4,

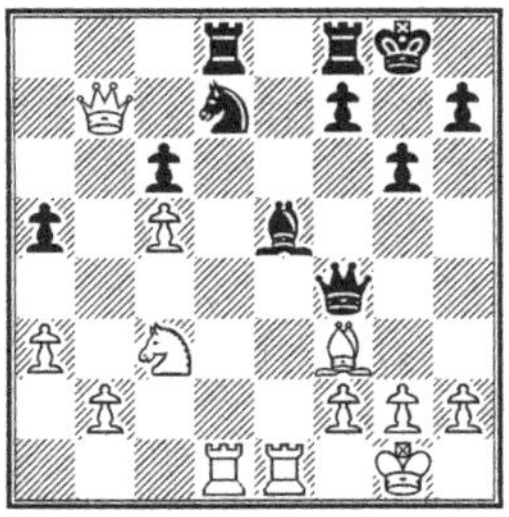

and now if he plays 23.♖×d7 ♕×h2+ 24.♔f1 ♖b8 25.♕ any 25...♖×b2 and 26...♕h1 mate.

25.♘d1

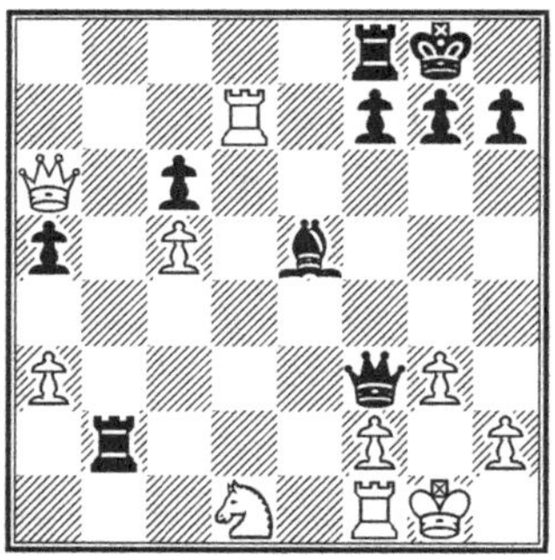

25...♖b3

Perhaps more energetic was 25...♖b5, *when if* 26.a4 ♖×c5 27.♕b6 ♕a3 *Black has the better game and an extra pawn. But White could also play* 26.♘e3 *when if* 26...♖×c5 27.♕a7 ♖b5 28.a4 ♖b4 29.♕×a5=.

26.♕×a5 ♖×a3 27.♕d2 g6 28.♖e7?

CT: Both players are very short of time. The right move which Black expected was 28.♖e1, because now Black can probably win with 28...♖d3 and 29...♗d4.

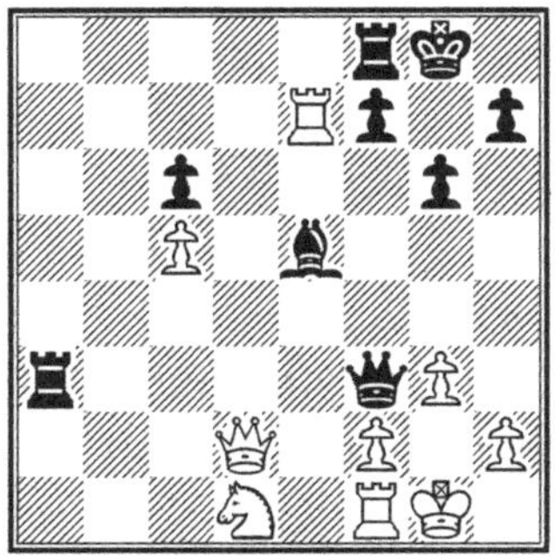

28...♗f6??

Black in turn errs seriously. Torre's line above, 28...♖d3 *followed by* 29...♗d4, *was correct, e.g.* 28...♖d3 29.♕c2 ♗d4 30.♕e2 *(if* 30.♖fe1?? ♖×d1 31.♕×d1 ♗×f2+ 32.♔f1 ♕f6!−+*)* 30...♕×e2 31.♖×e2 ♖b8∓.

After the text, White can win. Torre makes no mention of this.

29.♖e3! ♖×e3 30.♘×e3?

Returning the favor! White would have won with 30.f×e3 ♕h5 31.♖×f6.

30...♖d8 31.♕c2 h5

After the clock-induced errors, Black has emerged with only a small advantage, so the game moves rapidly toward a draw.

32.♖e1 h4 33.g×h4 ♗×h4 34.♕e2 ½–½

CT: Black's position is still advantageous. Here White proposed a draw, which was accepted to avoid a prolonged endgame, as the winning procedure is clearly very laborious.

On his return from Russia, Torre kept quite busy, giving simultaneous exhibitions all along the eastern seaboard. The February 1926 *ACB* reported:

> On the afternoon of February 6, Carlos Torre was the guest of the Newspaper Club of New York and played against twenty-three opponents with the result that he won 17, lost 2 and drew 4. A number of Commercial Chess League members participated. H.W. Hoke of the New York Edison company and W.A. Freudiger of the Chase National Bank were the victors ... At the Empire City Chess Club of New York, on February 13, Torre encountered twenty adversaries and made a score of 12 wins, 2 losses and 6 draws. The winners were David Feuerzeig and Benjamin Fox.

The March *ACB* reported:

> Playing against fifteen members of the Portland Chess Club, at the Falmouth Hotel, Portland, Maine, Carlos Torre made a score of 13 wins and 2 draws, which were obtained by R.B. Cooke, secretary of the club, and Dr. J. Melnick ... After his performance in Portland, Torre visited Durham, New Hampshire, where, at the Faculty Club of the University of New Hampshire, me met and defeated ten opponents, including ... A.E. Pillsbury ... a nephew of the late Harry N. Pillsbury.
>
> Carlos Torre visited the Boston Chess Club on Washington's Birthday and gave a simultaneous exhibition on 20 boards, winning 13, drawing 3 and losing 2. H.C. Mowry and C.C. Lee were two winners ... The following day Torre and Frank K. Perkins played an exhibition game for a small purse which was donated by Julius Helburn. The game ended in a draw after four hours' play, each side having made 24 moves.
>
> Playing in brilliant but accurate fashion, with a strong grip on every board, young Carlos Torre defeated a strong field of twenty players at the Providence [Rhode Island] Chess Club on Saturday evening, March 20, by a score of 19½ to ½, being the best score yet obtained at that club by a visiting chess master. S.M. Goldstein, who holds the best record in the state against simultaneous players, was the only one to draw his game ... The simultaneous exhibition was preceded by a short talk on chess, illustrated by the Gotthilf-Torre game *[sic; s/b Torre-Gotthilf]* from the Moscow Tournament. Torre presented a copy of his book, "The Development of Chess Ability," to Mr. Goldstein for drawing his game.

And the May-June *ACB* stated "Playing against 20 opponents in the rooms of the Philidor Chess Club, prior to his departure, Carlos Torre made a score of 18 wins and 2 draws. Not one of his adversaries was able to win from him." There was also, in the November issue, a belated mention of a simul in Atlanta, Georgia.

Finally the simuls were set aside, and Torre, for the first time in over ten years, made ready to revisit his native land.

Carlos Torre's Return to Mexico

When it was learned that Carlos Torre would sail from New Orleans on the Honduran steamer *Granada*, and arrive at Veracruz on April 19, 1926, a committee was formed in Mexico City, its honorary chairmen being señores Bello, Araiza, and Soto Larrea. The committee was formed to finance Torre's expenses in the Mexican capital, and to organize simultaneous exhibitions and a quadrangular tournament for the championship of Mexico.

Torre in Mexico, 1926. Behind him are José Joaquín Araiza and Manuel Soto Larrea.

Also, the "Círculo de Ajedrez de Yucatán" (Yucatán Chess Circle), whose president was don Carlos Somorrostro, sent a telegram to the mayor of Veracruz, which read as follows: "Mr. President of the Town Council: We have the honor of conveying to you, as the highest civil authority of that thrice heroic city and port, our humble request that upon the disembarkation in your city of the eminent and learned Mexican chess master, Mr. Carlos Torre Repetto, from the steamship *Granada* which is to set sail today from New Orleans, you will greet him most warmly and welcome him in the name of the Yucatán Chess Club, offering him at his arrival our affectionate regard and our enthusiastic admiration for his notable triumphs, and that you further convey to him that, counting beforehand on his acquiescence, we are working eagerly that he might come here, toward which end we extend our most cordial invitation."

The very night of his arrival in Veracruz, Torre gave a simultaneous exhibition organized by a local club, "El Centro de Dependientes." Playing 34 boards, he won

29 games, drew 3 and lost 2. The winners were Hugo del Cueto and B.R. Apendini. On most boards he essayed romantic openings, such as the King's and Evans Gambits; on none did Torre play his favorite 1.d4. Some of these games were made available to the author by señora Julieta Viuda de Repetto Milán, but after a brief examination it was decided not to include them in this collection, as they were all played by virtual novices. The next day Torre played on 27 boards, winning all games. At the exhibition's end, the assembled aficionados gave a standing ovation to the Yucatán grandmaster.

Games 82 through 85 are light offhand games: three of them belong to simultaneous exhibitions and the other is an exhibition game. GM Reuben Fine once said that offhand games rarely had any intrinsic value. He was specifically referring to Paul Morphy's games, since nearly 80% of Morphy's known games were offhand encounters. Fine was on the whole right: a master playing an offhand game rarely makes a serious effort to concentrate, mainly because he is aware that the opposition is weak. Thus a deep analysis is apt to disclose a large number of imprecise moves and oversights. However, offhand games, like blitz games, can be very entertaining and attractive for spectators. In particular, a massive simultaneous display of a strong master against thirty or forty amateurs is a most thrilling scene to watch. Velasco will never forget a massive simultaneous display by Bent Larsen in Mexico City, in December 1972, where the famous Danish grandmaster effortlessly and smilingly crushed forty adversaries in less than two hours; he was able to spot the most amazing combinations and sacrifices at a glance! Most grandmasters are able to do that, and Carlos Torre was not an exception. The following two games are typical of a simultaneous display.

Game 82

Torre-Bringas

Simul, Veracruz, 20 April 1926

Bishop's Opening [C23]

1.e4 e5 2.♗c4 ♗c5 3.b4

One must go back a quite a few years to find many examples of this opening.

3...♗b6

The gambit was usually accepted back in the Good Olde Days, play continuing 3...♗×b4 4.f4 in McDonnell-de La Bourdonnais, match, 1834 (0-1, 30), Dubois-Lecrivain, Paris, 1855 (1-0, 16), Mongrédien-Morphy, match, 1859 (½-½, 25), and in five simul games by Steinitz 1895-96.

4.♘f3 d6 5.c3

Varying from Morphy-Freeman, blindfold simul, Birmingham, 1858, where 5.d4 was played.

5...♘f6 6.d3 h6 7.♗e3 ♘c6 8.♘bd2 ♗e6 9.0–0 0–0 10.a4 ♗×e3 11.f×e3 ♗×c4 12.♘×c4 ♕e7 13.♘h4 ♘×e4?

Black thinks he has an interesting little combination. Unlike most of Torre's simul opponents, Bringas was not a beginner, in fact he was the champion of the Mexican state of Veracruz. But this try is unsound.

14.♘f5! ♕e6 15.d×e4 ♕×c4??

15...g6 was much less egregious.

16.♕g4! g6 17.♘×h6+ ♔g7

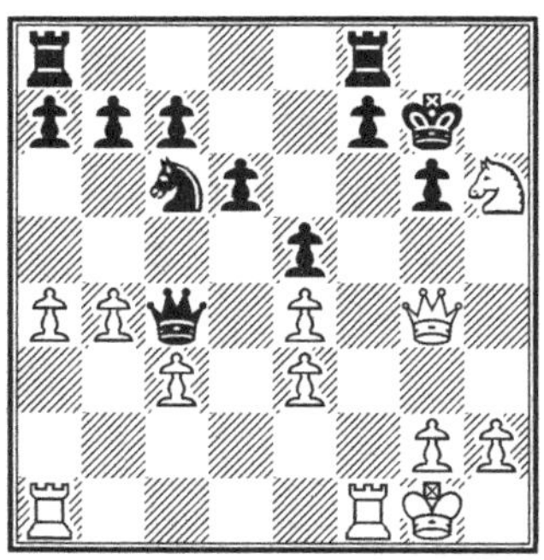

18.♕h4?!

Torre misses a win by 18.♘f5+ ♔g8 19.♖f3 d5 20.♕g5 ♕×e4 21.♖af1 and Black must give up his Queen to forestall mate.

18...♖h8??

18...f5!

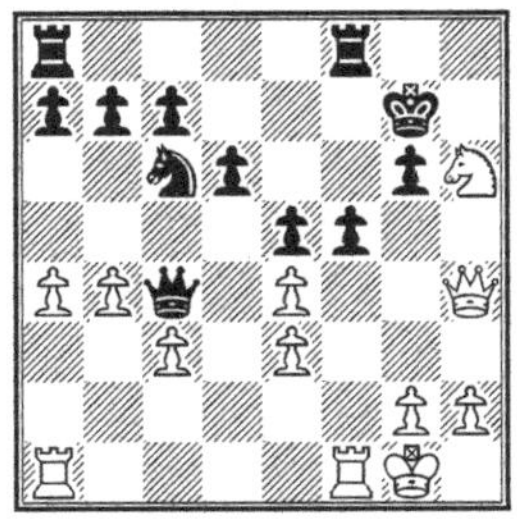

would force White to sue for peace, *e.g.* 19.♘×f5+ ♖×f5 20.♖×f5 g×f5 21.♖f1 ♕×e4 22.♕g5+ ♔h7 23.♕h5+ ♔g7 24.♕g5+ etc.

19.♕f6+! ♔×h6 20.♖f3 1-0

After 20...♕e6 21.♖h3+ ♕×h3 is forced.

That same day Carlos Torre left Veracruz for Mexico City, where he arrived the afternoon of April 21st. On Sunday the 24th he gave a simul against 35 opponents of generally much higher caliber than those he had faced earlier. Many of these were frequent café and club players, among them J. Brunner, Alvarez Tostado and a lawyer named Cárdenas. There were no beginners. Torre won 24 games, drew 9, and lost only 2. The session lasted just over four hours. We present one game from that exhibition where, interestingly, Torre's opponent had the audacity to use against him his own favorite defense.

Game 83

Torre-Peschard

Simul, Mexico City, 24 April 1926

French Defense [C12]

1.e4 e6 2.d4 d5 3.♘c3 ♘f6 4.♗g5 ♗b4 5.e5 h6 6.♗d2 ♗×c3 7.b×c3 ♘e4 8.♕g4 ♔f8 9.h4 ♘×d2 10.♔×d2 ♘d7?!

Black's basic idea in the McCutcheon (and for that matter in most variations of the French) is to obtain active counterplay on the queenside.

Therefore he should play 10...c5 and 11...♘c6. After the text move, White can proceed unmolested with his kingside demonstration.

11.♖h3 f5 12.♕f4 c5 13.g4 g6 14.g×f5

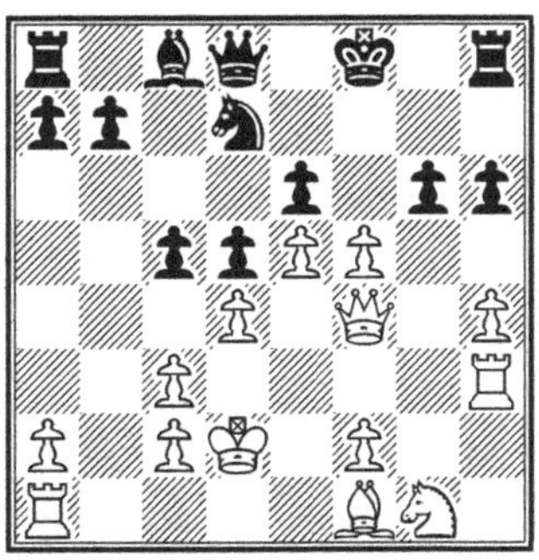

14...e×f5?

A serious mistake, but even after the most precise defense, Black's position would be very difficult to handle, *e.g.* 14...g×f5 15.♘e2 ♕a5 16.♖g3 ♘b6 (if 16...♔f7? 17.♕f3 △18.♕h5+) 17.♖g6 ♗d718.♕g3 (simply 18.♖×h6 is also good) 18...♖e8 19.d×c5 ♕×c5 20.♘d4 ♔e7□ 21.a4 ♔d8 22.a5 etc.

15.h5!

15.♖g3 or 15.♘f3 are also very strong.

15...♕g5?

Apparently Black believed that after the exchange of Queens, White's attack would lose momentum. But he probably did not realize that the ensuing ending would be hopeless for him. At any rate, resistance would have been a thankless and hopeless task.

16.♕×g5 h×g5 17.h×g6

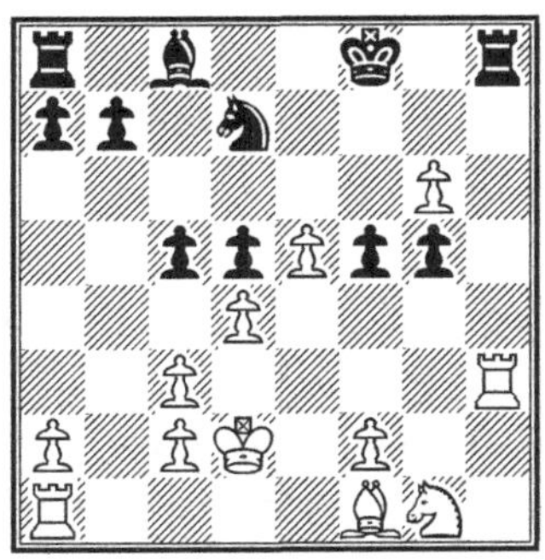

17...♖×h3

Or 17...♖g8 18.♖h5 ♖×g6 19.♘f3 ♘b6 (if 19...g4 20.♘h4 ♖g8 21.♘×f5+−) 20.♘×g5 c×d4 21.c×d4 ♗d7 22.♗d3 ♖g7 23.♖ah1 and Black is bereft of decent moves.

18.♘×h3 g4 19.♘f4 c×d4 20.c×d4 ♔g7 21.♗g2 ♘f8 22.♗×d5 ♘×g6 23.♘×g6 ♔×g6 24.e6! ♔f6 25.♖h1 ♔e7
Of course if 25...♗×e6 26.♖h6+.

26.c4
And now if 26...♗×e6 27.♖e1.

26...♔d6 27.♖h6 ♔e7 28.♔e3 a5 29.♔f4 1-0

Torre's stay in Mexico City drew out to more than three months. During May he gave almost no simuls, because they invariably exhausted him and he received scant remuneration for them. The *ACB* reported "Recent advices from Mexico City state that, owing to the indisposition of Carlos Torre, the tournament for the chess championship of Mexico was postponed." That postponement meant that Torre had to decline an invitation to play in the Lake Hopatcong tournament, held 7 to 21 July, which Capablanca won ahead of Kupchik, Maróczy, Marshall, and Edward Lasker.

However, Torre did play various exhibition games against and in consultation with the best players of the Distrito Federal. Of these, we have chosen one which contains an interesting combination and in which Torre's opponent showed a good knowledge of opening theory. It also has two things hard to explain: Torre's 26th move, and White's resignation.

Game 84

Arancegui-Torre

Exhibition game, Mexico City, 5 May 1926

Ruy López [C91]

1.e4 e5 2.♘f3 ♘c6 3.♗b5 a6 4.♗a4 ♘f6 5.0–0 ♗e7 6.♖e1 b5 7.♗b3 d6 8.c3 0–0 9.d4 ♗g4
As played in CB's oldest game in this line, Olland-Loman, Haarlem 1901 (½-½, 35). Soon 9.h3 became customary to prevent the pin, first in Tarrasch-Schlechter, Monte Carlo 1902 (1-0, 65), and then in tens of thousands of games since.

10.♗e3 e×d4 11.c×d4 ♘a5 12.♗c2

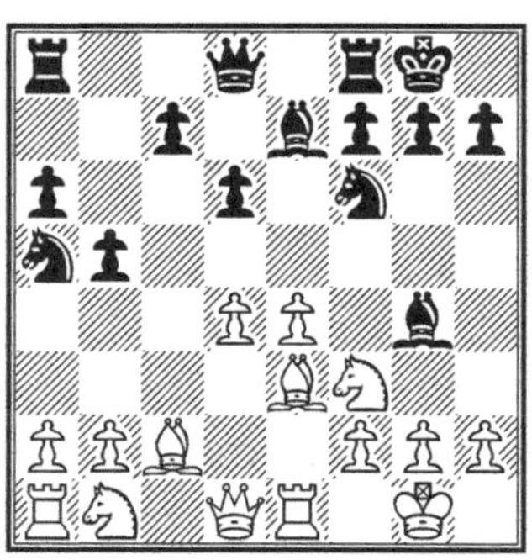

12...♘c4
In Yates-Bogoljubow, New York 1924,

Black equalized with 12...c5 13.♘bd2 (better 13.d×c5 d×c5 14.♘bd2 according to R. J. Fischer) 13...c×d4 14.♗×d4 ♘c6 15.♗e3 d5 16.e×d5 ♘b4.

13.♗c1 c5 14.b3 ♘a5

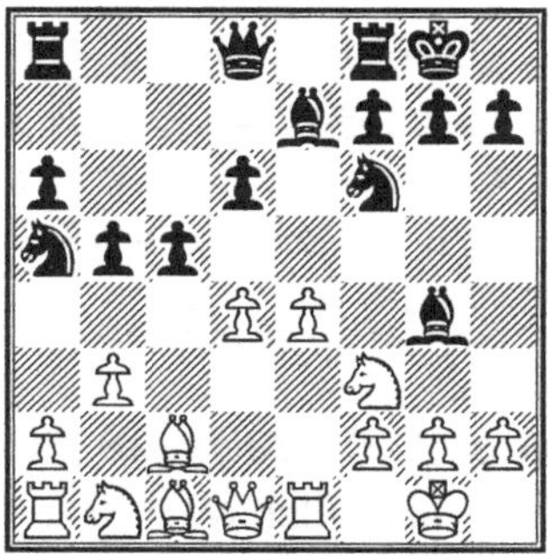

This position has an interesting history. It first occurred at London 1922, in a famous game between Capablanca and Bogoljubow. The World Champion played 15.♗b2 and won in very good style, so everyone took it for granted that 15.♗b2 was White's best move in this position. Nevertheless, forty years later, the American genius Bobby Fischer managed to find an improvement: 15.d5!, depriving Black's Knight of its retreat at c6[1]. Thus Fischer defeated Victor Korchnoi in 1962, and demonstrated that after 15.d5 White has virtually a winning advantage. Korchnoi himself became utterly convinced of it, as did Tal, Bronstein and other grandmasters. However, there was also a group of grandmasters who were skeptical and made efforts to improve on Black's game. Smyslov, Portisch and Gligoric were among those who still believed that after 15.d5 Black's game should be defensible, but they failed to prove their point. The variation was played subsequently in the games Korchnoi-Portisch, Sousse Interzonal 1967 (1-0, 44), Tal-Gligoric, Candidates Match 1968 (1-0, 66), and Bronstein-Smyslov, Petropolis Interzonal 1973 (1-0, 33). In all these games Black tried to find an improvement at different stages of the game, but to no avail. Therefore, it was virtually conceded that the diagrammed position could be labeled "White to play and win," starting with Fischer's 15.d5. Contemporary grandmasters have almost entirely given up this variation as Black, ChessBase showing only 49 games with it, White scoring +25 -9 =15.

15.♗b2 ♘c6

15...c×d4 is somewhat more accurate.

16.e5 ♘d7 17.e×d6 ♗×d6 18.d×c5 ♘×c5 19.h3 ♗h5 20.♘bd2 ♘b4 21.g4?

White could have equalized with 21.♘e4. The text is a serious error that should lose quickly.

21...♘×c2 22.♕×c2 ♗g6 23.♕c3 f6 24.♖ad1

1 It bears mentioning that 15.d5 had been played much earlier, in Rivlin-Botvinnik, training match, Leningrad, 1925 (0-1, 43). However, Botvinnik tended to keep his training games secret, so Fischer probably was not aware of it.

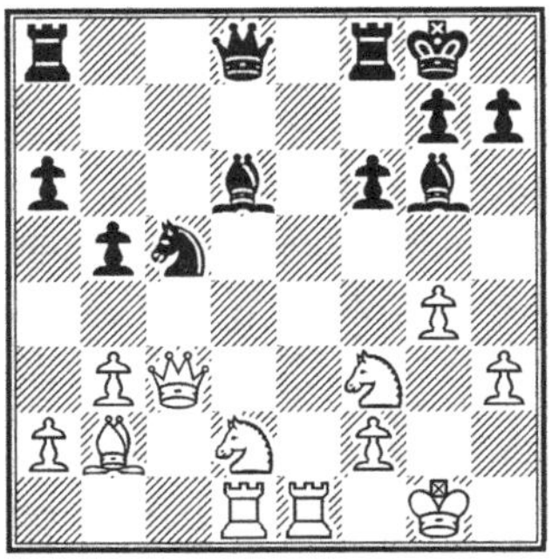

24...♖c8!

The best move on the board. Also very strong was 24...♘d3, *viz.* 25.♘e4 (if 25.♖e2 ♖c8 26.♕d4 ♖c2−+) 25...♗b4 26.♕×d3 ♕×d3 27.♖×d3 ♗×e1 28.♘×e1 ♗×e4−+.

25.♕d4 ♘d3! 26.♖e6

Since White's mistake at move 21, Torre has played only optimal moves. But now he goes badly astray.

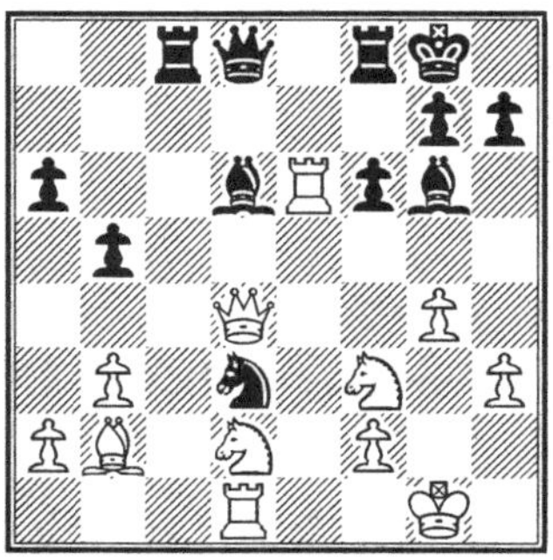

26...♘×b2?

Amazing that Torre should play this, which lets the game slip to equality, when he had so many winning moves to choose from. A few sample lines:

(a) 26...♗c5 27.♕×d8 ♖c×d8 28.♗a1 ♗×f2+ 29.♔f1 ♘f4 30.♖×f6 ♖×f6 31.♔×f2 ♖ff8 (-6.93/22);

(b) 26...♗b4 27.♕×d8 ♖f×d8 28.♗a1 ♘c5 29.♖e2 ♗c2 (-7.30/27);

(c) 26...♗e5 27.♕×d8 ♖c×d8 28.♗×e5 f×e5 29.♖×a6 e4 30.♘×e4 ♖×f3 (-3.69/25);

(d) 26...♗b8 27.♖e3 ♘f4 28.♗a3 (28.♔h2?? ♘e2+) 28...♘×h3+ 29.♔f1 ♕×d4 30.♘×d4 ♖fd8 31.♘2f3 ♖c2 32.♖e2 ♖×e2 33.♔×e2 ♘f4+ 34.♔f1 ♗a7 35.♗b2 ♗d3+ 36.♔g1 ♗e2 37.♖e1 ♗×f3 38.♘×f3 ♖d3 39.♘h4 ♖g3+ 40.♔f1 ♖h3 (-8.84/24).

27.♖×d6 ♘×d1 28.♖×d8 ♖f×d8

The two Rooks will have no perceptible advantage over the Queen.

29.♕b6 ♖e8 30.♕×a6 ♘c3 31.a4 b×a4 32.b×a4 ♘e4 33.a5 ♖c1+ 34.♔g2 ♖c2 35.♘×e4□ ♗×e4 36.♕b5 ♖ec8 37.♔g1 ♗a8?!

If 37...♗×f3 38.♕b3+ ♔h8 39.♕×f3. Best was 37...♖2c5 38.♕e2 ♗×f3 39.♕×f3 ♖×a5, with an almost certain draw (-0.65/31).

38.a6 ♖2c3? 0-1

Best was 38...♗×f3 39.♕b3+ ♔h8 40.♕×f3 ♖2c7 with a draw (-0.28/28).

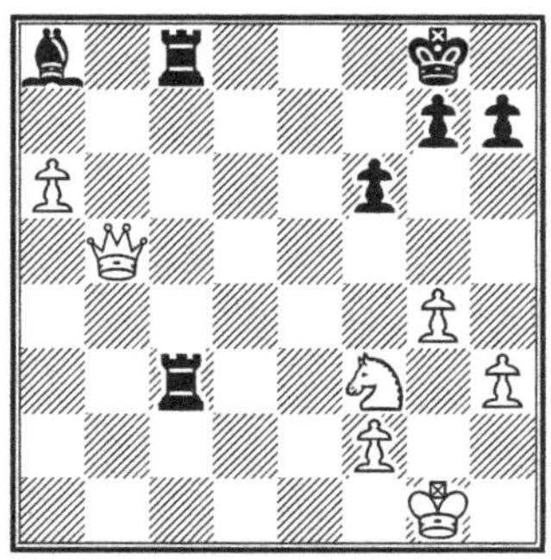

White's resignation is incomprehensible. With 39.♘d4! he would have done no worse than draw, and may have had winning chances. Stockfish sees best play as continuing 39...♖3c5 40.♕d7 ♖5c7 41.♕d6 ♔h8 42.♔h2 (42.♘e6?? ♖c1+ 43.♔h2 ♖h1+ 44.♔g3 ♖c3+ and mate shortly) 42...h6 43.♘e6 ♖c1 44.♕d4 (+1.40/25). One wonders if Arancegui overstepped the time limit?

On May 22, 1926, Torre gave a simultaneous exhibition on 32 boards, with the result of 29 wins and 3 draws. There is no record of any further simuls in the capital after that date, and probably there were none. The next game is the only one from that event to survive, its score having been saved by relatives of Carlos Torre.

Game 85

Torre-Mont

Simul, Mexico City, 22 May 1926

Evans Gambit Declined [C51]

On May 22, 1926, Torre gave a simultaneous exhibition on 32 boards, with the result of 29 wins and 3 draws. There is no record of any further simuls in the capital after that date, and probably there were none. This game is the only one from that event to survive, its score having been saved by relatives of Carlos Torre.

1.e4 e5 2.♘f3 ♘c6 3.♗c4 ♗c5 4.b4 ♗b6 5.a4 a6 6.♗b2

An oldie, going back to Rivière- De Boisterte, Paris 1881 (1-0, 35). Played four times in the 1914 Baden-bei-Wien gambit tournament, after which it disappeared for nearly 50 years. Later it cropped up now and then in the games of the late Russian GM Evgeny Sveshnikov, *e.g.* vs. Giorgiev, President's Cup, Elista 1998; vs. Miles at Nova Gorica Open 2000; and vs. Yashtylov at St. Petersburg 2000.

6...d6 7.b5 a×b5 8.a×b5 ♖×a1 9.♗×a1 ♘ce7 10.d4 e×d4 11.♗×d4 ♗×d4 12.♕×d4 ♘f6 13.♘c3 0–0 14.0–0 ♗e6 15.♖d1 ♗×c4 16.♕×c4 ♕c8 17.e5 d×e5 18.♘×e5 ♘f5 19.♘d5 ♘×d5 20.♕×d5 ♕e6?

Black has managed to keep things very even so far, and with 20...♘e7 they would have remained so. But the text is a serious positional mistake, leading to an ending highly unfavorable for Black.

21.♕×e6 f×e6 22.♖d7 ♖c8 23.c4! ♔f8

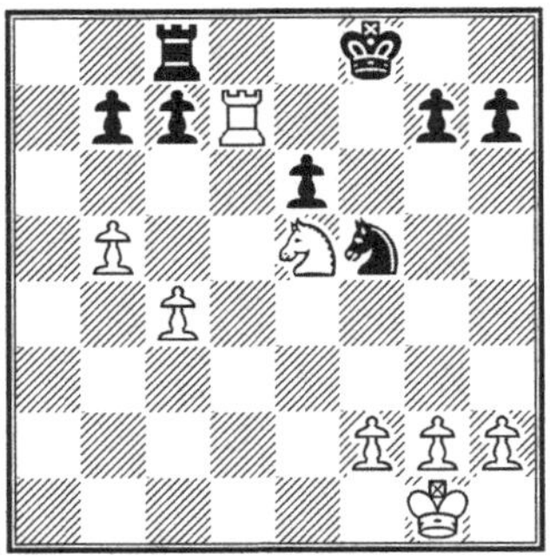

24.♖f7+
Better 24.g4 immediately, when if 24...♘e7 25.h4 ♔e8 26.f4 etc., or 24...♘h6 25.f3 and Black is effectively a piece down (+7.17/23), or 24...♘h4 25.f4 h5 26.h3 h×g4 27.h×g4 ♔g8 28.♔f2 ♔h7 29.♘f7 ♘g6 (if 29...♔g6 30.♔g3) 30.♘g5+ ♔g8 31.♘×e6+−, or 24...♘d6 25.b6! ♘e8 26.c5 c×b6 27.c×b6 ♖c5 (if 27...♖b8 28.g5 and Black is paralyzed; White can just march his King up the board and win as he pleases) 28.f4 ♖b5 29.♖f7+ ♔g8 30.♖×b7+−.

24...♔g8 25.g4 ♘d4
If 25...♘d6 26.♖e7.

26.♖d7 ♘e2+ 27.♔g2 ♘f4+ 28.♔f3 g5 29.h4
29.♘f7 was more efficient, but it matters little.

29...♖f8 30.♔g3 ♘e2+ 31.♔g2 ♘f4+ 32.♔h2 g×h4
If 32...♘g6 33.♘×g6 h×g6 34.♖×c7 g×h4 (if 34...♖×f2+ 35.♔g3 ♖c2 36.h×g5 and White can win at leisure (+8.30)) 35.♔g2 ♖f4 (or 35...♖f7 36.b6) 36.g5 ♖f5 37.b6 ♖×g5+ 38.♔h3 ♖f5 39.♖×b7+−.

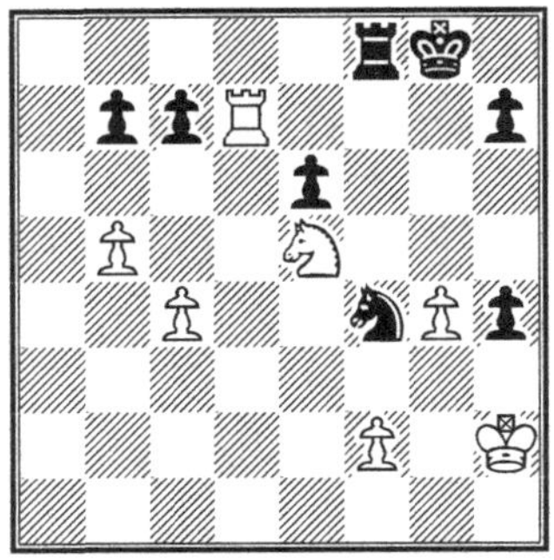

33.♖×c7 ♘g6 34.♘×g6 h×g6 35.♖×b7
35.♔g2, keeping the f-pawn, was considerably better.

35...♖×f2+ 36.♔h3 ♖c2?
36...g5 would have made the win a bit harder by enabling some annoying checks, *viz.* 37.b6 ♖b2 38.c5 ♖b3+ 39.♔g2 ♖b2+ 40.♔f1 ♖b1+ etc.

37.b6
"A Rook on the seventh rank confining the enemy King to the back rank, plus a passed pawn, win against any power on earth," wrote the late Correspondence Chess World Champion Cecil Purdy.

37...♖×c4 38.♖c7 ♖b4 39.b7 1-0
A game won by Torre without apparent effort, thanks to his better positional judgment and superior endgame technique.

The Chess Championship of Mexico

Over June 22-30, 1926, in Mexico City, Torre participated in a quadrangular tourney with Manuel Soto Larrea, Agustín Freyria, and Colonel José Joaquín Araiza. The event, billed as the Championship of Mexico, was organized by Araiza (pronounced ah-RYE-sah), who was then the best player in the Mexico City Federal District. Araiza was good enough to win a simul game from Alekhine in 1929, and in tournaments he drew against Tartakower, Spielmann, Vidmar, Maróczy, Reshevsky, Denker, Fine, Horowitz and Kashdan. Soto Larrea was also strong, producing in a long career some brilliant attacking games, some of which were included in Irving Chernev's The 1000 Best Short Games of Chess. *Freyria was the weakest of the four: though he did manage a win against Soto Larrea, against Torre he was not able to last more than 20 moves. Torre wrote brief notes to the games, which became the tournament book,* El Torneo de Ajedrez para el Campeonato de la República Mexicana. *By the good graces of Guy van Habberney of Belgium, we were able to obtain pdf scans of that rare item. We divide its coverage of the tournament into two parts. Here we present some pages from the original, a translation of Agustín Garza Galindo's intro, and the six games involving Torre, with both his notes and our own Stockfish 14 analysis. In Chapter VIII we give the six games between the other three participants, with Torre's notes.*

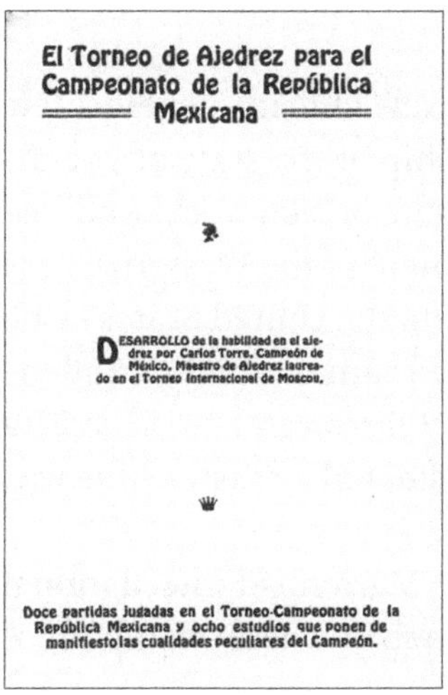

El Torneo de Ajedrez para el Campeonato de la República Mexicana

DESARROLLO de la habilidad en el ajedrez por Carlos Torre, Campeón de México. Maestro de Ajedrez laureado en el Torneo Internacional de Moscou.

Doce partidas jugadas en el Torneo-Campeonato de la República Mexicana y ocho estudios que ponen de manifiesto las cualidades peculiares del Campeón.

Original title page

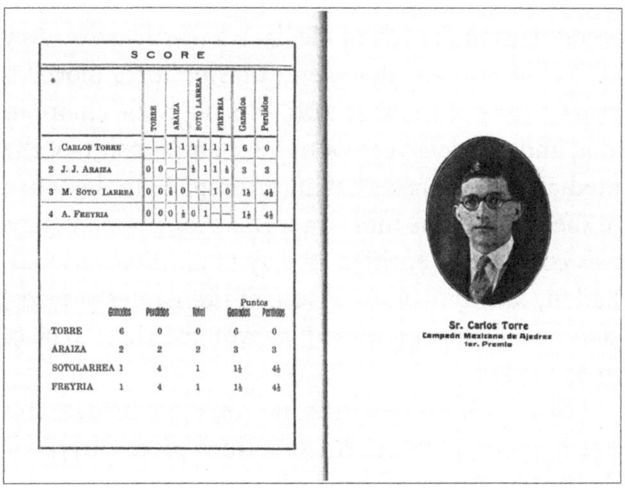

SCORE

	TORRE		ARAIZA		SOTO LARREA		FREYRIA		Ganados	Perdidos
1 CARLOS TORRE	—	—	1	1	1	1	1	1	6	0
2 J. J. ARAIZA	0	0	—	—	½	1	1	½	3	3
3 M. SOTO LARREA	0	0	½	0	—	—	1	0	1½	4½
4 A. FREYRIA	0	0	0	½	0	1	—	—	1½	4½

	Ganados	Perdidos	Total	Puntos Ganados	Puntos Perdidos
TORRE	6	0	0	6	0
ARAIZA	2	2	2	3	3
SOTOLARREA	1	4	1	1½	4½
FREYRIA	1	4	1	1½	4½

Sr. Carlos Torre
Campeón Mexicano de Ajedrez
1er. Premio

Frontispiece

Prologue

I have been given the privilege of writing a few words by way of a prologue to this important work, written by the chess master Carlos Torre, because my love of the noble game, and the desire to seek, even in what was just my pastime, the advice of those who know best, led me one day to translate a series of articles by the then World Champion, Dr. Emanuel Lasker, which, published in book form, later came into the hands of Carlos Torre, who obtained from it instruction and inspiration. He responded by inviting me to put my name next to his in this book. I take advantage of the honor that the master has given me, to make readers aware of some biographical data and other facts related to his chess career.

Carlos Torre was born in Mérida, capital of the state of Yucatán, on 29 November 1904, and as a child of six or seven, learned the movements of the symbolic chess pieces on the battleground of the mind, symbolized also by the sixty-four squares of the board. In a peaceful home he watched the tremendous face-to-face struggles contested by his father and the older sons, with the consequence of stirring up the interest of the child who, as soon as he became a young man, would win awards that would enable him to dispute, with great probability of success, the chess scepter with another master, also of Latin race, José R. Capablanca, son of Cuba, who, with the nobility inherited from Spain, already recognizes in the young Mexican a worthy adversary.

While still an adolescent, master Torre moved to New Orleans, where a few years ago — November 1923 — he won the championship of the state of Louisiana, and the next year won the championship of the state of New York. And immediately afterwards having triumphed in the tournament of the Western Chess Association — the most important tournament played in the United States — he was considered entitled to play in an international tournament, and in Baden-Baden, having won over 50% of the games played *[sic; Torre scored 5-4 in decisive games, while drawing eleven]*, he won the right to be considered a master. This was in April 1925.

Now with his new title, he could participate in the Marienbad international tournament, in which he took third place with F.J. Marshall, chess champion of the United States of America.

Suddenly considered a figure of the first rank in the chess world, he was invited to the international tournament at Moscow, a titanic struggle where twenty-one masters competed, and Torre took fifth place. It bears mentioning that he was only a half-point behind the US Champion, and the first, second and third places were held by the masters Bogoljubow, the former world champion Emanuel Lasker, and the current world champion José R. Capablanca, respectively. Individually Torre drew his game with the champion Capablanca, and he obtained a very difficult victory against the ex-champion Lasker.

He came to place these laurels before the country that gave him birth, along the way gaining two new tokens of glory: in a simultaneous exhibition, he was pitted against forty generals, chiefs, and officials of the Mexican Army, with the brilliant result of winning 34 games, drawing six and not losing a single one. The Secretary of War and Navy, General Joaquín Amaro, was one of the contestants who managed to draw his game.

And to conclude his progress through Mexico he, in a memorable contest of which this work leaves an enduring testimony, won the title of champion of the Republic, without losing a single game.

In referring to this tournament, we would not do justice if we did not state that it could only be brought to a successful conclusion by the effort, enthusiasm and spirit of a skillful organizer, the learned engineer General Manuel Mendoza, to whom the chess fans in Mexico give testimony of their gratitude.

When a fighter, in chess or any other field, takes up the motto of Carlos Torre, of surpassing himself in each new fight, of playing better each new game, and when from his lips, that speak sincerely, we have heard that he had never played better chess than when he played in Mexico, we can predict that very soon our country will be proud that one of its sons has taken the chess scepter.

Lic. Agustín Garza Galindo
Mexico City, August 1926

Game 86

Torre-Soto Larrea

Mexican Championship, Mexico City, 22 June 1926

Queen's Gambit Declined [D30]

According to Mexican IM Raúl Ocampo Vargas, Manuel Soto Larrea was, at various times, a fighter in the Mexican Revolution of 1910-1920, the chief of police in the Distrito Federal, a brigadier general in the Mexican Army, and a figure in Mexican politics.[1] Torre's conduct of this game is virtually flawless, and his notes are clear, simple, and instructive, leaving very little to add. His notes, here and in subsequent games, are indicated by "CT:"; Kingston's Stockfish-assisted notes by "TK:"; and notes by Velasco, retained from the first edition, by "GV:". Question marks and exclams were placed by the translator Kingston; Torre used none.

1.d4 ♘f6 2.♘f3 d5 3.c4 e6 4.♗g5 ♘bd7 5.e3 c6 6.♘bd2 ♗e7 7.♗d3 d×c4

CT: Black wants to annoy White by the harmonious development of his pieces, but he does not have sufficient vitality to initiate aggressive tactics so early in the game, and in consequence he fatally weakens his c-pawn.

8.♘×c4 b5?

TK: Very bad positionally. Much better was 8...c5.

9.♘ce5 ♘×e5 10.♘×e5 ♗b4+ 11.♔e2! ♕d5?

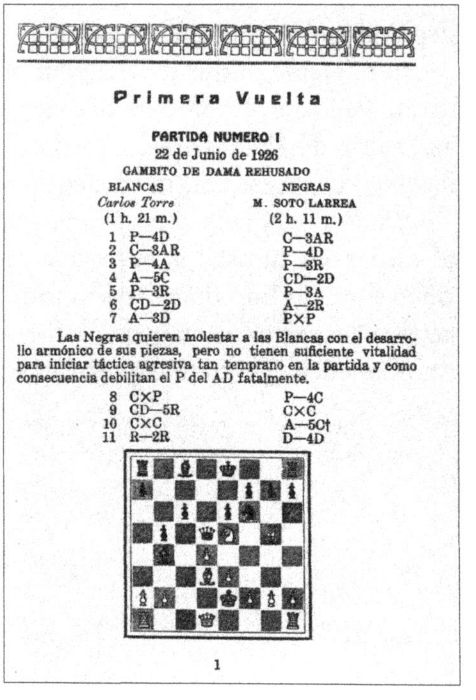

Primera Vuelta

PARTIDA NUMERO 1

22 de Junio de 1926

GAMBITO DE DAMA REHUSADO

BLANCAS	NEGRAS
Carlos Torre	M. SOTO LARREA
(1 h. 21 m.)	(2 h. 11 m.)
1 P—4D	C—3AR
2 C—3AR	P—4D
3 P—4A	P—3R
4 A—5C	CD—2D
5 P—3R	P—3A
6 CD—2D	A—2R
7 A—3D	P×P

Las Negras quieren molestar a las Blancas con el desarrollo armónico de sus piezas, pero no tienen suficiente vitalidad para iniciar táctica agresiva tan temprano en la partida y como consecuencia debilitan el P del AD fatalmente.

8 C×P	P—4C
9 CD—5R	C×C
10 C×C	A—5C†
11 R—2R	D—4D

1

TK: Making a bad game worse; lesser evils were 11...♗d7, 11...♗b7, or 11...♕b6.

12.♕c2

1 Per http://chesscom-chesscoach.blogspot.com/2007/10/hace-60-aos-vii.html. Considering the credibility of Ocampo in *Torre x Torre*, we do not guarantee the accuracy of this information.

CT: To augment the pressure on the enemy's weak point. TK: Stockfish agrees completely, and says White already has a winning position (+3.60/28).

12...♗b7 13.♗×f6 g×f6 14.♗e4 ♕d6 15.♗×c6+ ♗×c6 16.♕×c6+ ♕×c6 17.♘×c6 ♗d6

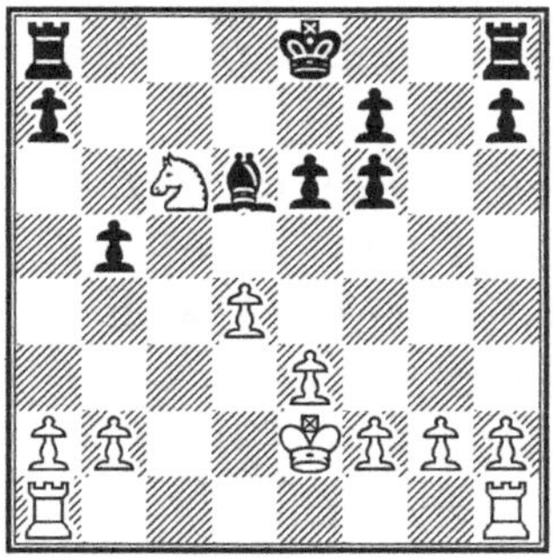

18.a4

CT: This move has a double objective: (1) Secure the c4 square for the Knight in the variation 18...b×a4 19.♖×a4 ♔d7 20.♘a5 followed by ♘c4 and ♖h1-a1; naturally not 20.♘×a7 ♖hb8, as White's situation would not be good. And (2) Invite the disadvantageous advance of the b-pawn, a completely weak move that blocks the action of the Bishop; furthermore a white Rook would later take up a dominant position on c4.

18...b4 19.♖hc1 ♔d7

CT: It would be an error to try to trap the Knight with 19...a5, as White plays 20.♘×a5.

20.♘a5 ♖hc8 21.♘b3 ♖×c1 22.♖×c1 ♖c8 23.♖×c8 ♔×c8 24.♔d3 ♔c7

TK: If 24...♗×h2? 25.g3 and Black soon loses the Bishop. But White now prevents ...♗×h2 because he wants to activate his King.

25.g3 ♔c6 26.♘a5+

CT: To oblige the King to come to b6, where it will be further away from the defense of its pawns.

26...♔c7 27.♔c4 ♔b6 28.♘b3 a5

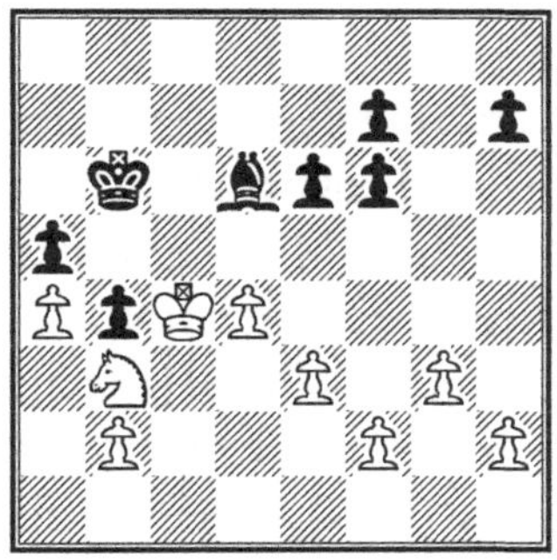

29.♘c5

CT: Of course e3-e4 and d4-d5 would produce a passed pawn, but it would also increase the scope of the black Bishop. Therefore it is more correct to maneuver with the Knight, in order to provoke Black to advance his pawns, restricting the Bishop's scope and enhancing the power of the Knight to destroy the pawns.

29...♔c6 30.♘e4 ♗e7 31.f4

CT: The pawns occupy the same color squares as the Bishop to limit its radius of action. Black cannot reply 31...f5, because then 32.♘g5 would force him to exchange pieces, increasing White's dominance.

31...h6 32.♘f2
CT: Threatening 33.♘g4, but if Black replies 33...h5, then 34.g4 would lead to a passed h-pawn for White.
TK: 33.♘g4 is indeed a good idea, but if 32...h5 33.g4, Black can avoid creating a passed pawn by 33...h4. Not that it would ultimately matter.

32...f5 33.♘d3 f6 34.♘c5 e5
CT: How limited is the Bishop's scope!

35.♘b3
CT: Illustrating a very useful principle: pawns should not be advanced without good reason, as then they may block the action of their own pieces. If the white pawn had carelessly been moved to b3, it would not be so easy to win.

35...♗d8
CT: If 35...e×f4 simply 36.g×f4 ♗d8 37.♘c5 to continue with ♘c5-e6-g7.

36.f×e5 f×e5 37.d×e5 ♗g5 38.♘d4+
CT: Simplifying the position; a white pawn will Queen. This is a very instructive game, and possibly the most classical of the entire tournament.

38...♔d7 39.♘×f5 ♔e6 40.♘d4+ ♔×e5 41.♘f3+ ♔e4 42.♘×g5+ h×g5 43.h4 ♔×e3 44.h×g5 ♔d2 45.b3 1-0
Time used: Torre 1 hr. 21 min., Soto Larrea 2 hrs. 11 min.

Game 87

Torre-Araiza

Mexican Championship, Mexico City, 23 June 1926

Barry Attack [D00]

José Joaquín Araiza (1900-1971) was the only contestant able to give Torre any worthwhile opposition. Of Torre's six games in the tournament, this one has the best play by his opponent.

1.d4 ♘f6 2.♘f3 g6 3.♘c3
CT: Black having played 2...g6, White is not obligated to play 3.c4.

3...d5 4.♗f4
TK: The Barry Attack, seen already in Torre-Frink (Game 4) and Torre-Yates, Baden-Baden 1925 (Game 49).

4...♗g7 5.e3 ♗f5
CT: This happily resolves the problem of developing the Bishop.

6.♗d3
CT: The best way to obtain an advantage in development.

6...♗×d3 7.♕×d3 c6

CT: Otherwise White would play 8.♕b5.

8.e4 d×e4 9.♘×e4 ♘bd7 10.0–0 ♘×e4 11.♕×e4 ♘f6 12.♕d3 0–0 13.♖fe1

CT: The only advantage White has been able to get from the opening is pressure on the e-file.

13...♘d5 14.♗g5 ♗f6 15.♗×f6 ♘×f6 16.♕e3

CT: In order to move the Queen to h6, where threats to the black King will gain time to bring the Rooks and Knight to good posts, and in this way maintain an advantage.

16...♖e8 17.♕h6 e6 18.♖ad1 ♕d6 19.♘e5 ♕f8

CT: Black moves his Queen here to avoid all danger.

20.♕h4 ♕e7 21.♕h6 ♕f8 22.♕h3 ♘h5

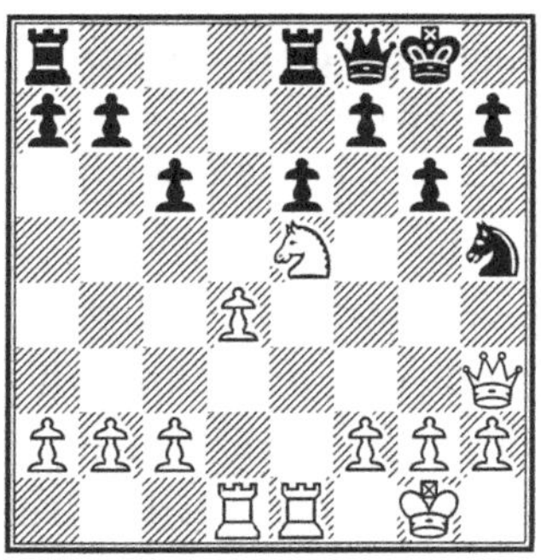

23.♕f3

CT: Not 23.g4 ♘f4 24.♕f3 g5. The text, however, poses a threat that virtually requires Black to make a weakening move.

23...f5?

TK: Torre's comment notwithstanding, there was no need yet to make such a committal, weakening move.
Better 23...♖ad8, or 23...♕e7 △ ...♘f6.

24.♕b3! ♖e7 25.♘d3

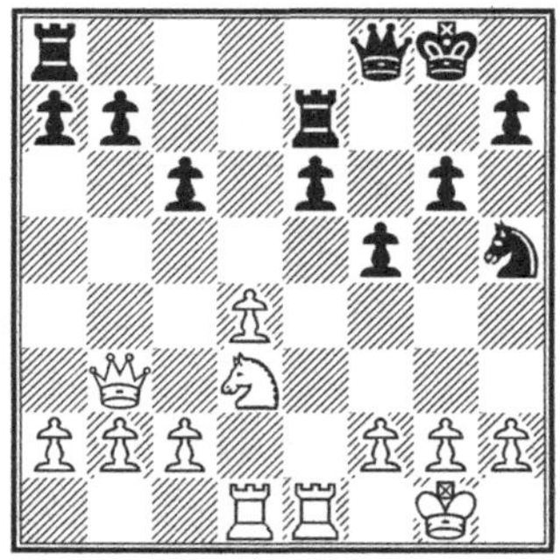

GV: If the reader is familiar with the games of Capablanca, he will have noticed a striking similarity with the plan followed by White in this game and that of the Cuban grandmaster in his game vs. Rafael Blanco at Havana, 1913. White harassed Black's kingside with simple threats, until he compelled him to play the weakening move ...f5, which left a hole on e5 and a backward pawn on e6. After that, Capa was able to win in a very speedy and instructive fashion. The fact that light-squared Bishops hadn't been exchanged in that game made no important difference. For the sake of comparison we give the score of that game:

Capablanca-Blanco, Havana, 1913:
1.e4 e6 2.d4 d5 3.♘c3 d×e4 4.♘×e4 ♘d7 5.♘f3 ♘gf6 6.♘×f6+ ♘×f6 7.♘e5

♗d6 8.♕f3 c6 9.c3 0–0 10.♗g5 ♗e7 11.♗d3 ♘e8 12.♕h3 f5 13.♗×e7 ♕×e7 14.0–0 ♖f6 15.♖fe1 ♘d6

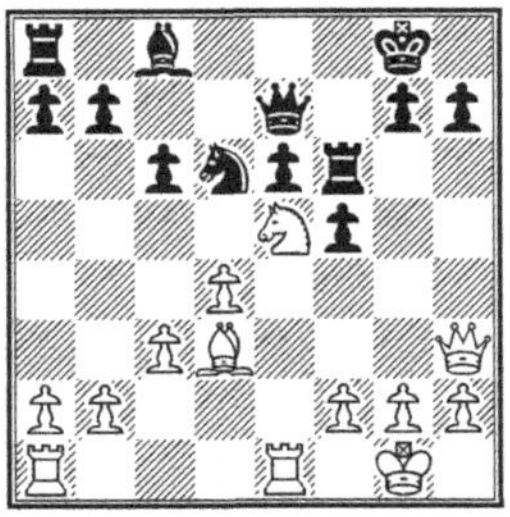

16.♖e2 ♗d7 17.♖ae1 ♖e8 18.c4 ♘f7 19.d5 ♘×e5 20.♖×e5 g6 21.♕h4 ♔g7 22.♕d4 c5 23.♕c3 b6 24.d×e6 ♗c8 25.♗e2 ♗×e6 26.♗f3 ♔f7 27.♗d5 ♕d6 28.♕e3 ♖e7 29.♕h6 ♔g8 30.h4 a6 31.h5 f4 32.h×g6 h×g6 33.♖×e6 1-0

Returning to Torre-Araiza (from previous diagram, **25.♘d3**):

25...♕f6 26.♖e5 ♖d8
CT: Black defends himself very ably. He will move this Rook to d5 to exchange it off, thereby reducing the pressure on e6.

27.♖de1
TK: Somewhat better was 27.c3, defending the d-pawn before doubling Rooks.

27...♖d5?!
TK: Black might have made things a bit easier on himself with 27...♖×d4 28.♖×e6 ♖×e6 29.♖×e6 ♕f7 30.♖e8+ ♔g7 31.♕c3 ♕c4.

28.♘c5?!
TK: Much stronger were 28.c3 or 28.♕a4.

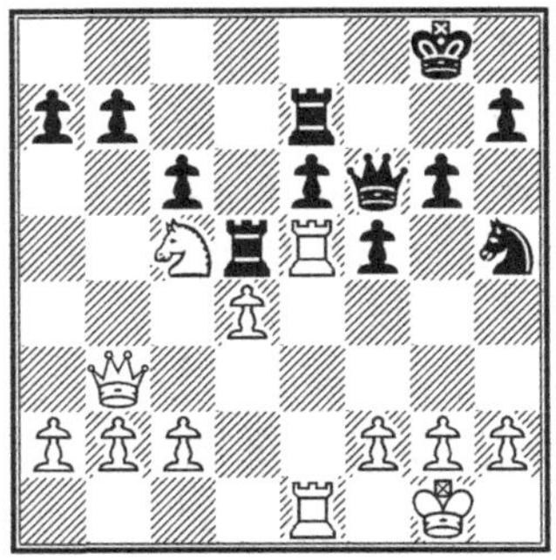

28...♘g7?
CT: 28...♘f4 would be answered by 29.♕e3 ♕g5 30.g3.
TK: 28...♘f4 was actually best, play then continuing 29.g3 b6 30.♘a6 ♘h3+ 31.♔g2 ♘g5 32.♘b4 ♖d6 33.h4 ♘f7 when White must play 34.♘d3! to retain a significant advantage (-1.84/27). And after 28...♘f4 29.♕e3, rather than 29...♕g5?, Black should play 29...b6 30.♕×f4 b×c5 31.d×c5 ♕×e5 32.♕×e5 (32.♖×e5?? ♖d1+) 32...♖×e5 33.♖×e5 ♔f7, when Black has some chance of drawing the Rook ending (+1.55/28).

29.♕e3?!
CT: Having driven the black Knight away from the vicinity of the white King, it might have been more precise to play 29.♕a4 inviting the reply 29...a6; then the position of the Knight on c5 would be decisive in the ending. It would not be prudent to play 29.♘×b7 ♖×d4, as then there would not be time to bring the Knight to a5, because the Queen would take the Rook.

TK: Actually 29.♘×b7! was quite playable, even best, as after 29...♖×d4 White has 30.♕c3! ♖d5 31.♘c5 and Black is all tied up (+2.80/27). Less good is 31.♘a5?! c5. 29.♕a4 is best met by 29...b6. With the text White begins a series of sub-optimal moves.

29...♖×e5 30.d×e5 ♕f7!

CT: This will enable Black to dispute the d-file.

31.♖d1?!

TK: Better 31.b4, and if 31...b6 32.♘b3 △33.♘d4. With the text White's advantage has shrunk greatly, about 200 centipawns down to +0.81/24.

31...b6!□ 32.♘b3 ♖d7 33.♖d3 c5

CT: To prevent 34.♘d4, but generally when one has a slightly inferior position, closing one line will open others. The best response was 33...♖×d3 34.♕×d3 ♕c7, with a more energetic defense.

34.♘d2 ♕e7 35.♘c4 ♘e8

CT: 35...♕d8 was superior.

36.♕d2 ♖×d3 37.♕×d3 ♘c7 38.♕d6

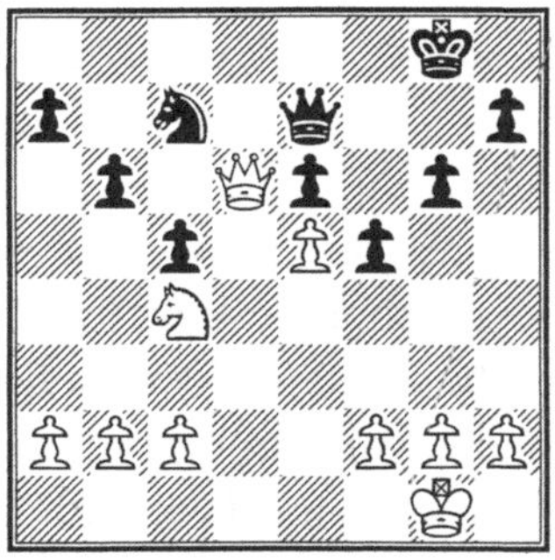

38...♔f7?

CT: 38...♘d5 was decidedly better; now White has gained both space and time.

TK: Indeed, after 38...♘d5 the game is virtually even (+0.29/30). It also bears mentioning that 38...♔f8 (+0.60/27) was also much better than the text, which is the losing move.

39.♕c6!□ ♘e8

CT: There was still some hope with 39...♘d5.

TK: Stockfish disagrees: +4.27/30 after 40.♘d6+.

40.♘d6+ ♔f8

CT: If 40...♘×d6 41.e×d6 ♕d8 42.♕c7+ with an ending very favorable to White.
TK: Even more favorable would be 42.f4.

41.♕c8
CT: Creating a position of "Zug's Zwang" *[sic]*, which happens quite often with pawns, but very seldom when there are major pieces.

41...h6 42.♔f1 h5 43.h4 a6 44.c4 a5 45.a4 1-0
Time: Torre 2 hrs. 15 min., Araiza 2 hrs. 25 min.

Game 88

Torre-Freyria

Mexican Championship, Mexico City, 24 June 1926

Dutch Defense [A92]

Torre's notes here must be viewed as either perplexing or amusing. Freyria played the opening so badly that Torre had a won game by move eight. His advantage just kept building to overwhelming proportions (nudging around +9.00 per Stockfish), and he was never in the slightest danger, but in his notes he called a black blunder "bold and daring," and kept saying that Black was the attacker, playing masterful moves that posed very difficult problems. He also criticized himself severely for a move that was actually quite strong. It is hard to believe Torre actually thought himself in danger, either during the game or when analyzing later. One strongly suspects he wanted to add some *faux* drama to a very one-sided game, to intrigue readers or to spare Freyria's feelings.

1.d4 f5 2.♘f3 ♘f6 3.g3
CT: The most modern method against the Dutch Defense, making it very difficult for Black to develop his Bishop to b7, which is the only diagonal this piece has at its disposal. Furthermore the Bishop on g2 does much in defense of the kingside, which is where Black tends to set his sights in this opening.

3...e6 4.♗g2 ♗e7 5.c4 0-0 6.♘c3 ♘c6?
TK: Better 6...d5 followed by 7...c6, or vice versa.

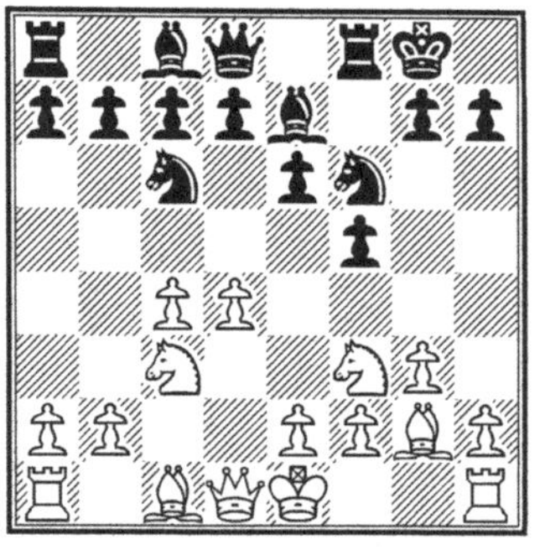

7.0–0

TK: White could already make trouble with 7.d5!. If then 7...♘a5 (Worse is 7...e×d5 8.c×d5 ♘b4 9.a3 ♘a6 10.♘d4 (+2.57/24), and of course 7...♘b8 is just a red-faced admission of error.) 8.b3 ♗b4 9.♗b2 ♘e4 10.♖c1 ♕f6 11.♕d3 with a very strong position for White (+1.73/24).

7...♕e8

CT: Beginning an attack that is premature, because Black has only two pieces developed, in that the ♗e7 cannot yet be considered an active piece. 7...d6 or 7...d5 to free the Queen's Bishop have their drawbacks, but are preferable.

8.♘b5

CT: Attacking the exact point weakened by Black's last move.

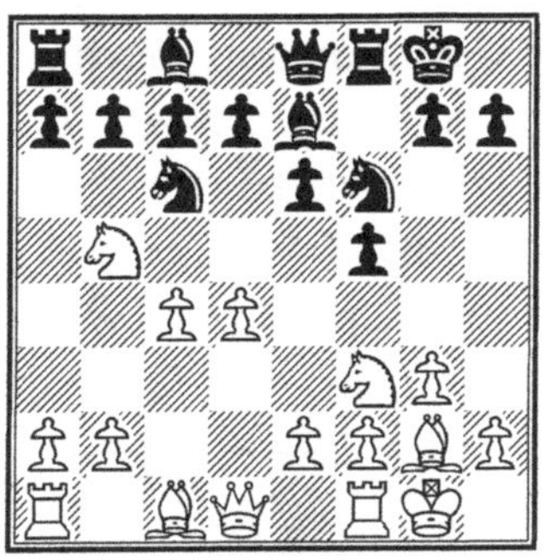

8...♕h5??

CT: A bold and daring move, completely forced on Black by the position he finds himself in, since if 8...♗d8 or 8...♕d8 White continues 9.d5 and 10.d6 and then Black has a very inferior position devoid of hope.

TK: Was Torre trying to spare Freyria's feelings? Objectively, 8...♕h5?? is just foolhardy, not bold and daring.

9.d5 ♘d8 10.♘×c7 ♗d6

CT: There is no other choice, as White threatened 11.d6.

11.♘×a8 e×d5

CT: If 11...e5 12.c5.

12.♕d4

CT: Threatening to eliminate all attacking chances by 13.♕h4, thus forcing Black's next move.

12...f4 13.c×d5

CT: It would not be very prudent to play 13.♗×f4 ♘e6, but now we threaten it to induce Black to play 13...f×g3, when with 14.f×g3 White develops his King's Rook and stands ready to attack.

13...g5

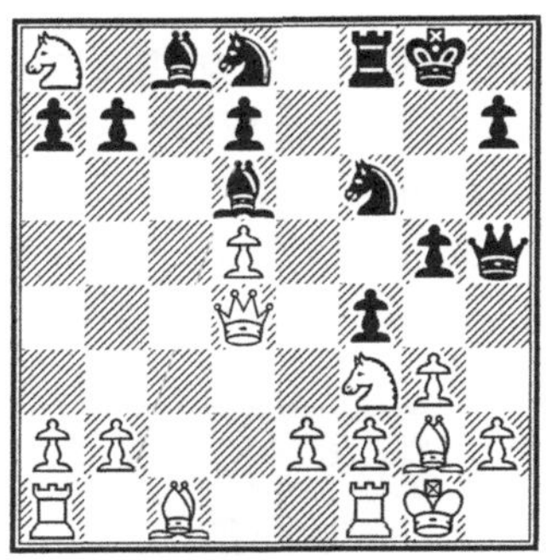

14.♗d2

CT: A serious lack of precision. White wants to move the Bishop to the a1-h8 diagonal, which will completely immobilize Black, and in this manner nullify

any possibility of attack. Certainly the text move threatens 15.♖c1, but in any event White must move the pawn to b4, 14.b4 so as to reply to 14...f×g3 with 15.f×g3, and it is more important to get the Bishop on the long diagonal than to threaten ♖a1-c1-×♗c5. White should have played 14.b4 to get the Bishop on said diagonal in two tempi rather than three. Furthermore White's defense is difficult. This is a lesson, that even in a position of advantage one should play with absolute precision.
TK: Torre is far too hard on himself. There is nothing wrong with the text move, and 14.b4 would have been only slightly better, if at all (Stockfish rates both in the +8.50 to +9.00 range). He greatly overstates Black's attacking chances, and there was no need to hurry with getting the Bishop on the a1-h8 diagonal.

14...b6
CT: A masterful move which indirectly attacks the position of the King and the Queen, posing White with a delicate problem.
TK: Carlos, calm down. Even a move that does not deter ...♗d6-c5, say

15.♗c3, is just fine because if then 15...f×g3 White simply replies 16.h×g3 and 16...♗c5 is nothing more than a minor annoyance.

15.b4 ♗a6 16.♖ae1
CT: Best, because it would not be prudent to allow that Bishop into the game.
TK: 16.♖fe1 was more natural, but it matters not.

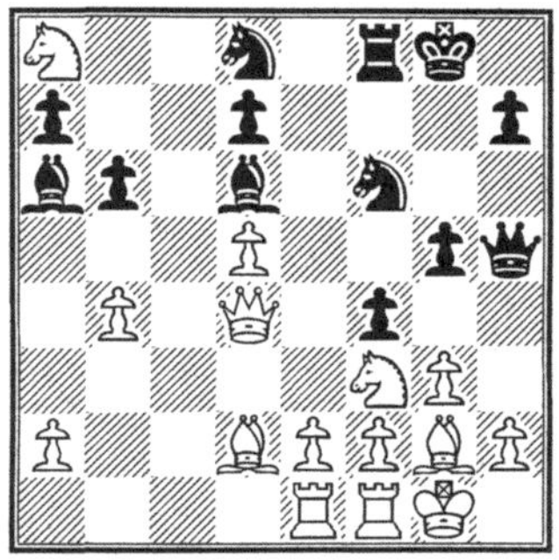

16...♗b7
CT: Black's hoped-for 16...g4 is rejected after a long analysis convincing him that it would not resolve in his favor: 17.♗×f4 (it would be fatal to move the Knight as that would lose the Queen) 17...g×f3 18.♗×f3 ♘g4 19.♗×g4 ♕×g4 20.f3

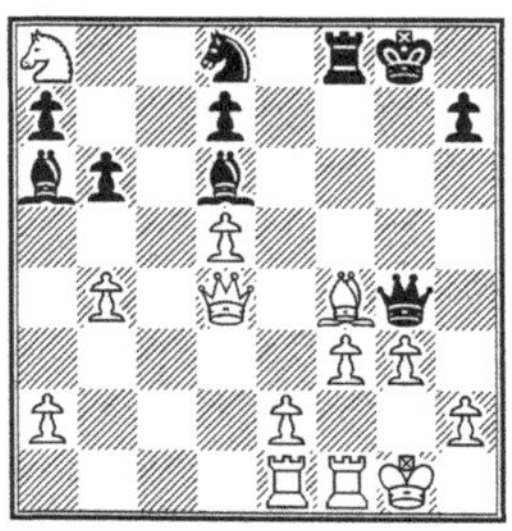

20...♖×f4 21.♕×f4 ♗×f4 22.f×g4 ♗e3+ 23.♔g2 ♗b7 24.♘c7 and White

escapes. Or 20...♕g6 21.♗×d6 ♕×d6 22.♖c1 ♗×e2 23.♖f2 ♗×f3 24.♖cf1.
TK: We offer only one improvement, at the end of the second variation: rather than 24.♖cf1, which runs into slight difficulties after 24...♘c6 and 25...♘e5, best is 24.♖×f3! ♖×f3 25.♕g4+ and 26.♕×f3.

17.♗c3
CT: Finally! The attack has changed hands.
TK: It never left Torre's grasp.

17...♗×a8 18.♘e5 ♕h6
CT: The best defense against the threat of 19.♘×d7.

19.♗f3
CT: Decisive, defending against 19...♘g4, 19...g4 or 19...f3, and preparing 20.e3 to bring the Rooks into the game. It also threatens 20.♗g4.

19...♘f7 20.♘c4 1-0
Time: Torre 1 hr. 25 min., Freyria 2 hrs. 22 min.

Game 89

Soto Larrea-Torre

Mexican Championship, Mexico City, 28 June 1926
Vienna Game (by transposition) [C55]

A good game by Torre, with good notes.

1.e4 ♘f6 2.♘c3
CT: One would think 2.e5 is more appropriate, as otherwise after 2...e5 White must settle for playing a Vienna Game.

2...e5 3.♗c4 ♘c6 4.♘f3
CT: 4.d3 would better conserve the advantage of the first move. Also 4.f4 is worth considering.

4...♘×e4 5.♘×e4
CT: Any other continuation would be less advantageous.

5...d5

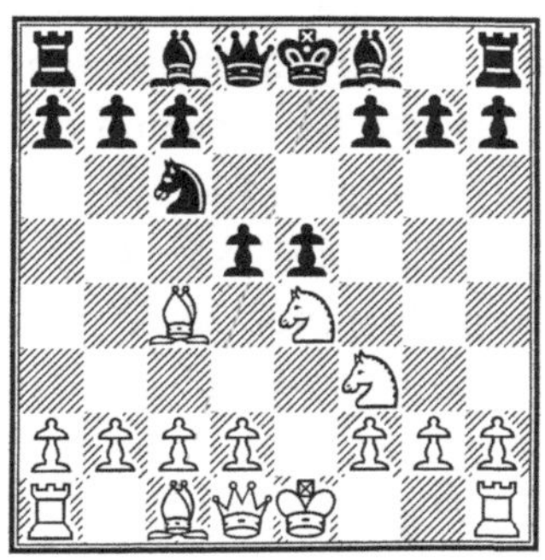

CT: If now 6.♗b5 d×e4 7.♘×e5 ♕d5.
TK: Stockfish evaluates that at only -1.30/25 after 8.♗×c6+ b×c6 9.d4, and offers an improvement: 7...♕g5! 8.d4 (if 8.♘×c6 ♕×b5, or 8.♗×c6+ b×c6 9.d4 ♕×g2 10.♖f1 ♗h3 11.♕e2 ♕×f1+ 12.♕×f1 ♗×f1 13.♔×f1 c5 (-5.96/26)) 8...♕×g2 9.♖f1 ♗d6 10.♘×c6 a6

11.♗a4 0–0 12.♘e5 ♗×e5 13.d×e5 ♗g4 14.f3 e×f3 15.♕d2 f2+ 16.♕×f2 ♕e4+ 17.♗e3 ♕×a4 (-4.11/27).

6.♗d3 d×e4 7.♗×e4 ♗d6 8.d4

CT: 8.d3 might be better, even though the Bishop on e4 would not be entirely well after 8...♘e7.

8...e×d4

CT: This opens the Bishop's diagonal, furthering Black's development.

9.♘×d4 0–0 10.♗e3

CT: If 10.♘×c6 ♕h4 or 10...♕e8, with advantage.

TK: 10...♕h4 is indeed advantageous, but 10...♕e8 yields nothing after 11.♕e2 b×c6 12.♗d3=.

10...♕h4! 11.♗×c6 b×c6

CT: Black will have an untenable pawn ending, but there is ample compensation in his two Bishops and in the effective use of the b-file, which will be the key to the position. On the other hand, White cannot castle with security.

12.♕d3 ♗g4

TK: Black could win a pawn by 12...c5 13.♘f5 ♗×f5 14.♕×f5 ♕b4+ 15.c3 ♕×b2 16.0–0, but this would mean giving up the Bishop pair and allowing White to castle safely, *i.e.* losing two of the three advantages Torre just mentioned.

13.♔f1?

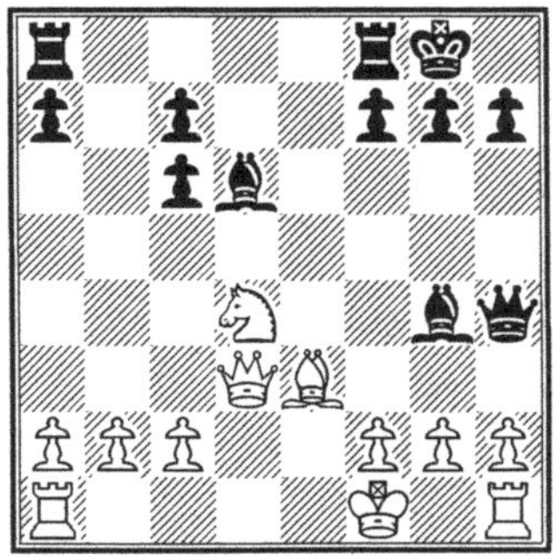

CT: A surprising move, but castling could have fatal consequences, *e.g.* 13.♘e2 ♖ab8 14.0–0–0 ♗×e2 15.♕×e2 ♕a4 16.♔b1 ♖×b2+ 17.♔×b2 ♕a3+ 18.♔a1 ♕c3+ 19.♔b1 ♖b8+ 20.♔c1 ♗a3#.

TK: The text must be considered the losing move. The least evil was 13.♘f5 13...♗×f5 (if 13...♕f6?! 14.♘×d6 c×d6 15.0–0=) 14.♕×f5 ♕b4+ 15.c3 ♕×b2 16.0–0 and while White still stands worse, he is not yet lost (-1.27/24).

13...♖ab8

CT: This move deserves special attention. At first 13...c5 seems advantageous, to be followed by ...c4-c3, but this would only serve to block Black's own pieces.

14.f3 ♗d7 15.♘b3 c5

CT: Threatening 16...♗b5 or 16...c4.

16.c4 ♗e6 17.♖c1 ♖b4 18.f4

CT: Naturally White does not want to lose a pawn and allow entry to the Rook, but this move has its drawbacks, as it not only weakens the f-pawn but also blocks the action of his Bishop.

18...♕f6

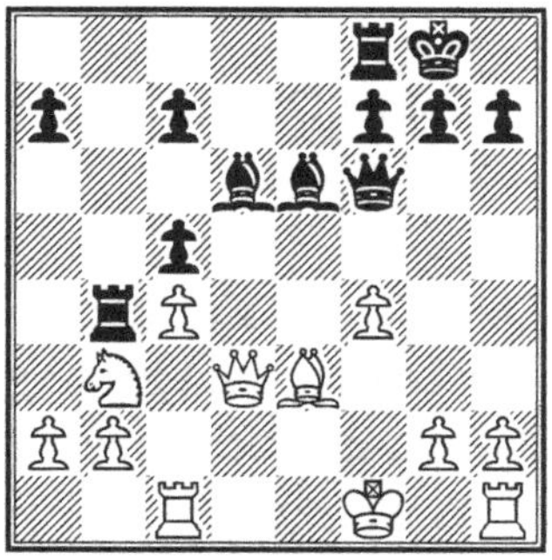

CT: It would be a mistake to play 18...♗×f4 due to 19.♕e4. Now Black threatens 19...♕×b2 followed by 20...♕×c1+ and 21...♗×c4, or if 19.g3 ♕×b2 20.♖c2 ♕b1+ 21.♔g2 ♗×c4, winning quickly.
TK: In that last line, even stronger would be 21...♗h3+ 22.♔×h3 ♕×h1.

19.♕c3 ♕f5
CT: Having such a good game it is not expedient to exchange pieces.

20.♕c2 ♗×c4+ 21.♔g1

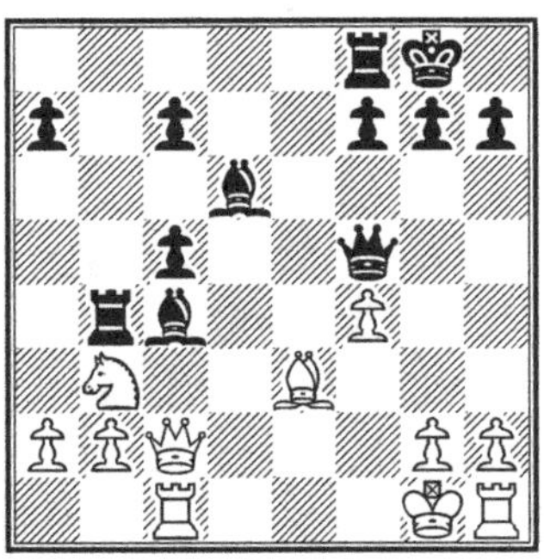

21...♗d3
GV: This brute-force move is strongest, but a more elegant variation bears mentioning: 21...♗×f4!, leaving the Queen *en prise* in the style of Game 18, Torre-Banks. Forced then is 22.♕×f5 ♗×e3+ 23.♕f2 ♖e8! 24.♖c2 ♗d3 25.♕×e3 ♖×e3 26.♔f2 ♗×c2 27.♔×e3 ♗×b3 28.a×b3 ♖×b3+ 29.♔e4 ♖×b2, with an easily won ending.

22.♕f2 ♖e8 23.h3
CT: Having nothing better, White gives his King an escape square.

23...♖be4 24.g4 ♕f6

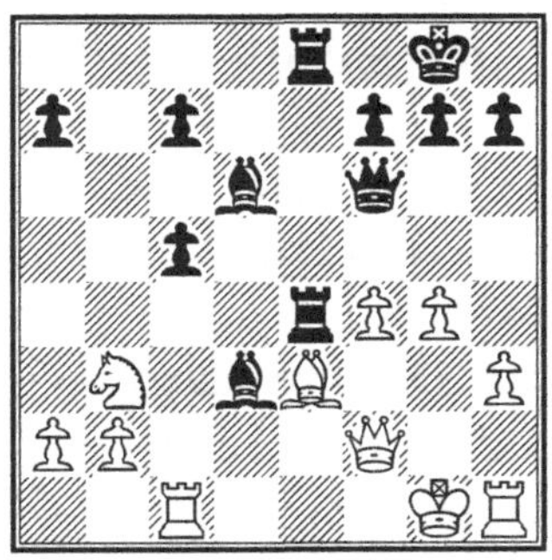

CT: If 24...♕d5, White defends himself with 25.♕f3.
TK: Which is equally futile. Stockfish's evaluation is now at about -9.00 or worse no matter what White tries.

25.♗d2 c4 26.♗c3 ♕×f4 27.♕×f4 ♗×f4 28.♘d2 ♖e2 0-1
CT: If 29.♖d1 ♗e6+ and mate shortly.
Time: Soto Larrea 2 hrs. 10 min., Torre 1 hr. 10 min.

Game 90

Araiza-Torre

Mexican Championship, Mexico City, 29 June 1926

English Opening [A16]

Torre's worst game of the tournament, and his worst annotations as well. Over moves 16-20 he made four mistakes that left him with a clearly losing position, but Araiza made worse errors in turn, including a gross blunder at move 25, that let Torre turn a humbling defeat into a lucky victory.

1.♘f3 ♘f6 2.c4 g6 3.g3 ♗g7 4.♘c3 d5 5.c×d5 ♘×d5 6.♗g2 0–0

CT: A positional error, because White can start a strong attack by 7.h4 without risk.

Better to play, like Rubinstein, 6...c5 and 7...♘c6, and not castle until White has done so.

7.♕b3 ♘b6 8.d3 ♘c6

CT: There is no time for 8...c5 because White is threatening to gather his pieces against the kingside.

9.♗g5 ♗e6

CT: Inviting the reply 9...h6, which would weaken the position.

10.♕c2 ♕d7

CT: Trying to oppose the attack by means of development.

11.h4 ♗g4 12.♘h2

CT: White wants to play safety first. More aggressive would be 12.h5, but also decidedly more complicated.

12...♗f5 13.♕d2 ♖ad8 14.♖d1

CT: Naturally he does not castle long, because he would later be exposed to a strong attack.

14...♕e6

CT: Threatening 15...♖×d3.

15.♕e3 ♕×e3

CT: Confident of reaching an endgame, Black does not examine 15...♘e5, which would make it difficult for White to find any strong continuation.

TK: Stockfish disagrees, seeing the position after 16.0–0 ♖fe8 17.♗h6 as favoring White (+0.79/25).

16.♗×e3

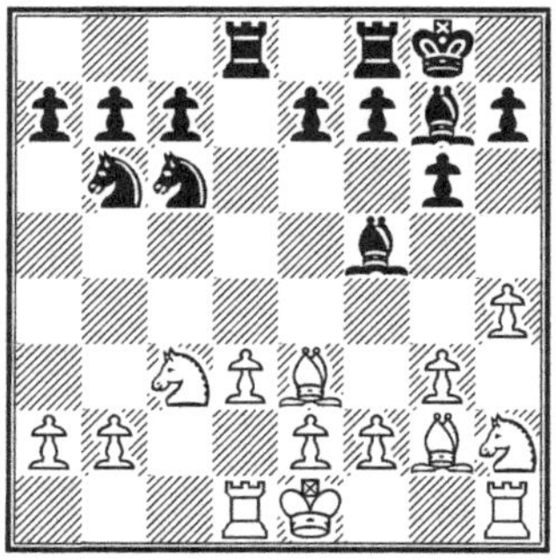

16...♘b4?

CT: The kingside attack has been repulsed. Now the difficulty lies in defending against the threat of 17.♗×c3, which would leave Black with an indefensible pawn position. Clearly better was 16...♘d4; if then 17.♗×d4 ♗×d4 18.♗×b7 ♖b8 Black, by virtue of the isolation of White's kingside Knight and Rook, may be able to recover his pawn with correct play.
TK: Torre is correct about the relative merits of 16...♘d4 vs. 16...♘b4, but he does not seem to realize that the text is a rather serious error that could have lost the game.

17.♗c5

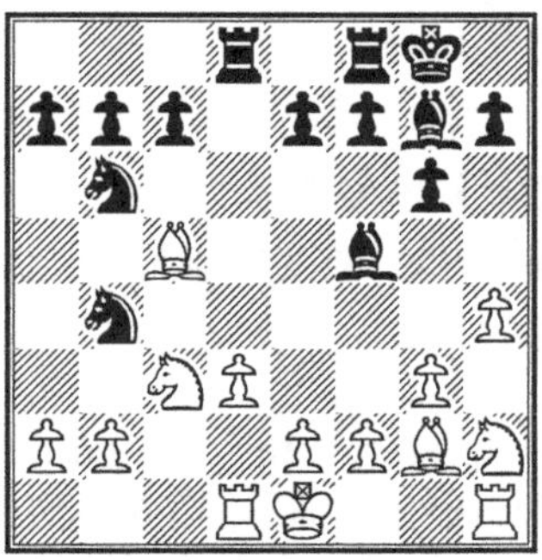

17...♗×c3+?
CT: There is nothing better, because if the Knight retreats to d5, White loses a piece after e2-e4.
TK: It bears mentioning that if 17...♘d5 White must first play 18.♘×d5, and only after 18...♘×d5 does he play 19.e4. More importantly, 17...a5 was a lesser evil than the text; after 18.♗×e7 ♘c4 19.♗×d8 (if 19.d×c4?? ♗×c3+ and 20.♖d2 is forced, since if 20.b×c3 ♘c2+ 21.♔f1 ♖×d1 #) 19...♘×b2 20.♖c1 ♖×d8 Black is not quite so bad off as in the actual game.

18.b×c3 ♘×a2?
TK: Torre's third bad move in a row. Better was 18...♘4d5, when to retain his advantage White must find 19.♗×d5 ♘×d5 20.♖c1! (if 20.e4? ♘×c3 21.♖c1 ♘×a2 22.♖c2 ♗e6 23.♗×e7 ♖×d3 24.♗×f8 ♔×f8=) 20...b6 21.♗a3 c5 22.e4+−.

19.♗×e7 ♘×c3

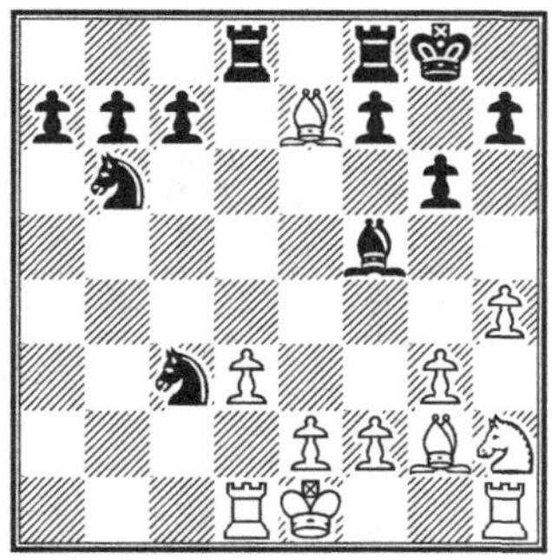

20.♖d2?
CT: White does not play 20.♖c1, because Black replies 20...♘×e2. The correct way to ensure success was 20.♗×d8 ♘×d1 21.♗×c7 ♘c3 22.♗×b7 with an extra pawn and the better position.
TK: This analysis can be improved considerably. Torre is quite correct about 20.♗×d8, but after 21...♘×d1, best is 21.♗f6! cutting off the ♘d1's escape. Then after, say, 21...♘d7 22.♗a1 ♘×f2 23.♔×f2 ♘c5 24.♗f6 (△25.♗e7) White has a Bishop for two pawns and the better position (+5.61/27). With White's Bishops and Rook roaming

free, Black will be unable to make much use of his passed pawns. Victory for White is assured with reasonably good technique. With the text move, however, White's advantage has disappeared.

20...c6?!

CT: This powerful resource nullifies the ♗g2, while Black's four pieces can maneuver on the queenside.

TK: This is actually Torre's fourth bad move in the last five. With 20...♘ba4, intending 21...b5, Black could have almost equalized.

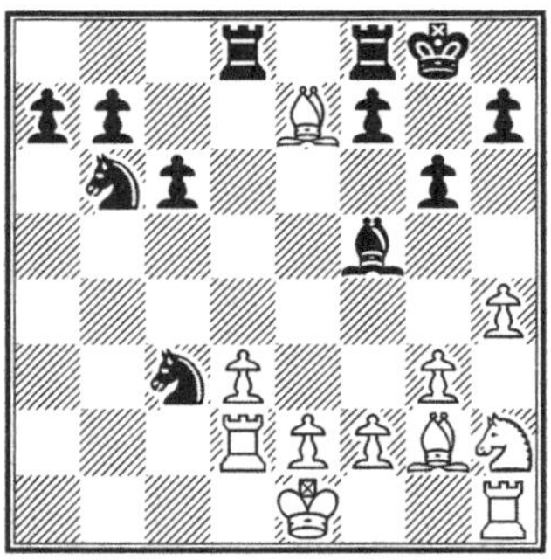

21.♗×d8

CT: White makes sure of gaining the Exchange; despite this his situation is not at all advantageous. Completely discouraged, from now on he plays moves that without being obvious errors, lead to failure.

TK: White did not need to rush this capture. Better first was 21.h5!?, White finally playing what Torre was worried about back at move 12. If then 21...g×h5? 22.♘f1 ♗g6 23.♘e3 △f2-f4-f5. Best play after 21.h5 seems to be 21...♖fe8 22.♗×d8 ♖×d8 23.h×g6 h×g6 24.♘f3 a5 25.♖b2 ♘b5 26.♘g5 a4 27.♖h8+ ♔×h8 28.♘×f7+ ♔g7 29.♘×d8 a3 30.♖c2, when Stockfish thinks White will somehow cope with the advanced a-pawn and have slightly better chances in the endgame (+0.92/25). There are other lines where White brings his inactive Rook into the game by ♖h1-h4, another virtue of 21.h5.

21...♖×d8 22.0–0 a5 23.♖c1

TK: Better was 23.♖b2 ♘b5 24.♖a1 a4 25.♘f3 getting all his pieces involved, when White may still be all right (+0.68/24).

23...♘b5 24.♘f1

TK: ⌓24.e4 ♗e6 25.♘f3=.

24...a4 25.♗×c6??

TK: Completely unwarranted desperation! With 25.♖b2 or 25.♘e3 White could still put up a fight. It is hard to understand why Torre made no comment on this move, and how he could have thought White's play from move 21 on was "without obvious errors."

25...♖c8 26.♗×b5? ♖×c1 27.♔g2 ♗e6 28.d4 a3 0–1

Time: Araiza 1 hr. 10 min., Torre 1 hr. 34 min.

Game 91

Freyria-Torre

Mexican Championship, Mexico City, 30 June 1926

Alekhine's Defense [B05]

In Mexico City's Lake Xochimilco, there lives a kind of salamander, the axolotl, which retains its gills into adulthood and never leaves the water. This game gives the impression that Freyria knew little more about chess than an axolotl knows about hang-gliding.

1.e4 ♘f6 2.e5 ♘d5 3.d4 d6 4.e×d6
CT: More prudent than 4.f4, but it may be better to force the Knight to retreat to b3 with 4.c4.

4...♕×d6
CT: Black can equally well play 4...e×d6 or 4...c×d6, but he prefers to capture with the Queen to guide the game into little-known lines, besides using the Queen post as a base of operations. White amiably allows this plan to take effect, creating no difficulties for Black.

5.♘f3
CT: Now it was definitely stronger to play 5.c4 ♘b6 6.♘c3 with Black probably continuing 6...c6.

5...♗g4 6.♗e2 ♘c6 7.0–0 0–0–0 8.c3 ♘f4
CT: Inviting the exchange of one of White's Bishops, and uncovering the action of the Rook.

9.♗×f4 ♕×f4

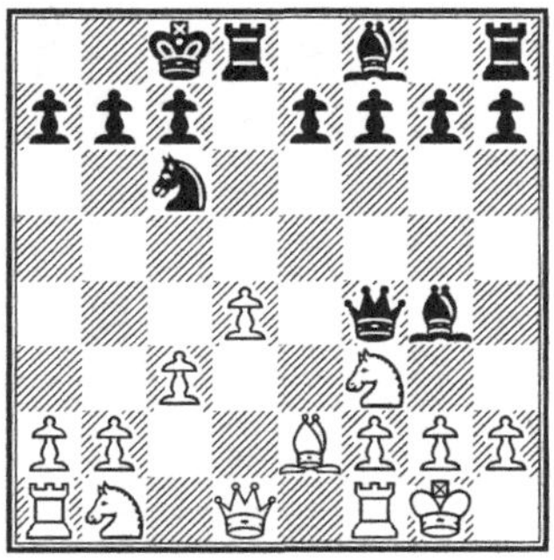

10.♕b3
CT: This can be considered an effort at counter-attack, though premature, because his pieces are undeveloped. Nevertheless, a defensive move like 10.♘bd2 would not be satisfactory, as Black will still gain an advantage with 10...e5.
TK: Stockfish suggests 10.h3 ♗h5 11.♖e1, when if 11...e5? 12.♘×e5 ♗×e2 13.♕×e2 ♘×e5 14.♕×e5 ♕×e5 15.♖×e5 and White has won a pawn.

10...e5 11.d×e5??
CT: Slightly preferable was 11.d5, but in any event Black would maintain his position, furthermore with the threat of ...e5-e4 and development of the King's Bishop to c5. On the other hand White may feel inclined to play c3-c4, which would markedly reduce his Bishop's scope.

TK: Torre is guilty of gross understatement. 11.d5, which leads to equality, was more than "slightly preferable" compared to the text, which is a blunder.

11...♘×e5

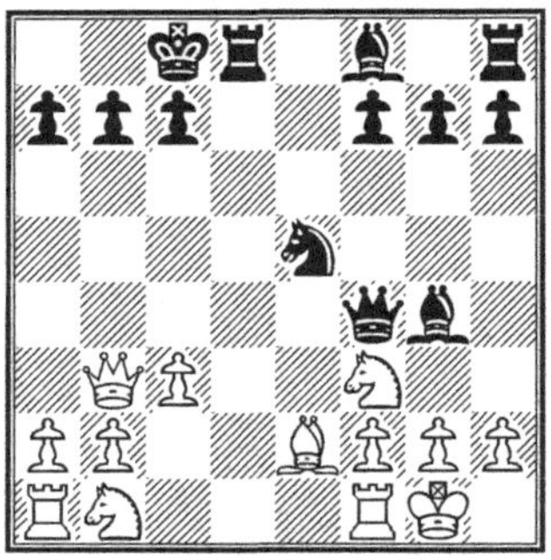

12.♘×e5??
TK: The least evil, though evil it still certainly would be, was 12.♘d4 ♖×d4 13.c×d4 ♗×e2 14.d×e5 ♗×f1 15.♔×f1 ♕c1+ 16.♔e2 ♗e7 17.♕c3 ♕g1 18.g3 ♖d8 19.♕e1 ♕×h2 20.♘c3, when White's material loss is limited to a pawn, though he still has many problems (-2.36/24). As with move 25 in the previous game, it is puzzling that Torre should say nothing about how bad the text move is.

12...♗×e2 13.♘×f7
CT: This is not a mistake, but a lost position. Black has superior development while White's Knight, Rook and Queen are inactive.

13...♗c4 14.♕a4 ♕×f7 15.♕×a7 ♗×f1 0–1
CT: Of no use would be 16.♕a8+ ♔d7 17.♕×b7 ♗c5. A game conducted good-naturedly by Sr. Freyria. Time: Freyria 25 min., Torre 25 min.

Page 108 of the July-August 1926 *ACB* reported on the championship tournament as follows:

> According to a special cable dispatch from Mexico City to the Bulletin on July 1, Carlos Torre of New York clinched his right to the chess championship of his native land, to which he had returned for the purpose of competing in the national tournament arranged especially for his benefit. The other three contenders, none of whom was a match for him, were J.J. Araiza, M. Soto and Augustín Freyria ... At the conclusion of the tournament Brigadier General Manuel Mendoza, acting in behalf of Torre as his manager, issued through the Bulletin a challenge to Frank J. Marshall to play a match for the Pan-American championship.

In that same issue Marshall discussed his conditions for the match, which were much like Capablanca's London Rules: a match of six games up, draws not counting; after 20 games the higher number of wins to decide, or in case of a tie at that point, the next win decides. Purse of $4,000, 20% of which to be Marshall's fee, the rest divided 60/40 between winner and loser. Time limit 40 moves in 2½ hours. Alas, due to Torre's breakdown the match did not come to fruition; it would have been a most interesting encounter.

Responding to an invitation from the Zacatecas Chess Club, Carlos Torre left Mexico City on July 20, 1926 for that city, then an important chess center of Mexico. Not only did Zacatecas have an active club, but it also produced the two most important chess-related periodicals published in Mexico at the time: the *Boletín de Ajedrez* and the *Revista Mexicana de Ajedrez*. Torre later agreed to contribute analyzed games and articles on various openings to the *Boletín*. Zacatecas was home to a magnificent chess club and many fans of the game, who gave Torre a warm welcome. On July 21st, he gave a simultaneous exhibition on 40 boards, scoring +36 =2 -2. The following two games are from that event.

Game 92

Torre-Zesati

Simul, Zacatecas, Mexico, 21 July 1926

Caro-Kann Defense [B13]

A game strongly played by Torre until move 24, when he inexplicably left a pawn *en prise*, the loss of which would have thrown his advantage away. But his opponent failed to capitalize. Further errors at moves 28 and 31, might also have led to a draw.

1.e4 c6 2.d4 d5 3.e×d5 c×d5 4.♗d3

This variation, which goes back to Schottländer-Weiss, Nuremberg 1883, has often been chosen by masters in simuls, as it is easy to play for White but requires skillful handling by Black, and it can allow White quickly to gain an idea of his (presumably unknown) opponent's strength. Attorney Roberto Zesati was, in fact, one of the strongest Zacatecan players, who a few years later would win the city championship.

4...♘c6 5.c3 ♘f6

Since most of the punch of this variation (from White's viewpoint) is based on the idea of playing ♗c1-f4 and ♘b1-a3 threatening ♘b5, in more recent years Black has been anticipating this by 5...♕c7!, as in Illescas-Anand, Linares 1994: 5...♕c7 6.♗g5 ♘f6 7.♘d2 ♗g4 8.♘gf3 e6 9.♗h4 ♗d6 10.♗g3 ♗h5 11.♗×d6 ♕×d6 12.0–0 0–0 13.♖e1 ♖ab8!∓ and Black eventually won. In fact, though, the move 5...♕c7 goes back at least as far as 1925, when the German master Carl Carls used it to defeat Mieses and Thomas at Baden-Baden.

6.♘f3

6.♗f4 at once is more incisive.

6...♗g4 7.♗f4 a6 8.♘bd2 e6

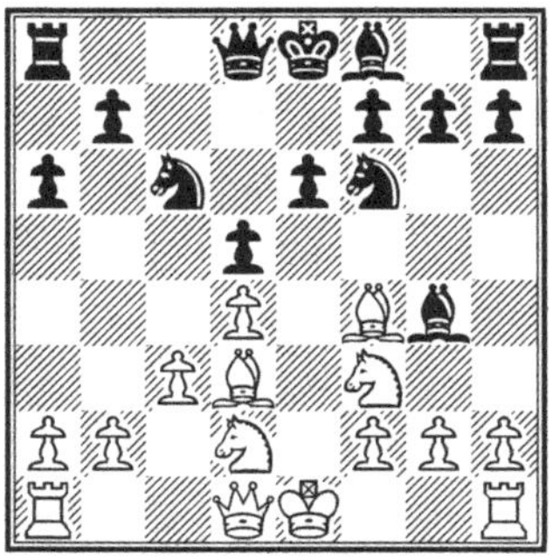

9.♕b3

The main line is 9.0–0, for example 9...♗d6 10.♗g3 (or 10.♗×d6 ♕×d6 11.♕e1 ♘d7 12.♕e3 ♗h5 13.♖fe1 ♗g6 14.♗f1 0–0 15.♘e5=, Rakic-Bagirov, 1983) 10...0–0 11.♕e1 ♘e7 12.♘e5 ♗f5 13.f4 ♗×d3 14.♘×d3 ♘f5 15.♗f2 ♗e7 16.♘e5 ♖e8 17.g4 ♘d6 18.♗e3 ♘fe4=, Smilga-Petrosian, Leningrad 1946 (0-1,46); or 9...♗e7 10.♖e1 ♗h5 11.♘f1 0–0 12.♘g3 ♗g6 13.♘e5 ♘×e5 14.♗×e5 ♘d7 15.♗f4 ♖c8 16.♘f1 ♘b6 17.♗×g6 h×g6 18.♘d2 ♕d7=, Pimenov-Makogonov, Moscow Trade Unions Ch 1936.

9...♕c8 10.0–0 ♗e7 11.♖ae1

Or 11.♖fe1 0–0 12.♘e5 ♗h5 13.♘df3 ♗g6 14.♘×g6 h×g6 15.♘e5 ♘×e5 16.♗×e5 ♕d7 17.♕d1 with attack, Hansen-Mogensen, Denmark 1994 (1-0, 38).

11...♘d7 12.♕c2 ♗×f3?!

An error that could have had serious consequences. Better 12...♗h5 to preserve the Bishop and allow it to retreat to g6.

13.♘×f3 h6

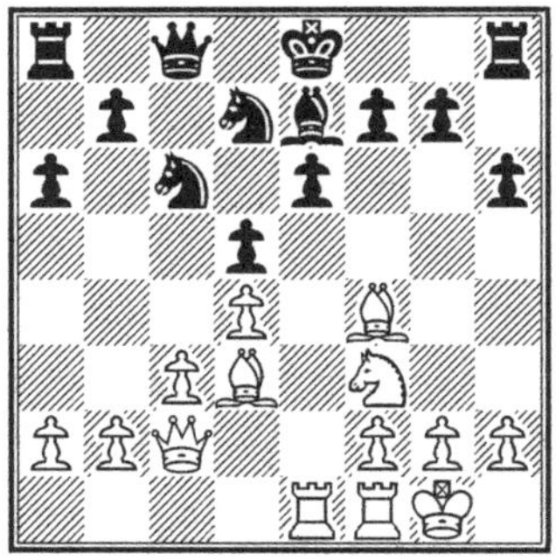

14.♕d2

Somewhat better was 14.♕e2 g5 15.♗g3 ♕d8 16.b4 h5 17.h3 ♖g8 18.a4, with Knight's pawn thrusts impending on opposite wings. White's is the stronger, however, *e.g.* 18...g4 19.h×g4 h×g4 20.♘d2 ♖g7 21.b5 a×b5 22.a×b5 ♘a5 23.♖a1 (+1.36/26).

14...♘f8?!

Played with the idea of exchanging some minor pieces, to relieve White's increasing pressure. He might also have considered 14...♕d8, as his Queen is clearly very clumsily placed on c8. Stockfish recommends 14...g5 15.♗g3 ♕d8 16.h3 with play much as in the previous note, though White will still want to bring his Queen to e2, making his 14th move a lost tempo.

15.♘e5

Though it runs contrary to general principles to give up a Bishop for a Knight, 15.♗e5 was probably better. After 15...♘×e5 16.♘×e5 ♘d7 (not 16...f6?? 17.♗g6+ ♘×g6 18.♘×g6 ♖g8 19.♘f4 and 20.♘/♖×e6+–)

17.f4 White has a very strong position (+2.07/25), much like in Torre-Verlinsky (Game 79).

15...♘×e5?

Another error, worse than at move 12. Correct was 15...♘d7 when White must either retreat the Knight back to f3, or play 16.♘×d7 ♕×d7, enabling Black to castle queenside.

16.♗×e5 ♗f6 17.f4!

An instructive move. White intends to open up the position by means of f4-f5. This is one of the most important principles that Paul Morphy taught by example: when the opponent's King remains uncastled, our first thought must be to open the central lines.

17...♕c6?

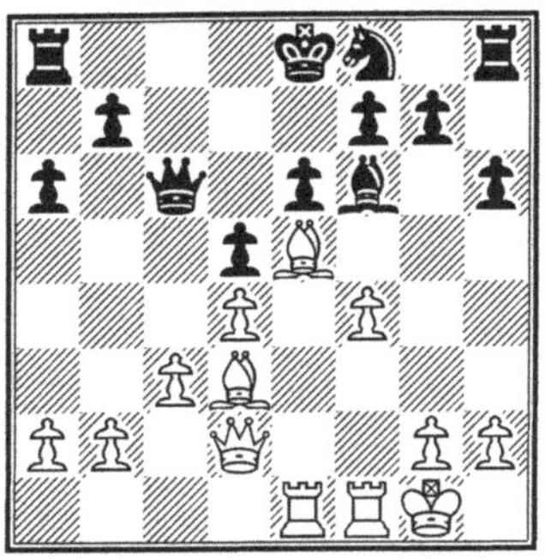

Black is reduced to playing least evils, but this is greater rather than lesser. 17...♘d7 was necessary.

18.f5

Good, but stronger still was 18.♗×f6 g×f6 19.f5 e5 (if 19...0–0–0? 20.f×e6 f×e6 21.♖×f6 is hopeless) 20.d×e5 ♘d7 21.e×f6+ ♔f8 22.♕e3 ♕×f6 23.♖f4 ♖c8 24.♖d4/♖b4 etc. (+4.55/24).

18...♗×e5 19.♖×e5 f6?

Another greater evil. Least was 19...0–0–0.

20.♖e2 ♔f7

Necessary now. If 20...e5?? 21.d×e5 0–0–0 22.e6 (+6.86).

21.♕f4 ♖e8 22.♖fe1 g5 23.♕f3

White's advantage is now so great that any reasonable Queen move preserves the win. Best, though, was 23.f×e6+ ♘×e6 24.♕f5.

23...h5

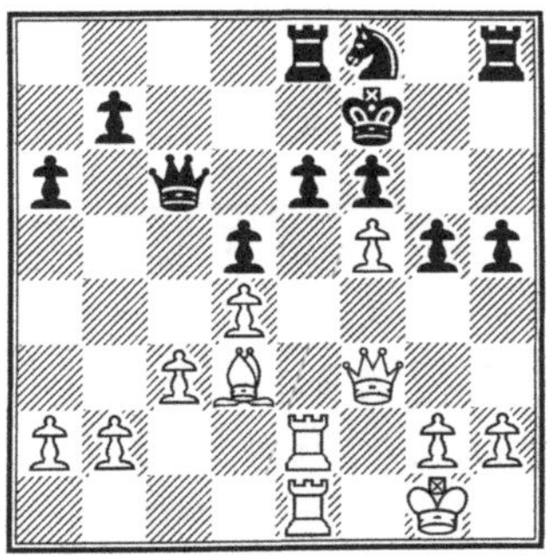

24.b3?

Intended to support the advance c3-c4, but Torre, playing on 40 boards at once, seems to have overlooked that this puts his c-pawn *en prise*.

If he wanted to push the c-pawn (not the best idea in this position, but far from the worst and much better than the text), best to do so immediately: 24.c4 g4 25.f×e6+ ♖×e6 26.♕×d5 ♕×d5 27.c×d5 ♖×e2 28.♖×e2 ♘g6

29.♖c2 ♖d8 30.♖c7+ ♘e7 31.♖×b7 and wins.

24...b5??
As perplexing as White's 24th move was, Black's is equally if not more so. With the obvious 24...♕×c3! he could have halted White's attack and sent most of White's advantage up in smoke. One wonders if, after 25.f×e6+, Torre and Zesati envisioned 25...♘×e6/♖×e6 26.♗g6+, winning Black's Queen. But of course Black can play 25...♔g7, evading the potential check, and after 26.e7 ♘g6 27.♖e3 ♕×d4 the game is virtually even. But with the text Black, like a defensive back who intercepts a pass and then fumbles, has restored the *status quo ante*.

25.c4 g4

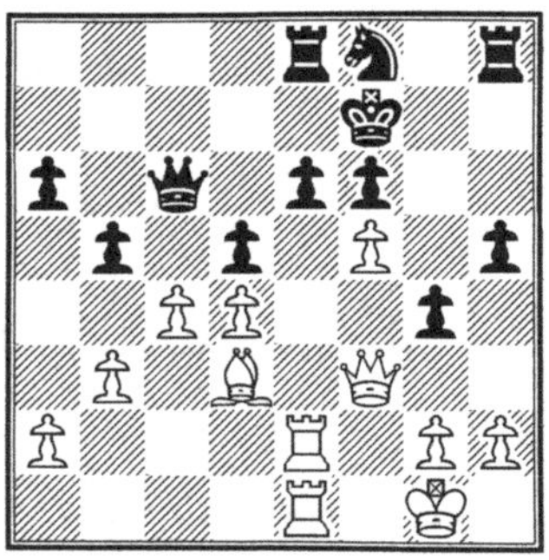

26.♕f4
Strongest was 26.f×e6+ ♖×e6 (if 26...♘×e6?? 27.♕f5) 27.♖×e6 ♕×e6 28.♕f2 ♕c6 29.c5 (+4.00/26). But the text is a close second. In a simul the master, forced to play quickly, will often make second- or third-best moves (He just needs to avoid ones like 24.b3?).

26...b×c4 27.b×c4 d×c4 28.♖c2?!
Wrong Rook! Correct was 28.♖c1. The text gives Black another shot at redemption.

28...e×f5!
Had White play 28.♖c1, this could be countered by 29.♖×c4 +−.

29.♗×c4+ ♔g7 30.♖×e8 ♕×e8 31.♕×f5?!
Letting his advantage slip further. Best was 31.♗×a6.

31...♕e1+ 32.♗f1

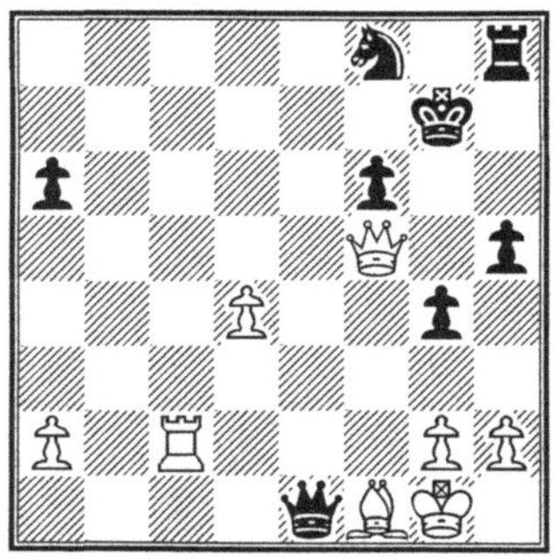

32...♕e6??
Missing his last chance. His best shot at survival was 32...♕e3+ 33.♕f2 ♕e7 (if 33...♕e6? 34.♖c7+ ♘d7 35.♕g3 ♖d8 36.♗d3 (+2.67/33)) 34.♗×a6 ♕d6 (+1.03/24). Now Torre finishes him off with deadly precision.

33.♖c7+! ♔h6 34.♕f4+ ♔g6 35.♗d3+ f5 36.♗×f5+! ♕×f5 37.♖g7+ ♔f6 38.♖f7+ 1-0
One must wonder if Torre's mistakes in this game indicate the aforementioned fatiguing effect simuls had on him.

Game 93

Torre-Solís

Simul, Zacatecas, Mexico, 21 July 1926

King's Gambit [C33]

1.e4 e5 2.f4 e×f4 3.♘c3 ♕h4+ 4.♔e2

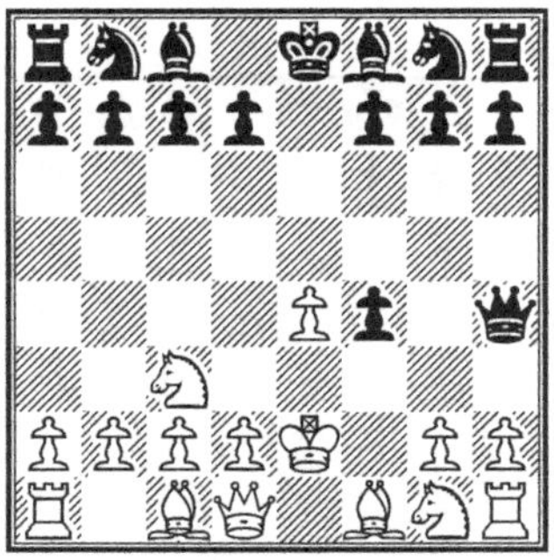

Torre again shows his simul penchant for speculative, romantic openings. Though it somewhat resembles the Steinitz Gambit (1.e4 e5 2.♘c3 ♘c6 3.f4 e×f4 4.d4 ♕h4+ 5.♔e2), this line is known as the Keres Gambit, based on Estonian GM Paul Keres' use of it in correspondence play in the 1930s. Obviously Keres (ten years old in 1926) was not the first to play it; in fact, it goes back at least to Mason-Rosenthal, Paris 1878 (0-1, 28). The fact that Torre and Keres managed to win with this line is probably due more to their chess strength and the relative weakness of their opponents, than to the intrinsic worth of the gambit.[1]

4...d6

Perhaps too conservative. Mason-Rosenthal went in quite the other direction with 4...d5! 5.♘×d5 ♗g4+ 6.♘f3 and now, instead of 6...♘a6 as played by Rosenthal, or 6...♗d6 by Furman, Stockfish recommends 6...♘c6!? 7.♘×c7+ ♔d8 8.♘×a8 ♘e5 9.♕e1 ♘×f3 10.♕×h4+ ♘×h4+ 11.♔e1 g5, and though White is temporarily up ♖+♙-for-♘, Black is seen as nearly winning (-1.34/25).

5.♘f3 ♗g4 6.♘d5?

Correct was 6.d4, but Torre is aiming for complications rather than correctness.

6...♘a6

Making the same mistake as Rosenthal. Bold and best was 6...♘c6! 7.d4 (if 7.♘×c7+ ♔d8 8.♘×a8 ♘e5 etc. as in the above note, with results even more favorable for Black (-2.60/25)) 7...0–0–0∓/–+.

With the text Black's advantage disappears.

7.d4 0–0–0 8.♗×f4 ♖e8?!

1 The gambit was also seen in Mackenzie-Judd, match, Toledo, 1887 (1-0, 24), and was played twice by Flamberg in one of the Triberg "prison tournaments" 1914-15. Most surprisingly, it was played in Spassky-Furman, USSR Ch semi-final, Tallin 1959 (1-0, 31).

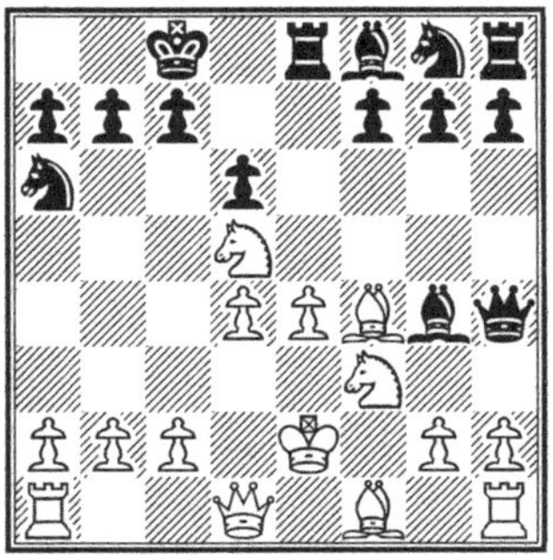

The game was quite even, but now it starts tending to White's favor.
Better 8...♘f6, or 8...c6 9.♗g3 ♕h5 10.♘f4 ♕h6 11.♔f2 ♘c7=.

9.♔d2! ♖×e4?
The exchanges this initiates do not work out well for Black. Better was 9...♕h5.

10.♘×h4

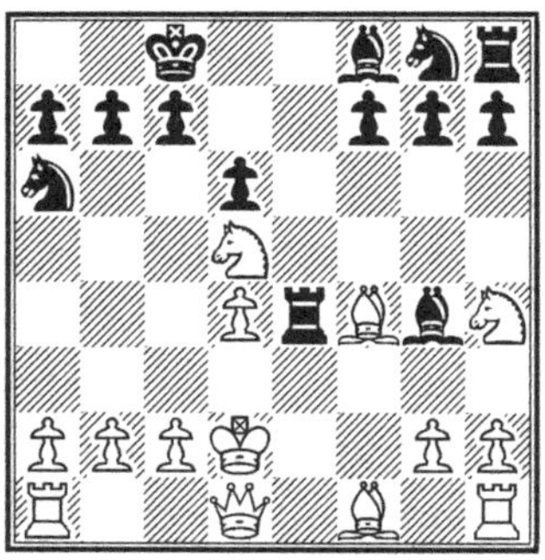

10...♖×d4+??
Patzer sees a check, patzer gives a check.
Necessary was 10...♗×d1 11.♖×d1 c6 12.♗×a6 b×a6 13.♘f5 c×d5 14.♖hf1 ♖e6, which would leave Black down only one pawn, though his development still suffers.

11.♔c3 ♖×d1 12.♖×d1 ♗×d1 13.♗×a6 ♗h5
13...b×a6 14.♖×d1 was worse.

14.♖e1! f6
Of course if 14...b×a6?? 15.♖e8+ ♔d7 16.♖×f8.

15.♗d3 g5

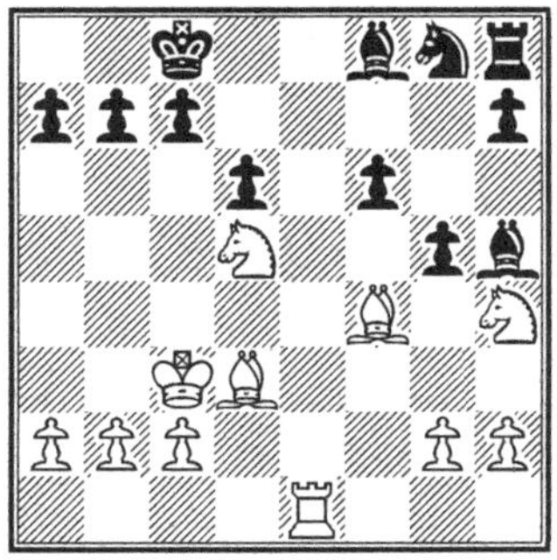

16.♗f5+?
Another simul-sloppy move, which like 24.b3 in the previous game might have wasted White's advantage.
Best and still winning was 16.♘g6 ♗×g6 17.♗×g6 h×g6 18.♖e8+ ♔d7 19.♖×f8 g×f4 20.♖×g8! ♖×g8 21.♘×f6+ and 22.♘×g8+−.

16...♔d8
Now ♖e1-e8+ is impossible.

17.♗g3 g×h4 18.♗×h4 c6
⌓18...♗f7=

19.♘f4 ♗g6?!
Again, 19...♗f7 was preferable. The text throws the advantage back to White.
20.♘e6+!

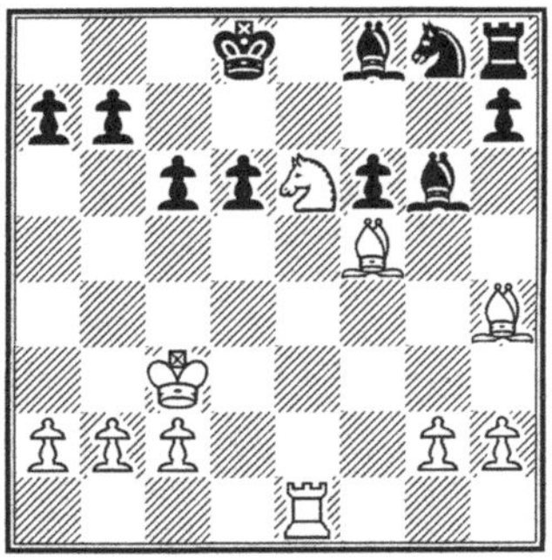

20...♔e7??
And now this blunder loses the game. Holding the line was 20...♔e8!, when if 21.♘g5+?? ♘e7−+. White would have to settle for 21.♘×f8+ ♔×f8 22.♗h3 d5, when winning is not at all certain (+1.14/26).

21.♘g5+! ♔d8 22.♗×g6 f×g5 23.♖e8+ ♔d7 24.♖×f8 h×g6 25.♗×g5

A remarkable position: Black is devoid of useful moves, almost in *Zugzwang*.

25...♖h5

There was nothing better. 25...♖×h2 26.♖×g8 ♖×g2 27.♖×g6 also loses, obviously.

26.h4 ♘h6 27.♖f4 ♘g8
Even after Black has "developed" his kingside pieces they have nowhere to go, *e.g.* 27...♘f5 28.g4. White's advantage is clearly decisive; further comments are superfluous.

28.♖f7+ ♔e6 29.♖g7 ♖h8 30.♖×g6+ ♔d7 31.g4 ♘e7 32.♖g7 ♖e8 33.h5 ♔e6 34.♗×e7 ♖×e7 35.♖×e7+ ♔×e7 36.g5 1-0

Torre gave a second exhibition in Zacatecas on July 23rd, but no games from that are known to have been preserved.

At the end of July 1926, Torre received an invitation from the Yucatán Chess Club to visit his native city and give exhibitions there. He came to Mérida, Yucatán in the early part of August, giving at least two simuls there, one on 30 boards (a clean sweep, +30 =0 -0), and another on 60 with a score of +52 =8 -0. He also played the following exhibition game against consulting allies, señores B. Ortiz and A. Nava, then considered the two best chess players of the Yucatán province (though in fact they proved rather weak opposition).

Game 94

B. Ortiz and A. Nava – Torre

Consultation game, Mérida, 4 August 1926

King's Indian Defense [E70]

1.d4 ♘f6 2.c4 g6 3.♘c3 ♗g7

This scheme of development leads to either the King's Indian or Benoni Defense. It was not often played in the 1920s, being deemed too *outré* even for most Hypermoderns, though Torre already had some experience with it (Game 40, Rabinovich-Torre for example), and a few adventurous masters such as Yates, Euwe and Lajos Steiner were also trying it out. The following year, Marshall essayed it against Nimzovich and Capablanca at New York 1927, but he was so badly outplayed in those games that the popularity of this scheme faded, until several decades later the Russians brought it to new life. Nowadays, of course, it is one of the most popular and most thoroughly analyzed openings.

4.e4 d6 5.♗e3

Other contemporary variations: 5.g3 0–0 6.♗g2 e5 7.♘ge2 ♘c6 8.0–0 e×d4 9.♘b5 ♖e8 10.f3 ♗e6 11.♕a4 ♘d7 12.♘f4±, Rubinstein-Blümich, Breslau 1925 (1-0, 35); and 5.♘f3 c5 6.d5 0–0 7.h3 ♘bd7 8.♗d3±, Vajda-L. Steiner, Debrecen 1925 (½-½, 55).

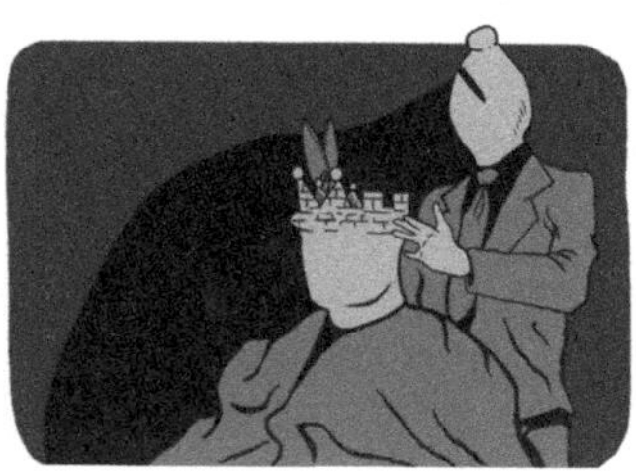

5...0–0

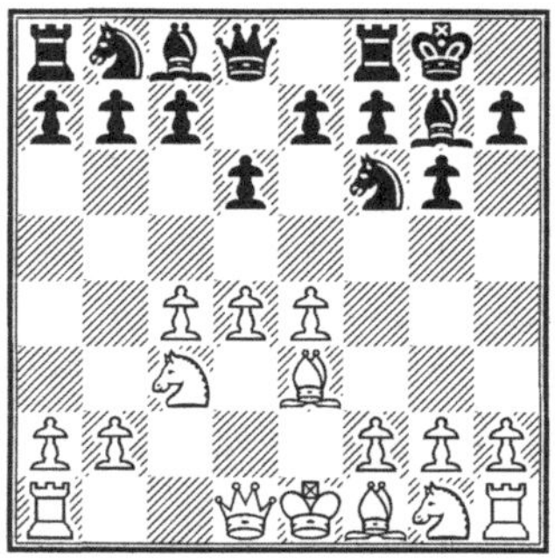

6.♗d3?!

A routine move that loses the first-move advantage. Perhaps best is 6.f3, for example 6.f3 e5 7.d5 (or 7.d×e5 d×e5 8.♕×d8 ♖×d8 9.♖d1 ♖×d1+ 10.♔×d1 c6 11.♘ge2 ♗e6∓, Schelfhout-Euwe, Amsterdam 1925, 0-1, 53) 7...c6 8.♕d2 c×d5 9.c×d5 ♘e8 10.0–0–0 f5 11.♔b1 ♘d7 12.♘h3 a6 13.e×f5 g×f5 14.g4 f×g4 15.♘g5 ♘ef6 16.♗d3 ♕e7 17.f4 e4 18.♘g×e4±, Alekhine-Euwe, match, Holland, 1926 (1-0, 35).

6...♘g4! 7.♘ge2?

Much better was 7.♕d2, 7.♕e2, or 7.♕c1, so as to recapture with the Queen after 7...♘×e3.

7...♘×e3 8.f×e3 c5

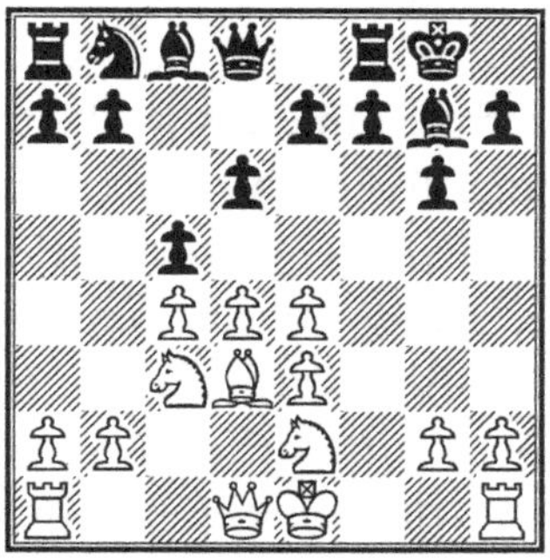

9.0–0

And now the least evil was 9.d5, though then after 9...♘d7 10.0–0 ♘e5 (demonstrating one of the drawbacks of no longer having an f-pawn) 11.h3 ♗d7 Black's advantage is considerable (-2.57/24).

9...♘c6 10.♗c2?

White just keeps digging a deeper hole.

Better 10.d5 transposing to the previous note variation.

10...♗g4 11.♕d2

11.d5 was still preferable.

11...c×d4

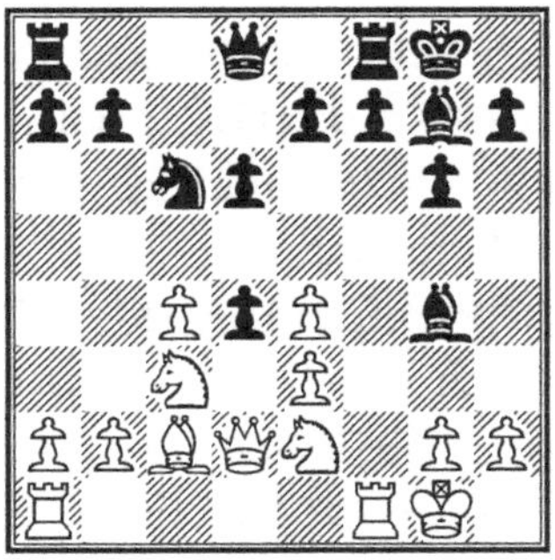

12.e×d4

Slightly less egregious was 12.♘×d4 ♘×d4 13.e×d4 ♕b6 14.e5 d×e5 15.♘d5 when White might muddy the waters enough to get counterplay (but probably not: 15...♕×b2 -3.48/26).

12...♘×d4

Perhaps a bit stronger was 12...♕b6 13.♔h1 ♗×e2 14.♘×e2 ♘×d4 15.♘×d4 ♕×d4 (-3.31/25), but Torre's straightforward approach is quite good enough too.

13.♘×d4 ♕b6 14.♔h1

Better 14.e5 d×e5 15.♘d5 as mentioned above.

14...♕×d4 15.♕×d4 ♗×d4

Though Black is nominally only a pawn up, his two active Bishops greatly augment his advantage (-4.36/27 at this point).

16.♘d5 ♗e2 17.♘×e7+ ♔g7 18.♖fe1 ♗×c4

It is well nigh impossible for White to avoid loss of another pawn.

19.♖ed1 ♗×b2 20.♖ab1 ♗e5 21.♖×b7 ♗×a2 22.♘c6 ♖fc8 23.♗a4 a5 24.g3 ♗e6 25.♔g2 h5 26.♘d4 ♗×d4!

Black could have kept his Bishops by 26...♗g4 but then White would have some counterplay, for example 27.♖f1 ♖f8 28.♘c6 ♗f6 29.♗b3. Therefore, Black rightly decides to simplify and rely on his material advantage.

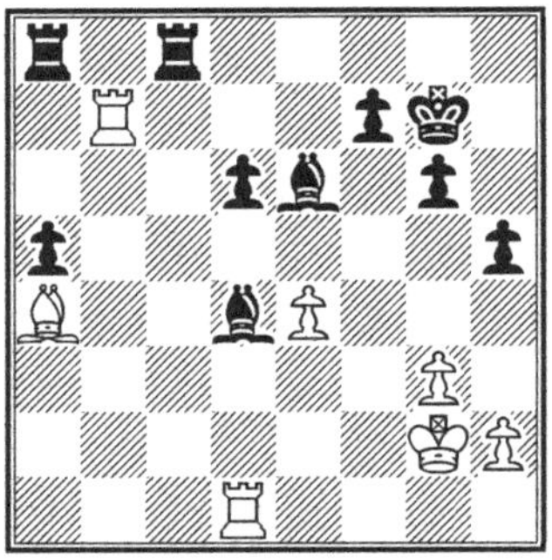

27.♖×d4 ♖ab8 28.♖×b8 ♖×b8 29.♖×d6 ♖b4 30.♗c6 ♖b6 31.♔f2 White cannot stop Black's King from emerging; if 31.e5?? ♖×c6 32.♖×c6 ♗d5+ and 33...♗×c6.

31...♔f6 32.♔e3 ♔e5 33.♖d5+ ♗×d5 34.♗×d5 a4 0-1

Later the same day as the preceding game, Torre gave a simultaneous exhibition at the Mérida Chess Club. Though no record remains of how many boards Torre played, or with what overall result, there have survived two charming miniatures from that display. The first was included in Chernev's *The 1000 Best Short Games of Chess*. The second, obviously played against a novice, features an entertaining variation on Legall's Mate.

Game 95

Torre-Ponce

Simul, Mérida, 4 August 1926

King's Gambit [C33]

Torre seems to have played this game aiming for light-hearted fun, with little regard for objective soundness.

1.e4 e5 2.f4 e×f4 3.♘c3 g5 4.h4

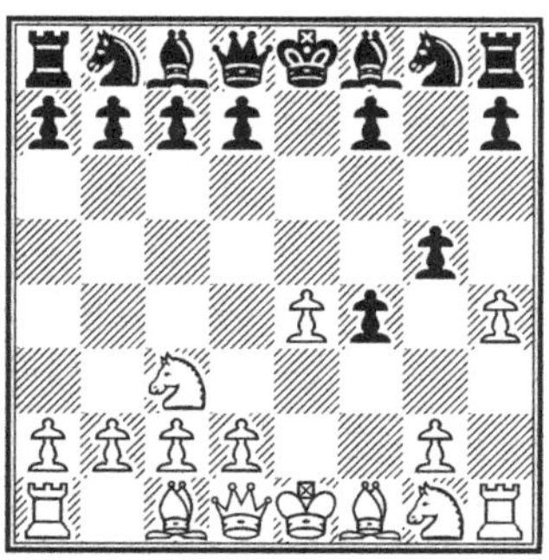

Another form of the Keres Gambit. In a 1935 correspondence game the great Estonian played 4.d4 d6 [Panuzzo-Zuraski, e-mail 1994 saw 4...♗b4 5.♘f3 ♗×c3+ 6.b×c3 d5? (⌓6...d6±) 7.♘e5?! (7.e×d5! ♕×d5 8.c4+−) 7...♕d6? 8.♕h5! ♕f6?? 9.e×d5 ♘d7 10.♗b5 ♕e7?? 11.0–0+− (1-0, 34)] 5.♗c4 h5 6.h4 ♘c6 7.♘d5 ♘a5?! 8.♗e2 c6 9.♘c3 d5 10.e×d5 c×d5 11.♘f3 g4 12.♘e5 ♗h6 13.0–0 f3??, and White was winning in Keres-Tatarski, 1935 (14.♗×f3! g×f3 15.♕×f3 ♗e6 16.♘×f7 etc.).

In a much older game White tried 4.♘f3 g4 5.♘e5 ♕h4+ 6.g3! (6.♔e2?? d6 7.♘c4 f3+ 8.♔d3 ♘a6−+) 6...f×g3 7.♕×g4 g2+? (⌓7...♕×g4 8.♘×g4 d5=) 8.♕×h4 g×h1♕ and now 9.♕h5! would have won in Taylor-NN, Thorpe 1874. What can we say — this is a crazy opening!

Continuing the game from the previous diagram (**4.h4**):

4...♗g7 5.♗c4

⌓5.h×g5±

5...h6?

A wasted move typical of very weak players. Correct was 5...♘c6.

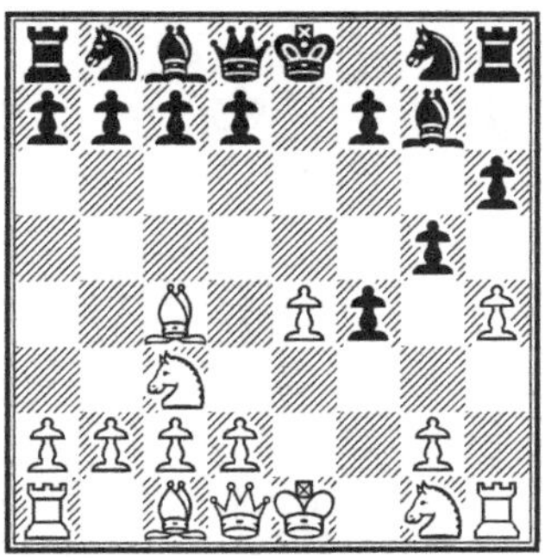

6.♕h5?!

Not good, but as we said Torre is playing light-heartedly.

Strongest was either 6.d4 ♘c6 7.h×g5 ♘×d4 8.♗×f4 d6 9.g×h6 ♘e6 10.♗×e6 ♗×e6 11.♕d2 ♗×h6 12.♗×h6 ♕f6 13.♗g5 ♖×h1 14.♗×f6 ♖×g1+ 15.♔f2 ♖×a1 16.♗h4 (+1.44/26), or 6.h×g5 ♕×g5 7.♘d5 ♘f6! (if 7...♕×g2?? 8.♕f3+−, or 7...♔d8 8.♔f1±/+−) 8.♘×c7+ ♔d8 9.♘×a8 d5 10.d3! (if 10.♗b5 ♘×e4=, or 10.♗e2?? ♘×e4 11.g4 ♘g3−+) 10...d×c4 11.♕f3 ♗g4 12.♕×f4 ♕×f4 13.♗×f4 ♘a6 14.♘f3 (+1.42/25).

6...♕e7 7.h×g5?

Committing White to an objectively unsound but interesting Queen sac. Better was 7.♕e2 c6 8.d4∓. But what the heck; the text at least has the virtue of complicating the game past Black's limited ability to cope.

7...h×g5 8.♕×h8

Forced; anything else is far worse, *e.g.* 8.♕×f7+ ♕×f7 9.♗×f7+ ♔×f7 10.♖×h8 ♗×h8 (-6.08).

8...♗×h8 9.♖×h8 ♔f8□ 10.b3?

Objectively a bad bet, but setting a clever trap. Best was 10.♖h7 d5 11.♗×d5 ♗e6 12.♗×b7 ♘a6 13.♗×a6 ♗f5∓.

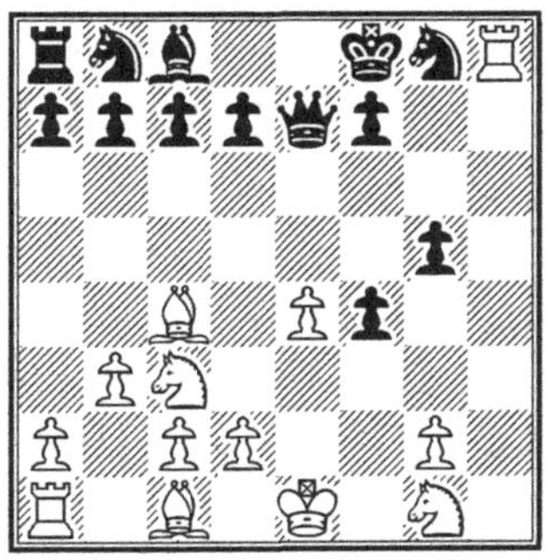

10...♔g7??

Black duly falls right into the trap. Correct was 10...d5! 11.♗×d5 c6 12.♗c4 b5 13.♗e2 b4 14.♘d1 ♕×e4 (-3.92/25).

11.♗b2! ♔×h8??

As Cecil Purdy wrote: "We all play a lot of rotten chess; some more than others, but very often the true motive behind weak moves lies in an exaggerated materialistic attitude." The least evil was 11...♕f6, but it would still lose, *viz.* 12.♖h2 ♔f8 13.0–0–0 ♕g6 14.♘d5 b5 15.♗d3 etc. (+4.24/23).

12.♘d5+ ♔h7 13.♘×e7 ♘×e7 14.♗×f7 ♘bc6 15.♘f3 ♔h6

Walking into a forced mate, but Black was lost whatever he tried.

16.♔f2 ♘g6 17.♖h1+ ♘h4 18.♘×h4 g×h4 19.♗f6! 1-0

Game 96

Torre-Subikursky

Simul, Mérida, 4 August 1926

Bishop's Opening [C25]

1.e4 e5 2.♗c4 c6 3.♘c3 d6 4.♘f3 ♗g4 5.d4 ♘d7 6.d×e5

A trap that seems to work 90% of the time in simuls.

An alternative was 6.h3 e×d4 7.♕×d4 ♗×f3 8.g×f3 ♕f6 9.♕×f6 ♘g×f6 10.♗e3 ♗e7 11.0–0–0 0–0±, Donev-Conquest, Liechtenstein 1993 (0-1, 51).

6...♘×e5?

A typical mistake, played innumerable times. Correct was 6...d×e5=.

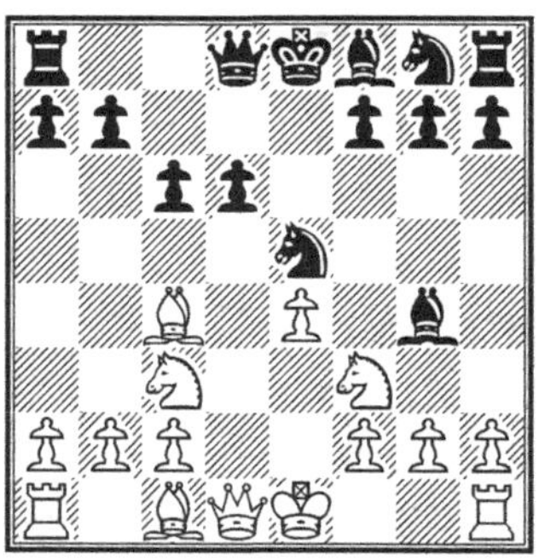

7.♘×e5! ♗×d1 8.♗×f7+ ♔e7 9.♗×g8!

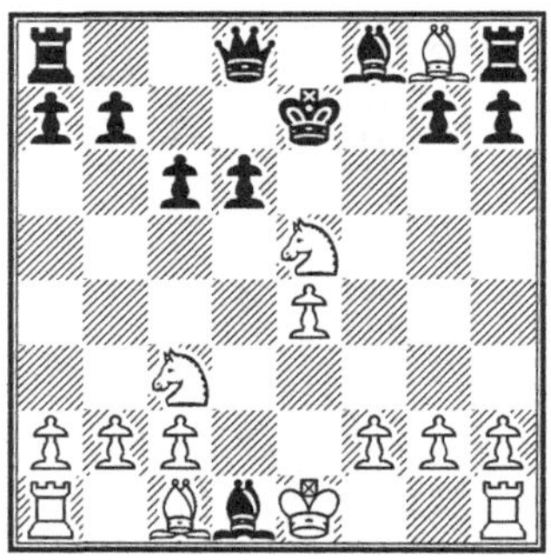

Threatening 10.♗g5+. In an archetypal Legall example White would give mate by ♘c3-d5, but here the pawn on c6 requires a variation on the theme.

9...♕a5??

Black apparently would rather be checkmated than return the Queen and go to an ending a pawn down.

After 9...d×e5 10.♗g5+ ♔e8 11.♗×d8 ♖×d8 12.♖×d1 ♖×g8 13.♖×d8+ ♔×d8 White would probably have managed to win very easily, considering his opponent's strength.

10.♗g5+ ♔e8 11.♗f7# 1–0

As a curious final note to this game, it should be mentioned that one identical to it from beginning to end was once lost by Filiberto Terrazas, a former member of the Mexican Chess Olympic team, and author of the first "biography" of Carlos Torre, *El Aguila Caída* (*The Fallen Eagle*), which is actually sort of a historical novel mixing fiction with fact and pretending to give an account of Torre's life under a fictitious name. As to how a member of a national Olympic team could possibly play such a game, perhaps not even Robert L. Ripley would have been able to answer.

Game 97

Allies-Torre

Consultation game, Progreso, 11 August 1926

French Defense [C11]

After leaving Mérida, Torre headed for the nearby port city of Progreso, where he stayed until August 11. The following consultation game, played the same day as his departure for New Orleans, was the last of his Mexican tour. The white pieces were conducted by señores E. Gordillo, F. García Andrade, V. Sabido and G. Díaz.

1.e4 ♘f6 2.♘c3 d5 3.e5 ♘fd7
Allowing transposition to a well-known line of the French. More in the spirit of Alekhine's Defense would be 3...d4.

4.d4 e6 5.♘f3 ♗e7 6.♗d3 c5 7.♗e3?!
Better 7.d×c5 ♘×c5 8.0–0 as in Fischer-Blaine, simul, Toledo, Ohio, 1964 (1-0, 32).

7...♘c6 8.♗b5?!
There is no justification for a second move of the Bishop at this early stage.

8...0–0 9.♗×c6 b×c6 10.0–0 ♖b8
Better first 10...c×d4 and if 11.♕×d4 then 11...♖b8∓, or if 11.♘×d4 ♗b7∓.

11.b3 f6?!
Attractive, as it attacks White's center at every possible point, but 11...c×d4 was still best.

12.♘a4
12.e×f6 would make it an even game. The text validates White's 11th move.

12...f×e5 13.d×e5 ♕c7 14.♖e1 ♖f5

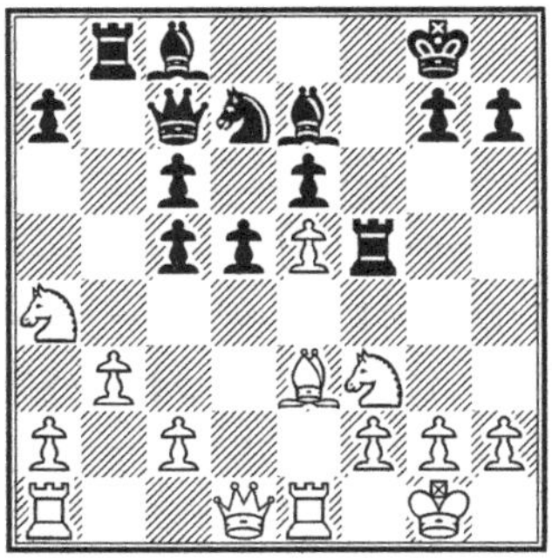

15.♗c1?

Losing a pawn without compensation. Better was 15.c4, and if 15...d4 16.♗d2= (if 16...♘×e5 17.♖×e5 ♖×e5 18.♗f4 ♖e1+ 19.♕×e1 ♕×f4 20.♕a5±, or 15...♗a6 16.♖c1 ♖bf8 17.♕e2=, or 15...d×c4 16.b×c4 ♘×e5 17.♘×e5 ♖×e5 18.♘c3=, as Black's extra pawn, being doubled, isolated, and blockaded, is worthless.

15...♘×e5 16.♘×e5 ♖×e5 17.♖×e5 ♕×e5 18.♗a3

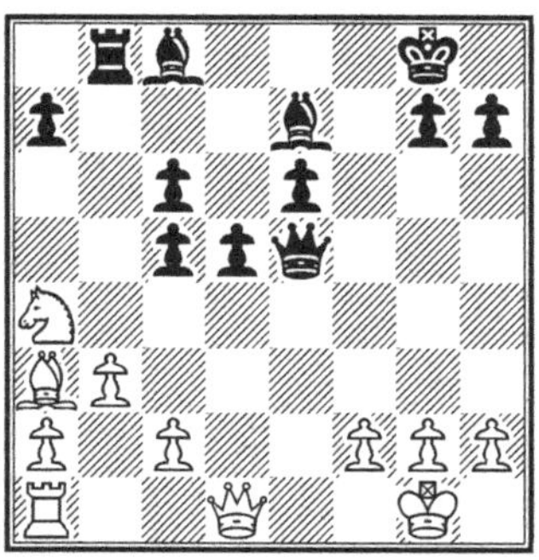

18...d4?!

This could have wasted Black's advantage. Best was 18...♗d6 19.g3 c4 20.♗×d6 ♕×d6 and if

(a) 21.f4 c5 22.♕e1 ♗a6 and Black has consolidated his extra pawn (-0.99/23), or

(b) 21.b×c4? ♖b4 22.c5 ♕e5 23.c3 ♖c4 24.♖b1 ♗a6 25.a3 ♗b5 26.♖b4 ♖e4! 27.♖×e4 ♕×e4 28.♘b2 ♗e2 29.♕c1 (if 29.♕e1? ♕c2–+) 29...♗g4 (△30...♗h3) 30.♕f1 ♕c2 31.♘d3 ♕×c3 etc. winning, as Black's Queen goes pawn-picking.

19.♘b2?!

A complementary mistake. Now Black gets the right idea.

19...♗d6 20.g3 ♕d5 21.♘c4 e5

21...♗c7, retaining the Bishop pair for the time being, was arguably better.

22.♕h5

The straightforward 22.♘×d6 was preferable, as White has nothing to fear from 22...♗h3 23.f3 ♕×d6 24.♕e2 (△25.♕c4+) 24...♖b5 and it will be a while before Black can even think about cashing in his extra pawn. And the remaining Bishops are of opposite color.

22...g6

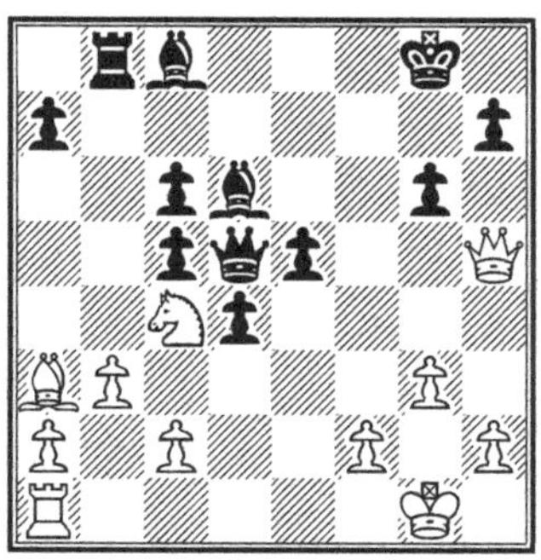

23.♕h4??

This is the losing move, turning a wasted tempo into a wild attacking gesture that backfires. The retreat 23.♕e2 was necessary, when after 23...♗a6 White is not much worse off than in the previous note variation.

23...♗e7! 24.♕h6

If 24.♕×e7 ♗h3–+.

24...♗g5!!

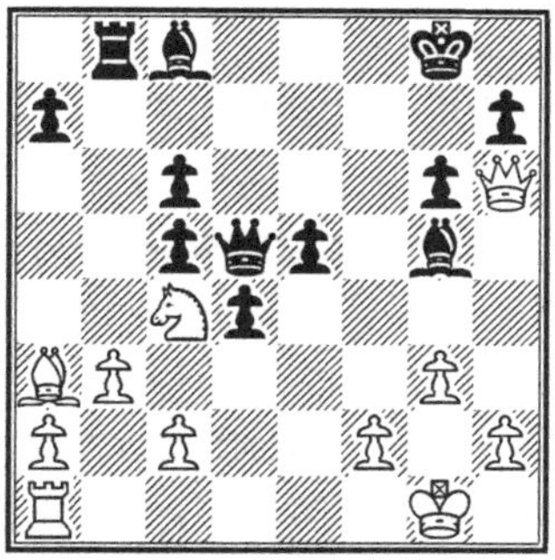

A well-calculated deflection. White's only decision now is whether he wants to be checkmated with or without his Queen on the board.

25.♕×g5 ♗h3 26.f3 ♕×f3 27.♕d2 ♖f8 28.♗×c5 ♕f1+ 0–1

While the concluding combinations of the last three games were clever, they were all based on serious mistakes by Torre's less than master-class opponents, rather than exemplary play on his part. This was not the best of omens as he now returned to master-level competition in Chicago.

Carlos Torre Returns to the United States

Torre departed Mexico August 11 aboard the Norwegian steamship *Gunni*, and returned to New Orleans. From there he left almost immediately for Chicago, where a tournament began August 21. This was a rare event for the time: a tournament featuring players of international stature on American soil in a city other than New York. In addition to Torre there were his familiar adversaries Marshall and Kupchik, other strong New York players such as Oscar Chajes and Charles Jaffe, German-American master Edward Lasker, old veterans such as the Hungarian Geza Maroczy and the former U.S. Champion Jackson Showalter, and promising young masters such as Isaac Kashdan. The front page of the September-October *American Chess Bulletin* read:

TWENTY-SEVENTH WESTERN CONVENTION AT CHICAGO

Chicago, accustomed to doing things in a big way, surpassed herself in the matter of the 27th annual convention of the Western Chess Association, held in that city from August 21 to September 2 in the Red Room on the 19th floor of the Hotel La Salle, and the result was a memorable meeting which will take high rank in American chess history. Aside from the several international tournaments of the first rank held in this country, no more important competition has ever been held here than the national masters' tournament in which the best talent available, 13 players in all, competed ...

In addition ... there were no less than 22 participants for the annual tournament for the Western championship, which was won last year by A. Kupchik of New York, and the year before by Carlos Torre of Mexico. Both of these experts were engaged in the masters' tournament ...

The programme was a most strenuous one and called for a round each day for the masters ... Moreover there were no spare days on which to play off the adjourned games.

The entry list for the national masters tournament: 1. F.J. Marshall, New York; 2. J.L. Isaacs, Chicago; 3. Edward Lasker, New York; 4. Charles Jaffe, New York; 5. I Kashdan, New York; 6. Samuel D. Factor, Chicago; 7. A.J. Fink, San Francisco; 8. Oscar Chajes, New York; 9. Newell W. Banks, Detroit; 10. A.J. Kupchik, New York; 11. Carlos Torre, Mexico City; 12. Geza Maróczy, Budapest; 13. Jackson W. Showalter, Georgetown, Ky.

At his best Torre would probably have been considered the tournament favorite, but as we have seen, after the lengthy tour in Mexico, playing against mostly quite inferior opposition, he was no longer in top form. This became evident in the first round.

Game 98

Jaffe-Torre

Western Association Masters, Chicago 1926, round 1, 21 August

Queen's Pawn, Double Fianchetto Defense [A48]

Russian-born Charles Jaffe (1879-1941, historical Elo 2430) was one of New York's best players, not in Marshall's class but not far below the likes of Kupchik. Though not prominent internationally, he had some big-league experience, having played for example at Carlsbad 1911 and Havana 1913, as well as numerous New York events involving world-class players. Some noteworthy scalps were on his belt, including Levenfish, Burn, Janowski, Marshall, Spielmann, and once even Capablanca.

This game is one of the most complicated in this whole collection. The players themselves were clearly baffled at several points, and it proved quite difficult for us to analyze even with computer assistance. Annotations here differ from the first edition probably more than in any other game. Around moves 20-26 possible variations sprouted like the Hydra's heads, making final conclusions difficult or impossible. Thus the reader should consider some of the lines presented here as suggestive and illustrative rather than definitive.

1.d4 ♘f6 2.♘f3 g6 3.e3 b6 4.c4 ♗b7 5.♘c3 ♗g7 6.♗d3 d6 7.e4 ♘bd7 8.0-0 e5 9.d5 ♘c5 10.♗c2 a5 11.♖e1 ♗c8 12.h3 h6 13.♗e3 ♘h5

Black might have castled here, but Torre is maneuvering to build up kingside pressure on a potentially open h-file, in which case the King's Rook belongs on h8. He achieves this, with White's cooperation.

14.♘h2 ♗f6 15.♕d2 ♗g5!

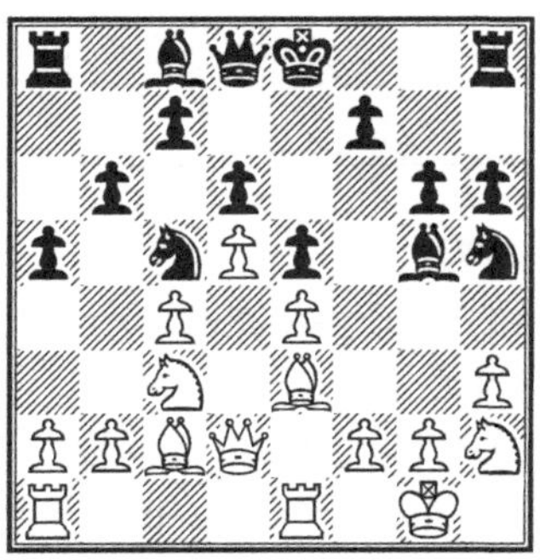

16.♗×g5?

Opening the h-file for Black is not a good idea. Better 16.♘f3 (16.♕d1 is also OK), when Black has nothing better than 16...♗×e3 17.♕×e3 ♘f4 18.♘e2 g5, and the kingside push looks more threatening than it actually is.

16...h×g5 17.♖e3 ♗d7 18.♖ae1 ♔f8

Preparing to get the King off the back rank so the Rooks can be connected. Also playable was 18...g4!? 19.h×g4 ♕g5! 20.f3 (if 20.♘e2 0–0–0∓, and if 20.g×h5?? ♕×h5 21.♔f1 ♕×h2–+) 20...♘g3∓.

19.♗d1?

This gives Black's next move added punch. Much better was 19.♘e2.

19...♘f4! 20.♖g3

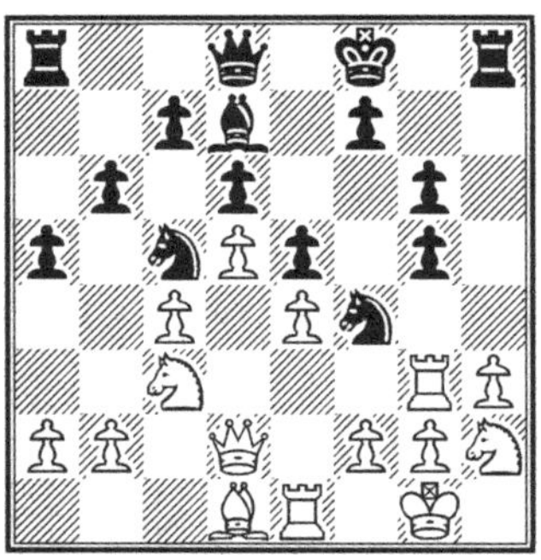

20...♔g7?!

Not bad, but probably winning was 20...f5!, *viz.*:

(a) 21.♗c2 g4 22.♘e2 ♘h5 23.♖a3 g×h3 24.g3 (24.g×h3?? f4–+) 24...♘f6 and Black's attack should break through (-2.81/26);

(b) 21.b3 (if 21.a3 a4 preventing b2-b4) 21...g4 22.e×f5 (if 22.h×g4?? ♕h4–+) 22...g×f5, and 23.♘×g4 or 23.♗×g4 is forced (either about -3.50/24);

(c) 21.e×f5 g×f5 22.♘f3 ♖g8 23.h4 g×h4 24.♖×g8+ ♔×g8 25.g3 (The only remotely playable move. If, say, 25.♘e2 ♘fd3 26.♖f1 ♕f6 27.♘e1 ♘×e1 28.♖×e1 f4 △ 29...h3 (-5.81/23)) 25...h×g3 26.f×g3 ♘h3+ 27.♔h2 f4 28.g×f4 ♘×f4 29.♘e2 ♕f6 etc. (-3.23/27).

21.♗g4?

This just wastes a tempo and hands a winning opportunity back to Black. Necessary was 21.♖ee3, when Black has to thread his way through a host of complications to stay on top, *viz.* 21...♖h6 22.b3 f5 23.a3:

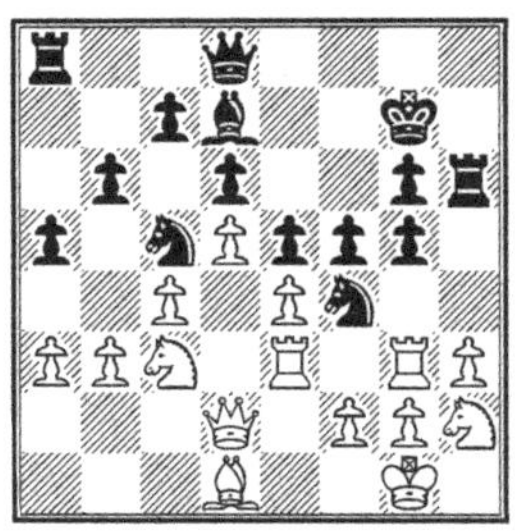

(a) Wrong is 23...g4 24.e×f5 g×h3 25.♘e2 ♘h5 26.♘g4 ♖h8 (if 26...♘×g3 27.♖×g3 ♖h5 28.f6+ ♔f7 29.♘h6+ ♖×h6 30.♕×h6 and the worst is over for White, -0.61/24.) 27.♗c2 ♗×f5 (if 27...g×f5?? 28.♘×e5+ ♘×g3 29.♖×g3+ ♔f8 30.♘g6+ ♔f7 31.♘×h8+ ♕×h8 32.♖×h3+–) 28.♗×f5 ♕g5 29.♘×e5 ♘×g3 30.♘×g3 d×e5 31.♗×h3 ♘×b3 32.♕e1 ♘d4 33.♖×e5 and White is out of the woods (-0.08/24);

(b) Best seems to be 23...a4 24.b4 ♘b3 25.♕b2 (not 25.♗×b3? a×b3 26.e×f5 g×f5 27.c5 g4 -2.65/24) 25...♘d4 26.♘b5 ♗×b5 27.c×b5 and Black's advantage, though still there, is no longer overwhelming (-1.43/26).

21...♕e7?

Incomprehensible. Could Torre be that rusty after his Mexican sojourn? Evidently. The obvious 21...f5! should win, *viz.* 22.e×f5 g×f5 23.♗d1 ♕f6 and:

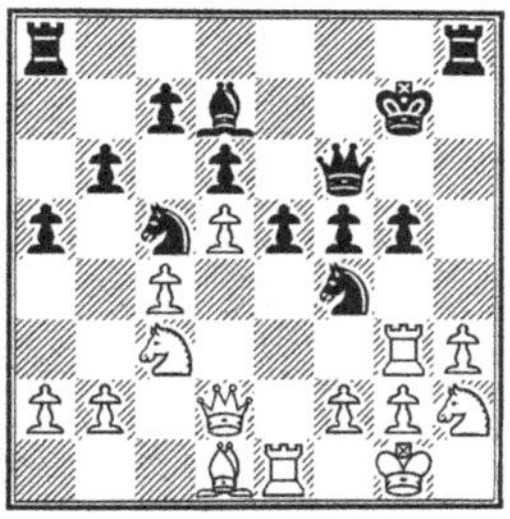

(a) 24.♘b5 ♗×b5 25.c×b5 ♖ag8 26.b3 ♔f8 27.♗c2 g4 28.a3

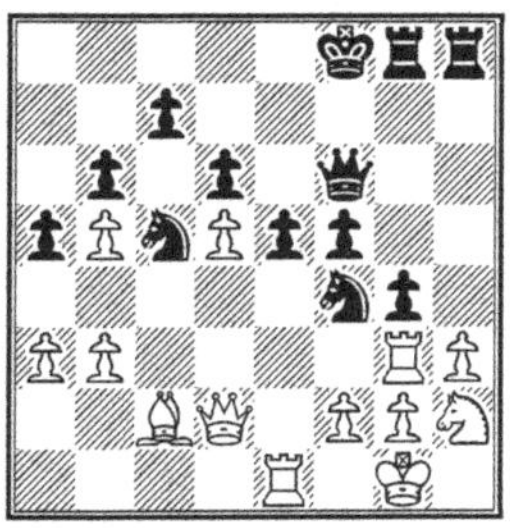

28...♕f7 (28...g×h3 29.♖×g8+ ♖×g8 30.g3 ♘g2 is interesting, but not 28...♕h4?! 29.b4! a×b4 30.a×b4 g×h3 31.♖×g8+ ♖×g8 32.g3□ ♘e4 33.♗×e4 f×e4±) 29.b4 g×h3! 30.♖×g8+ ♖×g8 31.g3 (of course not 31.b×c5?? ♖×g2+ and mate shortly) 31...a×b4 32.a×b4 ♘cd3 33.♖e3 e4 and Black has White locked down;

(b) 24.♖ee3 ♔f7 (not 24...♕h6? 25.♖×g5+ ♕×g5 26.♖g3=) 25.b3 ♖ag8 26.a3 g4 27.b4 ♘a6 28.b×a5 b×a5 29.♘b5 ♘h5 30.h×g4 ♘×g3 31.♖×g3 ♕h6 32.♕×h6 ♖×h6 33.♖h3 ♖×h3 34.g×h3 f×g4 35.h×g4 ♗×b5 36.c×b5 ♘c5 and the dust settles with a ♖-vs-♗+♙ ending winning for Black (-5.53/23).

It would not have been necessary for Torre to calculate all this before deciding on 21...f5; he need merely have observed that it would force the Bishop's retreat and enable his kingside onslaught to get rolling all the quicker. But Torre seems not to have sensed the strength of ...f7-f5 at all until it was too late.

Returning to the game:

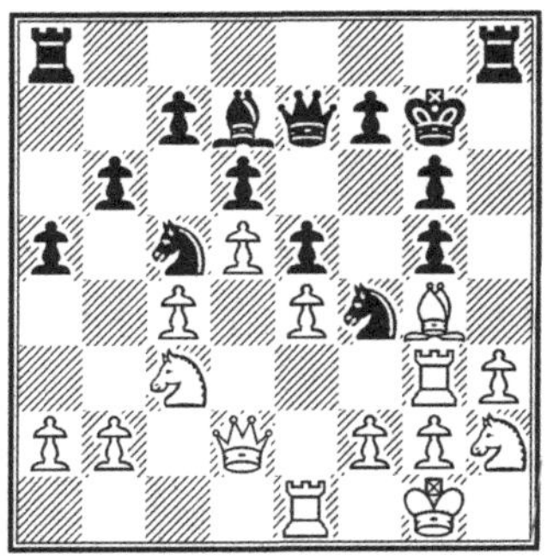

22.♗×d7 ♘×d7

The computer still sees Black as having an advantage, but one far from winning (-0.72/24).

23.♘e2 ♖h5 24.♘×f4

Somewhat better was 24.♕c2 or 24.b3.

24...g×f4 25.♖a3 ♖ah8 26.♔f1

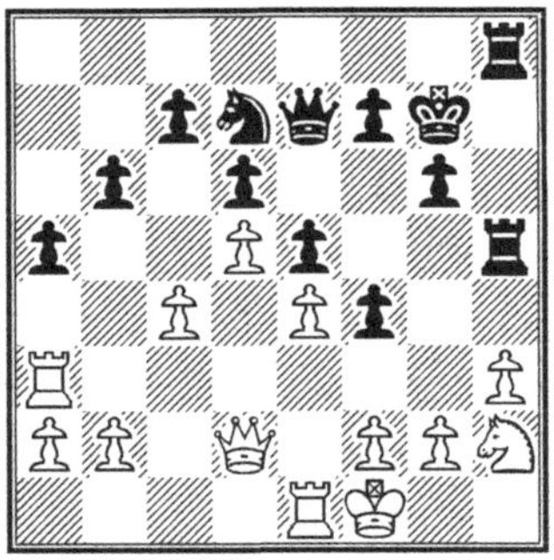

26...f5

This is nowhere near as effective now as back at move 20 or 21. Black's best try seems to be 26...♘c5, White's best reply 27.♘f3,

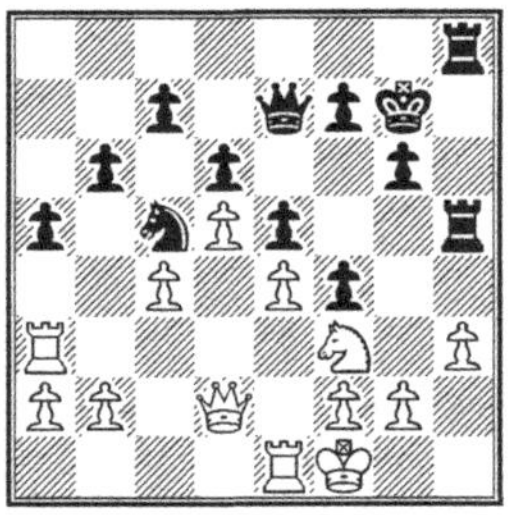

and now the best policy for both sides is to mark time, playing waiting moves until an opportunity arises. If Black rushes things he gets nowhere, *e.g.* 27...g5?! 28.♘h2=, or 27...f5?! 28.e×f5 ♖×f5= (but not 28...g×f5? 29.♕×f4). Thus a waiting move such as 27...f6 seems in order:

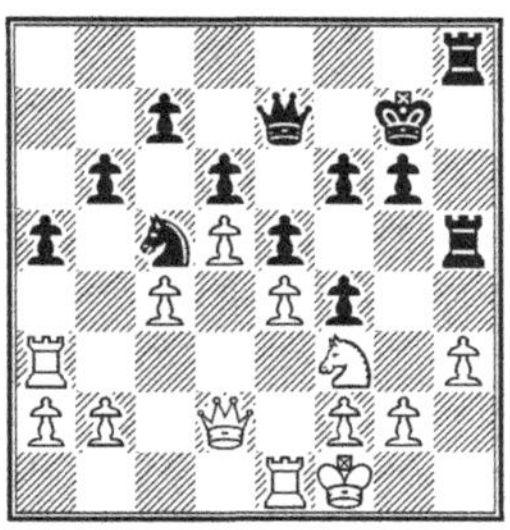

If White tries for counterplay he can run into trouble, *viz.* 28.b4 a×b4 29.♖a7 ♖b8 30.a4 (if 30.♕×b4 ♘d3 31.♕a4 ♘×e1 32.♔×e1 −+) 30...♖hh8 and now 31.♕×b4 is forced anyway, as anything else is much worse: 31.♖e2 ♖a8 32.♖×a8 ♖×a8 33.♕×b4 ♖×a4 −+. But White must also be careful which waiting moves he plays, as not all are created equal, *e.g.* 28.♖c3?! ♔f8 29.♕d1 f5 30.♘d2 (if 30.e×f5 g×f5 31.♘d4 ♖g5 32.♘e6+ ♘×e6 33.d×e6 ♖hg8 -4.64/31) 30...♕f6 31.b3 (or 31.♘f3 ♘×e4) 31...g5

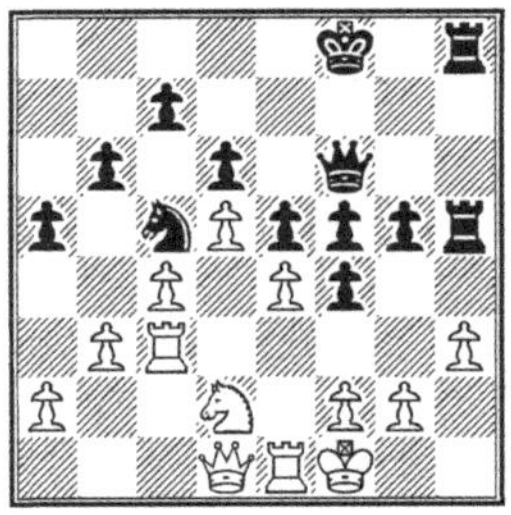

32.a3 [if 32.e×f5 e4! 33.♘×e4 ♘×e4 34.♖f3 g4 35.♖×f4 g×h3 36.g×h3 (36.♖f×e4?? h2) 36...♘c5 −+] 32...g4 33.b4 g×h3 34.g×h3 ♘×e4 35.♘×e4 f×e4 36.♕g4□ (if 36.♖×e4? ♕f5 −+) 36...e3! 37.♕c8+ ♔g7 38.♕×c7+ ♔g6 39.♕d7 e4! 40.♖c2 ♖f5 and White is obviously crushed (-7.23).

Therefore something like 28.♖e2 is called for, *e.g.* 28...♕d7 29.♘e1 f5 30.e×f5 g×f5 31.f3 ♕f7 32.♘d3 ♘×d3 (32...♖×h3? looks superficially attractive but leads only to loss: 33.g×h3 ♖×h3 34.♖g2+) 33.♖×d3 ♕g6∓.

But the text move renders this all academic. The game is now effectively even. Black does have a space advantage, which probably explains Stockfish's evaluation of about -0.65, but space is meaningful only if it can be used purposefully.

Returning to the game:

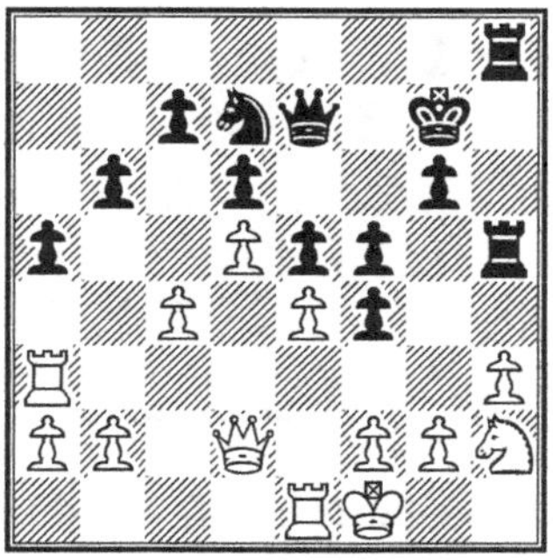

27.e×f5 ♖×f5
If 27...g×f5?! 28.♕×f4.

28.♘f3 ♕f7 29.b4 a×b4 30.♕×b4 ♘c5 31.♘d2 f3?
There is nothing Black can accomplish by this pawn sacrifice. One wonders why Torre, as he did so often at Baden-Baden, did not just propose a draw; very likely Jaffe would have accepted. But by 1926 Carlos Torre was not the up-and-coming unknown any more. He knew well that he already had a reputation, and thus might have felt it his duty to fight in every game to the last drop of blood, as it were. Furthermore, it is easy to say with hindsight that he was rusty, but he himself may not have been aware of it. It was better just to continue the aforementioned waiting policy with, say, 31...♕e7.

32.♘×f3 e4?
And now Torre presses too hard. The game was about dead even, and Black should have played 32...♖f4 or 32...♖f8, keeping it thus.

33.♕b2+!□
Now the game turns in White's favor. Torre may have overlooked this move, which defends f2 with tempo and enables the Knight to find a safe square.

33...♔h7 34.♘d4! ♖f4

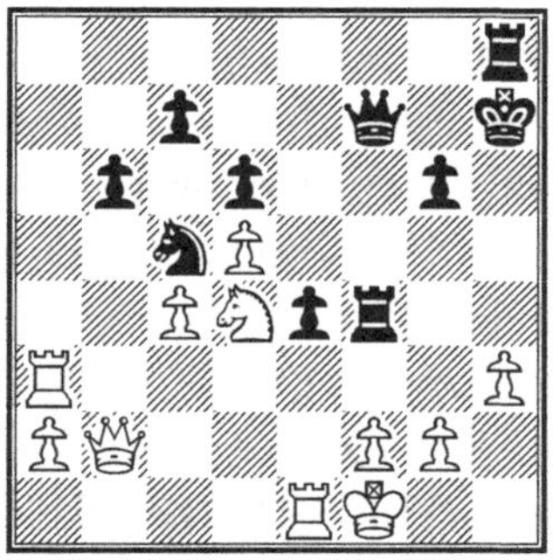

35.♕d2
Better 35.♖e2 and if then 35...♖f8 36.♔g1 ♘d3? 37.♕d2 ♘c5 (not 37...♘×f2?? 38.♘e6! +−) 38.♖ae3 +−.

35...♖f8
The game is once again even.

36.f3 ♕g7?
Beginning a series of errors by both sides, with time pressure no doubt a factor.
Better was 36...b5 37.♕e2 (37.c×b5 ♕×d5 is also equal, but not 37.♘×b5?? e×f3 38.g3 ♖×c4−+) 37...b×c4 38.♕×c4=.

37.♖ee3?!

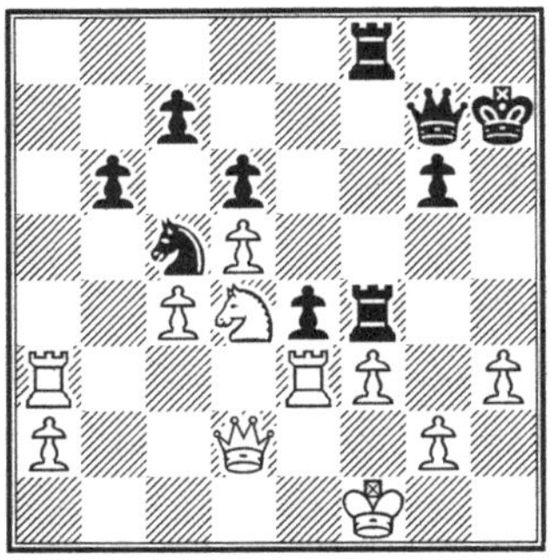

Another case of Wrong Rook. Correct was 37.♖ae3! e×f3 38.♘×f3 (+2.08/27).

37...♕h6?!
But Torre errs in turn. He could have virtually forced a draw by 37...e×f3, *viz.* 38.♘×f3 ♘e4 39.♕e1 ♘g5 40.♖e7 ♖8f7 41.♖×f7 ♕×f7 42.♔g1 ♘×f3+ 43.♖×f3 ♖×f3 44.g×f3.

38.♔g1! ♕h4 39.♔h2 ♕h5?
Better 39...♕f6.

40.♖e2
Second best. With 40.g3 ♖4f7 41.f4 White could have neutralized Black's pressure on the f-file and been well on his way to winning (+2.46/28).

40...♖8f7?
Torre too pulls a Wrong Rook. Better 40...♖4f7 41.♖ae3 ♕g5.

41.f×e4?!
Winning was 41.♘e6 ♘×e6 42.d×e6 ♖7f6 43.♖a7 and White finally gets his long-desired and decisive queenside invasion. The best Black could do then is 43...♕e5 44.♖×c7+ ♔g8 45.♕d5 ♖×e6 46.♖c6 ♖f5+ 47.♕×e5 ♖f×e5 48.f×e4 +–.

41...♕e5??

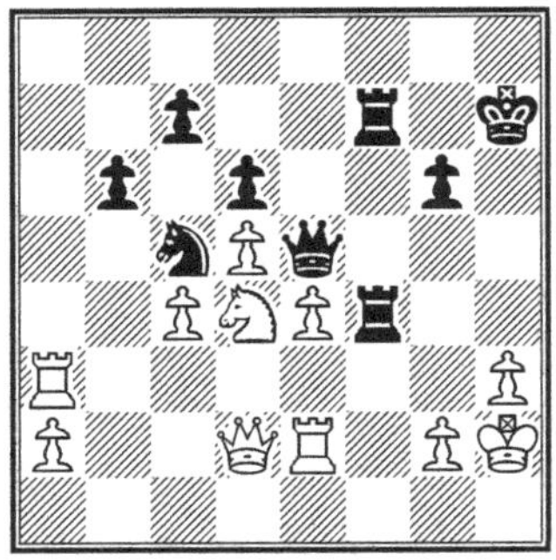

The least evil was 41...♘×e4 42.♕c2□ ♘g5 43.♘e6 ♘×e6 with advantage for White after either 44.d×e6 ♖e7 45.♖ae3±, or 44.♖×e6 ♖f2 45.♕e4 ♖2f4 46.♕d3±, but not yet a clear win.

42.♘c6! ♕h8??
Less bad was 42...♕f6.

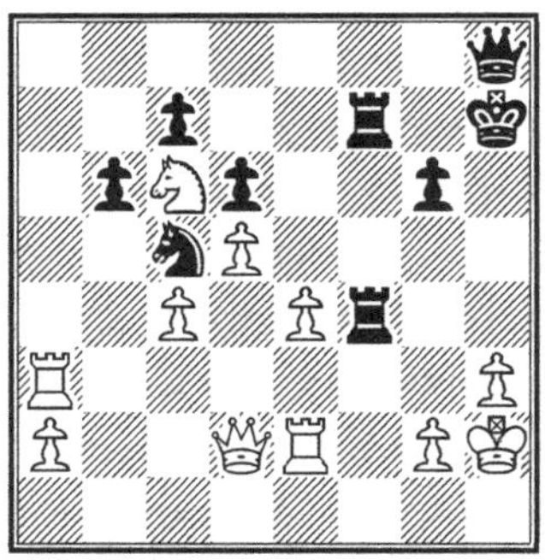

43.♖e1?!
The march of folly continues. Crushing was 43.e5! d×e5 44.♘×e5 ♖f8 45.d6! ♘e4 (if 45...c×d6?? 46.♖a7+ ♔h6 47.♘f7+ etc.) 46.♕d5 ♘×d6 47.♘×g6!

winning, since if 47...♔×g6 48.♖g3+ ♔h6 49.♕g5+ ♔h7 50.♕h5#.

43...♕f6?

Necessary was 43...♘×e4, though then after 44.♕c2 ♘c5 45.♖g3 ♕f6 46.♘d8 ♖d7 47.♘e6 ♘×e6 48.♖×e6 ♕f5 49.♕c3 Black remains on the defensive.

44.e5!

Jaffe finally gets the right idea and stops the comedy of errors.

44...d×e5 45.♘×e5 ♖f2

45...♘e4 would resist a bit harder.

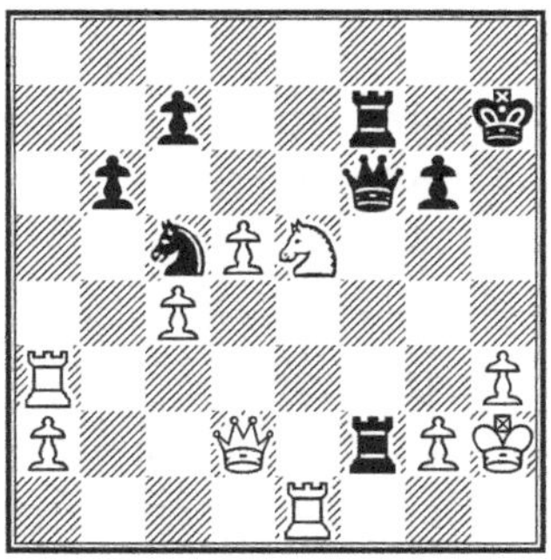

46.♕d4

White has a happy choice of four strong Queen moves.

Best was 46.♕c1, followed by 46.♕e3, the text, and 46.♕d1, all rated between +6.15 and +4.65. But not 46.♕c3? ♘e4 47.♕d4 ♕f4+ 48.♔g1 ♖f1+ 49.♖×f1 ♕×f1+ 50.♔h2 ♕f4+ etc., draw.

46...♘d7 47.♖f3! ♖×f3 48.♘×f3 ♕d6+ 49.♔g1 ♖f4 50.♖e7+

A good way to simplify while still retaining a winning edge.

50...♕×e7 51.♕×f4 ♘f6 52.♘g5+ ♔g8 53.♘e6 ♘e8 54.♕g4 ♕f6 55.h4 ♘d6

Better 55...♔f7.

56.h5

Missing 56.♘×c7 ♕a1+ 57.♔h2 ♕e5+ 58.g3 and White is safely up three pawns.

56...♕a1+ 57.♔h2 ♕e5+ 58.♘f4 g5 59.♕e6+

Forcing the exchange of Queens and putting the final result beyond all doubt. But Torre plays on stubbornly. One wonders if he was trying to play himself back into form, or just hoping for a lucky break like he got against Tartakower at Baden-Baden. Jaffe does not give him one.

59...♕×e6 60.♘×e6 ♘×c4 61.♘×c7 ♔g7 62.♘b5

This drops a pawn needlessly. Better 62.♔g3 ♔h6 63.♔g4.

62...♔h6 63.g4 ♘e3 64.♔g3 ♘×d5

Despite this, White is still winning.

65.♔f3 ♘b4 66.a3 ♘d3 67.♔e4 ♘f2+ 68.♔f5

Now comes some indecisive fiddling before White finally finds the winning path.

68...♘d3 69.♔e4 ♘f2+ 70.♔f3

♘d3 71.♘d4 ♘e5+ 72.♔g3 ♘c4 73.♘b5 ♘e5 74.♘d6 ♔g7 75.a4 ♔h6 76.♘f5+ ♔h7 77.♘e3 ♔g7 78.♘d5 ♘c4 79.♔f3 ♔h6

If 79...♘e5+ 80.♔e4! ♘×g4 81.♔f5 ♘h6+ 82.♔×g5 +−.

80.♔e4 ♘d2+ 81.♔d3 ♘f3 82.♔e4 ♘d2+ 83.♔f5 ♘c4 84.♔f6 1-0

A very difficult game and a hard loss, one in which Torre, reverting to the tendency seen in his games at Baden-Baden with Réti, Spielmann and Rabinovich, again was unable to find winning lines at crucial points. However, all this work does seem to have snapped him somewhat back into form, as the next round he started a ten-game unbeaten streak.

Game 99

Torre-Kashdan

Western Association Masters, Chicago 1926, round 2, 22 August

London System [A46]

After 1923, Frank Marshall avoided risking his U.S. Champion title in a match, and there was no regularly scheduled tournament championship until 1936. Starting about 1927, Isaac Kashdan (1905-1985, IM title 1950, GM 1954, historical Elo 2570) was generally considered the best American player until the rise of Fine and Reshevsky in the mid-1930s. Kashdan's status was at least tacitly recognized by his being placed at first board on U.S. Olympic teams, in which events he scored +52 -5 =22, a record better than any other American GM of any era, including Fischer. He also has another unique distinction, as the only American GM to appear on Groucho Marx's television show *You Bet Your Life*. When challenged by Marx to bet $100 on a chess game between them, Kashdan calmly offered to play blindfolded, which caused the normally unflappable Groucho's jaw to drop.

In 1926 Kashdan was just a year or two shy of his peak period, and with his careful, scientific style he proved very difficult for Torre to make any headway against. But our new analysis has uncovered a hitherto unsuspected winning opportunity Torre had.

1.d4 ♘f6 2.♘f3 c6 3.♗f4 d6

Yet again we already have a position not seen before in serious competition. Nor would it recur until 1958. Earlier games had seen 3...g6 in Schapiro-Kupchik, Lake Hopatcong 1923 (0-1, 48), and 3...d5 in König-Prokes, Four City match, Vienna, 1925 (1-0, 55).

4.h3

With e5 now unavailable, a retreat must be made for the Bishop.

4...♗f5 5.♘bd2 ♘bd7 6.e3 h6 7.♗c4 e6 8.♖c1 ♗e7 9.♕e2 d5
One of the reasons the London System waned in popularity is that it easily allows Black a comfortable equality. Given that Kashdan's weakness lay in handling complications, it was psychologically preferable for Torre to seek more aggressive lines; however in 1926 he likely was not familiar with Kashdan's style. Also, after the exhausting marathon with Jaffe, he may have been seeking an easy draw.

10.♗d3 ♘e4 11.♘e5 0–0 12.0–0 ♘×e5 13.♗×e5 ♘×d2 14.♕×d2 ♗×d3 15.♕×d3 f5
On 15...♗d6 16.♗×d6 ♕×d6 17.c4 ♖fd8 18.c×d5 e×d5 White would have a clear plan, namely to play a minority attack against the so-called Carlsbad pawn structure. The plan would involve something like ♖c1-a1, possibly ♖f1-b1/c1, and then b2-b4-b5, supported by a2-a4, and so forth. Good examples are Capablanca-Golombek, Margate 1939, and Evans-Opsahl, Dubrovnik 1950.

16.f4 ♗f6 17.♕e2 ♗×e5 18.d×e5 ♕e7 19.♔h2 ♔h7 20.g4
White tries to make something out of nothing, but it will be to no avail. The position is too barren to permit either player any interesting idea (for the time being).

20...g6 21.♖g1 ♖g8 22.♖g3 ♖g7 23.c4 ♖f8 24.c×d5
It is hard to say with which pawn Black must now recapture: if he takes with the c-pawn, then White will have the open c-file at his disposal, whereas if he takes with the e-pawn, then White would get a passed pawn that could be dangerous in the ending.

24...e×d5
If 24...c×d5 25.g5 h5 is an almost certain draw.

25.g×f5 g×f5
25...♖×f5 was equally good.

26.♖×g7+ ♕×g7 27.♖g1 ♕f7 28.♕e1 ♖e8 29.♕b4 ♕e7 30.♕d4 b6 31.a4 ♖d8 32.a5 c5 33.♕d3

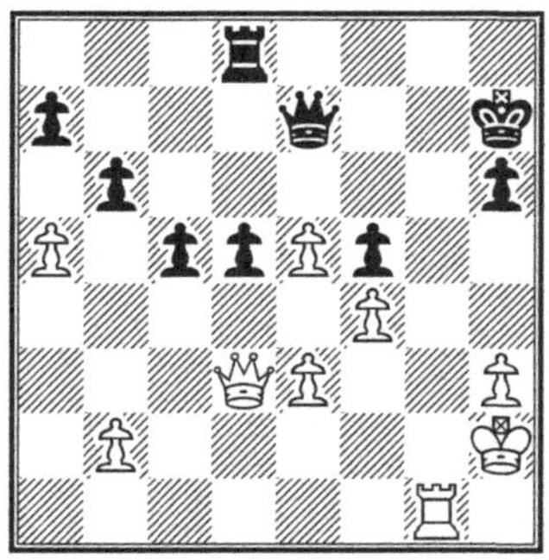

33...♕e6?
A subtle but potentially serious mistake. Better 33...♕f7 or 33...♕d7, keeping both the f- and a-pawns defended, with equality either way.

34.a×b6
A routine move which Torre, apparently already reconciled to a draw,

probably made without much thought. Instead 34.♕a6! could have made things very interesting:

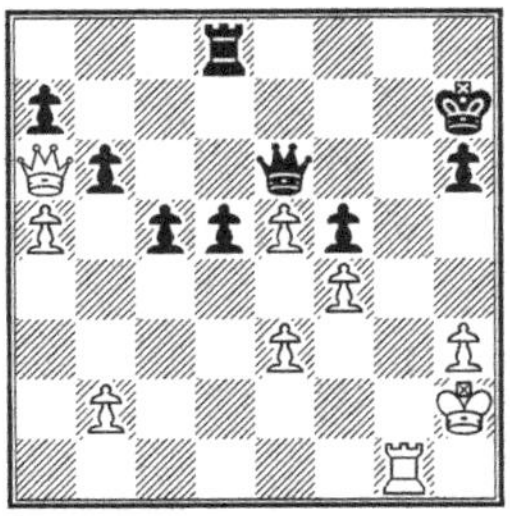

This move creates two threats. One of course is 35.♕×a7, but also, depending on how Black responds, there can be an invasion by the Queen into Black's two back ranks, with potential mating threats. Black must choose very carefully.

(a) An example of a careless choice is 34...♕d7?? 35.a×b6 a×b6 36.♕×b6 ♖g8 (if 36...♖c8?? 37.♕g6+ ♔h8 38.♕×h6+ ♕h7 39.♕f6+ ♕g7 40.♕×g7#) 37.♖×g8 ♔×g8 38.♕×c5+−;

(b) Less bad but still losing is 34...d4? 35.e×d4 c×d4 36.♕×a7+ ♖d7 and:

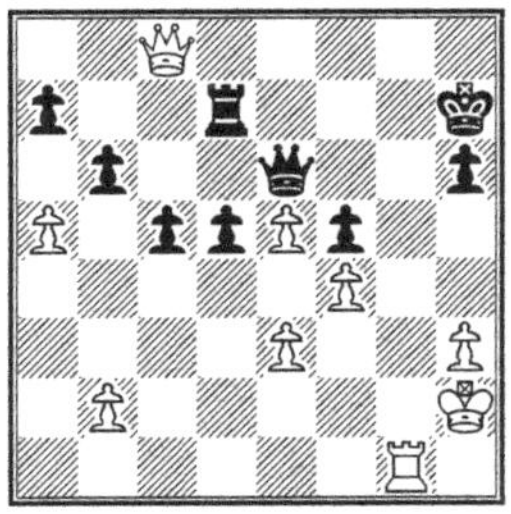

(b1) Not 37.♕×b6?! ♕×b6 38.a×b6 ♖b7 39.♖d1 ♖×b6 40.♖×d4 ♖×b2+ 41.♔g3 ♖b3+ etc. with a draw (+0.69/44);

(b2) Winning is 37.♕a6! d3 [Anything else is much worse, *e.g.* 37...♖c7? 38.♖g2 ♕c4 (if 38...♖c6?? 39.♕b7+ and mate swiftly) 39.♕×b6+−.] 38.♕×b6 ♕×b6 39.a×b6 ♖b7 40.♖d1 ♖×b6 41.♖×d3 Now the position of White's Rook on the 3rd rank instead of the 4th (as in variation b1) makes a major difference, as after 41...♖×b2+ 42.♔g3 Black cannot give check *ad nauseam*, and White wins (+7.84/27);

(c) The toughest defense is 34...♖d7, but then White has 35.♕c8!:

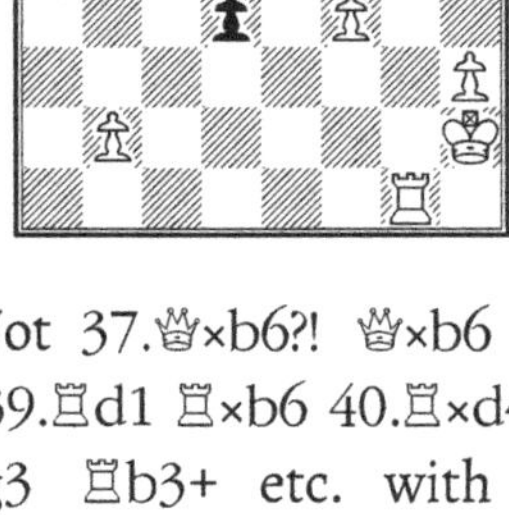

Again Black must choose carefully:

(c1) 35...d4? 36.e×d4 c×d4 37.♖g8! ♖e7 38.♖h8+ (38.♕×e6? ♖×e6 39.♖d8 b×a5 40.♖×d4 ♖b6 only draws now (0.13/32)) 38...♔g6 39.♕f8! ♖g7 40.h4 ♕f7 (if 40...h5 41.♖×h5! ♔×h5 42.♕×g7+−) 41.♕d6+ ♔h5 42.♖×h6+ (definitely *not* 42.♕×h6+? ♔g4 43.a×b6 a×b6 44.♕×b6?? ♕c4! and mate in six! White would have to play 44.♕c6 and settle for a draw.) 42...♔g4 43.♕×d4+−;

(c2) 35...♕f7 36.♖g8! ♖c7 37.♖h8+ ♔g7 38.♕a8 ♖e7 39.a×b6 a×b6 40.♖d8 b5 41.♕c6 c4 42.♕×d5 ♕×d5 43.♖×d5 ♖b7 44.♖c5 ♖d7□ 45.♖×b5 ♖d3 46.♖c5 ♖×e3 47.♖×c4 ♖b3 48.♖c3! (if 48.♖c2 ♖f3 49.♖c4 ♖b3 and 50.♖c3 is necessary anyway) 48...♖xb2+ 49.♔g3 and wins (+8.28/26);

(c3) Best is 35...♖e7 36.♕xe6 ♖xe6 37.♖d1 bxa5 38.♖xd5 ♖b6:

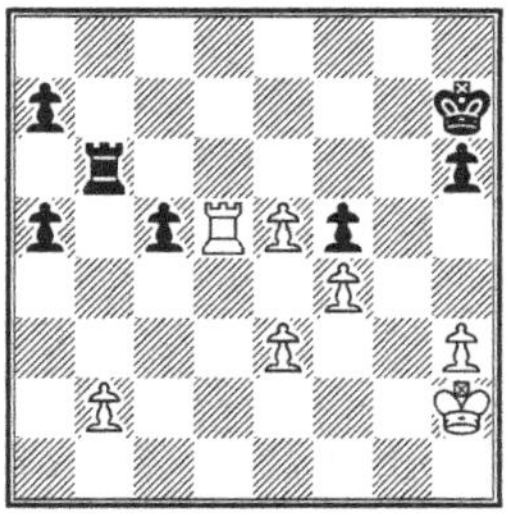

Now 39.♖xc5?! seems natural, but ultimately does not work: 39...♖xb2+ 40.♔g3 ♖b3 41.♖xa5 (or 41.♔f3?! a4 42.♖a5 ♖b4 +1.30/31) 41...♖xe3+ 42.♔g2 h5 43.♖xa7+ ♔g8 44.♖a6 h4 45.♖f6 ♖g3+ 46.♔f2 (46.♔h2 is no better) 46...♖xh3 47.♖xf5 and now 47...♖c3, 47...♖b3, or 47...♖a3 should hold the draw (+1.94/36; compare to variation (b1).

The reader should keep in mind that while in the opening or middle game such an evaluation might signify a winning advantage, in a Rook ending like this it merely reflects the fact that White has more pawns. The engine sees no way for White to force a win.

But the win is there. Going back to the above diagram, correct is 39.♔g3! ♖xb2 40.e6 ♔g6 41.e7 ♔f7 42.♖xf5+ ♔xe7 43.♖xc5 ♖b3 44.♔f3 a4 45.♖a5 a3 46.f5 ♔d6 47.♔f4 ♔c6 48.♖xa7□ ♔b6 49.♖a8□ ♔b7 50.♖a4 ♔c6 51.e4! ♖xh3 52.f6 ♔d7 53.f7 ♔e7 54.♖a7+ ♔f8 55.e5 ♖h2 56.e6 and Stockfish announces mate in 24.

It is wonderful when the computer reveals such unsuspected possibilities in old games. It would have been even more wonderful if Torre had hit on this, but it is understandable that he did not. The game concluded

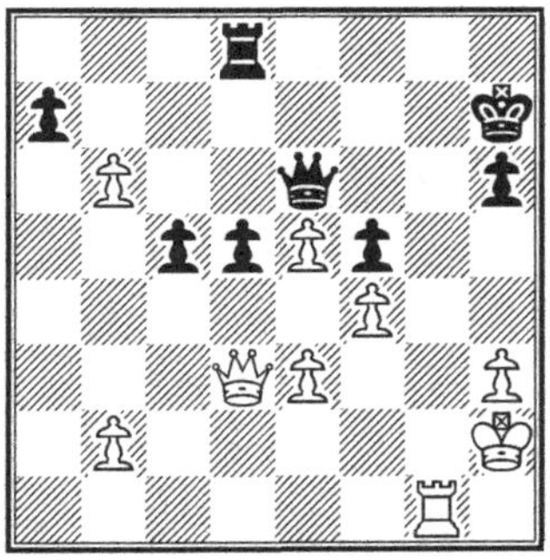

34...axb6 35.♕a6 ♖g8 36.♕b7+ ♔h8 37.♖xg8+ ♔xg8 ½-½

Game 100

Factor-Torre

Western Association Masters, Chicago 1926, round 3, 23 August

Grünfeld Defense [D90]

We met Samuel Factor earlier, in Game 26. Torre has a bit more trouble with him this time.

1.d4 ♘f6 2.♘f3 g6 3.c4 ♗g7 4.♘c3 d5 5.c×d5 ♘×d5 6.e3
As in Game 30, Kupchik-Torre.

6...0–0 7.♕b3
This seems to be the first time for this move. Kupchik had played 7.♗c4.

7...♘×c3 8.b×c3

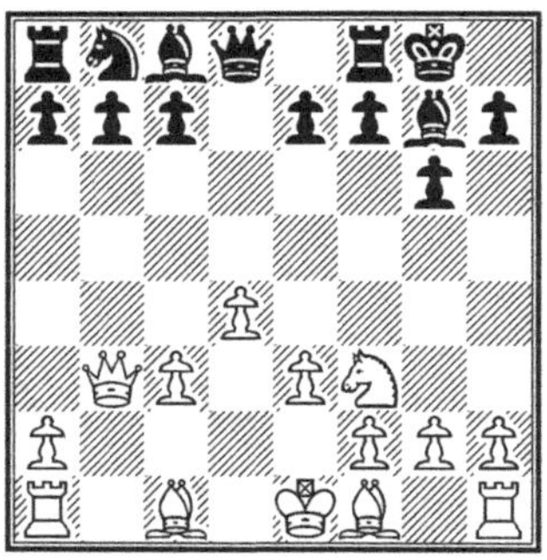

8...b6
One of the two best replies. What would become the main line was seen in Goglidze-Botvinnik, Moscow 1935: 8...c5 9.♗e2 ♕c7 10.0–0 b6 11.a4 ♘c6 12.♕a3 ♘a5 13.♘d2 ♗b7 14.♘b3 c×d4 15.c×d4 ♘c4 16.♕b4 ♖fc8 17.a5 e5 18.a×b6 ♘×b6 19.♘a5 ♗d5 20.♗b2 ♗f8 21.♕b5 a6 22.♕d3 e4 23.♕b1 ♕c2 24.♗a3 ♗×a3 25.♖×a3 ♕×e2 26.♕×b6 ♖ab8 27.♕d6 ♕×f1+ 28.♔×f1 ♖b1+ 0-1.

9.♗e2 ♗b7 10.0–0 ♘d7 11.♗a3 ♖e8 12.♖ad1 e6 13.♘e1 ♘f6 14.♗b5 c6 15.♗e2 ♕c7 16.♘d3 ♖ad8 17.♖fe1 ♘d7

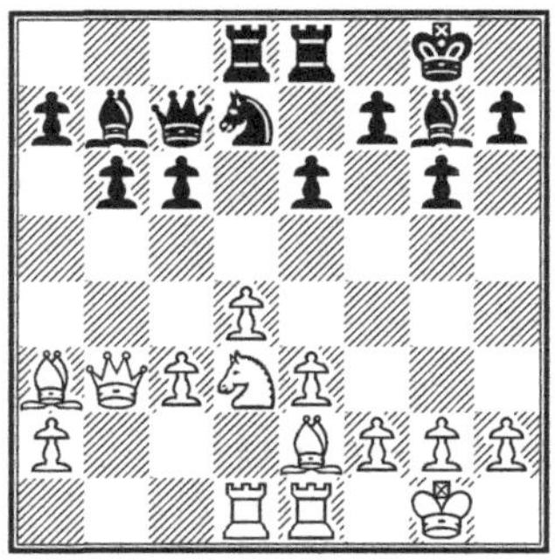

To this point both players have been concentrating on development, without trying to set difficult problems for each other. But now White becomes concerned about the prospect of 18...e5, and takes steps to prevent it.

18.f4?!
Better 18.c4, and if 18...e5 19.d5 e4 20.♘f4=, or 18...c5 19.d×c5 b×c5 20.♗b2 e5 21.♗a1=.

18...c5
Threatening 19...c4.

19.♘e5 ♘×e5 20.f×e5
The better recapture.

20...♖c8 21.♖c1?
Best was 21.c4 with only a slight positional inferiority. The text has a tactical flaw.

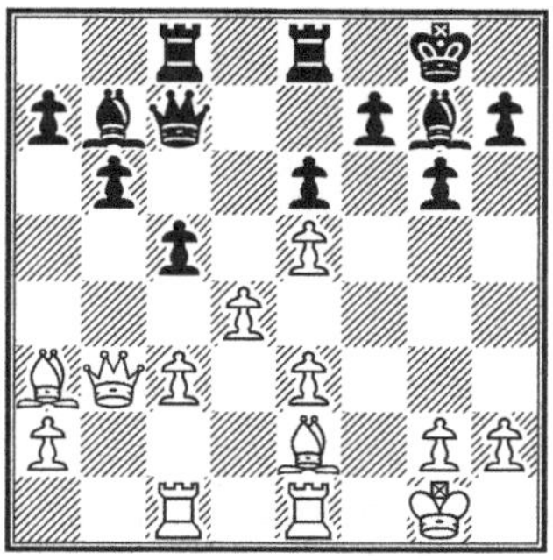

21...♖ed8
Not bad, but strongest was 21...♗h6!, when a likely line is 22.♗b5 ♖ed8 23.♕d1 [If 23.♖cd1? c×d4 24.c×d4 ♕c2! (△25...♕×g2#) 25.♗f1 ♕×b3 26.a×b3 ♖c3 27.♖d3 ♖dc8 with a dominant position (-3.53/25).] 23...a6 24.♗d3 ♕c6 25.♖c2 ♕a4 26.♗c1 b5 with a strong queenside initiative (-1.89/25).

22.♗f3?
Much less bad was 22.♖cd1 or 22.♕b2.

22...♗h6?!
As in the Jaffe game, Torre's tactical acumen seems absent. Strong last move, this now allows White equality. Correct was 22...♗×f3 23.g×f3 ♕e7,

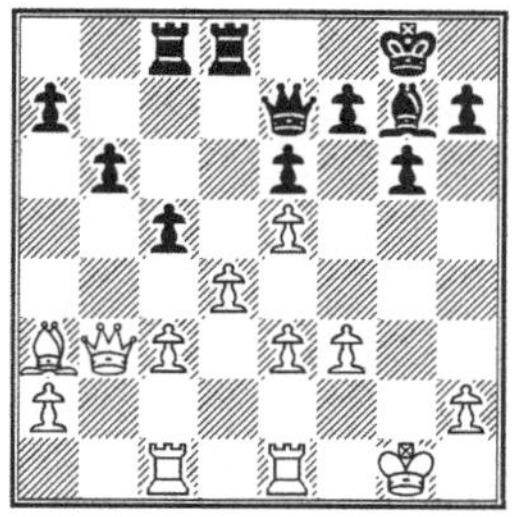

when Black can move on either wing depending on how White replies, *e.g.* 24.♖e2 ♕g5+ 25.♔h1 ♗h6 with kingside activity, or 24.♖c2 ♗f8 (△25...c4!−+) 25.♗c1 b5 etc. on the queenside.

23.♕b5?
But Factor does not see his chance, which was 23.♗×b7 ♕×b7 24.♗×c5!=.

23...♗d5
Another second-best move. Strongest was 23...♗×f3 24.g×f3 a6 25.♕e2 (not 25.♕×a6?? ♖a8) 25...♕d7 26.♔g2 ♕a4 27.♕b2 ♕a5∓.

24.♗×d5 ♖×d5 25.♕b3 ♖dd8
So that White cannot play 26.e4.

26.♗b2 ♕b7 27.♖cd1 ♕e4
Better 27...b5 to discourage 28.c4.

28.c4! ♗g7
Torre must have considered this and his next move a harmless time-gaining repetition, but it actually allows White to improve his position some. Better 28...♖c7 or 28...♖d7, intending to double Rooks on the d-file immediately.

29.♖f1 ♗h6

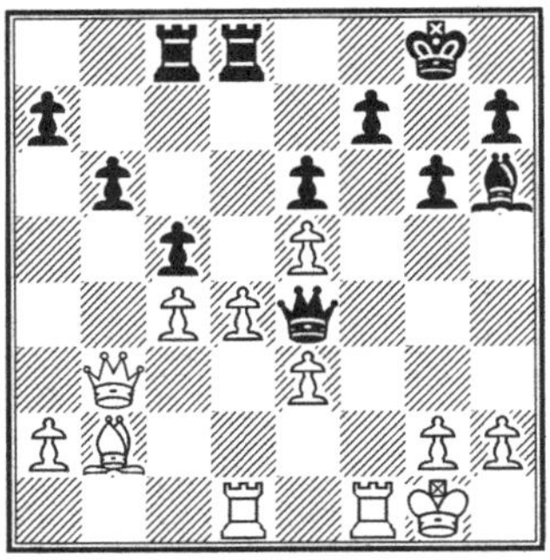

30.♖f3

30.d5!? would have solved the worst of White's problems; if 30...♕xe3+ 31.♔h1 ♕xb3 32.axb3 exd5 33.cxd5 and though Black has an extra pawn the game is virtually even (-0.21/26). Black could do a bit better with 30...b5 31.♕xb5 (if 31.d6?! ♕xc4) 31...♗xe3+ 32.♔h1 ♖b8 33.dxe6 fxe6 (not 33...♖xb5?? 34.exf7+) 34.♗c1! ♗xc1 35.♖xd8+ ♖xd8 36.♖xc1 ♕xe5 and though Black is a pawn up, winning will be problematic as long as Queens stay on the board.

30...♖d7?

Now was the time for 30...cxd4 31.exd4 and only then 31...♖d7. The text lets White completely off the hook.

31.a4?

Torre can only be glad that Factor was equally oblivious that day. 31.d5! was the ticket to equality. The text gives Black a winning shot, which this time he sees.

31...cxd4 32.exd4?

32.♖xd4 was the correct recapture; there would follow 32...♕c6 33.♖xd7 ♕xd7 34.♗d4 and White's position, though not enviable, may still be tenable (-1.93/32).

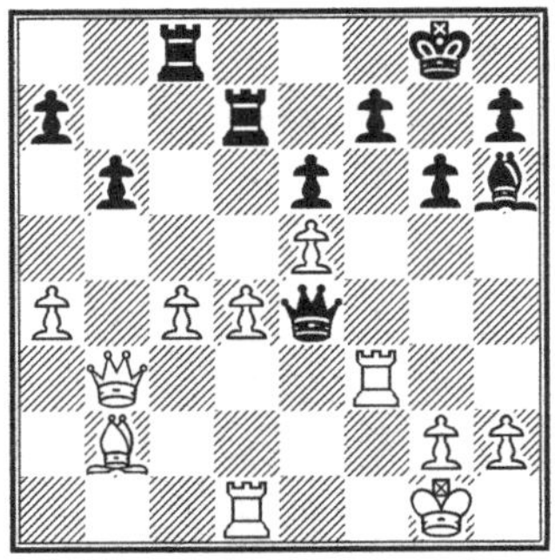

32...♕e2!

Threatening 33...♖xc4, against which White has no real defense. The Torre we know and love has finally shown up!

33.♖fd3

If 33.♖dd3 ♖dc7 34.♖f2 ♕e4 35.♖c3 (35.♖c2?? ♕e1#) 35...♖xc4! 36.♖xc4 ♕e1+ 37.♖f1 ♗e3+ and wins.

33...♖dc7! 34.d5

No longer salvific, but there was nothing better.

34...♖xc4 35.dxe6 ♖c2!

Striking while the iron is hot! 35...fxe6?! is much less good, as it immobilizes the ♖c4 for the moment.

36.exf7+ ♔g7!□ 37.f8♕+

White throws in two meaningless spite checks before throwing in the towel.

37...♖xf8 38.e6+ ♖xb2 0-1

In the 4th and 5th rounds, Torre drew with Fink and Chajes, giving him only an even score for five games. In the 6th round, he finally moved to +1 against Newell Banks. In contrast to his startling 1924 Queen sacrifice against Banks (see Game 18), Torre this time played in a highly positional style, missing some tactical opportunities, but ultimately giving a fine lesson in the technique of winning with a centralized Knight against a bad Bishop. Under computer examination the game proved to have unplumbed depths, labyrinthine complexities, subtle nuances, unnoticed errors and unsuspected resources for both sides, requiring many hours of probing with Stockfish before firm conclusions could be reached — and necessitating an almost complete revision of the first edition's annotations!

Game 101

Torre-Banks

Western Association Masters, Chicago 1926, round 6, 26 August

Torre Attack [A46]

1.d4 ♘f6 2.♘f3 e6 3.♗g5 c5 4.e3 c×d4 5.e×d4 ♘c6

Banks tries something new. At Moscow two of Torre's games reached this position, versus Lasker and Grünfeld, but in both Black continued 5...♗e7 and developed the Queen's Knight at d7.

6.♘bd2 ♗e7 7.c3 ♘d5

Banks again goes his own way. Exactly two months earlier, at Budapest 1926, Réti–Znosko-Borovsky got here by transposition, but continued 7...d5. In later games 7...0–0 would be most usual, followed by 7...b6. None of the four moves is notably better or worse than the others.

8.♘e4 ♗×g5 9.♘f×g5 0–0 10.h4

Torre disregards the rule of avoiding such pawn moves during the development stage.

Slightly better was 10.♕d2, but 10.♕h5 would be premature and easily repulsed by 10...h6∓.

10...h6 11.♘f3

11...♘f6

If 11...♘f4?! 12.♕d2 pretty much

dictates that the Knight go back to d5; if instead 12...♕c7 13.♘f6+!? g×f6 14.g3, when if 14...♘d5?? 15.♕×h6 d6 16.♗d3 f5 17.g4+−, or 14...♘g6? 15.♕×h6 ♘ce7 16.h5 ♘f5 17.♕d2 ♘ge7 18.g4 ♕c6□ 19.♗e2 ♘g7 20.0–0–0 with a winning attack (+3.81/24), or 14...♘e7 15.g×f4 and White can work up an attack on the g-file.

12.♗d3 ♘×e4 13.♗×e4 d5 14.♗d3

14.♗c2 was also possible, in fact preferable, as then White could play 15.♕d3, forcing the weakening move ...f7-f5, leaving a hole on e5 and a backward pawn on e6. See Capablanca-Blanco, given in the notes to Game 87.

14...♖e8 15.♕e2?

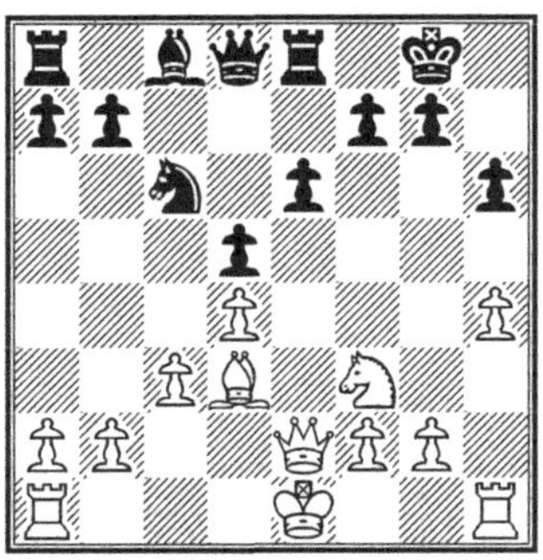

White wants to prevent 15...e5, but this in fact allows and augments it. Correct was 15.0–0. Torre should have recalled the general rule advising against having one's Queen and King on the same file as an enemy Rook, no matter what other pieces may be in between.

15...♕d6?!

Banks misses 15...e5!. White is then in a bad way however he captures the pawn, *viz.* 16.♘×e5? f6 17.♗g6 ♖e7−+, or 16.d×e5 ♗g4! 17.♕d2 ♘×e5 18.♘×e5 ♖×e5+ 19.♔f1 ♕f6 20.♖e1 ♖×e1+ 21.♕×e1 ♖d8 22.♕d2 d4 23.c4□ (23.c×d4?? ♕×d4 loses the Bishop) 23...♖e8 with much the better game for Black (-1.69/25).

16.♗b5?!

Stockfish definitely prefers 16.♘e5, but Torre apparently wants to do that without allowing ...♘c6×e5. He need not have worried, as after 16...♘×e5? 17.d×e5 ♕c5 18.♖h3! △19.♖g3, White can work up a nice attack (+2.22/26). The text is an unnecessary finesse that evens the game.

16...♗d7 17.0–0

Given White's early h2-h4, one would have expected 17.0–0–0, but both are about equally good.

17...♖ac8?!

Banks again misses a chance for 17...e5, with equality for Black after either 18.d×e5 ♘×e5 19.♗×d7 ♘×d7, or 18.♗×c6 e×d4 19.♕d3 b×c6 (19...♗×c6 20.♘×d4 is also even) 20.c×d4.

18.♖fe1

This shuts the door on ...e6-e5 for the time being, and forces Black into a slower buildup to achieve it.

18...♖e7 19.♖ad1 ♘b8?!
Best was 19...f6 intending ...e6-e5 soon. The text just drives the Bishop back to where it belongs.

20.♗d3
Torre is not about to let Black trade off his bad Bishop.

20...♗e8 21.♗b1
Intending ♕e2-c2/d3, to set up mate threats, and to uncover pressure on the d-pawn in the event of ...e5 and d×e5.

21...♘d7 22.♘e5! f5?
A rather serious mistake. Better 22...♘f8 when if, say, 23.♕g4 f6 24.♘d3 ♗g6 25.♘f4 ♗×b1 26.♖×b1 Black has nothing to fear.
Also not bad was 22...b5 23.a3 a5, aiming for a minority attack on White's Carlsbad pawn structure.

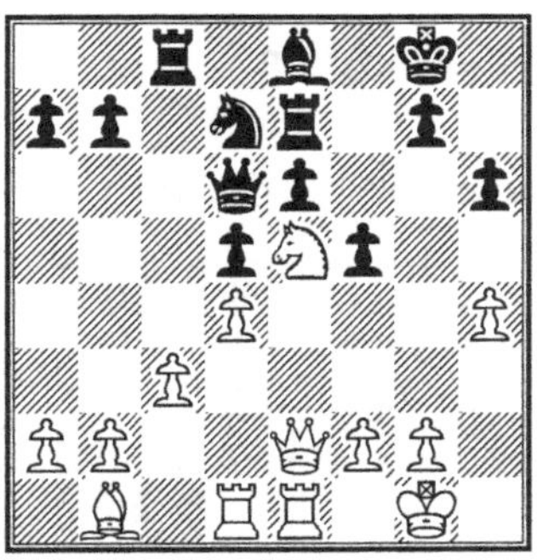

23.c4
Objectively, a distant second-best. Surely Torre saw that he could play 23.♘×d7 ♗×d7 24.♗×f5 winning a pawn, and which Stockfish considers worth much more than that (about +3.50). In the first edition we speculated that Torre felt that the counterplay Black might have had on the open f-file made that line problematic. Putting various lines stemming from 24.♗×f5 under the Lidless Eye helped us understand Torre's decision. Despite the high evaluations, none of Stockfish's variations led to further material gain within the next ten moves or even more. Whatever was justifying the +3.50 was rather far off. No wonder then that a human player, who does not have the benefit of seeing a running numerical score with each move, would opt for a different sort of advantage with which he feels more comfortable.

23...♘f6?
Better 23...b6 to prevent the next move, though then White still stands better after 24.♘×d7 ♗×d7 25.♗×f5 d×c4 26.d5 e5 27.♗b1 ±.
Even worse than the text would be 23...♘×e5 24.d×e5 ♕b4 25.c×d5 ♕×h4 26.d6 (+2.78/25).

24.c5!
The previous move ended any chance for Black to start a minority attack, and now this mobilizes White's queenside majority. This strategy is seen most clearly in the Gunderam variation of the Caro-Kann Defense, 1.e4 c6 2.d4 d5 3.e×d5 c×d5 4.c4 ♘f6 5.♘c3 e6 6.c5!, with which Kingston has won a number of games.

24...♕c7 25.b4 a6 26.♗d3

A strong alternative was 26.♗c2, intending a2-a4 and b4-b5, getting the pawns on the march. That scenario will not arise for another 22 moves.

26...♗h5 27.f3 ♖f8 28.♖b1

28.♕e3 or 28.♕d2, with the aim of inhibiting Black's next move, actually is not terribly effective: after 28...g5 29.h×g5 h×g5 30.♕×g5+ ♖g7 Black is glad to have the use of the g-file for counterplay.

28...g5 29.h×g5 h×g5

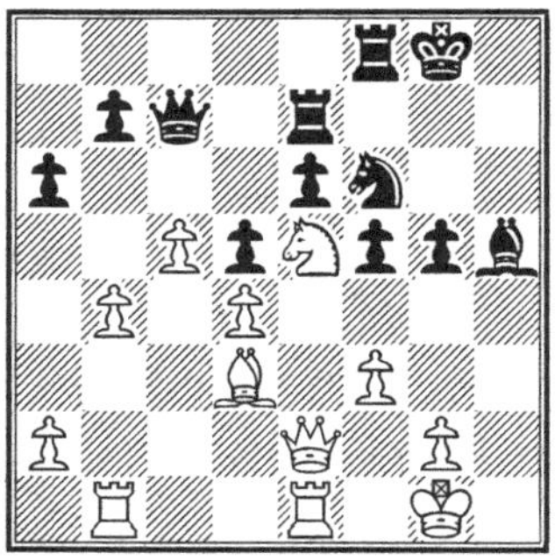

30.g3?!

Played with the idea of closing the kingside altogether and confining the action to the center and the queenside. But the kingside will not be completely closed: the h-file is still open, and Black can use it. It was better to push on the queenside immediately with 30.b5 and if

(a) 30...g4? 31.b×a6 g×f3 32.g×f3 ♖g7+ 33.♔h1 b×a6 34.♖g1 and it's White who goes on a kingside attack (+5.19/23); or

(b) 30...a×b5 31.♖×b5 ♗e8 32.♖b3 ♖h7 33.♖eb1 ♗c6 34.♕e3 g4 (if 34...♖g7? 35.♘×c6 ♕×c6 36.♖b6+−, or 34...♘d7 35.♘×c6 ♕h2+ 36.♔f1 b×c6 37.♕×e6+) 35.f×g4 ♘e4 36.g×f5 ♖×f5 37.♖f1 ♖×f1+ 38.♗×f1 (+4.53/31).

30...g4 31.f4

Seemingly giving up control of e4, but this was obligatory after 30.g3 anyway. Torre considered the weakness illusory, and was actually inviting ...♘f6-e4.

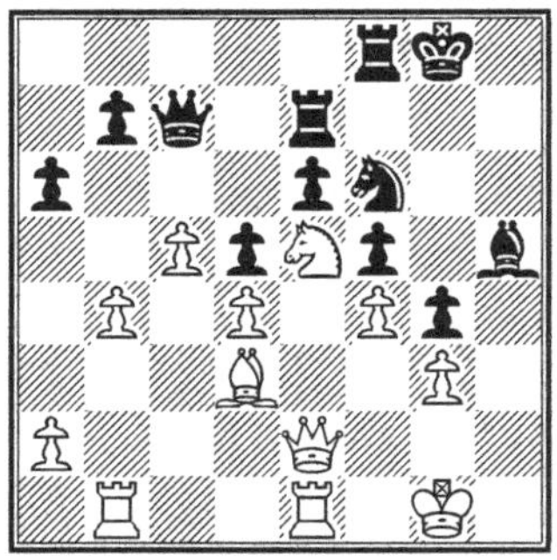

Before seeing the next actual move, it's worth examining other possibilities latent in this position:

(a) Not good is 31...♘d7 32.♘×d7 ♕×d7 33.b5 a×b5 34.♖×b5 ♕e8 35.♖b6

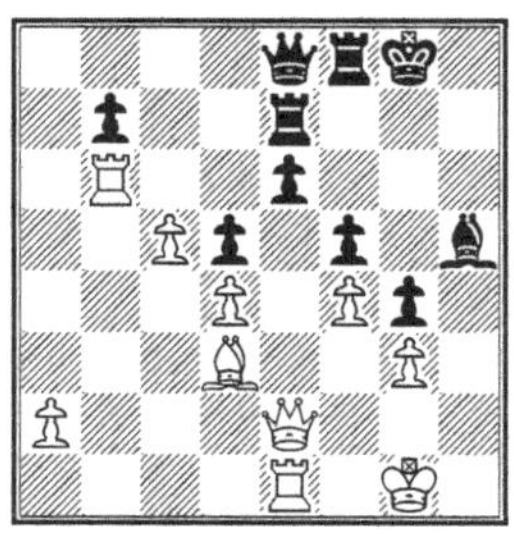

and both the b-pawn and the e-pawn will be targets (+3.21/28);

(b) If 31...♘e4 32.♗×e4 d×e4 33.♕c4±, much as in the actual game, but with more advantage for White;

(c) By far the most interesting is 31...♖h7 32.♔g2 ♔g7 33.♖h1 ♖fh8 34.b5 a×b5□ (not 34...a5?? 35.b6 ♕c8 36.c6 +7.46/24) 35.♗×b5 ♔g8 (Necessary to keep the b-pawn adequately defended; if instead, say, 35...♗f7 36.♖×h7+ ♖×h7 37.♕b2 ♕d8 38.♗e2 ♘d7 39.♘×d7 ♕×d7 40.♕×b7.) 36.♕b2 ♕e7 37.♕b4 ♗e8 38.♗×e8 ♕×e8:

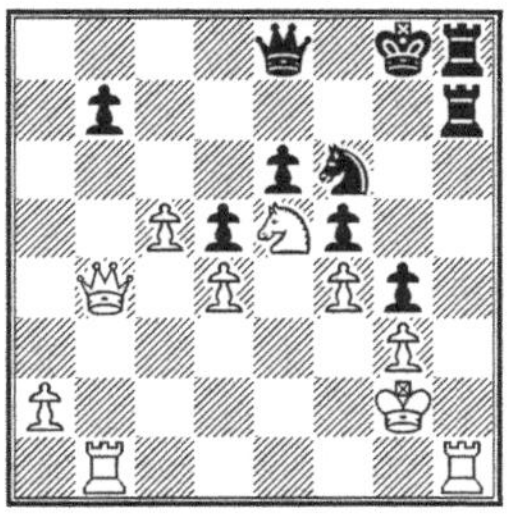

Now 39.c6 looks attractive, to make the a-pawn passed. However, it does not seem to work out: 39...b×c6 40.♖×h7 ♖×h7 41.♕d6 ♘e4 42.♕b8 ♕f8 43.♕×f8+ ♔×f8 44.♖b8+ ♔g7 45.♖b7+ ♔g8 46.♖×h7 ♔×h7 47.a4 ♘c3 48.a5 ♘b5 49.♘×c6 ♘c7 and it's a draw (0.26/46).

The way to success seems to be the cryptic, counter-intuitive 39.♖h4!?:

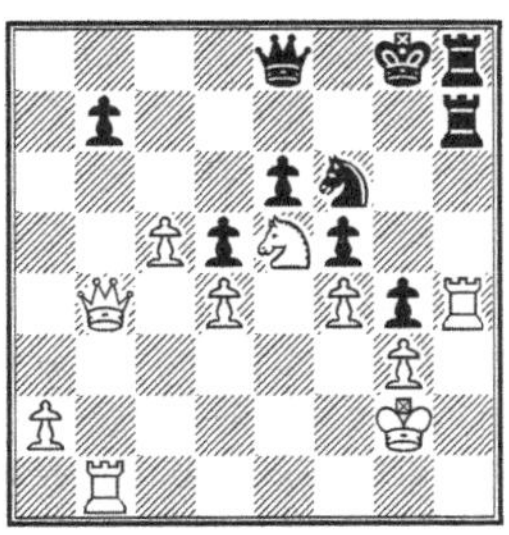

The computer then sees all lines heavily in White's favor (+4.00 or more), except for these five:

(c1) 39...♖×h4 40.g×h4 ♖×h4 41.♕×b7 ♖h3 42.♕b8 ♖c3□ 43.♕×e8+ ♘×e8 44.♖b8 ♔f8 45.c6 and White should win (+3.73/28);

(c2) 39...♖c7 40.♖×h8+ ♔×h8 41.♕a5 ♖h7 42.a4 ♘g8 43.♖h1 ♖×h1 44.♔×h1 ♘e7 45.♕d8 ♕×d8 46.♘f7+ ♔g8 47.♘×d8 and again, it looks like White should win (+3.45/27);

(c3) 39...♕d8 40.♕b6 ♕e8 41.♖×h7 ♖×h7 42.c6 b×c6 43.a4 ♘d7 44.♕×c6 ♖e7 45.♕d6□

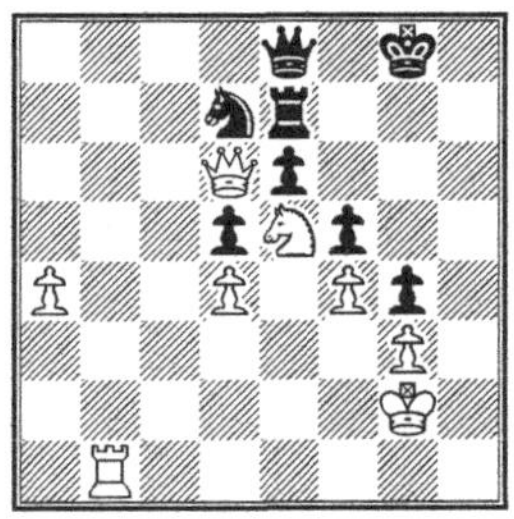

45...♘×e5 (if 45...♘f8 46.♔f2 ♖h7 47.♖b8 ♕e7 48.♕×e7 ♖×e7 49.♖×f8+ ♔×f8 50.♘g6+ ♔f7 51.♘×e7 ♔×e7 52.♔e3 and Stockfish announces mate in 20) 46.♖b8 ♘c4 47.♖×e8+ ♖×e8 48.♕c7 and White should win (+3.74/24);

(c4) A tricky line is 39...♖g7 40.♖×h8+ ♔×h8 41.a4 ♖c7 42.a5 ♔g7 43.c6 ♕h8

44.♕a3 (not 44.c×b7?? ♖c2+ 45.♔g1 ♕h2+ 46.♔f1 ♕f2#) 44...b×c6 (44...♕h3+?? 45.♔g1 accomplishes nothing) 45.a6 ♘e4 46.♔g1! ♕a8 (if 46...♕h3?? 47.♖b7+−) 47.♖b6 ♕a7 48.♕b4 (48.♖×c6?? ♕×d4+) 48...♔h6□ (49.♖b8 was threatened) 49.♔h2 ♖c8 50.♔g2 ♘f6 51.♕b1 ♘h5 52.♘×g4+! f×g4 53.♖b7+−;
(c5) The most difficult line is 39...♘e4 40.♕b6 ♖×h4 41.g×h4 ♖h7 42.a4 ♖e7 43.♕a7

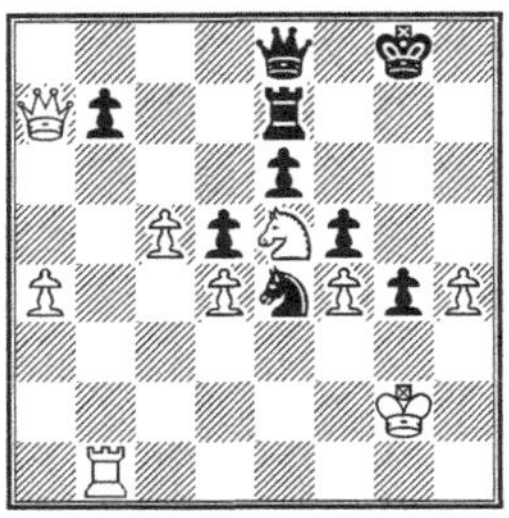

43...♕c8 [if 43...b5 44.♕a6 ♕h5 (if 44...b×a4? 45.♘c6 threatening both 46.♘×e7 and 46.♖b8) 45.a×b5 ♕×h4 46.♕c8+ ♔g7 47.♕f8+! ♔×f8 48.♘g6+ ♔g7 49.♘×h4+−] 44.c6 ♘d6□ 45.♕c5 ♕d8 46.♘d7 forcing 46...♖×d7 47.c×d7 ♕×d7 48.h5 (if 48.♖a1 ♕d8 0.00, or 48.♕b4 ♕c6 0.00) 48...♕×a4 49.♕×d6 ♕c2+ 50.♔g3 ♕×b1 51.♔h4 g3□ 52.♔g5 and Stockfish says White should win the Queen ending (+6.35/34); if 52...g2 53.♕d8+ forces mate in six.

These variations indicate some of the pitfalls Black could get into. Whether by luck or skill, Banks happened to choose what was probably the best move at this point.

From the position of the diagram after **31.f4**, that was:

31...♗e8 32.♔g2 ♘e4

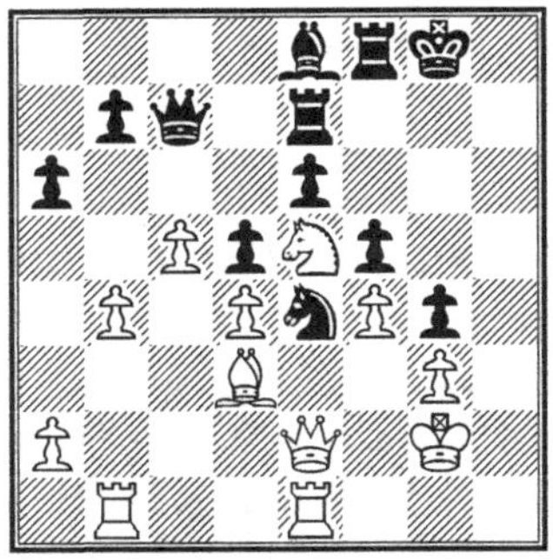

At this point in the first edition we wrote: "A typical positional mistake whose consequences will be felt only in the long run. This opportunity to exchange was precisely what White was looking for, as it gives him permanent positional pluses: centralized Knight vs. bad Bishop, queenside pawn majority, and control of the only open file." On the whole this is more or less true. But we continued "Materially, Black is equal, but positionally, he is doomed. From this point on, Torre conducts the game with machine-like accuracy." The first sentence is debatable, the latter definitely wrong.

33.♗×e4?!
As will be seen, this works only because of later errors by Black. Preferable was 33.♕b2!?, which retains White's advantage (+1.79/25).

33...d×e4 34.♖h1 ♖h7?
Correct was 34...♖f6=.

35.♖×h7 ♔×h7

Somewhat better was 35...♕×h7 36.♖h1 ♕g7.

36.♖h1+ ♔g7

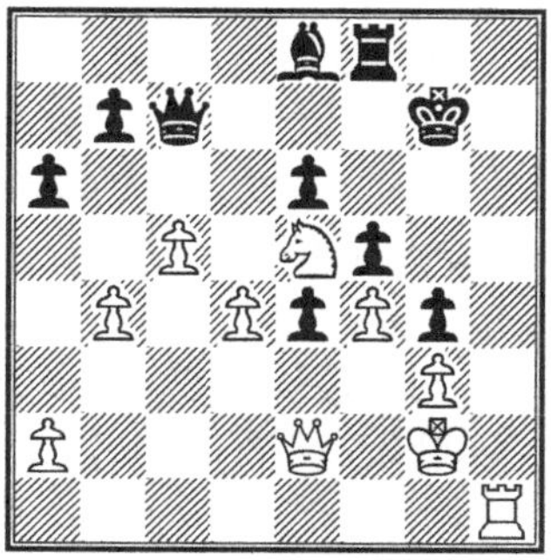

37.♕c4?

Torre's worst move of the game, putting the win in serious doubt.

Best and winning was 37.d5! e×d5 38.♕b2:

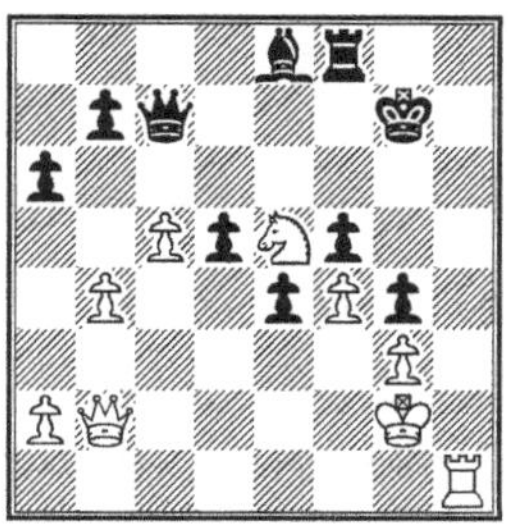

White threatens mate starting with either 39.♘d7+ or 39.♘×g4+. There is no good defense, *viz.*:

(a) 38...♔g8?? 39.♘×g4 and mate in 10;

(b) 38...♖f6 39.♔g1 d4 40.♕h2 ♔f8 41.♕h8+ ♔e7 42.♖h7+ etc.;

(c) 38...♕d8 39.♘d7+ ♖f6 40.♘×f6 ♕×f6 41.♖h7+ etc.;

(d) 38...d4 (relatively best) 39.♕×d4 ♖f6 40.♔f2 a5 41.b5! ♗×b5 42.♖h5 ♕e7 43.♖g5+ ♔h7 (if 43...♔f8?? 44.♘g6+, or 43...♔h6 44.♕d1! ♕×c5+ 45.♔g2 ♔h7 46.♘×g4+−) 44.♕d5!,

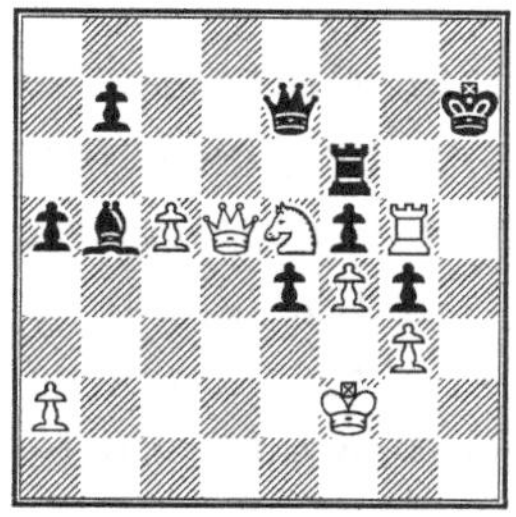

threatening 45.♕g8+, and Black cannot avoid serious material loss, *e.g.*:

(d1) 44...♖e6 45.♖h5+ ♔g7 46.♖×f5;

(d2) 44...♔h6 45.♘×g4+! f×g4 46.♖h5+ ♔g7 47.♕g5+ ♔f7 48.♖h7+;

(d3) 44...♕f8 45.♖h5+ ♖h6 46.♕×b7+ etc.;

(d4) 44...♖f8 45.♘g6 ♗c6 46.♕e5 ♕×e5 47.♘×f8+ ♔h6 48.♖g6+ ♔h5 49.f×e5.

Going back a bit, also quite strong was 37.♕b2, forcing 37...♕d8 38.d5 ♕×d5 39.♘×g4+ e5 40.♕×e5+ ♕×e5 41.♘×e5 (+3.28/24). But the text lets Black equalize.

37...♖f6 38.♔f2

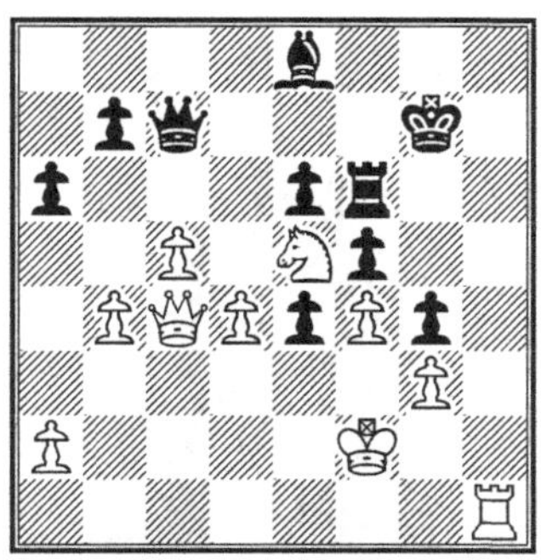

38...♔g8?

A subtle but definite error, from which Black never recovers. 38...♕d8 was absolutely necessary, and after 39.♔e3 ♕d5 the game is virtually even (+0.20/28). But after the text White is definitely winning, and in fact we enter a phase of the game where he can choose between several winning lines at various points. Perhaps Torre does not exhibit "machine-like accuracy," but he does not need to.

39.♔e3!

Best, not because it prevents a potential ...e4-e3+ (which is not really to be feared), but because it prepares to bring the Queen to the h-file.
39.d5! would again also win:

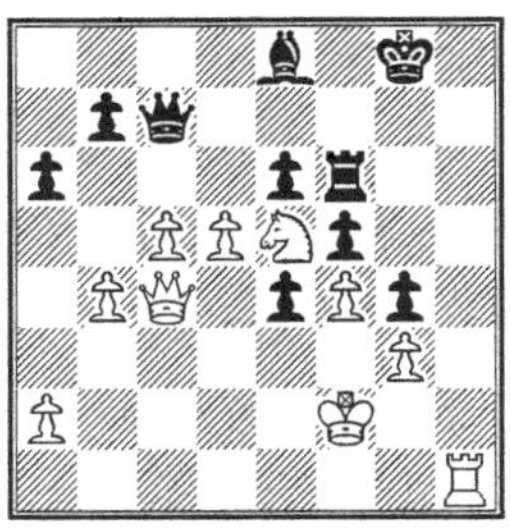

39...e×d5 40.♕×d5+ ♔g7 41.♕d4 a5 42.b5 ♕e7 (if 42...♗×b5 43.♖h5) 43.a4 ♕e6 44.♘c4 ♗f7 45.♖c1 ♕c8 46.♘e3 (46.♘×a5 is OK) 46...♔g6□

47.♘g2 ♗e8 (if 47...♗e6 48.♘h4+ ♔f7 49.c6 b×c6 50.♖×c6) 48.c6! b×c6 49.b6 ♕d7 50.♘h4+ ♔h7 51.♕×d7+ ♗×d7 52.♖c5+−.

39...♕e7 40.♕c2

Strongest was 40.d5 e×d5 41.♕×d5+ ♔g7 42.♕d4. The text is also strong and preserves the win, as would about a dozen other moves.

40...♕f8 41.♕h2 ♕g7 42.♕h4 ♗b5 43.♕h5 ♖f8 44.♘g6 ♖f6 45.♘e7+!

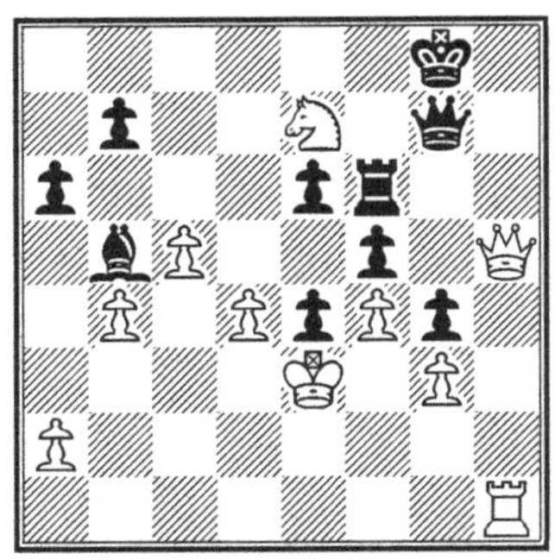

45...♔f8

Of course if 45...♕×e7 46.♕h8+ ♔f7 47.♖h7+ ♔g6 48.♕g8+ ♕g7 49.♕×g7#.

46.♘c8!

Equally good was 46.♕g5!, *e.g.* 46...♕×g5 47.f×g5 ♖f7 48.♘g6+ ♔g8 49.♖h8+ ♔g7 50.♖h6 ♗d7 51.♘f4 and either 51...♔g8 52.♘×e6+−, or 51...♖e7 52.♘h5+ ♔f7 53.♖h7+ ♔e8 54.♘f6+ ♔d8 55.♖×e7 ♔×e7 56.♘×d7 ♔×d7 57.a4+−.

46...♗c6 47.♘d6

A Knight securely posted on the sixth rank is effectively as strong as a Rook, so White may be considered to be up the Exchange.

47...♖g6 48.a4 ♔e7
If 48...♗×a4 49.♘×b7.

49.b5 a×b5 50.a×b5 ♗d5 51.♕h7 ♔f8 52.♕h4

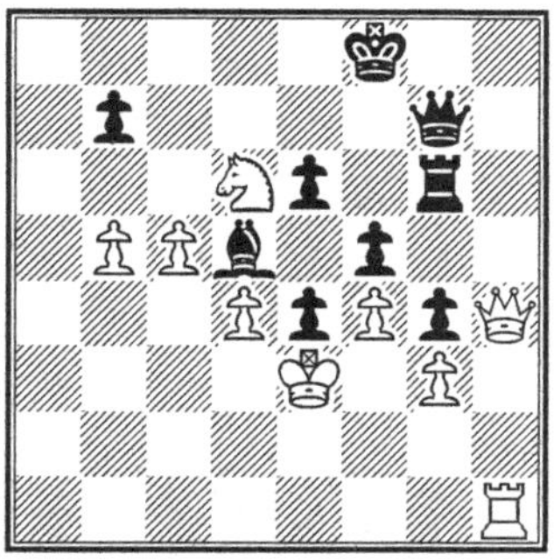

Gaining a little clock time before forcing the Queen exchange.

52...♖f6 53.♕h8+ ♕×h8 54.♖×h8+ ♔g7 55.♘e8+! ♔×h8 56.♘×f6 ♗c4 57.c6 b×c6 58.b×c6

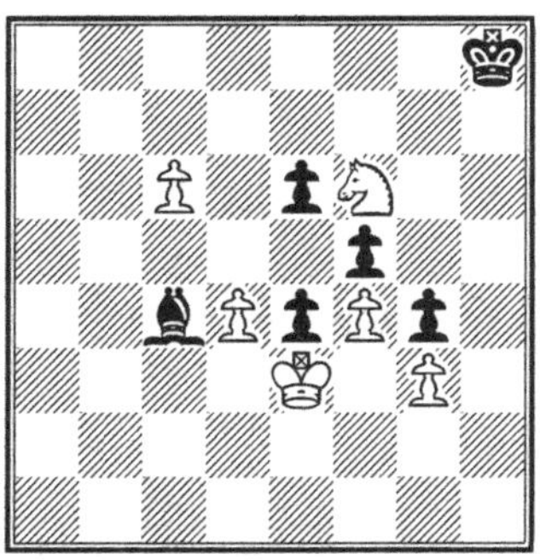

The game is now reduced to its bare essentials, and further comment is unnecessary.

58...♔g7 59.c7 ♗a6 60.♘e8+ ♔f7 61.♘d6+ ♔e7 62.c8♕ ♗×c8 63.♘×c8+ ♔d7 64.♘b6+ ♔c6 65.♘c4 ♔d7 66.♔d2 ♔c6 67.♔c3 ♔d5 68.♘e3+ ♔d6 69.♔b4 ♔c6 70.♔c4 ♔d6 71.♔b5 ♔e7 72.♔c6 ♔f7 73.♔d7 ♔f6 74.♔e8 1-0
Mate in at most 11 is inevitable.

Its slight imperfections notwithstanding, this was an outstanding positional game. The skeptical reader might say, "True, but Karpov has played many games as good or better." Agreed, but Karpov has played in hundreds of international tournaments, and has exchanged ideas with scores of grandmasters for decades. In contrast, Carlos Torre played in only four international tournaments in his whole life, and had little opportunity to exchange ideas with or receive the advice of other grandmasters. Taking this into account, a game such as this stands out all the more.

In the next round, Torre played a draw with his old rival Kupchik, then had a bye. The rest clearly seemed to do him good, as after it he won four games in a row, against Maróczy, Showalter, Marshall and Isaacs, putting him in first place.

Game 102
Torre-Maróczy

Western Association Masters, Chicago 1926, round 9, 29 August
Queen's Gambit Accepted [D21]

Around the period 1900-1906, Hungarian master Geza Maróczy (1870-1951, historical Elo 2620, GM title 1950) may well have been the second-best chess player in the world, after Lasker. He and Lasker had in fact signed a world title match agreement in 1906, but various circumstances aborted the match. Though Maróczy's ambition for the game declined somewhat after that, he remained remarkably strong and consistent; according to analysis by Elo his performance remained in the 2500-2620 range from 1905 until 1935.

In style Maróczy was strongly positional, favoring the endgame. Here Torre introduces early complications not to his taste, but this succeeds far too well: for much of the game neither player had any idea what was going on, and they traded mistake after mistake.

1.d4 e6 2.♘f3 d5 3.c4 d×c4 4.e4
White's deferring of the gambit makes this possible; after 1.d4 d5 2.c4 c×d4, 3.e4 is not advisable. Relatively untried at the time, the text goes back to Janowski-Taubenhaus, match, Paris, 1905 (0-1, 48). Before that White had always played 4.e3. Torre may have noticed that Capablanca played 4.e4 against Zubarev and Bogoljubow at Moscow 1925, winning both times, perhaps explaining his use of it here. It was also seen in P. Johner-Rubinstein, Dresden 1926 (0-1, 38), four months before the present game. Historically it has done quite well, White scoring +143 -67 =66 in 277 games on ChessBase.

4...c5

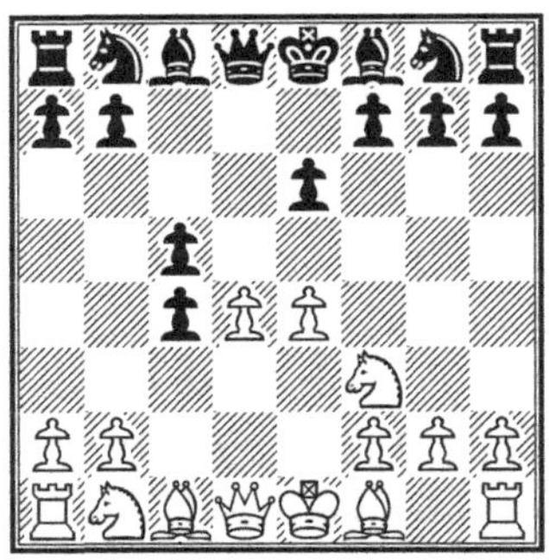

As played by Zubarev, Bogoljubow and Rubinstein in the aforementioned games. 4...b5 came to be the preferred move, as for example in Vallejo Pons-Kasparov, Linares 2005 (0-1, 28).

5.♗×c4
As in Capablanca-Bogoljubow. Against Zubarev the Cuban tried 5.d5 e×d5 6.e×d5 ♘f6 7.♗×c4 ♗d6 8.0–0 (8.♕e2+!?±) 8...0–0 9.♗g5 ♗g4 10.♘c3 ♘bd7=.

5...a6

Maróczy varies from Capa-Bogo, which continued 5...c×d4 6.♘×d4 ♘f6 7.♘c3 ♗c5 8.♗e3 ♘bd7? 9.♗×e6! f×e6 10.♘×e6 ♕a5? (⌓10...♕b6±) 11.0–0! ♗×e3? 12.f×e3 and 1-0, 32, one of the more complex games in chess history. In the tournament book, Bogoljubow wrote extensive analyses trying to prove the sacrifice unsound, but Capablanca must not have shared this opinion, since three years later he repeated it against the Hungarian Havasi and again won brilliantly. We will add that Stockfish thoroughly endorses Capablanca's view (+5.58/24 after 12.f×e3).

6.0–0 c×d4 7.♘×d4 b5

The aforementioned Capablanca-Havasi, Budapest 1928, continued 7...♘f6 8.♘c3 ♗c5 9.♗e3 ♘bd7 10.♗×e6!! f×e6?? (10...0–0 is less bad) 11.♘×e6 ♕a5 12.♘×g7+ ♔f7 13.♘f5 ♘e5 14.♕b3+ and White won in 27 moves.

8.♗b3

8.♗e2 may have been slightly better, but Black's next move renders that academic.

8...♘f6

Preferable was 8...♗b7, as in Makarov-Ibragimov, Smolensk 1991 (1-0, 53).

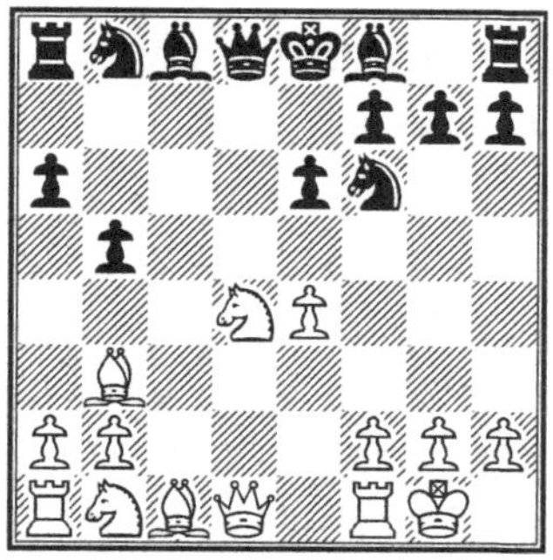

9.a4

Torre misses his first likely winning chance. Highly disruptive would have been 9.e5!, *viz.*

(a) 9...♘e4 10.♘c3 ♘×c3 11.b×c3 (+2.28), or

(b) 9...♘fd7 10.♘c3 (playable also is 10.♗×e6!? f×e6 11.♘×e6 ♕b6 12.♘f4 +1.82/26) 10...♘×e5 11.♖e1 ♘g6 12.♕f3! (+4.69/32), or

(c) 9...♘d5 10.♕f3 ♖a7 11.♘c3 ♘×c3 12.b×c3 ♖d7 13.♕g3 ♗b7 14.a4 ♘c6 15.a×b5 ♘×d4 16.c×d4 a×b5 17.♖d1 (+3.20), or

(d) 9...♗c5 10.e×f6 ♗×d4 11.f×g7 ♖g8 12.♕f3 ♖a7 13.♗e3 ♗b7 14.♕f4 ♗×g7 15.♖d1 (+3.50).

9...b4?

This allows Torre another opportunity for the pawn thrust. It is well known that Maróczy was never fond of complications, but in this situation he could hardly avoid them. Some probably better alternatives:

(a) 9...♘×e4 10.♘c3 ♘c5 11.a×b5 ♗e7 12.♗c4 0–0 13.b4 ♘b7 14.b×a6 ♕c7

15.♕b3 ♘d6 16.♗e2 ♗f6 17.♖d1 ♗×a6 18.♗×a6 ♘×a6 19.♗f4 ♖fd8, and while the position favors White (+1.59/27), material is even and Black can put up a good fight;

(b) 9...♗b7 10.a×b5 a×b5 11.♖×a8 ♗×a8 12.e5 ♘e4 13.♘×b5 ♗c5 14.♕g4 ♘d7 15.♕×g7 ♔e7 16.♗g5+ ♘×g5 17.♕×g5+ ♔e8 18.♘d6+ ♗×d6 19.♕×d8+ ♔×d8 20.e×d6 ♘c5 and Stockfish thinks Black has some compensation for his two-pawn deficit (+1.07/25);

(c) 9...♗c5 10.♗e3 ♗×d4 11.♗×d4 ♗b7 12.a×b5 a×b5 13.♖×a8 ♗×a8 14.♘c3 ♘×e4 15.♘×e4 ♗×e4 16.♖e1 ♗f5 (16...♗b7?? 17.♕g4!+−) 17.♗×g7 ♖g8 with even material, though White has some advantage with his Bishop pair (+1.62/27).

10.e5

Also strong was 10.♗e3 ♘×e4 11.♘d2 ♘c5 12.♕h5 ♘×b3 13.♘2×b3 ♗e7 14.♖ac1 with more than adequate compensation for the pawn (+2.19/25).

10...♘d5?

Better 10...♘e4 or 10...♘fd7.

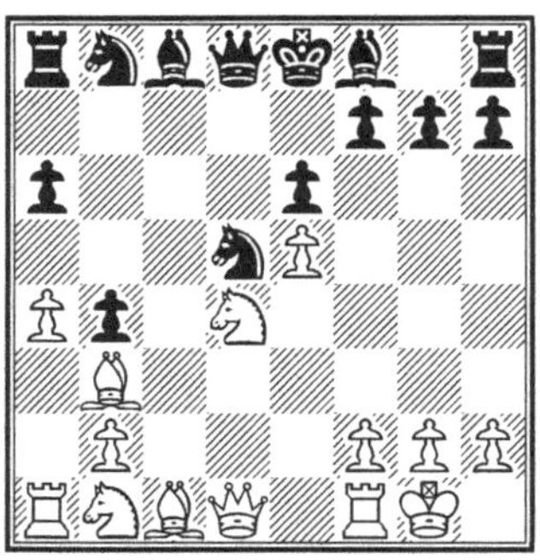

11.♕g4!

Very strong. It may have been even stronger to preface this with 11.♘d2, *viz.* 11...♗e7 12.♕g4 0–0 13.♘e4 ♔h8 14.♘g5 ♕c7 15.♕e4 ♗×g5 (if 15...g6? 16.♘×f7+! ♖×f7 17.♘×e6! ♗×e6 18.♗×d5+−) 16.♗×g5 ♘c6 17.♘×c6 ♕×c6 18.♗c2 g6 19.♖ac1 with a winning attack (+4.54/26).

11...h5

If 11...♗b7 White can either continue developing with 12.♘d2, or strike with 12.♘×e6 f×e6 13.♕×e6+ ♗e7 14.♖d1, winning back his piece with interest.

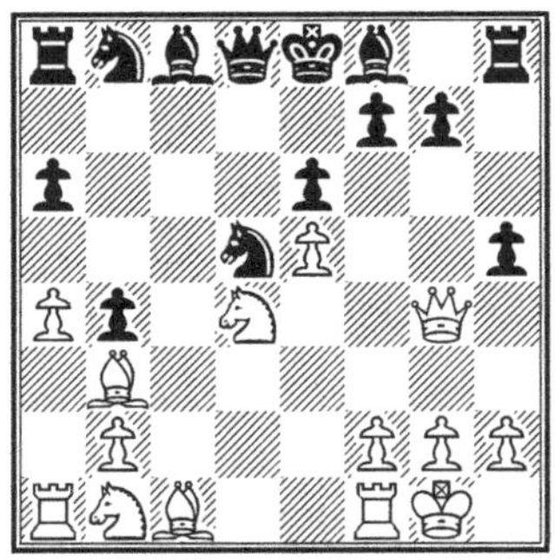

12.♕e4?!

After two strong moves, Torre plays a distant second-best. With Black still uncastled the Queen does not threaten much from here, and she will be vulnerable to threats herself.

Winning was 12.♕g3. If then:

(a) 12...♗b7 13.♘d2 ♘c6 14.♘×c6 ♗×c6 15.♘c4 ♖c8 16.♗g5 h4 17.♕g4 ♕c7 (if 17...♗e7 18.♘d6+) 18.h3 and Black can do little but wait for the hammer to fall (+6.38/29);

(b) 12...♕b6 13.♘f5! g6 14.♗×d5 e×d5

15.♘d6+ ♗xd6 16.exd6 0–0 17.♗e3 and there can be no doubt that White's attack will get through (+4.16/24);
(c) 12...♗d7 13.♗g5 ♗e7 14.♗xe7 ♘xe7 15.♖d1 (much stronger than 15.♕xg7) 15...♕c7 16.♘d2 ♘bc6 17.♘4f3 ♘f5 18.♕f4 0–0 19.♖ac1 ♖ad8 20.♘e4 ♗c8 21.♘d6 (+5.80/27).

12...♗b7!

A natural reply, potentially threatening the ♕e4.

13.♖d1?!

Another subpar move. Better 13.♘d2, or 13.a5 threatening 14.♗a4+.

13...♕c8?

Black could have solved the worst of his problems with 13...♗e7:

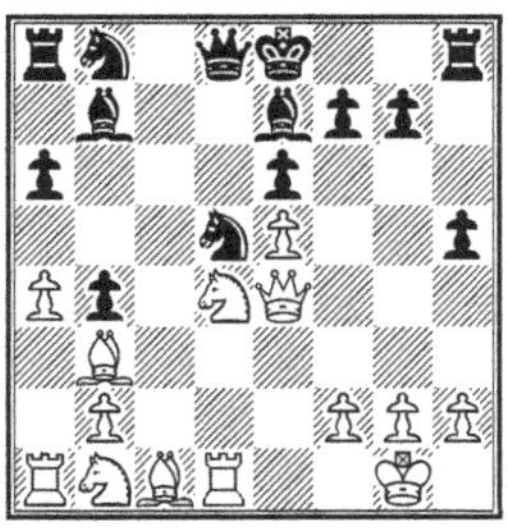

Then 14.♘xe6 fxe6 15.♕g6+ ♔d7 16.♘d2 ♕e8 (-0.47/24) was not to be feared, nor 14.♘f5 exf5 15.♕xf5 ♕d7 16.♕f3 0–0 17.♗xd5 ♗xd5 18.♖xd5 ♕e6=. Relatively best for White would be 14.♘d2 ♘d7 15.♘c4, but after 15...♘c5 16.♕e2 his attack is over and his advantage much diminished (+0.63/25).

14.♕d3?

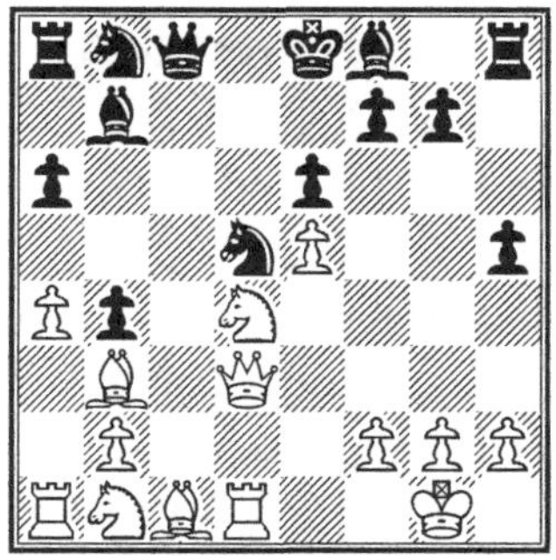

With this White's advantage completely disappears. 14.♘d2! would have maintained it, best play then proceeding 14...♗e7 15.♕d3 ♘d7 16.♕g3 (finally getting the Queen back to where she belonged at move 12!) 16...g6 17.♘c4 intending ♘c4-d6+ as in earlier analysis (+1.74/25).

14...♗e7?

But this, best a move ago, is now bad. Equalizing was 14...♘d7!, and if:

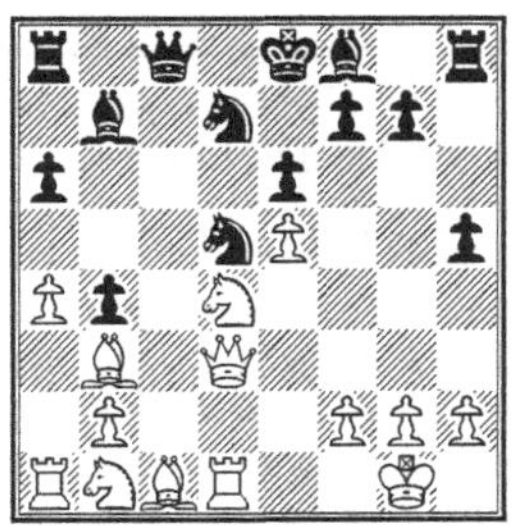

(a) 15.♘d2 ♘xe5 16.♕g3 ♕b8=;
(b) 15.♗g5 ♘xe5 16.♕g3 ♕b8 17.♘d2 ♘g4=;
(c) 15.♘xe6 ♘xe5!□ 16.♕d4 ♕xe6 17.♗xd5 ♗xd5 18.♕xd5 ♕xd5 19.♖xd5 f6=;
(d) 15.♕g3? h4 16.♕g5 g6 17.♘f3 ♘c5 18.♗xd5 (if 18.♗c2? ♗e7 19.♕g4 b3−+) 18...♗xd5 19.♘bd2 ♖h5

20.♕g4 h3 21.♘c4 ♕c6 22.♘d6+ ♗×d6 23.e×d6 ♖d8 24.♗e3 h×g2 25.♘h4 ♕×d6 26.♗×c5 ♕×c5 27.♘×g6 ♖×h2! 28.♔×h2 ♕×f2 29.♔h3 f×g6 30.♕×g6+ ♕f7−+.

In each case the capture of White's e-pawn is key. White cannot defend it without letting the initiative pass to Black, *e.g.* 15.♘f3 ♘c5 16.♕c2 ♗e7∓, or worse 15.f4? ♘c5 16.♕c4 ♘×b3 17.♕×c8+ ♖×c8 18.♘×b3 ♖c2−+, or variation **(d)** above.

Returning to the game:

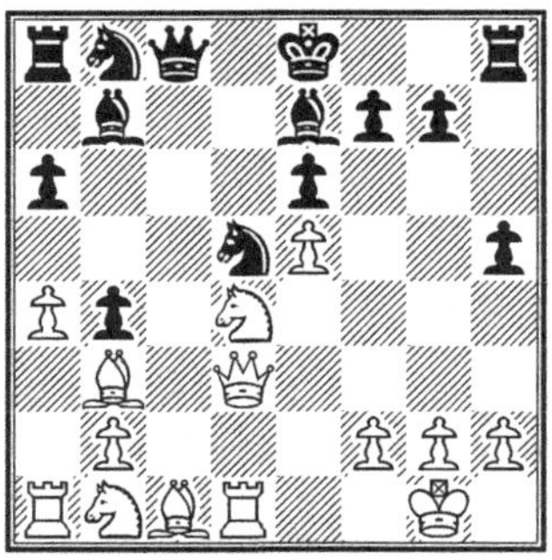

15.♘d2! ♘d7 16.♘e4?

But again Torre fails to see his chance, which was 16.♕g3! g6 17.h4 ♘c5 18.♗c2 ♕d8 19.♘2f3 (+2.00/25).

16...♘×e5

16...♕b8 produces deadeye equality, 0.00/35, but the text should be an adequate defense too, if properly followed up.

17.♕g3 ♘g4??

17...♘g6! was correct, *viz.* 18.♗g5 0–0 19.♗×e7 ♘g×e7 20.♕g5 ♘g6 21.♘d6 ♕d7 22.♘×b7 ♕×b7 23.♘×e6 f×e6 and either 24.♖×d5 ♘f4, or 24.♗×d5 e×d5 25.♕×g6 ♕f7 with only a minimal advantage for White in either case.

18.♗g5?

This is getting ridiculous. How did Torre miss 18.f3, winning a piece?

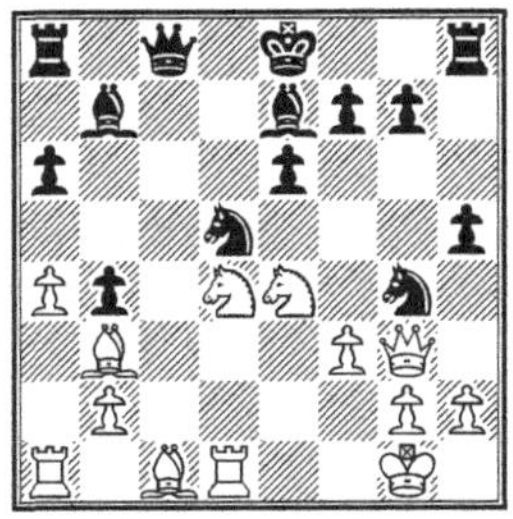

The attacked Knight must stay put, since if 18...♘gf6?? 19.♗×d5 ♘×d5 20.♕×g7 ♖f8 21.♗g5 (+7.06/25), or 18...♘ge3?? 19.♗×e3 ♘×e3 20.♕×g7 ♖f8 21.♘×e6! f×e6 22.♕g6+ ♖f7 23.♗×e6 ♕×e6 24.♕×e6+−, or 18...♘h6 19.♕×g7 ♖g8 20.♕×h6+−.

Neither is 18...e5 any good: 19.f×g4 e×d4 20.♖×d4 ♕e6 (if 20...♘f6 21.♘d6+ ♗×d6 22.♕×d6 ♕c6 23.♕×c6+ ♗×c6 24.g5+−) 21.♗g5 ♖d8 (not 21...♗×g5?? 22.♘×g5 ♕f6 23.♖e4+ ♔f8 24.♘×f7!+−) 22.♗×e7 ♕×e7 23.♖ad1 0–0 24.g5! etc.

Relatively best is the obviously losing 18...♕b8 19.♕×b8+ ♖×b8 20.f×g4 h×g4 (+3.61/27).

18...♕b8!

Now Black is again off the hook.

19.♗×e7 ♕×g3 20.h×g3 ♔×e7 21.♘c5 ♗c8

Better was 21...♖a7 22.♘×b7 ♖×b7=.

22.♖ac1 a5 23.♘c6+ ♔e8?

An error as bad as move 17. Best was 23...♔f6 24.♗×d5 e×d5 25.♖×d5 and Black's King is out of danger with even material.

24.♗×d5 e×d5 25.♖×d5

White is clearly winning now, but just wait — more mistakes are on the way!

25...♗e6 26.♖e1

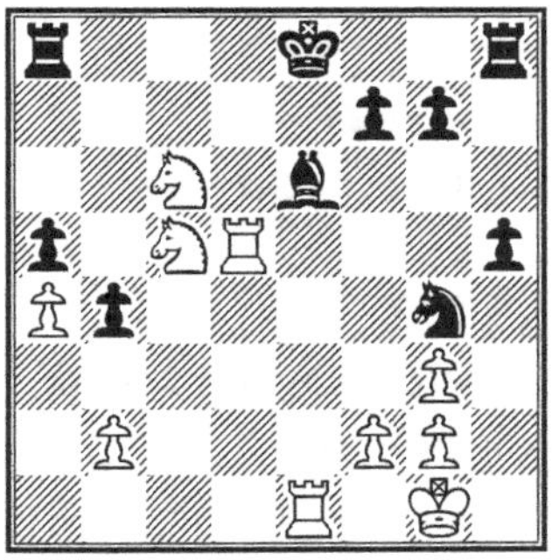

26...♖h6

If 26...♔f8 27.♘×e6+ f×e6 28.♖×e6 ♖h6 29.♖×h6 g×h6 30.♖d8+ ♖×d8 31.♘×d8 ♘e5 32.♘b7 ♘c4 33.b3 ♘e5 34.♘×a5 +−.

27.♖d6

Good, but clearly better was 27.♖g5 ♔f8 28.f3 ♘f6 29.♘×e6+ f×e6 30.♖×e6+−.

27...♔f8 28.f3

This is not nearly so effective now as in the note to move 18.

28...♗f5! 29.♖d8+ ♖×d8 30.♘×d8 ♘f6

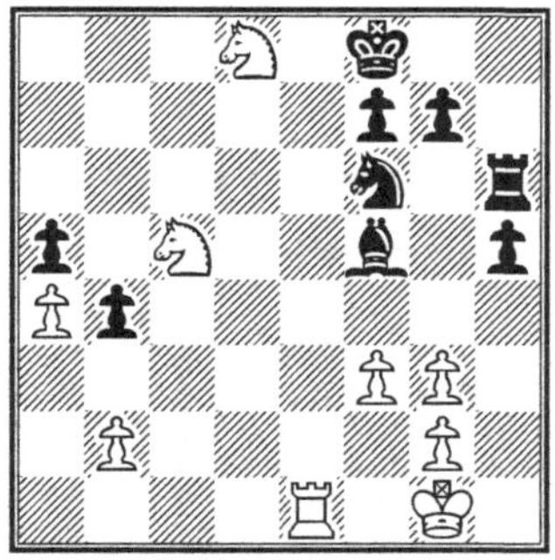

31.♘db7?

Another serious error by Torre.

Still winning was 31.♖d1 ♔e8 32.♘db7 ♘d7 33.♘d6+ ♖×d6 34.♖×d6 ♘×c5 35.♖d5 ♘×a4 36.♖×f5 ♘×b2 37.♖×a5.

31...♘d7!

This equalizes (0.29/30).

32.♘×d7+ ♗×d7 33.b3 ♖c6! 34.♘×a5 ♖c3?!

Maróczy was noted for his skill in Queen endgames, but it seems he was not quite so good with Rooks on this day. He could have maintained equality with 34...♖c5, *viz.* 35.♘b7 (if 35.♘c4 ♗×a4=) 35...♖c3 36.a5 ♗c6! 37.a6 ♖×b3 38.♘a5 ♖c3 39.♖b1 ♖c5 40.♘b3 ♖c2 (0.00/32).

The text needlessly gives up Black's b-pawn, leaving him not quite lost but in significantly worse shape than after 34...♖c5.

35.♖e4 ♖c5

This further worsens Black's plight. Better 35...♗e6 36.♖×b4 g5. If then 37.♘b7 ♗×b3, or 37.♖b5 g4 38.♖×h5 g×f3 39.g×f3 ♖×f3, with drawing chances either way.

36.♘b7 ♖c1+ 37.♔h2 ♗c6 38.♖×b4 ♖c2 39.♔h3 g5

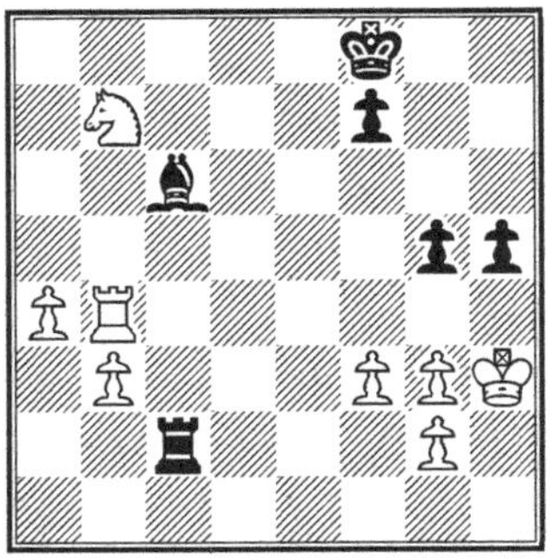

40.a5?!

Giving Black one last chance to draw. Correct was 40.♘d6 ♗d7+ 41.♔h2 g4 42.♖f4 ♗e6 43.f×g4 h×g4 44.b4+–.

But fortunately for Torre, this is the next-to-last mistake.

40...g4+??

As the fabric of space-time might have said after the Big Bang, "That's torn it!".

Black had two ways to draw: 40...♖a2 41.♖b6 ♗×b7 42.♖×b7 ♖×a5 (0.15/38), or 40...♖c1 (threatening mate) 41.♔h2 ♖a1 42.♘d8 ♗e8 43.♘b7 ♗c6 etc., drawing by repetition.

41.f×g4 ♗×g2+

Merely a spite check.

42.♔h4 1-0

One of Torre's less impressive games, but a point's a point.

Game 103

Showalter-Torre

Western Association Masters, Chicago 1926, round 10, 30 August

Alekhine's Defense [B03]

If Maróczy represented the generation before Torre's, Jackson W. Showalter (1860-1935, historical Elo 2470), was from another era altogether. Called "The Kentucky Lion" for both his chess prowess and his prominent mane of hair and sideburns, Showalter was probably the best American-born player between Morphy's retirement and Pillsbury's rise. In the years 1891-96 he won five matches for the US title. In an 1897 title match he played Pillsbury unexpectedly tough, going down +8 -10 =3. He regained the US title after Pillsbury's death in 1906, finally losing it to Marshall in 1909. After some international competition circa 1896-1900, Showalter stuck to American tournaments. Chicago 1926 was his last important event.

Frankly, Torre's play in this game was if anything worse than against Maróczy. In that game he kept missing wins but was never in serious danger of losing.

Here he was busted, but managed to pull off a Marshall-style swindle.

1.e4 ♘f6 2.e5 ♘d5 3.d4 d6 4.♗c4
Yet again, at a very early stage, we reach a position then new to serious chess. With the theory of Alekhine's Defense in its infancy in the 1920s, all sorts of approaches were tried. Showalter seems to have been the pioneer of this line, playing it also against Marshall in this event. Later it was taken up by Canal, and Lajos Steiner. It has never been very popular, occurring in less than 4% of the games on ChessBase, well behind 4.♘f3 (55%) and 4.c4 (35%), but it has been tried by Tal, Hort, Spassky, and Nepomniatchi, to name a few greats.

4...♘b6 5.♗b3 d×e5
This came to be the main variation.

6.♕f3
Forcing 6...e6 and avoiding an exchange of Queens.

6...e6 7.d×e5

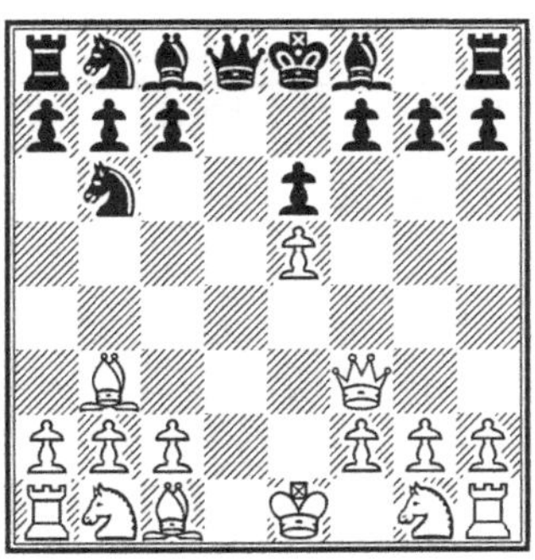

7...♘c6
The immediate 7...a5 is playable; a very one-sided example is Gufeld-Vasyukov, Kislovodsk 1968: 8.c3?! (△8.a4) 8...a4 9.♗c2 ♗d7 10.♕g3 ♗b5 11.♗g5 ♕d5 12.♘d2?! ♘c6 13.f4?? ♘c4 14.♕d3?? ♘×b2 (even stronger was 14...♘a3!) and 0-1, 33.

8.♕g3 a5 9.c3
This ultimately entails sacrifice of the e-pawn. As we saw in the previous game, Torre-Maróczy, that can be effective, but here White's prospects for compensation are not as good.
Better was 9.a4, when the ♗b3 keeps Black's Knight off c4. True, Black can then force its exchange for a Knight, 9...♘d4 10.♘c3 ♗d7 11.♘f3 ♘×b3 12.c×b3, but the position is still even.

9...a4 10.♗c2 ♘c4 11.♘f3 ♕d5 12.0–0

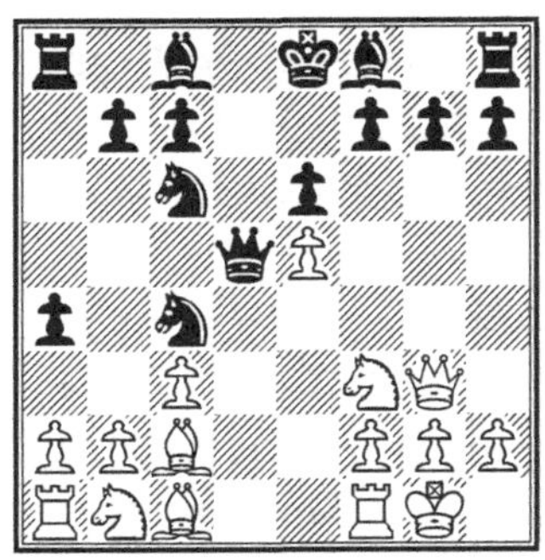

12...♘4×e5?
Wrong Knight! The correct capture was 12...♘6×e5 13.♘×e5 ♕×e5, when if 14.♗f4 ♕c5=.

13.♘×e5 ♕×e5
If 13...♘×e5 14.♖d1 ♕c5 (14...♕a5

15.♗f4 f6 16.♘d2 works out similarly) 15.♗e3 ♕a5 16.♗f4 f6 17.♘d2 ♗d7 18.b4 a×b3 19.♘×b3 ♕a3 20.♗×e5 f×e5 21.♕×e5 ± .

14.♗f4

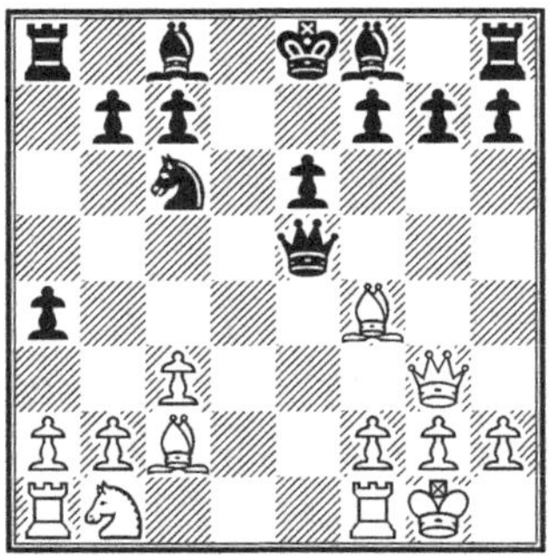

14...♕h5
Probably the best square for the Queen. If 14...♕b5 15.♗d3! and Black's Queen will be chased from pillar to post while White develops, *e.g.* 15...♕×b2? 16.♘d2 ♕×c3 17.♘c4 ♗c5 18.♖ac1 ♕f6 19.♗g5 ♕d4 20.♖fd1 ♕d5 21.♗b1 ♘d4□ 22.♔h1! and White has way more than ample compensation for his two pawns (+2.24/26).

15.♘a3?!
Better either 15.♖e1 f6 16.♗×c7 ± , or simply 15.♗×c7 ± . If the game was still in Showalter's home preparation, he clearly had not yet worked out all the bugs.

15...f6??
But neither had Torre! There was no need to prepare for advancing the e-pawn. Necessary and good was 15...e5! 16.♖fe1 and then 16...f6=.

The text is incomprehensible.

16.♗×c7 e5

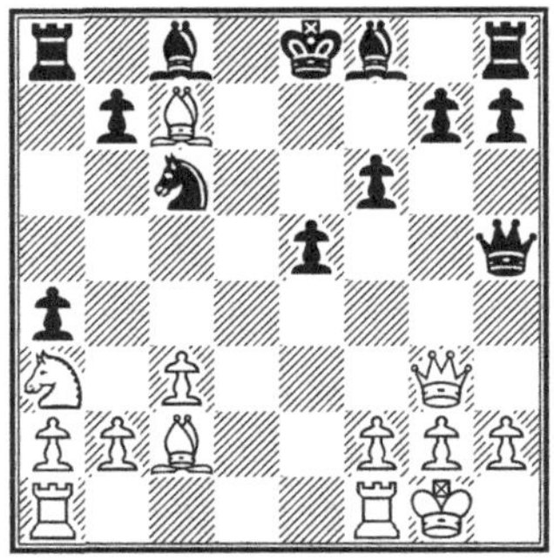

If there was ever a case of closing the church door after the Bishop had gone, this was it. White is now winning (+2.76/27).

17.♘c4
Sub-optimal. Best was 17.♘b5 (△18.♗b6+−) 17...♔f7□ 18.♗e4 ♗e6 19.♕d3 ♗e7 20.♗b6 f5 21.♗d5 etc. (+3.82/28).

17...♗f5
Best. If instead 17...♗e6 18.♘b6 ♖a7 19.♖ad1 ♗e7 20.♗d6 (+2.75/26).

18.♗×f5 ♕×f5

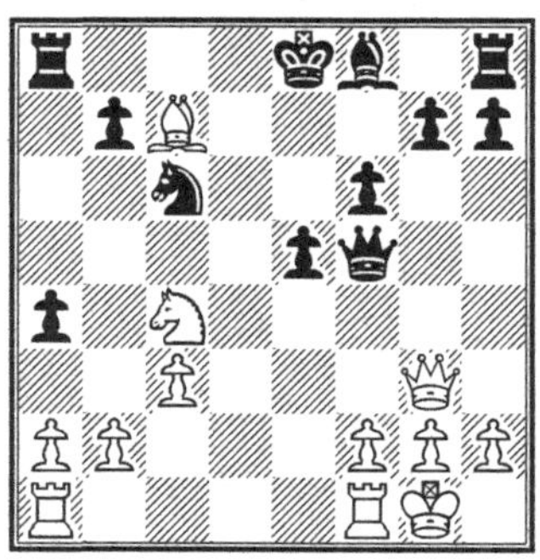

19.♘d6+?
White still had a decent advantage, but this throws it away.
Best was 19.♖ad1 and White should still win with correct play (+1.99/28). Also good was 19.♘b6 ♖a6 20.♖ad1 (+1.79/25).
The *WSZ* commented wryly "The sly fox Showalter believed he had lured his young opponent into a trap, and now made ready to spring it."

19...♗×d6 20.♕×g7??
Necessary was the prosaic 20.♗×d6 when a draw is likely.

20...♗f8!!□
This hard-to-foresee backward move wins a piece or traps the Queen.

21.♕×h8
If 21.♕g3 Black just banks his extra Knight.

21...♔f7
Says the *WSZ* "How great then was [Showalter's] astonishment when he realized he had trapped himself!"

22.h3 ♖e8 23.g4 ♕g6 24.♖ad1 ♗e7 25.♕×e8+ ♔×e8 0–1
The *ACB* commented "A lucky win for Torre, who was outplayed in the early part of the game."

Game 104

Torre-Marshall

Western Association Masters, Chicago 1926, round 11, 31 August

Semi-Slav Defense [D31]

This was the last of the eight tournament games between Torre and Marshall. The final total was +3 -1 =4 in favor of Torre. Marshall makes it easy for him here, trying a very ill-conceived opening experiment.

1.♘f3 d5 2.c4 c6 3.d4 e6 4.♘c3
Starting out as a Réti Opening, we have transposed to the Semi-Slav. Already this was a well-established line, first seen in Mason-Ware, Philadelphia 1876, and later played by Gunsberg, Chigorin, Showalter, and by Pillsbury from both sides, to name only a few early prominent names. The moves most frequently seen at this point have been 4...♘f6 (43% of the time), 4...d×c4 (34.6%), and 4...f5 (13.4%). Marshall chooses a very seldom played line.

4...♗b4
Only the second time this rare move had been tried. The first was Marshall-Chigorin, Barmen 1905 (0-1, 65). Perhaps that result prompted Marshall to try it here. Objectively it is dubious, and historically it has not done

well, White scoring +145 -51 =32 in 228 games on ChessBase.

5.♕b3

Probably best. Against Chigorin, Marshall tried 5.a3 ♗×c3+ 6.b×c3, ill-advisedly playing right into the Russian's well known preference for Knights over Bishops.

5...c5?

If the previous move was dubious, this is bad beyond doubt. Almost any other move that does not lose the Bishop was preferable.

6.c×d5! e×d5 7.d×c5! ♘c6

If 7...♗×c5 8.♕×d5 with already a virtually won game.

8.a3

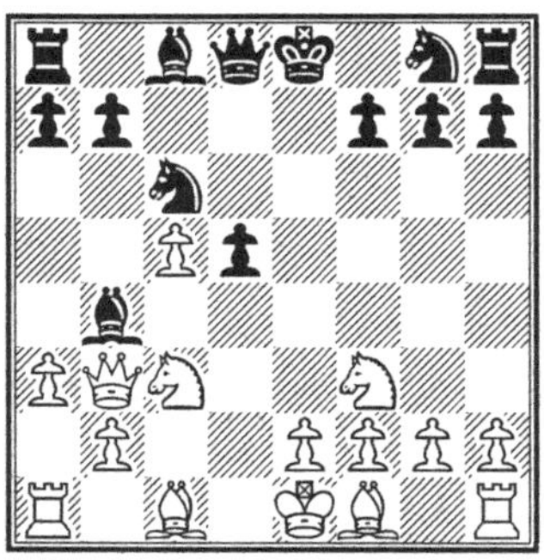

8...♗×c5

If 8...♗×c3+ 9.♕×c3 ♘f6 10.e3 0–0 11.b4 (+2.23/24).

9.♕×d5 ♕b6

Black has no compensation for his lost pawn, and must of course avoid exchanging Queens.

10.e3 ♘ge7?

Marshall just keeps digging a deeper hole. 10...♘f6 was much less unfavorable.

11.♕d1

11.♕d2 was a bit stronger (about +4.25), but this also wins.

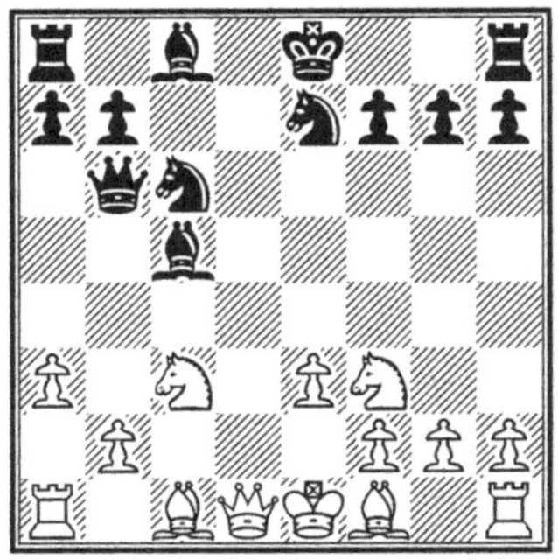

11...♕c7?

11...a5 12.♘a4 ♕a7 13.♕c2 ♗b6/♗d6 was the least evil, but evil it still was (+3.55/29). The text takes Stockfish's evaluation up past +6.00.

12.b4 ♘×b4

If 12...♗b6 13.♘b5 ♕d8 14.♘d6+ ♔f8 15.♗c4 (+6.69).

13.a×b4

13.♘b5! was also very strong, *e.g.* 13...♕b6 14.a×b4 ♗×b4+ 15.♗d2 ♗×d2+ 16.♕×d2 0–0 17.♗e2 (+6.50).

13...♗×b4 14.♕a4+ ♘c6 15.♗d2 0–0 16.♗b5

Besides having an extra piece, White now can finish his development very quickly and get all his forces to their best squares.

16...a5 17.0–0 ♖d8 18.♖fc1 ♗g4 19.♘d4

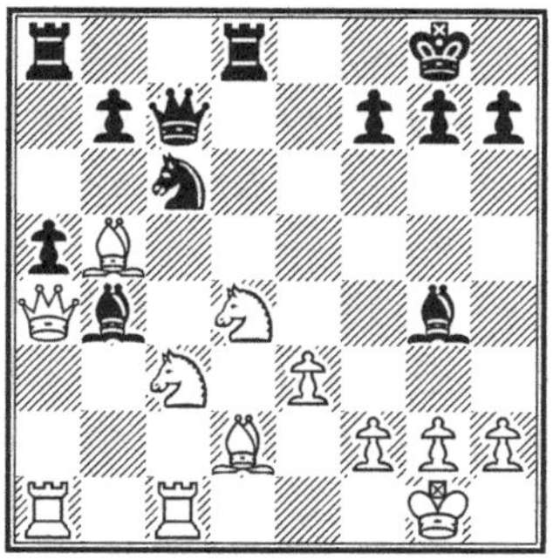

19...♕b6
If 19...♘×d4 20.e×d4 ♕e7 (if 20...♖×d4?? 21.♘e2) 21.♘d5! ♖×d5 22.♗×b4 etc. Marshall might well have resigned already, but he plays on, perhaps hoping for a swindle. Torre gives him no chance.

20.♗×c6 b×c6 21.♕×c6 ♕×c6 22.♘×c6 ♖×d2 23.♘×b4 ♖c8 24.♘bd5 ♔f8 25.♖×a5 ♗e6 26.♖ca1 f5 27.h3 g5 28.♖b1 h5 29.♖b6 ♗×d5 30.♖×d5 ♖×d5 31.♘×d5 ♔g7
The *ACB* remarked "Resignation is overdue."

32.♖f6 f4 33.e×f4 ♖d8 34.♖f5 g4 35.h×g4 h×g4 36.♖g5+ ♔h6 37.♘e3 1–0

Game 105

Isaacs-Torre

Western Association Masters, Chicago 1926, round 12, 1 September

Alekhine's Defense [B03]

Lewis J. Isaacs (1878-1967), a Lithuanian émigré, was one of Chicago's best players. In this event he was rather outclassed, losing nine times. Here he does extend Torre well into the endgame before succumbing, but along the way both players make enough mistakes to lose several times over.

1.e4 ♘f6 2.e5 ♘d5 3.c4 ♘b6 4.d4 d6 5.e×d6
For once we have a variation of Alekhine's Defense that was already well-established in 1926. See Game 69, Zubarev-Torre, for theoretical background.

5...c×d6
Varying from the Zubarev game, where Torre played 5...e×d6.
The text had recently been seen in Yates-Alekhine, Dresden 1926 (½-½, 37), and Yates-Takacs, Budapest 1926 (0-1,22).

6.♘f3
Finally breaking new ground. Yates had played 6.♗e3 in the two aforementioned games.

6...♕c7?

An experiment about as ill-advised as Marshall's in the previous game. This move, routine in a Sicilian, looks rather strange here; in fact we know of only one other example, Petryk-Motrenko, Sakharov Memorial, Kiev 2005 (1-0, 45). Stockfish does not like it, giving White an advantage of about +2.00 after 7.♘c3.

Normal here would be 6...♗g4, seen about 75% of the time, or 6...g6 at 21%.

7.b3

White's reply is equally unusual; the Queen's Bishop is seldom fianchettoed against Alekhine's Defense, usually going instead to e3. After Stockfish's preferred 7.♘c3, it looks like Black is in serious trouble, *viz.*:

(a) 7...g6 8.♗f4 ♗e6□ 9.♘b5 ♕c8 10.d5 ♗d7 11.♕d4 ♖g8□ 12.c5! dxc5 13.♕e4 (△14.♘d6+) 13...♗xb5 14.♗xb5+ ♘8d7 15.♘e5 g5 16.♕f5 ♖g7 17.♗xg5 +−;

(b) 7...♗g4 8.♗f4 e5 9.c5 ♘6d7 10.♘b5 ♕c6□ 11.cxd6 ♗xd6 12.♖c1 ♕e4+ 13.♗e2 0–0□ 14.♗g3 ♗b4+ 15.♔f1!□ exd4 16.h3 ♗h5□ 17.♘c7 ♘c6 18.♘xa8 ♖xa8 19.♘xd4 ♗xe2+ 20.♘xe2 and wins (+3.37/25).

Fortunately for Torre, Isaacs never seems to realize what an edge he had in the opening, and he continually fails to capitalize.

7...g6 8.♗b2 ♗g7 9.♘c3 0–0 10.♗e2 ♘8d7 11.0–0 ♘f6 12.h3 ♗d7 13.♕d2

13.d5 was definitely worth considering here (+1.82/25); it is much less effective by the time White gets around to it.

13...♖ad8 14.♖ae1?!

Again, 14.d5 was best, eyeing a potential ♘c3-b5-d4, or opening the d-file after ...e7-e6/e5.

14...♖fe8

And better here was 14...e6, to blunt a potential d4-d5.

15.♗d1?!

Missing his last chance to play d4-d5 with any effect.

15...e5! 16.d5 ♘h5

Intending 17...f5.

An alternative was 16...♘c8, intending ...♘c8-e7-f5; if 17.g4 to prevent that, then 17...a6 △18...b5 with queenside counterplay.

17.♔h2 f5

Stockfish endorses this kingside initiative. The one drawback is that Black cannot easily get his Queen's Knight involved.

18.g3

Something of a wasted move, as Black had no intention of moving his Knight to f4. Slightly better was 18.♘g5 ♘f6 (forced, else 19.♗×h5) 19.f4 h6 20.♘f3 e×f4 21.♕×f4±.

18...♖f8 19.♘g5 ♘f6 20.f4

This or 20.a4 is best.

20...e4?

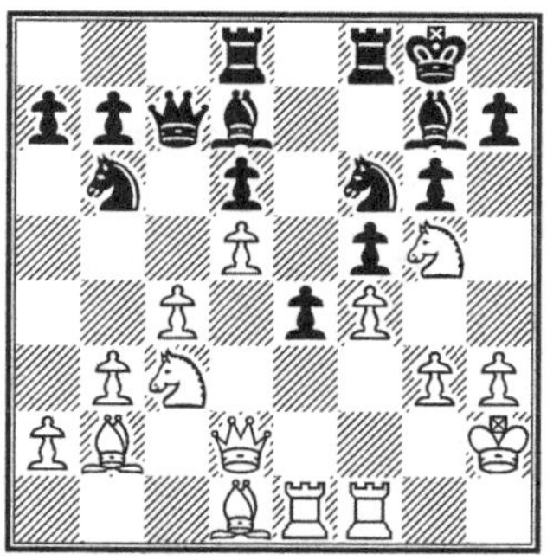

Torre's second major error (but by no means his last). Presumably intended to threaten trapping the ♘g5 by taking away f3 as a retreat, this is a serious mistake that could have lost the game. Best was 20...♖de8, when White stands better but not winning (+1.19/28 after 21.♗a3).

21.h4?

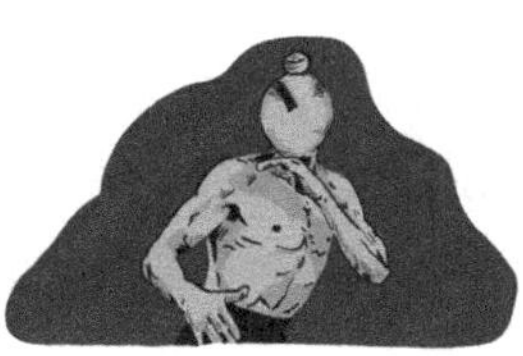

Isaacs, apparently fearing for his Knight, hastens to give it another retreat. Other than putting a piece *en prise*, he could hardly have found a worse move.

Instead he had a great chance, 21.g4!,

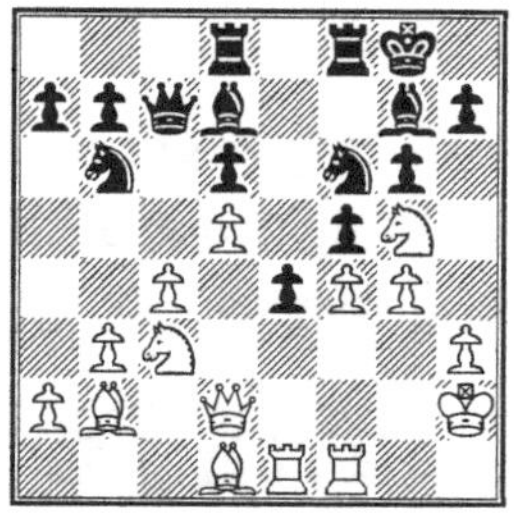

when suddenly the roof starts falling in on Black:

(a) 21...♖de8 22.g×f5 ♗×f5 23.♘b5 ♕e7 24.♘d4 ♗c8 25.a4 a5 26.♗f3 (+4.56/28);

(b) 21...h6 22.♘b5 ♕c8 23.♘e6! ♗×e6 24.d×e6 ♕×e6 25.♘d4 ♕d7 26.g×f5 g×f5 27.♖g1 △28.♕g2 with a ferocious attack (+5.69/33);

(c) If 21...a6, to prevent 22.♘b5, then 22.g×f5 ♗×f5 (22...g×f5?? 23.♖g1 is much worse) 23.♗c2 ♖de8 24.♘c×e4 ♗×e4 25.♗×e4 ♘×e4 26.♘×e4 ♗×b2 27.♕×b2 ♘d7 (27...♘c8?? 28.♘f6+) 28.♕a3 and Black's d-pawn falls and with it the game (+4.64/25).

All other defensive tries are worse.

As will be seen, in this game the players share a strange mirror-image form of chess blindness: they keep missing strong Knight's pawn advances, White on one wing, Black on the other.

Returning to the game (**21.h4?**):

21...h6
The game is now even.

22.♘h3 ♖fe8 23.♔g2?!
A future g3-g4 was still not out of the question for White, so why put the King where he blocks the g-file?

23...♖c8 24.♖e3 ♘a8
Getting the Knight out of the way of the queenside pawns.

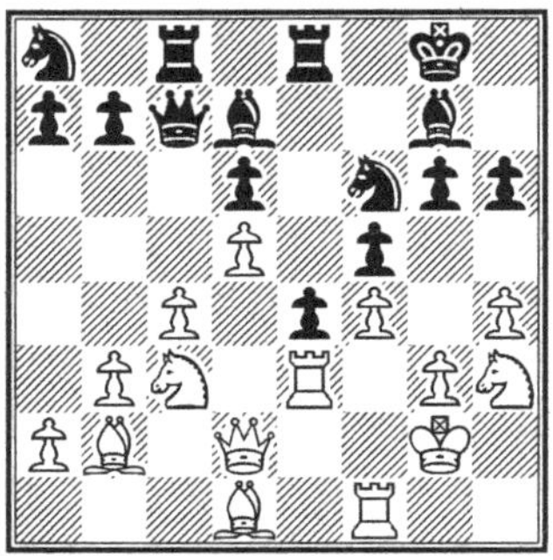

25.♖fe1?
White's second serious error. Correct again was 25.g4. While it would have none of the impact as at move 21, White would be OK after 25...f×g4□ 26.♘f2 ♕a5 (if 26...♗f5? 27.♖fe1 and ♘c3×e4± very soon) 27.♗c1 b5 28.♘c×e4 ♕×d2 29.♗×d2 b×c4 30.♘×f6+ ♗×f6 31.♘×g4=.
Also, after 25.g4, 25...b5 could be answered by 26.g5 h×g5 27.f×g5 ♘h7 28.h5 with a strong attack brewing again.

25...a6?
As in the Showalter game, Torre makes an unnecessary preparatory move before a desired pawn advance, and thereby misses a shot: 25...b5! 26.c×b5 ♘b6:

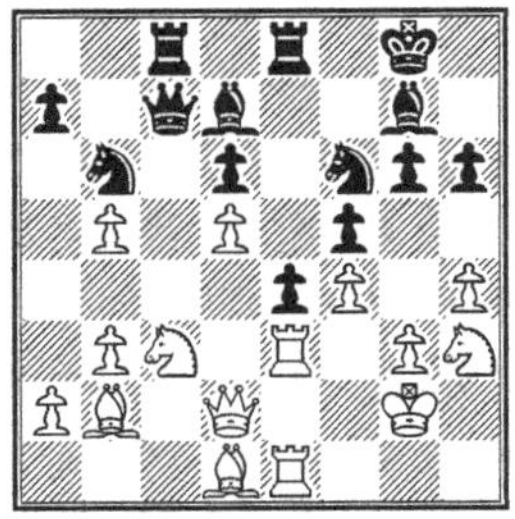

Now if 27.a4? ♕b7 28.♔h2 ♘b×d5 29.♘×d5 ♕×d5 30.♕g2 ♕c5 and Black's passed e- and d-pawns will be a major force (-2.93/24).
If 27.g4 f×g4 28.♘f2 ♗f5 29.♘c×e4 ♘×e4

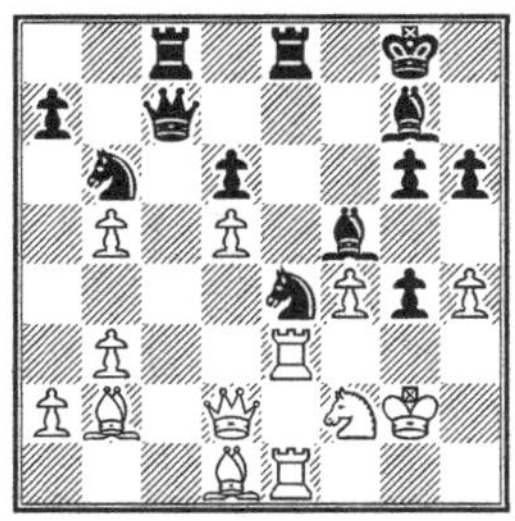

30.♖×e4 [if 30.♘×e4?? ♗×b2 31.♕×b2 ♘×d5 32.♘f6+ ♘×f6 33.♕×f6 ♕b7+ 34.♔h2 (or 34.♔g1 ♕b6 35.♔f2 ♖c1−+; if 34.♔f2 ♕b6 △35...g3+) 34...g3+ 35.♔×g3 ♖×e3+ 36.♖×e3 ♕h1−+] 30...♗×e4+ 31.♘×e4 ♗×b2 32.♕×b2 ♘×d5 33.♕d2 ♕f7 -3.38/35.

Returning to the game (**25...a6?**):

26.a4?
This not only misses an opportunity, but risks losing.
Instead, 26.g4! now would be quite strong again, *viz.*

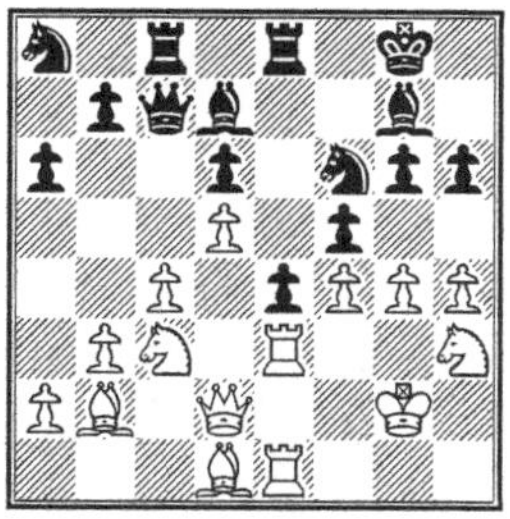

(a) 26...b5 27.g5 h×g5 28.f×g5 ♘h7 [if 28...♘h5? 29.♗×h5 g×h5 30.♘f4 (+5.23), or 28...♘g4?? 29.♗×g4 f×g4 30.♘f2 (+7.24)] 29.h5 and Black's kingside is caving in (+2.19/25);
(b) 26...f×g4 27.♘f2 ♕a5 28.♗c1 ♘h5 29.♘c×e4 ♘×f4+ 30.♔g1 ♕×d2 31.♗×d2 h5 (31...♗e5?? 32.♘×g4 ♗×g4 33.♗×g4 ♖cd8 34.♘×d6!) 32.♘×d6 ♖×e3 33.♗×e3 ♖f8 34.♘fe4 with a dominating position for White (+2.74/26).

26...♕c5?

And as in the Maróczy game, Torre just keeps matching his opponent mistake for mistake.
Again, 26...b5! was the move. If then:

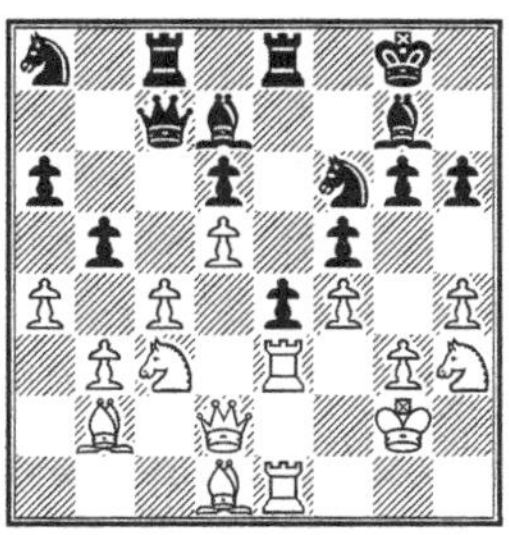

(a) 27.g4? f×g4 28.♘f2 b×c4 29.♘f×e4 ♖×e4! 30.♖×e4 (if 30.♘×e4? ♘×e4 31.♖×e4 c3–+) 30...♘×e4 31.♖×e4 c×b3 (-2.70/23);
(b) 27.c×b5 a×b5 28.a×b5 ♘b6 29.g4 ♕c5 30.g5 ♘f×d5 31.♘×d5 ♕×d5 32.♕f2 ♗×b2 33.♕×b2 h5 (-2.95/26);
(c) 27.a×b5 (least evil) 27...a×b5 28.♘×b5 ♗×b5 29.c×b5 ♕c5 30.b4 ♕×b5 and Black will soon also pick up the d-pawn (-1.96/24).

27.♘b1?

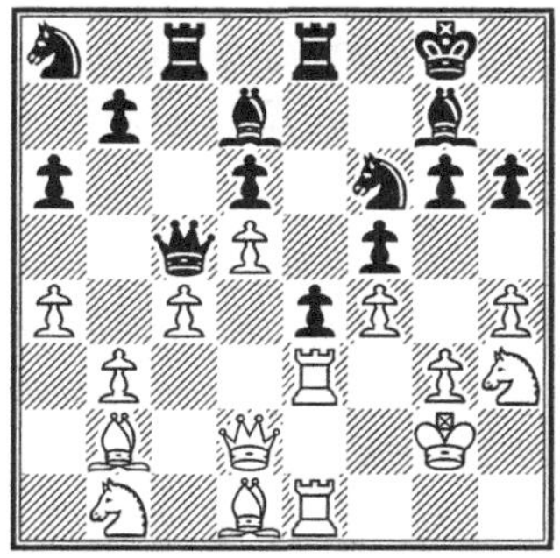

What a march of folly: five bad moves in a row, three by White, two by Black. 27.g4 was still best and very likely winning, *viz.* 27...b5 28.g5 h×g5 29.f×g5 ♘h7 30.h5 and:

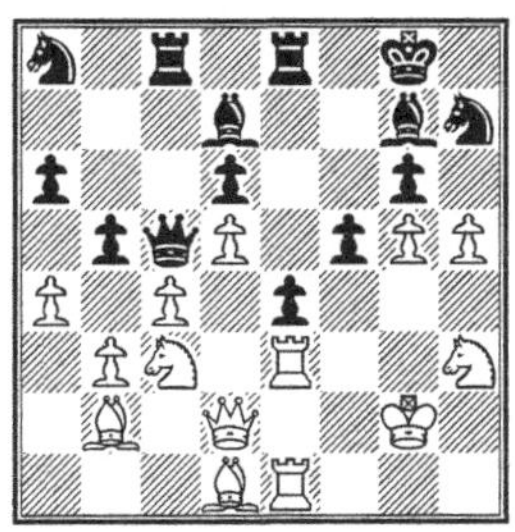

(a) 30...b×c4 31.h×g6 ♘f8 32.♘f4 ♘b6 33.♘h5 ♖e5 34.♘f6+ ♗×f6 35.g×f6 f4 (35...♘×g6?? 36.♖g3+–) 36.♖×e4 ♘×g6 37.♖×e5 d×e5 (37...♘×e5?? 38.♕×f4+–) 38.a5 (+4.16/24);
(b) 30...g×h5 31.♘f4 b×c4 (31...♘×g5?? 32.♖g3) 32.♘×h5 ♕d4□ 33.♕f2 ♖e7 34.g6 ♘f8 35.♘×g7 ♖×g7 36.♘×e4!

♖×g6+ 37.♔f1 c3 38.♗×c3 ♖×c3 39.♘×c3 (+4.72/27);
(c) 30...♗e5 31.♕f2 g×h5 32.♘f4 b4 33.♘a2 ♖e7 [if 33...♘c7 34.♗×h5 ♖e7 35.♘g6 ♖g7 36.♘×e5 d×e5 37.♗×e5 ♖×g5+ 38.♖g3 ♕×f2+ 39.♔×f2 ♖×g3 40.♔×g3 (+6.40/27)] 34.♘×h5 ♗×b2 35.♕×b2 (+6.65).

Returning to the actual game from the previous diagram (**27.♘b1?**):

27...b5
Finally Torre finds the right move, but it is only good for equality now, or at best a small advantage.

28.♗d4 ♕c7

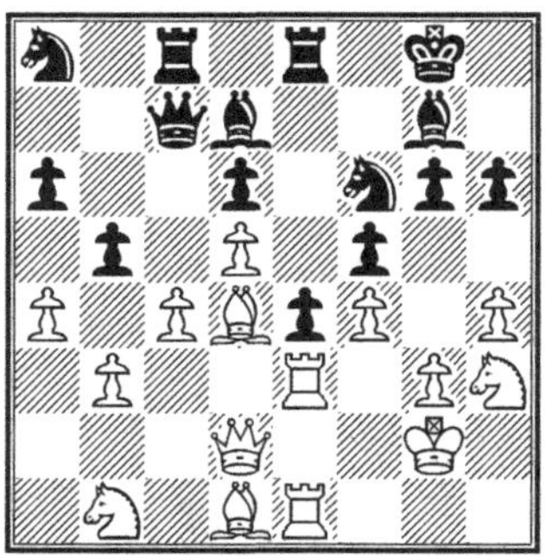

29.a×b5?!
This just helps to open lines for Black on the queenside, where he has massed most of his forces.
Better 29.♘a3, when if 29...b×a4 30.b4 ♘b6 31.♗e2 (-0.26/26), or 29... b×c4 30.♘×c4 ♘×d5 31.♗×g7 ♘×e3+ 32.♖×e3 ♔×g7 33.♘×d6 ♖cd8 34.♖c3 ♕b8 35.♘×e8+ ♗×e8 36.♕b2 ♔g8 with near-equality (-0.39/26).

29...a×b5 30.♕b2 ♖f8 31.♘d2?!
Better 31.♘a3 or 31.♗e2.

31...♘b6 32.♗e2

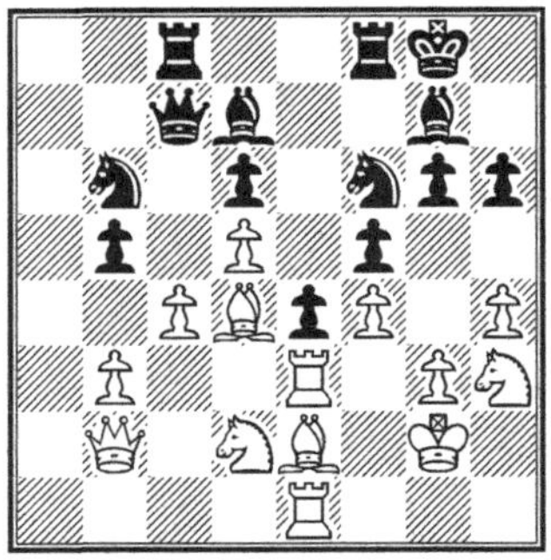

32...b×c4?!
32...♖b8!, with a veiled threat to White's Queen, would have been very hard to meet:
(a) 33.♖c1 b×c4 34.b×c4 ♘g4 35.♗×g7 ♘×e3+ 36.♔g1 ♘b×d5 37.♕d4 ♖f7 38.♗×h6 ♕b6 39.♕×b6 ♘×b6 and Black is safely up the Exchange;
(b) 33.♕a1 ♖a8 34.♕b2 b×c4 35.b×c4 ♘a4 36.♕a1□ ♕a5 37.♖d1 ♘c5 38.♕×a5 ♖×a5 39.♘b3 ♖a2 40.♗×c5 d×c5 41.♘f2 (41.♘×c5?? ♘g4–+) 41...♗a4 42.♖b1;
(c) Relatively best would probably be 33.♔g1 b×c4 34.b×c4 (if 34.♗×c4? ♘×c4 35.♘×c4 ♗b5 36.♖c1 ♘×d5–+) 34...♘b×d5 35.♖b3 ♖×b3 36.♘×b3 ♘e7 (-1.60/24).
The text once again makes it an even game.

33.b×c4 ♘a4 34.♕a1 ♖b8 35.♘f2 ♘e8
Exchanges favor Black, due to his superior pawn structure and protected

passed pawn. In fact, if now only Kings and pawns remained, Black would win easily. But we are a long way from that situation.

36.♗×g7 ♘×g7 37.♖a3 ♕a5?!
This just helps White bring his Knight to a good square. Better 37...♘c5=.

38.♘b3 ♕b4 39.♘d4 ♖fc8 40.♘b5?
Having just gotten this Knight to its best possible square, Isaacs discards it like a used Kleenex. Much better was 40.♖b3, 40.♖c1, or 40.♖d1.

40...♗×b5 41.c×b5

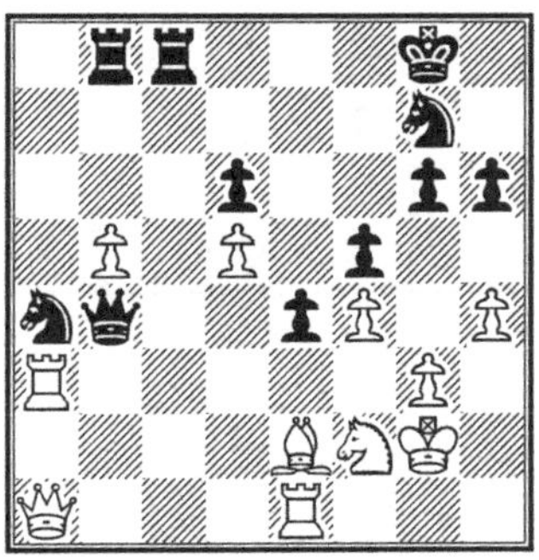

41...♘b6?
Torre misses another chance: 41...♘c3! and 42.b6 ♖c5 43.♖a7 ♕×b6−+, or 42.♖a5? ♕d4 43.♘d1 ♘×e2 44.♖×e2 and Black wins with either 44...♕d3 or 44...♕×a1 45.♖×a1 ♖×b5.
But now the game is yet again even.

42.♖a7 ♕c3 43.♖c1?!
White had little choice but to exchange Queens, but the right way to do it was 43.♕×c3 ♖×c3 44.♘d1 ♖c5 45.♘e3=.

43...♕×a1 44.♖a×a1?
And now a Wrong Rook recapture. Correct was 44.♖c×a1 and White stands only slightly worse (-0.44/28).

44...♘e8?!
But what's this? 44...♘×d5 was straightforward and strong. If then 45.♗c4, thinking to pin and win the Knight, there comes 45...♖×c4 46.♖×c4 ♘e3+.

45.♖c6?!
Best was 45.♘d1 and after 45...♘×d5 White can play 46.♗c4! because e3 is now covered. The best Black would have is 45...♖×c1 46.♖×c1 h5 47.♖c6 when a draw seems likely (-0.52/30).

45...♔f8

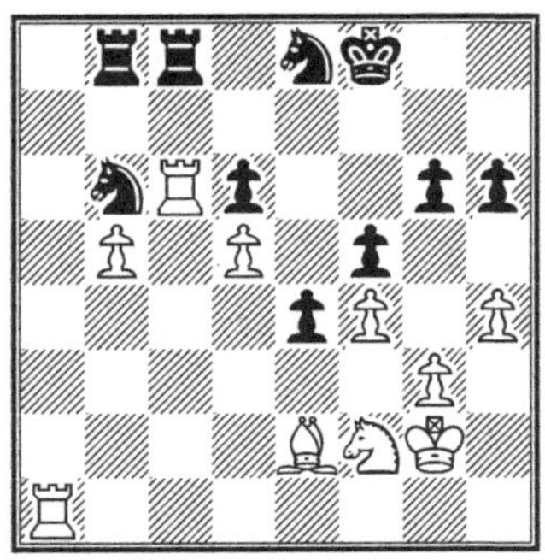

46.♖ac1?
Correct was 46.h5 when after either 46...g×h5 47.♗×h5, or 46...♘×d5 47.♖×c8 ♖×c8 48.h×g6 White is not too bad off (about -0.50). And if 46...g5 47.f×g5 h×g5 he may even be slightly better (+0.82/27).

46...♖d8! 47.h5
One move too late for this.

47...g×h5 48.♗×h5 ♘f6

Definitely second best. Much better was 48...♘×d5.

49.♗e2 ♘f×d5 50.♖a1?

This restores to Black the degree of advantage he had before his inferior 48th move.

Correct was 50.♘d1, and if 50...♘e7 51.♘e3! ♘×c6 52.b×c6 ♖a8 53.♖b1 ♘a4 54.♖b7=.

50...♘e7! 51.♖c7 ♘bd5! 52.♖cc1

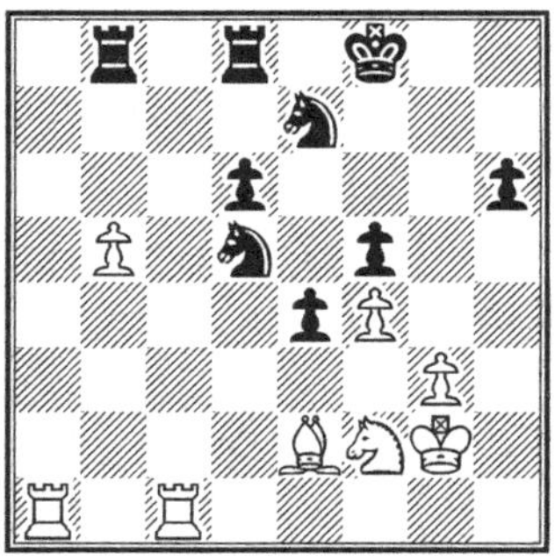

52...♖dc8

Another distantly second-best move. Stronger was 52...♘e3+ 53.♔h3 ♘7d5, and if 54.♖c6 then 54...♖b6 55.♖×b6 ♘×b6, blockading White's passed pawn, and preparing to push the d-pawn.

53.♘d1

Better first 53.♖×c8+ ♖×c8 and then 54.♘d1.

53...♖×c1 54.♖×c1 ♖a8 55.♔f2 ♖a2 56.♖b1 ♘c8?!

This jeopardizes Black's winning chances. Best was 56...♘b6.

57.♖c1?

Now Black is on top again. After 57.♖b2! the Lidless Eye sees little chance of Black winning (-0.85/31).

57...♘cb6! 58.♖c6 ♔e7 59.♘e3?

This makes it all the easier for Black. Better 59.♔f1.

59...♘×e3 60.♖×b6 ♘d1+ 61.♔e1 ♘c3 62.♖b7+ ♔d8! 63.♗c4 ♖b2 64.b6 e3

This or 64...d5 are both very strong.

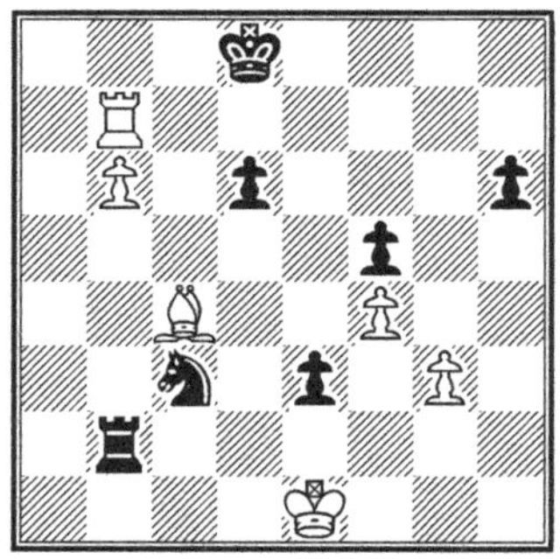

65.♗d3??

White caps all his errors with a final blunder, though it hardly matters.

Less egregious was 65.♖b8+ ♔d7 66.♗d3, when if 66...♖d2? 67.♗×f5+=. But Black still wins with 66...♖h2 67.♖b7+ ♔e6 68.♔f1 e2+ 69.♗×e2 ♘×e2 etc.

65...♖d2!

Threatening 66...♖×d3 and 66...♖d1#. Stockfish announces mate in 19 at most.

66.♖b8+ ♔e7 67.♔f1 ♖×d3 68.b7 ♖d1+ 69.♔g2 ♖b1 0-1

Torre now entered the 13th and final round a half-point ahead of the field. His opponent was to be the German-born naturalized American master Edward Lasker, a very good player (historical Elo 2470), but who at the moment had a minus score and who in his previous two serious tournaments (New York 1924 and Lake Hopatcong 1926) had finished 10th of 11 and 4th of 4, respectively, with a combined score of +3 -15 =10. These indications, and the fact that Torre would play White, all seemed to presage at worst a draw for Torre and thus shared or even clear first.

As the game progressed, however, it became clear that Torre was not at his best. He chose the Réti Opening, a line in which he had no special expertise. He blundered at move 8, and could have lost a piece, but Lasker failed to capitalize. That kept the game even, until an error by Black at move 16 let Torre get the upper hand. But he let his advantage gradually slip away, and then at move 25 he made a serious miscalculation that gave Black a won game. Still, Lasker seemed to be in almost as much of a funk as Torre. The two mixed good and bad moves, reaching a theoretically drawn position in an ending of ♗+♘+5♙-vs-♖+4♙. Finally, at move 37 Torre made an irrecoverable error, and turned over his King after move 48.

That Torre lost has prompted certain questionable explanations. According to Reuben Fine, Torre had been promised career support by the Mexican government. Hooper and Whyld, in *The Oxford Companion to Chess*, were even more specific, saying a position teaching chess at the National University of Mexico was to be his. Furthermore, they say that just before the final round at Chicago that day, he received two letters. One informed him that the teaching offer was rescinded, and the other that his fiancée had married another man. Under these twin blows, so the story goes, a crestfallen and broken-hearted Torre could not play his best, and so lost. (Though it bears mentioning that Torre's play was no worse than in several other games of the tournament.)

A compellingly romantic plot-line, that would play well in a paperback novel. Such in fact may literally be its source: the above paragraph mirrors the plot of the aforementioned "historical novel" *El Aguila Caída* (*The Fallen Eagle*) by Filiberto Terrazas, which is loosely based on Torre's life. Its details are questionable. That Torre was esteemed by his countrymen would not necessarily translate into financial support. Mexico in 1926 was not the USSR, and government support for even its best chess player, along the lines of Cuba's for Capablanca, was improbable at best (for a boxer or bullfighter perhaps, but not a chess player). Furthermore, Torre had little or no romantic involvement with women throughout his life.

Kingston later researched the matter further, and reported his findings to historian Edward Winter, who published them in *Chess Notes*, item #5767, in September 2008.[1] Here is that item in full:

> In 1999, I worked with Gabriel Velasco on an English version of his book *Vida y Partidas de Carlos Torre* (Mexico City, 1993). It was published as *The Life and Games of Carlos Torre* (Milford, 2000). In my role as translator/editor I naturally compared Velasco's work with other sources, including the entry on Torre in *The Oxford Companion to Chess*. I first noticed a minor error in *The Oxford Companion*'s account: the 1926 Chicago tournament at which the episode of the letters supposedly occurred was not the "Western championship." The tournament in which Torre played Edward Lasker was the Chicago Masters. See page 111 of the September-October 1926 *American Chess Bulletin*.
>
> A more significant difference was that *The Companion*'s tale of the emotionally painful letters which Torre supposedly received before his game with Lasker was conspicuously absent from Velasco's account. When I asked him about this, he expressed the opinion that the letters never existed. He pointed to two big improbabilities: one, that the Mexican government would offer financial support to a chessplayer, and two, that Torre, who was not noted for romantic involvement with women, would have been engaged.
>
> Velasco also pointed out that Filiberto Terrazas' novel *El Aguila Caída*, written in 1962 and based on Torre's life, featured the letters story prominently. Velasco regarded that book as more fiction than biography, and the episode of the letters as just one of its romantic embellishments. And I was struck by the fact that Terrazas' tale of heartbreak closely mirrored another fictionalized biography, Frances Parkinson Keyes' *The Chess Players* (1960), based on the life of Paul Morphy, in which a refused marriage proposal contributes to Morphy's withdrawal from chess. Therefore, before the discussion of the Torre v Lasker game in *The Life and Games of Carlos Torre* we added a passage highly skeptical of the letters' existence (see page 281).
>
> It is perhaps a pity that Velasco did not ask Torre about all this in his 1977 interview, but there is Torre's statement, "After the tournament in Chicago, in 1926, my health was shattered due to dietary difficulties. In fact, I suffered a nervous breakdown." (See page 292 of *The Life and Games of Carlos Torre*.)
>
> I asked Kenneth Whyld what sources he had used for the Torre

1 See https://www.chesshistory.com/winter/winter50.html.

entry in *The Companion*. At first he was unable to supply specifics, saying that some 20 different sources were consulted, some contradictory, and that it was a perennial problem for an encyclopedist to know which to believe. In further correspondence, however, he mentioned a source that not only referred to the letters but even gave a name to the supposed faithless fiancée: Susanna. The writer of this information? Gabriel Velasco himself.

What happened is this: Velasco began working on his Torre book in the 1970s. He consulted Whyld at that time about the possibility of an English edition, even sending him the manuscript. At that early point in his research, Velasco believed Terrazas' story of the letters and the jilting fiancée, and had treated them as fact in his MS. Whyld then took this as an authoritative source. By the time *The Companion* was published, Velasco and Whyld were no longer corresponding, so Whyld never learned of Velasco's change of mind until I contacted him in 1999.

I have confirmed all this recently with Velasco. On 18 September 2008 he wrote to me:

"I consider the *Oxford Companion* account false, in view of the testimony which was told direct to me by the late dean of chess in Mexico, Alejandro Báez Graybelt, who was the most reliable source for everything concerning Torre's life. Señor Báez assured me that the story was merely an invention, or, as you called it once, 'a story typical of a paperback novel.' What is true, of course, is that Torre suffered a nervous breakdown, returned to Mexico at the end of the year, took an ill-paid job in a drug-store, and played no more serious chess."

Now on to the Torre-Lasker game.

Game 106

Torre-Lasker

Western Association Masters, Chicago 1926, round 13, 2 September

Réti Opening [A09]

Edward Lasker (born 1885 in Kempen, Prussia (now Kępno, Poland), died 1981 in New York; IM title 1963, historical Elo 2470), had been playing high-level tournament chess since 1908. In 1914 he emigrated to the United States, and became one of America's top players, winning five US Opens 1916-1921, and eventually playing a US Championship match with Marshall in 1923, losing narrowly +4 -5 =9. At the legendary New York 1924 tournament he finished 10th of 11, but played well against many of the greats, for example a 103-move draw against Emanuel Lasker (to whom he was distantly related). An engineer by profession, he invented a mechanical breast pump which is credited with saving the lives of many premature infants. He played tournament chess well into the 1950s, and authored several fine books, from one of which, *Chess for Fun and Chess for Blood* (1942), we take many of the annotations below.

It bears mentioning that this may have been the second encounter for these two; ChessBase purports to have a Torre-Ed. Lasker game from November 1921 in New Orleans, which the latter won in 41 moves. Torre would have been just 17.

1.♘f3 d5 2.c4 d×c4 3.♘a3

In the *ACB*, C.S. Howell called this "unnatural looking ... a hyper-modern product." Yet it already had a high-level track record, appearing in Réti-Janowski, New York 1924 (1-0, 43), Euwe-Spielmann, Wiesbaden 1925 (½-½, 56), Müller-Bergman, Breslau 1925 (0-1, 24), Tartakower-Spielmann, Moscow 1925 (1-0, 26), Réti-Nimzovich, Semmering 1926 (0-1, 69), and Réti-Havasi, Budapest 1926 (1-0, 35).

3...e5

Howell said "We do not recall having seen this before. It seems to be rather a good counter." Lasker wrote "I wanted to avoid a closed game and preferred to test a new line of play which had been introduced by Spielmann [at Moscow 1925] ... I did not consider it likely that [Torre] would have expected this defense and presumed that he had rather planned and studied other variations in preparation for this game." The Russian theoretician Mark Taimanov recommends 3...c5 4.♘×c4 ♘c6 5.b3 f6 6.♗b2 e5=.

4.♘×e5

The best and most common reply. Less good are 4.♕a4+ ♗d7 5.♕c2 ♗×a3 6.b×a3, or 4.♘×c4 e4!.

4...♗×a3 5.♕a4+
Not 5.b×a3?? ♕d4−+.

5...b5 6.♕×a3
If 6.♕×b5+?? c6.

6...♗b7 7.b3
Better 7.♕g3 ♕f6 (else 8.♕×g7) 8.b3 with good prospects for White (+1.20/26).
The text allows Black to force either an awkward white retreat or the exchange of Queens.

7...♕d6!

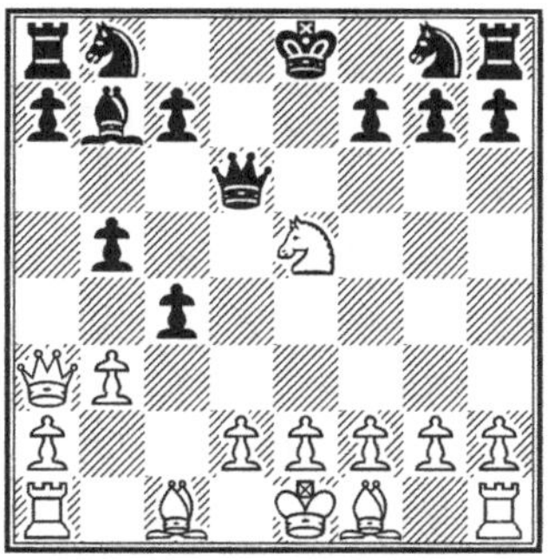

8.♗b2??
This is either an attempted trap, or simply a blunder. Lasker says Torre thought for almost ten minutes here, which would seem to rule out error due to haste. Black can now play 8...c3, winning a piece for two pawns.
White had four playable moves: 8.♕×d6, 8.♘f3, 8.♕b2, or 8.f4, after each of which he stands slightly better.

8...f6?
But Lasker misses his chance. He writes that 8...c3, suggested later by Marshall, "never occurred to me." Yet he adds "But I am not sure whether it was not just what Torre had hoped I would play ... Perhaps White had seen the move and thought he would have obtained a very dangerous attack with 9.d×c3 ♕×e5 10.c4 ♕g5 11.h4 ♕h6 12.♖h3 followed by ♖h3-e3 and ♕a3-c5. However, 10...♕e7 would have refuted this line of play. I did not consider 8...c3 in the game at all, but thought only of getting my pieces developed as fast as possible."

9.♕×d6
Arguably better was 9.♘f3, and if 9...b4 10.♕a4+ ♗c6 11.♕a5 c×b3 12.a×b3±, while if 9...♕×a3 10.♗×a3 Black's castling is hindered.

9...c×d6 10.♘f3

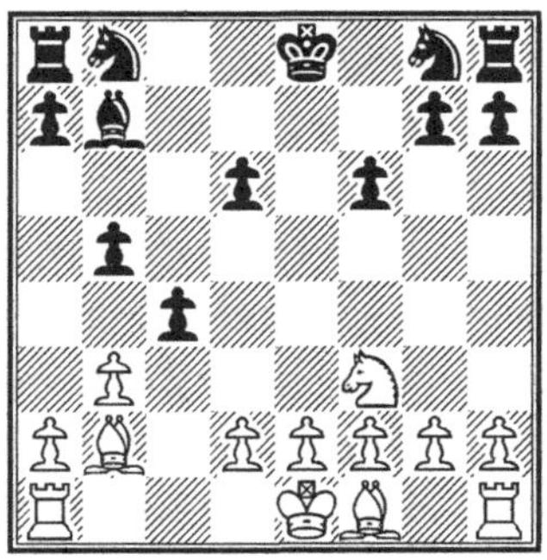

10...c×b3
Lasker notes "If in this position I had played the obvious move 10...♘d7 ... I would have run into trouble through 11.♘d4 a6 12.b×c4 b×c4 13.♘f5." Trouble indeed: Stockfish pegs that at about +6.60.

11.♘d4! a6?!

The lesser evil was 11...b×a2 12.♘×b5 ♔d7□ 13.♖×a2 a6 14.♘d4±.

12.a×b3 ♔d7 13.♘f5

Not bad, but best was 13.f3!?, blocking the action of Black's Bishop. Likely then is 13...♘e7 14.g3! ♘bc6 15.♗h3+ ♔e8 16.♔f2, when White's Bishops are both well posted, his Rooks soon will be, and he has potentially dominant center pawns to advance (+1.73/26).

13...g6

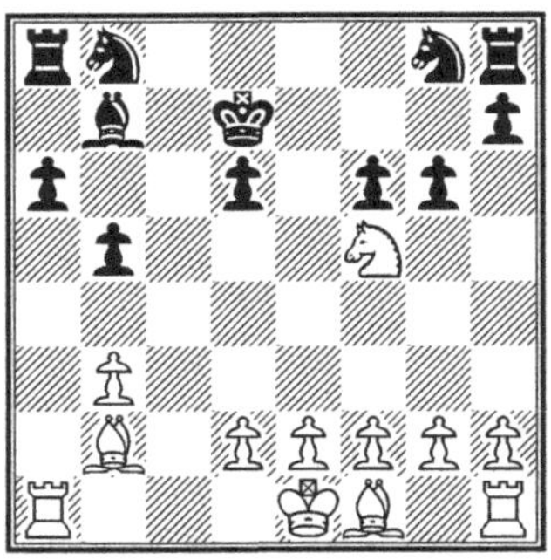

Lasker writes "we must come to the conclusion that the white army is not in very good condition. White's King's wing is still sadly undeveloped, and as long as I control the long diagonal with my Bishop White will have to resort to complicated maneuvers to get his King's Bishop out. To develop my own King's wing I need only place my King on e6 or e7, protecting my f-pawn." Stockfish does not quite agree, pegging the position at +1.00/29.
However, Lasker's comments do highlight the reasons why the previous note's line was better for White.

14.♘e3 ♔e6 15.♖c1

Lasker says "Threatening to invade the seventh rank, the heaven of Rooks." Stockfish still thinks 15.f3 was better, or perhaps the unorthodox 15.h4 h5 16.♖h3.

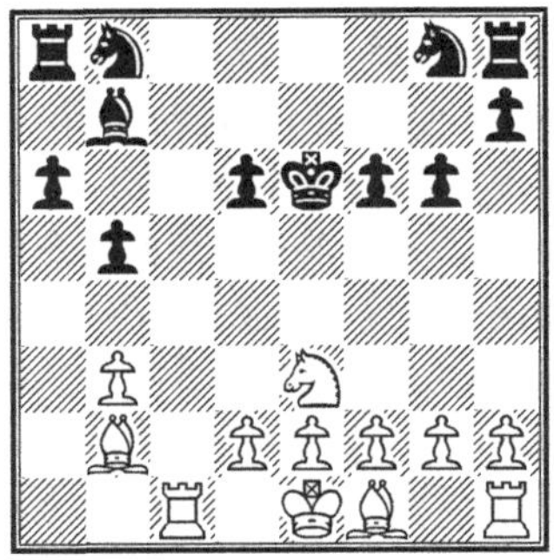

15...♘c6?

Lasker, belatedly realizing this was a mistake, writes "This gives White the opportunity for which he has been praying, to develop his King's Bishop and connect his Rooks through castling. I should have kept my Bishop unobstructed by playing 15...♘d7. There was no harm in letting White's Rook reach c7 because White could not maintain him there, due to the inability of his King's Rook to reach the c-file. After 15...♘d7 16.♖c7 ♖b8 17.f3 ♘e7 18.g3 ♖hc8 19.♗h3+ f5 20.♖×c8 ♖×c8 21.♔f2 White's King's Bishop would still have been out of play for quite a while, and I could have kept control of the c-file with 21...♘c5

22.b4 ♘b3." Stockfish has a few bones to pick with Lasker's analysis. Better than 17.f3 is 17.♗d4!,

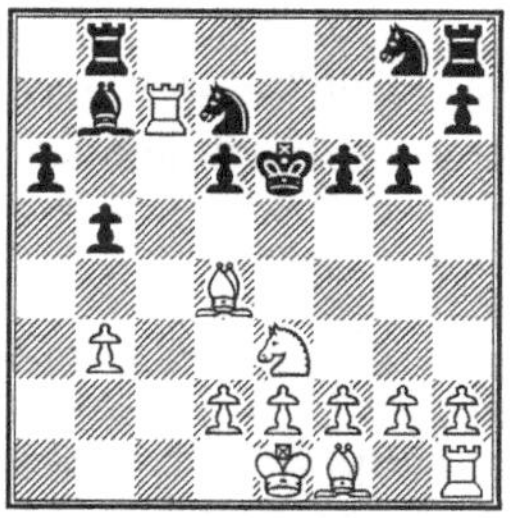

threatening 18.♗a7 and forcing 17...♗a8, when White can play 18.g3! ♗×h1 19.♗h3+ f5□ 20.♗×h8 ♘e7 21.♗b2 and he's in good shape (+0.95/25). Better than 21.♔f2 is 21.g4!,

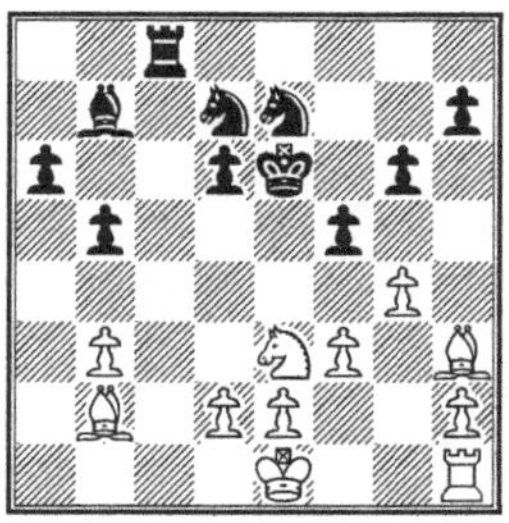

forcing 21...f4 22.g5+ ♘f5 23.♘g2 ♖c2 24.♘×f4+ ♔f7 25.♘d3 and again White is in even better shape (+1.55/27) and the "quite a while" his King's Bishop was supposed to be out of play has proven quite short. Finally, at Black's 22nd move,

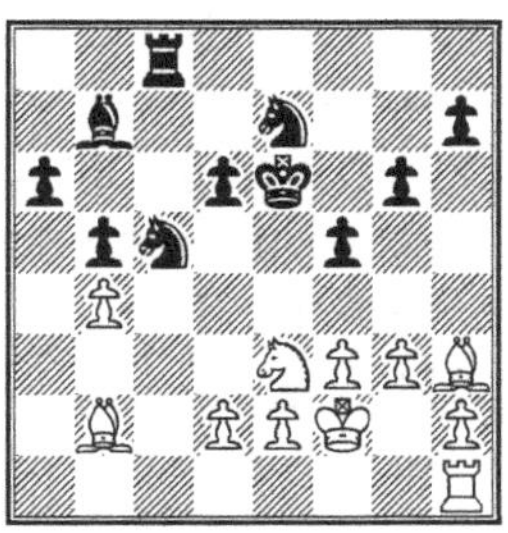

22...♘a4 is correct, with an even game after any reasonable move by the ♗b2. Lasker's 22...♘b3? loses a pawn, *viz.* 23.♗c3 d5 24.♖b1 d4 25.♖×b3 d×c3 26.♖×c3.

16.g3

Much stronger here, perhaps even winning, was 16.g4,

threatening 17.g5+−. Likely lines then are:

(a) 16...♘b4 17.♖g1 ♖c8 18.♖×c8 ♗×c8 19.g5 ♔f7 20.♖g3 (+2.51/28);

(b) 16...♘a5 17.♖g1 ♖c8 (not 17...♘×b3?? 18.♖c7 ♖b8 19.g5+−) 18.♖×c8 ♗×c8 19.b4 ♘c6 20.g5 ♔f7 21.♘d5 ♗e6 22.♘c7 ♘×b4 23.♘×e6 ♔×e6 24.♗h3+ ♔f7 25.♖g4 ♘c6 26.♖e4 (+4.17/35);

(c) 16...h6 17.f4 ♘ge7 [if 17...♘a5? 18.♖c7! ♘e7 (not 18...♗×h1?? 19.f5+ g×f5 20.g×f5#) 19.f5+ g×f5 20.g×f5+ ♔f7 21.♖g1 (+4.38/25)] 18.♗g2 ♖hc8 19.f5+ g×f5 20.g×f5+ ♔f7 (if 20...♘×f5?? 21.♘×f5 ♔×f5 22.0–0+ ♔e6 23.♖×f6++−) 21.♗f3 ♘d8 22.♗h5+ ♔f8 23.0–0 (+2.53/25).

The text retains some advantage for White, but a much smaller one.

16...♘ge7 17.♗h3+ ♔f7 18.0–0

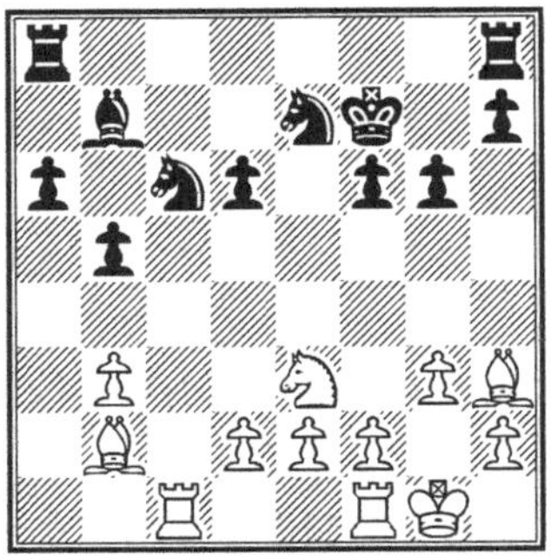

18...h5
Lasker: "The object of this move was to restrict the mobility of White's Knight. Had I played 18...♖hd8 immediately, White might have annoyed me with 19.♘g4 f5 20.♘h6+ ♔f8 21.♗f6 ♖dc8 22.e4." Stockfish does not think much of that variation, and considers 19.f4 best after 18...♖hd8.

19.♖c2?!
It was natural for Torre to want to double Rooks, but a much better way was 19.d4 d5□ 20.♖c5 ♖hd8 21.♖fc1.

19...♖hd8
Lasker writes "White has now temporarily obtained control of the c-file. My aim will naturally be to oppose my Rooks in that file and then to take advantage of my extra pawn on the Queen's wing and of the weakness of White's b-pawn. I thought White could do very little to prevent this maneuver, and I thought I might as well first restrict the mobility of White's Queen's Bishop by advancing my d-pawn to the fifth."

20.♖fc1 d5 21.♖c5
Better was 21.d4 or 21.d3. Lasker comments "Probably he did not want to block his Bishop with d2-d4 and would rather have a pawn of mine on that square, attacked by his Bishop."

21...d4 22.♘g2?!
This forces White to trade off his light-squared Bishop. Better 22.♘f1 intending 23.d3 and 24.♘d2. If 22...d3 23.e4 ♗c8 24.♗g2, retaining the Bishop.

22...♗c8 23.♗×c8 ♖a×c8
All White's advantage is gone now. The game is entirely even.

24.♘f4 ♘a5

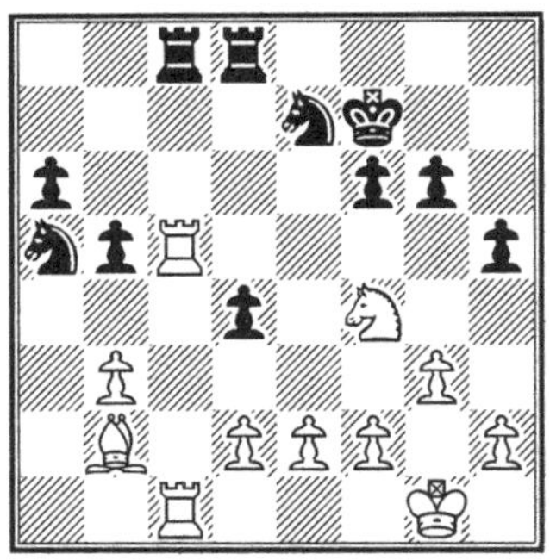

25.♖c7??
A dreadful miscalculation. Correct was 25.b4, of which Lasker writes "the ending ensuing after 25...♘b3 26.♖×c8 ♖×c8 27.♖×c8 ♘×c8 was distinctly unfavorable for him due to the constant threat which the black pawn majority on the Queen's wing constitutes." Stockfish does not agree, rating that position at -0.09/30. After 28.♘d5 intending 29.♘c7, Black would not get

his hoped-for two connected passed pawns, thus White would have good drawing chances.
Lasker also says "A very strong alternative I had after 25.b4 was 25...♘c4. White would have had to exchange one Rook on c8 as otherwise I would exchange myself and again emerge with the two connected passed pawns. The continuation might have been 26.♖×c8 ♘×c8 27.♖c2 ♘e7 28.♗c1(?) ♘c6 29.♘d3 ♖a8 and 30...a5." However, 28.♗c1? is not at all forced; better is 28.d3 with an even game whether Black takes the Bishop or not (-0.28/30 after 28...♘×b2 29.♖×b2).

But the text, which loses the Exchange, renders all that moot. Lasker says "Torre scared me for a moment with a move I had not expected at all ... After much hard work I saw that with a counter-sacrifice I could stop the attack and regain the initiative as follows:"

25...♘×b3 26.♗a3 ♘×c1 27.♖×e7+ ♔g8 28.♘×g6

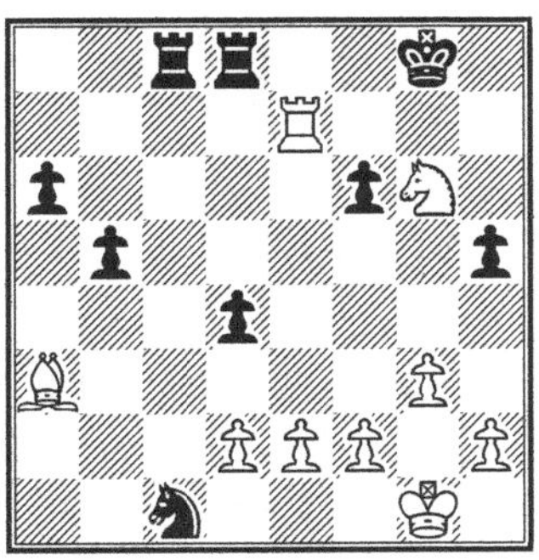

28...♖e8?!

Lasker mistakenly gives this a double-exclam, but it actually loses most of Black's newly gained advantage. Best was 28...d3! and if 29.e×d3 ♘×d3 30.♖a7 ♖a8 31.♖c7 ♘e5 (-4.89/23), or 29.e3 ♘b3 30.♗b2 ♖c6 (-4.47/23), or 29.e4 ♘b3 etc. as after 29.e3, but if 30.♗b2 definitely *not* 30...♘×d2?? 31.♗×f6! and mate in five.

29.♖×e8+ ♖×e8 30.♗×c1 d3?
Another mistaken exclam from Lasker. He writes "The point of the combination. White cannot take on account of ...♖e1+ etc. The following ending had to be calculated with precision." True, and Lasker miscalculates right off the bat.
Correct was 30...♖×e2 31.♔f1□ ♖e8 32.♘f4 a5 33.♗b2 b4 (33...♖d8? 34.♘e6=) 34.♘d3 ♔f7□ 35.h3 ♔e6 36.♗×d4 ♖d8□ 37.♘c5+ ♔d5 38.♗×f6 ♖f8 39.♗h4 ♖g8 (39...♔×c5?? 40.♗e7+) 40.♘d3 ♔c4 and Black should win, though it is not exactly a lead-pipe cinch (-1.86/24).

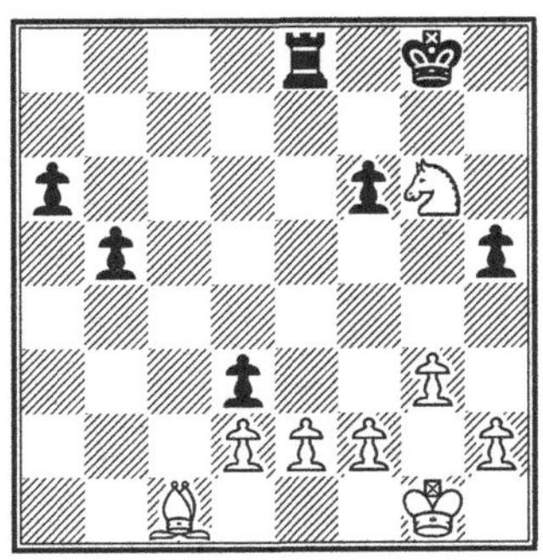

31.e3?
Very sub-optimal. Correct was 31.♔f1! and if

(a) 31...d×e2+ 32.♔e1 b4 33.♘f4 a5 (33...b3? 34.♘d5±) 34.♘×e2 a4 35.♔d1 (-0.43/26); or
(b) 31...b4 32.♘f4 d×e2+ 33.♔e1 transposing to (a); or
(c) 31...a5 32.♘f4 b4? 33.♘×d3 ♖c8 34.♔e1 ♖c2 35.♔d1 b3 36.♗a3! ♖a2 37.♗b2 a4 38.♗×f6 a3 39.♘b4 b2 40.♔c2!□ ♖a1 41.♗×b2!□ a×b2 42.♔×b2 and all the winning chances are White's (+1.97/27 after 42...♖e1).

31...b4?!
Another imprecision. Best was 31...♖e4

32.♘f4 ♖d8 33.♗b2
33.♔f1 was about equally good.

33...a5 34.♗×f6

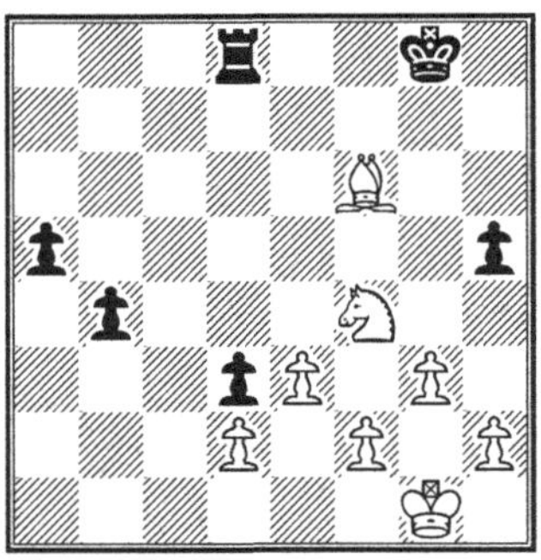

34...♖d7
34...b3 or 34...♖d6 were perhaps slightly better.
34...♖c8?, hoping next for 35...♖c2, hits a snag in the form of 35.♘×d3 ♖c2 36.♗d8 ♖×d2 (if 36...a4 37.♘×b4 ♖×d2 38.♗f6 +3.18/30) 37.♗×a5 ♖×d3 38.♗×b4 and it's White who has the winning chances (+2.50/27).

35.e4!□ a4 36.♘d5□ ♖b7

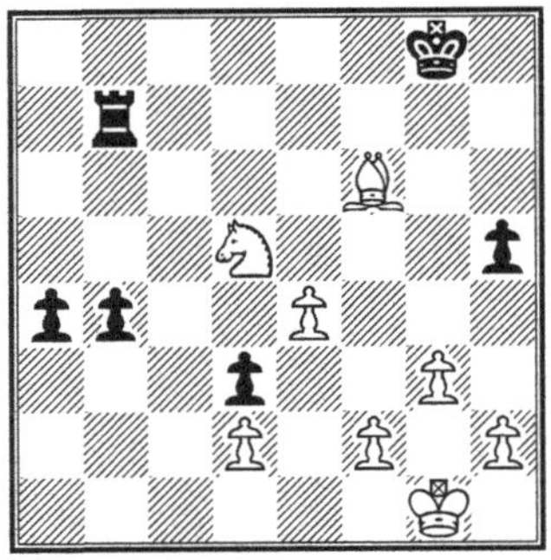

37.f3?
Here, finally, we have the losing move. Stockfish indicates that two moves could have held the draw:
(a) 37.♗d4 ♖b5 (the only move not rated 0.00 or worse) 38.♘c7!□ ♖b8 39.♘d5 ♔f7 40.♗e5!□ ♖b7 41.♔g2 ♔e6 42.♗b2 (42.f4? a3−+) 42...a3 43.♗c1 ♖b8 (△44...♖c8) 44.♘×b4! ♖×b4 45.♗×a3 ♖×e4 46.♗c5 ♖e2 47.♗e3 (0.00 *ad infinitum*);
(b) 37.♗e5 and:

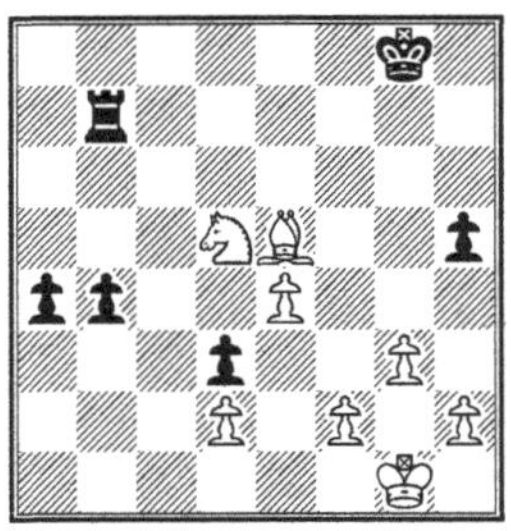

(b1) 37...♔f7 38.♔g2 ♔e6 39.♗b2 ♖b8 40.♘f4+ ♔d6 41.♘×d3 ♔c6 42.f4=;
(b2) 37...a3 38.♗d6! and either 38...b3 39.♗×a3 ♖a7 40.♗b2 ♖a2 41.♗c3 b2 42.♗×b2 ♖×b2 (0.00), or 38...a2 39.♗e5□ b3 40.♗b2 (0.00);
(b3) 37...b3 38.♗b2 ♖a7 (38...a3

39.♗×a3 b2 40.♘c3 b1♕+ 41.♘×b1 ♖×b1+ 42.♔g2 favors White (+0.68/27), though a draw is more than likely) 39.♗a3 ♖b7 40.♗b2 etc., draw.

Lasker, perhaps too intent on showcasing his "precision," makes no comment at move 37. Nor does Howell in the *ACB*.

37...a3!

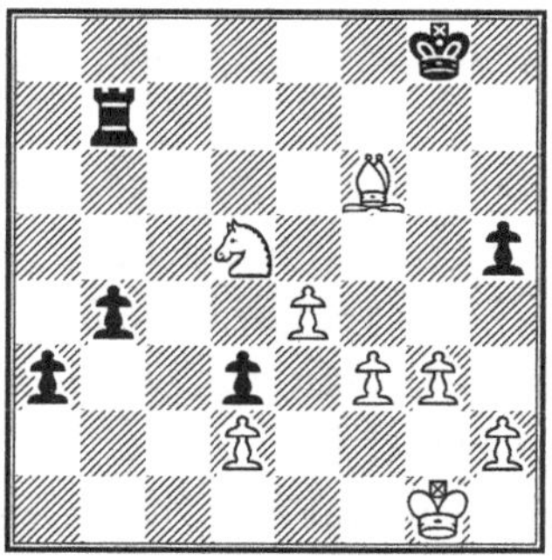

The only winning move.

38.♘×b4 ♖×b4 39.♔f2 ♔f7 40.♗h8 ♖b8 41.♗d4 a2 42.♔e3 ♔g6 43.h4 ♖b1 44.♔×d3

44...♖g1

A finesse, the desirability of which escaped Howell, who commented "Black can well afford to enjoy himself and take his time." Lasker, writing 16 years later, replied pointedly "This is perhaps the only move to force a clear win, a fact which apparently escaped the annotators of this game who at the time thought I was merely taking my time to enjoy myself." It does appear that more direct play might have sufficed: 44...a1♕ 45.♗×a1 ♖×a1 46.♔e2

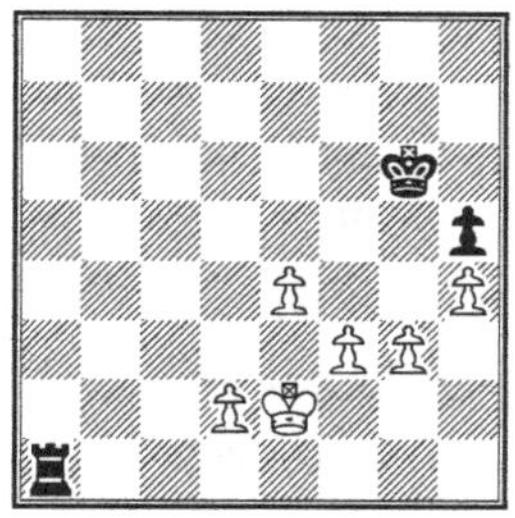

is rated -4.57/34 by Stockfish, but the ♖+♙-vs-5♙ ending could have been much more difficult for a human player to win.

45.♔e3??

Making it easy for Black. But after 45.♗e5 Black can either enter the aforementioned ♖+♙-vs-5♙ ending by 45...a1♕ 46.♗×a1 ♖×a1, or go for ♕+♙-vs-♗+4♙ by 45...♖×g3 46.♗×g3 a1♕ (-5.38).

45...♖×g3 46.♔f4 ♖h3 47.♔e5 ♖×f3 48.♔e6 ♖d3 0-1

Here is what the *ACB* had to say about the last round, from page 112 of its September-October 1926 issue:

An Eventful Final Round

In a special dispatch to the *Brooklyn Eagle* the following description of the finish is given:

Such a breakneck finish as that which brought to a conclusion the masters' tournament at the Western Chess Association meeting, and which ended in the victory of Frank Marshall of New York yesterday, has rarely been witnessed in a chess competition of this importance. Wednesday night Carlos Torre, the 21-year-old Mexican champion, a member of both the Manhattan and Marshall Chess Clubs, laid his head on his pillow and indulged in sweet dreams of the morrow. The morrow came and with it an unlooked for defeat by Edward Lasker, to whose credit it must be said that he put forth his best and played one of the finest games of his life.

It was exactly the "break" that the United States champion needed to enable him to slip in ahead of his young rival and carry off the chief prize with a score of 8½-3½, while Torre, at 8-3 *[sic; s/b 8-4]*, was tied by Geza Maróczy. The Hungarian, too, had the opportunity to get to 8½, but was prevented by L.J. Isaacs, who drew with him. Still another player to be disappointed was Charles Jaffe, who, like Marshall, started the final round with 7½. There he stayed, for Kupchik defeated and tied him for fourth prize.

Still another victim who fell just outside of the ring of prize-winners was Isaac Kashdan, the youthful champion of the Rice-Progressive Chess Club of New York. He was brilliantly defeated by Newell W. Banks of Detroit, the draughts professional and one of the conquerors of Marshall. The only other competitor to win from Marshall was Torre. In addition, Marshall had drawn games with Jaffe, Factor and Lasker.

It was a particularly hard ordeal for Torre to have the laurel snatched from his out-stretched hand at the last minute. He lost a game to Jaffe in the first round, after which he did not lose again until yesterday's all-important game with Lasker. But Torre is still young and can afford to wait.

In fact, however, Torre's time was up. The Lasker game marked the end of his short but brilliant international chess career. Torre himself summed up the tournament matter-of-factly in a 1927 interview for the Yucatán magazine *Anahuac*: "I believe my failure to gain first place in this tournament was due in large part to the excessive tiredness produced by my games in Mexico, as I had never played so continuously as then, and many were the simultaneous exhibitions I had to give, one after the other ..." For more of that interview, see Chapter III.

Back in New York after the tournament, Torre's eating habits became compulsive. Despite the demanding nature of tournament play, he had never bothered much about his health or diet, sometimes going for weeks without a hot meal or well-balanced nutrition. He had always had an immoderate fondness for sweets, sometimes eating a dozen pineapple sundaes in a day, but those who knew him in New York at this time report that he was eating almost nothing but candies and fudge. This could only have compounded the stress he already felt from the pressures of chess competition.

All this resulted in a nervous breakdown, a brief psychosis, which manifested itself when Torre began to undress on a Fifth Avenue bus. This would have occurred sometime during the first full week of October, since the *New York Sun* of Saturday, October 16, 1926 talks of Torre falling ill "last week." The *Brooklyn Eagle* of October 21 specifically says that Torre had a nervous breakdown. He was hospitalized for some time in New York. During this time he resolved to return to his native country. After his release, he booked passage on a steamship of the Ward line. On October 23, 1926, he left New York, sailing to Progreso, Yucatán via Havana. He lived out the remaining 51 years of his life in Mexico, still retaining a strong interest in chess, but never again playing a serious game. For more on that period of his life, see chapters III, IV, V and IX.

Odds and Ends

Our next game, with the possible exception of his Moscow 1925 tilt with Emanuel Lasker, is surely the best-known game Torre ever played. But did he actually play it? First, the game itself, as it was presented in the November 1925 issue of the *ACB*, with Torre's own notes:

Chess in New Orleans

Game 107

E.Z. Adams-Torre

New Orleans, 1920

Philidor's Defense [C62]

1.e4 e5 2.♘f3 d6 3.d4 e×d4 4.♕×d4 ♘c6 5.♗b5 ♗d7 6.♗×c6 ♗×c6 7.♘c3

Morphy played 7.♗g5, his adversaries answering 7...f6. Later they discovered the strong 7...♗e7.

7...♘f6 8.0–0 ♗e7 9.♘d5 ♗×d5 10.e×d5 0–0 11.♗g5 c6 12.c4 c×d5 13.c×d5 ♖e8 14.♖fe1 a5

To preserve the pawn after ...♖a8-c8, or perhaps to enable ...a5-a4 and ...♖a8-a5. It is a bit too slow.

15.♖e2 ♖c8

But now it was essential to play 15...h6. After this move the game is hopelessly lost as White will now demonstrate in a manner that is as masterly as it is pleasing. The coming moves are a study.

16.♖ae1! ♕d7 17.♗×f6!

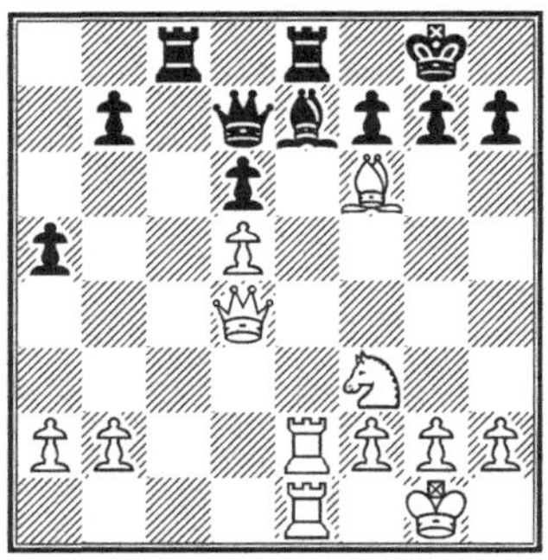

17...♗×f6

After 17...g×f6 18.♖×e7, but of course aside from this the game could not be saved.

TK: This is the one flaw in Torre's notes. After 18.♖×e7 ♕×e7! gets Black out of trouble, since if 19.♖×e7?? ♖c1+ and mate shortly. Better would be, say, 18.g3 or 18.h3, when White has much the better game because of Black's poor pawn structure.

18.♕g4! ♕b5 19.♕c4!
He must block the QR before attempting to win the Queen with a2-a4. Otherwise there would come ...♕×e2. For the same reason he does not play ♕×b7, until after having removed the Rook from e2.

19...♕d7 20.♕c7!

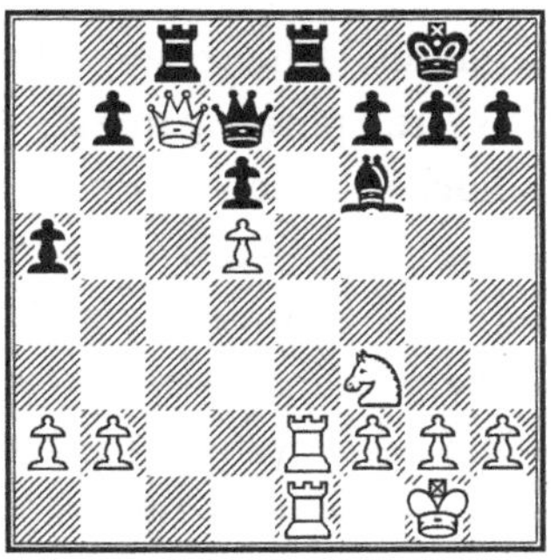

20...♕b5 21.a4! ♕×a4 22.♖e4!! ♕b5 23.♕×b7! 1–0
Played between E.Z. Adams and Carlos Torre in New Orleans during 1920.

While some authors (*e.g.* Fine in *The World's Great Chess Games*, 1951) have presented this as an actual, serious encounter, there is strong, almost conclusive evidence that it was not. Velasco once casually queried Torre on it. After 57 years he could not quite recall the details, but what he said implied that from his viewpoint it really didn't matter if it had been a skittles game or post-mortem analysis, so long as the combination was extremely original and beautiful. Torre's friends, the late Alejandro Báez, and Pedro Busto Undiano, knew him well when his memory was more reliable. Both of them assured Velasco that the game in fact was never played; rather the whole idea had occurred to Torre after analyzing a skittles game. They said that Torre could find no better way to make the beautiful possibilities he saw known to the public than by inventing a game, so he decided to pretend he had lost it to his teacher Edwin Adams, for whom he had great affection.

Furthermore, chess historian Edward Winter, in Chess Notes #1366, published a letter, dated November 1920, from Adams to Hermann Helms (see page 18). It discusses Torre, but makes no mention of the game. In the opinion of historian and publisher Dale Brandreth (from whom Winter acquired the letter), if the game had been played any time up until 22 November, 1920, Adams would surely have mentioned it.

The next game, which appeared in Chernev's *The 1000 Best Short Games of Chess*, casts further doubt. Compare the quality of Black's play here to that of White in the previous game. One must ask: could the brilliant tactician of Game 107 possibly be the same weak amateur who loses here?

Game 108

Torre-Adams

Offhand, New Orleans, 1920

French Defense [C13]

1.e4 e6 2.d4 d5 3.♘c3 ♘f6 4.♗g5 d×e4 5.♘×e4 ♗e7 6.♗×f6 ♗×f6 7.♘f3 c6 8.c3 ♕c7

Better 8...0–0.

9.♗d3 ♘d7 10.♕e2 b6 11.g4 c5 12.d×c5 ♘×c5 13.♘×c5 ♕×c5 14.g5 ♗×c3+

Too greedy. Black will win both Rooks but lose his King.

Correct was 14...♗×g5 with approximate equality.

15.b×c3 ♕×c3+ 16.♕d2 ♕×a1+ 17.♔e2 ♕×h1

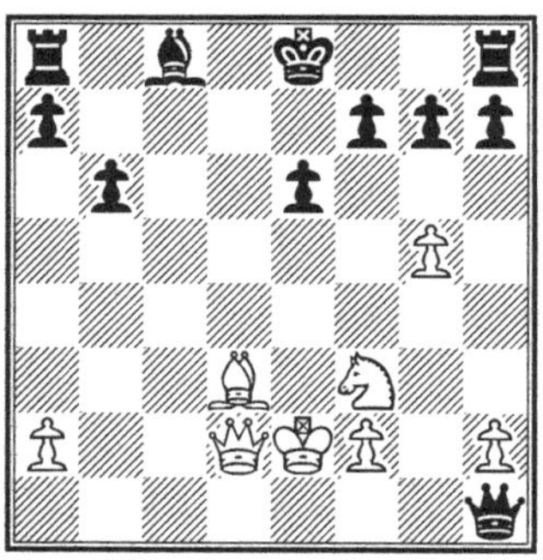

18.♗b5+ ♗d7

Or 18...♔e7 19.♕b4+ ♔d8 20.♕d6+ ♗d7 21.♕×d7#.

19.♕×d7+ ♔f8 20.g6 h×g6 21.♘g5 1–0

Finally, if any more evidence is needed, we note that in his aforementioned correspondence with Winter, Dale Brandreth also gave two other Adams games, which he rightly describes as "true patzer games":

Adams-Lockett, New Orleans, 1925: 1.e4 e6 2.d4 b6 3.f3 ♗b7 4.♗d3 ♕h4+ 5.g3 ♕h5 6.♗e3 ♗d6 7.e5 ♗×e5 8.d×e5 ♕×e5 9.♔f2 ♕×b2 10.♘d2 ♘f6 11.h3 ♘h5 12.♘e2 0–0 13.♗d4 ♕a3 14.♘c4 ♕e7 15.♕d2 d5 16.♘e5 c5 17.♗e3 c4 18.♘×c4 d×c4 19.♗×c4 ♕f6 20.♘g1 ♕×a1 0-1

Morton-Adams, New Orleans, 1934: 1.e4 e5 2.♘f3 ♘c6 3.♗c4 ♗c5 4.b4 ♗×b4 5.c3 ♗a5 6.d4 e×d4 7.0–0 ♗b6 8.c×d4 d6 9.d5 ♘a5 10.♗b2 ♘f6 11.♗d3 0–0 12.♘c3 ♗g4 13.♔h1 ♗d4 14.♕d2 ♗b6 15.♘e2 c5 16.♘g3 c4 17.♗c2 ♖c8 18.♘d4 c3 19.♗×c3 ♘c4 20.♕c1 ♘e5 21.♕b2 ♕c7 22.♘b5 ♕c5 23.♖ac1 ♘c4 24.♕b3 a6 25.♘d4 ♗a5 26.♘df5 ♗×f5 27.♘×f5 ♖c7 28.♗×f6 ♕a3 29.♗×g7 ♖fc8 30.♗f6 ♕×b3 31.♗×b3 b5 32.♗×c4 1-0

In 1934 the future American grandmaster Reuben Fine visited Torre in Monterrey. They played two friendly exhibition games, one of which is known to be preserved:

Game 109

Torre-Fine

Monterrey, 1934

Caro-Kann Defense [C11]

1.e4 c6 2. d4 d5 3.f3 e6 4.♘c3 ♘f6 5.♗e3 ♗e7 6.e5 ♘fd7 7.f4 c5 8.♘f3 ♘c6 9.♗b5 ♕b6 10.0-0 0-0 11.♔h1 a6 12.♗×c6 b×c6 13.♘a4 ♕a5 14.c3 c×d4 15.c×d4 c5 16.♖c1 c4 17.g4 f6 18.♖f2 f×e5 19.f×e5 ♗b7 20.♕c2?

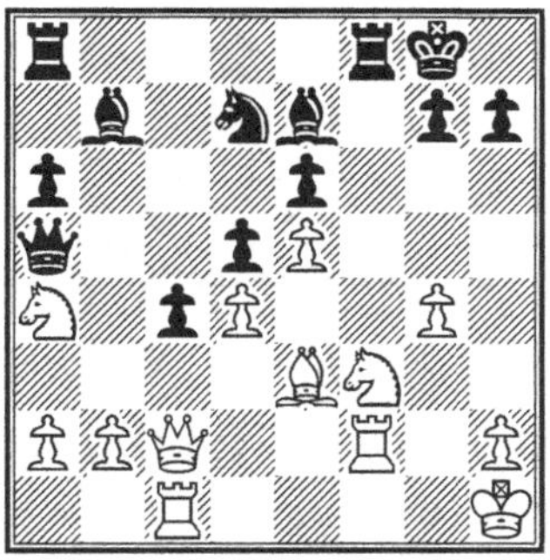

△20.♘c3

20...♗c6 21.♘c3 ♘c5! 22.♖cf1
If 22.c×d5 d4!.
22...♘d3 23.♖g2 ♘×e5 24.d×e5 d4 25.♘e4 d×e3 26.♔g1 ♕d5 27.♘c3 ♕d3 28.♕×d3 c×d3 29.♖g3 e2 0-1

In his book *The World's Great Chess Games* (1951) Fine wrote of these games

"In chess he was no longer the old Torre." Yet later, in *The Psychology of the Chess Player* (1957), he would say "After eight years away from tournament competition he might have been expected to be somewhat rusty; actually, from a technical point of view he had lost little of his skill."[1]

Our last Torre game is an offhand effort against the promising young master and future U.S. Champion Herman Steiner, played presumably at the Manhattan or Marshall Chess Club. Though far from a perfect game (it was probably played at the then-popular time limit of ten seconds per move), it features Torre's delightful tactical gift and serves as a fitting conclusion to this chapter.

1 Fine devotes one page to Torre in *The Psychology of the Chess Player*, but we include nothing more because that page is full of factual errors. For example Torre is said to have been born in New Orleans, and moved to New York at age 11; also to have never left Monterrey once he settled there. Fine at least corrected the first two errors in the 1976 edition of *TWGCG*.

Game 110

H. Steiner-Torre

Offhand, New York, 1925

Giuoco Piano [C54]

1.e4 e5 2.♘f3 ♘c6 3.♗c4 ♗c5 4.c3 ♘f6 5.d4 e×d4 6.c×d4 ♗b4+ 7.♘c3 ♘×e4 8.0–0

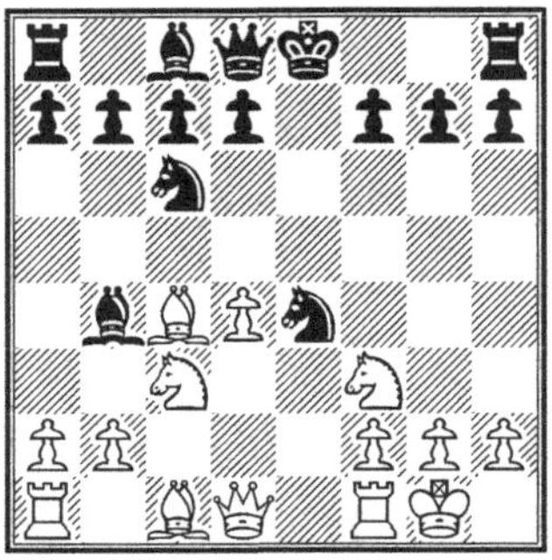

8...♗×c3

8...♘×c3 is a much riskier alternative, as this ancient example indicates: 9.b×c3 ♗×c3 10.♕b3 ♗×a1?? 11.♗×f7+ ♔f8 12.♗g5 ♘e7 13.♘e5 ♗×d4

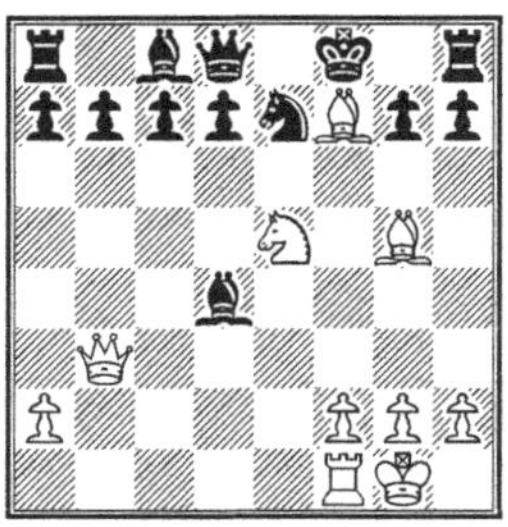

14.♗g6! d5 15.♕f3+ ♗f5 16.♗×f5 ♗×e5 17.♗e6+ ♗f6 18.♗×f6 g×f6 19.♕×f6+ ♔e8 20.♕f7#, Greco-NN, 1620.

9.b×c3 d5 10.♗b5 0–0 11.♕b3?!

A dubious experiment. Book is 11.♕c2.

11...♕f6 12.♘d2?

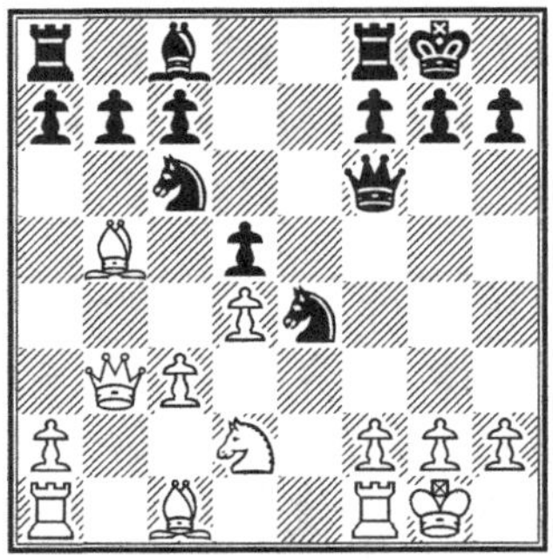

12...♗f5

If this game was played at ten seconds per move, it would explain both players missing 12...♘×c3! 13.♕×c3 ♘×d4, threatening both 14...♘e2+, winning the Queen, and 14...♘×b5, winning back the piece with at least two pawns interest.

13.♘×e4 d×e4 14.f3 ♕g6 15.♗f4 ♖ae8 16.f×e4

There was nothing wrong with 16.♗×c7, with an even game.

16...♗×e4 17.♖f2 ♖e7 18.♖af1

On 18.d5 Black could play 18...♘e5! with a promising attack, for example 19.♕b4 ♘f3+ 20.♔h1 ♘h4 21.♕×e7 ♗×g2+ 22.♔g1 ♘f3+ 23.♖×f3 ♗×f3+

24.♔f2 ♕g2+ 25.♔e3 (25.♔e1?? ♕b2+−) 25...♗xd5 and Black has three pawns and a terrific attack for the sacrificed piece.

18...h6 19.♗c4 ♔h7 20.♗g3 f5 21.♕xb7 ♘xd4 22.♕xa7 ♘e6 23.♕a3 ♖fe8 24.♖e1 ♖d7 25.♗xe6?

△25.♕b4∓

25...♕xe6 26.♕b3 ♕c6

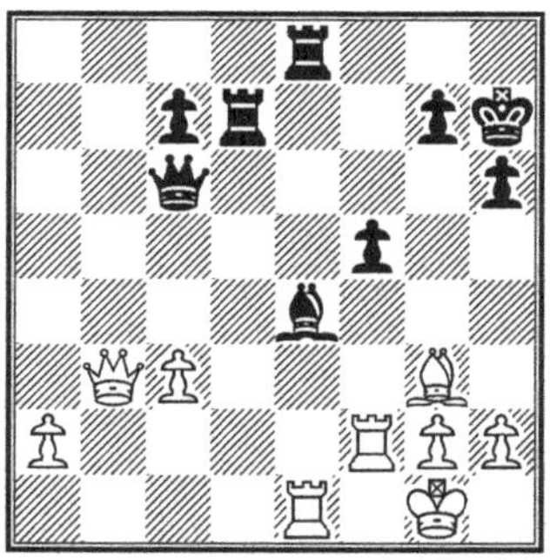

27.♖xf5??

Overlooking Black's very strong reply.

27...♖d2!

Also winning was 27...♗xf5! 28.♖xe8 ♖d2 29.♕g8+ ♔g6 30.♗f2

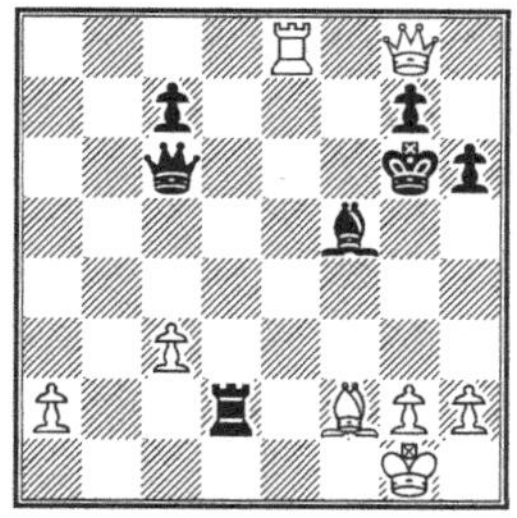

30...♖d1+!□ 31.♖e1 ♖xe1+ 32.♗xe1 ♕b6+ 33.♔h1 ♕e3 and White's Bishop is lost.

28.♕b5??

A blunder, but even after 28.♖f2 ♗c2! Black would win: 29.♖xd2 ♖xe1+ 30.♗xe1 ♗xb3 31.axb3 ♕xc3−+.

28...♖xg2+ 29.♔f1 ♕xb5+ 30.♖xb5 ♖f8+ 0–1

Mate is unavoidable.

Chapter III

Interviews with Carlos Torre Repetto

Anahuac Interview, 1927

Torre gave an interview to the Yucatán magazine Anahuac *some time in 1927, not long after he had returned to Mexico from New York. We did not have access to the full interview, but extensive excerpts were found in the book* 64 Variaciones Sobre un Tema de Torre *by Germán de la Cruz (about which see Chapter IV). The interview is highly interesting on several counts: (1) It adds important details to our knowledge of Chicago 1926 and its aftermath; (2) Torre sounds entirely lucid and clear-headed, not at all like someone in the throes of mental illness; and (3) He sounds very determined to return to international chess soon, and very pugnacious in defense of his rights as incumbent Mexican champion. Everything in quotes is from Torre; a few questions from the* Anahuac *reporter are interspersed here and there. We begin with Torre discussing the last part of his 1926 Mexican tour.*

"My games in the interior of Mexico being done, I had the great pleasure of returning to Yucatán, and giving my personal greetings to the city where I was born, Mérida, and offer a demonstration of the level I had reached in the game of chess ... To my regret my stay in Mérida was short, as I had to arrive in Chicago in time to take part in the Pan-American Tournament *[sic]* that would take place in the month of September, in which I would face Marshall, Jaffe, Lasker, Maróczy and others.

"In this tournament, despite the fatigue and vicissitudes of travel, I played with a good deal of luck, making moves the analysts called 'masterful,' but nevertheless, and for reasons I could not explain, I made some bad moves, which allowed Marshall to obtain 8½ points as opposed to 8 points for Maróczy and myself, tied for 2nd and 3rd place. I had beaten these two good players, Marshall and Maróczy, in our individual games ... My record was: six games won, four drawn, and two lost of the twelve games I played ... I stood better in the four drawn games, but in the endings, some bad moves I made let them be drawn. And the two losses were first to Jaffe and secondly to Lasker. I believe my failure to gain first place in this tournament was due in large part to the excessive tiredness produced by my games in Mexico, as I had never played so continuously as then, and many were the simultaneous exhibitions I had to give, one after the other, simuls of 20, 30, up to 42 boards.

"When I was in Mexico, arrangements were made by General Mendoza for a match between Marshall and me, for the Championship of America, play to begin the first of January 1927, the first ten games in New York and the last ten in Mexico. Upon my return to New York, after the Chicago tournament, I went together with Marshall to see Mr. George E. Roosevelt[1], who offered to contribute five hundred dollars, and also to serve as arbiter for the New York segment, the five hundred to be added to the two thousand dollars raised for the match from North American sources. Meanwhile General Mendoza, the arbiter in Mexico, would obtain an equal amount, for a total prize fund of five thousand dollars. This match would have taken place, but my illness made it impossible, at least for the time being."

Q: To what do you attribute your illness?

"To several different causes. Excessive mental labor, which effectively cost me first prize at Chicago, when I had it won; worries of a financial nature; and the tremendous effort I put in to reading and understanding perfectly the theory and philosophy of Dr. Lasker in his book *Lasker's Manual of Chess*. It was written in German, a language I had learned a bit in my time in Germany. I had to refer constantly to the dictionary to decipher it word by word and absorb perfectly its meaning. All this was the cause of my sickness. So great was the effect of cerebral labors and the different kinds of problems I had to solve, that everything started spinning in my head. It was as though a filing cabinet, with everything in order, was for whatever reason set tumbling, leaving not one thing in its proper place."

Q: It is known that you had a few drinks before you felt ill.

"Effectively. I was with some friends on 11th Street in New York, drinking a few glasses of wine, and that was my last lucid moment. After that I remember absolutely nothing, until I found myself on the ship bound for Yucatán. That I remember, along with my arrival."

Q: What are your current projects?

"To organize in Mérida a tournament, for next June, inviting all the states of the Republic to take part in the Championship of the Mexican Republic. I say in June

1 George Emlen Roosevelt (1887-1963), wealthy banker and philanthropist, a cousin of Theodore Roosevelt.

because in this month last year in Mexico City the National Championship was held, which title I won. Many good players can participate, principally Colonel Manuel Soto Larrea, Agustín Freyria and Joaquín Araiza, from the capital, and Sr. Modesto Castellón and the young Vásquez from Yucatán, and all those who come from other states. If it should happen that fortune favors me again, and I win the championship, and I see that my brain is not weakened, I will, after appropriate training, venture again into international competition, until I attain the place I long for.

"Concerning the tournament last year in Mexico City, I wrote a book, which I entrusted to General Mendoza, who had arranged with the Secretary of Education that it be published for free, giving me the income from its sales, but later my illness came on, and nothing has been said to me about it since, almost as if it has been forgotten. No one has informed me of anything about said book. But now I am going to get in touch with the center to find out what has been done.

"I have just recently learned that the chess club bearing my name, in Mexico City, has issued an announcement of a tournament for the championship of the Republic. This should not be, it is not just, because I still exist, and as I am the incumbent title-holder, the tournament should be held where I choose, and I want it to be in Mérida and on conditions that I stipulate. All the members of that club are good friends of mine and I hold them in very high esteem for all the considerations they gave me when I was among them. But that does not mean they can take away the right legitimately mine. I know perfectly well that my reappearance will upset the workings of that club, but at the same time, I like to believe they should, out of feelings of justice and humanity, be content that I return to the board."

Q: Who, in your opinion, are the strongest international players?
"Capablanca, Dr. Lasker, Alekhine, Bogoljubow and Nimzovich."

Q: And who would you say is the #1 contender?
"They are all of almost the same strength, and I consider myself closer to them now than when I first encountered them."

A very interesting conclusion to the interview; Torre sounds anything but resigned to retirement, and eager to take on the players he named and defend his national title. As near as we can make out from information given in the film Torre x Torre *(see chapter IX), he suffered a relapse into mental illness some time after this interview, dashing any hopes for a return to competition.*

See also Chapter V, the article "Carlos Torre Refused to Return to the United States," for a bit more from this interview.

Interview by Gabriel Velasco, 1977

Moving ahead 50 years from the Anahuac *interview, we give here excerpts from a conversation between Gabriel Velasco and Carlos Torre which took place in Mérida, Yucatán, on August 10th, 1977, at the home for the aged in which Torre had lived since 1973. This was a pleasant locale, surrounded by flower gardens, and managed by attentive nuns. Velasco recalls:*

"When I arrived after a lengthy bus trip from Mexico City, it was about 8:00 in the morning. I had never seen Carlos Torre in person, and could have recognized him only if he still resembled that thin youth wearing small, round tortoise-shell glasses that I had seen in photographs from the 1920s. I asked a nun if she could be so kind as to lead me to señor Carlos Torre. She responded that he was still at breakfast, but that she would call for him in some 10 or 15 minutes.

"What would the great Yucatecan chess master look like after more than 50 years? Would he be so changed as to be unrecognizable? How should I present myself and what questions should I ask? Would Torre be lucid enough for me to conduct a proper interview?

"All these questions and more ran through my mind during anxious minutes of waiting, when finally before me there appeared an old man, thin and smiling. He wore a casual suit, of heavy material despite the hot Yucatán summer, but he had an agreeable and friendly manner. There could be no doubt that this was the legendary grandmaster whose biography I had been set on writing since my days of post-graduate study in Kiev, Ukraine, in 1976. I introduced myself and apologized for interrupting his breakfast. I noticed he had in his pocket a book with a white jacket. Unexpectedly he brought it out and used it as a conversation-starter."

Carlos Torre (CT): How much do you think this book cost me? Only four pesos! I bought it from a friend, but I think that's ridiculous, because the plastic cover alone is worth six pesos.

Gabriel Velasco (GV): *Is it by chance a chess book? Or a novel you are reading, maestro?*
CT: Neither of those things. It is a scientific work, in fact a scholarly text. I read it to amuse myself, and find it quite entertaining.

After explaining to Torre my interest in his life, games, and memories, I put to him the questions I had formulated prior to the interview.
GV: *Can you tell me, maestro Torre, at what age and under what circumstances you learned to play chess?*

CT: I believe I was six years old when I learned the moves of the pieces and the object of the game. It was my father, whose name was Egidio, who taught me to play chess. He was a good player and I recall that he played by correspondence.

GV: *How many brothers and sisters did you have?*
CT: We were seven, four men and three women. I was the next to last. But today, apart from me, only two sisters survive. One of them lives 20 kilometers from here, and the other has lived in New Orleans since 1915. She married a North American and I believe she has even forgotten how to speak Spanish.

GV: *Of all the great chess games you played in your youth, which would you say is your favorite?*
CT: I believe the game I have always recalled with greatest fondness was the one I won against the English master Yates at the tournament of Marienbad 1925. The winning plan was very subtle and profound, and began with exchanging a Bishop for a Knight, which in that position appeared unnecessary. In the final analysis, that exchange proved to be the key to the plan, and execution of the plan turned out very nicely. An additional delight for me were the admiring words expressed by Nimzovich at the end of the game. Few joys can compare to those felt by a young chess player when he receives the sincere congratulations of a recognized grandmaster.

GV: *And now a question which I must ask you: why did you retire when your career had begun in such brilliant fashion? Were there special reasons which compelled you to lay aside active chess in 1926, before you were even 22 years old?*
CT: After the tournament in Chicago, in 1926, my health was shattered due to dietary difficulties. In fact, I suffered a nervous breakdown. A young, single man, with scant and unstable financial resources, far from his family and in fragile health, is always prone to nervous depressions. The travel and lifestyle involved in high-level tournaments is intense, and maddening. I preferred to return to my country to work with my brother at something more stable. In the end I abandoned chess competition, but never my love for this beautiful game.

GV: *During your formative years as a chess player, which masters exerted the strongest influence on your style of play?*
CT: Without a doubt, Doctor Emanuel Lasker, but I also learned much from the study of the famous games of Morphy, Steinitz, Mason, and Tarrasch. My first chess books were those of Mason, and I believe they exerted an influence on my style.

GV: *Whom do you consider the best chess players in history?*
CT: The world champions. And before them Morphy and Philidor. I knew Rubinstein in his declining years, but in his youth he reached a formidable level of skill. In 1925, Capablanca told me that Rubinstein was already finished.

GV: *Turning to other things, in some of his books, the American grandmaster Reuben Fine told some curious anecdotes about you, for example, that you almost never slept well, that you would eat great amounts of ice cream or sweets, and that you used to tell your fellow grandmasters that they should keep away from women, because they cost a lot of money.*
CT: Good grief! He said that? It would seem that Fine has exaggerated a great deal. Truly, I believe that the majority of anecdotes told in chess are greatly exaggerated. Certainly, I did sleep little compared to the ordinary chess master, who would go to bed at 3:00 or 4:00 AM and get up at noon. I used to go to bed at 3:00 AM, but I could not help waking up at 7:00 or 8:00 in the morning. Those are indeed short hours for sleep, but I did not feel that it affected my chess play. The comments about women, I do not recall making those, but since you mention it, no one can doubt that they do indeed cost a lot of money. But, well ... they are a necessary evil. That great ancient Greek philosopher, Socrates, put it succinctly: "Whether one marries, or does not marry, one will regret it."

GV: *What recollections do you have of the chess player who was world champion during the years you were an active master? I refer to the Cuban, José Raúl Capablanca.*
CT: He was a chess player of extraordinary talent. My impression was that he played for the endgame. It did not matter to him that the game might be prolonged to 60 or 80 moves or more. He saw or felt what was to be done in every position, and carried it out. In my judgement, a proof of his prodigious intuition is the game he played against Bogoljubow at Moscow 1925. The Cuban grandmaster reflected only for a few seconds before playing an extremely complicated piece sacrifice that in the end proved correct. I am convinced that Capablanca never analyzed the consequences of that move. He knew intuitively that it was correct and simply did it.

GV: *Then would you agree that the Capablanca of the 1920s was superior to the Alekhine of the 1930s?*
CT: I would not say that. The fact is that they played a match and Alekhine won it convincingly. Perhaps some five or ten years earlier, Capablanca would have won easily. Furthermore when they did play and Alekhine won, Capablanca

disappointed many by making errors that he never did before. Perhaps by 1936, Capablanca was once again superior to Alekhine, but also Botvinnik, Fine, Flohr, Keres and Reshevsky were as well. Even Max Euwe proved himself superior to Alekhine in 1935.

GV: ***Many have attributed the decline in Alekhine's play to his immoderate love of alcohol.***
CT: Perhaps some years before the war, but not when I knew him. To me, he was a very focused and disciplined man, with an enormous capacity for work, and a prodigious memory. Really it is astounding the number of games and positions he knew from memory. His chief virtue was the capacity to calculate variations mentally, something he had developed playing many blindfold games. In the calculation of variations Alekhine was very superior to Capablanca and everyone else.

GV: ***And what of Dr. Lasker?***
CT: Dr. Lasker was a most practical and rational chess player. His style was much more like that of Capablanca than that of Alekhine. A practical player with a fine intuition can save a lot of time and energy, which permits him to play his games quickly and stay at a high level, even at an advanced age.

GV: ***Did you admire any other master we have not yet mentioned?***
CT: Yes, Efim Bogoljubow. He was a formidable chess player and furthermore he made notable contributions to the development of chess theory. It was Bogoljubow who proposed dividing the chess board into the kingside, queenside, and center. Also he wrote the first scientific treatment of the openings.

GV: ***Whom did you consider the tougher opponent: Spielmann or Marshall?***
CT: Spielmann, without doubt, even though Marshall was a very good chess player, besides being a fine person and great friend.

GV: ***Many remember you for your famous victory against Dr. Lasker at Moscow 1925, where you sacrificed your Queen and showed the power of the "windmill" or "see-saw." Do you consider that game the best you ever won?***
CT: To tell the truth, I do not consider it a good game, because both of us committed various errors. There are many other games in which I take more pride, such as, for example, my victory against the Russian Gotthilf at Moscow 1925. Also I take great pleasure in the way I prevailed with only a small material advantage against Winter at Detroit 1924.

GV: ***Which was the most difficult game you ever played in your life?***
CT: Perhaps the one I won against Whitaker in the Western Championship of 1924. At first, the position was equal, then I offered a draw, but to my surprise Whitaker refused it. Therefore I decided to steel myself and exploit to the maximum any small imprecision by my opponent. From there developed a very hard-fought and tense struggle. About 20 moves later my opponent, in an inferior position, offered me a draw, but it was already too late. I was determined to win, and I did win, even though it required an almost superhuman effort.

GV: ***And what of your two brilliant victories against Viennese grandmaster Ernst Grünfeld in 1925?***
CT: The first was merely an opening trap that the Viennese master fell into through carelessness. The second, at the Marienbad tournament, was indeed a complicated game, and Dr. Lasker included it with commentary in his *Manual of Chess*.

GV: ***And your victory against Sammy Reshevsky in the Western Championship at Detroit?***
CT: Well, yes, it was a good game, but Reshevsky was even younger than I and had not yet reached the maturity of his best years.

GV: ***Have you followed events in the chess world since your retirement, or have you stayed completely away from it?***
CT: From time to time chess players visit me and give me recent chess magazines or books, which allow me to stay informed on what is happening in the world. But I read them only superficially.

GV: *Well, maestro Torre, I do not wish to impose on your time. I am grateful that you have allowed me this interview. It has been an honor to meet personally the man who was the greatest Mexican chess player of all time.*

Chapter IV

64 Variaciones Sobre un Tema de Torre

(64 Variations on a Theme of Torre)

We became aware of this book from the film Torre x Torre. *The author, Germán de la Cruz, was a medical doctor by profession. As a chess player he was around Elo 2000 to 2200; he was quite active in chess in both Mexico and the USA, and in 1972 he played fourth board for the Mexican Olympic team. He first met Carlos Torre in 1969, and they became good friends, conducting an extensive correspondence from then on. His friendship with Torre inspired him to write this book, which saw two editions, in 1982 and 1991. Running to about 220 pages, it is a rambling mix of annotated games, some by Torre, some by famous GMs, some by de la Cruz himself; plus general chess instruction, chess history, and stories about Torre. The excerpts it has from the 1927* Anahuac *interview have been placed in Chapter III; here we give extracts from the narrative portions relevant to Torre, plus some games and game fragments not already seen above. The somewhat disjointed nature of the narrative comes from the book itself; typically the passages about Torre are not in chronological order, and each is followed by several pages of games, instruction or history, with no clear connection to the anecdotes. We have rearranged our paraphrased excerpts into a roughly chronological order.*

De la Cruz met Torre in July of 1969 in Mérida. Torre took him to a house on 69th Street, a magnificent residence in the colonial style "This is my house," Torre said. When de la Cruz congratulated him, he quickly explained: "Here in Mérida, one's house is not where one lives, but rather where one is born, and I was born right here on the 29th of November in 1904."

From 1927 to 1950 Torre resided in the northern part of Mexico.[1] The forced retirement from master chess, plus his economic difficulties, affected his mental well-being. For a while he was looked after by a brother who was a pharmacist. These were the hardest times. Dedicated entirely to chess, and without the

1 As near as we could piece together from available sources, Torre stayed in Mérida from late 1926 into 1927, then some time later in 1927 he was taken to a friend's ranch in the state of Tamaulipas, which borders on the Gulf Coast south of Texas. In the late 1920s or very early '30s he relocated west to the neighboring state of Nuevo León, also bordering Texas.

possibility of living by other means, he suffered severe mental disturbances. He later made contact with Arturo Elizondo in Monterrey, and Elizondo got him admitted to an "ad hoc" clinic where he received treatment, including electroshock therapy.

While Torre lived in the north of Mexico, he thought about returning in some way to chess activity, but his mental troubles prevented this. Thus when he arrived in Mexico City *circa* 1950, his ambitions were no longer the same, though he hoped to continue in chess in some way. Alejandro Báez, and the journalist Bello Córdoba, received Torre soon after he arrived from Monterrey. Báez recalls that in both dress and physical appearance he presented a sad picture.

During the 1950s, Torre played many simultaneous displays in the Federal District. Báez relates that he would offer draws in all the games, even when the position was clearly in his favor.

Torre never retired from chess activities. From 1950 to 1960 he played simuls of 30 or more boards, and conducted classes for his closest disciples. He also carried out academic activities at the University of Mérida in the decade 1960-1970. He once said "If they cut off a finger I will live; if they cut off a foot I will live; but if they cut off my head I cannot live. By the same token if they separate me from chess I could not live." And so it was up to his death. He would comment on and analyze games from the championships until the end of his days.

By the time Torre left the capital and returned to the land of his birth, he had fully recovered his mental health. In Mérida he was able to fit in socially among friends and relatives. In the *Revista de la Universidad de Yucatán*, November-December 1964, there was an article about him, prompted by his 60th birthday. From it we know that he was studying philosophy, and also algebra under the engineer Rachó.

But by 1969, when de la Cruz visited Torre for the first time, he had stopped giving classes, whether by his own choice or the university's is not made clear. Torre lived then at 535 68th Street in Mérida, together with his sister and brother-in-law, Professor Manuel Agüero. De la Cruz says "One could detect in the Maestro some disenchantment over his retirement from the university, which meant a hard blow to his chess activities. I believe it was due to this that he insisted I write to him on chess matters, and we maintained a correspondence until his death."

At his retirement Torre was granted (according to his sister) a pension of 100 pesos per month, a pittance corresponding to the minimum wage. Along with it came the title "Prócer de la Patria" (Hero of the Nation).

De la Cruz once asked Torre about his religion. The reply was evasive: "On my father's side I am atheist, and on my mother's side I am Catholic." In his first letter to Cruz, July 1969, he said he was studying Mohammed, but a few months later, in October, he wrote "some girls are giving me classes about the Lord Jehovah," presumably referring to the Jehovah's Witnesses. But a bit later he said "Solomon is not so wise; his Ecclesiastes has no value."

Around 1973 a Carlos Torre Chess Club was formed in Apaseo el Grande, Guanajuato. De la Cruz and others proposed to organize a tournament in celebration of Torre's 70th birthday, for November 1974, with Torre present at the event. He accepted in principle, but in a later letter he said "Would it not be better to use that money in a noble cause?" He ended up not coming, but the next year, he did show up at the National Open Championship (as a spectator, not a participant).

On Benito Juárez Day, 21 March 1978, de la Cruz was talking with Marcel Sisniega[1] about Torre's death, news of which they had just received. Sisniega said "How would a match between Torre and Anatoly Karpov turn out?" De la Cruz replied that Karpov had reached his peak, but Torre had not. Sisniega insisted he was speaking of Torre at his best. De las Cruz replied that we have only speculations, and as Don Quixote had said, "All comparisons are odious."

We turn now to the Torre games de la Cruz presents. The one below came from the book *Latin American Chess Masters* by Hans Cohn.

Game 111

Allies (six in consultation) - Torre

Monterrey(?), 1933(?)

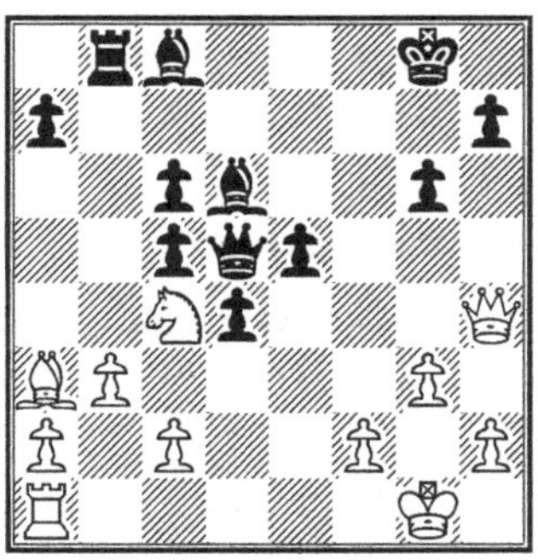

23...♗e7!! 24.♕h6

If 24.♕×e7 ♗h3–+ as in the game.

24...♗g5!! 25.♕×g5 ♗h3 26.f3 ♕×f3 27.♕d2 ♖f8 0-1

Mate in at most 3 is inevitable.

Cruz gives a game, Dupré-Torre, as being from the 1925 New York State Championship. In fact it is almost certainly a spurious, fictitious game. Torre played in the 1924 NYSC but not

1 Marcel Sisniega Campbell (1959-2013), nine-time Mexican champion who earned the IM title in 1978 and the GM title in 1992.

1925's, and no one named Dupré played in either. So we have omitted it. The provenances of the other games below seem at least plausible, and we have no grounds for rejecting them.

Game 112

Torre, Cervera, & Solís - Ponce, Rubio, & Solís

Mexico City(?), 1929

King's Gambit Accepted [C33]

The location given for this consultation game seems inconsistent with de la Cruz's statement that Torre lived in northern Mexico 1927-1950, but we have left it as is. Torre plays in a rather cavalier style.

1.e4 e5 2.f4 e×f4 3.♘c3 g5 4.h4 ♗g7 5.♗c4 h6

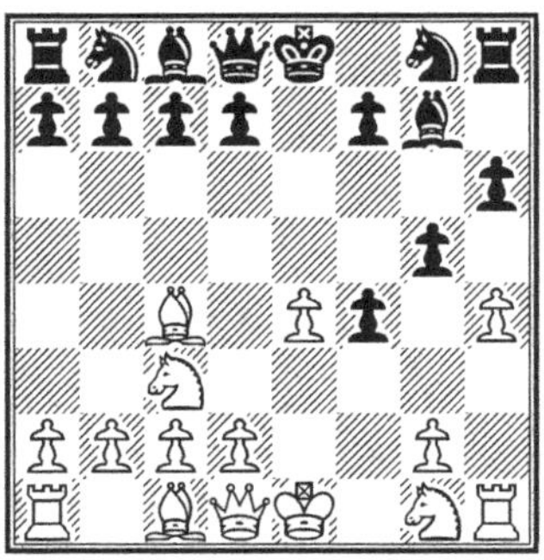

6.♕h5?!
Best was 6.h×g5!, when if 6...h×g5?? 7.♖×h8 ♗×h8 8.♕h5 ♕f6 9.♘d5 ♕h6 10.♘×c7+.

6...♕e7 7.h×g5?
Committing White to an unsound Queen sacrifice.

7...h×g5 8.♕×h8 ♗×h8 9.♖×h8 ♔f8 10.b3
Given two undeserved exclams by Cruz.

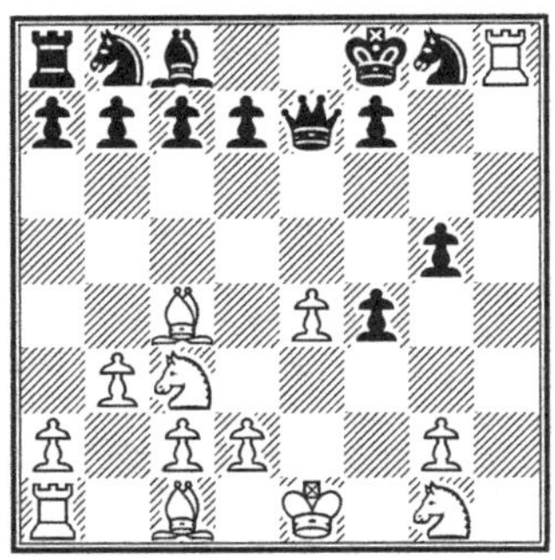

10...♔g7?
The losing move. Correct was 10...d5! 11.♗×d5 c6 12.♗c4 b5 13.♗e2 b4 14.♘d1 ♕×e4 15.♘f3 ♕×c2−+.

11.♗b2! ♔×h8??
From bad to worse. 11...♕f6 was necessary.

12.♘d5+ ♔h7 13.♘×e7 ♘×e7 14.♗×f7
"This Bishop, together with the other, imprisons the King at the edge of the board; and all in stateliness the Rook will give the *coup de grace*" (Cruz).

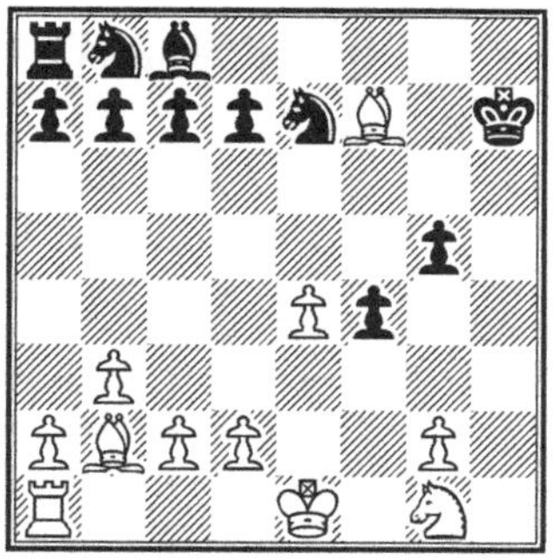

14...♘bc6 15.♘f3 ♔h6?
The least evil was 15...♘d8, but Black would still be quite lost.

16.♔f2 ♘g6 17.♖h1+ ♘h4 18.♘×h4 g×h4 19.♗f6
and mate next move. **1–0**

Game 113

Torre-Allies (4-man team)

Consultation simul, Mexico City, date unknown

This fragment features a nice windmill combination in which, unlike Torre's game with Lasker at Moscow 1925, a Knight is the active piece instead of a Rook.

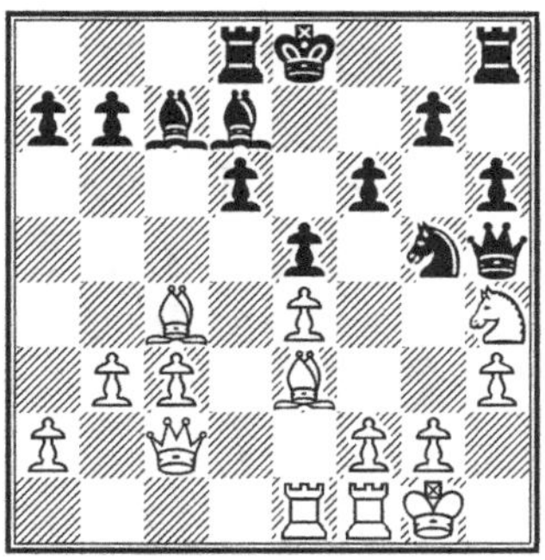

26.♘f5! ♔f8?
Better either 26...♗×f5 27.e×f5 d5±, or (probably best) 26...♘×h3+ 27.g×h3 ♕×h3±.

27.f4 ♘e6?
27...♘×h3+ was the only remotely playable move, though Black is still losing then.

28.f×e5 d×e5 29.♖d1 ♔f7??
29...♕f7 was less bad.

30.♗e2 ♕g6 31.♘h4 ♕h7 32.♗h5+ ♔e7

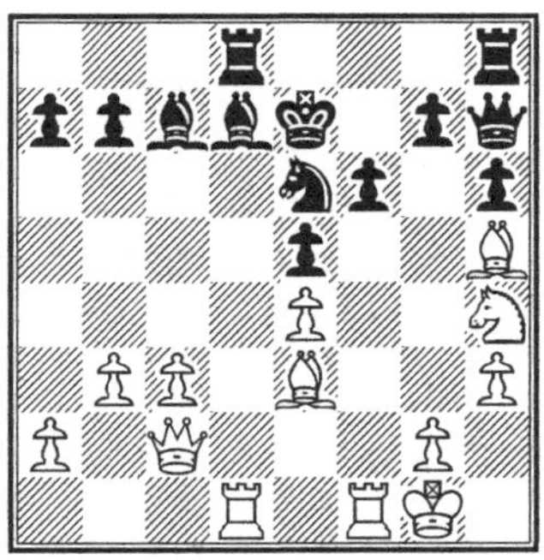

Now comes the windmill.

33.♘g6+ ♔f7 34.♘×e5+ ♔e7
Or 34...♔f8 35.♘×d7+ ♔e7 36.♕d3+−.

35.♘g6+ ♔f7 36.e5 ♕g8 37.♘×h8+ ♔e7 38.♘g6+ ♔f7 39.♘f4+ ♔e7 40.♘d5+ ♔f8 41.e×f6 g5 42.♘e7 ♕h8 43.♕g6 ♗e8 44.♖×d8 ♘g7 45.♕f7# 1–0

Game 114

Woo-Torre

Offhand, Monterrey, 1933

Mexican Defense [A53]

Here we see Torre reprising the defense he first sprung on Sämisch at Baden-Baden 1925.

1.d4 ♘f6 2.c4 ♘c6 3.♘c3 d6 4.e4 e5 5.d5 ♘e7 6.f4?!
Better, say, 6.♗g5 or 6.♗e2.

6...e×f4 7.♗×f4 ♘g6
This gain of tempo shows the flaw in 6.f4?!. Black already stands equal.

8.♗e3 ♗e7 9.♕d2 0–0 10.♘f3 ♗g4 11.0–0–0 ♖e8 12.h3 ♗d7 13.♗d4 a6

14.e5?
Better to keep the center closed and prepare a flank attack by 14.♗d3, 15.g4 etc. As it turns out, the white King's Bishop will never move.

14...d×e5 15.♘×e5 ♘×e5 16.♗×e5 b5 17.d6?
White continues his near-suicidal opening of the center, clearing the c- and d-files for Black to threaten his King. Better 17.a3 or 17.♗d3 with only a small advantage for Black.

17...c×d6 18.♗×d6 ♗×d6 19.♕×d6 ♕a5! 20.a3 ♖ac8

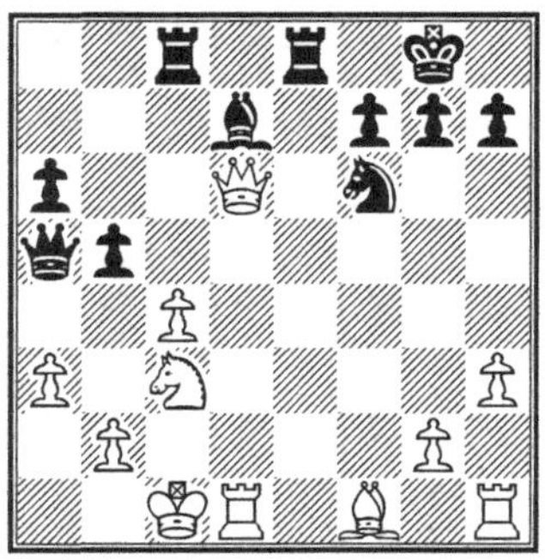

21.♘d5?
The final error. After 21.♕b4 White could still fight on.

21...♘×d5 22.♖×d5

If 22.♕×d5 ♗e6 23.♕d2 ♕c7 and 24...b×c4−+.

22...♗e6

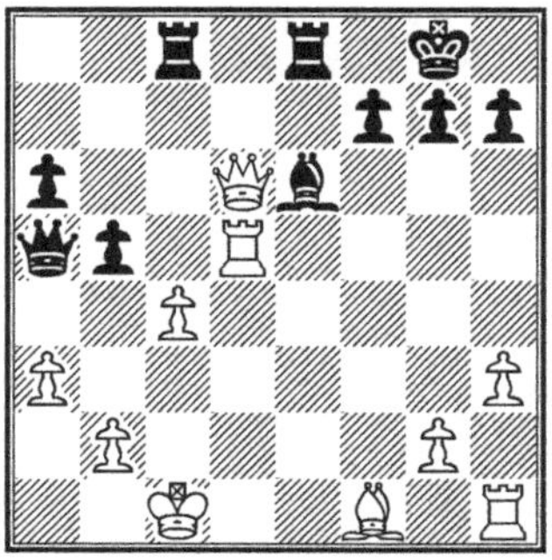

23.♖c5

If 23.♖e5 ♖ed8 24.♕b4 ♕c7 25.♕c3 a5! 26.♕e3 b4 27.a×b4 a×b4 28.♖×e6 (forced, as Black threatened 28...♗×c4 29.♖c5 ♗b3!! 30.♖×c7 ♖d1#) 28...♕a5!! 29.♗d3 (29.♖e5?? ♕a1+ 30.♔c2 ♕d1#) 29...♕a1+ 30.♔c2 ♕×h1−+.

23...♕e1+ 0–1

Chapter V

Remembrances of Carlos Torre

We present here, in English translation, several articles from two Mexican newspapers, the Diario Yucatán (Yucatan Daily) *and the* Diario del Sureste (Southeast Daily). *Jorge A. Balam Díaz had a regular column, El Mirador Ajedrecista (The Chess Spectator), in the former paper. We are grateful to Juan Obregón, co-director of the film* Torre x Torre, *for supplying these to us.*

Don Carlos Torre Repetto: A Chess Player Until Death

by Jorge A. Balam Díaz, from the Diario Yucatán, Sunday, 19 March 1989

Each year, a new Yucatan delegation departs, enthusiastically, for the National Open Chess Championship, but upon their arrival at the venue none had or will have a reception as unpleasant as that of 11 years ago. Nor a return so bitter.

Hours after parting in Mérida from the international grandmaster Carlos Torre Repetto, who was actively involved in arrangements to get financial backing for the group, the Yucatan players arrived in the capital of the Republic and went immediately to the event venue to register their enrollment, not suspecting what awaited them.

What they were told by the directors of the Mexican Chess Federation took them completely by surprise. At first it seemed to them a joke in very bad taste, and then a product of unfounded rumors which they hastened to dispute. However, the grim, serious tone of the organizers finally convinced them, and a sepulchral silence came over them.

"We are very sorry. The loss of Maestro Carlos Torre is a great blow to Mexican and international chess. Please accept our deepest condolences," said one of the functionaries who had welcomed the peninsular delegation, which included, among others, José Alayola Montañez, Carlos Manzur Simón, Miguel Cab Canul, Daniel Mena Briceño, and the writer of these lines.

Profoundly surprised, the local players hastened to brand this a big mistake: "This is not true, don't worry. This is all false information. We just left the Maestro in Mérida only a few hours ago ..."

With a sad and compassionate look, another of our informants insisted "He died yesterday, apparently of a heart attack," he exclaimed while showing us a copy of a sports newspaper in which a brief note of the passing of Carlos Torre was reported.

Then everyone fell silent. For more than a minute no one could speak a word. Everyone remembered moments spent, as little as day ago, with Maestro Torre, his accomplishments from more than half a century before, when he shook the world of the 64 squares with his genius, his historic confrontations with such legendary figures as Capablanca and Alekhine, his famous "windmill" that vanquished Emanuel Lasker, and which carved his name in golden letters in the chess pantheon, for the many works of art he produced in his brief, brilliant tournament career.

At last we reacted when another of those present proposed a minute of silence in memory of the only international grandmaster Mexico had had in the scientific game. The homage was repeated during the national assembly and the declaration inaugurating the championship.

The chess world dressed itself in mourning, for Don Carlos Torre Repetto was in truth a great of the board, as the greatest players of his epoch recognized.

But if his strength as a player was great, even greater was his quality as a person. A profound thinker, a lover of philosophy and letters, Don Carlos Torre considered himself the most humble of mortals. He always had on his lips an ingenious phrase or advice for the players.

He never tired of talking chess, for despite his retirement it was always his passion. He was born with it in his blood, and he died with it. He never ceased trying to promote the scientific game, and he never tired of repeating to players the importance of studying theory. His entire life was an example of dedication to the art of chess.

Before the delegation had left for the metropolis, most of them, students at the University, had gone before the Town Council, the Governor of the State, and various chess lovers, trying to gain funds to cover their expenses. Don Carlos Torre, knowing his presence would help influence acceptance of our proposals, was good enough to accompany us.

At the last of our visits, to Don Vicente Solís Azanar, an old friend of Carlos Torre and now also deceased, on whose offices we looked as if on the heights of The Louvre, our esteemed companion, enthusiastic for the success of our efforts, even put up a little money of his own to help with expenses.

It was to the Maestro's greatest satisfaction that in our group traveled two representatives of the fair sex: the then state champion Lizbet King Park and Gladys Brito Valle. He showed considerable enthusiasm for the way the game was acquiring fans among the feminine ranks.

During his stay in Moscow *[sic; s/b Leningrad]*, toward the end of 1925 *[sic; s/b early 1926]*, the Yucatan master wrote a treatise on the game, *The Development of Chess Ability*, a short work but worth its weight in gold even in our day, in that its principles have not lost validity. With this work he demonstrated that he was, besides an outstanding player, a great psychologist and remarkable teacher.

To show this, we transcribe here a passage: "If we resolve to play each time very much better than we did the last; to play the opening with greater precision, the middle game with higher consciousness, the ending with more directness, to see further ahead with finer accuracy, to evolve a greater masterpiece; the inner effort will prove very cumulative, and our progress will surpass our happiest dreams. Assuredly, if we play in this manner a number of times twenty, we will improve far more than we would from two years indifferent daily playing."

This one paragraph is a faithful reflection of his personality. Even though in his day he was hailed as a genius, his brief competitive career did not enable him to conquer the world title, but this never mattered for him. In reality, he never considered that his goal. He, as one comes to understand in his work, searched always for the truth on the board. Not the triumphs, but rather the perfection, the art.

He was truly a chess player who did not seek personal glory, nor did he think about himself, but about others, about spreading the game, and always, up to his last hours, he did what he could to increase the ranks of players. In sum, Don Carlos Torre Repetto always was what we want to be: a chess player ... until death.

Carlos TORRE Repetto

IN MEMORIAM

Carlos Torre Refused to Return to the United States

by Jorge A. Balam Díaz, Diario Yucatán, Thursday, 29 November 1990

Chess magazines in the United States are starting to speculate on the possibility that the scientific game's scepter may return to North American soil in the not too distant future, by means of the naturalization of the game's new phenomenon, the young Tartar Gata Kamsky, who emigrated some months ago from the Soviet Union.

Similar prospects were contemplated by North Americans 66 years ago when, profoundly impressed by the sensational performances of the young Yucatecan Carlo Torre Repetto, they proposed, by tempting offers that very few sportsmen would refuse, that he become a naturalized US citizen.

But the Yucatecan was not one to give up for dollars, however many there might be, his legitimate pride in being Mexican, so he refused the offer. Those who knew the Mexican grandmaster know that he did not even pause to consider the possibilities and great advantages that representing the biggest power in the world would have brought him in chess battles.

We could say much about the great love Torre professed for Mexico and his little homeland, but best to let the Yucatan genius do it himself, in an anecdote he told in an interview he gave the magazine *Anahuac* in 1927, when the ill-fated Torre had already retired from international competition:

"After the Chicago tournament, members of the Marshall Club of New York, where I had immediately moved back, made advantageous proposals for me to become a naturalized American citizen, proposals I turned down flat, because I have always said, and I repeat now, that my triumphs, those in the past and those I may have in the future, I want to be for my Mexico, for it gives me pride to be the only champion to come out of our beautiful homeland to contend with the top-rank players in the world, and for this reason no proposal, however tempting it might be, would make me deprive my country of this satisfaction.

"In Moscow, in Baden-Baden and in Marienbad, my joy would be immense when I saw in the newspapers, after my name, that of Mexico, and many times the emotion brought tears to my eyes. And I could never forget the satisfaction I felt in that last Czechoslovakian city when, after having won against the champion of England, Yates, in an encounter marvelous in the difficulty of attack and defense, I went out for a walk to clear and distract my brain, and went along the streets in the company of the tournament director Mr. Gunsberg and his wife, when we saw coming toward us, without a hat and his hair in disorder, the great player Nimzovich, who came shouting 'Torre ist ein grosser meister' *[Torre is a great master]*. Long live Mexico!"

Prophetic words from Nimzovich, the originator of hypermodern chess, many years before the official titles of International Master and Grandmaster would be created, a distinction the Yucatecan ultimately received while still alive about two decades ago.

Few could describe their love for Mexico with such emotion as Torre himself did, and few but Nimzovich were qualified to have such faith in the ability of the young Yucatecan, to whom today, Thursday, the Yucatecan and national chess communities pay homage on the 86th anniversary of his birth.

A Street to Be Named for Carlos Torre Repetto

from the Diario del Sureste, Friday, 29 June 1990

100 years ago, on 29 June 1890, there was founded the first chess association in Yucatan, named the "Lonja Meridiana Club," whose headquarters was in the social club of that name, on 62 x 63 Street in this city, and according to chess publications it was established along these lines:

One of the signs for Torre's street

First President: Ing. Néstor Rubio Alpuche; Vice-President Federico Casares; Secretary: José Rosado Sansores; Pro-secretary: Miguel Nogués; Treasurer: Pastor Milán; Assistant Treasurer: Rafael Trava Rendón.

For this reason all Yucatecan chess players are jubilant, the reason we celebrate with great joy as a part of this commemoration, the naming of the street "GMI Carlos Torre Repetto" — which goes from the roundabout at San Fernando Monumento to Bandera — in honor of our celebrated countryman, who to date has been the greatest Mexican chess player.

Torre, a Prophet in His Own Land

by Jorge A. Balam Díaz, Diario Yucatán, Thursday, 26 December 1990

A couple of years ago, two Dutch players showed up at the central chess club "Lic. Vicente Solís Aznar" and, after contesting a few games with the local players, someone asked them if they knew of master Carlos Torre Repetto, to which they responded immediately in the affirmative, embellishing their answer with brief tales of feats by the Yucatecan genius.

It should be no surprise that players from a country so far away would know of Torre, whose meteoric performance in the golden age of chess was very well known. What should be surprising is that in our own country so little should be known about the greatest Mexican chess player of all time.

And we must recognize, though we may not like it, that the president of the Mexican Chess Federation, Dr. Jorge Martín del Campo, was entirely right when, hours after arriving recently in this city to participate in the third Carlos Torre Memorial Tournament, he stated that the Yucatan master was better known in the Soviet Union than in Mexico.

Nevertheless, Yucatecans can affirm proudly and categorically, that it is not valid for the cradle of the only grandmaster the country has had. In Yucatan, many people, whether chess players or not, still know that Carlos Torre was a legendary figure of the scientific game. Perhaps they do not know that in his time of splendor he became immortalized by defeating the ex-world champion Emanuel Lasker in a famous game known as "the windmill," or that he drew another famous battle with the then universal monarch José Raúl Capablanca, and with Alexander Alekhine, another who would take the chess crown, but they certainly know that he was an illustrious Yucatecan.

In any other quarter, except in the chess media, very little is known, too little about the man who raised the flag of Mexico so high in the fascinating world of chess in the decade of the 1920s. If in these places one asks about Torre of someone who is not a chess player, they simply will not have the least idea of who one is talking about.

An inflexible law of life states that no one is a prophet in his own land, and in Yucatan this rule was perfectly applicable for long decades in Torre's case. But this is no longer true in our state, in that every day more Yucatecans take pride in his name being given to a busy street in Mérida.

With the annual memorial tournament celebrating our countryman and the restructuring of the fund undertaken by the Yucatan Chess Association, it is only a question of time before have an exception to the rule, and grandmaster Carlos Torre Repetto becomes a prophet in his own land.

Chapter VI

A Clash of Opposites

Taylor Kingston

We reproduce here an article which appeared in the Autumn 2001 issue of the British chess magazine Kingpin. *After reading John S. Hilbert's biography of Norman Tweed Whitaker, we realized that in Torre's game with Whitaker at Detroit 1924, rarely had two such different men sat across the board from each other, inspiring the theme for this article. We have left game annotations as they were; they may differ from those in the main part of this book.*

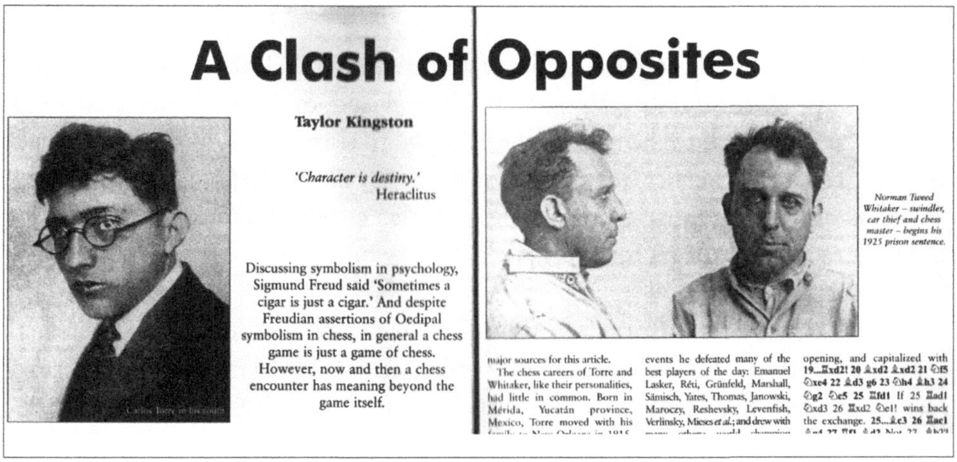

A Clash of Opposites

Taylor Kingston

'Character is destiny.'
Heraclitus

Discussing symbolism in psychology, Sigmund Freud said 'Sometimes a cigar is just a cigar.' And despite Freudian assertions of Oedipal symbolism in chess, in general a chess game is just a game of chess. However, now and then a chess encounter has meaning beyond the game itself.

Norman Tweed Whitaker – swindler, car thief and chess master – begins his 1925 prison sentence.

major sources for this article.

The chess careers of Torre and Whitaker, like their personalities, had little in common. Born in Mérida, Yucatán province, Mexico, Torre moved with his

events he defeated many of the best players of the day: Emanuel Lasker, Réti, Grünfeld, Marshall, Sämisch, Yates, Thomas, Janowski, Maroczy, Reshevsky, Levenfish, Verlinsky, Mieses *et al.*; and drew with

opening, and capitalized with **19...♖xd2! 20 ♗xd2 ♗xd2 21 ♘f5 ♘xe4 22 ♗d3 g6 23 ♘h4 ♗h3 24 ♘g2 ♘e5 25 ♖fd1** If 25 ♖ad1 ♘xd3 26 ♖xd2 ♘e1! wins back the exchange. **25...♗c3 26 ♖ae1**

Part of the article as it appeared in Kingpin

"Character is destiny." — Heraclitus

Discussing symbolism in psychology, Sigmund Freud said "Sometimes a cigar is just a cigar." And despite Freudian assertions of Oedipal associations in chess, in general a chess game is just a game of chess. However, now and then a chess encounter has meaning beyond the game itself.

Fischer-Spassky 1972, with its dramatic Cold War overtones, is an obvious example. Stylistic opposites, for example Tarrasch-Nimzovich and Petrosian-Tal, or temperament opposites, such as Alekhine-Capablanca, can also seem especially meaningful, a clash of hostile archetypes.

Such games are not found only at the highest levels. Our subject here is hardly one of the most important games in chess history, but it has definite symbolic significance. The players are Carlos Torre (1904-1978) and Norman Whitaker (1890-1975). Their one game against each other was nothing so earth-shaking as Fischer-Spassky or Alekhine-Capablanca, but it still represents a meeting of near-diametrical opposites.

Rarely have two chess figures had less in common. The career of one was brief but often brilliant, while the other's was long but without much major success. One ultimately found the competitive aspects of chess intolerably stressful, while the other reveled in dispute. One avoided women to save money, the other seduced women for their money. One was mild-mannered, sensitive and law-abiding; the other was extroverted, callous, and an habitual felon. One spent time in mental hospitals, the other years in jail. One sought beauty in chess as an art form, while the other sought egotistical self-glorification through the game. One is remembered today with honor, while the other left a mixed legacy with many negatives.

Both have the subject of recent biographies. Gabriel Velasco's *The Life and Times of Carlos Torre* (Russell Enterprises, 2000) is a revised, expanded version of a 1993 Spanish work, which this writer was privileged to translate. John Hilbert's *Shady Side: The Life and Crimes of Norman Tweed Whitaker, Chess Master* (Caïssa Editions, 2000), is one of the most thorough biographies ever devoted to a chess figure. These were major sources for this article.

The chess careers of Torre and Whitaker, like their personalities, had little in common. Born in Mérida, Yucatán province, Mexico, Torre moved with his family to New Orleans in 1911. There his chess talent bloomed. By the early 1920s he was the best player in Louisiana, and in 1924 he moved to America's chess capital, New York City. There he made an immediate impression, beating many strong players, including US champion Frank Marshall, and winning the state championship. He won at Detroit 1924 by a wide margin over many of America's best. His play was noticed in Europe, and in 1925 Torre played in three major international tournaments: Baden-Baden, Marienbad and Moscow, where he finished, respectively, 10th of 21, =3rd of 16, and =5th of 21, with a combined score of +19 -9 =27. In these and other events he defeated many of the best players of the day: Emanuel Lasker, Réti, Grünfeld, Marshall, Sämisch, Yates, Thomas, Janowski, Maróczy, Reshevsky, Levenfish, Verlinsky, Mieses *et al*; and drew with many others: world champion Capablanca, challenger-to-be Alekhine, Nimzovich, Rubinstein, Spielmann, Tartakower, Tarrasch, Rabinovich, Colle, Kashdan *et al.* Here are some examples of his creative play:

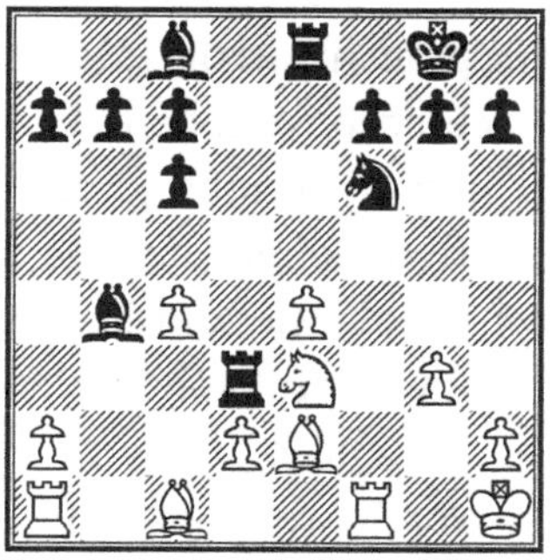

At Marienbad 1925, Torre (Black) outplayed Réti in the opening, and capitalized with

19...♖×d2! 20.♗×d2 ♗×d2 21.♘f5 ♘×e4 22.♗d3 g6 23.♘h4 ♗h3 24.♘g2 ♘c5 25.♖fd1
If 25.♖ad1 ♘×d3 26.♖×d2 ♘e1! wins back the Exchange.

25...♗c3 26.♖ac1 ♗g4 27.♖f1 ♗d2
Not 27...♗b2? 28.♖ce1 ♖×e1 29.♘×e1 ♘×d3 30.♘×d3 ♗e2 31.♖f2.

28.♖c2 ♗a5

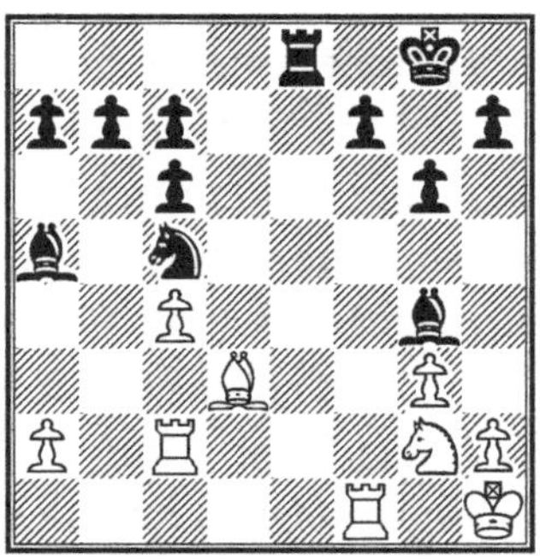

Surprisingly the white Bishop has no escape square, and Black achieves a decisive material advantage.

29.♘f4 ♘×d3 30.♘×d3 ♗e2 0-1

Torre showed an artistic, experimental attitude in many of his games. Here in **Torre-Banks**, Detroit 1924,

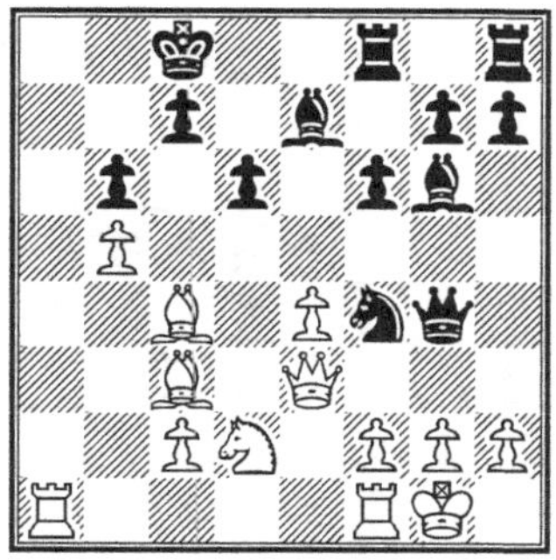

though Black threatens an unsubtle mate, White's advantage is clear and most easily realized by 22.♕g3, when 22...♕×g3 23.f×g3 traps the Knight, or if 22...♘e2+ 23.♗×e2 ♕×e2 24.♕h3+ f5 25.♗×g7. Either way White wins with little trouble, which Torre surely saw. Instead, though, he played the startling

22.♕×f4!!
This too led to a relatively easy win after

22...♕×f4 23.♗e6+ ♔b7? 24.♗d5+ c6 25.♗×c6+ ♔c8 26.♖a8+ ♔c7 27.♖a7+ ♔c8 28.g3 ♕g4 29.♖fa1 ♔d8 30.♗d4 1-0.
However, had Black played 23...♔b8 instead of ♔b7?, White's task would have been much harder; in fact it took several weeks of intensive computer-assisted research for Velasco and I to produce 2½ pages of fine-print analysis which, we believe, finally establish

that the sacrifice was sound. That Torre would risk such complications shows, I believe, not only his intuitive genius, but also his striving for beauty and creativity, not just the amassing of points.

Another example is **Torre-Verlinsky**, Moscow 1925:

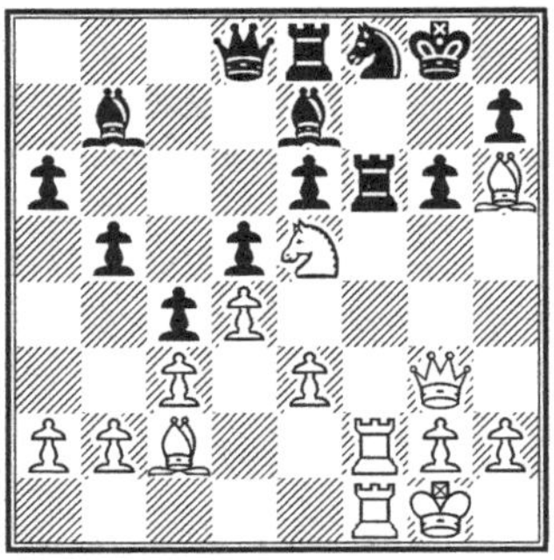

White's position is overwhelming, and the prosaic 22.♘g4 or 22.♖×f6 ♗×f6 23.♕f4 win, but Torre played it more like Anderssen:

22.h4 ♖f5 23.♗×f5 ♗×h4

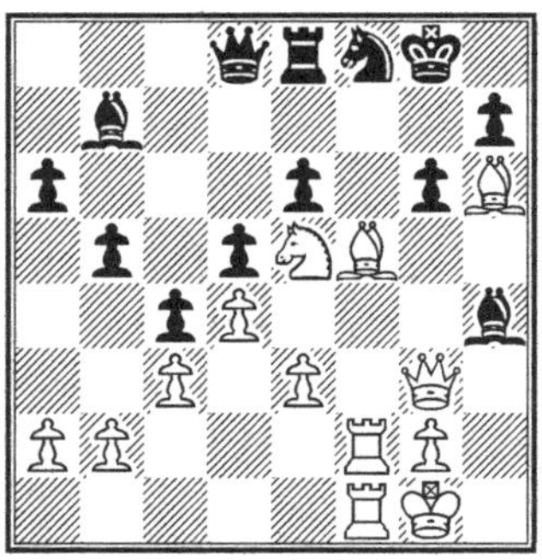

24.♗×g6!! ♗×g3
Or 24...♘×g6 25.♖f7 and mate in 5.

25.♗f7+ ♔h8 26.♗×e8 ♗×f2+ 27.♖×f2 1-0

Had Torre played Marshall for the US Championship in the mid-1920s he might well have won; he held a +2 -0 =2 edge in their serious games. In the Western Hemisphere he was second only to Capablanca, and in the world at large he was probably in the top 10 or 12 by the end of 1925. Nimzovich called Torre "a new genius," Lasker wrote of him as "a future world champion," and the young man received a hero's welcome on a tour of his native Mexico in 1926.

Norman Whitaker was not so early a bloomer as Torre. Born 14 years earlier, he learned chess the year Torre was born. Growing up in Philadelphia, then America's second chess city, he became by his late teens one of its best club and collegiate players. However in 1911 he left under a cloud, being censured by its chess patriarch, Walter Penn Shipley, and expelled from its premier club, the Franklin. This foreshadowed many ugly disputes in which Whitaker would be involved. Moving in 1913 to Washington DC to work as a patent attorney, he won several regional tournaments. In 1916 he played a match with former US champion Jackson Showalter, losing badly 6-1, but defeating him 5½-2½ two years later. He played well in several Western Chess Association events, the closest thing the US had to a championship tournament in those days, his best results being 2nd (to Showalter) in 1915, $=2^{nd}$-4th (with Hahlbohm, Morrison and Edward Lasker, behind Kostic) in 1918, 2nd (to Factor) in 1922, and =1st (with Mlotkowski) in 1923, with a combined score of +51 -14 =8 in six WCA championships over those years.

Whitaker's most noteworthy successes were Atlantic City 1921, where he scored 8-3 to finish 2nd of 12, half a point behind Janowski but well ahead of Marshall, and Kalamazoo 1927, the first National Chess Federation Championship, where he scored 6½-1½ and took clear first over Kupchik, Mlotkowski, Reshevsky, Herman Steiner and others. Though certainly not bad, Whitaker's games there do not make the same aesthetic impression as Torre's; his style is more one of opportunism and *Sitzfleisch*. For example, at Atlantic City,

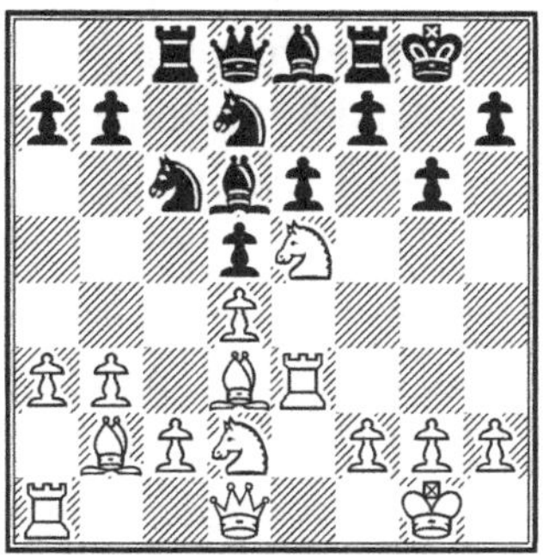

an incautious Janowski overreached with

14.c4?! ♗×e5!

Seeing that 15.d×e5 d4 16.♖e1 ♘d×e5 drops a pawn, Janowski sank deeper with

15.♖×e5? ♘c×e5 16.d×e5 ♘c5 17.♗c2 d×c4 18.♘×c4 ♕×d1+,

and Whitaker ground out an endgame win.

And here,

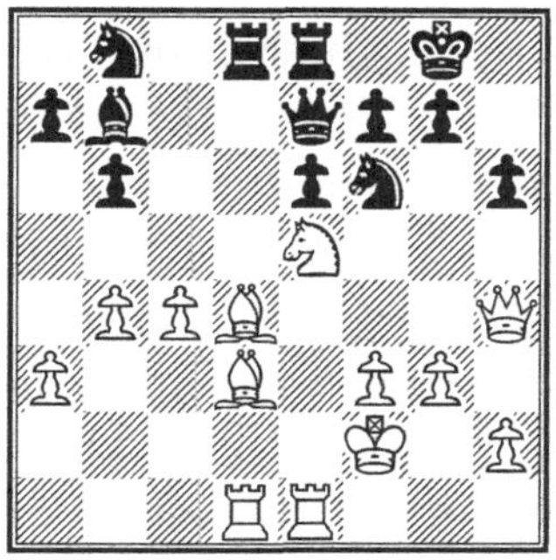

against Herman Steiner at Kalamazoo, Whitaker benefited from the egregious

27...g5?? 28.♕×h6 ♖×d4 29.♕×g5+ ♔f8 30.♕h6+ ♔g8 31.♕g5+ ♔f8 32.♕h6+ ♔g8 33.♗h7+ ♘×h7 34.♖×d4 f5?? 35.♕g6+ ♔f8 36.♖h4 1-0

In his only major international event, the 1928 FIDE Amateur Championship at The Hague, Whitaker made a respectable score, 9½-5½, to finish behind Euwe, Przepiórka and Mattison, joint 4th-6th with Golmayo and Treybal. For the 1920s Whitaker was among America's top 10, or even top five, below Marshall and Torre but up with Edward Lasker, Abraham Kupchik and a few others. However, that decade was about the last of high-level chess for Whitaker. He was being surpassed by the younger Kashdan, Steiner, Horowitz and Dake, and much to his angry displeasure, he was omitted from the 1930 and 1931 Olympic teams.

A major reason was that Whitaker had begun his criminal career. He committed his first felony, car theft, in 1921. He spent major portions of the years 1925-1950 behind bars and virtually all of 1932-1946 away from organized chess. His crimes were not violently or grossly evil, but showed a self-centered amorality about money, property and honesty. He felt little obligation to keep promises, tell factual truth, respect the feelings or possessions of others, or honor debts. His solipsistic outlook led to everything from petty thefts to major frauds. In between those extremes, he bounced checks, welched on business debts, dodged the military draft, used aliases, filed false insurance claims, stole cars, tampered with odometers of cars he owned legally, dealt in narcotics, attempted extortion, and seduced, swindled and jilted women. In one especially callous case, he courted one woman and stole her money for a honeymoon with another woman, then bragged about it openly.

The one major exception to his pattern of money-related crime was the sexual molestation of a 12-year-old girl, committed when he was 59. However, his most famous crime was the scheme of one Gaston Means, a notorious swindler compared to whom Whitaker was a novice. In 1932, when the baby of aviator Charles Lindbergh was kidnapped, Means convinced a wealthy, gullible heiress that for $104,000 he could secure release of the child. Whitaker joined in, posing as a gangster. Neither had any contact with the real kidnappers, but before the credulous heiress caught on she gave out the money. Shortly thereafter Means and Whitaker were arrested, but the money was never recovered, and of course the baby was dead. Their heartless ploy of using the tragedy for their own selfish ends was seen as particularly detestable.

In chess, Whitaker's amorality took the form of an egotistical assertion of his own status, and a persistent, grudgeful malice when it was not recognized. In one petty example, he barred Arthur Dake from entering a tournament, simply because Dake had been chosen over him for the Olympic team. He would continually barrage organizers with complaints phrased in seemingly general terms but which were actually personal grievances. More significantly, he made life miserable for the fledgling US Chess Federation during 1946-56. By this time Whitaker had spent years away from chess, including some in Alcatraz prison with Al Capone. His skill had declined badly, as evince by the 1948 US Championship, where he scored 6-13, finishing 16th of 20, 9 points behind winner Herman Steiner. Yet Whitaker insisted that his 1920s record still entitled him to elite status, and he vilified anything indicating otherwise, including the new USCF ratings, which in 1950 put him only at 2245, designated then as "expert" level, not even master. Angered by these and other perceived slights, he filed numerous protests and lawsuits, eventually settled out of court at a cost the cash-poor USCF could ill afford. Whitaker even attempted to split the USCF on racial lines, supporting segregated, whites-only tournaments. To give him his due, Whitaker did a lot in those years to organize tournaments, promote chess and teach it to youngsters, but overall he seems to have done more damage than good.

Whitaker's egotism could color his annotations. Consider Whitaker-Collins, Chicago 1930, for which he received a prize and which he annotated for the *Los Angeles Times*. In this position,

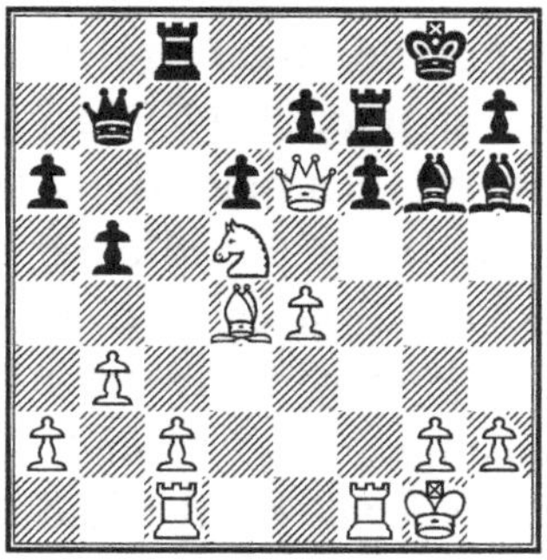

he played
30.♖cd1,
commenting "Best." Play continued

30...♖×c2 31.♖×f6!
Whitaker's punctuation.

31...e×f6 32.♘×f6+ ♔h8 33.♕e8+ ♖f8 34.♘g4+ 1-0.
Whitaker praises his own 30.♖cd1, but ignores the fact that 32...♔h8?? was a serious blunder, and that 32...♔g7! would probably have at least drawn, *viz.* 33.♕×d6? ♗e3+! 34.♗×e3 ♖×f6 35.♗h6+ (35.♗d4?? ♖×g2+!!) 35...♔×h6 36.♕×f6 ♕×e4, or 33.♘g4+ ♔f8 and either 34.♘×h6?! ♕e7 35.♕×e7+ ♖×e7 36.♖f1+ ♔e8, or 34.♕×d6+ ♕e7 35.♕b8+ ♕e8 36.♕d6+ ♕e7 etc., draw. Thus 30.♖cd1 and 31.♖×f6 were not "best," and better winning chances lay in 30.♘×e7+ ♕×e7 31.♕×c8+ ♖f8 32.♕×a6 ♗×c1 33.♖×c1 ♗×e4 34.♖e1. Whitaker so relished his "brilliancy" that he was not objective.

In contrast, Torre's annotations tended to be self-critical. For example, against Kupchik, New York Metropolitan League 1925,

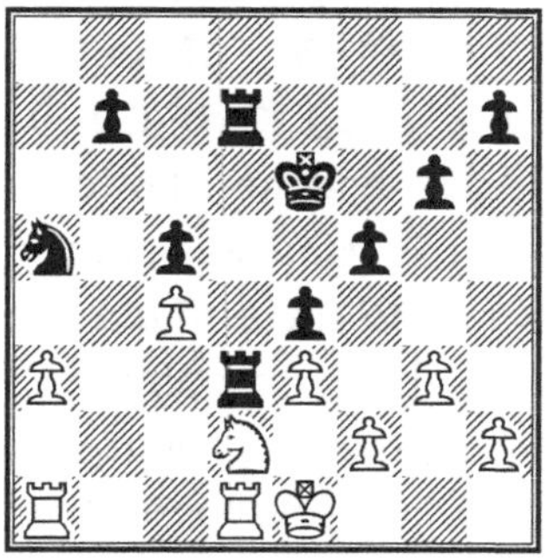

Torre played 27...b5. Annotating later, he castigated himself, writing "Entirely wrong. Black has played a fine positional game and has built a winning position; now he should simply continue with 27...♖c3. But he will

play a combination, his knowledge to the contrary notwithstanding." But 27...b5! was in fact the best move on the board.

Torre's lack of egotism is shown by the apocryphal game "Adams-Torre, 1920." In this famous combination, Edwin Z. Adams, an important figure in New Orleans chess but a player of no great ability,

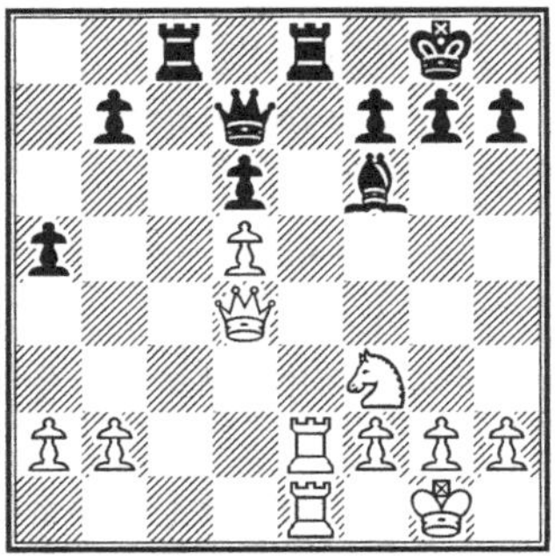

supposedly found the brilliant

18.♕g4! ♕b5 19.♕c4! ♕d7 20.♕c7!! ♕b5 21.a4!! ♕×a4 22.♖e4 ♕b5 23.♕×b7!! 1–0.

All available evidence, however, indicates that this game was never actually played; rather Torre found the main idea in analysis. To publicize it, and to honor Adams, his friend and chess mentor, Torre composed the game. Unlike Alekhine, who was known to falsify game scores to make himself look better, and unlike Whitaker, Torre here portrayed himself falsely as a loser, for the sake of showing something beautiful.

There is even a similar thread in their openings. Torre was not the first to play 1.d4 ♘f6 2.♘f3 e6 3.♗g5, but his use of it, especially his famous win over Lasker at Moscow 1925, led to its being called the Torre Attack. He did introduce to international play 1.d4 ♘f6 2.c4 ♘c6, against Sämisch at Baden-Baden 1925, and it was dubbed the Mexican Defense in his honor. In neither case, though, did Torre insist on these names; they were others' ideas. In contrast, Whitaker insisted that a line of the French, 1.e4 e6 2.d4 d5 3.♗e3, should be called "the Whitaker variation," despite the fact that Alapin and Mieses were playing it when Whitaker was a toddler.

Thus the differences between Torre and Whitaker. We now come to their one confrontation. As mentioned earlier, though Marshall was then US Champion by match play, the Western Chess Association championship, held more or less annually, was an unofficial US invitational tournament championship, limited to state champions and other strong players. The 1924 event was held in Detroit, Michigan. Torre, as New York champion, was invited. Though Whitaker's legal troubles had him in and out of court, he came too, and as 1923's co-winner he was a favorite. But this was a Torre triumph: he scored +12 =4 to finish 1st by 2½ points, with Whitaker, Hahlbohm and Factor joint 2nd and a young Reshevsky 5th. Torre had some walkovers, but not against Whitaker. Their game turned out to be the hardest fought of his career.

Rather than repeat this game all over again, we refer readers to Game 22 in the main part of the book. The annotations there are much better than what the article had in 2001.

Torre said this game "required an almost superhuman effort." Usually in chess there is no "good" or "bad" guy, but in this case it is hard not to feel that justice prevailed.

Their paths never crossed again. Torre went to Europe in 1925 and was feted in Mexico in 1926. Yet later that year, after a tournament in Chicago, he suffered a nervous breakdown. Due to insomnia, dietary problems and an oversensitive nature, he found competitive chess too stressful. He returned to Mexico to live in relative obscurity, and never again played serious chess. Nevertheless he retained an interest in the game, eventually becoming a sort of elder statesman and inspirational figure for the Yucatán chess community. FIDE also remembered him: in 1963 he was awarded the title of International Master, and in 1977, a few months before his death, Grandmaster.

Whitaker played chess the rest of his life, though in decreasingly important tournaments. He did gain the IM title in 1965, after years of self-promotion, including matches with old GMs. One, Fritz Sämisch, told of playing "a mad old American man who ... [was] trying to buy an international title." Sämisch had let him draw the match — "Why should I destroy the fool's life dream?" Whitaker continued to try various scams, which got progressively more sleazy and hare-brained. Though GM Arnold Denker has portrayed Whitaker as a wily, charming rogue who made a lot of money, in fact he was a rather inept con-man, and his thefts and scams netted him much more hard time than hard cash.

For all their differences, Torre and Whitaker had a flaw in common: difficulty in coping with real life. For Torre this harmed only himself, while with Whitaker the damage was to both himself and others. Torre's overly sensitive nature led him to shun competition, in chess and life; he retreated into honest but mostly menial labor for his more financially successful brothers. Whitaker spat on normal social conventions like honest work, yet he failed to succeed outside them, and he was often a financial burden to those close to him, especially his long-suffering wife. It is perhaps a pity that Torre and Whitaker could not have exchanged some traits. With some of Whitaker's thick-skinned assertiveness, Torre might have continued in chess and fulfilled Lasker's prophecy. With some of Torre's sensitivity and honesty, Whitaker might have stayed on the right side of the law. In the end, neither could avoid Heraclitus' dictum, and both died poor.

They are remembered quite differently. Whitaker's posthumous image, never bright, will be dimmed further by the Hilbert book, which gives many more sordid details than we have space for here. In Mérida, on the other hand, three chess clubs and a street are named after Torre, and the annual Carlos Torre Memorial Tournament has honored his name since 1987. As with the outcome of their game, it seems only just.

Chapter VII

The Development of Chess Ability

While Torre was in Leningrad, professor Konstantin Derzavin proposed that Torre write a book describing how he was able to make such rapid progress in chess in such a short time. Another Russian player, Abram Model, who would become Botvinnik's trainer in the late 1920s, was also curious to know if Torre had a secret or specific method of study that allowed him to become such a strong master so quickly. Model, Solomon Gotthilf, and Torre discussed that topic in Leningrad at the beginning of 1926. As a result, Torre in just two weeks produced this booklet, published first in Russian with a print run of 3,000 copies, later in Spanish as *El Desarollo de la Habilidad en el Ajedrez*, and in English as *Development of Chess Ability*, put out by the *American Chess Bulletin* and selling for 80 cents. We were fortunate to obtain a copy of the latter, now quite rare, and we present its contents in their entirety.

The booklet, only 32 pages all told, consists of eight games (called "studies" by Torre), ranging from the 1923 Louisiana Championship, to the 1926 Leningrad Quadrangular. Though all these games (except Study 6, Torre-Rokhlin) have been presented already in the main body of this book, we reprise them here with only Torre's own annotations, undistracted by computer kibitzing.

CARLOS TORRE

Development
of
CHESS ABILITY

By CARLOS TORRE

"An educational essay on development,
applied to chess."

Prof. Constantin Derzavin
Leningrad, U.S.S.R., 1926

Copyright 1926
By AMERICAN CHESS BULLETIN

PUBLISHERS
AMERICAN CHESS BULLETIN
150 Nassau Street
New York

DEDICATION:

In friendly dedication to Messrs. Edwin Z. Adams of New Orleans, Louisiana, Constantine Rasis of Detroit, Michigan, and Professor Constantin Derzavin of Leningrad, U.S.S.R.

FOREWORD

In this day of intensive chess study, made necessary by the multiplied congresses of international importance, it is little short of a miracle for anyone but a seasoned expert to force his way into the charmed circle of what have come to be known as "grand-masters." Yet this is what has taken place before our very eyes during the past year. A child of genius, a young Mexican by birth and resident of the United States for over ten years, has accomplished the seemingly impossible. With a latent talent given full opportunity to develop, with an eight years' sojourn in the home of the illustrious Paul Morphy for a romantic background, and then the hard knocks in the practical school of New York City, Carlos Torre blossomed forth and at 21 adorns acceptably the mystic garden of Caïssa.

That this youth, who feels himself at home in combat with the most famous exponents of the game the world has known, has a message to convey goes without saying. To reach his present high estate has required, aside from native talent, real determination and perseverance. Above all was essential a systematic course of regular study.

Anyone who will take but a casual glance at the literature of which the ancient pastime can boast and the quantity coming continually from the presses will appreciate what that means. A mere contemplation of it is apt to be discouraging to the tyro dreamily ambitious.

Our author, captivated at first like most of us by the beauties of romanticism, took pains to acquaint himself with the Steinitzian school, to the followers of which have gone most of the worthwhile prizes for two generations past. The hypermoderns held no secrets from him when, in the spring of 1925, he set out for Europe on conquest bent.

How to develop ability at chess is the subject of this little booklet treated by Mr. Torre in his own way. The marked success which has attended his brief career thus far fits him to tell a story well worth listening to. Eager youth everywhere will lend a ready ear. To the more mature also it will make strong appeal, as the message is delivered through the medium of actual games played by the author himself. A good game is a perennial source of joy to the true lover of chess and, like a work of art, never grows stale. The specimens chosen for exemplification here are, as our author puts it, annotated conversationally rather than analytically. His aim is the presentation of clear and simple truths.

HERMANN HELMS.
New York, February 5, 1926.

NOTE: It was my good fortune to make friends in Leningrad with Professor Constantin Derzavin and his wife, who arranged to have me write the present work for the Krolenko Publishing House of that city. That eminent Russian writer on chess, Professor A.A. Smyrnoff, undertook the happy translation of the original manuscript, although of course I had the opportunity to go more carefully over the same on the SS Lithuania.

CARLOS TORRE.
March 1, 1926.

Study One

The following was the deciding partie in the Championship Tournament held in New Orleans, Louisiana, in November, 1923. It was a double round affair with eight players. The leader of the white pieces is the foremost player of the state.

[Note: For the sake of indexing, we have assigned numbers to these games in sequence with the rest of this book.]

Game 115

Labatt-Torre

Louisiana State Championship, New Orleans 1923

Queen's Gambit Declined [D67]

1.d4 d5 2.♘f3 ♘f6 3.c4 e6 4.♗g5 ♗e7 5.e3 ♘bd7 6.♘c3 0–0 7.♖c1 c6

This mode of development was perfected by Capablanca. The idea is to develop the QB in due course at b7, where it may become far more useful than White's KB.

8.♗d3 d×c4 9.♗×c4 ♘d5 10.♗×e7

This little book is not intended to be a treatise on the Opening, so we need not dwell on the various continuations at this point.

10...♕×e7 11.0–0 ♘×c3 12.♖×c3 b6 13.♕e2 ♖d8 14.♗d3

As it is White's intention to exchange this Bishop at a6, it would have been far wiser to develop the King's Rook to d1 or c1.

14...♗b7 15.♗a6

True, White would obtain a very good, perhaps winning game with 15.♗e4, but we need not concern ourselves with moves that are only incidentally good.

15...♗×a6 16.♕×a6 c5 17.♕e2

As a result of the loss of time on the 14th move, which did not help his game in any manner, White has no longer an Opening advantage. This neglect we must guard against. If we are to develop our ability, there should be no wasted effort. Rather, let us cultivate the habit of playing throughout the game the very best moves we can find — the moves that help our game the most. And let there be no *conscious* violation.

17...♖ac8 18.♖fc1 ♖c7 19.d×c5 ♖×c5 20.a3 g6 21.g3

It would have been more prudent to play 21.h3.

21...e5

The advance of this pawn, otherwise

hardly justified, is very strong now because of the hole at f3.

22.b4 ♖×c3 23.♖×c3 e4 24.♘d4 ♘e5 25.♘c6

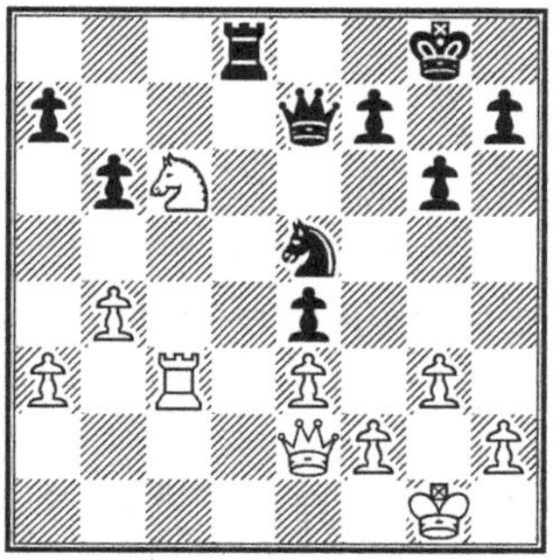

White has thought to eliminate all danger with the exchange of the Knights.

25...♕c7

It would not do to check with the Knight, for White would simply take it off. But with this move Black gets a very strong pin, enabling him to take advantage of the weakness at f3.

26.♕c2

Nor would other moves be much better.

26...♘f3+ 27.♔f1 ♖d3

Now there is no defense against the threat to double on the d-file.

28.h3 ♕d7 0–1

Study Two

In the playoff for the New York State Championship in October, 1924, I had to win the following game in order to tie the match, which I subsequently annexed. For this reason I consider this the most meritorious game I have won.

Game 116

Torre-Jennings

New York State Championship playoff, game 2, New York, 1924

Queen's Gambit Declined [D30]

1.d4 ♘f6 2.♘f3 d5 3.c4 e6 4.♗g5 ♘bd7 5.e3 c6 6.♘bd2

Avoiding the ordinary form of the Cambridge Springs variation, which may prove very troublesome.

6...♕a5 7.a3 d×c4

Black exchanges before playing ...♗d6, as he does not fancy c4-c5.

8.♗×c4 ♗d6 9.0–0 e5

Castling would be safer, although White still retains his opening advantage; in the simplest manner with ♗c4-d3, threatening to exchange Black's most useful piece.

10.♕b3 0–0

The complications ensuing from 10... e4 11.♘e5 would favor White, having the better development.

11.d×e5 ♗×e5 12.♘×e5 ♕×e5

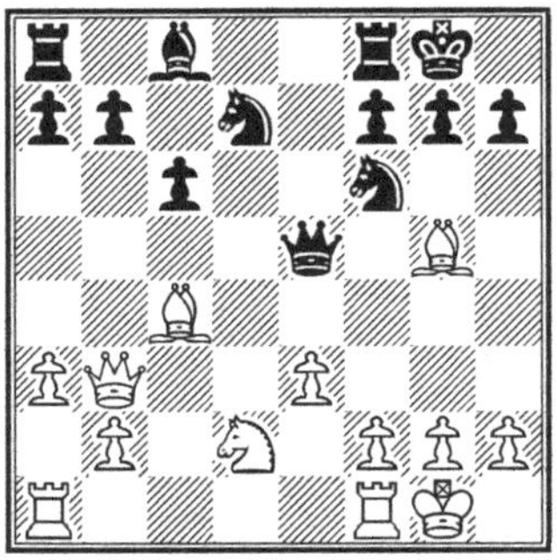

13.♘f3

Here White takes the simpler course, content with a slight advantage for the coming ending. Far more complicated would be the advance 13.f4.

13...♕c7 14.♗f4 ♕b6 15.♗d6 ♕×b3 16.♗×b3 ♖e8 17.♘g5 ♘d5 18.e4 h6 19.e×d5

19.♘×f7 loses after 19...♖×e4.

19...h×g5 20.♖fe1 ♘f6 21.♖×e8+ ♘×e8 22.♗e7 c×d5 23.♗×d5 ♘c7 24.♗e4 f6 25.♖c1 ♘e8 26.♗d5+ ♔h7 27.b4 ♔g6 28.♖c4 ♖b8 29.h4 g4

Black's position was not very wholesome in any event, but here he should have exchanged. In his inferior position he creates a very material weakness at g4. Furthermore, he keeps a good possible square from his Bishop.

30.h5+

This move is intended to invite the advance of the g7-pawn, when the weakness on the King's side will be all the more accentuated.

30...♔h7 31.♗f7 ♗f5 32.♖c5 g6 33.h×g6+ ♗×g6 34.♗e6 b6 35.♖c4 ♖b7 36.♗d8 ♗h5

We see that White's Bishops have increased their range, whereas Black's Bishop is completely hemmed in.

37.♖d4 ♔h6 38.♔h2 ♔g5 39.♗d7

Threatening 40.♖d5+ and 41.♖×h5.

39...♖b8 40.♗e7

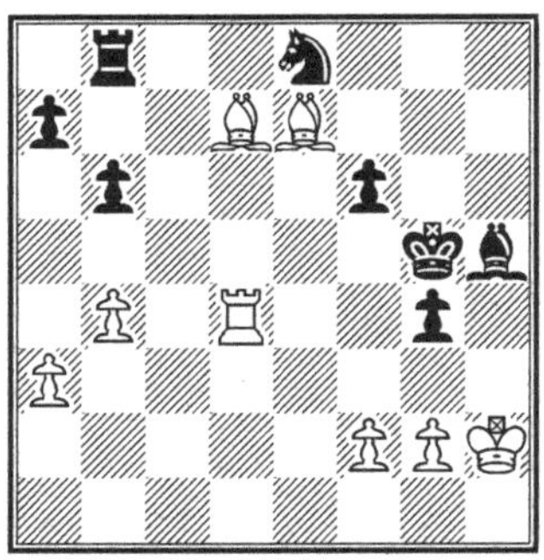

40...♔h6

Foreseeing that his efforts to save the King's side are only landing him in greater difficulties, Black endeavors to carry out an orderly retreat. But this is not to be accomplished after the mistake on the 29th move.

41.b5

This settles it. White rightly turns his attention to the Queen's side which has been weakened by the removal of the Bishop.

41...♔g7 42.♗c6 ♗g6 43.♖d7 ♗f5 44.♖×a7 ♔g6 45.a4 ♘g7 46.♗d6 ♖h8+ 47.♔g1 ♖d8 48.♗c7 ♖d1+

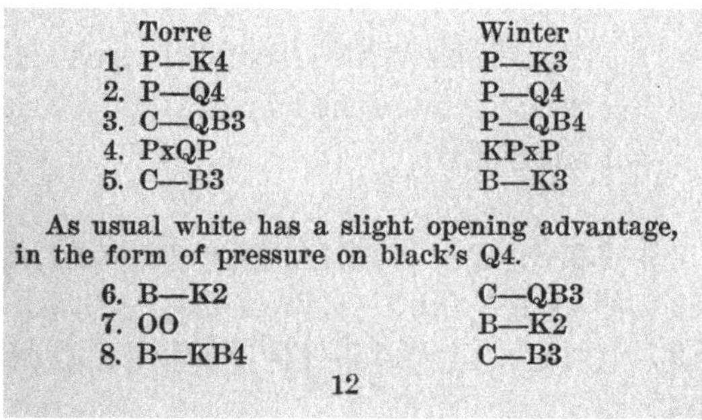

Torre	Winter
1. P—K4	P—K3
2. P—Q4	P—Q4
3. C—QB3	P—QB4
4. PxQP	KPxP
5. C—B3	B—K3

As usual white has a slight opening advantage, in the form of pressure on black's Q4.

6. B—K2	C—QB3
7. OO	B—K2
8. B—KB4	C—B3

12

49.♔h2 ♗e6 50.a5 ♘f5 51.a×b6 ♖d3 52.b7 g3+ 53.♗×g3 1–0

What we see exemplified in this game may be summed up as follows: When your opponent has a weakness, he may sufficiently protect it, but probably only at the expense of creating a minus elsewhere on the board. This minus is to be located and exploited, in order to take advantage of the original weakness.

An odd feature of Torre's booklet is that he used the letter "C" to stand for the Knight, rather than "Kt" which was common at the time, or "N" which became standard later. "C" is used for the Knight — Caballo, i.e. horse — in Torre's native Spanish, but it is strange that the ACB would leave it that way in the English-language edition. Another oddity is "OO" for castling.

Study Three

Game 117

Torre-Winter

Western CA Championship, Detroit 1924

French Defense [C10]

The following game I believe to be the best I won in the Western Championship Tournament held in Detroit, Michigan, in September, 1924. The leader of the black pieces is one of the oldest and strongest players of that city.

1.e4 e6 2.d4 d5 3.♘c3 c5 4.e×d5 e×d5 5.♘f3 ♗e6

As usual White has a slight opening advantage, in the form of pressure on d5.

6.♗e2 ♘c6 7.0–0 ♗e7 8.♗f4 ♘f6 9.d×c5 ♗×c5 10.♘b5 ♖c8 11.♘bd4 0–0 12.♘×c6
To take with the pawn would lose the Exchange.

12...♖×c6 13.♘d4 ♖c8
Black may of course play 13...♗×d4 14.♕×d4 ♖×c2 15.♗d3.

14.♗g5 h6 15.♗h4 a6
He wants to play ...♖f8-e8, which would now be answered by ♗e2-b5, but his policy is rather slow.

16.c3 ♖e8 17.♗f3 ♗e7 18.♖e1 ♕b6 19.♖b1 ♗d8 20.♕d3 ♘h7 21.♗×d8 ♖c×d8 22.♖e2 ♘g5 23.♖be1 ♘e4 24.h3
Here White could well play 24.♗×e4 d×e4 25.♕×e4 and after 25...♗×a2 26.♕×e8+ with advantage in material.

24...♗d7 25.♗×e4 d×e4 26.♖×e4 ♖×e4 27.♖×e4 ♕×b2
Black played 23...♘e4 with the idea of exchanging the weak d-pawn for the b-pawn, and White has evolved a plan that will meet this more than halfway. But incidentally the gain of the Exchange was here possible through 27... ♗f5. There were about eighty spectators watching the game and they all saw it; enlightening the players later of the fact. This may be of interest in showing the working of the chess mind.

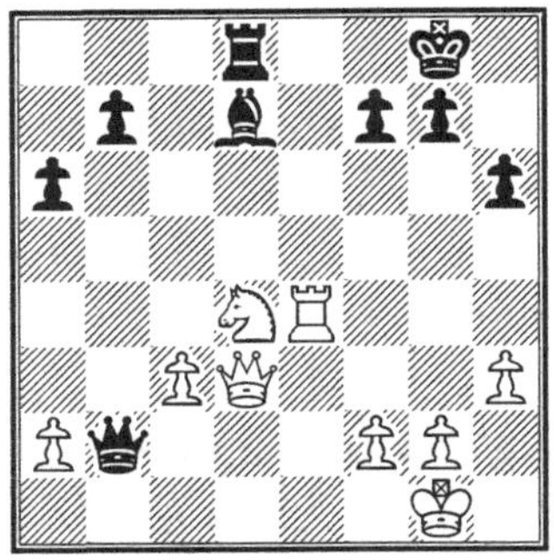

28.♘f5
We see that White has not merely exchanged pawns; he has obtained a very telling pin.

28...♕c1+ 29.♔h2 ♕g5 30.♖d4 g6 31.♘e3 ♕e7 32.♘g4 ♔g7 33.♖d6 ♗×g4 34.♕d4+ f6 35.♖×d8 ♗e6 36.♕d6 ♕f7

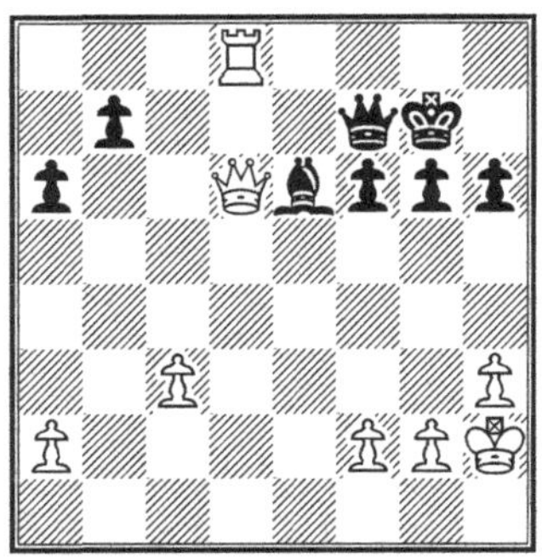

37.c4
A good move, to give the white pieces more scope.

37...g5 38.c5 ♔g6 39.c6 b×c6 40.♕×c6 ♗×a2 41.♕c2+ f5
If now or on the next move he plays the

King back to g7, White plays the Rook to the c-file.

42.♖d6+ ♗e6

White now plays the Queen to e5 in three moves.

43.♕c8 ♔f6 44.♕h8+ 1–0

Study Four

Game 118

Kupchik-Torre

Metropolitan League Team Ch, New York 1925

Grünfeld Defense [D71]

Shortly after my match with Kupchik, we contested the following game in New York, in March, 1925.

1.d4 ♘f6 2.c4 g6 3.♘c3 ♗g7 4.g3 d5 5.c×d5 ♘×d5 6.♗g2 ♘×c3 7.b×c3 c5 8.♘f3 ♘c6 9.♗b2

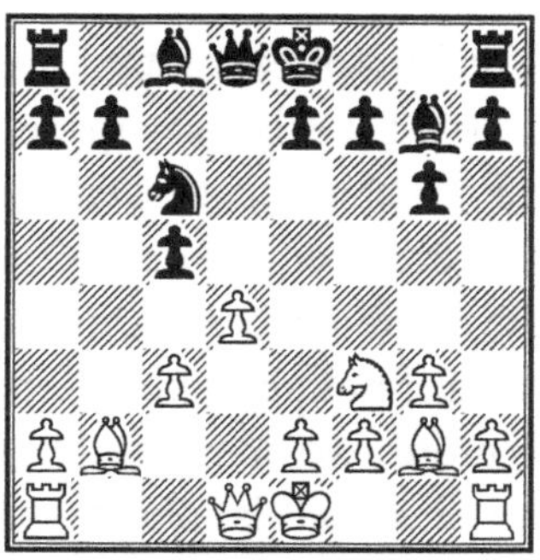

9...♕b6

With this move Black goes right straight for the ending, on the strength of his next move, which gives him a very marked advantage.

10.♕b3 ♗e6 11.♕×b6 a×b6 12.a3 0–0 13.0–0 ♗d5

Increasing his advantage by exchanging White's only useful piece.

14.♖fd1 ♖fd8 15.e3 ♘a5

The threat of this Knight coming to c4, which would prove very cramping, forces the exchange of Bishops. Also, it enables Black to obtain possession of the d-file.

16.♘d2 ♗×g2 17.♔×g2 e5

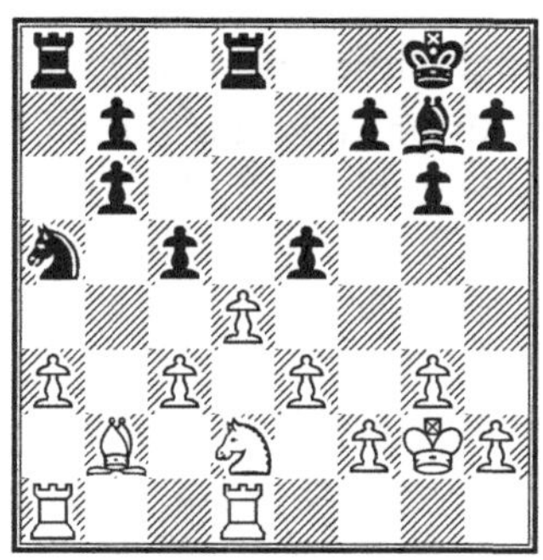

Whereas White's Bishop is completely hemmed in, this move is intended to increase the strength of the black Bishop.

18.d×c5 b×c5 19.♖ab1

Otherwise White would have to bear in mind the possibility of ...♖×d2 and ...♘a5-c4.

19...f5 20.c4

In liberating the Bishop White must chain the Knight.

20...♖d3 21.♔f1 ♖ad8 22.♔e2 e4 23.♗×g7 ♔×g7 24.♖a1 ♔f6 25.♔e1 ♔e6 26.♔e2 ♖8d7 27.♔e1

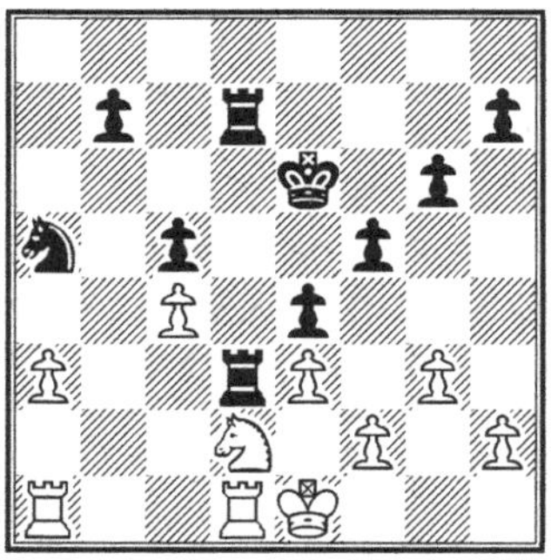

27...b5

Entirely wrong. Black has played a fine positional game and has built a winning position; now he should simply continue with 27...♖c3. But he will play a combination, his knowledge to the contrary notwithstanding. That is probably why the great masters — Capablanca, Lasker, Alekhine — lose so few games. Regardless of the judgment of other masters, they will seldom play against their own judgment.

28.c×b5 c4 29.♖ac1 c3 30.♘f1 ♘b3 31.♖×d3 ♖×d3 32.♖c2 ♔d5 33.g4 ♔c4 34.g×f5 g×f5 35.♘g3 ♔×b5 36.♘×f5 ♔a4 37.♘g3 ♘d2 38.♔d1

The position has been very difficult for the last ten moves and now White makes a surprising move, running into a discovered check.

38...♘f1+ 39.♔c1 ♘×g3 40.h×g3 ♔×a3 41.♖e2 ♔b3 0–1

For Black will play ...♖d6-d3, and then switch the Rook to the h- and a-files, to queen the pawn.

If we are to learn anything from this game, let it raise our appreciation of beauty in chess. Let us endeavor to curb our impulse for forced brilliancy; for to give it rein would retard our development if not altogether deform it. Furthermore, we may render incongruous that which is inherently beautiful.

Study Five

Game 119

Réti-Torre

Marienbad 1925

English Opening [A20]

I have selected the following game played in the Marienbad International Tournament, because it contains a most instructive problem to work out.

1.c4 e5 2.♘f3 e4 3.♘d4

Interesting would be to retreat the Knight to g1. Black would then be playing the Sicilian a move to the good. But whether or not it is a good move, that is the question. Nevertheless it is not an opening to be sought after for White.

3...♘c6 4.♘×c6

Here it would be wiser to play 4.♘c2, though in any event he has no longer an advantage; to Tournament exchange distinctly helps Black's position.

4...d×c6 5.♘c3 ♘f6 6.g3 ♗c5 7.♗g2 ♗f5 8.0–0 0–0 9.♔h1 ♕d4

The threat is 10...♘g4, and after 11.f3 ♕g1+.

10.♕b3 ♖fe8 11.♘d1 ♖ad8 12.♘e3

In his inferior development White rightly refuses to chase after pawns.

12...♗c8 13.♕c2

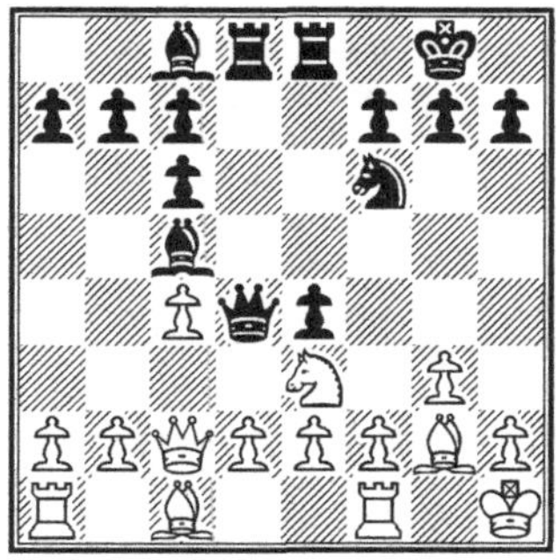

13...♕e5

Insufficient, for the reason that he merely transfers the Queen to another square where it exerts as much pressure, but no more. Black has the superior game; yet the white pieces are so placed that they can just repel all Black's threats. We must, therefore, find the continuation that will bring additional pressure to bear on the white camp. This can be accomplished with the advance of the h-pawn. So 13...h5 14.♖b1 h4 15.b4 ♗f8, leaving White with a very difficult game to hold together.

14.f3 ♕h5 15.b4

But now Mr. Réti, getting short of time, overlooks that his e-pawn is to fall. With 15.b3 White would have a very playable game. In truth, Black may very easily run into a bad position.

14...♗×b4 16.f×e4 ♕×e2 17.♗f3 ♕d3 18.♕×d3 ♖×d3 19.♗e2 ♖×d2

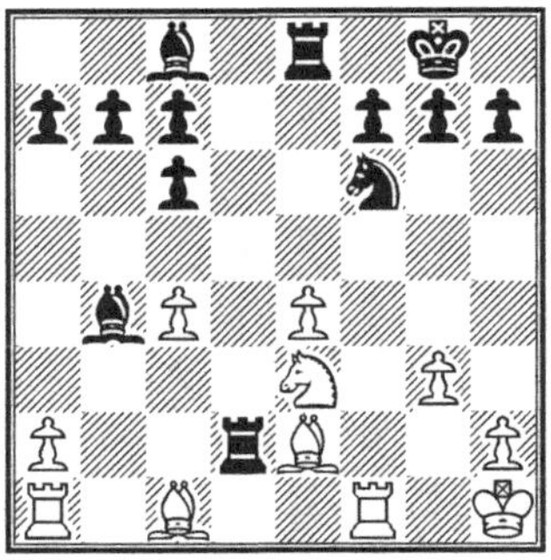

The simplest. Aside from the three pawns he obtains for the Exchange, his Bishops will prove very strong.

20.♗×d2 ♗×d2 21.♘f5 ♘×e4 22.♗d3

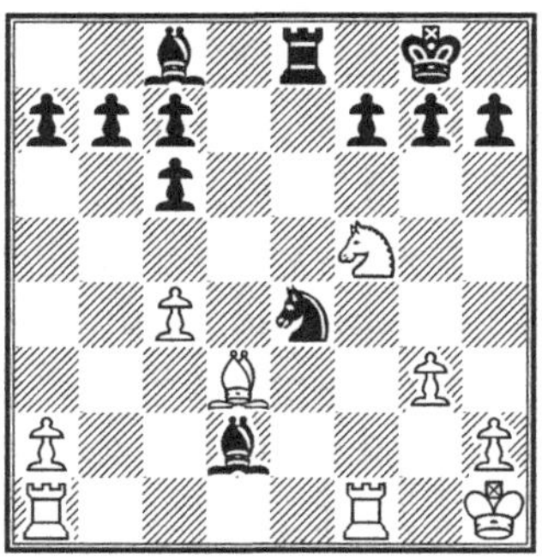

22...g6

Black now commences a series of moves to win back the Exchange.

23.♘h4 ♗h3 24.♘g2 ♘c5
When your opponent has not the b-pawn, the square c5 is most useful for the Knight.

25.♖fd1
To move the other Rook would lose the Exchange right off.

25...♗c3 26.♖ac1 ♗g4 27.♖f1 ♗d2

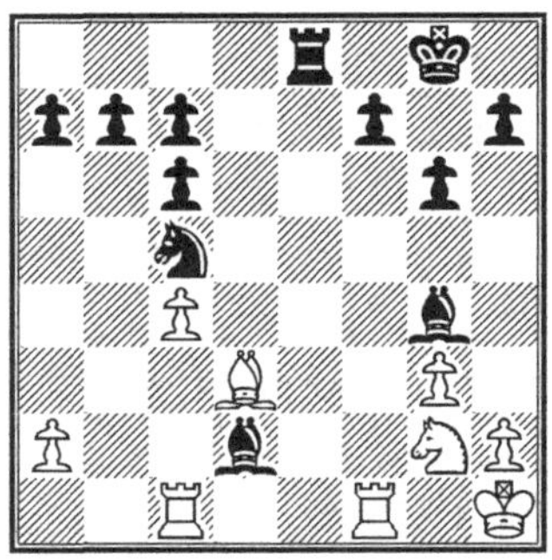

Not so convincing would be 27...♗b2 28.♖ce1 ♖×e1 29.♘×e1 ♘×d3 30.♘×d3 ♗e2 31.♖f2.

28.♖c2 ♗a5
The white Bishop is most curiously "mated" in the center.

29.♘f4 ♘×d3 30.♘×d3 ♗e2 0–1

Study Six

Game 120

Torre-Rokhlin

Leningrad Quadrangular 1926

Torre Attack [A47]

Having played a good game and obtained an advantage is not in itself sufficient. We should endeavor to find the continuation that will bring our advantage home in the most exact and precise manner, even if it does involve a little risk. The too safe course may be all wrong. In Capablanca's words, in some positions it may be the wisest and quickest way "to go right into the melee." An example from the Quadrangular Young Masters Tournament held in Leningrad, January, 1926, will bear this out.

1.d4 ♘f6 2.♘f3 e6 3.♗g5 c5 4.e3 c×d4

This system of play was originated and developed by Sämisch of Berlin.

5.e×d4 ♗e7 6.♘bd2 d6 7.♗d3 ♘bd7 8.0–0 b6 9.♖e1 ♗b7 10.c3 0–0 11.♘f1 ♖e8 12.♘g3 ♕c7

13.♘d2 h6 14.♗e3 ♘d5 15.♘h5 f5 16.♕b3 ♔h8

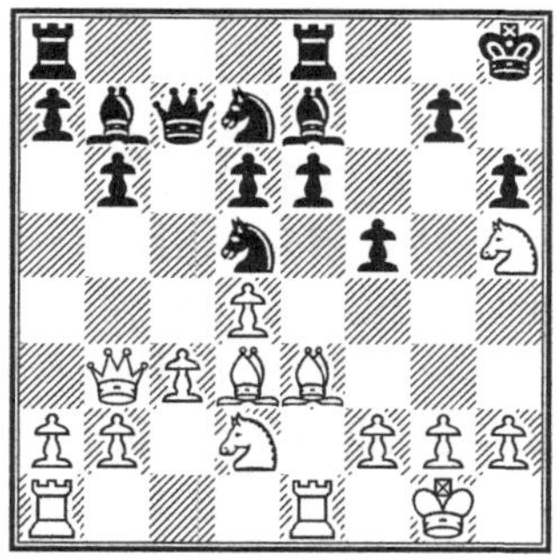

The white pieces have been placed right to meet the advance of the black pawns, therefore 17.♘f4 ♘×f4 18.♗×f4 e5 19.♕f7 ♗f6 20.♕h5 winning. Many and very instructive are the possibilities after 17.♘f4. But instead White played

17.f3

Whereupon Black got quite a good game with

17...♗h4

Completely reversing matters. The result of this Tournament was Gotthilf, 4-2; Rokhlin and Torre, 3-3; and Model, who played the best chess, but was guilty of this very omission, 2-4.

Study Seven

Game 121
Torre-Gotthilf
Moscow 1925

Slav Defense [D13]

This partie, played in the recent Moscow International Masters Tournament, is the most classical game I have won to date.

1.d4 d5 2.c4 c6 3.♘c3 ♘f6 4.♘f3 ♗f5 5.c×d5 c×d5 6.♕b3 ♕b6
The World's Champion played the more conservative 6...♗c8. If that is the best procedure at Black's disposal after his 4th move, the variation is to be shunned.

7.♘×d5 ♘×d5 8.♕×d5 e6 9.♕b3 ♕×b3 10.a×b3 ♗c2

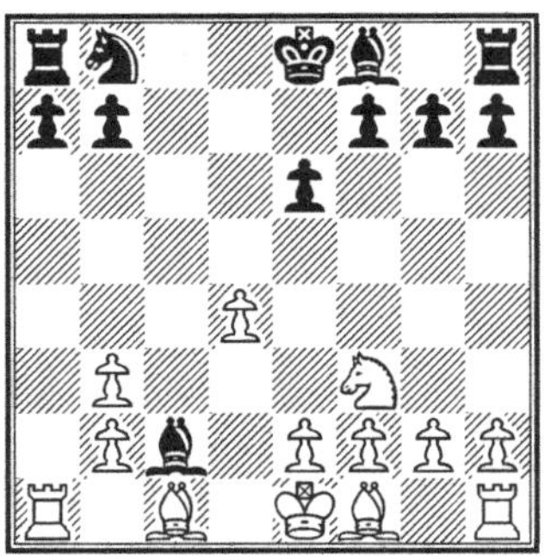

If White can hold his extra pawn, he will have a very good game, having some pressure on the a-file, and in addition controlling the center.

11.♗d2 ♗×b3
My partie with Opocensky in the first round in Marienbad went somewhat as follows: 11...♘c6 12.♗c3 ♗b4 13.♘d2 ♗g6 14.e3 0–0 15.♗b5 ♗e7 16.♔e2 ♖fd8 17.♖a4 ♖dc8 18.♖ha1 a6 19.♘c4 ♖ab8 20.♗×c6 ♖×c6 21.♘e5 ♖c7 22.♖c4 ♖bc8 23.♘×g6 h×g6 24.♔d3, with ♗c3-a5 to come. But in the actual game White played 22.♘×g6 h×g6 23.♖c4, and now Black obtained splendid drawing chances, playing 23...♖d7 and bringing the Rook to d5 and b5. This will help us to realize that we must play the best, to win even a won game.

12.e4
In this partie Black has played more consistently, in winning the pawn that he went after. But his Bishop is closed in and White is threatening ♗f1-b5+ and ♘f3-e5. Also ♗d2-c3 and ♘f3-d2.

12...f6 13.♗c3 ♗c2 14.♘d2 ♘d7 15.♗b5 a6 16.♔e2 ♖c8 17.♗×d7+ ♔×d7 18.♖hc1 b5 19.♖×c2 b4 20.♖×a6 b×c3 21.♖×c3
In this manner Black's only developed piece is exchanged. It is always wise to exchange the most valuable pieces of

your opponent. Compare with Game No. 4, where White has a dead Bishop at b2. But the moment it becomes useful, it is immediately exchanged.

21...♖×c3 22.b×c3 ♗d6 23.♘c4 1–0

The beauty of this game, very simple in its essence, lies in its harmony — harmony of conception, harmony in execution. For beauty and harmony are one. In the commencement White had a very simple plan, to take advantage of Black's doubtful 4th move. And the play is the natural unfolding of one sound idea.

Study Eight

Game 122

Model-Torre

Leningrad Quadrangular 1926

Queen's Indian Defense [E14]

Our last example will be taken from the Leningrad Tournament mentioned previously.

1.d4 ♘f6 2.c4 b6 3.♘c3 ♗b7 4.♘f3 e6 5.e3 ♗e7 6.♗d3 d6 7.0–0 ♘bd7 8.e4 e5

The Nimzovich defense. It is not so very good as there are too many pawn moves. Further, Black has holes at f5 and c6; and the KB is not happily placed.

9.♕e2 0–0

10.d5

After forty minutes deliberation White commits himself to this advance with the plan to advance the f-pawn and the massing of the forces on the black King. Such far reaching moves are to be played only after a profound understanding of the position, enabling one to judge the probable success of the plan in consideration.

10...♘c5 11.♗c2 a5 12.♘e1 ♘fd7 13.♘d1 ♗c8 14.♘e3

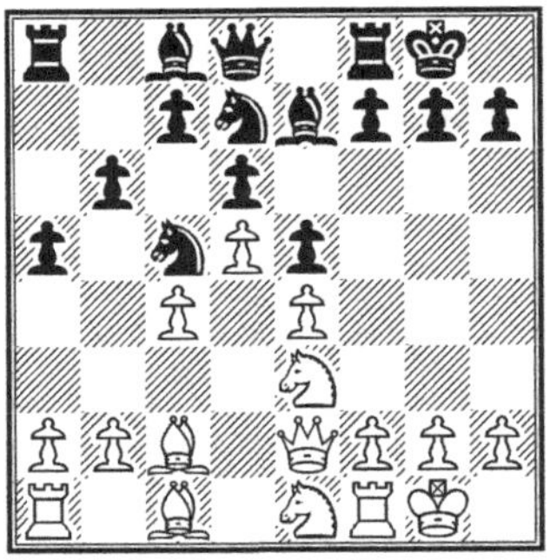

14...♗g5

Black's counter plan is now equally clear. The diagonal d8-h4 is sufficiently controlled by the Queen, so he wants to exchange White's powerful QB, with consequent utilization of the superior disposition of the other Bishop.

15.♘f5 g6 16.f4

White is a very fine player and will not deviate from his course. Naturally after 16.♘g3 ♗f4, but after the text, the black game simply flourishes. Nevertheless, this habit of going through with our plan is to be cultivated for it will develop our ability to evolve an ever sounder conception.

16...e×f4 17.♘d4 ♘e5 18.h3 ♗d7 19.b3 ♕e7

Wiser than 19...♕f6, which on account of the Bishop coming to b2 and the position of White's KR, would bring trouble.

20.♗×f4

He can save the pawn with another move, whereupon Black plays ♖a8-e8, always with manifest advantage.

20...♗×f4 21.♖×f4 ♕g5 22.♖f2 ♗×h3 23.♘ef3 ♘×f3+ 24.♘×f3 ♕g3 25.♕d2 ♗g4

Certainly more prudent than 25...♗×g2.

26.♕g5 f6 27.♕h6 ♗×f3 28.♖×f3 ♕e5 29.♖e1 ♖ae8 30.♖h3 ♖f7

Of some importance in preference to 30...♖e7, as will be seen shortly.

31.♖ee3 ♕a1+ 32.♔h2 ♕c1 33.e5 ♕×c2 34.e×f6 ♘e4

To exchange Rooks first would be even a little simpler. But if Black had to play 34...♖ef8, White would force a most beautiful win with 35.♖e7 and 36.♕g7+.

35.♖h4 ♘×f6 36.♖×e8+ ♘×e8 0–1

If this study should prove more pleasurable and instructive than the preceding examples, we may safely conclude that it exemplifies a higher art of chess — chess, not as a disconnected sequence of moves, but as the outworking of two ideas extending throughout the game.

Summary

The reader will have perceived that it has not been my intention to annotate the parties analytically, but rather conversationally, with the view of making clear some simple truths that may help us in the development of our ability.

This chapter, the continuation of the foregoing, is written for younger players aspiring to become masters, or at least very proficient in the art of chess. May it help you to the realization of your ambition.

Let us clearly and distinctly realize that to become learned in the openings, or skillful in the endings is not development. For there is no development without harmony. Our first endeavor then must be to play all parts of the game equally well; that is, to play chess.

Now let us decide how we are to play in order that our ability may be developed to an ever higher level.

If we resolve to play each time very much better than we did the last; to play the opening with greater precision, the middle game with higher consciousness, the ending with more directness, to see further ahead with finer accuracy, to evolve a greater masterpiece; the inner effort will prove very cumulative, and our progress will surpass our happiest dreams.

Assuredly, if we play in this manner a number of times twenty, we will improve far more than we would from two years indifferent daily playing.

For that which is cumulative must be progressive, and the continued greater effort will develop our ability in a compoundly progressive ratio.

Hitherto we have largely concerned ourselves with the borrowing of variations from books. But development without the inner effort will not come. The key word to our development then will be: Continued Greater Effort.

Consciousness is the virtue of the grand masters. The highest consciousness, combined with a superior knowledge, are embodied in the play of the World's Champion, Capablanca. So we see that consciousness and knowledge go hand in hand.

Let us, therefore, never make a move in the hope that it will come out all right, that it will prove the strongest. For we cannot develop in ignorance or at best it will not be the highest development.

Rather, let us cultivate the habit to know the why and wherefore we are playing, to see the combination through before making it. And let us ever satisfy ourselves that it is the best procedure.

Yes, let us keep away permanently from this most dangerous temptress, this "Good Enough Policy" which rarely wins games.

For beauty in chess, which is soundness of conception, allied with harmony in execution, lies not in her path.

The most wondrous combinations of the grand masters are the culmination of the most simple and direct play. These brilliant combinations that pervade our being with a higher sense of goodness, do not happen. They are evolved.

Eventually, if we put forth the inner effort, we will also be able to play the far-reaching positional plans exemplified in the games of the most modern masters.

To be conscientious, to be sincere, to will — is to develop.

CARLOS TORRE

January, 1926 Leningrad, U.S.S.R.

Chapter VIII

Others' Games from the 1926 Mexican Championship

We give here the six games between Araiza, Freyria and Soto Larrea, as annotated by Torre in the tournament book. Other than being translated into English and algebraic notation, the notes are just as Torre wrote them; we have even tried to maintain a semblance of his style. A few diagrams have been added. To minimize interference with the flow of Torre's ideas, we have added computer-assisted corrections or additions only where we deemed them absolutely necessary; these are in italics.

Game 123

Araiza-Freyria

Mexican Championship, Mexico City 1926, round 1, 22 June

Queen's Gambit Declined [D67]

1.d4 d5 2.♘f3 e6

There is no reason to obstruct the movements of the Queen's Bishop so early.

3.c4

White could have continued 3.♗f4 with a good game.

3...c6 4.♘c3 ♘f6

After Black's third move, 4...♘d7 would be more attractive, so as to reply to 5.♗g5 with 5...♗e7.

5.♗g5 ♘bd7

An interesting game would result from 5...h6 6.♗×f6 ♕×f6 etc.

6.e3 ♗e7

6...♕a5 would be the Cambridge Springs Defense, which has recently been rehabilitated.

7.♖c1 0–0 8.♗d3 d×c4 9.♗×c4 ♘d5 10.h4

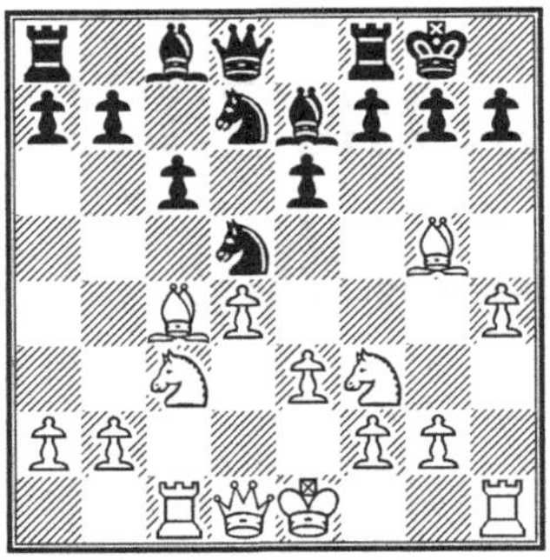

10.♗×e7 ♕×e7 11.0–0 could give White a slightly better game. 10.♘e4 would also be well played.

10...♖e8

In our judgement he should have proceeded to complete his development by 10...♘×c3 11.♖×c3 b6 and 12...♗b7, disregarding White's tactic for the moment.

11.e4 ♘5b6

11...♘×c3 etc. would still provide the opportunity to get his pieces out.

12.♗b3

Superior to 12.♗d3, because the attack is not about the King, but rather the enemy's dark squares, which will become weak after the exchange of Bishops.

12...♘f8 13.♕d2 ♗d7 14.e5 ♘d5

Black obtains a Knight well posted on d5, but it is not enough to equalize the position, since White reserves the option of trading it off at an opportune moment.

15.♗×e7 ♕×e7 16.♘e4 ♖ed8 17.♘d6 ♗e8 18.h5

Foreseeing Black's reply, keeping his pieces from getting out, and threatening a5-a6.

18...f6 19.♔f1

A simple but effective move.

19...f5 20.♖h3 ♖d7 21.♔g1

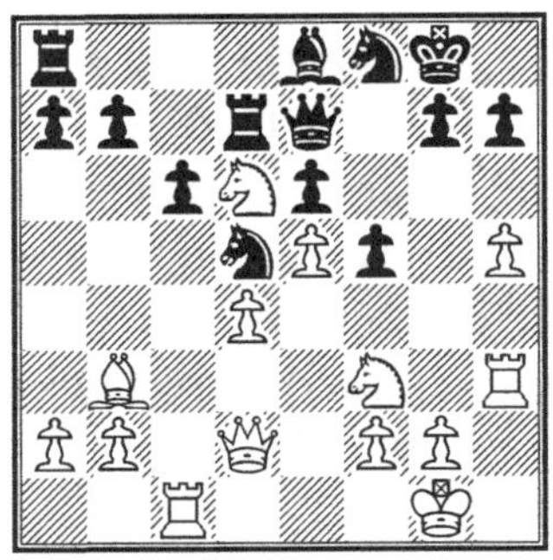

21...♖×d6

Desperately seeing that White will go on improving his position.

If 21...♖ad8 22.♗×d5 c×d5 23.♘c8 ♕f7 24.♘g5 winning the Queen. This is very beautiful!

22.e×d6 ♕×d6 23.♗×d5 e×d5

Already short of time, he disregards 23...♕×d5, so as to continue 24...♖d8 etc., obtaining a counter-attack on White's one weak point, which was Black's only hope. But with the text move the pawn on d4 is placed very strongly.

24.♖e1 ♗d7 25.♖e5 ♘e6

25...f4 first was somewhat better.

26.♘g5 ♖f8 27.♘×e6 ♗×e6 28.♕e2 ♗f7 29.♖×f5 ♗e6 30.♖×f8+ ♔×f8 31.♖f3+ ♔g8 32.♕e3 ♕d7 33.♕f4 ♕c8 34.h6 1–0

Finally executing the threat. A positional game classically conducted by White.

Time: Araiza 1 hr. 28 min., Freyria 2 hr. 16 min.

Game 124

Freyria-Soto Larrea

Mexican Championship, Mexico City 1926, round 2, 23 June

Sicilian Defense [B56]

1.e4 c5 2.d4 c×d4 3.♘f3 ♘c6

If Black had defended the pawn with 3...e5, White would get a strong attack with 4.♗c4, similar to what he obtains in some variations of the Scotch.

4.♘×d4 ♘f6 5.♘c3 d6

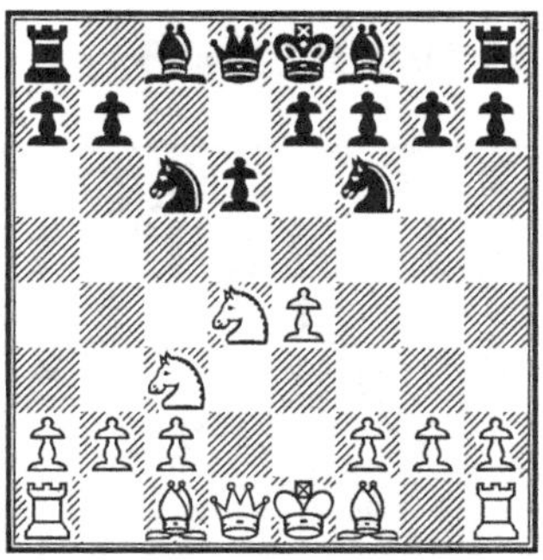

6.♗b5

White's innovation does not look judicious, as there is no advantage in trading the Bishop for the Knight, and if he plays ♘d4×c6 he loses a tempo, because Black, by capturing with the pawn, forces the Bishop to retreat. And if White makes no exchanges, his pieces suffer from a lack of support.

6...♗d7 7.0–0 g6 8.♗e3 ♗g7 9.♕d2

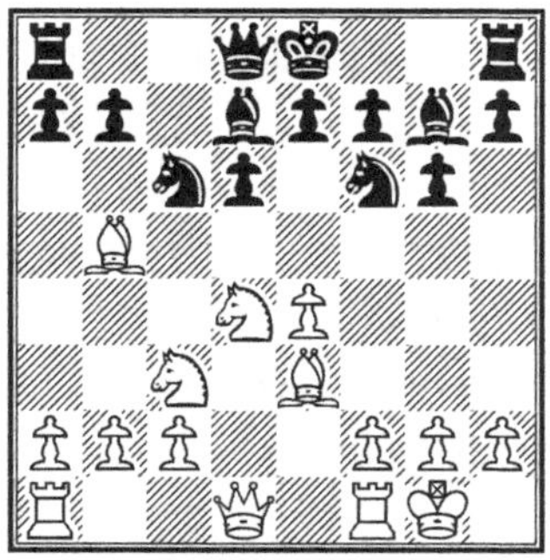

A premature move. White by virtue of being first to move would still have particularly good play by 9.f3.

9...♘g4

Black takes the offensive with this energetic move, gaining at least an advantage in the position of his two Bishops.

10.♘ce2

White's difficulties begin, although truly there was no need to turn them into disaster so quickly.

10...♘×e3 11.♕×e3 0–0 12.c3
A grave error; he could have avoided material loss by 12.♗×c6, but Black would then undoubtedly sense the strength of his two Bishops. In this way the game would have had some theoretical value, even though there is no doubt who had the advantage.

12...♘×d4 13.♘×d4 ♗×d4 14.♕×d4 ♗×b5 15.♖fd1 ♕c7 16.♕e3 ♕c5 17.♕g3 ♗c6
The game is now not of great interest, but one may study the precise way in which Black goes about gaining space to make his advantage decisive.

18.♖e1 f5 19.e5 f4 20.♕h4 d×e5 21.♖ad1 ♖ad8 22.♕g4 ♖×d1 23.♕e6+ ♔g7 24.♖×d1 ♖f6 0–1
Time: Freyria 1 hr. 8 min., Soto Larrea 36 min.

Game 125

Araiza-Soto Larrea

Mexican Championship, Mexico City 1926, round 3, 24-25 June

King's Indian Defense [E61]

A very engrossing game. From move 41 on, however, the ending was beyond the players' and Torre's comprehension, and so we felt compelled to comment.

1.d4 ♘f6 2.c4 g6 3.♘f3 ♗g7 4.♗f4 d6 5.h3
Not wanting his Bishop to be in the least danger on f4.

5...♘bd7 6.♘c3 0–0 7.e3 c5
With 7...♖e8 he would have forced the reply 8.♗e2, and then he could have continued 8...b6 and 9...♗b7 etc.

8.d5
All in all, what follows is a very daring maneuver, but Black saw far ahead.

8...♕a5 9.♕d2
The best way to counter Black's threat.

9...♘h5 10.♗h2 ♗×c3

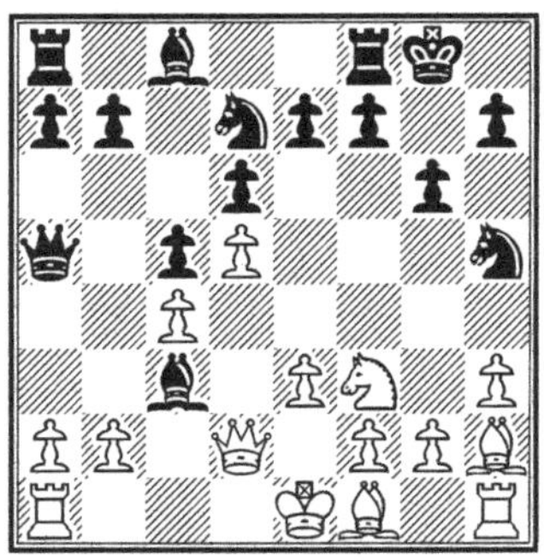

It is dangerous to start the exchanges with this Bishop, but Black understands that his opponent will not be able to keep both his Bishops.

11.b×c3 ♘df6 12.♗d3
With 12.g4 he could have retained

both Bishops and the position would be very interesting. For Black's part he would have to play ...f7-f5 later, to obtain maximum scope for his pieces.

12...♗f5
A move Black had foreseen when he began his maneuver.

13.g4
A great lack of precision. With 13.♗×f5 g×f5 14.g4 he would have attained a very advantageous position.

13...♗×d3 14.♕×d3 ♘g7 15.0–0 ♘d7
15...h5 would invite 16.g5, which would block the action of White's Knight and Bishop.

16.e4 ♘b6
He judiciously avoids opening the position with 16...f5.

17.♖fb1 f6 18.♗f4 g5 19.♗e3 ♕a6 20.♖b5 ♘d7 21.♖ab1

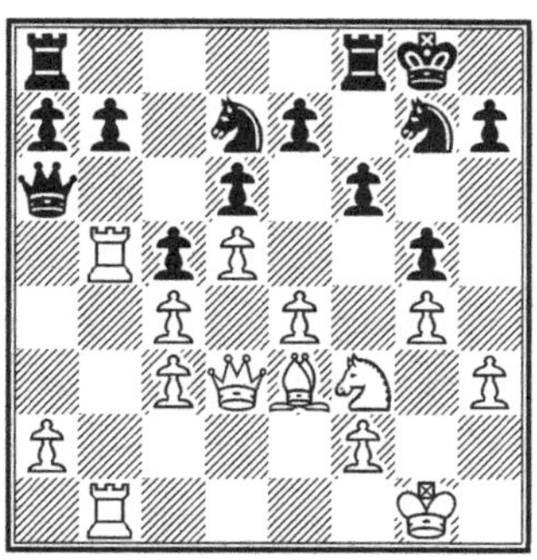

21...b6
Very interesting would be 21...♕×a2 22.♖5b2 ♕a4 23.♖×b7 ♖ab8, as then White would be invited to play "va banque" on the kingside.

22.♖5b2 ♖f7 23.♘d2
It would not be good to sacrifice the Bishop by 23.♗×g5 f×g5 24.♘×g5 ♘e5 etc.

23...♘e5 24.♕e2

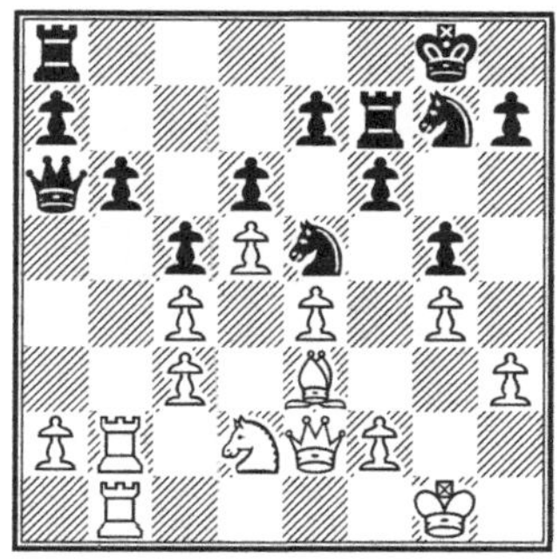

24...♘e8
Possibly better was 24...♘g6, and if 25.♖f1 e5 with good prospects.

25.f4 g×f4 26.♗×f4 ♕c8
26...♘g6 still looked good.

27.♗×e5 f×e5
Preferable was 27...d×e5 so as to bring the Knight to d6, whereas now Black is playing practically a pawn down with an inferior position.

28.♖f1 ♖×f1+ 29.♘×f1 ♘g7 30.♘g3 ♕e8 31.♕f1
Better was 31.♕f3, to continue 32.♖f2 advancing the kingside pawns. Without committing palpable errors White now starts losing the advantage he used to have.

31...♕g6 32.♖f2 ♕g5 33.♔g2 ♕e3 34.♖f3 ♕d2+ 35.♕f2 ♕×f2+ 36.♖×f2 ♖f8 37.♖×f8+ ♔×f8 38.g5 ♔f7 39.h4 ♔g6 40.♔h3 e6 41.♔g4

A move incomprehensible and unjustifiable. With 41.d×e6 ♘×e6 42.♘f5 he would have again gained a small advantage.

Actually after 41.d×e6 ♘×e6 *the advantage is gained by* 42.♔g4!, *and it is not small:*

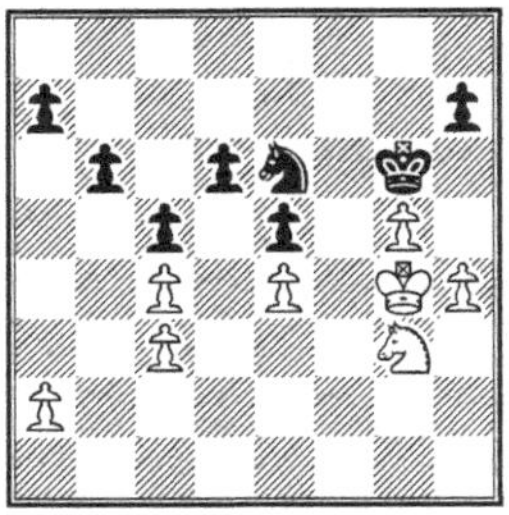

Forced then is 42...♘f4 43.h5+ ♔f7 44.♘f5 ♔e6 45.♘×d6! ♔×d6 46.g6! ♘×g6 (*if* 46...h×g6 47.h6+–) 47.h×g6 h×g6 48.♔g5 *and wins. But the text move also wins, and does not deserve the harsh criticism Torre gives it.*

Returning to the game:

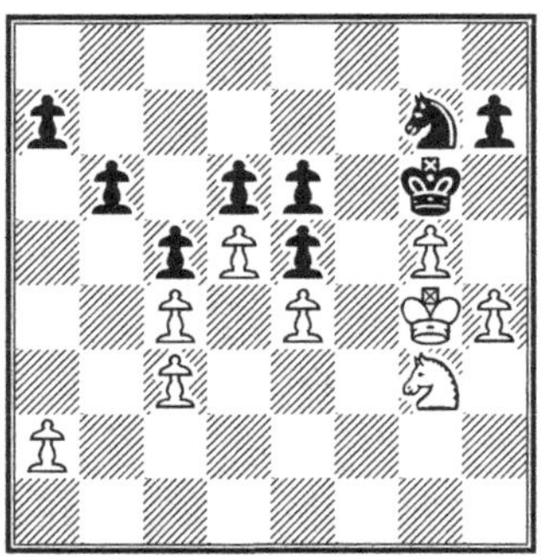

41...e×d5 42.c×d5 b5 43.h5+
△43.♘f5!+–

43...♔f7 44.♘f5 ♘e8

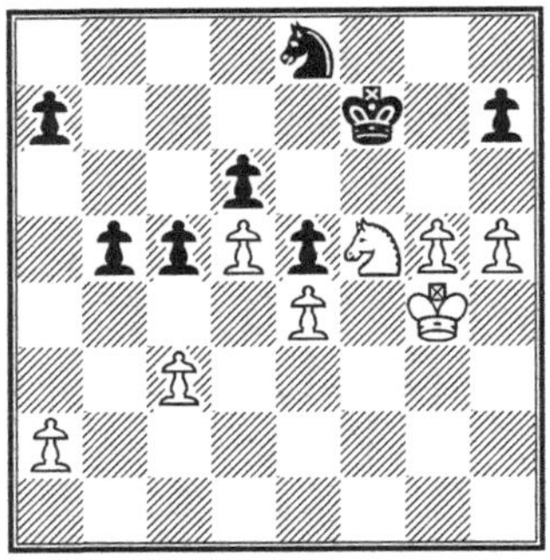

If 44...♘×f5 45.♔×f5, Black wins by playing 45...c4, but if White takes the Knight with the pawn there is no advantage and the game looks like a draw.

Actually White is definitely winning after 45.e×f5,

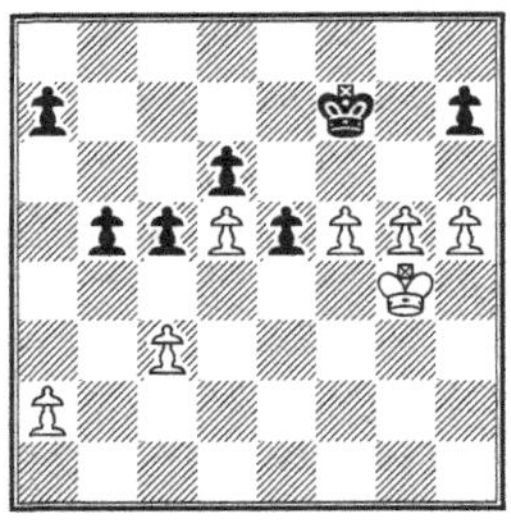

viz. 45...a5□ *and either* 46.f6 b4 47.c×b4 c4 48.♔f5! c3 49.g6+ h×g6+ 50.h×g6+ ♔g8 51.♔e6 c2 52.f7+ ♔g7 53.♔e7 c1♕ 54.f8♕+ ♔×g6 55.♕f6+ ♔h5 56.♔×d6+–, *or* 46.g6+ h×g6 47.h×g6+ ♔f6 48.♔h5 e4 (*if* 48...♔g7 49.♔g5+–) 49.♔h6 e3 50.g7 e2 51.g8♕ e1♕ 52.♕f8+ *and mate in* 12.

Returning to the game:

45.♘e3

With 45.♔f3 he would have secured the draw, as Black then could not move either the Knight nor the King advantageously.

Actually it is the text move that makes it a draw; after 45.♔f3 Stockfish still likes White (+3.95/27).

45...a5 46.h6

A grave error, which fortunately his adversary did not capitalize on, as with 46...♔g6 he would probably win.

The text is fine, and 46...♔g6 would not win.

46...b4

This should lose. 46...♔g6 or several other moves would hold the draw.

47.c×b4 c×b4 48.♘c4 a4 49.♔f5

A move he could not make had Black moved his King correctly.

Black should actually have been quite happy to see this, rather than 49.a3! when White wins,

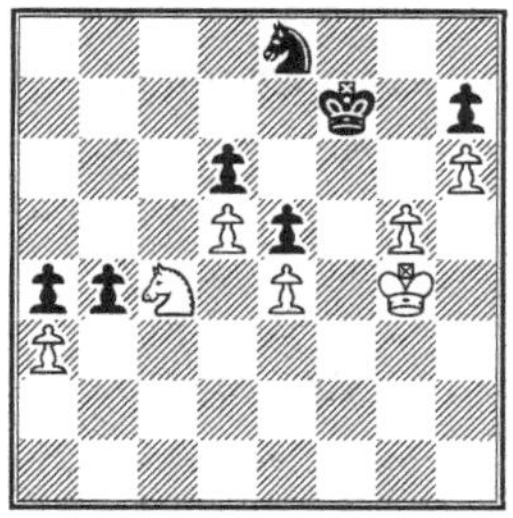

e.g. 49...b3 50.♔f5 ♔g8 51.♔e6 etc., or 49...♔g6 50.a×b4 *etc., or* 49...b×a3 50.♘×a3 ♔g6 51.♘c4

and Black is in Zugzwang: *if* 51...♘c7 52.♘×d6 a3 53.♘c4 a2 54.♘×e5#, *or* 51...♔f7 52.♔f5 *etc.*

Resuming the game from the position after **49.♔f5**:

49...b3

Here Black could have capitalized on the deficient moves 45.♘e3 and 46.h6, by 49...a3, with which he could try to win.

50.a×b3

Torre's last note was quite correct about 49...a3, but now White could have won with 50.a3.

50...a×b3 51.♘b2 ♘c7 52.♘c4 ♘b5 53.g6+ ♔g8

53...h×g6+ 54.♔g5 b2 55.♘×b2 ♘c3 would have been simpler.

54.g×h7+
Now White, with 54.g7 or 54.♔f6, would have made it harder for Black to draw.

54...♔×h7 55.♔e6 ♔×h6 56.♔d7 ♔g5 57.♔c6 ♘c3 58.♔×d6 ♔f4 59.♔c5 ♘×e4+ 60.♔b4 ½–½
A game very difficult to conduct correctly. *Indeed!*
Time: Araiza 2 hr. 30 min., Soto Larrea 2 hr. 55 min.

Game 126

Freyria-Araiza

Mexican Championship, Mexico City 1926, round 4, 28-30 June

Sicilian Defense [B73]

1.e4 c5 2.d4 c×d4 3.♘f3 ♘c6 4.♘×d4 ♘f6 5.♘c3 d6 6.♗e2 g6 7.♗e3 ♗g7 8.0–0 0–0 9.h3 ♗d7 10.♕d2 a6 11.♖ad1 ♕c7 12.♘f3

Generally this Knight goes to b3; this innovation by Sr. Freyria, envisioning kingside aggression as fast as possible, as usual deserves special study.

12...♖ac8 13.♗h6 ♘d8
To open a line for the Queen's Bishop and transfer the Knight to a good square on e6.

14.♗×g7 ♔×g7 15.♘h2 ♘e6 16.e5

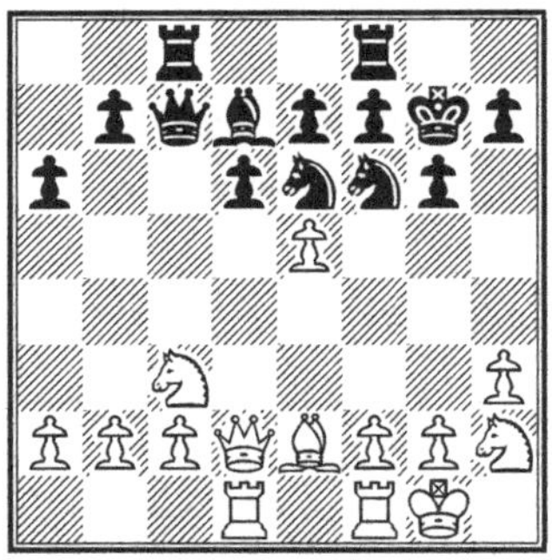

Up to here White has played creatively and masterfully, but now he rushes things; he should first have played 16.♘g4, creating difficulties for the opponent and holding in reserve the threats e4-e5 or ♘c3-d5. Having undertaken a line of attack, Black is in a position to search for how and where to defend himself.

16...d×e5 17.♘g4 ♘×g4

It would not do to allow 18.♕h6+ followed by 19.♘×f6 and 20.♘c3-d5. Furthermore 17...♗c6 would block the Rook and Queen.

18.♗×g4
If 18.♕×d7, Black would retreat his Knight to f6.

18...♖fd8
Black has happily finished his development a pawn up.

19.♘d5

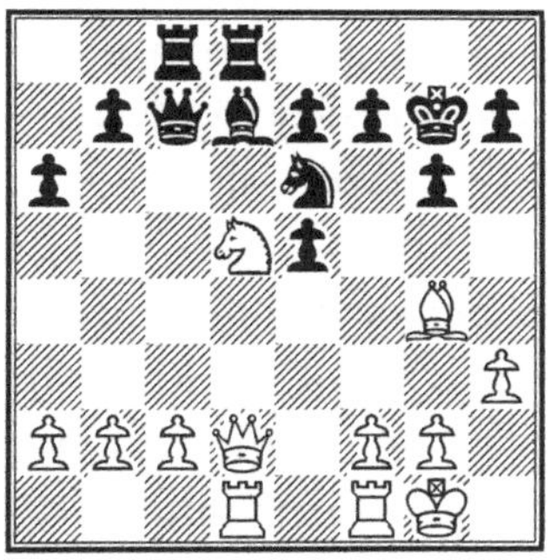

19...♕c5
The move 19...♕×c2 leads to very complicated variations, but 20.♕e3 would be best, and if 20...♕×b2 21.♘×e7 ♖b8 22.♖d2 ♕b5 23.♘d5 f6 24.♘b6 leaving Black in dire straits, but 19...♕d6 would save a move and allow him to preserve his advantage: 20.♕e3 ♘d4 21.♘×e7 ♕×e7 22.♖×d4 ♗×g4 23.♖×d8 ♕×d8 24.h×g4 ♖×c2 25.♕×e5+ ♕f6.

This note has several major errors. In the first variation, after 23.♘d5 f6,

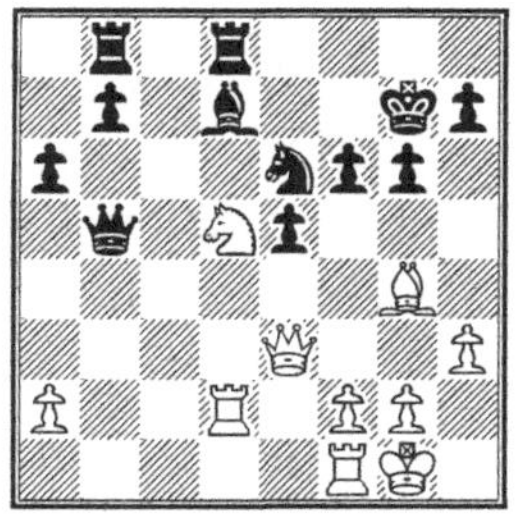

Torre's 24.♘b6? leaves White, not Black, in dire straits, viz. 24...♗c6! 25.♗×e6 (if 25.♖×d8 ♘×d8–+) 25...♖×d2 26.♕×d2 ♕×b6–+.
But White can win with 24.♖fd1! ♕c6 25.♘×f6! ♔×f6 26.♖d6 ♕c7 27.♕h6! ♗c8 28.♕h4+ ♔g7 29.♖×d8 ♘×d8 30.♕×d8 ♕×d8 31.♖×d8 and 32.♖×c8+–.
In the second variation, after 20.♕e3 ♘d4,

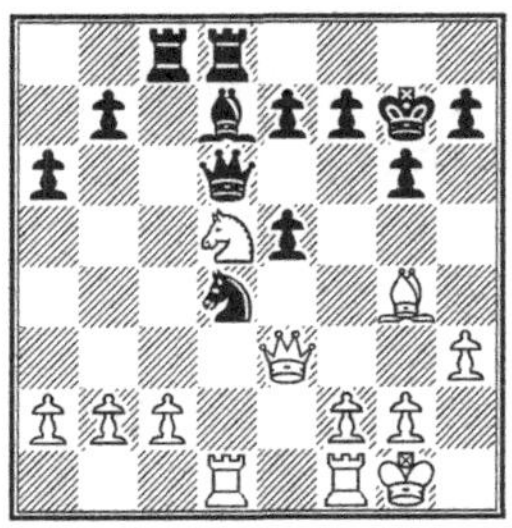

the least evil for White is 21.♘b6 ♕×b6 22.♕×e5+ ♕f6 23.♕×d4∓. Torre's 21.♘×e7(??) is refuted not by 21...♕×e7 but by 21...♖×c2!, with capture of the Knight on e7 later.

20.♕e1
A precise response to Black's inexactitude.

20...♕d6

This move is actually bad. 20...f6 would have posed more difficult problems for White in trying to improve his position; if he plays 21.b4 ♕×c2 22.♖d2 he would have been able to win easily. Nevertheless Black had a worthwhile defense with 20...♕a7 21.♘×e7 ♖b8 etc., which would have made White's triumph more difficult.

We strongly suspect typographical errors in this note. To begin with, in the original text the first variation is wrongly numbered, starting 20.b4 *instead of* 21.b4, *and the sentence containing it is sloppy in grammar and punctuation. Much more importantly, each variation is given the evaluation the other should have. The line beginning* 20...f6 *leads to an even game, while* 20...♕a7 *loses. It is hard to believe Torre did not know this, so we are inclined to think the typesetter somehow got the variations out of order.*

Here is the original text:

Returning to the game:

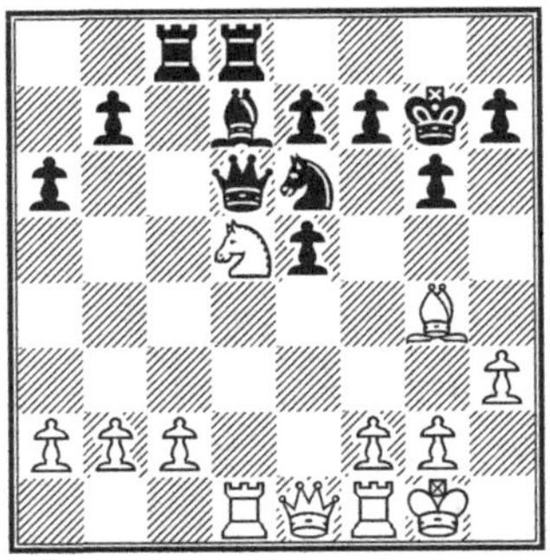

To simplify the position advantageously.

21...♕c7

Now it is not good to take the cat by the claws[1] and play 21...♕×d1 because of 22.♘h5+, which does not let Black gain a tempo because later he must make a move defending his pawn on e5: 22...g×h5 23.♗×d1 f6 24.♕b4 ♔f8, although then it would not be easy to demonstrate how White would win.

20 D—1R

Respuesta precisa a la inexactitud de las Negras.

D—3D

En la actualidad esta movida es mala, 20...., P—3A; hubiera puesto en condiciones más difíciles a las Blancas de mejorar su posición si juegan 20 P—4C, D×PA; 21 T—2D, y habrían podido ganar facilmente. Sin embargo las Negras tienen una defensa de valor con 20...., D—2T; 21 C×P, T—1CD; etc. que dificultaría el triunfo de las Blancas.

25

1 A literal translation of Torre's "tomar el gato por las uñas"; an English equivalent might be "take the bull by the horns."

Black does well to play 23...f6, since 23...♔f6, to use the g-file, would be answered by 24.♕e3 and 25.♖e1.

22.♘×d7 ♖×d7 23.♖×d7 ♕×d7 24.♕×e5+ ♔g8 25.♖d1 ♕c7 26.♕×c7 ♖×c7 27.♗×e6 f×e6 28.c3

Señor Freyria plays the ending very well but not well enough to win. This is regrettable, as otherwise the Student Reader would have gained some profitable ideas.

28...♔f7 29.♔f1 e5 30.♔e2 ♔e6 31.♔e3 ♖c6 32.♔e4 ♖c4+ 33.♔e3 ♖c8 34.♖d3 ♖f8 35.c4 ♖c8 36.b3 ♖c6 37.♔e4 ♖c5 38.♖d8 ♖a5 39.a4 ♖c5 40.g4 ♖c6 41.a5 ♖c5 42.♖d5 ♖×d5 43.c×d5+ ♔d6 44.h4

44...e6(??)

A serious mistake that could have lost the game and allowed Freyria to show off some "profitable ideas." Correct was 44...h6 45.b4 e6 46.d×e6 ♔×e6 47.h5 g×h5 48.g×h5 ♔f6 49.♔d5 ♔f5 50.♔c5 ♔e4 51.♔b6 ♔f3 52.♔×b7 ♔×f2 53.b5 e4 *(if* 53...a×b5?? 54.a6+− *)* 54.b×a6 e3 55.a7 e2 56.a8♕ e1♕ *and Black should be able to survive the Queen ending (+1.61/31).*

45.d×e6 ♔×e6 46.h5(?!)

46.f4! *would have won. Forced then is* 46...e×f4□ 47.♔×f4:

Now two main variations:

(a) 47...♔f6 48.g5+ ♔f7 49.♔e5 ♔e7 50.b4! *(a nice waiting move) and either* 50...♔f7 51.♔d6+− *or* 50...♔d7 51.♔f6+− *; and*

(b) 47...h6 48.g5 *and either* 48...h5 49.♔e4 ♔d6 50.♔d4 ♔c6 51.♔e5 *etc., or* 48...h×g5+ 49.♔×g5 ♔f7 50.♔h6 ♔f6 51.b4! *(again that key waiting move)* ♔f7 52.♔h7 ♔f6 53.♔g8 ♔e6 54.♔g7 ♔f5 55.♔f7 ♔g4 56.♔×g6 ♔×h4 57.♔f6 *etc.*

46...g×h5 47.g×h5 h6 48.b4 ½–½

Time: Freyria 2 hr. 30 min., Araiza 2 hr. 27 min.

Game 127

Soto Larrea-Freyria

Mexican Championship, Mexico City 1926, round 5, 29 June

Dutch Defense [A85]

1.d4 f5 2.♘f3

The move 2.e4 has fallen into disuse since variations have been found that strengthen the defense, for example 2...f×e4 3.♘c3 ♘f6 4.♗g5 ♘c6 etc.

2...♘f6 3.c4

The modern way is 3.g3, followed by ♗f1-g2. Even so the deployment White uses here has not been completely discarded.

3...e6 4.♗g5 ♗e7 5.♘c3 b6 6.e3 ♗b7 7.♗d3 0–0 8.0–0

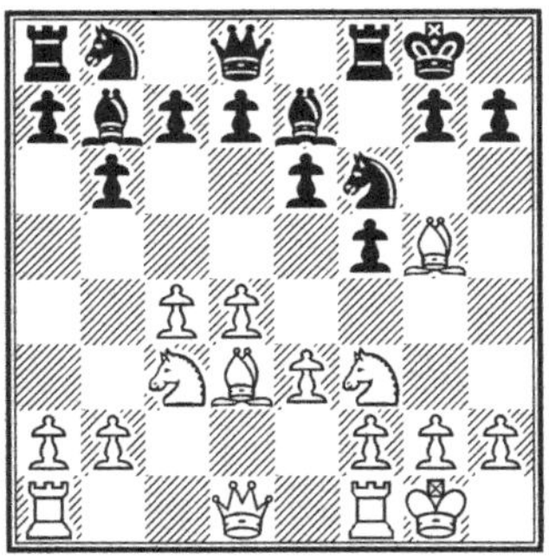

8...♘a6

Well played, since he must develop his pieces before pressing forward. 8...♘e4 would be premature.

9.a3

Black's position is too strong, so time should not be wasted on such moves, since the Queen's Knight's intention is to occupy the c5 square and not b4. White should have played 9.♕e2 etc.

9...c5 10.♕e2 ♘g4

The best move, and superior to 10...h6 or 10...♘e4, the latter being disadvantageous since it would block the action of the powerful ♗b7.

11.♗×e7 ♕×e7 12.h3

To eliminate the possibility of the Knight occupying the excellent square e5, as would happen after Black has played ...e6-e5.

12...♘h6

To be ready to answer 13.e4 with 13...f4, without loss of tempo.

13.e4 f4 14.e5

This grants greater scope to the ♗b7, and to the black King's Knight and Rook. Nevertheless it is necessary because it gives scope equally to the white pieces.

It would be the gravest error to play 14.d5 e5 followed by ...d7-d6, which leaves White with a dead Bishop.

14...c×d4 15.♘b5

Superior to 15.♘e4, which allows 15...♘f5 impeding the Knight's entry to d6.

But 15.♗e4 ♗×e4 16.♘×e4 ♘f5 17.♖ad1 deserves special consideration.

15...♘c5 16.♘d6

More prudent would be 16.♘b×d4, as the effectiveness of the Knight on d6 is more apparent than real.

16...♗×f3 17.♕×f3 ♘×d3 18.♕×d3 f3

The attack Black initiates with this move is the ideal culmination of the deployment he propounded in his opening.

19.g3 ♕g5 20.♕×d4 ♕h5 21.♔h2

Even though 21.♕h4 would repulse the attack, the endgame would be very disadvantageous.

21...g5

In complete harmony with his foregoing play, he wants to take the King's position by storm.

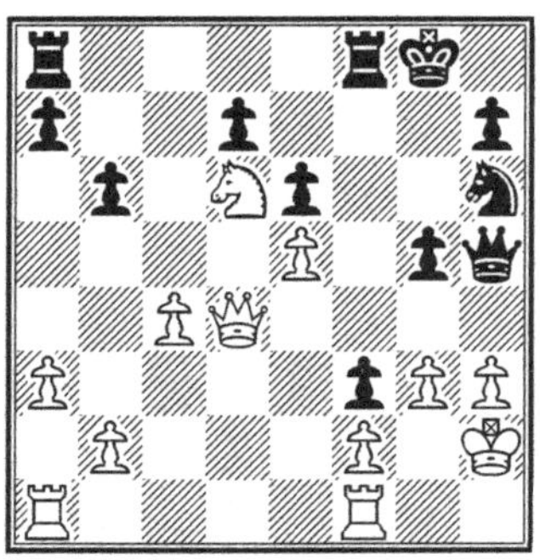

22.g4

It seems that the best defense would be 22.♖h1 ♖ad8 23.♖ad1 which is in all ways superior to 23.♘e4 ♕g6. Still Black would remain with a good position.

Torre might have noted that the text is a major blunder. The alternative line he gives would have defended adequately, with no sign of Black being able to attain an "ideal culmination."

22...♕h4

Shutting in his Queen on the conviction that the King's position must collapse in the end.

23.♖g1 ♖f4 24.♘e4

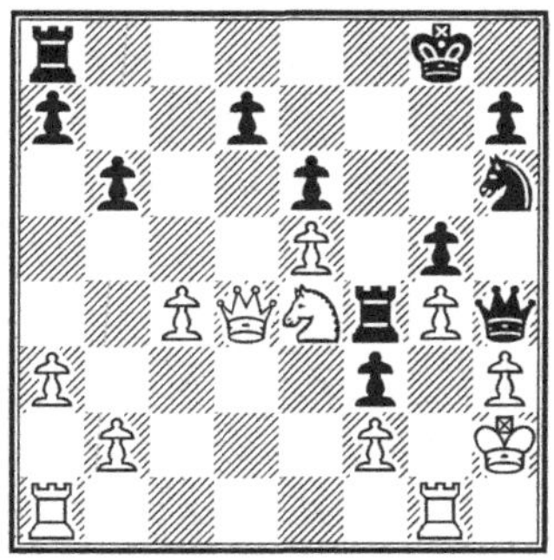

24...♖af8

This move accomplishes nothing, nor does it defend against the counterthreat ♘e4-f6+.

Meanwhile 24...♔h8 would have decided the game: 25.♖g3 ♘×g4+ 26.♔h1 ♘h6 threatening 27...♖×e4 or 27...♘f5. Or 25.♕×d7 ♘×g4+ 26.♖×g4 ♖×g4 27.♘g3 ♕×h3+ 28.♔×h3 ♖h4#. Or 25...♖×g4 26.♖e1 ♖×g3 27.f×g3 ♘g4+ 28.♔g1 ♕×h3 29.♕d2 f2+! 30.♘×f2 ♕×g3+ 31.♔f1 ♘h2+ 32.♔e2 ♕f3#. *Very good analysis!*

25.♖af1

The alternative 25.♖g3 was a better defense against Black's inexact play, continuing ♖a1-g1, ♕d3-d3 and ♘e4-f6. *The text was actually best.* 25.♖g3 *fails to* 25...♘×g4+ 26.♔g1,

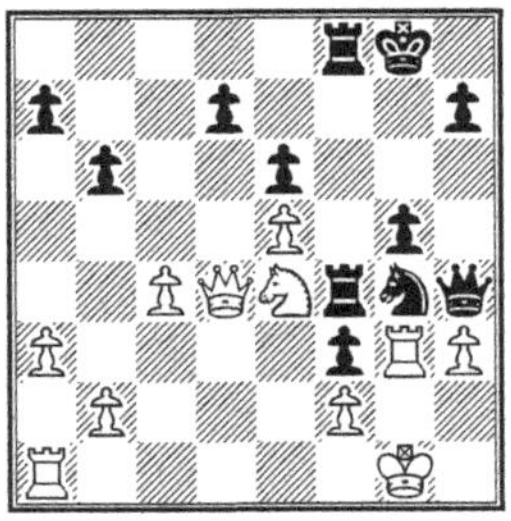

and either 26...♘h6 27.♕×d7 ♘f5 28.♘f6+ ♔h8 29.♔h2 ♖d4 *etc., or* 26...♘×f2 27.♕×f2 ♖×e4 28.♖×f3 ♖×f3 29.♕×f3 ♖e1+ 30.♖×e1 ♕×e1+ 31.♔g2 ♕×e5 *with a very winnable Queen ending.*

25...♔h8

This actually proves to be a serious error. Worth considering was 25...♔g7, even though White would be in position to defend better thanks to the veiled pressure of his Rook against the enemy, playing ♖g1-g3.

26.♕d6

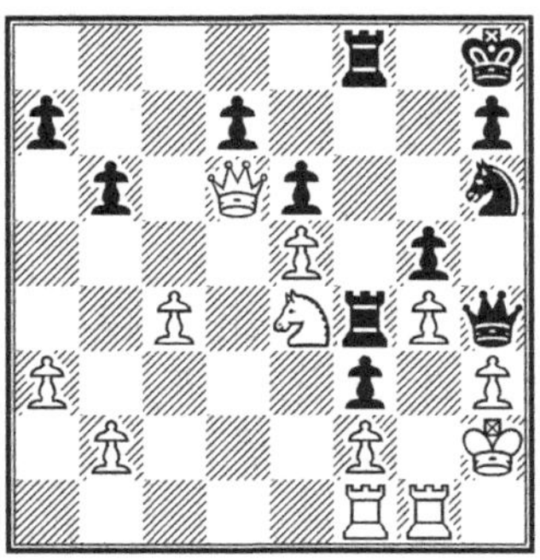

Effectively utilizing the lack of precision in Black's last few moves to get his Knight to f6, defending against all threats, which the adversary will not be easily able to coordinate because his Queen is shut in.

26...♖8f7

Making no comment, Torre fails to note how bad this move is. Necessary was 26...♔g8 or 26...♔g7, *when the best White has is* 27.♘f6 ♖8×f6 28.e×f6+ ♔g6 29.♕d3+ ♔×f6 30.♖g3 ♘×g4+ 31.♔g1 ♘e5 32.♕d6 *with a draw (0.00/25).*

27.♘f6 ♖×c4

So as to threaten 28.♖c2, but it is evident that the attack is minor.

28.♕b8+

White should have replied 28.♖g3, which is the key to his position. It is regrettable that he did not suspect the defensive strength of this move.

The text is by far best, and should win for White. After 28.♖g3 *Black could blunt White's attack with* 28...♖c8.

28...♔g7

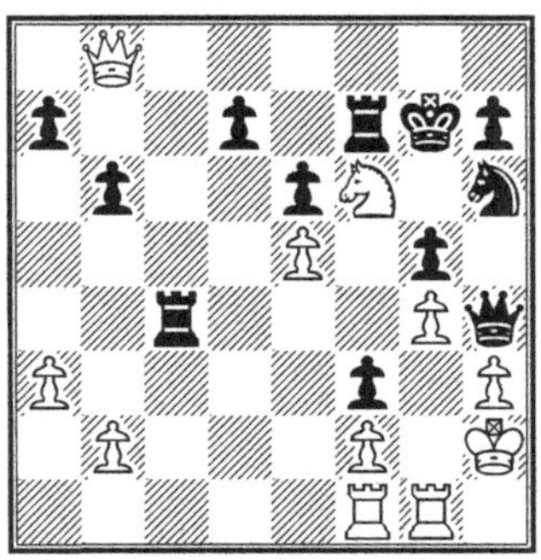

29.♘e8+
An error in calculation due to not having analyzed his position properly. It could not be a good move to remove the Knight from the vicinity of the Rook, but this move is a logical consequence of the previous move. 29.♖g3 was still good.
Indeed, 29.♖g3 *wins. Because of the threat to his rear posed by the white Queen, Black cannot play* 29...♘×g4+?? 30.♖×g4 ♖×g4 31.♕g8+ *and mate shortly, or* 29...♖×g4 30.♘×g4 ♘×g4+ 31.♖×g4 ♕h5+−.

29...♔g6 30.♘d6
Another error with lamentable consequences.
It is unimportant; the game was totally lost already. After the only move that does not allow a quick mate, 30.♘f6, *Black wins with* 30...♖×f6 31.e×f6 ♘×g4+ *etc.*

30...♘×g4+ 31.♖×g4 ♖×g4 32.♕g8+ ♖g7 0–1
A difficult game, full of vicissitudes. Time: Soto Larrea 1 hr. 40 min., Freyria 2 hr.

Game 128

Soto Larrea-Araiza

Mexican Championship, Mexico City 1926, round 6, 30 June

Slav Defense [D12]

1.d4 d5 2.♘f3 ♘f6 3.c4 c6 4.e3
There are two very good alternatives, 4.♘c3 or 4.c×d5.

4...♗f5 5.♘c3
Having shut in his Queen's Bishop, it was necessary to play 5.♕b3 to have a good game.

5...e6 6.♗d3
Now 6.♕b3 is not strong, because after 7.c×d5 Black replies 7...e×d5, obtaining thereby a slightly superior game.

6...♗×d3 7.♕×d3 ♘bd7 8.0–0 ♗b4

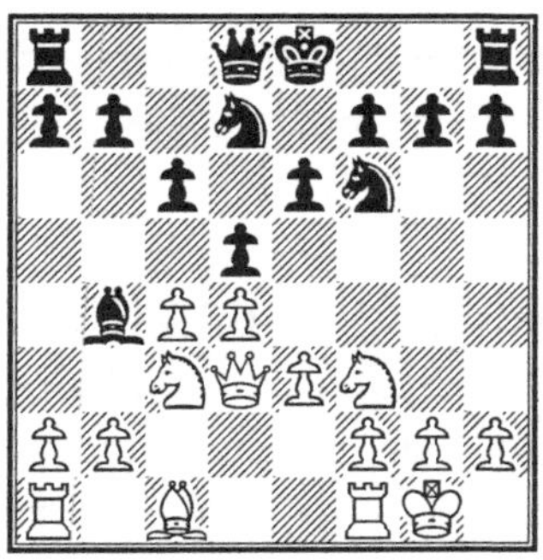

Impeding e3-e4 which would put the Bishop into action.

9.b3 ♗×c3
A premature exchange; castling was better.

10.♕×c3 ♘e4 11.♕d3
White lets himself be shut in more. 11.♕b4 would have given better play.

11...f5

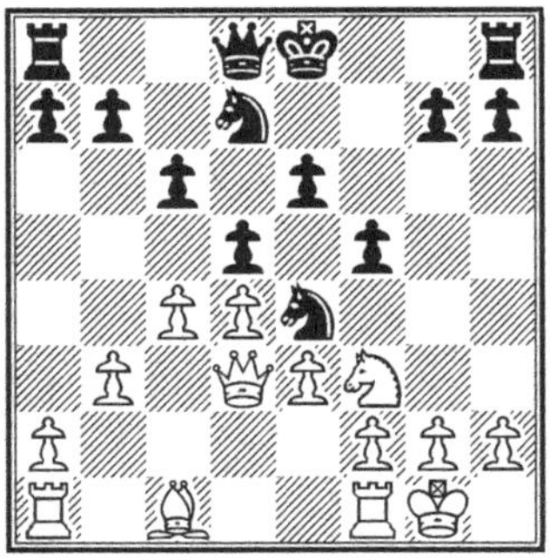

12.♘d2
If 12.♗a3, the continuation might be 12...♕a5 13.b4 d×c4 14.♕×e4 f×e4 15.b×a5 e×f3 16.g×f3 etc.
There is a need to remove the Knight from e4, but it would be better without exchanges, because after them his Bishop would not be very effective. Better for example 12.♘e1 0–0 13.f3 ♘ef6 14.♗a3.

12...0–0 13.f3 ♘×d2 14.♕×d2
The move 14.♗×d2 would have forced 14...♘f6, enabling a queenside advance by 15.b4 etc. White has gone for a wait-and-see plan.

14...♖f6 15.♗a3 ♕c7 16.♕f2
If 16.e4 d×e4 17.f×e4 f×e4 18.♕g5 ♕b6, retaining a small advantage.

16...♖g6
To prevent 17.♕g3, but this gives White an opportunity to free himself.

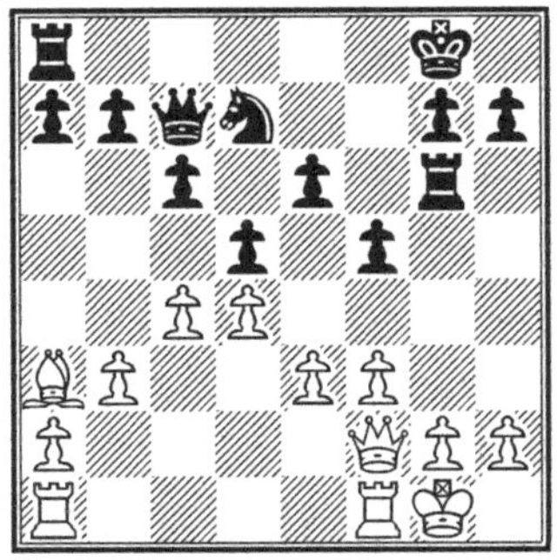

17.c×d5
A serious error that opens up lines to the King for Black. 17.e4 was the last chance to free himself: 17...f×e4 18.f×e4 d×e4 19.♕f7+ ♔h8 20.♖ae1, with an excellent game.
Torre's descriptive notation is ambiguous in this variation; the first two moves read 17.P-K4 PxP 18.PxP PxP. *Black has three possible pawn captures at move 17 and each side has two at move 18. We have had to infer what was actually played. If our continuation is correct, then after* 17...f×e4 18.f×e4 *Black should play* 18...♖f6, *preventing* 19.♕f7+ *and retaining an even game.*

17...e×d5 18.♗e7
18.e4 would still be opportune; the position must be opened for the Bishop.

18...♘f6 19.♗a3
If 19.♗×f6 ♖×f6 etc., Black would have a small advantage due to the weak position of the pawn on e3. The text move is in harmony with White's spirit.

19...♖e8 20.♖ae1 ♖h6

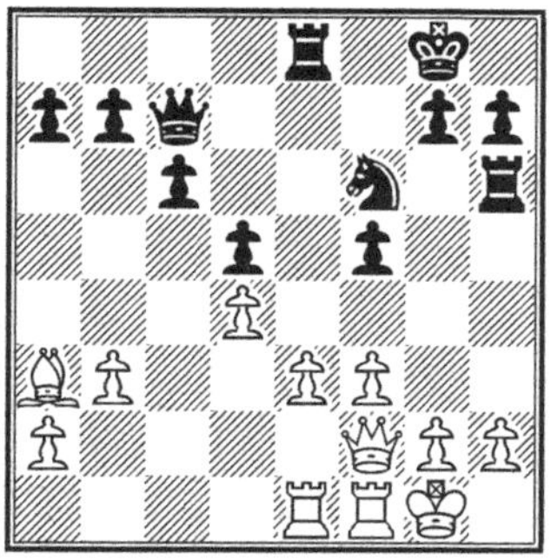

An excellent maneuver. White's only strongpoint is his pawn on f3, and this weakens it indirectly.

21.g3

If 21.♕g3 ♕×g3 22.h×g3 ♘h5 23.♔f2 (if 23.g4 ♘g3 24.♖f2 ♖h1#) 23...♖g6 24.♖h1 ♘×g3 25.♖h3 f4 26.e×f4 ♖×e1 27.♔×e1 ♘f5 etc. But 25.♖h4 gives White more options. Possibly White is positionally lost.

21...♖g6 22.♔h1 h6 23.♕c2 ♖g5 24.♖g1 ♕d7 25.♗c1 ♖h5 26.♕g2 g5

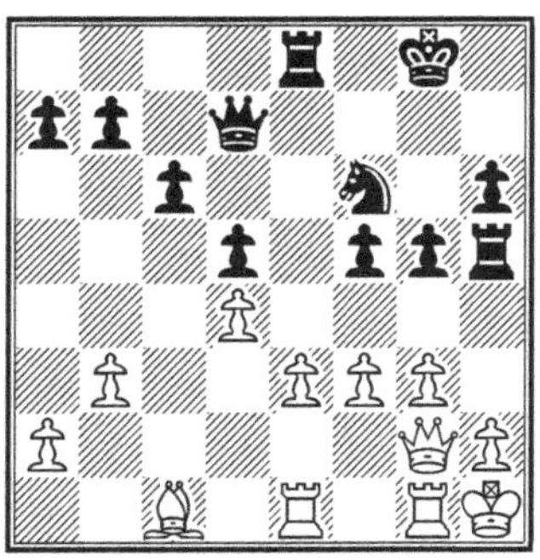

Delightfully, the f3-pawn will disappear, and the greatest weaknesses in White's position will be starkly evident.

27.g4

Just when there was nothing to do but wait, White makes an aggressive move that gives his Queen and Rook a bit more scope, but on a closed file. The position is thus: Black will play ...g5-g4[1], and if f3-f4 then ...♖h3 and ...h6-h5-h4. Decidedly best then was for White to return his King's Rook serenely to f1, to try to shut in the ♖h5 in the most profitable manner; we would say 27.♖gf1 g4 28.f×g4 ♘×g4 29.h4 so as to continue with ♖f1-f4 and ♕g2-f3, when Black's problem would be more complex.

27...f×g4 28.e4

If 28.f×g4 ♖h4 and the pawn cannot be defended.

28...d×e4 29.f×e4 g3

Exact play. 29...♕×d4 30.♗b2 would be an error.

30.♕×g3 ♘×e4 31.♕g2 ♕d5 32.♕f3

32.♖gf1 would still make victory for Black infinitely more laborious.

32...♖h3 0–1

Time: Soto Larrea 2 hr. 7 min, Araiza 1 h5. 15 min.

1 This corrects a typo. The original text read "las Negras jugarán P-3C," i.e. ...P-N3 or ...b7-b6, which would make the whole variation absurd. Clearly ...P-5C, i.e. ...g5-g4, was intended.

Chapter IX

The Documentary Film Torre x Torre

This movie, released in 2019, shows that nearly 100 years after his retirement from chess, interest in Carlos Torre still lives on. Written and directed by Roberto Garza and Juan Obregón, under the aegis of the Mexican production company Artegios, it has had only limited theatrical releases, but can be viewed on the on-demand video website vimeo.com, for a small fee. The trailer can be seen at no charge here:

https://vimeo.com/ondemand/torrextorre/440730589?autoplay=1.

With certain caveats, discussed at length below, we recommend it highly to readers of this book. Many languages are used — primarily Spanish, but also Russian, German, English, and Czech — but there is an option for English subtitles, which this writer, who has much greater facility with written Spanish than spoken, found very helpful. Quotes we give below are verbatim transcriptions of those subtitles.

Clocking in at one hour, forty-five minutes, the film consists mainly of interviews with people who knew Torre firsthand, along with others who have done research on him. The locales shown are mostly in Mexico, but we also see New Orleans, New York City, Baden-Baden, Marienbad, Moscow, Leningrad (now St. Petersburg), and Chicago. Those interviewed include nephews, nieces and in-laws of Torre; friends such as Filiberto Terrazas, Amador Terán Terán, Germán de la Cruz, FM Alfonso Ferriz Carrasquedo, and IM Raúl Ocampo Vargas; Russian historians Andrey Voronkov, Vadim Fybersovich, and GM Yuri Averbakh; Gabriel Velasco, co-author of this book; American master Jude Acers of New Orleans; and even a nun who cared for Torre in the Mérida nursing home where he spent his last years. There are brief appearances by former world champions Viswanathan Anand and Veselin Topalov in which, interestingly, they both speak Spanish rather than Urdu or Bulgarian.

The film begins at the end, in a sense, with friends and family describing Torre's return to Mexico in October 1926, after his nervous breakdown in New York. They describe the obvious mental problems he suffered from around that time. Amador Terán describes him as acting like a zombie, silent, with his eyes fixed on the ground. Some time in 1927 Torre was taken to Terán's ranch, Villagrán, where it was thought the outdoor environment might aid his recovery. He later was cared for by his older brother Egidio, a pharmacist, and improved greatly. In response to queries in 1931 from the Mexican Chess Federation about the possibility of Torre returning to serious chess, Egidio wrote to Augustín Garza Galindo (writer of the prologue to Torre's book on the 1926 Mexican Championship) as follows:

> I am the older brother of Carlos, who resides here under my care. Carlos is in a condition of perfect physical health, and very close to normal mentally. In my medical opinion, however, I do not judge it advisable for him to return to involvement in chess activities.

Various recurrences of mental problems are described. During one such episode we are told that Torre devised a new set of material values for the chess pieces: pawn 1.00, Knight 2.83, Bishop 2.97, Rook 4.05, Queen 7.81, King 3.48, first move 0.01, with an advantage of 0.25 needed to win.

Finally after about 30 minutes, the film turns to Torre's international tournaments. We see the actual tournament venues at Baden-Baden, Marienbad, Moscow and Leningrad. Most interesting is the segment about Moscow 1925. Several clips from the Russian film *Chess Fever* show Torre in live action, along with Capablanca, Marshall, Sämisch and other participants. Interesting anecdotes are told, *e.g.* how Torre, who arrived in Moscow unprepared for Russian winter weather, got a decent coat.

In the Leningrad segment we see the actual apartments where Torre wrote *Development of Chess Ability* over a period of two weeks. All through the Russian segments of the film people speak of how well Torre was received by the Russian public, with esteem, admiration and affection, perhaps second only to what they felt for Capablanca.

The last part of the film covers Torre's later years. We are told of his kindness, gentleness, pacifism, simplicity, modesty, and generosity; his respectful attitude toward people regardless of their social or economic status, his deep interest in philosophy, religion, science, Buddhism, and Freemasonry. Also his continued interest in chess, how he still enjoyed casual blitz games and almost always won, and how he helped and encouraged young players in Mérida's chess clubs.

So it is very much to the film-makers' credit that they give such a broad-based, interesting, informative and sympathetic portrait of Torre. However, not all the interviewees are equally credible, and not everything they say should be believed. The directors made a conscious choice to let them all have their say, without challenging or correcting anything. As co-director Garza told us "Through the interviews we made, we realized that there is a lot of jealousy surrounding this enigmatic character. Many of the interviewees are at odds with each other because each has his own version of events and considers himself the highest authority on the subject. We decided to believe them all and contrast their testimonies, leaving it up to the viewer to decide."

So there are various inconsistencies and factual errors. Most are minor, for example:

- ♖ A tour guide at the home of Paul Morphy in New Orleans is shown saying that Morphy never lost a game of chess in his life, and that he won an international tournament at the age of 13. In fact Morphy lost many games, and never played in any international tournament. This would be a terrible howler in a book about Morphy, but it has no bearing on Torre, and is minor in the overall context of the film.
- ♖ Raúl Ocampo says that Torre defeated both Tartakower and Rubinstein in tournament play. In fact his record against the former was +0 -0 =3, against the latter +0 -1 =2.
- ♖ Ocampo also says that Marshall was a world title challenger several times. In fact he played only one title match, against Lasker in 1907.
- ♖ Ocampo says that Edward Lasker invented the iron lung. While Lasker was an engineer and inventor, that was not his invention. Rather, he invented a mechanical breast pump.
- ♖ The term "grandmaster" is used somewhat loosely. Alfonso Ferriz Carrasquedo relates that "A Grandmaster arrived [in Mérida], his name was Lebedev, so he went to the Mérida chess club to play a game, and they told him that there was no one to play. Without mentioning the name, they asked him if he wanted to play against maestro Torre. So they played some games, and Torre won all of them, so Lebedev said 'How is this possible? Who are you?' and he answered 'My name is Carlos Torre.' So he

said 'Oh maestro, I didn't know ... I didn't recognize you! But you are very famous.'" *Chess International Titleholders 1950-2016* lists only three players named Lebedev, 2 FMs and a CM, all born after Torre died. There was a Russian master named Sergei Lebedev (1868-1942), rated by Elo at 2440, who was active circa 1900-1914. Whether he visited Mexico, we do not know.

- Germán de la Cruz says that Torre attended a tournament in the city of Torreón, Mexico, which included Cuban GMs. He played blitz against the Cubans, and won every game. Again, perhaps some such thing occurred, but Cuba did not have an official GM until Silvino García Martínez in 1975, just three years before Torre died. We could find no record of him ever playing in Torreón, nor in fact of there ever being an international tournament in that city.

Not for nothing did Torre himself say "Truly, I believe that the majority of anecdotes told in chess are greatly exaggerated." Yet these are not terribly important; they are the sort of "tall tales" and "good stories" that often develop around famous people, and can be excused.

Some dubious opinions are expressed, for example:

- Jude Acers asserts that the story of the two heart-breaking letters Torre supposedly received before the last round at Chicago 1926 is true. He claims to have been told this by Edward Lasker "before he died." We remain skeptical, for reasons explained in our account of that tournament in Chapter II.

- Ferriz Carrasquedo and Terrazas say Torre's mental ills were due to syphilis. Ferriz speculates this may have resulted when the Mexican generals he associated with in 1926 wanted to show him a good time. In rebuttal, Germán de la Cruz (a medical doctor) categorically rejects the syphilis hypothesis, and gives sound medical reasons why that diagnosis could not be correct.

- De la Cruz relates that he once asked Torre "Is it true that Alekhine died poisoned?", to which Torre replied "I was the only one who got away." It is hard to make sense of this. Torre's answer has no connection to the question. He "got away" from what? The notion of any link between his 1926 nervous breakdown, and Alekhine's death in Portugal 20 years later, is extremely implausible.

♜ However dubious the above opinions may be, they are completely outdone by Ocampo's account of Chicago 1926 and its aftermath. Here it is in full, transcribed directly from the film (odd translations and all):

Imagine a guy who is sponsored to play in Germany, suddenly he goes to play in the Soviet Union, and returns to Mexico with Mrs. Kollontai, Diego Rivera[1], and he hangs out with all the Mexican revolutionaries. Obviously, everybody thought that he was a communist. He goes to the United States and they say "How can it be possible? We sponsored and protected him, and now he turns against us." He noticed that he left his baggage one way, and they appeared in a different way. He realized he was being spied. Besides, people from the American Workers Union told him that he was being watched by American security agencies. Also, the Soviet security agencies did the same.

So he was caught between two groups that harassed him. So he thought they were helping his opponents, because that game was crucial to win the tournament, and he realized that they didn't want him to win. They began to talk in Yiddish, and Torre couldn't understand. He spoke some German, but not Yiddish, which is a combination of German and Hebrew.

He protested about the cheating that he believed Lasker did, and when they gave him his prize, he got it, and then returned the envelope, and asked the organizer about his objection, it seems that he got a bad answer, using bad words. Something like "We won't pay any attention to you, stupid." So Torre threw the envelope at him and hit him in the nose. Immediately, six bodyguards appeared and beat Torre. They try to detain him and Torre resisted, so they injected him a drug they used against every person that offered resistance of being deported from the United States. From that moment, no one knows anything. Torre arrived to Mexico three weeks later, and didn't remember anything. He didn't remember what happened. He only said "I was at the award ceremony and don't know what happened, and now I am here."

In the Soviet files, there is a record indicating that he received a letter, but it was encrypted. The code was something like "Did you deliver my love roses?" and he answered something like "Yistinet." That's why they say that, but that phrase, "yistinet," was used by the Russians to say "I didn't copy" or something like that. He was incriminated for "anti-American" activities, so they turned Torre's ejection order from the United States because they alleged that he distributed Soviet propaganda among the American workers.

1 Alexandra Mikhailovna Kollontai (1872-1952) was a Russian politician and diplomat who served as the USSR's ambassador to Mexico 1926-27. Diego Rivera (1886-1957) was a prominent artist and member of the Mexican Communist Party.

> But we have to corroborate it, because I've never seen the original letter. Terrazas mentions it, but I don't know if he saw it ... The fact is that he was expelled from the United States and he didn't remember what happened.

Ocampo further says Nikola Tesla was given the same drug as Torre, claiming "the Director of Migration Services said that at Geneva. When I heard that I called him and said 'Can you find out if Torre was in that list?'" Finally he adds "I do sustain that Torre was a victim of a migration issue, and that he suffered an attack by the Chicago magnates to take him out of international chess."

We scarcely know where to begin addressing this rambling hodge-podge of falsehoods, fabrications, fallacies and folderol; some claims are so ridiculous that they can be dismissed out of hand; for example Torre was never indicted, let alone "incriminated" for anything in the USA, least of all "un-American activities." The idea of him becoming involved in politics, of any stripe, is implausible at best. The notion of Edward Lasker somehow cheating is absurd. There was a span of over seven weeks, not three, between the end of the Chicago tournament and Torre's return to Mexico. The "yistinet" letter, if it actually existed, seems totally irrelevant. And of course Torre himself paints a totally different picture in the 1927 *Anahuac* interview in Chapter III.

And if any more contrary evidence is required, there is the *American Chess Bulletin*'s account of the closing ceremony at Chicago 1926, which is found on pages 113-114 of the September-October 1926 issue:

> **The Banquet in the Red Room**
>
> At the conclusion of play in both tournaments on the afternoon of September 2, a banquet, attended by about seventy-five persons, was held in the Red Room in the evening, with Maurice S. Kuhns acting as toastmaster. Others at the speakers' table were: F.H. Wade, F.E. de Vries, Charles Westcott, Francis Edler, W.E. Sparrow, Samuel D. Factor, S.W. Addleman, Harry E. Heick, T.P. Dudley, H. Helms and S.S. Bell.
>
> The chairman announced the list of special prizes, including one each from the Kalamazoo and Bethlehem Chess clubs and the *American Chess Bulletin*. These were added to later when both Edward Lasker and Lewis J. Isaacs handed over the consolation money due them for their scores in the masters' tournament to be devoted to prizes for the two best games played.
>
> Samuel D. Factor, introduced as "the Western Chess Association," received generous applause, as did all the other players as they came up to receive their shares of the prize fund. The real ovation of the evening, however, was reserved for Jackson W. Showalter, the veteran of the tournament and

now in his 67th year, and as a special compliment the chairman stepped over to the table at which the Kentuckian was seated and shook him warmly by the hand.

Speeches were made by Judge Jacob E. Dittus, Charles Westcott, Francis Edler, H. Helms, S.S. Bell, Marshall, Maróczy, Torre, Lasker and Banks. The six prize winners in the western finals also received their awards in due order. Chairman Kuhns then outlined his views upon a national association. The motion of Judge Dittus to submit the matter to the Western Chess Association was seconded and carried.

This account describes a normal, friendly, unremarkable final ceremony. Nothing about Torre lodging a protest, or being insulted, or throwing anything in anyone's face, nothing about six bodyguards beating Torre up or injecting him with drugs. No "Chicago magnates" wanting to take Torre out of international chess.

Since *ACB* editor Hermann Helms was actually there, one would expect that some report of the events Ocampo describes would have made it into the *ACB*, and that Helms, who had promoted and championed Torre since he first arrived in New York, would be outraged at the violence allegedly visited on him. Why no such report, no outrage? Obviously, because what Ocampo describes is completely false and never happened. His ramblings are the sort of nonsensical conspiracy theory, spun out of thin air, that one sees all too often these days.

Ocampo's fantasies notwithstanding, *Torre x Torre* is a good piece of documentary film-making, highly informative and well worth watching, as long as one maintains skepticism at appropriate points. It enables one to see Torre as a man of flesh and blood, mind and soul, and not just a player of chess games. We recommend it highly.

Chapter X

A Final Assessment of Torre as a Chess Player

Some concluding remarks on the question: Had Torre not suffered his nervous breakdown, and wanted to continue high-level play, would he have fulfilled the expectations that grew around him, in particular the prophecies of Emanuel Lasker and Augustín Garza Galindo, that he would become World Champion?

A very problematic question, and one that requires looking beyond the won/lost record to a close examination of the quality of Torre's play. That is just what we have been doing throughout this book, putting his games under the probing scrutiny of the Lidless Eye. And so we can formulate a very well supported "Devil's Advocate" case. A summary of the main flaws revealed by Stockfish:

- ♖ Torre committed serious miscalculations, even outright blunders, in several games, e.g. against Winter at Detroit; against Rubinstein, Tartakower, Bogoljubow and Carls at Baden-Baden; again vs. Rubinstein at Marienbad; against Bogoljubow, Romanovsky and Yates at Moscow; against Rokhlin at Leningrad; and against Showalter, Isaacs and Edward Lasker at Chicago.

- ♖ Too often Torre fell into lost positions, and avoided losing only by dint of his opponent's mistakes. Examples are Reshevsky at Detroit; te Kolsté, Sämisch, Tartakower and Nimzovich at Baden-Baden; Sämisch, Marshall and Haida at Marienbad; Lasker and Rabinovich at Moscow; Showalter and Isaacs at Chicago; and Araiza at Mexico City.

- ♖ Conversely, Torre often missed wins: against Réti, Spielmann, Rabinovich and Nimzovich at Baden-Baden, Rubinstein at Marienbad, Ilyin-Zhenevsky at Moscow, and Jaffe at Chicago. And while he did win against Whitaker at Detroit, Kupchik in the Metropolitan League, and Opocensky and Grünfeld at Marienbad, in all those games he let winning positions slip to draws, only salvaging full points with the help of later errors.

- ♖ He indulged too much in reckless opening experiments, as against Sämisch at Baden-Baden, and Levenfish and Zubarev at Moscow.

- ♖ His sense of danger was underdeveloped, as seen with Haida and Levenfish, and his first two games with Sämisch.

The reader might think we are trying to prove that Torre should never have won any games at all, but of course we are not. That might have happened had he played a match with Stockfish, but his opponents were all fallible human beings like himself, and the flaws described here could be found in many players' games, and are often seen in the rough-and-tumble of tournament play with clocks ticking.

But in considering whether Torre could have become world champion, these flaws are quite relevant. Such defects would not go unnoticed and unpunished in a match with Capablanca or Alekhine. We have put their games under the Lidless Eye also, and while they too are imperfect, such failings are far less frequent, and their alertness in detecting and capitalizing on them is sharp. One can be deceived by Torre's plus score in his games with Alekhine, Lasker, and Capablanca. In the first case Torre benefited from a dubious opening experiment Alekhine never repeated, and in the second from Lasker's distraction at having his stage play produced.

Against Capablanca Torre did produce a strong, impressive, near-perfect effort to hold the world champion to a draw in a very difficult 56-move game, but could he sustain that kind of effort, game after game in a match? Torre's physical conditioning was clearly inadequate, as his second-half collapse at Moscow showed, and as Tartakower attested.

Thus it is clear that before he could have had any realistic chance at the title, Torre would have needed more experience to work out his flaws, and a program of proper diet and exercise to get himself in shape and increase his endurance.

Beyond that, there would still be the problem of financial backing. Capablanca required a challenger to raise $10,000 (almost $160,000 in 2022 dollars) to get a title match. After winning the title in 1927 Alekhine imposed the same condition. Could Torre have raised such a sum?

And there was one more important factor that Torre lacked: ruthless ambition. To become a world champion, an iron-willed, single-minded egotism is a big help, prime examples being Alekhine, Botvinnik, Fischer, Karpov and Kasparov. Nicer guys, such as Euwe, Smyslov and Spassky did not keep the title for long. Torre was definitely the nice guy type. He would never say, as Fischer did, "I like to see their egos crack." As we have said several times in this book, Torre loved chess as art much more than as a competitive sport. As noted earlier, in his later years he would often offer a draw in offhand or simul games where he had a winning position. Even if his health had stayed good, he was probably too gentle and sensitive a soul to take the chess crown.

Finally, in reading Torre's two booklets, *Development of Chess Ability and El Torneo de Ajedrez para el Campeonato de la República Mexicana*, we noted one more possibly relevant psychological factor. In the former book he wrote:

> If we resolve to play each time very much better than we did the last; to play the opening with greater precision, the middle game with higher consciousness, the ending with more directness, to see further ahead with finer accuracy, to evolve a greater masterpiece; the inner effort will prove very cumulative, and our progress will surpass our happiest dreams.

And in his prologue to the latter book, Augustín Garza Galindo wrote:

> When a fighter, in chess or any other field, takes up the motto of Carlos Torre, of surpassing himself in each new fight, of playing better each new game, and when from his lips, that speak sincerely, we have heard that he had never played better chess than when he played in Mexico, we can predict that very soon our country will be proud that one of its sons has taken the chess scepter.

For a professional chess master, this "resolve to play each time very much better than we did the last" cannot be just lip service, a feel-good affirmation like Émile Coué's "Every day in every way I'm getting better and better." It requires hard work. Torre took it seriously, perhaps too seriously, as indicated by his needlessly harsh self-criticism in annotating his game with Kupchik. And there must be tangible results, otherwise the motto, however noble an ideal it may be, is of no practical value.

Try as he might, Torre was not showing the improvement his motto demanded. Yes, he had played qualitatively and quantitatively better at Marienbad, and in the first half at Moscow, compared to Baden-Baden. But in the latter half at Moscow, and at Chicago, the quality of his play had worsened. While Torre did not have Stockfish to grade his play, he was surely aware of this to some extent. One wonders — and here we are admittedly speculating — if the glib prophecies of Lasker and Garza Galindo weighed on Torre, and contributed to his desire to withdraw from serious chess when he realized the difficulties involved. This sort of "too much too soon" effect has been seen over and over, not just in chess but with young pop music and movie stars. At the time of this writing ballyhoo similar to what developed around Torre is growing around the Iranian chess prodigy Alireza Firouzja; it remains to be seen whether he will go the way of Torre, or of Magnus Carlsen.

Assuming Torre had maintained good health, and somehow summoned up sufficient ambition and financial backing to challenge Capablanca or Alekhine in the later 1920s, we suspect his score would be no better than Bogoljubow's in his two matches with the latter (15½-9½ in 1929, 15½-10½ in 1934), if even that good. This is no disparagement of Torre; Alekhine and Capablanca were simply that strong, standing, along with Lasker, head and shoulders above everyone else back then.

On the other hand, there were some non-title match opponents Torre might have played — Spielmann, Colle, Tartakower, Réti, Marshall and perhaps Nimzovich come to mind — with definite winning chances, and with every likelihood of producing lively, sparkling chess.

But again, this is all speculation. John Greenleaf Whittier wrote "For all sad words of tongue and pen, the saddest are these, 'It might have been.'" Let us not dwell too much on the sad aspects of Torre's all-too-short career; rather let us enjoy and appreciate what he was able to do, and remember him as a fine contributor to chess, both in his playing days and in retirement. That the reader may do that has been our goal in writing this book.

Index of Players

(numbers refer to games)

Index of Openings by Name

(numbers refer to games)

Index of Openings by ECO code

(numbers refer to games)

General Index

Bibliography

- Alekhine, Alexander, *My Best Games of Chess 1908-1937*, Russell Enterprises, Inc., Milford CT, 2013
- *American Chess Bulletin* yearbooks 1924, 1925, and 1926, Hermann Helms publisher, New York
- Bronstein and Fürstenberg, *The Sorcerer's Apprentice*, Cadogan Books, London, 1995
- Chernev, Irving, *The 1000 Best Short Games of Chess*, Simon and Schuster, New York, 1963
- Coles, R.N., *Dynamic Chess* (2nd edition), Dover Publications, Inc., New York, 1966
- De Firmian and Korn, *Modern Chess Openings* (13th edition), David McKay Company, Inc., New York, 1990
- Denker & Parr, *The Bobby Fischer I Knew and Other Stories*, Hypermodern Press, San Francisco, 1995
- Divinksky, Nathan, *Life Maps of the Great Chess Masters*, International Chess Enterprises, Seattle WA, 1994
- Elo, Arpad, *The Rating of Chessplayers, Past and Present*, Arco Publishing, New York, 1978
- Fine, Griffith and Sergeant, *Modern Chess Openings* (6th edition), David McKay Company, Inc., Philadelphia, 1939
- Fine, Reuben, *The Psychology of the Chess Player*, Dover Publications, Inc., New York, 1967
- Fine, Reuben, *The World's Great Chess Games*, Dover Publications, Inc., New York, 1976
- Forster, Hansen & Negele, *Emanuel Lasker: Denker, Weltenbürger, Schachweltmeister*, Excelsior Verlag, Berlin 2009
- Gaige, Jeremy, *Chess Personalia: A Biobibliography*, McFarland & Co., Jefferson NC, 1987
- Gaige, Jeremy, *Chess Tournament Crosstables*, 1921-1930, self-published, Philadelphia, 1974
- Hannak, D. J., *Emanuel Lasker: The Life of a Chess Master*, Dover Publications, Inc., New York, 1991
- Hilbert, John S., *Shady Side: The Life and Crimes of Norman Tweed Whitaker, Chess Master*, Caissa Editions, Yorklyn DE, 2000

♙ Hooper & Whyld, *The Oxford Companion to Chess*, Oxford University Press, New York, 1996

♙ Keyes, Frances Parkinson, *The Chess Players*, Farrar, Straus and Cudahy, New York, 1960

♙ Kingston, Taylor, *Edgard Colle, Caïssa's Wounded Warrior*, Russell Enterprises, Inc., Milford CT, 2021

♙ Lasker, Edward, *Chess for Fun & Chess for Blood*, Dover Publications, Inc., New York, 1962

♙ Lasker, Emanuel, *Lasker's Manual of Chess*, Russell Enterprises, Inc., Milford CT, 2008

♙ Nimzovich, Aron, *My System*, David McKay Company, Inc., New York, 1947

♙ Orlov, Georgi, *The Black Knights' Tango*, B. T. Batsford, Ltd., London, 1998

♙ Soltis, Andrew, *Soviet Chess 1917-1991*, McFarland & Co., Jefferson NC, 2000

♙ Summerscale, Aaron, *A Killer Chess Opening Repertoire*, Everyman Chess, London, 1998

♙ Tartakower, Savielly, *Die Hypermoderne Schachpartie*, Wiener Schachzeitung, Vienna, 1924

♙ Velasco, Gabriel, *Vida y Partidas de Carlos Torre*, Incaro, Mexico, D.F., 1993

Websites:

♘ https://new.uschess.org/chess-life-digital-archives (*Chess Life* and *Chess Review* magazines)

♘ Various Wikipedia entries

The Modernized
Anti-Sicilians
Volume 2
Moscow Variation & Sidelines
Ravi Haria

THE PRACTICAL ENDGAME BIBLE
Guidelines for the Fundamentals of the Endgame
Boroljub Zlatanovic

The Power of Middlegame Knowledge
The Exchange
Sacrifice Unleashed
Georg Mohr

Thinkers' Chess Academy
with Grandmaster
Thomas Luther
Volume 3
Test Your Chess Knowledge
Crucial Exercises to Sharpen Your Understanding
Thomas Luther

Supreme Chess Understanding
Statics & Dynamics
Wojciech Moranda

A Complete Opening Repertoire
for Black after 1.d4 Nf6 2.c4 e6!
Ragozin & Anti-Catalan
2 Dariusz Swiercz

The Nimzo and Bogo
Indian
Revisited
Lukasz Jarmula

The Modernized
Barry Attack
Vladimir Okhotnik

Extended & Revised Edition
The Taimanov Bible